The Encyclopedia of Eastern Philosophy and Religion

The Encyclopedia of Eastern Philosophy and Religion

Buddhism • Hinduism • Taoism • Zen

Buddhism & Taoism
Ingrid Fischer-Schreiber
University of Vienna

Tibetan Buddhism
Franz-Karl Ehrhard
University of Hamburg

Hinduism
Kurt Friedrichs
President, German Vedanta Society

Zen
Michael S. Diener
Japanologist, Tokyo

This edition is reprinted by Barnes & Noble, Inc.,
by arrangement with Shambhala Publications, Inc.

1999 Barnes & Noble Books

ISBN 0-7607-1597-1

Printed and bound in the United States of America

99 00 01 02 MC 9 8 7 6 5 4 3 2 1

RRD-H

Contents

Introduction

This encyclopedia presents the basic terminology and doctrinal systems of the four great wisdom teachings of the East—Buddhism, Hinduism, Taoism, and Zen—in a clearly understandable form. Like all pioneering endeavors of this kind, it is bound to have shortcomings. These, it is hoped, will be outweighed by its benefits.

It is evident that the roughly four thousand entries that could be included in this volume do not cover the entire range of concepts presented by the four doctrinal systems. Each of these systems has produced its own tremendous body of literature and terminology. To study the entirety of Buddhist literature alone would require several human lifetimes. Thus this encyclopedia is not intended for the use of a few academic specialists. It is rather intended to help general readers find their way through a thicket of unfamiliar terms and concepts that are frequently encountered today in widely varied fields of interest—in the sciences, in the media, in the health professions, in psychotherapy, in the study of meditation, and in psychophysical training.

Difficulties in the preparation of a work such as this arise from several sources. For one, these concepts are expressed in at least five Asian languages (Sanskrit, Pali, Tibetan, Chinese, and Japanese), which are as different from one another as they are from English, so that the translation and transliteration or romanization of the words are complex. Difficulties arise also and perhaps primarily from the subject matter of the wisdom teachings themselves. "Wisdom" is meant here primarily in the Buddhist sense of *prājña*: that is, not as a mere intellectual achievement but rather as immediately experienced intuitive wisdom, whose essence is insight into the true nature of the world as well as eschatological matters.

We are thus not dealing with an accumulation of factual knowledge in the form of the objective dates and measurements of natural science in the Western sense. This is true even though the research methods of Eastern religion are no less pragmatic than those of Western science (their results have shown incomparably greater coherence and stability over millennia and across all cultures than the few lasting "facts" of the natural sciences); however, the essence of the *insights* that have been gained through their methods, as all wisdom teachings repeatedly stress, cannot be conveyed in a conceptual, rational manner.

Thus the terms used always point to "generally valid" human experiences; yet their real content can ultimately be grasped only through immediate personal experience. By analogy, the *meaning* of the concepts "sweet" and "sour" can never be conveyed by chemical analysis, no matter how detailed; but biting into a pear or a lemon makes sweet and sour immediately experienceable. Only someone who has had this experience is in a position to use these concepts with knowledge of their meaning.

The insights that are the subject of this encyclopedia are thus to be gained on the path of immediate experience, not through measurements or philosophical speculations. The method entails looking within, the exploration of consciousness through meditative techniques. Even in Western science, consciousness is today proving itself ever more clearly to be the primary and critical factor in the struggle to know reality.

On this path, the spiritual researchers of the East have attained insight into areas and levels of consciousness that for the most part are completely unknown to the West and for which, therefore, the West has no concepts. In the absence of knowledge gained from inner experience concerning the meaning of the terms used in the wisdom teachings, up until now they have been fair game for the speculations, interpretations, and projections of Western scholars. For this reason, one is hard put to find two works of different authors in which the ideas treated here have been understood in the same manner. Even in cases where there is a foundation of actual experiential knowledge, linguistic expression has varied considerably. On top of this, for a long time nearly every Western scholar produced his or her own scheme for transcribing the Asian languages. As a result, a great number of different ways of writing individual terms is current.

This encyclopedia thus ventures into an area where, as far as the presentation of the material to Western readers is concerned, no fixed standards of form or content have yet been achieved—and indeed, perhaps none can be set. For this reason, there are bound to be criticisms. Such criticisms, it is hoped, will help to improve upon the pioneering attempt made in this volume to develop a unified terminology.

The difficulties described above are evident in the translations of original texts from Indian, Chinese, or Japanese literature. Thus the reader should keep in mind that a translation is an interpretation that reflects the translator's understanding, both in linguistic and substantive terms. Thus, for these often difficult texts, many translations, but not *one single correct* translation, are possible. For this reason, the Bibliography includes several translations of basic texts as far as this has been possible.

As concerns the terminology of Zen, the style of certain expressions might at first be puzzling; these have, however, been a matter of careful choice. The notion of "true nature," for example, points to a reality that is not to be dualistically conceived. "True nature" does not refer to a true nature as opposed to a false or untrue nature. "Nature" here is also not a substantive whose attributes and properties can be indicated by adjectives. True nature, as it is understood in Zen, is in fact *devoid of properties*; it is "the one mind without a second." It is to this reality that the expression points.

Furthermore, philosophico-religious theory has less importance in Zen than in the other teachings treated here. Thus the lives of the individual Zen masters, who represent an unbroken lineage of transmission of the Zen tradition going back to Buddha Shakyamuni (see the Ch'an/Zen Lineage Chart at the end of the book), play a greater role. What Zen is, is to a great degree exemplified in their lives. A relatively large space has therefore been devoted to their biographies. In the same way, certain developments and ideas that typify Zen are best clarified through the example of a particular Zen master. The length of a biographical article is thus not always an index of the importance of the person treated in it.

Guide to Using the Encyclopedia

The entries for all four subject areas—Hinduism, Buddhism, Taoism, Zen—are found together in the same alphabetical listing. The order of the entry titles is according to the letter-by-letter system of alphabetization, irrespective of word components: for example, *Ch'i-hai . . . Chih-i . . . Chih-kung,* and not, as in Chinese dictionaries, *Ch'i-hai . . . Ch'i-kung . . . Chih-i.*

The literal meaning of an entry title is given when it is different from the definition of the entry title or when a literal translation of the components of the entry title is an aid to understanding.

The inclusion of an entry title in one of the subject areas is indicated by **B** for Buddhism, **H** for Hinduism, **T** for Taoism, and **Z** for Zen. If the same concept is used in more than one of the subject areas but with different meanings—primarily Hinduism/Buddhism—then (in this case) both explanations are given one after the other, usually with the older, original meaning in the framework of Hinduism given first.

Zen, although frequently considered to be one among many schools of Buddhism, had its own independent development to such an extent that it is here treated as a separate subject area. This also corresponds to its own understanding of itself as "outside the orthodox teaching."

In the area of Buddhism, for the most part the literature makes use of the so-called hybrid Sanskrit form of Indian terms, even when there is an older Pali form. Thus the entry titles are also given in this form. If a Pali form different from the Sanskrit form often appears in the literature, it is added in parentheses. Pali forms appear as entry titles only where there is no Sanskrit form in common use. In cases where both forms are equally current, the reader is referred from the Pali to the Sanskrit form.

Zen in its essential form arose and flourished for the first time in China. Today, however, it survives primarily in Japan; thus the present language of Zen is Japanese. For this reason, as in the majority of the literature, Zen terms are given in their Japanese form. In the few cases where Chinese forms are also current, the reader is referred from them to the Japanese form (for example, *Kung-an* → *Kōan*). Personal names, however, are given in their original form; the reader is referred from the more common Japanese reading of the name to the original form (for example, *Rinzai Gigen* → *Lin-chi I-hsuan*).

In Chinese and Japanese there are many homonyms with different meanings. Since the transcriptions are based on pronunciation alone, one cannot tell that for each of these different words a different character is used in the original. Thus there are cases where the same entry title appears twice with a different literal meaning each time. In this case, it is not the *same* word with a different interpretation; rather these are different words (and characters) that are spelled the same way in the romanized form.

Transcription and Pronunciation

Sanskrit: Entry terms are rendered according to a simplified system of transliteration commonly used in nonscholarly literature. Where the scholarly transcription (B) diverges from this simple form (A), the former version is supplied in parentheses. The following differences will be noted:

A	B
ch (chakra)	c (cakra)
n, m (Sanskrit; Dipamkara)	ṃ (Saṃskrit; Dipaṃkara)
ri (Rigveda)	ṛ (Ṛgveda)
sh (Shiva; Krishna)	ś, ṣ (Śiva; Kṛṣṇa)
t, d, n, h	ṭ, ḍ, ṇ, ḥ

For pronunciation, the following simplified rules can serve as a general reader's guide:

a	pronounced	like *u* in *but*
ā		like *o* in *mom,* but longer
i		like *i* in *pick*
ī		like *i* in *pique*
u		like *u* in *rule*
ū		like *u* in *rule*, but longer
e		like *e* in *they*
o		like *o* in *go*
ai		like *ai* in *aisle*
au		like *au* in *how*

V is pronounced with the teeth lightly against the lower lip, so that the sound created is between English *v* and *w.*

A consonant followed by *h* (e.g., *kh, gh*) indicates "aspirated" pronunciation, a detail that can be ignored in nonscholarly contexts, as can the underdots employed in scholarly transcription to indicate retroflex *s, t, d,* or *n,* or to represent final-position aspiration (the *visarga ḥ*).

Chinese: Although the pinyin system of romanization was officially adopted by the People's Republic of China in 1979, the previously standard Wade-Giles system continues to be widely employed. Thus, in order to conform to the transcription most frequently encountered in scholarly literature, entry forms have been rendered in their familiar (Wade-Giles) form.

The following rules give approximate English equivalents for sounds as rendered in Wade-Giles:

ch	pronounced	j
ch'		ch
e		short *u* as in *fun*
j		like English *r* as in *ready*
k		g
k'		k
p		b
p'		p
t		d
t'		t
ts		dz
ts'		ts
hs		sh

Vowels are pronounced as in Italian or German.

Since readers may encounter pinyin in publications after 1950, a conversion chart is provided on pages xv–xvi. (Note: Syllables whose transliteration is the same in pinyin and Wade-Giles are not included.)

Japanese: The Hepburne system of transliteration employed in this encyclopedia—which is used in Japan itself as well as by the majority of international scholars—clearly indicates the Japanese syllables that make up each word.

Vowels are pronounced as in Italian or German; the addition of a macron (e.g., *kōan*) indicates a lengthened vowel.

The *u* of *tsu* is often elided, particularly in final position and preceding *k* or *t*. *Fu* is an aspirated sound (between English *f* and *h*). *Y* is pronounced discretely even in combination with consonants; e.g., *Tokyo* is pronounced Toh-kyoh (two syllables), not Toh-kee-oh (three syllables).

Tibetan: The extremely complicated scholarly transcription of Tibetan often appears unintelligible and unpronounceable to nonscholarly readers. The simplified system we have elected to use instead is based on principles of pronunciation and is, in fact, the form preferred in most scholarly literature. As in the case of Sanskrit, the scholarly transliteration of entry terms is provided in parentheses following this more familiar form.

Pinyin to Wade Giles

Pinyin	Wade-Giles	Pinyin	Wade-Giles	Pinyin	Wade-Giles
ba	pa	chuo	ch'o	gu	ku
bai	pai	ci	tz'u (ts'u)	gua	kua
ban	pan	cong	ts'ung	guai	kuai
bang	pang	cou	ts'ou	guan	kuan
bao	pao	cu	ts'u	guang	kuang
bei	pei	cuan	ts'uan	gui	kui
ben	pen	cui	ts'ui	gun	kun
beng	peng	cun	ts'un	guo	kuo
bi	pi	cuo	ts'o	he	he, ho
bian	pien	da	ta	hong	hung
biao	piao	dai	tai	ji	chi
bie	pieh	dan	tan	jia	chia
bin	pin	dang	tang	jian	chien
bing	ping	dao	tao	jiang	chiang
bo	po	de	te	jiao	chiao
bu	pu	deng	teng	jie	chieh
ca	ts'a	di	ti	jin	chin
cai	ts'ai	dian	tien	jing	ching
can	ts'an	diao	tiao	jiong	chiung
cang	ts'ang	die	tieh	jiu	chiu
cao	ts'ao	ding	ting	ju	chü
ce	ts'e	diu	tiu	juan	chüan
cen	ts'en	dong	tung	jue	chüeh, chüo
ceng	ts'eng	dou	tou	jun	chün
cha	ch'a	du	tu	ka	k'a
chai	ch'ai	duan	tuan	kai	k'ai
chan	ch'an	dui	tui	kan	k'an
chang	ch'ang	dun	tun	kang	k'ang
chao	ch'ao	duo	to	kao	k'ao
che	ch'e	e	eh	ke	k'e, k'o
chen	ch'en	er	erh	ken	k'en
cheng	ch'eng	ga	ka	keng	k'eng
chi	ch'ih	gai	kai	kong	k'ung
chong	ch'ung	gan	kan	kou	k'ou
chou	ch'ou	gang	kang	ku	k'u
chu	ch'u	gao	kao	kua	k'ua
chua	ch'ua	ge	ke, ko	kuai	k'uai
chuai	ch'uai	gei	kei	kuan	k'uan
chuan	ch'uan	gen	ken	kuang	k'uang
chuang	ch'uang	geng	keng	kui	k'ui
chui	ch'ui	gong	kung	kun	k'un
chun	ch'un	gou	kou	kuo	k'uo

Pinyin	Wade-Giles	Pinyin	Wade-Giles	Pinyin	Wade-Giles
le	le, lo	rang	jang	xue	hsüeh, hsüo
lian	lien	rao	jao	xun	hsün
lie	lieh	re	je	yan	yen
long	lung	ren	jen	ye	yeh
	lüeh	reng	jeng	yong	yung
lüe	lüo	ri	jih	you	yu
	lio	rong	jung	yu	yü
mian	mien	rou	jou	yuan	yüen
mie	mieh	ru	ju	yue	yüeh
nian	nien	ruan	juan	yun	yün
nie	nieh	rui	jui	za	tsa
nong	nung	run	jun	zai	tsai
	nüeh	ruo	jo	zan	tsan
nüe	nuö	shi	shih	zang	tsang
	nio	shuo	sho	zao	tsao
nuo	no	si	su, szu, ssu	ze	tse
pa	p’a	song	sung	zei	tsei
pai	p’ai	suo	so	zen	tsen
pan	p’an	ta	t’a	zeng	tseng
pang	p’ang	tai	t’ai	zha	cha
pao	p’ao	tan	t’an	zhai	chai
pei	p’ei	tang	t’ang	zhan	chan
pen	p’en	tao	t’ao	zhang	chang
peng	p’eng	te	t’e	zhao	chao
pi	p’i	teng	t’eng	zhe	che
pian	p’ien	ti	t’i	zhei	chei
piao	p’iao	tian	t’ien	zhen	chen
pie	p’ieh	tiao	t’iao	zheng	cheng
pin	p’in	tie	t’ieh	zhi	chih
ping	p’ing	ting	t’ing	zhong	chung
po	p’o	tong	t’ung	zhou	chou
pou	p’ou	tou	t’ou	zhu	chu
pu	p’u	tu	t’u	zhua	chua
qi	ch’i	tuan	t’uan	zhuai	chuai
qia	ch’ia	tui	t’ui	zhuan	chuan
qian	ch’ien	tun	t’un	zhuang	chuang
qiang	ch’iang	tuo	t’o	zhui	chui
qiao	ch’iao	xi	hsi	zhun	chun
qie	ch’ieh	xin	hsin	zhuo	cho
qin	ch’in	xian	hsien	zi	tzu (tsu)
qing	ch’ing	xiang	hsiang	zong	tsung
qiong	ch’iung	xiao	hsiao	zou	tsou
qiu	ch’iu	xie	hsieh	zu	tsu
qu	ch’ü	xin	hsin	zuan	tsuan
quan	ch’üan	xing	hsing	zui	tsui
que	ch’üeh	xiong	hsiung	zun	tsun
	ch’üo	xiu	hsiu	zuo	tso
qun	ch’ün	xu	hsü		
ran	jan	xuan	hsüan		

The Encyclopedia of Eastern Philosophy and Religion

A

Ābhāsa-Chaitanya 🅷 (Ābhāsa-Caitanya), Skt., lit. *ābhāsa:* "appearance, reflection," *chaitanya:* "consciousness"; absolute consciousness (→ *chit*), which is reflected in the human mind. The mortal, ego-bound individual (→ *jīva*) takes this reflection to be his own state of consciousness and thus impedes the discovery of absolute consciousness, which is identical with → *brahman.* If the *jīva* overcomes this limitation, he becomes aware of his true self (→ *ātman*) and its unity with brahman, and he attains liberation.

Ābhāsa-Vāda 🅷 skt.; the idea that the mortal individual (→ *jīva*), as a manifestation of *brahman,* is merely a thought projection of the internal organ (→ *antahkarana*).

Abhava 🅷 Skt.; 1. nonexistence, the absence of manifest objects; 2. release.

Abhaya-mudrā 🅱 Skt. → mudrā 5

Abhaya-Vachana 🅷 (Abhaya-Vacana), Skt., lit. *abhaya:* "fearlessness," *vachana:* "words"; words that can be uttered only when through spiritual knowledge one has overcome fear, the source of which is identification with the body.

Abheda-Bodha-Vākya 🅷 Skt., lit. *abheda:* "identity," *bodha:* "waking," *vākya:* "sentence, utterance"; a formula that invokes the supreme intelligence, the ultimate truth.

Abhibhāvāyatana 🅱 Skt. → eight masteries

Abhidhammika 🅱 Pali; a Buddhist monk who specializes in the study of → Abhidharma. This does not mean, however, that he is not familiar with the → Sūtra-pitaka and the → Vinaya-pitaka. The historical Buddha Shākyamuni is considered the first *abhidhammika,* even though the Abhidharma was compiled long after his death.

In early Buddhism the *abhidhammikas* of the → Theravāda school enjoyed greater respect than other monks. The Chinese pilgrim → Fa-hsien tells of a → stupa that was erected to the honor of the Abhidharma and was venerated by *abhidhammikas* on certain feast days.

Abhidharma 🅱 Skt. (Pali, Abhidhamma), lit. "Special Teaching"; the third part of the Buddhist canon (→ Tripitaka). The Abhidharma represents the earliest compilation of Buddhist philosophy and psychology. In it the teachings and analyses concerning psychological and spiritual phenomena contained in the discourses of the Buddha and his principal disciples are presented in a systematic order. It constitutes the dogmatic basis of the → Hīnayāna and → Mahāyāna. It took form in the period between the third century B.C.E. and the third century C.E. The final codification took place between 400 and 450 C.E. It is extant in different versions (Abhidharma of the → Theravāda and → Sarvāstivāda). The Abhidharma reflects the views of the individual Buddhist schools in that it gives interpretations and explanations of the concepts that appear in the sūtras. Its primary use is in the study of the teaching.

The Abhidharma of the Theravāda school, which received its definitive form from → Buddhaghosha, is written in Pali and consists of seven books: (1) the *Book of the Elements of Existence* (*Dhammasangani*), which contains an enumeration of both mental elements organized in relation to various meditations and material elements organized into groups; (2) the *Book of Classifications* (*Vibhanga*), which defines the aggregates (→ *skandha*), fields (→ *āyatana*), and faculties (→ *indriya*), etc.; (3) the *Book of Points of Controversy* (*Kathāvatthu*), which deals with 219 points of controversy significant for the history of the development of Buddhist thought; (4) the *Book of Individuals* (*Puggalapaññati*), which describes the different types of clerics and lay people; (5) the *Book of Elements* (*Dhātukathā*), which is concerned with the elements (→ *dhātu*); (6) the *Book of Pairs* (*Yamaka*), which derives its name from its treatment of questions in a "doubled"—i.e., positive and negative—fashion; and (7) the *Book of Causality* (*Patthāna*), which describes the relations existing between individual dharmas.

The Abhidharma of the Sarvāstivāda school, written in Sanskrit, is also composed of seven books, some parts of which are considerably different from those of the Theravāda school. The definitive version of this goes back to → Vasubandhu. The seven books of this Abhidharma are (1) the *Book of the Recitations of the Teaching* (*Sangītiparyāya*), which expounds the elements of the teaching as divided into monads, triads, etc.; (2) the *Book of Things* (*Dharmaskandha*), part of which is identical with the above-mentioned *Vibhanga* and defines aggregates, meditations, etc.; (3) the *Book of Descriptions* (*Prajñaptishāstra*), which gives proofs, in the form of songs, for numerous legendary events; (4) the *Book of Understandings* (*Vijñānakāya*), which contains a number of chapters on controversial points that recall the *Kathāvatthu,* as well as other chapters that recall the *Patthāna* and the *Dhātukathā* of the Theravada Abhidharma; (5) the *Book of Elements* (*Dhātukāya*), which essentially corresponds to the *Dhātukathā* of the Theravādins; (6) the *Book of Literary Treatises* (*Prakarana*), which deals with the definition of the various elements of the teaching and their division into categories; and (7) the *Book of the Starting Point of Knowledge* (*Jñānaprasthāna*), which treats various aspects of the teaching, such as propensities (→ *anushaya*), knowledge (→ *jñāna*), absorptions (→ *dhyāna*), etc.

Abhidharmakosha 🅱 (Abhidharmakośa) Skt., lit. "Treasure Chamber of the Abhidharma"; the most important compilation of the → Sarvāstivāda teaching, composed by → Vasubandhu in Kashmir in the fifth century C.E. It is composed of two parts: a collection of 600 verses (*Abhidharmakosha-kārikā*) and a prose commentary on these verses (*Abhidharmakosha-bhāshya*). It exists today only in Chinese and Tibetan versions. It is considered the highest authority in dogmatic questions.

The *Abhidharmakosha* reflects the transition from the Hīnayāna to the Mahāyāna view. It is the fundamental work of the Buddhist schools of China, where it contributed significantly to the spread of Buddhism. Nine points are treated in it: → *dhātu* (elements), → *indriya* (faculties), *loka* (worlds, modes of existence [→ *triloka*], → *karma*, → *anushaya* (propensities), *pudgala-mārga* (the path of liberation), → *jñāna* (*knowledge*), → *samādhi* (concentration), *pudgala-vinishaya* (theories about the individual). This last part constitutes an independent unit refuting the → Vātsīputrīya view of the existence of an independent entity.

Abhidharma-pitaka 🅱 (Abhidharma-piṭaka) Skt. (Pali, Abhidhamma-pitaka), lit. "Basket of the Special Teaching"; the third part of the Buddhist canon (→ Tripitaka), usually known by the short name → Abhidharma.

Abhijñā 🅱 Skt. (Pali, abhinnā); supernatural powers, abilities possessed by a buddha, bodhisattva, or → arhat. Generally, six types of *abhijñā* are distinguished. The first five are regarded as mundane and are attained by the realization of the four absorptions (→ *dhyāna*). The sixth is considered supramundane and can be attained only through the highest insight (→ *vipashyanā*). These powers are recognized by both the Hīnayāna and Mahāyāna. The six *abhijñās* are (1) → *riddhi*; (2) "divine hearing" (perception of human and divine voices); (3) perception of the thoughts of other beings; (4) recollection of previous existences; (5) the "divine eye" (knowledge of the cycles of birth and death of all beings); (6) knowledge concerning the extinction of one's own impurities and passions (→ *āsrava*), which signifies certainty of having attained liberation.

Abhimāna 🅷 Skt.; pride, arrogance, self-seeking; the characteristics of an ego that is identified with the body, that has removed itself from the unity of creation and believes itself to be a separate individual.

Abhimukti 🅷 🅱 Skt.; deliverance from the cycle of birth and death, which continues only as long as desires are present.

Abhinivesha 🅷 (Abhiniveśa), Skt.; 1. tendency, attraction; 2. love of life, clinging to life; 3. strong tenacity in pursuing a goal or an object.

Abhirati 🅱 Skt., lit. "Realm of Joy"; the paradise of the buddha → Akshobhya in the east of the universe. In Buddhism, the buddha paradises, the various hells, and the other realms of existence are considered not as locations but rather as states of consciousness, even though in folk belief they are often also regarded as places and geographical territories are ascribed to them. The compass directions ascribed to the various buddhas have symbolic and iconographic significance.

Abhisheka 🅱 (abhiṣeka) Skt., lit. "anointing," "consecration"; the process, central for the methods of the → Vajrayāna, in which the disciple is empowered by the master (→ guru) to carry out specific meditation practices. Thus in Tibetan Buddhism one speaks of the transmission of power (*dbang-bskur*). In the highest yoga Tantra (→ Tantra), there are four different and successive stages of initiation: (1) vase initiation (*kalābhisheka*); (2) secret initiation (*guhyābhisheka*); (3) wisdom initiation (*prajñābhisheka*); and (4) fourth initiation (*chaturābhisheka*). The vase initiation contains the initiation into the five aspects of the buddha families (→ *buddhakula*).

Generally an initiation is accompanied by the reading of the corresponding → *sādhana*, which authorizes the disciple to read and practice the corresponding text, as well as by an oral commentary by the master through which the proper mode of practice is assured.

Abhyāsa 🅷 Skt., lit. "repetition, repeated activity, practice"; the practice of spiritual disciplines.

Āchamana 🅷 (Ācamana), Skt., lit. "mouth purification"; the practice of sipping and spitting out water, whereby the worshiper symbolically cleanses not only what enters the mouth but also what leaves it, that is, one's speech. *Āchamana* is an aspect of → *pūjā*, the formal practice of worship, by means of which the

Hindu withdraws his thoughts from the world of the senses and directs them toward God.

Āchārya H B (ācārya) Skt.; teacher, master.
H a spiritual master who not only has mastered the philosophical systems but also has realized the truths they contain. The term is appended to the names of many great holy men.
B (Pali, ācāriya); one of the two kinds of spiritual leaders known in Buddhism; the second type of teacher is the → *upādhyāya.* Originally *āchārya* was understood to mean a master of the dharma, whereas the *upādhyāya* taught discipline and adherence to the rules. Every novice in a Buddhist monastery chose for himself these two kinds of teacher from among the older monks (→ *shrāmanera,* → *bhikshu,* → ordination).

In early Buddhist times the *upādhyāya* was considered the more important, reflecting the emphasis placed on the observance of rites and rules in the monastic community at that period. In the course of further development the role of the *āchārya* increased in importance and since the fifth century has been more important than that of the *upādhyāya.*

Achintya-Shakti H (Acintya-Śakti), Skt.; the unthinkable, divine force held in a → mantra; it cannot be comprehended by reason.

Ādesha H (Ādeśa), Skt.; to issue an order or instruction, to direct to something. It is primarily the → guru who gives directions for traversing the spiritual path and for overcoming obstacles along the way.

Ādhāra H Skt., lit. "container"; the form in which consciousness manifests itself, the physical-psychic instrument of the body and mind, which consists of the five sheaths (→ *kosha*) that envelop absolute consciousness (→ *ātman*).

Adharma H Skt.; absence of righteousness and virtue, the opposite of → *dharma*; a condition that arises through ignorance. It is characterized by the dominance of indolence (→ *tamas*) and greed (→ *rajas*).

Adhibūta H Skt. → Adhidaiva

Adhidaiva H Skt.; realm of the gods, the divine element, the supernatural, transcedental. In the *Bhagavad-Gītā* (7.30), Krishna speaks of *adhidaiva* and *adhibūta.* When the Pāndava prince Arjuna entreats Krishna to explain these terms to him (8.1), Krishna replies that the ground of all created entities (*adhibūta*) is mutable nature, whereas the ground of the divine elements (*adhidaiva*) is the cosmic soul.

Adhidevatā H, or Adhidaivata, Skt.; term used generally to refer to a divinity whom one invokes for protection.

Adhimātrā H Skt.; beyond all measure and conceptualization, the supreme; God, the Absolute (→ *brahman*).

Adhvaryu H Skt. → *Yajurveda*

Adhyāropa H Skt., lit. "false covering"; the superimposition of some false notion of reality. → Shankara gives the example of a rope that in the darkness is believed to be a snake. This error, which results from nescience (→ *avidyā*), is unremittingly alluded to in → Advaita-Vedānta. The scholar Sadānanda devotes the second chapter of his → *Vedāntasāra* to this topic. (See also → *vikshepa.*)

Adhyāsa H Skt.; error in perception; not seeing what really is; approximately identical in sense with → *vikshepa.* (See also → *adhyāropa.*)

Ādhyātma-Rāmāyana H Skt.; a spiritual interpretation of → Rāma's life; a work that expounds the *Rāmāyana* with concepts of nondualism and emphasizes the divine nature of Rāma. It forms a part of the *Brahmānda-Purāna* (→ Purāna).

Ādhyātma-Yoga H Skt., from *ādhyātma:* "the supreme *ātman,* the supreme Self"; 1. a yogic discipline that, through knowledge and realization of the Self, overcomes identification with the body and mind and produces the knowledge that man as → *ātman* is absolute consciousness and hence identical with → *brahman.* The superconscious state thus attained, in which the yogi becomes a → *jīvanmukta,* is called *ādhyātma-prasāda;* 2. a philosophical school in the tradition of → Shankara.

Ādhyātmika H Skt.; the spiritual path leading toward knowledge of the Self; also, the inner experience of an individual on the journey from mortality to immortality.

Ādi-buddha B Skt. → Samantabhadra

Ādi Granth H Hindi; holy scripture of the Sikhs (→ Sikhism). Begun by Guru Arjan in 1604, it was completed in 1705 by Guru Govind → Singh. The latter gave the scripture itself the name of Guru, whereupon it became known as *Guru Granth.* The compilation, written mostly in Hindi and comprising no less than 3,384 hymns (15,575 verses), is considered to be a manifestation of the mystic personality of the guru and hence to be the voice of the immortal spiritual teacher.

Aditi 🅷 Skt.; 1. unlimited space, eternity, infinite consciousness; 2. in the fem. form (Aditī), name of the mother of the → Ādityas.

Āditya 🅷 Skt.; sun, sun god; in the Vedas, identical at times with → Savitri or → Sūrya. As the source of light, warmth, and growth, the sun god is universally revered. To those of deeper vision, he is the symbol of the light of enlightenment, described in the Upanishads as "brighter than a thousand suns." The Ādityas, the sun deities, sons of → aditī, are the sons of infinite consciousness.

Ādityavarna 🅷 (Ādityavarṇa), Skt.; light of the color of the sun, perceived in a spiritual vision; a fact of spiritual experience.

Advaita 🅷 Skt., lit. "nonduality"; a state that can be ascribed to God or the Absolute alone. It is not accessible to reason, for the ego-bound mind in the waking condition cannot step out of the duality of the subject-object relationship. The concept of nonduality has acquired meaning in the West through the latest discoveries of nuclear physics. (See also → Advaita-Vedānta.)

Advaitānanda 🅷 Skt.; the bliss of knowledge of the Absolute.

Advaita-Vedānta 🅷 Skt.; one of the three systems of thought in → Vedānta; its most important representative is → Shankara. Advaita-Vedānta teaches that the manifest creation, the soul, and God are identical. Just as particle physicists have discovered that matter consists of continually moving fields of energy, so the sages (*rishis*) of Vedānta recognized that reality consists of energy in the form of consciousness (→ *chit*) and that human begins perceive a gross universe by means of gross senses, because of identification with the ego-limited body. That which is real and unchanging is superimposed in the mind (→ *vikshepa*) by the notion of an ever-changing manifest world of names and shapes (→ *nāmarūpa*).

Shankara's best-known example is the piece of rope that in the dark is taken for a snake. Anxiety, repugnance, heart palpitations are induced by a snake that was never born and never will die, but that exists only in one's mind. Once the rope is recognized under light as a rope, it cannot turn back into a snake. The initial error involves not only nescience of what is, but also the superimposition (*vikshepa*) of a notion that has nothing to do with what is. Advaita teaches that we in our ignorance continually superimpose the idea "snake" (the manifest world) on the "rope" (→ *brahman*). In a Skt. verse, Shankara says: "May this one sentence proclaim the essence of a thousand books: *Brahman* alone is real, the world is appearance, the Self is nothing but *brahman.*"

Ādya-Shakti 🅷 (Ādya-Śakti), Skt.; 1. the primal power, the original energy; 2. supreme, divine consciousness or divine omnipotence, which permeates all worlds; 3. epithet for the Divine Mother (→ Shakti).

Āgama 🅷 🅱 Skt., lit. "Source of the Teaching."
🅷 1. term referring generally to scripture; 2. a Tantra or other work having to do with the mystical worship of → Shiva and his → Shakti; 3. oral or written demonstration.
🅱 Mahayana name for collections of writings of the Sanskrit canon (→ *sūtra*), which coincides essentially with the Pali term → *Nikāya*. Four Āgamas are distinguished: (1) *Dīrghāgama* (*Long Collection*, comprising thirty sutras); (2) *Madhyamāgama* (*Medium Collection*, concerned with metaphysical problems); (3) *Samyuktāgama* (*Miscellaneous Collection*, dealing with abstract meditation); (4) *Ekottarikāgama* (*Numerical Collection*).

The contents of the Āgamas encompasses the basic teachings of the Hīnayāna, which the Buddha is supposed to have set forth in his first discourse (→ four noble truths, → eightfold path, → *nidāna*, → karma, etc.). Although the contents of the Hinayana Nikāyas coincides essentially with that of the Āgamas, a fifth Nikāya is known, the *Short Collection* (→ *Khuddaka-nikāya).*

Āgāmi-Karma 🅷 Skt.; future → karma, which arises through one's present actions and desires and must work itself out according to the law of causality. A further distinction is made between → *prārabdha-karma* (karma already initiated and now playing itself out) and → *sanchita-karma* (previously accumulated karma that has yet to be played out). The particular significance of *āgāmi-karma* lies in the fact that one can influence one's own future through present actions and desires.

Agni 🅷 Skt.; fire, one of the oldest and holiest objects of veneration in Hinduism. It appears in the heavens as the sun, in the air as lightning, on earth as fire. Agni is personified as one of the Vedic divinities, to whom many hymns are dedicated.

Agnihotra 🅷 Skt.; 1. daily ritual of a morning and evening milk oblation to → Agni; 2. the essence of the ritual, understood beyond the mere enactment of the rite, which in reality serves to prepare and sustain the practice of contemplation.

Agni-Vaishvānara 🅗 (Agni-Vaiśvānara), Skt.; the universal divine consciousness in which all worlds, people, and gods are held.

Agni-Yātavedas 🅗 Skt.; the fire of the forces of consciousness, described as the "knower of all births." It is the absolute consciousness, which as mental fire gives energy to the intellect and enables it to observe the comings and goings of → *māyā*.

Aham Brahman Asmi 🅗 (Aham Brahmāsmi), Skt., lit. "I am *brahman*"; one of the → *mahāvākyas*, the great precepts of the Vedas. It proclaims the absolute identity of the Self with → *brahman*. *Aham* is the true "I" (→ *ātman*) of every human being and must be distinguished from *ahamkāra* (I-consciousness).

Ahamkāra 🅗 (ahaṃkāra), Skt.; ego, I-consciousness, a part of the → *antahkarana*, the inner organ, which gives rise to all mental processes.

Ahamkāra is the motivator of thought that creates the notion that one is a unique entity separate from everything else. This subject-object duality gives rise to the illusory view whereby we see in *brahman*, the One without a second, the manifest world of multiple forms (→ *māyā*). All perceptions, feelings, desires, and acts of will are naturally and automatically related to *ahamkāra*.

Ahampratyaya 🅗 Skt.; a modification in the mind that results in I-consciousness. It consists in the belief *(pratyaya)* that one is the body and mind, so that the mind employs the absolute consciousness to create thought projections, all of which are associated with "I" (*aham*).

Ahimsā 🅗 🅑 (ahiṃsā), Skt., lit. "nonharming."
🅗 abstinence from injury of any living creature through thought, word, or deed; one of the five virtues on the first step (*yama*) of → Rāja-Yoga, as stipulated in the *Yoga-Sūtra* of → Patañjali; together these form the "Great Vow" (Mahāvrata).
🅑 In Buddhism "nonharming" of living beings is considered one of the most important aspects of the Buddhist spiritual attitude. The rule of vegetarianism for monks and nuns in most Buddhist cultures is based on this principle of ahimsā.

Aishvara-Yoga 🅗 (Aiśvara-Yoga), Skt.; the divine unity of which the *Bhagavad-Gītā* speaks, in which the Divine is one with all existence but as → Īshvara transcends all existence. *Aishvara* is the adjectival form of Īshvara.

Aishvarya 🅗 (Aiśvarya), Skt., lit. "sovereignty, majesty, supremacy"; one of the six characteristics of → Īshvara, the personal God.

Aitareya 🅗 Skt; name of an → Upanishad that belongs to the *Rigveda*. It propounds self-knowledge and describes the nature of the → *ātman*.

Ajantā 🅑 city in the western part of central India, famous for Buddhist grottoes dating from 200 to 700 C.E. The twenty-nine caves, which extend over a distance of 5.6 kilometers, hold the best-preserved Buddhist frescoes in the world. They represent the greatest monument to Buddhist painting in India and make it possible to follow its stylistic development over a full millennium.

The frescoes illustrate in part the life of the historical Buddha (→ Siddhārtha Gautama), as it is known from the sūtras (Prince Siddhārtha at the four gates, the temptation of Māra, entry into *parinirvāna*, etc.), and in part stories from the previous existences of the Buddha (→ *Jātaka*).

They give a detailed picture of life in India at the beginning of historical times. Four caves are so-called → *chaityas* and contain stupas.

Ajapa-Mantra 🅗 Skt.; the involuntary repetition of a → mantra, a sacred formula.

According to the view of → Hatha-Yoga, every creature unconsciously utters a prayer along with the sound of its inward and outward breath, in the form, respectively, of SO'HAM, "He am I," and HAMSA, "I am He."

Ajari 🅩 Jap.; translation of the Skt. word *āchārya*, title of a Buddhist master. In Japanese Buddhism *ajari* is used especially for an outstanding monk of the Tendai or Shingon schools of Buddhism (→ Mikkyō). In Zen the term *charya* or *sharya* is used not to mean "master" but rather as a polite form of address for any monk, much as the term *lama* is often loosely used today for any Tibetan monk.

Ajātasattu 🅑 (Skt. Ajātashatru [Ajātaśatru]); the king of Magadha mentioned in Pali texts, who reigned during the last eight years of the lifetime of Buddha → Shākyamuni and twenty-four years thereafter (ca. 494–462 B.C.E.). He was the son of Bimbisāra, whom he killed. Together with Devadatta, Ajātasattu developed a conspiracy against the Buddha, which was unsuccessful. Later he was converted and fostered Buddhism.

Ajātasattu's name means something like "Enemy before Birth," which, according to the legend, derives from his mother's wish to drink blood from the knee of her husband. This was interpreted by the astrologers to mean that her child would kill its father. Ajātasattu is described as an ambitious prince, who wanted to become ruler of the kingdom as quickly as possible and could not wait for the death of his father. Together with Devadatta, he contrived a double conspiracy: since Devadatta was eager to take over the leadership of the Buddhist order, he was to murder the Buddha, and Ajātasattu to kill his own father. The plot was discovered. Bimbisāra pardoned his son and ceded him the throne. Ajātasattu, nevertheless, did not feel secure with his father still alive and had him incarcerated and starved, together with his wife.

It is further reported in the texts that Ajātasattu later asked the Buddha for advice, as he was planning to conquer the northern, democratically ruled country of the Vajjī Confederation. The Buddha answered that the Vajjīs could not be overcome as long as they remained united. This response served the Buddha as occasion for a teaching on the advantages of a democratic government and the role of the → *saṅgha* as supporters of such a government. Through this teaching Ajātasattu was converted to Buddhism. According to tradition, Ajātasattu received a portion of the Buddha's ashes and erected a → stupa for them. Also, he is said to have built an immense hall for the first council.

Ājñā-chakra H B Skt. → chakra 6

Ajñāna H Skt.; nescience, ignorance. The term refers neither to a lack of knowledge at the empirical level nor to a lack of facts regarding the manifest world, but to the condition in which one takes oneself to be a mortal body and does not know that one, as the Self, is absolute consciousness (→ *brahman*). The consequences of *ajñāna* are the same as those of → *avidyā*. The opposite of nescience is → *jñāna*.

Akāma H Skt.; desirelessness. This state is identical to that in which there is no "I," for only the ego has desires.

Ākāsha H B (ākāśa), Skt.; the all-pervasive, space. H ether, the finest of the five elements; a substance that is said to fill and permeate the entire universe and to be the particular vehicle of life and sound.

B (Pali, ākāsa); in Buddhism understood not as in Hinduism as a substantial "ether" but as space. Two kinds of space are distinguished: (1) space limited by corporeality and (2) unlimited space. The former belongs to the corporeality aggregate (→ *skandha*); the latter is one of the six elements (→ *dhātu*), possesses no substance whatsoever, yet is the basic condition for any corporeal extension and is the container for all materiality manifesting through the four elements—earth, water, fire, air. It is emptiness, free from admixture with material things; unchangeable, imperishable, and beyond all description.

The interpretation of the concept *ākāsha* in the last sense varies in the individual Buddhist schools. The Sarvāstivāda school includes *ākāsha* among the unconditioned dharmas (→ *asamskrita*); it obstructs nothing, pervades everything without obstruction, and is free from changeability. The Mādhyamika school sees space as conditioned (→ *samskrita*); the first of the → four stages of formlessness is the endlessness of space; in the series of the ten total fields (→ *kasina*), *ākāsha* is the second to last.

Akrodha H Skt.; freedom from anger, animosity, or resentment, a state that is attained by control of one's thoughts and realization of "I"-lessness, for the ego alone produces the former conditions.

Akshara H (Akṣara), Skt., lit. "unchangeable"; the indestructible; an epithet for → *brahman*.

Akshara-Purusha H (Akṣara-Puruṣa), Skt.; the motionless soul, the uninvolved Self that detaches itself from the movements and modifications taking place in → *prakriti* (nature) and merely witnesses its processes.

Akshobhya B Z (Akṣobhya), Skr., lit. "Immovable"; the buddha who reigns over the eastern paradise Abhirati. In Buddhism, paradise is not understood as a location but rather as a state of consciousness; the compass directions ascribed to the buddhas have a symbolic and iconographic meaning (→ pure land).

Akshobhya as a monk is said to have taken a vow before the buddha who, endlessly long ago, reigned over Abhirati, never to feel disgust or anger towards any being. In carrying out this vow, he showed himself "immovable" and after endlessly long striving became Buddha Akshobhya and thereby the ruler of the Abhirati paradise. Whoever is reborn there can never fall back into lower levels of consciousness; thus all believers should seek to fulfill the promise kept by Akshobhya. Akshobhya symbolizes the overcoming of passions. He is iconographically depicted either with blue- or gold-colored upper body, sometimes riding on a blue elephant. His hands are in the earth-touching mudrā.

Aku-byōdō Z Jap., lit. "bad sameness"; a tendency to see things as the same in the sense of a misunderstanding of the enlightened experience of the sameness of the nature of all things (→ *byōdō*). In the Zen view, this sameness of nature

Akshobhya

is a transitional stage on the path to deeper enlightenment. One who remains stuck here and, because of the overwhelming experience of the sameness of nature of all things, overlooks their distinctness and uniqueness, falls into *aku-byōdō.*

Akushala 🅑 (akuśala), Skt., Pali; karmically unwholesome; anything connected with the unwholesome root (*akushala-mūla*) and thus with an effect bearing the germ of future suffering. The "unwholesome roots" are greed (*lobha*), hate (Skt., *dvesha*; Pali, *dosa*), and delusion or blindness (*moha*). Greed is attraction to a gratifying object and can be removed through the practice of generosity (→ *dāna*). Hate is ill will toward everything that stands in the way of gratification, and it is overcome through the cultivation of kindness (→ *maitrī*). Delusion refers to the inconsistency of an action or thought with reality and is overcome through insight. The three *akushala-mūlas* are the essential factors that bind a sentient being to the cycle of existences (→ samsara). The removal of these factors is necessary for the attainment of enlightenment. In symbolic representations, greed is depicted as a cock, hate as a snake, and delusion as a pig. (Also → *avidyā*, → *klesha*.)

Akushu-kū 🅩 Jap., lit. "falsely understood emptiness"; a misunderstanding of the teaching of emptiness (Jap., *ku*; Skt., → *shūnyatā*) which arises from the experience of → enlightenment. In this misunderstanding emptiness is understood as mere nothingness, as a negation of all existence. Emptiness, as it is spoken of in Zen, has nothing to do with this purely philosophical concept of nothingness. It is an emptiness that is not the opposite of the existence of all things and their properties but rather the basis of this existence, that engenders and bears it and, from the standpoint of complete enlightenment, is absolutely identical with it. Thus it says in the *Mahāprajñāpāramitā-hridaya-sūtra* (→ *Heart Sūtra*; Jap. *Maka Hannyaharamita shingyō*), which is often cited in Zen, "Form is no other than emptiness, emptiness is no other than form."

Alābha-Bhūmikātva 🅗 Skt.; the inability to practice in a consistent and steadfast manner; having no solid ground under one's feet, the sense that one cannot attain reality.

Ālambana 🅗 Skt.; support or aid for the practice of concentration, involving quiet, controlled breathing and the maintenance of a bodily condition that does not interfere with concentration.

Ālaya-vijñāna 🅑 🅩 Skt., lit. "storehouse consciousness"; central notion of the → Yogāchāra school of the Mahāyāna, which sees in it the basic consciousness of everything existing—the essence of the world, out of which everything that is arises. It contains the experiences of individual lives and the seeds of every psychological phenomenon.

The concept of *ālaya-vijñāna* constitutes the basis of the "mind-only" doctrine of the Yogāchāra and stands in the center of this school's theory of individuation, according to which the karmic seeds (*vāsanā*) of a past empirical individuality enter into the *ālaya-vijñāna*, whence they arise again to occasion thought activity. This individuated thinking is ridden with ignorance (→ *avidyā*) and egotism, which instigate its notion that it constitutes a real person in a real world. In this way ideation arises that causes this thinking that considers itself a person to create karma. These karmic impressions, once ripened (→ *vipāka*), call forth a new process of ideation. This cycle is ended through the removal of the concept that there is a world of objects separate from the mind. The *ālaya-vijñāna* is frequently equated with ultimate reality or "suchness" (→ *tathatā*); in other views it is regarded as the product of previous karma. (Also → Fa-hsiang school.)

Alchemy, Taoist 🅃 → *wai-tan,* → *nei-tan*

Ālvār 🄷 Tamil (S. Indian); the name means approximately "He who is master of the world through surrender to God"; the *ālvārs* are saints of the → Vaishnava tradition of South India.

Amanaska 🄷 Skt.; the state in which one is free from thoughts, desires, and cravings. It never occurs in the waking or dreaming condition, but only in deep sleep, unconsciousness, or → *samādhi,* and is spiritually fruitful in *samādhi* alone.

Amarakosha 🄷 (Amarakośa), Skt., lit. "immortal vocabulary"; the most important dictionary of classical Sanskrit, compiled by Amara-Simha, a Buddhist who lived sometime between the sixth and eighth centuries C.E.. No particular consideration is given in the work to Buddhist terminology.

The *Amarakosha,* whose entries are arranged by subject matter, was primarily created for the use of poets; however, in general it also represents a rich compendium of cultural information. Numerous commentaries exist as well as a supplement, the *Trikānda-Shesha.*

Amara-Purusha 🄷 (Amara-Puruṣa), Skt.; the immortal Self, the soul.

Amarāvatī 🄱 south Indian city; in the second and third centuries an important center for Buddhist art in which the beginnings of the Mahāyāna were reflected. These artworks constituted the transition between early Buddhist art and the → Gandhāra style and exercised a great influence on the art of Southeast Asia, above all on that of those areas known today as Sri Lanka, Indonesia, and Thailand.

The most important art monument in Amarāvatī is a stūpa in the eastern part of the city that, according to tradition, contains relics of the historical Buddha. The discovery of a pillar edict of Emperor → Ashoka (third century B.C.E.) permits the conclusion that the stūpa was erected by Ashoka.

Amarāvatī was the center of the → Mahāsānghika school. Pilgrims are said to have come there even from Pātaliputra. The renowned Chinese pilgrim → Hsüan-tsang (seventh century) reports that in Amarāvatī more than twenty flourishing monasteries existed.

Ambā 🄷 Skt., lit. "mother"; a name for → Shakti, the Divine Mother.

Ambedkar 🄱 Bhimrao Ramji, 1891-1956; Indian jurist and one of the fathers of the Indian constitution; founder of a movement to convert the members of the lowest caste of the Indian social system to Buddhism. Ambedkar, himself originally a Hindu, converted publicly to Buddhism in 1956 in Nagpur in a huge ceremony along with 500 thousand untouchables. Millions of untouchables have followed him since then, above all in areas where the Republican party, which was led by Ambedkar, is active. This alliance of religion and politics led to criticism of the movement, the critics of which regard it as purely a pragmatic association.

Ambedkar's book *The Buddha and His Dhamma* serves as a guide for his followers; in it he emphasizes the social revolutionary aspect of the Buddhist teaching, which is for him a purely rational religion. His work is continued by the Buddhist Society of India, which he founded.

Amida 🄱 🅉 Jap. → Amitābha

Amidism 🄱 🅉 generic term under which are comprehended all schools of Chinese and Japanese Buddhism that have made Amitābha the central point of their teaching. Included are the → Pure Land school, → Jōdo-shin-shū, and → Jōdo-shū.

Also → Shinran, → *nembutsu,* → pure land, → Sukhāvatī, → *tariki,* → Hui-yüan.

Amita 🄱 Skt. → Amitābha

Amitābha 🄱 🅉 (also Amita), Skt. (Jap., Amida), lit. "Boundless Light"; one of the most important and popular buddhas of the → Mahāyāna, unknown in early Buddhism. He is ruler of the western paradise Sukhāvatī, which is not to be understood as a location but as a state of consciousness (→ pure land). Amitābha is at the center of the worship of the Pure Land school of Chinese and Japanase Buddhism (→ Amidism). He symbolizes mercy and wisdom.

Iconographically, Amitābha is sometimes adorned with a crown of precious jewels; sometimes he is depicted with shaven head as the monk Dharmakara—who he was in a previous existence. Most often he is seated in the middle of a lotus blossom, symbol of purity. His hands form the meditation or teaching → mudrā. He often appears together with → Avalokiteshvara on his left and → Mahāsthāmaprāpta on his right, in which case Amitābha is seated and the two bodhisattvas stand. Another iconographic style shows him together with → Bhaishajya-guru-buddha. According to tradition Amitābha was a king who, having come in contact with the Buddhist teaching, renounced his throne and became a monk with the name

Amitābha

Dharmakara. He resolved to become a buddha and in this way to come into possession of a paradise in which the inhabitants would be assured a life of bliss through his merit until their final entry into nirvāna. He took forty-eight vows obliging him to sustain beings on the path to enlightenment. The most important of these vows are: the eighteenth—"If, O lord, after I have [once] attained enlightenment, beings of other world systems through hearing my name arouse the thought of supreme perfect enlightenment and recall me with a clear mind—if I should not, in the moment of their death having gone to them surrounded by a host of monks, stand before them as the venerated one in order to guard their minds from fear may I then not reach supreme perfect enlightenment"—and the nineteenth—"If, O lord, after I have [once] attained enlightenment, beings in the immeasurable, numberless buddha-fields through hearing my name should direct their thought to rebirth in [my] buddha-field and should thus bring the root of karmic merit to ripeness—if they should not be reborn in [my] buddha-field even if they had directed their thought only ten times [toward me and my buddha-paradise], may I then not reach supreme perfect enlightenment" (quoted from Schumann 1974, p. 168.) Through his meditative practice, he fulfilled his vow and became Buddha Amitābha, ruler of Sukhāvatī.

The veneration of Amitābha represents a significant turning point in the development of Buddhism. With it a new path to salvation opens that does not lead through an endless number of rebirths. Not by one's own force, as in the original teaching, but rather owing to help from outside through the liberating will of a buddha, the access to liberation becomes possible in a faster, easier way (→ *tariki*). Just calling on the name of Amitābha, especially in the hour of death, is enough to be reborn in a lotus blossom in the Sukhāvatī paradise. The formula of the Amitābha invocation is in Japanese *Namu Amida Butsu* (→ *nembutsu*) and in Chinese, *Namo o-mi-to-fo,* which roughly means, "Veneration to the Buddha Amitābha."

Amitābha-sūtra 🅱 Skt., lit. "*Sutra of the Buddha Amitābha*"; one of the three sutras that form the doctrinal basis for the Pure Land school in China and Japan. This sutra, also known as the short *Sukahāvatī-vyūha*, describes the simplest form of the practice of this school—recitation of Buddha Amitābha's name. If during a certain time the mind of the practitioner is filled only and alone with the name *Amitābha*, this uninterrupted concentration has the effect that Amitābha and his retinue will appear to the practitioner in the hour of his death. The practitioner will then not be confused by feelings of fear and will thus be able to be reborn in the pure land of the buddha Amitābha.

This sutra is extant only in Chinese translations; the most famous are those of → Kumārajīva and → Hsüan-tsang.

Amitāyurdhyāna-sūtra 🅱 Skt., lit. "Sutra on the Contemplation of the Buddha → Amitāyus, the Buddha of Boundless Life"; one of the three sutras that form the doctrinal basis of the Pure Land school. It gives a description of the pure land of the buddha Amitābha or Amitāyus and of the practice of this school: through leading a pure life, that is, through the observance of moral rules (→ *shīla*) and recitation of Amitābha's name, the potential results of all unwholesome deeds can be wiped away and one can attain rebirth in the pure land.

This sūtra gives the traditional view of the coming into being of the pure land, purported to have been already expounded by the historical Buddha: Queen Vaidehi, the mother of → Ajātasattu (who incarcerated her and her husband, King Bimbisāra) supplicated the Buddha, who had appeared to her, and questioned him concerning a place where she could lead a peaceful, happy life. The Buddha caused all the buddha-fields to appear before her and let her choose among them. Vaidehi decided for the pure land Sukhāvatī. Thereupon the Buddha instructed her in meditation suitable to bring about rebirth in this paradise. He taught her the following sixteen visualizations, which can effect realization of one of the nine stages of rebirth in the pure land, according to the makeup of the individual: contemplation of the setting sun; of water; of the ground; of wondrous trees; of healing waters; of the blissful world of wondrous trees; of the ground and water; of lotus thrones; of the forms of the three sacred ones (Amitābha, → Avalokiteshvara, → Mahāsthāmaprāpta); of the corporeal form of the buddha Amitāyus; of the bodhisattva Avalokiteshvara; of the bodhisattva Mahāsthāmaprāpta; of Amitābha in the blissful realm; of the middle and lower classes of birth. These visualizations permit the practitioner in this lifetime to see Amitābha and his companions Avalokiteshvara and Mahāsthāmaprāpta. This is interpreted as sure sign of rebirth in the pure land.

Amitāyus 🅱 Skt., lit. "Boundless Life"; manifestation of the buddha → Amitābha. He is iconographically depicted sitting, holding in his hands a vessel containing the nectar of immortality.

Amoghasiddhi 🅱 🆉 Skt., lit. "Who Unerringly Achieves His Goal"; one of the five transcendent buddhas. With him are associated the earthly buddha → Maitreya and the transcendental bodhisattva Vishvapani. Amoghasiddhi is usually depicted making the gesture of fearlessness (→ mudrā); his emblem is the double → *vajra.*

Amoghasiddhi

Amrita 🅷 (Amṛta), Skt., lit. "immortal"; the drought of immortality, the water of life; a concept frequently employed in the Vedas. The → *soma* is also often referred to by this term (→ Churning of the Ocean).

Amritattva 🅷 (Amṛtattva), Skt.; immortality, eternal life; attained not on the physical level but only through realization of the Self (→ *ātman*), which as absolute consciousness is identical with God (→ *brahman*).

Ānabodhi 🆉 twelfth patriarch in the Indian lineage of → Zen; probably identical with → Ashvaghosha.

Anāgāmin 🅱 Skt., Pali, lit. "never-returner"; designates those followers of the → Hīnayāna who are on the third stage of the supramundane path (→ *ārya-mārga*, → *ārya-pudgala*). They are free from the first five fetters (→ *samyojana*) of believing in an ego, doubt, clinging to rites and rules, sensual appetite, and resentment. An *anāgāmin* is never again reborn in this world.

Anāgārika 🅱 Pali, lit. "homeless one"; a man who enters upon a homeless life without, however, formally entering the Buddhist monastic order. At the time of the Buddha there existed in India numerous groups of *anāgārikas*, each of which possessed its own doctrinal tradition. One of them was the → *sangha.* In modern Buddhism → Dharmapāla was the first to make use of this term.

Anahana 🆉 the Japanese form of the Skt. word *ānāpāna*, which in Indian yoga refers to the regulation of the breath. In Zen the breath is not "controlled" or regulated, and *anahana* means the natural rhythmic flow of the breath. The practitioner is aware of the flow of the breath but does not try to influence it.

Whereas yoga is based on the point that the regulation of the breath has the effect of calming the mind, the Zen approach is that through the concentration of the mind in *zazen*, the breathing calms itself whereas the instrusive approach of intentionally influencing the breath leads rather to inner tension and distracts from actual Zen practice. Beginners in Zen often receive as their first practice "counting the breath" (→ *susokukan*), which, however, is not *ānāpāna* in the yoga sense (→ *prānāyāma*). Also → *ānāpānasati.*

Anāhata-chakra 🅷 🅱 Skt. → chakra 4

Anāhata-Shabda 🅷 (Anāhata-Śabda), Skt., lit. "unstruck sound"; a mystic sound, often also referred to as the music of the spheres, which can be perceived during the practice of meditation at a certain stage of spiritual development. Occasionally → OM is also referred to as *anāhata-shabda.* (See also → *chakra.*)

Ānanda 🅷 🅱 🆉 Skt., lit. "Bliss," "Absolute Joy." 🅷 The term refers not to the enjoyment of sense objects, which are transient, but to the bliss of a state that lies beyond all duality, all pairs of opposites. → Vedānta teaches that a state of consciousness that is free from thoughts and hence projects neither illness, old age, and death, nor anxiety, care, and suffering, is pure bliss. To define the abstract concept of → *brahman*, Vedānta uses the formula "*Sat-Chit-Ānanda,*" wherein "*Ananda*" is the unaffected absolute bliss that is experienced only in → *samādhi* and is the equivalent of divine consciousness. In the monastic orders of the → Shankara tradition, every → *sannyāsin* is given a name ending in *ānanda*, e.g., Vivekānanda.

B Z name of one of the most important disciples of the historical Buddha. He was a cousin of the Buddha and entered the Buddhist order two years after its founding. He became important for the history of Buddhism when in the twentieth year of the Buddha's teaching activity Ānanda became the Buddha's personal attendant. Ānanda was famous for his extraordinary memory, in virtue of which he was able to retain the Buddha's discourses. His exposition of the discourses formed the basis for the codification of the → Sūtra-pitaka at the first council. Ānanda is one of the → ten great disciples of the Buddha. In Zen Ānanda is considered the second Indian patriarch.

Ānanda is often extolled in the canonical writings for his humility and devotion toward the Buddha. He first took on the function of a personal attendant after the Buddha had assured him he would acquire no advantages as a result of his position. It was also Ānanda who foiled → Devadatta's assassination plot against the Buddha. Ānanda was more than any other an advocate for the cause of women. He gave dharma discourses in the presence of women, and it was at his intercession that Buddha consented to the founding of an order of nuns. Ānanda was reproached with this at the first council. He is said to have attained arhatship only after the death of the Buddha, immediately before the first council.

Ānandagiri H, an important disciple of → Shankara. He lived in the ninth or tenth century C.E. and composed one of the best available hagiographies of his master, the *Shankaravijaya* ("Shankara's Victory"), in which he describes Shankara's life as well as his disputes and debates with opponents. Anandagiri is also the author of the *Nyāyanirnaya*, a work of → Advaita-Vedānta that refutes the views of → Nyāya.

Ānandamaya-Kosha H (Ānandamaya-Kośa), Skt.; the final sheath that envelops the Self, also called the sheath of bliss, or causal sheath (→ *kosha*).

Ānandamayī Mā H, 1896-1982, born Nirmalā Sundarī Devī, in Kheora (East Bengal, now Bangladesh) to brahman parents. She was married at the age of twelve but from early childhood showed interest in spiritual life only. Within six years she had traversed all yogic practices leading to enlightenment, calling this process her "*līlā* of → sadhana." Following realization she received the name Ānandamayi Mā ("the mother filled with bliss"). A group of disciples and admirers soon assembled around her, and in 1929 they built a first ashram in Dacca. In 1932 she traveled to → Dehradun, at the foot of the Himalayas, where a second ashram was built in 1936. Over the next decades she traveled throughout India to bring comfort and aid to spiritual seekers of all classes. Numerous ashrams were erected in her name; the most prominent are in Calcutta, Benares, and Kankhal/Hardvar. She died on August 27, 1982, in her ashram in Dehradun. A selection of her sayings may be found in Ānandamayī 1982*b*.

Ānandamayī Mā attained realization without a guru and without studying the scriptures. True realization always yields insights into nonduality (→ *advaita*), and this experience is consistently expressed in her statements. She spoke of herself as "this body" or "this little sister." Her devotees called her in Hindi "Mātājī" ("Revered Mother") and in Bengali "Mā" ("Mother"). Her significance for the spiritual renewal of Hinduism is a powerful one. She never gave formal talks, but only answered questions; her answers were not based on reason but spontaneously arose from a higher state of consciousness whereby she was able to find the right words for the seeker of truth, whether believer, atheist, artist, or scholar, educated person or illiterate, beginner or advanced seeker. She often said that she did not speak to an "other." Her statements linked all faiths, philosophies, and yogic paths, but she herself stood above and beyond it all. She said, "This body is like a musical instrument; what you hear depends on how you play it."

Ānanda-Purusha H (Ānanda-Puruṣa), Skt.; term from the → Upanishads stating that one's true Self is nothing other than bliss.

Ānandatirtha H → Madhva

Ananta H Skt., lit. "infinite"; epithet for → Vishnu; description of the snake on whose body Vishnu slept.

Ānāpānasati B Pali; wakefulness during inhaling and exhaling, meditation on the breath. One of the most important preliminary exercises for attainment of the four absorptions (→ *dhyāna*). *Ānāpānasati* consists of counting the inhalations and exhalations, which has the effect of calming the mind. This exercise is the basic preliminary practice of meditation in the various schools of Buddhism. In *ānāpānasati* the breathing exercises so prized in yoga became exercises for wakefulness or → mindfulness (*sati*). The individual movements of the breath are consciously executed and attentively followed; however, the breathing is not "regulated." Then the attention is directed simultaneously onto other mental and physical processes.

In the *Sattipatthāna-sutta* this exercise is described as follows:

Breathing in a long breath, he knows, "I am breathing in a long breath"; breathing out a long breath, he knows, "I am breathing out a long breath." Breathing in a short breath, he knows, "I am breathing in a short breath"; breathing out a short breath, he knows, "I am breathing out a short breath." "Experiencing the whole body, I shall breathe in"—thus he trains himself; "Experiencing the whole body, I shall breathe out"—thus he trains himself. "Calming the activity of the body, I shall breathe in"—thus he trains himself; "Calming the activity of the body, I shall breathe out"—thus he trains himself. "Feeling a pleasant feeling, . . . feeling well-being, . . . experiencing the mind, . . . cheering up the mind, . . . collecting the mind, . . . freeing the mind, . . . contemplating the transitory, . . . contemplating release, . . . contemplating extinction, . . . contemplating renunciation, I shall breathe in"—thus he trains himself; "Feeling a pleasant feeling, etc., I shall breathe out"—thus he trains himself.

Anāthapindika 🅱 wealthy merchant from Shrāvastī, who lived at the time of the Buddha → Shākyamuni and was one of his most renowned lay followers. He acquired at great expense the → Jetavana Grove, where he had a monastery built for the Buddha and his students. This became the preferred sojourning place of the Buddha, where he would spend the greater part of the rainy season. In the sutras Anāthapindika is described as the greatest contributor of alms; a series of discourses in the → *Anguttara-nikāya* is addressed to him.

Anātman 🅱 Skt. (Pali, anatta); nonself, nonessentiality; one of the three marks of everything existing (→ *trilakshana*). The *anātman* doctrine is one of the central teachings of Buddhism; it says that no self exists in the sense of a permanent, eternal, integral, and independent substance within an individual existent. Thus the ego in Buddhism is no more than a transitory and changeable—and therefore a suffering-prone—empirical personality put together from the five aggregates (→ *skandha*).

In Hīnayāna, this analysis is limited to the personality; in Mahāyāna, it is applied to all conditionally arising → dharmas (→ *pratītya-samutapāda*). This freedom from self-nature (→ *svabhāva*) is called in the Mahāyāna → *shūnyatā* (emptiness).

According to the usual Hinduistic notion, the soul is the higher I or self (→ *ātman*) and is essentially characterized by permanence and freedom from suffering. In Buddhism, the personality, which according to its view arises out of the five *skandhas*—themselves impermanent—is not regarded as an eternal self but rather as the conventional ego of everyday experience.

Buddha himself, in answer to the question whether a self exists or not, never put forward a definite position so as not to cause new concepts to arise that would be irrelevant and obstructive for spiritual practice. Thus the teaching of no self is to be understood more as a fruitful pedagogical device than as a philosophical doctrine. Nevertheless in the course of the development of the Buddhist system of thought, this came more and more to be an unequivocal denial of the existence of a self. Only the → Vātsīputrīya school affirmed the concept of a self. This view was considered false by the other schools.

In Buddhism the methods for the attainment of liberation concentrate on doing away with the belief in an ego as the essential obstacle to the realization of nirvāna. Clinging to the concept of an ego is the primary cause of all passions and must be completely overcome. If one does not apprehend the impersonality of existence, does not recognize existence as a flux of arising and passing away of physical and mental phenomena in which there is no constant self, then one is unable to grasp the → four noble truths in their real significance and is unable to attain the insight that is essential for release.

Anātma-Vritti-Nirodha 🅷 (Anātma-Vṛtti-Nirodha), Skt.; the curbing of gross impulses; control over one's thoughts when they are in the form of anger, fear, greed, etc.

Anavasthi-Tattva 🅷 Skt.; lack of steadfastness in spiritual practice, brought about by the notion that one has already reached the highest level of → *samādhi*.

Andaja 🅷 🅱 Skt. → chatur-yoni

Anga 🅷 (Aṅga), Skt., lit. "limb, portion"; 1. the eight "limbs," or steps, of → Raja-Yoga; 2. one of the sacred texts of → Jainism. The Angas belong to the canonical writings that were laid down in their final form in the fifth century C.E. and are written in → Prakrit. Sanskrit terminology was later developed to defend Jainism against the orthodox schools of Hinduism.

Angkor Wat 🅷 🅱 temple complex in central Cambodia, considered the high point of classical

Khmer art and architecture. Built under King Suryavarman II (1113–50), Angkor Wat was initially a holy site consecrated to → Vishnu. Following the conversion of the succeeding Khmer kings to Buddhism, Angkor Wat served as a Buddhist holy place. After the destruction of Angkor by the Thais and the flight of the Khmer kings to Phnom Penh in the fifteenth century, Angkor Wat fell into oblivion and was covered by jungle. It was not rediscovered until the nineteenth century.

Ango 🅉 Jap., lit. "dwelling in peace"; a three-month period of intensive spiritual training in a Zen monastery during the rainy season in summer (hence also *ge-ango*, "summer *ango*"; or *u-ango*, "rain *ango*").

Anguttara-nikāya 🄱 Pali (Skt., *Ekottarāgama*, also *Ekottarikāgama*), lit. "*Graduated Collection*"; fourth collection of the Sūtra-pitaka. It is made up of texts organized numerically according to whether subjects treated appear singly or in groups. There are eleven sections. The sūtras included here, which are generally shorter than those in the other collections, are rich in enumerations and strongly recall the → Abhidharma.

Angya 🅉 Jap., lit. "wandering on foot"; the pilgrimage of a young Zen monk (→ *unsui*) who has completed the first phase of his training in a provincial temple to a Zen monastery, where he hopes to be accepted and receive training under a Zen master (→ *rōshi*).

Pilgrimage to a distant monastery, often through trackless terrain, was in ancient times not without peril. It was regarded as an opportunity for the *unsui* to put his physical strength and strength of character to the test, to develop presence of mind by overcoming unforeseen dangers, and, by meeting many different kinds of people in joyful as well as adverse circumstances, to ripen inwardly. In the prescribed equipage of an *unsui* is a round straw hat with a very low brim (Jap., *kasa*). This directs the gaze of the pilgrim onto the path before him; it prevents him from looking around, which would not be conducive to the mental concentration he is supposed to maintain during the entire pilgrimage. A black cloak, white woolen socks, and straw sandals are also part of his outfit. On his chest, the monk carries a bundle with his summer and winter robes, his eating and begging bowls (→ *jihatsu*), a razor for shaving his head, and some sūtra texts. On his back he carries a rolled-up straw raincloak (Jap., *mino*).

When the monk has come through all the difficulties of the pilgrimage and arrived at the monastery, he is often refused entrance in order to test the earnestness of his desire for spiritual training (→ *kokorozashi*). If—after days of persistance outside the monastery (→ *niwa-zume*), not rarely in rain and snow, or in the entrance hall of the monastery (→ *genkan*)—he is finally let in, then he must provide a further proof of his seriousness through a week of sitting (*zazen*) in a solitary cell under the most austere conditions (→ *tanga-zume*) before he is finally accepted into the monastic community.

Animitta 🄱 Skt., Pali; formlessness or absence of characteristics of all → dharmas; the mark of absolute truth, which is devoid of distinctions.

Aniruddha 🄷 🄱 Skt.

🄷, son of → Pradyumna and grandson of Krishna.

A Daitya princess named → Ushā fell in love with Aniruddha, and with the help of magic brought him to her chambers in the city ruled by her father, → Bāna. The king sent his henchmen to capture him, but Aniruddha destroyed them with an iron club. Bāna then used his occult powers to abduct Aniruddha. When Krishna, → Balarāma, and Pradyumna learned of this, they determined to rescue Aniruddha. A great battle ensued in which Bāna was supported by Shiva and Skanda, the god of war. Bāna lost nonetheless, but his life was spared through Shiva's intervention. With Ushā as his consort, Aniruddha returned to → Dvāraka.

🄱 one of the → ten great disciples of the Buddha.

Anīsh 🄷 (Anīś), Skt., lit. "no master"; one who is not free but bound by ignorance.

Anitya 🄷 🄱 Skt., lit. "impermanence."

🄷 Nothing is permanent; all is in flux and passing away; the characteristic of → *māyā*, whose one consistent attribute is change.

🄱 (Pali, anicca); transitoriness or impermanence is one of the three marks of everything existing (→ *trilakshana*). Transitoriness is the fundamental property of everything conditioned—that which arises, dwells, and passes away. From it derive the other two marks of existence, suffering and nonessentiality (→ *duhkha*, → *anātman*). Impermanence is the basis of life, without which existence would not be possible; it is also the precondition for the possibility of attaining liberation. Without recognition of *anitya* there is no entry into the supramundane path (→ *ārya-mārga*); thus the insight leading to "stream entry" (→ *shrota-āpanna*) is often said to be recognition of the transitoriness or impermanence of existence.

The nature of existence as suffering is based on impermanence because the phenomena that comprise impermanence—arising, dwelling, and passing away—are inherently painful. The impermanence of the five aggregates (→ *skandha*) explains nonessentiality, since nothing that is impermanent (and thereby of the nature of suffering) can constitute a self. This is because the Hinduistic conception of the self (which determined that of Buddhism) entails permanence and freedom from suffering. In the Mahāyāna, the emptiness (→ *shūnyatā*) of all → dharmas is concluded from their impermanence.

Anja 🅉 Jap.; the pronunciation customary in Zen of a word otherwise pronounced *gyōja:* this is Japanese for the Skt. term *achārin*, denoting a Buddhist ascetic or wandering monk. *Anja* is the term for a Zen monk who attends the → *rōshi.*

Añjali 🄷 Skt.; 1. one of the postures of → Hatha-Yoga, whereby the hands are clasped with fingers pointing upward; 2. the Indian manner of greeting by pressing the palms of the hands together.

Añjali-mudrā 🄱 Skt. → mudrā 9

Anjin 🅉 (also anshin), Jap., lit. "heart-mind [→ *kokoro*] in peace"; peace of mind, a state of consciousness that according to Buddhism, is possible only through the experience of → enlightenment. In Zen the practice of → *zazen* is seen as the shortest path to peace of mind.

A renowned kōan, the example 41 in the → *Wu-men-ku-an*, is concerned with peace of mind:

Bodhidharma sat facing the wall. The second patriarch, who had been standing in the snow, cut off his own arm and said, "The mind of your student still finds no peace. I entreat you, master, please give it peace."

Bodhidharma said, "Bring your mind here and I'll give it peace."

The second patriarch said, "I've looked for the mind, but finally it can't be found."

Bodhidharma said, "Then I have given it peace thoroughly!"

Annamaya-Kosha 🄷 (Annamaya-Kośa), Skt.; the sheath of the body, also called the food sheath, which envelops the Self. It is the sheath best known and dearest to us (→ *kosha*).

Annamāyā-Purusha 🄷 (Annamāyā-Puruṣa), Skt.; in taking on the food sheath (→ *annamaya-kosha*), the *ātman*, the Self, becomes materialized consciousness, or the physical person.

Annapūrnā 🄷 Skt., lit. "one who gives nourishment"; 1. epithet for the divine Mother; one of the two resident divinities of → Kāshī and → Vishvanātha; 2. name of a Himalayan mountain range in Nepal.

Anrakudō 🅉 Jap. → *nehandō*

An Shih-kao 🄱 Parthian monk of the second century C.E. who went to China around 148 and was the first to translate Buddhist scriptures into Chinese. The translations contained primarily material on the practice of → *dhyāna* and explanations of enumerated categories. With the help of these texts he founded the so-called Dhyāna school of early Chinese Buddhism (→ Dhyāna Buddhism).

An Shih-kao was the crown prince of Parthia and was intended to assume the throne at his father's death. However, he entered a monastery. Presumably he traveled to China as a fugitive. He lived there for more than twenty years.

An Shih-kao is the first historical figure of Chinese Buddhism. He initiated the systematic translation of Buddhist texts through so-called "translation bureaus." Records concerning the number of works he translated vary between 34 and 176. These works may be divided into two categories: (1) texts on the practice of *dhyāna*, which also treat preparatory techniques such as counting the breath (→ *ānāpānasati*), → *kasina* exercises, → mindfulness of body, and so forth; and (2) texts that treat enumerated categories like the five → *skandhas* and the six → *āyatanas*. An Shih-kao used many Taoistic terms in his translations in an effort to convey specialized Buddhist expressions in Chinese.

Anshin 🅉 → *anjin*

Antahkarana 🄷 (Antaḥkaraṇa), or Antarindriya, Skt., lit "inner organ, inner instrument"; that with which we think, feel, remember, and discriminate. It consists of → *manas*, → *chitta*, → *buddhi*, and → *ahamkāra*. A fine form of → *prakriti*, the *antahkarana* is lifeless, but becomes active and effective because of the consciousness of the *ātman* that is reflected in it.

Antara-Kumbhaka 🄷 Skt., suspension of breath following a full inhalation (→ *prānāyāma*); a term used in → Hatha-Yoga.

Antaranga-Sādhana 🄷 (Antaraṇga-Sādhana), Skt., lit. "inner spiritual exercises"; the final three of → Patañjali's eight steps of Yoga, namely, → *dhāranā*, *dhyāna*, and *samādhi*.

Antarātman 🄷 Skt.; the inner Self, the divine spark; that which interprets all experience, develops spiritual knowledge, and in time attains God-realization.

Antarindriya 🄷 Skt.; synonymous with → *antahkarana.*

Antarmukha 🄷 Skt.; turned inward, observation of inner events. Similarities exist between this concept and the fifth stage of → Rāja-Yoga, the withdrawal of the senses from exterior objects. Both serve as preparation for concentration and meditation.

Antaryāmin 🅷 Skt., lit. "inner leader"; God as the Lord within us, our real Self (→ *ātman*), which is identical with divine consciousness.

Anubhāva 🅷 Skt., lit. *anu:* "toward something," *bhāva:* "becoming, real being"; experience, direct perception, realization, certainty. The indirect knowledge of the divine that is obtained from sacred scripture, when realized through experience, leads to the certainty of direct knowledge and thereby to enlightenment. This entire process is summed up in the term *anubhāva.*

Anubhāvi-Guru 🅷 Skt., lit. "the guru is eyewitness." The guru is the witness of the highest truth, because he has experienced and realized it.

Anurādhapura 🅱 until the tenth century the capital city of Ceylon. In Anurādhapura are to be found the Mahāvihāra monasteries (one of the main seats of the → Theravāda school) as well as Abhayagiri Vihāra (focal point for a liberal Mahāyāna-influenced Buddhism). When the capital was moved elsewhere, Anurādhapura fell into oblivion and only in the nineteenth century were the temples, monasteries and stupas—valuable examples of Singhalese Buddhist art—rediscovered.

In Anurādhapura are two gigantic *dagobas* (→ stūpa), Ruwanweli and Thūparāma, the beginnings of which go back to pre-Christian times, and which represent the original prototype of the stūpa. A shoot from the → Bodhi-tree was purportedly planted in Anurādhapura.

Anuruddha 🅱 important Singhalese scholar of the → Theravāda, who lived between the eighth and twelfth centuries. He is the author of the renowned work *Abhidhammattha-sangaha* (*Collection of the Meanings of the Abhidharma*), which expounds the entire teaching of the Theravāda. In many ways it is similar to the *Visuddhi-magga* of → Buddhaghosa, though it is shorter and harder to understand. In it Anuruddha treats particularly topics of psychology.

Other, less important works are ascribed to Anuruddha, such as the *Nāmarūpaparichcheda* (*Concerning Name and Form, Which Constitute the Individual Entity*) and the *Paramatthavinichchaya* (Resolution Concerning the Supreme Meaning).

Anushaya 🅱 (anuśaya), Skt. (Pali, anusaya), lit. "tendencies"; in Buddhism there are seven tendencies or latent passions: sensual desire → kāma), recalcitrance, view (→ *drishti*), scepticism (*vichikitsā*), arrogance (*māna*), craving for existence (→ *bhava*), and ignorance (→ *avidyā*). These properties, which subsist unconsciously, are considered tendencies in that they tend ever and again to reappear and call forth new arisings of sensual desire.

According to the → Theravāda and the → Sarvāstivāda, these tendencies are mental in nature and are connected with the thinking process. They have an object and moral causes and are evil. According to the → Mahāsānghikas, → Vātsīputrīyas, → Dharmaguptakas, and others, the *anushayas* are separate from thinking and have no object and no moral cause. They are considered morally neutral.

Anushthāna 🅷 (Anuṣṭhāna) Skt.; the carrying out of religious practices and rites. Instructions for such practices are found in the portion of the Vedas known as the → Karma-Kānda.

Anussati 🅱 Pali; contemplation. Practices described in the Hīnayāna sūtras that bring about both release from the three unwholesome roots (→ *akushala*) of desire, hatred, and delusion and comprehension of, and joy in, the Buddhist teaching. Usually the term refers to the six contemplations: on the Enlightened One (→ Buddha), the teaching (→ dharma), the community (→ *sangha*), discipline (→ *shīla*), generosity (→ *dāna*), and heavenly beings (→ *deva*). To those are frequently added four further contemplations: on death, the body, mindfulness of inhaling and exhaling (→ ānāpānasati), and peace.

Anuttara-samyaksambodhi 🅱 (anuttara-samyaksaṃbodhi), Skt., lit. "perfect universal enlightenment"; full form of *samyaksambodhi* (enlightenment of a complete buddha) (→ *samyaksambuddha*).

Anuvyavasāya 🅷 Skt.; a higher form of perception that arises from steadfast, determined reflection of the Self (*ātman*); a direct perception of physical and psychic data that is not filtered through conceptual thought.

Anvaya 🅷 Skt.; a method of affirmation, that of logical connection; that which agrees with our own experience and contradicts neither our experience nor logic.

Anzen 🆉 Jap., lit. "peaceful Zen"; an expression for properly practiced → *zazen*, in which body and mind come to lucidly wakeful calm.

Apadāna 🅱 Pali → *Khuddaka-nikāya*

Apara-Prakriti 🅷 (Apara-Prakṛti) Skt.; the realm of lower nature, in which everything material (e.g., bodies, plants, and inanimate matter) becomes manifest.

Apara-Vairāgya 🅗 Skt.; the first stage of renunciation, whereby one attains purification, peace, and detachment.

Apara-Vidyā 🅗 Skt., lit. "lesser knowledge"; relative or indirect knowledge gained through the senses and intellect; knowledge of science, art, or literature, hence secondhand knowledge, as when one "knows" a city from maps and books without having actually walked through its streets. Its opposite is → *para-vidyā.*

Aparigraha 🅗 Skt.; the state of being without possessions, desirelessness; the state in which one is free from the craving to hoard; one of the five virtues on the first step of → Rāja-Yoga as stipulated in the *Yoga-Sūtra* of → Patañjali. The other four are: *satya* (truthfulness), *ahimsā* (harmlessness), *asteya* (not stealing), and *brahmacharya* (temperance, continence). Together they form the Great Vow (→ Mahāvrata) that is made for all steps.

Aparoksha 🅗 (Aparokṣa), Skt., lit. "perceivable, not hidden," also: present, visible; a designation for consciousness, which is present in every human being as waking, dreaming, and deep sleep. A short work by → Shankara is entitled *Aparokshānubhūti* ("The Direct Experience of Reality").

Apāya 🅑 Skt.; inferior modes of existence; four lower or evil forms of existence in the cycle of existence of beings (→ *gati*). These are the hell beings (→ *naraka*), hungry ghosts (→ *preta*), animals, and "titans" (→ *asura*). The latter are sometimes reckoned with the higher modes of existence. They are missing altogether in some schools of southern Buddhism. The first three inferior modes of existence are also called "the three woeful paths."

Apramāna 🅑 Skt. → *brahma-vihāra*

Apramatta 🅗 Skt., lit. "not careless"; to remain true to one's internal law without going astray; to refrain from carelessly wasting one's hard-attained human embodiment, the spiritual purpose of which is to achieve liberation.

Apratisamkhyā-nirodha 🅑 (apratisaṃkhyā-nirodha), Skt.; unconscious, effortless dissolution (→ *nirodha*), dissolution without productive cause, without the participation of wisdom (→ *prajñā*). One of the unconditioned dharmas (→ *asamskrita*) of the Sarvāstivāda and Yogāchāra schools.

Music and dance of the Apsarās. (Stūpa relief from Bhārhut, 1st century B.C.E.)

Apratishthita-nirvāna 🅑 (apratiṣṭhita-nirvāṇa), Skt., lit. "unfixed, active extinction"; in this type of nirvāna according to the Mahāyāna view, the liberated one renounces remainderless extinction and withdrawal from the cycle of existence. Nevertheless, he is not tied to the compulsions of the samsaric world (→ samsāra) because of remaining on in order to lead and sustain all beings on the path to liberation. *Aprathishtha-nirvāna* is the nirvāna of a transcendent bodhisattva.

An active liberated one is free from desire, hatred, and delusion and acts without creating further karmic bonds. He is independent of natural law and can manifest himself in any desired form.

Apsarā 🅗 Skt., lit. "moving in water"; the *apsarās* are the celebrated celestial nymphs of → Indra's heaven.

Aside from → Urvashī, the Vedas mention few *apsarās*. They first play a role in the great epics. The *Rāmāyana* and the Purānas trace their origin to the → Churning of the Ocean. As the apsarās emerged from the water, neither the gods nor the → *asurās* wished to marry them, despite their charm and youthful beauty. Thus they were created for all, and they received the name Sumad-Ātmajās ("daughters of joy").

Ārādhana 🅗 Skt.; 1. veneration of the Divine,

adoration of and surrender to God, the striving to reach God; 2. prayer and repetition of the divine name.

Ārambha-Vāda 🅷 Skt.; a theory according to which creation is based on causality, hence it is the effect of a cause.

Āranyaka 🅷 (Aranyaka) Skt., lit. "belonging to the woods"; the Āranyakas are supplementary texts to the → Brāhmanas, which in turn are appended to the Vedic Samhitās; thus each belongs to a specific Veda. Meant as reading matter for forest hermits, they contain mystic reflections as well as descriptions of important rites, and represent the point of departure for the → Upanishads.

The rites asnd cultic observances described in the Āranyakas were held to be particularly sacred; anyone who performed them prematurely, without proper authorization, ran the risk of forfeiting life and limb. Students were therefore given such instruction not openly in the village, but in the solitude of the forest.

Ārati 🅷, or Aratrika, Skt.; evening worship in the form of a → *pūjā* with flowers, incense, and → *bhajana*, whereby candles are swung in front of the image of a deity or a holy figure.

Arghya 🅷 Skt.; sacrificial offering to a divinity during ritual Hindu worship (→ *pūjā);* it involves the use of flowers, leaves of a sacred tree, sandalwood paste, *durva* grass, and rice.

Arhat 🅱 🆉 Skt. (Pali, arahat; Chin., → *lohan*; Jap., *rakan*); "worthy one," who has attained the highest level of the Hīnayāna, that of "no-more-learning" on the supramundane path (→ *ārya-mārga*), and who possesses the certainty that all defilements (→ *āsrava*) and passions (→ *klesha*) have been extinguished and will not arise again in the future. The fruition of arhatship is the nirvāna with a vestige of conditions (→ *sopadhishesha-nirvāna*). The arhat attains full extinction immediately following this life.

The arhat was the ideal of early Buddhism. In contrast to the bodhisattva of the Mahāyāna who wishes to free all beings, with the arhat the main emphasis is on striving to gain his own salvation. He is fully free from the ten fetters of the cycle of existence (→ *samyojana*), to wit, belief in an individual entity, skepticism, clinging to rites and rules, sensual desire, resentment, craving for refined corporeality and non-corporeality, arrogance, excitement, and ignorance. An arhat is seen as a person all of whose impurities are dissolved, whose wishes are fulfilled, who has laid down his burden, attained his goal, and freed his mind through perfect understanding.

Arhat

Ārjava 🅷 Skt.; honesty, uprightness; one of the *daiva-gunas,* the godly qualities (→ *guna*); Krishna describes them and sets them against the demonic qualities in *Bhagavad-Gītā,* chapter 16. *Ārjava* is mentioned in the first verse of the chapter.

Arjuna 🅷 Skt., lit. "white"; one of the five → Pāndava brothers aod the warrior hero of the *Mahābhārata.* A friend and disciple of the → *āvatara* Krishna, Arjuna received spiritual instruction on the battlefield of → Kurukshetra, where Krishna served as his charioteer. Arjuna exemplifies the spiritual seeker through whom God instructs all of humanity. The story of his instruction by Krishna is related in the *Bhagavad-Gītā.*

Āropa 🅗 Skt.; synonymous with → *adhyāropa*

Arpitamano-Buddhi 🅗 Skt.; a mind that has been surrendered to God's will, one that through spiritual practice has become free of egoistic impulses.

Artha 🅗 Skt.; wealth, possession; one of the four goals of human aspiration, which, according to Hindu tradition, are not reprehensible so long as in pursuing them one has regard for moral precepts and → *dharma.* The other three are: *dharma* (righteousness, virtue), → *kāma* (sensual desire), and → *moksha* (liberation).

Arthana-Chandata-Kriyā 🅗 (Arthana-Candata-Kriyā), Skt.; one of the eight occult powers that may be gained by advanced yogis; that which enables yogis to carry out anything they wish to.

Arunāchala 🅗 (Aruṇācala), Skt., lit. "red mountain" or "hill of light"; a holy mountain in present-day Tamil Nadu, South India. According to Tamil legend, it is older than the Himalayas.

At the foot of the mountain lies Tiruvannāmalai, site of the great Arunāchalasvara Temple, which is consecrated to Shiva. The Arunāchala became known to Westerners through → Rāmana Maharshi, who meditated in its caves for four years and subsequently established an ashram near Tiruvannāmalai.

Arūpadhātu 🅑 Skt. → *triloka*

Arūpaloka 🅑 Skt. → *triloka*

Arūpasamādhi 🅑 Skt., Pali → four stages of formlessness

Āryadeva 🅑 disciple of Nāgārjuna and author of various short writings belonging to the Mādhyamaka. Āryadeva was probably born in Ceylon in the third century. Under the name of Kanadeva he is considered as the fifteenth patriarch in the Indian lineage of Zen. He was purportedly killed by enemies of Buddhism. His works, which are only fully extant in Tibetan and Chinese versions, are commentaries on the writings of his teacher Nāgārjuna.

The *Chatuh-shataka* (the *Four Hundred*) explains in 400 verses the absence of substantiality (→ *anātman*, → *shūnyatā*) through the use of negative dialectic. The *Shata-shāstra* (*Treatise on the Hundred Songs*) exercised a great influence on Buddhism. In it Āryadeva attempts to refute various philosophical theories opposed to Buddhism. It is one of the foundational works of the → San-lun (Three Treatises) school of Chinese Mādhyamaka.

Aryaman 🅗 Skt.; 1. one of the → Ādityas; lord of yearning and striving for spiritual progress; 2. the aspiring forces of Truth; the light of divine consciousness, which acts as a force.

Ārya-mārga 🅑 Skt. (Pali, ariya-magga); sacred supramundane path. It consists of the four stages of holiness, each of which is divided in two according to whether the noble one (→ *ārya-pudgala*) treading the path is still on the way or has already attained a given level of holiness, the "fruit" (*phala*). The first stage of the supramundane path is that of the "stream enterer" (→ *shrota-āpanna*), the second that of the "once-returner" (→ *sakridāgāmin*), the third that of the "never-returner" (→ *anāgāmin*), and the fourth and last that of the "worthy one" (→ arhat).

Ārya-pudgala 🅑 Skt. (Pali, *ariya-puggala*), lit. "noble one"; persons who are on one of the four stages of the supramundane path (→ *ārya-mārga*).

Ārya-Samāj 🅗 Skt.; nineteenth-century social and religious reform movement in India. It was founded by Svāmi → Dayānanda and was influential primarily in North India.

Ārya-satya 🅑 Skt. → four noble truths

Asamprajñāta-Samādhi 🅗 Skt. → *samprajñāta-samādhi*

Asamskrita 🅑 (asaṃskṛta), Skt. (Pali, asankhata), lit. "unconditioned, unproduced," refers to everything that is completely beyond conditioned existence, beyond arising, dwelling, and passing away. It is the opposite of → *samskrita.* In the original teaching, only → nirvāna was regarded as unconditioned. To this view the → Theravāda and → Vātsīputrīya schools remained true. The other schools, however, in the course of further development interpreted this notion in various ways.

The → Mahāsānghikas had nine categories of unconditioned dharmas: two kinds of dissolution (→ *nirodha*), of which one is achieved through the ability to discriminate (→ *pratisamkhyā-nirodha*) and is equated with nirvāna and the other, attained without discrimination (→ *apratisamkhyā-nirodha*) or without the participation of wisdom (→ *prajñā*) is applicable to future passions that in the case of worthy ones no longer arise. Also included among the nine are space (→ *ākāsha*), the limitlessness of space, the limitlessness of consciousness, nothingness, that which is beyond conscious and unconscious, the content of the teaching on conditioned arising (→ *pratītya-samutpāda*), and the → eightfold path.

The Sarvāstivāda school had three kinds of unconditioned: space and the two above-mentioned kinds of dissolution. To these three dharmas the → Yogāchāra school adds also extinction through a state of immovability in heavenly meditation, the ending of thinking and sensing by an arhat, and suchness (→ *tathatā*).

Under the unconditioned the Dharmaguptakas subsume suchness and "continuity in things," by which they understand that which in their nature does not change and in virtue of which, for example, good deeds do not produce evil fruits; also certain absorptions.

Āsana 🅗 Skt.; 1. any of the various bodily postures of → Hatha-Yoga; 2. place or mat on which a spiritual aspirant sits. The *Bhagavad-Gītā* states that the place should be firm, neither too high nor too low, and must be peaceful and clean; according to Indian tradition, it should be covered with a mat of sacred grass, over which a deerskin and a cloth are laid. For the Western devotee, any seat will suffice that is comfortable and allows the meditator to forget about the physical body; 3. body position in meditation, the third stage of yoga as set forth by → Patañjali.

For the correct posture, the back, neck, and head must be held still in an unbroken straight line. Indian aspirants customarily prefer to sit on the ground with the legs crossed, a secure position in the event that one loses consciousness of the body.

Āsana-Jaya 🅗 Skt.; mastery of a bodily posture of → Hatha-Yoga; the ability to maintain a position without difficulty.

Asanga 🅗 🅑 (Asaṇga) Skt., lit. "Untouched," "Unbound," "Unfettered."

🅗 The state of a free soul (→ *ātman*) that knows it consists not of body and mind but of absolute consciousness.

🅑 name of a founder of the → Yogāchāra school. He lived in the fourth century C.E. and came from a brahmin family living in present-day Peshawar. His brother was → Vasubandhu. Asanga is said to have been converted to Buddhism by a monk of the Mahīshāsaka school but quickly to have turned to the Mahāyāna. Asanga, influenced by the → Sarvāstivāda school, departed from Nāgārjuna's view of absence of substantiality and advanced an idealistic doctrine. According to tradition, he received his teaching directly from Maitreya, the future Buddha. Some researchers see behind this tradition the historical figure → Maitreyanātha.

The most important works ascribed to Asanga (sometimes also to Maitreyanātha) are the → *Yogāchārabhūmi-shāstra* and the *Mahāyāna-sūtrālankāra* (*Ornament of the Mahāyāna Sūtras*); definitely by Asanga is the *Mahāyāna-samparigraha* (*Compendium of the Mahāyāna*), a treatise composed in prose

Asanga

and verse that expounds the basic teaching of the Yogāchāra. It is only extant in Chinese and Tibetan translations. This work consists of ten parts dealing with the storehouse consciousness (→ *ālaya-vijñāna*); the theory that everything is produced by the mind, that is, is pure ideation; the achievement of insight into pure ideation; the → *pāramitās*; the → *bhūmis*; discipline (→ *shīla*); meditation; wisdom (→ *prajñā*); higher undifferentiated knowledge; the teaching of the three bodies of a buddha (→ *trikāya*). Sometimes the *Guhyasmaja tantra* is also attributed to Asanga, which would make Asanga a significant figure in Buddhist Tantrism.

Asat 🅗 Skt., lit. "nonbeing, nonexistence"; often called the basis of the material world. The concept is an abstract one, since we, as the instrument of being, cannot imagine nonbeing and can only speak of an absence of objects. Hence, *asat* also refers to the unknowable that is beyond being, that which is inaccessible to speech or thought and which eludes any definition. It is the qualityless Absolute of → Advaita-Vedānta.

Asceticism 🅑 → *dhūta*

Ashoka 🅑 (Aśoka); king of the Maurya kingdom of northern India, who reigned 272–236 B.C.E. and died ca. 231. He is one of the most important figures in ancient Indian history. A bloody campaign in the east and costly victory over Kalinga in 260 brought him to a psychological crisis and caused him to enter Buddhism. He became a lay follower and resolved to commence a "reign of dharma." From his edicts one learns that he undertook journeys of inspection to all parts of his realm in order to establish uprightness and virtue (→ dharma) throughout the country. Special functionaries were appointed to watch over the well-being of his subjects; on the basis of his pacifistic attitude he propagated vegetarianism and forbade animal sacrifice. He maintained friendly relations with all neighbor states. Under his rule Buddhism gained a foothold also in Ceylon: → Mahinda, a son of Ashoka's, led the missionary activity there.

Sources for the life of Ashoka are Pali chronicles in which he is described as a Buddhist king; and archaeological finds, especially the stele and pillar edicts that come from Ashoka himself. From these it is clear that he supported, in addition to the Buddhist *sangha*, a number of other religious communities in consonance with his duty as a ruler. The word *dharma*, frequently used in the edicts, cannot necessarily be equated with the Buddhist concept of dharma. Ashoka's dharma contains none of the fundamental teachings of Buddhism; rather it is a moral teaching that drew its inspiration from the various religious currents of the time. The ideal of Ashoka is a moral, happy life for his subjects; it embraces generosity, compassion, refraining from killing, obedience, love of truth, inner insight, etc. Under Ashoka the first intervention of state power in the affairs of the Buddhist community took place. The community was threatened by a schism whereby some of the monks were excluded from the *sangha* and forced to return to lay life (→ Buddhist councils).

Āshrama H (Āśrama), Skt.; 1. or *āshram,* a center for religious study and meditation; it can be a private home, a villa, a hermitage, or a monastery. Anyplace where spiritual seekers gather is an *ashram.* 2. the four stages of life for a Hindu, according to Vedic precepts: → *brahmacharya,* → *grihashta,* → *vānaprastha,* → *sannyāsa.*

Āshraya H (Āśraya), Skt., lit. "domicile, refuge"; consciousness as the basis of all things manifest and unmanifest. *Āshraya* is a concept found in Vedānta after Shankara's time.

Ashtamangala B Skt. → eight auspicious symbols

Ashtānga-Yoga H (Aṣṭāṇga-Yoga), Skt., lit. "eight-limbed yoga." The term refers specifically to → Rāja-Yoga, which contains eight limbs (→ *anga*) or steps.

Ashtāvakra H (Aṣṭāvakra), Skt., lit. "crippled eightfold"; a sage, the sone of → Kahoda. Despite his physical deformity, he became the teacher of → Patañjali. Ashtāvakra is said to be the author of the *Ashtāvakra-Samhitā* (or *Ashtāvakra-Gītā*), a brief treatise in essay form on the perceptions and truths of Vedānta. It is considered a standard work of → Advaita-Vedānta. (English trans. by Hari Prasad Shastri, 1949.)

Ashta-vimoksha B Skt. → eight liberations

Ashubha H B (aśubha), Skt., lit. "unfavorable, unfortunate, impure, ugly"; the opposite of *shubha* ("favorable, fortunate, auspicious").

H symbolic term from the world of opposites; its meaning is relative and subjective.

B contemplation of the ten disgusting objects. One of the forty meditation exercises (→ *bhāvanā*) introduced in the → *Visuddhi-magga,* which coincide essentially with the practice of charnel-ground contemplation. It is sometimes referred to as *ashubha* and also as contemplation of the thirty-two parts of the body (→ *satipatthāna,* → contemplation of the body).

Ashvaghosha B (Aśvaghoṣa); Indian poet and Mahāyāna philosopher who lived in the first to second centuries and is considered one of the most important Buddhist authors. His most important works are the drama *Shāriputra-prakarana,* a fragmentarily extant life of the Buddha (→ *Buddha-charita*), and the epic *Saudarananda-kāvya.* Tradition also ascribes to him the → *Mahāyānashraddhotpāda-shāstra.*

Ashvaghosha was originally a brahmin and is said to have been converted to Buddhism by a monk named Parshva. All of his works contain easily graspable instructions and similes concerning the Buddhist teaching. The author recounts, for example, in the epic about "beautiful Nanda" the story about the young Nanda, who after his entry into a monastery remains in love with his wife and only after much instruction from the Buddha is cured of this love and renounces the world. Ashvaghosha is one of the four great Buddhist sages who are called the "four suns that illuminate the world." The other three are → Deva, → Nāgārjuna, and → Kumāralāta, a sage of the → Sautrāntika school.

Ashvattha H (Aśvattha), Skt.; 1. the fig tree venerated by Indians as sacred; 2. the Tree of Life, represented as having its roots in heaven and its branches and leaves on earth. The tree is symbolic of cosmic existence, which has its roots in the transcendent realms, while its branches extend into the world. → *Brahman,* the One without a second, has as cosmic existence two aspects: the roots of Ashvattha are the unmanifest Absolute, its trunk and branches are manifest being.

Ashvatthāman 🅗 (Aśvatthāman), Skt.; general of the → Kauravas. According to the *Mahābhārata*, at the end of the great final battle, Ashvatthāman and two compatriots were the sole survivors among the Kauravas.

Ashvatthāman's wrath against the → Pāndavas was great; he wished to wreak revenge on Drishtadyumna, who had slain his father, Drona. The three Kauravas crept into the Pāndava camp at night and found Drishtadyumna asleep. Ashvatthāman slew him together with other sons of the Pāndavas. The following morning, they fled, but Draupadī wanted her sons' murders to be avenged and the murderers destroyed. → Yudhishthira interceded for Ashvatthāman because he was a brahman, and Draupadī agreed to spare his life if she were given the protective jewel that he wore on his forehead. Arjuna, Bhīma, and Krishna pursued him, overtook him, and forced him to relinquish the jewel, which they brought to Draupadī. She gave it to Yudhishthira, who wore it afterward on his forehead.

Ashvin 🅗 (Aśvin), Skt., lit. "horse driver"; twin physician-gods named Nāsatya and Dasra, symbols of nervous strength and vital energy. These two divinities appear in the heavens before dawn in a golden carriage drawn by horses or birds and guide their vehicle over a golden path (Hiranyarūpa) down to earth, in order to protect humanity from suffering and misery and to lead human beings to enlightenment.

The Ashvins are married to the daughters of Light and, like Castor and Pollux, represent powers that convey the → *rishis* as in a ship to the opposite shore and guard them from drowning in the sea of ignorance. They rule over the joyous mental and vital powers, energies that lead upward by means of the wine of divine bliss (*ānanda*), which the Ashvins administer to human beings. They themselves further traverse the waters of heavenly bliss with the aid of → *soma,* the draught that dissolves all obstacles and leads to *brahman* and thereby to final emancipation.

Asparsha 🅗 (Asparśa), Skt.; nonimprisonment. This state is attained when, despite the subject-object relationship, the → *jīva* views itself merely as a witness, and imprisonment is no longer possible, because events are now seen merely as the play of → *māyā*, not as reality. The path to this state is called Asparsha-Yoga; its goal is the knowledge of transcendent, nondual reality.

Āsrava 🅑 Skt. (Pali, āsava), lit. "outflow, secretion," also "defilement" or "canker." Three cankers constitute the root of all suffering and the cause that beings are caught in the cycle of rebirth: the canker of desires (Skt., *kāmāsrava*; Pali, *kāmāsava*), of becoming (Skt., *bhavāsrava*; Pali, *bhavāsava*), and of ignorance (Skt., *avidyāsrava*; Pali, *avijjāsava*). The extinction of these three cankers means the attainment of arhatship.

The teaching of the cankers represents the final development in the historical sequence of different explanations for entanglement in the cycle of existence. It encompasses the two forms of thirst (→ *trishnā*) and ignorance (→ *avidyā*), which constitute the root of suffering in the teaching on conditioned arising (→ *pratītya-samutpāda*).

Asteya 🅗 Skt., lit. "not stealing"; one of the five virtues on the first stage (*yama*) of → Rāja-Yoga, as stipulated in the *Yoga-Sūtra* of Patañjali. They make up the Great Vow (→ Mahāvrata) that applies to all eight stages. The four remaining virtues are: *ahimsā* (harmlessness), *satya* (truthfulness), *brahmacharya* (continence), and *aparigraha* (possessionlessness).

Asthangika-mārga 🅑 Skt. → eightfold path

Āstika 🅗 Skt., lit. "orthodox, true to the Veda"; name for the six philosphical systems, or → *darshanas,* which are characterized as orthodox because they acknowledge the authority of the Vedas.

Asura 🅗 🅑 (also āsura), Skt., demon, evil spirit.
🅗 In the *Rigveda*, the word means "god" or the modifier "divine." Only later is the term used in hymns to represent dark powers, just as the battle of the *asuras* against the gods later becomes a favorite theme. Both the *asuras* and the gods, as well as human beings, are created by → Prajāpati.

In the fourth verse of the sixteenth chapter of the *Bhagavad-Gītā*, Krishna enumerates the demonic qualities in human beings, which he sets against the godly qualities. The demonic qualities plunge man into dark ignorance; the godly ones lead to illumination.

🅑 the "titans"; one of the six modes of existence (→ *gati*), sometimes reckoned among the higher modes and sometimes among the lower (→ *apāya*). In the sense of a higher or good mode of existence, *asura* refers to the lower gods who dwell on the slopes or summit of the world mountain Sumeru or in castles of air. Seen as a lower or evil mode of existence, the *asuras* are the enemies of the gods (→ *deva*). They belong to the sensual desire realm (→ *triloka*). In the classifications of many southern Buddhist schools, the *asuras* are entirely omitted.

Atharvaveda 🅗 Skt.; the fourth Veda (→ Vedas), devoted to the "knowledge of magic spells." It originated much later than the *Rigveda*, the

Sāmaveda, and the *Yajurveda,*, and was for some time not recognized as part of the Vedas, even though a portion of its 731 hymns derive from the *Rigveda.* The *Atharvaveda* was not strictly fixed in content; thus a series of mostly brief → Upanishads was appended to it. Many of these are apocryphal in character and actually represent textbooks for later schools of Hinduism. Only a few of these, in particular the *Mundaka, Prasna,* and *Māndūkya-Upanishads,* are recognized and utilized by Vedantists.

The *Atharvaveda* preserves many traditions of folk belief as well as atonement ceremonies, curses, and marriage and burial songs of the most ancient Indian priesthood, the Atharvan. The work can further be seen as the oldest document of Indian medicine, as it contains numerous magical spells against illness. The *Atharvaveda* was indispensable for priests serving at the court, since at that time (from the second century B.C.E.) magic and politics were closely conjoined.

Atīsha **B** (Atīśa), also Atīsha Dimpamkara Shrījñāna, 980/90–1055, Buddhist scholar of royal family who, particularly, systematized the method for generating enlightened mind (→ bodhicitta). As patriarch of Magadha and teacher at the great monastic university Vikramashīla, he was invited to Tibet and spent the last twelve years of his life there. Atīsha founded the → Kadampa school and his teaching tradition had a decisive influence on → Tibetan Buddhism, especially on the school of → Tsongkhapa. His most important disciple was the Tibetan Dromtön (1003–64).

The so-called second spreading of the Buddhist teaching in Tibet was initiated in the tenth century by the west Tibetan royal family. First they sent subjects of theirs to India, as, for example, the translator → Rinchen Zangpo; later they sought out suitable Indian masters and their choice fell on Atīsha. In the year 1042 Atīsha entered west Tibet. Soon, however, he transferred his principal seat to Netang in central Tibet, whence his teachings spread rapidly.

In his principal work *Bodhipathapradīpa* (*Lamp on the Way to Enlightenment*), he gave a general overview of the way of the Great Vehicle (→ Mahāyāna) and introduced a threefold classification of practitioners: persons who strive for a good rebirth, those who have their own enlightenment as goal (→ Hīnayāna), and those whose motive is the salvation of all sentient beings (→ bodhisattva).

A main object of Atīsha's was to stop random or careless propagation of religious texts. Also due to him was the spread of the cult of → Tārā. He combined in his teaching both great traditions of the → *prajñāpāramitā*: the tradition of deep insight into nothingness (→ *shūnyatā*) as it was developed by Nāgārjuna, and the teaching stemming from Asanga of the all-encompassing action of enlightened mind.

Ati-yoga **B** Skt. → *dzogchen*

Ātmabodha **H** Skt., lit. "knowledge of the Self"; a short but significant treatise of → Advaita-Vedānta; attributed to → Shankara, it is repeatedly cited in the literature of this philosophy. In sixty-eight slokas, or verses, the text presents the most important concepts of Advaitā, such as *ātman, brahman,* the superimposition of forms of the manifest world on Brahman, and the method that leads to knowledge of the Self and hence to liberation. (English trans. in Leggett, 1978 and Menon 1964.)

Ātma-Chintana **H** (Ātma-Cintana), Skt.; thoughts directed to the Self.

Ātmadāna **H** Skt.; surrender, the gift of the Self to the Divine. Only when God is acknowledged as the most precious commodity is such surrender (→ *bhakti*) possible.

Ātma-Darshan **H** (Ātma-Darsan), Skt.; a vision of the real Self (→ *ātman*).

Ātma-Droha **H** Skt.; indifferent or hostile attitude toward the Self, the → *ātman*; the mental attitude of materialists, atheists, and the ignorant.

Ātma-Jñāna **H** Skt.; knowledge of the Self, which according to Vedānta is synonymous with knowledge of God.

Ātman **H** **B** Skt.; according to the Hindu understanding, the real immortal self of human beings, known in the West as the soul. It is the nonparticipating witness of the → *jīva,* beyond body and thought and, as absolute consciousness, identical with → brahman. Philosophically ātman is known as → *kūtastha.* In virtue of its identity with brahman, its special characteristic marks (*ātmakara*) are identical with those of brahman: eternal, absolute being; absolute consciousness; and absolute bliss.

In Buddhism the existence of an *ātman* is denied: neither within nor outside of physical and mental manifestations is there anything that could be designated as an independent, imperishable essence. (Also → *anātman,* → *skandha.*)

Ātmānanda **H** Skt.; the bliss of the Self (→ *ātman*).

Ātmaprasāda **H** Skt.; the clarity, serenity, and peace of the divine Self, which arise only when identification with the body and the mind is relinquished.

Ātmarati 🅗 Skt.; the peaceful bliss of the divine Self in each of us, experienced only in deep meditation and in → *samādhi.*

Ātmasamarpana 🅗 (Ātmasamarpaṇa), Skt.; absolute surrender and submission to God.

Ātma-Shakti 🅗 (Ātma-Śakti), Skt.; the forces of the divine Self (→ *ātman*) in the human being. As an aspect of absolute consciousness, they are capable of accepting all thought projections, both those that lead to liberation and those that lead to imprisonment in the world of appearances.

Ātmavīrya 🅗 Skt.; the strength and power of the Self that arise from the awareness of being one with God.

Ātmayajña 🅗 Skt.; the sacrifice of the small self, or "I," considered to be the most important offering on the path from darkness to light, from death to immortality.

AUM 🅗 Skt., → OM

Aupapāduka 🅗 🅑 Skt. → *chatur-yoni*

Aurobindo Ghose 🅗 (Ghosh), called Shrī (or Śri) Aurobindo, 1872–1950; Indian spiritual leader, author of numerous works on yoga and the wisdom of the → *Bhagavad-Gītā.* An ashram that is now known worldwide arose around Shrī Aurobindo. He developed the system of → Pūrna-Yoga, or Integral Yoga, and contributed much to the spread of the Eastern religious spirit in the West with his writings, which were strongly influenced by Western thought due to the humanistic education he had received in England. Aurobindo regarded the classical Yoga systems of Hinduism as one-sided paths on the "ascent" to the divine, which he also called the "supramental," remarking that "in India and elsewhere, men have tried to reach it by raising themselves up to it; what was not attained was a method to integrate it into one's life" (*Letters on Yoga,* vol. 1; trans. from German ed.). In his Integral Yoga, Aurobindo strove to connect the "ascent" to divine consciousness with an opening to the "descent" of the divine principle into the material world, whereby man ultimately becomes a "superman" of supramental abilities.

Although Shrī Aurobindo was close to the Western spirit, he saw its limits quite clearly. He writes: "Thought, intellect, the mental grew to be regarded in the West more and more as the supreme means and even as the supreme goal; in philosophy, the thinking mind is the beginning and the end. Truth must be discovered here through intellectual examination and speculation; even spiritual experience is required to subject itself to the tests of the intellect if it wishes to be declared as valid. . . . Western thought is no longer dynamic, it has sought a theory, not realization . . . it turned into intellectual speculation without any practical method of attaining the truth with the help of spiritual experience, spiritual discoveries, and spiritual transformation. . . . In the process of overintellectualization of the mental realm in Europe, what was lost was the spiritual path, the way that leads past the intellect, the bridge from the outer being to the inmost self" (ibid.).

The goal of Integral Yoga, in contrast to traditional Hindu Yoga and the way of Western spirituality, is characterized by Aurobindo as follows: "Not by 'thinking through' the whole of reality, but by a conversion of consciousness is it possible to move from ignorance to knowledge, that knowledge by which we are known. The *integral* way to truth consists of turning from the outward to a direct and essentially inner consciousness, extending the consciousness beyond the limits of body and ego, raising it by means of inner will and aspiration and opening it to the light until in its ascent it transcends the mental; further, in bringing about a descent of the supramental divine through self-giving and surrender and the continuous evolution of mental, life, and body. This is what is called truth and the goal of our Yoga" (ibid.).

The chief works of Shrī Aurobindo include *The Divine Life* and *The Synthesis of Yoga.*

Aurobindo Ghose was born in Calcutta, the son of Krishna Dhan Ghose, a physician who was affiliated with the → *Brāhmo Samāj* and who had strong leanings toward Western thought. From his earliest years, Aurobindo was educated in a European-directed school; when he was seven his father sent him to England, where he attended the renowned Saint Paul's School and later received a scholarship to King's College, Cambridge. There he studied Latin, Greek, French, and German, and received a comprehensive humanistic education. When in 1893 his father died, he returned to India, where he became professor of English language and literature at Baroda College and later was named director of National College. As he had already done in England, Aurobindo actively worked for the liberation of India from British colonial power; ultimately he was imprisoned for a year for his underground activities.

It was during his term in prison that Aurobindo first had spiritual experiences; following his release in 1909, he abandoned his political activities and turned wholly toward the practice of Yoga, which over the years led him to even deeper religious experiences. In 1910 he was again threatened with arrest but escaped to the French enclave at Pondicherry, where he was to remain until his death. There he met Mira Alfassa, the daughter of a Turkish-Egyptian family who had grown up in France; from 1920 on she was Aurobindo's constant companion.

The Aurobindo ashram owes its inception to the energies of Mira Alfassa, now known simply as "the Mother." After Shrī Aurobindo's death, she also founded her own ashram-city, "Auroville," where devotees of Shrī Aurobindo and the Mother live and work, seeking to realize the teachings of Aurobindo by leading an active life in the world while governed by spiritual principles.

Avachcheda-Vāda H (Avacceda-Vāda), Skt.; the view that the → *jīva* is a form of → *brahman,* i.e., a manifestation of the Absolute, which, however, is limited due to ignorance (→ *avidyā*), which superimposes on the Absolute a veil of identification with the body and mind.

Avadāna B Skt., lit. "great deed"; Buddhist literary genre marking a transitional stage between Hīnayāna and Mahāyāna, in which strong tendencies towards glorification of the bodhisattva ideal are in evidence. The *avadānas* consist of legends about the previous lives of Buddhist saints that were recited by monks to lay believers. They were mainly intended to show that good deeds bring about good results, and bad deeds, bad results. Among the most important collections of such tales are the second-century *Avadāna-shataka* (*A Hundred Heroic Deeds*) and the especially popular *Divyāvadāna* (*Divine Deeds*).

Avadhūta H Skt.; a human being who has attained divine knowledge and has relinquished all ties to the world.

Avadhūt-Gītā H Skt., lit. "song of an illumined one"; a work consisting of 193 verses, composed by Mahātmā Dattatreya, who is presumed to have lived in the fourth century B.C.E.

Nothing is known of Dattatreya's life except that he lived long before Christ but after Krishna, and that he wrote this one work only. As brief as the *Avadhūt-Gītā* is, it summarizes in a nutshell the spirit of → *advaita* and the → Upanishads and thus is highly prized by advanced seekers.

Avalokiteshvara B Z (Avalokiteśvara), Skt.; one of the most important → bodhisattvas of the Mahāyāna. The literal meaning of *Avalokiteshvara* is variously interpreted. One interpretation is the "Lord Who Looks Down," in which the last component of the name is taken to be *īshvara,* "lord." Another interpretation is "He Who Hears the Sounds [Outcries] of the World" or also the "Sound That Illumines the World," in which *svara,* "sound" is regarded as the final component of the name. In any case, Avalokiteshvara embodies one of the two fundamental aspects of buddhahood, compassion (→ *karunā*), in virtue of which he is often given the epithet *Mahākarunā,* "Great Compassion." The other fundamental aspect of buddhahood is wisdom (→ *prajñā*), which is embodied by the bodhisattva → Mañjushrī. Avalokiteshvara is the power of the buddha Amitābha manifested as a bodhisattva and appears as his helper (→ Pure Land school). His limitless compassion expresses itself in his wonderful ability to help all beings who turn to him at times of extreme danger. In folk belief, Avalokiteshvara also protects from natural catastrophe and grants blessings to children.

The bodhisattva Avalokiteshvara in his eleven-headed, thousand-armed form

Iconographically, thirty-three different ways of depicting Avalokiteshvara are known, distinguished by the number of heads and arms as well as by the attributes held in the hands. Frequently he is shown with a thousand arms, a thousand eyes, and eleven faces. Usually adorning his head is a small image of Buddha Amitābha, which is his surest mark of recognition. In his hands he often holds a blue lotus blossom (hence his epithet *Padmapāni*, "Lotus Holder"), a rosary, and a vase of nectar. The numerous arms symbolize his ability to work for the welfare of sentient beings in a manner corresponding to any situation.

In his eleven-faced form, Avalokiteshvara wears as a crown the heads of nine bodhisattvas and that of a buddha; the latter is the head of Buddha Amitābha. Each triad of bodhisattva heads embodies compassion for suffering beings, wrath against evil, and joy concerning good. According to another view, the ten heads symbolize the ten stages of the career of a bodhisattva (→ *bhūmi*) and the fruition of buddhahood.

A legend explains the derivation of the eleven-faced, thousand-armed form. As Avalokiteshvara looked down on the suffering of the world, his head literally burst from pain; his spiritual father Amitābha put the pieces back together as nine new heads. The wish to help all beings caused Avalokiteshvara to grow a thousand arms, in the palm of each of which is an eye. Many depictions represent Avalokiteshvara as the helper of being in the six realms of existence (→ *gati*): Avalokiteshvara with a horse's head or riding on a lion rescues animals, the thousand-armed Avalokiteshvara rescues hell beings; the eleven-faced one, the → *asuras*.

In China Avalokiteshvara is venerated under the name → Kuan-yin, in Japan under the name Kannon (also Kanzeon or Kwannon), and in both countries is generally considered to be female. The Tibetan form of Avalokiteshvara is → Chenresi.

Āvarana **H** (Āvaraṇa), Skt., lit. "concealing"; the power of ignorance (→ *avidyā*) to cast a veil over *brahman* (see also → *vikshepa*).

Avasthā **H** Skt.; a plane or state of consciousness. There are four *avasthās*: → *jāgrat* (the waking state, also known in Vedānta as → *vaishvānara*), → *svapna* (dreaming sleep), → *sushupti* (deep sleep), and → *turīya* ("the fourth").

Avatamsaka-sūtra **B** Skt. → *Buddhāvatamsaka-sūtra*

Avatāra **H**, or Avatār, Skt., lit. "descent"; an incarnation of divine consciousness on earth. An *avatāra* is born not as the result of karma (as are ordinary human beings) but from an act of free will, and such a one is conscious of his divine mission throughout his life. He appears in order to establish new pathways for religious realization and to adapt them to the age in which he is born; he is able to confer divine knowledge upon his fellow human beings by a touch, a glance, or even through his silence. Because he is free from all bonds of the ego, he is beyond duality.

Vishnu in his avataric incarnation as Rāma.

According to the traditional Hindu view, it is Vishnu alone who is incarnated. Tradition speaks of ten incarnations: (1) Matsya, the fish; (2) Kūrma, the tortoise; (3) Varāha, the boar; (4) Narasimha, the man-lion; (5) Vāmana, the dwarf; (6) Parashu-Rāma, or Rāma the Ax Wielder; (7) Rāma of the *Rāmāyana*; (8) Krishna; (9) Buddha; (10) Kalki. Vishnu has not yet appeared in the last-named form, which he will assume only at the end of the Iron Age (→ *kaliyuga*), when he will arrive with drawn sword on a white horse to annihilate the wicked and restore → *dharma*. Independent of this tradition, however, Hindus also view Jesus as an *avatāra*.

Āvesha **H** (Āveśa), Skt.; the ability of advanced yogis to enter other bodies.

Avidyā **H** **B** **Z** Skt., lit. "ignorance, nescience." **H** As a Vedantic term, *avidyā* refers to both individual and cosmic ignorance. Individual ignorance is the inability to distinguish between the transient and the intransient, between the real and the unreal; cosmic ignorance is → *māyā.* Its effect is the same as that of → *ajñāna.*

B Z (Pali, avijjā); ignorance or delusion, that is, noncognizance of the → four noble truths, the three precious ones (→ *triratna*), and the law of → karma. *Avidyā* is the first part in the nexus of conditionality (→ *pratītya-samutpāda*), which leads to entanglement in the world of → samsāra as well as to the three cankers (→ *āsrava*). It is one of the passions (→ *klesha*) and the last of the ten fetters (→ *samyojana*).

Avidyā is considered as the root of everything unwholesome in the world and is defined as ignorance of the suffering-ridden character of existence. It is that state of mind that does not correspond to reality, that holds illusory phenomena for reality, and brings forth suffering. Ignorance occasions craving (→ *trishnā*) and is thereby the essential factor binding beings to the cycle of rebirth. According to the Mahayana view, *avidyā* with regard to the emptiness (→ *shūnyatā)* of appearances entails that a person who is not enlightened will take the phenomenal world to be the only reality and thus conceal from himself the essential truth.

Avidyā is differently expounded by the individual Mahāyāna schools. In → Mādhyamaka ignorance refers to the determination of the mind through a priori ideas and concepts that permit beings to construct an ideal world, that confer upon the everyday world its forms and manifold quality, and that thus block vision of reality. *Avidyā* is thus the nonrecognition of the true nature of the world, which is emptiness (*shūnyatā*), and the mistaken understanding of the nature of phenomena. In this way it has a double function: ignorance veils the true nature and also constructs the illusory appearance; the two condition each other mutually. In this system *avidyā* characterizes the conventional reality.

For the → Sautrāntikas and → Vaibhāshikas *avidyā* means seeing the world as unitary and enduring, whereas in reality it is manifold and impermanent. Ignorance confers substantiality on the world and its appearances. In the → Yogāchāra view *avidyā* means seeing the object as a unit independent of consciousness, when in reality it is identical with it.

Avidyā-Māyā H Skt., lit. "*māyā* of ignorance"; the illusion that leads to a dualistic view of the world. It results in anger, greed, and other driving feelings that bind us to the phenomenal world. Its opposite is *vidyā-māyā.* Both forms of *māyā* belong to the world of relativity. (See also → *māyā.*)

Aviveka H Skt.; the inability to discriminate, to distinguish between what is real and what is unreal, what is permanent and what is transitory, what leads to God and what leads to attachment to the world.

Avyakta H Skt., lit. "unmanifest"; latent, hidden, not objectified; the power that is present even when the world of appearances is not yet manifest.

Ayam Ātman Brahman H Skt., lit. "This Self is *brahman*"; one of the → *mahāvākyas,* the great Vedic precepts; it confirms that one's true self is not the body or mind but rather is identical with → *brahman.*

Āyatana B Skt., Pali; fields, especially the twelve sense fields, namely, the five sense organs (eye, ear, nose, tongue, body) and the objects corresponding to them (form, sound, odor, taste, bodily sensations), as well as the sixth sense organ (the thinking mind [→ *manas*]), and its objects (ideas or → dharmas). Sometimes also *āyatana* refers only to the objects of the sense organs (→ *shadāyatana*).

Āyurveda H Skt., lit. "the knowledge [science] of [long] life [or health]"; an ancient system of healing, sometimes regarded as an → Upaveda and specifically as a later supplement to the → *Atharvaveda.*

The standard texts of Āyurveda include the *Charaka-Samhitā,* composed by Charaka, a physician who lived around the first century C.E. (according to Stutley 1977), and the *Sushruta-Samhitā* of Sushruta, who lived approximately a century later. Both works declare Āyurveda to be of divine origin, although their authors differ regarding the details of its revelation. According to Charaka, → Indra revealed the Āyurveda to Bharadvāja, whose disciples included Ātreya Punarvasu, the legendary founder of the first school of Indian medicine. One of Ātreya Punarvasu's followers was Agnivesha, whose teachings form the basis of Charaka's work; hence, the *Charaka-Samhitā* is also known as the *Agnivesha-Tantra.* According to Sushruta, Indra revealed the Āyurveda to the Vedic king Divodāsa, whose teachings were passed on and formed the basis of the *Sushruta-Samhitā.*

Ayurvedic diagnosis and therapy are based on a system of three dynamic principles or "humors" (→ *dosha*) that are associated with the three basic qualities (→ *guna*) of the material principle → *prakriti.* Illness is caused by an imbalance in one or more *doshas,* which in combination also create the various constitutional types of human beings. The remedies, which work primarily through their taste (*rasa*), act either to strengthen or to pacify the *dosha,* and thus are used to restore the balance of forces in the organism.

Āyurveda is a holistic system of treatment, in which herbal therapy plays a major role, while the correct conduct of one's life in a religious sense is considered essential for the maintenance of health. For an introduction to the basic principles of Āyurveda, see Vasant Lad, *Ayurveda: The Science of Self-Healing* (Santa Fe, N.M., 1984).

B

Babu 🅗 Hindi, lit. "lord" also, a country squire or distinguished man. This title of respect usually follows one's first name, as in Girish Babu.

Bahiranga-Sādhana 🅗 (Bahiraṇga-Sādhana), Skt.; the development of a gradual distaste for the outer world, the beginning of the spiritual path. The first three stages of → Patañjali's yoga (*yama, niyama,* and *āsana*) are expedient means for the development of *bahiranga-sādhana.*

Bahirātman 🅗 Skt.; the outer self, body and mind; from *bahir:* "outer," and → *ātman*, the Self.

Bahir-Mukha 🅗 Skt., lit. "turning away, directed outward"; our mind is impelled by the senses to turn away from our true self (→ *ātman*) and toward the outer world of appearances. All the empirical sciences have arisen in this way.

Bāhya-Pūjā 🅗 Skt.; external form of devotion to divinities or → *avatāras,* resulting in the various → *pūjās* of Hinduism, with their basis in the → Karma-Kānda of the Vedas.

Bala 🅑 Skt., Pali, lit. "power"; five spiritual powers or faculties, developed through strengthening the five roots (→ *indriya*), that make possible the attainment of enlightenment. These powers are (1) the power of faith (→ *shraddhā*), which precludes all false belief; (2) the power of exertion (→ *vīrya*), which leads to overcoming all that is unwholesome through the application of the → four perfect efforts; (3) the power of mindfulness, that is, perfect mindfulness achieved through application of the four foundations of mindfulness (→ *satipatthāna*); (4) the power of → *samādhi*, that is, the practice of → *dhyāna* leading to the elimination of passions; (5) the power of wisdom (→ *prajñā*), which rests on insight into the → four noble truths and leads to the knowledge that liberates.

Balarāma 🅗, the elder brother of → Krishna. The *Mahābhārata* relates that → Vishnu pulled a white hair and a black hair from his head; these became Balarāma, whose skin was light, and Krishna, whose dark skin is represented iconographically by the color blue.

Bali 🅗 or Mahābali; a benevolent and virtuous → Daitya king, the son of → Vairochana and the husband of Vindhyavali. His capital city was Mahābalipura. Having been defeated in battle, he was permitted to decide whether to enter heaven accompanied by a hundred fools or to enter hell accompanied by one wise man. He chose hell, saying, "With the help of a sage I can easily turn hell into heaven, but a hundred fools will make even heaven into hell."

By his atonement and surrender, Bali vanquished Indra, the lord of the firmament, humbled other gods, and extended his dominion to cover heaven, earth, and the underworld. When the gods begged Vishnu for protection, he manifested himself in his dwarf incarnation (→ *avatāra*) in order to put a stop to Bali. The dwarf asked the king to grant him the space he could cover in three steps. When Bali granted him this boon, the dwarf covered heaven and earth in two steps, but out of respect for Bali's pure character allowed him to retain the lower regions (→ Pātāla). The origin of this legend is found in the *Rigveda,* where Vishnu traverses heaven, earth, and the lower region in three steps that symbolize the rising, zenith, and setting of the sun.

Bāmiyān 🅑 Buddhist holy place in Afghanistan with rock-cut caves dating from 300 to 600 C.E. It is composed of numerous small interconnected caves on different levels carved into a cliff face over more than two kilometers. The caves served as assembly rooms for monks living nearby and as → *chaityas.* The Buddhism of Bāmiyān, which was of the Mahāyāna type, was wiped out as a result of invasions by Islamic peoples and the Mongols (13th century).

Especially noteworthy are the domelike ceilings of

the caves, which have on them depictions of buddha paradises (→ pure land) with their ruling buddhas, sometimes in clear mandala form. Against the cliff face are two colossal Buddha figures, one thirty-five and one fifty-three meters tall, today in badly damaged condition. They were originally painted and gilded. The faces are missing; they were probably made of gilded wood. The various artistic representations indicate that the Buddha was understood as a personification of the universe and that the countless buddhas of all ages were considered to be manifestations of him. The style shows Sassanian, Indian, and Central Asian influence.

Bāna 🅗 (Bāṇa), a → Daitya, the eldest son of → Bali, also known by the names Tripura and Vairochi. He was Shiva's friend and Vishnu's enemy.

Bāna's daughter → Ushā fell in love with → Aniruddha, Krishna's grandson, and abducted him by means of her magical powers. Krishna, → Balarāma, and → Pradyumna wanted to rescue him but met resistance from Bāna, who was supported by Shiva and → Skanda, the god of war. Shiva was vanquished by Krishna, Skanda was wounded, and Bāna's many arms were knocked off by Krishna's missile weapon. Shiva then pleaded for Bāna's life, and Krishna spared him.

Bandha 🅗 Skt.; bondage, dependence, from *bandh:* to fetter or bind. Bondage to the sense objects of the manifest world is the greatest impediment to spiritual development.

Banka 🅩 Jap., lit. "evening section"; the evening sūtra recitation, part of the daily routine in a Zen monastery (→ *tera*).

Banka-zōji 🅩 Jap., lit. "*banka* cleanup"; cleaning of the interior rooms of a Zen monastery after the evening sūtra recitation (→ *banka*). A form of → *samu* that is part of the daily routine of a Zen monastery (→ *tera*).

Bankei Eitaku (Yōtaku) 🅩 also Bankei Kokushi, 1622–93; Japanese Zen master of the → Rinzai school; one of the most popular Zen masters of Japan and quite the most famous of his time.

In his early years Bankei wandered through Japan and sought out numerous Zen masters. Then for two years he retreated to a hermitage in order to do nothing but practice → *zazen.* During this time he neglected his health to such an extent that he had almost died of consumption when, one morning as he coughed up a clot of blood, he suddenly had an enlightenment experience. Later he became a disciple of the Chinese Zen master Tao-che Ch'ao-yüan (Jap., Dōsha Chōgen, ca. 1600–61) in Nagasaki, who led him to profound enlightenment and bestowed upon him the seal of confirmation (→ *inka-shōmei*). Since Bankei was the only student who had received the confirmation of this master, the latter advised him to make off during the night—as → Hui-neng and others in similar situations before him had done—in order to avoid bringing on himself the envy of his fellow students.

Since Bankei found that nobody understood his living words, spoken out of profound experience, he lived for many years in hiding before he gave himself out as a Zen master and thousands of students, monks and lay people, from all classes of society, thronged around him.

In 1672 Bankei was appointed abbot of the Myōshin-ji monastery in Kyōto by the imperial house. The power of his mind and his ability to present the truth of Zen in the language of the people in a way that was simple and widely comprehensible, contributed greatly to the revival of Rinzai Zen in Japan, which to a great extent had rigidified into concern with outer forms. In this regard Bankei was a precursor of the sixty-four-years younger → Hakuin Zenji. In spite of the large number of his studnts, Bankei confirmed only a few dharma successors.

Although he himself left no writings behind and forbade his students to record his teachings, a number of his presentations and dialogues were written down by followers. (A selection of them can be found in S. Waddell 1984.)

Bansan 🅩 Jap., lit. "evening devotion"; evening sūtra recitation in a Zen monastery; synonym for → *banka.*

Banzan Hōshaku 🅩 Jap. for → P'an-shan Pao-chi

Bardo 🅑 (bar-do), Tib., lit. "in-between state"; already in Hīnayāna and Mahāyāna works of around the second century there are indications of a concept of a state that connects the death of an individual with his following rebirth. This conception was further elaborated in the teachings of the → Vajrayāna. Finally, in the → *Nāro chödrug* and in the → *Bardo thödol,* six kinds of in-between states were differentiated: (1) the *bardo* of birth, (2) dream *bardo,* (3) *bardo* of meditation (→ *dhyāna*), (4) *bardo* of the moment of death, (5) *bardo* of supreme reality (→ *dharmatā*), and (6) *bardo* of becoming. While the first three *bardos* characterize the present life as a phase of "suspended states," the last three *bardos* encompass the forty-nine-day-long process of death and rebirth.

Bardo thödol 🅑 (bar-do thos-grol), Tib., lit. "Liberation through Hearing in the In-between State"; a text known as the *Tibetan Book of the Dead* composed of a group of instructions stemming from → Padmasambhava that were elaborated into a systematic teaching in the form of a → *terma* in the 14th century. The process of death and rebirth is set forth in this work as three phases or in-between states (→ *bardo*), which are closely connected with the three bodies of a buddha (→ *trikāya*): (1) in the *bardo* of the moment of death (*dharmakāya*) a dazzling white light manifests; (2) in the *bardo* of supreme reality (*sambhogakāya*) lights of five colors appear in the forms of mandalas, which emanate from the basic structure of the five → *buddhakulas*; (3) in the *bardo* of becoming (nirmānakāya) light phenomena of lesser brilliance appear that correspond to the six modes of existence (→ *bhavachakra*). All three phases offer the possibility, through hearing the appropriate instructions, for a being to recognize the nature of his own mind and so attain liberation (→ nirvāna).

Initiation cards used in the ritual reading of the *Bardo Thödol*. The symbols shown are the mystical jewel (*chintāmani*), lotus, double *vajra*, sword, *dharmachakra*, and bell (*ghantā*) with *vajra* handle.

A tradition of the *bardo* teaching is contained in the → *Nāro chödrug*, in the → *dzogchen* tradition, and in the → Bön school. This teaching was originally conceived as a meditation instruction for practitioners for whom the process of death offered the best possibility of consummating the → *sādhana* practiced during their lifetimes. In the course of centuries, however, it was expanded into a death ritual consisting of ceremonies and readings for the deceased. The death ritual is made up of several parts, in which are described, among other things, the process of dying, the appearances of light in the *bardo*, and the technique of searching out the place of rebirth.

The process of dying is presented in the *Bardo thödol* as a gradual dissolution of the body-mind organization, as a deterioration of the five → skandhas. With the falling away of external reality comes the *bardo* of the moment of death, in which the true nature of the mind is experienced as a brilliant light. If the dying person does not succeed in identifying with this experience, he falls into a state of unconsciousness for three or four days, during which time a so-called consciousness body is formed, which is the subject of the experiences to come.

In the following *bardo* of supreme reality (→ *dharmatā*), which lasts fourteen days, the consciousness perceives the forms of forty-two peaceful and fifty-eight wrathful deities (→ forms of manifestation). These appear as part of the unfolding of a mandala. The detailed description of these forms in the *Bardo thödol* is possible through the fact that a *sādhana* that encompasses the spectrum of human feelings is used to convey these experiences. The emptiness (→ *shūnyatā*) aspect is represented by the peaceful deities, and the luminosity or clarity aspect by the wrathful deities.

If the consciousness body fails also here to recognize these light appearances as its own projections, then the twenty-eight-day-long *bardo* of becoming begins. In the first three weeks of this in-between state, the consciousness relives its previous deeds (→ karma) and, in a manner corresponding to the development of that process, is prepared for the search, during the last seven days, for one of the six realms of rebirth.

There are already several translations of the *Bardo thödol* into English. The most noteworthy are Evans-Wentz 1960 and Fremantle & Trungpa 1987.

Bashashita 🅉 Jap. name for the twenty-fifth patriarch in the Indian lineage of → Zen.

Bashō Esei 🅉 Jap. for → Pa-chiao Hui-ch'ing

Baso Dōitsu 🅉 Jap. for → Ma-tsu Tao-i

Bassui Zenji 🅉 also Bassui Tokushō, 1327–87; Japanese Zen master of the → Rinzai school and one of the outstanding Zen masters of Japan. The death of his father when Bassui was seven years old drove him to try to resolve the question of his being. His intensive doubtful questioning (→ *dai-gedan*) led him to several enlightenment experiences, but he was never content with what he had attained but rather searched ever deeper. He began searching for a Zen master who could lead him to inner peace. At the age of twenty-nine, he received monastic ordination but did not, however, enter a monastery, since he felt no connection to the ritual activity and the comfortable life in many monasteries.

"On his numerous pilgrimages he stubbornly refused to remain overnight in a temple, but insisted on staying in some isolated hut high up on a hill or a mountain, where he would sit hour after hour doing zazen away from the distractions of the temple. To stay awake he would often climb a tree, perch among the branches, and deeply ponder his natural koan, 'Who is the master?' far into the night, oblivious to wind and rain. In the morning, with virtually no sleep or food, he would go to the temple or monastery for an encounter with the master" (Kapleau 1980, p. 165).

Finally he found a master who was right for him, Kohō Zenji. Kohō ultimately led him to profound enlightenment, in which "all his previous concepts, beliefs, and views were entirely annihilated in the fire of his overwhelming experience" and through which his profound doubt finally vanished. After receiving → *inka-shōmei* from Kohō, he continued his life of wandering and for many years opposed the efforts of Zen students to make him their master.

At the age of fifty he finally settled in a hermitage in the mountains, where students soon gathered around him. He now no longer drove them away. Finally he consented to become abbot of a Zen monastery and there, until his death, he led monks and lay people on the path of Zen. Shortly before passing away at the age of sixty, he sat upright in the lotus position and said to those assembled: "Don't be fooled! Look closely! What is this?" He repeated this loudly and then calmly died.

Bassui Zenji wrote little, nevertheless his "words of dharma" and the letters he wrote to a number of students are among the most penetrating writings in the literature of Zen. A translation of his "Dharma Talk" and some of his letters can be found in Kapleau 1980.

In a letter to "a man from Kumasaka," Bassui Zenji wrote: "All phenomena in the world are illusory, they have no abiding substance. Sentient beings no less than Buddhas are like images reflected in water. One who does not see the true nature of things mistakes shadow for substance. This is to say, in zazen the state of emptiness and quiet which results from the diminution of thought is often confused with one's Face before one's parents were born [→ *honrai-no-memmoku*]. But this serenity is also a reflection upon the water. You must advance beyond the stage where your reason is of any avail. In this extremity of not knowing what to think or do, ask yourself: 'Who is the master?' He will become your intimate only after you have broken a walking stick made from a rabbit's horn or crushed a chunk of ice in fire. Tell me now, who is this most intimate of yours? Today is the eighth of the month. Tomorrow is the thirteenth!"

Bathing of the Buddha 🅑 a ceremony, especially one performed in China on the birthday of the historical Buddha → Shākyamuni, which falls on the eighth day of the fourth month. In it a miniature image of Shākyamuni, sitting on a lotus throne with right hand pointing toward Heaven and left hand toward Earth, is bathed with water and flower offerings are made. The entire → *sangha* participates in this ceremony.

This custom, already known in India, is based on the tradition that immediately after his birth in the → Lumbini Grove, nine → *nāgas* sprinkled Siddhartha Guatma, later the Buddha Shākyamuni, with water.

Benares discourse 🅑 the first discourse of Buddha → Shākyamuni after his awakening (→ *bodhi*). It was given in Sarnath near Benares. The content of this first teaching was the → four noble truths and the → eightfold path. This first discourse is often referred to as "the first turning of the wheel of dharma" (*dharma-chakra*).

Ben'en 🅩 also Enni Ben'en or Enju Ben'en, also known as Shōichi (Shōitsu) Kokushi, 1202–80); an early Japanese Zen master of the Yogi lineage of Rinzai (→ Yōgi school). During a six-year stay in China he received the seal of confirmation (→ *inka-shōmei*) from the Chinese Zen master → Wu-chun Shih-fan (Jap., Bushun [Mujun] Shiban). After his return to Japan, he made a major contribution toward the establishment of Zen there.

At the age of eight Ben'en began to study the teachings of the → Tendai school and later of the → Shingon school of Japanese Buddhism. In 1235 he went to China and experienced enlightenment under Master Wu-chun. After the latter had confirmed him, he sought out other Zen masters of the Sung period in order to deepen his experience. In 1241 he returned to Japan and was active as a Zen master in various monasteries. He influenced the practices of the mystical schools of Tendai and Shingon through his style of Zen training.

In 1255 he became the first abbot of the Tōfuku-ji monastery in Kyōto; he also assumed leadership of monasteries like the Jufuku-ji in Kamakura and the Kennin-ji in Kyōto. All three monasteries belong to the → *gosan* of Kyōto or of Kamakura and are among the most important Zen monasteries in Japan. Ben'en had more than thirty dharma successors (→ *hassu*). Posthumously he received the honorific titles of Shōichi Kokushi, Kōshō Kokushi, and Jinkō Kokushi (→ *kokushi*).

Bengali calendar 🅗 , a calendar introduced at the beginning of the nineteenth century and still used today in India. It divides the year into the following lunar months: (1) Vaishākh, mid-April to mid-May; (2) Jyaishtha, mid-May to mid-June; (3) Āshad, mid-June to mid-July; (4)

Shrāvan, mid-July to mid-August; (5) Bhādra, mid-August to mid-September: (6) Āshvin, mid-September to mid-October; (7) Kārtik, mid-October to mid-November; (8) Āgrahāyan, mid-November to mid-December; (9) Paush, mid-December to mid-January; (10) Māgh, mid-January to mid-February; (11) Phālgun, mid-February to mid-March; (12) Chaitra, mid-March to mid-April.

Bhadrakalpika-sūtra B Skt., lit. "*Sūtra of the Fortunate Age*"; a Mahāyāna sūtra that contains the legends of the thousand buddhas of the fortunate age, of which → Shākyamuni is the fifth. It is the prototype of those sūtras that focus on the legendary lives of the buddhas, bodhisattvas, saints, deities, etc.

Bhaga H Skt.; 1. name of a god, one of the → Ādityas; 2. the divine enjoyer within a human being. The divine is pure bliss and immortal joy; it can dispel the nightmare of corporeality and death.

Bhāgatyāga-Lakshana H (Bhāgatyāga-Lakṣaṇa), Skt.; a process of discrimination and sorting out, in order to recognize what separates us from the Self. It is a mental procedure that must be carried out prior to meditation.

Bhagavad-Gītā H Skt., lit. "song of the exalted one"; a philosophical didactic poem, considered the "Gospel" of Hinduism. It constitutes the sixth book of the Indian national epic poem, the → *Mahābhārata,* which was composed between the fifth century B.C.E. and the second century C.E. In eighteen chapters (700 verses) the great warrior Arjuna receives a fundamental teaching in the face of the impending battle. Western readers may be puzzled by the fact that the teaching is set against the backdrop of a battlefield; yet aside from the fact that Arjuna's karma has sent him into battle, the battlefield serves as a symbol of the bitter conflicts that are waged between the good and evil forces within each human being, between the ego and one's higher nature.

In the dialogue, which is held on the renowned battlefield of → Kurukshetra, Krishna instructs his friend and disciple, Arjuna, regarding union with the highest reality. He shows him in turn the paths of knowledge (→ Jñāna-Yoga), devotion (→ Bhakti-Yoga), selfless action (→ Karma-Yoga), and meditation (→ Rāja-Yoga), the classic paths of yoga. The work presents a combination of teachings from the philosophic systems of Sānkhya, Yoga, and Vedānta.

The *Bhagavad-Gītā* has influenced the religious life of India as no other work has done. Acknowledging it to be a sacred text, the most prominent philosophers of various Vedantic schools have interpreted the work.

Bhagavān H Skt., lit. "noble, holy, the exalted one"; epithets for God, when a devotee is addressing the personal form of God, that is possessed of qualities such as omnipotence, omniscience, wisdom, majesty, and so forth. Great saints and holy figures are also often addressed by their devotees and disciples as Bhagavān (e.g., Bhagavān Shrī → Rāmana Maharshi).

Bhāgavata-Purāna H, also known as *Bhāgavatam,* Skt.; the "Purāna of devotees of the exalted one [Vishnu]," it is the most famous as well as the latest of the eighteen "old histories" (→ Purāna). Presumably composed in the tenth century, it is attributed by many commentators to → Vyāsa or his son Shukadeva and is considered by many to be equal in stature to the *Bhagavad-Gītā* and the Upanishads because of its poetic language and its philosophical depth. The *Bhāgavata-Purāna* expounds religious truths by means of stories featuring saints, seers, and kings, and devotes much space to the life of Krishna; hence it is considered particularly sacred by the → Vaishnavas.

Bhāgīrathī H Skt. → Gangā

Bhairava H Skt., lit. "frightening, the dreadful one"; 1. an epithet for → Shiva, frequently also the name of one of Shiva's divine companions; 2. a candidate for admission in a Tantric sect (→ Tantra).

Bhaishajya-guru-buddha B (Bhaiṣajya-guru-buddha), lit., "Medicine Teacher." He is frequently referred to as the "Medicine Buddha," but this epithet is not only awkward but also too narrow. He is a buddha who symbolizes the healing or perfecting quality of buddhahood. He reigns over an eastern paradise (→ pure land). Iconographically, he is usually depicted with a healing fruit in his right hand and his left in the gesture of protecting (→ mudrā) or resting in his lap in the meditation mudrā. He often appears as part of a triad with → Shākyamuni and → Amitābha, in which he is on the left, and Amitābha on the right, of Shākyamuni. In a sutra dedicated to him, only extant in Tibetan and Chinese, twelve vows are mentioned that Bhaishajya-guru made in a previous life and in the fulfillment of which he is aided by a great number of helpers, including buddhas, bodhisattvas, and the twelve generals of the → *yakshas.* He was of great importance in China, Tibet, and Japan (Jap., Yakushi Nyōrai).

The twelve vows are (1) to radiate his light to all beings, (2) to proclaim his power to all beings, (3) to fulfill the wishes of all beings, (4) to lead all beings into the Mahāyāna path, (5) to enable all beings to maintain the rules of discipline (→ *shīla*), (6) to heal all psychological and bodily illnesses and to lead all beings to enlightenment, (8) to transform women into men in their next rebirth, (9) to keep beings far from false teachings and to cause the truth to be recognized, (10) to save all beings from rebirth in an unfortunate age, (11) to provide food for the hungry, (12) to provide clothing for the naked.

Bhajana 🅷 , or Bhajan, Skt.; a form of worship of God or of an → *avatāra,* characterized by the use of music and singing.

Bhakta 🅷 Skt.; an adherent of the yogic path who aspires to God-realization through love and surrender to God (→ Bhakti-Yoga).

Bhakti 🅷 Skt.; love of God, surrender to the guru and to the chosen deity (→ *ishta-deva*). Hinduism distinguishes between various types and levels of *bhakti: guru-bhakti,* surrender to the guru; *vaidhi-bhakti,* a preparatory stage during which all instructions *(vidhi)* from one's guru for the practice of *bhakti* are followed; *rāga-bhakti,* a state in which the → *bhakta* thinks only of God. Everything reminds one of God and is related to God; *para-bhakti,* the supreme love of God, wherein nothing exists save God and the consciousness of unity with God; *prema-bhakti,* ecstatic love of God; → *mahābhāva,* intense, ecstatic love of God. These last three are different designations for the same state.

Bhakti-Mārga 🅷 Skt.; the path to knowledge and realization through the worship of a personal god.

Bhakti-Shāstras 🅷 (Bhakti-Śāstras), Skt.; all texts that have to do with the worship and veneration of God.

Bhakti-Sūtra 🅷 Skt.; a work composed by → Nārada on the love and worship of God.

The work contains eighty-four *sūtras;* these aphorisms, some of which are famous, do not discuss worldly love, whether of one's neighbor or sexual love, but rather discuss the path of *bhakti* as the simplest path for the present age. Like the divine *minne* of medieval Christianity, love of God as demonstrated by Nārada is the sole fulfillment of life and its chief goal. The individual sutras are extremely concise and in most editions are supplemented by the commentary of a spiritual teacher, since they are otherwise difficult to comprehend.

Bhakti-Yoga 🅷 Skt.; the path of love and surrender, one of the four primary yogic paths to union with God. After developing an intense love for the many aspects of God in a personal form—often in the form of some divine incarnation—the ego of the worshiper merges with the chosen ideal, the → *ishta-deva.* Bhakti-Yoga is the natural path to knowledge of God. Here the → *bhakta* has no need to suppress his feelings; rather, one intensifies them and directs them toward God. The majority of believers from the various world-traditions are fundamentally adherents of this path. Bhakti-Yoga distinguishes between five different devotional attitudes, or *bhāvas,* toward God.

The stages of Bhakti-Yoga are 1. *bhakti,* veneration; 2. → *bhāva,* mature love, an ecstatic state; 3. → *prema,* a state in which the devotee completely forgets the world as well as his own body; 4. → *mahābhāva,* the supreme manifestation of divine love. → Rādhā, Krishna's playmate, is considered its embodiment. Only → *avatāras* and → *īshvarakotis* can attain a state beyond *bhāva.* A competent, fundamental introduction to Bhakti-Yoga is in Vivekānanda 1955 *b.*

Bhārata 🅷 1. a king and saint in the → *Bhāgavata-Purāna,* the son of → Shakuntalā and progenitor of the Bhāratas, whose great battle is described in the famous epic poem the *Mahābhārata.* India was once named Bhāratavarsha for him, and Indians now refer to their country again as Bhārata. → Arjuna often bears the epithet Bhārata, which characterizes him as a member of the Bhārata clan or as a descendant of Bhārata. 2. a halfbrother of → Rāma; 3. an epithet for → Agni.

Bhāratavarsha 🅷 Skt. → Bhārata

Bhāratī 🅷 Skt.; the comprehensive word that brings all forth from its divine source; the breadth of wisdom and the magnitude of the consciousness of truth.

Bhārgavī-Varuni-Vidyā 🅷 (Bhārgavī-Varuṇi-Vidyā), Skt.; the knowledge of → Bhrigu (Bhārgavī-Varuni: from Bhrigu, the son of Varuna) that all matter is *brahman* but that one experiences *brahman* as the material universe through identification with one's material, mortal body. If through enlightenment such identification ceases, one realizes that the entire universe, in truth, is *brahman.*

Bhāskara 🅷 Indian philosopher who lived around 900 C.E., one of the main commentators on the → *Vedānta-Sūtra.* His work is entitled *Bhāskarabhāshya.* In it he represents the

Bhedābheda-Vāda, the teaching that identity lies at the basis of all differences (→ Dvaitādvaita-Vedānta); on many points he agrees with the views of → Nimbārka. He believes that full union with *brahman* is possible only after the death of the body.

Bhāva 🅷 Skt.; emotion, ecstasy; designation for any of five various devotional attitudes that a → *bhakta* may adopt in relation to his chosen deity (→ *ishta-deva*): 1. *shānta,* a serence, peaceful mood wherein one feels close to God without having developed a particular relationship to him; 2. *dāsya,* the attitude of servant to master or child to parent or guardian; 3. *sākhya,* the attitude of one friend to another; 4. *vātsalya,* the attitude of parent to child (e.g., that of Mary and Joseph toward Jesus); 5. *madhura,* the attitude of a wife or beloved toward her husband or lover. → *Bhāva* is also the designation for the second stage of → Bhakti-Yoga.

Bhava 🅱 Skt., Pali, "being, becoming"; used in Buddhism in three different contexts: (1) *bhava* as every kind of being in the three worlds (→ *triloka*): *kāmabhava* (being in the desire realm), *rūpabhava* (being in the realm of desireless form), *arūpabhava* (being in the formless realm); (2) *bhava* as the tenth link in the chain of conditioned arising (→ *pratītya-samutpāda*) means a process of becoming that is conditioned by identification with the components of individuality; (3) in the Mahāyāna *bhava* is brought into opposition with nothingness (→ *shūnyatā*) and is interpreted differently by different schools.

Bhava-chakra 🅱 (bhava-cakra), Skt., lit. "wheel of life"; a representation of the cycle of existence (→ samsāra) very widespread in → Tibetan Buddhism. The main types of worldly existence are divided into six segments of the wheel. The realms of the gods, of the antigods (or jealous gods, the "titans"), and of human beings constitute the upper part of the wheel. The realms of animals, hungry ghosts, and hell beings make up the lower half. Common to all these realms is the experience of suffering and death and the causes of these experiences. Death is symbolized by → Yama, the god of the Underworld, who holds the wheel of life in his claws. The causes of this cycle are represented by the animals found in the center of the wheel: the cock (desire), the pig (ignorance), and the snake (hate or aggression). A third iconographical element are the twelve factors of conditioned arising (→ *pratītya-samutpāda*), which form an outer circle and offer further philosophical explanation of the cycle of existence.

Bhava-chakra, the Wheel of Life

The symbology of the wheel of life can be interpreted on various levels. Originally the six realms of existence were viewed as concrete forms of existence (each characterized by a particular state of mind), into which beings were born in accordance with their → karma. The *Tibetan Book of the Dead* (→ *Bardo thödol*) takes this point of view and in certain places gives precise instructions on how to bring about rebirth in the higher realms (gods, antigods, and humans) and on how to avoid rebirth in the lower realms (animals, hungry ghosts, and hell beings). In a modern sense, these realms can also be understood as personality types or situations of life, each distinguished by a basic characteristic.

A later development in the depiction of the wheel of life are six forms of → Avalokitesvara shown in the six realms teaching the respective types of beings the way to liberation from the cycle of existence. Also with this sense the six syllables of the mantra of Avalokiteshvara (→ *om mani padme hum*) were assigned each to one of the realms of existence.

While in the six realms is shown the development of the world on the basis of the motives depicted in the center of the wheel, the outer circle symbolizes the causes created in individual life. The point of departure for both levels of explanation is ignorance (→ *avidyā*). The formula of conditioned arising is presented in the following pictures: a blind woman (ignorance), a potter (power of formation), monkey (consciousness), two men in a boat (name and form or mind and body), six-windowed house (the six senses), a couple embracing (contact), an arrow piercing an eye (sensation), a person drinking (craving), a man gathering fruit (grasping, attachment), copulation (becoming), a woman giving birth (birth), a man carrying a corpse (death).

Bhāvamukha 🅗 Skt.; a sublime state of spiritual experience wherein the seeker's consciousness hovers at the borderline between absolute and relative consciousness. With equal ease, the seeker can meditate on → *brahman* without qualities and participate in the activities of the world of appearances, which is viewed thereby as a manifestation of the Absolute. In technical terms, the seeker's consciousness moves between the *ājñā-chakra* and the *sahasrāra-chakra.* (See also → *chakra* and → *kundalinī.*)

Bhāvanā 🅑 Skt., Pali; meditation, mind development, all those practices usually designated as meditation. Two types of *bhāvanā* are distinguished: the development of tranquility (→ *shamatha*) and clear seeing (→ *vipashyanā*). Tranquility is the prerequisite for attaining clear seeing. According to the → *Visuddhi-magga* there are forty different exercises leading to the development of tranquility. They include absorption (→ *dhyāna*), contemplation (→ *samāpati*), and concentration (→ *samādhi*).

The forty exercises are ten → *kasina* exercises, contemplation of the ten disgusting objects (→ *ashubha*), the ten contemplations (→ *anussati*), the four → *brahma-vihāras*, the → four stages of formlessness, contemplation of the repugnance of food, and analysis of the four elements (→ *dhātu-vavatthāna*).

Bhāvanā-mārga 🅑 Skt. → Yogāchāra

Bhāva-Pratyaya 🅗 Skt.; complete control over the material world, by means of which a high → *samādhi* state is attained.

Bhavasāgara 🅗 Skt., lit. "ocean of becoming"; the world of change. The creation is in a state of constant flux and knows no rest. The true goal of human life is to surmount this unstable condition and to realize truth and inner peace.

Bhāva-Samādhi 🅗 Skt.; an ecstatic state attained through worship and love of God. In this state, the devotee retains a trace of the ego in order to enjoy God and his divine play. Rāmakrishna described this as "tasting sugar rather than becoming sugar."

Bhavatārinī 🅗 (Bhavatāriṇī), Skt., lit. "redeemer of the universe"; a name for the Divine Mother → Kālī, under which she is worshiped in the temple of Dakshineshvavra.

Bhāvaviveka 🅑 also called Bhavya; spokesman of the → Mādhyamaka who lived ca. 490–570. He was born in south India and went to Magadha, where he studied the teaching of Nāgārjuna. Then he returned to his homeland, where he quickly attained renown. In his works, which are only extant in Chinese and Tibetan translations, he attacks the theses of the → Yogāchāra. He founded the Svātantrika school, one of the two schools of Mādhyamaka, and opposed Buddhapālita, the founder of the Prāsangika school, using a positive dialectic. The development of his school led in the 8th century to the founding of the Svātantrika-Yogāchāra school by Shāntarakshita.

Bheda 🅗 Skt.; difference, disparity, division; the chief characteristic of our manifest world (→ *nāmarūpa*).

Bhedābheda-Vāda 🅗 Skt.; synonymous with → Dvaitādvaita-Vedānta

Bherī-Nāda 🅗 Skt.; the inner reverberation of the spoken syllable → OM or some other sound upon which one meditates.

Bhikshu 🅑 (bhikṣu), Skt. (Pali, bhikku); beggar, monk, male member of the Buddhist → *sangha* who has entered → homelessness and received full ordination. In ancient times the *bhikshus* formed the nucleus of the Buddhist community, since according to the early Buddhist view, only a person who had renounced the world could reach the supreme goal, nirvāna. The main activities of *bhikshus* are meditating and presenting the dharma. They are not allowed to work. Buddhist monks renounce the amenities of the world and lead a life of wandering. The basic principles of the monastic life are poverty, celibacy, and peaceableness. The lifestyle is governed by the rules layed down in the → Vinaya-pitaka.

Poverty expresses itself in the clothing of the monk, which consists of three parts (→ *trichīvara*) and is supposed to be made of rags. Possessions are limited to articles of daily use: alms bowl, razor, sewing needle, water filter, walking stick, and toothbrush. A *bhikshu* may not come into contact with money or other things of value; gifts and invitations may only be accepted under certain circumstances. He begs for his food in a daily begging round. For medicine he uses only animal urine.

In the beginning all *bhikshus* without exception led a life of wandering. During the rainy period, however, they were obliged to spend three months in a monastery (→ *vihāra*). According to tradition the reason for this was that during the rainy season a wandering monk could cause too much damage to the animal and plant worlds. During this period of repose, leaving the monastery was permitted only under certain conditions, as for visiting relatives or the sick. This period was ended with the *pravāranā* (Pali, *pavāranā*) ceremony, which consisted in asking forgiveness of the other monks for injuries caused during the period of common retreat.

In the course of the development of the *sangha*, the monks became sedentary and lived in monasteries. However, pilgrimages play an important role in the lives of monks up to the present day. The life of a modern monk corresponds essentially to that of a *bhikshu* in the time of the Buddha. Of course, with the spread of Buddhism, certain rules have been adapted to new social and geographical conditions. Chinese monks do physical labor, especially farming, which was forbidden to the early *sangha* since it involved killing sentient beings. Monks of particular schools of Tibetan and Japanese Buddhism marry and have families. Also the rules concerning the begging round and the acquisition of food have greatly changed.

Bhikshunī B (bhikṣunī), Skt. (Pali, bhikkunī); nun, fully ordained female member of the Buddhist → *sangha.* The order of nuns was founded by → Mahāprajāpatī Gautamī, the stepmother of the historical Buddha, after the death of her husband. → Ānanda interceded on her behalf and was reproached for this by the monks at the first council. Buddha himself was reportedly against creating an order of nuns, fearing for the moral state of the order. He is said to have been convinced that by consenting to the founding of the nuns' order he would diminish the lifespan of the Buddhist teaching from 1000 to 500 years.

The life of nuns is considerably more strictly regulated than that of monks. Nuns are dependent on monks for their education and for certain decisions. For the ordination of a nun to be valid it must be repeated in the presence of the order of monks; a nun may not reprimand a monk under any circumstances; the oldest nun must treat the youngest monk with deference. Acts punishable by exclusion from the order are much more numerous than in the order of monks; certain violations that in the monks' order bring only a limited suspension in the nuns' order are punished by definitive exclusion. The order of nuns has never played an important role in the Buddhist *sangha*; the number of nuns compared to that of monks is extremely small.

Bhīshma H (Bhīṣma), teacher of → Kauravas and the → Pāndavas; one of the warriors on the battlefield of → Kurukshetra who is mentioned in the *Mahābhārata* and the *Bhagavad-Gītā.*

Bhoga H Skt.; 1. enjoyment of sense objects, sensory pleasure; 2. food that is offered to a divinity.

Bhrānta H Skt.; confused, deluded, uncertain, dubious; error; a term referring to the unspiritual person's inability to discriminate (→ *viveka*). Such a person cannot perceive the line between reality and unreality, between the permanent and the transient. In → Shankara's terms, such people inevitably see a snake when only a rope is present. The consequences of such ignorance are fear and grief.

Bhrānti-Darshana H (Bhrānti-Darśana), Skt.; an understanding or vision that arises on a false basis and therefore is illusory.

Bhrigu H (Bhṛgu), a sage named in the Vedas, son of → Varuna; one of the seven great *Rishis* (→ *Maharishi*).

Bhrūmādhya-Dhrishti H (Bhrūmādhya-Dṛṣṭi), Skt., lit. *bhrū:* "eyebrow," *mādhya:* "in the middle," *drishti:* "to see"; an exercise in concentration in which the attention is directed to a spot between the eyebrows.

Bhūman H Skt., lit. "abundance, supreme being"; the highest goal of human life, absolute consciousness (→ *brahman*), with which the individual, as the → *ātman* (but not as the limited → *jīva*), is identical.

Bhūman-Vidyā H Skt.; knowledge of the infinite Self that contains everything and by its immortal character banishes darkness and care, disease and death.

Bhūmi B Skt., lit. "land"; each of the ten stages that the bodhisattva must go through to attain buddhahood. The individual stages are not described in the texts in an entirely consistent manner; the following exposition is based on the → *Dashabhūmika-sūtra* and the *Bodhisattvabhūmi.* The ten stages are as follows:

1. *Pramuditā-bhūmi* (land of joy). In this stage the bodhisattva is full of joy on having entered the path of buddhahood. He has aroused the thought of enlightenment (→ *bodhicitta*) and taken the bodhisattva vow. He especially cultivates the virtue of generosity (→ *dāna*) and is free from egotistical thoughts and the wish for karmic merit. Here the bodhisattva recognizes the emptiness of the ego and of all dharmas.

2. *Vimalā-bhūmi* (land of purity). Here the

bodhisattva perfects his discipline (→ *shīla*) and is free from lapses. He practices → *dhyāna* and → *samādhi*.

3. *Prabhākārī-bhūmi* (land of radiance). The bodhisattva gains insight into the impermanence (→ *anitya*) of existence and develops the virtue of patience (→ *kshānti*) in bearing difficulties and in actively helping all sentient beings toward liberation. He has cut off the three roots of unwholesomeness (→ *akushala*)—desire, hatred, and delusion. The attainment of this stage is made possible through ten qualities known collectively as "undertaking a firm resolve," which include determination, satiety with worldy life, and passionlessness. The bodhisattva achieves the four absorptions (*dhyāna*) and the → four stages of formlessness and acquires the first five of the six supernatural powers (→ *abhijñā*).

4. *Archismatī-bhūmi* (the blazing land). The bodhisattva "burns" remaining false conceptions and develops wisdom. He practices the virtue of exertion (→ *vīrya*) and perfects the thirty-seven requisites of enlightenment (→ *bodhipākshika-dharma*).

5. *Sudurjayā-bhūmi* (the land extremely difficult to conquer). In this stage the bodhisattva absorbs himself in meditation (*dhyāna*) in order to achieve an intuitive grasp of the truth. Thus he understands the → four noble truths and the → two truths . He has cleared away doubt and uncertainty and knows what is a proper way and what is not. He works further on the perfection of the thirty-seven requisites of enlightenment.

6. *Abhimukhī-bhūmi* (the land in view of wisdom). In this stage the bodhisattva recognizes that all dharmas are free from characteristics, arising, manifoldness, and the distinction between existence and nonexistence. He attains insight into conditioned arising (→ *pratītya-samutpāda*), transcends discriminating thought in the perfection of the virtue of wisdom (→ *prajñā*), and comprehends nothingness (→ *shūnyatā)*.

7. *Dūrangamā-bhūmi* (the far-reaching land). By now the bodhisattva has gained knowledge and skillful means (→ *upāya*), which enable him to lead any being on the way to enlightenment in accordance with that being's abilities. This stage marks the transition to another level of existence, that of a transcendent bodhisattva, one who can manifest himself in any conceivable form. After passing through this stage, falling back into lower levels of existence is no longer possible.

8. *Achalā-bhūmi* (the immovable land). In this stage the bodhisattva can no longer be disturbed by anything, since he has received the prophecy of when and where he will attain buddahood. He gains the ability to transfer his merit to other beings and renounces the accumulation of further karmic treasures.

9. *Sādhumatī-bhūmi* (the land of good thoughts). The wisdom of the bodhisattva is complete; he possesses the ten powers (→ *dashabala*), the six supernatural powers (→ *abhijñā*), the → four certainties, the → eight liberations, and the → *dhāranīs*. He knows the nature of all dharmas and expounds the teaching.

10. *Dharmameghā-bhūmi* (land of dharma clouds). All understanding (→ *jñāna*) and immeasurable virtue are realized. The *dharmakāya* (→ *trikāya*) of the bodhisattva is fully developed. He sits surrounded by countless bodhisattvas on a lotus in → Tushita Heaven). His buddhahood is confirmed by all the buddhas. This stage is also known by the name of *abhisheka-bhūmi*. Bodhisattvas of this *bhūmi* are, for example, → Maitreya and → Mañjushrī.

Bhūr 🅗 Skt.; a → *vyāhriti,* the first word of the → Gāyatrī. From this word, which was spoken by → Prajāpati at the dawn of creation, the earth (*bhū*) was created.

Bhūrloka 🅗 Skt.; the material world; the body and its material requirements constitute the earthly world for human beings.

Bhūta 🅗 Skt.; 1. creature; in general, everything that has become; 2. the five elements of the material world (→ *prakriti*).

Bhūta-Siddhi 🅗 Skt.; mastery over the elements and thus over → *prakriti.* As *prakriti* maifests itself in the three *gunas,* these must be brought under control.

Bhūtatathatā 🅑 Skt., "suchness of existents"; the reality as opposed to the appearance of the phenomenal world. *Bhūtatathatā* is immutable and eternal, whereas forms and appearances arise, change, and pass away. This concept is used synonymously in Mahāyāna texts with the absolute, or ultimate reality (→ *tathatā,* → *trikāya,* → buddha-nature).

Bhūtātman 🅗 Skt., the self-recalling self that knows what it truly is (from *bhūta:* "past," and → *ātman:* "Self").

Bhuva 🅗 Skt.; a → *vyāhriti:* the second word of the → Gāyatrī. Out of this word spoken by → Prajāpati, the atmosphere came into being.

Bhuvaneshvara H (Bhuvaneśvara), Skt., lit. "lord of the world"; 1. epithet for → Shiva; 2. a city in Orissa (present-day Bhubaneswar), the site of many beautiful temples dedicated to Shiva. The largest and best known of these is the Lingavaj temple, described by Babu Rajendra Lala in his great work on Orissa. In former times, the region around Bhuvaneshvara was a forest named Ekāmra-Kānana that is said to have been a favorite hunting ground of Shiva's.

Bhuvarloka H Skt.; the world of multifarious appearances, in which sensations, feeling, passions, and attractions exist as the result of desires. In this vital, nervous plane, located above our material earth, the gods associate with human beings. It is a vast and confusing region whose paths are many and difficult.

Bibhīshana H Skt. → Vibhīshana

Bīja H B Skt.; energy, seed, root power; the potential behind every material manifestation; particularly important in a *bīja* mantra (seed syllable), which is given by a guru. In the letters of a *bīja* mantra the nature of a particular aspect of the supreme reality is concentrated in the form of a symbolic sound. Such symbolic sounds, based on the experience of a spiritually accomplished person, have mystical, divine powers if they are received from a suitable, authentic guru. Every student of a guru receives such a mantra upon initiation.

Bimbisāra B king of Magadha at the time of the Buddha → Shākyamuni. At the age of thirty Bimbisāra heard a discourse of the Buddha and at once became a lay follower of his and an active fosterer of Buddhism. He gave the Buddha the bamboo forest Venuvana, where Buddha often remained with his students. Bimbisāra was killed by his son → Ajātasattu.

Bindu H Skt., lit. "particle, dot, spot"; a symbol for the universe in its unmanifest form. Because the metamorphosis of the unmanifest into the manifest world (i.e., the creation of something from nothing) is difficult to comprehend, the dot serves as an example of a starting point from which all lines and forms may emerge. In Tantra, the term refers to the male semen, out of which new forms and new life emerge.

Bodai Z Jap. pronunciation of the Chinese character used to translate the Sanskrit word → *bodhi* into Chinese. It means "complete wisdom," → enlightenment, → buddhahood, → *kokoro* ("enlightened mind"). In Zen *bodai* is generally used to refer to the wisdom that derives from enlightenment.

Bodaidaruma Z Jap. for → Bodhidharma

Bodaishin Z Jap., lit. "enlightenment mind"; aspiration toward → buddahood; resolve to find complete → enlightenment (see also → *hotsubodaishin*).

Bodh-gayā B (short form, Gayā), one of the four holy places of Buddhism, ninety kilometers south of Patna. Here the historical Buddha → Shākyamuni reached complete enlightenment after having meditated for forty-nine days under the so-called → bodhi tree. In Bodh-gayā the Mahābodhi Temple, built by a Singhalese king, still exists today, although in an altered form. (Also → Mahābodhi Society. For the sacred city of Hinduism, → Gayā.)

Bodhi H B Z Skt., Pali, lit. "awakened."
H perfect knowledge.
B Z *Bodhis* referred originally to the four stages of the supramundane path (→ *ārya-mārga*) and was attained through the completion of the thirty-seven prerequisites of enlightenment (→ *bodhipākshika-dharma*) and the dissolution of ignorance (→ *avidyā*), that is, through realization of the four noble truths.

In Hīnayāna *bodhi* is equated with the perfection of insight into, and realization of, the four noble truths, which perfection means the cessation of suffering. Here three stages of enlightenment are distinguished: the enlightenment of a noble disciple (→ *shrāvaka*), the enlightenment of one who sought only his own enlightenment (→ *pratyeka-buddha*) and the enlightenment of a buddha (→ *samyak-sambuddha*). The last is equated with omniscience (→ *sarvajñatā*) and is called *mahābodhi* (great enlightenment).

By contrast, in Mahāyāna *bodhi* is mainly understood as wisdom based on insight into the unity of → nirvāna and → samsāra as well as of subject and object. It is described as the realization of → *prajñā*, awakening to one's own → buddha-nature or buddha-essence (→ *busshō*), insight into the essential emptiness (→ *shūnyatā*) of the world, or omniscience and perception of suchness (→ *tathatā*).

The Mahāyāna also recognizes three kinds of *bodhi*: enlightenment for oneself (the enlightenment of an → *arhat*), liberation for the sake of others (enlightenment of a bodhisattva), and the complete enlightenment of a buddha. The individual Mahāyāna schools interpret this concept variously according to their views.

Bodhichitta B Skt., lit. "awakened mind"; the mind of enlightenment, one of the central notions of → Mahāyāna Buddhism. In the Tibetan tradition it is seen as having two aspects, relative and absolute. The relative mind of enlightenment is divided again into two phases (1) the intention and wish, nurtured by limitless compassion, to attain liberation (→ nirvāna) for the sake of the welfare of all beings and (2) actual entry into meditation, the purpose of which is the acquisition of the appropriate means to actualize this wish (→ bodhisattva). The absolute mind of enlightenment is viewed as the vision of the true nature (→ *shūnyatā*) of phenomena. The various methods for arousing the mind of enlightenment stem primarily from → Atīsha and entered into all schools of Tibetan Buddhism through him.

In addition, the systems of → Tantra developed the notion of the mind of enlightenment as a concrete physiological entity. The sublimation of the mind of enlightenment conceived as a "seed essence" leads to an enlightenment that can be directly experienced corporeally.

Bodhidharma B Z Chin., P'u-t'i-ta-mo or Tamo; Jap., Bodaidaruma or Daruma, ca. 470-543 (?); the twenty-eighth patriarch after → Shākyamuni Buddha in the Indian lineage and the first Chinese patriarch of Chan (→ Zen). Bodhidharma was the student and dharma successor (→ *hassu*) of the twenty-seventh patriarch Prajnādhara (Jap., Hannyatara) and the teacher of → Hui-k'o, whom he installed as the second patriarch of Zen in China. The event that marks the transmission of the → buddha-dharma from Prajnādhara to Bodhidharma is described in the → *Denkō-roku* as follows:

Once the twenty-seventh patriarch, the venerable Hannyatara, asked, "Among all things, what is formless?"

The master [Bodhidharma] said, "Nonarising is formless."

The patriarch said, "Among all things, what is the biggest?"

The master said, "The nature of dharmas is the biggest."

After Bodhidharma was confirmed by Prajnādhara as the twenty-eighth patriarch, according to tradition, he traveled by ship from India to south China. After a brief unsuccessful attempt to spread his teaching there, he wandered further to Lo-yang in north China and finally settled at the → Shao-lin Monastery on → Sung-shan (Jap., Sūzan, Sūsan) Mountain. Here he practiced unmovable → *zazen* for nine years, on which account this period is known as *menpeki-kunen* (→ *menpeki*), which roughly means "nine years in front of the wall." Here Hui-k'o, later the second patriarch of Zen in China, found his way to the master and, after an impressive proof of his "will for truth," was accepted as his disciple.

Bodhidharma, the "Barbarian from the West" (ink painting from Bokkei, 15th century)

The dates of Bodhidharma, who is said to have been the son of a south Indian brahmin king, are uncertain. There is a tradition that says that his teacher Prajnādhara charged Bodhidharma to wait sixty years after his death before going to China. If this is the case, Bodhidharma must have been advanced in years when he arrived in China. According to other sources, he was sixty years old when he arrived in China. Both these traditions are incompatible with the dates 470–543, which are given in most sources. After his arrival in what is today the port city of Canton, he traveled at the invitation of the emperor Wu of the Liang Dynasty to visit him in Nanking.

The first example in the → *Pi-yen-lu* reports the encounter between Bodhidharma and the emperor. Wu-ti was a follower and fosterer of Buddhism and had had several Buddhist monasteries built in his realm. Now he asked the master of buddha-dharma from India what merit for succeeding lives he [Wu-ti] had accumulated thereby. Bodhidharma answered curtly, "No merit." Then the emperor asked him what the supreme meaning of the sacred truth was. "Expanse of emptiness—nothing sacred," answered Bodhidharma. Now the emperor demanded to know, "Who is that in front of us?" "Don't know," replied Bodhidharma, who with this answer had really revealed the essence of his teaching to the emperor without the latter's catching on.

The encounter with Emperor Wu of Liang showed Bodhidharma that the time was not yet ripe for the reception of his teaching in China. He crossed the Yangtse—as the legend tells us, on a reed (this is a favorite subject in Zen painting)—and traveled on to north China, where he finally settled at Shao-lin Monastery.

It is not certain whether he died there or again left the monastery after he had transmitted the patriarchy to Hui-k'o. According to a legend given in the → *Ching-te ch'uan-teng-lu*, after nine years at Shao-lin Monastery he became homesick for India and decided to return there. Before departing, he called his disciples to him in order to test their realization. The first disciple he questioned answered, "The way I understand it, if we want to realize the truth we should neither depend entirely on words nor entirely do away with words; rather we should use them as a tool on the Way [→ *dō*]." Bodhidharma answered him, "You have grasped my skin." The next to come forward was a nun, who said, "As I understand it, the truth is an auspicious display of the buddha-paradise; one sees it once, then never again." To her Bodhidharma replied, "You have grasped my flesh." The next disciple said, "The four great elements are empty and the five → *skandhas* are nonexistent. There is in fact nothing to grasp." To this Bodhidharma responded, "You have grasped my bones," Finally it was Hui-k'o's turn. He, however, said nothing, only bowed to the master in silence. To him Bodhidharma said, "You have grasped my marrow."

According to another legend, Bodhidharma was poisoned at the age of 150 and buried in the mountains of Honan. Not long after his death, the pilgrim Sung Yun, who had gone to India to bring the sūtra texts back to China, met Bodhidharma on his way home in the mountains of Turkestan. The Indian master, who wore only one sandal, told the pilgrim he was on his way back to India; a Chinese dharma heir would continue his tradition in China. Upon his return to China the pilgrim reported this encounter to the disciples of Bodhidharma. They opened his grave and found it empty except for one of the patriarch's sandals.

The form of meditative practice the Bodhidharma taught still owed a great deal to Indian Buddhism. His instructions were to a great extent based on the traditional sūtras of Mahāyāna Buddhism; he especially emphasized the importance of the → *Lankāvatāra-sūtra*. Typical Chinese Zen, which is a fusion of the → Dhyāna Buddhism represented by Bodhidharma and indigenous Chinese Taoism and which is described as a "special transmission outside the orthodox teaching" (→ *kyōge-betsuden*), first developed with → Hui-neng, the sixth patriarch of Zen in China, and the great Zen masters of the T'ang period who followed him.

Bodhipākshika-dharma 🅱 (bodhipākṣika-dharma), Skt. (Pali, bodhipakkhiya-dhamma), lit., "things pertaining to enlightenment"; thirty-seven prerequisites for the attainment of enlightenment, which are divided into seven areas (1) the four foundations of mindfulness (→ *satipatthāna*); (2) the → four perfect efforts; (3) the four roads to power (→ *riddhipāda*); (4) the five roots (→ *indriya*); (5) the five powers (→ *bala*); (6) the seven factors of enlightenment (→ *bodhyanga*); (7) the → eightfold path.

Bodhiruchi 🅱 (Bodhiruci); north Indian Buddhist monk, who traveled to China in the year 508, where, together with Ratnamati, Buddhasanta, and others, he translated the → *Dashabhūmika-sūtra* into Chinese. He is considered the first patriarch of the northern branch of the → Ti-lun school of early Chinese Buddhism.

Bodhiruchi, however, also taught the doctrine of the → Pure Land school and in 530 acquainted T'an-luan with this teaching; the latter then became the first active spokesman of this school in China.

Bodhisattva 🅱 🆉 Skt., lit., "enlightenment being"; in Mahāyāna Buddhism a bodhisattva is a being who seeks buddhahood through the systematic practice of the perfect virtues (→ *pāramitā*) but renounces complete entry into nirvāna until all beings are saved. The determining factor for his action is compassion (→ *karunā*), supported by highest insight and wisdom (→ *prajñā*). A bodhisattva provides active help, is ready to take upon himself the suffering of all other beings, and to transfer his own karmic merit to other beings. The way of a bodhisattva begins with arousing the thought of enlightenment (*bodhicitta*) and taking the bodhisattva vow (*pranidhāna*). The career of a bodhisattva is divided into ten stages (*bhūmi*). The bodhisattva ideal replaced in Mahāyāna the Hīnayāna ideal of the → arhat, whose effort is directed towards the attainment of his own liberation, since this was found to be too narrow and ego-oriented.

The notion of the bodhisattva is already found in Hīnayāna writings, where it refers to the historical Buddha → Shākyamuni in his previous existences as they are described in the → *Jātakas*. In Mahāyāna the idea of the bodhisattva is rooted in the belief in future buddhas, who have long since existed as bodhisattvas.

The Mahāyāna distinguishes two kinds of bodhisattvas—earthly and transcendent. Earthly bodhisattvas are persons who are distinguished from others by their compassion and altruism as well as their striving toward the attainment of enlightenment. Transcendent bodhisattvas have actualized the *pāramitās* and attained buddhahood but have postponed their entry into complete nirvāna. They are in possession of perfect wisdom and are no longer subject to → samsāra. They appear in the most various forms in order to lead beings on the path to liberation. They are the object of the veneration of believers, who see them as showers of the way and helpers in time of need. The most important of these transcendent bodhisattvas are → Avalokiteshvara, → Mañjushrī, → Kshitigarbha, → Mahāsthāmaprāpta, and → Samantabhadra.

Bodhisattva-bhūmi 🅱 Skt., lit., "*Lands of the Bodhisattva*"; Mahāyāna work attributed to → Asanga, which describes the course of development of a bodhisattva (→ *bhūmi*).

Bodhisattva-shīla 🅱 (Bodhisattva-sīla), Skt.; rules of discipline of a bodhisattva; obligatory rules for a follower of Mahāyāna Buddhism, observed by monks and nuns as well as laymen. They are set forth in the → *Brahmajāla-sūtra*, where fifty-eight rules are to be found, of which the first ten are the most essential. These are refraining from (1) killing (2) stealing (3) unchaste behavior (4) lying (5) the use of intoxicants (6) gossip (7) boasting (8) envy (9)resentment and ill will and (10) slandering the three precious ones (→ *triratna*). Followers of Mahāyāna undertake to observe these rules in the framework of the so-called bodhisattva ordination, which is added to the Hīnayāna ordination formula (→ ordination). The ceremony comprises the assumption of *bodhisattva-shīla*, the burning in of scars (→ *moxa*) and the actual ordination ceremony, which is conducted by the abbot of a monastery.

The disciplinary and moral rules of the Mahāyāna differ in nature from those of the Hīnayāna (→ *shīla*); they are altruistically directed, while those of the Hīnayāna aim primarily at the attainment of personal merit; the latter can be taken without witnesses in the form of a personal vow. In contrast to Hīnayāna *shīla*, *bodhisattva-shīla* is more concerned with mental attitude than with the formal side of the rules. A violation of the rules in the Hīnayāna has as a consequence expulsion from the → *sangha* in every case; in the Mahāyāna this is not the case when the shīla is violated for the sake of the welfare of another being.

Bodhisattva vow 🅱 → *pranidhāna*

Bodhi tree 🅱 🅩 (*ficus religiosa*); the fig tree under which → Siddhārtha Gautama, the historical Buddha, attained complete enlightenment.

In → Bodh-gayā there is still today, located on the left side of the Mahābodhi Temple, a "grandchild" of the tree under which Siddhārtha meditated for forty-nine days. The original tree was destroyed in the 7th century by the Bengali king Shashanka; its offshoot fell victim to a storm in 1876. The tree venerated today is a scion of a sprout of the original tree, a sprout that → Ashoka had the king of Ceylon bring to his country in the 3rd century B.C.E. and that still stands today in the capital city of those times, → Anurādhapura.

Bodhyanga 🅱 (Bodhyaṅga), Skt. (Pali, bojjhanga), lit. "factors of enlightenment"; seven factors that lead to enlightenment (→ *bodhi*). They constitute the sixth element of the thirty-seven prerequisites for enlightenment (*bodhi-pākshika-dharma*) and consist of (1) mindfulness (→ *smriti*), (2) distinguishing right and wrong in accordance with the Buddhist teaching, (3) energy and exertion in the practice (→ *vīrya*), (4) joy concerning the view of the teaching (*prīti*), (5) pacification through overcoming the passions (→ *klesha*), (6) equanimity (→ *upekashā*), and (7) freedom from discrimination.

Body, speech, mind 🅱 Already in early Buddhism (→ Hīnayāna), the actions that produce → karma were subsumed under the categories of body, speech, and mind. The teachings of → Vajrayāna give this threefold division a new sense in that they regard various methods of meditation practice as sublimations of the three aspects. The goal of the transformation to be accomplished through → *sādhana* practice is the realization of the three bodies of a buddha (→ *trikāya*). This goal is reached through specific bodily postures and gestures (→ mudrā), concentration of the mind (→ *samādhi*), and the recitation of sacred syllables (→ mantra). These relationships and the intermediary role of speech, that is, of mantra, can be represented as follows:

Manifest Reality	*Means*	*Supreme Reality*
body	mudrā	nirmānakāya
speech	mantra	sambhogakāya
mind	samādhi	dharmakāya

This conception of the threefold division is symbolized in many ritual texts by the seed syllables *om ah hum*. They are focal points in the initiations necessary for the practice of the *sādhanas* and are frequently starting points in visualizations. Projected onto the practitioner, the white syllable *om* appears in the forehead and symbolizes body, the red *ah* corresponds to the throat center and speech, and the blue *hum* is in the heart, which in this system is equated with mind. The negative tendencies of these three levels of experience, which one is intended to transform, are connected with the three root causes of → samsāra: desire, hate, and ignorance. In their purified form, body, speech, and mind are likened to a → *dorje*, a sign that they have actualized their true nature. The symbology of body, speech, and mind also finds application in the consecration of *thangkas* (scroll paintings)—on the back side of a painting of, for example, Buddha, at the level of the forehead, throat, and heart centers the syllables *om ah hum* are placed.

The actual transformation of body, speech, and mind is encouraged in the → *mahāmudrā* and → *dzogchen* teachings through four special practices (*ngöndro*), the ritualized execution of which is precisely described in the various meditation manuals: (1) taking refuge (→ *kyabdro*) and arousing elightenment mind (→ *bodhicitta*); (2) the → *vajrasattva* practice of purification of body, speech, and mind; (3) accumulation of further merit through symbolic → mandala offerings; (4) integration of the individuality of the practitioner into the tradition represented by the master (→ guru).

Many other concepts of Tibetan Buddhism are connected with the principle of body, speech, and mind. Noteworthy is the repeated resolution of the opposition between body and mind through the communicative element of speech.

Bōkatsu 🅉 Jap., lit. "stick [and] shout"; expression for a type of Zen training customary in Zen since → Te-shan Hsüan-chien (Jap., Tokusan Senkan) and → Lin-chi I-hsüan (Jap., Rinzai Gigen). It consists of the skillful use of blows from a stick (→ *kyosaku*, → *shippei*) and a shout (→ *katsu*) by an experienced Zen master, who knows how to apply these at the right moment for the benefit of his students.

Te-shan (Tokusan) is as famous in the Zen tradition for his use of the stick as Lin-chi (Rinzai) is for his use of the shout. The great Japanese Zen master → Ikkyū Sōjun highly esteemed the legacy of Te-shan and Lin-chi in a time when the Zen of Japan was in decline and threatened to rigidify into outer forms. In the mocking tone so typical of Zen literature, Ikkyū, who himself was known as Crazy Cloud, in one of his poems contained in the → *Kyōun-shū*, sings the praises of his Chinese forefathers:

Crazy cloud
Crazy wind,
You ask what it means:
Mornings in the mountains
Evenings in the town
I choose
The right moment
For stick and shout
And make Tokusan
And Rinzai
Blush.

Bokujū Chinsonshuku 🅉 Jap. for → Mu-chou Ch'en-tsun-su

Bokuseki 🅉 Jap., lit. "traces of ink"; work of calligraphy from the hand of Zen masters and monks. The content of a *bokuseki* is usually "words of dharma" (→ *hōgo*) of the ancient Zen masters and patriarchs (→ *soshigata*). A *bokuseki* is not done with the intention of creating an art work; rather it is the outcome and expression of living Zen experience.

The "traces of ink" are executed by Zen monks practicing the way of calligraphy (→ *shōdō*) for the inspiration of their followers and sometimes at their request. The master who gives one of his students a calligraphy "communicates his heart-mind" (Jap., *kokoro-o ataeru*) to him. The *bokuseki* sometimes consist of a single character, sometimes of a word central to the Zen teaching, sometimes of a Zen poem or *hōgo*. The *bokuseki* of Zen masters like → Musō Soseki, → Ikkyū Sōjun, → Hakuin Zenji, and in our century, for example, → Yamamoto Gempo belong to the outstanding works of Japanese calligraphy. For a scene typical of those in which *bokuseki* come about, → Gyō-jū-za-ga.

Bokushū Chinsonshuku 🅉 Jap. for → Mu-chou Ch'en-tsun-su

Bokushū Dōmei 🅉 also Bokushū Dōmyō, Jap. for → Mu-chou Tao-ming

Bompu 🅉 Jap. → *bonpu-no-joshiki*

Bön 🅑 Tib. lit. "invocation, recitation"; a general heading in Tibetan Buddhism for various religious currents in Tibet before the introduction of Buddhism by → Padmasambhava. The word *bönpo* referred originally to priests with varying functions, as, for example, performing divination or burial rites for the protection of the living and the dead. In a later phase it referred to a theoretical doctrinal system developed that was strongly influenced by foreigners from the neighboring countries to the west. A special role in this was played by the Shangshung kingdom, usually considered to cover a geographical area corresponding to today's west Tibet. In the beginning of the 11th century Bön appeared as an independent school that distinguished itself from Buddhism through its claim to preserve the continuity of the old *bön* tradition. This school, which still exists, shares certain teachings with the → Nyingmapas.

The Tibetan tradition recounts that in pre-Buddhist Tibet the people with its chieftains, preeminently the king, was protected by three kinds of practitioners—the *bönpos*, the bards with their songs, and the practitioners of certain riddle games. With time the duties of the *bönpos*, who were held responsible for exorcism of hostile forces, changed and expanded. Later three aspects of this process were distinguished.

Revealed Bön represents the first, preliterary, stage. Practitioners of this *Bön* used various means in order to "tame the demons below, offer to the gods above, and purify the fireplaces in the middle." Divination with the help of strings and lots made the decisions of the gods visible.

With the murder of the legendary king Trigum began *irregular Bön*, the principal duty of which was the ritual burial of kings. This period, however, was also that of contact with non-Tibetan *bönpos* from the west and of the elaboration of a philosophical system.

In the phase of *transformed Bön* major portions of the Buddhist teaching were made part of this system, still without giving up the elements of the folk religion. This period coincides with the so-called first spread of the buddhist teaching between the 8th and 10th centuries and is also that in which appeared the teacher Shenrab, the founder of the actual Bön school.

The various teachings of this school were finally organized into a canon, the structure of which corresponds approximately to that of the Buddhist scriptures (→ Kangyur-Tengyur). The instructions of Shenrab were classified by later generations into nine vehicles (→ *yāna*). The first four vehicles are the "cause," the next four the "effect," and, parallel to the Nyingmapa school, the *bönpos* possess their own version of the → *dzogchen* teachings as the ninth vehicle.

Bonnō Z Jap., lit. "worldly care, sensual desire, passions, unfortunate longings, suffering, pain"; the (worldly) cares, suffering, and passions that arise out of a deluded (→ *Delusion*) view of the world. *Bonnō* is generally translated by "passions," but that, as the above-listed meanings of the Japanese word indicate, is too narrow a word. In the four great vows (→ *shiguseigan*), an adherent of Zen vows to eliminate these "passions," which obstruct the path to the attainment of enlightenment.

Bönpo B Tib. → *bön*

Bonpu-no-jōshiki Z Jap., lit. "everyman's consciousness"; ordinary consciousness as opposed to that of an enlightened person. Everyman's consciousness is characterized by → delusion, identification with an imaginary separate ego as subject opposed to "outside" objects, and, as a result of this, by the three poisons: aggression, desire, and stupidity (also ignorance, → *avidyā*). According to the Buddhist understanding, the *bonpu-no-jōshiki* is a sick state of mind, in which a person is not aware of his true nature or buddha-nature (→ *busshō*) and therefore remains imprisoned in the suffering-ridden cycle of life and death until he overcomes the deluded state of consciousness through → enlightenment and the realization of the experience of enlightenment in everyday life (→ *mujōdō-no-taigen*).

If the way of Zen is seen as a process that leads from delusion to enlightenment, then the above-described distinction between enlightened and unenlightened consciousness is appropriate. However, from the standpoint of enlightenment, "everyman's consciousness" is not different from enlightened consciousness. Enlightened and unenlightened consciousness— → samsāra and → nirvāna—are identical in nature. The distinction consists only in that the person living in *bonpu-no-jōshiki* does not realize his perfection, which is present in every moment.

The value in the Zen view of "ordinary consciousness" is expressed in a famous kōan from the → *Wu-men-kuan* (example 19). → *Heijōshin kore dō*.

Bonpu-Zen Z Jap. → five types of Zen 1

Borobudur B famous → stūpa in Java, built around the 9th century. Borobudur is a representation of the way of enlightenment in mandala form. This stūpa is comprised of five square, graduated terraces, on top of which are three circular platforms and a final stūpa. The walls of the terraces are adorned with reliefs and buddha figures; the round terraces hold a total of seventy-two stūpas.

Mandala-form ground plan of the stūpa of Borobudur

The mandalic character is clearly expressed by the arrangement of the buddha images on the first four terraces; they hold the respective buddhas of the four directions: → Akshobhya in the east, → Ratnasambhava in the south, → Amitābha in the west, → Amoghasiddhi in the north. The central buddha is → Vairochana, who is found on all sides of the fifth terrace.

The pilgrim who climbs the stūpa from below symbolically arrives at ever higher levels of the way to enlightenment: The lowest terrace shows in reliefs the world of desire (*kāmaloka*, → *loka*) and the realm of hell, that is, → samsāra. After that come reliefs that depict the life of the Buddha Shākyamuni and, higher up, illustrations pertaining to various sūtras, and symbols of the world of form (*rūpaloka*). The circular terraces symbolize the formless world (*arūpaloka*) and emptiness (→ *shūnyatā*).

Bosaṭsu 🅱 🆉 Jap. for → *bodhisattva*

Brahmā 🅷 Skt.; the first god of the → trimūrti, the Hindu trinity of Brahmā, Vishnu, and Shiva. Brahmā is God in his aspect as creator of the universe. Originally all three were accorded equal veneration, but in modern-day India → Brahmanism has diminshed in importance compared with → Vaishnavism, → Shaivism, and → Shaktism. The concept of Brahmā belongs to the realm of *māyā* (cf. Īshvara) and is by no means to be confused with → *brahman*. Brahmā is often depicted as having four faces and four arms that hold such symbols as the Vedas and prayer beads.

Brahmā. (Sandstone sculpture from Baset, Cambodia, 10th century)

Brahma-Chaitanya 🅷 (Brahma-Caitanya), Skt.; *brahman*-consciousness, also referred to as → *turīya*, the fourth, supraconscious state, which is experienced only in → *samādhi* and in which there is no longer any identification with the body and mind.

Brahmachāri 🅷 (Brahmacārin), Skt.; 1. a religious seeker who has submitted himself to spiritual disciplines and has taken the first monastic vows; 2. a young man on the first of the four stages of life according to the Vedas, that of → *brahmacharya*.

Brahmacharya 🅷 🅱 (brahmacarya), Skt.; continence, chastity.

🅷 1. continence in thought, word, and deed, one of the five virtues of the first stage (*yama*) of → Rāja-Yoga, as stipulated by the *Yoga-Sūtra* of → Patañjali; together these five constitute the Great Vow (→ Mahāvrata) that is undertaken for all eight steps. The other four virtues are *ahimsā* (harmlessness, noninjury of others), *asteya* (not stealing), *satya* (truthfulness), and *aparigraha* (noncovetousness, poverty); 2. an ordination ceremony at which a novice takes the first monastic vows; also, the attitude assumed by a → *brahmachāri* after taking such vows; 3. the first of the four stages (→ *āshrama*) into which a man's life is divided according to Vedic tradition. During this stage, the youth receives religious and worldly instruction from his parents and teachers. He develops his mental faculties and the virtues that lead to a spiritual life.

🅱 (Pali brahmacariya); holy conduct of life, leading a life in harmony with the Buddhist rules of discipline (→ *shīla*) and especially one of chastity. The lifestyle of a Buddhist monk.

Brahmajāla-sūtra 🅱 Skt., lit. "*Sūtra of the Net of Brahman*"; sūtra of Mahāyāna Buddhism that contains the basic teaching on discipline and morality (→ *shīla*) and that is therefore of major significance for Chinese and Japanese Buddhism.

It contains the ten rules of Mahāyāna, which are obligatory for every follower: avoidance of (1) killing, (2) stealing, (3) unchaste behavior, (4) lying, (5) use of intoxicants, (6) gossip, (7) boasting, (8) envy, (9) resentment and ill will, (10) slander of the three precious ones (→ *triratna*). Violation of these rules means expulsion from the → *sangha*.

The Brahmajāla-sūtra also contains a further forty-eight less important injunctions. In this sūtra, too, permission is given for self-ordination in cases where the requirements for an official → ordination cannot be fulfilled. The fifty-eight rules in the *Brahmajāla-sūtra* constitute the content of the bodhisattva vow, which every Mahāyāna monk takes after ordination.

Brahmajñāna 🅷 , or Brahmavidyā, Skt.; the transcendent knowledge of *brahman;* its realization. "One who knows *brahman,* becomes *brahman,*" proclaim the Upanishads, and the fourth chapter of the *Bhagavad-Gītā* states, "He who sees *brahman* in every action, shall attain *brahman.*" The highest goal of human life according to Hinduism is the realization of *brahman*; thus *brahmajñāna* is the summit of all knowledge. One who attains it is called a *brahmajñāni* (lit. "a knower of *brahman*").

Brahmakāra-Vritti 🅗 (Brahmakāra-Vṛtti), Skt.; devout thoughts concerning the knowledge of God and the experience of divine consciousness.

Brahmāloka 🅗 Skt.; a heaven or plane of existence where advanced spiritual aspirants go after death, there to dwell in the company of the divine.

Brāhmamuhūrta 🅗 Skt., lit. "Brahmā's hour"; the time of day that is most propitious for meditation; the hour at dawn or at dusk when night turns to day or day to night.

Brahman 🅗 Skt.; the eternal, imperishable Absolute; the supreme nondual reality of Vedānta (not to be confused with → Brahmā); *brahman* is a concept that has no equivalent in the religions of dualism, all of which feature a personal God. As absolute consciousness, *brahman* is an abstract concept that is not accessible to the thinking mind. In the process of any attempt to render it more concrete, *brahman* becomes → Īshvara.

Brahman is a state of pure transcendence that cannot be grasped by thought or speech. Hence Shrī Rāmakrishna's trenchant statement, "No tongue has ever defiled *brahman.*" Seekers employ linguistic approximations such as "the One without a second" or → Satchidānanda. Such phrases are meant to express that *brahman* is absolute being, absolute consciousness, and absolute bliss. Without *brahman* as absolute being, existence would not be possible, and *brahman* as consciousness makes it possible for us to perceive existence and bliss. *Brahman* as → *chit,* or absolute consciousness reflected in the → *jīva,* gives rise to mental consciousness, which in turn projects the entire manifest world of names and shapes (→ *nāmarūpa*). The Vedic utterance "Kham Brahm" (All is *brahman*) means that *brahman* alone exists, while we project upon it an imaginary world of notions, like the superimposition of the idea of a snake on a rope.

Brahman 🅗 Skt. (Brāhmaṇa), a member of the priestly class, the highest of the four castes (→ *varna*). In Vedic times, the brahmans were simply those priests who sang the hymns revealed to the → *rishis* and set down in the *Rigveda.* However, these hymns were never common property; rather they were transmitted orally from father to son in families of singers. As time went by and the people became increasingly estranged from the origins of these ancient hymns, the sense and understanding of their texts grew ever dimmer in the minds of the common people. Consequently, the brahmans, as the guardians of this spiritual treasure, grew in stature. To extend their control further, the brahmans supported the common belief that only through such ancient hymns, and the sacrificial rites associated with them, would proper communion with the gods be possible, such communion in turn being held to determine one's earthly happiness, the begetting of progeny, the accumulation of wealth, victory over one's enemies, and so forth.

The → *kshatriyas* opposed the dominance of the *brahmans,* and a bitter struggle for supremacy ensued between the two classes. The relationship between the two *rishis* → Vasishtha and → Vishvāmitra clearly reflects this struggle. Finally, the brahmans gained the upper hand. Just as the living religion threatened to turn to stone under their ambitious rule, the Buddha → Shākyamuni appeared and with his teaching overcame the dominion of the brahmans, freed the other castes from oppression, and brought reform to all of India. After more than a thousand years, Buddhism in turn lost its force in India and became frozen in a series of outer forms, whereupon → Shankara rose as the next great reformer. Returning to the profound teachings of the → Vedas and → Upanishads, he gave them new life through his commentaries and writings, his teachings, and the establishment of monastic orders.

Brāhmana 🅗 (Brāhmaṇa), Skt.; or Brāhmanam; each of the → Vedas includes a Brāhmana, a manual of instruction *(vidhi)* for the practical use of the material found in the → Samhitā. Appended to these are various explanatory texts *(arthavāda)* that have served as the point of departure for philosophical discussions, most of which originated toward the end of the Brāhmanas and which therefore have been compiled under the name → Vedānta ("end of the Veda"). This last category forms the content of the supplementary texts appended to the Brāhmanas, the so-called Āranyakas; the Upanishads were later derived from these and are thus each allocated to a specific Veda.

Brahma-Nadī 🅗 Skt.; a Tantric term for the channel of energy in the body through which the → *kundalinī* begins to rise.

Brahmā-Nāma 🅗 Skt.; a → *japa*-practice, the repetition of the name of Brahmā.

Brahmānanda 🅗 Skt., lit. "the bliss of *brahman*"; 1. according to the Vedantic view, *brahman* is absolute consciousness and admits no opposites; hence it must be pure, unclouded bliss; 2. one of the two major disciples of → Rāmakrishna (1863–1922); the other was Svāmi → Vivekānanda.

Svāmi Brahmānanda, born Rakhal Chandra Ghosh, joined Rāmakrishna in Dakshinesvara in 1881 and became his disciple. After the master's death, he renounced the world and, as Svāmi Brahmānanda, became the leader of the head monastery of the → Rāmakrishna Order, in Belur. In 1900, he became its president. He traveled throughout India, visiting the centers of the Rāmakrishna Mission and establishing new ones.

Brahmanaspati 🅷 (Brahmanaspati), Skt.; Brahmā as one of the three great divinities of the → *trimūrti.* He becomes creator through the word, bringing everything into existence by his cry. He gives expression to all existence, all vital movement, and all conscious knowledge.

Brahman-Bhāvanā 🅷 Skt.; identification of one's self with the supreme reality, the absolute consciousness (→ *chit*).

Brahmānda 🅷 (Brahmāṇḍa), Skt., lit. "the egg of Brahmā"; the universe, the manifest world.

Brahmānī 🅷 (Brahmāṇī), Skt.; 1. another name for → Durgā; 2. the wife of → Brahmā.

Brahmanirvāna 🅷 Skt.; dissolution and release in *brahman,* possible only in the state of → *nirvikalpa-samādhi,* in which even the last traces of duality are dissolved.

Brahmanism 🅷 1. a term used in the West for orthodox → Hinduism; 2. the worship of → Brahmā as the creator god. The notion of a creator god plays a much smaller role in India than it does in the West. In the Vedas, Brahmā is rarely mentioned as creator. Rather, Prajāpati is named lord of the creation, and Brahmā is at times accorded equal status; both gods emerged from → Hiranyagarbha. The *Nāsadāsīya,* the renowned creation hymn from the *Rigveda* (the oldest Veda), states that the gods appeared only after the creation (10.129.6). Not until the development of the → *trimūrti,* the Hindu trinity, which arose much later, is Brahmā venerated as a creator god; even here he shares his position with Vishnu, the maintainer, and Shiva, the destroyer, whereby each of the three takes a dominant role in turn, until Brahmā ultimately declines in importance.

Brahman Satyam, Jagat Mithyā 🅷 Skt.; this famous utterance of the teaching of → Advaita-Vedānta proclaims that *brahman* alone is real and the world is illusory, a superimposition.

Brahmarandhra 🅷 Skt.; the crown of the head. It is made accessible through certain yogic practices, so that the consciousness is able to ascend to higher planes. Symbol for the dematerialization of consciousness (→ *kundalinī).*

Brahma-Samādhi 🅷 Skt.; an illuminatory (→ *samādhi*) state of *brahman*-consciousness, supposed to be attained through → *japa,* the correct and steadfast practice of repetition of a mantra. However, there is no causal relationship between the period of practice or number of practices and illumination, a state that lies beyond causality.

Brahmasthiti 🅷 Skt.; a firm stand in that which is divine, from *sthā:* "to stand." The term refers to a firm foundation in God, by which any doubt regarding God's existence is dispelled. In one who has attained Brahmasthiti, faith in God as a "working hypothesis" has dissolved into the certainty that God is ever-present.

The closing lines of the second chapter of the *Bhagavad-Gītā,* in which Krishna describes those of constant wisdom, states: "Thus it is with the God-illumined. Never does such a one fall back into delusion. Even at the hour of death one lives in the light of truth. God and he are one" (2.72f.).

Brahma-Sūtra 🅷 Skt.; a collection of aphorisms and verses on the philosophy of Vedānta; also known as the *Vedānta-Sūtra.*

Brahmatejas 🅷 Skt.; the power and majesty of *brahman*; the fire or burning embers of the divine.

Brahma-Vastu 🅷 Skt.; the truth or reality of God. As long as it exists in the mind, it is not yet the ultimate truth, which is realized only in union with God (→ *brahman*), at which point it is beyond expression.

Brahmavid 🅷 Skt.; one who has seen and known God, an illuminated one, for whom God has become real; one who had the "*visio Dei,*" as the Christian mystics put it.

Brahmavid-Varishtha 🅷 (Brahmavid-Variṣṭha), Skt.; one who has attained supreme God-knowledge; the best of God-knowers.

Brahmavidyā 🅷 Skt.; knowledge of *brahman*; synonymous with → *Brahmajñāna.*

Brahma-vihāra 🅱 Skt., Pali, lit. "divine states of dwelling"; content of a meditation practice in which the practitioner arouses in himself four positive states of mind and radiates them out in all directions. The four *brahma-vihāras* are limitless kindness (→ *maitrī*) toward all beings; limitless compassion (→ *karunā*) toward those who are suffering; limitless joy (→ *muditā*) over the salvation of others from suffering; limitless equanimity (→ *upekshā*) toward friend and foe. Arousing these states of mind permits the practitioner to overcome ill will, gloating over others' misfortune, discontent, and passion.

In Mahāyāna the *brahma-vihāras* are included among the "perfect virtues" (→ *pāramitā*). These are states of mind required by the bodhisattva in order to lead all beings to liberation. Practicing the *brahma-vihāras* is said to bring about rebirth in the heaven of Brahma (→ *deva*). This belief explains the name *brahma-vihāra*. The *brahma-vihāras* are also known as the four immeasurables (Skt. *apramāna*; Pali *appamannā*).

The sūtra text on this meditation practice is: "There are four immeasurables. Therein, brothers, a monk radiates with a mind filled with kindness [compassion, sympathetic joy, equanimity] first one direction, then a second, then a third, then a fourth, above as well, and below, and all around; and feeling himself connected with everything everywhere, he irradiates the whole world with a mind filled with kindness [compassion, sympathetic joy, equanimity], with expansive, sublime, unconfined mind, free from malice and resentment (trans. from German edition of Nyanatiloka 1972).

Brahma-Yoga 🅗 Skt.; union with divine immortality, with the All, with everything that is manifest and unmanifest.

Brahmopāsana 🅗 Skt.; worship of Brahmā, or the divine (→ *upāsana*).

Brāhmo-Samāj 🅗 Skt.; a nineteenth-century Indian religious and social-reform movement. Marked by a theistic strain, it was devoted to the worship of the eternal, impenetrable, and immutable One, the creator and upholder of the universe.

The movement was founded by Ram Mohan Roy (1772-1833) and organized by Devendranāth Tagore (1817-1905). Membership was open to all, irrespective of religious denomination, caste, race, or nationality. In 1857 → Keshab Chandra Sen (1838-1884) became the third leader of the movement. He came under Christian influence, left Tagore's *samāj*, and founded the Sādhāran-Brāhmo-Samāj. Sen met several times with Shrī Rāmakrishna and died two years before Rāmakrishna, who had expressed great trust in him.

Braja 🅗 Skt. → Vrindāvan

Brihadāranyaka-Upanishad 🅗 (Bṛhadāranyaka-Upaniṣad), Skt., lit. *brihat:* "great," *āranyaka:* "of the forest"; an Upanishad belonging to the *White* → *Yajurveda*. Entitled "great" for its length and profundity, it is famous for the teaching on the Self that it contains as related by the sage Yājñavalkya to his wife, Maitreyī. The work teaches the absolute identity of *ātman* and *brahman*. Shankara wrote a commentary on it.

Brihaspati 🅗 (Bṛhaspati), synonymous with Brahmanaspati (Brahmaṇaspati), Skt., lit. "lord of prayer"; the creator of the word, who in the Vedas (as in the Gospel of John) stands at the origin of creation and is one with God. Through the word, Brihaspati conveys knowledge, conviction, and the faculty of the creative rhythm of expression.

With the help of the word, Brihaspati makes it possible to indicate things that lie beyond reason and can be grasped only through intuition. Moreover, by mastering all subtleties of language, one can gain influence and vanquish one's enemies by argument. Hence the great import accorded in Hinduism to the word. Brihaspati thus rose from his initial position as an unimportant deity to an increasingly higher rank.

Brindāban 🅗, or Brindāvan, Skt. → Vrindāvan

Buddha 🅑 🅩 Skt., Pali, lit. "awakened one." 1. a person who has achieved the enlightenment that leads to release from the cycle of existence (→ samsāra) and has thereby attained complete liberation (→ nirvāna). The content of his teaching, which is based on the experience of enlightenment, is the → four noble truths. A buddha has overcome every kind of craving (→ *trishnā*); although even he also has pleasant and unpleasant sensations, he is not ruled by them and remains innerly untouched by them. After his death he is not reborn again.

Two kinds of buddhas are distinguished: the *pratyeka-buddha*, who is completely enlightened but does not expound the teaching; and the *samyak-sambuddha*, who expounds for the welfare of all beings the teaching that he has discovered anew. A *samyak-sambuddha* is omniscient (*sarvajñatā*) and possesses the ten powers of a buddha (*dashabala*) and the → four certainties. The buddha of our age is → Shākyamuni (Also → Buddha 2).

Shākyamuni Buddha, the historical Buddha, is not the first and only buddha. Already in the early Hīnayāna texts, six buddhas who preceded him in earlier epochs are mentioned: Vipashyin (Pali, Vipassi), Shikin (Sikhī), Vishvabhū (Vessabhū), Krakuchchanda (Kakusandha), Konagāmana, and Kāshyapa (Kassapa). The

An early depiction of the Buddha with companions under the Bodhi-tree (sandstone sculpture from Mathurā, 2nd century)

buddha who will follow Shākyamuni in a future age and renew the → dharma is → Maitreya. Beyond these, one finds indications in the literature of thirteen further buddhas, of which the most important is → Dīpamkara, whose disciple Shākyamuni was in his previous existence as the ascetic Sumedha. The stories of these legendary buddhas are contained in the *Buddhavamsa*, a work from the *Khuddaka-nikāya.*

The life course of a buddha begins when he, as a bodhisattva in the presence of a previous buddha whose disciple he is, takes the bodhisattva vow to become an awakened one. After that he practices the ten → pāramitās for countless existences. Before his last birth, he dwells in the → Tushita Heaven. When he is reborn for the last time, the bodhisattva bears the thirty-two marks of perfection (→ *dvātrimshadvara-lakshana*) and the eighty minor marks. He is in possession of the thirty-seven preprequisites of enlightenment (→ *bodhipākshika-dharma*). The mother of this buddha dies seven days after his birth. At the appropriate time the incipient buddha enters into → homelessness, and after attaining enlightenment he founds an order. The course of his life is ended by his final extinction in nirvāna (→ *parinirvāna*).

2. The historical Buddha. He was born in 563 B.C.E., the son of a prince of the Shākyas, whose small kingdom in the foothills of the Himālayas lies in present-day Nepal. His first name was Siddhārtha, his family name Gautama. Hence he is also called Gautama Buddha. (For the story of his life, → Siddhārtha Gautama.) During his life as a wandering ascetic, he was known as Shākyamuni, the "Silent Sage of the Shākyas." In order to distinguish the historical Buddha from the transcendent buddhas (see buddha 3), he is generally called Shākyamuni Buddha or Buddha Shākyamuni.

3. The "buddha principle," which manifests itself in the most various forms. Whereas in Hīnayāna only the existence of one buddha in every age is accepted (in which case the buddha is considered an earthly being who teaches humans), for the Mahāyāna there are countless transcendent buddhas. According to the Mahāyāna teaching of the *trikāya*, the buddha principle manifests itself in three principal forms, the so-called three bodies (→ *trikāya*). In this sense the transcendent buddhas represent embodiments of various aspects of the buddha principle.

Among the transcendent buddhas are → Amitābha, → Akshobhya, → Vairochana, → Ratnasambhava, → Amoghasiddhi, → Vajrasattva, and many others. They are teachers of the bodhisattvas, and each reigns over a paradise (→ pure land). The transcendent buddhas are supramundane (→ *lokottara*), perfectly pure in spirit and body and possess eternal life and limitless power. According to the *trikāya* teaching they are so-called *sambhogakāya* buddhas, which according to some views are regarded as spiritual creations of the bodhisattvas, to whom their luminous images become so clear that they take on form as subjective realities or objectively present, unearthly beings of refined materiality. As *sambhogakāya* manifestations, they are the spiritual fathers of the *nirmānakāya* buddhas, the embodiments of the buddha principle in human form.

Around 750 C.E., as an outgrowth of the → Vajrayāna, a hierarchical schema developed, which admits, in addition to the *dharmakāya* (→ *trikāya*), which all buddhas have in common, five transcendent buddhas. Each of these buddhas is associated with an earthly buddha and a transcendent bodhisattva. The transcendent buddha Vairochana is associated with the earthly buddha Krakuchchanda and the transcendent bodhisattva → Samantabhadra; the transcendent buddha Akshobhya is associated with the earthly buddha Kanakamuni and the bodhisattva Vajrapāni; to Ratnasambhava belong Kāshyapa as earthly buddha and Ratnapāni as bodhisattva; the transcendent buddha Amoghasiddhi is associated with the earthly buddha Maitreya and the transcendent bodhisattva Vishvapāni. (Also → *buddhakula.*)

4. A synonym for the absolute, ultimate reality devoid of form, color, and all other properties—buddha-nature. When in Zen the question is posed, "What is a buddha?" this is neither a question about the historical dates of an earthly buddha nor a question concerning the philosophical and psychological nuances of the *trikāya* teaching; rather it is a question concerning the eternal, or timeless, truth of buddha-nature.

Buddhabhadra ▣ 359–429; monk of the → Sarvāstivāda school, born in Kashmir. In 409 Buddhabhadra went to China, where he translated important works of Mahāyāna Sanskrit literature into Chinese, in part together with → Fa-hsien.

Buddhabhadra entered the Buddhist order at the age of seventeen and was soon well known for his ability in meditation and in the observance of the rules of discipline. In his homeland he met the Chinese monk Chih-yen, who persuaded him to go to China. In 409 he arrived in Ch'ang-an where he became a spokesman for the doctrines of his teacher Buddhasena, a famous master of → dhyāna. He soon came into conflict with monks from the school of → Kumārajīva, who had the support of the imperial court. Buddhabhadra was compelled to leave the capital. In 410 Buddhabhadra reached the → Lu-shan, where he met Hui-yuan (→ pure land). In 415 he came to present-day Nanking. There he translated fundamental works of Buddhism: for example, the → Vinaya-pitaka and the *Mahāparinirvāna-sūtra*; between 418 and 421 he composed a sixty-volume version of the → *Buddhāvatamsaka-sūtra.*

Buddha-charita ▣ Skt., lit. "*Life of the Buddha*"; poetic work of → Ashvaghosha. It is the first complete life story of the Buddha → Shākyamuni from his birth to his *parinirvāna.* The *Buddha-charita* originally comprised twenty-eight songs, of which only thirteen are extant in Sanskrit. It also exists in a Tibetan translation.

Chinese pilgrims of the 7th century who traveled to India reported that the *Buddha-charita* enjoyed great popularity there and was frequently read and recited. The work resembles in its style classical Indian heroic poetry and is rich in poetical descriptions. It reflects the trend toward devotion (→ *bhakti*) to the Buddha as a cult figure and contributed to the widespread diffusion of Buddhism.

Buddhadatta ▣ scholar of the → Theravāda school who lived in the 4th to 5th centuries. He was of Tamil origin and was born in Uragapura in Ceylon. After long journeys to the capital Anurādhapura, he composed his works. Buddhadatta wrote commentaries to the → Vinaya-pitaka, the *Buddhavamsa* (→ *Khuddaka-nikāya*),the *Abhidhammāvtāra*, and the *Rūpārūpa-vibhāga*, the latter two being handbooks of the → Abhidharma, which set forth the teachings of the Theravāda in a concise, clear way.

Buddha-dharma ▣ ▣ Skt. (Jap., *buppō*); the "buddha law," "buddha teaching," "buddha norm"—generally, the teaching of the historical Buddha → Shākyamuni, which is based on enlightenment and is intended to lead to it; as such, buddha-dharma is a synonym for Buddhism. In Zen buddha-dharma (*buppō*) is not understood as a teaching that can be transmitted conceptually, as through writings and oral explanations, but rather as the conceptually ungraspable essential truth from the experience of which the teaching of the Buddha sprung and which is only accessible in the immediate realization of one's own enlightenment experience.

Buddhaghosha ▣ (Buddhaghoṣa), Pali, Skt., lit., "Buddha Voice"; scholar of the → Theravāda school. He was born to a brahmin family at the end of the 4th century in Magadha near → Bodh-gayā. After reading Buddhist texts, he converted to Buddhism and went to Ceylon, where, in the Mahāvihāra Monastery, he studied Theravāda teachings under the tutelage of the monk Sanghapala Thera. In Anurādhapura he wrote nineteen commentaries to canonical works, among others, the → Vinaya-pitaka and the → Nikāyas, and the *Dhamma-sangani* and the *Vibhanga* of the → Abhidharma. His principal work is the → *Visuddhi-magga* (*Way of Purity*), a complete exposition of the Theravāda teaching as taught at the Mahāvihāra Monastery.

Buddhahood ▣ ▣ expression for the realization of perfect enlightenment, which characterizes a buddha. The attainment of buddhahood is the birthright and highest goal of all beings. According to the highest teachings of Buddhism, as they are formulated, for example, in Zen, every sentient being has, or better, *is* already buddha-nature (Jap., → *busshō*); thus buddhahood cannot be "attained"; it is much more a matter of experiencing the factuality of this primordial perfection and realizing it in everyday life.

Buddhakula ▣ Skt., lit. "buddha family"; the five fundamental qualities of the sambhogakāya (→ *trikāya*), manifested in the mandala of the five → *tathāgatas.* They embody the properties of the five different aspects of wisdom (→ *prajñā*), but manifest themselves not only as positive energies, but also as negative states of mind. Since every phenomenon exhibits one of these five qualities, they are known as the "families" with which all phenomena are associated. This is a principle of organization much used in the → Vajrayāna; all iconography and symbology are based on it. The typology of the five buddha families also provides the basic framework for the deities visualized in → *sādhanas.* The lords of the five familes are → Vairochana, → Akshobhya, → Ratnasambhva, → Amitābha, and → Amoghasiddhi.

The first of the five *tathāgatas,* white in color and in the center of the mandala, is Vairochana. He represents the ignorance (→ avidyā) that is the origin of the cycle of existence (→ samsāra) and also the wisdom of the ultimate reality that is the basis of everything. Since as the central figure he is the point of origin of the mandala, his buddha family is called the *tathāgata* or buddha family.

On the east side of the mandala (which, following the Indian tradition, is below) is Akshobhya. He is the lord of the *vajra* family and his negative energy is aggression, which, however, can be transmuted into "mirrorlike wisdom." His body is blue in color.

In the southern part of the mandala (on the left side) is Ratnasambhava, yellow in color, the lord of the *ratna* family. He is associated with pride and its antidote, the wisdom of equanimity.

Above, in the west, appears Amitābha of the lotus or *padma* family. With his red color he symbolizes passion and longing, which corresponds to the wisdom of discriminating awareness.

On the right, northern, side is Amoghasiddhi of the karma family, green in color. The negative quality associated with him is envy or jealousy, which is related with all-accomplishing wisdom.

In particular Tantras, there are variations in this arrangement, particularly with regard to the placement of the buddha and *vajra* families. The *tathāgatas* possess further attributes beyond those mentioned and are accompanied by a feminine aspect.

Buddhamitra Z ninth patriarch in the Indian lineage of → Zen.

Buddhanandi Z eighth patriarch in the Indian lineage of → Zen.

Buddha-nature Z → *busshō*

Buddha-nature B (Skt. buddhatā); according to the Mahāyāna view, the true, immutable, and eternal nature of all beings. Since all beings possess this buddha-nature, it is possible for them to attain enlightenment and become a buddha, regardless of what level of existence they occupy.

The interpretation of the essence of buddha-nature varies from school to school; there is controversy over whether all beings and also inanimate entities actually possess buddha-nature.

The answer to the question whether buddha-nature is immanent in beings is an essential determining factor for the association of a given school with → Hīnayāna or → Mahāyāna, the two great currents within Buddhism. In Hīnayāna this notion is unknown; here the potential to become a buddha is not ascribed to every being. By contrast the Mahāyāna sees the attainment of buddhahood as the highest goal; it can be attained through the inherent buddha-nature of every being through appropriate spiritual practice.

Buddhapālita B → Mādhyamika

Buddha-shāsana B (buddha-śāsana), Skt. (Pali *buddha-sāsana*); buddha discipline, teaching of the Buddha. A term used in Asia for the Buddhist religion, which refers to the teaching, the rules of discipline or morality (→ *shīla*), devotional and meditative practices—all of which are said to stem from the Buddha. In a narrower sense, in the → Theravāda, *buddha-shāsana* designates the nine forms in which the message of the buddha is contained: sūtras; prose mixed with verse; verse (*gāthā*); ceremonial expressions (*udāna*); stories about the previous existences of the Buddha (*Jātaka*); words of the master (*itivuttaka*); extraordinary things; and analyses.

Buddhas of the three times B buddhas of the past, present, and future: Kāshyapa, → Shākyamuni, and → Maitreya. In most pictorial representations of the buddhas of the three times → Dīpamkara is the buddha of the past.

Buddhatā B Skt. → buddha-nature

Buddhavamsa B Skt. → *Khuddaka-nikāya*

Buddhāvatamsaka-sūtra B Z (Buddhāvataṃsaka-sūtra), short form *Avatamsaka-sūtra*, Skt., lit. "*Sūtra of the Garland of Buddhas*"; Mahāyāna sūtra that constitutes the basis of the teachings of the Chinese Hua-yen (Jap., Kegon) school, which emphasizes above all "mutually unobstructed interpenetration." In addition it teaches that the human mind is the universe itself and is identical with the buddha, indeed, that buddha, mind, and all sentient beings and things are one and the same. This aspect of the Mahāyāna teaching was especially stressed by the Chinese Ch'an (Jap., Zen) school, whence the frequent citations of the *Avatamsaka-sūtra* by these schools.

The *Buddhāvatamsaka-sūtra* is one of the → Vaipulya sūtras and is thus a collection of several individual writings, of which the longest is the → *Gandavyūha*; another important part is the → *Dashabhūmika*. The sūtra is extant only in Tibetan and Chinese translations. The oldest Chinese translation is from the 5th century. The teachings presented here are not spoken by Shākyamuni Buddha himself; he is present but remains silent most of the time. They are rather utterances of the dharmakāya (→ *trikāya*) aspect of all the buddhas. The silence of the Buddha corresponds to emptiness (→ *shūnyatā*), and the pronouncement of the teaching is born out of this silence as a manifestation of the true reality that is graspable by human consciousness. (Also → Hua-yen school, → Kegon school.)

Buddhehparatah 🅗 (Buddheḥparataḥ), Skt.; lying beyond reason; higher consciousness, intuition. Without intuition, spiritual experiences are not possible, and such experiences are more important than logic and reason.

Buddhi 🅗 Skt.; intelligence. The discriminatory element in the → *antahkarana,* that which categorizes all sensory impressions. In itself a lifeless instrument, *buddhi* draws upon the intelligence and consciousness of the → *ātman* and develops all human faculties, incluiding intuition.

Buddhīndriya 🅗 Skt. → *indriya*

Buddhism 🅑 the religion of the awakened one (→ buddha, → *buddha-dharma*); one of the three great world religions. It was founded by the historical Buddha → Shākyamuni in the 6th to 5th centuries B.C.E. In answer to the question concerning the cause of the entanglement of beings in the cycle of existence (→ samsāra) and the possibility of removing it—the central question for Indian philosophy at the time of the Buddha—he expounded the → four noble truths, the core of his teaching, which he had recognized in the moment of his enlightenment. Life is regarded by Buddha as impermanent (→ *anitya*), without essence (→ *anātman*), and characterized by suffering. The recognition of these three marks of existence (→ *trilakshana*) marks the beginning of the Buddhist path. The suffering-ridden quality of existence is conditioned by craving (→ *trishnā*) and ignorance (→ *avidyā*), through the clearing away of which liberation from samsāra can be attained. The entanglement of beings in the cycle of existence is explained in Buddhism by the chain of conditioned arising (→ *pratītya-samutpāda*). The termination of the cycle is tantamount to the realization of → nirvāna.

The way to this can be summarized in terms of the four noble truths, the eightfold path, training in discipline and morality (→ *shīla*), meditation (→ *samādhi*, → *dhyāna*), and wisdom and insight (→ *prajñā*).

The basic thought of Buddhism is summed up in the → Tripitaka. The Buddhist community (→ *sangha*) consists of monks and nuns (→ *bhikshu*, → *bhikshunī*) as well as lay followers (→ *upāsaka*).

The historical development of Buddhism can be divided into four major phases:

1. From the middle of the 6th to the middle of the 5th century B.C.E., the phase of early Buddhism, in which the teaching was expounded by the Buddha and diffused by his disciples.

2. The middle of the 4th century B.C.E. to the 1st century C.E., division into various schools on the basis of differing interpretations of the teaching (→ Hīnayāna, → Buddhist Councils).

3. The 1st to the 7th century C.E.; the rise of the Mahāyāna with its two major currents, → Mādhyamaka and → Yogāchāra.

4. After the 7th century; the emergence of Buddhist Tantra (→ Tibetan Buddhism, → Vajrayāna, → Tantra).

After the 13th century Buddhism became practically extinct in India, the country of its origin.

From about the 3d century, Buddhism began to spread outside of India, adapting itself to local conditions. Today Hīnayāna Buddhism of the → Theravāda school is to be found in Ceylon (Sri Lanka), Thailand, Burma, and Cambodia; Mahāyāna in China, Japan, Vietnam, and Korea; Vajrayāna in Tibet, Mongolia, and Japan.

Exact figures concerning the number of Buddhists in the world (150–500 million) cannot be given, since adherence to Buddhism does not preclude adherence to other religions.

Buddhism in Burma: According to tradition Burma came into contact with Buddhism during the reign of King → Ashoka (3d century B.C.E.). Another tradition says that Buddhism was brought to Burma by two merchants at the time of the Buddha. The merchants are said to have brought with them from India some of Buddha's hair, which is still preserved today in the Shwe-dagon Pagoda in Rangoon.

After the 5th century, there is evidence of a flourishing Buddhist life in Burma. Activity of the Theravāda and that of another school (probably the → Sarvāstivāda), which used Sanskrit, can be documented. In the 7th century both Hīnayāna and Mahāyāna (especially in the north) coexisted. In the following century, Buddhist

Tantrism penetrated Burma. In the 11th century the entire country was converted to Theravāda under the rule of King Anaratha. This spelled the end of Mahāyāna in Burma. The Theravāda gradually assimilated the indigenous folk belief in spirits called *nats* and gave it a Buddhist sense.

Pagan, in the north of the country, became the center of Buddhism. Burma maintained intensive contact with Ceylon. There, toward the end of the 12th century, the Buddhism practiced at the Mahāvihāra Monastery was declared obligatory for all Buddhists of Ceylon. This had a negative effect on Burmese Buddhism, since according to Burmese monks who had been in Ceylon, only those monks whose ordination had taken place at Mahāvihāra were legitimate. This met resistance within the Burmese *sangha* and resulted in the splintering of the community into several rival groups. In the 15th century King Dhammacheti unified the Burmese community under the auspices of the Mahāvihāra Monastery. Since then, this form of Theravāda has become the prevailing form of Buddhism in Burma.

The conquest of the country by the English in the 19th century greatly damaged the *sangha* and its organization. Only after the recovery of independence in 1947 could the old structures be restored with the help of the government.

In 1956 a council took place in Rangoon at which the full text of the Tripitaka was recited. Today about 85 percent of the population of Burma is Buddhist. Buddhism is the official religion of the country.

Buddhism in Cambodia: This region was in contact with a Sanskrit tradition of Buddhism in the 3d century C.E., probably that of the Sarvāstivāda school, which reached its zenith in the 5th and 6th centuries. An inscription from the year 791 found in the neighborhood of → Angkor Wat bears witness to the existence of the Mahāyāna in Cambodia. The country was also under the influence of Shaivism. The synthesis that developed out of the mixture of the two religions was characterized by the cult of the bodhisattva Lokeshvara, a fusion of Avalokiteshvara and Shiva. Later the Shaivite element seems to have been eliminated. However, again in the 13th century an upsurge of the Shiva cult took place, in the course of which the Buddhist *sangha* was exposed to severe persecution.

Records left by Chinese pilgrims show that during this time Theravāda was represented by numerous followers, while Mahāyāna was losing influence. The first inscription in Pali is from the year 1309; it makes clear that the Theravāda was under the protection of the royal house. Since that time it has been the dominant form of Buddhism in Cambodia. Toward the end of the 19th century the Dhammayut school of Thailand gained a foothold in Cambodia.

Buddhism in Ceylon: According to tradition, Buddhism was brought to Ceylon from India around 250 B.C.E. by → Mahinda and Sanghamitta, children of King Ashoka. The king of Ceylon, Devanampiya Tissa, himself became a Buddhist and built the Mahāvihāra Monastery, where he preserved the branch of the → Bodhi-tree that Mahinda and his sister had brought. This monastery remained for many centuries the center of orthodox Theravāda.

In the course of time various schools were formed. There was sometimes very vehement rivalry among them. A number of kings tried to end these disputes by convoking synods or by persecution of certain schools. The main antagonists were the monks of Mahāvihāra on one side and those of the Abhayagirivihāra and the Jetavanavihāra on the other. The latter party was under the influence of Indian schools; traces of Mahāyāna and Buddhist Tantrism can also be documented. The Theravāda gained the upper hand, to which result Buddhaghosha, one of the great scholars of the Theravāda, decisively contributed. His work marks Singhalese Buddhism to this day. The many-sidedness of Buddhism in Ceylon met a bitter end in the 12th century, when King Parakkambahu I convoked a synod and forced all hostile schools to adopt the Buddhism of Mahāvihāra.

The arrival of the Portuguese in Ceylon in the 16th century—who tried to introduce Catholicism by force—and that of the Dutch in the 17th century aroused national feeling and had a strengthening effect on Buddhism, which had been in the process of deterioration.

Several Singhalese kings undertook measures to give new impetus to Buddhism. They sent delegations to Burma (end of the 17th century) and Thailand (18th century) in order to gain support. As a result of this contact with foreign monks Burmese and Thai tendencies began to make themselves felt in the *sangha* in Ceylon. Thai monks introduced an aristocratic principle of selection, which aroused resistance in other strata of the population but established, in spite of this, one of the main enduring tendencies of Singhalese Buddhism. In 1802 a Burmese branch of the *sangha* emerged—Amarapura, the members of which came from the ordinary classes of the people. Both tendencies remain today, the Thai-inspired being the stronger.

More recently a third current developed, which is of Burmese origin and is characterized by particular strictness. In the 19th century the Buddhism of Ceylon was at its nadir; Western Buddhists, who formed new centers and organizations (→ Mahābodhi Society), contributed decisively to its revival.

By 1948 Buddhism was again a driving force in Singhalese culture and played a role in the achievement of national independence in that year. Today Singhalese Buddhism is influential in other Asian countries as well as in the West.

Buddhism in China: According to Chinese tradition Buddhism penetrated into China in 2 C.E. from Central Asia. In the beginning it was regarded as a variety of Taoism and associated with Lao-tzu. The latter is said to have left China riding on an ox in order to bring his teaching to the "barbarians" in the west. Thus Buddhism was understood as the barbaric version of Taoism. This equation of Buddhism and Taoism was probably based on the fact that both religions offer a teaching of salvation and the differences between the two were not known in this early phase. One reason for this was that the Chinese language did not possess a conceptual apparatus adequate for the abstract thought of Buddhism and therefore translations had to have recourse to the terminology of Taoism. The use of familiar concepts contributed significantly to the diffusion of Buddhism in China. The 3d century saw the beginning of lively translation activity; the most important Sanskrit texts were translated into Chinese. The preeminent figures of this period are → An Shih-kao, who primarily translated Hīnayāna sūtras, and Chih-lou Chia-ch'an, who devoted himself to the translation of Mahāyāna works.

In the year 355, permission was given for Chinese officials to enter the Buddhist *sangha*. This considerably advanced the establishment of Buddhism in China. In the 4th century the various Prajñāpāramitā schools (→ six houses and seven schools) emerged, the most important spokesman of which was → Chih-tun. In 399 → Fa-hsien was the first Chinese pilgrim to travel to India. A series of others was to follow (→ Hsuan-tsang, → I-ching).

In the 5th and 6th centuries Buddhism spread throughout China and received the support of the imperial house, which also encouraged the building of monasteries and the study of the teaching. At this time the renowned cave temples of → Yun-kang and → Lung-men were created. In the years 446 and 574–577 there were persecutions of Buddhism, which, however, did not hinder its rise. The translation of sūtras, thanks to the work of → Kumārajīva and → Paramārtha, reached a very high level. By this time all the important Hīnayāna and Mahāyāna texts existed in Chinese. The most important for the development of Buddhist philosophy were the → *Lankavatara-sūtra*, the → *Mahāparinirvāna-sūtra*, and the → *Satyasiddhi*, under the influence of which the → Satyasiddhi, → San-lun, and → Nirvāna schools were formed.

During the Sui and T'ang dynasties (end of the 6th to beginning of the 10th centuries) Buddhism in China reached its high point. The great schools of Chinese Buddhism made their appearance: → Hua-yen, → T'ien-t'ai, Chan (→ Zen), → Pure Land, → Fa-hsiang. The most important spokesmen of the Buddhism of this period were Hsuan-tsang, → Chih-i, and → Tu-shun.

The monasteries became so powerful economically that they represented a threat to the ruling house. Since the monasteries were exempt from taxes, many peasants gave them their properties and leased the land back. In that way the peasants were able to elude compulsory labor levies and military service, while the monasteries grew ever richer. For this reason in 845 there was a further persecution of Buddhism; the monasteries were dismantled, and the monks and nuns were obliged to return to worldly life. Buddhism in China never entirely recovered from this blow; nevertheless it had already left indelible marks on all areas of Chinese culture.

During the Sung Dynasty (10th–13th century), there came about a fusion of Buddhist, Confucian, and Taoist thought. Of the many Buddhist schools, in any broader sense only Ch'an (Zen) and Pure Land were still of any significance. The others were reduced to the status of objects of Buddhist philosophical study. Under the Ming Dynasty (14th–17th century) → Chu-hung brought about a synthesis of the Ch'an and Pure Land schools and a strong Buddhist lay movement developed.

Under the Manchurian Ch'ing Dynasty (17th to the beginning of the 20th century) → Lamaism made a major advance, but soon a strong decadent tendency became visible. The Buddhism of the 20th century is characterized by an effort toward reform (→ T'ai-hsü) and adaptation to modernity. Under Communist rule "religious freedom" subsisted nominally, but party functionaries made it clear that citizens did not have the freedom to believe anything that conflicted with the basic principles of Communist policy. Buddhists were permitted to continue their activities within the monasteries. During the land reform of 1950–52, however, most of the monasteries were dispossessed; and the monks, whose basis of livelihood was removed, for the most part returned to worldly life. After 1957 no further ordinations took place.

In 1953 the Chinese Buddhist Association was founded, the task of which was to convey to Buddhists the directives of the government and to report on their activities. In 1956 the Chinese Buddhist Institute was founded; its curriculum also included political training. Its task was to educate Buddhist scholars and monastic administrators.

During the Cultural Revolution (1966–76) many monasteries and other Buddhist monuments were destroyed. The last remaining monks left the monasteries. After the end of the Cultural Revolution still existing monasteries were renovated; the monks, in limited numbers, could return. The Chinese Buddhist Association resumed its activities; local associations were created in all the provinces. The Chinese Buddhist Institute in Peking and other large cities was again educating monks in Buddhist philosophy. These monks, after completing their three years of study, assume leadership positions in the monasteries.

Since 1981, the journal *Fa-yin* (*Voice of the Teaching*) has appeared. It has the task of supporting the government in its religious policies; however, it also gives practical instruction for Buddhist practice and discusses problems of Buddhist philosophy.

In Taiwan Buddhism is active predominantly in its popular Pure Land form; in addition, however, there is also lively interest in the Ch'an school. Besides this "orthodox" Buddhism there is also in Taiwan a folk Buddhism that is known as Chai-chiao (Religion of the Vegetarians), which includes Confucian and Taoist elements. Its followers are lay people and wear white robes. Also in Taiwan there is a strong revival movement that wishes to adapt Buddhism to modern times and that therefore particularly emphasizes its scientific qualities.

Buddhism in Indonesia: The first signs of Buddhism in Indonesia can be traced back, on the basis of Buddha statues, to the 3d century C.E. According to reports of the Chinese pilgrim → Fa-hsien, who visited Indonesia in 418, Buddhism had developed very little there. However, already by the end of the 5th century considerable progress is detectable, the effect of the efforts of Indian monks. In the 7th century Sumatra and Java were already important study centers for Buddhism, as can be learned from the reports of I-ching. The dominant current was Mahāyāna; in addition, however, there were also Hīnayāna communities, which probably belonged to the Sarvāstivāda school. In the 8th century Mahāyāna underwent a major upsurge under the Buddhist dynasty of the Shailendra. At this time, too, the famous stūpa of → Borobudur was built. Around the end of the 8th century the Buddhist Tantra spread in Indonesia. The Mahāyāna and especially Tantrism continued into the 15th century. Inscriptions show that King Ādityavarman (middle of the 14th century) was a follower of the → Kālachakra and was considered an incarnation of → Lokeshvara. At this time Indonesia cultivated lively intercourse with India, including with the monastic university → Nālandā. In Sumatra and Java there was fusion of Buddhist Tantra, Shaivism, and the cult of the king.

Through the inroads of Islam Buddhism vanished from Sumatra at the end of the 14th century and from Java in the early 15th. In the following century it had all but disappeared from all of Indonesia. Today only small Buddhist enclaves still exist. The immigrant Chinese are for the most part Buddhists. In addition there are tendencies in Indonesia toward a revival of Buddhism.

Buddhism in Japan: Buddhism was introduced into Japan from Korea in the year 522. In the beginning, as a foreign religion, it met with resistance but was recognized in 585 by Emperor Yomei. During the period of government of Prince Shōtoku (593–621) Buddhism was the official religion of Japan. Shōtoku decreed in 594 that the three precious ones (→ *triratna*) were to be venerated. He fostered the study of the Buddhist scriptures, himself composed important commentaries to several sūtras, and had monasteries built. He founded among others the famous monastery Hōryū-ji in Nara. Chinese and Korean monks were invited as teachers, and the first Japanese joined the Buddhist community. During this early period it was primarily the → Sanron school that spread.

During the Nara period (710–794) there were already six Buddhist schools in Japan, which were brought over from China and officially recognized in the 9th century: the → Kosha, → Hossō, Sanron, → Jōjitsu, → Ritsu, and → Kegon schools. Buddhism was firmly established in the imperial house, which especially took the teaching of the Kegon school as the basis of its government. The → *Sūtra of Golden Light* was of particular importance. The most famous monasteries in Nara stem from this time. During the Heian period (794–1184) the → Tendai and → Shingon schools gained in influence and became the dominant forms of Buddhism in Japan. The relationship of monks to the imperial house became even closer. Buddhism became de facto the state religion.

Around the middle of the 10th century Amidism began to spread; in the Kamakura period (1185-1333) it was organized into the → Jōdo-shū and the → Jōdo-shinshū. In 1191 → Zen came to Japan and has remained until today the most vital form of Japanese Buddhism. Two schools of Zen are of major importance: → Sōtō and → Rinzai.

In the 13th century the → Nichiren school emerged. In the following centuries, in part owing to the political situation, there were no significant new developments in Japanese Buddhism.

In the 19th century → Shintoism was elevated to the state religion. Since the Second World War there are clear signs of a renaissance of Buddhism in Japan. A whole series of popular movements have taken place, such as → Sōka Gakkai, → Risshō Koseikai, → Nipponzan Myōhōji, which, thanks to their concern for adapting Buddhism to modern times, have a very large following.

Buddhism in Korea: Buddhism entered Korea from China in the 4th century C.E. It attained its only high point in the 6th to 9th centuries during the three kingdoms of Koguryo, Paekche, and Silla and the united kingdom of Great Silla (668–935). During this time the most important schools of Chinese Buddhism gained a foothold in Korea. Of particular importance were the Ch'an (→ Zen), → Hua-yen, and esoteric Buddhism (→ Mi-tsung, → Shingon). Also the teachings of the → *Prajñāpāramitā-sūtra* were known early on in Korea. It is from this time that the most significant Buddhist art treasures of Korea stem.

During the Yi dynasty (1392–1910) → Confucianism became the state religion and Buddhist monks were forced to retreat into the mountains. Thus Buddhism lost influence with the people. Only after the end of Japanese rule (1945) did a revival of Buddhism begin. This took the form of a new movement within Buddhism (→ Won Buddhism).

In present-day South Korea there is no real discrimination between teachings of different schools. In the monasteries the meditation of the Rinzai school of Zen, repetition of Amitābha's name (→ *nembutsu*, → Pure Land school), and sūtra recitation are all practiced side by side. The recitation of → *dhāranīs* is also widespread, which goes back to the Tantrism that was prevalent in the middle ages. Among intellectuals Zen meditation is most popular; in rural areas the practice of the repetition of Buddha's name is predominant.

In Korea also, elements of the old autochthonous religion were assimilated into Buddhism. Mythological figures like Mountain God, Tiger, and the Deity of the Seven Stars are also to be found in rural Buddhist temples. Believers relate to the veneration of these deities as part of their religious practice.

Buddhism in Thailand: Concerning the beginnings of Buddhism in the area of present-day Thailand little is known. Archaeological sources permit the conclusion that Buddism came to Thailand from Burma in the 6th century C.E. The Buddhism that initially spread there was of the Hīnayāna type. Between the 8th and 13th centuries, the Mahāyāna appears to have been predominant, based on the evidence of buddha images of this period. Between the 11th and 14th centuries broad regions of Thailand were under the rule of the Hinduis Khmer. In the 13th century the Thai kings propagated the Theravāda. Relations with Ceylon strengthened the influence of this school, which became the dominant form of Buddhism. In 1882 a council was convoked by the king during which the entire Tripitaka was rehearsed. In the 19th century, with Mongkut (Rama IV), a king was in power who was himself a monk at the time of his enthronement. He laid the ground for modern Buddhism by initiating a reform movement within the Buddhist *sangha*. He founded the Dhammayut school, which lays special emphasis on the observance of the → Vinaya rules. The Dhammayuts have the greatest number of followers down to the present day. King Chulalongkorn (reigned 1868–1910) had an edition of the Pali canon published, which is one of the most important and complete. Later there were further reforms and Buddhism was subsumed under the pontificate of the king, who nominated himself as *sangharāja*, head of the Buddhist community. Today 95 percent of the population are Buddhists.

Buddhist councils 🅱 (Skt., samgīti); in the development of Buddhism, four councils are known, the history of which remains partially obscure. These councils were originally probably local assemblies of individual monastic communities that were later reported by tradition as general councils. The first council was that of Rājagriha, said to have taken place immediately after the *parinirvāna*, i.e., the death of the Buddha. The second council was held in Vaishālī approximately a century after that of Rājagriha, around 386 B.C.E. The third took place in Pātaliputra, present-day Patna, during the second century after the *parinirvāna* of the Buddha. This council is not recognized by the → Theravāda school which recognizes instead the so-called synod of the Pali school, which took place during the reign of King → Ashoka. The fourth council took place in Kashmir. Concerning this council, too, there are various opinions in the texts: some regard it as a general council convoked by King Kanishka, others as the synod of the → Sarvāstivāda school.

The purpose of the councils was generally to reconcile differences of opinion within communities as well as to present, reshape, and fix the canonical writings.

First council: Accounts of the first council are found in the → Vinaya-pitaka. This assembly was convoked by → Mahākāshyapa, who had detected tendencies within in the → *sangha* toward loss of discipline. In 480 B.C.E., 500 monks, all of them → arhats, came together in the vicinity of Rājagriha. Mahākāshyapa questioned → Upāli concerning the rules of discipline and → Ānanda concerning the doctrine. On the basis of Upāli's responses the Vinaya-pitaka was set down, and on the basis of Ānanda's the → Sūtra-pitka. The text, upon which all had agreed, was then recited.

At this council Añanda was the object of forceful reproaches by Mahākāshyapa, since at the time the council began Ānanda had not yet realized arhathood; this, however, took place during the council. Moreover, Ānanda had been empowered by the Buddha to eliminate certain less important rules; however, he had neglected to ask the Buddha for precise instructions concerning this matter. Another point of contention was Ānanda's advocacy of founding an order of nuns (→ *bhikshunī*). Ānanda's greatest failure, however, was considered to be that he had not entreated the Buddha to delay his entry into *parinirvāna*.

The historicity of this council, at least in the form described above, is doubted by many. Nevertheless, it is likely that the first collection of writings took place relatively early. This traditional account shows primarily how the individual school conceived of this process.

Second council: The second council is considerably better documented in the texts than the first and is generally recognized as a historical event. The reason for the convocation of the council, around 386 B.C.E., was disunity concerning matters of discipline. The Vaishālī monks had accepted gold and silver from lay adherents in violation of the Vinaya rules. Moreover, they were accused by Yasha, a student of Ānanda's, of nine further violations, including taking food at the wrong time, separate observance of the → *uposatha* by monks of a community, and drinking alcoholic beverages. On the other side, the monks expelled Yasha from the community because of his accusations. Yasha then sought support from influential monks in all areas to which Buddhism had spread. Finally a council, composed of 700 monks, all arhats, took place at Vaishālī. The monks of Vaishālī were found guilty by a committee composed of four monks from eastern and western regions, respectively. The Vaishālī monks accepted this judgment.

Records of this council are found in both the Pali and Sanskrit versions of the Vinaya-pitaka.

The Singhalese tradition (Theravāda) explains the schism between the → Sthaviras and → Mahāsānghikas on the basis of the conflict that led to the convocation of this council. According to their version, the monks of Vaishālī convoked a counter council in which they established themselves as Mahāsānghikas.

Third council: There are no records of this council in the Vinaya-pitaka. The records in other texts diverge markedly; nevertheless, most accounts give the reason for the convocation of the council as disagreement over the nature of an arhat. A monk from Pātaliputra, Mahādeva, put forward the following position: An arhat is still subject to temptation, that is, he can have nocturnal emissions. He is not yet free from ignorance (→ *avidyā*). In addition he is still subject to doubts concerning the teaching. Moreover, according to Mahādeva's view, an arhat can make progress on the path to enlightenment through the help of others and, through the utterance of certain sounds, he can further his concentration (→ *samādhi*) and thus advance on the path.

Differing views on these five points led to division of the monks into two camps. The council, which was intended to reconcile these differences, could only confirm the division.

Those who affirmed these five points, and who believed themselves to be in the majority, called themselves Mahāsānghika (Great Community). Their opponents, represented by the "elders," who were distinguished by outstanding wisdom and virtue, called themselves Sthavira.

The Pali school of Sri Lanka does not recognize this council. For them *third council* refers to the so-called synod of the Pali school of Pātaliputra that took place around 244 B.C.E., during the reign of King Ashoka. The occasion for this council was a conflict between the "authentic" Buddhist monks and those who insisted that the *sangha* be allowed to enjoy certain privileges. At the urging of Ashoka, Moggaliputta Tissa convoked the synod, in which those monks who rejected his position were excluded from the *sangha.* In his work *Kathāvatthu,* which is included in the → Abhidharma of the Theravāda school, he refuted the heretical views. At this synod also, the entire canon was read out.

Fourth council: This council seems also to have been the synod of a particular school, the Sarvāstivādins, rather than a general council. It is purported to have taken place under the reign of King Kanishka and to have served for a new interpretation of part of the → Abhidharma that was intended to forestall reformatory tendencies. According to various sources, this council was attended by 500 arhats as well as a like number of bodhisattvas. The principal role is ascribed to Vasumitra, who is said to have supervised the writing of the *Mahāvibhāshā,* a commentary on the Abhidharma. Because of the great importance later attained by the Sarvāstivādins, this synod came to be evaluated as a council having general authority.

Buddhi-Yoga [H] Skt.; self-knowledge, attained by the power of discrimination. In the *Bhagavad-Gītā* (2.49), the engagement of the → buddhi as the intelligence and discriminatory faculty is referred to as *buddhi-yoga* and is characterized as one of the most important prerequisites for the realization of God.

Buji-zen [Z] Jap.; an exaggerated, frivolous attitude towards the training and discipline of Zen. It comes about, for example, when someone, based on the mere thought that he is already Buddha, comes to the conclusion that he need not concern himself with practice, a disciplined life, or enlightenment. This is an attitude to which a misunderstanding, particularly of the teaching of the → Sōtō school of Zen (also → *mokushō* Zen), can lead.

Bukan [Z] Jap. for → Feng-kan

Bukka Zenji [Z] Jap. for → Fo-kuo-ch'an-shih

Bukkyō, [B] [Z] Jap., lit. "buddha teaching"; Buddhism, → *buddha-dharma.*

Bu'nan Shidō [Z] 1602–1676; Japanese Zen master of the → Rinzai school; a student and dharma successor (→ *hassu*) of Gudō Kokushi (d. 1661) and the master of → Dōkyō Eitan, the master of → Hakuin Zenji.

Buppō [B] [Z] Jap. for → *buddha-dharma*

Bushun Shiban [Z] Jap. for → Wu-chun Shih-fan

Busshin [Z] Jap., lit. "buddha-body" (Skt., buddhakāya). Busshin originally

Busshin [Z] Jap., lit. "buddha-mind" (for *shin,* → *kokoro*); 1. the great compassion by which a fully enlightened one (buddha) distinguishes himself. meant the physical body of the historical Buddha → Shākyamuni; in Mahāyāna Buddhism the meaning gradually shifted to "the limitless ability and

2. synonym for → *busshō.* potential that arises from the full realization of buddha-nature (→ *busshō*). It is in this sense that *busshin* is also used in Zen.

Busshin-in [Z] Jap., lit. "seal of buddha-mind"; another expression for → *inka-shōmei.* Short forms of *busshin-in* are *shin-in* and *butsu-in.*

Busshō [Z] Jap., lit. "buddha-nature"; a concrete expression for the substrate of perfection and completeness immanent in sentient beings as well as things. According to the Zen teaching, every person (like every other sentient being or thing) has, or better, *is* buddha-nature, without in general, however, being aware of it or living this awareness as one awakened to his true nature (a buddha) does. This awakening—and a living and dying that is a spontaneous expression from moment to moment of one's identity with buddha-nature—(→ *mujō-dō-no-taigen*) is the goal of Zen. (Also → Shō.)

As expounded by Hakuun Ryōko Yasutani, a Japanese Zen master of the 20th century, buddha-nature (also dharma-nature, → *hosshō*) is identical with that which is called emptiness (Jap., *ku*; Skt., → *shūnyatā*) in Buddhism. He further says, "With the experience of enlightenment, which is the source of all Buddhist doctrine, you grasp the world of ku. This world—unfixed, devoid of mass, beyond individuality and personality—is outside the realm of imagination. Accordingly, the true substance of things, that is, their Buddha- or Dharma-nature, is inconceivable and inscrutable. Since everything imaginable partakes of form or color, whatever one imagines to be Buddha-nature must of necessity be unreal. Indeed, that which can be conceived is but a picture of Buddha-nature, not Buddha-nature itself. But while Buddha-nature is beyond all conception and imagination, because we ourselves are intrinsically Buddha-nature, it is possible for us to awaken to it" (Phillip Kapleau 1980, 79).

Busso [Z] Jap., lit. "buddha patriarch(s)"; 1. the Buddha and the patriarchs (→ *soshigata*), the forefathers of Zen, with whom all the transmission lineages of all Zen schools originate (cf. Ch'an/Zen Lineage Chart).

2. the Buddha Shākyamuni as the founder of Buddhism.

Butsu B Z Jap. for → buddha

Butsuda B Z Jap. for → buddha

Butsudan Z Jap.; shrine or altar as found in a Buddhist temple or monastery, or, in miniaturized form, in many Japanese homes.

Butsuden Z Jap., lit. "buddha hall"; in large monastic complexes, a special building in which images of buddhas and bodhisattvas are placed and venerated.

Butsudō Z Jap., lit. "buddha way"; 1. the teaching of the Buddha, Buddhism. *Butsudō* is often used as a synonym for *buppō* (Skt., → buddha-dharma), but stresses more strongly the aspect of practical training on the path of enlightenment; 2. the path to → enlightenment or buddhahood; 3. complete enlightenment, buddhahood. In Zen, *butsudō* is particularly used in the last sense (for example, in the → *shiguseigan.*)

Butsugen-on Z Jap. for Fo-yen-yüan, → Kakushin

Butsuju Z → Myōzen Ryōnen

Buttō Kokushi Z Japanese Zen master, → Jakuhitsu Genkō

Byakue-Kannon B Z Jap., lit. "White-garbed Kannon"; a manifestation of the bodhisattva → Avalokiteshvara, who in Japan is called K(w)annon or Kanzeon and is often considered female and venerated as such. Byakue-Kannon is a favorite theme in Zen painting.

Byōdō Z Jap., lit. "sameness"; sameness of nature or nondistinction of all phenomena as experienced in → enlightenment.

Byōdō-kan Z Jap., lit. "view of sameness"; the experience that all things and beings are identical or nondistinct in their true nature or buddha-nature (→ *busshō*).

C

Celestial kings B (Chin., t'ien-wang; Jap. ‚shitennō; Skt., devarāja), also called world protectors; four demonic-looking figures, images of which are to be found in every Chinese and Japanese monastery. The celestial kings, who according to myth dwell on the world mountain → Meru are guardians of the four quarters of the world and of the Buddhist teaching. They fight against evil and protect places where goodness is taught. Their bodies are protected by armor and they wear helmets or crowns on their heads.

Each celestial king is associated with one of the directions. The guardian of the North (Skt., Vaishravana) has a green body. In his left hand he holds the parasol-like furled banner of the buddha-dharma; in the right hand he holds either a pagoda (in which → Nāgarjuna is said to have found the Buddhist scriptures near the sea palace of the → *nāgas*) or a silver mongoose vomiting jewels. He is the most important of the world guardians.

The guardian of the South (Skt., Virūdhaka) has a blue body. He brandishes a sword in his battle against darkness (i.e., ignorance, → *avidyā*). He protects the root of goodness in human beings. The guardian of the East (Skt., Dhritarāshtra) has a white body. He plays on a Chinese lute, the sound of which purifies the thoughts of men and brings them to tranquility.

The guardian of the West (Skt., Virūpāksha) has a red body. In his right hand, he has a serpent (*nāga*) before which he holds the wish-fulfilling gem (→ *chintāmani*). Although the *nāgas* desire to guard supreme treasures, this treasure deserves to be guarded only by enlightened beings and saints.

The four celestial kings have been known in China since the fourth century but have been venerated, in their present form only since the T'ang Dynasty. Each has ninety-one sons who help him to guard the ten directions as well as eight generals and other minions who care for the world quarter assigned to him.

The practice of placing images of the celestial kings in their own hall in a monastery derives from the following legend: In 742 Amoghavajra (→ Mi-tsung) invoked the help of the celestial kings by reciting → *dhāranīs.* Through their support they put an end to the siege of Hsi-an-fu by foreign peoples. The guardian of the North appeared to the soldiers with his retinue in the midst of clouds; mongooses bit through the bowstrings of the enemy. The guardian of the West repulsed the foe with his terrifying glance. As thanks for this, the emperor issued an edict prescribing that images of the celestial kings be placed in all monasteries.

Chāddar H Hindi; a long strip of cloth that is wound around the upper torso; a traditional form of Hindu garb.

Chadō 🅩 Jap., lit. "tea way"; one of the Japanese ways of training (→ *dō*), which in Japan is often also called *cha-no yū*, which means "hot tea water" or simply "tea." Both names indicate that it is not a matter of a ceremony that a subject executes *with* the tea as object, as the inappropriate translation "tea ceremony" would suggest. Here it is a question of *only tea*, a nondualistic state of consciousness to which this, as well as the other Zen-influenced Japanese training ways, leads. In *chadō*, many arts, such as pottery, architecture, and the way of flowers (→ *kadō*) come together to create a total work of art that lasts only momentarily, one in which all the human senses participate yet which stills the dualistic intellect.

Chai 🅣 Chin., lit. "fasting"; one of the most important festivals of religious Taoism (→ *tao-chiao*), known since its beginnings. In the official state ritual *chai* designates a fast before sacrifices. In Taoism the term refers to feasts held under the direction of a master, at which a specific number of pupils (between six and thirty-eight) participate. These feasts serve mainly for the confession of sins, which are considered to be the cause of all illness.

Every school of religious Taoism celebrates its own fasts. These are particularly important in the → *t'ai-p'ing tao*, → *wu-tou-mi tao*, and the → *ling-pao p'ai*. One of the best-known ceremonies is the *t'u-t'an chai*—a fast during which the participants smear themselves with charcoal.

Chai ceremonies are very complicated, so that those participating at them require detailed instruction. They are usually held in the courtyards of Taoist monasteries and may extend over several days. After a platform of strictly prescribed dimensions—its sides limited by ropes—has been erected, the participants, holding hands, step onto it. Their hair is tousled and their faces are covered with coal dust and dirt to signify their remorse. To the accompaniment of a drum, the master of the ceremony implores various deities to attend the feast. There follows a recitation of sins and their possible consequences. At this point the religious ecstasy of the participants reaches its peak. They throw themselves to the ground and roll in the dust to demonstrate their repentance. As the twelve vows of repentance are recited, the participants touch their foreheads to the ground and ask for their sins to be forgiven. The ceremony ends with further rituals. These collective repentance sessions are held three times daily, but participants are allowed only one meal each day. The resultant physical exhaustion produces a psychic collapse, which effects an inner purification.

Chaitanya 🅗 (Caitanya), Skt.; 1. spiritually awakened consciouness (i.e., not merely the common state of thinking consciousness); 2. in orders belonging to the → Rāmakrishna Mission, a name appended to that of an initiated → *brahmachāri*, as in *bhakti-chaitanya*, "he whose consciousness is full of devotion"; 3. Indian mystic (1485-1534), born in Nadia (Nabadwip), Bengal; he is also known under the names Gauranga, Gaur, Gorā, Nimai, and Krishna-Chaitanya.

Chaitanya was an outstanding scholar who abruptly renounced the world and became an ardent devotee of Krishna. The → Vaishnavas regard him as part incarnation of Krishna. The ecstatic love that he felt for God embraced sinners and saints of all castes and faiths. For Chaitanya, → Bhakti-Yoga was the simplest path to God-realization and → *japa* one of the most important practices.

Chaitanya-Purusha 🅗 (Caitanya-Puruṣa), Skt.; consciousness of the → *purusha*. Although man is essentially absolute consciousness (→ *chit*), the individual uses this consciousness to superimpose on the essential nature the notion that one is the body and mind, and thereby becomes the → *jīva*, who creates the manifest world (→ *māyā*) by means of thoughts.

Chaitya 🅑 (Caitya), Skt. (Pali, cetiya), lit. "sanctuary"; assembly hall of a Buddhist community for meditation and presentation of teaching.

The *chaitya* hall, which developed from cave monasteries, was originally a three-naved, rectangular room with rows of pillars on both sides and a → stūpa at its focal point in the apse. The stūpa contained relics or, more often, → sūtra texts written on palm leaves, bark, leaves of metal, etc. The *chaitya* hall lost its popularity early on and its function was taken over by a room containing a buddha image.

Chaitya-Purusha 🅗 (Caitya-Puruṣa), Skt.; according to the school of → Sānkhya, the universe is conceived by the union of the cosmic soul (→ *purusha*) and material nature (→ *prakriti*). The cosmic soul contains within itself all individual souls, which in turn are designated as *chaitya-purusha*.

Chakra 🅗 🅑 (cakra), Skt., lit. wheel, circle; 1. in Hinduism a circle of worshipers.

2. Term for the centers of subtle or refined energy (→ *prāna*, → *kundalinī*) in the human energy body (astral body). They concentrate, transform, and distribute the energy that streams through them. Though chakras have correspondences on the coarse, bodily level (for example, heart or solar plexus), these correspondences are not identical with them but belong to another level of phenomenal reality. The chakras are

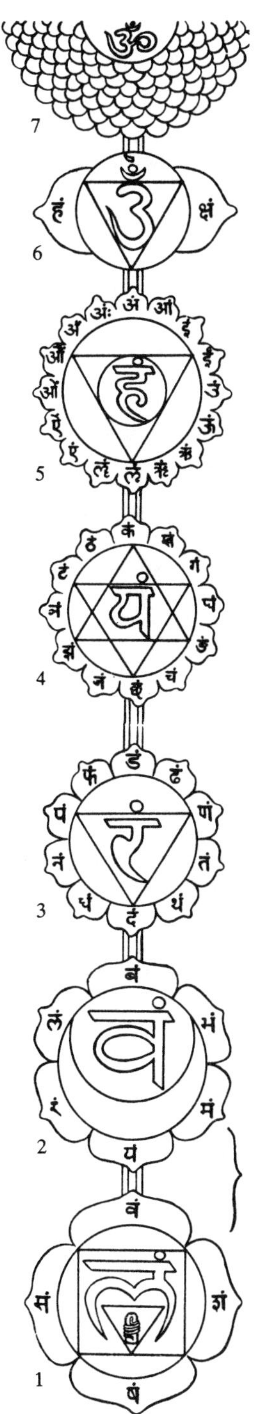

Diagram of the chakras with their most important symbols

points where soul and body connect with and interpenetrate each other. The seven principal chakras of Indian → kundalinī-yoga (these centers are known under other names in other cultures) lie along the → *sushumnā*, the principal channel of subtle energy, located in the spinal column, through which kundalinī rises in the course of spiritual awakening. The first six chakras are located within the coarse body and the seventh outside of it above the crown of the head. When the kundalinī is aroused, which is generally brought about by the special practices of a yoga based on this system, it rises from the first, i.e., lowest, chakra, activating one chakra after the other, up to the seventh and highest. In every chakra to which the yogi brings the kundalinī, he experiences a particular kind of bliss (*ānanda*), acquires a particular psychic power (→ *siddhi*), and realizes a particular form of knowledge. Thus the chakras are also known as centers of consciousness (*chaitanya*). From each chakra radiate a specific number of energy channels (→ *nādī*).

Mediumistically gifted persons who can see the human astral body describe the chakras as "lotus blossoms" with varying numbers of petals; this is the way they are traditionally depicted in illustrations. The number of petals of a given chakra corresponds to the number of *nādīs* radiating from it. These "lotus blossoms" are in circular motion, hence the impression of a wheel (for example, a whirling wheel of fire) and the name *chakra*. According to the system of kundalinī-yoga each chakra corresponds to specific psychophysical properties, which are expressed through various symbols (shapes, colors, mantric syllables, animal symbols, divinities, etc.). The seven principal chakras and their most important attributes are as follows

(1) *Mūlādhāra-chakra.* It is located at the lowest part of the *sushumnā* between the root of the genitals and the anus. In the *mūlādhāra-chakra* (in the unawakened state), the kundalinī, which is depicted as a coiled snake (whence the epithet "serpent power"), reposes, providing power and energy to the other chakras. Four *nādīs* radiate from this chakra, representing the four petals of the lotus. The symbolic shape is a square, its color is yellow, the associated seed syllable is *lam*, the animal symbol is an elephant with seven trunks, and the divinities are → Brahmā and Dākinī, Brahmā's → shakti.

The yogi who by spiritual practice penetrates to the *mūlādhāra-chakra* conquers the quality of earth (*prithivī-tattva*) and no longer fears bodily death. Concentrating and meditating on this chakra, he attains "complete knowledge of kundalinī and thus the means to arouse it. Arousing it, he receives the *darduri-siddhi*, the power to levitate and to control breath, consciousness, and seed. His *prāna* enters the central *brahma-nādī*. His sins are wiped away. He knows past, present, and future and enjoys natural bliss (*sahaja-ānanda*)" (trans. from German edition of Sivananda 1935).

(2) *Svādhishthana-chakra*. It lies in the energy channel *sushumnā* at the root of the genitals. It corresponds to *bhuvarloka*, and its bodily correspondence is the *plexus hypogastricus*, which controls the inner organs of elimination and procreation. From its center radiate six *nādīs*, or petals. The symbolic shape is the half-moon, its color is white, the seed syllable is *vam*, the animal symbol is the crocodile, the associated deities are → Vishnu with the lesser divinity Rākinī as shakti.

"One who concentrates and meditates on the *devatā* has no fear of water and completely masters the water element. He acquires various psychic powers, intuitive knowledge, complete mastery of his senses, and knowledge of the astral essences. Desire, wrath, greed, deception, pride, and other impurities are wiped away. The yogi becomes victorious over death [→ *mrityuñjaya-siddhi*]" trans. from ibid.).

(3) *Manipūra-chakra*. It lies within the energy channel *sushumnā* in the navel region. The corresponding bodily center, the solar plexus, controls liver, stomach, and so on. From this chakra radiate ten *nādīs*, the petals of this lotus. The symbolic shape is the triangle, its color is red, the seed syllable is *ram*, the animal symbol is the ram, the ruling deities are → Rudra and → Lākinī.

"The yogi who concentrates on this chakra attains *satala-siddhi* and is able to find hidden treasures. He is freed of all diseases and knows no fear of fire. "Even if he were thrown into a blazing fire, he would remain alive and without fear of death." (ibid.).

(4) *Anāhata-chakra*. It lies in the heart region within the *sushumnā* energy channel. The bodily center corresponding to it is the *plexus cardiacus*, which controls the heart. From this chakra radiate fifteen *nādīs*, the petals of this lotus. The symbolic shape is the double-triangle star, its color is grayish blue, the seed syllable is *yam*, the animal symbol the gazelle, the ruling deities → Īsha and Kākinī.

"In this center, the sound *anāhat* [→ *anāhata-shabda*], the sound of → *shabda-brahman*, is evident. One perceives it very distinctly when one concentrates on this center. Whoever meditates on this center completely masters the *vāyu-tattva* (quality of air), which is full of *sattvas* (harmonious properties). He can fly through the air and enter the bodies of others (*bhuchari-siddhi, kechari-siddhi, kaja-siddhi*). Cosmic love and other divine qualities come to him" (ibid.).

(5) *Vishuddha-chakra*. It lies in the *sushumnā nādī* at the lower end of the throat and is the center of the ether element. From this chakra, which corresponds to the bodily center, *plexus laryngeus*, radiate sixteen *nādīs*, the petals of this lotus. The symbolic shape is the circle, its color is white, the seed syllable is *ham*, the animal symbol an elephant with six tusks, the ruling deities are Sadā-Shiva and the goddess Shākinī.

"Concentration on the qualities (*tattva*) of this chakra is called *ākāshi-dhāranā*. One who practices this concentration will not perish even with the destruction of the cosmos (→ *pralaya*), for he attains complete knowledge of the four Vedas. He becomes a *trikāla-jñāni* [→ *trikāla-jñāna*] and knows past, present, and future" (ibid.).

(6) *Ājñā-chakra*. It lies in the *sushumnā nādī* and has its physical correspondence in the space between the eyebrows. In Western esoteric systems this chakra is known as the "third eye." This lotus has two petals, i.e., it has two *nādīs* radiating from its middle. Its color is milky white, the seed syllable is short *a*, the associated deities are Parama-Shiva in the form of → Hamsa and the goddess Hākinī. This chakra, the corresponding physical center of which is the *plexus cavernus*, is regarded as the seat of consciousness.

"One who concentrates on this chakra destroys all karma from previous lives. Thus the benefits of such meditation, which transforms the yogi into a *jīvanmukti* (→ *jīvanmukta*), one liberated in this lifetime, are indescribably significant. The yogi acquires all the higher and the thirty two lesser siddhis" (ibid.).

(7) *Sahasrāra-chakra*. This chakra is located above the crown of the head, thus outside the coarse body, above the upper end of the *sushumnā*. As the name of the chakra indicates, this lotus has a thousand petals, that is, a thousand, or countless, *nādīs* radiate from it. The physical correspondence of the *sahasrāra-chakra* is the brain, its seed syllable is *om*, the sacred

utterance (→ *pranava*). The fifty letters of the Sanskrit alphabet run twenty times around the thousand petals of this lotus so that this lotus blossom represents the totality of all seed syllables and all chakras, which the *sahasrāra-chakra*, set above all the other chakras, encompasses. It radiates light "like ten million suns" and belongs to a higher level of reality than the other six chakras, which as the six chakras (*shat-chakra*), constitute the chakras in the narrower sense of the word.

The *sahasrāra-chakra*, which is regarded as the abode of the god Shiva, corresponds to cosmic consciousness. "If the kundalinī is unified with the god Shiva in the *sahasrāra-chakra*, the yogi experiences supreme bliss (→ *paramānanda*), superconsciousness, and supreme knowledge. He becomes a → *brahmavid-varishta*, a perfect *jñāni* " (ibid.).

A detailed exposition of the chakras and their many aspects according to the teaching of kundalinī-yoga can be found in Arthur Avalon's *The Serpent Power* (see Woodroffe 1919).

Although developed by Hinduism, the system of the chakras also plays a role in Buddhism, especially Tantric Buddhism (→ Tantra, → Vajrayāna, → Tibetan Buddhism). In basic outline the system of energy centers (chakras) and connecting channels (*nādī*) is the same as in kundalinī-yoga. The symbolism connected with it, however, is taken from Buddhist iconography, and the meditation practice based on it is significantly different in many respects from that of kundalinī-yoga. An exposition of Buddhist chakra-yoga can be found in Govinda 1959.

Chakrabandha 🅷 (Cakrabandha), Skt.; a state in which all the → *chakras* are activated, thereby enabling the → *kundalinī* to rise to the seventh center of subtle energy (*sahasrāra*) and thus bring about illumination.

Chakravartin 🅱 (cakravartin) Skt., lit. "wheel ruler"; a ruler of whom it is said, "the wheels of his chariot roll unobstructedly everywhere," a world ruler. Four types of *chakravartin* are distinguished, symbolized by wheels of gold, silver, copper, and iron. *Chakravartin* later became an epithet for a buddha whose teaching is universal and whose truth is applicable to the entire cosmos.

Chakugo 🆉 Jap. → *jakugo*

Chamatkāra 🅷 (Camatkāra), Skt., lit. "astonishment"; a term referring to the uncommon or unusual, especially that which lies beyond the realm of the senses and thought; that which belongs to the realm of subtle consciousness and is revealed only through intuition.

Ch'an 🅱 🆉 Chin. for → Zen

Chañchala 🅷 (Cañcala), Skt., from *cañc:* "to hop, spring, flicker"; unsteady, unreliable, inconstant. The term refers to our usual ungoverned thought processes, which flit restlessly from one object to another, constantly misleading us and putting us in a state of agitation.

In the sixth chapter of the *Bhagavad-Gītā* → *Arjuna* says to Krishna, "The mind is verily restless, turbulent, strong, and obstinate, and as difficult to control as the wind" (6.34).

Chandas 🅷 , or Chhandas, Skt.; one of the six → Vedāngas, the science of prosody. It is concerned not only with the number and length of syllables but also with their "weight," that is, the value ascribed to any particular syllable.

An important authority on this subject was → Pingalā, author of the *Chandah-Sūtra* ("manual of prosody"). For a long time, the teachings of the → Vedas were transmitted orally; therefore, each syllable was treated with great attention so that it might be impressed deeply into the student's memory. The teachings were ultimately written down.

Chandī 🅷 (Caṇḍī), Skt.; a sacred text in which the Divine Mother (→ Shakti is described as "ultimate reality"; part of the *Shakta-Tantra,* it consists of thirteen chapters.

Chāndogya-Upanishad 🅷 Skt.; the "secret lesson of the Chāndogya school" is the second-oldest of the → Upanishads and belongs to the *Sāmaveda.* It presents the fundamental principles of → Vedānta, in particular the nature of one's true self (→ *ātman*), and contains the great precept → *Tat tvam asi* ("That thou art").

The work is made up of eight chapters that offer a wealth of ideas regarding the origin of the cosmos, the universal soul and the individual soul, and life in the afterworld. It also contains the famous conversation between the sage → Uddālaka Āruni and his son → Shvetaketu on cosmic unity, that is, the teaching that existence is in everything and that the universe is everywhere permeated by the Absolute.

Chandrakīrti 🅱 → Mādhyamika

Chandra-Nādī 🅷 (Candra-Nāḍī), Skt., lit. "channel of lunar energy"; an epithet for the → *idā.*

Chandrayama 🅷 (Candrayama), Skt.; a religious vow whereby one's food intake is decreased or increased according to the waning or waxing of the moon *(chandra).*

Ch'ang 🅃 Chin., lit. constant, enduring, eternal; concept of philosophical Taoism (→ *tao-chia*). *Ch'ang* designates the permanent, as opposed to the changeable, and is one of the symbols of the Tao. In the → *Tao-te ching* the term *ch'ang* is attributed to all laws that are universally applicable and not subject to change. Enlightenment (→ *ming*) consists in the realization of the unchangeable.

Chapter 1 of the *Tao-te ching* states "The Tao that can be expressed is not the eternal (*ch'ang*) Tao; the name that can be named is not the eternal name." And in Chapter 37, "The Tao abides (*ch'ang*) in nonaction [→ *wu-wei*], yet nothing is left undone" (Feng & English 1972). Concerning enlightenment as a realization of the nature of *ch'ang*, Chapter 16 says, "Things in all their multitude: each one returns to its root. Return to the root means stillness. Stillness means return to fate (its original state). Return to fate is the eternal (*ch'ang*) law." In a treatise on Lao-tzu, the philosopher Han Fei-tzu (3d century B.C.E.) describes *ch'ang* as follows:

"Things which now exist and then perish; which suddenly come into being and as suddenly die; which first bloom and then fade—such things are not *ch'ang*. Only that which was created simultaneously with the separation of Heaven and Earth, and will not perish before Heaven and Earth, can be called *ch'ang*."

Ch'ang-ch'ing Huai-hui 🅉 (Jap., Shōkyō [Shōkei] Eki), 756/59–815/18, Chinese Ch'an (Zen) master; a student and dharma successor (→ *hassu*) of Ma-tsu Tao-i (Jap., Baso Dōitsu). We encounter him in example thirty-one of the → *Pi-yen-lu*.

Ch'ang-ch'ing Hui-leng 🅉 (Jap., Chōkei Eryō) 854/64–932, Chinese Ch'an (Zen) master; a student and dharma successor (→ *hassu*) of → Hsüeh-feng I-ts'un (Jap., Seppō Gison). Ch'ang-ch'ing had twenty-six dharma successors; we encounter him in examples 8, 22, 23, 74, 76, and 93 of the → *Pi-yen-lu*.

The *Tsu-t'ang chi* recounts of Ch'ang-ch'ing, who had already become a monk by the age of thirteen and had already trained under other Ch'an masters before he met Hsüeh-feng, that at the beginning he had great difficulties with the Ch'an training. He came again and again for → *dokusan* to Hsüeh-feng but appeared in spite of earnest efforts to be making no progress. One day Hsüeh-feng offered to prescribe for him "medicine for a dead horse" if he would only take it. Ch'ang-ch'ing gave his assurance that he was ready to trust wholly in the advice of the master. Thereupon Hsüeh-feng told him that he should not come to *dokusan* any more and for several years should sit in meditation "like a wooden pillar in a blazing fire" (→ *zazen*); then he would surely experience enlightenment.

One night, after two and a half years of this kind of practice, his mind was restless and he could no longer remain in his spot. He stood up and took a walk around the monastery garden. Returning to the monk's hall, he drew up a bamboo shade and found himself looking into the light of a lamp. Suddenly he experienced enlightenment. Ch'ang-ch'ing later became a highly respected Ch'an master.

Chang-cho Hsiu-ts'ai 🅉 (Jap., Chōsetsu Yūsai); Chinese Ch'an (Zen) master of the T'ang period; a student and dharma successor (→ *hassu*) of → Shih-shuang Ch'ing-chu (Jap., Sekisō Keisho). We encounter him in example 39 of the → *Wu-men-kuan*.

Chang Chüeh 🅃 d. 184 C.E., founder of the Taoist school of → *t'ai-p'ing tao* (Chin., lit. "Way of Supreme Peace"). His teachings are based on the doctrines of the → *T'ai-p'ing ching* and stem from the → *Huang-lao tao* (Way of Huang-ti and Lao-tzu). Chang Chüeh aimed at establishing supreme peace, with particular emphasis on the peaceful equality of all individuals. This ideal brought his teachings great popularity at a time when the people were plagued by famine and suppressed by their rulers. Within ten years Chang Chüeh attracted several hundred thousand followers. A further factor contributing to his success was the holding of collective rites for the healing of sicknesses, which he claimed to be a consequence of sinful actions. These ritual practices centered around collective ceremonies of repentance (→ *chai*).

Between 165 and 184 C.E. his teaching expanded over eight provinces. He organized his followers on a strictly hierarchical basis, with himself at their head as celestial duke-general. In 184 C.E. he led the rebellion of the → Yellow Turbans, which was ruthlessly put down and during which he and his brothers Chang Pao and Chang Liang, who enthusiastically fought by his side, were killed.

Chang Chüeh's religious activities were triggered by a revelation of an approaching age of supreme peace, of paradise on Earth. This age was to begin on the day the Han Dynasty was succeeded by that of the Yellow Heaven of the *t'ai-p'ing tao* (yellow being the color of → Huang-ti, the Yellow Emperor, whom the followers of Chang Chüeh venerated). This was expected to happen in 184 C.E.

Nevertheless, Chang Chüeh's enormous popularity was above all due to his capabilities as a healer. In addition to conducting fasting and healing ceremonies, he made use of magic formulae and sacred water (Chin. *fu-shui*), which he blessed by pronouncing magic spells over it, while holding a bamboo staff with nine knots (nine being the number of Heaven). He would command the sick to kneel, touch the earth with their foreheads, and contemplate their sins and omissions. After that they drank of his sacred water. If the patient was healed, he was considered to be a practitioner of the Tao. Similar ceremonies were held by other schools of religious Taoism (*wu-tou-mi tao*).

Chang Hsien 🅃 Chin., lit. "Chang the Immortal"; traditional immortal (→ *hsien*). In popular belief Chang Hsien bestows male offspring. He is usually depicted as an old man aiming a drawn bow at Heaven. Frequently the Hound of Heaven (*t'ien-kou*), against whom he protects children, is shown by his side. He is, as a rule, accompanied by his son, who carries in his arms the boy-child whom Chang Hsien bestows on those who believe in him. Sometimes he is in the company of Sung-tzu niang-niang, the "lady Who Bestows Children."

Chang Hsiu 🅃 general of the Han Dynasty and founder of a movement in religious Taoism (→ *tao-chiao*) similar to that of the → *t'ai-p'ing tao* and the → *wu-tou-mi tao* and widespread throughout the province of Szechwan. The central practices of this school consisted in healing ceremonies, during which sacrifices were made to the three rulers (→ *san-kuan*), i.e., Heaven, Earth, and Water. Chang Hsiu was murdered by Chang Lu in 190 C.E.

Like other leaders of early Taoist movements, Chang Hsiu was of the opinion that illnesses were a consequence of evil deeds. As part of his "therapy" the sick were locked up in "convalescent homes," there to contemplate their transgressions. However, a complete healing was possible only if the sufferer listed his sins on three separate strips of paper, which were then submitted to the three rulers (Heaven, Earth, and Water) by being respectively left on a mountaintop, buried, and thrown into a river. The family of a patient had to pay five pecks of rice for his treatment.

Chang Hsiu organized his followers on a strictly hierarchical basis, the most important functions being performed by the presenters of liquid sacrifices (the *chi-chiu*), whose task it was to determine whether all believers followed the teachings of the → *Tao-te ching* —the root text of the Chang Hsiu movement, albeit interpreted in a manner peculiar to that school. The religious hierarchy was based on a military model: the *chi-chiu* were "officers" and their subordinates "demon soldiers."

Chang-hsiung 🅉 (Jap., Chōyū); Chinese master of the Fuke school of Zen → Kakushin.

Chang Liang 🅃 d. 187 B.C.E.; high-ranking official of the early Han Dynasty and traditional founder of religious Taoism (→ *tao-chiao*). He is one of the first immortals (→ *hsien*) mentioned in Taoist literature. It is said that to attain immortality he performed physical exercises (→ *tao-yin*) and abstained from eating grain (→ *pi-ku*).

Chang Lu 🅃 2d century C.E.; one of the founders of the → *wu-tou-mi tao* ("Five-Pecks-of-Rice Taoism"). Chang Lu was a grandson of → Chang Tao-ling. In 190 C.E. he succeeded with the help of → Chang Hsiu in establishing a strictly hierarchical politico-religious state, which lasted for thirty years. As a leader he emerged from the circle of his later followers, who venerated him as a miraculous healer. His teachings were based on the view that external well-being is dependent on morality, so that illnesses are ordained by the spirits in retribution for sinful actions. He organized mass ceremonies during which believers repented of their transgressions and thereby were cured of their afflictions. For every such cure Chang Lu charged a fee of five pecks of rice, hence the name of the religious school founded by him. He called himself a celestial master (→ *t'ien-shih*)—a title passed on by his descendants to this day.

The state founded by Chang Lu was organized on a strictly military basis. Local communities were led by the presenters of liquid sacrifices, known as libationers (*chi-chiu*), who officiated at healing ceremonies for the sick, during which sacrifices were made to the three rulers (→ *san-kuan*), i.e., Heaven, Earth, and Water. Chang Lu adopted these ceremonies from Chang Hsiu. Public life centered on communal dwellings (*i-she*) in which everyone was provided with food free of charge. A further characteristic feature of Chang Lu's rule was the manner in which transgressions were punished: in the case of the first three transgressions the sinner simply had to regret his evil deeds. A fourth transgression, however, called for active repentance; i.e., the guilty person might be ordered to meet the cost of repairing a thousand paces of public road, or effect the repair in person.

Chang Po-tuan 🅃 984-1082 C.E.; well-known Taoist master who combined the teachings of Taoism with those of Zen Buddhism and Confucianism. Chang Po-tuan was one of the most important representatives of the alchemical School of the Inner Elixir (→ *nei-tan*), whose aim consisted in attaining spiritual immortality. The inner elixir is not produced by a method of chemical transmutation but rather is said to consist in spiritual enlightenment, in a return to the source (→ *fu*). Chang Po-tuan explains his teaching in his *Wu-chen p'ien* (*Essay on the Awakening to the Truth*).

According to the *Wu-chen p'ien*, which is couched in the language of the School of the Outer Elixir (→ *wai-tan*), the ingredients of the inner elixir are "true lead" and "true mercury," i.e., the essences of yang and yin. The latter has to be caught and absorbed by the yang; Chang Po-tuan calls this the "marriage of yin and yang." A commentary on the *Wu-chen p'ien* describes the essence of yang to be that which is real, and the essence of yin as that which is unreal.

By lying on his bed at midnight of the winter solstice and meditating, the alchemical practitioner marries these two essences within his body with the help of the life energy (→ *ch'i*), thereby giving birth to an embryo (→ *sheng-t'ai*), which increases in size proportionate to the growth of yang. By this method the alchemist can attain immortality. The embryo referred to is the new "I," which, being enlightened and knowing no difference between subject and object, is immortal.

Ch'ang-sha Ching-ts'en 🅉 (Jap., Chōsha Keijin), d. 1868; Chinese Ch'an (Zen) master; a student and dharma successor (→ *hassu*) of → Nan-ch'üan P'u-yüan (Jap., Nansen Fugan). After Ch'ang-sha had received the seal of confirmation (→ *inka-shōmei*) from Nan-chüan, he wandered homelessly through China and expounded the buddha-dharma according to the circumstances he encountered. He had two dharma successors. We encounter him in example 36 of the → *Pi-yen-lu.*

There we find Ch'ang-sha in a → *mondō* with one of his students:

"One day Ch'ang-sha was wandering around in the mountains; then he turned back and came to the gate. The eldest of the monks asked him, 'Master, where did you go and where did you come back from?'

"Ch'ang-sha said, 'I'm coming from a walk in the mountains.'

"The elder monk said, 'How far did you go?'

"Ch'ang-sha said, 'First I followed the fragrance of the herbs; then I came back following falling flower petals.'

"The elder monk said, 'That sounds a lot like spring.'

"Ch'ang-sha said, 'It really goes beyond the autumn dew that drips from the lotus blossoms.' "

Ch'ang-sheng pu-ssu 🅃 Chin., lit. long-living, nondying; immortality, the goal of various Taoist practices. Immortality can be either physical or spiritual. The idea of physical immortality goes back to the very beginnings of Taoism and its attainment is the aim of most schools of religious Taoism (→ *tao-chiao*). The followers of the alchemical School of the Outer Elixir (→ *wai-tan*) strove to become immortals (→ *hsien*) by swallowing various life-prolonging substances. Other practices for attaining physical immortality were abstention from eating grain (*pi-ku*), various breathing exercises, gymnastics (→ *tao-yin*), meditation, and certain sexual practices (→ *fang-chung shu*). A person who is physically immortal ascends to Heaven (→ *fei-sheng*) in broad daylight or dies in appearance only; when his coffin is opened, it is found to be empty (→ *shih-chieh*).

The philosophical Taoism of → Lao-tzu and → Chuang-tzu strives for spiritual immortality, i.e., enlightenment and the attainment of oneness with the highest principle (→ Tao)—a state in which the distinction between life and death is dissolved and yin combines with yang. The followers of the inner elixir (→ *nei-tan*) also strive for spiritual immortality. Spiritual immortality implies not only freedom from life and death but also from time space and sexual identity; for that reason immortals may be depicted as either male or female.

Common immortality symbols found in Taoist-inspired art are a crane, a gnarled staff of wood, pine trees, peaches (→ Hsi wang-mu), the mushroom of immortality (→ *ling-chih*), the god of immortality (→ Shou-lao, → San-hsing), etc.

It may be difficult to determine which type of immortality a particular school or practice strives for, because many texts employ esoteric terminology that can be interpreted either way. Even some passages in texts of philosophical Taoists such as → Chuang-tzu and → Lieh-tzu can be taken as pointing toward physical immortality: descriptions of places such as → K'un-lun or the isles of the immortals (→ P'eng-lai, → Ying-chou, → Fang-chang), which are considered to be dwelling places of immortals, can be understood either abstractly or concretely. Ch'in Shih Huang-ti, the first Chinese emperor, organized several—albeit unsuccessful—expeditions with the aim of discovering the mysterious isles of the immortals and obtaining the draught of immortality. Some commentators consider such passages to be descriptive of a spiritual journey into the center or essence of man.

This ambiguity applies to alchemical texts in general; e.g., followers of the inner elixir (→ *nei-tan*) may employ the language of Outer Alchemy (→ *wai-tan*) to describe processes of consciousness. In the early stages of Chinese alchemy the inner and outer methods for achieving immortality were coexistent and of equal importance until ca. the 6th century C.E. when immortality increasingly came to be considered as being of a spiritual nature; instead of trying to manufacture a pill of immortality from gold, cinnabar, and other chemical substances, alchemists were almost exclusively concerned with developing the inner gold, the golden flower, the sacred embryo (→ *sheng-t'ai*). By the 13th century C.E. the Outer Elixir School had faded into insignificance, although its language continued to be used. The followers of the Inner Alchemy despised those who tried to attain immortality by the transmutation of chemical substances. The influence of Buddhism—above all, Zen—decisively contributed toward the spiritualization of the search for immortality, so that ancient alchemical texts were consistently interpreted in accordance with the teachings of the Inner Elixir School.

In the search for immortality specific sexual techniques played an important part in many schools of religious Taoism and were practiced in public (→ *ho-chi*) from the 2d to the 7th century, when they were forced to retreat to the private domain under the pressure of Confucianist morality but continued to be performed as a preliminary to Taoist meditation.

Chang Tao-ling ◼ also known as Chang Ling, 34-156 C.E.; founder of → *wu-tou-mi tao,* one of the most important schools of religious Taoism (→ *tao-chiao*). Toward the middle of the 2d century Chang Tao-ling practiced as a healer in Szechwan Province, curing the sick by the recitation of magical formulae and by serving them sacred water. His fee for each such treatment consisted of five pecks of rice, so that the school founded by him came to be known as Five-Pecks-of-Rice Taoism. His followers venerated him as a celestial master (→ *t'ien-shih*), a title borne by his descendants to this day.

According to legend, Chang Tao-ling carried out alchemical experiments over a period of many years and in the end even succeeded in producing a pill of immortality. Upon swallowing this pill, his face became as fresh and rosy as that of a young boy, despite the fact that he was sixty years old at the time. It is said that he received the instructions for producing such a pill and for healing the sick from → Lao-tzu in person, together with a book of spells for driving out demons. Chang worked as a healer to finance his expensive alchemical experiments and attracted a great number of followers. He died in Szechwan province at a ripe old age and allegedly ascended to Heaven in broad daylight (→ *fei-sheng*).

Chang Tsung-yen ◼ d. 1292 C.E.; celestial master (→ *t'ien-shih*) in the thirty-sixth generation. Chang was granted the title of celestial master in 1276 C.E. by the Emperor Khubilai, together with rulership over all Taoist believers south of the Yang-tse river. In 1288 C.E. the emperor again summoned him to court and demanded to see the jade seal and sword that, according to legend, had been passed from one celestial master to the next since the time of the Han Dynasty. The emperor considered the survival of these treasures to be a sign from Heaven and declared that the title and office of a *t'ien-shih* could be passed on by inheritance. The importance of the Chang family line in religious Taoism rests on this pronouncement (→ Chang Tao-ling).

Ch'an-na ◼ Chin. for Skt. *dhyāna*; → Zen

Ch'an-shih ◼ Chin. for → *zenji*

Ch'an-tsung ◼ Chin. (Jap., zenshū), lit. "the Ch'an school"; Ch'an (Zen) as a school of Buddhism (→ Zen, exoteric). The Chin. *tsung* (Jap., *shū*) is often translated as "sect." This overly stresses the sense of separating or splintering from the mainstream of a religion and—as the form *sectarian* shows clearly—has too negative a connotation. The various schools of Buddhism rather complement each other than contradict and conflict with each other; they are different manners of expressing the → buddha-dharma, suited for bringing people of different types onto the path. Officially in Japan there are only the → Rinzai school, the → Sōtō school, and the → Ōbaku school and no "Zen school"; nevertheless the term *zenshu* is used in Japan, like *ch'an tsung* in China, as a general concept.

Chao-chou Ts'ung-shen ◼ (Jap., Jōshū Jūshin), 778–897; one of the most important Ch'an (Zen) masters of China; a student and dharma successor (→ *hassu*) of Nan-chüan P'u-yüan (Jap., Nansen Fugan). The great Japanese master Dōgen Zenji, who applied the strictest possible standards in evaluating Zen masters, called him deferentially "Jōshū, the old buddha." Chao-chou had thirteen dharma successors, but since there were few who equaled him, let alone surpassed him, in profundity of experience, his lineage died out after a few generations.

The life story of Chao-chou is an especially good example of what Zen masters repeatedly stress—that enlightenment is only the *beginning* of real training on the path of Zen. Chao-chou had already experienced profound enlightenment at the age of 18; following that he trained himself for forty more years under his master Nan-ch'üan. After the latter's death, he set about wandering in order to deepen his experience further through → *hossen* with other Ch'an masters. It is said that during this period he sought out as many as eighty of the dharma successors of his "grandfather in Ch'an," → Ma-tsu Tao-i (Jap., Baso Dōitsu). Finally, at the age of 80, he settled in a small Ch'an monastery in the town of Chao-chou. There at last students gathered around him and he led them on the path of Ch'an until his death at the age of 120.

Chao-chou had a way of instructing his students that people called "Chao-chou's lip and mouth Ch'an." In a soft voice, often almost whispering, he answered his students' questions with short, simple pronouncements. His words were, however, very powerful; it is said they were able to cut through the deluded feeling and thinking of his students like a sharp sword. Many famous kōans originated with Chao-chou, among them the one used by Master → Wu-men Hui-k'ai (Jap., Mumon Ekai) as the first example in his renowned kōan collection, the *Wu-men-kuan.*

"A monk once asked Master Chao-chou: 'Does a dog really have buddha-nature, or not?'

"Chao-chou said, '*Wu*,' " [Jap., *mu*].

Since the time when words of the old masters began being used as a means of training (→ *kōan*), this so-called kōan *mu* has helped thousands of Zen students to a first enlightenment experience(→ *kenshō*, → *satori*). Still today it is given to many Zen students as their first koan.

We encounter Master Chao-chou in examples 1, 7, 11, 14, 19, 31, and 37 of the → *Wu-men-kuan*, as well as in examples 2, 9, 30, 41, 45, 52, 57, 58, 59, 64, 80, and 96 of the → *Pi-yen-lu*. The biography and the record of the words of Master Chao-chou are found in the *Chao-chou Chen-chi-ch'an-shih yü-lu hsing-chuan.*

For the incident that led to the enlightenment of the eighteen-year-old Chao-chou in a → *mondō* with his master Nan-ch'üan (*Wu-men-kuan* 19), → *Heijōshin kore dō*. For Chao-chou's famous answer to a monk's question about the meaning of Bodhidharma's coming out of the west (→ *seirai-no-i*), → *mondō*.

Chariyā-pitaka **B** Skt. → *Khuddaka-nikāya* → *ajari*

Charnel ground contemplation **B** (Pali, sīvathikā), a part of the practice of → mindfulness of body within the framework of the four foundations of mindfulness (→ Satipatthāna).

The sūtra text explaining this practice is as follows:

"Monks, it is as though a monk were to see a corpse that had been thrown on the charnel ground, one, two, or three days after death—bloated, bluish, festering—as though he saw this and related it to his own body: 'Also this, my own body, has a like destiny, a similar lot, and cannot evade it.' Or further, monks, as though the monk saw a corpse that had been thrown on the charnel ground as it was being devoured by crows, sea gulls, vultures, dogs, jackals, or by many kinds of worms, . . . as though he saw a skeleton held together by sinews on which flesh and blood still hung, . . . a bloodstained skeleton held together by sinews from which the flesh was gone, . . . bones loosed from the sinews, scattered in all directions, here a bone from the hand, there a bone from the foot, there a legbone, there the spine, there the skull, . . . bleached bones resembling shellfish, . . . heaped-up bones after the passage of many years, . . . mouldered bones, crumbling into dust: as though he saw this and related it to his own body: 'Also this body has such a destiny, a similar lot, and cannot evade it' " (Trans. from Nyanatiloka 1956).

Chārvāka **H** (Cārvāka), Indian philosopher whose precepts are founded upon skepticism and materialism. The writing presumed to be his principal work, *Bārhaspati-Sūtra* (ca. 600 B.C.E.), is lost to us, but citations from it are found in various eighth-century Buddhist and Jain texts (→ Jainism). The philosophical school named for him advocates the pursuit of happiness and perfection in the here and now.

Charya **Z** Jap. → *ajari*

Chatur-Āshrama **H** (Catur-Āśrama), Skt.; the four (*chatur*) life stages of a Hindu (→ *āshrama*).

Chatur-yoni **H** **B** (catur-yoni), Skt.; four (*chatur*) kinds of birth by which the beings of the six modes of existence (→ *gati*) can be reborn: (1) *jarāyuja*, born alive (mammals, humans); (2) *andaja*, egg-born (birds, reptiles); (3) *samsvedaja*, moisture- or water-born (fish, worms); (4) *aupapāduka*, born by metamorphosis, i.e., not by a "mother" but rather through the power of → karma alone. In the last way → *devas*, → *pretas*, → hell beings (→ *naraka*), and beings of a newly arisen world are born.

Chela **H** **B** really *cheta* (ceṭa), Skt., lit. "servant"; a general word for student, but especially a spiritual seeker who is expecting teaching from his guru and therefore serves him.

The relationship between guru and *chela* can only be fruitful if it goes beyond the mere teacher-student relationship in that the student manifests complete trust in his master. To make this possible, the student must first critically examine whether he has found the right master.

Ch'eng-huang **T** Chin.; protective deity of a city. In Taoist belief these deities ward off disasters and catastrophes and protect the inhabitants of cities under their care, who may also supplicate them. In periods of drought, the *ch'eng-huang* cause rain to fall and the sun to shine again after a thunderstorm. They grant a plentiful harvest and ensure the affluence of the citizens.

In addition, the *ch'eng-huang* act as guides of the souls of the departed. A Taoist priest who wishes to help the souls (→ *hun*, → *po*) of a dead person out of Hell, must inform the protective deity of the city by submitting a document.

The *ch'eng-huang* tradition dates back to ancient times and was adopted by Taoism, which admitted these city protectors to the ranks of its most important deities. As a rule, prominent citizens who devoted their energies to the public good were also venerated as *ch'eng-huang*. Toward the end of the 10th century it became the custom to accord to city deities the title *king* or *duke*, depending on the importance of the city in question. The feast day of a city deity was an important festival in the life of a city and was celebrated with parades, at which a statue of the *ch'eng-huang* was carried through the streets.

Cheng-i tao ◼ Chin., lit. "Way of Right Unity"; collective term for all Taoist schools that use talismans, amulets, etc. as part of their religious practice (→ *fu-lu p'ai*). Next to the → *ch'üan-chen tao* (Way of the Realization of Truth) the *cheng-i tao* was the most important branch of religious Taoism (→ *tao-chiao*) since the time of the Yuan Dynasty.

The beginnings of the *cheng-i tao* go back to the Five-Pecks-of-Rice Taoism (→ *wu-tou-mi tao*) founded by Chang Tao-ling during the Eastern Han Dynasty. During the T'ang and Sung dynasties the *cheng-i tao* school combined with the → *ling-pao p'ai* (School of the Magic Jewel) and several other schools. In 1304 C.E. one of Chang Tao-ling's descendants in the thirty-eighth generation was accorded the title *leader of right unity,* because he led several religious schools that made use of talismans. Since then all schools using talismans are considered to be part of the Way of Right Unity, in whose practices exorcisms, talismans, spells, and other magical elements play an important role. The priests of the *cheng-i tao,* unlike those of the *ch'üan-chen tao,* may marry. The *cheng-i tao* still has active followers in Taiwan and Hong Kong.

Cheng-i tao priests pass on their magical skills through inheritance. The believers visit the priests to obtain talismans, which protect the wearer against evil spirits, sorcery, sickness, fire, and other disasters. The → *tao-shih* of this school also officiate at various ceremonies, e.g., to cause the soul of a dead person to return into that person's body or to guide a dead person through Hell. Some *tao-shih* practice as spiritualists and soothsayers, basing their prophecies on astrology, physiognomy, or the *Book of Change(s)* (→ *I-ching*).

Ch'eng-kuan ◼ → Hua-yen school

Chen-hsieh Ch'ing-liao ◼ (Jap., Shingetsu Shōryō [Seiryō]), 1089–1151; Chinese Ch'an (Zen) master of the → Sōtō school; a student and dharma successor (→ *hassu*) of → Tan-hsia Tzu-ch'un (Jap., Tanka Shijun) and the master of Ta-hsiu Tsung-chüeh (Jap., Daikyū Sōkaku, 1091–1162), who was the grandfather in succession of → Dōgen Zenji.

Chen-jen ◼ Chin., lit. "true [pure] human being"; ideal figure of philosophical and religious Taoism. The term was first employed by → Chuang-tzu and refers to a person who has realized the truth within himself and thus attained the → Tao. The true man is free of all limitations, has abandoned all concepts and attained total freedom.

Chuang-tzu (chap. 6) describes the true or pure men as follows:

"The pure men of old acted without calculation, not seeking to secure results. They laid no plans. Therefore, failing, they had no cause for regret; succeeding, no cause for congratulation. And thus they could scale heights without fear; enter water without becoming wet; fire without feeling hot. So far had their wisdom advanced toward Tao. The pure men of old slept without dreams, and waked without anxiety. They ate without discrimination, breathing deep breaths. For pure men draw breath from their innermost depths; the vulgar only from their throats. The pure men of old did not know what it was to love life or to hate death. They did not rejoice in birth, nor strive to put off dissolution. Quickly come, and quickly go—no more. They did not forget whence it was they had sprung, neither did they seek to hasten their return thither. Cheerfully they played their allotted parts, waiting patiently for the end. This is what is called not leading the heart astray from Tao, nor to let the human seek to supplement the divine. . . . Such men are in mind absolutely free; in demeanour, grave; in expression, cheerful. If it is freezing cold, it seems to them like autumn; if blazing hot, like spring. Their passions occur like the four seasons. They are in harmony with all creation, and none know the limits thereof." (*See* Giles 1961.)

The → *Huai-nan-tzu* says that the pure man is "neither born, nor does he die; he is not empty, nor is he full." The *Book of Supreme Peace* (→ *T'ai-p'ing ching*) places the *chen-jen* above the immortals (→ *hsien*) and below the gods (→ *shen*) in the Taoist hierarchy.

Since the T'ang Dynasty *chen-jen* has been an honorary title of historical personalities and Taoist masters. The Emperor T'ang Hsüan-tsung bestowed upon Chuang-tzu the title "Pure Man from the Southern Land of Blossoms" (*Nan-hua chen-jen*) from which the title of his collected writings (*Nan-hua chen-ching*) derives.

Chenrezi ◼ (sPyan-ras-gzigs), Tib., lit. "looking with clear eyes"; the Tibetan form of → Avalokiteshvara, the bodhisattva of compassion. He is considered as the patron and protector of the "land of snow," and important events and personalities of → Tibetan Buddhism are regarded as connected with Chenrezi's action. Legend sees in him the founding father of the Tibetan people; also King Songtsen Gampo (reigned 620–49), who is responsible for the introduction of Buddhism into Tibet, is regarded as an incarnation of Chenrezi. Among the countless persons who over the centuries have been venerated as incarnations (→ *tulku*) of Avalokiteshvara are the → dalai lama and the → Karmapa.

The Sanskrit formula associated with him (→ *om mani padme hum*; Tib. form, *om mani peme hung)* was the first mantra introduced in Tibet and is most widespread there. In one of the most important iconographical forms, Chenrezi is represented standing with eleven heads and a thousand arms. In this form, he is the main focus of particular meditation practices (→ *sādhana)* that are connected with periods of fasting. In his best-known form, however, he has four arms and sits on a lotus; it is this manifestation to which → Thangtong Gyelpo devoted an imporant meditation practice.

Chen-ta-tao chiao ▣ Chin., lit. "Teaching of the True Great Tao"; school of religious Taoism founded in 1142 C.E. by Liu Te-jen. Based on the concepts of the → *Tao-te ching,* this school stresses the ideals of unmotivated action (→ *wu-wei*), contentment, and altruism. The adherents of the *chen-ta-tao chiao* strive toward the good and endeavor to avoid evil. Life-prolonging and magical practices play no part in this school, in which a strong Confucianist influence can be felt. The *chen-ta-tao chiao* reached its peak in the 13th century but faded out soon after.

Chen-tsung ▣ 968-1022 C.E.; Sung Dynasty emperor who, in 1012 C.E., instituted the veneration of the Jade Emperor → Yü-huang after allegedly having received a letter from him. In 1016 C.E. Chen-tsung granted the use of a large area of land on Dragon-and-Tiger Mountain (→ Lung-hu-shan) to the then heavenly master (→ *t'ien-shih*). It is said that this mountain continued to be an abode of heavenly masters until the year 1949. In addition, Chen-tsung promoted the compilation of the Taoist canon (→ *Tao-tsang*), which first appeared in print in 1019 C.E.

Ch'en T'uan ▣ ca. 906-89 C.E.; Taoist scholar well-versed in the teachings of both the inner and outer elixir (→ *nei-tan,* → *wai-tan*), Ch'en lived as a hermit on Hua-shan, one of the sacred Taoist mountains, where he is said to have carved the diagram of the ultimateless (*wu-chi-t'u*) into the rock face near where he meditated on the Inner Alchemy. Ch'en T'uan is also considered to be the creator of the diagram of primordial heaven (*hsien-t'ien-t'u*). These two diagrams influenced the neo-Confucian philosopher Chou I-tun as he worked on his diagram of the supreme ultimate (→ *t'ai-chi-t'u*).

Chang Chung-yüan interprets Ch'en T'uan's diagram of the ultimateless as follows:

"The diagram consisted of several tiers of circles describing the process of meditation. The first tier (bottom row in the illustration) was a circle labeled,

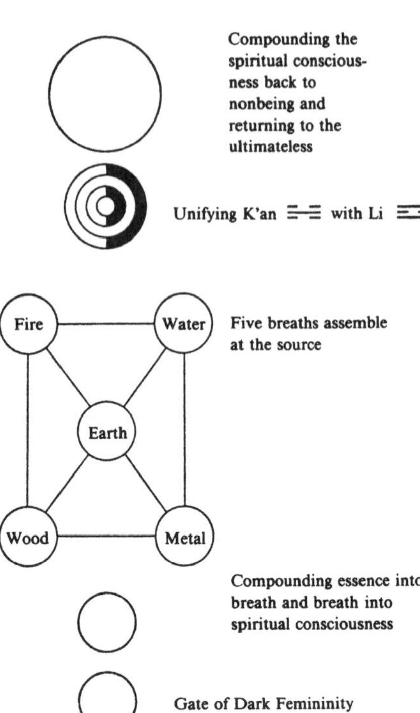

The Diagram of Ultimatelessness

in Lao-tzu's expression, 'The Gate of the Dark Femininity,' which is the Foundation of Heaven and Earth. The next tier is another circle, illustrating the process of compounding → Ching (essence) into → Ch'i (breath) and then into → Shen (spirit). *Ching, ch'i* and *shen* are the fundamental concepts of meditative breathing. . . . This tier [thus] shows how the energy from the lowest center of the body [→ *tan-t'ien*] is transformed into the circulation of breath and . . . further into spiritual consciousness. The following, or middle, tier of the diagram consists of the Five Elements [→ *wu-hsing*]: fire and wood on the left, metal and water on the right, and earth in the middle. They symbolise the five movers in the lesser circulation (of the breath), which ultimately reach the grand circulation. The fourth tier shows the unification of *k'an* and *li* in the form of a circle, which is divided into *yin* and *yang.* The fluctuation of *yin* and *yang* [represents] the grand circulation through the entire body. Both the five movers in the small circulation and *yin* and *yang* in the grand circulation lead to *shen,* or spiritual consciousness. The tier at the top of the diagram shows the compounding of *shen* back to *hsü,* or nonbeing.

"Thus all things return to ultimatelessness (*wu-chi*). The spiritual consciousness is the ultimate of the individual, and nonbeing is ultimatelessness. In other words: the spiritual consciousness is compounded back to absolute nonbeing, the origin of all things." (Chang 1963, p. 165)

Chetas 🅷 (Cetas), Skt.; intelligence, thinking consciousness.

Chetasika 🅱 (cetasika) Skt., Pali; factors of mind or consciousness, the mental concomitants connected with a simultaneously arising consciousness and conditioned by it. *Chetasika* is one of the categories of the → Abhidharma; it includes feeling (*vedanā*), perception, and fifty mental formations (→ *samskāra).*

Ch'i 🆃 Chin., lit. air, vapor, breath, ether, energy; also "temperament, strength, atmosphere"; central concept in Taoism and Chinese medicine. In the Taoist view *ch'i* is the vital energy, the life force, the cosmic spirit that pervades and enlivens all things and is therefore synonymous with primordial energy (→ *yüan-ch'i,* → *nei-ch'i*). In the human body *ch'i* is accumulated in an area near the navel, known as the ocean of breath (→ *ch'i-hai*), and must be carefully tended to prevent it from being wasted, which results in sickness or death.

Ch'i as life energy is a central concept in Taoist breathing exercises aimed at strengthening and increasing this energy (→ *hsing-ch'i,* → *fu-ch'i, yen-ch'i, lien-ch'i,* → *t'ai-hsi*). By training his *ch'i* a Taoist adept can acquire extraordinary abilities, which, incidentally, play an important part in the various martial arts. The meditative breathing techniques of the Inner Alchemy (→ *nei-tan*) also work with the *ch'i,* with the aim of purifying and transmuting it.

In his *Pao-p'u-tzu* the great Taoist alchemist → Ko Hung says concerning the importance of *ch'i,* "Man is in *ch'i* and *ch'i* is within each human being. Heaven and Earth and the ten thousand things all require *ch'i* to stay alive. A person that knows how to allow his *ch'i* to circulate (→ *hsing-ch'i*) will preserve himself and banish illnesses that might cause him harm."

In addition to this understanding of *ch'i* as cosmic energy, *ch'i* also designates the breath—the air we breathe in and out—and in this sense is known as outer *ch'i* (→ *wai-ch'i*). *Ch'i* is moreover an important element in the teachings of the neo-Confucianist philosopher → Chu Hsi, who distinguishes between *ch'i* as the material aspect of things and *li* as their principle, or inner aspect. Only in combination with the form-giving power of *ch'i* can this principle (*li*) manifest in the visible realm. In Chinese medicine *ch'i* designates the general life energy that circulates through the body along the so-called meridians and regulates the body's maintenance and growth. Disruptions or blockages in the circulation of *ch'i* are the cause of illness. In addition, *ch'i* designates the breath. In any case, these two aspects of *ch'i* are considered to be inseparable. Lastly, *ch'i* refers to the emotions and—in a more modern view—to the activity of the body's neurohormonal systems.

In the Taoist view the world is an expression of the Tao—i.e., the One in which yin and yang intermingle with the primordial *ch'i* (→ *yüan-ch'i*). Heaven and Earth came into being through the separation of yin and yang, and their renewed intermingling caused the ten thousand things—i.e., all things and creatures—(→ *wan-wu*) to appear.

A Taoist text—*The Experience of the Golden Flower*—contains the following passage: "Before Heaven and Earth were separate, there was only the indefinable ONE. This ONE was divided and yin and yang came into existence. That which received *yang-ch'i* rose up bright and clear and became Heaven; that which received *yin-ch'i* sank down heavy and obscure and became Earth; and that which received both *yin-ch'i* and *yang-ch'i* in right proportions became man." (Translated from Miyuki 1984, p. 185. *See also* Wilhelm 1938.)

Like human beings, Heaven and Earth breathe and as with human beings, the inhaled breath is clean, and the exhaled breath is stale. For that reason each day is divided into two periods. The period of the living *ch'i* (Chin. *sheng-ch'i*)—when Heaven and Earth inhale—runs from midnight to noon. The period of the dead *ch'i* (Chin. *ssu-ch'i*)—when Heaven and Earth exhale—from noon to midnight. According to the relevant Taoist teachings breathing exercises should only be performed during the living *ch'i* period, because only then can positive energy be absorbed.

Chid-Ābhāsa 🅷 (Cid-Ābhāsa), Skt., lit. "appearing like consciousness"; absolute consciousness (→ *chit*) reflected in mental activity and ignorance; the consciousness of the individual soul, or → *jīva.*

Chidākāsha 🅷 (Cidākāśa), Skt.; the realm of the all-pervading, absolute consciousness (→ *chit*), which is identical with → *brahman.*

Chidambaram 🅷 Skt.; 1. famed temple pilgrimage site in South India; 2. an epithet for God, who permeates everything with his consciousness.

Chidātman 🅷 (Cidātman), Skt.; consciousness of the → *ātman,* the Self. This consciousness (→ *chit*) is identical with → *brahman,* or absolute consciousness.

Ch'ien and K'un 🆃 Chin.; the first and second hexagram of the → *I-ching* (*Book of Change*[*s*]) or two of the eight trigrams (→ *pa-kua*). The *ch'ien* hexagram consists of six yang (unbroken) lines and the *ch'ien* trigram of three yang lines, thus representing pure yang, Heaven and the creative principle. The *k'un* hexagram consists of six and the *k'un* trigram of three yin lines and symbolizes pure yin, the Earth and the receptive principle:

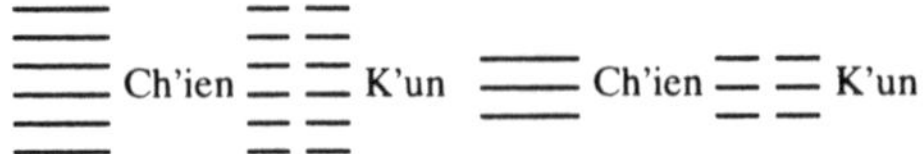

Ch'ien and *k'un* are the gateway to transformation and considered to be the parents of the remaining hexagrams, which are combinations of yin and yang lines. In the language of Taoist alchemy (→ *nei-tan, wei-tan*) *ch'ien* and *k'un* refer respectively to the furnace and cauldron (melting pot) or to the head and belly of the practitioner.

Ch'ien is furthermore associated with external features of the physical body such as the ears, eyes, nose, mouth, and tongue, whilst *K'un* is said to be related to the internal organs such as the heart, lungs, kidneys, and pancreas.

Chien-chen 🅱 Jap., Ganjin, 688–763; Chinese Vinaya master, who went to Japan at the invitation of the Japanese emperor and founded there the → Ritsu school (School of Discipline) in 754.

Chien-chen entered the → *sangha* as a child; he spent many years wandering and studied the entire Buddhist canon. In his home city Yang-chou he propagated his teaching, in which particular emphasis was laid on the rules of the Vinaya. He was invited to Japan in 742; however, the Chinese emperor, a convinced Taoist, denied him permission to go. Five secret attempts to leave China failed. During this time Chien-chen lost his eyesight. But in 754 he finally reached Japan where the Japanese emperor put a monastery in Nara at his disposal. All the members of the imperial family had themselves ordained by Chien-chen. He built an ordination hall on the Chinese model, which became the center for the Japanese → Ritsu school.

Chien-hsing 🆉 Chin. for → *kenshō*

Chien-yüan Chung-hsing 🆉 (Jap., Zengen Chūkō); a Chinese Ch'an (Zen) master of roughly the ninth century; a student and dharma successor (→ *hassu*) of → Tao-wu Yüan-chih (Jap., Dōgo Enchi). He appears in example 55 of the → *Pi-yen-lu.*

Chien-yüan is considered the dharma successor of Master Tao-wu, although according to example 55 of the *Pi-yen-lu,* he first came to a glimpse of enlightenment after the death of Tao-wu under Master → Shih-shuang Ch'ing-chu (Jap., Sekisō Keishō).

Ch'i-hai 🆃 Chin., lit. "ocean of breath"; a point situated two to three fingers' breadths below the navel near the lower cinnabar field (→ *tan-t'ien*), where → *ch'i,* the vital energy, is stored. The *ch'i-hai* is of special importance for a practice called embryonic breathing (→ *t'ai-hsi*), as well as in traditional Chinese medicine.

Chih-i 🅱 🆉 also called Chih-che (Jap., Chisha), 538–97, the actual founder of the → T'ien-t'ai school of Chinese Buddhism, who is considered its fourth patriarch.

Chih-i was the first in the history of Chinese Buddhism to elaborate a complete, critical, and systematic classification of the Buddhist teaching. He did this in order to explain the many and partially contradictory doctrines of Buddhism. As for Buddhist practice, he developed in his works the practice of → chih-kuan, which is still today one of the most widespread meditation practices in Chinese and Japanese Buddhism. His most important works are *Mo-ho chih-kuan* (*Great Shamatha-vipashyanā*), *Liu-miao fa-men* (*The Six Wondrous Gates of Dharma*), and *T'ung-meng chih-kuan* (*Shamatha-vipashyanā for Beginners*). These are among the most widely read works on meditation in China.

Chih-i is said already to have shown special gifts as a child. After hearing it only once, he could recite an entire sūtra by heart. According to his biography, he comprehended the past of all beings when he saw a valuable library destroyed by troops. This experience moved him to enter the monastic order and to become a student of the third patriarch Hui-ssu (515–77), under whom he studied Vinaya texts. In addition he occupied himself with the → *Lotus Sūtra* and learned various methods of → *dhyāna.* In 567 he went to Nanking, where he began teaching. In 576 he went into retreat on T'ien-t'ai Mountain (hence the name of his school). His fame was soon so great that the emperor commanded the tax revenues of an entire district to be used for the maintenance of his monastery. He received the honorary title of *chih-che* ("man of wisdom"). Chih-i died on T'ien-t'ai Mountain.

Chih-jen 🆃 Chin., lit. "perfected human being"; one of the names used by → Chuang-tzu to describe his ideal human being. *Chih-jen* is employed synonymously with → *chen-jen,* → *shen-jen* and → *sheng-jen.* A perfected human being has realized unity with the Tao and is free of all limitations and concepts.

The *Chuang-tzu* (chap. 2) describes the perfect man (through the words of Wang I) as follows: "The Perfect Man (*chih-jen*) is a spiritual being. Were the ocean itself scorched up, he would not feel hot. Were the Milky Way frozen hard, he would not feel cold. Were the mountains to be riven with thunder and the great deep to be thrown up by storm, he would not tremble. In such case, he would mount upon the clouds of heaven and, driving the sun and moon before him, would pass beyond the limits of this external world where death and life have no victory over man—how much less what is bad for him?" (Giles 1961).

Chih-kuan ■ Chin. (Skt., shamatha-vipashyanā; Jap., shikan); tranquility and insight; special meditation methods of the → T'ien-t'ai school. *Chih (shamatha)* refers to calming of restless mind and freeing it from distinctions; *kuan (vipashyanā)* refers to contemplation, examination, and insight into the truths of Buddhism. In some works, these methods, which are very widespread forms of meditation practice in China and Japan, are described in complete detail. An example is the *Tung-meng chih-kuan* (*Shamatha-Vipashyanā for Beginners*) by Chih-i.

This practice is divided into preparatory and main parts. The preparatory practices are divided into achievement of favorable preconditions; diminution of desires; overcoming hindrances (→ *nīvarana*); regulation of eating, sleeping, body, breath, and mind; observance of → *shīlas.*

In the main part the various kinds of *chih-kuan* are practiced. Three kinds of *chih* practice are distinguished: fixing the attention on the tip of the nose; taming the mind by interrupting rising thoughts as they begin; apprehension of conditioned arising (→ *pratītya-samutpāda*) and emptiness (→ *shūnyatā).*

Kuan can be practiced in five ways: contemplation of impurities (→ *ashubha*); contemplation of kindness (→ *maitrī*) in order to do away with hatred and resentment; contemplation of the limitations of the realms of existence (→ *gati*) in order to overcome belief in an ego; contemplation of the emptiness of all dharmas. These contemplations can be carried out during any bodily activity.

In the controlling of the six sense organs, which follows, *chih* represents recognition of the unreality of all existence and avoidance of the arising of repulsion and desire. *Kuan* is the turning inward of the mind during the process of perception in order to become aware of the formlessness of the mind. Definitive realization takes place through the meditation on the unreal, which leads to the realization of *shūnyatā*. This is possible through insight into the → Middle Way.

Chih-men Kuang-tsu ■ (Jap., Chimon Kōso), d. 1031; Chinese Ch'an (Zen) master of the → Ummon school; a student and dharma successor (→ *hassu*) of → Hsiang-lin Ch'eng-yüan (Jap., Kyōrin Chōon) and the master of → Hsüeh-tou Ch'ung-hsien (Jap., Setchō Jūken). Chih-men, whom we meet in examples 21 and 90 of the *Pi-yen-lu,* had thirty dharma successors. He was one of the first masters of the Ch'an (Zen) tradition to celebrate the words of the old masters in poetic form—an art at which his student Hsüeh-tou was even better than his teacher.

Example 90 of the *Pi-yen-lu* shows us Master Chih-men in a → *mondō* with one of his students:

"A monk asked Chih-men, 'What is the wisdom body?'

"Chih-men said, 'The Venus mussel bears the bright moon [in it].'

"The monk asked, 'And what is the effect of wisdom?'

"Chih-men said, 'The female hare gets pregnant.' "

Chih Tao-lin ■ → Chih-tun

Chih-tun ■ also known as Chih Tao-lin, 314–66; one of the most important monks of the 4th century and founder of the so-called Prajñā school of early Chinese Buddhism, the School of Appearance As Such (→ six houses and seven schools).

Chih-tun was the first to reinterpret *li*, a central notion in Chinese philosophy. According to the classical view, *li* means the cosmic order; Chih-tun, in contrast, saw in *li* the supreme truth, the ultimate principle, "suchness" (→ *tathatā*). This meaning for *li* was adopted by other schools in the course of the development of Buddhism in China (→ Hua-yen school). Chih-tun was also known as a student of the → *Chuang-tzu* and enjoyed great popularity in Taoist circles.

Chih-yen ■ → Hua-yen school

Chiji ■ Jap. → *inō*

Chi-kuan ■ Chin. for *kikan* (→ kōan)

Chikuhei ■ Jap. → *shippei*

Ch'i-kung ■ Chin., roughly "working the energy" (→ *ch'i*); physical exercises important in Chinese medicine. These health exercises combine Buddhist and Taoist elements and cover a wide range of practices, such as techniques for regulating the body, the mind (by reducing and quieting thought activity), and the breath (e.g. → *t'u-ku na-hsin*); movement exercises (e.g., → *t'ai chi chuan* and → *tao-yin*), self-massage, etc. In a wider sense the various martial arts (*wu-shu*) are also a form of *ch'i-kung.* Instructions for performing certain basic *ch'i-kung* exercises can be found in Zöller 1984.

Ch'i-kung exercises are usually classified as either active (*tung-kung*) or passive (*ching-kung*). The former are performed while standing, sitting, or lying down and are aimed at relaxing the body, regulating the breath, and turning the mind inward. They are also known as inner exercises (*nei-kung*). The active exercises consist of sequences of physical movements of the body and with which the consciousness and breath of the practitioner have to be coordinated. They are also known as outer exercises (*wai-kung*).

Ch'i-ming ◻ → Shih-shuang Ch'u-yüan

Chimon Kōso ◻ Jap. for → Chih-men Kuang-tsu

Ching ◻ Chin., lit. "semen, spermatozoa"; one of three life forces, the intermingling of which—according to Taoist teachings—is essential for the preservation of life. The other two are the breath, or vital energy (→ *ch'i*), and the mind, or consciousness (→ *shen*). *Ching* literally designates the semen of a man or the menstrual flow of a woman. In Taoist texts, however, it is not used in such a concrete sense but rather describes a subtle substance or essence, capable of combining with → *ch'i.*

Ching is produced in the abode of ching (*ching-she*) near the lower cinnabar field (→ *tan-t'ien*). If *ching* is present only in small quantities within the body, the person concerned will become ill; when the *ching* is exhausted, death ensues. For that reason, Taoist adepts strive to restrict the loss of *ching* by means of various sexual practices and techniques essentially based on avoiding ejaculation and to strengthen the *ching* (→ *fang-chung shu,* → *huan-ching pu-nao*) with the help of the female yin essence (→ yin-yang).

According to the most ancient Chinese dictionary, *ching* designates cleaned rice; it is additionally defined as "seed," and "source of life." The → *Huang-ti nei-ching* defines *ching* not only as "seed essence" but also as "essence of the [bodily] organs" and "germ of life." It is said that after conception the first to form is the *ching,* and only after that the brain and spinal cord.

Taoist practice knows several methods to strengthen and increase *ching.* The simplest of these states that a man should, as often as possible, have successive sexual intercourse with different—and preferably young and beautiful—female partners but not allow himself to ejaculate until the end of the final copulation. By this practice his essence is strengthened under the influence of the female yin, any illnesses are healed and the life force increases. The practice of allowing the semen to return to nourish the brain (*huan-ching pu-nao*) is considered to be more effective.

Ching-ch'ing Tao-fu ◻ (Jap., Kyōsei [Kyōshō] Dōfu), 863/68–937; Chinese Ch'an (Zen) master, a student and dharma successor (→ *hassu*) of → Hsüeh-feng I-ts'un (Jap., Seppō Gison). Ching-ch'ing had five dharma successors. We encounter him in examples 16, 23, and 46 of the → *Pi-yen-lu.*

Ch'ing-lung ◻ Chin. → *k'an* and *li*

Ch'ing-t'an ◻ Chin., lit. "pure conversation"; neo-Taoist school (→ *hsüan-hsüeh*) that originated in the 3d century C.E. *Ch'ing-t'an* refers to a refined form of conversation on the teachings of philosophical Taoism (→ *tao-chia*), particularly those of Lao-tzu and Chuang-tzu. In this way the followers of the *ch'ing-t'an* formed a basis for reinterpreting the Confucianist classics from a neo-Taoist point of view. The most important representatives of the school were → Wang Pi (226-49 C.E.), Kou Hsiang (?-ca. 312 C.E.), and Hsiang Hsiu (221-300 C.E.).

Wang Pi and several others held that Confucius (→ K'ung-tzu) was a greater Taoist than either Lao-tzu or Chuang-tzu, because he actually attained a state of nonbeing (→ *wu*), while Lao-tzu and Chuang-tzu contented themselves with talking about such a state. The *Ch'ing-t'an* School also shows Buddhist influences.

Ching-te ch'uan-teng-lu ◻ Chin. (Jap., *Keitoku Dentō-roku*), *"Record Concerning the Passing On of the Lamp, Composed in the Ching-te Period"*; the earliest historical work of Ch'an (Zen) literature, compiled by the Chinese monk Tao-hsüan (Jap., Dōsen) in the year 1004. It consists of short biographies and numerous anecdotes from the lives of the early masters of Ch'an up to → Fa-yen Wen-i (Jap., Hōgen Bun'eki), the founder of the → Hōgen school.

This thirty-volume work, in which the deeds and sayings of over 600 masters are recorded and more than 1000 masters are mentioned, is one of the most important source works of Ch'an (Zen) literature; many of the kōans that are found in later Zen literature were fixed in writing here for the first time. Selections from this work in English translation can be found in Chang 1969.

Ch'ing-yüan Hsing-ssu ◻ (Jap., Seigen Gyōshi), 660?–740; early Chinese Ch'an (Zen) master, a student and dharma successor (→ *hassu*) of → Hui-neng. Little is known of Ch'ing-yüan Hsing-ssu except that he was an outstanding student of Hui-neng and the master of → Shih-tou Hsi-ch'ien (Jap., Sekitō Kisen). The first main lineage of Zen goes back to the T'ang period and Ch'ing-yüan (see the Ch'an/Zen Lineage Chart). He received posthumously the honorific title of Hung-chi-ch'an-shih (Jap., Kōsai Zenji).

Chin-lien ◻ Chin., lit. "golden lotus"; → *ch'üan-chen tao*

Chinmātra ◻ (Cinmātra), Skt.; state of pure being (→ *sat*); a reference to → *brahman.* Prior to the manifestation of its primal energy (→ *shakti*), *brahman* is absolute being, without name or form.

Chinmātroham H (Cinmātroham), Skt., lit. "I am absolute pure being." Absolute being is difficult to grasp with the mind; Meister Eckhart referred to it as *Istheit* ("is-ness"). Since God is not an object and thus cannot be described, Hinduism refers to him with the term → *satchidānanda:* Absolute being, absolute consciousness, and absolute bliss. The phrase "*chinmātroham*" affirms that one's identity with God as being, consciousness, and bliss can be realized.

Chinmāyākosha H (Chinmāyākośa), Skt.; the sheath (→ *kosha*) in which the → *ātman's* state is still one of divine self-awareness; the sheath of divine consciousness.

Chinnamasta H Skt.; the Divine Mother (→ Shakti) in her creative and destructive aspects; a symbol for dissolution and return to the source (→ *brahman*).

Chin-niu Z (Jap., Kingyū); 8th- to 9th-century Chinese Ch'an (Zen) master; a student and dharma successor (→ *hassu*) of → Ma-tsu Tao-i (Jap., Baso Dōitsu). Chin-niu appears in example 74 of the → *Pi-yen-lu.*

Ch'in-shan Wen-sui Z (Jap., Kinzan Bunsui); Chinese Ch'an (Zen) master of the T'ang period; a student and dharma successor (→ *hassu*) of → Tung-shan Liang-chieh (Jap., Tōzan Ryōkai). We meet Ch'in-shan in example 56 of the → *Pi-yen-lu.*

In the → *Ching-te ch'uan-teng-lu* it is reported that Ch'in-shan, after already having entered a Ch'an monastery in his early years, went on pilgrimage with → Yen-t'ou Ch'üan-huo (Jap., Gantō Zenkatsu) and → Hsüeh-feng I-ts'un to seek out various Ch'an masters. At last the three of them came to → Te-shan Hsüan-chieh (Jap., Tokusan Senkan). While Yen-t'ou and Hsüeh-feng became outstanding students of his and his dharma successors, Ch'in-shan could not get used to Master Te-shan's extremely strict style of training. After the master had beaten him so hard that he had to be taken sick to bed, Ch'in-shan left and went to Master Tung-shan, under whom he also at last experienced enlightenment. Ch'in-shan is said to have become abbot of the monastery on Mount Ch'in at the age of twenty-seven.

Chintāmani H B (cintāmaṇi), Skt.

H 1. a mystical jewel with the power to fulfill its possessor's every desire; 2. an epithet for God; 3. the title, or part of the title, of numerous works in Sanskrit.

B 1. the wish-fulfilling jewel, attribute of various buddhas and bodhisattvas (→ *Kshitigarbha,* → Avalokiteshvara, → Ratnasambhava, etc.). 2. a symbol for the liberated mind.

Chin-tan T Chin., lit. "golden cinnabar"; the golden elixir, a variously interpreted concept in Taoist alchemy (→ *nei-tan,* → *wai-tan*). In texts predating the T'ang and Sung dynasties, *chin-tan* usually refers to the outer elixir. The adherents of the Outer Alchemy strove to produce gold from various chemical substances, which was to bestow immortality on those who swallowed it. In later texts *chin-tan* usually designates the inner elixir, and in this sense is synonymous with the sacred embryo (→ *sheng-t'ai*) and the golden flower of Inner Alchemy (→ *nei-tan*).

Chisha B Z also known as Chisha Daishi, Jap. for → Chih-i.

Chit H (cit), Skt.; absolute consciousness; an important concept in → Vedānta, it is sharply distinct from Western ideas of consciousness. Whereas Westerners essentially live by Descartes's "I think, therefore I am," states that "I am also when I am not thinking," as in the "unconscious" states of fainting, deep sleep, or → *samādhi,* also called → *turīya.* By contrast, thinking consciousness is present only in the states of waking and dreaming.

According to → Advaita-Vedānta, to be an atheist is impossible, since whoever doubts the existence of God does not doubt that he doubts; yet in order to doubt one must use *chit,* consciousness—which is just what the atheist is trying to deny: for *chit* is identical with God or → *brahman.* In the great play of the inner organ of mind (→ *antahkarana*), which projects the manifest world, a faint glow reflects the light of the *chit,* said to be "brighter than a thousand suns."

Chitam H (Cita) Skt.; a technical term for the seat of the unconscious, conscious, and superconscious. By means of yoga, the first two are mastered so that the superconscious may be made manifest.

Chit-Purusha H (Cit-Puruṣa), Skt.; the force of consciousness of the Self (→ *purusha*).

Chitrā-Nādī H (Citrā-Nāḍī), Skt.; a channel in the → *sushumnā* through which streams of spiritual consciousness, governed by → *sattva,* rise when the → *kundalinī* rises.

Chi-tsang B 549–623; a teacher of the Chinese → San-lun school, disciple of → Fa-lang. Chi-tsang wrote well-known commentaries on the three fundamental works of his school and a compendium of its teachings, as well as a treatise on the two truths (→ Mādhyamika) and commentaries on all the most important Mahāyāna sūtras. He is regarded as having brought the teaching of the San-lun school to completion.

Chi-tsang was born in 549 in what is now Nanking. His father, who became a monk shortly after the birth of his son, was a Parthian. Chi-tsang entered the San-lun Monastery at the age of seven. There he studied the Mādhyamika texts. When he received full ordination at the age of twenty-one, he was already renowned for his profound understanding. Because of political chaos he left his home city and settled further to the south. In this period he composed his commentaries. Chi-tsang's interpretation of the two truths is of particular importance. He formulated it in three stages:

Relative (worldly) truth	*Ultimate reality*
1. affirmation of existence	affirmation of nonexistence
2. affirmation of existence or nonexistence	negation of both existence and nonexistence
3. either affirmation or negation of existence and nonexistence	neither affirmation nor negation of both existence and nonexistence

Thus Chi-tsang reaches, through a series of negations, the level where nothing is affirmed and nothing negated; this is the highest level of the → Middle Way.

On the basis of his reputation as master of the San-lun school, in 606 Chi-tsang was invited by the emperor to the capital, Ch'ang-an, where more than ten thousand monks and lay people are said to have attended his presentation of the teachings. In consideration of his inestimable contribution to the development of Buddhism in China, Chi-tsang was included in the list of the ten most important monks of the Wu-te period (618–26). His Korean disciple Ekwan brought the San-lun school to Japan.

Chit-Shakti 🅗 (Cit-Śakti), Skt.; consciousness as the supreme energy, the force that gives rise to the universe. → Vedanta teaches that the manifest world consists solely of energy (→ *shakti*), which is identical with consciousness (→ *chit*). In our identification with the body, we use this consciousness to forge the idea of a material universe.

Chitta 🅗 🅑 (citta), Skt.

🅗 a level of the inner organ (→ *antahkarana*), designated as the substance of mind; it gives rise to perception and thinking.

🅑 1. As a synonym for → *manas* (thinking mind) and → *vijñāna* (consciousness) *chitta* designates the totality of mental processes and manifestations and is equated with thinking, discriminating mind.

2. In the → Abhidharma *chitta* was considered as separate from mental factors (→ *chetasika*), i.e., as sort of mental substance; this led to a substantialistic view of phenomena.

3. In the terminology of the → Yogāchāra, *chitta* has the same meaning as "storehouse consciousness" (→ *alaya-vijñāna*), the source of all mental activities. According to this view the universe is nothing but *chitta*, "pure consciousness." Here the term is used as a synonym for ultimate reality or suchness (→ *tathatā*), i.e., for concepts referring to the absolute.

Chit-Tapas 🅗 (Cit-Tapas), Skt.; divine self-awareness and infinite, all- achieving will; the sheath of → *chaitanya-purusha.*

Chittaprasāda 🅗 (Cittaprasāda), Skt.; contentment, serenity; stillness of mind.

Chitta-Shuddhi 🅗 (Citta-Śuddhi), Skt.; purification of thoughts and feelings.

Chitta-Vikshepa 🅗 (Citta-Vikṣepa), Skt.; the mind under the veil of distraction, confusion, and entanglement in ignorance.

Chittavritti 🅗 (Cittavṛtti), Skt., lit. "state of mind, emotion"; mental vibrations, thoughts; state or disposition of the substance of mind in the form of memories, desires, and feelings.

Chittavritti-Nirodha 🅗 (Cittavṛtti-Nirodha), Skt.; restraint of the movements of mind, control of thought; the eighth step in → Patañjali's → *Yoga-Sūtra,* to be equated with → *samādhi.*

Ch'iu Ch'u-chi 🅣 → *ch'üan-chen tao*

Chiu-feng Tao-ch'ien 🅩 (Jap., Kyūhō Dōken); Chinese Ch'an (Zen) master; → Ho-shan Wu-yin

Chiu-kung 🅣 Chin., lit. "nine palaces"; according to the teachings of the → Inner Deity Hygiene School, the human brain is divided into nine palaces, which are inhabited by different deities (→ *shen*) and arranged between the forehead and the nape of the neck in two rows, of four and five compartments. The most important of these are the first three palaces of the lower row, where → Huang-lao-chün and his assistants reside. The palace found at the center of the head is called → *ni-huan* (after the Buddhist term *nirvana*) and is the seat of the highest body deity, the Supreme One (T'ai-i).

In some Taoist texts *chiu-kung* refers to nine bodily

organs, namely the heart, kidneys, liver, lungs, pancreas, gall bladder, small intestine, large intestine, and bladder.

Chöd 🅱 (gcod), Tib., lit. "cut off, cut through"; along with Shijed, one of the two branches of the school of Tibetan Buddhism founded by the Indian ascetic Phadampa Sangye (d. 1117). Its theoretical basis is drawn from the *prajñāpāramitā* teachings but was expanded to include certain shamanistic elements. The central practice of Chöd is to cut away the false concept of ego (ātman) by offering one's own body to demons. This ritual was carried out especially in charnel grounds—the dwelling place of demons—in order to cut through the most dormant attachments to an ego. The most important disciple of Phadampa Sangye was Machig Labdrönme (1055–1145); through her the teaching of Chöd passed into the other Tibetan schools.

Phadampa Sangye, who because of his "bluish" skin color was regarded as south Indian, was a contemporary of → Milarepa and is said to have undertaken five journeys to Tibet. The Shijed—"Pacifying Pain"—school originated by him, generated a noteworthy literature but did not develop into an independent tradition.

The Chöd teaching, on the other hand, continued successfully and is to be found today in the Kagyüpa school. The point of departure for this teaching is the postulate of the *prajñāpāramitā* tradition that any appearance arises out of one's own consciousness. Particularly the fear of death and all other imaginations and deceptions are products of an uncontrolled thinking process.

The practice of Chöd sets itself the task of entirely cutting through this thinking process through the use of a radical meditation technique. It is composed of a preparatory moment, in which the practitioner presumes the existence of demons as real and intentionally invokes them and requests them to devour his body; and a second moment, in which he experiences them as emanations of the mind and recognizes their true nature (→ *shūnyatā*). This techniques is most effectively carried out in extreme environments such as charnel grounds, since it is in such places that demons and fright most easily arise. Here the Chöd aspirant settles in, equipped only with a trumpet made from a human thighbone and a drum.

The emphasis in Chöd is on actual practice. Thus Phadampa Sangye is purported to have said to Machig Labdrönme, "Go to the charnel grounds and to the mountains; leave studying behind you and become a wandering yoginī!"

Chōka 🅩 Jap., lit. "morning section"; the morning sūtra recitation; part of the daily routine of a Zen monastery (→ *tera*).

Chōkei Eryō 🅩 Jap. for → Ch'ang-ch'ing Hui'leng

Chörten 🅱 Tib. for → stūpa

Chōsan 🅩 Jap., lit. "morning devotion"; morning period of → *zazen* with which the day in a Zen monastery (→ *tera*) begins.

Chōsetsu Yūsai 🅩 Jap. for → Ch'ang-sha Ching-ts'en

Chōsha Keijin 🅩 Jap. for → Ch'ang-sha Ch'ing-ts'en

Chou-i 🅣 Chin., lit. *"Change(s) of the Chou Dynasty"*; a designation found in Chinese texts for the *Book of Change(s)* (→ *I-ching*), referring to both the root text and the commentaries (→ *Shih-i*).

Chou-i ts'an-t'ung-ch'i 🅣 Chin., → Wei P'o-yang

Chou Tun-i 🅣 → *t'ai-chi-t'u*

Chōyū 🅩 Jap. for Chang-hsiung; → Kakushin

Cho-yü 🅩 Chin. for → *jakugo*

Ch'u 🅣 Chin., lit. "kitchen," banquet; feasts held by followers of the → *t'ai-p'ing tao* and → *wu-tou-mi tao* schools to honor and thank priests for their help and ministrations in important family matters.

At these banquets the members of the community give the → *tao-shih* presents, the value of which varies with the nature of the occasion. The most lavish of these ceremonies is held to celebrate the birth of a son. It is attended by ten members of the community, and the present given to the priest consists of a hundred sheets of paper, several writing brushes, ink, etc.

Only five guests are invited to celebrate the birth of a daughter and the *tao-shih* is offered a straw mat, a broom, and a waste basket. These presents have to be handed to the priest within a month of the birth of a child if the family concerned does not wish to run the risk of losing merit. Similar feasts are held after the death of a relative and at the beginning of the new year. The believers ask to be blessed with wealth and children or even good fortune in general or promotion to a higher post. *Ch'u* are furthermore thought to be a way of curing illnesses and warding off misfortunes and disasters.

Ch'üan-chen tao 🅣 Chin., lit. "Way of the Realization of Truth"; one of two main streams of religious Taoism (→ *tao-chiao*), the other being the "Way of Right Unity" (→ *cheng-i tao*). The *ch'üan-chen tao* is also known as *chung-yang* (pure yang) and *chin-lien* (golden lotus).

The Way of the Realization of Truth is said to have been founded by Wang Ch'un-yang (1112-70 C.E.), who, according to tradition, in 1159 C.E. met a hermit who was a reincarnation of two immortals, Lü Tung-pin and Chung Li-ch'üan (→ *pa-hsien*), and from this hermit received secret verbal teachings, which came to form the basis of the school founded by him. In 1167 C.E. he established a monastery on Shantung peninsula, known as the Monastery for the Realization of Truth. According to Wang Ch'un-yang a Taoist realizes the truth by understanding his mind and realizing his true nature.

Ch'üan-chen tao is a synthesis of the basic tenets of the three great religions of China—Confucianism, Buddhism, and Taoism—with Zen Buddhist elements predominating. In his *Treatise on the Foundation of the Way for the Realization of Truth* (*Li-chiao shih wu-lun*), which outlines the practices of the school founded by him, Wang Ch'un-yang combines the teachings of the *Prajñāpāramitā sūtra* with those of the Inner Elixir School (→ *nei-tan*). Seven of his pupils—known as the seven enlightened ones of the North—initiated separate movements within the *ch'üan-chen tao.* One of them—Ch'iu Ch'u-chi—is said to have been well connected to the imperial court. He was a protégé of the Emperor T'ai-tzu (1206-27 C.E.), who founded the Yüan Dynasty and bestowed on Ch'iu the title *divine immortal* (*shen-hsien*). The wide dissemination of the *ch'üan-chen tao* was largely due to this imperial patronage.

In time, two movements within the *ch'üan-chen tao* gained special importance. The first of these was the *Lung-men* (lit. Dragon Gate) School, founded by Ch'iu and also known as the Northern School. One of its best-known texts is *The Secret of the Golden Flower* (→ *T'ai-i chin-hua tsung-chih*). Its main seat is the Monastery of the White Clouds (→ Pai-yün kuan). The second is the Southern School, which was founded by → Chang Po-tuan and died out near the beginning of the 18th century.

The followers of the *ch'üan-chen tao* aim at transcending the mundane world through experiencing the Tao. To this end they practice meditation without the use of external objects of faith, such as talismans (→ *fu-lu*) or methods employed by the followers of Outer Alchemy (→ *wai-tan*). The → *tao-shih* of the *ch'üan-chen tao* remain throughout their lives in strict celibacy.

The *ch'üan-chen tao* lays claim to five patriarchs: Wang Hsiao-yang (to whom the teachings were transmitted by → Lao-chün, a pupil of Lao-tzu); Chung Li-chüan; Lü Ch'un-yang; Liu Hai-shan (who is said to have initiated Chang Po-tuan, the founder of the Southern School); and lastly the actual founder of the *ch'üan-chen tao,* Wang Ch'un-yang.

The teaching and practice of the school are based on the following fifteen points of Wang Ch'un-yang's *Treatise on the Foundation of the Ch'üan-chen tao:*

(1) to live in a hermitage, where mind and body can find rest and peace and where →*ch'i* and → *shen* are brought into balance and harmony; (2) to follow the path of the clouds, i.e., to be untiring in the search for the Tao; (3) the study of books, letting their meaning deeply penetrate into oneself, as a result of which spontaneous insight arises and the "wisdom mind" manifests; (4) on the coagulation of elixir materials; (5) on the construction of a hermitage; (6) on winning Tao friends; (7) on correct sitting meditation; (8) on keeping one's soul in check and cultivating the mind of stillness; (9) on keeping one's nature in balance; (10) on fusing the five elements [→ *wu-hsing*]; (11) on the manifestation of spirit nature in life; (12) on sacredness; (13) on transcending the threefold world (i.e., the world of desire, the world of appearances, and the world of the unformed); (14) on nourishing the spirit; (15) on leaving the world. (Miyuki 1984, p. 62ff.)

Chuang chou ◻ → Chuang-tzu

Chuang-tzu ◻ 1. Taoist sage, ca. 369-286 B.C.E., also known as Chuang Chou; author of the Taoist classic, *Chuang-tzu.* He and → Lao-tzu are considered the founders of philosophical Taoism (→ *tao-chia*). Little is known about his life apart from the fact that he was born in what is now Ho-nan province, was married and held a minor administrative post in Ch'i-yüan. Being unwilling to serve under a prince or ruler, he lived in humble circumstances. His philosophy owes much to the teachings of Lao-tzu. He was a relentless critic of Confucianism.

A historical work dating from the Western Han Dynasty contains an anecdote that may serve as evidence of Chuang-tzu's strong sense of independence: "King Wen of Chou, having heard about Chuang Chou's talents, sent a messenger laden with expensive presents to invite him to join his court and offer him a post as minister. Chuang Chou laughed at the offer and said, 'A thousand pieces of gold is no mean sum, I readily admit, and the office of minister is no doubt an honorable one. But have you ever seen an ox on its way to be slaughtered? Having been carefully fattened over a number of years, it is bedecked with richly embroidered ribbons and led to a great temple. At that moment, that ox would dearly love to be a little pig to which no one pays any heed, but it is too late then. Leave me! Do not sully me! I would rather wallow joyfully in a dirty puddle than be led on a rope by the ruler of a kingdom. I live as I please and so shall never accept an official post' " (Kaltenmark 1981, p. 125ff.).

2. Taoist classic by Chuang-tzu (see 1 above), also known as *The Divine Classic of Nan-hua* (Chin. *Nan-hua chen-ching*). The *Chuang-tzu* consists of thirty-three chapters, the first seven of which are called the "inner" books and were

Chuang-tzu

actually written by Chuang-tzu. The fifteen "outer" and eleven "mixed" books, on the other hand, are believed to be the work of his disciples.

The themes dealt with by Chuang-tzu are in part identical with those to which Lao-tzu addresses himself in the → *Tao-te ching,* and the views of both authors on such matters as the nature of the → Tao and the → *te* essentially coincide. The *Chuang-tzu* furthermore attaches central importance to unmotivated action (→ *wu-wei*), stresses the relativity of all opposites, the identity of life and death, and the importance of meditation as a means of becoming one with the Tao. Nature herself is seen by Chuang-tzu as a never-ending transformation of appearances. He was thus one of the first to point to the illusory nature of the world.

However, the *Chuang-tzu* also shows the influence of non-Taoist movements, and → Hui Shih, Chuang-tzu's closest friend, played an important part in the development of its philosophy. The book contains numerous attacks on Confucius (→ K'ung-tzu) and his teachings. For example, Chuang-tzu rejected the Confucianist cardinal virtues of fellow-feeling (→ *jen*) and uprightness (→ *i*) as artificial concepts that could easily become no more than mere ideas without any correspondence to living reality.

The *Chuang-tzu* is valued both for its philosophical insights and as a work of great literary merit.

Chuang-tzu considers the harmony and freedom attainable by following our own nature the highest good a human being is capable of realizing. He further considers the egalitarianism of institutions that ignore the originality and uniqueness of people to be a major cause of human suffering. For that reason he is categorically opposed to "government by government," arguing instead that the world can only be kept in order by nongoverning, i.e., by a ruler adhering to the principle of unmotivated action. Book 7 of the *Chuang-tzu* gives the following description of an ideal ruler:

"The goodness of a wise ruler covers the whole empire, yet he himself seems to know it not. It influences all creation, yet none is conscious thereof. It appears under countless forms, bringing joy to all things. It is based upon the baseless and travels through the realms of Nowhere." Book 3 gives the following advice: "Resolve your mental energy into abstraction, your physical energy into inaction. Allow yourself to fall in with the natural order of phenomena, without admitting the element of self,—and the empire will be governed." Chuang-tzu rejects all distinctions between good and evil, claiming that there are no universally valid criteria by which to judge such matters. This view is reflected by the title of Book 2, "The Identity of Contrasts." He even considers life and death to be essentially identical, because they are part of the flow of everlasting change and transformation, rather than a beginning or end. This helps to explain his—in the Confucianist view—frivolous reaction to the death of his wife. He came to realize "that she had already existed in a previous state before birth, without form, or even substance; that, while in that unconditioned state, substance was added to spirit; that this substance then assumed form; and that the next stage was birth. And now, by virtue of further change, she is dead, passing from one phase to another, like the sequence of spring, summer, autumn and winter. And while she thus lies asleep in Eternity, for me to go about weeping and wailing would be to proclaim myself ignorant of these natural laws. Therefore I refrain."

Again and again the *Chuang-tzu* returns to the subject of longevity. It mentions a Master Kuang Ch'eng, who lived for twelve hundred years, and one called Kui who had in his possession a prescription that enabled him to gain the appearance of a child. Indeed, Chuang-tzu describes various methods for attaining immortality that came to be of paramount importance in later religious Taoism (→ *tao-chiao*). Book 1, for instance, tells of a divine sage living on Miao-ku-she mountain, "whose flesh is like ice or snow, whose demeanour is that of a virgin, who eats no fruit of the earth [→ *pi-ku*] but lives on air and dew [an allusion to various breathing techniques: → *hsing-ch'i*, → *fu-ch'i*] and, riding on clouds with flying dragons for a team [→ *fei-sheng*], roams beyond the limits of mortality. His being is absolutely inert. Yet he wards off corruption from all things, and causes the crops to thrive."

Although Chuang-tzu would not appear to attach particular importance to either physical (→ *tao-yin*) or breathing exercises, Book 1 points out that the pure men of old draw breath "from their uttermost parts" (lit. "with their heels"). This might be an oblique reference to the practice known as embryonic breathing (→ *t'ai-hsi*).

The *Chuang-tzu* moreover contains descriptions of such meditative practices as → *tso-wang* (in Book 6); and the dialogue (in Book 11) between the Yellow Emperor (→ Huang-ti) and Master Kuang Ch'eng-tzu can be seen as a complete instruction in a Taoist meditation technique that employs visualizations.

All such practices are said to result in the acquisition of supernormal powers. Those fully skilled in them are said to be immune against fire and water and capable of ascending to the clouds, riding through the air on dragons, healing the sick, and ensuring a rich harvest. With these teachings Chuang-tzu contributed toward the development of the cult of the immortals (→ *hsien*). (Quotes from Giles 1961.)

Ch'uan-hsin-fa-yao Z Chin.; abbreviation for the title of the work *Huang-po-shan Tuan-chi-ch'an-shih ch'uan-hsin-fa-yao*; → Huang-po Hsi-yün.

Ch'uan-teng-lu Z Chin.; → Ching-te ch'uan-teng-lu

Chü-chih Z (Jap., Gutei); Ch'an (Zen) master of about the 9th century; a student and dharma successor (→ *hassu*) of → Hang-chou T'ien-lung (Jap., Kōshū Tenryū).

Master Chü-chih, about whom hardly anything else is known, appears in a famous kōan from the → *Wu-men-kuan* (example 3).

The example goes as follows: "Master Chü-chih, whenever a question was posed to him, just held his finger up.

"Later on he had a boy [as an attendant]. Once an outsider asked the boy, 'What kind of dharma does the master teach?' The boy also just held up a finger.

"Chü-chih heard about it, immediately grabbed a kitchen knife, and cut the boy's finger off. The boy, overwhelmed with pain, ran away screaming. Then Chü-chih shouted to him to come back. The student turned his head around. Then Chü-chih once more held his finger up. All of a sudden the boy attained enlightenment.

"As Chü-chih was getting ready to depart from the world, he spoke to his students and said, 'I received the one-finger Ch'an from T'ien-lung. I used it my whole life long and never used it up.'

"As soon as he finished saying this, he passed away."

Chu Hsi T 1130-1200 C.E.; one of the most important philosophers in the history of China. He was a representative of neo-Confucianism, which predominantly concerned itself with metaphysical problems and was influenced by both Buddhism and philosophical Taoism (→ *tao-chia*). Under Chu Hsi the philosophical analysis of → *li* reached its highest level. He specifically investigated the relationship between *li* (the principle, or formal, aspect of a thing) and → *ch'i* (its material aspect) and considered the highest reality to be → *t'ai-ch'i*, the supreme ultimate.

Chu Hsi's philosophy is based on two concepts: *li*, the principle, and *ch'i*, the material. Anything beyond form he categorized as *li*, which in this sense can be taken as synonymous with the term *Tao*. *Ch'i*, on the other hand, is capable of bringing form into being. *Li* and *ch'i* are inseparable: wherever there is matter, *ch'i*, there must also be *li*, because without *li* the thing in question could not exist. Things are thus the instruments through which *li* finds expression. The specific *li* of a thing exists prior to that thing coming into being in the physical realm. The highest reality is *t'ai-ch'i*, which embraces the *li* of Heaven and the *li* of Earth. Thus each thing, apart from its own specific *li*, partakes of this ultimate reality.

For Chu Hsi the universe is the result of *ch'i*'s continually alternating phases of rest and movement. *Ch'i* at rest is *yin*, *ch'i* in motion is *yang* (→ yin-yang). Out of this the five elements (→ *wu-hsing*) arise, which, by their infinite combinations, give rise to the material world.

Chu-hung B Z 1535–1615; important Chinese monk of the Ming Dynasty who developed a practical path based on a combination of → Zen and → Pure Land and instigated a strong Buddhist lay movement.

Chu-hung proposed that in reciting the name of Buddha one should concentrate not only on the name but on the "supreme reality" behind it. Outside of the mind that recited the name of → Amitābha, there is no Amitābha; and besides Amitābha there is no mind. This was for Chu-hung another way of expressing the Zen view that outside the mind there is no Buddha. Through the recitation of Buddha's name this absolute mind can be actualized. Thus for Chu-hung there is no significant difference between this meditation and that of Zen.

Chu-hung married twice. He first entered the monastic order at the age of thirty-two and became a student of noted masters of various schools. He spent most of his life in the neighborhood of Hang-chou, where he built the Yün-chi Temple. In this monastery particular emphasis was laid on strict observance of the rules of the Vinaya. Through this Chu-hung wished to purify the → *sangha.* His effort to link the practice of the Pure Land school with that of Zen was based on his conviction that, although externally the followers of each school travel different paths, their inner attitude is the same. The recitation of Buddha's name (→ *nembutsu*), which banishes everything from the mind but the name of Amitābha, invokes the same state of mind as meditating on a kōan in Zen. Under Chu-hung's influence many lay followers began intensively to practice the recitation of Buddha's name and strictly to observe the rules of discipline without formally entering the monastic order.

Chu-i 🅃 Chin. → Wen-ch'ang

Chūkai 🅉 Jap., lit. "taking off the robes"; a rest break between periods of practice in a Zen monastery. In these breaks the monks can leave the → *zendō* and lie down to rest in the monastery dormitories.

Chulavamsa 🄱 Skt., → *Mahāvamsa*

Chu-lin ch'i-hsien 🅃 Chin., lit. "The Seven Sages of the Bamboo Grove"; a group of seven Taoist scholars and artists who lived during the 3d century C.E., the most important of them being the poet and musician Hsi K'ang (224-263 C.E.). His companions were Juan Chi (210-263 C.E.) and his nephew Juan Hsien, both of whom were also poets and musicians; Liu Ling (221-300 C.E.), a great lover of wine; and Hsiang Hsiu, Wang Jung, and Shan Tao. The seven gathered in a bamboo grove near Hsi K'ang's house to practice pure conversation (→ *ch'ing-t'an*). They sought harmony with the universe and oneness with the Tao by drinking wine. Their ideal consisted in following their impulses and acting spontaneously. Their outstanding collective characteristic was their sensitivity to the beauties of nature.

Hsi K'ang was born into a wealthy family and brought up in accordance with Confucian principles but felt strongly drawn toward Taoism. He practiced the technique, "nourishing the life principle" (→ *yang-hsing*). After extensive travels, during which he made the acquaintance of immortals (→ *hsien*), he and his wife settled in what is now Ho-nan and gathered a group of friends. A collection of anecdotes that conveys an idea of their life style is extant.

The two Juans were known for drinking wine from a large bowl, which they would occasionally share with the neighbors' pigs. Of Juan Hsien it is related that as a host, he offended against all principles of etiquette by leaving his guests and riding after his eloping mistress.

Liu Ling is said to have traveled in the company of a servant who always carried a bottle of wine and a spade so that he could instantly supply his master with drink or bury him without delay, if worst came to worst. Liu Ling would normally wear no clothes at home. To a somewhat dumbfounded Confucian visitor he explained that he considered the whole universe his home, and his room his trousers. He then asked the visitor what business he had in his trousers.

Chung-kuo-shih 🅉 (Jap., Chū-Kokushi), "master of the country Chung; an honorific title bestowed upon the Ch'an (Zen) master → Nan-yang Hui-chung by the imperial court during the T'ang Dynasty.

Chung Li-ch'üan 🅃 → *pa-hsien,* → *ch'üan-chen tao*

Ch'ung-yang 🅃 Chin., lit. "pure yang"; → *ch'üan-chen tao*

Chün-tzu 🅃 Chin., → K'ung-tzu, → *jen*

Churning of the Ocean, the 🄷 , Hindu mythology repeatedly mentions this event. It is a reference to the legend that following a great flood or deluge, many precious objects were lost in the ocean. In order to recover them, Vishnu in his incarnation as a tortoise (→ Kūrma) dived to the bottom of the ocean and allowed his back to serve as the base of Mount Mandara, around whose circumference the gods and demons wrapped the great serpent → Vāsuki. The gods then pulled on one end of the snake, while the demons pulled on the other end; in this way, they churned up the sea until all the objects in question rose to the surface, in particular → *amrita* (the water of immortality), → Dhanvantari (the physician of the gods, who bore the chalice containing *amrita*), → Lakshmī (the goddess of fortune and beauty), Kaustubha (a celebrated jewel), Surabhī (the cow of abundance), and others as well. However, a poison was also churned up in the process. In order to protect humanity, Shiva drank the poisonous substance, which dyed his throat blue.

Ch'u-yüan 🅉 → Shih-shuang Ch'ing-chu

Cinnabar field 🅃 → *tan-t'ien*

Confucianism 🅃 (*ru-chia,* Chin., roughly "School of Scholars"); a state doctrine combining philosophical, religious, and sociopolitical aspects reflected in the teachings of Confucius (→ K'ung-tzu). The original basis of Confucianism was the classical writings attributed to Confucius. The further development of the doctrine was decisively influenced by → Meng-tzu (ca. 372-289 B.C.E.), also known as Mencius, and Hsün-tzu (ca. 313-238 B.C.E.). Central to Meng-tzu's teaching is the belief in inherent goodness of human nature, bestowed by Heaven (→ *t'ien*) and reaching its ultimate perfection in Confucianist saints who, according to Meng-tzu, play an important role in maintaining and defending the so-called royal path (*wang-tao*) against erroneous views and moral decay. Hsün-tzu, on the other hand, argued that man was not inherently good and therefore had to be taught goodness. In addition he stressed the role of → *li* as a principle of cosmic order. The ritualistic practices of Confucianism are mainly based on two sections of the *Book of Rites* (*Li-chi,* → K'ung-tzu): the *Great Teaching* (*Ta-hsüeh*), which stresses the relationship between the individual and the cosmos, and the *Application of the Center* (*Chung-yung*), which describes the role of the saint as a mediator between Heaven and Earth.

Confucianism suffered for some time under the excesses of legalism, but reestablished its influence during the Han Dynasty. Under the emperor Han Wu-ti philosophical Confucianism was extended by the addition of various legalistic elements of considerable political significance and proclaimed an orthodox doctrine. The imperial academy began to employ scholars, who were responsible for the study and interpretation of the Confucianist classics. This development marked the beginning of the selection of state officials by conducting state examinations on Confucianist teachings.

An essential contribution to the development of a Confucianist state doctrine was made by T'ung Chung-shu, who combined the cosmological speculations of the → *yin-yang chia* and the teachings concerning the five elements (→ *wu-hsing*) with the political and socioethical elements of the Confucianist classics.

Between the 3d and 8th centuries Confucianism was penetrated by the teachings of other philosophical schools, mainly of Taoist and Buddhist origin. This led to a revival of mystical traditions within the proclaimed doctrine. The → *I-ching,* in particular, acquired its mystical significance during this period. In philosophy, the prevailing mechanistical correspondences between man and nature were replaced by a search for an inner connection with the → Tao, the primordial principle of the universe. In Western philosophical terminology this phase, marked by the revival of mystical traditions and their incorporation into the Confucianist canon, is known as neo-Confucianism. The so-called *Four Books* (*Ssu-chu*), i.e., the *Analects* of Confucius, the *Meng-tzu,* the *Ta-hsüeh,* and the *Chung-yung* came to be considered more important than the *Five Classics* of early Confucianism. The most significant neo-Confucianist innovation consisted in providing a metaphysical rationale for traditional ethics. In this context *li,* the cosmic principle, is of special importance and central to the teachings of → Chu Hsi, perhaps the most important representative of neo-Confucianism.

In the course of time philosophical speculations became increasingly predominant. The first openly critical writings date from the end of the Ming Dynasty, but it was not until the 19th century that the hollowness of orthodox Confucianist thought was clearly exposed under the scrutiny of Western philosophy.

Various reforms were followed by conservative reversals. The official state examinations were abolished in 1905; and with this Confucianism, as an orthodox state doctrine, came to an end.

After the proclamation of a republic it was recognized that Confucianism had exerted a significant influence on the way the Chinese, as a people, see themselves. It continues to be important as a personal philosophy of life.

Confucius 🅃 → K'ung-tzu

D

Dahara-Vidyā 🄷 Skt., lit. *dahara:* "small space," *vidyā:* "knowledge"; realization of the → *atman* in the inner region of the heart, the "city of *brahman.*"

Dai-anjin 🅉 also dai-anshin, Jap., lit. "great peace of mind"; a Zen expression for complete → enlightenment. (Also → *anjin.*)

Daibai Hōjō 🅉 Jap. for → Ta-mei Fa-ch'ang

Daie Sōkō 🅩 Jap. for → Ta-hui Tsung-kao

Dai-funshi 🅩 Jap., lit. "the great inflexible resolve"; firm resolve is regarded as one of the three "pillars" of the practice of → *zazen.* It is the inflexible determination to dispel "great doubt" (→ dai-gidan) with all the force of one's energy and will. The other two essentials are → *dai-shinkon* and *dai-gidan.*

The modern Japanese Zen master → Hakuun Ryōko Yasutani said about *dai-funshi* in his "Introductory Lectures on Zen Training," "Believing with every pore of our being in the truth of the Buddha's teaching that we are all endowed with the immaculate Bodhi-mind, we resolve to discover and experience the reality of this Mind for ourselves" (Kapleau 1980, p. 65).

Dai-gedatsu 🅩 Jap., lit. "great liberation"; 1. an expression for complete → enlightenment, the attainment of buddhahood; 2. a synonym for → nirvāna; through the "great liberation" the unity of nirvāna and → samsāra is realized.

Dai-gidan 🅩 Jap., lit. "great doubt"; inner condition of doubt-ridden questioning, one of the three "pillars" of the practice of → *zazen.* In Zen doubt does not mean scepticism but rather a state of perplexity, of probing inquiry, of intense self-questioning. The other two essentials are → *dai-shinkon* and → *dai-funshi.*

In his "Introductory Lectures on Zen Training," modern Japanese Zen master → Hakuun Ryōko Yasutani said about *dai-gidan*:

"Not a simple doubt, mind you, but a 'doubt-mass'—and this inevitably stems from a strong faith. It is a doubt as to why we and the world should appear so imperfect, so full of anxiety, strife, and suffering, when in fact our deep faith tells us exactly the opposite is true. It is a doubt which leaves us no rest. It is as though we knew perfectly well we were millionaires and yet inexplicably found ourselves in dire need without a penny in our pockets. Strong doubt, therefore, exists in proportion to strong faith" (Kapleau 1980, p.64).

Daigo-tettei 🅩 Jap., lit. "great [*dai*] satori [*go*] that reaches to the ground [*tettei*]"; profound → enlightenment, which differs in degree from less deep experiences of "glimpses of self-nature" (→ *kenshō,* → satori), even though all these experiences are the same in nature.

The essential content of *daigo-tettei* includes the experience of emptiness (Jap., *ku*; Skt., → *shūnyatā*), also known as "empty expanse" (→ Bodhidharma); the elimination of all antagonism; the experience that the form (Jap., *sugata*) of the cosmos and one's own form are identical, that form is no other than emptiness; the thoroughgoing dissolution of the small → ego.

Daijō 🅩 Jap. for → Mahāyāna

Daijō-kai 🅩 Jap., lit. "rules of the great vehicle"; rules for monastic and lay adherents of → Mahāyāna Buddhism. (Also → *jūjūkai.*)

Daijō-zen 🅩 Jap., → five types of Zen 4

Daikō Koke 🅩 Jap. for → Ta-kuang Chü-hui

Daikōmyō-zō 🅩 Jap., lit. "treasure house of the great beaming light"; 1. Zen expression for one's own true nature or buddha-nature (→ *busshō*), of which one becomes cognizant in the experience of → enlightenment. Also → *kenshō,* → satori.

2. The cloister on T'ien-tung Mountain in which the Chinese Ch'an (Zen) master → T'ien-t'ung Ju-ching (Jap., Tendō Nyojō) lived.

Daimin Kokushi 🅩 → Mukan Fumon

Dainichi Nōnin 🅩 also called Jimbō Zenji; 12th/13th-century Japanese Zen master of the Rinzai school; Nōnin, who was introduced to the teachings of the Tendai school (→ Mikkyō) on Mount Hiei, reached enlightenment without a master. He founded the Sambō-ji monastery in Settsu province and began to instruct students in the mind of Zen. To protect himself from the accusation that he was not part of the Zen tradition and had not been authorized by a master of the Zen lineage of transmission, he finally sent two students of his to China with writings concerning his Zen experience. There the students presented these to the Ch'an (Zen) master Yü-wang Cho-an (Jap., Ikuō Setsuan) of the → Rinzai school, who thereupon confirmed Nōnin's enlightenment.

The relatively short-lived school founded by Nōnin, in which elements of Zen and the Tendai school were mixed, was called the Nihon-Daruma school. Among Nōnin's most prominent students was Koun Ejō (1198–1280), who later became the second patriarch (→ *soshigata*) of the Sōtō Zen school of Japan.

Daiō Kokushi 🅩 → Shōmyō

Daioshō 🅩 Jap., lit. "great priest"; an honorific title of Zen masters.

In the framework of the daily recitations in a Zen monastery, the lineage of the tradition that runs from → Shākyamuni Buddha to the current Zen master of the monastery is recalled by reciting the names of the patriarchs (→ *soshigata*) and their dharma successors (→ *hassu*) in the order of "transmission from heart-mind to heart-mind." In this recitation the title *daioshō* is attached to the names of the Zen masters.

Daishi 🅩 Jap., lit. "great master"; Buddhist honorific title, usually

Daishi Z Jap., lit. "great death"; Zen expression for the death of → ego, which leads to "great rebirth" (profound enlightenment, → *daigo-tettei*). The bestowed posthumously; not to be confused with the *daishi* that crops up in feminine Zen names, which means "great sister." way that leads from great death to great rebirth is that of → *zazen*. Thus it is said in Zen, "At some time you must die on the cushion [→ *zagu*]." This expression does not refer to physical death, but rather to the death of the illusion of ego, of → delusion.

Dai-shinkon Z Jap., lit. "great root of faith"; the strong faith that is considered one of the three "pillars" of the practice of → *zazen*. The other two essentials are → *dai-gidan* and → *dai-funshi*.

In his "Introductory Lectures on Zen Training," the modern Japanese Zen Master → Hakuun Ryōko Yasutani says that *dai-shinkon* means "a faith that is firmly and deeply rooted, immovable, like an immense tree or huge boulder. It is a faith, moreover, untainted by belief in the supernatural or the superstitious. Buddhism has often been described as both a rational religion and a religion of wisdom. But religion it is, and what makes it one is this element of faith, without which it is merely philosophy. Buddhism starts with Buddha's supreme enlightenment, which he attained after strenuous effort. Our deep faith, therefore, is in his enlightenment, the substance of which he proclaimed to be that human nature, all existence, is intrinsically whole, flawless, omnipotent—in a word, perfect. Without unwavering faith in this the heart of the Buddha's teaching, it is impossible to progress far in one's practice." (Kapleau 1980, p. 64).

Daitō Kokushi Z also Kōsen Daitō Kokushi; posthumous honorific title bestowed by the imperial court on Japanese Zen master → Myōchō Shūhō, the founder of the → Daitoku-ji in Kyōto. (Also → Kokushi).

Daitoku-ji Z Jap., "Monastery of Great Virtue"; one of the largest Zen monasteries of Kyōto. It was built in 1319 by Akamatsu Norimura in order to house the many students who had gathered around the great Japanese Zen master → Myōchō Shūhō (also called Daitō Kokushi).

Daitoku-ji belonged for a time to the "Five Mountains" (→ Gosan) of Kyōto, but was eventually declared the monastery in which the health of the emperor was to be prayed for; thus it received a special status outside the Gosan.

In the middle ages Daitoku-ji was an important center of culture; great masters of the Way of tea (→ *chadō*) like Sen-no-Rikyū or Kobori Enshū taught there. In the course of centuries it developed into a monastic complex with many smaller monasteries as part of it, each under the leadership of its own abbot.

Daitsū Chishō Z Jap.; a buddha who appears in a metaphorical passage of the *Lotus Sūtra*. In Zen there is a famous kōan associated with this passage (example 9 of the → *Wu-men-kuan)*.

Daitya H or Daiteya, Skt.; Titan, decendant of the goddess → Diti. The Daityas were a race of demons and giants who waged war against the gods and interfered with the performance of sacrifices. They were vanquished and disappeared.

Daiun Sōgaku Harada Z 1870–1961; one of the most important Zen masters of modern Japan.

At the age of seven, he became a monk in a monastery of the → Sōtō school and trained later at Shōgen-ji, a monastery of the → Rinzai school. At forty he became a student and attendant of Dokutan Rōshi, then abbot of Nanzen-ji and the most respected Zen master of his time. After Master Dokutan had conferred the seal of confirmation (→ *inka-shōmei*) on him, he became the abbot of the Hosshin-ji monastery in Obama. Under his forceful leadership it became a stronghold of authentic Zen training in a modern Japan that was no longer rich in Zen masters.

His instructions for beginners in Zen became known also in the West through his student and dharma successor → Hakuun Ryōko Yasutani. The latter made them the basis for his "Introductory Lectures on Zen Training." (For an English translation, see Kapleau 1980.)

Daiva H Skt.; 1. divinity; 2. fate; omen; the influence of powers and forces that are distinct from the visible, mechanical workings of nature; 3. sacred action.

Daivī-Māyā H Skt.; there are two types of → *māyā*: (1) divine *māyā* (*daivī*), through which *brahman* manifests itself in the world of appearances; (2) lower *māyā*, which in the form of matter is taken to be real.

Daivi-Shakti H (Daivi-Śakti), Skt., lit. "divine power"; a mantra that is given to the student by a guru is considered to contain *daivi-shakti*.

Dākinī B Skt.; in Indian folk belief, a female demon to be found in the company of gods; in → Vajrayāna Buddhism, the inspiring power of consciousness, usually depicted in iconography as a wrathful naked female figure (→ forms of manifestation). As semiwrathful or wrathful → *yidam*, the dākinī has the task of integrating the powers liberated by the practitioner in the process of visualization (→ *sādhana*). In Tibetan, *dākinī* is translated as *khadroma. Kha* means "celestial space," emptiness (→ *shūnyatā*) become an image; *dro* has the meaning of walking and moving about; *ma* indicates the feminine gender in substantive form. Thus the *khadroma* is a female figure that moves on the highest level of reality; her nakedness symbolizes knowledge of truth unveiled. The homeland of the *dākinīs* is said to be the mystic realm of → Urgyen.

The *dākinī* Vajravarāhi with hook knife and skull cup, treading on the demon of ignorance

Daksha H (Dakṣa), Skt.; 1. an epithet for → Prajāpati, the lord of all created beings; 2. the name of a god, one of the → Ādityas; 3. the intuituve capacity for discrimination; the comprehending faculty of mind; 4. proficiency.

Dakshinā H , (Dakṣiṇā), Skt.; 1. the right side, on the right; 2. a milk cow; 3. gifts that one presents to a spiritual teacher in gratitude for his guidance and blessings. In Hinduism, one uses the right hand alone in giving something to another; 4. south; 5. the goddess of divine insight who rules over sacrificial actions and the distribution of sacrifical offerings.

Dakshinā-Agni H (Dakṣiṇāgni), Skt.; the third of the three sacrificial fires, the southern *(dakshinā)* fire of insight; a symbol of the god of intuition and the mind.

Dakshināchāra H (Dakṣiṇācāra), Skt., lit. *dakshinā:* "right," *āchāra:* "custom"; in Hindu Tantrism, a pure ritual (in contrast to other, darker Tantric practices), referred to as "right-hand practice." In Hinduism, the right hand is reserved for pure actions; impure actions may be carried out with the left hand alone.

Dakshinā-Mārga H (Dakṣiṇā-Mārga), Skt., lit. *dakshinā:* "right," *mārga:* "way"; in the Tantric worship of → Shakti, *dakshinā-mārga* is the way of knowledge, in contrast to *vāma-mārga* (*vāma:* "left"), the way of pleasure.

Dakshināyana H (Dakṣiṇāyana), Skt., lit. "southern path, southward way"; one of the paths that a human being may follow in his evolution on earth. It lead to the realm of the dead. Its opposite is → *devayāna.*

Dalai Lama B (dalai bla-ma), Mong. and Tib. lit. "teacher whose wisdom is as great as the ocean"; an honorary title bestowed by the Mongolian prince Altan Khan on the third head of the → Gelukpa school in 1578. This close connection with Mongolia brought the school of → Tsongkhapa into a position of political preeminence, which with the fifth dalai lama (1617–82) was consolidated into rulership over all of Tibet. Since this time, the Dalai Lama has been regarded as an incarnation of → Avalokiteshvara, and the → Panchen Lama has been venerated as his spiritual representative. Each Dalai Lama is considered a reincarnation (→ tulku) of the preceding Dalai Lamas.

The Dalai Lamas not only fulfilled their role as heads of state. Among them are also great scholars and poets filled with *joie de vivre*, like the sixth Dalai Lama. The fourteenth Dalai Lama, in exile since 1959, combines in his person a spiritual and political authority that is still binding for the Tibetan people.

The individual Dalai Lamas are as follows:

1. Dalai Lama Gendün Drub	(1391–1475)
2. Dalai Lama Gendün Gyatso	(1475–1542)
3. Dalai Lama Sönam Gyatso	(1543–1588)
4. Dalai Lama Yönten Gyatso	(1589–1617)
5. Dalai Lama Losang Gyatso	(1617–1682)
6. Dalai Lama Jamyang Gyatso	(1683–1706)
7. Dalai Lama Kelsang Gyatso	(1708–1757)
8. Dalai Lama Jampel Gyatso	(1758–1804)
9. Dalai Lama Lungtog Gyatso	(1806–1815)
10. Dalai Lama Tsültrim Gyatso	(1816–1837)
11. Dalai Lama Kedrub Gyatso	(1838–1856)
12. Dalai Lama Trinle Gyatso	(1856–1875)
13. Dalai Lama Tubten Gyatso	(1876–1933)
14. Dalai Lama Tenzin Gyatso	(born 1935)

Dama 🅷 Skt. → *shatkasampatti*

Dāna 🅱 Skt., Pali, roughly "gift, alms, donation"; voluntary giving of material, energy, or wisdom to others, regarded as one of the most important Buddhist virtues. *Dāna* is one of the six perfections (→ *pāramitā),* one of the ten contemplations (→ *anussati*), and the most important of the meritorious works (→ *punya*).

In Hīnayāna *dāna* is regarded above all as a means to overcoming greed and egoism and avoiding suffering a future life. In Mahāyāna *dāna* is associated with the virtues of kindness (→ *maitrī*) and compassion (→ *karunā*) and viewed as an essential factor in leading all beings to enlightenment.

The practice of *dāna* in the form of almsgiving to mendicant monks is still very widespread today in many → Theravāda countries. The lay follower gives food and clothing to the monk as well as money to the monastery; the monk, for his part, gives instruction and other spiritual help. This form of *dāna* has become in many cases a routine, understood mainly as a means of accumulating merit.

Dandin 🅷 (Daṇḍin), Skt., lit. "the one with the stick"; 1. a → *sannyāsin,* who carries a staff with him throughout his monastic life; 2. a brahman in the fourth life stage (→ *varna*); 3. or Dandi, one of the most famous writers in the Sanskrit language. He lived sometime between the sixth and eighth centuries C.E. andy left a "novel," *Dashakumāra-Charita,* which despite its incompleteness is highly valued. One of the few prose works extant in Sanskrit, it is marked by many fantastic and humorous embellishments and is stylistically so perfect that it is regarded as belonging to the category of *kāvyas,* or literary poems. Also important is Dandin's *Kāvyādarsha* ("Mirror of Poetry"), a three-volume handbook on Sanskrit poetics in verse form.

Dan-gyō 🆉 Jap. for *T'an-ching,* → *Liu-tsu-ta-shih fa-pao-t'an-ching*

Darani 🆉 Jap. for → *dhāranī*

Dardura-Siddhi 🅷 Skt., lit. *dardura:* "frog," *siddhi:* "supernatural power"; the power, achieved through yogic practices, to raise one's body off the ground, referred to in the West as "levitation." (See also → *divya-siddhis.*)

Daridrā-Shevā 🅷 (Daridrā-Śevā);, Skt., lit. *daridra:* "poor," *shevā:* "service, pledge, worship"; service to and care of the poor and needy.

Svāmi → Vivekānanda cast a completely new light on the matter of charity by pointing out what Hindus had not previously considered: that it was a privilege to serve the poor, since each human being is a manifestation of God; hence one is presented with the opportunity to serve and worship God in every needy fellow human being.

Darshana 🅷 🅱 (darśana), also darshan, Skt., lit. (1) "view, sight"; (2) "system."

🅷 1: paying respect to a holy man or a sacred site in order to receive blessings and purification from that presence. Every encounter with a guru or holy person can be regarded as *darshana.* 2: a name for the six doctrines (shad-darshana) that form the six schools of orthodox Hindu philosophy, namely → Nyāya; → Vaisheshika; → Sānkhya; Yoga (→ Rāja-Yoga); → Pūrva-Mīmāmsā, or Mīmāmsā; and → Vedānta, also called Uttara-Mīmāmsā. All six doctrines have the same goal: to liberate the soul from the round of births and deaths and to bring about union with God or the Absolute. They are all represented in the *Bhagavad-Gītā.*

🅱 (Pali, dassana); insight based on reason, which is capable of eliminating the passions (→ *klesha*) that are conceptual in nature, false views (→ *drishti*), doubt (→ *vichikitsā*), and clinging to rites and rules. The way of seeing *(darshana-mārga),* which leads from mere blind trust in the → four noble truths up to actual comprehension of them, transforms a → *dharmānusārin* or → *shraddhānusārin* into a "stream enterer" (→ *shrota-āpanna*).

Daruma 🅱 🆉 Jap. for → Bodhidharma

Daruma-ki 🆉 Jap., lit. "Daruma's day of death"; the death date of the first patriarch of Zen in China, → Bodhidharma (Jap., Daruma), which is commemorated in Zen monasteries on the fifth day of the tenth month.

Daruma-shū 🆉 Jap., lit. "Daruma school"; the name of the school of Buddhism that was brought by the Indian Master → Bodhidharma (Jap., Daruma) from India to China (another name for → Zen).

Daruma-sōjō 🆉 Jap.,lit. "the Daruma succession"; Zen expression for the authentic transmission of → buddha-dharma by the Indian master → Bodhidharma (Jap., Daruma) and his dharma successors (→ *hassu*), the patriarchs of the Zen lineage (→ *soshigata*).

Dashabala 🅱 (daśabala), Skt. (Pali, dasabala), lit. "ten powers"; designates ten abilities possessed by a buddha, which confer the following kinds of knowledge on him: (1) knowledge concerning what is possible and impossible in any situation; (2) concerning the ripening of deeds (→ *vipāka*); (3) concerning the superior and inferior abilities of other beings; (4) concerning their tendencies; (5) concerning the manifold constituents of the world; (6) concerning the paths leading to the various realms of existence; (7) concerning the engendering of purity and impurity; (8) concerning the contemplations, meditative states (→ *samādhi*), the → three liberations, and the absorptions (→ *dhyāna*); (9) concerning deaths and rebirths; (10) concerning the exhaustion of all defilements (→ *āsrava*).

Dashabhūmika 🅱 (daśabhūmika), Skt., lit. "On the Ten Lands"; independent part of the → *Buddhāvatamsaka-sūtra* in which the bodhisattva Vajragarbha, in Indra's paradise and in the presence of the Buddha, explains the course of development of a bodhisattva (→ *bhūmi*). A commentary on the *Dashabhūmika* by → Vasubandhu was the doctrinal basis of the → Tin-lun school of early Chinese Buddhism.

Dasharatha 🅷 (Daśaratha), Skt.; king of Ayodhya. He had three wives. His chief consort, Kausalyā, bore him the prince → Rāma, one of the ten incarnations of → Vishnu and the main character in the renowned epic the → *Rāmāyana*. Dasharatha's other sons were → Bharata, → Lakshmana, and Shatrughna.

Dāsya 🅷 Skt., lit. "servant"; one of the five possible emotional attitudes of a devotee, in which God is the master and the devotee the servant or child (→ *bhāva*).

Datsuma 🆉 Jap. transliteration of → dharma.

Dayānanda 🅷, Svāmi, 1824–1883, founder of the → Ārya-Samāj, a reformation movement important chiefly in North India. Svāmi Dayānanda was a great scholar whose interpretation of the Vedas was strictly monotheistic. He preached against idolatry and attempted to reestablish the ancient Vedic sacrificial rites. He held the Vedas to be the supreme religious authority and accepted their every word as literally true.

Deceptive appearances and sensations 🆉 - → *makyō*

Deha-Abhyāsha 🅷 (Deha-Abhyāśa), Skt., lit. *deha:* "body," *abhyāsha:* "proximity"; imprisonment in the body, identification with the body through ignorance.

Delusion 🆉 also deception, madness (Jap., *mayoi*); being deluded means being fully in error. Delusion refers to belief in something that contradicts reality. In Buddhism, delusion is approximately the same as ignorance (→ *avidyā*), a lack of awareness of the true nature or buddha-nature of things (→ *busshō*) or of the true meaning of existence.

According to the Buddhist outlook, we are deluded by our senses—among which intellect (discriminating discursive thought) is included as a sixth sense. Consciousness, attached to the senses, leads us into error by causing us to take the world of appearances for the whole of reality, whereas in fact it is only a limited and fleeting aspect of reality.

To the erroneous view to which the senses seduce us belongs also the belief that the world is outside of us (the subject-object split), whereas in reality it is our own projection. This, however, does not mean that the phenomenal world has no reality. When the Buddhist masters say that all phenomena are deceptive, they are referring to belief in the *objective* existence of things perceived by the senses and in their status as constituting the whole of reality. The goal of Buddhism is, following the example of Buddha Shākyamuni, to overcome this deluded view through enlightenment. Among the Buddhist schools, Zen particularly stresses the central importance of the enlightenment experience (→ enlightenment, → *kenshō*, → Satori).

According to the most profound teachings of Buddhism, which are at the core of Zen, delusion and enlightenment, phenomenal world and absolute reality, form and emptiness, → samsāra and → nirvāna are, however, completely one. One can come to this proposition, like many Buddhist schools, purely through logico-philosophical analysis, or like modern science, by drawing conclusions from experimental observations. However, Zen emphasizes that the delusion-supported and delusion-motivated thinking and striving of people, which leads to endless suffering in and on account of the phenomenal world, can ultimately only be overcome through one's own immediate experience of this unity (i.e., enlightenment).

Den'e 🆉 also Denne or Den-i, Jap. lit. "handing on the robe"; zen expression for the authentic transmission of → buddha-dharma in the lineage of Zen. In ancient times, the passing on of begging bowl and monastic robe was the symbolic confirmation of the transmission of buddha-dharma from a Zen patriarch *soshigata*) to a dharma successor (→ *hassu*). (Also → *inkashōmei*, → *Denkō-roku*.)

Dengyō Daishi B → Saichō

Den-i Z Jap., → Den'e

Denkō-roku Z short for *Keizan oshō denkō-roko*, Jap. lit. "*Account by the Monk Keizan of the Transmission of the Light*"; collection of episodes from transmission situations in the history of the lineage of the fifty-two patriarchs of the → Sōtō school, from → Mahākāshyapa to Eihei Jō (→ Dōgen) Zenji), as they were recounted by Master → Keizan Jōkin and written down by his students.

The *Denkō-roku* shows how the dharma was authentically transmitted from Shākyamuni Buddha through the patriarchs of the Sōtō school; with the → *Shōbōgenzō* it is one of the most important writings of this school. The *Denkō-roku* should not be confused with the *Dentō-roku* (→ *Ching-te ch'uan-teng-lu*).

Some typical examples of the "transmission of the untransmittable," which is characteristic of Zen, are the following episodes from the *Denkō-roku*:

The first patriarch, the Venerable Mahākāshyapa: Once, as the World-Honored One, winking an eye, twirled a flower between his fingers [→ *nengemishō*], Kāshyapa smiled. The World-Honored One said, "Mine is the treasure-house for the eye of true dharma, the wonderful mind of nirvāna. With that I entrust Mahākāshyapa."

The second patriarch, the venerable Ānanda, asked Venerable Kāshyapa, "Did the World-Honored One pass on anything else besides the gold brocade robe?"

Kāshyapa shouted, "Ānanda!"

Ānanda said, "Yes?"

Kāshyapa said, "Knock over the flagpole in front of the gate."

Ānanda experienced great enlightenment.

The fifty-second patriarch, Eihei Jō Oshō [→ Dōgen Zenji] came (for instruction) to master Gen.

One day when he asked him for instruction, he heard the kōan "Put a single hair simultaneously through many holes" and came immediately to enlightenment.

In the evening he prostrated and asked: "I have no question about the one hair, but what about the many holes?"

Gen smiled slightly and said: "You have put it through!"

The master [Eihei] prostrated.

Denne Z Jap., → *den'e*

Denshin Hōyō Z Jap. for *Ch'uan-hsin-fa-yao*, → Huang-po Hsi-yün

Dentō-roku Z Jap. for *Ch'uan-ten lu*, → *Ching-te ch'uan-teng-lu*

Deva H B Skt., Pali, lit. "shining one."
H 1. *brahman* in the form of a personal God; 2. a name for those divinities who inhabit a realm higher than that of human beings but yet are mortal; 3. a name appended to that of enlightened ones who have realized God.
B celestial being or god, name of inhabitants of one of the good modes of existence (→ *gati*) who live in fortunate realms of the heavens but who, like all other beings, are subject to the cycle of rebirth. The gods are allotted a very long, happy life as a reward for previous good deeds; however, precisely this happiness constitutes the primary hindrance on their path to liberation, since because of it they cannot recognize the truth of suffering (→ four noble truths).

There are in Buddhism twenty-eight divine realms, of which six are in the realm of desire (*kāmaloka, kāmadhatu*), eighteen in the realm of desireless form (*rūpaloka, rūpadhātu*; also called realm of pure form), and four in the realm of the bodiless (*arūpaloka, arūpadhātu*; also called realm of formlessness) (→ *triloka*).

In the realm of desire live (1) the four celestial kings, who are the protectors of the four directions and live on the slopes of Mount → Meru; (2) the thirty-three gods who live on the summit of Mount Meru, who were directly taken over from Hinduism along with their chief, → Shakra (see also → Indra); (3) the *yāmas* or *suyāmas*, who are in a state of continual happiness; (4) the "peaceful and contented gods" (→ *tushita*); (5) gods who take joy in magical creations; and (6) the gods who attempt to dominate each other, ruled by → Māra.

In the realm of desireless form are those gods who dwell in the four *dhyāna* heavens, which they have reached through their practice of the four → *dhyānas*; they are male and free from sexual desire but still possess visible bodies. On the lowest level here is → Brahmā.

The gods of the formless realm are absorbed in contemplation of the → four stages of formlessness.

Devadatta H B Skt., lit. "God-given."
H 1. a → *prāna*-stream created by yawning in order to supply oxygen to the body in a state of exhaustion; 2. the name of → Arjuna's conch; 3. the name of the white horse that → Kalki will ride.
B cousin of the Buddha → Shākyamuni, who joined the *sangha* after hearing a discourse of the Buddha. He became a highly respected member of the Buddhist community. Eight years before the death of the Buddha, however, he tried himself to become the head of the Buddhist order and planned to murder the Buddha. The attempt failed. Thereupon he brought about a schism among the monks of → Vaishālī.

In his assassination plan Devadatta could reckon with the help of the king of Magadha, → Ajātasattu. They had three attacks on the Buddha carried out: The first time, they hired a group of assassins, but these were so impressed by the Buddha that they became his followers. The second time, they tried to crush the Buddha with a boulder; however, the boulder stopped before it reached the Buddha. In their last attempt they set a wild elephant on him; the elephant, however, was tamed by the Buddha's kindness of mind.

Devadatta brought about the schism among the monks of Vaishālī by advocating rigorous asceticism and accusing the Buddha of living a pampered life. The Buddha left the choice to the monks which way to follow. Devadatta succeeded in getting 500 newly ordained monks on his side. At his death, however, Devadatta is reported to have said that the Buddha was his only refuge (→ *trisharana*). According to legend he was condemned to long sufferings in the hells.

Deva-dūta B Skt. for → divine messengers

Devakī H the mother of → Krishna and wife of → Vāsudeva; cousin of → Kansa. She is also occasionally mentioned as an incarnation of Aditī, mother of the sun gods.

Devarāja B Skt. → celestial kings

Devayāna H, or Uttarayāna, Skt. lit. "way of the gods"; the path beyond reason, which leads to higher consciousness; the path of wisdom and spiritual knowledge. Its opposite is → *dakshināyana.*

Devī H Skt.; 1. goddess. The word can be used to refer to any Hindu female divinity; often it is added to the name of the goddess, as in Lakshmī-Devī; 2. queen; 3. princess; 4. term of respectful address, added to the first name of an Indian woman.

Dhāma H Skt.; in Hindu mythology, originally a class of supernatural beings. In → Vaishnavism, it is a term for the transcendent plane of divine love, corresponding to the Christian idea of the "kingdom of God."

Dhammapada B Pali → *Khuddaka-nikāya*

Dhammapāla B → Theravāda scholar. He was born in Ceylon in the middle of the 5th century. At Mahāvihāra, the main monastery of the Theravāda, he wrote a number of commentaries on chapters of the → *Khuddaka-nikāya*, which are known under the name *Paramatthadīpanī* ("*Light of the Supreme Meaning*").

Dhanurveda H Skt., lit. "science of the bow"; a treatise on archery; part of the *Yajurveda*, it is ascribed to → Bhrigu or → Vishvāmitra. The *Agni-Purāna* also teaches this art, which every prince was expected to master.

Dhanvantari H 1. name of a Vedic deity to whom sacrifices were offered at twilight; 2. the physician of the gods. He was the teacher of medical science to whom the → *Āyurveda* is attributed. In another life he was the son of the *rishi* Dīrghatama. He was free from human frailties and in every lifetime was a master of universal knowledge. He is also known as Sudāpāni, lit. "one who bears nectar in his hands," as well as Amrita, lit. "The immortal one"; 3. a celebrated physician, one of the "nine jewels" at the court of King → Vikramāditya.

Dhāranā H (Dhāraṇā), Skt.; concentration, the sixth of the eight stages enumerated by → Patañjali in his *Yoga-Sūtra.* In → Rāja-Yoga, *dhārāna* constitutes an important prerequisite for the practice of deep meditation.

Dhāranī B Z Skt., lit. "holder [feminine]"; short sūtras that contain magical formulas of knowledge comprised of syllables with symbolic content (→ mantra). They can convey the essence of a teaching or a particular state of mind that is created by repetition of the *dhāranī.* They are in general longer than mantras.

Dhāranīs play an important role in Chinese, Tibetan, and Japanese Tantra (→ Shingon, → Vajrayāna).

Dharma H B Z Skt., lit. carrying, holding.

H a comprehensive term used to refer to that which determines our true essence; righteousness; the basis of human morality and ethics, the lawful order of the universe, and the foundation of all religion. Hindus call their tradition → *sanātana-dharma,* the "eternal religion."

For the individual, *dharma* is inseparable from one's → *karma,* since *dharma* can be realized by the individual only to the extent permitted by one's karmic situation.

B Z (Pali, dhamma; Chin., *fa*; Jap., *hō* or *datsuma*); central notion of Buddhism, used in various meanings. 1. the cosmic law, the "great norm," underlying our world; above all, the law of karmically determined rebirth.

2. The teaching of the → Buddha, who recognized and formulated this "law"; thus the teaching that expresses the universal truth. The dharma in this sense existed already before the birth of the historical Buddha, who is no more than a manifestation of it. It is in the dharma in this sense that a Buddhist takes refuge (→ *trisharana*).

3. Norms of behavior and ethical rules (→ *shīla*, → Vinaya-pitaka).

4. Manifestation of reality, of the general state of affairs; thing, phenomenon.

5. Mental content, object of thought, idea—a reflection of a thing in the human mind.

6. Term for the so-called factors of existence, which the → Hīnayāna considers as building blocks of the empirical personality and its world.

Dharma-chakra 🅱 (dharma-cakra), Skt. (Pali, dhamma-chakka), wheel of the teaching; in Buddhism a symbol of the teaching expounded by the Buddha, i.e., the → four noble truths, the → eightfold path, and the → Middle Way. The dharma-chakra is usually depicted with eight spokes representing the eightfold path. (Also → eight precious ones.) According to tradition the wheel of dharma was set in motion three times: (1) in → Sārnāth where the Buddha pronounced his first discourse after attaining complete enlightenment; (2) through the origination of the → Mahāyāna; (3) through the arising of the → Vajrayāna.

Dharmachakra-mudrā 🅱 Skt. → mudrā 3

Dharma contest 🆉 → *hossen*

Dharmadhātu 🅱 Skt., lit. "realm of dharma"; according to → Hīnayāna the nature of things, in the sense of a rule to which they hold. In the → Mahāyāna it developed into the notion of a true nature that permeates and encompasses phenomena. As a space or realm, then, the realm of dharmas is the uncaused and immutable totality in which all phenomena arise, dwell, and pass away. Finally the idea of a point of departure or center in relation to this realm became, for the symbology of the → Vajrayāna, extraordinarily effective; thus the → Shingon school devised a special mandala under the name of *vajradhātu.*

Dharmaguptaka 🅱 Skt., (Pali, Dhammaguttika), lit., "protector of the teaching"; Buddhist school belonging to the larger grouping of → Sthaviras. Developed out of the Mahīshāsaka school, it was founded by the Sinhalese monk Dharmagupta and was prevalent primarily in south India.

A major point by which this school is distinguished from others is its view concerning the nature of giving (→ *dāna*). The Dharmaguptakas maintain that only offerings made to the Buddha, and not those made to the → *sangha*, bring a great reward; the Buddha represents a far superior "field of merit" (→ *punya*).

The → Vinaya-pitaka of this school, which is structured into four parts, is considered authoritative by the schools of Chinese Buddhism. It was translated into Chinese in 105 C.E. by Buddhayashas. It contains 250 rules for monks and 348 for nuns.

Dharmakāya 🅱 🆉 Skt. → *trikāya*

Dharmakīrti 🅱 1. one of the most important Buddhist philosophers and one of the principal spokesmen of the → Yogāchāra. He came from south India (7th century) studied with → Dharmapāla at the monastic university → Nālandā and was an outstanding logician. His principal works *Pramānavārttika* (*Explanation of the Touchstones*) and *Pramānavishchaya* (*Resolve Concerning the Touchstones*) treat the basic questions concerning the nature of knowledge, its various forms, and its relation to the external world. The *Nyāyabindu* is a much-read, concise guide to logic.

2. Devarakshita Jayabāhu Dharmakīrti, who lived ca. 1400, was the head of the Buddhist spiritual community in his homeland, Ceylon. He composed the two most important works on the development of Buddhism in this area: *Nikāya-sangrahaya* and *Saddharmālankāraya.* These works are also considered the most important examples of Sinhalese literary prose.

Dharmānusārin 🅱 Skt. (Pali, dhammānusārin); follower of the teaching; one of the two kinds of aspirants to "stream-entry" (→ *shrotaāpanna*). The follower of the teaching, unlike the follower of the faith, does not enter the supramundane path because of his trust but rather on the basis of his intellectual understanding of the Buddhist teaching.

Dharmapāla 🅱 Skt. lit. "guardian of the teaching." 1. For the protection of its teaching and institutions against hostile forces, the → Vajrayāna called upon a group of deities, who can also be invoked by the individual practitioner in → *sādhana* practice. In addition to the actual *dharmapālas,* such as Mahākāla (Great Black One) and the wrathful form (→ forms of manifestation) of → Avalokiteshvara, there are also the so-called *lokapalas* (guardians of regions), taken from pre-Buddhist folk belief and bound by oath to the Buddhist teaching.

For the Vajrayāna Buddhist, the function of the dharmapālas lies in their ability to protect him from dangers and bad influences that might be obtstructive for his spiritual development. This principle of protection can only become effective when the practioner has received an empowerment for a personal → *yidam.*

Mahākāla, one of the *dharmapālas* (Tibetan woodblock print)

Mahākāla, among others a guardian of the Kagyü school and of the → dalai lamas, possesses a terrifying form and is represented with a black body. His principle task comprises four activities: pacifying, enriching, magnetizing, and destroying. These activities can be applied to both outer and inner hindrances.

The *lokapalas* in Tibetan Buddhism were transformed, particularly by the activity of → Padmasambhava, from deities of the → *bön* religion into Buddhist protective deities. They are for the most part embodiments of extreme forces of nature. Exceptions are the guardians of the four directions. These were taken over from Indian iconography; among them is also → Kubera, god of wealth.

2. Philosopher of the → Yogāchāra school, who lived in the 6th to 7th centuries. He was a disciple of → Dignāga. He became Dignāga's successor at the Buddhist university of → Nālandā and held the position of abbot. After that he went to → Bodh-gayā and became the abbot of the Mahābodhi Monastery. Dharmapāla died at the age of thirty-two. His literary work has been almost entirely lost.

He wrote, among other works, commentaries on the *Shata-shāstra* of → Āryadeva and on the *Vimshatikā* of → Vasubandhu which are extant in Chinese translation. Fragments are also found in the works of → Hsüan-tsang. Dharmapāla and his students stressed the idealistic side of the Yogāchāra, particularly, that the world is "nothing but a concept."

3. Sinhalese monk, 1865–1933, founder of the → Mahābodhi Society (1891), the objective of which was the restoration of the Mahābodhi Monastery in Bodh-gayā. Dharmapāla was the first monk in modern times to call himself a "homeless one" (→ *anāgārika*). In 1925 he founded the British Mahābodhi Society in London.

Dharma-Shāstra 🅷 (Dharma-Śāstra), Skt.; a term given to numerous ancient Indian law books. The "Laws of Manu," the → *Manu-Samhitā* (or *Mānava-Dharmashāstra*) is regarded as the basis for most other law books, such as the *Dharma-Smriti,* ascribed to → Yājñavalkya (and hence also called the *Yājñavalkya-Smriti*) and the *Dharma-Shāstra* of → Gotama. Probably even older than the Laws of Manu is the *Vasishtha-Dharmashāstra,* a work that is traditionally associated with the seer and *Rigveda* author → Vasishtha, although it appears to have been composed no earlier than the fourth century B.C.E. The *Dharma-Shāstras* were primarily conceived as a code of rules for the conduct of a brahman's life, but because of the broad catalog of duties and wise precepts they contained, they gradually became binding for the other upper castes as well.

Dharma successor 🆉 → *hassu*

Dharma-Sūtra 🅷 Skt., lit. "law guide"; a collection of instructions and principles for social and religious behavior.

Dharmatā 🅱 Skt.; nature of the → dharmas, the essence that is the basis of everything. Philosophical concept of the → Mahāyāna. Synonymous with → *tathatā,* → buddha-nature.

Dhashanjaya 🅷 (Dhaśaṇjaya), Skt.; the → *prāna* -stream that remains in the body after death and produces changes in the body.

Dhātu 🅱 Skt., Pali, lit., "region, realm, element"; a concept appearing frequently in compounds. It designates

1. one of the four elements (→ *mahābhūta*)
2. one of the six elements (i.e., the four *mahābhūta* plus → *ākāsha* and → *vijñāna*)
3. one of the three realms or worlds, i.e., the world of desire (*kāmadhātu*), the world of desireless form or pure form (*rūpadhātu*), and that of formlessness or bodilessness (*arūpadhātu*). (Also → *triloka.*)

4. one of the eighteen elements that determine all mental processes: (a) organ of sight, (b) organ of hearing, (c) organ of smell, (d) organ of taste, (e) organ of touch, (f) object of seeing, (g) object of hearing, (h) object of smelling, (i) object of tasting, (j) object of touch, (k) seeing consciousness, (l) hearing consciousness, (m) smelling consciousness, (n) tasting consciousness, (o) consciousness of touch, (p) mind element (*manodhātu*), (q) object of mind (*dharmadhātu*), (r) mind-consciousness element (*manovijñānadhātu*). Of these eighteen elements a–j are physical, k–p and r are mental, and q is either physical or mental in nature. Also → *āyatana*, → *shadāyatana*, → *vijñāna*.

Dhātu-Prasāda 🅗 Skt. lit. *dhātu:* "root, source," *prasāda:* "grace, clarity, serenity"; the peace and grace that come from within through purification of one's own being, which is pure consciousness.

Dhātu-vavatthāna 🅑 Pali; analysis of the elements of the body; one of the forty meditation exercises (→ *bhāvanā*) described in the → *Visuddhi-magga* in which one mentally dissects the body into its individual parts and recognizes that they are made of nothing but the four elements (→ *dhātu*)—the firm, fluid, heat-generating, and windy. Through this the practitioner's conception of a unitary permanent self disappears. (Also → *satipatthāna*, → contemplation of the body, → *anātman*.)

The following simile illustrates this practice in the *Visuddhi-magga* (11,28):

"*Bhikkus*, a *bhikku* reviews this body, however placed, however disposed, as consisting of elements: in this body there are the earth element, the water element, the fire element, and the air element. The meaning is this: just as though a clever butcher or his apprentice . . . had killed a cow and divided it up and were seated at the crossroads, . . . having laid it out part by part, so too a *bhikku* reviews the body, however placed, because it is in one of the four postures, and however disposed, because it is so placed—thus: 'In this body there are the earth element, the water element, the fire element, the air element.' What is meant? Just as the butcher—while feeding the cow, bringing it to the shambles, keeping it tied up after bringing it there, slaughtering it, and seeing it slaughtered and dead—does not lose the perception *cow* so long as he has not carved it up and divided it into parts, but when he has divided it up and is sitting there, he loses the perception *cow* and the perception *meat* occurs (he does not think, 'I am selling *cow*' or 'They are carrying *cow* away' but rather, 'I am selling meat' or 'They are carrying meat away'); so too this *bhikku*, while still a foolish ordinary person—both formerly as a layman and as one gone forth into homelessness—does not lose the perception *living being* or *man* or *person* so long as he does not, by resolution of the compact into elements, review this body, however placed, however disposed, as consisting of elements. But when he does review it as consisting of elements, he loses the perception *living being* and his mind establishes itself upon elements" (Nyanomoli 1976, vol. 1, pp. 380–381).

Dhenu 🅗 Skt.; 1. a cow (revered in India as sacred); milk; 2. the earth.

Dhītika 🅩 fifth patriarch in the Indian lineage of → Zen

Dhritarāshtra 🅗 (Dhṛtarāṣṭra), Skt.; the blind brother of → Pāndu. Both brothers renounced the throne, and a great battle, described in the *Mahābhārata*, was subsequently waged between their sons, the → Kauravas and the → Pāndavas. In old age, Dhritarāshtra withdrew with his wife, Gāndhārī, to a forest hermitage, where they later perished in a forest fire.

Dhruva 🅗 Skt.; 1. the North Star; 2. → *soma* that is expelled in the morning and offered in the evening; 3. a prince, of whom the *Bhāgavata-Purāna* relates that he was a great devotee of Vishnu.

Dhruva's father had two wives. As a young boy Dhruva was mistreated by his stepmother, who wished to secure the throne for her own son. Dhruva, who was modest and humble, declared that he desired only those honors that he himself had earned. Although he was a → *kshatriya*, he joined a group of → *rishis*, underwent strict spiritual disciplines, and became a *rishi*. His unshakable devotion to Vishnu caused the god to set him in the sky as the North Star. Because of his constancy, he is also called Grahādhara, "the support of the planets" (*graha:* "planet," *dhara:* "holding, bearing").

Dhūta 🅑 Skt., Pali, lit. "shaking off"; ascetic practices accepted by the Buddha that one may take on oneself by vow for specific periods of time in order to develop contentedness and will power and in order to "shake off" the passions.

Twelve such ascetic practices are known: (1) wearing patched robes, (2) wearing a robe made of three pieces (→ *trichīvara*), (3) eating only begged food, (4) eating only one meal a day, (5) refraining from all further food, (6) taking only one portion, (7) living in a secluded, solitary place, (8) living in a charnel ground, (9) living under a tree, (10) living in the open, (11) living in whatever place presents itself, (12) sitting only, never lying down.

Dhyāna 🅗 🅑 🅩 Skt.; meditation, absorption.

🅗 *Dhyāna* is one of the three final stages of → Patañjali's yoga, referred to as → *dhāranā, dhyāna*, and → *samādhi*. *Dhyāna* is the means by which *samādhi* is attained. The mind must be stilled so that absolute consciousness is free from any overlay. Patañjali refers to meditation as an unbroken stream of thought directed toward the object of concentration. Without *dhyāna*, higher states of consciousness cannot be achieved.

B **Z** (Pali, jhāna; Chin., ch'an-na or ch'an; Jap., zenna or zen); in general any absorbed state of mind brought about through concentration (→ *samādhi*). Such a state is reached through the entire attention dwelling uninterruptedly on a physical or mental object of meditation; in this way the mind passes through various stages in which the currents of the passions gradually fade away. *Dyāna* designates particularly the four stages of absorption of the world of form (*rūpadhātu*, → *triloka*), the condition for which is the removal of the five hindrances (→ *nīvarana*). These four absorptions make possible the attainment of supernatural powers (→ *abhijñā*). They prepare the way for knowledge of previous births and of the arising and passing away of beings and for the elimination of the defilements or cankers (→ *āsrava*). This is tantamount to liberation. Practice of each of the four *dyānas* also affects rebirth in the corresponding *dyāna* heaven (→ *deva*).

The first absorption stage is characterized by the relinquishing of desires and unwholesome factors (→ *akushala*) and is reached through conceptualization (*vitarka*) and discursive thought (*vichāra*). In this stage, there is joyful interest (*priti*) and well-being (*sukha*). The second stage is characterized by the coming to rest of conceptualization and discursive thought, the attainment of inner calm, and so-called one-pointedness of mind, which means concentration on an object of meditation. Joyful interest and well-being continue. In the third stage joy disappears, replaced by equanimity (→ *upekshā*); one is alert, aware, and feels well-being. In the fourth stage only equanimity and wakefulness are present.

In Chinese Buddhism the notion of *dhyāna* has a much broader application. It includes all meditation practices such as → *ānāpānasati*, → *kasina* exercises, contemplation of the body, and other similar techniques that have concentration or one-pointedness of mind as their objective. Thus it also includes all preparatory practices necessary for *dhyāna* in the narrower sense. From → Dhyāna Buddhism, which was brought to China by → Bodhidharma, among others, Ch'an (Zen) developed.

Dhyāna Buddhism, **B** **Z** general name for all schools of Buddhism that place particular emphasis on the practice of meditation (→ *dhyāna*) as the way to enlightenment (Skt., *bodhi*; Jap., satori). The main teachings of Dhyāna Buddhism found clear expression in → Zen, which developed in China in the 6th to 8th centuries from the encounter and mutual fruitful influence of Dhyāna Buddhism and Taoism.

Dhyāni buddha **B** Skt., roughly "meditation buddha"; five transcendent buddhas (also → buddha) who symbolize the various aspects of enlightened consciousness. The five are distinguished for the purposes of meditation, but basically they are manifestations of a single buddha principle. The five *dhyāni* buddhas are → Amitābha, → Amoghasiddhi, → Akshobhya, → Ratnasambhava, and → Vairochana.

Dhyāni-mudrā **B** Skt. → mudrā 1

Diamond Sūtra **B** **Z** (Skt., Vajrachchedika-prajñāpāramitā-sūtra; lit., "*Sūtra of the Diamond-Cutter of Supreme Wisdom*"); an independent part of the → *Prajñāpāramitā-sūtra*, which attained great importance, particularly in East Asia. It shows that all phenomenal appearances are not ultimate reality but rather illusions, projections of one's own mind. Every practitioner of meditation should regard all phenomena and actions in this way, seeing them as "empty, devoid of self, and tranquil." The work is called *Diamond Sūtra* because it is "sharp like a diamond that cuts away all unnecessary conceptualization and brings one to the further shore of enlightenment."

Digambara **H** Skt.; 1. lit. "clothed in air," i.e., naked. In Hinduism, the fact that a *sādhu* goes about naked means that he is no longer bound to his sexual identity; 2. the name of one of the two major sects of → Jainism.

Dīgha-nikāya **B** Pali (Skt., Dīrghāgama), lit., "*Long Collection*"; the first five → Nikāyas of the Sūtra-[or Sutta-]pitaka (→ Tripitaka). In the Pali version it is made up of thirty-four *suttas*; the Mahāyāna version (*Dīrghāgama*), which is extant in Chinese, contains thirty sutras; twenty-seven are common to both versions. The title (*dīgha*, "long") refers to the relatively great length of the individual *suttas*.

The most important of the thirty-four *suttas* in the Pali version are *Brahmajāla*, on philosophical theories and superstitions of early Buddhist times; *Sāmaññaphala*, on the six important non-Buddhist teachings of early Buddhist times and the rewards of monastic life; *Mahāpadāna*, legends of the six buddhas said to have existed before the historical Buddha; *Mahānidāna*, explanations of the chain of conditioned arising (→ *pratītya-samutpāda*); → *Mahāparinibbāna*, a description of the last weeks in the life of the historical Buddha → Shākyamuni and his entry into nirvana; *Singālovāda*, of particular importance for laymen, since it describes their duties as parents, teachers, students, and so on.

Dignāga 🅑 also Dinnāga, ca. 480–540; a principle teacher of the → Yogāchāra, who developed a logical-epistemological approach. Most of his works, which are only extant in Chinese or Tibetan translation treat themes of logic. The most important is the *Pramānasamuchchaya* (*Summary of the Means to True Knowledge*), which became a fundamental manual for the new approach. In addition Dignāga composed an important commentary on the → *Abhidharmakosha.* His main disciple was → Dharmakīrti.

Dignāga, who spent a long time at the monastic university → Nālandā, bases his approach on the idealistic teaching of the Yogāchāra. He admits two "touchstones" of knowledge → direct perception and logical conclusion. His analysis of the logical process in its various forms and of the relationship between logical steps was developed further by Dharmakīrti.

Dīkshā 🅗 (Dīkṣā), Skt. initiation by the guru of an aspirant into spiritual life. The pupil receives a mantra and is introduced to the ultimate spiritual truths.

Dīpamkara 🅑 (Dīpaṃkara), Skt. (Pali, Dīpankara), lit. "kindler of lights"; legendary buddha who is said to have lived an endlessly long time ago. Dīpamkara is considered the first of the twenty-four buddhas preceding the historical Buddha → Shākyamuni. The latter, in the form of the ascetic Sumedha, is said to have vowed in the presence of Dīpamkara to become a buddha. Thanks to his supernatural powers Dīpamkara recognized that after an endless number of ages had elapsed, Sumedha would become a buddha named Gautama; he proclaimed to the multitude the glorious future of the ascetic.

Dīpamkara is considered the most important of all the predecessors of the Buddha Shākyamuni. He symbolizes all the buddhas of the past and, particularly in China, he is depicted together with Shākyamuni and → Maitreya, the buddha of the future, as one of the "buddhas of the three times" (past, present, future).

According to tradition he was eighty ells tall, his retinue was composed of 84 thousand → arhats, and he lived 100,000 years. The stūpa that holds his relics is thirty-six → *yojanas* high. Legendary tales of his life abound.

Dīpāvali 🅗 , also Dīvāli or Devali, Skt.; a row of lamps or lights; the festival of lights that is held on the nights of the new moon during the month of Kārttika (mid-October to mid-November).

Dīpavamsa 🅑 (Dīpavaṃsa), Pali, lit. "History of the Island"; anonymous Pali chronicle from the 4th century C.E. It contains reports from the time of the historical Buddha concerning the colonization of Ceylon and continues up to the reign of King Mahāsena in the middle of the fourth century C.E. It provides valuable material on the Buddhist history of this period.

Dīrghāgama 🅑 Skt. → Āgama, → *Dīgha-nikāya*

Diti 🅗 the ancient Indian goddess of earth; less powerful than → Aditī, the goddess who rules over the entire solar system, Diti is consequently less frequently mentioned in the Vedic texts and less widely venerated. She is held to be the mother of the → Daityas (Titans).

Divine messengers 🅑 (Skt., deva-dūta); old age, sickness, and death are called "divine messengers" in Buddhism. Their role is to make people aware of the suffering and impermanence of existence and urge them onto the path to liberation.

Divine states of dwelling 🅑 → *brahma-vihāra*

Divya-Gandha 🅗 Skt., lit. *divya:* "heavenly," *gandha:* "aroma"; heavenly scents that are occasionally perceived during meditation.

Divya-Jyotish 🅗 (Divya-Jyotiṣ), Skt., lit. *divya:* "heavenly, " *jyotish:* "light"; a supernatural light that is occasionally perceived during meditation and is said to be a sign of spiritual progress.

Divya-Siddhis 🅗 Skt.; supernatural, occult powers that may arise during the practice of meditation. Authentic spiritual teachers warn their students against taking notice of or utilizing such powers, as they can interfere with one's spiritual development.

The inferior spiritual value of these *siddhis* is often pointed out by means of stories such as the following: Two brothers had studied with two different masters for twelve consecutive years. One day they met, and the older brother, who had studied the Vedas, asked the younger what he had learned. Just then they reached a river, and the younger brother crossed over by walking on the water. The older brother handed two copper pennies to a ferryman standing nearby and was transported over the river in turn, whereupon he remarked to the younger brother, "So this is what your twelve years of study is worth—two pennies!"

Dō 🅩 Jap., lit. "Way"; *dō* is the Japanese way of pronouncing the Chinese character for Tao. In Japanese Buddhism *dō* generally means following the Buddha on the way of → enlightenment (also → *butsudō*) and is used as a synonym for → buddha-dharma (which is usually translated as "Buddhism"). In this meaning *dō* is also used in Zen.

Based on this meaning, in Japan the various spiritual-practical "ways" of training permeated with Zen mind are known as *dō*. Among these are, for example, the Way of the sword (→ *kendō*), the Way of the bow (→ *kyūdō*), and the Way of tea (→ *chadō*).

Dōan 🅩 Jap.; the Japanese word *dōgyō*, which in colloquial language roughly means "traveling companion," in Zen is pronounced *dōan* and refers in this case to a companion on the way of → enlightenment. Zen students who submit to training under a Zen master (→ *Rōshi*) and dedicate themselves to the practice of → *zazen* call each other *dōan*.

Dōchō 🅩 Jap., lit. "head [*chō*] of the monk's hall [*dō* → *sōdō]"; the elder monk in a Zen monastery (→ tera*).

Dōgen Kigen 🅩 → Dōgen Zenji

Dōgen Zenji 🅩 also Dōgen Kigen or Eihei Dōgen, 1200–1253; Japanese Zen master who brought the tradition of the → Sōtō school to Japan; without any question the most important Zen master of Japan. He is also considered Japan's greatest religious personality and is venerated there by all Buddhist schools as a saint or bodhisattva. However, he is often misunderstood as having been a philosopher and referred to as the "most profound and original thinker" ever produced by Japan. What is missed here is that his writings, although they do treat man's most profound existential questions, do not represent a *philosophy* of life. What Dōgen writes does not originate in philosophical speculation and is not the result of a thought process but rather is the expression of immediate inner experience of the living truth of Zen.

In 1223 Dōgen traveled to China, where he experienced profound enlightenment under Master → T'ien-t'ung Ju-ching and received from him the seal of confirmation (→ *inka-shōmei*) of the lineage of Sōtō Zen (ch'an). In 1227 he

Dōgen Zenji (contemporary portrait)

returned to Japan and lived for ten years in Kyōto, first in the Kennin-ji monastery, then in the Kōshō(hōrin)-ji monastery. In order to protect his lineage from the influence of worldly power, which in the imperial city was often all too great, he withdrew to a hermitage in Echizen province (today Fukui province). From the hut in which he then lived gradually developed a large monastery, first called Daibutsu-ji, later → Eihei-ji. It is still today, with → Sōji-ji, one of the most important monasteries of Japanese Sōtō Zen. Dōgen's principal work, → *Shōbō-genzō,* is considered one of the most profound writings of Japanese Zen literature and as the most outstanding work of the religious literature of Japan.

In accordance with the teachings of the Sōtō school, Dōgen emphasizes that → *shikantaza* is the supreme and true form of → *zazen* (also → *mokushō* Zen, → Zen, esoteric). However, he by no means rejected training with the help of kōans, as favored by the → Rinzai school (also → *kanna* Zen), which can be seen from the fact that he put together a collection of 300 kōans, providing each one with his own commentary and obviously also used them in Zen training (*Nempyo sambyaku soku*, "*Three Hundred Kōans with Commentary*." Other works of Dōgen Zenji, which, unlike the *Shōbō-genzō*, are introductory in character, are the → *Fukan zazengi* and the → *Shōbō-genzō zuimonki*.

The most important stages of Dogen's development can be summarized as follows (Kapleau 1980):

"Born of an aristocratic family, Dōgen even as a child gave evidence of his brilliant mind. It is related that at four he was reading Chinese poetry and at nine a Chinese translation of a treatise on the → Abhidharma. The sorrow he felt at his parents' death ... undoubtedly impressed upon his sensitive mind the impermanence of life and motivated him to become a monk. With his initiatin into the Buddhist monkhood at an early age, he commenced his novitiate at Mount Hiei, the center of scholastic Buddhism in medieval Japan, and for the next several years studied the → Tendai doctrines of Buddhism. By his fifteenth year one burning question became the core around which his spiritual strivings revolved: 'If, as the sūtras say, our Essential-nature is Bodhi (perfection), why did all Buddhas have to strive for enlightenment and perfection?' His dissatisfaction with the answers he received at Mount Hiei led him eventually to → Eisai-zenji, who had brought the teachings of the Rinzai sect of Zen Buddhism from China to Japan. Eisai's reply to Dōgen's question was: 'No Buddha is conscious of its existence [that is, of this Essential-nature], while cats and oxen [that is, the grossly deluded] are aware of it.'

"... At these words Dōgen had an inner realization [→ *kenshō*] which dissolved his deep-seated doubt.... Dōgen thereupon commenced what was to be a brief discipleship under Eisai, whose death took place within the year and who was succeeded by his eldest disciple, → Myōzen [Ryōnen]. During the eight years Dōgen spent with Myōzen he passed a considerable number of kōans and finally received *inka.*

"Despite his accomplishment Dōgen still felt spiritually unfulfilled, and this disquiet moved him to undertake the then-hazardous journey to China in search of complete peace of mind [→ *anjin*]. He stayed at all the well-known monasteries, practicing under many masters, but his longing for total liberation was unsatisfied. Eventually at the famous T'ien-t'ung monastery, which had just acquired a new master, he achieved full awakening, that is the liberation of body and mind, through these words uttered by his master, Ju-ching: 'You must let fall body and mind.'

"... Later Dōgen appeared at Ju-ching's room, lit a stick of incense (a ceremonial gesture usually reserved for noteworthy occasions), and prostrated himself before his master in the customary fashion.

" 'Why are you lighting a stick of incense?' asked Ju-ching.

" 'I have experienced the dropping off of body and mind,' replied Dōgen.

"Ju-ching exclaimed: 'You have dropped body and mind, body and mind have indeed dropped!'

"But Dōgen remonstrated: 'Don't give me your sanction so readily!'

" 'I am not sanctioning you so readily.'

"Reversing their roles, Dōgen demanded: '*Show* me that you are not readily sanctioning me.'

"And Ju-ching repeated: '*This* is body and mind dropped,' demonstrating.

"Whereupon Dōgen prostrated himself again before his master as a gesture of respect and gratitude.

" 'That's "dropping dropped," ' added Ju-ching"

Even after this profound experience Dōgen continued his zazen training in China for another two years before returning to Japan, where he founded the Japanese tradition of Sōtō Zen that has flourished until the present day.

Dōgō Enchi 🅉 Jap. for → Tao-wu Yüan-chih

Dōitsu 🅉 Jap. for Tao-i, → Ma-tsu Tao-i

Dōjō 🅉 Jap., lit. "hall of the way"; hall or room in which one of the Japanese "ways" (→ *dō*) of spiritual-practical training is practiced; as, for example, the Way of the sword (→ *kendō*) or the Way of the bow (→ *kyūdō*). *Dōjō* is also used as a synonym for → *zendō.*

Dokugan-ryū 🅉 Jap. for Tu-yen-lung, → Ming-chao Te-chien

Dokusan 🅉 Jap., lit. "go alone [*doku*] to a high one [Sino-Jap., *san*; Jap., *mairu*]"; meeting of a Zen student with his master in the seclusion of the master's room. *Dokusan* is among the most important elements in Zen training. It provides the student an opportunity privately to present to his master all problems relating to his practice → *zazen* and to demonstrate the state of his practice in the encounter with the master so as to test the profundity of his Zen experience.

Many kōans have as their content → *mondōs* between master and student and thus give us information about *dokusans* of ancient times. The practice of giving individual instruction in this manner began, according to Zen tradition, with the "secret teachings" of → Shākyamuni Buddha and has been preserved in this "school of Buddha-mind" ever since. Although it was formerly customary in all Zen lineages, the practice has nearly died out today in the → Sōtō school and is basically still only cultivated by the → Rinzai school.

The content of *dokusan*, for several reasons, is subject to strict secrecy. First, *dokusan* requires from the student complete openness and honesty towards the master, which for many people is difficult in the presence of others. Second, in the *dokusan* the student demonstrates to the master his solution of a kōan; if other students were to witness this response, it could hinder them in their struggle for their own answer. Third, it is generally the case that the instruction of the master accords with the particular situation of an individual student; he might respond to externally similar manifestations of different students in entirely different ways, which might be a source of confusion for students who have not yet reached an understanding with the master. *Dokusan* can be given only by a person who has received → *inka-shōmei* from an authentic master and who has, moreover, been confirmed by him as → *hassu.*

Dōkyō Z Jap., → Ichien

Dōkyō Etan Z also Shōju Rōjin, 1642–1721; Japanese Zen master of the → Rinzai school, a dharma successor (→ *hassu*) of → Bu'nan Shidō and the master of → Hakuin Zenji.

Dölma B Tib. for → Tārā

Dorje B (rdo-rje), Tib., lit. "lord of stones." Originally, as lightning or thunderbolt (*vajra*), the weapon attributed to the Hindu god Indra, the source of the name of Tantric Buddhism (→ Vajrayāna). In this context it was interpreted as indestructible diamond. The *dorje* is the symbol of the clear immutable essence of reality that is the basis of everything. Its immaculate transparency, which nevertheless gives rise to a profusion of manifestations, corresponds to the concept of → *shūnyatā* stressed by → Nagārjuna. Also → *vajra.* In → Tibetan Buddhism the *dorje* is the masculine symbol of the path to enlightenment, standing for the → *upāya* (skillful means) aspect. The *drilbu*, or ritual bell, is the symbol of the feminine and stands for → *prajñā* (wisdom). Both together reflect the duality of phenomenal reality.

One of the most important → *buddhakulas* possesses as its basic quality the firmness of the *dorje. Dorje lopön* (diamond master) is a title for a teacher who has fully mastered the skillful means of the Vajrayāna and is able to pass them on to others.

A ritual implement related to the *dorje*, the origin of which has to do with the sacredness of metals, is the → *phurbu* (dagger). It particularly symbolizes the subjugation of demons (aggression) and was used by → Padmasambhava.

The secret mind of all the buddhas,
Omniscient wisdom
Transmitted by the symbol of eternal strength
and firmness
Clarity and emptiness, the *dorje* essence
Like heavenly space —
It is wonderful to see the true face of reality!

Dōsen Risshi Z Jap. for → Tao-hsüan Lü-shih

Dōshin Z Jap. for → Tao-hsin

Dōshin Z Jap., lit. "mind of the way"; 1. the longing and the resolve to attain → enlightenment; also → *kokorozashi*; 2. a novice in a Zen monastery (→ *tera*); also → *unsui.*

Dōshō B Z 629–700; Japanese Buddhist monk, who founded the → Hossō school of Buddhism in Japan in the 7th century. While he was in China, his Chinese master → Hsüan-tsang (Jap., Genjō), with whom he was studying → Yogāchāra philosophy, drew his attention to the Zen of the → Southern school. He decided to try to be the first Japanese monk to master this tradition as well. Once back in his homeland, he erected the first Zen meditation hall in Japan in a Hossō school temple in Nara. However, at this time there had as yet in Japan been no genuine transmission of the Zen tradition through a master who had received the "spiritual seal of the patriarchs" (→ *busshin-in*, → *inka-shōmei*) from an enlightened master in the Zen lineage.

Dōsu Z Jap., lit. "administrator [*su*] of the monk's hall [*dō*, → *sōdō*]"; the → *inō* of a Zen monastery or his living quarters.

Dragon King T → *lung-wang*

Draupadī H A daughter of Drupada, king of Pañchāla, and consort of the → Pāndavas.

Drig-Drishya-Viveka H (Dṛg-Dṛśya-Viveka), Skt., lit. "the distinction *(viveka)* between the seer *(drig)* and the seen *(drishya)*," the title of a Sanskrit tractate of forty-six *shlokas* that facilitates entry into the higher philosophy of → Vedānta. The origin of the work is associated with three names: Bhārati Tīrtha, → Shankara, and Svāmi → Vidyārahnya. Most likely the author was Bhārati Tīrtha, Vidyāranya's master and from 1328 to 1380 the head of the monastery founded by Shankara at Shringeri.

Taken individually, the *shlokas,* or verses, of the work are too abstract to be grasped by our normal consciousness, since we identify with the body and see no more than a gross, material universe, i.e., the snake in the rope. (In Shankara's famous example, a man in the dark takes a piece of rope to be a snake; in this same way, one who is deluded by the darkness of ignorance views the immortal *brahman* as the gross, transient universe.) The *shlokas* are meant to serve as pure meditation texts and thereby to awaken spiritual intuition. The *Drig-Drishya-Viveka* attempts to show that the seer (→ *sākshin*) has nothing whatever to do with what is seen. Absolute consciousness is used by the individual consciousness to split the One without a second (→ *advaita*) into subject and object, into seer and seen, thereby projecting a world of multiplicity, full of division and confusion (*māyā*). The treatise divides the embodied consciousness into the → *jīva* of the waking state, the *jīva* of the dream state, and the true *jīva.* Only the latter strives to know and realize its identity with *brahman.* When the aspirant recognizes his many false notions and asks, "Who then am I in reality?" the guru replies, "*Tat tvam asi:* Thou art *ātman-brahman*" (→ *Tat tvam asi*). This is the highest knowledge that has ever been expressed in words.

Drilbu 🅱 Tib.; ritual bell used in → Vajrayāna. See also → *dorje*.

Drishti 🅷 🅱 (dṛṣti), Skt.

🅷 a concept generally used in the sense of "vision, view, revelation; eye; worldview, theory."

🅱 (Pali, diṭṭhi), lit., "seeing, sight, view"; the seven so-called false views: belief in an ego or self, repudiation of the law of karma (→ karma), "eternalism" and nihilism, observing false → *shīlas*, regarding karma resulting from bad deeds as good, and doubting the truths of Buddhism. In another classification three types of false views are distinguished: belief in the causelessness of existence, in its inefficacy, and nihilism.

By *eternalism* is meant the view that there is an individuality independent of the → *skandhas* that is eternal, i.e., that continues to exist after death and the dissolution of the *skandhas*. By nihilism is meant the view that there is an individuality independent of the *skandhas* that is annihilated after death.

By *causelessness of existence* is understood denial of any cause for the purity or impurity of beings and fatalistic belief in predetermination. The belief in the inefficacy of existence denies that there is any karmic effectiveness to wholesome or unwholesome deeds. Nihilism in this context is the view that a person is dissolved into the elements after death.

These false views were pointed out by Buddha as being extremely reprehensible, because they were the basis for unwholesome behavior and led toward unfortunate rebirth.

Drugpa Künleg ('brug-pa kun-legs), Tib., lit. "Perfect Good Dragon" one of the best known "holy madmen" of Tibet (1455–1570). He received a religious education in the tradition of the Drugpa school of the → Kagyüpas but soon adopted the unorthodox life of a wandering ascetic. Regarded as an incarnation of the two Indian → *mahāsiddhas* Saraha and Shavaripa, Künleg composed spiritual songs in their style. He played an important role in the conversion of Bhutan to Buddhism. He owes his popularity with the Tibetan people to his great proclivity toward women and beer.

I am called the crazy dragon Künga Legpa
I am no vagabond who begs for food and clothing
I have left home and family behind me
To make the pilgrimage that never ends.
(Dowman 1982)

Duhkha 🅱 Skt. (Pali, dukkha); suffering; a central concept in Buddhism, which lies at the root of the → four noble truths. The characteristic of suffering is one of the three marks of existence (→ *trilakshana*).

Duhkha signifies not only suffering in the sense of unpleasant sensations; rather it refers to everything, both material and mental, that is conditioned, that is subject to arising and passing away, that is comprised of the five *skandhas*, and that is not in a state of liberation. Thus everything that is temporarily pleasant is suffering, since it is subject to ending. *Duhkha* arises because of desire and craving (→ *trishnā*) and can be overcome by the elimination of desire. The means to bring about the extinction of suffering is shown by the → eightfold path.

The nature of suffering is described in the first of the four noble truths as follows: "Birth is suffering; aging is suffering; sickness is suffering; dying is suffering; care, distress, pain, affliction, and despair are suffering; the nonattainment of what one desires is suffering; in short, the five aggregates [*skandhas*] connected with attachment are suffering."

Duhkha-Nirodha 🅱 (Duḥkha-Nirodha), Skt., lit. *duhkha:* "sorrow," *nirodha:* "annihilation"; the conquest or end of sorrow.

Durgā 🅷 Skt., lit. "the unfathomable one"; one of the oldest and most widely used names for the Divine Mother, the consort of Shiva.

Her ten-armed figure, standing on the back of a lion, symbolizes the great power that the Vedic texts describe her as wielding, either to punish or to confer grace on human beings. She destroys the demon of ignorance, nourishes the poor, and confers blessings of love and knowledge upon all those who strive for God-realization. The annual festival in the goddess' honor (Durgā-Pūjā) is held in the fall, and in Bengal lasts for at least five days. It opens with an invocation to call Durgā from her heavenly realm. On the last day of the festival, the image of Durgā that has been fashioned for the occasion is lowered into a river or the sea.

Dūrvā 🅷 Skt.; sacred grass used in the Hindu worship ritual (→ *pūjā*); it is drawn from its hull as a symbol of the spiritual aspirant's effort to sever the association of the → *ātman* with the body and mind.

Dvaita 🅷 Skt., lit. "duality"; the name of a philosophy that views the human body as separate from the creator god. The exoteric teachings of all religions and philosophies operate at this level of duality; only the mystics of the various world religions and the exoteric traditions associated with them have reached beyond the duality of creature/creator (→ Advaita-Vedānta). Our everyday consciousness is necessarily governed by subject-object dualism.

Dvaitādvaita-Vedānta 🅷 or Bhedābheda-Vāda, Skt., from *dvaita:* "duality," and → Vedānta; a philosophy of dualistic nondualism, chiefly represented by → Nimbārka. It teaches that *brahman* is one with the universe (nondualism) but takes on three distinct (dualistic) forms: (1) the inanimate world (→ *jagat*); (2) the individual soul (→ *jīva*); (3) the personal God (→ Īshvara), here represented by Vishnu.

Dvaitavāda 🅗 Skt. → Dvaita-Vedānta

Dvaita-Vedānta 🅗 Skt., from *dvaita:* "duality," → Vedānta; the third of the major philosophical schools of Vedānta, developed by → Madhva, who set his dualism (*dvaita*) against → Shankara's → Advaita-Vedānta. Dvaita-Vedānta, or Dvaitavāda, teaches that God and the individual soul are eternally separate and that the world is not illusion (→ *māyā*) but reality. The One and the many are eternally distinct from each other. Between the two schools of Dvaita and Advaita lies Rāmānuja's → Vishishtādvaita-Vedānta.

Dvandvamoha 🅗 (Dvaṃdvamoha), Skt., lit. *dvandva:* "pair, opposite," *moha:* "illusion"; the illusion of such pairs of opposites as happiness and sorrow, light and dark, and so on. The system of → Advaita-Vedānta regards such pairs as illusory because they can exist only in → *māyā. In* → *brahman,* the supreme reality, there are no contradictions and no opposites.

Dvāpara-Yuga 🅗 Skt. → *yuga*

Dvārakā 🅗 Skt.; a renowned sacred place at the western end of India. Its temple is dedicated to the worship of Krishna.

Dvātrimshadvara-lakshana 🅑 (dvātriṃśadvara-lakṣana), Skt.; the "thirty-two marks of perfection" of a → *chakravartin,* in particular a buddha, who is distinguished from ordinary men also in his external appearance.

The thirty-two marks are: level feet; sign of a thousand-spoked wheel on the soles of feet; long slender fingers; broad heels; curved toes and fingers; soft, smooth hands and feet; arched feet; lower body like an antelope's; arms reaching to the knee; virile member without narrowing in the foreskin; powerful body; hairy body; thick, curly body hair; golden-hued body; a body that gives off rays ten feet in every direction; soft skin; rounded hands, shoulders, and head; well-formed shoulders; upper body like a lion's; erect body; powerful, muscular shoulders; forty teeth; even teeth; white teeth; gums like a lion's; saliva that improves the taste of all foods; broad tongue; voice like Brahmā's; clear blue eyes; eyelashes like a bull's; a lock of hair between the eyebrows; a cone-shaped elevation on the crown of the head.

Some of these marks were particularly emphasized in artistic representations of the Buddha. The rays from the body, which according to the Indian view enlightened beings give off and which in the case of the Buddha symbolize his kindness and wisdom, are sometimes depicted as flames blazing out from the shoulders. Often also there is a halo over the head.

The lock of hair on the forehead between the eyebrows, curling to the right (*ūrnā*), out of which streams the light of wisdom that enlightens all beings, is usually depicted as a point of gold, a crystal, or a semiprecious stone. The cone-shaped elevation on the crown of the head (*ushnīsha*) is round in → Gandharan and Chinese art; in Cambodia it is conical, and in Thailand pointed or in the form of a flame.

Dvija 🅗 Skt., lit. "twice born"; the "twice-born" are the members of the three upper castes (→ *varna*) of Hindu society, the *brahmans,* the *kshatriyas,* and the *vaishyas.* Members of the fourth caste, the *shudras,* are not included.

Dyaus 🅗 Skt.; the threefold lower world of mind, along with its three heavens. The → *rishis* saw the world in many planes and often divided such planes further into three regions each. The "three heavens" of the human mind refer to the realm of pure light, the realm of pure thought, and the realm of pure spirituality.

Dyoya-Drishti 🅗 (Dyoya-Dṛṣṭi), Skt.; the third or divine eye (*drishti:* "eye"), which is located between the eyebrows and is identical with the *ājñā-chakra* (→ *chakra,* 6). It is the seat of intuition.

Dzogchen 🅑 (rdzogs-chen), Tib., lit., "great perfection"; the primary teaching of the → Nyingmapa school of Tibetan Buddhism. This teaching, also known as ati-yoga (extraordinary yoga), is considered by its adherents as the definitive and most secret teaching of Shākyamuni Buddha. It is called "great" because there is nothing more sublime; it is called "perfection" because no further means are necessary. According to the experience of *dzogchen* practitioners, purity of mind is always present and needs only to be recognized. The tradition of *dzogchen* was brought to Tibet in the eighth century by → Padmasambhava and Vimilamitra; in the 14th century it was synthesized by → Longchenpa into a unified system. The condensation of this system by Jigme Lingpa (1730–98) remains an authoritative expression of the great perfection tradition up to the present day.

The *dzogchen* teaching has its point of origin in → Samantabhadra, the truth of *dharmakāya* beyond space and time. It was directly transmitted to → Vajrasattva, an aspect of the *sambhogakāya* and through him came down to Garab Dorje (b. 55 C.E.), the *nirmānakāya* (→ *trikāya*). Garab Dorje wrote this teaching down for the first time in 6.4 million verses, which he left to his disciple Mañjushrīmītra. The latter classified them into three cycles: *semde* (mind class), *longde* (space class), and *mengagde* (oral instruction class), and his classification determined the exposition of the *dzogchen* teachings in the following centuries. Mañjushrīmītra's student Shrīsimha reedited the oral instruction class, and in this form the teaching was passed down to Jñānasūtra and Vimalamitra and via the latter reached Tibet.

A further tradition began with Padmasambhava, who received the great perfection teaching from the → *dākinīs*. Common to all expositions of *dzogchen* is the axiom that the mind, as self-existing intelligence, is by nature pure and undefiled. Because, however, this is not recognized, beings wander in the cycle of existences (→ samsāra). A method for breaking out of this cycle is direct experience of "naked," or "ordinary," mind, which is the basis of all activities of consciousness. This is the gateway to primordial knowledge, the union of emptiness (→ *shūnyatā*) and clarity. In addition to approaches of this kind that are oriented toward emptiness and intended to be applied without goal-oriented effort, there are also methods that place the emphasis on the clear light aspect of primordial knowledge. Their goal is realization of the "rainbow body," i.e., the dissolution of the physical body—that is, of the four elements that constitute the body—into light.

E

Easy path 🅱 → Jōdo-shū, → Pure Land school

Ego 🅩 in Buddhism the concept of an ego, in the sense of consciousness of one's self, is seen as composed of nonvalid factors, as → delusion. The concept of an ego arises when the dichotomizing intellect (the sixth sense, → *shadāyatana*) is confused into presupposing a dualism between *I* and *not-I* (or *other*). As a result we think and act as though we were entities separated from everything else, over against a world that lies outside of us. Thus the idea of an *I* becomes fixed in our subconscious, a self which produces thought processes like "I hate this, I love that; this is yours, this is mine." Nurtured by such conceptions, we reach the point where the *I* or ego dominates the mind; it attacks everything that threatens its dominance and is attracted to everything that seems to extend its power. Enmity, desire, and alienation, which culminate in suffering, are the ineluctable results of this outlook, which in Zen is cut through by the practice of → *zazen*. Thus in the course of Zen training under a → *rōshī*, who leads people on the path to → enlightenment (→ satori, → *kenshō*), the dominance of the ego illusion over the practioner's thinking and aspirations is gradually overcome.

Ehatsu 🅩 Jap. → *sanne ipatsu*

Eight auspicious symbols 🅱 (Skt., ashtamangala); eight symbols betokening the veneration of the universal monarch and by extension the veneration of the Buddha. In Chinese monasteries they are often placed on lotus pedestals before statues of the Buddha. The eight symbols are parasol (symbol of royal dignity, which shields from harm); two fish (Indian emblem of the universal monarch); conch shell (symbol of victory in battle); lotus blossom (symbol of purity); vase of sacred water (filled with the nectar of immortality); furled banner (emblem of the victory of spirituality); knot of eternity; wheel of the teaching (→ *dharma-chakra*).

Eightfold path 🅱 (Skt., ashtangika-mārga [aṣṭangika-mārga]; Pali, atthangika-magga); the path leading to release from suffering (→ *duhkha*), constituting the contents of the last of the → four noble truths. It is one of the thirty-seven limbs of enlightenment (→ *bodhipākshikadharma*) and encompasses all aspects of the threefold training (→ *trishiksha*). The eight parts of the path are (1) perfect view (Skt., *samyagdristhi*; Pali, *sammā-ditthi*), i.e., the view based on understanding of the four noble truths and the nonindividuality of existence (→ *anātman*); (2) perfect resolve (Skt., *samyak-samkalpa;* Pali, *sammā-sankappa*), i.e., resolve in

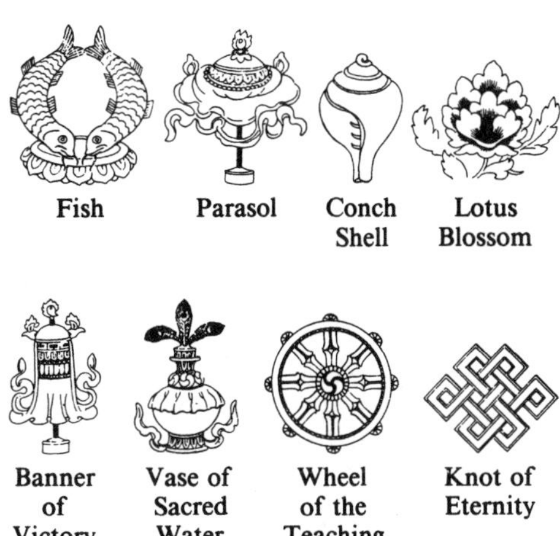

The eight auspicious symbols

favor of renunciation, good will, and nonharming of sentient beings; (3) perfect speech (Skt., *samyag-vāch*; Pali, *sammā-vāchā*), i.e., avoidance of lying, slander, and gossip; (4) perfect conduct (Skt., *samyak-karmānta*; Pali, *sammā-kammanta*), i.e., avoidance of actions that conflict with moral discipline (→ *shīla*); (5) perfect livelihood (Skt., *samyag-ājīva*; Pali, *sammā-ājīva*), i.e., avoidance of professions that are harmful to sentient beings, such as slaughterer, hunter, dealer in weaponry or narcotics, etc.; (6) perfect effort (Skt., *samyag-vyāyāma*, Pali, *sammā-vāyāma*), i.e., cultivation of what is karmically wholesome and avoidance of what is karmically unwholesome; (7) perfect mindfulness (Skt., *samyak-smriti*; Pali, *sammā-sati*), i.e., ongoing mindfulness of body, feelings, thinking, and objects of thought (→ *satipatthāna*); (8) perfect concentration (Skt., *samyak-samādhi*; Pali, *sammā-samādhi*), i.e., concentration of mind that finds its highpoint in the four absorptions (→ *dhyāna*).

In most books on Buddhism by Western authors, the Sanskrit word *samyak* (Pali, *sammā*) is translated "right." The Buddhist scholar Lama → Govinda (1898–1985) renders it with "perfect" in order to convey the original meaning of the word, which contains the sense of "wholeness" or "completeness." The Sanskrit and Pali do not refer to the opposition between right and wrong, as translation with "right" might lead one erroneously to assume.

The eightfold path does not actually represent a path on which linear progress is made, since in practice the first to be realized are stages 3–5, which belong to the *shīla* phase of the threefold training (→ *trishiksha*), then stages 6–8, the *samādhi* phase, and then finally 1–2, which belong to the *prajñā* phase. Right view is the immediate condition for entering upon the supramundane path of sacredness (→ *ārya-mārga*, → *ārya-pudgala*) and for attainment of nirvana.

The Mahāyāna gives an interpretation of the Hīnayāna eightfold path modified according to its doctrines. The Mahāyāna finds the Hīnayāna version too egoistic, since it is directed only towards one's own liberation. Because in Mahāyāna suffering arises out of ignorance (→ *avidyā*) of the emptiness (→ *shūnyatā*) of all → dharmas of any essential being, liberation can be attained only through the removal of this ignorance; not, however, only through ethically right conduct.

→ Bhāvaviveka interprets the eightfold path in the following typically Mahāyāna fashion: perfect view is insight into the *dharmakāya* (→ *trikāya*) of the perfect one; perfect resolve represents the coming to rest of all mental projections; perfect speech is the recognition that speech is rendered dumb in the face of the dharmas; perfect conduct is abstention from all deeds directed toward karmic gain; perfect living is the insight that all → dharmas are without arising or passing away; perfect effort means becoming intentionless; perfect mindfulness means giving up pondering on being and nonbeing; perfect concentration means being free from opinions in that one does not grasp onto ideas.

Eight liberations B (Skt., ashta-vimoksha [aṣṭa-vimokṣa]); a meditation exercise that moves through eight stages of concentration as an aid to overcoming all clinging to corporeal and noncorporeal factors. The eight stages are (1) cognition of internal and external forms (contemplation of things within and outside the body as impure in order to overcome attachment to forms); (2) cognition of forms externally but not internally (since there is no further attachment to forms internally, "contemplation of the external as impure" is practiced in order to reinforce this condition); (3) cognition of the beautiful (no attachment to the beautiful arises; contemplation of impurity is dropped); (4) attainment of the field of the limitlessness of space; (5) attainment of the field of the limitlessness of consciousness; (6) attainment of the field of nothing whatsoever; (7) attainment of the field of neither perception nor nonperception; (8) cessation of perception and feeling (→ *nirodha-samāpatti*. Liberations 1 and 2 correspond to the first stage of the → eight masteries, liberations 3 and 4 to the second stage. Liberations 4–7 are identical with the → four stages of formlessness.

Eight masteries B also eight fields of mastery (Skt., abhibhāvayatana; Pali, abhibhāyatana);

eight meditation exercises for mastery of the sphere of the senses through command of perception in relation to various objects. These exercises are already to be found in the earliest phase of Buddhism. The eight masteries are (1) perception of forms in relation to one's own body and of limited forms in the external world; (2) perception of forms in relation to the body and of unlimited external forms (these two stages permit the practitioner to conquer attachment to forms and correspond to the first of the → eight liberations); (3) perception of no forms in relation to one's own body and limited external forms; (4) perception of no forms in relation to one's own body and unlimited external forms (these two stages serve to strengthen concentration and correspond to the second stage of the eight liberations. In masteries 5–8 no forms are perceived in relation to the body, but externally blue, yellow, red, and white forms, respectively are perceived. These exercises aim at restraining attachment to beauty. Masteries 5–8 are identical with the third stage of the eight liberations and the fifth through eighth → *kasina* exercises.

"Perception of forms in relation to one's own body" means picking a limited (small) or unlimited (large) place on one's body and directing one's attention fully onto it, so that after some practice this object appears as a mental reflex. In masteries 3 and 4 one selects an external object (e.g., a flower). A limited, small object is supposed to be beneficial for mentally unsteady persons, a large one for mentally deluded persons, a beautiful one for persons inclined to reject things, and an ugly one for lustful persons.

Eight negations **B** **Z** → Nāgārjuna

Eihei-ji **Z** Jap., "Monastery of Eternal Peace"; one of the two principal monasteries of the Japanese → Sōtō school. It was founded in the year 1243 by → Dōgen Zenji and is located in Fukui province in north central Japan, which is known for its harsh winters. The other principal monastery of the Sōtō school is the → Sōjī-ji.

Eihei Kōroku **Z** Jap.; a collection of the sayings and instructions of the great Japanese Zen master → Dōgen Zenji. It was redacted after the master's death by Sen'e and other students.

Eihei Shingi **Z** Jap.; a written work of the great Japanese Zen master → Dōgen Zenji that treats the rules for behavior and the ideals of a Buddhist community (Skt., → *sangha*). (Also → *shingi*).

Eisai Zenji **Z** also Myōan Eisai (Yōsai) or Senkō (Zenkō) Kokushi (→ Kokushi), 1141–1215; Japanese Zen master of the Ōryō lineage of Rinzai Zen (→ Ōryō school), who was the first successfully to transmit the Zen tradition in Japan. Although his lineage did not last long, Eisai is considered the founder of the Japanese Zen tradition. He traveled twice (in 1168 and 1187) to China. During his second stay there, he received the seal of confirmation (→ *inka-shōmei*) from the Chinese master → Hsü-an Huai-ch'ang (Jap., Kian Eshō) of the Ōryō lineage. On his return to Japan he founded the Shōfuku-ji near Hakata in Kyūshu, the first monastery in Japan in which Rinzai Zen was practiced. Later he was appointed abbot of the Kennin-ji monastery in Kyōto, where he taught Zen and also the teachings of the Tendai and Shingon schools (→ Mikkyō). Later Eisai transferred the main center of his activities to Kamakura in the "shadow capital" of the shōguns. There in 1215 he founded the Jufuku-ji monastery. Kamakura became, along with Kyōto, the most important center of Zen in Japan (also → Gosan). As the first Zen master of → Dōgen Zenji, who later transmitted the Zen of the Sōtō school in Japan, Eisai is also important for that Zen lineage.

Eisai became a monk as a boy and studied the teachings of the → Tendai and → Shingon schools on Mount Hiei near Kyōto. During his first stay in China he visited the centers of the → T'ien-t'ai school but also came in contact with Ch'an (Zen) and felt drawn to it. He undertook his second journey in part in order to search for instruction in Ch'an. Having received confirmation as a master of the Rinzai tradition from Hsü-an Huai-ch'ang, he returned to Japan. There, by teaching the superiority of Zen over the teaching and practice of the Tendai school, he incurred the wrath of the established Tendai monks, who were able to effect a prohibition of the new school for a short time. However, in the Shōgun Minamoto Yoriie, who as a warrior was attracted to the toughness and rigor of Zen, he found a powerful protector and patron. The shōgun appointed him in 1204 as abbot of the Kennin-ji monastery in Kyōto, which thus became the first monastery in the capital where Zen was the primary teaching. Here it was also that Dōgen Zenji sought Eisai out. As a concession to the established Buddhist schools, but also as a result of his own development, the Zen that Eisai taught was strongly mixed with elements of Tendai and Shingon. The Japanese lineage of Zen that originated with him died out after a few generations. The fact that his most important student and dharma successor → Myōzen Ryōnen died in China in 1225 may have been an important factor in this outcome.

Other names under which Eisai Zenji is known are Myōun, Yōjō-bō, and Senkō Kokushi. Among his literary works are the *Kozen gokoku-ron*, the *Ichidai kyōron sōshaku,* and the *Kissa yōjō-ki,* in which he discusses basic questions of Buddhism.

Eka 🅉 Jap. for → Hui-k'o

Ekādashī 🄷 (Ekādaśi), Skt.; the eleventh day following the new moon or full moon, observed by orthodox Hindus as a day of prayer, meditation, and fasting. In monasteries, it is associated with the chanting of → Rām-Nam.

Ekāgattā 🄱 Pali → one-pointedness of mind

Ekāgra 🄷 🄱 also ekāgrata, Skt.; attention focused solely or alone (*eka*) on one object; situation in which all mental powers are concentrated on one object.

In Buddhism it is referred to as → one-pointedness of mind.

Ekāgratā 🄷 🄱 Skt. → *ekāgra,* → one-pointedness of mind

Ekaku 🅉 posthumous name of the Japanese Zen master → Hakuin Zenji

Eka-Tattvābhyāsa 🄷 Skt., lit. *eka:* "single," *tattva:* "truth, reality," *abhyāsa:* "repeated activity"; study of the one reality, the supreme consciousness, which permeates all beings as their inmost self.

Ekatva 🄷 Skt.; unity, all-embracing view; the ability to see the Self or the divine in all things and all things in oneself.

Ekavyāvahārika 🄱 Skt., → Hīnayāna, → Mahāsānghika

Ekayāna 🄱 also buddhayāna, Skt., lit. "one vehicle"; the buddha vehicle, the one teaching that leads to supreme enlightenment and the attainment of buddhahood. This term has two aspects: From a relative point of view, *ekayāna* refers to the bodhisattva or buddha vehicle as opposed to the → *shrāvaka* or → *pratyekabuddha* vehicle; these three together are called the "three vehicles" (→ *triyāna*), the teachings of which are applied in accordance with the ability of students. In the absolute sense, *ekayāna* refers to the ultimate reality, which includes and transcends all expedient and temporary teachings of the Hīnayāna and → Mahāyāna.

After the absolute buddha vehicle is expounded, none of the other methods remain valid, since only in it is the highest teaching of Buddhism expressed. This use of the concept of *ekayāna* is found in the → *Lotus Sūtra,* which claims to contain the most perfect teaching of Buddhism. It is the doctrinal basis of the → Hua-yen, or → Kegon, school and of the → T'ien-t'ai, or → Tendai, school.

Ekottarikāgama 🄱 Skt. → *Anguttara-nikāya*

Ellora 🄷 or Elura, cave and rock temple complex in the state of Maharashtra, India. It comprises thirty-four temples and monasteries dating from the fifth through the ninth centuries, including Hindu, Jain, and Buddhist sanctuaries. The most prominent is the Kailāsanātha temple (eighth century); chiseled from a single, freestanding block of stone, it is said to symbolize the "silver mountain" → Kailāsa, the seat of Shiva. Its stone reliefs depict especially Shiva's and → Durgā's battle against the demons, as well as the dance of Shiva, which represents the cosmic cycle of creation and dissolution.

Empō Dentō-roku 🅉 Jap.; one of the writings compiled by the Japanese Zen monk Shiban Mangen (1625?–1710), which contains the biographies of more than a thousand Zen monks.

Engaku 🅉 Jap., lit. "complete enlightenment"; the degree of → enlightenment attained by a buddha.

Engaku-ji 🅉 Jap., "monastery of complete enlightenment"; a famous Zen monastery in Kamakura that was founded in 1282 by the Chinese Ch'an (Zen) master → Wu-hsüeh Tsu-yüan (Jap., Magaku Sogen, also Bukkō Kokushi) under the patronage of Shōgun Hōjō Tokimune. It is the main monastery of the Engaku-ji lineage of the → Rinzai school in Japan and was among the five leading Zen monasteries in Kamakura (→ Gosan). Engaku-ji is one of the few Zen monasteries still active today in Japan; many smaller monasteries scattered throughout the country are under the administration of Engaku-ji.

Engaku-kyō 🅉 Jap. for → Yüan-chüeh-ching

Engo Kokugon 🅉 Jap. for → Yüan-wu K'o-ch'in

Enju Ben'en 🅉 → Ben'en

Enkan Seian 🅉 also Enkan Saian, Jap. for → Yen-kuan Ch'i-an

Enlightenment 🄱 🅉 the word used to translate the Sanskrit term → *bodhi* (lit. "awakened") and the Japanese → satori or → *kenshō.* A person awakens to a nowness of emptiness (Jap., *ku;* → *shūnyatā*) which he himself is—even as the entire universe is emptiness—and which alone enables him to comprehend the true nature of things. Since enlightenment is repeatedly misunderstood as an experience of light and experiences of light wrongly understood as enlightenment, the term *awakening* is preferable, since it more accurately conveys the experience. The emptiness experienced here is no nihilistic emptiness; rather it is something unperceivable, unthinkable, unfeelable, and endless beyond existence and nonexistence. Emptiness is no object that could be experienced by a subject, since the subject itself is dissolved in the emptiness.

The perfect enlightenment of → Shākyamuni Buddha is the beginning of the → buddhadharma, i.e., that which is known as Buddhism. Buddhism is basically a religion of enlightenment; without this experience there would be no Buddhism.

Although enlightenment (satori, *kenshō*) by its nature is always the same, nevertheless there are quite different degrees of this experience. If we compare the process to breaking through a wall, then the experience can vary between a tiny hole in the wall (a small *kenshō*) and the total annihilation of this wall as in the complete enlightenment of Shākyamuni Buddha—and all the degrees in between. The differences in clarity and accuracy of insight are enormous, even though in both cases the same world is seen.

Although this example makes the differences clear, it falls short insofar as it makes the world of enlightenment seem like an object that one as subject perceives. It also awakens the false impression that the world of enlightenment, emptiness, is separate from the world of phenomena. But this is not the case. In a profound experience it becomes clear that emptiness and phenomena, absolute and relative, are entirely one. The experience of true reality is precisely the experience of this oneness. "Form is no other than emptiness, emptiness no other than form," it is said in the *Prajñāpāramitā-hridaya-sūtra* (→ *Heart Sūtra*)—there are not two worlds. In profound enlightenment the ego is annihilated, it dies. Thus it is said in Zen, "You have to die on the cushion." The results of this "dying," of this "great death," is "great life," a life of freedom and peace.

Enni Ben'en Z → Ben'en

Ennin B usually called Jikaku Daishi, 793–864; important representative of the Japanese → Tendai school; student of → Saichō. He spent nine years in China, where he studied the teachings of various Buddhist schools. He described his experiences in a travel journal.

At the age of fifteen Ennin became a student of Saichō in the monastic center on Mount Hiei. After the latter's death he went in 838 to China, where he trained in various monasteries under renowned teachers. In 847 he returned to his homeland with 559 volumes of → sūtras and commentaries.

On Mount Hiei Ennin propagated the teaching of the Tendai and the → Shingon schools; he also taught the recitation of Buddha's name (→ *nembutsu*) of the → Pure Land school. He continued the work of his teacher Saichō in that he advocated the Mahāyāna → ordination and built his own ordination hall. Under Ennin the Tendai school experienced a major upsurge. The account of his pilgrimage in the China of the T'ang Dynasty provides valuable material for research into the Buddhism and the social situation of China during this period. There is an English translation of this journal: E. O. Reischauer, *Ennin's Diary* (New York, 1955).

E'nō Z Japanese for → Hui-neng

Ensō Z also ichi-ensō, Jap., lit. "circle"; the

Ensō by Tōrei (18th century), a student of Hakuin Zenji

circle as a symbol of the absolute, the true reality, → enlightenment. The circle executed with a single fluid brushstroke is a popular theme in Zen painting. It is said that the state of mind of the painter can be particularly clearly read in the manner of execution of such a circle—only someone who is inwardly collected and in equilibrium is capable of painting a strong and well-balanced circle.

Enza Z Jap., lit. "joyful sitting"; another expression for sitting in meditation (→ *zazen*).

E'shu Z Jap. → *inō*

E'shū Kempō Z Jap. for → Yüeh-chou Ch'ien-feng

F

Fa-hsiang 🅱 Chin. (Jap., → Hossō), lit., "Marks-of-Existence school"; important school of Chinese Buddhism, which continues the teaching of the → Yogāchāra and is based on the writings of → Vasubandhu and → Asanga. It was founded by → Hsüan-tsang (600–64) and his student K'uei-chi (638–82), who systematized the teaching. The most important book of the school is the *Vijñaptimātratā-siddhi* (Chin., *Ch'eng wei-shih lun, "Proof of Nothing-but-Cognition"*) by Hsüan-tsang, a compendious work in which the teaching of the school is presented in detail.

The central notion of the Fa-hsiang school is, Everything is only ideation. This means that the "external world" is only the product of our consciousness and possesses no reality. The world is purely mind. Things are only existent insofar as they are contents of consciousness. The Fa-hsiang school developed a teaching on eight types of consciousness in order to explain the process of ideation (→ *ālaya-vijñāna*). This school is presently undergoing a revival and is being intensively studied in China and Japan.

The Fa-hsiang school reduces all of existence to 100 → dharmas, which are divided into five groups: (1) mind or consciousness (→ *vijñāna*), (2) mental factors (→ *chetasika*), (3) form (→ *rūpa*), (4) dharmas independent of mind, (5) unconditioned (→ *asamskrita*) dharmas. While other schools consider mind to be a single dharma, the Fa-hsiang school distinguishes eight types of consciousness: (1–5) the five kinds of sense consciousness; (6) the → *manovijñāna*, i.e., the thinking consciousness that coordinates the perceptions of the sense organs; (7) → *manas*, the self-conscious "defiled" mind, which thinks, wills, and is the principal factor in the generation of subjectivity; (8) the storehouse consciousness (*ālaya-vijñāna*); see also → *shiki*.

When the self-conscious mind, *manas*, engages the storehouse consciousness, which is itself not active but resembles an ocean, the seeds (i.e., the impressions that have been created by actions and stored in the *ālaya-vijñāna*) revive and cause the arising of individual objects. *Manas* is the principle of discrimination that engenders the consciousness of an ego and thus the duality of subject and object. The experiences of the six senses are reported without interpretation to *manas*, which evaluates and orders the information they contain and returns commands to the six senses. At the same time *manas* stores new seeds or impressions in the in the *ālaya-vijñāna*. These seeds influence external manifestations, which in turn provide further new impressions.

Manas, the link between the senses and the storehouse consciousness, causes the conception of an ego to arise and thus "soils" the *ālaya-vijñāna*. In order to avoid this one must cut through the process of discrimination of the *manas* and enlighten it by developing the "wisdom of equality," which is beyond all duality. In this way one gains insight into the illusionary nature of the world (→ enlightenment).

Concerning the nature of dharmas, the Fa-hsiang school distinguishes three qualities corresponding to the "three levels of truth." These are (1) the level of the conceptualized nature of dharmas (→ *parikalpita*)—this is the level of the "false," illusory aspect of truth, which takes things as they appear to our senses; (2) the level of "contingent nature" (*paratantra*)—on this level dharmas enjoy only temporary existence, since everything that arises contingently (i.e., interdependently) possesses neither self-nature nor "reality"; (3) the level of the nature of ultimate reality—this is the level of "absolute reality," which is beyond all conditionality and relativity. Its characteristic is nonduality. It is suchness (→ *tathatā*), which transcends all appearances and specific characteristics. It is → nirvāna, the true state of the → *tathāgata*.

In order to reach this last level, one must work through various stages of spiritual development until one attains the wisdom of a buddha. This is realized when the first five types of consciousness have been transformed into the "wisdom of action," when the *manovijñāna* has been transformed into the "wisdom of insight," the *manas* into the "wisdom of equality," and the *ālaya-vinjñāna* into the "wisdom of the wondrous mirror." The Fa-hsiang school denies that all beings possess → buddha-nature and can attain buddhahood. An → *ichchantika*, according to this view, can never become a buddha. In this position the Fa-hsiang school stands opposed to other schools of the Mahāyāna, which contributed to its loss of prestige after the T'ang Dynasty.

Fa-hsien 🅱 ca. 337–422, Chinese monk and pilgrim, who left China in 399 and reached India via → Tun-huang, Khotan, and the Himālayas. There he gathered Buddhist scriptures, particularly various versions of the → Vinaya-pitaka. In 414 he returned to China by sea, where, together with → Buddhabhadra he translated the → *Mahāparinirvāna-sūtra* and the Vinaya-pitaka of the → Mahāsānghikas into Chinese. There he also composed his renowned travel account, the *Fo-kuo chi*, which is one of the most important sources of information on the history and culture of India as well as on the state of Buddhism in the fourth and fifth centuries. For an English edition, see *A Record of the Buddhist Countries*, trans. Li Yung-hsi (Peking, 1957).

Fa-hsien set a precedent that many other Chinese pilgrims were to follow. His particular importance lies in the fact that he was the first actually to reach India, to collect scriptures, to study the teaching under various masters, and return to China. His journey, begun together with four other monks, led him from Ch'ang-an (presently Hsi-an) by the southern route to the centers of Indian Buddhism (Benares, Gandhāra, Bodhgayā, Magadha, Patna), to Ceylon, where he spent two years; and finally to Sumatra and Java. Altogether he visited thirty different countries.

In Pātaliputra he found the Vinaya-pitaka of the Mahāsānghikas and the Sarvāstivādas as well as an edition of the *Mahāparinirvāna-sūtra*. In Ceylon he found the Vinaya-pitaka of the → Mahīshāsakas, which he also brought back to China.

Fa-jung **Z** (Jap., Hōyū), 594–657; an early Chinese Ch'an (Zen) master. Fa-jung, who is also called Niu-t'ou (Jap., Gozu) after the mountain on which he lived, founded the → Gozu school. He was a student of → Tao-hsin, the fourth patriarch of Ch'an (Zen); however, he was not confirmed by the latter as a dharma successor. Thus the Gozu school was not among the acknowledged Ch'an schools (→ *goke-shichishū*) in China.

Fa-jung was a Confucian scholar in his younger years. Nevertheless, he was attracted to Buddhism, underwent Buddhist meditative training, and eventually withdrew to a cave in the vicinity of a Buddhist monastery on Mount Niu-t'ou. It is said that the emanations of his enlightened mind were so powerful that the birds of the region came to make him offerings of flowers.

The → *Ching-te ch'uan-teng-lu* reports that Tao-hsin sensed that there was a holy man of great power living on Mount Niu-t'ou and went to look for him. After searching for a few days, he found Fa-jung on a cliff absorbed in meditation. Then suddenly Tao-hsin seemed to hear the roaring of a tiger reverberating from the cliff face, which startled him. "I see you're not rid of it yet," Fa-jung remarked—by which he certainly meant that Tao-hsin still showed traces of → ego. A little later, when Fa-jung got up from his meditation, Tao-hsin inscribed the Chinese character for *buddha* on the spot where he had been sitting. When Fa-jung came back to take his place again, he in his turn was startled and unwilling to sit down on the sacred name. "I see you're not rid of it yet," said Tao-hsin, smiling. Fa-jung, who as shown by his reaction was still caught in orthodox Buddhist conceptions and did not understand this comment on the part of the fourth patriarch, asked him to instruct him in its deep meaning—which Tao-hsin then did. It is said that after Tao-hsin left Fa-jung, no more birds came to the latter with flower offerings, a sign that his enlightenment now left no "traces" (→ *goseki*). Thus the fourth patriarch had brought him to a more profound level of enlightenment. Later, students gathered around Fa-jung and he taught them the → buddha-dharma in his style, thus founding the Gozu school of Ch'an (Zen). The teachings of this school were brought to Japan by the Japanese monk → Saichō. However, these teachings never became of major importance for the development of the Ch'an (Zen) tradition either in China or Japan and died out after a few generations.

Fa-lang **B** 507–81; important representative of the → San-lun school of Chinese Buddhism. In 528 he entered the Buddhist order and devoted himself initially to the practice of → *dhyāna* and the study of the → Vinaya texts. Later he occupied himself with the writings of the San-lun school. In 558 he went to the capital of those times (present-day Nanking), where he gathered thousands of students around himself, thus bringing the San-lun school great popularity. His student → Chi-tsang carried on the tradition after the death of Fa-lang.

Fan **T** Chin. → *fu*

Fang-chang **T** Chin., lit. "Square Fathom," also called Fang-hu ("Square Urn"); one of the three isles of the immortals off the east coast of China. They are the home of the immortals and the epitome of ultimate bliss. The search for these islands (→ P'eng-lai, → Ying-chou) is an important feature of religious Taoism (→ *tao-chiao*).

A Taoist text dating from the 4th or 5th century gives the following description of Fang-chang:

"The island of Fang-chang is in the exact center of the eastern ocean. Its four coasts, facing west, south, east, and north, form a perfect square, each side of which is five thousand miles long. The island is a favorite dwelling place of dragons. On it there are palaces of gold, jade, and crystal. . . . Immortals who do not wish to ascend to Heaven travel to this continent, where they receive their 'certificate of the primordial source of life.' Several hundred thousand immortals live there. They till the fields and plant the herb of immortality. . . . There are also rocks of jade and many springs, among them the 'Nine [life-giving] Springs.' The rulers of the land are married to princesses, who rule over water spirits, dragons, sea snakes, whales, and all other marine animals" (Bauer 1974, p. 151).

Fang-chung shu **T** Chin., lit. "arts of the inner chamber"; collective term for all sexual techniques said to lead to the realization of the → Tao and to the attainment of immortality (→ *ch'ang-sheng pu-ssu*).

The various Taoist sexual techniques aim at nourishing and strengthening the semen or essence (→ *ching*). For this the adept requires the energy of a sexual partner of the opposite sex, because a man can strengthen his yang only with the help of the feminine yin and vice versa. The most important methods for strengthening the *ching* are prevention of ejaculation and allowing the *ching* to return, in order to strengthen the brain (→ *huan-ching pu-nao*). There is historical evidence of collective sexual practices in early Taoist schools. The followers of Five-Pecks-of-Rice Taoism (→ *wu-tou-mi tao*) and of the Way of Supreme Peace (→ *t'ai-p'ing tao*) practiced the so-called unification of the breaths (→ *ho-ch'i*). These *fang-chung shu* have been known since the Han dynasty and were practiced both privately and publicly until about the 7th century, when they were forced to withdraw to the private sphere under the pressure of Confucianist morality. There is no mention of such practices in Taoist texts dated later than the Sung Dynasty, but it may be assumed that they continued up to the very recent past.

The philosophical foundation of the *fang-chung shu* is the widespread idea that the world came into being as a result of the marriage of Heaven and Earth—of yin and yang—a process that continually repeats itself in nature. Human sexual intercourse was seen as an opportunity to participate in this creative process both physically and psychologically and thereby experience the Tao.

An essential feature of these sexual practices is the exchange of energy. To strengthen his yang a man may—for example, during foreplay to sexual intercourse—partake of the special yin essence of the woman from the saliva under her tongue and from her breasts, thereby strengthening his own energy. The most powerful essences, however, are liberated during orgasm. The man absorbs these energies through his penis from the vagina of the woman, and the woman through her vagina from the penis of the man. This exchange of yin and yang produces good health and longevity.

In most cases, however, the aim of such practices goes further in that it consists in the accumulation of energy rather than its mere exchange. The Taoist adept must learn to prevent ejaculation of his semen in order to preserve all the *ching* within his body. At the same time, however, he endeavors to produce as many sexual climaxes as possible in his female partner with the aim of absorbing the female yin energy thereby liberated. A man may increase the effectiveness of this technique by having successive sexual intercourse with as many partners as possible. These partners, ideally, should be young and beautiful. The legendary Yellow Emperor (→ Huang-ti) is said to have had intercourse with twelve hundred concubines without any damage to his health, because he knew how to inhibit ejaculation.

A more advanced technique is described as "allowing the essence to return, in order to strengthen the brain." This technique was also used as a preliminary to meditative Taoist breathing exercises aimed at developing the sacred embryo (→ *sheng-t'ai*).

It cannot be denied, however, that in most cases these techniques constituted an exploitation of the female partners involved. For that reason a further tradition states that both partners should suppress orgasm and instead strive to unite at a higher level. We quote a relevant Taoist tract: "To live for a long time without aging, a man should indulge in amorous play with his female partner. He should drink the 'jade fluid,' i.e., swallow her saliva; in this way passion will be aroused in both the man and the woman. Then the man should press the *p'ing-i* spot with the finger of his left hand. (This spot is situated approximately 2.5 cm above the nipple of the right breast and is also referred to as 'yin present in yang.') Then the man should visualize in his (lower) cinnabar field (→ *tan-t'ien*) a bright essence, yellow within and red and white without. He should then imagine that this liquid separates into a sun and a moon, which move about in his abdomen and then rise within him until they reach the → Ni-huan point in his brain, where the two halves are once again united" (trans. from Colegrave 1980). This symbolic gathering back of the semen thus culminates in the fusion of the male and female principles represented by the sun and moon respectively.

The detailed instructions for practicing these sexual techniques were mostly kept secret or revealed in a language reminiscent of that employed by the Outer Alchemy (→ *wai-tan*), which could only be understood by initiates.

Not all Taoist schools approved of sexual practices as means of attaining enlightenment. The Way for the Realization of Truth (→ *ch'üan-chen tao*), among others, rejects them and teaches that sexuality has to become an exclusively inner experience. Chinese art is replete with sexual symbols. The peach, because of its clearly discernible notch, represents the female vulva; further symbols for the feminine are vases, clouds, open peony blossoms, mushrooms, the white tiger, kidney-shaped stones, etc. Masculine symbols are jade, sheep, phallus-shaped rock formations, the green dragon, the color green, and the phoenix bird.

Fang-hu 🅃 Chin. → Fang-chang

Fang-shih 🅃 Chin., lit. "master of prescriptions"; magician; precursor of Taoist sages and priests (→ *tao-shih*). The earliest reports about *fang-shih* date from the 3d century B.C.E. These magicians (shamans) lived mainly on the northeastern coast of China and were proficient in a great variety of arts (Chin., *fang-shu*) such as astrology, astronomy, spirit healing, prophecy, geomancy, sexual practices, the science of calendars, etc. They were in the possession of prescriptions for attaining immortality and were believed to be experts in the search for the isles of the immortals (→ P'eng-lai, → Fang-chang, → Ying-chou), which secured them the patronage of rulers. They made use of drugs and talismans (→ *fu-lu*), developed physical exercises and breathing techniques aimed at the prolongation of life, and enlisted the help of gods. For all these reasons they played an important part in the creation of religious Taoism (→ *tao-chiao*), their knowledge and proficiencies forming the basis of various streams within the *tao-chiao.* One of the most famous and influential *fang-shih* was → Li Shao-chün.

Fang yen-k'ou 🅑 Chinese → release of the burning mouths

Fa-shun 🅑 → Tu-shun

Fa-tsang 🅑 → Hua-yen school

Fa-yen-tsung 🅩 Chin. for → Hōgen school

Fa-yen Wen-i 🅩 (Jap., Hōgen Bun'eki), 885–958; Chinese Ch'an (Zen) master, a student and dharma successor (→ *hassu*) of → Lo-han Kuei-ch'en (Jap., Rakan Keijin) and the master of → T'ien-t'ai Te-shao (Jap., Tendai Tokushō). Fa-yen was one of the most outstanding Ch'an masters of his time; he was in the lineage of → Hsüan-sha Shih-pei (Jap., Gensha Shibi). The latter's dharma teaching was widely propagated by Fa-yen and as a result this lineage, which had hitherto been known as the Hsüan-sha school, was thereafter known as the Fa-yen school (Jap., → Hōgen school). Fa-yen had sixty-three dharma successors; we encounter him in example 26 of the → *Wu-men-kuan* as well as in example 7 of the → *Pi-yen-lu.*

Only a few of Fa-yen's voluminous writings are extant, among them a few poems and a treatise, the *Tsung-men shih-kuei-lu* on Ch'an and the signs already present in his time of the degeneration of the Ch'an schools of China. His sayings and instructions are recorded in the *Ch'ing-liang Wen-i-ch'an-shih yü-lu* (*Record of the Words of the Ch'an Master Wen-i from Ching-liang Monastery* [*in Ching-ling*]), compiled in the first half of the 17th century by the monks Yüan-hsin and Kuo Ning-chih.

Fa-yen became a monk at the age of seven. First he studied the Confucian classics and the Buddhist sūtras, particularly the → *Buddhāvatamsaka-sūtra,* the fundamental work for the Hua-yen school of Chinese Buddhism. Since, however, he was not contented by such philosophical study, he eventually sought instruction in Ch'an. His first Ch'an master was → Ch'ang-ch'ing Hui-leng (Jap., Chōkei Eryō). Although Fa-yen did not experience enlightenment under him either, he was already highly respected in the monastic community surrounding Ch'ang-ch'ing. Later, when he was on a pilgrimage (→ *angya*) with some companions, the group was forced by a storm to seek shelter in Ti-ts'ang monastery in Fu-chou. There they met the abbot, Lo-han Kuei-ch'en, who was also called Master Ti-ts'ang (Jap., Jizō), after the name of his monastery. Here the → *mondō* took place between Ti-ts'ang and Fa-yen that is cited under the rubric of Lo-han Kuei-ch'en. As we learn from the → *Ching-te ch'uan-teng-lu,* Fa-yen came to an enlightenment experience when he heard Ti-ts'ang's words *ignorance is the thickest.* Thereafter he and his three companions remained at Ti-ts'ang monastery to train further under Master Lo-han; they all later became important Ch'an masters.

Master Lo-han submitted Fa-yen, who was still strongly under the influence of his early intellectual studies and liked especially to cite and discuss passages from the *Buddhāvatamsaka-sūtra,* to very strict training. Repeatedly he swept aside Fa-yen's erudite pronouncements with the words, "That is not the buddhadharma." One day when Fa-yen wanted to leave and travel further, Lo-han accompanied him to the monastery gate. There he pointed to a stone and asked Fa-yen, "It is written, 'The three worlds are nothing but mind, the ten thousand things [all phenomena] are nothing but consciousness.' Tell me, is this stone in your consciousness or not?"

Fa-yen answered, "In consciousness."

Master Lo-han then said, "Why are you dragging such a stone around with you on a pilgrimage?"

Fa-yen did not know what to answer—and remained with Master Lo-han, who eventually led him to profound enlightenment.

Later when Fa-yen himself became active as a Ch'an master, his reputation spread quickly, and Ch'an monks thronged about him from all parts of the country. The number of monks gathered around him at Ch'iung-shou monastery in Lin-ch'uan is said never to have been less than a thousand. The dharma successors of Fa-yen spread his dharma teaching all over China and as far as Korea. The Ch'an school named after him flourished for three generations, however, then degenerated, and died out after the fifth generation.

Fei-sheng 🅣 Chin., roughly "ascending to Heaven in broad daylight"; a metaphor descriptive of the ultimate apotheosis of a follower of religious Taoism (→ *tao-chiao*) who has succeeded in transforming his nature by the performance of various exercises, and thus become an immortal (→ *hsien*).

Feng-hsüeh Yen-chao 🅩 (Jap., Fuketsu Enshō), 896–973; Chinese Ch'an (Zen) master of the → Rinzai school; a student and dharma successor (→ *hassu*) of → Nan-yüan Hui-yung (Jap., Nan'in Egyō) and the master of → Shou-shan Sheng-nien (Jap., Shuzan Shōnen). Feng-hsüeh is considered one of the greatest masters in the lineage of → Lin-chi I-hsüan (Jap., Rinzai Gigen), and, as Yang-shan Hui-chi (Jap., Kyōzan Ejaku) is said already to have prophesied, a worthy dharma heir of Huang-po Hsi-yün (Jap., Ōbaku Kiun), Lin-chi's master. We encounter Feng-hsüeh in example 24 of the → *Wu-men-kuan* and in examples 38 and 61 of the → *Pi-yen-lu.*

Feng-hsüeh studied the Confucian classics in his youth and wanted to take the examination for entry into the civil service. The fact that he did not pass it on the first try brought about a turning point in his life. He undertook a life of → homelessness and then entered a Buddhist monastery. There he underwent the strict discipline of the → Vinaya school and for the first time studied the scriptures of Mahāyāna Buddhism, especially the teachings of the T'ien-t'ai school. Mere philosophical speculation, however, left him unsatisfied; thus he set about searching for a master of Ch'an who could lead him to his own experience of the truths described in the scriptures. Since he was not lacking in intelligence, quick wit, and confidence, and since no one could easily get the better of him in debate, he prematurely considered himself enlightened; and it took a strict master like Nan-yüan to show him his limitations, thus making authentic training possible. Feng-hsüeh's development, which eventually led to enlightenment under Master Nan-yüan, is described in detail in Master Yüan-wu's presentation in example 38 of the → *Pi-yen-lu.*

Feng-kan **Z** (Jap., Bukan); Chinese Ch'an (Zen) master of the T'ang period (precise dates unknown, probably the middle of the 7th century). He was the abbot (→ *rōshi*) of the Kuo-ch'ing Monastery in the T'ien-t'ai Mountains. The little that is known of him comes for the most part from the foreword to the *Han-shan-shih,* a collection of the poetry of the hermits of → Han-shan. It also contains several poems attributed to Feng-kan.

Concerning his role as a subject of Zen painting, → Han-shan.

Fen-yang Shan-chao **Z** (Jap., Fun'yō Zenshō), 947–1024; Chinese Ch'an (Zen) master of the → Rinzai school; a student and dharma successor (→ *hassu*) of → Shou-shan Sheng-nien (Jap., Shuzan Shōnen) and the master of → Shih-chuang Ch'u-yüan (Jap., Sekisō Soen). It is said of Fen-yang that he wandered throughout China and sought out seventy-one masters in an effort to save what could be saved of the Ch'an tradition, which was then in decline. Thus his style of instruction synthesized elements from the various lineages that then survived in the Rinzai school.

Fen-yang was one of the first Ch'an masters to celebrate the sayings of the ancient masters in poetic form; in this way he founded the Ch'an-Zen tradition of eulogistic poetry (→ *ju*). (Also → Chih-men Kuang-tsu, → Hsüeh-tou Ch'ung-hsien.)

Five degrees (of enlightenment) **Z** (Jap., Go-i); a classification of degrees of realization of → enlightenment (also → *kenshō,* → satori) according to their depth, as established by the Chinese Ch'an (Zen) master → Tung-shan Liang-chieh (Jap., Tōzan Ryōkai). In order of increasing depths of enlightenment, these degrees are *sho-chu-hen, hen-chu-sho, sho-chu-rai, ken-chu-shi, ken-chu-to.* The characters *shō* and *hen* here represent polar aspects of reality, for example,

Shō represents	*Hen represents*
the absolute	the relative
the fundamental	the phenomenal
emptiness	form and color
sameness	difference
one	many
true nature	attributes

The five degrees indicate the following mutual relationships of *shō* and *hen*:

1. *Sho-chu-hen* (lit. "*hen* in the midst of *shō*"); on this level of experience the world of phenomena dominates, but it is experienced as a manifestation of the fundamental, our true nature.
2. *Hen-chu-sho* (lit. "*shō* in the midst of *hen*"); in this second stage of enlightened experience, the quality of nondistinction comes to the fore and the quality of manifoldness fades into the background.
3. *Sho-chu-rai* (lit. "[the one] coming out of the midst of *shō* [and *hen* as polarly related to it]"); this is an experience in which there is no longer any awareness of body or mind—both "drop completely away." This is the experience of emptiness (Jap., *ku,* Skt., → *shūnyatā*).
4. *Ken-chu-shi* (lit. "entering between the two [polar aspects]"); at this stage each thing is accorded its special uniqueness to the greatest degree; emptiness has vanished into phenomena.
5. *Ken-chu-to* (lit. "having already arrived in the middle of both"); on the fifth and highest level form and emptiness fully interpenetrate each other. From this state of mind arises self-evident, intentionless action, that is to say, action without any movement of brain or heart that instantaneously suits whatever circumstances arise (→ *fugyō-ni-gyō*).

Five elements **T** → *wu-hsing*

Five hellish deeds **B** also five deadly sins; five unforgivable deeds, which according to the traditional view immediately plunge their doers into the depths of hell (→ *naraka*). They are patricide, matricide, murder of an → arhat, injury of a → buddha, and the attempt to bring about a schism in the Buddhist monastic community (→ *sangha*).

Five hindrances **B** → *nīvarana*

Five-Pecks-of-Rice Taoism **T** → *wu-tou-mi tao*

Five periods and eight teachings **B** → *wu-tou-mi tao*

Five phases of transformation 🅃 → *wu-hsing*

Five types of Zen 🅉 a classification by the early Chinese Ch'an (Zen) master → Kuei-feng Tsung-mi of the most important categories of Zen. The notion *Zen* in this context stands generally for "meditative practice." The five types of Zen are:

1. *Bonpu* Zen (Jap., *bonpu* or *bompu*, "ordinary unenlightened person"); the type of → *zazen* that is practiced without religious motivation, as, for example, for the improvement of mental or bodily health.

2. *Gedō* Zen (Jap., *gedō*, "outside way"); betokens a type of Zen that is religious in character but follows teachings that are outside the Buddhist teachings. Yoga meditation or Christian contemplation, for example, would fall into this category. Also subsumed under *gedō* Zen are those meditative practices that are pursued purely for the sake of developing supernatural powers and abilities.

3. *Shōjō* Zen (Jap., *shōjō*, "small vehicle"; Skt., → Hīnayāna); a type of Zen that leads to the state of → *mushinjō*, a condition in which all sense perceptions are cut off and consciousness discontinued. If one remains in *mushinjō* until death occurs, then there is no rebirth and a kind of separation from the cycle of existence (→ samsāra) is achieved. Since *shōjō* Zen is directed only toward the attainment of one's own inner peace, it is regarded by Zen Buddhism, which belongs to Mahāyāna Buddhism, as not in agreement with the highest teachings of the Buddha. The last two of the five types of Zen, on the other hand, are considered in agreement with these teachings.

4. *Daijō* Zen (Jap., *daijō*: "great vehicle"; Skt. → Mahāyāna); the central characteristic of *daijō* Zen is self-realization (→ *kenshō*, → satori) and the actualization of the "great way" in everyday life (→ *mujōdō-no-taigen*). Since in self-realization the connectedness, indeed, the unity, of the self with all beings is experienced, and since the actualization of the "great way" in everyday life has to do with working for the welfare of all beings, this is a Zen of the Mahāyāna type.

5. *Saijōjō* Zen (Jap., *saijōjō*, "supremely excellent vehicle"); in this highest form of Zen practice, the way and path are fused into one. *Zazen* is understood here not so much as a means to "attain" enlightenment, but rather as a realization of the buddha-nature immanent in every being (→ *busshō*). It is said that this Zen was practiced by all the buddhas of the past and it is considered as the pinnacle and crown ornament of Buddhist Zen. This practice, also known as → *shikantaza*, is the Zen particularly fostered by → Dōgen Zenji.

The view occasionally put forward that *daijō* Zen refers to the practice of the → Rinzai school and *saijōjō* to that of the → Sōtō school is not entirely accurate. *Daijō* and *saijōjō* Zen mutually complement and interpenetrate each other and both forms of practice are practiced in both schools. In the Rinzai school the emphasis lies more strongly on bringing about self-realization with the help of kōans, while in Sōtō Zen the practice of *shikantaza* is preferred.

Kuei-feng Tsung-mi's classification of five categories of Zen reflects, moreover, a traditional Buddhist view that today—since Zen has spread beyond the bounds of Buddhist culture—must be modified. Thus a Muslim or Christian can practice *shōjō*, *daijō*, or *saijōjō* Zen within the framework of his own religious background, even though according to the classification of the five types of Zen, any non-Buddhist Zen would have to be classified as *gedō* Zen. This classification is thus valid particularly within the theoretical framework of Zen "Buddhism" (→ Zen, exoteric), whereas in connection with the view that Zen is the core experience presupposed by, and at the basis of, every religion, this classification has very little application.

Forms of manifestation (of Buddhist deities) 🄱 In → Tibetan Buddhism the distinction is possible between an angry or wrathful and a peaceful aspect of any deity in the pantheon; thus, for example, Avalokiteshvara (peaceful) and Mahākāla (wrathful). As a → *sādhana*, the deities symbolize the peaceful and aggressive or destructive disposition of the practitioner's consciousness. As the modern Tibetan meditation master Chögyam Trungpa stresses, "wrath" is not to be understood here as an egoistic emotion, nor "aggressive or destructive" in an evil, negative sense. The energies symbolized by the wrathful deities are as helpful and necessary to the realization of enlightenment as the peaceful ones. What is destroyed here are the illusions that hinder spiritual development, and what feels itself attacked and terrified is the illusionary ego of the practitioner.

The equal recognition in Tibetan Buddhism of wrathful energies and the major role played by wrathful deities depicted in terrifying forms of manifestation have often led in the West to the erroneous view that "demon worship" is prevalent in Tibetan Buddism.

Besides the five buddha families (→ *buddhakula*), the → Vajrayāna also speaks of the "hundred families of sacred peaceful and wrathful deities" (Tib., *zhi khro dam pa rigs brgya*). This enumeration of forty-two peaceful and fifty-eight wrathful deities, known particularly from the *Tibetan Book of the Dead* (→ *Bardo thödol*), is part of the Mahāyāna teachings (→ Nyingmapa) introduced into Tibet by → Padmasambhava. These deities are brought together in two → mandalas, which represent an expansion of the schema of the five buddha families. The archetype of the deities manifesting wrathful energies is Chem Chog Heruka.

Fo-t'u-teng 🅱 232–348; Buddhist monk of Central Asian derivation, who went to Lo-yang in 310 and built a religious center there. Because of his magical powers (foreseeing the outcome of military operations, making rain, etc.), he gained the confidence of the ruler and functioned as his advisor for more than twenty years.

He indefatigably stressed the importance of a sense of humanity, and of refraining from killing and tyranny. Through this he had a positive influence on the rulers of his time. Fo-t'u-teng advocated the propagation of Buddhism among the Chinese people in its most elementary form and by the simplest means. Under his influence the Chinese were for the first time officially permitted to join the Buddhist → *sangha* and to undergo monastic ordination. He is said also to have been responsible for the founding of the Chinese order of nuns (→ *bhikshunī*).

Four certainties 🅱 (Skt., *vaisharadya*); a characteristic mark of a buddha. The four certainties are (1) certainty that his perfect enlightenment is irreversible; (2) certainty that all defilements (→ *āsrava*) are exhausted; (3) certainty that all obstacles have been overcome; (4) certainty of having proclaimed the way of abandoning → samsāra.

Four famous mountains 🅱 four mountains in China that in Buddhism are regarded as the sacred places of the four great → bodhisattvas. According to tradition they appeared at these mountains to expound the teaching. They are (1) Wu-t'ai-shan (Shansi province), associated with → Wen-shu (Skt., → Mañjushrī); (2) P'u-t'o-shan (Chekiang province), considered the sacred mountain of the bodhisattva → Kuan-yin (Skt., → Avalokiteshvara); (3) O-mei-shan (Szechuan province), the sacred mountain of the bodhisattva P'u-hsien (Skt., → Samantabhadra); (4) Chiu-hua-shan (Anhwei province), the sacred place of the bodhisattva → Ti-ts'ang (Skt., → Kshitigarbha).

Four foundations (awakenings) of mindfulness 🅱 → *satipatthāna*

Four immeasurables 🅱 → *brahma-vihāra*

Four noble truths 🅱 (Skt., *ārya-satya*; Pali, *ariya-satta*); these are the basis of the Buddhist teaching. The four noble truths are (1) the truth of suffering (→ *duhkha*); (2) the truth of the origin (*samudāya*) of suffering; (3) the truth of the cessation (→ *nirodha*) of suffering; (4) the truth of the path that leads to the cessation of suffering.

The first truth says that all existence is characterized by suffering and does not bring satisfaction. Everything is suffering: birth, sickness, death; coming together with what one does not like; separating from what one does like; not obtaining what one desires; and the five aggregates (→ *skandha*) of attachment that constitute the personality.

The second truth gives as the cause of suffering craving or desire, the thirst (→ *trishnā*) for sensual pleasure, for becoming and passing away. This craving binds beings to the cycle of existence (→ samsāra).

The third truth says that through remainderless elimination of craving, suffering can be brought to an end.

The fourth truth gives the → eightfold path as the means for the ending of suffering

Nonrecognition of the four noble truths is ignorance (→ *avidyā*).

The discovery of the four noble truths by the Buddha constituted, according to the various traditions, his actual enlightenment (→ *bodhi*). Buddha expounded these truths in the → Benares discourse as his first teaching immediately after his enlightenment.

The sūtras explain the four noble truths in the following words:

"But what, O monks, is the noble truth of suffering? Birth is suffering; decay is suffering; death is suffering; sorrow, lamentation, pain, grief and despair are suffering; in short the five groups [aggregates] of existence connected with clinging are suffering.

"But what, O monks, is the noble truth of the origin of suffering? It is that craving which gives rise to fresh rebirth and, bound up with lust and greed, now here, now there, finds ever fresh delight. It is the sensual craving, the craving for existence, the craving for nonexistence or self-annihilation.

"But what, O monks, is the noble truth of the extinction of suffering? It is the complete fading away and extinction of this craving, its forsaking and giving up, liberation and detachment from it.

"But what, O monks, is the noble truth of the path leading to the extinction of suffering? It is the noble eightfold path that leads to the extinction of suffering, namely: perfect view, perfect thought, perfect speech, perfect action, perfect livelihood, perfect effort, perfect concentration" (trans. from Nyanatiloka 1972, pp. 151–152).

Four perfect exertions 🅱 (Skt., *samyak-prahānāni*; Pali, *sammā-padhāna*); one of the meditation practices recommended by the Buddha, the objective of which is to avoid unwholesome factors in the future and eliminate those that are present. The four perfect exertions are (1) the exertion of restraint (i.e., avoiding unwholesome factors); (2) the exertion of overcoming (unwholesome factors); (3) the exertion of developing (wholesome factors, especially the factors of enlightenment, → *bodhyanga*); (4) the exertion of maintaining (wholesome factors). The four perfect exertions are identical with the sixth element of the → eightfold path, right effort or exertion.

Four stages of absorption 🅱 → *dhyāna*

Four stages of formlessness 🅱 (Skt., Pali, arūpasamādhi); meditation practices from the early phase of Buddhism, the objective of which was to raise oneself stage by stage into increasingly higher levels of incorporeality. The four stages of formlessness are (1) the stage of the limitlessness of space (→ *ākāsha*); (2) the stage of the limitlessness of consciousness (→ *vijñāna*); (3) the stage of nothing whatever; (4) the stage of beyond awareness and nonawareness.

These practices, which the Buddha probably adopted from the ancient tradition of India, and which do not conform in nature to other Buddhist meditation practices, were in the course of further development assimilated, along with the four stages of absorption (→ *dhyāna*), into a larger series of practices. The four stages of formlessness constitute the fifth through eighth elements of the new series. The four stages of absorption, though they can lead to the attainment of supreme knowledge, are not accorded the highest place in this series, because all contents of consciousness are not eliminated in them. For this reason, from the point of view of the stages of formlessness, they are to be regarded as lower.

Fo-yen-yüan 🆉 (Jap., Butsugen-on); Chinese master of the → Fuke school; → Kakushin.

Fu 🆃 also *fan*, Chin., lit. "return"; a concept in the *Tao-te ching* to describe the natural movement of the Tao: "Returning (recurrence) is the motion of the Tao" (Chapter 40). The law underlying all appearances is that all things return to their origin. All things arise from the Tao and must return to it. In Taoist meditation practice, "returning to the root or source" is synonymous with attaining enlightenment.

This idea is expressed in Chapter 16 of the *Tao-te ching:* "Empty yourself of everything. Let the mind rest at peace. The ten thousand things rise and fall while the Self watches their return. They grow and flourish and then return to the source. Returning to the source is stillness, which is the way of nature. The way of nature is unchanging. Knowing constancy is insight. Not knowing constancy leads to disaster" (Feng & English 1972). The *Tao-te ching* describes the destination of this return in a number of ways: most frequently it is simply referred to as the Tao, but in some passages it is related to the idea of the homeland, the mother, or the root. In yet other passages it is seen as original simplicity (→ *p'u*), the limitless (→ *wu-chi*) or as an ideal primordial state of society (golden age). If the notion of a return refers to the Tao itself, what is meant is the return of the Tao to its primordial state of nonbeing, nonaction (→ *wu-wei*), and namelessness.

In the *Book of Change(s)* (→ *I-ching*) *fu* describes the process of a quality changing or being transformed into its opposite: when the yin (→ yin-yang) has reached its peak, the yang returns. This motion is symbolized by the hexagram *fu,* which consists of an unbroken yang line below five broken yin lines. In Chinese thought in general *fu* may symbolize the recurrence of the seasons and/or the succession of life and death.

Fubo-mishō-izen 🆉 Jap., lit. "before the birth of one's parents"; a Zen expression that points to one's true nature or buddha-nature (→ *busshō*); another expression for → *honrai-no-memmoku.*

Fu-ch'i 🆃 Chin., lit. "nourishing oneself by the breath"; Taoist breathing technique, in which the practitioner focuses his attention on the breath and allows it to penetrate and circulate in the five internal organs (→ *wu-tsang*). From there the breath is directed to flow through the feet, heart, neck, joints, and nine bodily orifices. In this way the body is nourished. This technique is a preliminary for embryonic breathing (→ *t'ai-hsi*).

A special form of *fu-ch'i* consists in absorbing the breaths of the five shoots, or sprouts (*wu-ya*): the → *ch'i* of the five elements (→ *wu-hsing*) is allowed to enter the corresponding internal organs by absorbing the breaths of the five heavenly directions (the fifth being the center). During this exercise the Taoist adept follows the breath with his mind and sees it enter the organs in question, where it mingles with the secretion or essence of that particular organ. In this way the breath is circulated through the body and can release its healing powers. The absorption of the breath of the five shoots results in a strengthening of the five internal organs.

Fudochi Shimmyō-roku 🅉 a written work of the Japanese Zen master → Takuan. It presents the principles of Zen practice by comparing the mental attitude of a Zen practitioner to that of a person practicing the Japanese Way of the Sword (→ *kendō*).

Fugen 🅑 🅉 Japanese for → Samantabhadra

Fugyō-ni-gyō 🅉 Jap., lit. "doing by not doing"; Zen expression for intentionless action, which leaves no trace in the heart-mind (→ *kokoro*) of the one acting, as is the case with profound → enlightenment. It is a manner of "doing" that is not premeditated but rather arises as an instantaneous, spontaneous reaction to given circumstances. A prerequisite for this is the development of → *jōriki*. But *jōriki* by itself is not sufficient for the attainment of the state of mind of *fugyō-ni-gyō*. For this it is also necessary that the person acting not be attached to the result of his action, indeed, that in acting he is not aware of himself in the sense of a limited → ego as the author of the act. This is not possible without enlightenment.

The notion of "doing by not doing" is already to be found in Taoism (→ *wu-wei*), which contributed significantly to the development of Zen.

Fuhōzō 🅉 Jap., lit. "treasure-house of dharma-transmission"; 1. the fact of the transmission of → buddha-dharma through a long lineage of patriarchs (→ *soshigata*) beginning with → Shākyamuni Buddha (see also the Ch'an/Zen Lineage Chart); 2. a person in the lineage of patriarchs deriving from the historical Buddha who transmits the dharma.

Fu Hsi 🅣 figure in Chinese mythology and husband of → Nü-kua. Fu Hsi is the first of China's three noble emperors. According to tradition he ruled either from 2852 to 2737 B.C.E. or from 2952 to 2836 B.C.E. Mankind is said to owe many inventions to him. He taught the use of the fishing net as well as ways of taming wild animals and the breeding of silkworms. He invented the set square, which became his emblem and with which Great Yü (→ Ta-yü) later measured the world. His most important creations, however, were music and the eight trigrams (→ *pa-kua*, → *I-ching*), said to be the basis of Chinese writing. Tradition furthermore ascribes to him the invention of casting oracles by the use of yarrow stalks. He is also said to have invented the one hundred Chinese family names and decreed that marriages may only take place between persons bearing differing family names. Fu Hsi is represented as a human being with the body of a snake. In Taoist temples he is usually portrayed holding a panel on which the eight trigrams are inscribed.

Fu jih-hsiang 🅣 Chin., lit. "absorbing the image of the sun into oneself"; Taoist heliotherapeutic technique practiced in combination with breathing exercises. The technique is confined to men; women absorb the image of the moon.

The Taoist adept practicing *fu jih-hsiang* writes the Chinese character depicting the sun in vermilion ink on a rectangular piece of green paper. Every morning thereafter, holding the paper in his left hand and facing east, he concentrates on this image until it is transformed into the sun itself. He then dissolves the green paper in water, which he drinks, knocking his teeth together nine times (→ *k'ou-ch'ih*), and swallows his saliva (→ *yü-chiang*).

Fukaku Zenji 🅉 Jap. for → P'u-chüeh-ch'an-shih

Fukan Zazengi 🅉 Jap., "*General Presentation of the Principles of Zazen*"; a written work of the great Japanese Zen master → Dōgen Zenji, which he composed after his return to Japan from China as a general introduction to the practice of → *zazen*. In it he stresses that *zazen* is no "means to enlightenment," since even after experiencing → enlightenment, one continues to practice *zazen*, which is the fundamental practice of all the buddhas (→ Zen, esoteric). This development continues without end.

Fukasetsu 🅉 Jap., lit. "the unsayable"; like the mystics of all cultures and ages, the Zen tradition also says that what is experienced in → enlightenment (also → *kenshō*, → satori) eludes all conceptual expression. Whoever has realized his true nature or buddha-nature (→ *busshō*) is "like a mute who has had a dream," as the Chinese Ch'an (Zen) master → Wu-men Hui-k'ai (Jap., Mumon Ekai) says in his exposition of the example 1 of the → *Wu-men-kuan* concerning the famous kōan Mu. The experience of *fukasetsu* is the basis for the admonition so typical of Zen not to fixate on the words of sacred scriptures, which can only be the "finger that points to the moon (true reality), but not the moon itself."

Thus in the characterization of Zen in four short phrases that is attributed to the first patriarch of Ch'an

(Zen) → Bodhidharma but according to the opinion of many Zen scholars really came from Master → Nan-ch'üan P'u-yüan (Jap., Nansen Fugan), it is said: "(1) special transmission outside the orthodox teaching [Jap., *kyōge betsuden*], (2) independence from scriptures [Jap., *furyū monji*], (3) and immediate pointing to the human heart [Jap., *jikishi ninshin*] (4) lead to realization of one's nature and to becoming a buddha [Jap. *kenshō jōbutsu*]."

The ineffability of Zen experience is what causes the Zen masters so readily to have recourse in → *mondō* or → *hossen* to wordless gestures as a means of communication that transcends verbal expression. As shown by the fact that Zen has produced a rich literature, Zen does not deny the usefulness of the written word; however, it is repeatedly stressed that no words can contain true reality or communicate it. Only a person who has been through the experiences expressed in the writings can read what is written there.

In the *Chuang-tzu*, the work by the great Taoist sage of the same name—who with his spiritual father Lao-tzu belongs as much among the Zen forefathers as do the early Indian patriarchs (→ *soshigata*)—is this saying of Lao-tzu's, which is often quoted by Zen masters in connection with *fukasetsu*: "If the Tao [→ *dō*] were something that could be presented, each man would present it to his lord. If the Tao were something that could be handed to somebody, each man would give it to his parents. If the Tao were something that could be told to others, everybody would tell it to his brothers."

However, such is not the case. It is only accessible to one's own immediate experience. That is why Lao-tzu also says at the end of the above section, "He who has not experienced [the Tao] in his heart, for him the gates of Heaven are not open."

Fukashigi 🅉 Jap., lit. "the unthinkable"; that which eludes every thought-conditioned, conceptual comprehension, i.e. which transcends thinking; the wondrous, the essentially inscrutable. According to the teachings of Zen, ultimate reality, true nature, or buddha-nature (→ *busshō*) is beyond thought, i.e., *fukashigi*. But though it is inconceivable and beyond intellection, it is nevertheless *experienceable*. The experience of the unthinkable is what is referred to as → enlightenment (also → *kenshō*, → satori).

Fukatoku 🅉 Jap., lit. "that which cannot be held onto," the "ungraspable"; insubstantial nature of all phenomena. According to the Buddhist understanding, all phenomena arise dependent upon direct and indirect causes (→ *innen*, → *pratītya-samutpāda*); thus they are devoid of any nontransitory substance and are ultimately "empty" (Jap., *kū*; Skt., *shūnyatā*) and thus *fukatoku*.

Fuke school 🅉 (Chin., P'u-hua-tsung or P'u-hua-ch'an; Jap., Fuke-shū); one of the less important secondary schools of the Chinese Ch'an (Zen) tradition, founded in the ninth century by an eccentric Chinese master, → P'u-hua (Jap., Fuke), a student of → P'an-shan Pao-chi (Jap., Banzan Hōshaku) and "grandson in dharma" of the great Ch'an master → Ma-tsu Tao-i (Jap., Baso Dōitsu). In this school, which does not belong to the → *goke-shichishū*, the chanting of sūtras as a meditative practice is replaced by the playing of a bamboo flute (Jap., *shakuhachi*).

The teachings of the Fuke school were brought to Japan during the Kamakura period by the important Japanese Zen master → Kakushin. Adherents of the school, who were for the most part lay people, made pilgrimages through the country wearing beehive-shaped bamboo hats, which hid their personal identities, and playing *shakuhachi*, the sound of which was to recall the buddha-dharma to the minds of believers. Such pilgrims were called → *kamusō*, "monks of emptiness." Toward the end of the Tokugawa (also called Edo) period, the Fuke school became a refuge for lordless samurai (Jap., *rōnin*), who often misused the pilgrim's hat in their dealings, just for concealment. In the Meiji period this school was officially prohibited.

Fuketsu Enshō 🅉 Jap. for → Feng-hsüeh Yen-chao

Fukyō 🅉 Jap., lit. "sūtra recitation"; Zen expression for the communal recitation of sūtras by monks in a Zen monastery.

Fu-lu 🅃 Chin.; magical talismans used by many schools of religious Taoism (→ *tao-chiao*). According to tradition, the first to use *fu-lu* was → Chang Tao-ling, to whom they were revealed by → Lao-tzu.

Fu-lu are strips of paper, metal, or bamboo, inscribed with lines that resemble Chinese writing, and are said to protect the wearer against illness and ward off demons. The use of such talismans was most widespread in the school of the → *cheng-i tao*.

Originally *fu-lu* were contracts written on small pieces of paper or metal and then split in two, so that each party would hold half of such a contract. The *fu-lu* employed by celestial masters (→ *t'ien-shih*) were magic formulae to guarantee that contracts entered into with deities would be honored. Taoist believers promised the deities to abstain from sinful actions, and the deities in return undertook to ensure that a believer making such a promise does not fall ill. The *fu-lu* symbolized these contracts. Later, however, they

Talisman (*fu-lu*) for establishing contact with spirits and achieving unity.

were used as contracts for all important transactions. According to → Ko Hung the wearing of *fu-lu,* when engaged in a special project such as a search for the draught of longevity, was of paramount importance. Without such a talisman one would be in danger of falling prey to the spirits, and the genies ruling the mountains would conceal the desired substances (herbs or minerals) from the seeker.

Nowadays *fu-lu* are mainly of psychological significance. They are believed to heal sicknesses, facilitate giving birth, and ward off misfortunes and disasters.

Fu-lu p'ai 🅃 Chin., lit. "School of Talismans" (→ *fu-lu*); collective term descriptive of all streams of religious Taoism (→ *tao-chiao*) in which the use of talismans for the purpose of curing illnesses and casting out demons has a central place. Among these movements are the Way of Supreme Peace (→ *t'ai-p'ing tao*), Five-Pecks-of-Rice Taoism (→ *wu-tou-mi tao*), and the Way of Right Unity (→ *cheng-i tao*).

All these schools had their origin in shamanic practices—the veneration of various deities, the use of spells, and the casting out of demons or evil spirits being common features. They were most widespread among the simple people and played an important part in several peasant uprisings.

Fu-mo ta-ti 🅃 → Kuan-ti

Fun'yō Zenshō 🅉 Jap. for → Fen-yang Shan-chao

Furyū-monji 🅉 Jap., lit. "not depending [on sacred] writings"; practitioner's nondependence on sacred writings—a characteristic of Zen.

Fusa 🅉 Jap., roughly "tea for all"; tea offering for the inhabitants of a Zen monastery made by supporters of the monastery.

Fusatsu 🅉 Jap.; Japanese way of reading the Chinese character that translates the Sanskrit word *upavasatha. Fusatsu* is a Buddhist ceremony originated by → Shākyamuni Buddha, held twice monthly in a Zen monastery, in which certain vows (→ *shiguseigan*) are renewed. *Fusatsu* requires confession of violations against Buddhist rules of behavior (→ *jūjūkai*) and acceptance of the → karma resulting from them.

Fusetsu 🅉 Jap., roughly "propagation of the words"; general term for the presentation of Buddhist teachings in a Zen monastery. (Also → *teishō*.)

Fushizen-fushiaku 🅉 Jap., lit. "not thinking good, not thinking bad"; Zen expression for transcending the dualistic worldview in which phenomena are distinguished in terms of "good" and "bad," desirable or repulsive, and judged on that basis. This is a state of mind that can only be actualized through the enlightened experience of the sameness of nature of all phenomena (→ enlightenment; also → *kenshō*, → satori).

The expression *fushizen-fushiako* comes from a famous story of the Ch'an-Zen tradition, which is given as example 23 of the → *Wu-men-kuan*. In it → Hui-neng, the sixth patriarch of Ch'an (Zen) appears. He had received from the fifth patriarch → Hung-jen the "bowl and robe" (→ *den'e*) and had thus been confirmed as his dharma successor (→ *hassu*) and installed as the sixth patriarch. He was pursued by the followers of → Shen-hsiu, who wanted to get these insignia of the patriarchate away from him by force. In the first part of example 23 of the *Wu-men-kuan* we hear further:

"The sixth patriarch was once pursued by the monk Ming to Mount Ta-yü. When the patriarch saw Ming coming, he put the robe and bowl on a rock and said, 'This robe represents faith. It should not be fought over with violence. I leave it to you to take it.'

"Ming immediately tried to pick it up, but it was

heavy like a mountain and could not be moved. Trembling and shaking, Ming said, 'I came to seek the dharma, not to get this robe. Please reveal it to me.'

"The patriarch said, 'Think neither good nor bad. In this moment, what is the primordial face [→ *honrai-no-memmoku*] of Ming the monk?'

"In that moment Ming suddenly experienced profound enlightenment."

Fushō 🅉 Jap., lit. "unborn"; Zen expression for the absolute, the true reality, in which there is no birth, no death, no becoming nor passing away, and no time in the sense of before and after.

Futan-kū 🅉 Jap., lit. "not just emptiness"; the insight that the true nature or buddha-nature (→ *busshō*) of all phenomena is neither existence nor nonexistence, but rather both and yet neither, depending on the viewpoint from which phenomena are regarded. A glimpse of the nondistinctiveness of relative and absolute, which transcends all logical or conceptual comprehension, is provided by the short formula from the *Mahāprajñāpāramitā-hridaya-sūtra* (Jap., *Maka hannyaharamita shingyō*, → *Heart Sutra*), "Form is nothing other than emptiness, emptiness is nothing other than form."

The expression *futan-kū* is used in opposition to *tankū* ("only emptiness"), the term used by Japanese Mahāyāna Buddhism to refer to those Buddhist schools that on the basis of logical analysis affirm the nonexistence of all phenomena and deny their simultaneous existence. The unity of form and emptiness is not something that can be reached by the path of logic (already, just emptiness alone is inconceivable); it can only be experienced in profound → enlightenment.

G

Gaki 🅉 Jap. expression for the "hungry ghosts" (Skt., → *preta*). In Zen monasteries it is customary to make a small food offering to the *gaki* before beginning to eat a meal.

Gakudō Yōjin-shū 🅉 Jap.; a written work of the Japanese Zen master → Dōgen Zenji, in which he put forward ten rules for beginners on the path of Zen.

Gampopa 🄱 (sgam-po-pa), Tib., lit. "man from Gampo," 1079–1153; also known as Dvagpo Lhaje, "Doctor from Dvagpo"; one of the central personalities in the tradition of the → Kagyüpa school. After the early death of his wife, Gampopa became a monk at the age of twenty-six and pursued the teaching of the → Kadampa school. Seeking for further instruction, he heard the name → Milarepa, found the latter and finally received from him the transmission of the → *mahāmudrā* teachings. After the death of Milarepa, Gampopa founded the monastic tradition of the Kagyüpa. In his most important work, *The Jewel Ornament of Liberation* (→ *lamrim*), he brought together the teachings of the Kagyüpa and Kadampa "as two streams flow into one."

Ganapati 🄷 Skt. → Ganesha

Ganda-vyūha 🄱 (Gaṇḍa-vyūha), Skt., lit. the cone shaped elevation on the crown of the Buddha's head; an independent part of the → *Buddhāvatamsaka-sūtra.* Said to have been taught by Buddha → Shakyamuni in Shravasti, this scripture is an account of the pilgrimage of young Sudhana, who is guided on his way to enlightenment by the bodhisattva → Manjushri and who requests the advice about his religious practice from fifty-three persons, including the imminent buddha → Maitreya. Finally he meets → Samantabhadra, through whose teaching he attains enlightenment and experiences reality. The last chapter concerns the vows of Samantabhadra, which constitute the basis of the life of a → bodhisattva and which comprise a fundamental text of the → Hua-yen (→ Kegon) school.

Gandhāra 🄱 the region in the extreme northwest of India, today including southern Afghanistan and parts of Pakistan, one of the greatest centers of Buddhist art and culture. During the first half of the 2d century C.E., the first depictions of the Buddha appeared here. These reflected the Mahāyāna view of the Buddha as embodiment of the absolute principle of existence, the personification of wisdom and kindness.

The art of Gandhāra, which was strongly influenced by eastern Roman art, reached its pinnacle between 130–50 and 430–50 C.E. It is characterized by an idealized style of representing the human form. In the course of its development a progressive spiritualization and formal abstraction can be detected. Of numerous monasteries—evidence that Buddhism was deeply rooted in the population—for the most part only the foundations are preserved. Most of the monasteries were probably destroyed in invasions by alien peoples in the 5th century. By the 7th century, according to accounts by the Chinese pilgrim → Hsüan-tsang, Buddhism in Gandhāra was extinct.

In contrast to the beginnings of Buddhist art, in Gandhāra Buddha was depicted as a person. Most depictions are in reliefs that illustrate his biography and the → *Jātaka* tales. He appears as a yogi in perfect physical and mental equilibrium. Sometimes he is also represented as a teacher, but always without action and inward-turned. Still other images showing the Buddha during his ascetic period, emaciated down to the skeleton, are starkly realistic. In Gandhāra a systematic symbology had already been elaborated. The representations show the typical posture of the hands (→ mudrā) and the marks of a buddha: short locks of hair curled to the right or a hair knotted in a snail shape, (i.e., the *ūrnā* and *ushnīsha*, → *dvātrimsha-dvara-lakshana)*.

Typical of Gandhāran art is the manner of representing the detail of Buddha's robe. In the early phase, the robe was shown as a calm, even flow of folds and smooth forms; later it took on a cool, graphic regularity that covered the body with an ornamental network of lines; finally the representation of the robe is reduced to engraved double lines.

Gandharva **H** **B** Skt.; the celestial *gandharva* of the Hindu Vedas is a deity who knows and reveals the secrets of the celestial and divine truth. He is a personification of the light of the sun. His task is to prepare the celestial soma drink for the gods. In later representations the *gandharvas* were a race of demigods—singers and musicians who took part in the banquets of the gods. It is in the latter sense that the concept is used in Buddhism.

Gandhi **H**, Mohandas Karamchand, called Mahātmā (Skt., "great soul"), 1869–1948, leader of the Indian movement for independence. His program of nonviolent resistance against discriminatory laws and above all against British colonial rule was based on the concepts of → *satyāgraha* (Skt., "holding fast to truth") and → *ahimsa* (Skt., "noninjury," i.e., nonviolence). In the Satyāgraha campaigns of 1920–22 and 1930–32, he called for a refusal on the part of his Indian countrymen to participate in the administration of British India and for passive resistance against the government. He was subsequently sentenced repeatedly to long periods of imprisonment. His ascetic mode of life, his unprejudiced intercession for the "untouchables" (pariahs) and for recognition of the ethical value of other religions (e.g., by study of Christ's Sermon on the Mount and Tolstoy's teachings) proved exemplary in bringing about a deepening reorientation of Hinduism and peaceful coexistence with the followers of Islam. On January 30, 1948, fatally injured by a shot from the gun of a Hindu fanatic, he sank to the ground with the words "O Rāma!"

Gandhi was born in Porbandar, on the Kathiawar Peninsula in Gujarat and belonged to the *vaishya*, or merchant, caste (the word *gandhi* means "shopkeeper, greengrocer"). He studied French, Latin, physics, and law in London from 1888 to 1891, and returned to India to establish himself as a lawyer. In 1893, he moved to South Africa, where he became a political leader of the India immigrant population. There his nonviolent battle against the British began. Back in India in 1914, Gandhi carried on this war, using every peaceful means possible from Hindu teachings to the point of total self-sacrifice, until in 1947 India became independent, albeit at the cost of the division of India and Pakistan, a move that Gandhi could not prevent.

Ganesha **H** (Gaṇeśa), or Ganapati, Skt.; son of → Shiva and → Pārvatī; god of wisdom and remover of all obstacles; he vouchsafes success on the secular as well as the spiritual plane. Many → *pūjās* begin with the veneration of Ganesha. His majesty is celebrated in the *Ganesha-Purāna.*

Ganesha is depicted as a small, squat yellow god with a prominent belly. He has four arms and an elephant's head, but only a single tusk. In one hand he holds a conch, in the second a disk, in the third a mace, and in the fourth a water lily. His steed is a rat.

Regarding his elephant head, the following legend (one of many) is related: His mother, Pārvatī, proud of her son, asked Shani (god of the planets) to look upon him, but she had forgotten about the effect of Shani's gaze. As Shani turned to regard the child, Ganesha's head burned to ashes. Responding to Pārvatī's distress, Brahmā advised her to replace the head with the first one she could find, which turned out to be that of an elephant. This legend and others regarding Ganesha and the loss of his tusk are told in the *Brahmā-Vaivarta-Purāna.*

Ganesha-Gītā **H** (Gaṇeśa-Gītā), Skt., a version of the *Bhagavad-Gītā* in which Krishna's name is replaced by that of → Ganesha. The text is

Ganesha. (Statue from Madras)

used by the Ganapatyas, a small sect that worships Ganesha, or Ganapati, as its chief deity.

Gangā 🅷 the river Ganges, which originates in the Himalayas at Gangotri and flows into the Bay of Bengal. It is as sacred to Hindus as is the Jordan river to Christians. A sip of Ganges water is often administered to the dying. Ganges water is also employed in every → *pūjā.*

In the *Rigveda,* the Ganges is mentioned only twice. According to the Purānas, Viyadgangā, the heavenly Ganges, sprang from Vishnu's foot and declared that she had been called from Heaven by the prayers of the great sage Bhāgīratha; hence she is also called Bhāgīrathī. Gangā was annoyed at having to leave heaven; to protect the earth from the impact of her fall, Shiva caught the falling river in his eyebrows and directed its course through his hair. For this deed he received the name Gangā-Dhara (lit. "holding the Ganges").

Ganjin 🅱 Jap. for → Chien-chen

Gantō Zenkatsu 🆉 Jap. for → Yen-t'ou Chüan-huo

Gārhapatya-Agni 🅷 Skt., lit. "householder fire"; the divine spark in man that is symbolically kindled by the householder by freeing the fire that is trapped in wood; the first of three sacred fires (the "circular" fire), it is kindled by the householder during sacrificial rites.

Garuda 🅷 🅱 (garuḍa), Skt.; a mythical bird, half man, half bird.

🅷 Garuda is the king of the birds, Vishnu's steed, and the archenemy of serpents. He inherited this last-named characteristic from his mother, who had fallen out with her neighbor Kadru, the mother of snakes. Garuda is depicted with the head, tail, and wings of an eagle and the torso and legs of a man. His face is white, his wings red, and his body golden. He is said to have stolen → *amrita* from the gods to ransom his mother's freedom from Kadru. → Indra discovered the theft and fought with Garuda. The *amrita* was won back, but Indra was vanquished and his thunderbolt shattered in the process.

🅱 In Buddhism *garuda* is occasionally used as a synonym for Buddha; in representations of the *dhyāni buddha* → Amoghasiddhi, *garuda* sometimes appears as his vehicle.

Gasshō 🆉 Jap., lit. "palms of the hands placed together"; Zen expression for the ancient gesture of greeting, request, gratitude, veneration, or supplication common in many cultures (particularly in the East).

In this gesture of "palms of the hands placed together" a state of mind is spontaneously manifested that suggests the unity of the antithetical forces of the phenomenal world.

Gāthā 🅱 → sūtra

Gati 🅱 🆉 Skt., Pali, lit. "mode of existence"; refers to the various forms of existence within which rebirth takes place and which constitute → samsāra. Three good, or higher, and three bad, or lower, modes of existence are distinguished. The good ones are humans, gods (→ *deva*), and the → *asuras*; the bad are animals, hungry ghosts (→ *preta*), and hell beings (→ *naraka*). These modes of existence are displayed in the three worlds or realms (→ *triloka*).

These three worlds are the worlds of desire, where the activity of the six lowest classes of gods and of humans and animals takes place; the world of desireless embodiment or "pure form," with seventeen types of gods; and the world of bodilessness or formlessness with four classes of *devas.* Between the various forms of existence there is no essential difference, only a karmic difference of degree. In none of them is life without limits. However, it is only as a human that one can attain enlightenment. For this reason Buddhism esteems the human mode of existence more highly than that of the gods and speaks in this context of the "precious human body." Incarnation as a human being is regarded as a rare opportunity in the cycle of a samsāra to escape this cycle and as a challenge and obligation to perceive this opportunity and strive toward liberation (→ *bodhi*, → enlightenment).

Gatsurin Shikan Z Jap. for → Yüeh-lin Shih-kuan

Gaudapāda H , a profound Advaitin (→ Advaita-Vedānta). He became well known through his commentary (→ *kārikā*) on the → *Māndūkya-Upanishad.*

Gaudapāda's Kārikā is divided into four sections. The first part is essentially a paraphrase of the Upanishad. The second part, Vaitathya (Skt., "untruth"), describes the untruth of empirical reality and the theories associated with it. The third part, Advaita, discusses nonduality and the identity of → *jīva* and *ātman.* The fourth part, Alātashānti (Skt., lit. *alāta:* "firebrand," *shānti:* "cessation"), points to the contradictions inherent in the concepts of causality. Just as a torch swung around creates the appearance of a fiery circle even though the flame itself does not change, so we project the manifest world with our thoughts. If the process of thinking ceases (i.e., if the "firebrand" is extinguished) only one point remains: pure consciousness, the realization of which is enlightenment itself.

Gaurānga H Skt. → Chaitanya

Gautama H → Gotama

Gautama Siddharta B → Siddharta Gautama

Gavishthira H (Gaviṣṭhira), Skt., lit. "steadfast in the light of illumination," from *gavishtha:* "sun"); a designation for the ancient → *rishis.*

Gayā H city in the North Indian state of Bihar, one of the seven sacred cities; a celebrated place of pilgrimage, which, however, has diminished in importance. Its temple, Vishnupāda, is dedicated to the lotus feet of Vishnu. As a sacred Buddhist site it is called Bodh-Gayā.

Gāyatrī H Skt.; 1. a meter of 3 x 8 syllables; 2. one of the most sacred verses of the *Rigveda,* an important mantra. The Gāyatrī calls upon the sun as → Sāvitrī, the begetter, and hence is also called Sāvitrī. Personified as a goddess, Sāvitrī is the wife of Brahmā and the mother of the four → Vedas as well as of those who are "twice-born" (i.e., members of the three upper castes of Hindu society). Of the various translations of the Gāyatrī, one of the most familiar is the following: "Let us meditate on the brilliant light of that one who is worthy of worship and who has created all worlds! May he direct our minds to the truth!" Hindus of the upper three castes are expected to recite this prayer thrice daily. Gāyatrī is also the name of the goddess who presides over this mantra.

Ge-Ango Z Jap. → ango

Gedatsu Z Jap., lit. "release, liberation"; 1. the liberation the experiencing of which is the goal of all Buddhists and all meditative training in Buddhism. *Gedatsu* is also used as a synonym for → enlightenment. 2. Another expression for meditative practice (→ *zazen*), since liberation is actualized through meditation. (Also → *dai-gedatsu.*)

Gedō Z Jap., lit. "outside way"; non-Buddhist religion or philosophy. (Also → five types of Zen 2.)

Gedō Zen Z Jap., → five types of Zen 2

Gelugpa B (dgelugs-pa), Tib., roughly "school of the virtuous"; the last to be established of the four main schools of Tibetan Buddhism, founded by → Tsongkhapa. This doctrinal tradition, pursuant to that of the Kadampa, lays particular emphasis on the observation of monastic rules (→ Vinaya-pitaka) and thorough study of authoritative texts. Principal among these is the literature on the stages of the path (→ *lam-rim*) and the systematic works on the various Buddhist doctrinal views (→ Siddhānta). Since the installation of the dalai lamas as heads of state in the 17th century, the Gelugpas have held political leadership.

The doctrinal system of the Gelugpas is based on the writings of Tsongkhapa and his two main disciples Gyaltshab (1364–1432) and Khedrub (1385–1483). After having had a vision of → Mañjushrī, Tsongkhapa formulated in voluminous commentaries the → Mādhyamika view that is regarded as authoritative for his school. In the meditation manuals composed by him, it is described in great detail how to arrive at this insight. Besides basic contemplations of the inadequacy of the cycle of existence (→ samsāra), the arousing of the mind of enlightenment (→ *bodhicitta*) is given a preeminent position. Only after having aroused *bodhicitta* can insight into the true reality of phenomena be gained.

Thus the actual spiritual practice consists in achieving concentration (→ *samādhi*). In his writings Tsongkhapa incisively demonstrated how this goal may be reached through the differentiated states of equilibrium of dwelling in tranquility (→ *shamatha*) and through special insight (→ *vipashyanā*). Also the teachings of the → Tantras are regarded by the Gelugpas as a special technique for the realization of this state of equilibrium.

Gematsu 🅩 Jap., lit. "end of summer"; the end of the → *ango*, the summer period of intensive training in a Zen monastery (→ *tera*).

Genjō-Kōan 🅩 Jap., roughly "*Enlightenment Appears in Everyday Life*" or "*Everyday Life is Enlightenment*"; a writing of the Japanese Zen master → Dōgen Zenji, which became a chapter in the → *Shōbō-genzō*. This text, which concerns the connection between practice (→ *zazen*) and → enlightenment, is one of the most important writings of the → Sōtō school of Japan. An English translation with commentary by a modern Japanese Zen master is Maezumi 1978.

Genkan 🅩 Jap., lit. "secret gate"; 1. entry; entry into Buddhism, setting out on the path of → enlightenment as shown by the various styles of training. 2. The entrance gate to the guest rooms (*tanga-ryō*) in a Zen monastery or the foyer at the entrance to the monastery; the entryway between the outside door and the living quarters of a Japanese house, corresponding roughly to our vestibule, though usually without door or wall separating it from the open foyer set one step higher.

Gensha-Shibi 🅩 Jap. for → Hsüan-sha Shih-pei

Genzen sambō 🅩 Jap., → *sambō*

Gesar 🅑 (Ge-sar), Tib., lit. "Lotus Temple." Name of a mythical hero who inspired the greatest epic of Tibetan Buddhism. This epic was diffused in the form of folk tales as far as Mongolia and was transmitted by professional singers or bards. The eastern Tibetan kingdom of Ling is given as the homeland of Gesar. The Gesar legends arose in the 11th century. At this time Buddhism began to prevail in the belief of the people over the → *Bön* religion and the main theme of the epic is the battle of Gesar against evil (i.e., *bön*). In these conflicts on behalf of the qualities of Buddhism Gesar is regarded as the embodiment of → Avalokiteshvara and of → Padmasambhava and his heros as incarnations of the → *mahāsiddhas*. Today Gesar is venerated as a warrior god and a god of wealth, and his consort as a → *dākinī*.

Following the style of spiritual songs, as composed, for example, by → Milarepa and → Drugpa Künleg, traveling singers transmitted the early, oral versions of the epic. The later legends surrounding the figure of Gesar arose as a rule on the basis of visions and revelations of Tibetan monks (→ lamas) of all schools.

The epic is divided into two main parts: the unhappy youth of the hero, who was despised by all, and his reign as mighty King Gesar. His special qualities single him out as the son of a god who is to bring order to the world once again. After his birth, nonetheless, he was exiled along with his mother and brought this exile to an end only at the age of fifteen. In a horse race, the winner of which was to become king of Ling, against all expectations he defeated his principal foe Khrothung, became king of Ling and received the former king's daughter Brugmo as his wife. Following this are battles against various demons. The last and most important episode is the conquest and conversion of the land of Hor.

All the legends composed in later generations were based on this episode. In these later legends Gesar converted countries like Iran and China, even descended into hell to confront the god of death, and in a version that first appeared in the twentieth century, conquered the land of Jar (i.e., Germany).

Based on the numerous legends, a cult of Gesar developed in Tibet, which produced a rich iconography. Temples were built, and offerings made, to Gesar as a warrior god. As a subduer of demonic powers, Gesar played a role comparable to that of Padmasambhava. As the bringer of future salvation, Gesar is associated with the kingdom of → Shambhala.

Getsurin-Shikan 🅩 Jap. for → Yüeh-lin Shih-kuan

Gettan Zenka 🅩 Jap. for → Yüeh-an Shan-kuo

Geza 🅩 Jap., lit. "summer sitting"; another term for → *ango*, the summer training period in a Zen monastery (→ *tera*).

Ghāt 🅗 Hindi; a place, usually provided with steps, where people can walk down to a body of water, primarily to bathe but also to wash clothes; certain of these are reserved for cremation ceremonies, so that the participants have access to water for cleansing themselves and for the scattering of the ashes.

Ghatākāsha 🅗 (Ghatākāśa), Skt., lit. *ghata:* "pot," *ākāsha*: "space"; the space contained by a pot. The example of the pot, which separates the inner, limited space from the outer, unlimited space, is frequently cited in philosophical expositions, as in explaining the distinction between the → *jīvātman* (i.e., the → *ātman* limited by a body) and the pure, unlimited *ātman*, which is identical with → *brahman*.

Ghrita 🅗 (Ghṛta), Skt., lit. "clarified butter"; Ghrita is used to fuel the butter lamps in → *pūjā* ceremonies. It is a symbol for clarity of mind and illumination. The threefold clarity represented by *ghrita* is that of → Indra, → sūrya, and → *soma*. It is the light of knowledge become form. Indra frees the divine light from dynamic mentality, Sūrya frees it from purely reflective mentality, and *soma* liberates it from attachment to the senses.

Gikū ▣ Jap. for → I-k'ung

Gītā ▣ Skt.; song; almost always used to refer to the → *Bhagavad-Gītā,* but there are also other important song-poems in Sanskrit literature, e.g., the *Avadhūt-Gītā,* the *Ashtāvakrā-Gītā,*, and the *Ganesha-Gītā.*

Gītagovinda ▣ Skt.; a lyrical poem in twelve cantos by Jayadeva (early twelfth century), the court poet of the Bengali king Lakshmanasena. The work celebrates Krishna's youth as Govinda, the shepherd boy in the forest of → Vrindāvan, and the love between Krishna and → Rādhā, who symbolizes the ardent love of the human soul for the divine (→ *bhakti*). The work is still performed today as a melodrama.

Go ▣ Skt.; 1. the cow, revered by Hindus as the granter of life; also, cow in general; 2. stars, rays; 3. earth.

Gō ▣ ▣ Jap. for → karma

Godō ▣ Jap., lit. "back hall"; 1. one of two sections of the meditation hall in a Japanese monastery. 2. The elder monk under whose supervision the *godō* section of the meditation hall is placed; in the → Sōtō school, the elder monk to whose charge supervision of the → zendō falls; the *godō* corresponds to the → *jikijitsu* in the → Rinzai school.

Gohō Jōkan ▣ Jap. for → Wu-feng Ch'ang-kuan

Go-i ▣ Jap., → five degrees (of enlightenment)

Goke-shichishū ▣ Jap., lit. "five houses–seven schools"; general term for the seven schools of Ch'an (Zen) during the T'ang period; these stemmed from five lineages ("houses" or "families").

The five houses and their founders are (1) the → Rinzai school of → Lin-chi I-hsüan (Jap., Rinzai Gigen); (2) the → Igyō school of → Kuei-shan Ling-yu (Jap., Isan Reiyū) and → Yang-shan Hui-chi (Jap., Kyōzan Ejaku); (3) the → Sōtō school of → Tung-shan Liang-chieh (Jap., Tōzan Ryōkai) and → Ts'ao-shan Pen-chi (Jap.,Sōzan Honjaku); (4) the → Ummon school of → Yu-men Wen-yen (Jap., Ummon Bun'en); and (5) the → Hōgen school of → Fa-yen Wen-i (Jap., Hōgen Bun'eki).

The seven schools are the above-mentioned five houses plus the two further schools into which the Rinzai school split after → Shi-shuang Ch'u-yüan. These two are (6) the → Yōgi school of → Yang-ch'i Fang-hui (Jap., Yōgi Hōe) and (7) the → Ōryō school of → Huang-lung Hui-nan (Jap., Ōryō E'nan). (See also the Ch'an/Zen Lineage Chart.)

Gokoku Keigen ▣ Jap. for → Hu-kuo Ching-yüan

Gokulika ▣ Skt. → Hīnayāna, → Mahāsānghika

Golden elixir ▣ → *chin-tan*

Goloka ▣ Skt., lit. 1. "place of cows"; 2. "heaven," especially Krishna's heaven; a later addition to the original seven → *lokas,* the → Vaishnava concept of a realm of eternal beauty and bliss; also, the eternal home of → Vishnu.

Gomati ▣ Skt., lit. "full of light"; a description of the dawn (also in the sense of a mental or spiritual dawning) as full of light; spiritually interpreted, the fullness of illumination.

Gomi(-no)-zen ▣ Jap., lit. "Zen of the five types of taste"; the five types of meditative practice in the sense of the → five types of Zen. The expression *gomi-zen* is used as the opposite of → *ichimi-zen.*

Gonkyū ▣ Jap., lit. "elder who has served"; an elder monk in a Zen monastery or a Zen master who has already led students on the way of Zen for many years and has retired from his activity as → *rōshi.*

Gonsen-kōan ▣ Jap. → kōan

Gopāla ▣ Skt., lit. "cowherd," a name for young Krishna, who as a youth lived among the cowherds in → Vrindāvan. Gopāla is often the chosen deity (→ *ishta-deva*) for those spiritual aspirants who take up the fourth of five possible emotional attitudes (→ *bhāva*) of a *bhakta* to God, i.e., the love that parents feel for their child (→ *vātsalya*).

Gopīs ▣ Skt., lit. "cowherdesses"; the milkmaids of → Vrindāvan, playmates and devotees of Krishna, particularly → Rādhā. They are models for, and symbols of, the soul's intense love of God.

Gorakh ▣ , a tenth-century prophet, a Tantric saint who founded his own sect and whose adherents call themselves Kaupatta yogis. Many have taken the name Gorakh.

Goroku ▣ (Chin., *yü-lu*), lit. "record of words";

collection of the instructions, discourses, and sayings of a Zen master. The title of the work is usually formed by adding-*goroku* or the short form-*roku* to the name of the master.

Gosan 🅉 also *gozan*, Jap. (Chin., Wu-shan), lit. "five mountains"; the Wu-shan in China was a league, institutionalized by the Sung emperor Ning-tsung, of the five most important Ch'an (Zen) monasteries in the cities Hang-chou and Ming-chou. This became the model for similar leagues of the most important Zen monasteries of the → Rinzai school in Kyōto and Kamakura. In the middle ages these became important centers of art and culture in Japan.

The following Zen monasteries belonged to the *gosan* of Kamakura: Kenchō-ji, Engaku-ji, Jufuku-ji, Jōchi-hi, and Jōmyō-ji. The *gosan* of Kyōto is comprised of Tenryū-ji, Shōkoku-ji, Kennin-ji, Tōfuku-ji, and Manju-ji. Nanzen-ji, another important Zen monastery in Kyōto, was partly under the jurisdiction of the *gosan* of Kyōto.

The word *mountain* (Chin., *shan*; Jap., *san* or *zan*) means in this context Ch'an or Zen monastery (in ancient times such monasteries were generally built on mountains). The names of the mountains were often given to the monasteries as well as to the ancient Ch'an or Zen masters.

Gosan-bungaku 🅉 Jap., lit. "Five Mountain Literature"; blanket term for the writings of the Zen masters of the five leading Zen monasteries (→ *gosan*) of Kyōto during the Ashikaga (or Muromachi) period (1338–1573). The founders of the Gosan-bungaku are considered to be the Chinese Ch'an (Zen) master → I-shan I-ning, who came to Japan in 1299, and his Japanese student → Sesson Yūbai. The best-known authors of the Five Mountain Literature were the genius → Musō Soseki—who, like I-shan I-ning, was not only an important Zen master but also an outstanding artist—and Zen masters Gen'e (1269–1352), Shūshin (1321–88), and Zekkai Chūshin (1336–1405), a student of Musō Soseki.

These authors particularly cultivated the Chinese art of poetry and neo-Confucian philosophy; they also contributed a great deal to the transfer of Chinese science and art to Japan. Some of them became known as painters and masters of the way of calligraphy (→ *shōdō*). Particularly Musō Soseki, through his writings, composed in simple, easily understood Japanese, contributed to the diffusion of this literature in Japan.

Goseki 🅉 Jap., lit. "trace of enlightenment"; in Zen it is said that profound → enlightenments leaves no traces behind. Of someone whose behavior suggests that he has experienced enlightenment, it is said thae he shows "traces of enlightenment," or, in the drastic style of expression so typical of Zen, that he "stinks of enlightenment." Only after the "stink" has fully settled and a person lives what he has experienced of enlightenment in a completely natural way—without being aware of being "enlightened" or giving any outward signs of it—only then in Zen is the authenticity of his enlightenment acknowledged.

Goso Hōen 🅉 Jap. for → Wu-tsu Fa-yen

Gosvāmī 🄷 Skt.; → Vaishnava priest. The *gosvāmīs* are brahmans and descendants of → Nityānanda, the companion of → Chaitanya.

Gotama 🄷, or Gautama or Satānanda, founder of the → Nyāya school (one of the six → *darshanas*) and author of an important Hindu law book (→ Dharma-Shāstra), whose twelve volumes discuss creation, transmigration, and liberation, and contain detailed instructions for the duties of each social class.

Gottan Funei 🅉 Jap. for → Wu-an P'u-ning

Govinda 🄷 Skt.; 1. a frequent term of address for Krishna, referring to his role as knower of earth and the senses and as protector of cows (*go:* "cow," but also "earth"); 2. a name for Vishnu, of whom Krishna is one incarnation (→ *avatāra*).

Govinda 🄱 Lama Anāgārika, 1898–1985; Buddhist scholar of German origin who was particularly engaged with the theory and practice of → Tibetan Buddhism (→ Vajrayāna). His books, translated into many Western languages, contributed to the diffusion of Buddhist thought in the West. Among his best-known publications are a personal account of his travels in Tibet (*The Way of the White Clouds*) and an introduction to the teachings of Vajrayāna (*The Foundations of Tibetan Mysticism*). Lama Govinda founded in the West the Buddhist order Ārya Maitreya Mandala.

Gozu school 🅉 (Chin. Niu-t'ou-tsung or Niu t'ou-ch'an; Jap. Gozu-shū); a secondary lineage of Chinese Ch'an (→ Zen), which does not belong to the traditional Zen schools (→ Goke-shichishu) in China. It derives from Master → Fa-jung (Jap. Hōyū), also known as Niu-t'ou (Jap. Gozu), a student of → Tao-hsin, the fourth patriarch of Zen in China. The school declined during the Song dynasty.

Granthi 🄷 Skt., lit. "knots"; the entanglements

of subtle nerve forces in the psycho-physical system that block the free flow of spiritual forces in the human being. These knots, which arise through ties to the lower elements of our being, create desires, passions, selfishness, etc.; they can be overcome only with the aid of spiritual exercises.

Great Vehicle 🅑 → Mahāyāna

Gridhrakūta 🅑 🅩 Skt. → Vulture Peak Mountain

Grihastha 🅗 (Gṛhastha), or Garhasthya, Skt., lit. "householder"; the second life-stage (→ *āshrama*) of a Hindu, that requiring marriage and a family. In Hinduism, marriage is a spiritual exercise wherein one not only expands one's consciousness but simultaneously learns a lesson in self-control.

Almost all known Hindu gods are represented as married. Children are regarded as a blessing, for they are the link between the living and the dead and guarantee the continuation of the culture of one's race. The householder maintains his connection to God through prescribed ritual (→ *Grihya-Sūtra*). He must fulfill his duty to his family, his society, and his nation according to his → *dharma*, the result of his caste (→ *varna*) and social position.

Grihya-Sūtra 🅗 (Gṛhya-Sūtra), Skt.; rules for home ritual and personal duties from birth to death. The best-known *Grihya-Sūtra* is that compiled by Gobhila.

Gritsamada 🅗 (Gṛtsamada), Skt.; a well-known → *rishi*; the chief author of *Rigveda II*, he is mentioned in many hymns in the *Rigveda*.

According to the *Vishnu-Purāna*, Gritsamada was a → *kshatriya* and a son of Sunahotra. In the *Mahābhārata* he is described as the son of Vītahavya, king of the Haihayas, who was a *kshatriya* but later became a *brahman*.

Gudakesha 🅗 (Guḍakeśa), Skt., lit. "he with the tuft of hair"; an epithet for → Arjuna, who is often addressed by this name in the *Bhagavad-Gītā*.

Gufu-shogyō-zen 🅩 Jap., lit. "fool's Zen"; Zen expression for the style of meditation in which one thinks about orthodox doctrinal ideas (for example, impermanence, egolessness, emptiness, etc.). Zen distinguishes true Zen practice (→ *zazen*) from this conventional style of meditation, ruling out preoccupation with religious notions, however holy they may be, in order to free the mind from dependence on thinking.

Guha 🅗 Skt., lit. "attacker"; 1. an epithet for → Skanda, the god of war; 2. an epithet for → Shiva; 3. a king of the Nishadhas and a friend of → Rāma.

Guna 🅗 (Guṇa), Skt., lit. "fundamental quality"; all objects of the manifest world (→ *prakriti*) are structurally composed of the three *gunas*: *sattva*, *rajas*, and *tamas*. As qualities of → *māyā*, the *trigunas* are dependent on → *brahman*, but veil the reality of *brahman*. If they are fully in balance, nothing appears—neither manifestation nor creation. Once this balance is disturbed, however, the creation appears. In the physical world, *sattva* embodies what is pure and subtle (e.g., sunlight), *rajas* embodies activity (e.g., a volcano), and *tamas* embodies heaviness and immobility (e.g., a block of granite).

From the point of view of human development, *sattva* is the nature of that which must be realized; *tamas* is the obstacle that opposes this realization; and *rajas* is the force that overcomes *tamas*. In terms of human consciousness, *sattva* is expressed as peace and serenity; *rajas* as activity, passion, and restlessness; and *tamas* as laziness, lack of interest, and stupidity. A person's character and mood are determined at any given time by the dominant *guna*. The spiritual aspirant must overcome *tamas* with *rajas* and *rajas* with *sattva*. For the realization of the → *ātman*, even *sattva* must be overcome. The → Vedānta refers to the *gunas* as "three thieves," a reference to the following story: Three thieves fell upon a merchant who was on his way home and robbed him. *Tamas* wanted to kill the merchant in order to destroy any trace of the crime. The other two hesitated, and *Rajas* said, "Lets's tie him to a tree. Whether or not he is found will depend on his *karma*." They bound him to a tree and hurried away. After a while, *Sattva* returned and cut the ropes. The merchant was overjoyed. "You've saved my life," he said. "Come back to the village with me and I'll reward you." "No, that won't do," replied *Sattva*. "The police know me to be a thief. The only thing I could do was to release you from your bonds."

Gunātīta 🅗 (Guṇātīta), or Trigunātīta, Skt., lit. "having transcended the *gunas*"; the three *(tri)* → *gunas* are the fundamental qualities of the manifest world (→ *prakriti*). One who has freed himself from the *gunas* has overcome the material world and realized *brahman*, and has thereby attained liberation (→ *moksha*), the goal of all spiritual aspirants in Hinduism.

Gunin 🅩 Jap. for → Hung-jen

Gupta 🅗 350-650 C.E., a dynasty of kings who governed Māgadha and under whose rule many temples were built. Art historians refer to this time as the Gupta period.

Guru 🅗 🅑 Skt.; teacher, particularly a spiritual

master. The Hindu tradition speaks of four stages of the guru principle: (1) parents, who provide us with this body and acquaint us with life and its problems; (2) the worldly teacher of school and university, the master of a craft, and all others who concern themselves with our education; (3) the spiritual master, who knows the way, explains to us the sense and purpose of life and the way to self-realization and also shows its dangers and obstacles; (4) the cosmic guru (→ *avatāra)* to which the spiritual master leads us and which as divine incarnation is fully enlightened.

Two questions are constantly asked about the guru: (1) whether a guru is necessary on the spiritual path and (2) what the meaning is of the unconditional obedience that one is supposed to show towards the guru. In response to the first question, the Indian teachers often give a very simple example. When you come to a strange city and want to find a particular street, there are two ways to do it: either you can try all the streets until you come to the one you are looking for, which, if you are unlucky, will be the last; or you can ask a native. He will show you the shortest way to the place you are seeking. A guru is a native who is in every way familiar with the realm of spirituality. Moreover the scriptures assure us that, from a certain point on, one's own self becomes the guru and takes over the guiding role. For this there is a word in Sanskrit, *antaryāmin,* lit. "inner leader."

As far as obedience to the guru is concerned, it is senseless if it is practiced from a sense of obligation against one's will. If one has the right relationship to the guru and trusts him completely, one will obey him out of trust and love, even when one does not immediately grasp the sense of his instruction.

Gurubhāva 🅷 Skt.; the spiritual power of a guru, which is effective only when a disciple is receptive.

Gurudeva 🅷 Skt.; 1. the highest level of guru, that of a divine incarnation (→ *avatāra*); 2. a name for God.

Gurukripā 🅷 (Gurukṛpā), Skt.; the mercy *(kripā)* of the guru, showered upon a chosen pupil.

Gurumantra 🅷 Skt.; a → mantra conferred by the guru during initiation; the student is asked to repeat it continually but to keep it a secret.

Guru Rinpoche 🅱 → Padmasambhava

Gutei 🆉 Japanese for → Chü-chih

Gyō-jū-za-ga 🆉 Jap., lit. "walking-sitting-lying"; an expression betokening that Zen practice should be maintained uninterrupted throughout all the business of daily life.

Gyō-jū-za-ga means the undivided attention, or mindfulness, that the Zen practitioner should devote to all his activities. The following famous anecdote form the life of the Japanese Zen master → Ikkyū Sōjun makes clear what fundamental importance the practice of mindfulness has in Zen:

One day a man of the people said to Zen Master Ikkyū, "Master, will you please write for me some maxims of the highest wisdom?"

Ikkyū immediately took his brush and wrote the word: "attention."

"Is that all?" asked the man. "Will you not add something more?"

Ikkyū then wrote twice running: "Attention. Attention."

"Well," remarked the man rather irritably, "I really don't see much depth or subtlety in what you have just written."

Then Ikkyū wrote the same word three times running: "Attention. Attention. Attention."

Half-angered, the man demanded: "What does that word attention mean anyway?"

And Ikkyū answered gently: "Attention means attention." (Kapleau 1980, pp.10–11)

Gyōrin 🆉 Jap. → *mokugyō*

Gyulü 🅱 (sgyu lus) Tib., lit. "illusion body"; in the → Vajrayāna the notion of a refined body that exists beyond the five aggregates (→ *skandha*), yet at the same time lies within them. As part of the → *Naro chödrug* and other Tantric traditions, it refers especially to a particular meditation technique with the help of which the ordinary body can be purified to the state of buddhahood.

H

Ha 🅷 Skt. → Hatha-Yoga

Hachi 🆉 Jap. → *jihatsu*

Haiku 🅉 Jap.; a sixteen-syllable Japanese poetic form with the syllable sequence 5–7–5. Matsuo Bashō (1644–94) is considered the greatest Japanese haiku poet and the founder of the classical art of haiku. He was an adherent of Zen and practiced → zazen under the guidance of Master Bu'cho (1643–1715). His best haiku, which became models for all later haiku poets, are permeated with the mind of Zen and express the nondualistic experience of Zen.

Hakuin Zenji 🅉 also Hakuin Ekaku (1689–1769), one of the most important Japanese Zen masters of the → Rinzai school. He is often referred to as the father of modern Rinzai Zen, since he gave new impetus to the Rinzai school—which had been gradually deteriorating since the 14th century—and reformed it. He systematized kōan training and emphasized once again the importance of → *zazen*, the practice of which had been more and more eclipsed by intellectual preoccupation with Zen writings. In his famous praise of *zazen* (→ *Hakuin Zenji zazen-wasan*), he extolls the importance of "sitting in meditation" for the actualization of → enlightenment, which is the goal of the way of Zen (also → *mujōdō-nō-taigen*). Hakuin's → *sekishu*, "What is the sound of one hand clapping?" is the best-known kōan stemming from a Japanese master. The ingenious Hakuin Zenji was not only an outstanding Zen master, but also an important painter, master of calligraphy (→ *shōdō*), and sculptor. His ink paintings are among the most renowned works of Zen painting.

At the age of seven or eight Hakuin visited a Buddhist temple with his mother. He heard a discourse by the temple priest in which the torments of hell beings as described in a sūtra were so graphically presented that young Hakuin could not shake off the horrifying vision of hell. He resolved to become a monk and to come to the state of a man whom "fire could not burn and water could not drown." His parents opposed his aspiration to become a monk, but at fifteen he left home and entered a monastery. There day and night he recited sūtras and venerated the buddhas. At nineteen he read the story of the great Chinese Ch'an (Zen) master → Yen-t'ou Ch'üan-huo (Jap., Gantō Zenkatsu). The thought that even so great a master of the → buddha-dharma could not escape a painful death caused him for a time to lose all faith in the truth of Buddhism. He absorbed himself in the study of literature in order to cover over his torturesome doubt.

After his first experience of enlightenment (→ kenshō, → satori) at the age of twenty-two, which came as he heard a sentence from a Buddhist scripture, his desire to attain peace of mind (→ *anjin*) only became deeper, and he dedicated himself with complete devotion to practice with the kōan → *mu*. Completely

Self-portrait of Hakuin with a fly whisk (*hossu*)

absorbed by this kōan, one day he experienced profound enlightenment upon hearing the sound of the temple bell. All his earlier fears and doubts were wiped away and he cried out, "Wonderful, wonderful! There's no cycle of birth and death that one has to go through! There's no enlightenment that one has to strive after! The seven hundred kōans transmitted from ancient times haven't the least worth!" His experience was so overwhelming that he believed it was unique in the world. "My pride rose up like a mighty mountain; my arrogance swelled like a tidal wave," he writes in one of his most famous letters (*Orategama* 3). He set off to see Master → Dōkyō Etan in order to tell him about his experience. But Dōkyō saw the nature of his state and did not confirm his experience. In the following years, during which he submitted Hakuin to severe Zen training, Dōkyō referred to him again and again as a "poor cave-dwelling devil" whenever Hakuin tried to tell him about his profound insights. Hakuin had further enlightenment experiences but was not confirmed by Master Dōkyō, who obviously saw the great potential of the young monk and wanted to drive him on to a more profound experience of Zen. Even though, as it seems, Hakuin never received → *inka-shōmei* from Dōkyō and truly understood his dharma teaching—as he himself said—only years after Dōkyō's death, today Hakuin is considered to have been Dōkyō's dharma successor (→ *hassu*).

Hakuin's style of Zen training, which was further developed in certain details by his student and dharma successor Tōrei Enji (1721–92), by the latter's dharma heir Inzan Ien (1751–1814), and by Takusu Kōsen (1760–1833), sets the standard up to the present time for the Rinzai school. According to Hakuin, there are three essentials of the practice of *zazen*: great faith (→ *dai-shinkon*), great doubt (→ *dai-gidan*), and great resolve (→ *dai-funshi*). He stressed the importance of kōan practice and arranged the traditional kōans into a system in which the practioner has to resolve kōans in a particular order according to their level of difficulty. The kōan *mu* and then later his *sekishu* he regarded as the best *hosshin-kōan* (→ kōan). After the successful conclusion of kōan training, marked by the conferral of a seal of confirmation, there should follow, as the masters of the Rinzai Zen in the tradition of Hakuin emphasize, a several-year period of solitary life, which serves for the deepening and clarification of the experience of the confirmed one before he makes his appearance as a master.

Hakuin also stressed the importance of a strictly regulated monastic life and—in the tradition of → Pai-chang Huai-hai—daily physical work. He regarded this work (→ *samu*) as part of meditation practice, which should continue during the everyday activity of the monastery and outside the monastery.

In his *Orategama* he writes on the importance of "practice in action":

What I am saying does not mean that you should do away with your sitting in stillness and place priority on finding an occupation in which you can continue your practice. What is worthy of the highest respect is pure kōan practice, which neither knows nor is affected by either stillness or activity. Thus it is said that the monk who is practicing properly walks but does not know that he is walking, sits but does not know that he is sitting. In order to penetrate to the depths of one's own nature and realize a true living quality that is preserved under all circumstances, there is nothing better than still absorption in the midst of activity. (Trans. from Yampolsky 1971, 15–16)

Hakuin was the abbot of several Zen monasteries, among them Ryūtaku-ji in Shizu-oka province, which has remained one of the most important Zen monasteries in Japan up to the present. Today it is one of the few monasteries in Japan in which authentic Zen in the manner of Hakuin is still a living tradition. Hakuin's voluminous writings are among the most inspiring of Japanese Zen literature. (Selected writings from his work are available in English translation in Yampolsky 1971, and Shaw 1963.)

Hakuin Zenji zazen-wasan 🅉 Jap., lit. "*Hakuin Zenji's Praise of Zazen*"; the poem of the great Zen master → Hakuin Zenji, frequently chanted in the Zen monasteries of Japan. It begins with the words *All beings are fundamentally Buddha* and continues by praising the practice of → *zazen* as the most effective means to awaken to this basic truth of Buddhism.

Hakushi 🅉 Jap. lit. "white paper"; an expression for the state of consciousness attained through the practice of → *zazen*, which is a precondition for the experience of "awakening" (→ enlightenment). It is, in the words of the Occidental mystic Meister Eckhart, "*leer und ledig aller Dinge*" ("empty and devoid of all things"). In order to realize this, as the Zen masters stress, all thoughts, ideas, images, concepts, opinions, and patterns of belief must disappear. The Japanese Zen master → Hakuun Ryōko Yasutani says about this, "As long as there is anything written, recorded, or pictured in your head or heart, you can't find any enlightenment. Throw everything away. Your mind must be as empty and spotless as a piece of white paper—*hakushi*."

Hakuun Ryōko Yasutani 🅉 1885–1973; important Japanese Zen master of the modern period. He was one of the first authentic Zen masters also to be active in the West. Ordained as a monk at the age of eleven, he trained in his younger years under several well-known Zen masters. After having taught high school in Tōkyō for sixteen years, he was accepted in 1925 as a student of → Daiun Sōgaku Harada, from whom he received the seal of confirmation (→ *inka-shōmei*) in 1943.

Between 1962 and 1969 he visited the United States several times at the invitation of followers, and there, as in Japan, he instructed Western students in Zen. Of his voluminous writings, best-known in Japan are primarily his presentations of the great kōan collections, the → *Pi-yen-lu*, the → *Wu-men-kuan*, and the *Ts'ung-jung-lu*. In the West he became known particularly through an introduction into Zen practice edited by Phillip Kapleau, which was to a great extent based on the teachings of Yasutani Rōshi and his dharma successor Kōun Yamada Rōshi: *Three Pillars of Zen* (Garden City, NY, 1980).

Like his master Harada Rōshi, Yasutani Rōshi made use in his style of Zen training of the → *shikantaza* practice of the → Sōtō tradition (→ *mokushō* Zen) as well as the kōan practice of the Rinzai tradition (→ *kanna* Zen).

Hakuun school 🅉 (Chin., Pai-yün-tsung; Jap., Hakuun-shū); an unimportant secondary lineage of Zen founded by the Chinese master Ch'ing-chüeh (Jap., Shōkaku), which is regarded as splinter group deviating from the true dharma tradition of Zen. It arose during the northern Sung Dynasty and died out during the Yüan Dynasty. Its name comes from that of the monastery where Ch'ing-chüeh lived.

Hakuun Shutan 🅩 Jap. for → Pai-yün Shou-tuan

Hamsa 🅗 (Haṃsa), Skt., lit. "swan"; 1. a name in the *Bhagavata-Purāna* for the "one caste," for in ancient times there was but one Veda, one God, and one caste; 2. in the *Mahābhārata,* a name for Krishna; 3. a name given to saints; also, a name used for → *paramahamsa.*

Han 🅩 Jap., lit. "board"; a wooden board measuring ca. 45 × 30 × 8 cm used in Zen monasteries, on which a rhythm is beaten three times a day: at dawn, at dusk, and before going to bed.

Often the following verse appears on the *han*:
Heed, monks!
Be mindful in practice.
Time flies like an arrow;
It does not wait for you.

Han-Chung-li 🅑 → Pa-hsien

Hang-chou T'ien-lung 🅩 (Jap., Kōshū Tenryū); a Chinese Ch'an (Zen) master of roughly the 9th century; a student and dharma successor (→ *hassu*) of → Ta-mei Fa-ch'ang (Jap., Dabai Hōjō) and master of → Chüchih (Jap., Gutei). We encounter Hang-chou in example 3 of the → *Wu-men-kuan.* (Also → Chü-chih.)

Han Hsiang-tzu 🅑 → Pa-hsien

Hanka-fuza 🅩 Jap.; term for the "half lotus position," in which only one foot lies on the upper thigh of the opposite leg.

Hanka-fuza is a meditation posture recommended to those who cannot maintain the full lotus position (→ *kekka-fuza*) for long periods of time without great pain, even though *hanka-fuza* is not as balanced and stable and thus not so conducive to absorption (→ *zazen*) as *kekka-fuza. Hanka-fuza* is also called *bosatsu-za*, or the "bodhisattva position."

Hannya 🅩 Jap.; one of the most important concepts in Zen; it means "wisdom" or "immediate intuitive insight." It is closely connected with meditation (Skt., → *dhyāna*, → *zazen*), and Zen meditation is based on the inseparability of *hannya* (Skt., → *prajñā)* and meditative practice. This inseparability has been particularly stressed in Zen since → Hui-neng.

Hannya shingyō 🅩 Jap., short form for *Maka hannyaharamita shingyō* (→ *Heart Sutra*).

Hannyatara 🅩 Jap. for → Prajñādhāra

Han-shan 🅩 (Jap., Kanzan); Buddhist layman of China of the T'ang period (precise dates unknown, probably the middle of the 7th century), who lived as a hermit on Mount Han-shan (Cold Mountain, or Cold Peak) in the T'ien-t'ai Mountains and is known by its name. He celebrated his unfettered lifestyle, bound to neither worldly nor orthodox religious rules, in poetry that he is said to have written throughout a wide area surrounding his hermitage on cliff faces, trees, and the walls of houses. These poems were later collected in an anthology called *Poems from Cold Mountain* (*Han-shan-shih*).

The two enlightened Zen laymen Han-shan and Shih-te (ink painting from Shūbun, 15th century)

From the poems of Han-shan it is clear that he was a practicing Ch'an (Zen) Buddhist who from time to time sought out the Ch'an master → Feng-kan (Jap.,

Bukan) at his monastery, Kuo-ch'ing, in the vicinity of Han-shan Mountain in order to receive → *Dokusan* from him.

In the kitchen of this monastery worked the foundling Shih-re (Jap., Jittoku) as a cook's helper. He became friendly with Han-shan and provided the hermit, who lived in complete poverty, with leftovers. According to the sayings of Master Feng-kan recorded in the foreword to the *Han-shan-shih*, Han-shan and Shih-te had realized the → buddha-dharma to a much greater degree than most of the monks in his monastery. In this way, Han-shan and Shih-te came in Zen literature to provide the fundamental images of enlightened Zen lay people, who—completely dependent on their own resources, without attachment to any particular school, never having undergone the strict discipline of a monk—trod the path of Buddha's lineage. Their cheerful equanimity and unorthodox lifestyle are seen as an expression of the unshakable confidence that leads to the experience of one's true nature.

Han-shan and Shih-te have been a favorite theme in Ch'an (Zen) painting in China as well as Japan. Another theme that is frequently improvised upon is that of the "four sleepers." Here the Ch'an master Feng-kan with a tiger that is said frequently to have accompanied him and Han-shan and Shih-te together make a picture of four sleeping figures all curled up together.

Hanuman 🅷 variant of → Hanumat

Hanuman-Nātaka 🅷 (Hanuman-Nāṭaka), or *Mahānātaka,* Skt., lit. "great drama of Hanumat"; one of the most remarkable works of Indian literature, in the form of a play in fourteen acts, although it could equally well be called an epic. Presumably written between the ninth and thirteenth centuries, it relates the adventures of the monkey king Hanumat and his subjects, courageous warriors who fought on the side of Rāma. Legend ascribes its authorship to Hanumat himself.

Hanumat is said to have chiseled the text into a rock that he then sank in the ocean. Only centuries later did Vikramāditya have the rock retrieved and the text copied, partially reconstructed, and distributed.

Hanumat 🅷, or Mahāvīra ("great hero") or Mahāvīr, Skt., lit. "the one with big jaws"; a monkey king. He could fly through the air and is a well-known figure in the *Rāmāyana.* With his monkey followers he supported → Rāma in his war against → Rāvana. Hanumat's deeds are represented in many paintings and sculptures. For his magic healing powers he is also called Yogāchāra. The *Rāmāyana* states: "The monkey chieftain is perfect, none is his equal in knowledge of the → Shāstras, scholarship, and interpretation of the texts." For the *bhakta,* the lover of God, Hanumat is the symbol of *dasya,* the emotional attitude of a devoted servant to his master (→ *bhāva).* Hanumat's adventures are described in the → *Hanuman-Nātaka.*

The monkey god Hanumat. (Copper statue from Mathurā)

Hanumat was of divine origin and possessed superhuman powers. In a single bound he sprang from India to Ceylon, tore out trees, pushed aside the Himalayas, seized hold of the clouds, and wrought many miracles. He is described thus: "His form is as large as a mountain and as high as a mighty tower, his skin is yellow and glows like molten gold, his face is red as a brilliant ruby and his tail mighty in length. He stands high on a rock and roars like thunder, he springs into the air and flies through the clouds with a rushing sound, while the ocean waves beneath him toss and roar." In one of his battles with Rāvana and the → Rākshasas, the demons greased his tail and set it on fire, but in the process their capital city, Lankā, went up in flames. Hanumat rendered great service to Rāma, acting as his powerful warrior and spy and accompanying the prince back to Ayodhyā. He was rewarded by Rāma with immortality and eternal youth.

Hara 🆉 also *kikai-tanden,* Jap., lit. "underbody, belly, gut"; in Zen the term has predominantly a spiritual meaning in the sense of a person's spiritual center.

Based on the experience that body and mind are one, the Zen master → Daiun Sōgaku Harada said, "You have to realize that the center of the universe is your belly-cave!" By *belly-cave* he meant *hara.*

Harada Rōshi 🅉 → Daiun Sōgaku Harada

Hari 🄷 Skt., lit. "dispeller of sins"; a name for God in the forms of Vishnu and Krishna, later used generally to mean the personal form of God (→ Īshvara). In the → *soma* sacrifice, the brown color of the *soma* draught is called *hari.*

Hari-Hara 🄷 Skt.; the combined epithets for Vishnu (Hari) and Shiva (Hara), used to make manifest the unity of the two divinities, a reference to → *advaita* belief.

A legend tells how God appeared to a devotee of Vishnu with two faces, one side that of Hari, the other that of Hara. The worshiper deliberately made his sacrifice to the Hari (Vishnu) side alone, but it was rejected by God. Thereupon he recognized his narrow-mindedness and was brought a step closer to illumination.

HARI OM 🄷 Skt.; a sacred formula (→ mantra) by which God's presence is called forth (→ OM).

Harivamsha 🄷 (Harivaṃśa), Skt., lit. "the race of Hari (or Vishnu)"; a religious epic that is regarded as a supplement to the → *Mahābhārata,* although it was composed much later. The work has three parts: the first is concerned with the Creator and the various legendary dynasties; the second describes the life and adventures of Krishna; the third discusses the future of the world and the corrupt times of the *kali-yuga* (→ *yuga*), the age in which we now live.

Harivarman 🄱 4th century Buddhist scholar from central India. After his entry into the → *sangha,* he turned to the teachings of the → Sarvāstivāda school but soon became discontent with them. For some years he deepened his knowledge of the Buddhist canon, then went to → Pātaliputra, where he studied the Mahāyāna texts of the Mahāsānghika school with the monks there. From this period comes his work *Satyasiddhi* (*Perfection of the Truth*), in which he developed the notion of emptiness (→ *shūnyatā*). This work became the basis for the Chinese → Satyasiddhi and the Japanese → Jōjitsu schools.

Harsha 🄷 (Harṣa), the name of two famous Indian poets. 1. The author of three action-filled dramas (*Nāgānanda,* "The Bliss of the Demon Snakes," *Priyadarshikā,* and *Ratnāvalī,* "The Rope of Pearls"), which draw on favorite themes from Indian legend and in part show Buddhist influence. Harsha was the emperor of a wide region in North India from 606 to 647. His adventurous life is described by the poet Bāna (seventh century) in the novel *Harsha-Charita.* 2. The epic poet and Vedantic philosopher Harsha, court poet under the twelfth-century king of Kanauj. He was celebrated under the honorific names Shrīharsha and Harshadeva as author of the great literary epic *Naishadha-Charita,* composed on the theme of the love between → Nala and Damayanti. He also wrote the philosophical work *Khandanakhanda-khādya* ("Tidbits of Love"), which debates the teachings of the → Nyāya school from the viewpoint of a Vedāntin.

Haryō Kōkan 🅉 Jap. for → Pa-ling Hao-chien

Hasan 🅉 Jap., roughly "interruption of (religious) practice"; term for a Zen student who in the course of his Zen training comes to an experience of → enlightenment (→ *kenshō,* → satori).

In a Zen monastery a *hasan* frequently celebrates his experience by providing a meal for the other monks, which is called *hasan-sai.* In Zen, however, it is repeatedly stressed that no matter how joyous such an experience may be, it is only a first step on the way of Zen and must be followed up by many other such steps. A person who dwells too long on such an experience and fails to persist vigorously in his practice (→ *zazen,* → kōan) falls quickly back into the state of mind in which the enlightenment experience is no longer a living experience but only a memory.

Hassu 🅉 Jap., lit. "dharma successor"; a Zen student who has reached at least the same degree of enlightenment as his master and who has been empowered by the latter to carry on his dharma teaching and in his turn to transmit the Zen tradition to an appropriate dharma successor. Only a student who has received → *inka-shōmei* from his master can be a *hassu.*

The great masters of Zen repeatedly emphasize that Zen is basically not teachable and cannot be conveyed; for this reason such notions as teaching, tradition, transmission, and so on must be regarded as makeshift expressions referring to a process that cannot be grasped conceptually. The function of a master can be roughly compared to that of a catalyst that instigates a chemical reaction without contributing in substance to the outcome of it; that is to say, in the presence of, and through the training given by, an enlightened master, the student can himself come to an enlightenment experience without the master actually "transmitting" anything or the student "receiving" anything. This is the process that is called "transmission." (Also → *Denkō-roku.*)

In the early Ch'an (Zen) tradition the student received from the master the latter's monastic robe and his begging bowl as confirmation of dharma-successorship. The expression "robe and bowl" thus became a metaphor in Zen literature for "transmission without the scriptures"; this kind of transmission is one of the chief features of Zen. (Also → *den'e.*)

Hatha-Yoga 🅗 (Haṭha-Yoga), Skt.; this yoga was originally a technique of Rāja-Yoga as taught by → Patañjali; with its help, the centers of psychic energy (→ *chakra*) are activated and thereby raise the → *kundalinī* to higher states of consciousness. Its most important practices are the → *āsana* and → *prānāyāma,* control of the → *prāna*-stream. Its main goal is to unite *ha* (the breath of the sun, known as *prāna*) with *tha* (the breath of the moon, known as *apāna*). The Hatha-Yogi thereby attains spiritual powers, and the *kundalinī* begins to rise through the six *chakras*. Hatha-Yoga utilizes various bodily postures and purification exercises. Its chief goal as pursued by modern-day adherents is physical health. When Westerners speak of yoga, they almost invariably mean this type, which is represented by many schools and teachers. The path of Hatha-Yoga is not to be confused with the traditional path of → yoga, which aims toward liberation and union with God.

Hatha-Yoga-Pradīpikā 🅗 (Haṭha-Yoga-Pradīpikā), Skt., lit. "light of severe yoga"; a standard work on → Hatha-Yoga by Svātmārāma (sixteenth century). In four chapters comprising 395 verses, the disciplines of Hatha-Yoga are related to → Rāja-Yoga and the two paths are shown to complement each other. Svātmārāma concludes that Rāja-Yoga begins where Hatha-Yoga leaves off.

Hatsu 🅩 Jap. → *jihatsu*

Hayagrīva 🅗 🅑 Skt., lit. "Horse's Neck."

🅗 Legend relates that a → Daitya by this name stole the Veda as it fell from the mouth of Brahmā, who was taking his sleep at the close of a cosmic age (→ *kalpa*). Vishnu in his incarnation as a fish (→ Matsya) slew Hayagrīva. According to another legend, Vishnu himself took on the form of Hayagrīva in order to retrieve the Veda after its theft by two Daityas.

🅑 (Tib., Tamdrin [rta-mgrin]); wrathful protector deity (→ forms of manifestation) belonging to the *padma* family (→ *buddha-kula*) of the → Vajrayāna; in this tradition he is often related to as a → *yidam.*

Heart-mind 🅩 → *kokoro*

Heart Sūtra 🅑 🅩 (Skt., *Mahāprajñāpāramitā-hridaya-sūtra,* Jap., *Maka hannyaharamita shingyō, roughly "Heartpiece of the* → *'Prajñāpāramitā-sūtra'*); shortest of the forty sūtras that constitute the *Prajñāpāramitā-sūtra.* It is one of the most important sūtras of Mahāyāna Buddhism and, particularly in China and Japan, it is recited by monks and nuns of almost all schools. The sūtra is especially emphasized in Zen, since it formulates in a particularly clear and concise way the teaching of → *shūnyatā,* emptiness, the immediate experience of which is sought by Zen practitioners.

The pith sentence of the *Heart Sutra* is, "Form is no other than emptiness; emptiness is no other than form," an affirmation that is frequently referred to in Zen.

Heijōshin kore dō 🅩 Jap., lit. "Ordinary mind is the way"; a famous Zen saying stemming from the Chinese Ch'an (Zen) master → Nan-ch'üan P'u-yüan (Jap., Nansen Fugen). It comes in the first part of a → *mondō* with → Chao-chou Ts'ung-shen (Jap., Jōshū Jūshin), which appears as example 19 of the → *Wu-men-kuan*:

Chao-chou asked Nan-ch'üan, "What is the Way?"

Nan-ch'üan said, "The ordinary mind is the Way."

Chao-chou said, "Should I apply myself to that or not?"

Nan-ch'üan said, "If you try to turn toward it, it'll get away from you."

Chao-chou said, "If I don't try to find it, how can I know the Way?"

Nan-ch'üan said, "The Way is not a matter of knowing or not knowing. Knowing is delusion. Not knowing is not distinguishing. When you have really reached the true way that is beyond all doubt, you will find out that it is as vast and limitless as the great emptiness. How could anything be right or wrong there?"

With these words Chao-chou came to a sudden enlightenment experience.

Heikan 🅩 Jap., lit. "closing the gate"; an expression for the Zen practice (→ *zazen*) that consists in "closing the gate" of distraction and cultivating inner concentration and "enlightenment mind"

(→ *bodaishin*). *Heikan* does not, however, mean that one no longer perceives external circumstances and thus is no longer able to tend to worldly needs and duties. It only means that one no longer permits oneself to be captivated by worldly cares, pains, and passions and thus to be distracted from spiritual practice.

The basic sense of *heikan* is conveyed by a poem by the Taoist-influenced Chinese poet T'ao Yüan-ming (also T'ao Ch'ien, 365–427) that is often quoted in Zen. It begins with these lines:

My house I built in the midst of people's dwellings,
But I do not hear the noise of horse and wagon.
You ask, how could that be possible?
Once your heart is resolved, then the place where you live is also peaceful.

Heitai-dōji 🅉 Jap., lit. "fire boy"; the boy in a Zen monastery who tends to the maintenance, lighting, and extinguishing of the lamps.

Hekikan-Baramon 🅉 Jap., lit. "Brahmin Who Looks at the Wall"; a popular name for → Bodhidharma, the first patriarch of Ch'an (Zen). Bodhidharma came from a brahmin family and in the → Shao-lin monastery spent nine years practicing *zazen* "facing the wall" (→ *menpeki*).

Hen-chū-shō 🅉 Jap. → five degrees (of enlightenment) 2

Heng O 🅃 also known as Ch'ang O; the lunar goddess of Chinese mythology and wife of the celestial archer, Shen I, who received the draught of immortality (→ *ch'ang-sheng pu-ssu*, → *hsien*) from the Royal Mother of the West (→ Hsi wang-mu). Heng O tried to abduct this draught from her husband, but he caught her before she could drink all of it. The draught gave her the power to ascend to Heaven, but, as she had not consumed all of it, she had to halt halfway up and settle on the moon. Shen I himself went to the abode of the immortals and became ruler of the sun. Heng O is usually portrayed sitting on a three-legged toad.

Henkū 🅉 Jap., lit. "one-sided emptiness"; term for the Buddhist doctrine, advocated particularly in the → Hīnayāna, that especially stresses the insubstantiality and thus the nonexistence of all phenomena (also called *tankū*, "only emptiness"). This does not describe the whole of reality, only half; thus it is called "one-sided." Also → *futan-kū*.)

Hieizan 🄱 🅉 Jap., lit. "Mount Hiei"; mountain near Kyōto on which → Saichō (also Dengyō Daishi, 766–822) built, in the 9th century, the principal monastery of the Japanese line of → T'ien-t'ai Buddhism (also → Tendai), which he founded. The great monastic complex became one of the most important centers of Buddhism in medieval Japan. It also accommodated masters of other Buddhist schools, particularly of the → Shingon and → Zen schools.

Himavat 🄷 Skt., lit. "snowy peak"; a symbol for the pinnacle of being; the divine forces in their supreme manifestation.

In myth, Himavat appears as the personification of the Himalayas; he is the father of → Umā and → Gangā.

Hīnayāna 🄱 🅉 Skt., "Small Vehicle"; originally a derogatory designation used by representatives of the → Mahāyāna ("Great Vehicle") for early Buddhism. The followers of Hīnayāna themselves usually refer to their teaching as the → Theravāda (Teaching of the Elders), in spite of the fact that strictly speaking, Theravāda was *one* of the schools within the Hīnayāna; it is, however, the only one still existing today. Hīnayāna is also referred to as Southern Buddhism, since it is prevalent chiefly in countries of southern Asia (Sri Lanka, Thailand, Burma, Kampuchea, Laos).

The Hīnayāna enumerates the traditions of eighteen schools that developed out of the original community; however, the texts make reference to many more.

At the third → Buddhist council the first schism took place, which split the original community into → Sthavira (Pali, Thera) and → Mahāsānghika factions. Between 280 and 240 B.C.E., the Mahāsānghika group divided into six schools: The Ekavyāvahārikas; the Lokottaravādins, who split from them; the Gokulikas, and the Bahushrutīyas, Prajñaptivādins, and Chaitikas, who split from the Gokulikas. The → Vātsīputrīyas (also called Pudgalavādins) separated themselves from the Sthaviras around 240 B.C.E. The Vātsīputrīya had four subdivisions: Dharmottarīya, Bhadrayānīya, Sammatīya, and Sannagarika (or Sandagiriya). Two other schools that splintered from the Sthaviras are the → Sarvāstivāda, out of which, around 150 B.C.E., came the Sautrāntikas, and the → Vibhajyavādins, who see themselves as orthodox Sthaviras. Out of this last school arose the Theravāda, Mahīshāsakas, and Kāshyapīyas; from the Mahīshāsakas came the → Dharmaguptakas.

The Hīnayāna school developed between the death of the Buddha and the end of the first century B.C.E. According to its adherents it represents the original, pure teaching as it was taught by the Buddha. Its doctrines are essentially based on the sūtras, which are said to have been spoken by the Buddha himself. The disciplinary rules compulsory for monks are contained in the → Vinaya-pitaka. In the → Abhidharma, the third part of the canon (→ Tripitaka), the teachings contained in the sūtras are analyzed and systematized.

The Hīnayāna presents primarily the path to liberation. Philosophical speculations have no role in this; on the contrary, they are considered a hindrance on the path. The Hīnayāna teaching provides an analysis of the human situation, the nature of existence, and the structure of individuality, and shows methods for the resolution of suffering (→ *duhkha*).

All schools of the Hīnayāna have in common a realistic view of existence. Suffering, from which one should liberate oneself, is seen as real. Liberation from the suffering-ridden cycle of rebirth (→ samsāra) and the attainment of nirvāna are seen as the supreme goal. This can only be achieved through one's own effort, by renouncing the world and overcoming it. For this, the adherent of Hīnayāna must enter into → homelessness, that is, lead a monastic life. For the layman, the attainment of nirvāna is not possible. The ideal figure of Hīnayāna corresponding to these principles is the → arhat, who through his own effort has attained release.

Hīnayāna avoids affirming anything about the ultimate goal of spiritual striving, nirvāna, beyond the experiential fact of enlightenment and the concomitant extinction of the illusion of an ego and its cravings.

The Buddha is regarded by these schools as a historical person, an earthly man and teacher, not as a transcendent being.

The essence of the teaching is expressed in the → four noble truths, the doctrine of dependent arising (→ *pratītya-samutpāda*), the teaching of → *anātman*, and the law of → karma. The basic practice of the Hīnayāna is described in the teaching of the → eightfold path.

From the Mahāyāna point of view, the Hīnayāna is called the "Small Vehicle" because, in contrast to the Mahāyāna, it has one's own liberation as goal rather than that of all beings. It is regarded as the first stage of the Buddha's exposition of the teaching, in which only a small part of the Buddhist teaching is given. Only later did the Buddha expound the complete teaching, the Mahāyāna. (Also → *ekayāna*, → *triyāna*, → Buddhism.)

Hindi 🅗 the vernacular spoken in much of North India, comprising two varieties (East Hindi and West Hindi) and numerous dialects. West Hindi, spoken by some 112 million people, is the official administrative language of India. It is transcribed in the Devanāgarī alphabet, which is also used for classical → Sanskrit.

Hinduism 🅗 the name used in the West to designate the traditional socioreligious structure of the Indian people. Those Indians who are not followers of the distinct teachings of Islam, → Jainism, or → Sikhism are generally referred to as "Hindus." In India this religious complex is called → *sanātana-dharma*, "the eternal religion," because it incorporated for centuries all aspects of truth. As a religion based on mythology, it has neither a founder (as do Buddhism, Islam, and Christianity) nor a fixed canon. Myriad local cults and traditions of worship or belief can be distinguished. Common to all Hindus, however, is the teaching of the law of → karma.

Ever since the penetration of the Indo-Aryan peoples into India and their subsequent introduction of the Vedic period, seers, saints, and → *avatāras* have discovered spiritual truths that were first laid down in the → *shrutis* and still represent the foundation and substance of Hindu life. The Indo-Aryans who came upon the Dravidian cultures of South India were receptive to their religious teachings, which in turn permeated the teachings of *sanātana-dharma*. The latter system, ever open to new insights, has thus maintained its living power in an unbroken line to the present day. Because the Indian mind was directed from the outset toward eternity, no significance was given to the temporal sequence of events and discoveries. For this reason, the historical dates given in Hindu accounts for saints, philosophers, schools, and so forth often diverge by as much as centuries. Nevertheless, a certain chronology can be determined in broad strokes.

The → Vedas and → Upanishads were followed by other sacred texts, although these no longer belonged to the category of *shruti* (revelatory scripture). Of these texts, the → Itihāsas, the most prominent are the two great epics, the → *Rāmāyana* and the *Mahābhārata*. The latter contains the *Bhagavad-Gītā*; one of the most sacred texts in Hinduism, it is known to every Indian and is often consigned to memory. The Itihāsas, more historical in character than the earlier texts, were followed by the → Purānas, whose vivid sagas and legends chiefly served to make the abstract teachings of the Vedas and Upanishads accessible to the people of later periods, most of whom were no longer able to understand the earlier works. The Purānas thus became the chief texts of → Vaishnavism, → Shaivism, and → Brahmanism.

Next in importance for the religious and spiritual development of Indian thought is → Tantrism. This teaching focuses primarily on the study of divine energy, which if rightly used can be of great help to aspirants on the path to illumination, but if misused can be highly dangerous.

The six philosophical doctrines, or → *darshanas*, were not fixed in writing until a relatively late date, but their origins are evident in Vedic times. In particular, the perceptions of Vedānta, regarded by Western scholars as the apex of Indian philosophy, can be traced through the entire history of Indian thought from the → *Rigveda* down to the reform movements of the past two centuries.

The six *darshanas* are collectively characterized as orthodox (*āstika*), because they acknowledge the authority of the Vedas. Yet alongside these there arose from early times teachings and schools that did not acknowledge the Vedas' authority and that are therefore known as *nāstika* (unorthodox). Of these, the most important are Jainism and Buddhism. For Hindus, the Buddha is not only a Hindu but an *avatāra*, an incarnation of divine consciousness on earth, in particular the ninth of the traditional ten *avatāras*. (The tenth has not yet appeared; see → Kalki.)

The most significant present-day Indian devotional movements are Vaishnavism, Shaivism, and → Shaktism; Brahmanism, to use a term frequently employed in the West in connection with India, plays no more than a minor role in Hinduism in the sense of a following devoted to the worship of Brahmā.

The influences of Buddhism, Islam, Christianity, Jainism, and the → Parsis were not without importance and contributed considerably to the gradual spread of Hinduism. A text as early as the *Rigveda* contains the fundamental statement "*Ekam sat vipra bahudhā vadanti*" ("Truth is one, many are its names"). The modern-day mystic → Rāmakrishna bore witness to truth as he practiced the various paths of individual religions in the course of his life and in each attained the same enlightenment.

Hiranyagarbha 🅗 (Hiraṇyagarbha), Skt., lit. "golden egg"; in the *Rigveda*, Hiranyagarbha is the source, the one God of all, who contains within himself heaven and earth and confers life and breath; he is the animating principle in all creatures, whom all the gods obey.

According to → Manu, Hiranyagarbha is identical with → Brahmā as the first manifestation of the male principle. Brahmā emerged from the unfathomable First Cause in the form of a golden egg that shone like the sun. Brahmā remained in the egg for a year; then he split it in two by sheer thought, and from the two half-shells created heaven and earth.

Hiranyaparakosha 🅗 (Hiranyaparakośa), Skt., lit. "golden sheath of the beyond"; the divine, golden, supreme sheath, the body of → Brahmā.

Hiranyavat 🅗 (Hiraṇyavat), Skt., lit. "golden treasure"; the fundamental substance of truth. *Hiranya* literally means "gold" and hence "wealth, treasure," but in compounds is often used symbolically to represent the radiant treasure of the divine light.

Hi-shiryō 🅩 Jap., lit. "that which is immeasurable by thought"; Zen expression for → enlightenment, which is experienceable but cannot be grasped in concepts; it is thus unthinkable. (Also → *fukashigi*, → *fukasetsu*.)

Hitopadesha 🅗 (Hitopadeśá), Skt., lit. "good advice, friendly instruction"; a collection of instructive tales and animal fables. Largely based on the older and more comprehensive → *Pañchatantra*, it is assumed to have been composed by a certain Nārāyana sometime between the tenth and fourteenth centuries in Bengal. Good-humored and edifying, it is still used today as a reader.

Hō 🅑 🅩 Jap. for → *dharma*

Ho! 🅩 Chin. for → *katsu*!

Ho 🅣 Chin., lit. "crane"; Taoist symbol of immortality (→ *Ch'ang-sheng pu-ssu*, → *shou*) and wisdom. Frequently, the crane is shown together with a pine tree and a rock, both of which are symbols of longevity. Taoist adepts who have attained immortality (→ *hsien*) ascend to Heaven riding on a crane (→ *fei-sheng*). The crane's red head is taken as a sign that it has preserved its vital energy and thus consists of pure yang (→ yin-yang).

Representations that show a crane flying towards a pavilion situated on a rock above the sea are symbols for the isles of the immortals (→ P'eng-lai, → Ying-chou, → Fang-chang). Pairs of cranes, on the other hand, are symbols of good fortune and an elegant literary style and thus represent the Lucky Star (→ *san-hsing*) and the deity of literature (→ Wen-ch'ang).

Hōbōdan-gyō 🅩 Jap. for *Fa-pao-t'an-ching*, → *Liu-tsu-ta-shih fa-pao-t'an-ching*

Hōbō Kokumon 🅩 Jap. for → Pao-feng K'o-wen

Ho-ch'i 🅣 Chin., lit. "unification of the breaths"; collective sexual orgies practiced since the time of the Han Dynasty by the Taoist school of the Way of Supreme Peace (→ *t'ai-p'ing tao*) and by Five-Pecks-of-Rice Taoism (→ *wu-tou-mi tao*). These practices continued until the time of the Sung Dynasty. *Ho-ch'i* aims at the unification of yin and yang (→ yin-yang), the female and male essence, respectively, thereby nourishing the life principle (→ *yang-hsing*). It is said that the practice of *ho-ch'i* can enable the practitioner to attain immortality.

Ho-ch'i ceremonies were held on the days of the new moon and the full moon. After performing the dances of the dragon (a symbol for yang) and of the tiger (symbol for yin) the participants withdrew to private chambers, where they endeavored to have sexual intercourse with as many different partners as possible.

We have no details of the precise *ho-ch'i* ritual, because all descriptions of it were deleted from the Taoist canon (→ *Tao-tsang*) under the pressure of Confucianist morality. The practice of *ho-ch'i* is based on the idea that male semen (→ *ching*), the essence of yang, can best be nourished by the female orgasm (yin). If a man has intercourse with many female partners, each of whom experiences an orgasm, but does not allow himself to ejaculate until the final copulation, he will accumulate a large quantity of yang. This has a positive effect on the duration of his life. It is said that the legendary Yellow Emperor (→ Huang-ti) had sexual intercourse with twelve hundred concubines yet suffered no damage to his health, because he was acquainted with the technique of *ho-ch'i*.

Hō'e 🅩 Jap., lit. "dharma clothing"; term for the robe of a Buddhist monk. In Zen the monastic robe is a symbol for the transmission of the → buddha-dharma "from heart-mind to heart-mind" (→ *ishin-denshin*) in the lineage of the patriarchs (→ *soshigata*), which goes back to Buddha Shākyamuni. A robe was given by the early Ch'an (Zen) patriarchs to their dharma successors (→ *hassu*) as a sign of confirmation (→ *inka-shōmei*). (Also → *den'e*.)

Hofuku Jūten 🅩 Jap. for → Pao-fu Ts'ung-chan

Hōgen Bun'eki 🅩 Jap. for Fa-yen Wen-i

Hōgen school 🅩 (Chin., Fa-yen-tsung; Jap., Hōgen-shū); a school of Ch'an (Zen) that belongs to the five houses–seven schools (→ *goke-shichishū*), i.e., to the great schools of the authentic Ch'an tradition. It was founded by → Hsüan-sha Shih-pei (Jap., Gensha Shibi), a student and dharma successor (→ *hassu*) of → Hsüeh-feng I-ts'un (Jap., Seppō Gison), after whom it was originally called the Hsüan-sha school.

Master Hsüan-sha's renown was later overshadowed by that of his grandson in dharma → Fa-yen Wen-i (Jap., Hōgen Bun'eki) and since then the lineage has been known as the Fa-yen (Jap., Hōgen) school. Fa-yen, one of the most important Ch'an masters of his time, attracted students from all parts of China. His sixty-three dharma successors spread his teaching over the whole of the country and even as far as Korea. For three generations the Hōgen school flourished but died out after the fifth generation.

Hōge-sō 🅩 Jap., lit. "freed-renunciate monk"; originally Buddhist monks during the Kamakura and Muromachi (or Ashikaga) periods in Japan, who, unburdened by any worldly possessions wandered through the country singing and dancing and begging for food. In the sense of one who has renounced all worldly possessions, *hōge-sō* is used to refer to an enlightened monk.

Hōgo 🅩 Jap., lit. "dharma word(s)"; the living truth of Buddhism, particularly the sayings relating to Zen of the patriarchs (→ *soshigata*) and the ancient masters of the Ch'an (Zen) tradition. Such sayings have been readily cited by later Zen masters in their → *teishō*. If they were also practitioners of the way of calligraphy (→ *shōdō*), they often made calligraphies of these sayings as an artistic expression of the Zen experience.

Ho Hsien-ku 🅣 → Pa-hsien

Hōjin 🅩 Jap. for *sambhogakāya*, → *trikāya*

Hōjō 🅩 Jap., lit. "ten-foot square"; 1. term for the cell of the elder monk of a Buddhist monastery. The expression is an allusion to the cell of the legendary Buddhist saint Vimalakīrti, who is said to have attained the degree of enlightenment of a buddha as a layman; this can be read in the → *Vimalakīrtinirdesha-sūtra*, 2. the abbot of a Buddhist monastery, 3. honorific title of the elder monk in a Zen monastery.

Hōju Enshō 🅩 Jap. for → Pao-chou Yen-chao

Hokke-kyō 🅑 🅩 Jap. for → *Lotus Sūtra*

Hō Koji 🅩 Jap., → P'ang Yün

Hokushū-Zen 🅩 Jap. for the Chinese *Pei-tsung ch'an*, i.e., "Northern School of Ch'an [Zen]," → Southern school.

Hōkyō 🅩 Jap., lit. "dharma bridge"; term for Buddhism, which is compared to a bridge that permits human beings to cross the river of life and death (→ samsāra).

Hōkyō-ki 🅩 Jap.; collection of the answers made by the Chinese Ch'an (Zen) master → T'ien-t'ung Ju-ching (Jap., Tendō Nyojō) to the Japanese monk who was later known as → Dōgen Zenji, the founder of the Japanese lineage of the → Sōtō school. The work was written down by Ejō, a student of Dōgen Zenji.

Hōkyō Zanmai 🅩 Jap. for → *San-mei-k'o*

Homa 🅗 Skt.; vedic ritual of sacrificial offering to a fire. The fire itself is venerated as a visible manifestation of the deity being worshiped. This is a ritual of inner purification, representing the spiritual offering to the deity of the worshiper's thoughts, words, and deeds.

Homelessness 🅑 (Skt., pravrajyā; Pali, pabbajjā); "entering into homelessness," that is, leaving behind one's family and abandoning all social ties, is the first step in the life of a Hīnayāna monk, who must turn away from the world in order to tread the path of liberation. With this step, symbolized by shaving the head and beard and putting on a yellow robe, one enters the novitiate (→ *shrāmanera*).

Entering into homelessness is described in various texts, for example, as follows:

"Full of hindrances is the life of a householder, a state of impurity; but like the open air, the life of homelessness. Not easy is it in the householder's state to lead an immaculate, holy life. What if I were now to shave hair and beard, put on the yellow robe, and go forth from the house into homelessness?" And after some time, giving up a small or a great fortune and a small or a large family, he shaves his hair and beard, dons the yellow robe, and goes forth from his house into homelessness (translated from German translation of Nya-natiloka 1976, 73)

Hōmon 🅩 Jap., lit. "dharma gate(s)"; the teachings of the Buddha, the founder of Buddhism. These teachings are here compared to a gate through which the practitioner enters the world of → enlightenment. In the four great vows (→ *shiguseigan*) adherents of Zen vow to realize all the teachings of the Buddha: *Hōmon muryō seigangaku* ("The gates of dharma are manifold; I vow to pass through all"). In this, however, the practitioner is aware that the gate does not lead from one world into another.

Hōnen 🅑 → Jōdo-shū

Honganji 🅑 Jap. → Jōdo-shin-shū

Honrai-no-memmoku 🅩 Jap., lit. "original [*honrai*] face [*memmoku*]"; this expression, translated as "original [or primordial] face [or countenance]," is a favorite metaphor in Zen, which points to the true nature or buddha-nature (→ busshō) of human beings and all things.

In the question form, "What is your original face?" or "What is your face before your parents were born?" this expression is the core of a favorite → kōan.

Honshi 🅩 Jap., lit. "root master"; 1. in Japanese Buddhism, generally, → Shākyamuni Buddha; 2. the founder of a Buddhist school; 3. the master from whom one received → *jukai*; 4. in Zen the master from whom one received → *inka-shōmei*. It can be the case that a Zen student receives instruction from several Zen masters in the course of his life; if he receives the seal of confirmation from one of these masters, this master is then, according to Zen tradition, his *honshi*.

Honsoku Jap., lit. "original rule"; another term for → kōan, which refers in kōan collections like the → *Wu-men-kuan* or the → *Pi-yen-lu* to the kōan itself as opposed to the preceding introduction or the succeeding "praise" (→ *ju*).

Hon'u-busshō 🅩 Jap., lit. "buddha-nature present from the beginning"; another expression for → *busshō*.

Hōrin-ji 🅩 Jap. for → Pao-lin-ssu

Ho-shang kung 🅣 Chin., lit. "Venerable of the River"; commentator of the *Tao-te ching* who, according to tradition, lived during the early period of the Han Dynasty at the time of the Emperor Wen (180–157 B.C.E.). Recent research, however, has shown that the commentary bearing his name dates from the end of the Han Dynasty (2d century C.E.). The reason for his name is that he lived in a hut on the bank of a river. In Taoism he is venerated as an immortal (→ *hsien*).

About Ho-shang kung's life there is only one well-known legend, which is quoted at the beginning of the commentary attributed to him: "Emperor Wen was fond of the writings of Lao-tzu, but there were many passages he was unable to understand, and he knew of no-one that might explain them to him. One day he heard reports of a venerable Taoist sage said to live in a straw-covered hut by a river, who devoted all his time to the study of the *Tao-te ching*. The emperor despatched a messenger to question him about the difficult passages in Lao-tzu's writings. Ho-shang kung, however, insisted that the emperor come to see him in person. Thereupon the emperor went to Ho-shang kung, but before questioning him about the incomprehensible passages berated him for his arrogance, saying: 'There is no place below heaven that does not belong to the king, and all who dwell upon this earth are vassals of the king. . . . You may possess the Tao but nevertheless are one of my subjects. . . . Could it be that by refusing to bow to my wishes you are overestimating your own status? Consider that I have the power to make anyone rich or poor, mighty or miserable.' At this Ho-shang kung rose from his seat and ascended high into the air, from where he addressed the emperor as follows: 'Since I am neither in heaven, nor among the people or on earth, am I still your subject?' Emperor Wen then realised that he was dealing with a supernatural being. He apologised most humbly and thereupon received from Ho-shang kung the *Tao-te ching* and Ho-shang kung's commentary" (trans. from Kaltenmark, *Lao-tzu und der Taoismus;* see Kaltenmark 1969).

Ho-shan Wu-yin 🅉 (Jap., Kasan [Kazan] Muin), d. 960; Chinese Ch'an (Zen) master, a student and dharma successor (→ *hassu*) of Master Chiu-feng Tao-ch'ien (Jap., Kyūjō Dōken), who was in turn a dharma successor of → Shih-shuang Ch'ing-chu (Jap., Sekisō Keisho). We encounter Ho-shan in example 44 of the → *Pi-yen-lu*. Ho-shan entered the monastery of → Hsüeh-feng I-ts'un (Jap., Seppō Gison) at the age of seven. After Hsüeh-feng's death, when Ho-shan was twenty years old, he became a student of Chiu-feng.

In example 44 of the *Pi-yen-lu*, we see him as he "beats the drum":

Ho-shan said during instruction, "Those in the basic school we call hearers; those in the higher school we call neighbors. He who has gone through both we call he who has gone beyond into the truth."

A monk came forward and asked, "So what is one who has gone beyond into the truth?"

Ho-shan said, "Baroom-boom-boom!"

The monk again asked, "I'm not asking about the idea consciousness in itself is buddha in itself, but what does not consciousness, not buddha mean?"

Ho-shan said, "Baroom-boom-boom!"

Once again the monk asked, "If a venerable one were to come here, how should we relate with him?"

Ho-shan said, "Baroom-boom-boom!"

Hossen 🅉 Jap., lit. "dharma contest"; the method typical for Zen of demonstrating the living truth directly, without recourse to discursive thinking or philosophical or religious doctrine. *Hossen*, like → *mondō*, consists of an exchange of words, questions and answers, gestures and responses between two enlightened people. While the *mondō* usually consists of one question and one answer, the *hossen* can develop into an extended encounter. Most → kōans consist of *hossen* or *mondō* that have been handed down by tradition.

In contrast to what the term *dharma contest* might suggest, a *hossen* is not a matter of debate; it is not a question of defeating an enemy in discussion or determining which partner is the "better man." The participants in a *hossen* speak from their Zen experience, which admits of no antagonism, no *I-you* split. They make use of these occasions only to test the depth of their own experience in an encounter with a person of greater spiritual power and in this way to train themselves further.

The *P'ang-chü-shih yü-lu* (→ P'ang-yün) contains a series of *hossen* of an enlightened layman of the T'ang period with renowned Zen masters, among them the following:

One day the Layman P'ang addressed Master Ma-tsu and said, "A person whose original face is not obscured bids you look up."

Ma-tsu looked straight down.

The Layman spoke, "You alone have achieved wondrous mastery at playing the stringless zither."

Ma-tsu looked straight up.

The Layman prostrated. Ma-tsu drew back.

"That's how one spoils it when one tries to be particularly clever," said the Layman.

Hosshin 🅉 Jap. for *dharmakāya*, → *trikāya*

Hosshin-kōan 🅉 Jap. → kōan

Hosshō 🅉 Jap., lit. "dharma-nature"; the true nature of the phenomenal world, which is experienceable in → enlightenment but eludes all description (→ *fukasetsu*, → *fukashigi*). It is identical with buddha-nature (→ *busshō*), with which it is used interchangeably.

Hossō school 🄱 Jap. (Chin. → Fa-hsiang school), lit. "school of the characteristics of dharmas"; school of Japanese Buddhism, continuation of the Chinese Fa-hsiang school (which in turn was based on the → Yogāchāra school of India).

The Hossō school was brought to Japan by the Japanese monk → Dōshō (629–700). He went to China in 653 and was there a student of → Hsüan-tsang for ten years. Hsüan-tsang was the founder of the Fa-hsiang school. Back in Japan Dōshō propagated the Hossō teaching at the Guan-go-ji monastery. His first student was Gyogi (667–748). The lineage founded by him was called the transmission of the teaching of the Southern Monastery.

In 716 the monk Gembo went to China and became a student of the Fa-hsiang master Chih-chou. Gembo also remained for ten years. After his return to Japan in 735, he taught at the Kōbuku-ji monastery. His student was Genju, who propagated the line of the teaching represented by Gembo. This line of transmission is known as that of the Northern Monastery. It is generally considered to be the orthodox line. The Hossō school never flourished in Japan to the extent that its counterparts had in India and China.

Hossu 🅉 Jap., lit. "little-animal broom"; flywhisk modeled on the whisk that the wandering Buddhist monks of India used to carry to sweep small creatures out of their paths so that they would not step on them. The *hossu* is a short staff of wood on which a horse or yak tail is fastened. In the Ch'an (Zen) monasteries of ancient China, it was an exclusive prerogative of the master to use such a flywhisk. Thus the *hossu* became a symbol of the "transmission from heart-mind to heart-mind" and as such it was passed down from a Zen master to his dharma successor (→ *hassu*).

As many kōans in Zen literature show, Zen masters occasionally used their *hossu* in a → *mondō* or → *hossen* to deliver a sudden blow to their interlocutor or, with a gesture transcending conceptual expression, to express true reality. Thus in the *Lin-chi-lu* we find the following examples of the use of the *hossu* by the great Ch'an master → Lin-chi I-hsüan:

Ta-chüeh came to see Lin-chi. The master raised his flywhisk. Ta-chüeh spread his sitting mat. The master threw his flywhisk to the ground. Ta-chüeh folded his sitting mat up and went into the monks hall.

A monk asked, "What is the essence of Buddhism?"

The master raised his flywhisk. The monk shouted, "Ho!"

The master also shouted, "Ho!"

The monk hesitated. The master struck him.

Hotei B Z Jap. for → Pu-tai

Hotoke B Z Jap. for → buddha

Ho-tse Shen-hui Z (Jap., Kataku Jin'e), 686–760 or 670–762; Chinese Ch'an (Zen) master of the T'ang period; a student of → Hui-neng and the founder of the → Kataku school. His decades-long advocacy of the tradition of Hui-neng and his relationship to the court of the T'ang emperor Su-tsung led in the middle of the 7th century to the official recognition of his master as the sixth patriarch, instead of → Shen-hsiu, who had hitherto been considered so. However, as with the case of Shen-hsiu, alliance with political power led not to an improvement in the fortunes of the lineage he founded but rather to its decline. The only important master produced by the Kataku school, in the fifth generation after Ho-tse Shen-hui, was Kuei-feng Tsung-mi (Jap., Keihō Shūmitsu), who is better known as the fifth patriarch of the Chinese Hua-yen (Jap., Kegon) school. The school died out without making a significant contribution to the development of Ch'an (Zen).

Ho-tse Shen-hui, initially a Taoist scholar, converted to Buddhism in his forties and in his search for a master ended up in the monastery of Hui-neng, the Pao-lin-ssu of Ts'ao-ch'i near the port city of Canton. Ho-tse was an outstanding student of the sixth patriarch until the latter's death five years later. He was confirmed as the sixth patriarch's dharma successor (→ *hassu*).

Almost two decades after the death of his master, Ho-tse convoked a gathering of the leading Zen monks in south China and proclaimed to them that Hui-neng had been the rightful heir of the fifth patriarch and that the then official sixth patriarch Shen-hsiu's claim was illegitimate. Then he traveled to the capitals in the north, Ch'ang-an and Lo-yang, and presented his claim there, which, considering imperial protection of Shen-hsiu and his successor, showed considerable courage on his part. Eventually, not least because of his great success as a Ch'an master, he so infuriated the religious establishment of the north against him that Emperor Hsüan-tsung banished him to south China. Later, after the An-Lu-shan Rebellion (755–57), the weakened T'ang imperial house remembered the popularity of Ho-tse and wanted to make use of it to reconsolidate its position. The tables now turned in favor of Ho-tse. He was installed once again as the abbot of Ho-tse monastery in Ch'ang-an (he had held this position earlier, before his banishment, and had assumed the name of the monastery) and eventually achieved so much influence at court that he was able to impose recognition of Hui-neng and of the → Southern school of Ch'an.

Ho-tse-tsung Z Chin. → Kataku school

Hotsu-bodaishin Z Jap., lit. "arousing the mind of enlightenment"; the resolve to reach supreme → enlightenment through actualization of the → bodhisattva path. An inner attitude made up of → *dai-shinkon* and → *dai-gedan*. (Also → *kokorozashi*.)

Hotsugammon Z Jap.; a combination of prayers and supplications prepared by → Dōgen Zenji for beginners in → *zazen*.

Ho-t'u and Lo-shu T Chin., lit. "diagram from the [Yellow] River and diagram from the River Lo"; two magical diagrams by which Confucianism explains the origin of the *Book of Change(s)* (→ *I-ching*) and the → *Hung-fan*. In all probability the two diagrams are the result of combining numerological speculations with the → yin-yang teachings of the *I-ching*, and they are in fact mentioned in a commentary known as *Hsi-tz'u* (→ *Shih-i*).

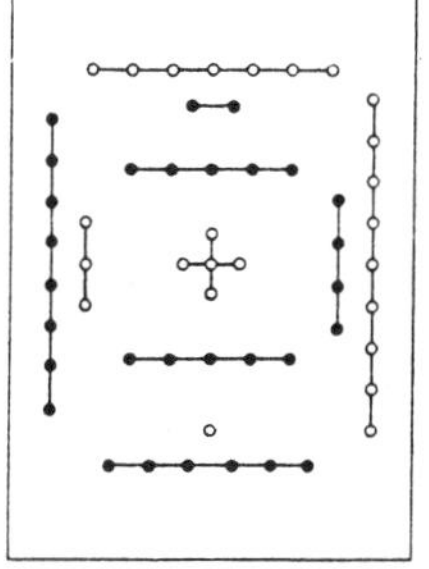

Ho-t'u

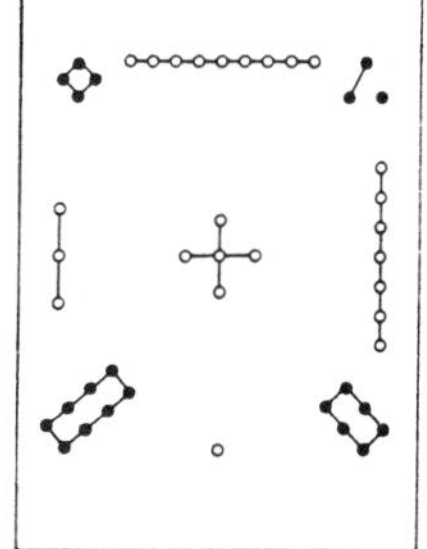

Lo-shu

The *Ho-t'u* is so constructed that its odd numbers as well as its even numbers add up to twenty, if the central five and ten are ignored.

In the *Lo-shu,* on the other hand, the sum of its horizontal and vertical rows, as well as its diagonals, is always fifteen. In both diagrams, even (yin) numbers are indicated by white and odd (yang) numbers by black circles.

In ancient times both diagrams were used for purposes of prophecy. In the Inner Alchemy (→ *nei-tan*) they serve to explain processes occurring within the body under the influence of the inner elixir.

There are conflicting reports about the origin of these diagrams. According to one tradition, Yü the Great (→ Ta-yü) received them from two fabulous animals. The *Ho-t'u* appeared on the back of a dragon-horse emerging from the Yellow River, and the *Lo-shu* on the back of a turtle from the River Lo.

Another tradition states that → Fu Hsi acquired the diagrams in the same manner and then derived the eight trigrams (→ *pa-kua*) from the *Ho-t'u.* According to yet another version, the *Lo-shu* originated with Yü and the *Ho-t'u* with Fu Hsi.

Until the 12th century the names of the two diagams were reversed, i.e., the present *Lo-shu* was known as *Ho-t'u* and vice versa. They were given their present designations by → Chu Hsi and have retained them to this day.

Hou-t'ien 🅃 Chin., lit. after Heaven, post-celestial, after time; a concept occurring in the *Book of Change(s)* (→ *I-ching*) to describe the phenomenal, i.e., the state following the creation of Heaven. *Hou-t'ien* can also refer to "form" or to that which is after birth.

In the *hou-t'ien* ordering of Emperor Wen's eight trigrams (→ *pa-kua*), these are not arranged according to their polar correspondences, i.e., in a precelestial order, but in accordance with their periodical return. In the Inner Alchemy (→ *nei-tan*) the physical forms of the three life forces (→ *ching,* → *ch'i,* → *shen*) are said to be postcelestial.

Hōyū 🅉 Jap. for → Fa-jung

Hsiang Hsiu 🅃 → *Chu-lin ch'i-hsien,* → *hsüan-hsüeh*

Hsiang-lin Ch'eng-yüan 🅉 (Jap., Kyorin Chōon), ca. 908–87; Chinese Ch'an (Zen) master; a student and dharma successor (→ *hassu*) of → Yün-men Wen-yen (Jap., Ummon Bun'en) and the master of → Chih-men Kuang-tsu (Jap., Chimon Kōso). Besides → Tung-shan Shou-chu (Jap., Tōsan Shusho) Hsiang-lin was the most important of the sixty dharma successors of Master Yün-men. He grew up in Szechwan in west central China. There he heard of the renowned masters of the → Southern school of Zen. Eventually he took up a life of wandering and covered a good 2000 kilometers on foot through trackless countryside before he reached the monastery on Mount Yün-men. Here he served Master Yün-men as attendant for eighteen years.

The only instruction that he received from Yün-men during these years, came as follows. From time to time Yün-men would call him: "Attendant Yüan!" Hsiang-lin would then answer, "Yes!" Yün-men then said only, "What is it?!" After eighteen years Hsiang-lin finally came with this "What is it?!" to profound enlightenment.

Returning to Szechwan, he took over the leadership of the Hsiang-lin monastery, the name of which was transferred to him, and for forty years led students on the way of Zen. He had three dharma successors. Before he passed away, at an advanced age, while sitting in meditation, he said to his students, "This old monk was forty years long in one piece!" We encounter him in example 17 of the → *Pi-yen-lu*:

A monk asked Hsiang-lin, "What is the meaning of the patriarch's coming out of the west [→ *seirai-no-i*]?"

Hsiang-lin said, "Tired from long sitting."

Hsiang-sheng hsiang-k'o 🅃 Chin., → *wu-hsing*

Hsiang-yen Chih-hsien 🅉 (Jap., Kyōgen Chikan), d. 898; Chinese Ch'an (Zen) master; a student and dharma successor (→ *hassu*) of → Kuei-shan Ling-yu (Jap., Isan Reiyū). Hsiang-yen appears in example 5 of the → *Wu-men-kuan.*

The story of the enlightenment of Hsiang-yen is often told in Zen, since it is instructive in many ways. Hsiang-yen was a scholar with comprehensive knowledge of Buddhist texts. He had already been a student of Pai-chang Huai-hai (Jap., Hyakujō Ekai) but had had no enlightenment experience under him. After Pai-chang's death, Hsiang-yen continued his training under Pai-chang's chief student Kuei-shan. One day the latter asked him about his "original face before the birth of his parents" (→ *honrai-no-memmoku*), but Hsiang-yen could think of no answer. Also when he looked the matter up in his books, sūtras, and learned commentaries, he could not find a single sentence that seemed to him a suitable answer. He returned in despair to his master and asked him to tell him the answer.

"I could easily give you the answer," Kuei-shan said, "but later you would reproach me for it."

Thereupon Hsian-yen said to himself, "An empty stomach cannot be filled with pictures of food"—and burned his books. Then, despairing that he could ever find enlightenment, he resolved to give up the study of Buddhism, and withdrew to a hermitage at Nan-yang with the intention of ending his days there taking care of the grave of "Master of the Country Chung" (→ Nan-yang Hui-chung).

One day, as he was sweeping the ground, a pebble rebounded from his broom and struck the trunk of a bamboo tree. At the sound of the pebble striking the trunk Hsiang-yen experienced enlightenment and broke out into resounding laughter. He returned to his hut, offered incense and prostrated in the direction of Mount Kuei. He said, "Master, your kindness is far greater than that of my parents. If you had given me the answer then, I never would have come to this joy."

As we learn in the → *Ching-te ch'uan-teng-lu*, he once later said to his students, "The way is realized through one's own inner awakening; that is not dependent on words. If you look at the invisible and limitless, where is there a gap there? How could you reach it through an effort of conceptual mind? [The Way] is simply a reflection of enlightenment, and that is also your entire daily task. Only the ignorant go in the opposite direction."

Hsien ■ Chin., immortal; ideal of religious Taoism (→ *tao-chiao*). *Hsien* designates a being who has attained physical immortality, is no longer subject to the "world of dust" and is a master of various magical skills.

Taoism teaches various ways of restoring to the body pure energies it possessed at birth and thereby attaining immortality (→ *ch'ang-sheng pu-ssu*). Some Taoists follow the alchemical path and strive to produce an elixir of immortality (→ *wai-tan*); others endeavor to reach their aim by special hygiene exercises (→ Inner Deity Hygiene School), breathing exercises (→ *hsing-ch'i*, → *fu-ch'i*, → *t'ai-hsi*, etc.), gymnastics (→ *tao-yin*), sexual techniques (→ *fang-chung shu*), fasting (→ *chai*) or meditation (→ *tso-wang*, → *shou-i*, → *ts'un-ssu*).

Taoist literature mentions various categories of immortals. The great alchemist → Ko Hung speaks of three such categories, namely celestial immortals, terrestrial immortals, and immortals who have separated from their dead body (→ *shih-chieh*). Terrestrial immortals live in forests or in the mountains, whereas celestial immortals dwell either in the Taoist Heaven (→ *t'ien*); on the isles of the immortals (→ P'eng-lai, → Ying-chou, → Fang-chang), which are situated in the eastern sea; or in the → K'un-lun Mountains toward the West.

Immortals are often portrayed riding on a crane, because according to an ancient belief cranes may live for a thousand years or longer. The vermilion red color of the crane's head is considered to be proof that the crane has preserved his life energy and consists of pure yang (→ yin-yang). That is why immortals are said to ascend to Heaven riding on the back of a crane (→ *fei-sheng*).

In the course of time famous and venerated historical personalities came to be admitted to the ranks of the immortals. The best-known *hsien* are the eight immortals (→ *pa-hsien*).

Immortals have for centuries been a favorite subject in Chinese art. Frequently they are portrayed as having a body covered with feathers. This points to an earlier interpretation of the word *hsien*, related to the development of the relevant Chinese pictogram: originally the pictogram for *hsien* was a sign that signified rising, ascending into the air. The present pictogram for "immortal" (consisting of the signs for "man" and "mountain") was not introduced until later, when immortals came to be seen as seeking the seclusion of the mountains or withdrawing to a paradisical island.

In Ko Hung's classification celestial immortals are accorded the highest stage of realization. He describes them as follows: "Some immortals ascend to the clouds, their body upright, and they fly among the clouds without the beating of wings; some glide across the cloudy vapor by harnessing a dragon and ascend up to the very steps of Heaven; some transform themselves into animals and roam through the azure clouds; yet others dive deep into rivers and oceans or flutter on wings to the peaks of famous mountains. . . . Their kind has attained an eternal life, free from death; but before they reach their goal they have to shed all human emotions and all ambitions about fame and glory. . . . They have abandoned their former nature and are pervaded by a new life energy" (trans. from W. Bauer, *China und die Hoffnung auf Glück* [Munich, 1974], 157). The terrestrial immortals prefer to live in the seclusion of the mountains. They are masters of various supernatural skills; e.g., they are able to conquer demons, walk through forests without being attacked by wild animals, make themselves invisible in moments of danger, etc. They are saints and retain their youthful appearance despite their great age. Occasionally they mingle with ordinary mortals to astonish them by their magical abilities and transmit to them long-forgotten knowledge. They have decided not to die and thus had to forgo the possibility of ascending to Heaven.

Hsien-t'ien ■ Chin., lit. "before Heaven, precelestial, before time"; a concept found in the *Book of Change(s)* (→ *I-ching*), describing the state that existed before the creation of Heaven, i.e., the absolute. *Hsien-t'ien* can also be understood to refer to the formless, i.e., that which exists before birth.

→ Fu Hsi's arrangement of the eight trigrams (→ *pa-kua*) is said to be precelestial. In his ordering of the trigrams, pairs of forces with a polar relationship face each other and hold each other in balance. The later ordering of the trigrams by the Emperor Wen is described as postcelestial (→ *hou-t'ien*).

In the Inner Alchemy (→ *nei-tan*) the purified cosmic state of the three life forces (→ *ching*, → *ch'i*, → *shen*) is described as precelestial.

Hsien-t'ien-t'u ▣ Chin. → Ch'en T'uan

Hsi K'ang ▣ Chin. → *chu-lin ch'i-hsien*

Hsin ▣ Chin. for Japanese *shin*, → *kokoro*

Hsin-chai ▣ Chin., lit. "fasting or abstinence of the heart"; a concept found in the writings of → Chuang-tzu to describe the purification of the mind, thereby making it possible to experience the Tao. Chuang-tzu describes this fasting of the heart as follows: "Unify your will. No longer hear with your ears, but with your heart. Nay, hear no longer with the heart but with the → *ch'i*. Auditory perception is limited by the ears, and even the heart [i.e., (self)-consciousness] is restricted by its attachments to certain external things; the *ch'i*, however, perceives through emptiness, and the Tao arises from emptiness. This emptiness is attained by [what I call] fasting of the heart" (trans. from Kaltenmark, *Lao-tzu und der Taoismus;* see Kaltenmark 1969).

In the official state religion *chai* denotes ritual fasting before sacrifices are offered. Chuang-tzu explains this to Hsing-ch'i by referring to a conversation between Confucius and his pupil Yen Hui, who is planning to civilize a tyrant. Confucius—here presented as a Taoist—points out the pitfalls and dangers of [self]-conscious will and action to Yen Hui and advises him to practice *hsin-chai* and thereby purify his mind. Only then would Yen Hui be able to influence the tyrant constructively: "Then you may enter the cage [i.e., enter the tyrant's service] and move therein without causing undue offence. If people are willing to listen, sing your song; if not, keep silent. You cannot influence men by force or guile. You are in the same cage with them and should live among them quite naturally. In this way you may be able to achieve something" (trans. from Wilhelm 1969).

Hsing-ch'i ▣ Chin., lit. "allowing the breath to circulate"; Taoist breathing technique by which the practitioner allows the breath to circulate through all parts of the body. *Hsing-ch'i* forms part of embryonic breathing (→ *t'ai-hsi*) as well as the practices of → *tao-yin*, → *t'u-ku na-hsin* and other methods of nourishing the body (→ *yang-sheng*). The *hsing-ch'i* practitioner directs his breath by the power of his mind. Each practitioner develops his own method of doing this: some see the breath as two white lines (it enters through the nostrils and circulates through the body in two separate and independent streams); others prefer to imagine that the breath is led by a small figure whose progress they follow in their mind. The breath is circulated within the body as slowly as possible, endeavoring to dispatch it to all parts of the body. By this method sicknesses may be cured and blockages dissolved.

Concerning *hsing-ch'i* practices → Ko Hung writes, "The absorption of medicaments and draughts is a basic requirement for attaining immortality. However, by practicing the circulation of the breath, the process can be accelerated. Even without medicaments or draughts a person can reach the age of a hundred years by just practicing *hsing-ch'i*. It nourishes the body within and helps to ward off external evils."

The *hsing-ch'i* practitioner should retire to a quiet room, lie on the floor, place a flat cushion under his head, and close his eyes. The practitioner should eliminate thoughts and sense perceptions, as well as all feelings and emotions. Then he should inhale and hold the breath for several heartbeats. A practitioner will not approach the state of immortality until he is able to let his breath circulate through his body for a thousand heartbeats.

Hsing-hua Ts'ung-chiang ▣ (Jap., Kōke Zonshō), 830–88; Chinese Ch'an (Zen) master; a student and dharma successor (→ *hassu*) of → Lin-chi I-hsüan and the master of → Nanyüan Hui-yung. Little is known concerning Hsing-hua besides that he was the dharma heir of Lin-chi through whom the lineage of transmission of the → Rinzai school passed. This lineage is still active in Japan.

Hsing-ming ▣ Chin., lit. "nature and life"; the spiritual nature and the life or fate of a human being. *Ming* stands for the substance of life and death, *hsing* for the root of spiritual consciousness. *Ming* is seen as the source of life-giving breath (→ *ch'i*), and *hsing* as the source of the mind (→ *shen*).

Both *hsing* and *ming* arise from the void (*hsü*) existing before birth: at the moment of birth this primordial energy separates into the two components *hsing* and *ming*. The aim of the Inner Alchemy School (→ *nei-tan*) consists in purifying the mind so as to be able to return to the void (*lien-shen fu-hsü*). In the symbolic language of the alchemists this process is described as the uniting of → *k'an* and *li,* or the heart and kidneys.

Hsing-yang Ch'ing-jang 🅉 (Jap., Kōyō Seijō [Shinjō]); Chinese Ch'an (Zen) master; a student and dharma successor (→ *hassu*) of Pa-chiao Hui-ch'ing. We encounter Master Hsing-yang, who flourished in the 10th/11th century, in example 9 of the → *Wu-men-kuan.*

Hsi-tang Chih-tsang 🅉 (Jap., Seidō Chizō), 734/35–814, Chinese Ch'an (Zen) master; a student and dharma successor (→ *hassu*) of → Ma-tsu Tao-i (Jap., Baso Dōitsu). Hsi-tang was an outstanding student of Ma-tsu; after the latter's death, the monks of the monastery requested Hsi-tang to assume leadership as abbot and to instruct them. We encounter Hsi-tang in example 73 of the → *Pi-yen-lu.*

Hsi Wang-mu 🅃 Chin., lit. "Royal Mother of the West"; Taoist figure that rules over the western paradise (of the immortals) in the K'un-lun Mountains. As the ruler of the immortals (→ *hsien*) she is portrayed as a young beautiful woman wearing a royal gown, sometimes also riding on a peacock. She lives in a nine-storied palace of jade, which is surrounded by a wall over a thousand miles long and of pure gold. The male immortals reside in the right wing of this palace, the female immortals in the left wing.

In her garden Hsi Wang-mu cultivates the peach of immortality; whoever partakes of this fruit is no longer subject to death. However, her miraculous peach tree forms only one peach every three thousand years, which then takes a further three thousand years to ripen. When it is ripe, the Royal Mother of the West invites all the immortals to a feast to celebrate their birthday and to partake of the miraculous peach, which bestows another lease of immortality. The feast has often been described in Chinese literature.

In the course of history the figure of Hsi Wang-mu has undergone considerable changes of meaning. In ancient texts, such as the *Shan-hai ching* (*Book of Mountains and Oceans*) she is described as a monster with a human face, the teeth of a tiger, and a leopard's tail. She was the goddess of epidemics, who lived in the West and ruled over the demons of the plague. By the beginning of the Christian era, however, she had become a noble lady. According to legend she presented gifts to several ancient Chinese rulers, at first of jade and later of the life-prolonging peach, which has ever since been her symbol.

In the Taoist view, the Royal Mother of the West arose from the purest air of the West and is representative of yin, the passive feminine principle, whereas Tung Wang-kung, her male consort—known as the Prince of the East—was born of the pure breath of the East and represents yang, the active male principle (→ yin-yang).

Hsi-yüan Ssu-ming 🅉 (Jap., Saiin Shimyō); Chinese Ch'an (Zen) master of about the 9th century; a student and dharma successor (→ *hassu*) of Ch'an master Pao-chou Yen-chao (Jap., Hōju Enshō), who was in turn a dharma successor of Lin-chi I-hsüan (Jap., Rinzai Gigen). We encounter Hsi-yüan in example 98 of the → *Pi-yen-lu.*

Hsü 🅃 Chin., → *hsing-ming*

Hsüan-hsüeh 🅃 Chin., lit. "secret mystical teaching"; a philosophical movement of the 3d and 4th centuries C.E., known as neo-Taoism, and based on the philosophical Taoism (→ *tao-chia*) of Lao-tzu and Chuang-tzu. The term *hsüan-hsüeh* as a concept goes back to the *Tao-te ching,* which describes the → Tao as the "secret of secrets."

The followers of the *hsüan-hsüeh* movement combine Taoist ideas with Confucianist principles. They consider Confucius (→ K'ung-tzu) to be the greater sage because he attained a higher level of insight than either Lao-tzu or Chuang-tzu.

The neo-Taoists developed and refined a special form of converse known as pure conversation (→ *ch'ing-t'an*). The most important representatives of the *hsüan-hsüeh* movement were → Wang Pi (226–49 C.E.), Hsiang Hsiu (221–300 C.E.), and Kuo Hsiang (?–ca. 312 C.E.), all of whom wrote important commentaries on the *Tao-te ching.*

Neo-Taoists see the Tao as literally nothingness, whereas Lao-tzu holds that the true Tao cannot be named. It follows from this that the Tao cannot be the cause of anything: to say that something was caused by the Tao would amount to saying that it was caused by itself. The *hsüan-hsüeh* philosophers thus refute the view that nonbeing (→ *wu*) can give rise to being (*you*).

Thus in neo-Taoism the Tao—the central concept of original Taoism—was increasingly replaced by the idea of Heaven (→ *t'ien*), which is said to be the totality of all that exists. To see the world from the point of view of Heaven means to transcend phenomena and differentiations. The identity of things is therefore a central tenet of neo-Taoism. To realize this identity, it is necessary to abandon all likes and dislikes and live in complete harmony with one's true self, uninfluenced by external factors. Such an attitude is said to lead to complete freedom and happiness.

Unlike Lao-tzu, the supporters of neo-Taoism do not condemn institutions and customs, providing these adapt themselves to social change and to the requirements of the times. They see change as a mighty force, which man is unable to perceive directly but to which everything is subject. Voluntary submission to this principle is known as → *wu-wei,* i.e., to let things take their course by not opposing or resisting the process of natural change.

Since the 5th century C.E. neo-Taoism has been strongly influenced by Buddhism and in consequence lost a great deal of its earlier importance.

Hsü-an Huai-ch'ang 🅩 (Jap., Kian Eshō; Chinese Ch'an (Zen) master of the Sung period who belonged to the Ōryō lineage of Rinzai Zen (→ Ōryō school). He was the master of → Eisai Zenji, who is regarded as the father of the Japanese Zen tradition.

Hsüan-sha Shih-pei 🅩 (Jap., Gensha Shibi); Chinese Ch'an (Zen) master; a student and dharma successor (→ *hassu*) of → Hsüeh-feng I-ts'un (Jap., Seppō Gison) and the master of → Lo-han Kuei-ch'en (Jap., Rakan Keijin). Hsüan-sha was one of the most important of the fifty-six dharma successors of Master Hsüeh-feng and as master of the master of → Fa-yen Wen-i (Jap., Hōgen Bun'eki) one of the forefathers of the → Hōgen school. In the *Ching-te ch'uan-teng-lu,* this is still called the Hsüan-sha school. Hsüan-sha had thirteen dharma successors; we encounter him in Master Wu-men's commentary to example 41 of the → *Wu-men-kuan,* as well as in examples 22, 56 and 88 of the → *Pi-yen-lu.*

Hsüan-sha was a fisherman until his thirtieth year, an illiterate of whom it is said that he could not even read the four characters with which the then current coins were marked. Nevertheless, one day he abandoned his boat and entered the Ch'an monastery of Ling-hsün of Fu-jung-shan (Lotus Mountain). He received full monastic ordination from a master of the → Vinaya school and led for some years thereafter a strict ascetic life in the mountains. Once when he came to see Master Ling-hsün, he met Hsüeh-feng, who was only thirteen years his senior. He attached himself to Hsüeh-feng in 872 in order to help the latter build his monastery on Hsüeh-feng Mountain. On one of the pilgrimages that Hsüan-sha henceforth undertook in order to meet other Ch'an masters, he stubbed his toe on a stone on a mountain path and, with the sudden pain, experienced enlightenment.

Between Master Hsüeh-feng and his student and helper Hsüan-sha there developed such a close relationship that finally they could understand one another entirely without speaking. Later when Hsüan-sha himself became active as a Ch'an master, it is said that he was able to express Hsüeh-feng's dharma teaching more simply and directly than his master. Hsüan-sha passed away in the same year as his master.

Hsüan-tsang 🅑 also called San-tsang, Sentsang, "Tripitaka," or T'ang-seng, 600–664; important Chinese monk and pilgrim; one of the four great translators of Sanskrit texts of Chinese Buddhism. He was cofounder of the → Fa-hsiang school, the Chinese form of → Yogāchāra. Hsüan-tsang spent sixteen years (629–45) on a pilgrimage to India, where he studied at Nālandā and visited all important Buddhist sites. He reported his experiences in his famous travel account *Ta-t'ang hsi-yu chi,* which provides important dates for research on the history and archaeology of India as well as on the situation of Buddhism in the 7th century.

After his return to China Hsüan-tsang translated the fundamental works of the Yogāchāra into Chinese, for example, the → *Prajñāpāramitā-sūtra* in 600 volumes; the → *Yogāchāra-bhūmi-shāstra,* the → *Abhidharmakosha,* the *Mahāyāna-samparigraha* of → Asanga, the *Trimshikā* and *Vimshatikā* of → Vasubandhu. In addition he wrote the *Vijñaptimātratā-siddhi* (Chin., *Ch'eng wei-shih lun*), in which he synthesized and commented upon the work of ten renowned Yogāchāra masters. It is a complete presentation of the Yogāchāra.

Hsüan-tsang was born in what is today Honan province. At the age of thirteen he became a novice in the monastic order and at twenty-one became a monk. He studied the important Mahāyāna writings under a wide variety of teachers. Since, however, individual teachers interpreted these works in different ways, Hsüan-tsang decided to go to the west, to India, where he hoped to find a competent teacher.

In 629 he quit the capital Ch'ang-an without the emperor's permission. His route led through Kan-su, Tun-huang, Turfan (where he was the recipient of significant aid in the form of letters of recommendation to various rulers), further to Tashkent, Samarkand, and Bactria, then over the Hindu Kush to Gandhāra. In 631 Hsüan-tsang reached Kashmir. In 633 he undertook the perilous journey to the holy sites of Buddhism (Kapilavastu, Kushinagara, Vaishālī, Bodh-gayā), and finally reached the Buddhist monastic university Nālandā. There under the abbot Shīlabhadra, he studied texts of the Yogāchāra. After two years he left Nālandā to continue to Ceylon. However, he soon returned to the monastic university, where he now engaged himself principally in the study of Indian philosophy.

His erudition rapidly became so renowned that he received invitations from many rulers. He was victorious in a number of debates with representatives of the Hīnayāna and also of Brahmanism.

In 645 he returned to Ch'ang-an by the southern route, bringing with him 520 Hīnayāna and Mahāyāna texts. In the following years he devoted himself entirely to his translation work and translated altogether 75 works. In addition he translated Lao-tsu and the → *Mahāyānashraddhotpāda-shāstra* into Sanskrit. His translations are outstanding for their high literary level. He was a principal participant in the creation of an adequate Buddhist terminology in Chinese.

Hsüan-tsang's experiences on his pilgrimage provided the material for a famous Chinese novel of the 16th century, *The Journey to the West* (*Hsi-yu chi*) by Wu Ch'eng-en, in which Hsüan-tsang appears as the monk San-tsang, who goes through fantastic adventures (trans. Anthony C. Yu, Chicago 1980).

Hsüeh-feng I-ts'un ■ (Jap., Seppō Gison), 822–908; one of the most important Chinese Ch'an (Zen) masters of ancient China; a student and dharma successor (→ *hassu*) of → Te-shan Hsüan-chien (Jap., Tokusan Senkan). Hsüeh-feng, who is one of the forefathers of the → Ummon and → Hōgen schools in China, is said to have had fifty-six dharma successors, among whom the best known are → Hsüan-sha Shih-pei (Jap., Gensha Shibi) and → Yün-men Wen-yen (Jap., Ummon Bun'en). We encounter Hsüeh-feng in example 13 of the → *Wu-men-kuan* and in examples 5, 22, 49, 51, and 66 of the → *Pi-yen-lu.*

By far the most renowned kōan with Hsüeh-feng is example 5 of the *Pi-yen-lu,* which is as follows:

"Hsüeh-feng said in instructing the assembled: 'The whole great earth, taken between the fingers, is of the same size as a grain of rice. I throw it down before you. A paint bucket that you don't grasp. Beat the drum, spare no effort, search, search!' "

Hsüeh-feng already wanted to become a monk at the age of nine, but was held back by his parents. When at the age of twelve he visited his father at Yu-chien monastery in P'u-t'ien, he saw the Vinaya master there and declared, "That is my master," and stayed at the monastery. His first Ch'an master was Ling-hsün, a "dharma grandchild" of → Ma-tsu Tao-i (Jap., Baso Dōitsu). After Hsüeh-feng had been fully consecrated as a monk, he wandered through the country, visited many Ch'an masters, and served in a number of monasteries as kitchen master (→ *tenzo*). In example 13 of the *Wu-men-kuan* we see him as a *tenzo* in the monastery of Te-shan, whose dharma successor he is considered to be, although at the time of Te-shan's death he still had not experienced profound enlightenment. Only after Te-shan had passed away did Hsüeh-feng experience profound enlightenment, at about the age of forty-five, in a → *mondō* with his dharma brother → Yen-t'ou Ch'üan-huo (Jap., Gantō Zenkatsu), who was also a student of Te-shan. The circumstances surrounding this experience as well as more about the life of Hsüeh-feng we learn in Master Yüan-wu's discourse concerning example 5 of the *Pi-yen-lu.*

At about fifty years of age Hsüeh-feng gave into some monks who were seeking instruction from him and settled on Mount Hsüeh-feng (from which his name comes). From the brushwood huts that he and his students built there soon grew a large monastery; for within ten years 1,500 monks had gathered around him. The monastic community lived following Hsüeh-feng's model—he was known for his care and earnestness in practice and all other matters. The community became known throughout China for its diligence and for a lifestyle concerned only with the essential. A number of Hsüeh-feng's dharma successors, as well as their dharma successors, became important masters of Ch'an.

Hsüeh-tou Ch'ung-hsien ■ (Jap., Setchō Jūken), 982–1052; Chinese Ch'an (Zen) master of the → Ummon school; a student and dharma successor (→ *hassu*) of → Chih-men Kuang-tsu (Jap., Chimon Kōso). Hsüeh-tou, a "great-grandson in dharma" of master Yün-men Wen-yen (Jap., Ummon Ben'en) was one of the last great masters of the Ummon school of Ch'an. He is known especially as the master who compiled the hundred kōans that constitute the basic material of the → *Pi-yen-lu,* after the → *Wu-men-kuan* the best-known collection of kōans. He also celebrated the examples of the ancient masters in praises (→ *ju*), which are among the most profound poems of Ch'an (Zen) literature. Here and there are also to be found short commentaries (→ *jakugo*) that Hsüeh-tou added to certain kōans (for example, *Pi-yen-lu* 18).

Hsün-tzu ■ Chin. → Confucianism

Hsü-t'ang Chih-yü ■ (Jap., Kidō Chigu), 1189–1269; Chinese Ch'an (Zen) master of the Yōgi lineage of Rinzai Zen (→ Yōgi school). He was the master of → Shōmyō, who brought his dharma teaching to Japan. In their effort to preserve Rinzai Zen in Japan from decline, great Japanese masters like → Ikkyū Sōjun and → Hakuin Zenji, who stood in the lineage of Hsü-t'ang, repeatedly appealed to the strict Zen of this great Chinese master, while referring to themselves as his dharma heirs.

Hua-hu ching ■ Chin., lit. *"Classic [Treatise] on the Conversion of Barbarians";* Taoist work, dating from ca. 300 C.E., in which the missionary activities of → Lao-tzu "in the West of China" (i.e., India) are described. The *Hua-hu ching* claims that the Buddha was a pupil of Lao-tzu and Buddhism therefore a variant of Taoism.

The *Hua-hu ching* figures prominently in the early controversies between Taoists and Buddhists, the Taoists citing it as proof of their superiority over the followers of Buddhism and demanding that Taoism be accorded the status of an official religion. The Buddhists countered by moving the Buddha's date of birth back to the 11th century B.C.E.: Lao-tzu could not possibly have converted a person that lived several centuries before him.

Huai-hai 🅉 → Pai-chang Huai-hai

Huai-nan-tzu 🅃 Chin., philosophical treatise dating from the 2d century B.C.E.; more specifically, a collection of writings by scholars gathered around Liu An, the prince of Huai-nan, who later became involved in a conspiracy against the ruler and committed suicide in 122 B.C.E.

Like the → *Lü-shih ch'un-ch'iu,* the *Huai-nan-tzu* is an analytical compilation of the teachings of philosophical schools prevalent during the 2d century. It accords special emphasis to Taoist ideas. Of particular importance are its chapters on the origin of the cosmos, because they are clearer and more lucid than relevant passages in other works. In addition, the *Huai-nan-tzu* deals with the doctrine of the five elements (→ *wu-hsing*) and with the → yin-yang.

The *Huai-nan-tzu* originally consisted of twenty-one "inner" chapters, which contain Taoist teachings, and thirty-three "outer" chapters devoted to the philosophies of other schools. The thirty-three "outer" chapters are lost. The third of the "inner" chapters describes the genesis of the universe as follows:

"Before Heaven and Earth took on form, there was a state of amorphous formlessness. This is known as the great beginning [→ *t'ai-shih*], which gave rise to an empty expanse, from which emerged the cosmos, which produced the (no longer unlimited or infinite) primordial breath [→ *yüan-ch'i*]. That which was lucid and light gathered to form Heaven, and that which was heavy and opaque combined to form Earth. The joining of the light and the opaque was effortless, whereas the fusion of the heavy and opaque was difficult. That is why Heaven was formed before Earth.

"The essences of Heaven and Earth formed yin and yang, and their concentrated essences in turn gave rise to the four seasons. The scattered essences of the four seasons produced the ten thousand things. The hot yang energy, having accumulated over a long period of time, produced fire, the essence of which became the sun. The cold yin energy, similarly accumulated over a long period of time, produced water, the essence of which became the moon. The purified essences of sun and moon gave rise to the stars and planets. Heaven received the sun, moon, stars and planets, while Earth received water, rivers, soil, and dust."

Huan-ching 🅃 Chin., lit. "allowing the semen to return"; Taoist sexual practice aimed at prolonging life, in which the practitioner causes his essence (→ *ching*) to intermingle with his breath (→ *ch'i*) and then to circulate through his body, dispatching it from the lower to the upper cinnabar field (→ *tan-t'ien*), with the aim of nourishing the brain (*pu-nao*). Before *huan-ching* can be practiced the adept must increase and strengthen his *ching* by refraining from ejaculation during sexual intercourse (see next entry).

Huan-ching pu-nao 🅃 Chin., lit. "allowing the semen to return [in order to] strengthen the brain"; Taoist sexual technique (→ *fang-chung shu*) for strengthening the *ching* essence and prolonging life.

When practicing *huang-ching pu-nao* the man firmly grips the root of his penis between two fingers prior to ejaculation, while deeply exhaling through the mouth and grinding his teeth (→ *k'ou-ch'ih*). This causes the semen to ascend to the upper cinnabar field (→ *tan-t'ien*) in the brain. *Huang-ching pu-nao* should only be practiced on certain days and at certain hours of the day. In addition, the practitioner should be in a state of meditative absorption.

The alleged reason for the rejuvenating effect of this practice is that the semen (*ching*) can combine with the vital energy (*ch'i*). There are divergent views as to where in the body this fusion of *ching* and *ch'i* occurs. Some maintain it takes place in the respiratory tract, to which the essence ascends; others say it occurs in the lower cinnabar field, to which the breath descends. Once combined, the semen and the vital energy circulate through the body until they once again rise from the lower to the upper cinnabar field—more precisely, that part of it known as → *ni-huan,* whereby the brain is repaired. Some Taoists practice *huang-ching pu-nao* as a preliminary to meditative breathing exercises of the Inner Alchemy School (→ *nei-tan*).

Taoists are convinced that this method of preventing ejaculation was already known at the time of the legendary Yellow Emperor (→ Huang-ti), who is said to have had successive sexual intercourse with twelve hundred concubines, suffering no damage to his health. In any case, it is certain that the practice was widespread by the time of the Han Dynasty.

Most Taoist works stress that the essential generating factor of this technique is the primordial essence of the semen rather than the semen itself. The process of the *huan-ching pu-nao* practice begins at the moment an erection becomes manifest and sexual energy is aroused. In the Taoist view an erection need, however, not always be dependent on sexual arousal; rather it is taken to indicate that energy is present in sufficient quantity to circulate freely through the body. Furthermore, an erection may occur during meditation if the practitioner reaches a state free of thought and desire. *Huan-ching pu nao* can thus also be practiced by Taoists who reject sexual techniques involving a partner of the opposite sex.

Huang-chin 🅣 Chin., lit. "yellow cloth," "Yellow Turbans"; a term descriptive of the followers of the Way of Supreme Peace (→ *t'ai-p'ing tao*) founded by → Chang Chüeh. They wore around their heads a yellow cloth in honor of the Yellow Emperor (→ Huang-ti) who, together with → Lao-chün, was considered the original founder of the *t'ai-p'ing tao* movement as a whole.

A rebellion organized in 184 C.E. by the followers of the Way of Supreme Peace has gone down in history as the Rising of the Yellow Turbans (*huang-chin ch'i-i*).

Huang-ch'üan 🅣 Chin., lit. "yellow springs"; the Underworld, to which yin souls (→ yin-yang, → *p'o*) return after death. The *huang-ch'üan* is traditionally believed to be a watery place, situated in the North. That is why in ancient times the dead were buried in the northern part of the town and with their heads pointing north.

Huang-lao 🅣 Chin., lit. "Yellow-old"; Taoist deity. The *Huang* component refers to → Huang-ti, the Yellow Emperor, and the *lao* component to → Lao-tzu. Religious Taoism (→ *tao-chiao*) considers both as its founders, and they have been jointly venerated as Huang-lao since ca. 200 B.C.E. Later, Huang-lao developed into one of the most important deities of early Taoism, → Huang-lao-chün, the main deity of the Way of Supreme Peace (→ *t'ai-p'ing tao*).

Huang-lao-chün 🅣 Chin., lit. "Ancient Yellow Lord"; important deity of early Taoism and main god of the Way of Supreme Peace (→ *t'ai-p'ing tao,* → Huang-lao). The common people considered Huang-lao-chün to be the ruler of the world, who descends to Earth to guide and assist mankind. From the beginning of the world he is said to have appeared, again and again, in the shape of Taoist masters to spread the teachings about the Tao. One of his incarnations was → Lao-tzu.

Huang-lung Hui-nan 🅩 (Jap., Ōryō [Ōryū] E'nan), 1002–69; Chinese Ch'an (Zen) master of the → Rinzai school; a student and dharma successor (→ *hassu*) of → Shih-huang Ch'u-yüan (Jap., Sekisō Soen) and the master of → Hui-t'ang Tsu-hsin (Jap., Maidō Soshin), Yün-kai Shou-chih (Jap., Ungai Shichi), and Pao-feng K'o-wen (Jap., Hōbō Kokumon). Master Huang-lung founded the → Ōryō school of Rinzai Zen that bears his name, one of the two lineages into which the Rinzai-school tradition of Master Shih-shuang divided. The Zen of the Ōryō lineage was the first school of Zen to be brought to Japan, at the end of the 12th century, by → Eisai Zenji.

Huang-lung p'ai 🅩 Chin. for → Ōryō school

Huang-mei 🅩 Jap. Obai; another name for → Hung-jen (Jap. Gunin), the fifth patriarch of Zen in China. Huang-mei is the name of the mountain on which Hung-jen lived.

Huang-po Hsi-yün 🅩 (Jap., Ōbaku Kiun), d. 850; one of the greatest Chinese Ch'an (Zen) masters; a student and dharma successor (→ *hassu*) of → Pai-chang Huai-hai (Jap., Hyakujō Ekai) and master of → Lin-chi I-hsüan (Jap., Rinzai Gigen). Huang-po had thirteen dharma successors; as the master of Lin-chi he is one of the forefathers of the → Rinzai school. His teachings and instructions were recorded by the functionary and scholar P'ei Hsiu (Jap., Haikyū) under the title *Huang-po-shan Tuan-chi-ch'an-shih ch'uan-hsin-fa-yao* (for short, *[Huang-po] Ch'uan-hsin-fa-yao*), which is one of the most profound texts of the Ch'an (Zen) tradition. (For an English translation see Blofeld 1958.) We encounter Huang-po in example 2 of the → *Wu-men-kuan* and in example 11 of the → *Pi-yen-lu.*

Huang-po left his home in his early years and became a monk in a monastery on Mount Huang-po near his home village. His biography describes him as a stately man well over six feet tall with a bead-shaped protuberance on his forehead and a sonorous voice. He is said to have been of simple and pure character. One day he set out to see Master → Ma-tsu Tao-i (Jap., Baso Dōitsu), but when he got to his monastery he heard that Ma-tsu had already died. He stayed nevertheless and became a student of Ma-tsu's dharma successor Pai-chang.

We learn of the nature of the communication between these two Ch'an giants in an anecdote recorded in the → *Ching-te ch'uan-teng-lu*:

"One day Pai-chang asked Huang-po where he had been. He answered that he had been gathering mushrooms at the foot of Mount Ta-hsiung. Pai-chang asked, 'Did you see the tiger?'

"Immediately Huang-po roared like a tiger. Pai-chang grabbed an axe and raised it as though to strike the tiger. Huang-po gave Pai-chang a sudden slap. Pai-chang laughed uproariously.

"Back at the monastery, Pai-chang told the assembled monks, 'At the foot of Mount Ta-hsiung there's a tiger. You should be careful; he already bit me today.' " It is said that with these words Pai-chang confirmed Huang-po as his dharma successor.

Later, after Huang-po had already lived for a period of time at the monastery of → Nan-ch'üan P'u-yüan (Jap., Nansen Fugan), he settled at the Ta-an monastery in Hung-chou. The prime minister P'ei Hsiu, who was one of his students, had a large Ch'an monastery built and asked Huang-po to move there. Huang-po named the monastery after the mountain he had lived on as a young monk, Huang-po-shan, and this name eventually was applied to him.

The spirit in which he instructed his students speaks from example 11 of the *Pi-yen-lu*:

"Huang-po once said while instructing the assembled, 'You're a bunch of dregs-lickers. If you're still on pilgrimage, where are you going to be today? Don't you know that in the entire T'ang empire there are no Zen teachers?'

"Now there was a monk there who came forward and said, 'Why then are students accepted from all over and why are they given instruction all over the place?'

"Huang-po said, 'I didn't say there's no Zen, only that there are no Zen teachers.' "

Huang-ti ■ Chin., lit. "Yellow Emperor"; one of the legendary emperors, whose life span is variously given as 2697–2597 B.C.E. or 2674–2575 B.C.E. He is venerated as one of the founders of religious Taoism (→ *tao-chiao*) and furthermore credited with the creation of mankind, the invention of writing, the compass, the pottery wheel, and the breeding of silkworms. In addition, the Yellow Emperor is considered to have been a determining influence in establishing the Chinese social order, in that he allocated a name to each family. Lastly he is the alleged author of the → *Huang-ti nei-ching,* the first medical treatise in the history of China.

According to one tradition Huang-ti spontaneously came into being as a result of the fusion of energies that marked the beginning of the world. He created man by placing earthen statues at the cardinal points of the world, leaving them exposed to the breath of the world's beginning for a period of three hundred years. When they were totally pervaded by the energy of that breath, the statues were able to speak and move. In this way the various races of mankind came into being. Since the Warring States Period, Taoists have associated Huang-ti with the cult of the immortals. On his travels to the Sacred Mountains, Huang-ti met Master Kuan Cheng, who initiated him in the practices for the realization of the Tao. This encounter is described by → Chuang-tzu (Book 11, Chapter 3) as follows (Kuan Cheng speaking): "See nothing; hear nothing; let your soul be wrapped in quiet, and your body will begin to take proper form. Let there be absolute repose and absolute purity; do not weary your body nor disturb your vitality–and you will live forever. For if the eye sees nothing and the ear hears nothing, and the mind thinks nothing the soul will preserve the body and the body will live forever. Cherish that which is within you and shut off that which is without; for much knowledge is a curse. Then I will place you upon that abode of Great Light, which is the source of the positive Power (*yang*) and escort you through the gate of Profound Mystery, which is the source of the negative Power (*yin*)" (Giles 1961). At the age of 100 Huang-ti was possessed with magical powers and produced the golden elixir (→ *chin-tan*). He attained immortality on Ching Mountain, whereupon he ascended to Heaven riding a dragon (→ *fei-sheng*) and became one of the five mythological emperors, who rule over the five cardinal points (the fifth being the center, ruled by Huang-ti).

Huang-ti nei-ching ■ Chin., lit. *"Inner Classic of the Yellow Emperor";* first medical treatise in the history of China. Although the *Huang-ti nei-ching* is ascribed to the Yellow Emperor (Huang-ti), in all probability it dates from the 3d or 2d Century B.C.E. The basic theories of Chinese medicine contained in the *Huang-ti nei-ching* have retained their validity to the present day. The title of the work is generally translated as *The Yellow Emperor's Classic of Internal Medicine.*

Huang-t'ing ching ■ Chin., lit. *"Classic Treatise on the Yellow Hall* [or *Castle*]"; 3d century Taoist treatise describing the most important deities of the body (→ *shen*) and their functions. In addition, the *Huang-t'ing ching* contains instructions for breathing exercises, above all on letting the breath circulate through the body. (→ *hsing-ch'i*), sexual practices (→ *fang-chung shu*), and other techniques aimed at attaining immortality. The earliest known mention of the term *yellow castle* occurs in an inscription dating from the year 165 C.E. in honor of → Lao-tzu: "Enter into and depart from the cinnabar hut, ascend from and descend to the yellow castle" (Homann 1971, p. 57).

The somewhat ambiguous term *yellow castle* refers primarily to the notion of a center and to the connections that can be established—by following the instruction of the *Huang-t'ing ching*—between the centers of Heaven, of man, and of the Earth. In the case of man, the term *yellow castle* (as employed in the *Huang-t'ing ching*) refers to the heart as the central organ and ruler over thoughts and emotions. Other texts, however, associate the term with the pancreas.

The repeated recitation of the *Huang-t'ing ching* is said to ward off evil, allow the adept to regain his former youthful appearance, and to bestow physical invulnerability. Such recitation, moreover, causes the various deities of the body to appear before the inner eye of the practitioner and helps him to contact these deities so as to obtain instructions on how to attain immortality. In the Taoist view, the effectiveness of the *Huang-t'ing ching* is due to the fact that it reveals the actual names of the deities; by reciting their names the deities can be invoked.

Huan-tan ■ Chin., lit. "recycled cinnabar"; a term used by Taoist alchemists to describe a life-prolonging elixir obtained by a method of cyclic transformation: cinnabar powder is heated and thereby turned into mercury. As a result of the consequent oxidation of the mercury, the alchemist obtains a vermilion-colored oxide, which explains the origin of the term *cinnabar.* As a rule, this process was repeated nine times, thereby producing *chiu-huan-tan,* the "nine times recycled Elixir."

For the followers of the Inner Elixir School (→ *nei-tan*) the term *huan-tan* designates the → *ch'i* produced and accumulated in the body. This *ch'i* is capable of transforming aged body tissue to resemble that of a new-born child. In this way, the adherents of this school believe it to be possible to attain physical immortality.

Hua T'o ■ Taoist physician of 2d/3d century C.E. He was a renowned surgeon, the first anaesthetist in Chinese medicine, and made an important contribution to the development of Taoist gymnastic exercises (→ *tao-yin*).

According to Hua T'o physical exercise effects a removal of negative energies resulting from eating grain (→ *pi-ku*), and ensures the unimpeded circulation of blood. *Tao-yin* exercises are capable of restoring a youthful appearance to the aging body. Hua T'o is furthermore credited with the invention of the *ch'i-kung* exercise known as "movements of the five animals" (*wu-ch'in-hsi*), which consists of imitating the movements of a tiger, a stag, a bear, a monkey, and a bird, thereby stimulating and balancing the flow of → *ch'i* within the body and enhancing the practitioner's health. (For a detailed description of this exercise, see Zoller 1984, p. 256 ff.)

Hua-tou ■ Chin. for → Wato

Hua-yen school ■ Chin. (Jap. → Kegon school; Skt., Avatamsaka school), lit. "Flower Garland school"; important school of Chinese Buddhism, which derived its name from the title of the Chinese translation of the → *Buddhāvatamsaka-sūtra.* It was founded by Fa-tsang (643–712), but its earliest beginnings go back to the monks → Tu-shun (557–640) and Chih-yen (602–68), who are considered the first two patriarchs of the Hua-yen school. Further important representatives were Ch'eng-kuan (737–820), under whom the school gained great influence, and who was regarded by his successors as an incarnation of → Mañjushrī. The fifth patriarch of the school was → Tsung-mi (780–841), who is considered the outstanding master of the school. The Hua-yen school was brought to Japan in the year 740 by Shen-hsiang (Jap., Shinshō). There it was propagated under the name *Kegon.*

This school teaches the equality of all things and the dependence of all things on one another. Its teaching is known as the "teaching of totality," since according to the Hua-yen view all things participate in a unity and this unity divides itself into the many, so that the manifold is unified in this one. The fundamental teaching of Hua-yen is the notion of the "universal causality of the → *dharmadhātu,*" i.e., that everything in the universe arises simultaneously out of itself. All → dharmas possess the six characteristics universality, specificity, similarity, distinctness, integration, and differentiation. They are in either a state of "suchness" (→ *tathatā*), the static aspect of which is emptiness (→ *shūnyatā*), or the realm of "principle" (*li*), the dynamic aspect of which is the realm of phenomena (*shih*). These two realms are so interwoven and dependent on each other that the entire universe arises as an interdependent conditioning.

The teachings of Hua-yen have as their point of departure the theory of causation by the universal principle, or dharmadhātu. According to this, all dharmas of the universe are dependent on one another and condition each other, and none can subsist on its own.

All dharmas are empty: both aspects of this emptiness, the static (*li,* absolute) and the active (*shih,* phenomena) interpenetrate each other unobstructedly; every phenomenon is identical to every other.

This view is illustrated by Fa-tsang in his celebrated simile of the golden lion. The lion symbolizes the phenomenal world of *shih,* the gold the "principle," or *li,* which possesses no form of its own but rather can take on any form according to circumstances. Every organ of the lion participates in the whole result—that it is made of gold. In every part the whole is present and conversely. Thus all phenomena are manifestations of one principle and each phenomena encompasses all others. Gold and lion exist simultaneously and include each other mutually, which according to

Fa-tsang means that each thing in the phenomenal world represents the principle, *li.*

This view is explained in the division of the universe into four realms and in the thesis of the sixfold nature of things. The four realms of the universe are as follows: (1) the realm of reality, of phenomena; (2) the realm of the principle, the absolute; (3) the realm in which phenomena and principle mutually interpenetrate; (4) the realm in which all phenomena exist in perfect harmony and do not obstruct each other; this is the "ideal" world.

The sixfold nature of things is explained by Fa-tsang in his simile in the following manner: (1) the characteristic of universality corresponds to the lion as a whole; (2) that of specificity he explains with the organs of the lion, which all fulfill a specific function and are distinct from the lion as a whole; (3) similarity consists in the fact that they are all parts of the lion; (4) distinctness is expressed in the distinct functions that the organs fulfill; (5) the characteristic of integration he explains through the fact that all organs together make up the lion; (6) the nature of differentiation is explained by the fact that every organ takes its own particular place.

Like the → T'ien-t'ai school, the Hua-yen undertakes a division of the Buddha's teaching into different categories. It makes a fivefold division: (1) the teaching of the → Hīnayāna as it appears in the Āgamas; (2) elementary teachings of the → Mahāyāna as advocated by the → Fa-hsiang and → San-lun schools, which see all dharmas as empty because they arise in a conditioned fashion—these schools of the Mahāyāna are considered elementary because they deny that all beings possess → buddha-nature; (3) the definitive teaching of the Mahāyāna, as presented by the T'ien-t'ai school—on this level all things are considered empty, but also their seeming existence is admitted; (4) the "sudden" teaching, according to which enlightenment is attained suddenly (and not gradually)—this is the stage of → Zen; (5) the "rounded out" teaching of the Mahāyāna, the teaching of the Hua-yen school.

The Hua-yen school distinguishes itself from the other Mahāyāna schools in an important point. It concentrates on the relationship between phenomena and phenomena and not on that between phenomena and the absolute. All things are in complete harmony with one another, since they are all manifestations of one principle. They are like individual waves of the same sea. From this point of view everything in the world, whether animate or inanimate, is an expression of the highest principle and is thus one with buddha-mind.

Hu-ch'in Shao-lung 🅉 (Jap., Kukyū [Kokyū] Jōryū), 1077–1136; Chinese Ch'an (Zen) master of the Yōgi lineage of Rinzai Zen (→ Yōgi school); a student and dharma successor (→ *hassu*) of the great master → Yüan-wu K'o-ch'in (Jap., Engo Kokugon). Through Master Hu-ch'in passes the transmission lineage of Zen of → Hakuin Zenji, the great renewer of Rinzai Zen in Japan.

Hui-k'o 🅉 (Jap., Eka), 487–593; the second patriarch of Ch'an (Zen) in China. He was the dharma successor (→ *hassu*) of → Bodhidharma and the master of → Seng-ts'an. According to tradition Hui-k'o came to → Shao-lin monastery in about his fortieth year to ask Bodhidharma for instruction. It is said that initially Bodhidharma did not acknowledge him and Hui-k'o stood for several days in the snow in front of the cell (or cave) where the first patriarch was practicing *zazen* "facing the wall" (→ *menpeki*). In order to prove his earnestness to the Indian master of → buddha-dharma and to induce the latter to accept him as a student, Hui-k'o finally cut his own left arm off and presented it to Bodhidharma, who thereupon accepted him as a student. A renowned kōan, example 41 of the → *Wu-men-kuan*, gives an account of the encounter between Bodhidharma and Hui-k'o:

> Bodhidharma sat facing the wall. The second patriarch, who had been standing in the snow, cut his own arm off and said, "The mind [heart, consciousness] of your student has still found no peace. I entreat you master, give it peace."
>
> Bodhidharma said, "Bring the mind here and I'll pacify it."
>
> The second patriarch said, "I have searched for the mind, but in the end it can't be found."
>
> Bodhidharma said, "Then I have completely pacified it."

After six years of intensive meditative training under Bodhidharma, the latter confirmed Hui-k'o through → *inka-shōmei* as his dharma successor and transmitted the patriarchate to him. Thus Hui-k'o became the twenty-ninth patriarch of the Ch'an (Zen) tradition (see Ch'an/Zen Lineage Table), or as is more usually said, the second patriarch of Ch'an (Zen) in China.

The state of affairs marked by this transmission is presented in the *Denkō-roku* as follows:

> The twenty-ninth patriarch Taisō Daishi [a Japanese name for Hui-k'o] served the twenty-eighth patriarch. One day he [Hui-k'o] went to the patriarch and said, "I have already ceased having anything to do with outer circumstances."
>
> The patriarch [Bodhidharma] said, "Hasn't everything been extinguished?"
>
> The master [Hui-k'o] said, "It hasn't been extinguished."
>
> The patriarch said, "What proof is there for that?"
>
> The master said, "Since I am always aware of it, no word can touch it."
>
> The patriarch said, "That is just the spiritual body, known to all the buddhas. Have no doubt about it!"

Pui-k'o, who was originally called → Seng-k'o, had the reputation of a scholar who was well versed in the writings of Confucianism, Taoism, and Buddhism.

His book knowledge, however, gave him no satisfaction; and he felt himself ever more attracted to the practice of meditation, through which he could acquaint himself with the profound contents of the scriptures through his own experience. After Bodhidharma had transmitted the patriarchate to him and had died or left Shao-lin monastery, it is said that Hui-k'o remained there for a time and then disappeared, because he did not yet want to accept students. Rather he wanted to train further and to study the → *Lankāvatāra-sūtra*, the importance of which Bodhidharma had stressed. It is said that during this period he lived among simple working people in order to develop the humility that should mark a master of the buddha-dharma. After a few years of the wandering life, he settled in Yeh-tu in north China and there taught the buddha-dharma according to his style. Here he probably met Seng-ts'an.

Hui-k'o's unorthodox lifestyle and his great success as a master at last aroused the anger and envy of orthodox Buddhist circles, which intrigued against him and forced him to flee to south China to escape official persecution. Later he returned to the north and continued to live there until he died at the age of 106. According to some traditions, he was executed because he had once again aroused the envy of influential Buddhist priests. They induced the authorities to charge him with heresy and to condemn him to death.

Hui-neng 🅩 (Jap., E'nō), also called Wei-lang, 638–713; the sixth patriarch of Ch'an (Zen) in China; a student and dharma successor (→ *hassu*) of → Hung-jen. Hui-neng was one of the most important Ch'an masters. He gave Ch'an, which had hitherto been strongly marked by traditional Indian Buddhism, a typical Chinese stamp. Thus he is sometimes regarded as the real father of the Ch'an (Zen) tradition. He never transmitted the patriarchate formally to a successor; thus it came to an end. Nonetheless Hui-neng had several outstanding students and dharma successors. From two of them, → Nan-yüeh Huai-jang (Jap., Nangaku Ejō) and → Ching-yüan Hsing-ssu (Jap., Seigen Gyōshi) stem all the major lineages of Ch'an (→ *goke-shichishū*).

Hui-neng is considered the author of the only Chinese work that later was attributed the status of a sūtra, the *Sūtra [spoken] from the High Seat of the Dharma Treasure*, or, as it is usually known, the *Platform Sūtra* (→ *Liu-tsu-ta-shih fa-pao-t'an-ching*), which contains some of the most profound passages in Zen literature. We also learn from this sūtra, called for short the *T'an-ching* (Jap., *Dan-gyō*), various details of

Hui-neng tears up the sūtras (water-color by Liang-k'ai, 12th century)

the life of the sixth patriarch. Hui-neng came from a poor family, had hardly any formal education, and had to support his widowed mother by gathering and selling firewood. One day he heard, in front of a house he had just serviced with wood, someone reciting the → *Diamond Sūtra*. Hearing the sentence, "Let your mind flow freely without dwelling on anything," he had an enlightenment experience. He learned that the man who had recited the sūtra had come from Hung-jen and decided to go see him. When he reached the monastery led by Hung-jen on Mount Huang-mei, Hung-jen immediately recognized his potential but had Hui-neng begin as a helper in the kitchen, where he split firewood and cranked the rice mill. The most famous episode of his life, which concerns the transmission of the patriarchate and the division of Ch'an into a Northern and a → Southern school, is, in broad outline, as follows:

When the aged fifth patriarch saw that the time had come to transmit the patriarchate to a successor, he requested the monks of the monastery to express their experience of Ch'an in a poem. Only → Shen-hsiu, the most intellectually brilliant of his students and the head monk, highly esteemed by all the monks of the monastery, wrote such a poem. In it he compared the human body with the → Bodhi-tree (under which Shākyamuni Buddha attained complete enlightenment) and the mind with a stand holding a mirror that must be continuously cleaned to keep it free of dust. When Hui-neng, who was working in the kitchen, heard this poem, he composed as an answer the following verse:

Fundamentally *bodhi* is no tree
Nor is the clear mirror a stand.
Since everything is primordially empty,
What is there for dust to cling to?

Hung-jen, who recognized in Hui-neng's lines a level of experience far deeper than that of Shen-hsui, fearing Shen-hsui's jealousy, sent for Hui-neng secretly in the middle of the night and gave him robe and bowl (→ *den'e*) as a sign of confirmation. Thereby he installed Hui-neng, who in contrast to Shen-hsiu was not seeking this position, as the sixth patriarch, well knowing the difficulties for the transmission of his dharma teachings that would arise from this move. At the same time Hung-jen charged Hui-neng to leave the monastery immediately and to go into hiding in south China so as to be safe from the reprisals that were to be expected from Shen-hsiu and his followers.

After about fifteen years of living in hiding, Hui-neng, who as yet was still not even ordained as a monk, went to Fa-hsin monastery (Jap., Hōshō-ji) in Kuang-chou, where his famous dialogue with the monks who were arguing whether it was the banner or the wind in motion, took place. This dialogue is recorded as example 29 in the → *Wu-men-kuan.* When Yin-tsung, the dharma master of the monastery, heard about this, he said to Hui-neng, "You are surely no ordinary man. Long ago I heard that the dharma robe of Huang-mei had come to the south. Isn't that you?" Then Hui-neng let it be known that he was the dharma successor of Hung-jen and the holder of the patriarchate. Master Yin-tsung had Hui-neng's head shaved, ordained him as a monk, and requested Hui-neng to be his teacher.

Thus Hui-neng began his work as a Ch'an master, first in the Fa-hsin monastery, then in his own monastery, the Pao-lin-ssu near Ts'ao-ch'i, not far from the port city of Canton. He founded the Southern school of Ch'an, while Shen-hsiu and his students propagated the teachings of the Northern school and also claimed the successorship of the fifth patriarch. In a manner corresponding to the respective inclinations of the two founders, the Southern school stressed reaching enlightenment through a sudden, intuitive leap into intellect-transcending immediacy of experience (→ *tongo*), whereas the Northern school advocated a gradual approach to enlightenment with the help of intellectual penetration of the meaning of the sūtras (→ *zengo*). In the "competition" between the partisans of sudden and gradual enlightenment, the Southern school eventually proved itself the more vital. While the Northern school died out after a few generations, a great number of profoundly enlightened masters in succession from Hui-neng bear witness to the legitimacy of the attribution of the patriarchate, and thus the lineage of the true dharma, to Hui-neng.

With Hui-neng, who as an uneducated layman received the transmission of the patriarchate against all conventions of the religious establishment, a decisive step was made toward the assimilation of Indian → Dhyāna Buddhism into the Chinese mind-set, as well as toward the development of a native Chinese Ch'an that was at least as strongly marked by Taoism as by Buddhism. It was this Southern school with its radical rejection of mere book learning (a view already exemplified for centuries by Taoist sages), and its practical down-to-earthness combined with dry humor, so typical of the Chinese folk character, that produced all the great lineages of Ch'an. With Hui-neng and his students and dharma successors began the golden age of Ch'an. During the T'ang, and the following Sung, period, it produced numerous outstanding Ch'an masters, whose deeds and sayings are still an inspiration today and (as → kōans) an important means of training on the way of Zen.

Hui Shih 🅃 ca. 370–310 B.C.E.; a philosopher of the Warring States Period, who represented the School of Names, which concerned itself with the problem of the relationship between names and reality. Hui Shih was a friend of Chuang-tzu, in whose writings his thoughts have come down to us. Within the philosophical School of Names Hui Shih represented a faction supporting the unification of opposites. His central idea is that of the unity of the universe, forming a single whole. This thought finds expression in the equation of varying concepts of size: "There is nothing beyond the infinitely great, which I call the Great One [→ T'ai-i]; there is nothing within the infinitely small, which I call the Small One [Hsiao-i]" (trans. from Kaltenmark, *Lao-tzu und der Taoismus;* see Kaltenmark 1969).

Hui Shih sees all differences and opposites in relative terms: thus Heaven and Earth are not to be considered as different from each other. This proposition finds its direct and most positive expression in a nondifferentiating love for all things. Hui Shih's celebrated paradoxes aim at questioning deeply rooted notions concerning the qualities of things and the nature of beings.

The writings of Hui Shih have not been preserved in their entirety; fragments of his teaching are found in the → *Chuang-tzu,* → *Lieh-tzu,* and → *Lü-shih ch'un-ch'iu.*

Book 33 of the *Chuang-tzu* contains some of Hui Shih's most famous paradoxes:

"That which is without dimension cannot be piled up, yet it measures a thousand li."

"Heaven and Earth are equally low. Mountain and marsh are equally level."

"The sun at noon is the sun setting; when an animal is born, it dies."

"The Center of the World is north of Yen and south of Yueh (Yen was the northernmost and Yueh the southernmost region of ancient China)." A commentator has interpreted this last paradox as expressing the idea that the world is infinite and its center everywhere. (Quotes from Giles 1961.)

Hui-t'ang Tsu-hsin 🅉 (Jap., Maidō Soshin), 1025–1100; Chinese Ch'an (Zen) master of the Ōryō lineage of Rinzai Zen (→ Ōryō School); a student and dharma successor (→ *hassu*) of → Huang-lung Hui-nan (Jap., Ōryō E'nan) and the master of → Ssu-hsin Wu-hsin (Jap., Shishin Goshin). Through Hui-t'ang passes the lineage that produced the first school of Zen in Japan, transmitted there by → Eisai Zenji.

Hui-tsung 🅃 1082–1135 C.E.; Sung Dynasty emperor and one of the staunchest supporters and promoters of Taoism. During his reign numerous Taoist temples and monasteries (→ *kuan*) were built. He referred to himself as "nobleman of the Tao" and bestowed upon the Jade Emperor (→ Yü-huang)—an important Taoist deity—the title *Shang-ti* (god). In addition he greatly encouraged the compilation of the Taoist canon (→ *Tao-tsang*).

Hui-yüan 🄱 336–416; important Chinese monk, student of → Tao-an, founder of the → Amitābha cult and the White Lotus Society; first patriarch of the → Pure Land school. Among his most important works is a treatise on → karma (*San-pao-lun*) in which he confronts the problem of the ripening of deeds (→ *vipāka*) and of the immortality of the "soul." Of importance for the Chinese *sangha* was that, at Hui-yüan's urging, monks were freed from their worldly duties toward the emperor.

Hui-yüan studied the teachings of Confucius, of Chuang-tzu, and of Lao-tzu before he was ordained as a monk at the age of twenty-one by Tao-an and occupied himself intensively with the → *Prajñāpāramitā-sūtra*. In his interpretation of the work he used Taoist concepts for the sake of better understanding. In 381 he went to Lu-shan, where a monastery was built for him and his already numerous students. Hui-yüan was to spend the rest of his life on Lu Mountain. During this period Lu-shan became one of the most important centers of Buddhism and distinguished itself by its model discipline. At Hui-yüan's invitation, the Kashmiri monk Sanghadeva came to Lu-shan and translated the most important works of the → Sarvāstivāda into Chinese. Over many years Hui-yüan carried on a correspondence with → Kumārajīva, in which he posed many questions concerning especially the *dharmakāya* of the Buddha (→ *trikāya*) and the difference between an → arhat and a → bodhisattva.

In 402 Hui-yüan assembled a group of 123 followers in front of an image of Buddha Amitābha. They took a vow to be reborn in the western paradise → Sukhāvatī and, according to tradition, formed the White Lotus Society. Hui-yüan is thus considered the founder of the Pure Land school. Hui-yüan was also one of the first of the Chinese monks to recognize the importance of the practice of → *dhyāna* on the path to enlightenment.

Hu-kuo Ching-yüan 🅉 (Jap., Gokoku Keigen), 1094–1146; Chinese Ch'an (Zen) master of the Yōgi lineage of Rinzai Zen (→ Yōgi school); a student and dharma successor (→ *hassu*) of → Yüan K'o-ch'in (Jap., Engo Kokugon) and the master of → Huo-an Shih-t'i (Jap., Wakuan Shitai).

Hun 🅃 Chin., "breath soul," spirit soul; one of two souls said to reside in each human being, the other being the so-called body soul (→ *p'o*). The life and health of a person depend on the harmonious interplay of these two souls, or energies. When *hun* and *p'o* separate, death ensues.

Each human being has, in fact, three *hun,* which are considered to be higher souls that form at birth, after the seven *p'o* souls. The *hun* represent the *yang* energy (→ yin-yang), the active force, and regulate the higher physical functions. At death, they leave the body and return to Heaven. They are also capable of manifesting in another form or shape, because they may leave the body of a person, without that person dying, e.g., when someone loses consciousness or faints. This view is also reflected by the old custom of "recalling the *hun*" (*chao-hun*), in which the souls of people who have drowned, lost consciousness, or been hanged are beckoned to return and thereby revive their former bodies.

Hung-chih Cheng-chüeh 🅉 (Jap., Wanshi Shōgaku), 1091–1157; Chinese Chan (Zen) master of the → Sōtō school; a student and dharma successor (→ *hassu*) of → Tan-hsia Tsu-ch'un (Jap., Tanka Shijun). Master Hung-shih is particularly known for his confrontations (obviously carried out in a friendly spirit) with the Rinzai master → Ta-hui Tsung-kao (Jap., Daie Sōkō) concerning the advantages of the → *mokushō* Zen fostered by the Sōtō school over the → *kanna* Zen of the Rinzai school. That this difference of opinion, which is sometimes made much of by later overenthusiastic followers of the two schools, did not go so deep for the two masters is shown by the fact that Master Hung-chih, before his death, entrusted Master Ta-hui with the completion of his work, the → *Ts'ung-jung-lu.*

Hung-fan 🅃 Chin., lit. great plan, great norm; a chapter of the *Book of Writings* (*Shu-ching*), a classic Confucian treatise, which contains the first exposition of the teaching of the five elements (→ *wu-hsing*).

The *Hung-fan* considers the five elements (water, fire, wood, metal, and earth) to be concrete substances instead of—a later view—abstract energies, and teaches that the world of nature is dependant on the world of man: the inadequate conduct of a ruler will cause abnormal phenomena in nature. Later, this view was more fully developed by the Yin-Yang School (→ *yin-yang chia*).

Hung-jen 🅉 (Jap., Gunin or Kōnin), 601–74; the fifth patriarch of Ch'an (Zen) in China; the dharma successor (→ *hassu*) of → Tao-hsin (Jap., Dōshin) and the master of → Hui-neng (Jap., E'nō) and → Shen-hsiu (Jap., Jinshū). According to tradition Hung-jen met the fourth patriarch at age fourteen and impressed Tao-hsin, already at this first encounter, by his deep realization of Zen mind.

The dialogue between the fourth and the (later) fifth patriarch is passed down in the → *Denkō-roku.* In it the two great masters punned on the characters for *name* and *nature* which are pronounced almost the same. Since the play on words with their double meanings cannot be reproduced in English, in the following translation *name* is used for both the words, read in Japanese *sei* and *sho*:

"The thirty-second patriarch [counting from Shākyamuni Buddha] Daiman Zenji [honorific title for Hung-jen] met the thirty-first patriarch [Tao-hsin] on the road to Ōbai.

"The patriarch [Tao-hsin] asked, 'What is your family name?'

"The master [Hung-jen] said, 'Although I have a name [*sei*], it is nonetheless no ordinary name.'

"The patriarch said, 'What kind of name is it then?'

"The master said, 'It is buddha-nature.'

"The patriarch said, 'Don't you have a family name?'

"The master said, 'I don't, since that nature is empty.'

"The patriarch was quiet and noted that he was a dharma vessel.

"And he gave him the dharma robe."

With the passing along of the robe (→ *den'e*), the fourth patriarch confirmed Hung-jen as his dharma successor and installed him as the fifth patriarch in the lineage of Ch'an (Zen). After the death of his master, Hung-jen founded the monastery on Mount → Huang-mei (Jap., Ōbai) in which the memorable episode concerning the dharma succession of the sixth patriarch took place (→ Hui-neng), which split Ch'an (Zen) into a Northern and a → Southern school.

Hungry ghosts 🄱 → *preta*

Huo-an Shih-t'i 🅉 (Jap., Wakuan Shitai), 1108–79; Chinese Ch'an (Zen) master of the Yōgi lineage of Rinzai Zen (→ Yōgi school); a student and dharma successor (→ *hassu*) of Hakuo Ching-yüan (Jap., Gokoku Keigen). We encounter Master Huo-an in example 4 of the → *Wu-men-kuan.*

In this famous kōan Huo-an plays on the fact that → Bodhidharma, who in the Ch'an (Zen) tradition is often called the "barbarian from the west," according to tradition had a thick, dark beard. In all Zen paintings he is depicted as a tough-looking bearded figure. However, this example goes, "Huo-an said: 'How is it that the barbarian from the west has no beard?' "

Hyakujō Ekai 🅉 Jap. for → Pai-chang Huai-hai

Hyakujō Shingi 🅉 Jap. for → *Pai-chang ch'ing-kuei*

I

I 🅃 Chin., roughly honesty, uprightness, duty; a concept in

I 🅃 Chin., lit. "change, transformation" → *I-ching* Confucianist philosophy. To act in accordance with *i* means to respond to the demands of a situation from a sense of moral obligation and without any thought of gain (*li*). *I* and *li* are total opposites. Uprightness is one of the five cardinal virtues of Confucianism (→ *wu-ch'ang,* → K'ung-tzu).

The *Analects* (*Lun-yü*) of Confucius state (4.16), "A noble man understands what is moral; a small man understands what is profitable."

Ichchā-Mrityu ▣ (Icchā-Mṛtyu), Skt., lit. "death according to desire"; the ability to surrender one's life at will, not by committing suicide but by conceiving the hour of death in the mind.

Ichchantika ▣ (iccantika), Skt., lit. "unbeliever"; designates a person who has cut all the wholesome roots (→ *kushala*) in himself and has no wish to attain buddhahood. The question as to whether or not an ichchantika possesses → buddha-nature led to differences of opinion, particularly in the schools of Chinese Buddhism. More rarely the term refers to a → bodhisattva who has taken the oath not to attain buddhahood before all beings have found release.

Ichibō ▣ Jap., lit. "one stick"; Zen expression for the use of the stick (→ *kyosaku*, → *shippei*) by a Zen master for the benefit of his students. (Also → *bōkatsu*).

Ichien ▣ also called Dōkyō or Muju, 1226–1312; a Japanese monk of the → Rinzai school, a student of → Ben'en (Shōichi Kokushi). Ichien wandered through Japan and trained under masters of various Zen schools. He is the author of the *Shaseki-shū* (*Collection of Sand and Stone*), a popular anthology of frequently humorous Buddhist stories and legends, which Zen masters are fond of quoting in their teaching.

Ichi-ensō ▣ Jap. → Ensō

Ichiji-fusetsu ▣ Jap., lit. "not a [single] word said"; a Zen expression referring to the fact that the Buddha (and the patriarchs, → *soshigata*) in all his instruction never made use of a single word to describe ultimate reality (see also → *busshō*), since it is "not sayable" (→ *fukasetsu*). In consideration of this fact, the Buddha after his complete → enlightenment even did not want to teach at all; finally, however, compassion for beings trapped in the cycle of life and death (→ samsāra) moved him, as the Zen masters say, "to fall into the grass," that is, to come down from the level of true insight to that of "everyman's consciousness" (→ *bonpu-no-jōshiki*) for the purpose of giving those who wished to listen to him at least a "finger-point" on the way leading to enlightenment and insight into the true nature of reality.

Thus Zen regards all the teaching of the Buddha in the sūtras and all the instructions and writings of the Zen masters only as "a finger pointing to the moon [the truth], not the moon itself." Insight into ultimate reality can be transmitted (→ *hassu*), if at all, only in an intimate process that is called in Zen "transmission from heart-mind to heart-mind" (→ *ishin-denshin*).

This is the reason that Zen refers to itself as a "special tradition outside the [orthodox] teaching" (→ *kyōge-betsuden*), stresses its nondependence on [sacred] writings (→ *furyū-monji*), and prefers to "point directly to the human heart-mind [→ *kokoro*]" rather than relying on verbally transmitted "teachings," which each person understands only in a manner corresponding to his or her momentary state of mind—i.e., perceives only the projection of him- or herself.

Ichiji-kan ▣ Jap., lit. "one-word barrier"; Zen expression for a → *wato* that consists of one word.

Famous "one-word barriers" are the *mu* of the Chinese master → Chao-chou Ts'ung-shen (Jap., Jōshū Jūshin), (example 1 of the → *Wu-men-kuan*) or the *kan* of the Chinese master → Yun-men Wen-yen (Jap., Ummon Bun'en) from the following kōan (example 8 of the → *Pi-yen-lu*):

"Toward the end of the summer period [→ *ango*] Ts'ui-yen said in his instruction to the monks, 'The whole summer long I've spoken to you, you younger and older brothers; look here if Ts'ui-yen still has his eyebrows.'

"Pao-fu said, 'With people who steal, the heart is full of fear.'

"Ch'ang-ch'ing said, 'They've grown!'

"Yun-men said, 'Stop!' [Jap., *kan*, "barrier"].

Ichiji Zen ▣ Jap., lit. "one-word Zen"; a Zen practice in which a single word of a master (→ ichiji-kan) is taken as a → kōan. The Chinese master → Yun-men Wen-yen (Jap., Ummon Bun'en) is particularly famed in the Zen tradition for his *ichiji-kan*.

Ichimi-shabyō ▣ Jap., lit. "one-taste pouring of the bowl"; Zen expression for the authentic transmission of the → buddha-dharma from a Zen master to his dharma successor (→ *hassu*). Also → *ishin-denshin*, → *ichimi-zen*.

Ichimi-zen ▣ Jap., lit. "one-taste Zen"; authentic Zen, the Zen of the Buddha and the patriarchs (→ *soshigata*). "One taste" refers to the experience of nondistinction (of form and emptiness); see also → enlightenment. The expression is used in opposition to → *gomi(-no)-zen*.

Ichinen-fushō ▣ Jap., lit. "a thought not arising"; in Zen it is said that the state of mind of a person in whom no deluded thought arises is that of a buddha. *Ichinen-fushō* refers to this state of consciousness free of all deluded thoughts, concepts, feelings, and perceptions, which is reached through the practice of → *zazen* and at the same time *is zazen* in its purest form. Thus it is also said, "Five minutes *zazen*, five minutes a buddha."

Ichinen-mannen 🅩 Jap., lit. "one moment of consciousness [→ *nen*], ten thousand years"; this expression of Japanese Buddhism, in which the number ten thousand simply means a limitlessly large number, refers to the experience common to mystics and saints of all cultures that in the world of → enlightenment there is no time in the everyday sense. Thus from the point of view of enlightened consciousness, one moment of consciousness is eternity.

I-ching 🅑 635–713; one of the most important translators of Buddhist texts from Sanskrit to Chinese and a renowned pilgrim, who in 671 traveled to India by sea and spent more than twenty years there. At the monastic university Nālandā he studied the teachings of Hīnayāna and Mahāyāna Buddhism and began the translation of important religious works into his mother tongue. In 695 I-ching returned to his homeland, bringing more than 400 Buddhist texts. Together with Shikshānanda he translated, among other works, the → *Buddhāvatamsaka-sūtra* and the → Vinaya-pitaka of the Mulasarvāstivāda school. Altogether I-ching translated fifty-six works in 230 volumes. Besides the account of his travels, he composed a collection of biographies of fifty-six monks who had made the pilgrimage to India, most of them by sea.

I-ching 🅣 Chin., lit. *"Book of Change(s)"*; a Chinese book of wisdom and oracles, dating from the transition period between the Yin and Chou dynasties. The essential philosophy of the *I-ching* is based on Confucianism, but there are also Taoist ideas present. The *Book of Change(s)* is based on the idea of two polar energies, by whose activities all things are brought about and come into being. Initially, these two energies were simply called the light and the dark, but later were referred to as yin and yang (→ yin-yang). The interaction of yin and yang produces change (*i*), which is to be understood as the movement of the → Tao.

The basic structure of the *Book of Change(s)* is formed by the eight trigrams (→ *pa-kua*), which consist of three broken and/or unbroken horizontal lines. The various combinations of these trigrams in pairs produce the sixty-four hexagrams. The root text of the *Book of Change(s)* describes the individual hexagrams and their lines, representing states or tendencies of transformation, and explains the social and political aspects of whatever sign is under discussion. The various commentaries (→ *Shih-i*) on this root text were added later and are Confucianist interpretations.

In all probability the *I-ching* was originally used as a manual of prophecy. When oracles were first cast in China, the answer to a question would be simply *Yes* or *No,* indicated by either an unbroken (——) or a broken (– –) line. In the face of the complexity of reality, this method of prediction soon proved inadequate, and this led to the introduction of trigrams and hexagrams composed of broken and/or unbroken lines.

These trigrams and hexagrams reflect events in Heaven and on Earth, and the prediction is based on the transformation of one state into another. The relevant processes are described in concise sayings that refer to basic cosmic or social situations. Change is inherent in the hexagrams themselves, because they are said to be in a continuous state of motion, so that one or several lines may change into their opposite and thus into another of the sixty-four hexagrams. This makes it possible to embrace the whole of reality in the prediction.

Traditionally, oracles were cast by throwing fifty yarrow stalks or—in a simplified procedure—three coins. The best-known translations of the original Chinese text of the *I-ching,* containing also a description of the method of obtaining a prediction, are Wilhelm 1967 (an English translation of Wilhelm's German translation) and Blofeld 1965.

The hexagrams of the *I-ching* were adopted by the followers of the Inner Alchemy (→ *nei-tan*), to symbolize various internal processes (→ *ch'ien* and *k'un,* → *k'an* and *li*).

In the traditional view the *Book of Change(s)* goes back to → Fu Hsi, who is said to have invented the eight trigrams and some of the sixty-four hexagrams. The remaining hexagrams allegedly originated with King Wen, one of the founders of the Chou Dynasty. Some scholars say both the trigrams and the hexagrams should be attributed to King Wen, while others hold that King Wen created the trigrams, and the Duke of Chou the hexagrams. The main commentary (also called the *Ten Wings*) on the root text is attributed to Confucius (→ K'ung-tzu) but in actual fact stems from a later period, in all probability the early Han Dynasty.

The *I-ching* is the only philosophical work to survive the burning of the books ordered in 213 C.E. by Ch'in Shih-huang-ti, the first historical emperor of China, who himself consulted the *I-ching* as a book of prophecy. The *I-ching* was commonly used for purposes of divination at the time, both by the → *fang-shih* and the followers of the → *yin-yang chia.* Subsequently it came to be considered primarily a book of wisdom and of the official state doctrine.

The *I-ching* has been used for casting oracles since the time of the Chou Dynasty. During the Han Dynasty methods of prediction by the use of emblems and numbers began to spread and reached their highest popularity in Confucianist circles during the Sung Dynasty. The most common—and at the same time, most reliable—method of putting a question to the oracle was by throwing fifty yarrow stalks. This method symbolizes the harmony between the macrocosmic order of nature and the microcosmic order at the precise moment of consultation.

I-chuan 🅃 Chin., lit. *"Commentary on the Changes";* another name for the *Ten Commentaries* on the *Book of Change(s)* (→ *I-ching*). For further details → *Shih-i.*

Idā 🄷 (Iḍā), Skt.; one of the major channels of subtle energy (→ *nāḍī*) that furnish the entire body with the life force (→ *prāna*) by transporting it to various places in the body. The *idā,* which takes up *prāna* through the left nostril and is cooling and soothing, corresponds to the parasympatheticus of the sympathetic nervous system. Its counterpart is the → *pingalā.*

In the *Rigveda, idā* is nourishment, refreshment, or a milk libation, later a stream of praise, personified as the goddess of speech and sacrifice, the adviser to → Manu. Many texts ascribe to her the disposition of sacrificial rites.

Idam 🄷 Skt., lit. "this." The → *rishis* (seers, illuminati) of the → Upanishads often use the pronoun "this" to stand for this universe as the revelation of God in manifest form, as contrasted to "that" *(tat),* the undescribable, omnipresent reality that underlies, permeates, and transcends the visible world. The latter term appears in the celebrated formula → *Tat tvam asi.*

Ignorance 🄱 🅉 → *avidyā,* → delusion

Igyō school 🅉 (Chin. kuei-yang-tsung; Jap. *igyō-shū*); a school of Ch'an (Zen) that was among the "five houses–seven schools," i.e., the great schools of the authentic Ch'an tradition. The name of the school derives from the initial characters of the Japanese names of its two founders, → Kuei-shan Ling-yu (Jap., Isan Reiyu) and his dharma successor → Yang-shan Hui-chi (Jap., Kyōzan Ejaku).

Typical for the method of instruction of the Igyō school was the use of a system of ninety-seven symbols, each inscribed in a circle. This system, which is said to have originated with Hui-neng, the sixth patriarch of Ch'an (see also → Tan-yuan Ying-chen), has not been preserved but did influence the development of the ten oxherding pictures (→ *jūgyū[-no]-zu*) as well as the → five degrees (of enlightenment) of Master Tung-shan. It seems to have represented some sort of secret language through which persons with profound experience of Ch'an could communicate with each other concerning the basic principles of the teaching. Since the masters were aware that this system could easily degenerate into a mere formalized game, it was evidently transmitted to only a few students under a seal of strict secrecy. In the middle of the 10th century the Igyō lineage merged with the lineage of the → Rinzai school and from that time no longer subsisted as an independent school.

I-hsuan 🅉 → Lin-chi I-hsuan

Ikkyū Sōjun 🅉 1394–1481; Japanese Zen master of the → Rinzai school. He is known in the history of Zen quite as much for his profound wit as for his profound realization of Zen. Because of his unconventional lifestyle, he is often referred to as a kind of Puck of Zen, and is definitely the most popular figure of Zen in Japan. In the manner of a holy madman, he mocked the deteriorating Zen of the great monasteries of his time. Many authentic and legendary tales are in circulation concerning his life and his indifference to social convention. He was an outstanding painter, calligrapher (→ *shōdō*), and poet. In his poems recorded in the → *Kyōun-shū,* he praised the great masters of ancient times, lamented the decline of Zen, and sang the praises of wine and physical love. Two typical poems of Ikkyū, who often called himself "the blind ass," are as follows:

Who among Rinzai's students
Gives a hoot
About the authentic transmission?
In their school
There's no shelter
For the blind ass
Who, on the road
With staff and straw sandals,
Finds truth.
There they practice Zen on sure ground,
Comfortably leaning back,
For their own profit.

Ten days
In the monastery
Made me restless.
The red thread

On my feet
Is long and unbroken.
If one day you come
Looking for me,
Ask for me
At the fishmonger's,
In the tavern,
Or in the brothel.

In 1420, while meditating by night in a boat on a lake, at the sudden caw of a crow Ikkyū experienced enlightenment. Confirmed by his master as his dharma successor (→ *inka-shōmei*), like his master Ikkyū kept monastic life at a distance. Initially he lived as a hermit on Mount Jōu and later in his "hut of the blind ass" (Jap., *katsuro-an*) in Kyōto. In 1474 he was appointed by the imperial house as abbot of Daitoku-ji. He could not avoid this appointment; however, he lived not in Daitoku-ji but in Shūon-an, a small temple in his home village of Maki, where, until his death, in his unconventional style, he instructed those who sought him out in the truth of Zen. Ikkyū, who in bitterness over the state of the Zen of his day once tore up his own certificate of confirmation as a Zen master, himself confirmed no dharma successor.

Ikshvāku 🅗 (Ikṣvāku), Skt.; the son of the Manu → Vaivasvata, whose father was the sun god Vivasvat. Krishna mentions all three in the *Bhagavad-Gītā* (4.1).

Ikshvāku was the progenitor of the solar race and ruled over Rāma's capital city, Ayodhyā. The eldest of his hundred sons was → Vikukshi. The *Rigveda* mentions Ikshvāku only once in reference to the race of Ikshvāku that made its home in North or Northwest India.

I-k'ung 🅩 (Jap., Giku); Chinese Ch'an (Zen) master of the → Rinzai school, who in the middle of the 9th century at the invitation of Empress Tachibana Kachiko went to Japan to teach Zen, first in the imperial palace and later at the monastery of Danrin-ji in Kyōto, which was built for him. I-k'ung, however, found in Japan no suitable students, not to mention dharma successors (→ *hassu*), and returned several years later to China. Until the 12/13th century (→ Eisai Zenji, → Dōgen Zenji, → Kakushin), there were no further attempts to bring Zen to Japan.

Ina 🅩 Jap. → *inō*

Indra 🅗 god of the firmament, the personified atmosphere. In the Vedas he is the supreme deity, yet he was born of a father and mother. Lord of the weather, he sends down rain, thunder, and lightning. He is revered as the dispenser of rain, the source of fecundity, and feared as the lord of storms. More hymns in the Vedas are dedicated to Indra than to any other god with the exception of → Agni.

Indra is described as a golden being with enormously long arms. His forms are without number, for he can assume any shape. He rides in a gleaming golden carriage drawn by two brown horses whose manes toss in the wind. His weapon is the thunderbolt (→ *vajra*) that he wields in his right hand. He also uses arrows, a huge lance, and a net to catch his enemies. The → *soma* libation is especially prized by Indra, who consumes vast quantities of it. In later mythology, Indra drops from his supreme position to the second level of gods, but remains lord over this group. The *Rāmāyana* reports that → Rāvana, the king of Lankā, fought victoriously against Indra in his own heaven, whereupon Rāvana's son (→ Indrajit) carried him off to Lankā. The → Purānas contain many stories about Indra in which he figures primarily as Krishna's rival. Mythology relates that Indra was the father of → Arjuna. His importance gradually diminished with time, as Krishna rose as an object of devotion. Indra is also known under many other names.

Indrajit 🅗 Skt., lit. "conqueror of Indra"; an epithet given by → Brahmā to Meghanāda, the son of → Rāvana. Together with his father he fought → Indra, and Meghanāda, upon whom Shiva had conferred the magical ability to become invisible, shackled the god and bore him off to Lankā. The gods, led by Brahmā, wished to free Indra, but were able to do so only by promising immortality to Indrajit.

Indriya 🅗 🅑 also jñānendriya and buddhīndriya; Skt., lit. "sense organ."

🅗 any of the forces of → Indra that enable us to perceive the manifest world (→ *nāmarūpa*). The *indriyas* consist of the five organs of sense: ear, eye, nose, skin, tongue; and the five organs of action: larynx, hand, foot, and the organs of excretion and procreation. The eleventh *indriya* is thought. The *indriyas* furnish → *manas* with impressions of the outer world and thus belong to the realm of the → *antahkarana*.

🅑 Twenty-two psychological and physical capabilities or faculties: (1–6) the six bases (→ *āyatana*, → *shadāyatana*); (7–8) the masculine and feminine potentialities that distinguish the sexes; (9) the vital faculty, which determines all physiological phenomena; (10–14) the faculties of pleasure, pain, joy, sadness, and indifference; (15–19) the five mental roots that form the basis for the development of the five powers (→ *bala*), namely, the root of faith (→ *shraddhā*), of energy or exertion (→ *vīrya*), of mindfulness, of concentration (→ *samādhi*), of wisdom (→ *prajñā*); (20) the supramundane faculties—the certainty of being able to know what is not yet known, which comes at the beginning of the supramundane path (→ *ārya-mārga*); (21) supreme knowledge, which is reached at the moment of actualizing stream-entry (→ *shrota-āpanna*); finally (22) the faculty of him who possesses perfect knowledge, the faculty of an → arhat.

Indriyasamvara 🅑 (indriyasaṃvara, Skt., lit. "guarding of the sense organs"; a meditation technique that leads to pure, objective observation and is intended to prevent emotions such as sympathy, antipathy, desire, hate, etc., from arising as result of the stimuli of perception. Guarding the sense organs also serves to make concentration (→ *samādhi*) possible.

Indriyasaṃvara is a practice preparatory for actual meditation and must also be practiced outside of the purely meditative context during the business of everyday life. It is a discipline (→ *shīla*) of purity obligatory for monks and nuns.

The practice of guarding the sense organs has been described in the following words: "When a monk sees a form [→ *rūpa*] with the eye, hears a sound with hearing, smells a smell with smelling, tastes a taste with the tongue, feels something tangible with the body, or knows a representation [→ dharma] with the mind, he heeds neither the generality nor the details. Before that takes place whereby the evil, unwholesome representations of craving and repulsion stream in upon one who is not guarding the organ of the eye, etc.—before that, he seeks to guard the organ of the eye, etc.; before that, he guards the organ of the eye, etc., and achieves the guarding of the organ of the eye, etc. Through practicing this guarding of the sense organs, he perceives an inner happiness without distraction" (trans. from Frauwallner 1954, p. 165ff).

Inga 🅩 Jap., lit. "cause-fruit"; cause and effect in the sense of the Buddhist law of cause and effect (→ karma, also → *innen*). In Zen, the basis of which is the immediate realization of the true nature of reality, which transcends the categories of time and space as well as linear connections within time and space, it is said, *Inga ichinyo* ("Cause and effect are one").

Ingen Hōgo 🅩 Jap., lit. "*Dharma Words of Ingen* [Chin., Yin-yuan]"; collection of the discourses and sayings of the Chinese Ch'an (Zen) master → Yin-yuan Lung-ch'i, who founded the → Ōbaku school in Japan in the middle of the 17th century.

Inka-shōmei 🅩 also *inka*, Jap., lit. "the legitimate seal of clearly furnished proof"; the legitimate seal of confirmation that authentic → enlightenment has been clearly shown. A Zen term for the official confirmation on the part of a master that a student has completed his training under him. In the case of masters who use the → kōan system, this means that the student has mastered all the kōans specified by his master to the master's complete satisfaction. If a master does not use kōans, the conferral of *inka* means that he is content with his student's level of genuine insight. Only after receipt of this confirmation—and when other requirements established at the master's discretion, such as, for example, the ability to lead other people, have been fulfilled—is a person following an authentic Zen tradition entitled to lead other students on the way of Zen, to proclaim himself his master's dharma successor (→ *hassu*), and to be addressed as → *rōshi*. However, even when training under the master has officially concluded with the conferral of *inka*, this does not mean that Zen training is over. The deeper the insight of a Zen master, the clearer it is to him that Zen training is endless; it extends over numberless lives. Thus it is said in Zen that even the Buddha, who attained complete and perfect enlightenment, is still training.

With *inka* the master confirms that the student has reached at least the same degree of enlightenment as himself and thenceforth can stand on his own feet. Nevertheless, it is said in the Zen tradition that a master should constantly be concerned that his students surpass him in depth of realization. If the student is only equal to the master, there is the danger that the → dharma teaching of the master will decline increasingly in following generations and his dharma successors and their dharma successors will only have "the miserable stamp of a miserable stamp."

Inkin 🅩 Jap.; a small bowl-shaped bell with a cushion beneath it, which is placed on a wooden pedestal and struck with a small metal striker.

The *inkin* is sometimes used in Zen monasteries to signal the beginning or end of → *zazen* periods or is rung at the beginning of recitations.

Innen 🅩 Jap., lit. "direct inner cause and indirect outer effect [i.e., cause and occasion]"; this notion is used in Zen as well as in other schools of Buddhism in Japan in relation to the Buddhist understanding of the "law of cause and effect" (→ karma), according to which every event takes place in dependence on direct and indirect causes. *Innen* is sometimes translated as "occasion–condition–cause" in order to indicate the multifaceted meaning of this concept.

Inner Deity Hygiene School 🅣 a movement within religious Taoism (→ *tao-chiao*) which allocated deities (→ *shen*) to the various parts and organs of the human body. By means of right nourishment, appropriate invocations, and meditation practices these deities were induced to protect the body and grant the practitioner immortality. The inner deities are identical with the deities inhabiting the Taoist heavens. The basic philosophical tract of this movement, which flourished between the 2d and 6th century C.E., is the → *Huang-t'ing ching.*

The inner pantheon—like the outer—consists of 36,000 deities. The most important of these reside in the three vital centers of the body, i.e., the three cinnabar fields (→ *tan-t'ien*). They are the three ones (→ *san-i*) who are ruled by the Supreme One (→ Tai-i). A further important inner deity is → Ssu-ming, the Ruler of Fate.

The allocation of deities to the various organs of the body is not uniform and varies from one text to the next; in the course of time more and more deities were admitted to the pantheon. Each practitioner has a special relationship with one of these deities and is capable of establishing direct contact with it; the higher this deity is placed in the overall hierarchy of the *shen* the greater the benefit the practitioner can derive from his association with it.

The followers of the Inner Deity Hygiene School consider the presence of these 36,000 deities within the body of a prerequisite for life: if the deities leave the body, the person in question dies. Taoist adepts employ various methods to prevent the deities from leaving the body.

A practitioner may try to visualize the deities (→ *nei-kuan*) and keep a specific diet: he will neither eat meat nor drink wine, because the deities are said to dislike the smell of both. In addition, he may abstain from eating grain (→ *pi-ku*), which is said to serve as nourishment for the three worms, the enemies of the deities (→ *sun-ch'ung*).

However, all these practices are of no avail if the practitioner leads an immoral life, in which case the deities will withhold their support. In this way good deeds and charitable works, such as the construction of roads and bridges, the establishment of orphanages, and similar projects became a very important aspect of religious practice.

During the 6th century C.E. the Inner Deity Hygiene School was displaced by the School of the Magic Jewel (→ *ling-pao p'ai,* → *Ling-pao ching*) and the consequent externalization of the inner deities.

Inner Elixir 🅃 → *nei-tan*

Inō 🅉 also ina, e'shu, or chiji, Jap.; a monk who is charged with the supervision and leading of ceremonies in a Zen monastery.

Integral Yoga 🄷 → Aurobindo, → Pūrna-Yoga

Iro-futo 🅉 Jap., lit. "unreachable by the path of thought"; another expression for → enlightenment. (Also → *fukashigi.*)

Isan Reiyū 🅉 Jap. for → Kuei-shan Ying-lu

Īshā 🄷 (Īśā), Skt.; 1. the name given to Jesus by Hindus; 2. the name of an Upanishad of the *White* → *Yajurveda.* Its eighteen verses make it perhaps the shortest Upanishad, but it is highly valued. It is named for its opening words and thus is also known as the *Īshāvasya.* Most Indian collections of the Upanishads begin with the *Īshā,* but its chronology places it at a relatively late date in the sequence of the Upanishadic texts. It contrasts the empirical perception of reality (→ *avidyā*) with the perception of the one reality, → *ātman* or → *brahman.* → Shankara wrote a commentary on the *Īshā.* Its best-known mantras are SO'HAM and SO'HAM ASMI, both of which translate as "He am I," meaning that the *ātman,* one's self, is identical with *brahman* or God.

I-shan I-ning 🅉 (Jap., Issan Ichinei), 1247–1317; Chinese Ch'an (Zen) master of the → Rinzai school. After the overthrow of the Sung Dynasty by the Mongols, he was sent by the Mongolian emperor Ch'en-ts'ung to Japan to try to renew relations with Japan, which had been broken off following the Mongol attempts at invasion. When he landed in Japan in 1299, the Shōgun Hōjō Sadatoki had him imprisoned as a spy. I-shan, however, was soon able to convince the shōgun of his pure intentions. He was appointed as the tenth abbot of the → Kenchō-ji monastery in Kamakura and in 1302 was made abbot also of Engaku-ji. In 1312 he went at the wish of Emperor Go-uda to Kyōto to become the third abbot of Nanzen-ji monastery. He is known not only as a Zen master but also as a painter and a master of the way of calligraphy (→ *shōdō*).

Together with his student → Sesson Yūbai, I-shan is also considered the founder of the "literature of the five mountains" (→ *gosan-bungaku*). → Musō Soseki, who was for a time one of his students, contributed significantly toward making the Zen monasteries of Kyōto centers of art and science, in which a strong Chinese influence was detectable.

Ishin-denshin 🅉 Jap., lit. "transmitting mind [*shin,* → *kokoro*] through mind"; a Zen expression for the authentic transmission of → buddha-dharma from master to students and dharma successors (→ *hassu*) within the lineages of transmission of the Zen tradition (also → *soshigata,* → *inka-shōmei*). This term, which is usually translated "transmission from heart-mind to heart-mind" became a central notion of Zen. It comes from the *Sūtra [spoken] from the High*

Seat of the Dharma Treasure (*Platform Sūtra,* → *Liu-tsu ta-shih fa-pao-t'an-ching*) of the sixth patriarch of Ch'an (Zen) in China, → Hui-neng. He points out that what is preserved in the lineage of the tradition and "transmitted" is not book knowledge in the form of "teachings" established in sacred scriptures but rather an immediate insight into the true nature of reality, one's own immediate experience, to which an enlightened master (→ enlightenment, → *rōshi*) can lead a student through training in the way of Zen (→ *zazen*).

Ishta-Deva 🅗 (Iṣṭa-Deva), Ishta-Devatā, or Ishta, Skt., lit. *ishta:* "1. beloved; 2. desire," *deva:* "god," *devata:* "divinity"; commonly translated as "chosen deity." One who enters the path of → Bhakti-Yoga needs a concrete object to whom one can offer one's worship and devotion. It can be a divinity, some particular manifestation of God, a saint, an → *avatāra,* or some other figure to whom the devotee is especially attracted.

Devotees who are initiated by a guru are often given an appropriate *ishta-deva* along with their mantra, since a true guru can judge which aspect of the divine will be most compelling and hence of greatest value to the disciple.

Ishta-Mantra 🅗 (Iṣṭa-Mantra), Skt., lit. "chosen mantra"; to practice → *jpa* when a mantra has not been received from a guru, various traditional mantras are available, such as OM NAMO NĀRĀYANĀYA ("OM! Honor to God, the guide within!") or OM NAMAH SHIVĀYA ("OM! Honor to Shiva!").

Īshvara 🅗 (Īśvara), Skt., lit. "lord of the universe" (from the root *ish:* "to rule, reign"); the concept of a personal god as creator of the world. → *Brahman* is Īshvara in its relation to the manifest world and as the object of our worship; in Svāmi → Vivekānanda's words, "Īshvara is the supreme interpretation of the Absolute (*brahman*) by human thought." (See also → Aishvara-Yoga.)

The God of Christianity and of Islam, as well as all the deities of Hindu mythology, are aspects of Īshvara. Our human reason can conceive of divinity only within some form; thus, we need the concept of Īshvara, which in the view of → Advaita-Vedānta is merely a superimposition on *brahman.* The most widely disseminated form of Īshvara in Hindu thought is the → *trimūrti,* the trinity of Brahmā, Vishnu, and Shiva.

Īshvarakoti 🅗 (Īśvarakoti), Skt., a free, perfect soul that is reborn on earth in order to help humanity realize the ultimate spiritual truths. Such a soul displays some of the characteristics of an → *avatāra.*

Īshvara-Pranidhāna 🅗 (Īśvara-Pranidhāna), Skt.; surrender of all activity in thought, word, and deed to God, an effort that is required at the second stage of → Patañjali's Yoga but is also an important element in → Bhakti-Yoga and → Karma-Yoga.

Issan Ichinei 🅩 Jap. for → I-shan I-ning

Isshi-injō 🅩 Jap., lit. "one-master seal confirmation"; training of a Zen student by a single master (→ *roshi*). The necessity of *isshi-injo* has been stressed, particularly in Japanese Sōtō Zen (→ Sōtō school) since the 17th century, in order to counteract the tendency of Zen student to go from master to master. In Zen training it is not a question of teaching and learning objectifiable knowledge, the type of logically graspable knowledge that anyone who learns it can pass on to anyone else willing and able to learn it (→ *fukasetsu*). In this case it is a matter of transmission of the → buddha-dharma "from heart-mind to heart-mind" (→ *ishin-denshin*) by an enlightened Zen master (→ enlightenment) to his student. Here the master-student relationship is of special significance.

There are no codifiable rules for Zen training; rather each *rōshi* relates to the needs of students on the basis of his own realization of Zen and in his uniquely personal way. Thus a training begun by one master cannot be seamlessly continued by another. The differences in the external form of the training (though not of the essential content) resulting from different styles of leadership and instruction of different Zen masters would tend to confuse rather than help a student who had not yet ripened to a deep experience of Zen.

Thus it is important for a Zen student, after he has found a master suited to him, to commit himself unreservedly and exclusively to his authority. If he comes to the point of equaling the realization of his master, which the latter will confirm through → *inka-shōmei,* then it is useful for him to seek to deepen his realization of Zen through → *mondō* and → *hossen* with other Zen masters.

Itihāsa 🅗 Skt., lit. "So it was"; legends in poetry and prose, heroic sagas, mythological tales. The best-known works in this genre are the *Mahābhārata* and the *Rāmāyana.*

Ittai 🅩 Jap., lit. "one body"; the experience of being one and identical with nondualistic nature of the truth experienced in → enlightenment, which is not a truth opposed to or varying from other truths. It is the one true nature of reality in which there are no dualistic counter-distinctions, no "true" and no "false" in the logical-philosophical sense.

Ittai 🅉 Jap., lit. "one truth"; the one truth the grasping and actualization of which is the goal of Zen training. This expression points to the entire cosmos that one comes to in profound → enlightenment. All phenomena are then nothing other than one (one's own) body. (Also → *sambō).*

Ittai-sambō 🅉 Jap. → *sambō*

J

Jābāli 🄷 a priest under King → Dasharatha who espoused skepticism. According to the *Rāmāyana,* he attempted to force his views upon → Rāma, who energetically rejected them, whereupon Jābāli claimed to have advocated atheism only in order to test Rāma; in reality, he said, he was religious and pious. He was a logician and probably belonged to the school of → Nyāya.

Jada-Prakriti 🄷 (Jaḍa-Prakṛti), Skt.; inanimate, unconscious nature, in which → *tamas* is dominant (→ *prakriti*).

Jada-Samādhi 🄷 (Jaḍa-Samādhi), Skt., from *jada:* "stiff, apathetic, dull"; a condition in which thinking is suspended, i.e., a temporarily inactive state of consciousness. It corresponds more or less to the state of dreamless sleep, which everyone has experienced but of which we have no awareness. The state is called *jada-"samādhi,"* but it is not true → *samādhi,* since thought is merely suspended and absolute consciousness is not experienced.

Jagannātha 🄷 Skt., lit. "lord of the world"; a name for → Vishnu. Jagannātha is worshiped chiefly in Bengal. A famous temple devoted to his worship is located in Puri (state of Orissa). Large numbers of pilgrims congregate there, particularly for the festivals of Rathayātrā ("car-procession") and Snānayātrā ("bathing-procession").

The following legend is related about the image of Jagannātha: Krishna was slain by a hunter, and his corpse lay rotting under a tree. A pious man discovered the bones and placed them in a box. Vishnu ordered King Indradyumna to have a statue of Jagannātha constructed so that it might hold Krishna's bones. → Vishvakarma, the divine architect, accepted the assignment with the stipulation that he not be disturbed during his work. After fifteen days, however, the king grew impatient and called upon him. Enraged, Vishvakarma abandoned the work before he had formed the hands and feet of the statue. Indradyumna then prayed to Brahmā, who promised to make the image famous. Brahmā gave it eyes and a soul and, acting as chief priest, took charge of its consecration.

Jagat 🄷 Skt.; the universe, the manifest world.

Jāgrat 🄷 Skt.; one of the four → *avasthās,* the waking state, in which a person thinks and acts immediately upon awakening. In this state of consciousness, which is used by the intelligence to perceive outer objects and to enjoy, the senses and mind are turned outward. The term *jāgrata-avasthā* refers to the perception of all four states of consciousness: *jāgrat,* → *svapna* (the dreaming condition), → *sushupti* (deep sleep), and → *turīya* (lit. "the fourth").

Jahānaka 🄷 Skt. → *mahāpralaya*

Jahnu 🄷 Skt.; 1. a holy man whose meditation was disturbed by the roaring sound of the Ganges rushing by and who therefore swallowed its waters. He later regretted his deed and allowed the water to flow out of his ear. Thereafter, the Ganges was also known as Jahnavi, "daughter of Jahnu"; 2. the name of a cave in the Himalayas out of which the Ganges flows.

Jai 🄷 Skt. → *jaya*

Jaimini 🄷 a sage, student of the Veda-Vyāsa (→ Vyāsa). He is said to have received the → *Sāmaveda* from his master and to have distributed and interpreted it. He is probably not identical with the scholar Jaimini, author of the → *Mīmāmsā-Sūtra,* who founded the philosophical school of → Mīmāmsā.

Jainism 🄷 (Skt. Jaina), an unorthodox Indian religion that rejects the authority of the Vedas.

Its tradition refers to twenty-four teachers, or → *tīrthankaras,* also called *jinas* (lit. "the conquerors"). The last of these and the founder of Jainism was → Mahāvīra, a contemporary of the Buddha. Jains do not believe in God. Their religion teaches that divinity dwells within every soul, and perfect souls are venerated as the Supreme Spirit. Liberation is attained through right belief, right knowledge, and right action, whereby the practice of noninjury of living beings is particularly stressed.

Jakugo **Z** also chakugo, Jap., lit. "words of arrival"; short, powerful pronouncement expressing the true understanding of the content of a → kōan or part of a kōan.

In kōan collections like the → *Pi-yen-lu* there are frequently *jakugo* that were originally "incidental remarks" on the part of the compiler, frequently a well-known Ch'an or Zen master, and that later were interpolated into the text of the kōan.

In the Japanese → Rinzai school it has been customary since the time of → Hakuin Zenji for Zen students to add one or more *jakugo,* often in poetic form, to their "solution" of a kōan as a further expression of their penetration of its meaning. These short poetic expressions are not necessarily composed by the student; they can be well-known sayings or lines of poetry from Zen or secular literature.

The main source for such quotations was the → *Zenrin-kushū,* an anthology of quotations from Chinese sources, which Hakuin Zenji had often consulted in his youth. The *jakugo* should not be confused with the "praise" (→ *ju*).

Jakuhitsu Genkō **Z** 1290–1367; Japanese Zen master of the → Rinzai school. He was ordained as a monk at fifteen and soon thereafter became a student of the Zen master Buttō Kokushi (→ Kokushi) in Kamakura.

Later Jakuhitsu went to China, where he sought out Master Ming-pen and other Ch'an (Zen) masters of the Rinzai school of the Yuan period. All of these confirmed his profound realization of Zen. Jakuhitsu was the last well-known Japanese Zen master to go to China, where Ch'an was already in decline.

Once when his master was sick, Jakuhitsu, who was taking care of his treatment, asked him about the "last word" (a question about the living truth of Zen). Buttō Kokushi hit him, and in this instant Jakuhitsu experienced enlightenment. He was then eighteen years old.

Jakujō **Z** Jap., lit. "stillness [and] peace"; complete inner stillness and inner peace, freedom from ignorance (→ *avidyā,* → delusion) and the (worldly) care, suffering, and passion resulting from it (→ *bonnō*). A notion pointing to the state of → *jakumetsu.*

Jakumetsu **Z** Jap., lit. "stillness-extinction"; Japanese pronunciation of the two characters by which the Sanskrit term *nirvāna* is translated into Chinese. *Jakumetsu* means a state of total peace beyond birth and death, arising and passing away, time and space, beyond all conditions and qualities, a state of consciousness in which a fully awakened one (i.e., a buddha; also → enlightenment) lives. This state admits of no definition—also not the one attempted here—in that it cannot be grasped by thought (→ *fukashigi*) or words (→ *fukasetsu*). Any positive proposition concerning it, even from the point of logic alone, is impossible, since it is an attempt to limit the limitless (Lat., *definere*). The only propositions concerning *jakumetsu* that are possible are negative propositions saying that it is "not this, not that" (Skt., *neti, neti*) or that it is beyond all categories of thought and understanding.

According to the highest teaching of Buddhism, particularly as it is propounded in Zen, *jakumetsu* is → nirvāna but nevertheless completely one with → samsāra: that which is limitless, unconditioned, and devoid of qualities is identical with that which is limited (characterized by form), conditioned (subject to cause and effect, i.e., → karma), and with the phenomenal world of countless qualities. Nirvāna itself is already unthinkable; the unity of nirvāna and samsāra can only be realized in enlightenment. The realization of complete enlightenment means that a buddha can live in the world of appearance (samsāra) in complete peace (*jakumetsu,* nirvāna). Thus nirvāna is not realized only after death in some kind of "world of the beyond" that is different from "this world."

Jamgon Kongtrul **B** ('jam-mgon kon-sprul), 1813–99, "kind protector, incarnation from Kong"; one of the most important scholars of → Tibetan Buddhism of the 19th century. Imbued with the teachings of the → Bön school as a child, he also received monastic ordination from both the → Nyingmapa and → Kagyü schools. Together with the → Sakyapa teacher Jamyang Khyentse Wangpo (1820–92) he created in East Tibet an atmosphere of general religious tolerance (→ Rime) and also exercised political influence. His five most important written works are deferentially known as the Five Treasures. His *Nges-*

don sgron-me, a meditation manual, appeared in English translation under the title *The Torch of Certainty.*

Jamgon Kongtrul with hands in the Vitarka Mudrā

At the age of thirty Jamgon Kongtrul had received instruction in over sixty teachings and had completed the study of them. At this time he was also recognized as a → *tulku.* On the basis of his knowledge of the Bön and Nyingmapa traditions, he began to collect all the → *terma* traditions available at this time. He finished this task at the age of fifty-nine. This collection was later printed in sixty volumes and is one of his five principal works.

His concern that all traditions of Tibetan Buddhism be regarded as of equal value also became apparent in his other works. Besides religious literature, they contain treatises on painting and medicine. Jamgon Kongtrul's connection with the Karma-Kagyü school is evidenced by his writing new commentaries on its teachings as well as meditation manuals that are in use to this day. His influence was strengthened still further after his death as various reincarnations of him were recognized. The most influential of these incarnations were Zhechen Kongtrul (1901–60) and Pälpung Kongtrul (1904–53).

Janaka 🅗 1. king of Videha, the father of → Sītā. He is the ideal → Karma-Yogi of ages past. By means of desirelessness and the selfless actions he offered as a sacrifice to God, Janaka attained perfection. He serves as an example of how one can continue to live serenely in the world after liberation. The sage → Yājñavalkya was Janaka's priest and adviser.

The → Brāhmanas report that Janaka resisted the dominance of the brahmans and claimed the right to offer sacrifices without the intervention of priests. He prevailed in this claim. Because of his pure, righteous life, he became a brahman and one of the → *rājarishis.* Janaka is also called Sīradhvaja (lit. "the plow-bannered"), because his daughter Sītā (lit. "furrow") sprang fully formed from a furrow as Janaka was plowing and preparing a sacrifice in order to obtain progeny.

Japa 🅗, or Japam, Skt., lit. 1. "whisper, murmur"; 2. "rose"; repetition of a sacred name or sacred formula (→ mantra) as a form of meditation. The repetition may be spoken aloud or sounded in the mind. Any name of God or a mantra received from one's guru may be used. *Japa* is an important exercise for calming and clarifying the mind, whereby the use of a rosary (→ *mālā*) or a chain of beads can be of great help. Three types of *japa* are distinguished: 1. repetition out loud (*vaikhari-japa*); 2. repetition in the mind *(mānasika-japa*); 3. silent repetition with the lips (*upānshu-japa*).

Jarāyuja 🅗 🅑 Skt. → *chatur-yoni*

Jātakas 🅑 Pali, lit. "birth stories"; a part of the → *Khuddaka-nikāya.* The 547 *Jātakas* are by themselves the biggest section of the → *Sūtra-pitaka.* The birth stories detail the previous lives of the Buddha and of his followers and foes. They show how the acts of previous lives influence the circumstances of the present life according to the law of → karma.

Many of the *Jātakas* are Indian folk tales from pre-Buddhist times, adapted by the Buddhists for their purposes. The most important part of each *jātaka* is considered to be the verse containing the moral of the story. In the strictest sense, these verses alone are the canonical part of the *Jātakas.* The *Jātakas,* which have inspired numerous artistic representations, particularly in the form of reliefs on stūpas and pagodas, enjoy great popularity among the lay people of Southeast Asian countries, for whom they convey the basic concepts of the teaching. The *Jātakas* are extant, not only in Pali, but also in a Chinese translation that is based on a lost Sanskrit version. English translations of the *Jātakas* are available in anthologies of Buddhist myths and tales.

Jaya 🅗, or Jai, Skt./Hindi: "Hail!" or "Victory to Him!" or "Glory to Him!"; an interjection often used in → *pūjā* and chanted in chorus, e.g., in phrases extolling gods and holy persons, as "Jai Shrī Guru Mahārāj" or "Jai Shrī Durgā."

Jen 🅣 Chin., roughly humanity, love of fellow man; central virtue of → Confucianism and the most important characteristic of the ideal man (*chün-tzu,* lit. "duke's son") in the teachings of

Confucius (→ K'ung-tzu). *Jen* is the manifestation of pure untarnished human nature in accordance with the requirements of morality (→ *li*). Its basis is a natural sympathy for one's fellow beings, its expression the maintenance of mutuality (*shu*) and loyalty (*chung*).

In the *Analects* (*Lun-yü*) Confucius states (6.28), "To apply one's own wishes and desires as a yardstick by which to judge one's behavior toward others is the true way of *jen.*" Asked about the essence of *jen,* the master replied, "To love your fellow men."

The roots of *jen* are piety (*hsiao*), i.e., the veneration shown by children for their parents in life and after their death, and fraternal obedience (*ti*), i.e., the subordination of the younger brother to the older: "A noble person will cultivate the root; if the root is rooted firmly, the path will grow. Piety and obedience: these are the roots of *jen.*" An analysis of the pictogram for *jen* allows us to arrive at a deeper understanding of the term: the pictogram consists of the sign for "human being" and the sign for "two." *Jen* thus embraces all the moral qualities governing—and expressed by—the ideal behavior of one human being toward another.

Jetavana B monastery in Shrāvastī (India), which the wealthy merchant → Anāthapindika established for the historical Buddha. It became the Buddha's favorite sojourning place and he spent nineteen rainy seasons there. The oldest monastery of China → Pai-ma-ssu is built on the model of the Jetavana Monastery.

Jigme Lingpa B → *dzogchen*

Jihatsu Z also *hatsu, hachi,* Jap.; a wooden bowl that serves a Buddhist monk both for eating and as a begging bowl. (Also → *oryōki*).

Jikijitsu Z Jap.; in the → Rinzai school the elder monk who is charged with the supervision of the → *zendō.* (Also → *godō*).

Jikishi-ninshin Z Jap., lit. "direct pointing [to the] human heart-mind [*shin,* → *kokoro*]"; expression for the style of presenting the → buddhadharma characteristic of Zen, without recourse to conceptual thought or to action motivated by a dualistic view of the world. (Also → *fukasetsu*).

Jikishi-tanden Z Jap., lit. "direct pointing–a transmission"; another expression for → *inshin-denshin,* the transmission of the buddha-dharma from heart-mind (→ *kokoro*) to heart-mind, which is the basis of the Zen tradition.

Jina H Skt. → Jainism, → *tīrthankara*

Jiri Z Jap., lit. "thing-principle"; the relative and the absolute, the phenomenal world and the true nature of reality, the many and that which is devoid of distinctions.

Jiriki B Z Jap., lit. "one's own power"; an expression referring to the endeavor to attain → enlightenment through one's own efforts (for example, → *zazen*). Jiriki is usually used in counterdistinction to → *tariki,* which roughly means "the power of the other." This refers to the fact that the adherents of some Buddhist schools place their trust in the notion that the mere belief in Buddha (generally, his manifestation as → Amitābha) and calling upon his name will bring about rebirth in a buddha paradise (→ Pure Land) and thus the liberation of the believer (→ Amidism). This is an approach that places the power of the buddha principle to liberate human beings in the foreground. Thus it is characterized as *tariki,* "power of the other." In contrast, other schools of Buddhism, such as Zen, place the emphasis on the ability to actualize enlightenment and achieve liberation through one's own efforts, i.e., through meditative training. This is characterized as *jiriki.*

On a deeper level, as is stressed in Zen, every sentient being and thing from the very beginning is endowed with buddha-nature (→ *busshō*). From this point of view, the opposition of *jiriki* and *tariki* must be regarded as an artificial one, which, though indicating a differing emphasis in religious practice, is ultimately not valid. On the one hand, on a *tariki* path one's own effort is also necessary in order to open oneself to the liberating power of the supposed "other"; on the other hand, the practitioner's "own effort" on a *jiriki* path is nothing other than a manifestation of the "power of the other."

Jishō Z Jap., lit. "self-nature"; another expression for the buddha-nature (→ *busshō*) that is immanent in everything existing and that is experienced in self-realization (→ *kenshō*). (Also → *sho.*)

Jishō-shōjō-shin Z Jap., lit. "the pure-clear heart-mind [*shin,* → *kokoro*] of self-nature [→ *jishō*]"; a term for the primordial perfection, buddha-nature (→ *busshō*) that is immanent in all beings and does not need to be "attained." This perfection is always present—a fact, however, that is obscured by → delusion in "everyman's consciousness" (→ *bonpu-no-jōshiki*).

Jīva H Skt., from *jīv,* "to live"; one who lives in the body, a mortal being; the embodied self that identifies with body and mind; as ego, it creates the notions of duality and causality and thereby becomes bound to the cycle of birth and death. (See also → *jīvātman*.)

Jīva is → Īshvara, but only in the sense of his partial manifestation. From the point of view of philosophy, it is *brahman* that manifests itself as the individual self through → Shakti. The *jīvas* are infinite in number, the true Self (→ *ātman*) is only One.

Jīvakoti 🄷 Skt., lit. "highest mortal"; a human being who after realizing *brahman* is not born again, in contrast to → *īshvarakoti*.

Jīvanmukta 🄷 Skt., lit. "one liberated while still alive"; one who is still in the body but has freed himself from the bonds of ignorance (→ *avidyā*) and → *māyā*. Such a one has given up identification with the body and mind and has attained liberation (→ *mukti*). As the Self (→ *ātman*), he knows that he is one with *brahman*.

Jīvanmukti-Viveka 🄷 Skt., lit. "liberated while still in the body by means of discrimination"; an important work by → Vidyāranya (fourteenth century), it describes in five chapters the path to illumination. The work calls upon the authority of the Vedas, from which it draws proof for the possibility of liberation; it calls for the overcoming of all desires, explains how thoughts must be eliminated and the mind must be bypassed in order to achieve liberation, and ends with a description of the renunciation of one who is illuminated (→ *vidvat-sannyāsa*).

Jīvātman 🄷 Skt.; the → *ātman* manifested as the embodied self. He dwells in the body and uses it as an instrument, but knows that in reality he is the *ātman*.

Jizō 🄱 🅉 Jap. for → Kshitigarbha

Jizō 🅉 Jap. for Ti-ts'ang, → Lo-han Kuei-ch'en

Jñāna 🄷 🄱 Skt., from the root *jñā*, "to know." 🄷 1. general knowledge; 2. spiritual wisdom and illumination; knowledge of the ultimate reality; the transcendent realization that → *ātman* and → *brahman* are one.

Jñāna is the purely intellectual, logical path of divine knowledge; because of the advanced development of mental faculties in modern times, this path seems to be simple, clear, and logical, but in its practical application it is one of the most difficult paths. The process of → *neti, neti* ("not this, not this") demands an uncompromising discriminatory faculty, one that puts aside everything belonging to → *māyā* as unreal, including all of one's desires and notions, until *brahman* is left as the only reality. It is a dry, abstract way to God, only which → Rāmakrishna once described with the remark, "I don't want to be sugar but only to taste sugar."

🄱 (Pali, ñāna); intellectual knowledge concerning phenomena and the laws governing them and concerning the right definition of all → dharmas. *Jñāna* is a component of → *prajñā* (wisdom).

Mahāyāna Buddhism understands by *jñāna* the mastery of all the rational contents of the teaching as they are presented in the Hīnayāna scriptures. *Jñāna* is actualized at the tenth stage of the development of a bodhisattva (→ *bhūmi*).

Jñāna-Kānda 🄷 (Jñāna-Kāṇḍa), Skt.; the portion of the Veda dealing with knowledge; it develops the system of → Vedānta in the form of the Upanishads and other → *shrutis*. The other part of the Veda is the → Karma-Kānda.

Jñāna-Karma-Samuchchaya-Vāda 🄷 (Jñāna-Karma-Samuccaya-Vāda), Skt., lit. *jñāna:* "knowledge," *karma:* "action," *samuchchaya:* "as well as"; a theory represented by Bhartriprapañcha, → Rāmānuja, and other philosophers; it states that only the combination of knowledge and action can lead to liberation.

Jñāna-Mudrā 🄷 Skt.; a hand gesture (→ *mudrā*) in which the index finger and thumb touch, while the remaining fingers are held outstretched, a symbol for → *jñāna*. The index finger symbolizes the individual soul, the thumb is the cosmic soul. The union of the two is the symbol for true knowledge.

Jñāna-Yoga 🄷 Skt.; the way of knowledge, one of the four primary yogas, that which leads to God through intellectual analysis and knowledge. Through discrimination (→ *viveka*), the entire manifest world is known to be transitory and unreal, and it is recognized that only one unchanging, imperishable, eternal reality exists: *brahman*. This path requires not merely a sharp mind but detachment, renunciation, and clarity of thought as well. In Jñāna-Yoga, every form of ignorance (→ *avidyā*) must be overcome. The meditation of the Jñāna-Yogi is directed to the qualityless Absolute (*brahman*), with which the *atman* is identical. An introduction to Jñāna-Yoga is Vivekānanda 1955*a*.

Jñānendriya 🄷 Skt. → *indriya*

Jñāni-Bhakta 🄷 Skt.; a particular type of devotee: the lover of God who also possesses knowledge of the ultimate reality; one who has united within himself a purely intellectual knowledge of God (*jñāna*) and a pure love of God (→ *bhakti*).

Jñānin 🅗 Skt.; 1. an adherent of → Jñāna-Yoga, one who seeks to realize God by means of logic and discrimination (→ *viveka*); 2. a nondualist, i.e., one who follows a nondualist religion or philosophy (→ *advaita*); 3. a knower of → *brahman*.

Jōbutsu 🅩 Jap., lit. "becoming a buddha"; an expression in Zen for the realization of one's own buddha-nature (→ *busshō*). According to the understanding of Zen, a man cannot *become* a buddha, because he always already is a buddha, that is, his true nature is identical with buddha-nature. However, a man caught in "everyman's consciousness" (→ *bonpu-no-jōshiki*) is not aware of this fact and thus it seems to him as though he "becomes" a buddha when he realizes his buddha-nature for the first time. A synonym for *jōbutsu* is → *jōdō*.

Jōdō 🅩 Jap., lit. "ascent [into the Zen] hall"; ceremonial entrance of

Jōdō 🅩 Jap., lit. "realization of the way"; another term for → *jōbutsu*. the → *rōshi* into the → *zendō* for the purpose of holding a → *teishō*.

Jōdo school 🅑 → Jōdo-shū

Jōdo-shin-shū 🅑 Jap., lit. "True School of the Pure Land." The short form is Shin-shū (Shin school). A school of Japanese Buddhism that was founded by → Shinran (1173–1262) but first organized as a school by Rennyo (1414–99). It is based on the → *Sukhāvatī-vyūha*, the core of which is the forty-eight vows of Buddha Amitābha (Jap., Amida). The essence of the Jōdo-shin-shū teaching lies in the formula for venerating Amida (→ *nembutsu*), in whom are unified all the virtues of a buddha. The recitation of this formula permits the believer to be reborn in the → Pure Land of Amida and to realize buddhahood, even if he has accumulated bad karma. This is possible through the active help of Amida. The most important element in the practice is thus the unshakable belief in the power of Buddha Amida.

The Jōdo-shin-shū has no monastic aspect; it is purely a lay community. A peculiarity of the school is that the office of abbot of the main temple and thus also the function of head of the school is hereditary. Today the Jōdo-shin-shū is the most important school of Buddhism in Japan and consists of two factions: Ōtani and Honganji. The main temples of both are in Kyōto. This division took place in the 17th century as a result of differences in the manner of performing rituals. Both factions maintain large universities.

In contrast to the → Jōdo-shū, in which the recitation of Amida's name serves essentially for the strengthening of trust in Amida, the Shin school sees in it an act of gratitude on the part of the individual. This arises from the insight that the buddha Amida exerts his entire force for the sake of saving this individual. In the Shin school only Amida is venerated; he may not, however, be called upon for the sake of purely private interests.

The Jōdo-shin-shū represents the most extreme form of the "easy path," in which the practitioner relies on the "power of the other," (→ *tariki*), i.e., of Amida. Besides the absolute trust in Amida, no other effort of one's own is required to attain enlightenment. Trust and reliance toward Amida alone effect liberation.

In this school, the old Buddhist idea of adapting oneself to the world to the greatest possible extent is logically extended: If members of the school live like all other men, i.e., as lay people, they avoid building up barriers between themselves and the world around them. Thus the Shin school is inclined to do away with all religious rules. Thus, for example, marriage is a way to participate in the life of ordinary people as well as to serve the Buddha.

Jōdo-shū 🅑 Jap., lit. "School of the Pure Land"; school of Japanese Buddhism derived from the → Pure Land school of China. The Jōdo-shū was brought to Japan, along with other Buddhist teachings, by the monk → Ennin (793–864), who studied in China the teachings of the → T'ien-t'ai, → Mi-tsung, and Pure Land schools. Ennin propagated the practice of reciting the name of Amida (→ *nembutsu*). Important representatives of the early period of this school were Kūya (903–72), called the Sage of the Streets, and Genshin (942–1017). In their time recitation of Amida's name was a component of the practice of all Buddhist schools, especially of the → Tendai and → Shingon schools.

In the 12th century Hōnen (1133–1212) founded the actual Jōdo school. He wanted in this way to open up an "easy path" for the distressed people of the "last times." He succeeded in assembling a great host of followers around him and forming them into a powerful organization. Since he considered his teaching the supreme one, he alienated the representatives of other Buddhist schools and was condemned to exile in a remote area at the age of seventy-four.

The doctrinal basis of his schoool is provided

by the three most important texts of the Pure Land school: → *Sukhāvatī-vyūha*, → *Amitābha-sūtra*, → *Amitāyurdhyāna-sūtra*. The practice of the Jōdo-shū consists exclusively of reciting the name of Amida in the formula *Namu Amida Butsu* ("Veneration to Buddha Amida"). This is essential in order to strengthen faith in Amida, without which rebirth in the Pure Land of Amida (→ Sukhāvatī), the goal of the practice, is impossible. The adherents of the Jōdo-shū, unlike those of the Jōdo-shin-shū, enter the monastic life.

Kūya was the first adherent of the Amida cult who propagated it publicly. The Sage of the Streets moved through the streets dancing and singing, to a melody invented by himself, the formula for the veneration of Amida, beating rhythm on a bowl. Ryōnin, who belonged to the Tendai school, is known particularly for propagating the invocation formula through folk songs. He was strongly influenced by the totalistic philosophy of the Tendai and → Kegon schools and developed the "all-pervasive *nembutsu*": if a person recites the name of Amida, it redounds to the benefit of all men; in this way one can participate in the worship of others. Ryōnin's exposition of the teaching gained great influence at the imperial court. After his death the teaching was continued by his students.

Genshin, a monk on Mount Hiei, a center of the Amida school, was persuaded that there must be a means for the liberation of all beings. He expounded such a method in his work on the belief in Amida, in which ten sections described the tortures of the hells (→ *naraka*) and the benefits of the Jōdo practice. He believed he understood the two essential features of human nature—repulsion and fear of hell and longing for rebirth in the Pure Land. This became one of the most influential works in the history of Japanese Amidism. Genshin, however, was not only a writer; he tried through painting and sculpture to bring his message also to uneducated people. Still, however, the veneration of Amida did not constitute an independent school but was part of the practice of other Buddhist schools.

Only with Hōnen was this belief institutionalized as the Jōdo school. In his work, *Senchakushū*, on the vows of Amida, Hōnen presented unequivocally the view that calling upon Amida represented the highest of all religious practices. He distinguished—following the doctrine of T'ao-ch'o (7th century), a representative of the Chinese Pure Land school—between the "sacred" (or "difficult") path of traditional methods, which require strict discipline and effort, and the "path of the Pure Land" (or "easy path"), which requires only faith in Amida and the recitation of his name. Hōnen was of the opinion that in an age of religious decadence, the majority of humanity is not capable of following the "sacred path"; their only chance is the second path, based on the compassion and help of Amida, on the "power of the other" (→ *tariki*).

Jōjitsu school 🅱 Jap., lit. "School of the Perfection of Truth": name of the Japanese branch of the → Satyasiddhi school. This teaching was brought to Japan in 625 by Ekwan, a Korean monk who had studied this school in China. Since then, this teaching has been studied in Japan by students of many Buddhist leanings but never regarded as an independent school, rather as part of the → Sanron school (Skt., → Mādhyamika; Chin. → San-lun school).

Jō Jōza 🆉 Jap. for → Ting Shang-tso

Jōkin 🆉 → Keizan Jōkin

Jōriki 🆉 Jap., lit. "power of mind"; that particular power or force that arises from the concentrated mind and that is brought about through training in → *zazen*. Jōriki makes possible continuous presence of mind as well as the ability, even in unexpected or difficult circumstances, spontaneously to do the right thing.

According to the modern Japanese Zen master → Hakuun Ryōko Yasutani, *jōriki* is "more than the ability to concentrate in the usual sense of the word. It is a dynamic power which, once mobilized, enables us even in the most sudden and unexpected situations to act instantly, without pausing to collect our wits, and in a manner wholly appropriate to the circumstances. One who has developed jōriki is no longer a slave to his passions, neither is he at the mercy of his environment. Always in command of both himself and the circumstances of his life, he is able to move with perfect freedom and equanimity. . . . While it is true that many extraordinary powers flow from jōriki, nevertheless through it alone we cannot cut the roots of our illusory view of the world. . . . Concomitantly there must be satori-awakening." (Kapleau 1980, 49–50)

Since *jōriki* and the "miraculous powers" (→ *siddhis*) that can arise from it constitute for many people an extraordinary lure, the great Chinese master → Shih-t'ou Hsi-ch'ien (Jap., Sekitō Kisen) stressed, "In our school the realization of buddha-nature takes priority and not mere devotional practices or the accumulation of awakened powers."

Jōshin 🆉 Jap.; from *jo* (=*sadameru*), "determine, establish, decide, resolve," and *shin*, → *kokoro*; the "collected mind," a state of consciousness in which the mind is fully and integrally collected and absorbed by one thing with which it has become one. This collectedness is not concentration in the conventional sense, which usually refers to a directedness from here (subject) to there (object)—and thus, in contrast to collectedness is a dualistic state—and is generally brought about by active pushing. In contrast to this, collectedness is characterized by "passive" though wakeful receptivity. The ability to "collect the mind" is an essential prerequisite for the practice of → *zazen.*

Jōshū Jūshin 🅉 Jap. for → Chao-chou Ts'ung-shen

Ju 🅉 Jap., lit. "eulogy, song of praise"; in its general meaning *ju* is the translation of the Sanskrit word *gāthā*, which refers to the expression of Buddhist wisdom in the form of a poem. In Zen the term is predominantly used for the "eulogies" that compilers of kōan collections such as the → *Pi-yen-lu* and the → *Wu-men-kuan* or other Zen masters added to particular examples (→ kōan) in such collections, in which they expressed their insight into the kōan. Another term for *ju* is → *juko.*

Some of these eulogies are among the most sublime works of Buddhist poetry in the Chinese language, especially the eulogies that the great Chinese Ch'an (Zen) master Hsüeh-tou Ch'ung-hsien (Jap., Setchō Jūken) added to the hundred kōans collected by him. Master → Yuan-wu K'o-chin (Jap., Engo Kokugon) made these the basis of his *Blue Cliff Record* (*Pi-yen-lu*).

Juan Chi 🅃 → *chu-lin ch'i-hsien*

Juan Hsien 🅃 → *chu-lin ch'i-hsien*

Ju ching 🅃 Chin., lit. "to enter into the silence"; the cultivation of quietude prior to Taoist meditation. To cultivate this stillness the adept withdraws to a quiet place, closes his eyes, eliminates all distracting thoughts, and empties his mind. Only then is he ready to begin his actual meditation.

Jūgyū(-no)-zu 🅉 Jap., lit. "*Ten Oxen Pictures*"; representation of the stages of the Zen way or of the different levels of realization of enlightenment shown in ten pictures of an ox (or water buffalo) and his herder. The ten pictures, usually each painted in a circle, and the accompanying texts—short explanations and poems—became popular in Japan in the 14th/15th century and have been handed down in many versions. The best-known stems from the Chinese Ch'an (Zen) master K'uo-an Chih-yuan (or Shih-yuan; Jap., Kakuan Shien), fl. 1150. The stages depicted are (1) seeking the ox; (2) finding the tracks; (3) first glimpse of the ox; (4) catching the ox; (5) taming the ox; (6) riding the ox home; (7) ox forgotten, self alone; (8) both ox and self forgotten; (9) returning to the source; (10) entering the marketplace with helping hands. This cycle with accompanying text can be found in Kapleau 1980.

The Sixth Oxherding Picture: Riding the Ox Home

There are earlier versions of the oxherding pictures consisting of five or eight pictures in which the ox is black at the beginning, becomes progressively whiter, and finally disappears altogether. This last stage is shown as an empty circle. "This implied that the realization of Oneness (that is, the effacement of every conception of self and other) was the ultimate goal of Zen. But Kuo-an, feeling this to be incomplete, added two more pictures beyond the circle to make it clear that the Zen man of the highest spiritual development lives in the mundane world of form and diversity and mingles with the utmost freedom among ordinary men, whom he inspires with his compassion and radiance to walk in the way of the Buddha" (Kapleau 1980, 313).

Juhotsu 🅉 Jap.; roughly "upright hossu"; the wordless gesture of a Zen master of raising his flywhisk (→ *hossu*) as an expression of the ineffability (→ *fukasetsu*) of Zen realization.

Ju-i 🄱 🅃 🅉 Chin. (Jap., nyoi), lit. "as one wishes"; name for the "wish-fulfilling scepter," a frequent attribute of Taoist or Buddhist saints or masters.

The *ju-i* is carved from bamboo, jade, bone, or other materials. The upper end usually has the form of the immortality mushroom (→ *ling-chih*). It is easily wielded. Also → *kotsu.*

Jui-yen Shih-yen 🅉 (Jap., Zuigan Shigen); 9th century Chinese Ch'an (Zen) master; a student and dharma successor (→ *hassu*) of → Yen-t'ou Chuan-huo (Jap., Gantō Zenkatsu). Almost nothing is known of Jui-yen's life. He appears in a famous kōan, recorded as example 12 of the → *Wu-men-kuan*: Master Jui-yen called himself every day, "Master!" And he also answered himself, "Yes!" And again, "Are you awake?" he asked, and answered, "Yes! Yes!" "Don't let yourself be deceived by others." "No! No!"

Juji-sambō 🅩 Jap. → *sambō*

Jūjūkai 🅩 also jūjūkinkai, Jap., lit. "the ten main precepts"; the ten main precepts of → Mahāyāna Buddhism, of which there is an exoteric and an esoteric form:

1. In their exoteric form the *jūjūkai* forbid: (a) taking life, (b) stealing, (c) being unchaste, (d) lying, (e) selling or buying alcohol (i.e., causing others to drink or drinking oneself), (f) talking about others' bad deeds, (g) praising oneself and deprecating others, (h) giving spiritual or material help reluctantly, (i) aggression, (j) slandering the three precious ones (Skt., *triratna*, → *sambō*). These precepts are, with the exception of the chastity precept, the same for monks and laymen.

Observance of the precepts is not only important for ethical reasons. The precepts are the basis of spiritual practice; one cannot progress on the path of spiritual training if heart and mind are not free from the inner malaise brought about by a careless lifestyle that is in violation of these precepts. Regardless of their level of commitment, few novices are able to maintain every precept; thus infringements in various degrees are inevitable. Such infringements, however, do not impede progress on the way of → enlightenment, provided that one confesses them, genuinely regrets them, and endeavors thereafter to live in accordance with the precepts. As progress on the path is made and increasing power, purity, and insight come about through meditative practice (→ *zazen*), infringements become less. However, according to the Buddhist understanding what does bring about lasting impairment and has a disastrous effect on the possibility of spiritual progress is loss of faith in the Buddha, in the truth that he revealed through his complete enlightenment (→ *dharma*), and in the corroborative teachings of the patriarchs (→ *sangha*). In this case, it is said, complete enlightenment and therewith the dissolution of the fundamental root of unwholesomeness, i.e., ignorance (→ *avidyā*) and → delusion, is impossible.

2. In the *jūjūkai* in their esoteric form, one vows (a) not to desist from the true dharma, (b) not to give up seeking enlightenment, (c) to covet nothing and be niggardly with nothing, (d) not to be lacking in compassion toward all beings, (e) not to speak ill of any of the Buddhist teachings, (f) not to be attached to anything, (g) not to harbor false views (h) to encourage people to seek enlightenment, (i) to present the teachings of Mahāyāna also to adherents of → Hīnayāna, (j) always to practice charity toward → bodhisattvas.

Jukai 🅩 Jap.; 1. lit. "receiving [*ju*] the precepts [*kai*]"; the reception and acknowledgment of the Buddhist precepts (→ *kairitsu*, → *jūjūkai*) through which one officially becomes a Buddhist.

2. lit. "granting [*ju*] the precepts [*kai*]"; the ceremonial initiation into Buddhism. In this ceremony one commits oneself to be completely devoted to the three precious ones (Skt., *triratna*, → *sambō*) and the ten main precepts, to cleave to Buddhism, to avoid all evil, to do good, and to work for the salvation of all beings (→ bodhisattva vow). *Jukai* is regarded as a major step on the path to buddhahood.

Juko 🅩 Jap., lit. "praise of the ancients"; another word for → *ju*.

Jvāla-Mukhī 🅗 Skt., lit. "mouth of fire"; a well-known pilgrimage site in the Punjab, at the foothills of the Himalayas, where fire rises from the earth. According to legend, to was ignited by → Satī, consort of Shiva. Satī (lit. "true wife"), who later threw her own body into the same flames, gave her name to the practice of self-immolation of widows in India.

Jyotis 🅗 Skt., lit. "light, brightness"; the shining spiritual light of higher consciousness, which bridges the gap between knowledge and action and brings about not simply a feeling of happiness but absolute bliss (→ *ānanda*).

Jyotisha 🅗 (Jyotiṣa), Skt.; the science of astronomy, one of the → Vedāngas. Its object is the establishment of the most propitious season and day for sacrificial rites. This Vedānga presumably first evolved in the third century B.C.E.

K

Ka H Skt.; 1. the first consonant of the → Sanskrit alphabet; 2. the interrogative pronoun "Who?" It was later elevated to a divinity. By the time the → Brāhmanas were composed, the poetic character of the Vedic hymns, and the questions they contained regarding an unknown god, were no longer understood; thus the authors of the Brāhmanas took the interrogative "Ka" to stand for a specific god.

Wherever they touch upon interrogative verses, the *Taittirīya-, Kaushītaki-,* and *Shatapatha-Brāhmana* state that Ka is → Prajāpati, lord of all created beings. Hymns and sacrifices to the gods were named *kāya.* By Pānini's time, the word was so firmly established that rules for its explanation were introduced. In the later Sanskrit literature of the → Purānas, Ka appears as an acknowledged god, and the Laws of → Manu mention a form of marriage, *kāya,* that is generally known as Prajāpati-marriage. The *Mahābhārata* identifies Ka as → Daksha.

Kabīr H, Indian poet and mystic, ca. 1440-1518; he lived in North India at a time following the invasion of Islam, when Hindus and Muslims were attempting to approach one another's beliefs and spiritual practices. His adoptive parents, poor weavers of Benares, belonged to a low caste in both Hinduism and Islam and were thereby freed from the burden of religious duties. This background greatly influenced Kabīr's poetry and songs, which are sung even today by Muslims and Hindus alike. (These are collected under the title *Bījak,* meaning "the seed.")

Kabīr's mentor was → Rāmānanda. Like all mystics, he was forced to traverse a "dark night of the soul" before attaining enlightenment. His unconventional manner of speaking directly about God and his criticism of the superficiality of spiritual dignitaries provoked such anger that he was forced to leave Benares; thereafter, he roamed from place to place with his followers, singing and praising God. For Kabīr God was the all-pervading supreme spirit who dwells in all beings and yet transcends all forms. At the same time, like the medieval mystics of the West, he viewed God as the soul's eternal beloved, who can be known by pure love alone. Legend relates that after his death Hindus and Muslims fought over the manner in which the body was to be disposed of. When they lifted the shroud, however, they found beneath it nothing but a heap of flowers.

Kadampa B ('ka'-gdams-pa), Tib., lit. "oral instruction"; a school of → Tibetan Buddhism founded by → Atīsha. After the degeneration of Buddhism in Tibet in the 10th century, this school saw the correct exposition of the traditional writings as its primary task. The most important teachings of the Kadampas became known by the name *lo-jong* ("training the mind"). This school did not survive as an independent tradition, but the Kadampa transmissions were absorbed by the other schools, particularly by the → Gelugpa school.

The most important contribution of the Kadampas to the spiritual life of Tibet was a group of clearly conceived programs of practice that are still taught today with the purpose of training the mind. Its point of orientation is the → bodhisattva ideal, and it is regarded as a special method for arousing enlightenment mind (→ *bodhicitta*).

Although at the time of Atīsha these teachings were only transmitted orally, later on texts that were easy to memorize were composed. The two best known are "Eight Verses on Training the Mind" by the Kadampa Geshe Langri Thangpa and "Seven Points of Mind-Training." One of the most important figures in the early Kadampa school was Dromtön (1008–64), who is the author of the following verse:

If you hear words that are unpleasant to you
Then quickly heed the echo's sound.
If your body receives injury
Recognize in that your previous deeds.

Kadō Z Jap., lit. "Way of flowers"; one of the Japanese ways of training (→ *dō*) permeated by the mind of Zen, which contribute to the development of their practitioners. In *kadō,* which is often called *ikebana* (lit. "pond flower"), the idea is not to "arrange flowers," which would presuppose a subject operating on flowers as an object. Rather one is concerned to actualize a nondualistic state of mind in which the flower itself reveals its nature.

Kagyüpa B (bka'-rgyud-pa), Tib., lit. "oral transmission lineage"; one of the four principal schools of → Tibetan Buddhism. The central teaching of this school is the "great seal" (→ *mahāmudrā*) and the six dharmas of → Nāropa (→ *Nāro chödrug*). The teachings were brought to Tibet from India in the 11th century by → Marpa. → Gampopa, a student of → Milarepa's, organized them into the Kagyüpa school. From this school is derived that of the → Karma Kagyü and others. The school places particular value on the direct transmission of instruction from teacher to disciple.

The Kagyü transmission has its point of origin in Vajradhara (holder of the vajra), an embodiment of the dharmakāya (→ *trikāya*) and passed from → Tilopa to Nāropa. Marpa the Translator brought these teachings to Tibet, and his student Milarepa succeeded in mastering them all after years of ascetic practice. In the 12th century the physician Gampopa integrated the doctrines of the → Kadampas into the Kagyü tradition and formed it into an independent school, which was named after the birthplace of its founder, Dagpo-Kagyü. Already in the next generation four further schools developed out of this: (1) Kamtshang or Karma Kagyü, (2) Tsälpa Kagyü, (3) Baram Kagyü, (4) Phagmo Drupa Kagyü. The last of these divided into eight subschools of which the Drugpa Kagyü and the Drigung Kagyü still exist.

A further school associated with the Kagyü, was founded by Khyungpo Naljor (1310–?). It bears the name Shangpa Kagyü and possesses a special *mahāmudrā* transmission, which originated with Nāropa's sister Niguma. Through the effort of the → Rime movement, this tradition still exists.

Kaidan-Seki **Z** Jap., lit. "*kaidan* stone"; a stone tablet set up in front of Zen monasteries which bears the inscription: "Meat, fish, and alcohol prohibited." *Kaidan* is the ordination hall in a monastery in which monks are initiated into Buddhism (→ *jukai*) and thereby receive the Buddhist precepts (→ *kairitsu*, → *jūjūkai*).

Kaifuku Dōnei **Z** Jap. for → K'ai-fu Tao-ning

K'ai-fu Tao-ning **Z** (Jap., Kaifuku Dōnei) d. 1113; Chinese Ch'an (Zen) master of the Yōgi lineage of Rinzai Zen (→ Yōgi school); a student and dharma successor (→ *hassu*) of → Wu-tsu Fa-yen (Jap., Goso Hōen) and the master of Yueh-an Shan-kuo (Jap., Gettan Zenka).

Kaigen **Z** Jap., lit. "opening the eye"; 1. expression for the experience of awakening (→ enlightenment), in which one receives insight into the world of true reality. The genuine insight of a student or master on the way of Zen is often called his "dharma eye." 2. Term for a ceremony in which the representation of a buddha or bodhisattva is consecrated by a Buddhist master. It is said that a representation (whether a sculpture or painting) is first filled with "life" when it is given eyes. Thus in a formal act the master actually or symbolically adds the eyes to the representation and confirms by this "opening of the eyes" that the representation is an expression in form of the formless buddha-nature (→ *busshō*) that is venerated in it.

Kaijō **Z** Jap., lit. "opening of silence"; the matinal awakening of the monks in a Zen monastery by striking a wooden board (→ *han*) or gong (→ *umpan*). The term is also used for the termination of periods of sitting meditation (→ *zazen*) through a sounded signal.

Kaikeyī **H** wife of King → Dasharatha and mother of his third son, → Bharata. When Dasharatha was wounded in battle, she nursed him back to health and was therefore granted two boons. She later claimed her due, demanding that the king banish Prince → Rāma, so that her own son, Bharata, would take his place.

Kailāsa **H** **B** also Kailāsh or Rajatādri, Skt., lit. "Silver Mountain"; a mountain in the Himālayas famous in myth and legend. The paradise of Shiva is said to be there. For Hindus it is the most holy mountain. It is the object of many pilgrimages, hymns, and legends.

In Buddhism too, Kailāsa is venerated as a sacred mountain.

Kaimyō **Z** Jap., from *kai*, "Buddhist precept" (→ *kairitsu*, → *jūjūkai*) and *myō*, "name"; 1. the Buddhist name that a monk or lay person receives at his initiation into Buddhism (→ *jukai*) from the master giving the initiation. For a monk in a monastery, this name replaces his ordinary given name. This symbolizes the monk's turning away from (worldly) cares, suffering, and passions (→ *bonnō*); with the taking of a vow he begins a new life directed entirely toward the realization of awakening (→ enlightenment).

2. a posthumous Buddhist honorific title for lay people and monks that can be bought in present-day Japan at a high price.

Kairitsu **Z** Jap., lit. "precepts and rules"; term in Japanese Buddhism for the Buddhist precepts (→ *jūjūkai*), which one receives and acknowledges through → *jukai*, the ceremonial initiation into Buddhism.

Kaisan **Z** Jap., lit. "mountain founder"; term for the founder of a Zen monastery. In ancient times Ch'an (Zen) monasteries were usually located on mountains, and the name of the mountain was generally applied to the monastery (and also to the first abbot of this monastery); thus the Japanese *san* stands in this context for "monastery." The term *kaisan* is also used for the founder of a Buddhist school. The memorial ceremony for the anniversary of the death of the founder of a monastery or Buddhist school is called *kaisan-ki*.

Kaivalya **H** Skt., lit. "exclusivity, uniqueness, complete release"; a term that is primarily used in → Rāja-Yoga to designate the state of the soul that realizes that it is perfect and depends on neither the gods nor the realm of atoms. Such a state is attained when consciousness has become as pure as the → *ātman* itself.

Kaivalya-Mukti 🅗 Skt., lit. "absolute release"; it brings about release from all matter and freedom from all further rebirth. This liberation from any form of embodiment is the goal of → Rāja-Yoga.

Kaivalya-Pāda 🅗 Skt.; the fourth and final part of → Patañjali's *Yoga-Sūtra;* it discusses final liberation.

Kajishō 🅩 Jap., lit. "What does its nature look like?" A question frequently used in Zen, which asks about the nature i.e., the true nature, or buddha-nature (→ *busshō*), of things.

Kakunen-daigo 🅩 Jap., lit. "unrestricted great satori"; another expression for → daigo-tettei. (Also → satori).

Kakushin 🅩 also Shinchi Kakushin, 1207–98; Japanese Zen master who brought the → *Wu-men-kuan* to Japan and contributed significantly to the establishment of → kōan practice in that country (→ *kanna* Zen). He first practiced the esoteric Buddhism of the Shingon school (→ Mikkyō) on Kōya-san (Mount Kōya) and also found a Zen master there, a student of → Eisai Zenji named Gyōyū. He trained under various Zen masters, including → Dōgen Zenji, and in 1249 traveled to China.

In China he trained initially under masters Fo-yen-yuan (Jap., Butsugen-on) and Chang-hsiung (Jap., Chōyū) of the → Fuke school. From Chiang-hsiung he learned to play the bamboo flute (Jap., *shakuhachi*), which in the Fuke school took the place of reciting sūtras. Eventually he came to the most important Chinese Ch'an (Zen) master of the time, → Wu-men Hui-k'ai (Jap., Mumon Ekai), who belonged to the → Yōgi school of Rinzai Zen. Kakushin fast became one of his most outstanding students. Master Wu-men conferred upon him the seal of confirmation (→ *inka-shōmei*) and installed him as his dharma successor (→ *hassu*). When Kakushin returned to Japan in 1254, Master Wu-men gave him as a gift a copy of the *Wu-men-kuan*, which he had compiled, written in his own hand.

After his return to Japan, Kakushin first stayed at Mount Kōya, then a short time later founded in Wakayama prefecture the Zen monastery Saihō-ji, which he later renamed Kōkoku-ji. Kakushin was summoned to Kyōto several times by Emperor Kameyama and his successor Go-Uda. There he lived in the Shōrin monastery but always returned to Kōkoku-ki.

Kakushin brought the Rinzai Zen of the Yōgi school to Japan and is considered one of the most important Zen masters. He led many students via the path of kōan training to → enlightenment. His teaching style, however, also contained elements of esoteric Shingon Buddhism. In addition, he brought the teaching of the Fuke school to Japan. His dharma successor in the fourth generation, Zen master → Shun'o Reizan published in 1405 the Japanese edition of the *Wu-men-kuan* that is authoritative down to the present day.

Kakushin received the posthumous honorific title *hōto* (*hottō*) *zenji* from Emperor Kameyama and from Emperor Go-Daigo the honorific title *hōtō* (*hottō*) *emmyō kokushi* (also → *kokushi*).

Kāla 🅗 Skt., lit. "time"; a name for → Yama, the god of death. The → *Atharvaveda* speaks of Time as the cause and ruler of all things: "It is he who caused the worlds to come into being and holds them. He is the father of all things. There is no power greater than he."

The *Vishnu-*, *Bhāgavata-*, and *Padma-Purāna* state that → Brahmā exists in the form of time, but the Purānas do not view time as an aspect of the first cause (→ *brahman*). In the *Bhagavad-Gītā*, Krishna says, "I am time."

Kāla-Bhairava 🅗 Skt., lit. *kāla:* "time; black," *bhairava:* "terrible"; → Shiva in his terrible aspect as time, which devours all; chiefly observed by two Shiva sects in Kashmir. Elsewhere in India, Shiva's destructive aspect is usually represented by the "black goddess" → Kālī, who is also worshiped throughout India as the "Divine Mother." In one passage of the *Bhagavad-Gītā,* Krishna states: "I am all-devouring time" (10.32). In a commentary on this verse, Sarvepalli Radhakrishnan writes, "Kāla, or Time, is the first mover of the universe. When one thinks of God as Time, he is the one who ceaselessly creates and destroys. Time is an ever-moving stream."

Kālachakra 🅑 (kālcakra), Skt., lit. "*Wheel of Time*"; the last and most complex Buddhist → tantra (10th century). It is said to have been written down by the mythical King Suchandra of → Shambhala. In the Kālachakra teaching a special time reckoning and astronomy play a major role. The *Kālachakra Tantra* was introduced into Tibet in 1027 and it is considered the basis of the Tibetan calendar. A unique feature of the meditation system of the *Kālachakra*

Tantra is its derivation of its teaching from an *ādi-buddha* (primordial buddha), with whom the number of the buddha families (→ *buddha-kula*) is raised to six. The "tenfold powerful → mantra" symbolizes the Kālachakra teaching.

According to Tibetan tradition, the *Kālachakra Tantra* was transmitted through seven kings of Shambhala and twenty-five authorized "proclaimers." At the time of the twelfth proclaimer the teaching reached India and soon thereafter, Tibet. One of its most important lineages of transmission passed through the scholar Butön (1290–1364) to → Tsongkhapa and the *Kālachakra Tantra* is still practiced in the → Gelugpa school.

The Tantra itself consists of three parts—outer, inner, and other. The outer part has as its focus the physical world; it describes the arising of the universe and develops a geography and astronomy. The emphasis here is on the time reckoning and the mathematics necessary for it. In contrast, the inner part describes the structure of the psychological world, for example, the function of the → *nādīs*. The "other" part is devoted to a → *sādhana* in which deities are visualized. All three parts are regarded as different aspects of the *ādi-buddha* principle (→ Samantabhadra).

The *Kālachakra Tantra* also teaches a series of six meditation practices, which, it is true, correspond in number to the → *Nāro chödrug* and were also the subject of commentaries by Nāropa; however, it has only the technique of → *tumo* (inner heat) in common with the six Nāropa yogas.

Kali 🅗 Skt.; 1. personification of evil in the *kali-yuga (→ yuga)*; 2. in the game of dice, the "snake-eyes," the worst possible cast; a symbol of bad luck.

Kālī 🅗 or Kālikā, Skt., lit. "the black one"; in the Vedas the name is associated with → Agni, the god of fire, who had seven flickering tongues of flame, of which Kālī was the black, horrible tongue. This meaning of the word has meanwhile been replaced by the goddess Kālī, the grim consort of Shiva and his → Shakti, also known as the Divine Mother.

As the Divine Mother, Kālī is usually represented dancing or in sexual union with → Shiva. Whereas Shiva represents the transcendental aspect, Kālī symbolizes the dynamic aspect, primal energy. As Bhavatārini, the redeemer of the universe, she stands upon the supine form of her spouse, Shiva. Kālī wears a belt made of dismembered arms and a necklace of skulls; of her four arms, the lower left hand holds the bloody head of a demon, the upper left hand wields a sword. With her upper right hand she makes a gesture of fearlessness, while the lower right hand confers benefits. She destroys ignorance, maintains the world order, and blesses and frees those who strive for the knowledge of God. Kālī is the symbol of dissolution and destruction. She is worshiped particularly in Bengal. Her best-known temples are in Kālighāt and Dakshineshvara, where → Rāmakrishna was once the priest of Kālī.

Kālī in her destructive aspect. (Indian painting, 18th century)

Kālidāsa 🅗, the most important early Indian poet and dramatist. Little is known regarding his life (fourth/fifth century). He is said to have been one of the "nine jewels" at the court of King → Vikramāditya and to have been supported by the Gupta rulers. His works were the first to be translated from Sanskrit into Western languages, thereby making Indian literature known in Europe. Among his chief works are the literary epics *Kumāra-Sambhava* and *Raghuvamsha*; a third epic, *Setubandha*, is traditionally ascribed to him (→ Rāmasetu). Purely lyrical in character are the works *Meghadūta*, a kind of poetic geography of India in 111 stanzas, and *Ritusamhāra*, another purported title whose authorship is not certain. However, Kālidāsa attained greatest popularity and greatest renown in the history of world literature as a dramatist. His *Shakuntalā*, a play in seven acts that won the enthusiasm of Goethe, has been translated into many languages. Its plot, a fairytale-like love story, is based on an episode from the

Mahābhārata. His two other major plays, *Mālavikāgnimitra* and → *Vikramorvashīya,* deal with topics from the time of the legendary royal dynasties; they feature political and amorous intrigues and the intervention of Indra and other gods.

Kālikā 🅷 synonymous with → Kālī

Kālikā-Purāna 🅷 (Kālikā-Purāṇa), Skt.; one of the eighteen Upa-Purānas. In 9,000 stanzas arranged in ninety-eight chapters, it discusses the worship of → Shiva's bride in her various forms as Girijā, → Devī, → Kālī, → Mahāmāyā, and others. The text belongs to the → Shakti tradition, which stresses worship of the feminine divine forces.

Kali-Yuga 🅷 Skt. → *yuga*

Kalki 🅷 or Kalkin, Skt., lit. "white horse," the tenth → *avatāra,* who is yet to appear. The white horse symbolizes the strength (of the horse) and the power (of the color white, which unites in its being all colors of the spectrum) that Kalki will possess. He will vanquish Yama, or Death, and will resolve all opposites as well as overcome darkness. He will be the divine man, at one with infinite divinity.

Kalpa 🅷 🅱 🆉 Skt.; world cycle, world age.
🅷 a day and a night in the life of → Brahmā; according to Vedic scripture, a period of time that comprises four cosmic ages (→ *yuga*) and lasts for a total of 4,320,000 human years.
🅱 🆉 (Pali, kappa); term for an endlessly long period of time, which is the basis of Buddhist time reckoning. The length of a kalpa is illustrated by the following simile: suppose that every hundred years a piece of silk is rubbed once on a solid rock one cubic mile in size; when the rock is worn away by this, one kalpa will still not have passed.

A kalpa is divided into four parts: the arising of a universe, the continuation of the arisen universe, the demise of that universe, the continuation of chaos. In the period of the arising of a universe, individual worlds with their sentient beings are formed. In the second period sun and moon come into being, the sexes are distinguished, and social life develops. In the phase of universal demise, fire, water, and wind destroy everything but the fourth → *dhyāna.* The period of chaos is that of total annihilation.

The four phases constitute a "great kalpa" (*mahākalpa*). This consists of twenty "small kalpas." A small kalpa is divided into ages of iron, copper, silver, and gold. During the generational period of a small kalpa, human lifespan increases by one year every hundred years until it has reached 84 thousand years. At the same time, the human body increases in size to 84 hundred feet. In the period of decline of a small kalpa, which is divided into phases of plague, war, and famine, human lifespan decreases to ten years, and the human body to one foot.

Kalpa-Sūtra 🅷 Skt.; a collection of rules for Vedic ceremony, one of the → Vedāngas. Instructions for ritual performance in the form of short, technical rules. (See also → *sūtra.*)

Kalpataru 🅷 Skt., lit. "wish-fulfilling tree"; 1. a name for God; 2. the heavenly tree of Hindu mythology that fulfills all wishes that are expressed by those standing beneath it.

Kalyānamitra 🅱 (kalyāṇamitra), Skt. (Pali, kalyāna-mitta), lit. "noble friend"; a friend who is rich in experience of Buddhist doctrine and meditation, who accompanies and helps one and others on the path to enlightenment.

The historical Buddha → Shākyamuni highly esteemed the value of a friend on the path: "This entire religious life consists of good friendship. . . . A monk who is a good friend, a good companion, a good comrade, from such a one it can be expected that he develops and cultivates the → noble eightfold path [to enlightenment for himself and also for his fellow monks]" (trans. from German ed. of Schumann 1974).

Kalyāna-Shraddhā 🅷 (Kalyāṇa-Śraddhā), Skt.; unshakable faith, one of the four "perfections of the heart." The other three are *saumyatva* (gentleness, benevolence), *tejas* (fiery spirit), and *prema-sāmarthya* (the power of love). All four are concepts in the system of → Pūrna-Yoga as developed by → Aurobindo.

Kāma 🅷 🅱 Skt., Pali; sensual desire, longing, sexual pleasure.
🅷 The *Rigveda* represents desire as the first movement of the Absolute toward manifestation: "Desire arose in him who is the source of consciousness, whom the sages through examination have found in their hearts and who unites absolute being with the manifest world."

This form of *kāma*—here not sexual desire but the impulse to create good—is praised in a hymn of the *Atharvaveda* in which *kāma* is elevated to the rank of creator and god. "Kāma was the first to be born. Neither gods nor fathers nor men are his equal." In another passage in the same Veda, *Kāma* is described as the first desire as well as the power to fulfill wishes. Elevated as the god of love in the form of Kāma-Deva, similar to the western figures of Eros and Cupid, he is portrayed in the *Taittirīya-Brāhmana* as the son of → Dharma, the god of justice, and → Shraddhā, the goddess of faith. In the → *Harivamsha,* he is the son of → Lakshmī; another text describes him as having emerged from the heart of → Brahmā. Kāma's mysterious origins and his universal influence have given rise to the many names and attributes he bears.

[B] one of the characteristics of existence in the lowest of the three realms constituting the universe (→ *triloka*), the realm of sensual desire (*kāmaloka*). Kāma refers to desire toward sensually satisfying objects and to the joy taken in these things. In Buddhism it is seen as one of the primary obstacles on the spiritual path. Five types of sensual desire are distinguished, corresponding to the five sense organs: desire toward form, sound, smell, taste, and bodily feeling.

Kāma is one of the three kinds of craving (→ *trishnā*), one of the five hindrances (→ *nīvarana*), and one of the defilements (→ *āsrava*).

Kāmadhātu [B] Skt. → *triloka*

Kāmadhenu [H] Skt. → Surabhī

Kamalashīla [B] → Mādhyamika

Kāmaloka [B] Skt. → *triloka*

Kāma-Sūtra [H] Skt., approx. "manual of the erotic art"; a basic text for the → Shaktism of → Vātsyāyana. Visual representations from the text are found in sculptures and certain Indian temples. Best known of these are the sculptures of the temple of Konarak in Orissa, built in the thirteenth century by King Narahimsa to honor the sun god → Sūrya. Although competent translations of the text have been published, many available works bearing the title "Kāma-Sūtra" have virtually nothing to do with the work composed "in modesty and supreme reverence" by Vātsyāyana.

Kāminikāñchana [H] (Kāminikāñcana), Skt., lit. "women and gold"; a collective term referring to desire, greed, and other human passions; an expression often used by → Rāmakrishna.

Kāmya [H] Skt., lit. "desirable, pleasant" (from *kāma:* "desire"). The term has particular significance in the first part of the → *Katha-Upanishad* (2.1-2): "The good is one thing, the pleasant another. These two, serving different ends, prompt our actions. Those who choose the good attain salvation. Those who seek the pleasant miss the goal. Both the good and the pleasant offer themselves to mankind. The wise, examining both, distinguishes between them and chooses the good over the pleasant. The fool, driven by fleshly desire, chooses the pleasant."

Kanāda [H] (Kanāda), Skt.; a sage, founder of the philosophy of → Vaisheshika. He presumably headed a school for priests in the second century B.C.E. and is regarded as the author of a first version of the *Vaisheshika-Sūtra.* The first systematic work of the Vaisheshika school, it contains a theory of the atom.

K'an and Li [T] Chin.; the twenty-ninth and thirtieth hexagrams of the → *I-ching*; two of the eight trigrams (→ *pa-kua*). The trigram *k'an* consists of a broken, an unbroken, and another broken line: ☵. The hexagram *k'an* is a duplication of that trigram: ䷜. The trigram *li* consists of an unbroken, a broken, and another unbroken line: ☲. The hexagram *li* is a duplication of that trigram: ䷝.

K'an and *li* represent a combination of yin and yang (→ yin-yang), which are symbolized by the trigrams and hexagrams *ch'ien* ☰ ䷀ and *k'un* ☷ ☷ ䷁ ䷁. They furthermore represent the function of the → Tao, which pervades Heaven (*ch'ien*) and Earth (*k'un*), i.e., the macrocosm and the microcosm. As stated in the *Book of Change(s)*, yin and yang cannot be fixed or brought to rest, but circulate in the spaces between the lines of a hexagram and thus give rise to the remaining hexagrams. Together with *ch'ien* and *k'un* they are said to be the parents of the remaining hexagrams.

In the writings of Taoist alchemists (→ *nei-tan,* → *wai-tan*) *k'an* and *li* designate the ingredients of the elixir (of life).

In the texts of the Inner Alchemy (→ *nei-tan*) there is frequent mention of the fusion of *k'an* and *li;* this fusion produces the sacred embryo (→ *sheng-t'ai*) in the body of the Inner Alchemy practitioner: the broken yin line of *li* descends and unites with the ascending yang line of *k'an.* The upward movement of the yang line symbolizes the purification of the essence (→ *ching*) and the energy (→ *ch'i*); the downward movement of the yin line symbolizes the crystallization of the spirit (→ *shen*).

Common alchemical symbols for *k'an* are: the white tiger (*pai-hu*), the crescent moon, and the hare; in addition, *k'an* is associated with winter, the North, water, the color black, the kidneys, and lead.

Li is symbolized by the green dragon (*ch'ng-lung*), the sun, or a crow and is further associated with summer, the South, the color red, the heart, fire, and mercury.

One of the most important texts of the Inner Alchemy School—the *Chou-i ts'an-t'ung-ch'i* of → Wei P'o-yang states:

"The transformation rests on *k'an*—the nature of which is symbolized by water, the abysmal, the heart, the soul, light, and reason [*logos*]—and *li*—the nature of which is symbolized by fire, that which clings, brightness, and nature in its glorified state; and these two, *k'an* and *li,* are functions, respectively, of the creative and the receptive.

"These two functions have no fixed position; they weave and knit to and fro between the six empty positions. Coming and going are not bound by energy; above and below float freely, they sink into the hidden, they disappear into the twilight.

"The transformation and exchange (of *k'an* and *li*) occur in the six empty spaces between the lines of the hexagram. They embrace myriads of manifestations and thus become the great principle of the Tao" (trans. from Miyuki 1984).

Kāñchi 🅗 (Kāñcī), Skt.; one of the seven holy cities of India, some 70 km to the south of Madras (present-day Conjeeveram or Kanchipuram). It is said to have been the site at one time of 108 Shiva temples.

Kan Chi 🅣 → Yü Chi

Kanchō 🅩 Jap.; a title introduced by the Meiji government in 1872 for the head of a Buddhist school. In Zen it designates the abbot of a Zen monastery under the jurisdiction of which a number of submonasteries is placed.

Kānda 🅗 (Kāṇḍa), Skt., lit. "section, part"; chiefly used for the division of the Vedas into the → Karma-Kānda, or section on ritual action, and the → Jñāna-Kānda, the portion relating to knowledge.

Kandōnin 🅩 Jap., lit. "person of the way of leisure"; a person who through profound → enlightenment has gained total freedom; a profoundly enlightened Zen master.

Kangi-zatori 🅩 also gangi-zatori, Jap., lit. "graduated satori"; an expression for approaching profound → enlightenment (also → satori) through a succession of a number of small experiences of → *kenshō*. In the history of Zen, the notion of "graduated enlightenment" is associated particularly with the Northern school, which stems from → Shen-hsiu (Jap., Jinshū), a student of the fifth patriarch of Ch'an (Zen) in China. (Also → *zengo,* → Southern school.)

Kangyur-Tengyur 🅑 (Bka'-gyur Bstan-'gyur), Tib., lit. "Translation of the Word of Buddha–Translation of the Teaching of Buddha." The canon of → Tibetan Buddhism, consisting of more than 300 volumes. It contains all the Buddhist works translated into Tibetan from a Sanskrit original and exists in several versions, which differ as to the ordering of the works. The Kangyur, the collection of the instructions of Buddha → Shākyamuni, consists of ninety-two volumes containing 1,055 texts. The Tengyur, the Indian works of commentary, fills 226 volumes and contains 3,626 texts.

The Buddhist scriptures of India are to a great extent only extant in Tibetan and Chinese translation. In the first period of Buddhism in Tibet, many works were translated; however those for which later there remained no Sanskrit original were not included in the canon. Only in the 11th century did a systematic treatment of the translations begin. The result was the Kangyur and Tengyur. The Kangyur is divided into six parts: (1) → Tantra, (2) → Prajñāpāramitā, (3) Ratnakūta, (4) → Avatamsaka, (5) Sūtra (Hīnayāna and Mahāyāna teachings), (6) → Vinaya.

The Tengyur is divided into three large sections: (1) → *stotras,* (2) commentaries on the Tantras, (3) commentaries on the sūtras. The commentaries on the sūtras contain works from the *prajñāpāramitā* literature, from the → Mādhyamika and → Yogāchāra schools, as well as from the → Abhidharma. There are also treatises on logic, poetry, medicine, and grammar. In close connection with these translations, there developed in Tibet a voluminous literature exhibiting the same encyclopedic character.

K'an-hua-ch'an 🅩 Chin. for → Kanna Zen

Kanna Zen 🅩 Jap. (Chin., K'an-hua-ch'an), lit. "Zen of the contemplation of words"; an expression coined in the lifetime of the Chinese master → Ta-hui Tsung-kao (Jap., Daie Sōkō, 1089–1163) to designate the style of Ch'an (Zen) that regarded the → kōan as the most important means of training on the way to awakening (→ enlightenment, → *kenshō,* → satori). Kōans were used as a means of training starting from the middle of the 10th century; however Ta-hui, a student and dharma successor (→ *hassu*) of → Yuan-wu K'o-ch'in (Jap., Engo Kokugon), the compiler of the → *Pi-yen-lu,* contributed significantly to the establishment of kōan practice as a means of training in the → Rinzai school as well as to the definitive form it took. Since that time *kanna* Zen has been practically synonymous with the Zen of the Rinzai lineage. The practice of the → Sōtō school became known as → *mokushō* Zen.

Kannō-Dōkō 🅩 Jap., roughly "mutual exchange of feeling"; in Zen the direct and immediate communication between master and student in a → *dokusan* or → *mondō* or between masters in → *hossen.* This is an instantaneous, nondualistic accord of thought, feeling, and action that is experienced, no longer as an exchange between two different persons, but rather as a unitary event. This is generally possible only in a state of heightened, collected attention, as is brought about, for example, by the practice of → *zazen.*

Kannon 🅱 🆉 also Kanzeon or Kwannon, Jap. for → Avalokiteshvara.

Kansa 🅷 (Kaṃsa), Skt.; a tyrannical king of Mathurā, cousin of Devakī, the mother of Krishna. He married two daughters of Jarāsandha, the king of Magadha.

Kansa drove his father away, and upon learning of the prediction that a son born to Devakī would slay him, he attempted to have all her children killed. Balarāma, her seventh son, was secretly taken to Gokula. When Krishna, her eighth son, was born, his parents took him and fled. The king then ordered the destruction of all male children. Kansa pursued Krishna, but at last Krishna slew him. He is also referred to as Kalānkura ("the crane") and is numbered among the → *asuras.*

Kan-shiketsu 🆉 Jap., lit. "dry shit stick"; a Zen expression designating a person who is attached to the world of appearance. *Kan-shiketsu* is the → *wato* of a famous kōan (example 21 of the → *Wu-men-kuan*). The expression stems from a time in China in which a wooden stick was used instead of toilet paper.

Kanva 🅷 (Kaṇva), Skt.; the name of a → *rishi* to whom several hymns in the *Rigveda* are ascribed. He is listed as one of the seven great *rishis,* and is said to have brought up → Shakuntalā as his daughter. The same name is shared by various other figures.

Kanyā-Kumārī 🅷 Skt., lit. "young maiden, virgin"; in South India, → Durgā, the Divine Mother, is worshiped under this name in the form of a young girl. The famous temple of Kanyā-Kumārī is located at the southernmost tip of the Indian subcontinent, on Cape Komorin (a name derived from Kumārī).

Kanzan 🆉 Jap. for → Han-shan

Kanzan Egen 🆉 also Musō Daishi, 1277–1360; Japanese Zen master of the → Rinzai school, a student and dharma successor (→ *hassu*) of → Myōchō Shūhō (also Daitō Kokushi). Following Myōchō, who founded the most important Zen monastery of Kyōto, Daitoku-ji, Kanzan Egen was the second abbot of the monastery. Later he was the first abbot of Myōshin-ji, also in Kyōto, a monastery built for him by the abdicated emperor Go-Komatsu.

After he had received from Myōchō the seal of confirmation (→ *inka-shōmei*), following the example of his master, Kanzan went into retreat for many years in the mountains in order to deepen his realization. During this time he worked as a laborer during the day and sat in meditation (→ *zazen*) at night.

Kanzen Egen received a number of posthumous honorific titles from the Japanese imperial house. Among them are: *musō daishi, honnu enjō zenji, busshin kakusho zenji, daijō shōō zenji, hōmu ryōkō zenji.*

Kanzeon 🅱 🆉 also Kannon or Kwannon, Jap. for → Avalokiteshvara

Kāpāla 🅷 Skt., lit. "made of skulls"; followers of Shiva, who worship him as the "terrible one." Shiva's → Shakti, in the form of his consort → Kālī, wears a chain of skulls around her neck.

Kapila 🅷 , founder of the → Sānkhya philosophy; a → *rishi* about whose life no details are known. His works have also been lost. The *Tattvasamāsa* ("summary of the truth"), a text that consists of only fifty-four words and is ascribed to him, holds no key to the origins of Sānkhya, its earliest authentic text is the so-called *Sankhya-Kārikā* of Īshvarakrishna, which undoubtedly dates back to sometime before 500 C.E.

Kapilavastu 🅱 Skt. (Pali, Kapilavatthu); home city of the historical Buddha → Siddhārtha Gautama, located at the foot of the Himālayas in present-day Nepal. Kapilavastu was the capital of the kingdom of the → Shākyas. The Buddha was born in Lumbinī near Kapilavastu and spent his childhood and youth in Kapilavastu.

As seen in the texts, the Buddha frequently visited his home city even after his enlightenment and presented several discourses there. As a result his father Suddhodana attained the level of stream-entry (→ *shrota-āpanna*). The Buddha's son → Rāhula was accepted into the monastic order as a novice (→ *shrāmanera*) there.

In Kapilavastu in 1898 reliquaries of the Buddha have been found. In a → stūpa an urn with burial offerings was discovered and a stone box with five vessels in it. One of these, a soapstone urn, bore the following inscription: "This urn with relics of the sublime Buddha of the Shākya clan is a donation of Sukiti and his brothers, along with their sisters, sons, and wives" (trans. from German ed. of Schumann 1974).

Kapimala 🆉 13th patriarch in the Indian lineage of → Zen

Kārana-Purusha 🅷 (Kāraṇa-Puruṣa), Skt.; the self in every human being; a term from the → Pūrna-Yoga of → Aurobindo, it is synonymous with → *ātman* and → jīvātman.

Kārana-Sharīra 🅗 (Kāraṇa-Śarīra), Skt., lit. *kārana:* "cause," *sharīra:* "body, sheath"; the third of the → *sharīras* that envelop the Self, also known as the causal sheath. It is identical with the → *ānandamaya-koshā*, the bliss sheath (→ *kosha*).

Kāranopādhi 🅗 (Kāraṇopādhi), Skt.; synonymous with → *kāranā-sharīra.* In → Rāja-Yoga, the → *sharīras* are also designated as → *upādhis.*

Kārikā 🅗 Skt.; a commentary to a sacred scripture in verse form. The best-known *kārikā* is → Gaudapāda's *kārikā* on the → *Māndūkya-Upanishad.*

Karma 🅗 🅑 🅩 Skt., lit. "deed."

🅗 Karma is understood as 1. a mental or physical action; 2. the consequence of a mental or physical action; 3. the sum of all consequences of the actions of an individual in this or some previous life; 4. the chain of cause and effect in the world of morality.

Each individual's karma is created by that person's → *samskāras.* This potential directs one's behavior and steers the motives for all present and future thoughts and deeds. Thus every *karma* is the seed for further karma. Its fruits are reaped in the form of joy or sorrow according to the type of thought or action accomplished.

Although every human being creates his own limitations through his past thoughts and actions, once having formed these tendencies he has the option of continuing to follow them or resisting them. This freedom of will and possibility of free choice are a reflection in each person of the freedom of the → *ātman,* the consciousness within. Surrender to God, the creation of good karma, and the dissolution of bad karma act to loosen the bonds imposed by the law of karma. Once enlightenment is attained, no new *karma* is produced. Three types of karma are distinguished: → *āgāmi-karma,* → *prārabdha-karma,* and → *sanchita-karma.* In the Vedas, karma also refers to ritual worship and philanthropic actions.

🅑 🅩 (Pali, kamma). Universal law of cause and effect, which according to the Buddhist view takes effect in the following way: "The deed (karma) produces a fruit under certain circumstances; when it is ripe then it falls upon the one responsible. For a deed to produce its fruit, it must be morally good [→ *kushala*] or bad [→ *akushala*] and be conditioned by a volitional impulse, which in that it leaves a trace in the psyche of the doer, leads his destiny in the direction determined by the effect of the deed. Since the time of ripening generally exceeds a lifespan, the effect of actions is necessarily one or more rebirths, which together constitute the cycle of existence (→ samsāra)" (trans. from German translation of A. Bareau 1964, 41).

The effect of an action, which can be of the nature of body, speech, or mind, is not primarily determined by the act itself but rather particularly by the *intention* of the action. It is the intention of actions that cause a karmic effect to arise. When a deed cannot be carried out but the intention toward it exists, this alone produces an effect. Only a deed that is free from desire, hate, and delusion is without karmic effect. In this connection it should be noted that also good deeds bring "rewards," engender karma and thus renewed rebirth. In order to liberate oneself from the cycle of rebirth, one must refrain from both "good" and "bad" deeds.

The teaching of karma does not constitute determinism. The deeds do indeed determine the *manner* of rebirth but not the *actions* of the reborn individual—karma provides the situation, not the response to the situation.

Karma Kagyü 🅑 (kar-ma bka'-brgyud), Tib., lit. "Oral Transmission Lineage of the *Karmapas*"; a subdivision of the Kagyüpa school, founded in the 12th century by Düsum Khyenpa (the first → *karmapa*). The doctrinal tradition of the Karma Kagyü is very closely bound up with the lineage of the *karmapas.* This school owes its name to a black crown, made from the hair of → *dākinīs*, which embodies the beneficial activity (karma) of all the buddhas. The Karma Kagyüs were strongly supportive of the → Rime movement and are now one of the most successful Buddhist schools in the West.

The first *karmapa* (1110–93) founded the three main monasteries of the school and chose Tsurphu as his residence. With the second *karmapa* (1204–83) the influence of the Karma Kagyüs spread as far as Mongolia. The third *karmapa* (1284–1339) composed one of the most important books of teaching of his school and produced a synthesis of the → *mahāmudrā* and → *dzogchen* doctrines. Like the two *karmapas* preceding him, the fifth *karmapa* (1384–1415) was the teacher of the emperor of China and received from him the so-called black crown (also → *karmapa*). The eighth *karmapa* (1507–54) distinguished himself as an author on all areas of Buddhist philosophy. The ninth Karmapa (1556–1603) composed basic meditation texts of the school. The sixteenth *karmapa* (1924–1982), after the occupation of Tibet by the Chinese, succeeded in preserving the teachings of his school and in transferring his residence to Rumtek in Sikkim.

The *karmapas* were supported in their work by three other important incarnation lineages (→ *tulku*): that of the *shamar tulkus*, whose name is derived from a red crown, the *situ tulkus*, and the *gyaltshab tulkus*. One of the most important figures of the Karma Kagyü in the 19th century was → Jamgon Kongtrul, whose writings encompassed all areas of knowledge.

Karma-Kānda H (Karma-Kāṇḍa), Skt.; the portion of the → Vedas that deals with rituals, sacrifices, and ceremonies, which in turn were later philosophically interpreted by the school of → Pūrva-Mīmāmsā.

This ritual portion, also called Karma-Mārga, consists of the → Samhitās and the → Brāhmanas. The other part of the Vedas is → Jñāna-Kānda, the portion dealing with knowledge.

Karmapa B Skt. and Tib., roughly "man of buddha-activity"; the spiritual authority of the → Karma Kagyü school and the oldest → *tulku* lineage of Tibetan Buddhism. The appearance of the *karmapa* as an embodiment of compassion was prophesied by both → Shākyamuni Buddha and → Padmasambhava. In sixteen incarnations he worked for the welfare of all sentient beings—since the 15th century particularly through a special ceremony in which, through wearing a black crown, he shows himself as an embodiment of → Avalokiteshvara.

The biographies of his individual incarnations portray the *karmapa* as scholar, ascetic, artist, and poet. The most important function of the *karmapa* is the unbroken transmission of the Vajrayāna teachings. The incarnations of the *karmapa* extend over a period of more than 800 years:

1. Karmapa Düsum Khyenpa (1110–93)
2. Karmapa Karma Pakshi (1204–83)
3. Karmapa Rangjung Dorje (1284–1339)
4. Karmapa Rölpe Dorje (1340–83)
5. Karmapa Deshin Shegpa (1384–15)
6. Karmapa Tongwa Dönden (1416–53)
7. Karmapa Chödrag Gyatso (1454–1506)
8. Karmapa Mikyö Dorje (1507–54)
9. Karmapa Wangchuk Dorje (1556–1603)
10. Karmapa Chöying Dorje (1604–74)
11. Karmapa Yeshe Dorje (1676–1702)
12. Karmapa Changchub Dorje (1703–32)
13. Karmapa Düdül Dorje (1733–97)
14. Karmapa Thegchog Dorje (1798–1868)
15. Karmapa Khachab Dorje (1871–1922)
16. Karmapa Rigpe Dorje (1924–82)

Karmaphalatyāga H Skt., lit. *karma:* "action," *phala:* "fruit, result, reward," *tyāga:* "surrender, release"; renunciation of all fruits of one's actions, as stipulated in the → *Bhagavad-Gītā*; it is the most important practice in → Karma-Yoga.

Karma-Yoga H Skt.; one of the four chief types of yoga, or path to union with God. Karma-Yoga consists of selfless conduct, whereby the spiritual aspirant offers every action together with its results as a sacrifice to God. In the third chapter of the *Bhagavad-Gītā,* Krishna says to Arjuna: "For those of clear mind there is the path of knowledge, for those who work there is the path of selfless action. No one will attain perfection by refusing to work. No one can refuse to act; everyone if forced to act by the *gunas.* Therefore you must perform every action as a sacrifice to God, free from all attachment to the results thereof. In this way man attains the supreme truth through work, without care for its fruits. The ignorant act for the fruits of action. The wise act equally, but without desire for reward."

The aspirant who ultimately knows himself to be the → *ātman* and not bound by the → *gunas,* which produce all actions, regards himself as the observer rather than as the one who acts. An introduction to Karma-Yoga is in Vivekānanda 1955*b*.

Karmendriya H Skt., lit. *karma:* "activity," *indriya:* "organ"; the five organs of action are (1) speech, (2) the hands, (3) the feet, (4) the organs of excretion, (5) the organs of reproduction.

Kartavyam-Karma H Skt.; an action that must be carried out according to the law of → karma; an obligation that cannot be avoided.

Kartritva-Abhimāna H (Kartṛtva-Abhimāna), Skt.; the false notion that the self is the one who acts, an idea that arises when one identifies the self with the body (*abhimāna:* "false supposition").

Kārttikeya H Skt.; 1. the planet Mars; 2. a name of → Skanda, the god of war.

In the *Mahābhārata* and the *Rāmāyana,* Kārttikeya is known as the son of Shiva. He had no mother; he emerged when Shiva offered his seed to the fire and it was taken up by the Ganges. Kārttikeya was then born; he is thus also called Agnibhū and Gangāja. His steed is the peacock Paravāni. In one hand he holds a bow, in the other an arrow.

Karunā H B Z (karuṇā) Skt., Pali; compassion, active sympathy, gentle affection.

H all actions that help to diminish the sufferings of others.

B Z the outstanding quality of all bodhisattvas and buddhas; one of the four → *brahma-vihāras.* Compassion extends itself without distinction to all sentient beings. It is based on the enlightened (→ *bodhi*) experience of the oneness of all beings. *Karunā* must be accompanied by wisdom (→ *prajñā*) in order to have the right effect. The virtue of compassion is embodied in the bodhisattva → Avalokiteshvara.

Karunā is often translated as "pity" or "sympathy"; since these notions tend to suggest passive attitudes that do not contain the quality of active help that is an essential part of *karunā*, the concept of "compassion" is more suitable.

Karunā and *prajñā* are the principal virtues for adherents of the Mahāyāna, whereas in the Hīnayāna wisdom is regarded as the most important factor on the path to enlightenment. In the schools of → Amidism in China and Japan, the compassionate approach finds expression in the "saving grace" of → Amitābha.

Kārya-Brahman 🅗 Skt., *kārya* lit. "acting"; → *brahman* as the effective cause of the universe. *Brahman* is not only the abstract cause but through his → Shakti, he is also the effective cause of the universe, without which the manifest world would not have appeared.

Kashaku 🅩 Jap., lit. "hanging up (ka = kakeru) the priest's staff (shaku → shakujō)"; entry of a monk into a Zen monastery, after completing the → *angya*, for the purpose of training under a → *rōshi*.

Kashāya 🅗 (Kaṣāya), Skt., lit. "passion"; the subtle influence that is left as a residue in consciousness in the form of → *samskāra* following enjoyment of the senses.

Kāshī 🅗 (Kāśī), Skt.; an earlier name for present-day Vārānasī (or Benares, as it was named by the British). A celebrated site of pilgrimage on the Ganges, it is one of the seven sacred cities of India. The chief object of veneration there, aside from → Annapūrnā (in the temple named for her), is Shiva, who is worshiped as lord of the universe under the name → Vishvanātha in the temple of that name. Benares is also called the city of Shiva.

Many Hindus come to Kāshī to die, because death in the "golden city," as it is called in mythology, means liberation. It is said that whoever dies in Benares is granted a vision of Shiva in which the god whispers, "That which you see is my embodiment in *māyā*. I take on this form for the sake of those who worship me. But now behold: I am about to enter the unseen, → *satchidānanda*." With these words, Shiva dissolves his form, allowing the dying person to glimpse *brahman* and thereby attain liberation. Various saints have described this vision of Benares as a golden city in which Shiva moves among the dying, whispering into their ears.

Kashyapa 🅗 (Kaśyapa), Skt.; a Vedic sage to whom numerous hymns, particularly creation hymns, are ascribed.

In the *Mahābhārata*, the *Rāmāyana*, and the Purānas, he is described as the son of → Brahmā and the father of Vivasvat, who in turn was the father of → Manu. *Kashyapa* means "tortoise," a symbolical reference to the doctrine that everything was created from water; hence the saying that "all creatures are the progeny of Kashyapa." The *Atharvaveda* states that "Kashyapa, the self-born, emerged from Time" (Time being identical with → Vishnu). Because he is the father of all, he is often called → Prajāpati. He is one of the seven great → *rishis* and was the priest of → Parashu-Rāma and Rāmachandra (→ Rāma).

Kāshyapa 🅑 🅩 1. the buddha of the world age preceding the present one. Also → buddha 1.

2. → Mahākāshyapa

Kasina 🅑 Pali, lit. "total field"; term for the ten "total fields" that serve as objects of meditation, i.e. as supports for concentration of the mind. In this process, the mind is exclusively and with complete clarity filled with this object and finally becomes one with it (→ *samādhi*). If one continues in the exercise, every activity of the senses is nullified and one enters the state of the first absorption (→ *dhyāna*). The ten *kasinas* are earth, water, fire, wind, blue, yellow, red, white, space (→ *ākāsha*), consciousness (→ *vijñāna*). In the form of an earthen disk, a water bowl, a burning staff, a colored disk, etc., these are employed as meditation objects.

Kassapa 🅑 🅩 Pali → Mahākāshyapa

Kataku Jin'e 🅩 Jap. for → Ho-tse Shen-hui

Kataku school 🅩 (Chin., Ho-tse-tsung; Jap. Kataku-shū); a school of Ch'an (Zen) founded by → Ho-tse Shen-hui (Jap., Kataku Jin'e), a student of the sixth patriarch (→ Hui-neng). In contrast to the traditional Indian "meditation Buddhism" (→ Dhyāna Buddhism), in which → Bodhidharma, the first patriarch of Ch'an stood and in contrast to the Zen of Hui-neng's predecessors of the Northern school of Ch'an (→ Southern school), Ho-tse emphasized that → enlightenment could not be realized *gradually* with the help of meditative techniques. According to him the true practice of Zen consisted rather in "mental nonattachment" (Chin., *wu-hsin*, also translated as "no mind" or "non-thought," → *mushin*), which leads to direct insight into one's own nature (→ *kenshō*) and thus to *sudden* enlightenment. Although Ho-tse made an essential contribution toward the official recognition of Hui-neng and his Southern school, the Kataku school founded by him did not belong to the "five houses–seven schools" (→ *goke-shichishū*) and died out after a few generations.

The only well-known master produced by this lineage was → Kuei-feng Tsung-mi (Jap., Keihō Shūmitsu), who is actually less known as a Ch'an master than as the fifth patriarch of the → Hua-yen school of Chinese Buddhism (Jap., → Kegon school). After his death Ho-tse received the honorific title Chen-tsung-ta-shih (Jap., Shinshu Daishi).

Kathaka 🅗 Skt.; 1. an interpretation of the → *Yajurveda* that takes a position between the *Black* and the *White Yajurveda*; 2. a term used to refer to someone who publicly reads and explains the scriptures, a common occurrence in India, since many people cannot read.

Katha-Upanishad 🅗 (Kaṭha), or Kathaka, Skt.; an Upanishad belonging to the *Black* → *Yajurveda,* in which → Nachiketa's instruction by Yama, the god of death, is described.

Katsu! 🅩 also kwatsu!, Jap., (Chin., *ho!*); a shout without a single meaning, which is used by Zen masters much in the way the stick (→ *kyosaku*) is used. It also serves in encounters between masters (→ *mondō,* → *hossen*) as a means of expression transcending words and concepts. Like a blow of the stick at the right moment, a powerful cry by the master at the right moment can help the Zen student to achieve a breakthrough to enlightened vision (→ enlightenment, → *kenshō,* → satori).

According to tradition, such a cry was first used by the great Chinese master → Ma-tsu Tao-i (Jap., Baso Dōitsu), who was known for his thunderous voice. Also famous for his skillful use of "stick and shout" was → Lin-chi I-hsuan (Jap., Rinzai Gigen), who distinguished four types of *ho!*: "Sometimes it is like the diamond sword of a *vajra* king; sometimes it is like the goldenhaired lion that creeps forward in a crouch; sometimes it is like a lure stick with a tuft of grass dangling on the end; sometimes it is no *ho* at all."

The *Lin-chi lu* contains numerous episodes in which Master Lin-chi makes use of stick and shout. Two examples follow:

A monk asked, "Master, where does that song you're singing come from? What is that melody?"

The master said, "When I was still with Huang-po, I asked him three times and three times he hit me." The monk hesitated. The master shouted *Ho!*, hit him, and said, "One can't drive a nail into empty space."

A monk asked, "What is the essence of Buddhism?"

The master raised his flywhisk [→ *hossu*]. The monk shouted *ho!*

The master also cried *ho!* The monk hesitated, the master struck him.

Kattō 🅩 Jap., lit. "[thicket of] creeping vines"; a Zen expression used to refer to oververbose explanations of the → buddha-dharma. It is also used to refer to hanging on words and their literal meaning. By *kattō* Zen (also *moji* Zen) is meant a Zen that hangs on the words of the scriptures rather than directly grasping their deeper meaning.

Kātyāyana 🅗 an important writer of the third/second century B.C.E. who completed → Pānini's grammar and is identified with → Vararuchi, author of the *Prākrita-Prakāsha* ("The Original Light"). According to legend, Kātyāyana was once Shiva's companion in the form of → Pushpadanta; as punishment for eavesdropping on Shiva's conversation with → Pārvatī and relating the conversation elsewhere, he was reborn in a human body.

Katyāyana 🅑 → ten great disciples of the Buddha

Kaupīna 🅗 or Kaupīn, Skt.; the loincloth worn by *sādhus* and ascetics as a symbol of renunciation.

Kauravas 🅗 Skt., lit. "descended from Kuru"; a clan who attacked the → Pāndavas and drove them from their territory. Later the Pāndavas returned, conquered the Kauravas with the help of Indra, Arjuna, and Balarāma, and repossessed their realm. In this great battle, which is described in the *Mahābhārata,* Krishna acts as Arjuna'a charioteer; just before the battle Krishna instructs Arjuna as the latter hesitates to fight. This conversation before the two approaching armies forms the content of the famous → *Bhagavad-Gītā.*

Kaushītaki 🅗 (Kauṣītaki), Skt.; 1. a → Shākhā of the *Rigveda*; 2. the name of a → Brāhmana and → Āranyaka; 3. the name of an Upanishad of the *Rigveda* that primarily deals with the doctrine of the → *ātman.*

Kautsa 🅗 a rationalistic philosopher who lived sometime before → Yāska, the author of the → *Nirukta*; he regarded the Vedas as meaningless and described the → Brāhmanas as mistaken in their interpretations. Yāska opposed his objections.

Kavi 🅗 Skt., lit. "poet, seer"; someone who unveils the supreme light of knowledge from personal insight. → Aurobindo noted: "The *rishis* of ancient India were knowers of the divine as well as *kavis,* poet-seers, who expressed the eternal truths which they intuitively grasped in poetic hymns that are now known as the *Rigveda.*"

Kāyagatā-sati 🅱 Pali → mindfulness of the body

Kazan Muin 🆉 Jap. for → Ho-shan Wu-yin

Kedārnāth 🅷 Skt.; a Himalayan peak, one of the four holy places of India (the other three are → Dvārakā, → Puri, and → Rāmeshvara), a well-known site of pilgrimage that is accessible only in summer. Its temple holds one of the twelve great *lingas,* worshiped as Kedārnāth (a name for → Shiva). Another temple in which Shiva is venerated as Kedārnāth is in → Kāshī.

Kegon-kyō 🅱 🆉 Jap. for → *Buddhāvatamsaka-sūtra*

Kegon school 🅱 Japanese, lit. "School of the Flower Garland"; school of Japanese Buddhism corresponding to the Chinese → Hua-yen school. It was brought to Japan from China around 740 by Shen-hsiang (Jap., Shinshō). The first Japanese representative of the Kegon school was Roben (689–722).

Emperor Shōmu (724–48) wanted to rule Japan according to the principles of Kegon. He had the Tōdai-ji (Great Eastern Monastery) built in Nara, in which there is a colossal image of the buddha → Vairochana (Jap., Birushana). This monastery is still today the center of the Kegon school.

The Kegon school was of extraordinary importance for the development of Japanese Buddhism. The fundamental sūtra for this school, the → *Buddhāvatamsaka-sūtra* (Jap., *Kegon-kyō*) was politically construed and taken as a confirmation of the ideal of the unity of the state and of the national-political coloration of Japanese Buddhism.

Keihō Shūmitsu 🆉 Jap. for → Kuei-feng Tsung-mi

Keitoku Dentō-roku 🆉 Jap. for → *Ching-te ch'uan-teng-lu*

Keizan Jōkin 🆉 1268–1325; after → Dōgen Zenji, the most important Zen master of the → Sōtō school of Japan; he is also referred to as the fourth patriarch (→ *soshigata*) of the Japanese Sōtō Zen. Keizan Jōkin founded the Sōji-ji, one of the two principal monasteries of the Japanese Sōtō school and composed the → *Denkō-roku,* which is among the most important writings of Sōtō Zen. Other writings of Keizan Jōkin are the *Keizan shinki*, the → *Zazen yōjinki*, the *Sankon zazen setsu*, and the *Kyōjukaimon.*

Kekka-fusa 🆉 Jap.; term for the lotus position (Skt. *padmāsana*), which in Oriental traditions is regarded as the most appropriate sitting posture for meditation. This is the posture in which the Buddha is depicted.

In the lotus position the legs are crossed, the right foot rests on the left thigh, the left foot on the right thigh, the back is straight, and the hands rest with the palms turned up on the heels of both feet. Unlike in most Buddhist schools, in the practice of → *zazen*, the left palm rests on the right; this is an expression of the dominance of the passive over the active side of the body in the practice of meditation.

Kena-Upanishad 🅷 or *Talavakāra-Upanishad,* Skt.; an Upanishad belonging to the → *Sāmaveda.* The work speaks of → *brahman* without attributes, that which cannot be approached through reason; yet all creatures long to transcend the limits of reason and become one with *brahman.*

Kenchō-ji 🆉 Jap.; monastery of the Japanese → Rinzai school, the first abbot of which was the Chinese Ch'an (Zen) master → Lan-ch'i Tao-lung (Jap., Rankei Doryū). It is located in Kamakura and belongs to the Five Mountains (→ Gosan) of this center of Zen in Japan. The Kenchō-ji is one of the few Japanese monasteries in which monks are still trained today in the authentic Zen tradition.

Ken-chū-shi 🆉 Jap., → five degrees (of enlightenment) 4

Ken-chū-to 🆉 Jap., → five degrees (of enlightenment) 5

Kendō 🆉 Jap., lit. "Way of the sword"; fencing in the Japanese style, in which the sword is wielded with both hands. Especially in medieval Japan, in which the art of sword fighting was held in particular esteem and was almost necessary for survival, but also on into modern times it was customary for adepts of kendō to train in Zen in order to develop presence of mind, the ability to react spontaneously (→ *jōriki*), and fearless readiness to die. Some Japanese Zen masters were at the same time outstanding masters of the sword.

In a text by the Zen master → Takuan, in which he compares the mental attitude of a practitioner of Zen with that of a sword fighter, we find: "From the point of view of the right understanding of *ken,* not only Zen but also the great law of Heaven and Earth as well as all the laws of the universe are nothing other than kendō; and conversely, from the point of view of Zen, not only *ken* but also everything in the universe is nothing more than the motion of waves on the ocean of Zen. More incisively put, the unity of *ken* and Zen refers to that stage in which there is neither *ken* nor Zen, and yet we cannot find anything in the universe that is not *ken* and not Zen" (trans. from Fumio Hashimoto, cited in Dürckheim 1979, p. 37).

Kenshō Z Jap., lit. "seeing nature"; Zen expression for the experience of awakening (→ enlightenment). Since the meaning is "seeing one's own true nature," *kenshō* is usually translated "self-realization." Like all words that try to reduce the conceptually ungraspable experience of enlightenment to a concept, this one is also not entirely accurate and is even misleading, since the experience contains no duality of "seer" and "seen" because there is no "nature of self" as an object that is seen by a subject separate from it.

Semantically *kenshō* has the same meaning as → satori and the two terms are often used synonymously. Nevertheless it is customary to use the word *satori* when speaking of the enlightenment of the Buddha or the Zen patriarchs and to use the word *kenshō* when speaking of an initial enlightenment experience that still requires to be deepened.

Kenshō-jōbutsu Z Jap., lit. "[self-]realization–becoming a buddha"; concise description of the goal of Zen training, which is meant to lead the practitioner, with the help of → *zazen* and kōan training, to the experience of awakening (→ enlightenment, → *kenshō*, → satori) and through limitless deepening of this experience eventually to the complete enlightenment of a buddha.

"Becoming a buddha" is to be understood here in experiential terms, since according to the teaching of Zen every sentient being is fundamentally already a buddha, that is, endowed with immaculate buddha-nature (→ *busshō*) and thus perfect. However, one who is not enlightened (→ *bonpu-no-jōshiki*) is not aware of this identity with buddha-nature. Thus for him it seems that he "becomes a buddha" when in enlightenment he realizes his true nature for the first time.

Kentan Z Jap., lit. "looking at the → *tan*"; a round made by Zen masters through the → *zendō* along the rows of → *zazen* practitioners early in the morning during the first set of sitting periods of a day of → *sesshin*. By making this round the master gets an impression of the state of mind of the practitioners, each of whom greets him with a *gasshō*.

Kentsui Z Jap., lit. "tongs [and] hammer"; a Zen expression for the manner in which a Zen master trains his students. It is, as many examples of the ancient masters (→ kōan) show, not for the faint-hearted. This frequently harsh-seeming way of training is, however, an expression of great compassion on the part of the master, who through it helps his students to realize their deepest potential and to progress as far as it is possible for them on the path to awakening (→ enlightenment).

Kesa Z Jap., lit. "coarse wool shawl"; originally the shoulder cloth that is part of the habit of a Buddhist monk. In Zen this cloth of coarse material (ordinarily patchwork) is stylized into a bib made of pieces of brocade,which symbolizes the patchwork robe. It is worn by Zen masters and Zen priests on festive occasions or during → *sesshin*.

Keshab Chandra Sen H 1838–1884, a well-known Indian reformer, the third leader of the → Brāhmo-Samāj.

Keshab was influenced by Christianity and wished to reform the Samaj accordingly. For this reason he separated from Devendranāth → Tagore in 1868. He believed he had received a divine commission to create a new interpretation of God's law, which he named *navavidhān* (Lit. "new administration"). Of particular interest are his meetings with → Rāmakrishna.

Ketsuge Z Jap., lit. "beginning the summer"; the first day of → *ango*, the summer training period in a Zen monastery.

Kevala Asti H Skt., lit. "Thou art alone," meaning that one has nothing to do with the multifarious forms of the manifest world (→ *namarūpa*), but rather is solely → *ātman*.

Kevalādvaita-Vedānta H Skt., *kevala*, lit. "unique, perfect"; the unqualified nondualism of → Shankara, who taught that God and the individual are one in transcendence. All else is → *māyā* and thus unreal.

Khadroma B Tib. for → *dākinī*

Kham Brahm H Skt., lit. "all is *brahman*"; an → Advaita expression from the Vedas; it states that nothing else exists but → *brahman*, because everything is *brahman*. Every other view is an illusory superimposition of thoughts on *brahman*.

Kheyala ꟷ Skt.; a sudden, unexpected mental movement in the form of desire or will, attention, memory, or knowledge. The sages also interpreted *kheyala* as an unfathomable act of God, such as his division into the multiplicity of creation. When an enlightened, egoless being feels, thinks, and moves, this manifestation of spontaneous divine will in a human body is *kheyala.*

Khuddaka-nikāya 🅱 Pali, lit. "*Short Collection*"; fifth part of the Sutta- or → Sūtra-pitaka, consisting of fifteen "short" sections: (1) *Khuddaka-pātha*, collection of rules and prescriptions for ceremonies, etc.; (2) *Dhammapada*, 426 verses on the basics of the Buddhist teaching, enjoying tremendous popularity in the countries of → Theravāda Buddhism (it is arranged in twenty-six chapters); (3) *Udāna*, eighty pithy sayings of the Buddha; (4) *Itivuttaka*, (lit. "thus was it spoken"), treatments of moral questions that are ascribed to the Buddha; (5) *Sutta-nipāta*, one of the oldest parts of the canonical literature, of high literary worth; (6) *Vimāna-vatthu*, collection of eighty-three legends that show how one can achieve rebirth as a god (→ *deva*) through virtuous action; (7) *Peta-vatthu*, concerning rebirth as a hungry ghost after an unvirtuous life; (8) *Thera-gāthā*, collection of 107 songs (*gāthā*) that are ascribed to the "oldest" monks (→ *thera*) (these are from the earliest Buddhist times); (9) *Therī-gāthā*, seventy-three songs of the female elders (→ *theri*), who became famous through their virtue; (10) → *Jātaka*; (11) *Niddesa*, commentary to the *Sutta-nipāta* (see no. 5); (12) *Patisambhidā-maggā*, analytical treatments in the style of the → *Abhidharma*; (13) *Apadāna*, stories about the previous existences of monks, nuns, and saints renowned for their beneficient action; (14) *Buddhavamsa*, tales in verse about the twenty-four buddhas who preceded Buddha → Shākyamuni; (15) *Chariyā-pitaka*, collection of tales that take up themes from the *Jātaka*. They show how the Buddha in his previous existences realized the ten perfections (→ *pāramitā).*

Ki 🆉 Jap., lit. "action"; in Zen the unique fashion that each master has of training his students, which arises from his particular personality and the depth of his realization of Zen.

Kian Eshō 🆉 Jap. for → Hsu-an Huai-ch'ang

Kiangsi Tao-i 🆉 → Ma-tsu Tao-i

Kichijō-ji 🆉 Jap.; a monastery of the → Sōtō school in Kyōto, which was founded in 1457 by Ōta Dōkan and was in the Tokugawa period among the most important centers of Zen in Japan.

Kidō Chigu 🆉 Jap. for → Hsu-t'ang Chih-yu

Kikai tanden 🆉 Jap. → *hara*

Kikan-kōan 🆉 Jap. → Kōan

Kimō-tokaku 🆉 Jap., lit. "hair of a tortoise (and) horn of a hare"; a Zen expression referring to the belief in something that does not really exist, i.e., belief in a permanent substance in phenomena or → ego as a subject that is separate and different from objects "out there." (Also → delusion.)

Kingyū 🆉 Jap. for → Chin-niu

Kinhin 🆉 Jap.; Zen walking as it is practiced in Zen monasteries between sitting periods (→ *zazen*).

In the → Rinzai school the walking is done fast and energetically, frequently at a jog, while in the → Sōtō school *kinhin* is practiced in a "slow-motion" tempo. In the lineage of Zen started by the modern Zen master → Daiun Sōgaku Harada, a pace between these two extremes is practiced.

Kīrtana 🅷 or Kīrtan or Sankīrtan, Skt.; communal chanting, singing, and dancing in honor of God; it plays a major role in → Bhakti-Yoga especially, as such behavior heightens the *bhakta's* feelings and thereby brings him further along the path to God.

Kissako 🆉 Jap., lit. "drink [a bowl of] tea"; a Zen saying, originally of the great Chinese Ch'an (Zen) master → Chao-chou Ts'ung-shen (Jap., Jōshū Jūshin). It points to the fact that life based on Zen realization is not something "special" that is separated from everyday affairs.

Klesha 🅷 🅱 (kleśa) Skt., lit. "trouble, defilement, passion."

🅷 a term from → Patañjali's yoga philosophy. His *Yoga-Sūtra* lists five "plagues," i.e., impediments on the way to → *samādhi.* They are ignorance (→ *avidyā*), egoism, love, hate, and thirst for life; *avidyā* is the root of the other four.

🅱 (Pali, kilesa); refers to all the properties that dull the mind and are the basis for all unwholesome (→ *akushala*) actions and thus bind people to the cycle of rebirth (→ samsāra). The attainment of arhathood (→ arhat) signifies the extinction of all *kleshas*.

The *kleshas* are subject to very different analyses. In the → *Visuddhi-magga* ten *kleshas* are enumerated: desire or craving (→ *trishnā*), hate, delusion, pride, false views, (→ *drishti*), doubt (→ *vichikitsā*), rigidity, excitability, shamelessness, lack of conscience. The division into *mūlaklesha* and *upaklesha* is also often found. By *mūlaklesha* is understood desire, hate, delusion, pride, doubt, false views (for example, belief in an ego, eternalism, nihilism, denial of the law of karma, persistance in these false views, and the belief that false views can lead to liberation). *Upakleshas* are the passions that are bound up with the *mūlakleshas*. Sometimes the five hindrances (→ *nivārana*) are also included with them.

The false views can be eliminated merely by insight (→ *darshana*); the other passions that are based on desire, hate and similar emotional factors and are not, like the false views, intellectual in nature take longer and are more difficult to eliminate. One can get rid of them through regular meditation practice (→ *bhāvanā*), such as that of → *dhyāna*, → *samāpatti*, and concentration (→ *samādhi*).

Kōan 🅉 Jap., lit. "public notice"; the Chinese *kung-an* originally meant a legal case constituting a precedent. In Zen a kōan is a phrase from a → sūtra or teaching on Zen realization (→ *teishō*), an episode from the life of an ancient master, a → *mondō* or a → *hossen*—whatever the source, each points to the nature of ultimate reality. Essential to a kōan is paradox, i.e., that which is "beyond" (Gk., *para*) "thinking" (Gk., *dokein*), which transcends the logical or conceptual. Thus, since it cannot be solved by reason, a kōan is not a riddle. Solving a kōan requires a leap to another level of comprehension.

Pictorial representation of a famous kōan: Nach'üan kills the cat (*Mumonkan* 14; ink painting by Sengai)

Kōans have been used in Zen as a systematic means of training since around the middle of the 10th century. Since the kōan eludes solution by means of discursive understanding, it makes clear to the student the limitations of thought and eventually forces him to transcend it in an intuitive leap, which takes him into a world beyond logical contradictions and dualistic modes of thought. On the basis of this experience, the student can demonstrate his own solution of the kōan to the master in a → *dokusan* spontaneously and without recourse to preconceived notions. The word or expression into which a kōan resolves itself when one struggles with it as a means of spiritual training is called the → *wato* (Chin., *hua-tou*). It is the "punch line" of the kōan. In the famous kōan "Chao-chou, Dog," for example, *mu* is the *wato*. Many longer kōans have several *watos*.

There are all told about 1,700 kōans, of which present-day Japanese Zen masters use only 500 to 600, since many are repetitions or are not so valuable for training purposes. Most of these kōans are in the great collections, the → *Wu-men-kuan* (Jap., *Mumonkan*), the → *Pi-yen-lu* (Jap., *Hekigan-roku*), the → *Ts'ung-jung-lu* (Jap., *Shōyō-roku*), the *Lin-chi-lu* (Jap., *Rinzai-roku*), and the → *Denkō-roku*.

In general kōan practice is associated with the → Rinzai school (→ *kanna* Zen), however kōans have also been used, both in China and Japan, in the → Sōtō school (→ *mokushō* Zen). To begin with, kōan practice prevents a student from falling back after a first enlightenment experience (→ enlightenment, → *kenshō*, → satori) into "everyman's consciousness" (→ *bonpu-no-jōshiki*); beyond that, it helps the student to deepen and extend his realization.

Within the system of kōan training adopted by the Rinzai school, five types of kōan are distinguished: *hosshin-*, *kikan-*, *gonsen-*, *nantō-*, and *go-i-kōan*.

1. *Hosshin-kōan* (*hosshin*, Jap., "dharmakāya," → *trikāya*) are kōans that help a student to make a breakthrough to enlightened vision and to become familiar with the world of true nature, buddha-nature (→ *busshō*).

2. The *hosshin-kōan* relates with the world of "nondistinction," however the student should not get stuck on this level of experience. The *kikan-kōan* (Jap., *kikan*, "support, tool") is meant to train the student in the ability to make distinctions within nondistinction.

3. The *gonsen-kōan* (Jap. *gonsen*, "pondering words") is concerned with the deepest meaning and content of the sayings and formulations of the ancient masters, which lies beyond lexical definition and conceptual representation.

4. The *nantō-kōan* (Jap., *nantō*, "difficult to get through") are basically those kōans that, as the name implies, are particularly hard to solve.

5. When the student has mastered the kōans of the first four classes, then, through the kōans of *go-i*, the → five degrees (of enlightenment) of Master → Tung-shan Liang-chieh (Jap., Tōzan Ryōkai), the genuine insight he has developed is once more fundamentally worked through and put to the test.

After a first glimpse of enlightenment (often through the use of the kōan "Chao-chou, Dog"), the kōan training "in space" (Jap., *shitsu-nai*) begins. At the end of kōan training comes the time to become acquainted with the real meaning of rules and precepts like the → *jūjūkai* and with the different levels of meaning of the "three precious ones" (→ *sambō*). When a student has mastered the different levels of kōans to the satisfaction of his master, he has fulfilled an essential requirement for receiving → *inka-shōmei.*

Kobō-Daishi B → Kūkai

Kobusshin Z Jap., lit. "old buddha's heart-mind"; deferential term for the mind of a profoundly enlightened Zen master (→ enlightenment).

Kobutsu Z Jap., lit. "old buddha"; originally, a buddha of an earlier world age. In Zen the expression is used, like → *kobusshin,* as a deferential epithet for a great Zen master.

Ko Hung T 284–364 C.E.; influential Taoist alchemist and theoretician, author of the *Pao-p'u-tzu,* an encyclopedia of methods and practices for attaining immortality. The esoteric chapters of the *Pao-p'u-tzu* describe procedures for changing one's outer appearance, making talismans, producing spells and magical formulae, etc. Ko Hung, in compiling the *Pao-p'u-tzu,* made use of all Taoist texts known to him. This explains a number of contradictions between entries. The exoteric part is not confined to Taoist texts but also contains Confucianist ideas.

Ko Hung's major contribution consisted in systematically arranging all known teachings on how to attain immortality and in combining these with the central teachings of → Confucianism (→ K'ung-tzu). He emphasizes that immortality cannot be attained by physical, sexual, or meditative practices alone; the practitioner must also train himself in the Confucianist virtues (→ *wu-ch'ang*). Ko Hung therefore had a decisive influence on the moral orientation of Taoism. He opposed the neo-Taoist → *ch'ing-t'an* movement (→ *hsüan-hsüeh*), which he considered to be totally devoid of any religious value.

In addition, Ko Hung was a prominent physician. One of his treatises contains the first known descriptions of smallpox and psittacosis.

In the *Pao-p'u-tzu* Ko Hung argues that immortality can only be attained through the workings of the secret elixir of Life (→ *nei-tan,* → *wai-tan*); physical exercises and sexual practices are merely methods for prolonging life. Alchemy furthermore made it possible to acquire certain supernatural abilities, such as walking on water, calling back the dead, securing whatever official post one desired, etc. In addition, Ko Hung describes the preliminary spiritual exercises for attaining immortality. The most important of these is the veneration of the Supreme One (→ T'ai-i), of the Spirit of the Hearth (→ Tsao-chün), and of → Lao-tzu.

Ko Hung classifies immortals hierarchically according to their practices. He allocates the highest rank to those who have ingested elixirs of gold or jade and performed twelve hundred meritorious deeds. They rise to Heaven in broad daylight (→ *fei-sheng*) but may remain in this world if that is their wish: in that case they make it their task to explain the teachings of Confucius to the common people and to initiate advanced adepts into the secrets of alchemy. Other immortals do not have such a choice, although they liberate both themselves as well as others. They withdraw from the world to devote themselves exclusively to hygiene exercises.

Ko Hung was renowned for his profound knowledge of the classics. He held several high military and public posts, which gained him the respect of Confucianists. He also played an important part in the successful suppression of a peasant uprising. After that he turned his back on public life and withdrew to the mountains near Canton to devote himself to alchemical practices.

Kōke Zonshō Z Jap. for → Hsing-hua Ts'ung-chiang

Kokoro Z Jap. (Sino-Jap., *shin*) Japanese way of reading the Chinese character *hsin,* which can be translated by "heart, spirit, consciousness, soul, mind, outlook, sense, interiority, thought," and so on. In Zen it means, depending on the context, either the mind of a person in the sense of all his powers of consciousness, mind, heart, and spirit, or else absolute reality—the mind beyond the distinction between mind and matter (→ *busshō*), self-nature, or true nature.

Kokorozashi Z Jap., lit. "will, volition, intention, plan, outlook, goal, ambition, wish, hope, resolve"; in Zen, particularly by → Bassui Zenji, it is used, not in the everyday sense, but rather more as Meister Eckhart uses it. This kind of will is inherently a longing for the truth, for reality; it is the instinct to commit oneself to the path of awakening (→ enlightenment) and to continue on it endlessly.

Kokushi B Z Jap., lit. "teacher of the nation" or "master of the country"; honorific title for the Buddhist teacher of a Japanese emperor; the Japanese equivalent for the Chinese → Kuo-shih.

Kokushittsū Z Jap., lit. "bucket of black paint";

a Zen expression meaning the state of total darkness in which a practitioner of meditation (→ *zazen*) sometimes finds himself before a breakthrough to an experience of awakening (→ enlightenment, → *kenshō*, → satori).

Kokyū Jōryū Z Jap. for → Hu-ch'in Shao-lung

Kokyū-no-daiji Z Jap., lit. "great experience of one's own self"; another expression for the experience of awakening (→ enlightenment, → *kenshō*, → *satori*).

Komusō Z Jap., lit. "emptiness monk"; a monk of the → Fuke school who wanders through the countryside playing the bamboo flute (*shakuhachi*). *Komusō* wear beehive-shaped bamboo hats, which hide their faces and thus their identities.

Konagāmana B Skt.; buddha of a previous world age; also → buddha 1.

Kōnin Z Jap. for → Hung-jen

Kosha H (kośa), Skt., lit. "sheath, covering." The *Taittirīya-Upanishad* describes five *koshas* that envelop the → *ātman*. The first, outermost sheath is *annamaya-kosha*, the material sheath or food sheath. The second, *prānamaya-kosha*, is the subtle or vital sheath that animates and maintains the body and mind. So long as this vital sheath is present, the organism will remain alive. The gross manifestation of this sheath is the breath. The third sheath is *manomaya-kosha*, the mental sheath that receives all sensory impressions. The fourth is *vijñānamaya-kosha*, the intelligence sheath, with its faculties of discrimination and will. The fifth is *ānandamaya-kosha*, called the sheath of bliss, because in it man is closest to the *ātman*. The *ātman* remains apart from these sheaths and is untouched by their qualities.

Koshala B (Kośala); an Indian state at the time of the historical Buddha → Shākyamuni, located in the territory of present-day Nepal. The capital was Shrāvastī. Koshala was the most powerful state in North India until it was absorbed by Magadha in the third century. Buddha often sojourned in the capital of Koshala, especially in the → Jetavana Monastery.

Kosha School B from Skt. *kosha* (Chin., chushe; Jap., kusha); the actual meaning is "School of the → *Abhidharmakosha*"; a school of Chinese Buddhism based on the *Abhidharmakosha* of → Vasubandhu, which was translated into Chinese by → Paramārtha and → Hsüan-tsang. The Kosha school belongs by its doctrine to the "realistic" schools of the Hīnayāna, since it takes as its point of departure the existence of all → dharmas in the past, present, and future.

The school existed as such only during the T'ang Dynasty; it is mentioned in an official document of 793 only as a part of the idealistic → Fa-hsiang school, since no one actually belonged exclusively to the Kosha faction. In the 7th and 8th centuries the Kosha teachings were brought to Japan.

The Kosha school sees dharmas as building blocks of existing things and divides them into two catagories: conditioned (→ *samskrita*) and unconditioned (→ *asamskrita*). Dharmas exist forever, however the things constituted by them are transitory. Thus the substance of each thing passes from the past to the present and from the present to the future. This does not mean, however, that the school admitted the existence of a permanent self, an → ātman.

The conditioned dharmas are divided by the Kosha school into four groups: (1) form (eleven dharmas), i.e., matter; (2) consciousness (one dharma); (3) mental factors (forty-six dharmas, including among others, perception, will, intellect, trust, and ignorance, → *chetasika*); (4) and elements, which are to be subsumed under neither matter nor mind (fourteen dharmas, including birth, death, name, transitoriness, etc.). The unconditioned dharmas are space (→ *ākāsha*), → *pratisamkhyā-nirodha*, and → *apratisamkhyā-nirodha*. The seventy-five dharmas are connected with one another in our world in a way that is explained by a scheme of causal connection in which six principal and four secondary causes differentiate an effect.

Kōshū Tenryū Z Jap. for → Hang-chou T'ien-lung

Kotsu Z Jap., lit. "bones," also *nyoi* (Jap. for → *ju-i*); the scepter, about 35 cm long, of a Zen master (→ *rōshi*), which is bestowed on him by his master as a sign of his mastership.

The scepter has a slight S-shaped curve, like a human spinal column. The rōshi uses the *kotsu*, for example, to emphasize a point in a → *teishō*, to lean on when sitting, or also occasionally to strike a student.

K'ou Ch'ien-chih T 365–448 C.E.; Taoist master, initially a follower of the Five-Pecks-of-Rice School (→ *wu-tou-mi tao*). After → Lao-tzu had appeared to him in several visions, K'ou Ch'ien-chih brought about various reforms within the Five-Pecks-of-Rice School with the aim of eliminating its sexual practices. In 415 C.E. he assumed the title Celestial Master (→ *t'ien-shih*). As a result of his endeavors Taoism was accorded the status of an official state religion. In addition, K'ou Ch'ien-chih initiated the persecution of Buddhists in Northern China during the seven years from 438 to 445 C.E.

In K'ou Ch'ien-chih's visions Lao-tzu predicted that K'ou would cleanse Taoism of the false teachings of → Chang Chüeh and abolish the practice of "combining the breaths" (→ *ho-ch'i*) as well as the payment of five pecks of rice to priests as a fee for performing certain ceremonies. Lao-tzu furthermore taught him how to perform certain → *tao-yin* and breathing exercises. K'ou stressed the importance of good deeds in the life of a Taoist. The newly reformed Taoism became known as the New Way of the Celestial Master or the Northern Way of the Celestial Master.

K'ou feared the competition of Buddhist teachings and rituals and, together with the reactionary Confucianist Ts'ui Hao, convinced the emperor of the Northern Way Dynasty that Buddhism constituted a danger to the state. In consequence Taoism was proclaimed a state religion. In 438 C.E. the emperor, influenced by K'ou, passed a law forbidding any man aged over fifty to become ordained as a Buddhist monk. In 441 C.E. the majority of Buddhist monasteries and temples were closed down. In 444 C.E. Buddhist monks were forbidden to lead a nomadic life; in 445 C.E. all the monks in the capital were killed, and soon after, the remaining monks in Northern China. It must be said that K'ou objected to such radical measures, but his Confucianist ally was determined to "kill the evil ones in order to help the good." Taoist temples were constructed in the capital, and the emperor assumed the title of True Prince of Supreme Peace.

K'ou-ch'ih T Chin., lit. "chattering of teeth"; Taoist health exercise consisting of clapping one's teeth together thirty-six times. It is performed as a preliminary to most breathing exercises and other hygiene practices and is said to stimulate the production of saliva (→ *yü-chiang*) and, according to the Inner Deity Hygiene School, attract the attention of the body deities (→ *shen*).

Kōyō Seijō Z also Kōyō Shinjō, → Hsing-yan Ch'ing-jang

Kozen gokoku-ron Z Jap.; a written work of the Japanese Zen master → Esai Zenji, who was the first to transmit the Zen tradition successfully in Japan. He wrote it as a response to accusations from rival Buddhist schools; in it he explains that the adoption of the Zen teachings could only redound to Japan's benefit. The *Kozen gokoku-ron* was the first book about Zen written in Japan.

Krakuchchanda B Skt., a buddha of a previous age of the world; also → buddha 1.

Kria-Yuga H Skt. → *yuga*

Krishna H (Kṛṣṇa), Skt., lit. "black" or "dark blue"; a symbol for the infinite space of the universe. The name Krishna appears in the *Rigveda,* but without reference to the later divinity. The earliest reference to Krishna as the son of → Devakī is found in the → *Chāndogya-Upanishad,* where he is described as a scholar.

Krishna's birth from the side of the Divine Mother. (Relief, 11th century)

The later god Krishna is the most celebrated hero of Indian mythology and the best known of all the deities. He is the eighth incarnation of → Vishnu. This hero and → *avatāra,* around whom so many fables, legends, and tales arose, lived at a time when the Hindus had not yet left northwest India. He is a prominent figure in the *Mahābhārata,* and as the "Divine One" he instructs → Arjuna in the → *Bhagavad-Gītā,* the most famous "song" of Hinduism. Here Arjuna addresses Krishna as the supreme, universal consciousness, as divine yet present before the gods, as unborn and omnipresent.

The elevation of Krishna to the rank of deity was established still more clearly in the → Purānas, particularly in the → *Bhāgavata-Purāna,* which presents Krishna's life story from his infancy in great detail. The various stories contained in the *Bhāgavata-Purāna* were later widely disseminated by the publication of a translation into Hindi under the title *Prem-Sāgar* ("ocean of love").

Concerning Krishna's birth, the *Mahābhārata* and the *Vishnu-Purāna* relate that Vishnu plucked two of his hairs, a white and a black one, which entered the wombs of Rohinī and Devakī. From the white hair → Balarāma was created, from the black hair, Krishna. From his early days among the shepherds in → Vrindāvan to the battlefield at → Kurukshetra, where he appeared as Arjuna's charioteer and teacher, he destroyed countless demons and foes and fought myriad battles. A vast literature is devoted to the narration of these adventures.

Krishna-Chaitanya H → Chaitanya, 3.

Krita-Kritya H (Kṛta-Kṛtya), Skt., lit. "the one who has fulfilled what was to be done"; one who has perceived the realization of God as the sole purpose of life and has attained liberation.

Kritātman 🅷 (Kṛtātman), Skt., lit. *krita:* "perfect," *ātman:* "self"; a perfect soul.

Krita-Yuga 🅷 Skt. → Yuga

Kriyā 🅷 Skt., lit. "deed, operation, effort"; effective practice of the path of → yoga; any practice aimed at the attainment of higher knowledge.

Kshānti 🅷 🅱 (kṣānti), Skt., lit. "patience."
🅷 1. the bearing of outer circumstances and the termperaments of others; 2. patience with oneself; 3. patience arising from spiritual knowledge, which leads to freedom from attachment.
🅱 (Pali, khanti); one of the ten perfections (→ *pāramitā*). *Kshānti* includes patience in bearing aggression and injury from other beings, in bearing adversity without being drawn away from the spiritual path, as well as patience in following difficult points of Buddhist doctrine through to comprehension.

Kshara 🅷 (Kṣara), Skt.; perishable, changeable, inconstant; the divine in the constantly changing, transitory form of the universe, as opposed to *akshara,* the imperishable (→ *brahman*).

Kshara-Purusha 🅷 (Kṣara-Puruṣa), Skt., lit. *kshara:* "the perishable," *purusha:* "world soul"; the imperishable consciousness in the transitory manifest world and in the cosmic process of becoming. *Purusha* is a key concept in → Sānkhya philosophy.

Kshatriya 🅷 (Kṣatriya), Skt.; the second caste (→ *varna*) of Hindu society, that of warriors, princes, and kings. Its duty was the protection of the community; it is symbolized by → *rajas,* the → *guna* of activity.

Kshetrajña 🅷 (Kṣetrajña), Skt., lit. "one who knows the field"; one who knows everything that takes place on the field of life in body and mind. The term appears in the thirteenth chapter of the → *Bhagavad-Gītā.*

Kshitigarbha 🅱 🆉 (Kṣitigarbha), Skt., lit. "womb of the earth"; a → bodhisattva who is venerated in folk belief as a savior from the torments of hell and helper of deceased children. Sometimes he is also regarded as a protector of travelers. He is the only bodhisattva portrayed as a monk, however also with an *ūrnā*—one of the thirty-two marks of perfection (→ *dvātrimshadvara-lakshana*)—on the forehead. His attributes are the wish-fulfilling gem (→ *chintāmani*) and a monk's staff with six rings, which signifies that Kshitigarbha stands by all beings in the six realms of existence (→ *gati*). In China Kshitigarbha is known as → Ti-ts'ang, in Japan as Jizō.

Kuan 🆃 Chin., lit. seeing, beholding; designation for a Taoist monastery or nunnery. *Kuan* were constructed on the pattern of Buddhist monasteries. In the early days of Taoism they were the abode of either celibate monks (→ *tao-shih*) or lay priests and their families. Under → Sung Wen-ming (6th century C.E.) these *kuan* were turned into strict monasteries or nunneries, so that married Taoist teachers (*shih-kung*) and their families had to live outside the monastery walls.

Tradition explains the use of a term meaning "seeing" or "beholding" to designate a monastery or nunnery as follows: In ancient times (i.e., some centuries before the Christian era) when → Yüan-shih t'ien-tsun walked upon the Earth in the shape of → Lao-tzu to teach people the Way [→ Tao] there lived in Western China a fervent believer in the Tao. His name was → Yin Hsi, the Guardian of the [Mountain] Pass. He built himself a hut from brushwood to practice "seeing." According to one tradition Yin Hsi was informed by a supernatural manifestation of light in the eastern sky that Lao-tzu was approaching his mountain pass. Another tradition says that Yin Hsi was an astrologer who gazed at the stars, which told him that Lao-tzu would be passing his way. He set out to meet Lao-tzu, became his pupil, and received from him the → *Tao-te ching.* Yin Hsi's hut was thus a precursor of Taoist monasteries.

Kuang-tsu 🆉 → Chih-men Kuang-tsu

Kuan-ti 🆃 Chin., lit. "Emperor Kuan"; Taoist war god, who opposed all disturbers of the peace. He had the task of protecting the realm against all external enemies and internal rebels and began to be venerated sometime in the 7th century C.E. He was also worshipped as a protector of state officials, who accorded him special veneration. In popular religious belief he was known primarily for casting out demons and was called Fu-mo ta-ti, the Great Ruler Who Banishes Demons. He is portrayed as a nine-foot tall giant with a two-foot-long beard. His face is scarlet, his eyes like those of a phoenix, and his eyebrows like silkworms. Frequently he is shown standing beside his horse, in full armor and carrying a halberd. Sometimes, however, he is portrayed as a military mandarin, in a sitting position, unarmed, stroking his beard with one hand and in the other holding one of the classic Confucianist works, the *Spring and Autumn Annals* (*Ch'un-ch'iu*).

The deity Kuan-ti is a historical personality, namely the 3d-century general Kuan Yü, who served under the founder of one of the three realms and, in 220 C.E., was executed on the orders of a hostile ruler. His life story forms the theme of one of the most popular Chinese novels and of many plays.

The cult around Kuan-ti as a deity is of a relatively recent origin and was strongly influenced by Buddhist ideas. Kuan-ti has even been described as a Bodhisattva. During the 7th century C.E. he was one of the protectors of Buddhist temples and monasteries. In the 16th century he was accorded the title Great Just Emperor Who Assists Heaven and Protects the State and admitted to the Taoist pantheon. In the 19th century the then emperor bestowed upon him the title Military Emperor and elevated him to the level of Confucius (→ K'ung-tzu).

Temples were erected in his honor throughout the realm, and imperial officials made offerings to him on the thirteenth day of the first and fifth month of each year. This practice continued until the end of the Chinese empire (1911 C.E.). Furthermore, Kuan-ti was called upon during spiritualist seances to guide the brush of the medium and provide, inter alia, information about people who had died, prophecies concerning the future, and knowledge about divine recompense or retaliation for good or evil deeds.

Kuan-yin 🅱 also Kuan-shi-yin, Chin., lit. "Who Contemplates the [Supplicating] Sound of the World"; Chinese version of → Avalokiteshvara. Kuan-yin, along with → Samantabhadra, → Kshitigarbha (→ Ti-ts'ang), and → Mañjushrī (→ Wen-shu) is one of the four great bodhisattvas of → Buddhism and is the object of particular veneration.

Kuan-yin in typical pose (wooden figure, 12th century)

Kuan-yin manifests himself in any conceivable form wherever a being needs his help, especially when someone is menaced by water, demons, fire, or sword. In addition, Kuan-yin is the bodhisattva to whom childless women turn for help. In the → *Sukhāvatī-vyūha*, Kuan-yin is one of the companions of Buddha → Amitābha.

In more recent representations, Kuan-yin is often depicted with feminine features, an effect of Taoistic and Tantric influences.

Many kinds of iconographical representation are known (→ Avalokiteshvara). The one most frequent in China is the thousand-armed, thousand-eyed bodhisattva. In many representations, Kuan-yin has a child on one arm or appears in the company of a maiden who holds a fish basket or is together with → Wei-t'o, the protector of the teaching. Still other depictions show Kuan-yin standing on clouds or riding on a dragon in front of a waterfall. As Kuan-yin of the Southern Sea, he stands on a cliff in the midst of flaming waves and rescues shipwrecked persons from the sea, which symbolizes → samsāra. Kuan-yin usually holds a lotus blossom or a willow twig and a vase containing heavenly dew or the nectar of immortality.

According to the folk belief of eastern China, Kuan-yin dwells on the island P'u-t'uo-shan, which is the bodhisattva's sacred place.

In China Kuan-yin was depicted up until the time of the early Sung Dynasty as a man, and in the grotto paintings of → Tun-huang is even shown with a mustache. From approximately the 10th century on, the figure of Kuan-yin in a white robe (Pai-i Kuan-yin) with feminine facial traits is predominant. This development is probably due, on the one hand, to the admixture of Taoistic folk religious ideas since the Sung period, an admixture from which Buddhism in China suffered considerable losses in intellectual and cultural level. On the other hand, it can also be connected with the incursion of Tantric elements. In Tantric Buddhism, the two essential aspects of enlightenment, compassion (→ *karunā*) and wisdom (→ *prajñā*), are symbolized by masculine and feminine genders, respectively; every buddha and bodhisattva is associated with a female companion. That of Avalokiteshvara is White → Tara, of which name the Chinese *Pai-i Kuan-yin* is the literal translation. The figure of Kuan-yin in a white robe was taken up by Chinese folk religion and restyled into the figure of Kuan-yin the provider of children.

This bodhisattva figure is surrounded by a great number of legends. According to the best known, Kuan-yin is Miao-shan (the Wondrously Kind One), the third daughter of King Miao-chung. Against the will of her father, she enters the White Sparrow Monastery. Her father tries by every means to persuade her to return to worldly life. Finally he intends to kill her by the sword. However, in this moment the lord of hell (→ Yama) appears and leads her away to the Underworld, where she soothes the torment of the damned and transforms hell into a paradise. Thereupon Yama releases her and she is reborn on the island P'u-t'uo-shan, where she protects seafarers from storms (hence she is considered patron of seafarers). When her father becomes gravely ill, she heals him by placing a piece of her own flesh on the diseased area. Out of gratitude, her father has an image made in her honor; because of a verbal misunderstanding between the king and the sculptor, the latter created a statue with a thousand arms and a thousand eyes, still today the most popular form of the bodhisattva.

Kubera 🅗, also Kuvera, Skt.; 1. god of the spirits of darkness; god of treasures and wealth; 2. guardian of the North (on the compass).

Kuei 🅣 Chin., lit. ghost, spirit, demon; spirit of the dead formed of the negative yin components (→ yin-yang) of a person's soul—i.e., the *p'o* souls—after death.

The term *kuei* applies to all dead souls except those of members of one's own family. *Kuei* are feared, because they are believed to be capable of avenging injustices or insults suffered by them when they were alive. This particularly applies to the *kuei* of people who die by drowning or hanging or die a long way from home but also to the souls of those for whom no ancestral tree (→ *tzu*) has been erected. They are the so-called hungry ghosts.

Offerings of paper money are made to placate the *kuei* and accumulate merit in their world: at these sacrificial ceremonies bundles of bank notes, issued by the "bank of the Lower World," are burned, sometimes also houses constructed of paper. In the seventh month of each year a feast of the hungry ghosts is celebrated, at which the community endeavors to appease these lost souls by ceremonial sacrifices.

According to popular belief the clothes worn by *kuei* have no hems. Their body casts no shadow so that people can perceive them only as a breath of air. The *kuei,* on their part, perceive living humans as a dim red light. Their voices do not sound like those of the living. In the teachings of the inner elixir (→ *nei-tan*) it is said that the sacred embryo (→ *sheng-t'ai*) must consist of pure yang, because even the presence of a minute trace of yin in the embryo renders it susceptible to falling victim to the *kuei.*

K'uei-chi 🅑 also Kui Ji (632–682); important Chinese monk; student of → Hsüan-tsang and co-founder of the → Fa-hsiang school.

K'uei-chi became a monk at the age of 17 and at 25 a member of the translation bureau of Hsüan-tsang. He worked on the translation of the *Vijñaptimātratā-siddhi*, the key work of the Fa-hsiang school, on which he also composed a commentary. In this and other writings, he systematized the teaching of his master.

Kuei-feng Tsung-mi 🅩 (Jap., Keihō Shūmitsu), 780–841; great Chinese Ch'an (Zen) master who was trained in the Chinese → Kataku school. He is known less as a Zen master than as the fifth patriarch of the → Hua-yen school (Jap., → Kegon school) of Buddhism. This school, in China as well as in the early period in Japan, always stood in close relationship to Zen. Kuei-feng wrote many books.

For his significance in the Hua-yen school, see → Tsung-mi, the name used for him in that school.

Kuei-shan Ling-yu 🅩 also Wei-shan Ling-yu (Jap., Isan Reiyū), 771–853; great Chinese Ch'an (Zen) master; a student and dharma successor (→ *hassu*) of → Pai-chang Huai-hai (Jap., Hyakujō Ekai) and the master of → Yang-shan Hui-chi (Jap., Kyōzan Ejaku) and → Hsiang-yen Chih-hsien (Jap., Kyōgen Chikan). Kuei-shan was quite the best known Buddhist master of his time in southern China. The monastic community that gathered about him numbered 1,500, and he had forty-one dharma successors. He and his principal student Yang-shan founded the Igyō school, the name of which comes from the initial characters of their names (→ Igyō school). Kuei-shan appears in example 40 of the → *Wu-men-kuan*, as well as in examples 4, 24, and 70 of the → *Pi-yen-lu*. His sayings and teachings are recorded in the *T'an-chou Kuei-shan Ling-yu-ch'an-shih yü-lu* (*Record of the Words of Ch'an Master Kuei-shan Ling-yu from T'an-chou*). Kuei-shan became a monk at the age of fifteen and first trained in a monastery of the → Vinaya school of Buddhism. At the age of twenty-two he came to Pai-chang, became his student, and under him realized profound enlightenment. Even after his enlightenment he trained further under Pai-chang and served for twenty years in his monastery as head cook (→ *tenzo*). He is Pai-chang's most important dharma successor and received from him his → *hossu* as a token of confirmation (→ *inka-shōmei*). This *hossu* plays a role in the famous → *hossen* with Master Te-shan *(Pi-yen-lu* 4). When Master Pai-chang was looking for a suitable abbot for a newly founded monastery on Mount Kuei-shan, the following incident, which appears as example 40 of the *Wu-men-kuan*, took place:

Master Kuei-shan, when he was training under Pai-chang, worked as head cook. Pai-chang wanted to select an abbot for the Kuei-shan monastery. He opened the matter up to the head monk and all the monks, indicating that they should speak and the right one would go. Thereupon Pai-chang held up a jug, placed it on the floor and asked, "This you should not call *jug*; so what do you call it?"

Then the head monk said, "One can't call it a wooden sandal."

Now Pai-chang asked Kuei-shan. Kuei-shan immediately knocked the jug over and went away.

Pai-chang said, laughing, "The head monk lost to Kuei-shan," and he directed that Kuei-shan should found the new monastery.

Thus empowered, Kuei-shan went to Mount Kuei-shan, the name of which he later assumed, built himself a hut, and did nothing other than train himself further there. He built no buildings, offered teaching to no students. Only after seven or eight years did anyone notice him; students began to gather around him and soon a large monastery came into being.

Kūkai 🅑 called Kōbō Daishi, 774–835; founder of the → Shingon school of Japanese Buddhism. Kūkai studied the esoteric teaching (→ Mi-tsung) under Hui-kuo in China. After his return to Japan, he founded a monastery on Mount Kōya, which became the center of the Shingon school. His most important works are a treatise on Confucianism, Taoism, and Buddhism, which he composed at the age of seventeen and revised six years later, and *Ten Stages of Religious Consciousness*, composed originally at the command of the emperor, in which he sets forth the basic principles of the Shingon teaching.

Kūkai also founded a school of art and science that was open to persons from all social classes and included both worldly and religious studies. Besides Buddhism, Confucianism and Taoism were also taught. He is also renowned as a painter, woodcarver, and engineer.

Kūkai laid particular emphasis on the study of Sanskrit, for in his opinion only in this language could the true meaning of the → mantras and → *dhāranīs,* which are of great importance in Shingon, be expressed. He is also the first to have introduced Shintō deities (in the form of bodhisattvas) into Buddhism. Later his successors developed the system of Ryobu-shintō, in which Buddhism and Shintoism are combined.

Kūkai came from an aristocratic family. In 791 he entered a Confucianist college and there, in the same year, composed his treatise on the great teachings of his time. In it he stresses the superiority of Buddhism over Confucianism and Taoism, the limitations of which he showed. According to Kūkai, Buddhism includes all the most valuable elements of both Confucianism and Taoism. *Ten Stages of Religious Consciousness* was by far the most significant of the six works presented to the emperor by the representatives of the Buddhist schools existing in Japan at the time. It consists of ten chapters, which describe the individual stages in the development of religious consciousness. In it Kūkai attempts, for the first time in the history of Japanese Buddhism, to expound the teaching of a school while taking into account the doctrines of other, also non-Buddhist, schools.

The first stage focuses on the world of animals, who cannot control their passions and whose lives are devoid of any religious exertion.

The second stage is that of Confucianism, which teaches worldly virtue, but knows no religious goal.

The third stage is that of Taoism, the followers of which believe in a blissful heaven that can be reached through the practice of certain kinds of meditation.

The fourth stage corresponds to the → *shrāvaka* vehicle of the Hīnayāna, which recognizes the non-reality of the self (→ *anātman*) as consisting only of the five → *skandhas*.

The fifth stage is that of the → *pratyekabuddhas,* who, through the insight of conditioned arising (→ *pratītya-samutpāda*), recognize the impermanence and nonessentiality of all things and so prevent the arising of new karma.

The sixth stage is that of the → Hossō school (→ Yogāchāra). The seventh stage corresponds to the → San-ron school (→ Mādhyamika), the eighth to the → Tendai school (→ T'ien-t'ai), the ninth to the → Kegon school (→ Hua-yen). The tenth stage is that of the Shingon school, which, in contrast to the first nine stages which only cure "illnesses of the mind," contains the real truth.

Kukyū Jōryū 🅩 Jap. for → Hu-ch'in Shao-lung

Kuladevatā 🅗 Skt., lit. "family divinity"; among Hindus it is traditional for each family to worship God under a particular aspect and name. Thus, for example, → Rāma may be worshiped in one family as Ramchandra and in another as Raghuvir, or → Krishna may be venerated as Govinda or Gopāla (the child Krishna). Many families also have a family guru who will generally give spiritual guidance to the members of the family. (They may also receive some particular initiation from another guru, however.)

Kumārajīva 🅑 344–413, China's most important translator of Sanskrit texts. Kumārajīva, who came from a noble family from Kucha (in present-day Sinkiang), first studied the teachings of the Hīnayāna and later became an adherent of the Mahāyāna. In 401 he went to Ch'ang-an (today's Xi'an), where he undertook his translation activities with the help of thousands of monks. In 402 he received the title of "teacher of the nation" (→ *kuo-shih*).

The most important of Kumārajīva's translations are the → *Amitābha-sūtra* (402), the → *Lotus Sūtra* (406), the → *Vimilakīrtinirdhesha-sūtra* (406), and the *Shata-shāstra* of → Āryadeva (404), as well as the *Mādhyamaka-kārikā* (409), the *Mahāprajñāpāramitā-shāstra* (412), and the *Dvāda-shadva-shāstra* (409), which were written by the founder of Mādhyamaka, → Nāgārjuna. In translating the last three works, Kumārajīva made a major contribution to the propagation of the → Mādhyamika school in China (→ San-lun).

Kumārajīva entered the Buddhist monastic order, together with his mother, a princess, at the age of seven. Both went to Kashmir, where for three years they studied under the most renowned of Hīnayāna teachers. After that they lived for a year in Kashgar, where Kumārajīva studied astronomy, mathematics, and occult sciences in addition to Buddhism. There he also came in contact with the Mahāyāna, to which he was later to dedicate himself exclusively. After his return to Kucha, his reputation as a scholar reached even to the imperial court. In 384 he was taken prisoner when the Chinese conquered Kucha and for seventeen years held captive by a general who was hostile to Buddhism. Finally in 402 he went to Ch'angan, where with the support of the emperor he was able to undertake his translation work. Kumārajīva decisively improved the methods of translation prevailing in China before his arrival. He himself spoke fluent Chinese and his colleagues possessed excellent knowledge of Buddhism and Sanskrit. The procedure for translation was as follows: Kumārajīva explained the meaning of the text twice in Chinese; then the monks discussed the content of the material and tried to translate it into literary Chinese; Kumārajīva then compared the translation to the original again and again until a definitive version was arrived at.

Kumārajīva was concerned, unlike other translators, to convey the essence of a sūtra and avoided word-by-word translation. He also dared to shorten the texts and adapt them to Chinese tastes.

Kumāralāta 🅉 19th patriarch of the Indian lineage of → Zen

Kumārī 🄷 Skt., lit. "virgin"; a name used to designate → Sītā as well as → Durgā. In the temple of Kanyā-Kumārī on the southernmost tip of India, the Divine Mother (→ Shakti) is worshiped as a virgin.

Kumārila Bhatta 🄷 (Kumārila Bhaṭṭa), or Kumārila Svāmin, Skt.; a celebrated teacher of → Mīmāmsā philosophy who wrote a commentary on Jaimini's → *Mīmāmsā-Sūtra.* An opponent of the Buddhists, he is said to have won them over by arguments and the power of persuasion. He was born before → Shankara and reportedly immolated himself in the saint's presence.

Kumbhaka 🄷 Skt; 1. retention of the breath between exhalation (*rechaka*) and inhalation (*pūraka*) and vice versa. A practice employed by → Rāja-Yoga and → Hatha-Yoga; 2. suspension of the breath, effected by one of two methods. First, the breathing exercises of → *prānāyama* can create a level of concentration that results in *kumbhaka.* Second, by the use of spiritual practices in which the mind is not occupied with the breath but with surrender to the object of meditation, a high level of concentration is acheived and supension of the breath occurs by itself. In this case, *kumbhaka* arises naturally and there is no risk of bodily injury. In his work *Kundalini-Yoga* (1935) → Shivānanda states that *kumbhaka* increases the amount of → *prāna* in the body.

Kumbha-Melā 🄷 Skt., lit. *kumbha:* "water-pot" (as carried by → *sādhus* as a symbol of renunciation). *melā:* "assembly"; a famous gathering of *sadhus* near Allahabad every twelve years. Another meeting is held every four years in Hārdvār; others, less well known, take place every three years in various holy cities in India.

Kundalinī 🄷 (Kuṇḍalinī), Skt., lit. "snake," also called "serpent power," because this sleeping spiritual force in every human being lies coiled at the base of the spine. Once awakened, it rises through a series of centers (→ *chakra*) and finds expression in the form of spiritual knowledge and mystical visions.

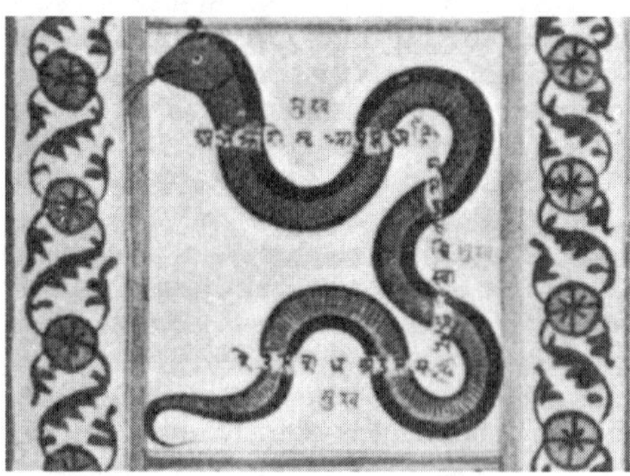

Representation of the serpent (Kundalinī) as a symbol of microcosmic energy.

Tantric philosophy teaches that the human body contains six centers of subtle energy (*chakras*), referred to as "lotuses," through whose channels the *kundalini* rises. The first center, *muladhara* ("root center"), with four red petals, is located at the base of the spinal column and governs the organs of excretion and reproduction; second is *svadhisthana* ("self-place"), with six vermilion petals, which governs the intestines; third is *manipura* ("full of radiance"), with ten blue petals, hear the solar plexus; fourth is *anāhata* ("soundless sound"), with twelve scarlet petals, in the region of the heart; next is *vishuddha* ("purity"), in the area of the throat, with sixteen dark crimson petals; sixth is *ājñā* ("the Guru's command"), between the eyebrows, with two white petals. The *kundalinī* rises through these centers from the base of the spinal column to the top of the head, where the thousand-petaled seventh *chakra, sahasrāra* ("the seat of Shiva") is located, streaming radiant white light. At this point the wakened spiritual energy develops its full majestic force in the form of enlightenment (→ *samādhi*).

According to the descriptions given by those who have experienced the rising of *kundalinī*, this can take place in one of five ways: like an ant creeping forward; like a fish swimming happily in the ocean; like a monkey that in a single leap reaches the crown of the head; like a bird hopping from one branch to the next; or like a snake moving upward in zigzag motion.

A standard work on *kundalinī* and Kundalinī-Yoga is by Arthur Avalon (see Woodroffe 1919).

Kundalinī-Shakti 🅷 (Kuṇḍalinī-Śakti), Skt., lit. "serpent power"; the cosmic energy that lies sleeping at the base of the spinal column; it can be awakened by the practice of spiritual exercises and made to rise through the → *chakras.* (See also → *kundalinī,* → Kundalinī-Yoga.)

Kundalinī-Yoga 🅷 (Kuṇḍalinī-Yoga) or Tantra-Yoga, Skt.; the goal of this path is to awaken the spiritual power that in every human being lies sleeping at the base of the spinal column (→ *kundalinī*) so that it rises through the six centers (→ *chakras*) located along the spine, until this energy reaches the seventh center at the top of the head and there unites with Shiva, the divine, thereby activating all the divine forces that sleep in human beings; they are then manifested as wisdom and bliss. This process is effected through purification exercises, training of the breath, and the practice of various positions of → Hatha-Yoga, certain → *mudrās*, and intense concentration. (See also → *chakra.*) An introduction to the theory and practice of Kundalinī-Yoga by the Indian master → Shivānanda is *Kundalinī-Yoga* (1935).

Kung-an 🅩 Chin. for kōan

K'ung-fu-tzu 🅣 → K'ung-tzu

Kung Sun-lung 🅣 Chinese philosopher of the Warring States Period. He belonged to the School of Names, which studied the relationship between name and reality, and was a contemporary of → Chuang-tzu and → Hui Shih. His main pursuit consisted in the "correction of names," i.e., the restoration of a proper correspondence between names and realities. (Also → K'ung-tzu.)

A well-known paradox of Kung Sun-lung states that "a white horse is not a horse": he argued that there was an essential difference between the terms *horse* and *white horse,* because the former was general and the latter specific. For that reason he considered them to be different names, i.e., separate concepts.

By his analysis of the determinateness of all concepts and the differences between them he made an important contribution to the development of logic in Chinese philosophy.

K'ung-tzu 🅣 551–479 B.C.E., also transcribed as *K'ung-fu-tzu;* Confucius, founder of the first Chinese wisdom school, whose teachings were a determining influence on public life in China, Japan, and Korea until the time of the 20th century. Confucius set himself the task of salvaging the ideals of the ancients from the general decline. He reformulated and systematically ordered the thoughts and ideas contained in the classical writings, which tradition later accredited to him. The central concepts of his philosophy were → *jen* (humaneness, love of fellow men) and → *li* (morality, uprightness, custom). He considered these to be the indispensable virtues of a princely person (*chün-tzu*), the Confucianist ideal. His political views were essentially based on the idea that order can only be brought about by the correction of names (*cheng-ming*) so that all things will correspond with the qualities ascribed to them by their names (appellations). In other words, a prince has to behave like a prince.

Confucius had a strong sense of his heavenly vocation and voluntarily submitted to the celestial mandate (→ *t'ien-ming*), the will of Heaven. His teachings are preserved in the *Analects* (*Lun-yü*).

K'ung-tzu was born into a noble family in Lu (now Shantung) province and grew up in humble circumstances. At the age of fifteen he decided to pursue a career as state official; when he was twenty years old he held an official post as storekeeper and later became a supervisor of the royal lands. Under various teachers he studied the thoughts and customs of the ancients

Portrait of K'ung-tzu.

and soon gathered a group of pupils around him. At the age of fifty he held the post of justice minister, but political intrigues forced him to abandon it and go into exile. He spent several years traveling through various provinces in the hope that his views on political and social reform would find favor, because he was convinced that they were capable of renewing the world. At the age of sixty-seven he was allowed to return home, where he died in 479 B.C.E.

According to tradition, K'ung-tzu, toward the end of his life, wrote a number of works which have come to be considered the classic teachings of → Confucianism. He is credited with the authorship of the *Shi-ching* (*Book of Songs*), the *Shu-ching* (*Book of Writings*), and the *Ch'un-ch'iu* (*Spring and Autumn Annals*), the first Chinese historical work. In addition, parts of the → *I-ching* and the *Chia-yü* (*Instructive Discourses*) are attributed to him. The *Yüeh-ching* (*Book of Music*) and the *Li-ch'i* (*Book of Rites*) are said to have been edited by him. His pupils—of whom there were approximately three thousand—compiled his sayings in the *Analects* (*Lun-yü*). (All the above works have been translated into the major European languages.)

The central concept of his teachings was that of *jen* (humaneness, loving-kindness toward one's fellow men): "Do not unto others what you would not have them do unto you" (*Analects* 15.23). The practice of *jen* is governed by *li* (morality): "To conquer oneself and turn to *li;* that is humaneness" (*Analects* 12.1). This concept of humaneness and benevolence furthermore embraces the virtues of conscientiousness (*chung*) and reciprocity (*shu*). Social intercourse is governed by the five relationships (→ *wu-lun*), which regulate moral behavior and allocate a proper place to each member of society. The five relationships are those between father and son, husband and wife, older and younger brother, ruler and subject, and friend and friend. To bring order into the world it is necessary to first create order within the family, and then within the territorial provinces. Once that is done, the realm will naturally fall into order. Order within the family depends on the respect and piety shown by children toward their parents.

Confucius adopted a somewhat reserved attitude toward the religious ideas of his time. His philosophy contains no religious speculations, although he felt that he had a heavenly (→ *t'ien*) vocation. It was not his intention to abolish ancestor worship—the basis of the official religion of the time—and he went so far as to include it, together with the rites of mourning, in the duties of piety toward ancestors. He refused to pronounce on the fate of the dead: "We do not even know what life is; how then can we know anything about death?" Confucianist philosophy has little room for superstition. The respect Confucius held for the official cult of ancestor worship was based on ethical rather than religious considerations. He was of the opinion that it made no sense to ask the deities for their help. In his view the will of Heaven could not be changed by our prayers.

His ideas about government are simple: if the ruler is righteous and honest, so will his subjects be. Reforms must begin at the top. When asked what would be the first measure he would take if he were appointed to govern, Confucius replied, "Correct the names; because if the names are incorrect, the words will not be correct either; and if the words are incorrect, actions will not be properly carried out; and if the actions are not properly completed, rites [*li*] and music cannot flourish; if rites and music do not flourish, punishments will not fit the crime; if punishments do not fit the crime, the common people will not know where to put hand and foot. Therefore a noble person takes care to ensure that names are properly used in speech and that what he says will in all circumstances be practicable. A noble person will not tolerate disorder in his words. That is what matters" (*Analects* 13.3).

And elsewhere, "Let the prince be prince, the minister minister, the father father, and the son son" (*Analects* 12.11).

The first step toward the correction of names thus consists in the prince behaving like a prince, whereby all remaining names are also put in order and society, too, can be restored to order. Every name contains qualities that correspond to the essence of the thing referred to by that name. If a ruler follows the → Tao of a ruler he will rule in accordance with the essence and qualities of a ruler and not merely in name. There is then a harmonious correspondence between name and external reality. Confucius therefore states that everyone—father, son, wife, etc.—must act in accordance with the duties arising from his or her appellation. He further considered it to be his task to give rulers a true idea of their calling so that they might live up to and act in accordance with the requirements of rulership.

Although the Confucian model of society had no immediate effect on the society of his time, it became—for over two thousand years—a model and example for the people of China, Japan, and Korea, in that their whole life was oriented toward Confucianist ideas. (Also → Confucianism.) (Quotes from Opitz 1968.)

K'un-lun 🅃 mountain range in Western China, glorified as a Taoist paradise. It is the abode of the Royal Mother of the West (→ Hsi wang-mu) and of the immortals (→ *hsien*). The K'un-lun—one of the ten continents and three islands in Taoist cosmology—is said to be three (or nine, according to some texts) stories high. Whoever is capable of ascending to its top gains access to the heavens. The K'un-lun furthermore extends three (or nine) stories below the Earth, thereby connecting the subterranean watery realm—the dwelling place of the dead—with the realm of the gods. In the K'un-lun the Royal Mother of the West grows the peaches of immortality, which Taoists have again and again set out to discover in countless expeditions.

The → Inner Deity Hygiene School equates K'un-lun with the human head.

According to tradition the first to visit this paradise was King Mu of Chou, who there discovered a palace of the Yellow Emperor (→ Huang-ti) and erected a stone memorial. He was then received by the Royal Mother of the West.

The K'un-lun has been a popular subject of Chinese literature since the early days of the Han Dynasty. According to the → *Huai-nan-tzu* "the mountains' Hanging Garden, Cool Breeze and Fenced Paulonia Gardens form the municipal parks of K'un-lun City, and the lakes to be found in these parks are plenished by yellow water, which, after flowing through the park, returns to its source. This water is known as cinnabar water, and whoever drinks it becomes immortal.... One may also attain immortality by climbing the first and lowest of the three mountains of K'un-lun—the mountain called Cool Breeze. Whoever reaches the top of the second mountain, called Hanging Garden and twice as high as the first, will become a spirit capable of magic and of commanding wind and rain. Those who climb the third and highest mountain . . . can step from its peak directly into Heaven and become a spirit of the gods (→ *shen*), because they have reached the palace of the Supreme Celestial Emperor (Ta-ti)" (Bauer 1974).

Kuntī 🄷 or Pritha, Skt., the wife of → Pāndu and mother of → Yudishthira, Bhīma, and → Arjuna; the last is often referred to by Krishna in the *Bhagavad-Gītā* as "Kuntī's son."

Kuntī was the daughter of the Yādava king Sura. She showed great reverence to the saint Durvāsa and was granted the boon that she might choose any god to father her child. She chose the sun god and bore a son, → Karna, whom she set out on the bank of the Yamunā.

Following the end of the great battle (→ *Mahābhārata*), Kuntī withdrew to the forest with → Dhritarāshtra, the brother of her husband Pāndu, and the latter's wife, Gāndhārī; all three perished in a great forest fire.

Kuo Hsiang 🅃 → *hsüan-hsüeh*

Kuo-shih 🄱 🅉 Chin. (Jap., → *kokushi*), lit. "teacher of the nation" or "master of the country"; honorific title bestowed by the Chinese imperial house on outstanding Buddhist masters, especially those considered by emperors as their teachers.

Kūrma 🄷 Skt., lit. "tortoise"; → Vishnu's second incarnation (→ *avatāra*). Symbolically, the amphibian tortoise represents the vital, physical human being whose keenest desires for immortality are churned from the ocean with Kūrma's help.

Kūrma-Purāna 🄷 (Kūrma-Purāṇa), Skt.; this Purāna contains 17,000 verses in which → Vishnu, in the form of a tortoise, explains the four aims (*purushārtha*) of life: *artha* (wealth), *kāma* (pleasure), *dharma* (duty), and *moksha* (liberation).

Since Kūrma is the name of an → *avatāra* form of Vishnu, it might readily be assumed to be a → Vaishnava text; however, it is traditionally listed among the Shaiva-Purānas, because the text has chiefly to do with the worship of → Shiva and → Durgā.

Kurukshetra 🄷 (Kurukṣetra), Skt., lit. "the field of the Kurus"; a region near present-day Delhi, where the great battle between the → Kauravas and the → Pāndavas was fought (→ *Mahābhārata*).

It was here that Krishna instructed → Arjuna in knowledge of the divine. Kurukshetra is also regarded as a symbol of the battlefield of life, where one must take up arms against the ego and one's lower nature.

Kusha 🄷 (kuśa), Skt.; a sacred grass, used to cover the place of meditation and also employed in worship rites.

Kushala 🄱 (kuśala) Skt. (Pali, kusala), lit. "wholesome"; any activity based on the wholesome roots (Skt., kushala-mūla; Pali, kusala-mūla), i.e., the absence of passion, aggression, and delusion. The opposite is → *akushala*.

Ku-shen 🅃 Chin., lit. "Spirit of the Valley"; a

deity mentioned in the → *Tao-te ching* and said to be identical with the mysterious Primordial Mother (Hsüan-p'in), who herself is a symbol of the → Tao. According to Chapter 6 of the *Tao-te ching,* "The Valley Spirit never dies; it is the woman, primal mother. Her gateway is the root of heaven and earth. It is like a veil barely seen. Use it; it will never fail" (Feng & English 1972).

This passage has been cited by later followers of religious Taoism (→ *tao-chiao*) to justify various sexual practices, the alleged purpose of which was to attain immortality.

In the *Tao-te-ching* the valley is a symbol of the Tao or the → *te.* It signifies emptiness or the void (→ *wu*) and also points towards the place to which all waters flow. It can thus be understood as a general symbol for the true Taoist's philosophy of life.

In a narrow sense *ku* designates a mountain spring. This allows the possible conclusion that the Spirit of the Valley may originally have been a spirit of springs.

Kushinagara 🅱 (Kuśinagara), also Kushinara; present-day Kasia in the state of Uttar-Pradwsh; one of the four sacred places of Buddhism. This is where the Buddha → Shākyamuni entered → *parinirvāna.*

After his death, his mortal remains were burned outside Kushinagara. According to tradition, part of the relics were preserved in a → stūpa in Kushinagara. The city thus became one of the most important Buddhist places of pilgrimage. However, by the time the Chinese pilgrim → Hsüan-tsang visited Kushinagara in the 7th century, it had already been destroyed.

Kwatsu 🆉 also kwatz, Jap. → katsu

Kyabdro 🅱 (skyabs-'gro), Tib., roughly, "taking refuge." For all schools of → Tibetan Buddhism, the ritual act of taking refuge is a strict prerequisite for any kind of relationship with the Buddhist teaching (→ dharma). In → Hīnayāna and → Mahāyāna, the three objects of refuge are (1) the → Buddha, (2) the teaching (dharma), and (3) the spiritual community (→ *sangha*). These grant protection to the spiritual seeker and are known as the three precious ones (→ *triratna*). Unreserved recognition of these three principles and devotion to them is expressed through the formal taking of refuge. The "diamond vehicle" (→ Vajrayāna) expands the formula by adding the guru (→ lama), and in certain schools the refuge is sixfold. In that case, to the three precious ones are added the "three roots": (4) guru, (5) personal deity (→ *yidam*), and (6) powers of inspiration (→ *dākinī*).

The importance of the notion of Buddha as guru or master and the community of monks as bearers of his teaching was recognized quite early and eventually came to be regarded as a basic point in the Buddhist worldview. With the development of the various Mahāyāna schools, the importance of the historical Buddha diminished and universal buddhahood assumed primary importance. Finally in the Vajrayāna the spiritual teacher was seen as the embodiment of this buddhahood.

The Buddhist → Tantras continually point to the central role of the guru, who has the ability to explain and carry out difficult practices. The position of the guru as fourth refuge and the view that he is the embodiment of the three precious ones is an integral part of the Vajrayāna practices.

At around the time the Buddhist Tantras were transmitted to Tibet, refuge in the guru was formalized, and the biographies of → Nāropa and of → Milarepa provide a clear illustration of this principle. Also → Atīsha stressed the special importance of the lama or guru and of taking refuge. Hence he received the epithet Kyabdro Pandita (the Taking-Refuge Pandit).

In the following centuries taking refuge, together with arousing enlightenment mind (→ *bodhicitta*), became established as practices preparatory for all other Vajrayāna practices in the systems of meditation techniques of the individual Tibetan Buddhist schools. The following words are attributed to Nāropa himself: "My mind is the perfect Buddha, my speech is the perfect teaching, my body is the perfect spiritual community.

Kyō 🅱 🆉 Jap. for → sūtra

Kyōge-betsuden 🆉 Jap., lit. "special tradition outside the [orthodox] teaching"; the transmission of the → buddha-dharma from heart-mind to heart-mind (→ ishin-denshin) in the tradition of Zen, which is not to be confused with the transmission of the teaching of Buddha through sacred scriptures. (Also → *fukasetsu*).

Kyōgen-Chikan 🆉 Jap. for → Hsiang-yen Chih-hsien

Kyōrin Chōon 🆉 Jap. for → Hsiang-lin Ch'eng-yuan

Kyosaku 🆉 also keisaku, Jap., lit. "wake-up stick"; flattened stick, 75 to 100 cm in length, with which the "sitters" in Zen monasteries are struck on the shoulders and back during long periods of → *zazen* in order to encourage and stimulate them.

The *kyosaku* is always used to help, *never,* as is often wrongly supposed, to punish. It symbolizes the sword of wisdom of the bodhisattva → Mañjushrī, which cuts through all delusion; thus it is always respectfully handled. It helps to overcome fatigue, awakens potential, and can, used just at the right moment, bring a person to an experience of awakening (→ enlightenment, → *kenshō*, → Satori).

Kyōsei Dōfu 🅉 Jap. for → Ching-ch'ing Tao-fu

Kyōun-shū 🅉 Jap., lit. "*Anthology of the Mad Cloud*"; anthology of the poetry of the Japanese Zen master → Ikkyū Sōjun, who gave himself the literary name *Mad Cloud.* The poems collected here are written in the Chinese style (Jap., *kambun*); in them Ikkyū celebrates the great Zen masters of ancient times, laments with biting mockery the decline of Zen in the Japan of his times, castigates corrupt priests and their foibles and compares their lifestyle to his own nonconformist life, which spanned the worlds of hermitage and brothel. The poems about his lover, the blind serving-woman Shin, are among the most beautiful erotic poems in Japanese literature. A typical poem from the *Kyōun-shū* is as follows:

The status and wealth
Of the Zen world is great,
Horrendous is its decline.
Naught but false priests,
No true masters.
One should get hold of a boatpole
And become a fisherman.
On the lakes and rivers
These days
A fresh headwind is blowing.

Kyōzan Ejaku 🅉 Jap. for → Yang-shan Hui-chi

Kyūdō 🅉 Jap., lit. "Way of the bow"; the "art of archery," one of spiritual-physical training ways (→ *dō*) of Japan, the practice of which is permeated by the mind of Zen. The spiritual roots of *kyūdō* are treated in Eugen Herrigel's book *Zen in the Art of Archery* (New York, 1971), which is among the best books written by a Westerner on the spirit of Zen.

Kyūhai 🅉 Jap. → *sampai*

Kyūhō Dōken 🅉 Jap. for Chiu-feng Tao-ch'ien, → Ho-shan Wu-yin

L

Laghiman 🄷 Skt., lit. "lightness"; a special psychic ability (→ *siddhi*). Yogic practices can result in a weightlessness that causes the body to float in air. This phenomenon, which has been attested to on numerous occasions (as in the case of Theresa of Ávila), is known in the West as levitation. If consciousness is increasingly directed away from the physical realm toward the spiritual, the gravity of the physical body may ultimately fall away altogether.

Lakshana 🄷 (Lakṣaṇa), Skt., lit. "favorable sign, mark"; 1. signs of self-realization; 2. five elements associated with the Purānas, the legends of ancient times.

According to the Sanskrit scholar Amara-Simha, each Purāna should include five *lakshanas*, or particular themes: (1) the creation of the world; (2) its dissolution and renewal; (3) the origin and genealogy of the gods, partriarchs, and heroes; (4) the rule of the → Manus (the original lawgivers) in the various stages of societal development; and (5) the life and works of the progeny of Manu. The → Purānas are invariably written in verse and presented in the form of a dialogue between an enlightened master and his disciple, whereby other dialogues and observations are interspersed in the text. However, not all Purānas adhere to the principle of five *lakshanas.*

Lakshana-Vākya 🄷 (Lakṣaṇa-Vākya), Skt.; unerring, ultimate knowledge, based solely on the reality of God and the transitory nature of the world.

Lakshmana 🄷 (Lakṣmaṇa), Skt.; son of King → Dasharatha and his wife Sumitrā. He was the half-brother of Rāma, and as his close friend accompanied him into exile. He was extremely devoted to Rāma's wife, → Sītā.

Lakshmana's wife was Ūrmilā, the sister of Sītā. They had two sons, Angada and Chandraketu. While Rāma and Lashmana were living in the wilderness, a *rākshasī*, one of → Rāvana's sisters, fell in love with Rāma. He sent her to Lakshmana, who in turn sent her back to Rāma. Rebuffed, she attacked Sītā, who was protected by Rāma. Lakshmana was asked by his brother to disfigure the *rākshasī*, and he thereupon cut off her nose and ears. The mutilated female demanded that her brother avenge her, and a mighty battle broke out, in the course of which Sītā was abducted by Rāvana. Lakshmana accompanied Rāma in the search for Sītā and supported him in his struggle against the demon king. When the war was ended, Lakshmana withdrew to the forest by the river Sarayū and offered homself to the gods, who sent down a shower of blossoms and took him up into paradise.

Lakshmī 🅷 (Lakṣmī), Skt.; in the *Rigveda* the word means only "fortune." In the *Atharvaveda* it is personified as a feminine being who brings fortune as well as misfortune. Later Lakshmī, or Shrī, becomes the goddess of fortune, the consort of → Vishnu, and the mother of → Kāma. She is said to possess four arms, but because she is a symbol of beauty she is usually portrayed with only two arms, one of which bears a lotus blossom. No temples are dedicated to her, but she is constantly worshiped as the goddess of surplus and of happiness, and hardly suffers neglect.

Legend relates that Lakshmī rose like Aphrodite from the foam of the ocean as it was churned by the gods and → *asuras* (–Churning of the Ocean). She was perfect in her beauty. According to another legend, she lay on a lotus blossom at creation. The → *Vishnu-Purāna* states that she was born several times from the ocean spray. As Vishnu appeared in his incarnation as Vāmana, Lakshmī emerged from a lotus blossom; When he was born as → Parashu-Rāma, she was his consort, Dharanī. When he was born as Rāma, she was → Sītā. When he appeared as Krishna, she was Rukminī.

Lakshya 🅷 (Lakṣya), Skt., lit. 1. "expressed figuratively," 2. "goal"; the choice of an → *ishta-deva* ("chosen deity"), upon whose form the concentration or meditation of the aspirant is directed.

Lalitavistara 🅱 Skt., lit. *"Detailed Representation of Play"* (i.e., the life of Buddha); text from the transition period between → Hīnayāna and → Mahāyāna, which describes the previous two lives of Buddha up until his first dharma discourse. This biography of Buddha, dating some time from the second century B.C.E. to the second century C.E., had several authors. It probably originated with the → Sarvāstivāda school and was later reworked from a Mahāyāna point of view.

Lama 🅱 (bla-ma), Tib., lit. "none above"; in → Tibetan Buddhism a religious master, or guru, venerated by his students, since he is an authentic embodiment of the Buddhist teachings. The term *lama* is used for the Sanskrit *guru* in the traditional Indian sense, but includes still further meanings. For the → Vajrayāna, the lama is particularly important, since his role is not only to teach rituals but also to conduct them. As spiritual authority, he can be the head of one or several monasteries and possess political influence (→ *tulku*). The spiritual "value" of the lama is indicated by the honorific title *rinpoche* ("greatly precious"), which is bestowed upon especially qualified masters. Today, however, *lama* is often used as a polite form of address for any Tibetan monk, regardless of the level of his spiritual development.

Since the lama plays a very prominent role in Tibetan Buddhism, this form of Buddhism is sometimes known in the West as Lamaism. In this context the Western colloquial equation of lama and monk is misleading. The lama is regarded as an embodiment of Buddha himself, while a monk is only a resident of a monastery who is studying the Buddhist teachings.

In order to master the Vajrayāna teachings as a layman or monk, it is absolutely necessary to receive instruction from one or more lamas. Following the highest doctrinal point of view, as for instance that of → *mahāmudrā* or → *dzogchen*, meditation practice should concentrate from the beginning on the person of the lama, whether he is physically present or not. In his presence the behavior of the student is highly ritualized and unconditional obedience to the master is stressed.

The lama has the function of transmitting the Buddhist tradition not only to his students; he also makes the transmitted teachings available to all the people by performing public rituals. Here he acts as protector against hostile influences (demons) and makes use of the most widely varied means for this purpose. Among the best known are the so-called lama dances and the recitation of the → *Bardo thödol.*

The traditional training of a lama includes many years of study of the various disciplines of Buddhist philosophy and meditation. Only after the completion of a so-called retreat of more than three years was the lama finally authorized to refer to himself as such and to transmit his knowledge to others.

Lamaism 🅱 the Buddhism of Tibet, prevalent at various times also in China and Mongolia (→ Tibetan Buddhism, → Vajrayāna).

Lamdre 🅱 (lam-'bras), Tib., lit. "path [and] goal"; a cycle of → Vajrayāna teachings transmitted especially by the → Sakyapa school. The Vajrayāna-specific tendency to see the goal of the path in the path itself comes clearly to expression in this teaching. The root text of the Lamdre system is based on the oldest Buddhist → Tantras and was brought to Tibet in the 11th century by the translator Drogmi. The first head of the Sakyapa school composed various commentaries on it, thus creating the foundation of the Sakyapa Lamdre tradition.

The Indian → *mahāsiddha* Virūpa is considered the originator of the Lamdre teaching. He gave his student Nagpopa the root text, the so-called *Vajra Verses*. This text is very short and is understandable only with the help of oral instructions. The basis of Lamdre is the experience that as to their true nature, the cycle of existence (→ samsāra) and liberation therefrom (→ nirvāna) are not different.

This insight, however, is only to be gained when the true nature of the mind is known through enlightenment. In Lamdre the mind is defined in threefold fashion: (1) the mind is clear or luminous, (2) the mind is empty (→ shūnyatā), (3) the mind is the unity of these two aspects. Only the realization of all three aspects guarantees understanding of the path as goal.

In the Sakyapa school the Lamdre teachings are inconceivable without the practice program of "training the mind," which developed at the same time as the similar teaching of the → Kadampa school. The best known of these practices is letting go of the four attachments. This practice also originated with the first head of the Sakyapas, Sachen Künga Nyingpo (1092-1158), who wrote them down after having a vision of → Mañjushrī.

Lamrim B (lam-rim), Tib., lit. "stages of the path"; term for a group of doctrinal manuals that give a complete description of the individual stages of the spiritual path. The oldest Lamrim work of → Tibetan Buddhism is the *Jewel Ornament of Liberation* by the Kagyü teacher → Gampopa (1079-1153), who was considerably influenced by the → Kadampa school. On the model of these teachings, → Tsongkhapa, the founder of the Gelugpa school, composed in the 14th century his *Graded Path to Enlightenment*. In the other schools this genre of literature enjoyed the same popularity, as evidenced, for example, by *Instructions on the All-Encompassing Good Teaching* by the Nyingma master Pältrül Rinpoche (1809–?). All these works are practical introductions to all aspects of the Buddhist teaching.

Gampopa's *Jewel Ornament of Liberation* is divided into six main sections: (1) The point of departure is the so-called → *tathāgata-garbha* teaching, i.e., the view, prevalent already in early Buddhism, that in every sentient being → buddhahood is already present as a basis—this view, however, led in later centuries to serious controversies and is no longer found in Tsongkhapa's classical work; (2) human existence offers the best opportunity to realize this latently present buddhahood; (3) the indispensible condition for such a process is the instruction of a "spiritual friend" (→ guru, → lama)—the spiritual friend and the student possess distinctive qualities; (4) the means to achieve buddahood are the instructions of the master—these concern the deficiencies of the cycle of existence (→ samsāra), the law of → karma, the function of love and compassion, the arousing of enlightenment mind (→ *bodhicitta*), the six perfections (→ *pāramitā*), the five paths (→ *pañcha-mārga*), and the ten stages (→ *bhūmi*). (5) The various teachings lead the practitioner to a goal that is experienced on different levels (→ *trikāya*). (6) This goal is not just his own welfare; rather he finds the meaning of his own life only in working for other sentient beings.

The structure of the other great Lamrim works corresponds generally to that of the Gampopa text; there are only different points of emphasis. Thus the focal point of the *Great Exposition of the Stages of the Path* is "dwelling in tranquility" (→ *shamatha*) and "clear insight" (→ *vipashyanā*), while the work of Pältrül Rinpoche contains elements of the → *dzogchen* tradition. As manuals for the guidance of lay people or the training of monks, these works have kept their effectiveness up to the present day.

Lan-ch'i Tao-lung Z also Lan-hsi Tao-lung (Jap., Rankei Dōryū), 1203–68 or 1213–78, Chin. Ch'an (Zen) master of the Yōgi lineage of Rinzai Zen (→ Yōgi school). He trained under several famous Ch'an masters of Chekiang province, among them → Wu-chun Shih-fan (Jap., Bushun [Mujun] Shiban). In 1246 he traveled to Japan. There he lived initially in Kyōto but went to Kamakura in 1247 at the invitation of Shōgun Hōjō Tokiyori. There, under the shōgun's patronage he founded Jōraku-ji monastery and, in 1253, the Kenchō-ji, one of the most important Zen monasteries of Kamakura (also → Gosan), of which he was also the first abbot.

Lan-ch'i was also active intermittently in the Kennin-ji in Kyōto, where he instructed the abdicated emperor Go-Saga in → buddha-dharma. Lan-ch'i was one of the outstanding Ch'an masters who contributed towards bringing the Ch'an tradition to Japan and adopted Japan as their homeland. He died in Kenchō-ji in Kamakura and received posthumously the honorific title daikaku zenji.

Lan-hsi Tao-lung Z → Lan-ch'i Tao-lung

Lankā H (Laṇkā), Skt.; early name of the island Ceylon (which today bears the name Sri Lanka); also, the former name of its capital.

In the *Rāmāyana* the mighty walls of Lankā are described. Lankā was said to have been built of gold by → Vishvakarma as a residence for → Kubera, but then to have been conquered by → Rāvana. In the *Bhāgavata-Purtāna*, the island is described as the tip of Mount → Meru, which the wind god broke off and threw into the sea.

Lankāvatāra-sūtra B Z (Laṇkāvatāra-sūtra), Skt., lit. "*Sūtra on the Descent to Sri Lanka*"; Mahāyāna sūtra that stresses the inner enlightenment that does away with all duality and is raised above all distinctions. This experience is possible through the realization of the → *tathāgata-garbha* (also → *busshō*) that is immanent in all beings. In this sūtra is also found the view that words are not necessary for the transmission of the teaching. Here the relationship to the doctrine of Zen is clear; thus this sūtra is one of the few traditional Mahāyāna texts, along with the → *Diamond Sūtra* and the → *Mahāyānashraddhotpāda-shāstra*, that exercised a major influence on this school. It is said to have been given by → Bodhidharma, the first Chinese patriarch of Zen, to his student → Hui-k'o. Also the teaching of gradual enlightenment (→ *zengo*) of → Shen-hsiu can be traced back to the *Lankāvatāra-sūtra*.

The sūtra consists of nine chapters of prose mixed with verse and one chapter in verse. It was translated for the first time into Chinese in the 5th century. The scene of this sūtra is an assembly in Sri Lanka at which the Buddha, at the invitation of a king, responds to various questions posed to him by the bodhisattva Mahāmati and proclaims a → Yogāchāra-related doctrine.

Lan Ts'ai-ho 🅃 → *pa-hsien*

Lao-chün 🅃 Chin., lit. "Master Lao"; also called T'ai-shang lao-chün ("Supreme Master Lao"); name of → Lao-tzu in his deified form. Together with → Yüan-shih t'ien-tsun and → T'ai-shang tao-chün, Lao-chün is one of the highest deities of religious Taoism (→ *tao-chiao*).

The deification of Lao-tzu began in the 2d century B.C.E. He already was a legendary figure at the time and was reported to have lived to an unusually ripe old age. During the Eastern or Late Han Dynasty he became one of the most important deities of Taoism. Some followers of the Tao considered him to be an emanation of the primordial chaos. It is said that he reincarnated many times as a human being in order to teach mankind. He is reputed to have been initiated into the secret practices of longevity characteristic of most later Taoist sects.

Although Lao-chün is generally acknowledged to have been a revealer of sacred writings and a teacher of mankind, not all Taoists look upon him as their highest deity. Often he is placed below Yüan-shih t'ien-tsun and some Taoists have gone so far as to question his divinity altogether, e.g., → Ko Hung, who believed him to be an extraordinary human being but not a god.

Lao-na Tsu-teng 🅉 (Jap., Rōnō Sotō); ca. 12th century Chinese Ch'an (Zen) master of the Yōgi lineage of Rinzai Zen (→ Yōgi school); a student and dharma successor (→ *hassu*) of → Yueh-an Shan-kuo (Jap., Gettan Zenka) and the master of → Yueh-lin Shih-kuan (Jap., Gatsurin Shikan).

Lao Tan 🅃 early Taoist designation for → Lao-tzu. *Tan* means "long ears," a symbol of longevity (→ Li Erh).

Lao-tzu 🅃 Chin., lit. "Old Master," also known as → Lao Tan or → Li Erh; traditionally considered to be the author of the → *Tao-te ching* and a contemporary of Confucius (6th century B.C.E. → K'ung-tzu). The biography of Lao-tzu in the *Historical Records* (*Shih-chi*), dating from the 2d/1st century B.C.E., mentions that he was born in Hu-hsien in the state of Ch'u (now Honan Province). His family name was Li, his first name Erh, and his majority name Tan. Most philosophical texts refer to him as either Lao-tzu or Lao Tan.

Lao-tzu riding a water buffalo. (19th-century wood carving)

According to the *Shih-chi* Lao-tzu was keeper of archives at the court of the king of Chou when he first met Confucius. This encounter has frequently been described but cannot be considered historical. Disputes at the royal court prompted Lao-tzu to resign from his post. He traveled west and at the mountain pass of Hsien-ku met → Yin Hsi, the Guardian of the Pass, at whose request he wrote the *Tao-te ching,* consisting of five thousand pictograms. After that his traces vanish.

Although tradition considered Lao-tzu to be the author of the *Tao-te ching,* scholars have established that this work cannot have been written before the 4th or 3d century B.C.E. and thus did not originate with Lao-tzu.

The author of the *Shih-chi* tells us that "Lao-tzu lived in accordance with the Tao and the *te.* He taught that one should live anonymously and in obscurity" (trans. from Kaltenmark, *Lao-tzu und der Taoismus;* see Kaltenmark 1969). His simple view of life also is reflected in a dialogue between him and Confucius: "When Confucius went to the land of Chou, he questioned Lao-tzu about the observance of the rites (→ *li*). Lao-tzu replied, 'The bones of those of whom you speak have long since turned to dust; only their words have been preserved for us. In any case, if time and fortune favor a person, he will travel to court in a carriage. If they do not favor him, he will roam about in unpretentious attire. I have heard it said that a good merchant will conceal his wealth and act as if he were poor. A noble person with sufficient inner virtue may give the appearance of a fool. Therefore, give up your high-handed manner, your desires, your vanity, and your zeal—for they are of no use to you.' Confucius then withdrew and said to his pupils, 'I know that birds can fly, that fish can swim, and that quadrupeds can roam about on the earth. Roaming animals may be caught in a pit or cage, fish with a net or rod, and birds can be shot down with an arrow. The dragon however cannot be caught by such cleverness. It wings towards Heaven on wind and clouds. Today I have seen Lao-tzu. He is like a dragon!" (trans. from Kaltenmark, *Lao-tzu und der Taoismus;* see Kaltenmark 1969).

Religious Taoism (→ *tao-chiao*) has admitted Lao-tzu to the Taoist pantheon. He is venerated as either → T'ai-shang lao-chün, Tao-te t'ien-tsun (Celestial Noble of the Tao and Te), or Lao-chün and is considered to be the founder of religious Taoism. He is, moreover, the subject of numerous legends. His disappearance after traveling west is explained by his having allegedly traveled to India, where he met the Buddha, who became his pupil—a claim Taoists are wont to make in their disputes with Buddhists (→ *Hua-hu ching*).

Laughing Buddha **B** **Z** (Chin. Mi-lo-fo); Chinese style of depicting the buddha → Maitreya, which originated in the 10th century. The image of the Laughing Buddha is to be found in the hall of the four → celestial kings in Chinese monasteries. He is usually shown sitting with the right leg partly raised (the characteristic sitting posture for Maitreya), with a fat naked belly, wrinkled forehead, and a broad smile. Usually he is surrounded by a group of children. According to tradition, this figure is the monk Pu-tai, who is considered an incarnation of the future Buddha Maitreya.

Laughing Buddha, standing form (wooden statuette)

Several Chinese ideals are embodied in this figure. The fat belly symbolizes wealth; his smile and his relaxed sitting posture indicate his equanimity and contentment with himself and the world. The children around him show his great love of children, one of the principal Chinese virtues.

Laya **H** Skt.; dissolution, melting, disappearance; the merging of the individual soul in the Absolute; union with God.

Laya-Samādhi **H** Skt., from *laya*: "merging," i.e., with the supreme consciousness; also called → *turīya* ("the fourth").

Laya-Yoga **H** Skt.; the path of union with God through intense worship and veneration, which lead to the awakening of the → *kundalinī.*

Lei-kung **T** Chin., lit. "Thunder Duke"; god of thunder. In the Taoist pantheon Lei-kung is an official in the Ministry of Thunder, which forms part of the celestial administration.

Lei-kung is portrayed with the beak, wings, and claws of an eagle owl. His body has the shape of a human and is blue. He wears a loin cloth and carries a drum, which he beats with a hammer to produce thunder. His image can be found in many Taoist temples.

Li B Chin., roughly "principle, the absolute, cosmic order," → Chih-tun, → Hua-yen school

Li T Chin., roughly rites, customs, morality; central concept of Confucianism (also → K'ung-tzu); the rules governing interhuman relations as well as ceremonies and how to act in a given situation. *Li* also serves as a means of expressing man's inherent benevolence (→ *jen*). It is the right expression of the right view. The concept of *li* is extensively discussed in a Confucianist classic known as *Li-chi* (see Chai & Chai 1965; Legge 1964).

In the *Analects* (*Lun-yü*) of Confucius we read (8.2), "Deference that lacks form [*li*] becomes servility, caution without form becomes timidity, courage without form becomes rebelliousness, honesty without form becomes rudeness."

To apply these rules correctly and distinguish between that which is proper and that which is not requires wisdom (*chih*), i.e., the ability to discriminate without confusion. → Meng-tzu (also transcribed as *Mencius*), a famous Confucianist of the 4th century B.C.E., writes concerning this wisdom, "When it is a question of whether or not to accept a gift or favor, it is less selfish not to accept. If there is doubt as to whether or not one should make a present, it is more considerate not to make one. If it is a question of whether or not to die, it is more courageous not to die" (trans. from Wilhelm 1982).

In pre-Confucianist China *li* mainly governed the performance of religious rituals or ceremonies connected with the veneration of ancestors. Because of the tremendous importance of these rituals in the political life of the country, *li* gradually came to be applied to the notion of correct behavior in general, instead of remaining confined to the proper performance of such rituals.

Liang-chieh Z → Tung-shan Liang-chieh

Liang-i T Chin., two forms or basic energies, a concept in the *Book of Change(s)* (→ *I-ching*). The two basic energies referred to are the yin and yang (→ yin-yang). According to one commentary—*Hsi-tz'u* (11.5)—there is in the *Changes* the supreme ultimate (→ *t'ai-chi*), which produces the two basic energies. The basic energies in turn give rise to the four images (→ *ssu-hsiang*) and these in turn to the eight trigrams (→ *pa-kua*).

The same idea is expressed in Chapter 42 of the → *Tao-te ching:* "The Tao begot one. One begot two. Two begot three. And three begot the ten thousand things" (Feng & English 1972).

Li-chiao shih-wu-lun T Chin., → *ch'üan-chen tao*

Lieh-tzu T Taoist philosopher of the Warring States Period and the alleged author of a work named after him but also known as the *Ch'ung-hsü chen-ching* (roughly, "True Book of the Expanding Emptiness"). Scholars have however established that this is a much later work, dating from the Chin Dynasty. Lieh-tzu was fond of transmitting his ideas and thoughts by reinterpreting ancient folk tales and myths. A characteristic feature of his view of life was that nature and life were mechanical processes, not admitting of free will. To further illustrate his ideas he made reference to the basic themes of Confucius (→ K'ung-tzu) as well as the → *Tao-te ching* and the → *I-ching.* Chapter 7 of the *Lieh-tzu* is devoted to the teachings of → Yang Chu. (An English version of Lieh-tzu's work has been published in Giles 1912. See also Wilhelm 1981b.)

The *Lieh-tzu* contains the earliest known reference to the isles of the immortals (→ P'eng-lai, → Fang-chang, →Ying-chou), the abode of the → *hsien.* During the later period of religious Taoism (→ *tao-chiao*), these descriptions led to numerous expeditions being dispatched, although there can be little doubt that Lieh-tzu meant them to be understood allegorically, i.e., referring to soul journeys.

Little is known about Lieh-tzu's life. He lived for forty years in one place and remained relatively unknown. He questioned Kuan-yin-tzu (→ Yin Hsi) concerning the Tao and had several other teachers. After nine years of Taoist practices he was able to rise on the wind. In Chapter 2 of the work accredited to him Lieh-tzu describes his state of mind after becoming one with the Tao: "After nine years of study I can set my mind completely free, let my words come forth completely unbound as I speak. I do not know whether right or wrong, gain and loss, are mine or others. I am not aware that the old Master Shang-tzu is my teacher and that Pai-kao is my friend. My self, both within and without, has been transformed. Everything about me is identified. My eye becomes my ear, my ear becomes my nose, my nose my mouth. My mind is highly integrated and my body dissolves. My bone and my flesh melt away. I cannot tell by what my body is supported or what my feet walk upon. I am blowing away, east and west, as a dry leaf torn from a tree. I cannot even make out whether the wind is riding on me or I am riding on the wind" (Chang Chung-yuan 1963, p. 87).

Lien-ch'i T Chin., lit. "melting the breath"; Taoist breathing exercise, in which the breath is allowed to flow unimpeded through the whole of the body instead of being directed along certain channels (→ *hsing-ch'i*). The practice of *lien-ch'i* is thought to be helpful in curing illnesses, acquiring supernatural abilities, and attaining immortality.

To practice *lien-ch'i* the adept withdraws to a quiet room, discards all restrictive clothing and lies down on a firm support, legs and arms extended. He harmonizes the breath (→ *t'iao-ch'i*) and swallows it (→ *yen-ch'i*), endeavoring to hold it for as long as possible (→ *pi-ch'i*). At the same time he strives to eliminate all thoughts and to calm the mind. The breath is then allowed to roam freely throughout the body without any intervention on the part of the practitioner. When he can no longer hold his breath, he opens his mouth and permits the breath to escape slowly.

The exercise is best performed after practicing → *fu-ch'i* and should be repeated ten times; a well-trained practitioner is capable of repeating it fifty times or more. If *lien-ch'i* is properly performed the breath is felt throughout the body; blockages are loosened and dissolved and the pores opened. The best indication for the effectiveness of the practice is perspiration. Because of its strong effect, *lien-ch'i* should be practiced at intervals of five to ten days.

Lien-tan ■ Chin., lit. "melting the cinnabar"; a method of Taoist alchemy for attaining immortality (→ *ch'ang-sheng pu-ssu*).

Originally *lien-tan* referred to a procedure in which various substances such as gold, cinnabar, mercury, and lead were melted over a trivet with the aim of producing the golden elixir (→ *chin-tan*). It was believed that whoever ingested this elixir would become immortal. Later this form of *lien-tan* came to be considered an outer elixir (→ *wai-tan*) practice and was gradually replaced by an inner elixir (→ *nei-tan*) practice, in which the adept fuses the life energy (→ *ch'i*), the semen (→ *ching*), and the mind (→ *shen*) within his body, thereby producing the sacred embryo (→ *sheng-t'ai*), the symbol of spiritual immortality.

Li Erh ■ according to Chinese historical sources the true name of → Lao-tzu, ascribed to him by the historian Ssu-ma Ch'ien (2d–1st century B.C.E.) on the basis of the ancestral tree of a family from Shantung by the name of Li, which was attached to an early biography of Lao-tzu.

Although this assertion cannot be proven historically, the family name Li, in Chinese tradition, became so closely linked with Lao-tzu that the later emperors of the T'ang Dynasty bearing that name looked upon Lao-tzu as their original ancestor.

Li Hsüan ■ → *pa-hsien*

Līlā ■ Skt., lit. "play"; the divine play in the manifest world. The creation is described by the → Vaishnavas as God's *līlā*. *Līlā* is the relative state, in contrast to → *nitya*, the Absolute.

Līlāmāyā ■ Skt., the play (→ *līlā*) of "deception" of the manifest world (→ *māyā*); Krishna employs *līlāmāyā* to draw all beings to him by means of his love and so to lead them to liberation.

Lin-chi I-hsüan ■ (Jap., Rinzai Gigen), d. 866/67; Chinese Ch'an (Zen) master; a student and dharma successor (→ *hassu*) of the great master → Huang-po Hsi-yun (Jap., Ōbaku Kiun) and the master of Hsing-hua Ts'ung-chiang (Jap., Kōke Zonshō) and Pao-chou Yen-chao (Jap., Hōju Enshō). At the time of the great persecution of Buddhists from 842 to 845, he founded the school named after him, the Lin-chi school (Jap., Rinzai school) of Ch'an (Zen). During the next centuries, this was to be not only the most influential school of Ch'an but also the most vital school of Buddhism in China. With the → Sōtō school, it is one of the two schools of Zen still active in Japan. In the tradition of → Ma-tsu Tao-i (Jap., Baso Dōitsu), his "grandfather in Zen," Lin-chi made use of such supportive means as the sudden shout *ho!* (Jap., *katsu*!) and unexpected blows of the stick (*shippei*, → *kyosaku*) as well as of the flywhisk (→ *hossu*). Of these he was best-known for his use of the shout (regarding his classification of the shout into four types, → *katsu!* and → *bōkatsu*!).

With Lin-chi's style of Zen training, which represents in many regards a synthesis of the methods of his predecessors in dharma, the development that received its decisive impetus from → Hui-neng, the sixth patriarch, came for all practical purposes to completion. This is the development that from the Chinese form of → Dhyāna Buddhism produced the unmistakably distinct school of Ch'an (→ Zen), contrasting sharply with the orthodox Buddhist schools. The single new element in methodology that entered Zen after Lin-chi was the → kōan (also → *kanna* Zen, → Yun-men Wen-yen, → Ta-hui Tsung-kao), and it is particularly the Rinzai school that preserved all the traditional elements of training.

We encounter Lin-chi, who had twenty-one dharma successors, in examples 20 and 32 of the → *Pi-yen-lu*. His sayings and teachings have been preserved in the *Lin-chi-lu* (Jap., *Rinzai-roku*), "*Record [of the words] of Lin-chi*" (English translation: Irmgard Schloegl, *The Record of Rinzai* [London 1975].)

In example 32 of the *Pi-yen-lu*, a (for Lin-chi) typical → *mondō*, we find

"The head monk Ting asked Lin-chi,"What is the great meaning of Buddha's dharma?"

Lin-chi came down from his seat, grabbed him, hit him with his hand, and pushed him away. Ting stood there stunned. The monk next to him said, "Head Monk Ting, why don't you prostrate?" Ting, as he prostrated, experienced profound enlightenment.

Lin-chi came from Nan-hua in what is now the province of Shantung. He entered a Buddhist monastery as a boy and devoted himself to study of the → Vinaya school and the sūtras. In his early twenties, however, he began to feel an urgent need to grasp the deep meaning of the scriptures through his own experience. He set out on the easily two thousand- kilometer-long pilgrimage to the south of China in order to seek instruction from a master of the → Southern school of Ch'an. Eventually he arrived at the monastery of Huang-po, where for about three years he lived as a monk among many others and visited the public dharma discourses of Huang-po. → Mu-chou Ch'en-tsun-nu (Jap., Bokushū Chinsonshuku), who was then acting as the head monk in Huang-po's monastery, recognized the potential of young Lin-chi and advised him to try to seek out Huang-po for → *dokusan*. The experiences that Lin-chi then had, which eventually led to his enlightenment are reported in Master Yuan-wu's introduction to example 11 of the *Pi-yen-lu*.

After his enlightenment Lin-chi trained further under Huang-po. Later he returned to the north, where he was invited to settle at Lin-chi monastery, the name of which later was applied to him. Here he soon gathered monks and lay people around him, whom he led on the way of Zen. Little is known of Lin-chi's dharma successors, which may well be due to the political and social chaos in northern China at the end of the T'ang period and in the Five-Dynasty period, and may also be an aftermath of the above-mentioned repression of Buddhism.

The great masters of Ch'an and Zen have always attempted to cover their traces, and in these uneasy times it may have seemed more than ever appropriate to the dharma successors of Lin-chi not to be publicly known. Some of them, e.g., the Recluse of T'ung-feng Mountain (encountered in example 85 of the *Pi-yen-lu*, lived as hermits and had few or no students. Since the framework of formal monastic and clerical organization was never essential for the Zen transmission "from heart-mind to heart-mind" (→ *inshin-denshin*), the Zen tradition survived the time of repression better than any of the other Buddhist schools in China. It continued as an undercurrent and resurfaced powerfully after a few generations, becoming in the Sung period the predominant religious tradition. The Rinzai school, which assimilated all the still-living lineages of Zen besides that of Sōtō Zen, also gradually declined in China after the 12th century, but before it did, it was brought to Japan, where it continues up to the present day.

Lin-chi-tsung 🅩 Chin. → Rinzai school

Linga 🅗 (liṇga), or Lingam, Skt.; usually a stone pillar in the form of a phallus, in which symbolic form → Shiva is generally worshiped. Still unknown in the Vedas, it is mentioned frequently in the *Mahābhar̄ata*, where it is described as a simple stone pillar or a cone of any type of material. In the West this little-understood sign has been related purely to sexual symbolism. Yet much in religion appears to contradict reason, including the fact that Shiva, originally the god of destruction, is worshiped in the form of a symbol of generative force.

In the *Shiva-Purāna* and the *Nandi-Upa-Purāna*, Shiva states: "I am present everywhere, but especially in twelve forms at twelve holy places." These are the twelve great *lingas*: (1) Somanātha, "lord of the moon," in Gujarat; (2) Mallikārjuna, "the mountain of Shrī"; (3) Mahākālesvara in Ujjain; (4) Omkāra in Omkāra-Māndhāttā on the Narmadā; (5) Amareshvara, "god of gods," in Ujjain; (6) Vaidyanātha, "lord of physicians," in Deogarh, Bengal; (7) Rāmeshvara, "lord of Rāma," on the southernmost tip of India. This *linga* is said to have been erected by Rāma himself. The temple is well preserved and is one of the largest and best known in all of India; (8) Bhīmashankara in Dracharam; (9) Vishveshvara, or Vishvanātha, "lord of the universe," in Benares, also known as Jyotir-Linga (Light Linga); (10) Tryambaka, "the three-eyed one," on the banks of the Gomati; (11) Gautamesha, "lord of Gautama"; (12) Kedārnātha, high in the Himalayas, where Shiva is worshiped in the form of a block of stone.

Linga-Purāna 🅗 (Liṇga-Purāṇa), Skt.; this Purāna, comprising 11,000 stanzas, is said to have received the name *linga* from Brahamā himself. The text has little to do with the symbol of the phallus, but is entirely spiritual and mystical in nature. As Maheshvara, "the great god," Shiva explains the four goals of life: *artha* (wealth), *kāma* (pleasure), *dharma* (duty), and *moksha* (liberation).

Linga-Sharīra 🅗 Skt. → *sūkshma-sharīra*

Lingāyat 🅗 (Liṇgāyat), or Vīrashaiva, Skt.; the name of a South Indian sect of Shiva-worshipers. The sect is unorthodox (i.e., its members do not recognize the authority of the Vedas). Shiva is worshiped through the symbol of the → *linga* as the manifest omnipotence of the divine. The Lingāyat scriptures are collected in the *Shūnyasampādana*, a work on the philosophy of *shūnya*, the "void" (i.e., of all distinctions, a reference to the Absolute), and *sampādana*, realization or attainment of enlightenment. The sect believes that only mystics can achieve this goal.

The Lingāyat sect flourished in South India in the

twelfth century but thereafter declined in importance, as its rejection of the Vedas and of the brahmans as the ruling priestly caste resulted in its not being included in the system of → Vedānta. Its members view the *linga* as the sole sacred symbol and hence are opposed to pilgrimages, sacrificial rites, and image worship. They accept the monism of Vedanta as well as its theory of → *māyā* as cosmic illusion. Shiva is revered as the eternal principle that is free from all qualities and identical with the supreme Self (→ *paramātman*). Lingāyats seek the company of holy men but possess no temples, and their priests do not perform → *pūjā*. Their initiation ceremony features the symbol of the *linga* rather than the sacred thread of the brahmans.

Ling-chih ◼ Chin., lit. "magic herb"; Taoist plant of immortality. The *ling-chih* is portrayed variously as grass, or as a trufflelike mushroom. It grows on the isles of the immortals (→ P'eng-lai, → Ying-chou, → Fang-chang). Like many others, Ch'in Shih-huang-ti, the first historical emperor of China, dispatched expeditions to gain possession of this magic herb, the ingestion of which is said to confer immortality for at least five hundred years.

In Taoist art the *ling-chih* symbolizes the female yin energy (→ yin-yang). Often, in popular illustrations, a stag or crane is shown holding the *ling-chih* in his mouth or beak—a twofold symbol of immortality.

Ling-pao ching ◼ Chin., lit. *"Scriptures of the Magic Jewel";* a body of writings forming the doctrinal basis of the School of the Magic Jewel (→ *ling-pao p'ai*), an independent stream of religious Taoism (→ *tao-chiao*). The *Ling-pao ching* describes the hierarchy of the Taoist pantheon, the rites by which believers may summon the various deities, and also contains instructions on how to conduct funeral ceremonies, etc. The oldest sections of the *Ling-pao ching* date from the 3d century; those explaining the Taoist doctrine, from the 4th and 5th centuries. Because of a commentary by the Taoist scholar → Sung Wen-ming (ca. 550 C.E.) the *Ling-pao ching* became an authoritative text of religious Taoism.

According to Taoist tradition these writings came into being spontaneously at the beginning of the world and were in the form of golden signs written on small tiles of jade. Their meaning is communicated to the deities at the beginning of each aeon by the Celestial Venerable of the Primordial Beginning (→ Yüan-shih t'ien-tsun), who alone is capable of reading them. Some of these deities have passed the teachings on to certain human beings, which is how they are said to have come into the possession of → Chang Tao-ling.

Ling-pao p'ai ◼ Chin., lit. "School of the Magic Jewel"; a branch of religious Taoism (→ *tao-chiao*) that developed in the 4th/5th century C.E. and was based on the scriptures of the Magic Jewel (→ *Ling-pao ching*).

The School of the Magic Jewel reformed rites and practices to bring them into line with its own teaching, which was strongly influenced by Buddhism. It teaches that a person's salvation (or liberation) largely depends on the help that person is able to obtain from the venerable celestial deities (→ *t'ien-tsun*). This constitutes a simplification of the original Taoist doctrine. The deities are projected out from within the body (→ Inner Deity Hygiene School) and rule the whole universe. The Magic Jewel School owed its rapid spread to this simplification. The most important practices of the school were so-called fasting ceremonies (→ *chai*).

Li Shao-chün ◼ ?–133 B.C.E.; Taoist sorcerer (→ *fang-shih*) who declared the aim of the Taoist path to be the attainment of immortality by alchemical methods. He himself claimed to be immortal and to have visited the isles of the immortals (→ P'eng-lai, → Ying-chou, → Fang-chang). He also knew prescriptions for prolonging life, performed hygiene exercises, and abstained from eating grain (→ *pi-ku*). In addition, he introduced the veneration of the deity of the hearth (→ Tsao-chün). He died of an illness. Taoist literature records his death as the first example of a separation from the corpse (→ *shih-chieh*).

In 133 B.C.E. Li Shao-chün persuaded the emperor Han Wu-ti to permit experiments, the aim of which consisted in transforming cinnabar into gold. These were the first recorded alchemical experiments in the history of mankind. The transformed cinnabar, however, was not ingested, as was the case later. Instead it was fashioned into crockery. Anyone eating from such crockery would enjoy a long life (but not immortality) and behold the immortals of the isles of P'eng-lai. Li promised the emperor immortality, if, upon beholding the → *hsien*, he were to perform certain sacrifices.

According to Li Shao-chün cinnabar could not be transformed into gold without the help of Tsao-chün, the hearth deity. These alchemical practices thus marked the beginning of the cult of the hearth deity, which continues to this day.

Li T'ieh-kuai ◼ → *pa-hsien*

Liu-chia ch'i-tsung ◼ Chin. → six houses and seven schools

Liu-fu ◼ Chin., lit. "six containers"; six bodily organs—stomach, gallbladder, small intestine, large intestine, bladder, and the alimentary and respiratory tracts (these two being classed as one)—of particular importance in Taoist breathing and hygiene exercises.

Liu Ling ■ → *chu-lin ch'i-hsien*

Liu Te-jen ■ → *chen-ta-tao chiao*

Liu T'ieh-mo ■ (Jap., Riū Tetsuma), ca. 9th century; a profoundly enlightened Buddhist nun; a student of → Kuei-shan Ling-yu (Jap., Isan Reiyū). Her family name was Liu, and she acquired the nickname T'ieh-mo, "iron millstone," because she was renowned in the Zen circles of her time for "grinding to bits" like an iron millstone anyone who confronted her in dharma battle (→ *hossen*). In example 24 of the → *Pi-yen-lu*, we see her in a *hossen* with her master, Kuei-shan.

The kōan goes as follows:

"Liu-T'ieh-mo came to Kuei-shan. Kuei-shan said, 'So old cow, you've come.' Tieh-mo said, 'Tomorrow will be the big festival on Mount T'ai; the abbot will go there?' Thereupon Kuei-shan relaxed his body and lay down. Immediately T'ieh-mo went out and departed."

Liu-tsu-ta-shih ■ (Jap., Rokuso Daishi); lit. "Sixth Patriarch, Great Master"; an honorific title by which Hui-neng, the sixth patriarch of Ch'an (Zen) in China, is referred to in many writings.

Liu-tsu-ta-shih fa-pao-t'an-ching ■ short title, *T'an-ching*, (Jap., *Rokuso daishi hōbōdan-gyō*, for short, *Dan-gyō*), lit. "*The Sutra of the Sixth Patriarch [spoken] from the High Seat of the Dharma Treasure,*" often known as the *Platform Sutra*; basic Zen writing in which the biography, discourses, and sayings of → Hui-neng are recorded. (An English translation by Charles Luk appeared in *Ch'an and Zen Teachings* (See Lu 1962); another English translation is *The Platform Sūtra* (Wing 1963).

Lobha ■ Skt. → *akushala*

Lohan ■ ■ Chin. (Skt., arhat; Jap., rakan); holy one, saint, the ideal of the → Hīnayāna. In the passage of Buddhism to China the conception of the → arhat underwent a particular development and became one of the most important elements in Chinese Buddhism, even of the Mahāyāna schools. Representations of the arhat in China are known since the 7th century, but they became popular only in the ninth or tenth centuries. The prime vehicle for the veneration of arhats was the Ch'an (→ Zen) school, at that time the most important Buddhist school in China. Because of its emphasis on the human side of things and its aversion to any worship of deities, it saw in these saints, who had attained liberation through their own effort, beings corresponding to the mind of Ch'an (Zen).

Sitting Lohan (ceramic, 110 cm, 12th century)

Magical abilities (→ *abhijñā*) were attributed to the *lohans* as the fruit of their wisdom. In the course of the development of their iconography they took on the appearance of demonic sorcerers or other weird figures and were elevated to a superhuman level. At the same time, however, they continued to be depicted also in a simple, human form. In Chinese and Japanese monasteries groups of 500 *lohan* images are found, arranged in special halls, and also groups, originally of sixteen, now mostly of eighteen, located left and right on the short walls of the main halls of the monasteries. Each individual *lohan* has unique features that are characteristic of him and that are highly expressive.

The depictions of 500 *lohans* derives from the canonical descriptions of the first → Buddhist council, at which 500 arhats were present. Also the council of Kashmir is said to have been attended by 500 arhats. Many legends developed concerning the 500 *lohans.* They are said to dwell in 500 caves near a lake in the K'un-lun Mountains and to have brought the Buddha to this place at the invitation of the dragon king. In various places in China one finds caves and halls of the 500 *lohans.* In every Chinese monastery one encounters the group of sixteen or eighteen *lohans.* According to legend, 800 years after the Buddha's death, the arhat Namdimitra proclaimed in Sri Lanka that the Buddha had confided the teaching to sixteen *lohans* in order to ensure its preservation. These *lohans* are considered immortal and dwell with their students in various regions of the world on sacred mountains where they preserve the teaching. Only when the time has come in which the → buddha-dharma is in its final decline will the sixteen *lohans* gather, place the relics of the Buddha in a → stūpa, and raise themselves up into the air and enter nirvāna, while the stūpa sinks to the bottom of the world.

In the 10th century the series of sixteen *lohans* was expanded to eighteen. They are each known by name. Among them, for example, are the Buddha's important disciples. However, some of them have been replaced by new figures, such as → Bodhidharma or even Marco Polo; thus the original group has changed. In any case their names are without significance—they are often named on the basis of their characteristic features: the *lohan* with the Buddha in his heart (a sign he will be reborn as a buddha), the *lohan* with the long eyebrows (sign of a long life), the *lohan* who is scratching his ear (indication of the divine ear, *abhijñā*), the *lohan* who tames the dragon (creative mind) or the tiger (sensuality), etc.

Lo-han Kuei-ch'en 🅩 (Jap., Rakan Keijin), also Ti-ts'ang (Jap., Jizō), 867/69–928; Chinese Ch'an (Zen) master; a student and dharma successor (→ *hassu*) of Hsuan-sha Shih-pei (Jap., Gensha Shibi) and the master of → Fa-yen Wen-i (Jap., Hōgen Bun'eki).

Lo-han Kuei-ch'en is known particularly for several → *mondō* with his principal student Fa-yen that have been handed down in the Zen texts. One of them is found as example 20 of the → *Ts'ung-jung-lu* (Jap., *Shōyō-roku*):

"Ti-ts'ang asked Fa-yen, 'Head monk, where are you going?'

"Fa-yen said, 'I'm rambling aimlessly around.'

"Ti-ts'ang said, 'What's the good of rambling around?'

"Fa-yen said, 'I don't know.'

"Ti-ts'ang said, 'Not knowing is closest.' "

Lo-han Tao-hsien 🅩 (Jap., Rakan Dōkan), 9th century; Chinese Ch'an (Zen) master; a student and dharma successor (→ *hassu*) of → Yen-t'ou Ch'uan-huo (Jap., Gantō Zenkatsu) and the master of → Ming-chao Te-chien (Jap., Meishō [Myōshō] Tokken).

Loka 🅗 Skt., lit. "world"; a term used in reference to the traditional division of the universe into various worlds, generally a threefold division (*triloka*) into heaven, earth, and hell (or the underworld). These are continually referred to as "the three worlds."

Another classification lists seven higher worlds: (1) *bhūr-loka*, the earth; (2) *bhuvar-loka*, the space between the earth and the sun, the region of the → *munis*, → *siddhis*, etc.; (3) *svar-loka*, the heaven of → Indra; (4) *mahar-loka*, the residence of → Bhrigu and other sages; (5) *jana-loka*, the home of → Brahamā's sons Sanaka, Sānanada, and Sanatkumāra; (6) *tapar-loka*, where the → Vairājas reside; (7) *satya-loka* or *brahmā-loka*, the realm of Brahmā; after attaining this last world, one is no longer reborn. Seven netherworlds, collectively known as → *pātāla*, correspond to these seven higher worlds.

The schools of → Sānkhya and → Vedānta mention eight *lokas*, including both higher and lower regions: (1) *brahmā-loka*, the world of supreme gods; (2) *pitri-loka*, the realm of the → *pitris*, → *rishis*, and → *prajāpatis*; (3) *soma-loka*, the region of the moon and the planets; (4) *indra-loka*, the region of lower divinities; (5) *gandharva-loka* the region of heavenly spirits; (6) *rākshasa-loka*, the realm of the → *rākshasas*; (7) *yaksha-loka*, the realm of the *yakshas*; (8) *pisācha-loka*, the realm of devils and demons.

Lokapāla 🅗 🅑 Skt., lit. "world-protector."

🅗 Guardian deities who rule over the eight cardinal and intermediate points of the world; → Indra, over the East, → Agni, over the Southeast, → Yama, over the South, → Sūrya, over the Southwest, → Varuna, over the West, → Vāyu, over the Northwest, → Kubera, over the North, → Soma, over the Northeast.

Each of these guardian deities protects his realm with the help of an elephant, also known as *lokapāla*. The eight elephants (listed in the same order as the regions given above) are Airāvana, Pundarīka, Vāmana, Kumuda, Añjana, Pushpadanta, Sārvabhauma, and Supratīka.

🅑 the protectors of the world-quarters of the four cardinal directions; protectors of the world and the Buddhist teaching. Images of the lokapālas are often placed as guardians at the gates of Buddhist monasteries.

Lokāyata 🅗 Skt.; the materialistic school of Hindu philosophy (→ Chārvāka).

Lokeshvara 🅑 (Lokeśvara), Skt., lit. "lord of the world"; name of a buddha and of → Avalokiteshvara.

In Cambodia Lokeshvara is considered the embodiment of the supreme principle of the world and as incarnated in the ruler.

Lokeshvararāja 🅑 (Lokeśvararāja), Skt., roughly "king of the world", buddha of a previous age before whom → Amitābha in one of his lives took forty eight vows to become a buddha.

Lokottara 🅑 Skt. (Pali, lokuttara), roughly "supramundane"; all that is connected with the path to liberation or that is directed toward the attainment of → nirvāna is regarded as supramundane. In particular *lokottara* is a designation for the individual stages of the "supramundane path" (→ *arya-mārga*), i.e., the path and fruit of steam-entry (→ *shrota-āpanna*), of once-returning (→ *sakridāgāmin*), never-returning (→ *anāgāmin*), and of arhatship (→ arhat, → nirvāna).

In the → Mahāyāna the Buddha is considered a supramundane being who is mentally and physically absolutely pure and possesses eternal life and limitless power.

Lokottaravādin [B] Skt. → Mahāsānghika, → Hīnayāna

Longchenpa [B] (kloṅ-chen-pa), 1308–64; a Tibetan master who held the honorific title of "omniscient." Master and scholar of the → Nyingmapa school. Longchenpa played a special role in the transmission of the → *dzogchen* teachings, having synthesized the traditions of— Padmasambhava and Vimalamitra into a coherent system. In his relatively short life he composed 270 works, of which the most important are known as the Seven Treasures. His works are distinguished by extraordinary profundity and great lucidity and are a shaping influence on the Nyingmapa tradition up to the present time.

At the age of eleven, Longchenpa received his first ordination. He spent the following years in intensive study. Besides the teachings of his own school, he studied also those of the → Sakyapa school and was a student of the third → *karmapa*, Rangjung Dorje (1284–1339). Two events determined his further spiritual development: After a vision of Padmasambhava and his consort → Yeshe Tsogyel, he entered into direct contact with the *dzogchen* transmission of the → *dākinīs* and wrote this experience down as a → *terma*. In the person of Master Kumārarāja (1266–1334), he had a further meeting with the *dzogchen* teachings, this time those of the tradition of Vimalamitra. After he had revised these, he combined both lines of transmission into a single system.

Although Longchenpa was the abbot of the Samye Monastery of central Tibet, he spent most of his life traveling or in retreat. He rebuilt or founded various monasteries, especially in Bhutan, where he was obliged to spend a decade in political exile. Longchenpa's teachings were reorganized by Jigme Lingpa (1730–98). In the resultant form they were finally transmitted to the teachers of the → Rime movement.

Lotus [H] [B] (Skt., padma); plant of the water lily family (*nelumbo nucifera*, also *nelumbium speciosum*).

[H] 1. a symbol for the various centers of consciousness (→ *chakra*) in the body; 2. the rounded lotus petal is regarded as a symbol of nonattachment. Just as the lotus floats on the water and yet remains dry, so should the spiritual aspirant live in the world without being affected by it, "in the world, but not of it"; 3. iconographically, the lotus is a symbol of beauty and sacredness; for this reason reference is often made to the "lotus eyes" and "lotus feet" of saints and deities. Brahmā is often represented sitting on a lotus blossom that emerges from the navel of Vishnu, who also is seated on a lotus.

[B] In Buddhism the lotus is a symbol of the true nature of beings, which remains unstained by the mud of the world of → samsāra and by ignorance (→ *avidyā*) and which is realized through enlightenment (→ *bodhi*). Often the lotus is also a symbol of the world with the stem as its axis. Iconographically, it is a form of the seat or → throne of the buddha. The lotus is also the identifying attribute of → Avalokiteshvara. In the → Pure Land school it is the symbol of the Buddha's doctrine.

Lotus school [B] → T'ien-t'ai school

Lotus Sūtra [B] [Z] (Skt. *Saddharmapuṇḍarīka-sūtra*, i.e., "Sūtra of the Lotus of the Good Dharma"); one of the most important sutras of Mahāyāna Buddhism, especially popular in China and Japan. The schools of → T'ien-t'ai (Jap., Tendai) and → Nichiren are based on its teaching; it is, however, recognized by all other Mahāyāna schools, since it contains the essential teachings of the Mahāyāna: the doctrines of the transcendental nature of the Buddha and of the possibility of universal liberation. It is considered in the Mahāyāna as that sūtra that contains the complete teachings of the Buddha, in contrast to the Hīnayāna sūtras, which contain it only partially. It is said to have been expounded by the Buddha at the end of his period of teaching. It was written down in about the year 200.

The *Lotus Sūtra* is a discourse of the Buddha on → Vulture Peak Mountain before an endlessly large throng of various kinds of sentient beings. In it the Buddha shows that there are many methods through which a being can attain → enlightenment (also → *bodhi*) but which have only temporary validity and in their nature are all one: the "vehicles" of the → *shrāvakas*, → *pratyekabuddhas*, and bodhisattvas are different from one another only insofar as they are adapted to the varying capabilities of beings. The Buddha taught these three vehicles (→ *triyāna*) as skillful means (→ *upāya*). In reality, however, there is only one vehicle, the buddha vehicle, which leads to enlightenment and includes both Hīnayāna and Mahāyāna.

This view is illustrated by the well-known simile of the burning house from which a father wants to save his playing children. Since they will not heed his call, he promises them, each according to his inclination, a wagon yoked with an antelope, a goat, or a buffalo if they will drop their game and leave the house. When, as a result of this trick, they have been rescued from the house, he makes them each a gift of a very valuable wagon drawn by a white buffalo.

The *Lotus Sūtra* also stresses the importance of faith (→ *shraddhā*) on the path to liberation, as a result of which the buddhas and bodhisattvas can offer their help. A separate chapter is devoted to the bodhisattva → Avalokiteshvara in which the notion of help from the bodhisattvas is particularly clearly expressed.

In the *Lotus Sūtra* the Buddha is not presented as a historical person, but rather as a manifestation of the *dharmakāya* (→ *trikāya*), which exists eternally. Every being participates in this transcendental nature of the Buddha (→ buddha-nature, → *busshō*) and can thus become a buddha, i.e., awaken to his true nature.

Lumbinī 🅱 one of the four sacred places of Buddhism (→ Sārnāth, → Bodh-gayā, → Kushinagara), which is believed to be the place of birth of the historical Buddha → Shākyamuni. Lumbinī was near the capital of the → Shākya kingdom, Kapilavastu, and lies in the territory of present-day Nepal.

In Lumbinī there is a stone column that King → Ashoka had erected there on the occasion of a pilgrimage in the year 249 B.C.E. The inscription reads, "Twenty years after his coronation King Devānapiya Piyadasi [i.e., Ashoka] came here and commemorated his veneration, because the Buddha, the sage of the Shākya clan, was born here. He had a stone relief and a stone column set up to show that here a venerable one was born. He exempts the village of Lumbinī from taxes and (reduces) its tribute in kind (from the usual quarter) to an eighth."

Lung 🆃 Chin., lit. "dragon." In Taoism, the dragon represents the yang principle (→ yin-yang) and is often portrayed surrounded by clouds or water (both symbols of yin).

Chinese mythology knows five types of dragon: celestial dragons, who guard the abodes of heavenly deities; dragon spirits, who rule over wind and rain but can also cause flooding; earth dragons, who cleanse the rivers and deepen the oceans; treasure-guarding dragons; and finally imperial dragons, who have five claws instead of the usual four.

Lung-gom 🅱 (rlung-gom), Tib., roughly "mastery of the energy currents"; a meditative practice in Tibetan Buddhism connected with control of the breath in yoga (*prānāyāma*) and mindfulness of the breathing process in early Buddhism (→ *satipatthāna*). As a practitioner in the practice of inner heat (→ *Nāro chödrug*) concentrates on the element of fire in the corresponding psychic center (chakra), so the element of air plays the most important role for the practitioner of *lung-gom*. In the terminology of the → Vajrayāna, air (Tib., *lung*) refers to specific energy currents that regulate bodily function. In the particular geographical conditions of Tibet, the mastery of the energy currents was used, among other things, to cover long stretches on foot effortlessly and in the shortest possible time.

Lung-hu 🆃 Chin., lit. "dragon [and] tiger"; symbols, respectively, for yang and yin (→ yin-yang) in Taoist alchemy (→ *nei-tan,* → *wai-tan*).

In the teachings of the Inner Alchemy it is said that the dragon arises from *li* (→ *k'an* and *li*), i.e., "out of the fire"; the tiger (yin) is associated with *k'an,* which is associated with water. For that reason the tiger is said to arise from the water. The fusion of *k'an* and *li* leads to the realization of → Tao.

The dragon's color is green; it is further associated with the East, the liver, wood, and spring. The tiger's colour is white, and it is associated with the West, the lungs, metal, and autumn.

Lung-hu-shan 🆃 Chin., lit. "Dragon [and] Tiger Mountain"; famous Taoist mountain (situated in Chiang-shi Province), which from the 3d century C.E. until 1949 was the abode of the celestial masters (→ *t'ien-shih*), the descendants of → Chang Tao-ling and the subsequent patriarchs of Five-Pecks-of-Rice Taoism (→ *wu-tou-mi tao,* → *tao-chiao*).

Lung-men 🅱 Chin., lit. "Dragon Gate"; Buddhist grottoes thirteen kilometers south of Lo-yang in the Chinese province of Honan. The grottoes of Lung-men, → Yun-kang, and → Tun-huang, are the three greatest Buddhist sacred grottoes of China.

Work on the Lung-men caves began in 494, after the transfer of the capital to Lo-yang, and lasted until the time of the Sung Dynasty. There are over 21 hundred caves, 750 niches, over forty chiseled pagodas, and approximately 100 thousand statues. In order of the number of representations, these statues depict → Amitābha, → Avalokiteshvara, → Shākyamuni, → Maitreya, → Ti-tsang, and other buddhas and bodhisattvas. Most of the representations of Amitābha are from the time of the T'ang Dynasty, when the Amitābha cult of the → Pure Land school reached its peak.

The most important are the Ku-yang and Pin-yang grottoes. In the former, which was begun in 495 and finished in 575, there are sculpted images of Shākyamuni and Maitreya. The style of representing Maitreya is based on the *Vimilakīrtinirdesha-sūtra.* Reliefs show scenes from everyday life.

The Pin-yang caves, the work on which was supported by the imperial family, depicts in its frescoes scenes of members of the imperial house paying obeisance to the Buddha, who is accompanied by two bodhisattvas as well as by → Ānanda and → Mahākāshyapa. The sculptures in these caves are based primarily on → *Jātaka* tales. As described in an inscription, the work on the middle of the three Pin-yang caves was accomplished between 500 and 523 by 802, 366 craftsmen.

Lung-men School 🅃 → *ch'uan-chen tao*

Lung-t'an Ch'ung-hsin 🅉 (Jap., Ryūtan [Ryōtan] Sōshin), 9th century; Chinese Ch'an (Zen) master; a student and dharma successor (→ *hassu*) of → T'ien-huang Tao-wu (Jap., Tennō Dōgo) and the master of → Te-shan Hsuan-chien (Jap., Tokusan Senkan). Little is known of Lung-t'an other than that as a youth he often brought offerings of rice cakes to Master Tao-wu of T'ien-huang Monastery and eventually became his student. In example 28 of the → *Wu-men-kuan* we encounter Lung-t'an in a → *mondō* with his principal student Te-shan (for this *mondō*, → Te-shan Hsuan-chien).

Lung-wang 🅃 Chin., lit. "dragon king[s]"; mythological figures who, in the Taoist view, are ruled by the Celestial Venerable of the Primordial Beginning (→ Yüan-shih t'ien-tsun), to whom they ascend once a year in order to submit their reports. The *lung-wang* have jurisdiction over rain and funerals; during a drought they are supplicated to produce rain. If mistakes or omissions occur at a funeral ceremony, which might result in misfortunes or disaster for descendants of the person that has died, the dragon kings are similarly implored to help. Taoism distinguishes between various types of *lung-wang:* the celestial dragon kings, the dragon kings of the four oceans, who live in splendid palaces at the bottom of the sea, and the *lung-wang* of the five cardinal points.

Lung-ya Chü-tun 🅉 (Jap., Ryūge Koton), 834/35–920/23; Chinese Ch'an (Zen) master; a student and dharma successor (→ *hassu*) of → Tung-shan Liang-chieh (Jap., Tōzan Ryōkai). Lung-ya had five dharma successors; we meet him in example 20 of the → *Pi-yen-lu.*

Lung-ya entered a monastery in his home city of Kiangsi as a boy. Later he went on a pilgrimage and sought out some of the leading Ch'an masters of his time, among them → Ts'ui-wei Wu-hsueh (Jap., Suibi Mugaku) and → Te-shan Hsuan-chien (Jap., Tokusan Senkan). At last he came to Master Tung-shan and became his student. One day he asked Tung-shan, "What is the meaning of the patriarch's coming out of the west [→ *seirai-no-i*]?"

Tung-shan replied, "I'll tell you when Tung-shan Creek runs uphill."

At these words Lung-ya experienced enlightenment.

Exulted by this experience, he set out wandering again in order to confront other Ch'an masters in → *hossen* with this same question and through these encounters to deepen his realization further. During this period of wandering he came once again to Master Ts'ui-wei and also to → Lin-chi I-hsuan (Jap., Rinzai Gigen); example 20 of the *Pi-yen-lu* gives an account of both these meetings. (For this kōan, → *zemban.*) After eight years of wandering, at the request of the military governor of Hu-nan, he assumed the leadership of a monastery on Mount Lung-ya (from which his name comes) south of Lake Tung-t'ing, where soon not less than 500 students gathered about him.

Lü Pu-wei 🅃 → *Lü-shih ch'un-ch'iu*

Lu-shan 🅑 Chin., lit. "Mount Lu"; center of Buddhism in the present-day province of Kiangsi that flourished in the period after 380. Among the renowned monks who lived on Lu-shan were → Hui-yüan and → Tao-sheng. On Lu-shan Hui-yüan founded the White Lotus Society and provided the intial impetus for the → Amitābha cult.

The first monastery on Lu-shan is said to have been built in 367; before this time the mountain was a refuge for Taoist hermits. A renowned healer is said to have lived there, who at the age of 300 became one of the immortals.

Another legend tells that in his travels → An-shih-kao converted on Lu-shan a giant serpent who was the reincarnation of a friend from a previous life and was worshiped on the mountain as a god.

Lü-shih ch'un-ch'iu 🅃 Chin., lit. *"Spring and Autumn of Master Lü";* Philosophical work dating from the 3d century B.C.E. and compiled by Lü Pu-wei (?–235 B.C.E.), a rich merchant of the Warring States Period, who is said to have assembled as many as 10,000 scholars of the various philosophical schools at his court and recorded their teachings in his annals. The *Lü-shih ch'un-ch'iu* contains Taoist, Confucianist, Legalist, and Mohist ideas. (See Wilhelm 1979.)

Lü-tsung 🅑 Chin., roughly "school of discipline"; school of Chinese Buddhism originated by Tao-hsüan (596–667). The basis of this school is the disciplinary code of the → Dharmaguptakas, contained in the *Vinaya in Four Parts* (Chin., *Ssu-fen-lü*).

The emphasis of the practice of this school is on strict observance of the Vinaya rules, which, according to the *Dharmaguptaka-vinaya*, consists of 250 rules for monks and 348 for nuns. Although this Vinaya is of Hīnayāna origin, it was also regarded as authoritative by the Mahāyāna schools of China. The teachings of this school were brought to Japan in 745 by → Chien-chen (→ Ritsu school).

In founding this school Tao-hsüan wished to make clear that in Buddhism the observance of the monastic rules is an essential part of practice. He also stressed the importance of the correct performance of → ordination and in his monastery he firmly established the formalities for the consecration of a monk.

Lü Tung-pin 🅣 → *pa-hsien*

M

Mādhava 🅗 Skt., lit. "spring; the delightful one"; 1. a name for → Vishnu as well as for → Krishna. Devotees of Vishnu are also called Mādhavas; 2. → Madhva.

Madhu 🅗 Skt.; in the mythology of the → Purānas the personification of darkness, one of the two primal forces that emerged from the primal chaos as "firstborn"; the personification of the other primal force, that of light, was → Brahmā. These two divinities were among the most important → *devas* of the Vedic period. They fought each other constantly, but neither was able to destroy the other. In later Hindu cosmology Madhu was slain by Vishnu in his manifestation as Krishna, and Brahmā became one element in the Hindu trinity (→ *trimūrti*).

Madhura-Bhāva 🅗 Skt.; one of the five attitudes that may be assumed by a → *bhakta* toward his chosen deity (→ *ishta-deva*), that of a wife or beloved toward her husband or lover. (See also → *bhāva*.)

Madhu-Vidyā 🅗 Skt., lit. *madhu*: "honey, *soma*," *vidya*: "knowledge"; knowledge, attained with the aid of *soma* (the "secret honey"), concerning the divine play (→ *līlā*) that arises through the creative power (→ *shakti*) or *brahman*; also knowledge of the joy (also referred to as the "secret honey") in knowing this play, which despite all variations maintains its unity, harmony, and balance, since *brahman* is its foundation.

Madhva 🅗, also known as Madhvāchārya, Mādhva, and Ānandatīrtha, 1199-1278; chief representative of the dualist philosophy of → Dvaita-Vedānta, the third of the three major schools of Vedantic thought. He postulated five great distinctions: (1) between God and the individual soul; (2) between God and matter; (3) between the individual soul and matter; (4) among individual souls; (5) among the individual elements of matter. For Madhva, three separate substances have existed eternally: God, the soul, and the world. Although all three are real and eternal, the latter two are subordinate to and dependent upon God. The independent reality (→ *brahman*) is the absolute creator of the universe (identified by Madva with Vishnu), who manifests himself in various forms and from time to time is incarnated as an → *avatāra*.

Madhva was born in a vilage near Udipi, South India; he came to know the Vedas while still young and became a → *sannyāsin* early on. After spending several years in prayer and meditation as well as in study and discussion, he began to teach and sermonize. He founded a temple devoted to Krishna in Udipi, where he continued to work until his death. His chief works are commentaries on the → *Vedānta-Sūtra*, the → *Bhagavad-Gītā*, several → Upanishads, and especially the → *Bhāgavata-Purāna*. His *Anuvyākhyāna* contains a defense of his commentary on the *Vedānta-Sūtra*.

Mādhyamaka 🅑 Skt.; the teaching of the → Middle Way, advocated by the → Mādhyamikas.

Mādhyamaka-kārikā 🅱 Skt. → Nāgārjuna

Mādhyamika 🅱 Skt., representative of the school of the Middle Way (from *madhyama*, "the middle"); a school of Mahāyāna Buddhism founded by → Nāgārjuna and → Āryadeva, which attained great importance in India, Tibet, China, and Japan (→ San-lun school, → Sanron school). Besides the founders, the most important representatives of the school were Buddhapālita (5th century), → Bhāvaviveka (6th century), Chandrakīrti, Shāntirakshita, and Kamalashīla (8th century). The last three exercised a particularly great influence on the development of *mādhyamaka* in Tibet.

The name of the school refers to the Middle Way, which describes the position taken by the school in relation to the existence or nonexistence of things. With the help of eight negations (→ Nāgārjuna), any affirmation about the nature of things is rejected as inaccurate and thus the illusionary character and the relativity of all appearances is shown. Since all phenomena arise in dependence upon conditions (→ *pratītya-samutpāda*), they have no being of their own and are empty of a permanent self (→ *svabhāva*).

Emptiness (→ *shūnyatā*) has a twofold character in the Mādhyamika school. On the one hand it is emptiness of a self (also "egolessness"); on the other hand it means liberation, because emptiness is identical with the absolute. To realize emptiness means to attain liberation. This is accomplished by purifying the mind of affirmation and negation. For the Mādhyamikas, *shūnyatā* is the ultimate principle; it is often identified with *dharmakāya* (→ *trikāya*). Because of its teaching concerning the radical emptiness of all things, the Mādhyamika school is also called Shūnyatāvāda (Teaching of Emptiness).

The absolute can, however, only be realized by working through "relative truth" in order to reach the "absolute" or "supreme truth". Here we encounter the notion of "the two truths" peculiar to this school. The relative, "veiled" truth (→ *samvriti-satya*) is the reality of everyday life. From its relative point of view, the conventional outlook is valid and appearances are real. This view is characterized by duality. The truth in the highest sense (→ *paramārtha-satya*) is devoid of manifoldness; opposites have no meaning in it. "Realities" grasped by the intellect are not ultimately real, but they have relative value. Thus emptiness of all things does not mean devaluation of human experience. This is shown by the lifestyle of a Mādhyamika: externally he seems to accept the world with its suffering as real; he follows the moral precepts (→ *shīla*) and exerts himself to support other beings on the way of liberation. On the other hand, however, he knows that such action is fundamentally only of relative value.

Further development of this basic line of thought, which is found in the work of Nāgārjuna, came about through advances in the field of logic and under the influence of the second great current of the Indian Mahāyāna, the → Yogāchāra. Perfecting of logical method obliged the Mādhyamikas to provide valid proofs of their teaching. The Yogāchāras treated in their doctrine a number of points that the Mādhyamikas had left open, for example, the question of how the phenomenal world arises.

The first Mādhyamika of importance after Nāgārjuna was Buddhapālita, who composed a commentary on Nāgārjuna's principal work, the *Mādhyamaka-kārikā*. In it he subjected the positions of opponents and their "undesirable consequences" (*prasanga*) to a deductive reductio ad absurdum. From this method comes the name of the school founded by him, the Prāsangika school.

Bhāvaviveka applied the teaching of the Yogāchāra and the logic developed by → Dignāga. He made use in his style of argumentation of the "marks of right logic," which gave the name to his school, the Svātantrika. He also confronted his opponents in his arguments and produced a critique of the method of Buddhapālita. A decisive point for the development and enrichment of the Mādhyamika philosophy was Bhāvaviveka's adoption into his system of the Yogāchāra psychology and doctrine of liberation. He adopted these teachings with certain changes, particularly with regard to the nature of consciousness, which he regarded as part of the world of appearances.

Chandrakīrti was concerned to reinstate the original teaching of Nāgārjuna. He regarded himself as the successor of Buddhapālita and rejected the new elements introduced by Bhāvaviveka, especially the latter's use of logical propositions that in his opinion violated the basic tenet of Mādhyamika not to affirm any positive position.

A further, more important, representative of this school was Shāntideva (7th/8th century), who is famous for two works: the *Bodhicharyāvatāra* (see Matics 1970), in which he describes the path of a bodhisattva, and *Shikshāmuchchaya (Collection of Teachings)*, in which he enumerates a series of rules that a bodhisattva should observe as he travels on the path.

The Mādhyamika philosophy has played an important role in → Tibetan Buddhism since the last quarter of the 8th century. Its influence was initially due to the work of the Indian scholar Shāntirakshita and his student Kamalashīla. These two were representatives of the Yogāchāra-Mādhyamika school then active in India, which had adapted elements of the Yogāchāra to the teaching of Nāgārjuna. Kamalashīla is said to have taken part in a debate with followers of Ch'an Buddhism (→ Zen); after Kamalashīla's victory in this debate, the Tibetan king declared the Indian exposition of the Mādhyamika teaching authoritative in Tibet.

In the 11th century, with the "second spread of the Buddhist teaching" in Tibet, the Mādhyamika school of Chandrakīrti gained in importance. At about the same time a new interpretation of Mādhyamaka was developed by the Shentong (Tib., lit. "Emptiness of Other") school, which represents a synthesis with the school of → Asanga. From the standpoint of this school, the other schools were subsumed under the point of view of *rangtong* ("emptiness of self"). Between the 11th and 14th centuries the entirety of the Mādhyamika teaching in all its versions was assimilated in Tibet and further developed. With the definitive establishment of the four main schools of Tibetan Buddhism between the 14th and 16th centuries, the development of this teaching reached its pinnacle. In the following centuries it continued to be the subject of further study and commentary within the individual doctrinal traditions. At last, in the → Rime movement of the 19th century further attempts were undertaken to reorganize the various interpretations of Mādhyamaka.

The various philosophical theories of the Mādhyamika are given in the → Siddhānta literature. As a complement to this literature, in Tibet practical handbooks were composed which were particularly concerned with meditative practice, the goal of which was a direct and immediate realization of the Mādhyamika teachings.

Magadha 🅑 north Indian kingdom of the time of the historical Buddha → Shākyamuni. The capitals were → Rājagriha and → Pātaliputra, successively. Among the kings of Magadha were → Bimbisāra and his son → Ajātasattu, and → Ashoka. Magadha was the country of origin of Buddhism, from which, after the third → Buddhist council, it spread to other parts of India.

Under the rulership of Ashoka, Magadha reached its greatest level of expansion. Between the language of Magadha, Magadhi, and the → Pali of the Buddhist canon, there is a relationship, the nature of which has yet to be completely clarified.

Magic Jewel School 🅣 → *ling-pao p'ai*

Mahābhārata 🅗 Skt., lit. "the great epic (of the battle) of the descendants of → Bhārata"; next to the → *Rāmāyana* the second monumental (and most voluminous) epic of Hindu or Indian literature. It consists of 106,000 verses in eighteen books (*parva*). Its authorship is ascribed to the mythical sage → Vyāsa; however, between the fifth century B.C.E and the second century C.E. a great many authors and "compilers" (Skt. *vyāsa*) indubitably worked on the text, which gradually came to include the greater part of India's popular myths, fables, and fairy tales.

The battle between the Pāndavas and the Kauravas. (Woodcut from a 1907 edition of the *Mahābhārata*)

The story's main theme is the battle between two related Bhārata families, the evil → Kauravas and the virtuous → Pāndavas, for the kingdom divided up by the blind king → Dhritarāshtra. The most important philosophical section is the → *Bhagavad-Gītā*, in book 6, which contains Krishna's instructions to → Arjuna just before the beginning of the eighteen-day battle whose dramatic events form the focal point of the *Mahābhārata*. Popular narrative elements include the romance between → Nala and Damayantī in the "Book of the Forest" and the highly poetic story of the faithfulness of → Sāvitrī, with its description of the victory of love over death.

"The key to the understanding of this immense work is seen by Indians to lie in its moral intention to portray the triumph of virtue and the subjugation of vice. The accounts of legends, cultures, myths, and traditions that are preserved in this work offer a profound look into India's past. They bear witness to a unique, early inquiry into the hidden truths of religion and contain the beginnings of philosophical speculation. No other work except the Bible has had such influence on the moral education of a culture." (Helmut Hoffmann)

Mahābhāva H Skt.; intense, ecstatic love for God, the highest manifestation of love, as personified by → Rādhā.

Mahābhūta H B Skt., lit. mahā, "great"; bhūta, "element."
H The five elements—ether, air, fire, water, and earth—from which are derived the five → *tanmātras.*
B Synonym for → *dhātu*, an element in the sense of the four elements that constitute all corporeality—the firm, the fluid, the heating, and the moving elements. The analysis of the body that makes clear that it is constituted by the *mahābhūtas* is a meditative practice, the goal of which is to overcome the concept of an ego and to come to the recognition of everything corporeal as transitory, unreal, and characterized by suffering.

Mahābodhi Monastery B → Bodh-gayā, → Dharmapāla 2, 3, and → Mahābodhi Society.

Mahābodhi Society B lit. "Society of Great Enlightenment"; a society founded by the Sinhalese monk → Dharmapāla in the year 1891, which contributed decisively to the revival of Buddhism in India. The goal of the Mahābodhi Society was to regain → Bodh-gayā from the Hindus, to make it once again a center of Buddhism, and to build a university there for monks from all over the world.

At the time the Mahābodhi Society was founded, the Buddhist sacred site of Bodh-gayā was under Hindu control and in a state of decay. In October 1891 the society convoked an international Buddhist conference in order to secure the support of Buddhists of other countries for its Bodh-gayā project. In 1892 the society began publishing the periodical *The Mahābodhi Society and the United Buddhist World*, which became the essential instrument for diffusion of its concerns among Indian intellectuals and English people resident in India. Because of resistance on the part of the British authorities and the Hindus, a long legal proceeding in Bodh-gayā had to be undertaken, which only reached a conclusion in 1949 with the attainment of Indian independence. From that point on Buddhists and Hindus assumed common responsibility for the maintenance of the sacred sites at Bodh-gayā.

The Mahābodhi Society today maintains schools, hospitals, and other social institutions, has centers throughout the world, and has undertaken the translation and publication of Pali texts.

Mahādeva H B
H Skt., lit. "the great god," a name frequently given to → Shiva.
B → Buddhist council

Mahākāla H B Skt., lit. "great time" or "great black one."
H 1. an aspect of → Shiva as a personification of the dissolving force of the universe; 2. one of the twelve great → *lingas*, situated in a celebrated Shiva temple in Ujjayinī.
B → *dharmapāla* 1

Mahākārana H Skt., lit. "the great cause"; a name for the transcendent reality, the Absolute.

Mahākāshyapa B Z (Mahākāśyapa), Skt. (Pali, Mahākassapa); also in short form, Kāshyapa (Kassapa); outstanding student of the historical Buddha → Shākyamuni. He was renowned for his ascetic self-discipline and moral strictness and, thanks to these qualities, took over leadership of the → *sangha* after the death of the Buddha. Mahākāshyapa is considered the first patriarch of → Zen.

At the first → Buddhist council, which Mahākāshyapa convoked in order to counteract tendencies toward a less strict lifestyle within the *sangha*, differences of opinion arose between him and → Ānanda, another principal disciple of the Buddha. Ānanda was supposed not to be permitted to attend the council, because he had not yet attained → arhathood. Mahākāshyapa also accused him of having favored the founding of the order of nuns (→ *bhikshunī*), and of not having asked the Buddha for precise instructions concerning the elimination of certain disciplinary rules. Mahākāshyapa also accused Ānanda of not having supplicated the Buddha to prolong his earthly existence.

In Chinese monasteries in the main hall, one often finds images of Mahākāshyapa to the right of the image of the Buddha, and of Ānanda, the second patriarch of Zen, to the left. For the view that Mahākāshyapa is the first patriarch of Zen, → *nenge-misho.*

Mahāmaudgalyāyana B Skt. (Pali, Mahāmoggalana); short form, Maudgalyāyana (Moggalana); one of the most important disciples of the Buddha → Shākyamuni. Mahāmaudgalyāyana, who came from a Brahman family, entered the Buddhist community together with the friend of his youth, → Shāriputra, and soon became famous for his supernatural abilities (clairvoyance and magic). The images of Mahāmaudgalyāyana and Shāriputra are often found in Buddhist monasteries next to that of the

Buddha. Both were murdered shortly before the death of the Buddha by enemies of Buddhism. Mahāmaudgalyāyana is one of the → ten great disciples of the Buddha.

Mahāmāyā 🅗 Skt., lit. "the great sorceress"; a name for → Kalī and → Durgā; also a term used to refer to the veiling of → Brahman by his → Shakti.

Mahāmudrā 🅑 Skt., lit. "great seal"; one of the highest teachings of the → Vajrayāna, which in Tibet is transmitted especially in the → Kagyupa school. The Tibetan term for *mahāmudrā, phyag-rgya chen-po,* is described as realization of emptiness (→ *shūnyatā*), freedom from → samsāra, and the inseparability of these two. As a meditative system, the teaching of *mahāmudrā* was revealed to the *mahāsiddha* → Tilopa by → Samantabhadra, an embodiment of the *dharmakāya* (→ *trikāya*), and through → Nāropa, → Marpa, and → Milarepa reached Tibet. The "ordinary" practice of *mahāmudrā* begins with "dwelling in peace" (→ *shamatha*) and leads to the transformation of every experience by the qualities of emptiness and luminosity (or clarity). It has sometimes been called "Tibetan Zen." The "extraordinary" practice of *mahāmudrā* is an extension of this method through the → *Nāro chödrug.*

The teachings of *mahāmudrā* are divided in the Tibetan tradition into three aspects: view, meditation, and action.

1. The view is defined as the insight that the timeless true nature of the mind is the unity of emptiness and luminosity. Every phenomenon bears the "seal" of this experience.

2. The essence of meditation is the direct, effortless experience of the nature of the mind. This is attained through two types of preparatory practices. The first consists of four practices involving the contemplative realization of the principles of the preciousness of a human birth, impermanence, the law of → karma, and the unsatisfactoriness of the cycle of existence (→ samsāra). The second type consists of four special practices involving particular types of → *sādhanas* and serves to purify → "body, speech, and mind."

3. The experience of *mahāmudrā* leads to a spiritual freedom that eventually leaves behind all convention and manifests itself most vividly in the activity of the "sacred fool" (→ Drukpa Kunleg). The Karmapa Rangjung Dorje (1284–1339) wrote on the practice of *mahāmudrā,*

> The ground of purification is the mind itself, indivisible luminosity, and emptiness;
> The means of purification is the great *vajra* yoga of *mahāmudrā*;
> What are to be purified are the transitory contaminations of confusion;
> The untainted pure fruit is the *dharmakāya*—may I realize all this.

Mahāparinibbāna-sutta 🅑 Pali, lit. "*Sūtra Concerning the Great* → *Parinirvāna*"; part of the → *Dīgha-nikāya.* This sūtra of Hīnayāna Buddhism deals with the last years of the life of the historical Buddha (→ Siddhārtha Gautama), his death, as well as with the cremation of his body and the distribution of the relics. It was composed by a number of authors over a long period of time starting around 480 B.C.E.. It is available in several English translations. It should not be confused with the → *Mahāparinirvāna-sūtra.*

Mahāparinirvāna-sūtra 🅑 Skt., lit. "*Sūtra Concerning the Great* → *Parinirvāna*"; a collection of Mahāyāna sūtras, which takes its name from the first of these; it has been handed down only in Chinese translation. The work deals primarily with the doctrine of → buddha-nature, which is immanent in all beings; however, it also treats other central notions of Mahāyāna Buddhism. In the Chinese canon (→ Tripitaka), it is reckoned with the → Vaipulya-sūtras. It should not be confused with the → *Mahāparinibbāna-sūtra.*

Mahāprajāpati Gautamī 🅑 stepmother of the historical Buddha (→ Siddhārtha Gautama), by whom he was raised following the death of his mother Māyādevi a few days after his birth. After the death of her husband, Mahāprajāpatī requested the Buddha's consent to the foundation of an order of nuns (→ *bhikshunī*). The Buddha was seemingly against this, fearing for the discipline of the order as a whole. Only at the urging of his student → Ānanda is he said to have yielded and then predicted that the foundation of the nuns' order would shorten the period of survival of the teaching from 1,000 to 500 years.

Mahāprajñapāramitā-hridaya-sūtra 🅑 Skt. → *Heart Sūtra*

Mahāprajñāpāramitā-sūtra 🅑 Skt. → *Prajñāpāramitā-sūtra*

Mahāpralaya 🅗, also called Jahānaka and Sanhāra, Skt., lit. "great dissolution"; the total dissolution of the universe at the end of a → *kalpa,* when the seven → *lokas* and their inhabitants, saints, gods, and even Brahmā disappear.

Mahāpurānas 🅗 (Mahāpurāṇas), Skt., lit. "the great → Purānas"; a term referring to the *Vishnu-Purāna* and the *Bhāgavata-Purāna,* the two great Purānas of the → Vaishnavas.

Mahāpurusha 🅗 (Mahāpuruṣa), Skt., lit. "the great soul"; the world soul as the highest being, a name for → Vishnu. Important sages and saints are often addressed by devotees as Mahāpurusha.

Maharishi 🅗 (Maharṣi), Skt., lit. "great seer"; the ancient seers and saints to whom the truths of the Vedas were revealed and from whom the hymns derive. The seven great → *Rishis* are also referred to as Maharishi. In modern times it is a title of respect given to illumined ones, as in → Rāmana Mahar(i)shi.

Mahāsamnipāta-sūtra 🅑 Skt., lit. "*Sūtra of the Great Assembly*"; one of the → Vaipulya sūtras of Mahāyāna Buddhism preserved in the Chinese canon (→ Tripitaka). This collection of sūtras of the 6th century C.E. is heterotgeneous in nature; however, many of the texts stress the emptiness (→ *shūnyatā*) of the worlds. The work exhibits Tantric influence and is rich in → *dhāranīs* and mantras.

Mahāsānghika 🅑 (Mahāsāṅghika) Skt., adherent of the "Great Maha Community [→ *sangha*]"; one of the two Hīnayāna schools into which the original Buddhist community split at the third → Buddhist council in Pātaliputra, at which this group declared itself in favor of the five theses concerning the nature of an → arhat. In the course of further development the Mahāsānghikas further split into the Ekavyāvahārikas (which produced the Lokottaravādins) and the Gokulikas (which divided into the Bahushrutīyas, Prajñaptivādins and the Chaitikas).

The schools of the Mahāsānghikas are considered to have prepared the ground for the idealistic ontology and buddhology of the → Mahāyāna. One already finds with them the theory that everything is only a projection of mind, the absolute as well as the conditioned, nirvāna as well as samsāra, the mundane as well as the supramundane. According to this view, everything is only name and without real substance. This idealistic view opposes the realistic theories of the → Sthaviras.

The Mahāsānghikas consider the Buddha to have a supramundane (→ *lokottara*), perfectly pure body and mind. As a further development, he was seen as inhering transcendentally, above the world. This became the basis for the Mahāyāna notion of a supernatural, transcendent buddha. The Mahāsānghikas ascribe to him a limitless body, limitless power, and perpetual life. He is omniscient (→ *sarvajñatā*) and abides in eternal → *samādhi*.

The Mahāsānghikas also maintain the view that a → bodhisattva can voluntarily be reborn in the lower modes of existence (→ *gati*) in order, for example, to soothe the torments of the hell beings (→ *naraka*), to expound the teachings, and to awaken the factors of wholesomeness in beings.

Mahāshūnya 🅗 (Mahāśūnya), Skt., lit. "the great emptiness"; in → Vedānta, *mahāshūnya* is the emptiness of nonduality, in which there are no objects to permit a dual relationship between subject and object, between seer and seen.

Mahāsiddha 🅑 Skt., roughly "great master of perfect capabilities." In the → Vajrayāna, this term refers to an ascetic who has mastered the teachings of the → Tantras. He distinguishes himself through certain magical powers (→ *siddhi*), which are visible signs of his enlightenment. Best known is the group of eighty-four mahāsiddhas. They represent a religious movement, which developed in India from the 8th to 12th centuries against the background of, and in opposition to, the monastic culture of Mahāyāna Buddhism. Among the eighty-four *mahāsiddhas* were men and women of all social classes; their model of highly individual realization strongly influenced Tibetan Buddhism. Also of importance were their spiritual songs.

The biographies of the eighty-four *mahāsiddhas*, preserved in Tibetan translation, describe personalities like Chatrapa the beggar, Kantali the tailor, and Kumaripa the potter. However, King Indrabhūti and his sister Lakshmīnkarā are also among them, as are scholars like Shāntipa. What is common to all of them, regardless of background, is the manner in which, through the instruction of a master, they transformed a crisis in their lives into a means for attaining liberation. Then, through unorthodox behavior and the use of paradoxes, they expressed the ungraspability of ultimate reality.

The trait of combining degraded social circumstances with the highest level of realization is found in the biography of Mahāsiddha Tandhepa, for example. He gambled away all his possessions at dice; however, through the instruction that the world was just as empty as his purse, he attained enlightenment and entered nirvāna.

The songs of the *mahāsiddhas*, known as *dohas*, are rich in poetic imagery and speak directly to the power of imagination. The *doha* tradition was continued in Tibet by → Milarepa and → Drukpa Kunleg, among others. The greatest influence was exercised by the dohas of the arrowsmith Saraha, who expresses the spiritual experience (→ *mahāmudrā*) of the *mahāsiddhas* in the following words: "Whoever understands that from the beginning mind has never existed realizes the mind of the buddhas of the three times."

Mahāsthāmaprāpta 🅑 Skt., lit. "one who has gained great power"; an important → bodhisattva of Mahāyāna Buddhism, who brings men the knowledge of the necessity of liberation. In China and Japan Mahāsthāmaprāpta is, with Avalokiteshvara, often depicted as a companion of Buddha Amitābha. In such representations, Mahāsthāmaprāpta appears to the right of Avalokiteshvara and symbolizes the latter's wisdom. Mahāsthāmaprāpta is often depicted with a pagoda ornamenting his hair.

Mahātattva 🅗, or Mahat, Skt., lit. "the great fundamental principle"; the great cosmic intelligence that arose at the Creation.

Mahātma 🅗 Skt., lit. "great soul"; term of respect given to important spiritual teachers and leaders. The term is known through Mahātma → Gandhi.

Mahāvairochana-sūtra 🅑 Skt., lit. *"Sūtra of the Great Radiant One"*; sūtra of Mahāyāna Buddhism, a fundamental work for the Tantric Buddhism schools of China (→ Mi-tsung) and Japan (→ Shingon). It was translated into Chinese around 725 by Shubhākarasimha, one of the three great Tantric masters who traveled to China. It contains the essential Tantric teachings.

Mahāvākya 🅗 Skt., lit. "Great Sentence"; the important Vedic precepts, also known as → *mantra*, which proclaim that → *brahman* and the self of man are identical.

Each of the four Vedas contains a great precept: (1) → *Prejñānam Brahma* ("Consciousness is Brahman") appears in the *Aitareya Upainishad* of the *Rigveda*; (2) → *Aham Brahman asmi* ("I am Brahman") is found in the *Brihadāranyaka Upanishad* (*Yajurveda*); (3) → *Tat tvam asi* ("That art thou") is in the *Chāndogya Upanishad* (*Sāmaveda*); (4) *Ayam ātman Brahma* ("This self is Brahman") is mentioned in the *Māndūkya Upanishad* (*Atharvaveda*).

Mahāvamsa 🅑 (Mahāvaṃsa) Pali, lit. *"Great Story"*; Pali chronicle of Sinhalese history, ascribed to Mahānāma (6th century). The *Mahāvamsa* contains accounts from the time of the historical Buddha (→ Shākyamuni), of the colonization of Ceylon, and of the period up to the 4th century C.E..

The *Chūlavamsa* (*Little Story*) is a supplement to the *Mahāvamsa*. It was composed during different periods by many authors and gives an overview of Sinhalese Buddhism until the 18th century. These "stories" are important sources for the study of early Buddhism in India and Ceylon.

Mahāvastu 🅑 Skt., lit. "the great event"; a work of the Lokottaravādin (→ Mahāsānghika) school of Hīnayāna Buddhism. The work stems from the beginning of the Common Era and deals with individual previous existences of the historical Buddha → Shākyamuni. It contains early descriptions of the career of a bodhisattva (→ *bhūmi*); thus it is considered as marking the transition between Hīnayāna and Mahāyāna.

Mahāvibhāshā 🅑 Skt. → Vaibhāshika

Mahāvidyās 🅗 Skt.; ten divinities who are worshiped because they can lead one to the knowledge of → Brahman. These are Kālī, Tārā, Shodashī, Bhuvaneshvarī, Bhairavī, Chinnamastā, Dhūmāvatī, Vagalā, Mātangī, and Kamalā. All ten are personifications of Brahman's → Shakti; the way to the knowledge of Brahman, and hence to ultimate illumination, is often made more accessible to the spiritual aspirant through the worship of his Shakti.

Mahāvīra 🅗, or Mahāvīr, Skt., lit. "great hero"; 1. name of the saint who established → Jainism as a religious community. He lived in the sixth/fifth century B.C.E. and was the last of the great teachers of Jainism who bear the title → Tīrthankara; 2. a name for → Hanumat.

Mahāvrata 🅗 Skt., lit. "great vow"; Patañjali's *Yoga-Sūtra* (2.31) refers to → *yama*, the first step in → Rāja-Yoga, as the "Great Vow" that holds for all eight steps. In other words, it is the indispensable prerequisite for the successful practice of yoga, from which no caste, place, time, or other circumstance provides exception.

In terms of their fundamental significance for the spiritual path, *yama* and → *niyama* (the second step of Rāja-Yoga) may be compared in a sense with the Ten Commandments of the Jewish and Christian traditions. However, the latter precepts are less systematically associated with the spiritual path; rather, they serve as general principles for the daily life of Jews and Christians.

Mahāyāna 🅑 🅩 Skt., lit. "Great Vehicle"; one of the two great schools of Buddhism, the other being the Hīnayāna, "Small Vehicle." The Mahāyāna, which arose in the first century C.E., is called Great Vehicle because, thanks to its manysided approach, it opens the way of liberation to a great number of people and, indeed, expresses the intention to liberate all beings.

Hīnayāna and Mahāyāna are both rooted in the basic teachings of the historical Buddha → Shākyamuni, but stress different aspects of those teachings. While Hīnayāna seeks the liberation of the individual, the follower of the Mahāyāna seeks to attain enlightenment for the sake of the welfare of all beings. This attitude is embodied in the Mahāyāna ideal of the → bodhisattva, whose outstanding quality is compassion (→ *karunā*).

The Mahāyāna developed from the Hīnayāna schools of the → Mahāsānghikas and Sarvāstivādins (→ Sarvāstivāda), which formulated important aspects of its teaching. From the Mahāsānghikas came the teaching, characteristic of the Mahāyāna, of the transcendent nature of a buddha, as well as the bodhisattva ideal and the notion of emptiness (→ *shūnyatā*). Seeds of the → *trikāya* teaching can be recognized in the doctrine of the Sarvāstivādins.

The Mahāyāna places less value on monasticism than the Hīnayāna; by contrast to early Buddhism, here the layperson can also attain → nirvāna, in which endeavor he can rely on the active help of buddhas and bodhisattvas. In this approach to Buddhism, nirvāna does not mean only liberation from samsāric duress (→ samsāra), but beyond that also the realization that by one's very nature one is liberated and inseperable from the absolute. The buddha principle (→ buddha-nature, → *busshō*) that is immanent in all beings becomes more important than the person of the historical Buddha.

The Mahāyāna divided into a series of further schools, which spread from India to Tibet, China, Korea, and Japan. In India arose the → Mādhyamika school, founded by → Nāgārjuna, and the → Yogāchāra school, founded by → Asanga. Parallel to the development of → Tantra in Hinduism, in Buddhism also a magic-oriented school appeared, the → Vajrayāna, which today flourishes primarily in → Tibetan Buddhism.

The most important Mahāyāna schools in China were Ch'an → Hua-yen, → T'ien-t'ai, and the → Pure Land school. These schools were further developed in Japan as Zen → Kegon, → Tendai, and → Amidism, respectively.

The teachings of the Mahāyāna are contained in the Mahāyāna sūtras (→ sūtra) and → *shāstras*, among which are some of the most profound writings of Buddhism.

Mahāyānashraddhotpāda-shāstra B Z (Mahāyānaśraddhotpāda-śāstra) Skt., lit. *"Treatise on the Awakening of Faith in the Mahāyāna"*; Mahāyāna work from the 5th/6th century, attributed by tradition to → Ashvaghosha, who, whoever, lived in the 1st/2nd century. Because it is only extant in a Chinese version from the year 557, the *Mahāyānashraddhotpāda-shāstra* is often regarded as a purely Chinese work. The *Awakening of Faith* is a commentary on Mahāyāna Buddhism that explains the basic notions of the teaching and is used, particularly in China, as an introduction to the Mahāyāna. It is one of the few sūtras that is also of importance for → Zen.

The *Mahāyānashraddhotpāda-shāstra* is divided into five chapters: (1) the reasons for the composition of the work: in order to free all beings from suffering, to spread the true teaching, to support those on the path, to awaken faith in beginners, to show means for remaining free of bad influences, to teach proper methods of meditation, to present the advantages of reciting the name of → Amitābha, to provide an introduction to → *dhyāna* (also → Zen); (2) explanation of the most important Mahāyāna terms; (3) exposition of the Mahāyāna: on the threefold nature of the "essence of the mind," on enlightenment and nonenlightenment, on ignorance, refutation of false teachings and preconceptions, presentation of the proper methods leading to enlightenment, on the merits and virtues of a bodhisattva; (4) Mahāyāna practice: development of faith through the practices of generosity, discipline, patience, exertion, wisdom, and → *shamatha-vipashyanā*; (5) advantages of Mahāyāna practice.

Mahā-Yoga H Skt., lit. "the highest union"; the wholly abstract union of every individual with all other individuals, of every object with all other objects, and of all individuals and objects with the universal One (→ *brahman*).

Maheshvara H (Maheśvara), Skt., lit. "Great → Īshvara"; a name for → Shiva.

Mahinda B Buddhist monk of the 3d century B.C.E.. He is thought to have been the son of King → Ashoka. Mahinda was the leader of the mission to Ceylon that took place around 250 B.C.E. and that resulted in the conversion of the Sinhalese king, Devānam-piya Tissa. The latter had built the "great monastery" Mahāvihāra in his capital, → Anurādhapura, where a branch of the → Bodhi-tree, brought by Mahinda from the mainland, was preserved. Mahinda died in Ceylon at the age of sixty. A → *chaitya* was built over his mortal remains.

Mahīshāsaka B (Mahīśāsaka), Skt.; → Hīnayāna school, which split off from the school of the → Vibhajyavādins in the second century B.C.E. and later produced the → Dharmaguptaka school. Among the school's teachings was the reality of the present but not of the past and future.

Maidō Soshin Z Jap. for → Hui-t'ang Tsu-hsin

Maitreya B Z Skt. (Jap. Miroku), lit. "Loving One"; in the teaching of the five earthly buddhas, already present in the Hīnayāna but first fully developed by the Mahāyāna, the embodiment of all-encompassing love. He is expected to come in the future as the fifth and last of the earthly buddhas. The cult of Maitreya is very widespread in Tibetan Buddhism. His Heaven (→ Pure Land) is *tushita* ("the joyful"), after which the Tibetan saint → Tsonghkapa named the first monastery he founded. As the world teacher to come, Maitreya is expected to appear in around 30 thousand years.

Maitreya, the buddha of the next world age (Tibetan block print)

He is depicted iconographically on a raised seat with his feet resting on the ground as a sign of his readiness to arise from his seat and appear in the world. If the five earthly buddhas (Krakuchchanda, Kanakamuni, Kāshyapa, → Shākyamuni, and Maitreya) are seen as analogous to the five buddha families (→ *buddhakula*), then Maitreya's qualities correspond to those of the karma family of all-accomplishing wisdom.

Maitreyanātha B one of the founders of the → Yogāchāra school. He is believed to have lived in the 4th–5th centuries. The historicity of Maitreyanātha is a matter of controversy; however, the latest research shows him to have been the master of → Asanga. According to tradition, Asanga received the inspiration for his teaching direct from the buddha → Maitreya. Maitreya here might well mean Maitreyanātha, however, if this were the case, then Maitreyanātha would be the actual founder of the Yogāchāra school.

The following works are respectively ascribed either to Maitreyanātha or Asanga, depending on the viewpoint of the scholar: the *Abhidharma-samuchchaya ('Collection of the Abhidharma'*), which presents the teaching of the Yogāchāra in the form of classifications; the *Mahāyānasūtralankāra ('Ornament of the Sūtras of the Mahāyāna')*; the *Madhyanta-vibhanga ('Differentiation of the Middle and the Extremes')*, a short didactic treatise; the → *Yogāchārabhūmi-shāstra.*

Maitreyī H Skt.; one of the two wives of the sage → Yājñavalkya. As the sage prepared to withdraw to the forest to lead a life of renunciation, he wished to divide his property between his two wives. Maitreyī asked him if she could attain immortality by means of this property or by all the wealth in the world. When her husband replied that she could not, she countered that she had no wish but to be taught by him regarding the way to immortality. The dialogue that follows, in which Yājñavalkya fulfills Maitreyī's wish, is one of the highlights of the → *Brihadāranyaka Upanishad.*

Maitrī B Skt. (Pali, mettā), lit. "kindness, benevolence"; one of the principal Buddhist virtues. *Maitrī* is a benevolence toward all beings that is free from attachment. *Mettā* is the subject of a meditative practice of the → Theravāda in which kindness is to be developed and aggression overcome. In it the feeling of kindness is directed first toward persons who are close to one and then gradually extended toward persons and other beings who are indifferent and ill-disposed toward oneself (*mettā* meditation). The notion of *maitrī* is developed particularly in the → *Mettā-sutta. Maitrī* is one of the four divine states of dwelling (→ *brahma-vihāra*).

Maitrī-karunā B Skt., lit. "kindness [and] compassion"; two principal Buddhist virtues that are the basis of the spiritual attitude of a → bodhisattva. They manifest as part of a bodhisattva's wish to bring all beings to liberation.

Three types of *maitrī-karunā* are distinguished: (1) kindness and compassion toward beings in a general sense; (2) kindness and compassion resulting from the insight into the egolessness of all dharmas that is proper to → *shrāvakas*, → *pratyekabuddhas*, and bodhisattvas starting from the lowest stage of their development (→ *bhūmi*); (3) the *mahāmaitrī-*

karunā ("great goodness and compassion") of a buddha, which is without distinction or condition.

Majjhima-nikāya B Pali (Skt. *Madhyamāgama*), lit. "*Middle Collection*"; the second collection (→ Nikāya, → Āgama) of the → Sūtra-pitaka. In the Pali version, it consists of 152 sūtras of medium length and in the Chinese translation of the lost Sanskrit version, of 222 sūtras; 97 sutras are common to both. According to tradition, this collection was recited by → Shāriputra at the first → Buddhist council.

Maka hannyaharamita shingyō Z Jap. for *Mahāprajñāpāramitā-hridaya-sūtra,* → *Heart Sūtra.*

Ma-ku Pao-che Z also Ma-yu Pao-che (Jap., Mayoku Hōtetsu), Chinese Ch'an (Zen) master of the T'ang period; a student and dharma successor (→ *hassu*) of → Ma-tsu Tao-i (Jap., Baso Dōitsu). Ma-ku appears in example 31 of the → *Pi-yen-lu.*

Makyō Z Jap., roughly "diabolic phenomenon," from ma (akuma), "devil" and kyō, "phenomenon, objective world." *Makyō* are deceptive appearances and feelings that can arise in the practice of → *zazen.* These phenomena include visual hallucinations as well as hallucinations involving the other senses, such as sounds, odors, etc., also prophetic visions, involuntary movements, and, rarely, even levitation. All these phenomena, whether frightening or seductive, are not "diabolic" so long as the practitioner pays them no heed and continues undistracted in his practice.

In a deeper sense, for Zen the entire experienced world of the unenlightened person—the world of "everyman's consciousness" (→ *bonpu-no-jōshiki*)—is nothing but *makyō*, a hallucination. The true nature, or buddha-nature (→ *busshō*), of all phenomena is experienced only in → enlightenment.

Mālā H B Skt., lit. "garland, rose"; also called *japamālā.*

H The prayer beads customarily used in the practice of → *japa.* They consist generally of 108 *rudrāksha* or *tulasī* berries.

B a string of beads that is used to count repetitions in the recitation of → mantras, → *dhāranīs*, and the name of Buddha (→ *nembutsu*). The number of beads in a Buddhist *mālā* is 108.

Mampuku-ji Z also Manpuku-ji, Jap.; main monastery of the → Ōbaku school, founded by the Chinese Zen master → Yin-yuan Lung-ch'i (Jap., Ingen Ryūki). It is located in Uji, south of Kyōto and is one of the most outstanding examples of Chinese temple architecture in Ming period style in Japan.

Māna B Skt. → *anushaya*

Manana H Skt., lit. "consider, reflect"; critical reflection on all truths that have been heard or read; the second of three means to knowledge as propounded by → Vedānta. The first stage is → *shravana*, the reading, hearing, and perception of spiritual truths; the third is → *nididhyāsana*, allowing what has been heard and considered to penetrate through meditation.

Manas H B Skt.

H The capacity of thought; one aspect of the → *antahkarana*, the "inner organ." Through *manas* we receive impressions of the outer world, which are then presented to the → *buddhi.* It enables us to doubt, to make decisions, and to translate our will into action.

B (Pali, mano); roughly "mind" or "intelligence". In the broadest sense *manas* means all mental faculties and activities—the intellectual function of consciousness. As the sixth of the six bases (→ *shadāyatana*, → *āyatana*), *manas* is the basis for all mental functioning and acts as controller of the first five "bases." As the human rational faculty, *manas* is considered a special "sense" that is suited to rational objects as the eye, for example, is suited to visible objects. In → Yogāchāra *manas* is the seventh of the eight types of consciousness.

Mānasika-Japa H Skt. → *japa*

Mānava-Dharmashāstra H Skt. → *Manu-Samhitā*

Mandala H B (maṇḍala), Skt., lit. "circle, arch, section."

H 1. The voluminous collection of verses that makes up the *Rigveda* is divided into ten mandalas ("song cycles"); 2. a mystical drawing used in → Tantra, a diagram constucted of squares and circle, symbols of cosmic forces that are employed in the practice of meditation.

B a symbolic representation of cosmic forces in two- or three-dimensional form, which is of considerable significance in the Tantric Buddhism of Tibet (→ Tibetan Buddhism, → Vajrayāna). Representations of mandalas, which are often depicted on → *thangkas*, are used primarily as supports for meditation—the picture can be used as a reference for a particular visualization. The meaning of mandala in Tibetan Buddhism can be derived from the Tibetan translation of the Sanskrit word by *dkyil-khor*, which roughly means "center and periphery." A mandala is thus understood as the synthesis of numerous distinctive elements in a unified scheme, which through meditation can be recognized as the basic nature of existence. Apparent chaos and complexity are simplified into a pattern characterized by a natural hierarchy.

Basic form of a mandala

In the Vajrayāna, representations of mandalas also function as a kind of two-dimensional shrine on which the meditator sets ritual objects, as for instance a → *dorje*. Here an empowerment to practice a particular → *sādhana* is required, since the mandala is the environment of a particular deity who dwells at its center. The ritual objects or offerings are connected with a particular quality of the deity, which the ritual action invokes.

In the Vajrayāna, the external world as well as the body and one's own consciousness can be seen as mandalas. The form of the mandala, which is determined by tradition, is in its basic structure a square palace with a center and four gates in the four cardinal directions. Mandalas can be represented in four ways: (1) painted (*thangka*), (2) drawn with colored sand, (3) represented by heaps of rice, or (4) constructed three-dimensionally (usually in cast metal). If a wrathful deity (→ *yidam*, → forms of manifestation) is the central figure, the mandala, as a symbol of the impermanence of existence, is surrounded by charnel grounds. The outer rim of the representation usually consists of circles of flame in the five basic colors, which symbolize the five buddha families (→ *buddhakula*) and the protection granted by them.

Māndūkya-Upanishad 🅷 (Māndūkya-Upanisad), Skt.; an → Upanishad belonging to the → *Atharvaveda*; it discusses the syllable → OM and the four states of consciousness (waking, dreaming, deep sleep, and → *turiyā*). → Gaudapāda wrote his famous → *kārikā* on this Upanishad in the eighth century.

Manipūra-chakra 🅷 🅱 Skt. → chakra 3

Mañjughosha 🅱 (Mañjughoṣa), Skt., lit. "Gentle-voiced One"; another name for → Mañjushrī.

Mañjushrī 🅱 🆉 Skt. (Jap., Monju), lit. "He Who Is Noble and Gentle"; the bodhisattva of wisdom, one of the most important figures of the Buddhist pantheon. He first appears in the *Ārya-mañjushrī-mūlakalpa*, a work dating from before the 4th century. Usually Mañjushrī is iconographically depicted with two lotus blossoms at the level of his head, on which his attributes—a sword and a book of the *prajñā-pāramitā* literature—are placed. These attributes stand for the wisdom embodied by Mānjushrī, which dispels the darkness of ignorance.

Mañjushrī with his attributes, the sword of wisdom and the sutra

In Tibetan Buddhism, great scholars, for example, → Tsongkhapa, are considered incarnations (→

tulku) of Mañjushrī. Homage is frequently made to Mañjushrī under the name of Manjughosha ("the Gentle-voiced One") at the beginning of philosophical texts, especially of → Mādhyamika texts. He is thus the symbol for the experience of enlightenment as manifested in intellectual exposition.

In his wrathful form (→ forms of manifestation), Mañjushrī is called Yamāntaka ('Subduer of the Lord of Death') and appears as a bull-headed deity. In this form he is one of the most important → *yidams* of the → Gelugpa school.

Manomaya-Kosha 🅗 (Manomaya-Kośa), Skt. the third of the five sheaths that surround the → *ātman*; the sheath of mind. (See also → *kosha*.)

Manomaya-Purusha 🅗 (Manomaya-Puruṣa), Skt.; the individual (*purusha*) who identifies himself with the "sheath of mind" (→ *manomaya-kosha*). He takes himself to be a mental being and remains in ignorance, believing there to be nothing higher for him to attain.

Manorājya 🅗 Skt., lit. "fantasy": daydreaming, allowing the thoughts to drift: a habit that impedes spiritual progress, as it diverts one from concentration.

Manorata 🅩 twenty-second patriarch of the Indian lineage of → Zen.

Manovijñāna 🅑 Skt. (Pali, manovinnāna); the consciousness of which the "sixth sense," the mind (→ *manas*), is the basis and of which the objects are all material and mental appearances. The *manovijñāna* includes psychological processes such as knowing, conceiving, judging, etc. It is the basis of the first five types of consciousness, i.e., of the consciousnesses of seeing, hearing, smelling, tasting, and touching (→ *āyatana*).

Mantra 🅗 🅑 also mantram, Skt.

🅗 1. a name for God or an → *avatāra* corresponding to the → *ishta-deva* (chosen deity) of the pupil; with this name he is initiated by his guru into spiritual life. The mantra, which is held to be one with God, contains the essence of the guru's teachings. The pupil is asked to keep it a sacred secret and continually to meditate on this aspect of God. Regular repetition of the mantra (→ *japa*) clarifies thought and with steady practice will ultimately lead to God-realization (see also → *bīja-mantra*); 2. term referring to a → *mahāvākya*; 3. term for a sacred Sanskrit text as well as for the section of the → Vedas containing hymns about sacrifical actions.

🅑 a power-laden syllable or series of syllables that manifests certain cosmic forces and aspects of the buddhas, sometimes also the name of a buddha. Continuous repetition of mantras is practiced as a form of meditation in many Buddhist schools (for example, → Amidism, → *nembutsu*); it also plays a considerable role in the → Vajrayāna (see also → Tibetan Buddhism). Here mantra is defined as a means of protecting the mind. In the transformation of → "body, speech, and mind" that is brought about by spiritual practice, mantra is associated with speech, and its task is the sublimation of the vibrations developed in the act of speaking. Recitation of mantras is always done in connection with detailed visualizations and certain bodily postures (→ mudrā) as prescribed in the → *sādhanas*.

In the Tibetan tradition, the function of mantra is defined differently for the individual classes of the Tantras. In reciting, for example, concentration on the sacred written form of the syllables is distinguished from concentration on their sound. In concentrating on the written form of the syllables, the meditator can visualize them in the space before him or within his own body. In the case of concentrating on the sound, the recitation can consist in actual utterance of the mantra or in mental representation of its sound. In the fifth chapter of the *Subāhupariprichchā*, we find:

At the time of reciting:
Neither too fast nor too slow,
Neither too loud nor too soft.
It should be neither speaking
Nor distraction.

Mantrayāna 🅑 Skt. → Vajrayāna

Mantra-Yoga 🅗 Skt.; the yogic path that aims to achieve union with God or → *brahman* by means of repetition (→ *japa*) of a → mantra. The → Purānas state that in our age *japa* is an easy way to *brahmavidyā*, the knowledge of *brahman*.

Manu 🅗 Skt., lit. "man"; the progenitor of humanity. In the tradition of myth, the concept of Manu is rather the symbol for a mental being that stands between the divine and the human and characterizes the awakening faculty of mind (*man*: "to think") in the human being.

According to the → Vedas, the Manus represent the earliest divine lawgivers, who established sacrifical acts and religious ceremonies. In the → Purānas the name Manu is used particulary to refer to fourteen successive rulers who inhabit the ethereal realms, from where they guide the conscious life of human beings. The Manu of the present age is the seventh and bears the name → Vaivasvata ("the sun-born"). The celebrated law book called the → *Manu-Samhitā* purportedly derives from Manu; even today it serves as the basis for the religious and social behavior of Hindus.

Manu-Samhitā 🅗 (Manu-Saṃhitā), also *Mānava-Dharmashāstra* or *-Smriti*, Skt.; the law book of → Manu. It is said to go back to ancient times and to derive from → Manu; however, it bears signs of the work of various hands. One of the authors is held to be → Vaivasvata.

This work, the first and most important of those designated as → *smriti*, is the foundation of Hindu society and arose before the philosophical schools. It was first disseminated by the Mānavas, a group of brahmans who followed the *Black* → *Yajurveda*. The work deals not only with laws but with many other aspects of the old Hindu community as well. It originally consisted of twenty-four chapters containing a total of 100,000 verses, which were reduced to 12,000 by → Nārada. Sumati reduced them further to 4,000; today only 2,685 verses are extant.

Mao-shan p'ai 🅣 Chin., lit. "School of Mount Mao"; one of the talisman schools (→ *fu-lu p'ai*) of religious Taoism (→ *tao-chiao*). The Mount Mao movement was founded in the 6th century by → T'ao Hung-ching and is based on the teachings of the brothers Mao (2d century), whom T'ao venerated.

Its doctrinal basis is the *Scriptures of the Magic Jewel*. Its followers endeavored to summon the deities and banish evil spirits by the use of spells and talismans. They abstained from eating grain (→ *pi-ku*), practiced → *tao-yin*, and carried out alchemical experiments. The Mao-shan movement flourished during the Sui and T'ang dynasties and in the 13th century was absorbed by the Way of Right Unity (→ *cheng-i tao*).

Mao Tzu-yuan 🅑 → White Lotus school

Māra 🅑 Skt., Pali, lit. "murder, destruction"; although actually the embodiment of death, Māra symbolizes in Buddhism the passions that overwhelm human beings as well as everything that hinders the arising of the wholesome roots (→ *kushala*) and progress on the path of enlightenment.

Mara is the lord of the sixth heaven of the desire realm (→ *triloka*, → *deva*) and is often depicted with a hundred arms, riding on an elephant.

According to legend, the Buddha → Shākyamuni was attacked by Māra as he was striving for enlightenment, because Māra wanted to prevent him from showing men the way that liberates from suffering. Māra first called up a horde of demons, but Shākyamuni did not fear them. Then he sent his most beautiful daughter to seduce Shākyamuni, but before Shākyamuni's eyes she turned into an ugly hag, whereupon Māra admitted conclusive defeat.

Marana 🅑 (Maraṇa) Skt., Pali, lit. "death"; in addition to death in the conventional sense, in Buddhism *marana* refers to the arising and passing away of all mental and physical phenomena.

This momentariness of existence is described in the *Visuddhi-magga* in the following words: "In the highest sense, beings have only a very short instant to live, only so long as a moment of consciousness lasts. Just as a wagon wheel, when rolling as well as when standing still, at any time rests on a single point of its rim, just so the life of beings endures only for the length of a single moment of consciousness. When this is extinguished, so also is the being extinguished. For it is said: The being of the last moment of consciousness lived, now lives no longer, and will also not live again later. The being of the future moment of consciousness has not lived yet, now also does not yet live, and will only live later. The being of the present moment of consciousness did not live previously, lives just now, but later will not live anymore" (trans. from Nyanatiloka 1976, . . . 125).

Mārdava 🅗 Skt., "gentleness, friendliness, kindness"; one of the *daiva-gunas*, the godly qualities, that Krishna enumerates in the sixteenth chapter of the *Bhagavad-Gītā* (5.1-3).

Mārga 🅗 Skt., lit. "path"; the path of the various forms of yoga, always meant in the sense of a spiritual path leading to union with God.

Marks of perfection 🅑 → *dvātrimshadvara-lakshana*

Marpa 🅑 the "Man from Mar," 1012–97, renowned yogi from southern Tibet, also called the Translator. By making three journeys to India, he brought back to Tibet the teachings of → *mahāmudrā* and the → *Nāro chödrug*. Marpa was the master of → Milarepa and was a principal figure in the lineage of transmission of the → Kagyupa school. He is seen as the ideal of the married householder who devotes himself to spirituality without neglecting his worldly obligations.

Marpa studied Sanskrit in his early years. After exchanging all his possessions for gold, he undertook the onerous journey to India. There he met the → *mahāsidda* → Nāropa, who instructed him for sixteen years. Returning to Tibet, Marpa devoted himself intensively to the work of translating the texts he had brought back into Tibetan, led the life of a farmer, and married Dagmema, who bore him several sons.

In search of further teaching, he traveled a second time to India. Upon his return he accepted Milarepa as his student. He subjected the latter to trials of utmost difficulty before transmitting to him the secret teachings.

On account of a particular special teaching and in

spite of his advanced age, Marpa set off for the third time to India. There he met → Atīsha and came together for the last time with his master Nāropa. Marpa made use of dreams to see the future, and foresaw the founding of the Kagyupa school. (An English translation of a Tibetan biography of Marpa is Chögyam Trungpa, *The Life of Marpa the Translator: Seeing Accomplishes All* [Boulder, 1982].)

Marut 🅷 Skt.; the storm gods; they are given a significant role in the Vedas, which represent them as the friends and allies of → Indra.

Many origins have been given for the Marut: they are the sons of → Rudra, sons or brothers of Indra, or the sons of the ocean or the heaven or earth. Armed with lightning and thunderbolts, they ride on the wind and command the storms. Many legends arose to explain the Vedic passages that describe the Maruts as sons of Rudra.

Master of the country 🅱 🆉 → *kokushi*, → *kuo-shih*

Master's staff 🆉 1. *ju-i*. 2. → *kotsu*

Mathurā 🅷 🅱 an ancient city on the right bank of the Yamunā in present-day Uttar-Pradesh (north India).

🅷 The birthplace of → Krishna and one of the seven holy cities of Hindu India. The *Vishnu-Purāna* states that it was originally named Madhunvana, after the demon Madhu, who ruled there. When Shatrughna, the twin brother of → Lakshmana, conquered the city, it was renamed Muttra, later Mathurā (not to be confused with Madura or Madurai in present-day Tamilnadu, South India).

🅱 Between 150 and 250 C.E. Mathurā was a center of Buddhist art and culture. There, at the same time as in → Gandhāra, the first buddha images were made. Here the Buddha was depicted standing, in the form of a → *yaksha*.

His body is blocklike and compact, athletic; he wears a smooth pleatless robe that leaves the greater part of his body bare. He is not, as in Gandhāran art, abstracted from the world, but seems ready to proclaim the teaching to a world in need of liberation.

Under the influence of Gandhāran art, the figure of Buddha became slenderer and more gentle, and the smooth-fitting robe became a monastic garment falling in symmetrical folds, through which the lines of the body traced themselves. In this style of depiction, the Buddha radiates an aristocratic sense of humanity and formal harmony.

Ma-tsu Tao-i 🆉 (Jap., Baso Dōitsu), also Kiangsi (Chiang-hsi) Tao-i, 709–788, one of the most important Chinese Ch'an (Zen) masters; a student and the only dharma successor (→ *hassu*) of → Nan-yueh Huai-jang (Jap., Nangaku Ejō). He was the master of many great Ch'an masters, among whom the best-known are → Pai-chang Huai-hai (Jap., Hyakujō Ekai), → Nan-ch'uan P'u-yuan (Jap., Nansen Fugan), and → Ta-mei Fa-ch'ang (Jap., Daibai Hōjō). More than any other Ch'an master after → Hui-neng, Ma-tsu exercised a shaping influence on the development of Ch'an (Zen) in China. He made use of training methods such as the sudden shout (Chin., *ho!*; Jap., *katsu!*), wordless gestures, as for example with the → *hossu*, and unexpected blows of the stick (→ *shippei*, → *kyosaku*). He knocked his students to the ground, pinched their noses, and shot sudden questions and paradoxical answers at them in order to shake them out of the routine of "everyman's consciousness" (→ *bonpu-no-jōshiki*), liberate them from well-worn ruts of conceptual thinking, and enable them, through a collapse of their habitual feeling and thinking brought on by a sudden shock, to come to the experience of → enlightenment. The power of his mind and the effectiveness of his style of training are attested by the fact that as tradition tells us, he had 139 dharma successors. Ma-tsu appears in examples 30 and 33 of the → *Wu-men-kuan* and in examples 3, 53, and 73 of the → *Pi-yen-lu*.

Ma-tsu must have been impressive on the basis of his appearance alone. It is said he had a glance like a tiger's and a gait like a buffalo's; he could cover his nose with his tongue, and on the soles of his feet were marks in the shape of wheels. In his youth Ma-tsu enjoyed the benefits of strict training under a second-generation dharma successor of the fifth patriarch, → Hung-jen. After the death of his master, he settled at a hermitage on Mount Heng, where day after day he sat absorbed in meditation (→ *zazen*). Here his famous meeting with his later master Nan-yueh took place. (On this meeting, → Nan-yueh Huai-jang.)

We see him in a → *mondō* with → Pai-chang Huai-hai, the most important of Ma-tsu's dharma successors for the further development of Ch'an (Zen), in example 53 of the → *Pi-yen-lu*. This kōan is a typical example of Ma-tsu's training style:

Once when the great master Ma-tsu was out walking with Pai-chang, they saw wild ducks flying by.

The great master said "What is that?"

Pai-chang said, "Wild ducks."

The great master said, "Where have they flown to?"

Pai-chang said, "They flew away."

Thereupon the great master pinched the end of Pai-chang's nose.

Pai-chang cried out in pain.

The great master said, "Why didn't they fly away?"

As we do not find out in this kōan but can learn from the → *Ching-te ch'uan-teng-lu*, at the last words of Ma-tsu, Pai-chang realized enlightenment.

In the *Ching-te ch'uan-teng-lu* we also find an example of Ma-tsu playing together with a great contemporary Shih-t'ou (for this, also → Shih-t'ou Hsi-ch'ien) at training Ch'an monks:

"Teng Yin-feng came to take leave of Master [Ma-tsu]. The master asked him where he was going and he [Teng] informed him he was going to Shih-t'ou.

" 'Shih-t'ou [lit. rock pinnacle] is slippery,' said Ma-tsu.

" 'I've outfitted myself with a balancing pole that I know how to make use of at all times,' answered Teng Yen-feng.

"When he reached his destination, he circumambulated Shih-t'ou's seat once, shook his stick, and said, 'What's that?'

"Shih-t'ou cried, 'Good heavens! Good heavens!'

"Teng Yin-feng said nothing more. He returned to Ma-tsu and reported to him what had happended. Ma-tsu charged him to return to Shih-t'ou; there, in case Shih-t'ou shouted 'Good heavens!' again, he was to blow and hiss twice.

"Teng Yin-feng returned to Shih-t'ou. He repeated what he had done before and again asked, 'What's that?'

"Thereupon Shih-t'ou blew and hissed twice. Again Teng Yin-feng departed without a further word. He reported the incident to Ma-tsu, whereupon Ma-tsu said he had after all warned him that Shih-t'ou was slippery."

Many well-known Zen sayings come from Ma-tsu, including the two answers he gave to the question, What is Buddha? (→ *mondō*). Also famous are his → *hossen* with the enlightened Layman → P'ang-yun, which are recorded in the *P'ang-chu-chih yu-lu*. Ma-tsu's comments and teachings are preserved in the *Kiangsi Tao-i-ch'an-shih yu-lu* (*Record of the Words of Ch'an Master Tao-i from Kiangsi*).

Matsya H Skt., lit. "fish"; Vishnu's → *avatāra* incarnation as a fish, first mentioned in the *Shatapatha-Brāhmana*, part of the *White* → *Yajurveda*, in connection with the Hindu saga of the Great Flood (similar to the biblical story of the flood).

According to the → Purānas, Vishnu was incarnated in the form of the fish *avatāra* in order to protect Vaivasvata, the seventh → Manu, from being destroyed by a great flood. A tiny fish slipped into Manu's hand, begging him for protection. Manu guarded him carefully. The fish then grew so rapidly that only the ocean was large enough to hold him. Manu recognized him as Lord Vishnu, worshiped him, and was then instructed by the god about the approaching flood. At Vishnu's instruction he built a ship that held himself, the → *rishis*, and the seeds of all living beings. The ship was held over the waters in safety on the gigantic horn of the fish until the floods receded. The *Bhāgavata-Purāna* adds that Vishnu instructed Manu and the *rishis* in the true teaching of the soul and → *brahman*. The *Matsya-Purāna* is so named because Vishnu is said to have relayed its 14,000 verses to Manu in the form of a fish. However, much of its text is taken from the → *Mahābhārata*.

Mauna H Skt.; 1. the state of consciousness of a → *muni*; 2. silence, oath of silence, an ascetic practice to further one's spiritual development.

Māyā H B Z Skt., lit. "deception, illusion, appearance."

H A universal principle of → Vedānta; the foundation of mind and matter. *Māyā* is the force (→ *shakti*) of *brahman* and hence is eternally, inseparably united with *brahman*, just as heat is united with fire. *Māyā* and *brahman* together are named → Īshvara, the personal God who creates, maintains, and dissolves the universe. As ignorance or cosmic illusion, *māyā* draws a veil over *brahman* and also veils our vision, so that we see only the diversity of the universe rather than the one reality. *Māyā* has two aspects: → *avidyā* (ignorance) and *vidyā* (knowledge). *Avidyā* leads man away from God and toward worldliness and imprisonment by materiality, which in turn leads to passion and greed. *Vidyā* leads to God-realization and finds expression in spiritual virtues. Both aspects are active in the realm of time, place, and causality, and hence are relative. Human beings transcend *avidyā* and *vidyā* by realizing *brahman*, the Absolute.

B Z The continually changing, impermanent phenomenal world of appearances and forms, of illusion or deception, which an unenlightened mind takes as the only reality. The concept of māyā is used in opposition to that of the immutable, essential absolute, which is symbolized by the *dharmakāya* (→ *trikāya*). The recognition of all → dharmas as māyā is equivalent to the experience of "awakening" (→ enlightenment, → *bodhi*) and the realization of → nirvāna. According to the highest teachings of Buddhism, as they are fomulated, for example, in Zen, it is not actually an illusion or deception to regard the phenomenal world as real; the deception consists rather in taking the phenomenal world to be the immutable and only reality and thus to misplace the view of what is essential. Fundamentally, the relative and the absolute are one and identical, and māyā (Jap., *mayoi*, → delusion) and *bodhi* (enlightenment) are one.

Māyāvāda 🅷 Skt.; the doctrine of → Advaita-Vedānta that the world is only → *māyā* (i.e., unreal), because it is created by the power of illusion of the mind. Adherents of this doctrine are called *māyāvādins.*

Mayoi 🆉 Jap., lit. "error, delusion, deception"; → delusion

Mayoku Hōtetsu 🆉 Jap. for → Ma-ku Pao-che

Ma-yu Pao-che 🆉 → Ma-ku Pao-che

Meditation 🅷 🅱 🆃 🆉 general term for a multitude of religious practices, often quite different in method, but all having the same goal: to bring the consciousness of the practitioner to a state in which he can come to an experience of "awakening," "liberation," "enlightenment." Esoteric schools of various religions, i.e., schools practically concerned with individuals' *own* religious experience, have developed different "ways" geographical circumstances as well as to the psychological dispositions and personality types of different individuals or groups. If an individual religion comes to a conclusion concerning a specific unwholesome state of mind of people in a culture which it is its goal to cure, then the "medicine" to accomplish the cure will be the path of meditative training developed within that religion. Such training, while not a goal in itself, should also not be regarded as a mere means to an end; for, as many religious traditions stress, "the path *is* the goal." At the same time, however, it is said that it is futile to hang on to a method when the goal has already been reached, as though one were to carry a boat about after one had already crossed the river.

A common mark of all forms of meditation is that practice of the meditation concentrates the mind of the practitioner, calms and clarifies it like the surface of a turbulent body of water, the bottom of which one can see only when the surface is still and the water is clear. This is accomplished through different techniques, depending on the method of training—for example, by physical or breathing exercises as in hatha-yoga, by concentration on symbolic forms (for example, mandalas, *thangkas*, yantras) or sounds (mantra) as in Indian Tantra or Tantric Buddhism, on feelings such as love or compassion, on pictorial representations (visualization), on a kōan in Zen, or by resting in collected, contentless wakefulness in the practice of *mahāmudrā*, *dzogchen*, or Zen (*shikantaza*).

Diligent practice of meditation leads to a nondualistic state of mind in which, the distinction between subject and object having disappeared and the practitioner having become one with "god" or "the absolute," conventions like time and space are transcended in an "eternal here and now," and the identity of life and death, phenomenal and essential, samsāra and nirvāna, is experienced. If this experience, in the process of endlessly ongoing spiritual training, can be integrated into daily life, then finally that stage is reached which religions refer to as salvation, liberation, or complete enlightenment.

Meishō Tokken 🆉 Jap. for → Ming-chao Te-chien

Mempeki 🆉 Jap. → Menpeki

Meng-tzu 🆃 also known as Meng K'o and latinized as *Mencius;* Confucianist philosopher, 372–289 B.C.E., Meng-tzu is representative of the idealistic branch of Confucianism. His basic thesis postulates that man is inherently good. (See Legge 1861–1872, 1964; Wilhelm 1982.)

Meng-tzu argued that human beings are inherently capable of experiencing pity, shame, and modesty and have an inborn sense of right and wrong. These inherent qualities generate benevolence (→ *jen*), uprightness (→ *i*), morality (→ *li*), and wisdom. They are what distinguishes man from the animals and have to be further developed and cultivated. In this context Meng-tzu stressed the importance of education and the environment. The above seed qualities find their perfect expression in the Confucianist saint. Meng-tzu further emphasized that all rulers must possess proper ethical qualifications; only a wise man can be a true ruler. If a king lacks these qualifications, the people—by virtue of being the most important element in the state—have a right to rebel. This view influenced Chinese politics up to the 20th century.

Menju-kuketsu 🆉 Jap., roughly, "receiving privately the transmission of the oral secret"; an expression referring to the transmission of the → buddha-dharma from heart-mind to heart-mind (→ *inshin-denshin*), from a Zen master to his student.

Menpeki 🆉 also Mempeki, Jap., lit. "facing the wall"; a Zen expression referring to the *menpeki-kunen*, the nine year's of sitting absorbed in meditation at Shao-lin Monastery of → Bodhidharma, the first patriarch of Ch'an (Zen) China). Menpeki became practically a synonym for → *zazen.*

In the → Sōtō school it is customary to practice *zazen* facing the wall, whereas monks in a monastery of the → Rinzai school sit facing the center of the → *zendō*. In many Zen paintings of Bodhidharma, the patriarch is shown sitting facing the wall of a cliff.

The expression *menpeki* should, however, not be understood as describing the outer circumstances of *zazen* practice alone—in a deeper sense it designates the state of mind of the practitioner. On the one hand, the practitioner wants to make progress on the path of Zen and experience → enlightenment. On the other hand, in the practice of Zen, all props and stays, all conceptions of a path and a goal, are taken away from him. Thus he finds himself in a situation where he is unable to make a single "step forward," as though he were standing in front of a massive wall. This situation and the despair arising from it can bring the practitioner to the point where finally he lets go of all thoughts, wishes, conceptions, and goals and in a sudden intuitive leap breaks through the wall, i.e, realizes that such a wall never existed.

Men-shen 🅃 Chin., lit. "gods of the doorway"; deities in syncretistic Chinese folk religion who, as guardians of the gate, protect the double doorway of a domestic dwelling or public building. *Men-shen* are commonly believed to have been Ch'in Shu-pao and Hu Ching-te, two generals of the T'ang Dynasty emperor T'ang T'ai-tsung—who have been venerated as guardians of the doorway since the 13th/14th century. According to legend they also defended the 6th emperor against attacks by demons while he was asleep, and popular belief continues to consider it their task to keep away or ward off ghosts and evil spirits. They figure as protectors in many folk tales.

The doorways of private and public buildings are ornamented with color prints of the two *men-shen*. They are usually shown in military uniform and/or armor, with tiny banners affixed to their shoulders to signify their rank. They are armed with a rapier or halberd. Their facial expression is appropriately terrifying. The veneration of *men-shen* is not part of a specific cult; people simply fix their picture to the front entrances to their houses at the beginning of the new year. The back door is guarded by the less popular deity Wei Ch'eng, a former minister of the emperor T'ang T'ai-tsung.

Meru 🄷 🄱 also Sumeru, Skt.; the "world mountain" that according to ancient Indian cosmological conceptions stands at the center of the universe and is the meeting place or dwelling place of the gods. The notion of Meru is common to both Hinduism and Buddhism; however, the cosmological systems associated with it in the two religions are different.

🄷 According to the Hindu view, the heavenly Ganges (→ Gangā) springs forth from the pinnacle of Meru to divide into four earthly currents, which flow up to the four corners of heaven. At Meru's peak lies the four-cornered golden city of → Brahmā; at its spurs are located the eight cities of the eight → *lokapālas*. The heaven or realm (→ *loka*) of Krishna and Vishnu also lie on Mount Meru. Seated beneath Meru are the seven lower worlds; in the lowest of these resides the giant snake Vāsuki, who bears Meru and the other worlds and with its fiery breath destroys them all at the close of the world-age (→ yuga).
🄱 According to the Buddhist view, Meru is surrounded by seas and continents; under these lie the hells and the realm of the hungry ghosts (→ *preta*). Above Meru are the realms of the high → *devas* and the gods of the realms of "pure form" (Skt., *rūpaloka*, → *triloka*), as well as the formless realm and finally the buddha-fields (→ pure land). A detailed presentation of the Buddhist Meru world-system can be found in Tatz & Kent 1977.

Mettā-sutta 🄱 Pali, lit. "Sūtra on Kindness"; Hīnayāna sūtra the theme of which is the development of kindness (→ *Maitrī*, *brahma-vihāra*). It is one of the most popular texts of the → Theravāda and is recited daily by the monks and lay people of this school.

The text of the *Mettā-sutta* (also called "Unlimited Friendliness") is as follows (Conze 1968, p.185):

This is what should be done by the man who is wise, who seeks the good, and knows the meaning of the place of peace.

Let him be strenuous, upright, and truly straight, without conceit of self, easily contented and joyous, free of cares; let him not be submerged by the things of the world; let him not take upon himself the burden of worldly goods; let his senses be controlled; let him be wise but not puffed up, and let him not desire great possessions even for his family. Let him do nothing that is mean or that the wise would reprove.

May all beings be happy and at their ease! May they be joyous and live in safety!

All beings, whether weak or stong—omitting none—in high, middle or low realms of existence, small or great, visible or invisible, near or far away, born or to be born—may all beings be happy and at their ease!

Let none deceive another, or despise any being in any state! Let none by anger or ill-will wish harm to another!

Even as a mother watches over and protects her child, her only child, so with a boundless mind should one cherish all living beings, radiating friendliness over the entire world, above, below, and all around without limit. So let him cultivate a boundless good will towards the entire world, uncramped, free from ill-will or enmity.

Standing or walking, sitting or lying down, during all his waking hours, let him establish this mindfulness of good will, which men call the highest state!

Abandoning vain discussions, having a clear vision, free from sense appetites, he who is made perfect will never again know rebirth.

Middle Way 🅱 (Skt. madhyamā-pratipad; Pali, majjhimapātipadā); generally, a term for the way of the historical Buddha → Shākyamuni, which teaches avoidance of all extremes—like indulgence in the pleasures of the senses on one side and self-mortification and asceticism on the other. More specifically, it refers to the → Mādhyamika school founded by → Nāgārjuna, which refrains from choosing between opposing positions, and in relation to the existence or nonexistence of all things, treads a middle way.

In the Hīnayāna, the → eightfold path is seen as a middle way, since in following it, both wallowing in sense pleasures and asceticism are avoided, and it leads to release from suffering. This attitude is expressed in the texts in the following words: "Two extremes . . . are to be avoided by him who has entered into → homelessness: giving oneself over to sense pleasure, which is low, debased, worldly, ignoble, and meaningless; giving oneself over to self-mortification, which is full of suffering, ignoble and meaningless. The Perfect One avoided these two extremes and found the Middle Path, which opens the eyes, produces knowledge and leads to peace, insight, enlightenment, and nirvana; to wit, perfect knowledge, perfect outlook, perfect speech, perfect action, perfect livelihood, perfect effort, perfect mindfulness, and perfect concentration" (*Samyutta-nikāya* 56, 11).

Sometimes Middle Way also refers to the absence of eternalism or nihilism as well as of belief in the being or nonbeing of the world.

In Mādhyamika, the Middle Way is most clearly expressed in the so-called eight negations (→ Nāgārjuna) that analyze the nature of things: no elimination, no production, no destruction, no eternity, no unity, no manifoldness, no arriving, no departing.

In → Yogāchāra the Middle Way consists in not accepting the existence of all things (since in reality external things do not exist), nor postulating the nonexistence of all things (since on the basis of ideation they do indeed exist).

In → T'ien-t'ai (also → Tendai) the Middle Way is based on the recognition that all things are empty because they possess no independent reality; at the same time they have temporary validity, since as phenomena they have a certain duration. The synthesis between emptiness (→ *shūnyatā*) and phenomenal existence is the truth of the Middle Way.

Mien-pi 🆉 Chin. for → *menpeki*

Mikkyō 🅱 🆉 Jap., lit. "the secrect teaching"; Japanese term for so-called "mystical," or Tantric, Buddhism (Skt., → Vajrayāna). This form of Buddhism reached Japan at the beginning of the 9th century with Saichō (also Dengyō Daishi), the founder of the Japanese Tendai school, and Kūkai (also Kōbō Daishi), the founder of the Shingon school. Saichō settled on Hiei-san and Kūkai on Koya-san, two mountains in the vicinity of the old imperial city of Kyōto. The monasteries that were built on the two mountains became the main seats of the two schools.

Milam 🅱 (rmi-lam), Tib., lit. "dream"; one of the "six doctrines of Nāropa" (→ *Nāro chödrug*) in the practice of which dream images are used for spiritual development. One aspect of this "dream yoga" is exercising conscious influence on dreams. Through the practice the practitioner is brought to recognize the world of the waking state as merely a dream.

Milarepa 🅱 (Mi-la-ras-pa), Tib., roughly "Mila who wears the cotton cloth of an ascetic," 1025–1135; by far the most famous saint of Tibet. After trials of the utmost difficulty imposed on him by his master → Marpa, he received the complete teachings of the → *mahāmudrā* and of the → *Nāro chödrug*. His diligent and exemplary exertion in the realization of these teachings brought about the founding of the → Kagyupa school. The biography of Milarepa, composed in the 15th century, with all the spiritual songs it contains, is still today one of the greatest sources of inspiration in → Tibetan Buddhism. (English translation: see Lhalungpa 1984.)

Milarepa was born in western Tibet near the Nepalese border. When he was seven his father died and the family property fell into the hands of greedy relatives, who treated Milarepa and his mother badly. In order to revenge these injuries, Milarepa learned to master the destructive forces of nature and killed many people with a fierce storm. Wishing to atone for this deed, Milarepa turned to the → Nyingmapa teacher Röngtön, but the latter sent him to Marpa. Milarepa became Marpa's student at the age of thirty-eight, but for six years had only the role of a servant. During this period Marpa subjected Mila to extraordinarily harsh—seemingly cruel—training, which brought him to the end of his forces and to such despair that he was near suicide.

After Milarepa's evil deeds (→ karma) had been purified in this fashion, Marpa began preparing him for a life of solitude. He transmitted to him the teachings of Nāropa, laying particular emphasis on the practice of "inner heat" (Tib., *tummo*, → *Nāro chödrug*). Clad only in a thin cotton cloth, Milarepa lived for many years in complete seclusion in icy mountain caves in the Himalayas and devoted himself to his

Milarepa in his meditation cave in the Himalayas

meditative practice. After a period of nine years of uninterrupted solitude, he finally began to accept students and to teach the people through his songs. The most important of Milarepa's students was the physician → Gampopa.

Milinda 🅑 → *Milindapañha*

Milindapañha 🅑 Pali, lit. "The Questions of [King] Milinda"; the most important noncanonical work of the → Theravāda, composed in the form of a dialogue between the monk → Nāgasena and King Milinda (also Milindo), the Greek Menander, who in the first century B.C.E. conquered northern India from Peshawar to Patna. As a result of his conversations with Nāgasena, Milinda is said to have converted to Buddhism. (English translation: see Rhys Davids 1963.)

The *Milindapañha* seems to have served as a propaganda text for the conversion of the Greeks in northwest India. It was probably composed around the beginning of the common era. It has been preserved in Pali and in two Chinese translations. King Milinda's questions concern the basic teachings of Buddhism, particularly the doctrines of rebirth, → *anātman*, and the law of → karma. Nāgasena answers them with the help of noteworthy similes.

Mīmāmsā 🅗 (Mīmāṃsā), Skt., lit. "investigation"; name of two schools of Hindu philosophy. The older of the two is → Pūrva-Mīmāmsā, usually called Mīmāmsā; the later is → Uttara-Mīmāmsā, generaly known as → Vedānta. In contrast to Uttara-Mīmāmsā, which is concerned with knowledge of the truth, Pūrva-Mīmāmsā is primarily concerned with ritual. In general, the performance of rites precedes any quest for knowledge and is the preparation for such a quest. The actual performance of sacrifical rites depends upon correct interpretation of the Vedic texts, and decisions are made regarding the many questions of interpretation as they arise. The ritual instructions scattered throughout the → Brāhmanas are often so unclear that they cannot be understood without further investigation. → Jaimini attempted in his → *Mīmāmsā-Sūtra* to systematize all the various rules and precepts; thus, he is held as the founder of the Pūrva-Mīmāmsā school.

Even today Pūrva-Mīmāmsā plays a major role in Hindu life, since worship and the performance of sacrifices are held to bring about the fulfillment of every type of desire, whether spriritual (for which the ritual is preparatory cleansing) or everyday material desires.

The light of spiritual truth held in the Vedas finds its expression in the rhythmic perfection, the consummate style and the sublime poetry of the verses that are recited within the framework of Pūrva-Mīmāmsā. They are said to have been the basis for the Greek mystery rites performed by Orphic and Eleusian cults, which in turn prepared the ground for the thought of Pythagoras and Plato.

Mīmāmsā-Paribhāshā 🅗 (Mīmāmsā-Paribhāṣā), Skt., lit. "a clear presentation of Mīmāmsā"; a treatise on → Pūrva-Mīmāmsā, by Krishna Yajvan. Little is known about the author. Some familiarity with → Mīmāmsā is necessary for an understanding of the philosophical literature of Hinduism. This work is a particularly useful introduction, as it is the shortest, most easily comprehensible treatise on the most important questions regarding ritual, an extract from Jaimini's → *Mīmāmsā-Sūtra*. (An English translation is Mādhavānanda 1948.)

Mīmāmsā-Sūtra 🅗 (Mīmāṃsā-Sūtra), Skt.; → Jaimini's *sutra*, the foundation work of the school of → Mīmāmsā, is preceded by a long history of interpretations of Vedic sacrifical rites. In twelve chapters, Jaimini summarizes all the interpretations then current. The first chapter is of particular philosophical value, as it treats the sources of Vedic knowledge and their validity. Jaimini attempts to justify each section of the Vedas. His work is dated no earlier than the fourth century B.C.E.

Mīmāmsā-Vārttika ▣ (Mīmāṃsā-Vārttika), Skt., a treatise by → Kumārila Bhatta on the philosophy of → Mīmāmsā.

Mindfulness ▣ (Skt., smriti [smṛti]; Pali, sati). Practicing mindfulness in Buddhism means to perform consciously all activities, including everyday, automatic activities such as breathing, walking, etc., and to assume the attitude of "pure observation," through which clear knowledge, i.e., clearly conscious thinking and acting, is attained. In the practice of perfect mindfulness (→ eightfold path), one begins by rendering conscious the individual activities of the body. Then one extends mindfulness to sense data, thinking, and the objects of thinking. The intention of mindfulness practice is to bring the mind under control and to a state of rest. This practice brings insight into the transitory, unsatisfying, and essenceless nature of all existence and is thus the basis for all higher knowledge. Mindfulness is systematically taught through the practice of → *satipatthāna*, which is extraordinarily popular in the countries of the → Theravāda.

Mindfulness of the body ▣ (Pali, kāyagatā-sati); mindfulness directed toward the body. Part of the four foundations of mindfulness (→ *satipatthāna*). It consists of mindfulness of inhalation and exhalation (→ ānāpānasati) and of bodily posture (sitting, lying, walking, standing); lucid attention to all bodily activities; contemplation of the thirty-two parts of the body; analysis of the elements of the body (→ *dhātu-vavatthāna*); → charnel ground contemplation. Often the term *mindfulness of body* refers only to the contemplation of the thirty-two parts of the body.

In the → *Satipatthāna-sutta*, the contemplation of the thirty-two parts of the body is described in the following words: "And further, monks, a monk reflects on this very body enveloped by the skin and full of manifold impurity from the sole up, and from the top of the head-hair down, thinking thus: 'There are in this body hair of the head, hair of the body, nails, teeth, skin, flesh, sinews, bones, marrow, kidney, heart, liver, midriff, spleen, lungs, intestines, mesentery, gorge, faeces, bile, phlegm, pus, blood, sweat, fat, tears, grease, saliva, nasal mucus, synovial fluid, urine.' "

Ming ▣ Chin., lit. "luminosity"; Taoist enlightenment. According to Lao-tzu this enlightenment consists in the realization of the law of return to the source (→ *fu*). This law, to which all beings are subject, is characterized by the eternal and enduring (→ *ch'ang*). To know and understand it is a characteristic of the saint, who lives in accordance with it, by returning to the → Tao and realizing its simplicity, unity, and emptiness.

Chapter 16 of the → *Tao-te ching* (Feng & English 1972) explains as follows:

Empty yourself of everything
Let the mind rest at peace.
The ten thousand things rise and fall while the Self watches their return.
They grow and flourish and then return to the source.
Returning to the source is stillness, which is the way of nature.
The way of nature is unchanging (*Ch'ang*).
Knowing constancy is insight (*Ming*).
Not knowing constancy leads to disaster.
Knowing constancy, the mind is open.
With an open mind, you will be openhearted.
Being openhearted, you will act royally.
Being royal, you will attain the divine.
Being divine, you will be at one with the Tao.
Being at one with the Tao is eternal.
And though the body dies, the Tao will never pass away.

Ming ▣ Chin., roughly, fate, destiny, celestial mandate; a concept of → Confucianism, in which *ming* originally denoted the celestial mandate, i.e., the will of Heaven (→ *t'ien*) and later referred to the totality of all energies and conditions of the universe that are beyond the influence of the human will. The successful outcome of an action therefore essentially depends on *ming*.

To understand *ming* means to act in accordance with the requirements and obligations of a given situation, without being concerned about the success or failure of such action. To know *ming* means to accept the inevitability of the world as it is. This acceptance is considered one of the outstanding characteristics of the ideal man of Confucius.

Ming-chao Te-chien ▣ (Jap., Meishō [Myōshō] Tokken), Chinese Ch'an (Zen) master of about the 10th century; a student and dharma successor (→ *hassu*) of Master → Lo-han Tao-hsien (Jap., Rakan Dōkan). We encounter Ming-chao, who is also called the One-eyed Dragon (Chin., Tu-yen-lung; Jap., Dokugan-ryū) because he lost his left eye, in example 48 of the → *Pi-yen-lu*.

The master was active for forty years on Mount Ming-chao, the name of which was applied to him. He attracted many students and his words were in everyone's mouth in the Ch'an (Zen) circles of ancient China.

Ming-men T Chin., lit. "door of destiny"; a location situated between the kidneys of the human body and considered to be the source of the vital energy (→ *ch'i*).

Ming-ti B reigned 58–75; Chinese emperor of the Han Dynasty. According to legend, a dream of the emperor's was decisive for the spread of Buddhism in China. Ming-ti saw in his dream a golden deity hovering before his palace. The following morning he ordered his ministers to determine the identity of this deity. One of them reported that he had heard of a sage in India who had attained liberation and realized Buddhahood. He possessed a golden body and could fly. Emperor Ming accepted this interpretation of his dream and sent emissaries to the west to learn more about this sage. They returned with the → *Sūtra in Forty-two Sections* to house which the emperor had a temple built. This is said to have been the beginning of the spread of Buddhism in China. This story cannot, however, be regarded as historically founded.

Mīrā Bāī H North Indian princess and mystic poet, 1498?-1546, who renounced the world out of her great love for → Krishna. Her literary work (*Padāvalī*) consists of hundreds of poems in the form of various → *rāgas*. She wrote in her mother tongue, Mārwārī Hindī, interspersed with many words in Gujarātī and Panjābī. Her poems and songs are extraordinarily popular because of the passionate devotional surrender they express, and they are still sung today by Indians of all classes.

Early in life Mīrā Bāī felt drawn to the teachings of the → Vaishnavas, from whom she learned of God's love and mercy. Taking the name Giridhara-Nagar, she began to worship God in the form of Krishna. Her love for the all-encompassing Lord was so great that she spent her time exclusively in worship and praise of him, much to the distress of her husband and her family, who tormented her in every way possible to divert her from this activity. Nevertheless she remained steadfast, and when, upon the death of her husband, her father-in-law ordered her to follow the custom of self-immolation (see → *satī*), she refused, because she regarded herself not as a widow but as the bride of the universal soul. In spiritual ecstasy she sang and danced before the temple image of the Lord and went into → *samādhi*. People began to view her as a saint. Finally, she left the palace, spent several years in → Vrindāvan and → Mathurā, and then remained at the Krishna temple in → Dvārakā until her death.

Miroku B Z Jap. for → Maitreya

Mishaka Z Jap. name for the sixth patriarch of the Indian lineage of → Zen.

Mitra H Skt.; name of a sun god. In the Vedas, Mitra, lord of the day, is associated with → Varuna, ruler over the night. Together they maintain and govern heaven and earth, protect the world, encourage the pious, and punish sinners.

Mi-tsung B Chin., lit. "School of Secrets"; Tantric school of Chinese Buddhism, which was brought to China in the 8th century by three Indian masters of → Tantra: Shubhākarasimha (Chin., Shan-wu-wei, 637–735); Vajrabodhi (Chin., Chin-kang-chih, 663–723); and Amoghavajra (Chin., Pu-k'ung, 705–774). Shubhākarasimha, on whom was bestowed the title "teacher of the nation," translated the → *Mahāvairochana-sūtra*, the basic scripture of the school, into Chinese. Amoghavajra transmitted the magical formulas (→ mantra, → *dhāranī*) appertaining to it.

Important elements of the practice of this school are the recitation of mantras, the use of → mudrās and → mandalas, and of empowerment cermonies (→ *abhisheka*). The esoteric teachings of the Mi-tsung were transmitted only orally from master to disciple, which explains why the school never became widespread in China. After the death of Amoghavajra, who was the personal teacher of the three emperors, it quickly decreased in importance, since no more Tantric masters came to China from India.

This school was systematized and brought to Japan by → Kūkai, a Japanese monk and student of the Mi-tsung master Hui-kuo, who was in turn a student of Amoghavajra. The school is known as → Shingon in Japan, where it is one of the most important Buddhist schools. (Also → Mikkyō.)

Miu Chi T → T'ai-i

Mo-chao Ch'an Z Chin. for → *mokushō* Zen

Mo-chia T Chin. → Mo Ti

Moha H B Skt., roughly "bond, attachment, deluded love, deception"; derived from the verb *muh*, "become confused."

H one of the asura gunas, that is, the ungodly or—as Krishna says in the *Bhagavad-Gītā* (6, 10)—demonic qualities.

B → *akushala*

Mohism T → Mo Ti

Moji Zen Z → *kattō*

Moksha H (Mokṣa), Skt.; the final liberation and release from all worldly bonds, from → karma and the cycle of life and death (→ *samsāra*) through union with God or knowledge of the ultimate reality. *Moksha* is the highest of the four goals of human life; the other three are → *artha* (wealth), → *kāma* (pleasure), and → *dharma* (duty). For the spiritual aspirant, the realization of *moksha* is the sole aim of life.

Mokuan Shōtō 🅉 Jap. for → Mu-an Hsing-t'ao

Moku-funi 🅉 Jap., lit. "silent non-two"; a Zen expression indicating that the nondualistic nature of reality, the true nature, or buddha-nature (→ *busshō*), inherent in all phenomena, is best expressed through silence.

The expression comes from the *Vimalakīrtinirdesha-sūtra*, in which the bodhisattva → Mañjushrī praises the layman Vimalakīrti, whom Zen holds in particularly high esteem, saying that his silence is a better expression of nonduality than any exposition of the teaching. In Zen one also speaks in this context of the "thundering silence" of Vimalakīrti. Scholars generally consider Vimalakīrti a legendary figure.

Mokugyō 🅉 Jap., lit. "wooden fish," also gyōrin; a wooden drum originally carved in the form of a fish, but which today usually has a bell-like form. The *mokugyō*, which is struck with a stick with a padded head, is used in Japan in the recitation of sūtras in Buddhist monasteries.

In Buddhism fish, since they never sleep, symbolize the resiliency and wakefulness necessary on the path to → buddhahood.

Mokusa 🄱 Jap. → *moxa*

Mokushō Zen 🅉 Jap. (Chin., *mo-chao ch'an*), lit. the Zen of silent enlightenment; an expression that came into being during the lifetime of the Chinese Ch'an (Zen) master → Hung-chih Cheng-chueh (Jap., Wanshi Shōgaku, 1091–1157) to distinguish the style of meditative practice favored by the → Sōtō school from the "Zen of the contemplation of words" (→ *kanna* Zen) that at the same time became the practice typical of the → Rinzai school. *Mokushō* Zen stresses primarily the practice of → *zazen* without the support of such means as → kōans; i.e., it stresses that form of practice later called → *shikantaza* by the great Japanese Zen master → Dōgen Zenji.

Although *kanna* Zen was associated with the Zen of the Rinzai school and *mokushō* Zen with that of the Sōtō school, the Sōtō school also uses kōans and the practice of the Rinzai school always contains elements of *mokushō* Zen.

Mondō 🅉 Jap. (Chin., *Wen-ta*), lit. "question [and] answer"; Zen dialogue between masters or between master and student in which one party asks a question concerning Buddhism or some existential problem that has profoundly disquieted him and the other, without recourse in any way to theory or logic, responds in a way that invokes the answer from the deepest layers of his partner's heart-mind (→ *kokoro*; also → *hossen*).

Many *mondō* handed down by tradition later became → kōans. Three famous examples of such *mondō* are the following:

"A monk asked master Tung-shan, 'What is Buddha?' Tung-shan said, 'Three pounds of flax' [Jap., *masagin*]."

"Ta-mei once asked Ma-tsu, 'What is Buddha?' Ma-tsu said, 'Not mind, not Buddha.' "

"A monk asked Chao-chou 'What is the meaning of the patriarch's coming from the west?' Chao-chou said, 'The oak over there in the garden.' "

Monji-hōshi 🅉 Jap., lit. "scriptures dharma master"; Zen expression referring to a Buddhist teacher who is attached to the literal sense of the teaching of the Buddha in its traditional written form (→ sūtra) without understanding or actualizing its deeper sense.

Monju 🄱 🅉 Jap. for → Mañjushrī

Monna 🅉 Jap., lit. "question word"; a question posed by a Zen student to his master in a → *mondō*.

Mosshōryō 🅉 Jap., lit. "unthinkable, unspeakable"; Zen expression referring to the true nature of reality. (Also → *fukashigi*, → *fukasetsu*.)

Mosshōseki 🅉 Jap., lit. "leaving no trace"; as a flying bird leaves no trace in the sky and a swimming fish no trace the water, according to the Zen view, the person who has realized → enlightenment should live leaving no trace. By this is meant that he should live with a complete naturalness to which no trace of his knowledge of having attained "enlightenment" clings.

This is the state of "second naturalness" (the "first naturalness" is the state of innocence of an infant, a state from which the infant soon falls); basically it is the discovery of the primordial naturalness, which is present even before the "first naturalness".

Attainment of the state of *mosshōseki* presupposes realization of profound enlightenment. Nevertheless, one who still betrays traces of this enlightenment, or as it is said in Zen, who "stinks of enlightenment," has not yet entirely integrated the enlightenment he has experienced into his everyday life. (Also → *goseki*).

Mo Ti 🅃 also known as Mo-tzu (Master Mo),

about 468–376 B.C.E.; opponent of Confucius (→ K'ung-tzu) and founder of Mohism (Chin., *mo-chia*). His doctrines are contained in a work known as *Mo-tzu,* which in all probability was compiled by his pupils around 400 B.C.E. (see Graham 1978; Mei 1929; Watson 1967).

Mo Ti initially studied the teachings of Confucius (→ K'ung-tzu), but was unable to agree with his definition of morality (→ *li*). He thus developed his own philosophy, the central idea of which was an all-embracing love, not confined to the family or clan (as in the case of Confucius) and subject to the will of Heaven (→ *t'ien*). In his philosophy Mo Ti personifies Heaven and sees it as a supreme being, which will intervene unfavorably in the lives of men who do not love each other. Mo Ti furthermore bases his doctrine on the existence of spirits and demons, who also punish those who do not live in accordance with the principle of all-embracing love and reward those who do.

Mo Ti rejects offensive warfare, criticizes the elaborateness of Confucianist rites, and considers the cultivation of music—an important feature of Confucianist doctrine—as a mere waste of time. For about two centuries, Mohism held its own against the teachings of Confucius but later was gradually displaced by it. The followers of Mo Ti were tightly organized in groups, some of which continued to study problems of logic and dialectics and even matters of technology, which led to an elaboration of certain materialist aspects of Mohism.

Mo-tzu 🅃 Chin. → Mo Ti

Moxa 🄱 Jap., actually *mokusa*, lit. "burn herb"; the burning in of scars, by means of a small cone of incense, on the head of a monk or nun at the end of the → ordination ceremony. This was a widespread custom in China. The number of scars, depending on the monastery, was between three and twelve.

There was also a more general practice of *moxa* cultivated by ascetic monks in China. They made burns representing, for example, a → *mālā* of 108 beads, a swastika, or the Chinese character for *buddha* on their chests. Burning in of these symbols was also accomplished with small cones of herbs. During this extremely painful procedure, monks recited a formula of veneration to the Buddha or a bodhisattva, asking for his assistance.

Mrityuñjaya-Siddhi 🄷 (Mṛtyuñjaya-Siddhi), Skt., from *mrityu*: "death," *jaya*: "conquer"; one of the → *siddhis* that may be gained by the rising of → *kundalinī*. One who achieves this is given the title Mrityuñjeya, "Victor over Death." (See also → *chakra*.)

Mu 🅉 Jap. (Chin., *wu*), lit. "nothing, not, nothingness, un-, is not, has not, not any"; the → *wato* of the famous kōan "Chao-chou, dog," often called the kōan *mu*. This kōan (→ *Wu-men-kuan* 1) is as follows:

A monk asked master Chao-chou respectfully, "Does a dog really have buddha-nature or not?" Chao-chou said, "*Mu.*"

The task of the Zen student, while practicing → *zazen* with this *mu*, is to come to an immediate experience, beyond any intellectual signification, of its very profound content. Since this kōan is extraordinarily apt as a *hosshin-kōan* (→ kōan), it is often the first kōan received by a Zen student from his master. When the student has mastered it, it is said that he has become acquainted with "the world of *mu*." In the course of Zen training this *mu* is to be experienced and demonstrated on ever deeper levels.

Mu-an Hsing-t'ao 🅉 (Jap., Mokuan Shōtō), 1611–1684, Chinese Ch'an (Zen) master of the → Ōbaku school. He was the student and dharma successor (→ *hassu*) of → Yin-yuan Lung-ch'i (Jap., Ingen Ryūki), whom he followed to Japan in 1655.

In Japan Yin-yuan founded the Ōbaku school and in 1664 installed Mu-an as its second patriarch. In 1671 Mu-an founded the Zuishō-ji monastery in the neighborhood of Edo (present-day Tōkyō). As its first abbot, he contributed greatly to the diffusion of the Ōbaku school in Japan.

Mu-chou Ch'en-tsun-su 🅉 (Jap., Bokushū [Bokujū] Chinsonshuku), also Mu-chao Tao-tsung or Mu-chou Tao-ming (Jap., Bokushū Dōmei [Dōmyō]), ca. 780–877; Chinese Ch'an (Zen) master; a student and dharma successor (→ *hassu*) of → Huang-po Hsi-yun (Jap., Ōbaku Kiun). Mu-chou was one of the most important students of Huang-po. It was he who first recognized the great potential of → Lin-chi I-hsuan (Jap., Rinzai Gigen) and recommended to his master to accept the young Lin-chi as a student. Mu-chou is also known as the strict master of → Yun-men Wen-yen (Jap., Ummon Bun'en).

It is reported concerning Mu-chou that he always kept the door of his room shut. If a monk came for → *dokusan*, Mu-chou was able to discern the monk's state of mind by the sound of his step. If he considered this state of mind promising, he called out, "Come in!" grabbed hold of the monk as soon as he entered, shook him, and shouted, "Say it! Say it!" If the monk hesitated only for an instant, he shoved him out and slammed the door behind him. This very sequence of events befell Yun-men one day, but his leg caught in the door when Mu-chou slammed it. The leg broke and Yun-men shouted *ouch!* with pain. In that very moment he came abruptly to enlightenment.

We encounter Mu-chou in example 10 of the → *Pi-yen-lu.*

In the → *Ching-te ch'uan-teng-lu* we learn that Mu-chou settled at the Lung-hsin monastery in Mu-chou after he had taken leave of Huang-po. He "effaced his traces" and did not let himself be recognized as a master. He made straw sandals and secretly placed them out in the street for the poor. People found out only after many years that the sandals came from him and then gave him the nickname *Straw-Sandal Ch'en.* When Buddhist scholars came to ask him questions, he answered instantaneously. His pronouncements were short and followed no orthodox teaching. Thus those with little understanding laughed at him; only persons of deeper insight grasped what he was saying. Eventually his reputation spread; students gathered around him and Mu-chou became known as a strict Zen master. In example 10 of the *Pi-yen-lu* we see him in → *mondō* with a monk:

> Mu-chou asked a monk, "Where do you come from?"
> Immediately the monk shouted, *ho!* [→ *katsu!*]
> Mu-chou said, "Now the old monk [himself] has had a *ho* from you."
> The monk again shouted, *ho!*
> Mu-chou said, "A third *ho* and a fourth *ho*, and then what?"
> The monk said nothing more.
> Mu-chou hit him and said, "What a scoundrel!"

Mu-chou Tao-ming 🅉 (Jap., Bokushū Dōmei [Dōmyō]), → Mu-chou Ch'en-tsun-su

Mu-chou Tao-tsung 🅉 → Mu-chou Ch'en-tsun-su

Muditā 🅑 Skt., Pali, roughly "sympathetic joy"; one of the → *brahma-vihāras. Muditā* means sympathetic joy in the happiness of other beings. The practice of *muditā* helps to overcome taking pleasure in others' misfortunes and to eliminate the sense of separation between self and other. As one of the "four immeasurable states of a buddha," *muditā* manifests particularly as limitless joy over the liberation of others from suffering (→ samsāra.)

Mudrā 🅗 🅑 Skt., lit. "seal, sign"; a bodily posture or a symbolic gesture.

🅗 The *mudrās* of ritual worship (→ *pūjā*) in Hinduism are meant to connect outer actions with spiritual concepts. They also assist in concentration of the mind on God, comparable to the Christian gestures of kneeling and folding one's hands to pray.

🅑 In Buddhist iconography every buddha is depicted with a characteristic gesture of the hands. Such gestures correspond to natural gestures (of teaching, protecting, and so on) and also to certain aspects of the Buddhist teaching or of the particular buddha depicted. Mudrās acquired special significance in the Mahāyāna, especially in the esoteric schools (→ T'ien-t'ai, → Mi-tsung, → Vajrayāna). Here mudrās accompany the performance of liturgies and the recitation of → mantras. They also help to actualize certain inner states in that they anticipate their physical expression; thus they assist in bringing about a connection between the practitioner and the buddha visualized in a given pratice (→ *sādhana*).

The most important mudrās are (1) *dhyāni* mudrā (gesture of meditation), (2) *vitarka* mudrā (teaching gesture), (3) *dharmachakra* mudrā (gesture of turning the wheel of the teaching), (4) *bhūmi-sparsha* mudrā (gesture of touching the earth), (5) *abhaya* mudrā (gesture of fearlessness and granting protection), (6) *varada* mudrā (gesture of granting wishes), (7) *uttarabodhi* mudrā (gesture of supreme enlightenment), (8) mudrā of supreme wisdom, (9) *añjali* mudrā (gesture of greeting and veneration), and (10) *vajrapradama* mudrā (gesture of unshakable confidence).

1. *Dhyāni mudrā.* In this mudrā, the back of the right hand rests on the palm of the other in such a way that the tips of the thumbs lightly touch one another. The hands rest in the lap. The right hand, resting on top, symbolizes the state of enlightenment; the other hand, resting below, the world of appearance. This gesture expresses overcoming the world of appearance through enlightenment, as well as the enlightened state of mind for which → samsāra and → nirvāna are one.

In a special form of this mudrā, the middle, ring, and little fingers of both hands lie on top of one another and the thumb and index finger of each hand, touching each other, form a circle, which here also symbolizes the world of appearance and the true nature of reality. This hand posture is often found in representations of the Buddha → Amitābha, hence it is also called the "meditation mudrā of Amitābha."

2. *Vitarka mudrā.* The right hand points upward, the left downward; both palms are tuned outward. The thumb and index finger of each hand form a circle. The right hand is at shoulder level, the left at the level of the hips. In a variant of this teaching gesture, the left hand rests palm upward in the lap, and the right hand is raised to shoulder level with its thumb and index finger forming a circle. In a further form of this mudrā, the index and little fingers of both hands are fully extended, the middle and ring fingers somewhat curved inward. The left hand points upward, the right downward.

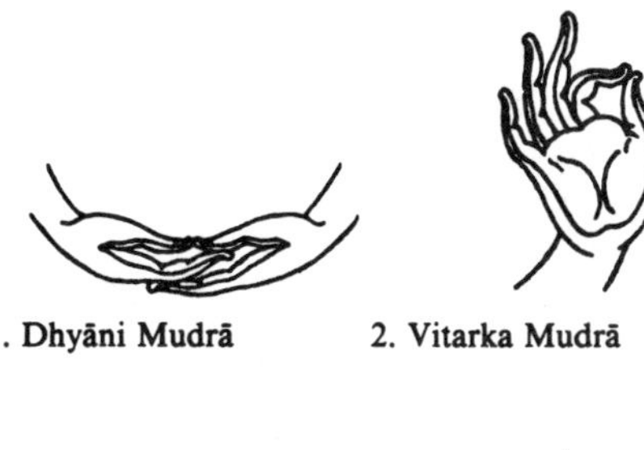

1. Dhyāni Mudrā 2. Vitarka Mudrā

3. Dharmachakra Mudrā

4. Bhūmisparsha Mudrā

5. Abhaya Mudrā

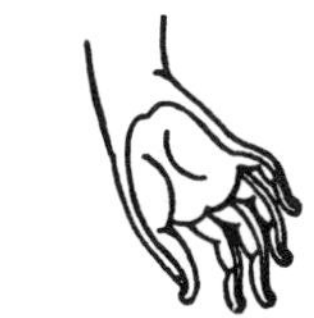

6. Varada Mudrā

7. Uttarabodhi Mudrā

8. Mudrā of Supreme Wisdom

9. Añjali Mudrā

10. Vajrapradama Mudrā

The ten most important mudrās

The *vitarka* mudrā is found most frequently in representations of Amitābha but also in representations of → Vairochana and others.

3. *Dharmachakra mudrā.* The left palm is tuned inward (toward the body), the right outward, and the circles formed by the thumbs and index fingers of each hand touch one another.

The *dharmachakra* mudrā is found primarily in representations of → Shākyamuni, Amitābha, Vairochana, and → Maitreya.

4. *Bhūmisparsha mudrā.* The left hand rests palm upward in the lap; the right hand, hanging over the knee, palm inward, points to the earth. Sometimes the left hand holds a begging bowl. This is the gesture with which the Buddha summoned the Earth as witness to his realization of → buddhahood. It is considered a gesture of unshakability; thus → Akshobhya (the Unshakable) is usually depicted with this mudrā.

5. *Abhaya mudrā.* Here the right hand is raised to shoulder height with fingers extended and palm turned outward. This is the gesture of the Buddha Shākyamuni immediately after attaining enlightenment. → Amoghasiddhi is also frequently depicted with this mudrā.

6. *Varada mudrā.* The right hand, palm facing out, is directed downward. When Shākyamuni is depicted with this mudrā, it symbolizes summoning Heaven as witness to his buddhahood. This mudrā is also seen in representations of → Ratnasambhava. In a variant, the thumb and index finger of the downward-extended hand touch one another. Frequently the *abhaya* and *varada* mudrās are combined: the right hand makes the gesture of fearlessness, the left that of wish granting. Standing buddha figures are often shown in this posture.

7. *Uttarabodhi mudrā.* Both hands are held at the level of the chest, the two raised index fingers touch one another (and form the point of a → *vajra*), the remaining fingers are crossed and folded down; the thumbs touch each other at the tips or are also crossed and folded. This mudrā is frequently seen in images of Vairochana.

8. *Mudrā of supreme wisdom.* The right index finger is grasped by the five fingers of the left hand. This mudrā, characteristic of Vairochana, is the subject of many interpretations in esoteric Buddhism, most of which have to do with the relationship between the empirical world of manifoldness and the principle that is its basis—the unified world principle, the realization of unity in the manifold as embodied in the Buddha.

9. *Añjali mudrā.* The palms are held together at the level of the chest. This is the customary gesture of greeting in India. Used as a mudrā, it expresses "suchness" (→ *tathatā*).

10. *Vajrapradama mudrā.* The fingertips of the hands are crossed.

Mugaku Sogen 🅩 Jap. for → Wu-hsueh Tsuyuan

Mu-ichimotsu 🅩 Jap., lit. "not one thing"; an expression that originated with → Hui-neng, the sixth patriarch of Ch'an (Zen) in China. It points to the fact no phenomenon has a permanent substance as its basis—all things are nothing other than manifestations of emptiness (Jap., *ku*; Skt., → *shūnyatā*). There exists "not one thing."

Mui-no-shinnin 🅉 Jap., lit. "genuine person without rank"; an expression that originated with the great Chinese Ch'an (Zen) master → Lin-chi I-hsuan (Jap., Rinzai Gigen). It refers to a person who has realized profound enlightenment, or indicates the true nature, or buddha-nature (→ *busshō*) that is immanent in every person.

Mujaku 🅉 Jap. for → Wu-cho

Muji 🅉 Jap., lit. "the [written] character *mu*; term for the kōan → *mu.*

Mujōdō-no-taigen 🅉 Jap., lit. "the embodiment [*taigen*] of the unsurpassable way [*mujōdō*]"; expression for the embodiment of → enlightenment (also → satori, → *kensho*) as lived in everyday life; realization of buddha-nature (→ *busshō*) to which no trace of intention, no thought of "enlightenment" and its "realization," still clings. This means continuing uninterruptedly in the "*samādhi* of innocent playfulness."

This state does not arise of itself from satori, but requires long training after the occurrence of satori. As many Zen masters say, "One or two lives are not enough for that." The path that leads to living spontaneously what one has experienced is a long one.

Mujū 🅉 Jap. → Ichien

Mujun Shiban 🅉 Jap. for → Wu-chun Shih-fan

Mukan Fumon 🅉 also Daimin Kokushi (→ *kokushi*), d. 1293; Japanese Zen master of the → Rinzai school; his first master was → Ben'en (also Shōichi Kokushi); later Mukan traveled to China where he trained for twelve years under a Rinzai Zen master and received the seal of confirmation (→ *inka-shōmei*) from him.

After returning to Japan, he became abbot of the Tōfuku-ji monastery in Kyōto and thus the third-generation successor of Ben'en. In 1293 he was appointed the first abbot of the → Nanzen-ji monastery in Kyōto by Emperor Kameyama; however, he died before he could assume this post.

Muktānanda, Svāmi 🄷, 1908-1983; born in South India, he followed the path of → Siddha-Yoga, taught in the West as well as in the East, and was venerated as a holy man.

Svāmi Muktānanda went on pilgrimage at the age of eighteen, and studied → Vedānta and other sacred texts under various teachers. In 1947 he met his guru, Svāmi Nityānanda; later he became head of the Gurudev Āshram in Ganishpuri, near Bombay. His teaching addresses the true self (→ *ātman*) of man and its identity with absolute consciousness (→ *brahman*).

Mukti 🄷 Skt. → *moksha*

Mūlādhāra chakra 🄷 🄱 Skt. → chakra 1

Mūlaprakriti 🄷 (Mūlaprakṛti), or → Avyakta, Skt., lit. *mūla*: "origin, root," *prakriti*: "nature"; the primal element, from which all forms have developed. The first slight vibrations of life are created by the mutual influence of → *parabrahman* and *mūlaprakriti*, divine, transcendent Being and the first divine form. *Mūlaprakriti* is the seed form of → *prakriti*, that is, of all forms from the most subtle to the grossest.

Mūlāvidyā 🄷 Skt., from *mūla:* "origin, root," → *avidyā:* "ignorance"; the primal ignorance, metaphysically the primal cause of the creation of the universe.

Mumon Ekai 🅉 Jap. → Wu-men Hui-k'ai

Mumonkan 🅉 Jap. for → *Wu-men-kuan*

Mumukshutva 🄷 (Mumukṣutva), Skt., from *mumukshu:* "striving for liberation"; serious and constant longing for liberation, one of the four prerequisites for the spiritual aspirant that → Shankara mentions in his work *Tattva-bodha* ("The knowledge of truth"). The other three are: → *viveka* (discriminatory faculty), → *vairāgya* (detachment), and → *shatkasampatti* (the "six great virtues").

Mundaka-Upanishad 🄷 (Muṇḍaka-Upaniṣad), or *Mantra-Upanishad,* Skt.; an Upanishad belonging to the → *Atharvaveda*; it is highly prized for its purity and clarity of expression. It consists of three sections. The first describes the preparation for the knowledge of → *brahman;* the second contains the teaching of *brahman;* the third indicates the way to *brahman.*

Muni 🄷 🄱 Skt.; a pious person, scholar, or saint of more or less divine nature, who through asceticism and spiritual practice has reached a high level of consciousness.

This term is also used as a title for → *rishis* and authors of important texts, as, for example, Pānini and Vyāsa. The *munis* have for the most part used their supernormal powers beneficially but occasionally also to curse gods and men.

Mushin 🅉 Jap., colloquial, lit. "innocence"; in Zen an expression for detachment of mind, a state of complete naturalness and freedom from dualistic thinking and feeling. (Also → *mosshōseki*).

Mushinjō 🅉 Jap., from mu, "not, no," shin, "heart-mind, consciousness," and jō (= sadameru), "establish, decide, determine, resolve"; Zen expression for a kind of trance, a state brought about by meditation, in which consciousness ceases to function and the mind becomes completely vacuous. (Also → five types of Zen 3.)

Musō Daishi Z honorific title for → Kanzan Egen

Musō Kokushi Z → Musō Soseki

Musō Soseki Z also Shōkaku Kokushi, known as Musō Kokushi (→ *kokushi*), 1275–1351; famous Japanese Zen master of the → Rinzai school, who made a major contribution to the spread of Zen in Japan. He became a monk at the age of eight and first devoted himself to study of the → sūtras and the teachings of the mystical schools of Buddhism (→ Mikkyō). Then he underwent Zen training and eventually received the seal of confirmation (→ *inka-shōmei*) from Master Ken'ichi (also Bukkoku Kokushi, ?–1314). During long and eventful years of wandering he lived in various monasteries and hermitages, where he dedicated himself to sitting in meditation. At last he was appointed abbot of → Tenryū-ji, one of the monasteries of the → Gosan of Kyōto. In this post he became one of the central figures in the Buddhist culture of the imperial city.

Zen master Musō Soseki (contemporary portrait)

Musō Soseki was one of the leading authors of the Literature of the Five Mountains (→ Gosan-bungaku), which played a major role in the transplantation of Chinese science and art to Japan. His name is associated with the foundation of numerous monasteries, and he was the abbot of several influential Zen monasteries, among them, → Nanzen-ji. At his instance Shōgun Ashikaga Takauji had "Zen monasteries for the gratification of the country" (Jap., *ankoku-ji*) built in sixty-six Japanese localities, from which Zen spread throughout the country. Among his principal works are the *Muchū-mondō*, in which the principles of Zen are presented in the form of questions and answers. He is also famous as a master of the Way of calligraphy (→ *shōdō*) and of the art of garden design. He received the title of Musō Kokushi from Emperor Go-Daigo, and posthumously the honorific title Musō Shōgaku Shinshū Kokushi from Emperor Kōmyō.

Myōan Eisai Z → Eisai Zenji

Myōchō Shūhō Z also Shūhō Myōchō, known as Daitō Kokushi (→ *kokushi*), 1282–1338; Japanese Zen master of the → Rinzai school; a student and dharma successor (→ *hassu*) of → Shōmyō (known as Daiō Kokushi) and the master of → Kanzan Egen (also Musō Daishi). These three Zen masters are the founders of the → Ō-tō-kan school, a particularly important lineage of Rinzai Zen in Japan. Myōchō was the founder and first abbot of → Daitoku-ji in Kyōto, one of the most important Zen monasteries in Japan.

Myōchō entered the monastery of Enkyō-ji on Mount Shosha in Hyōgo province at the age of ten. Later he trained under master Ken'ichi, the abbot of Monju-ji in Kyōto. In Master Shōyō, whom he met in Kyōto and followed to Kamakura, he finally found the master who was to lead him to enlightenment. He was confirmed by Shōyō as his dharma successor at the age of twenty-five. Myōchō returned to Kyōto and, following the counsel of his master, "effaced his traces" for roughly twenty years before he came forward as a Zen master. It is said that during this time he lived in utmost poverty among the beggers under Kyōto's Gojō Bridge.

At last he settled in a hermitage on a hill on the edge of Kyōto, where soon many students gathered around him. The press of persons seeking instruction from him on the way of Zen was soon so great that a great monastery, Daitoku-ji, was built to house them. From the abdicated emperor Hanazono, who was among his students, he received the honorific title of *kōzen daitō kokushi*. Daitoku-ji was soon declared the monastery in which the emperor's health was to be prayed for and, in the classification of the → Gosan of Kyōto, placed above them. Myōchō received posthumously the honorific titles of *daiijun kyōshi kokushi* and *genkaku kōen kokushi* from the imperial house.

In spite of the great esteem in which he was held already during his lifetime, Daitō Kokushi remained a man of utmost humility. At a time several generations after Daitō when Rinzai Zen in Japan was in the grips of decline, → Ikkyū Sōjun, one of Daitō's most important dharma heirs in the Ō-tō-kan lineage, sang the praise of the great Zen master in a poem with the title "Written on the Last Page of a Biography of Daitō" (trans. from Shuichi & Thom 1979):

Far
Over the heavens
Streams Daitō's light.
Before his monastery
They throng in gorgeous sedan chairs
Trying to see the master.
No one remembers the time
When he lived from wind
And slept on water
Twenty years
Beneath the Gojō Bridge.

Myōhō-renge-kyō 🅑 🅩 Jap. for → *Lotus Sūtra*

Myōshō Shūhō 🅩 → Myōchō Shūhō

Myōshō Tokken 🅩 Jap. for → Ming-chao Te-chien

Myōzen Butsuju 🅩 → Myōzen Ryōnen

Myōzen Ryōnen 🅩 also Myōzen Butsuju, 1184–1225; early Zen master of the Ōryo lineage of Rinzai Zen (→ Ōryo school); a student and dharma successor (→ *hassu*) of → Eisai Zenji and after Eisai the second Zen master of → Dōgen Zenji. In 1223 Myōzen went with Dōgen to China, where he died after three years in T'ien-t'ung Monastery (Jap., Tendō-ji).

N

Nachiketa 🅗 (Naciketa), Skt.; the story of the young boy Nachiketa appears in the *Taittirīya-Brāhmana* and in the → *Katha-Upanishad.* Its philosophical significance lies in Nachiketa's request of → Yama, the god of death, for the secret of immortality. In order to test him, Yama initially witholds the answer. Only when he is convinced of Nachiketa's determination and maturity does Yama impart his teaching regarding this essential question.

Nachiketa's father, Vājashravasa, wanted to attain heaven and thus promised a great sacrifice. His son said that Vājashravasa had not given all that he had and asked, "To whom do you give me?" His father, annoyed, replied, "To Death." Nachiketa then entered the realm of Death but had to wait three days for the arrival of Yama, who thereupon offered him three boons. Nachiketa first wished that his father would forgive him. This was granted. Then he asked for instruction concerning the fire sacrifice, by means of which one attains heaven. Yama taught him this and added that the sacrifice would henceforth be named for him. As his third boon he asked what happened to man after death. Yama replied that even the gods could not solve this riddle, and tried to offer the boy all the treasures of → *māyā* in place of the boon he had asked for. But Nachiketa, not allowing himself to be disconcerted, insisted on his original wish, whereupon the god of death taught him the secret of immortality.

Nāda 🅗 Skt., lit. "sound, tone"; vibratory energy manifested as sound; inner, mystical sound. *Nāda-bindu* refers to the original vibration, the primal sound, from which the universe unfolded. *Nāda-brahman* is a term used to refer to the sound symbol → OM, the sound of → *brahman.* Illumined ones who have reached a very high level are said to be able to perceive this sound.

Nadī 🅗 🅑 (naḍī) Skt., lit. "tube, vessel, vein"; the *nadīs* are the energy channels through which → *prāna*, which is necessary for life, passes to all parts of the body. (Also → chakra).

Nāga 🅗 🅑 Skt., lit. "serpent."

🅗 1. A snake, especially the cobra, depicted as a mystical, semidivine being with a human face, the tail of a snake, and the raised head of a cobra. 2. Followers of a snake cult widespread in India. 3. A people, traces of whom can be found in the history of the Indian subcontinent. Certain mountains bear their name, and Nāga-Dvīpa was one of the seven subdivisions of the ancient country Bhāratavasha (India). The Nāagas were clearly not Hindus; they are thought to have been Scythes. Their name, which probably reflects their practice of snake veneration, has been retained in such place names as Nāgpur.

🅑 the "dragon," a beneficent half-divine being, which in spring climbs into the heavens and in winter lives deep in the Earth. *Nāga* or *mahānāga* ("great dragon") is often used as a synonym for the Buddha or for the sages who have matured beyond rebirth. *Nāgarāja* ("dragon king" or "dragon queen") are water deities who govern springs, rivers, lakes, and seas. In many Buddhist traditions (for example, → Tibetan Buddhism) the *nāgas* are water deities who in their sea palaces guard Buddhist scriptures that have been placed in their care because humanity is not yet ripe for their reception.

Nagara 🅗 Skt., lit. "city"; India contains seven sacred cities, wherein Hindus can attain eternal bliss (→ *ānanda*). They are (1) Ayodhyā; (2) → Mathurā; (3) → Gayā; (4) Kāshī (Benares); (5) → Kānchī (Conjeeveram); (6) Avantī (Ujjayinī); and (7) → Dvārakā. All seven are visited by pilgrims.

Nāgārjuna 🅑 🅩 one of the most important philosophers of Buddhism and the founder of the → Mādhyamika school. Hardly any reliable dates for his life (2d/3d century) are known. Numerous works are attributed to him that were probably written by various other authors. His most important authentic work is the *(Mūla-) Mādhyamaka-kārikā* (*Memorial Verses on the Middle Teaching*). It contains the essentials of Nāgārjuna's thought in twenty-seven short chapters (400 verses). Nāgārjuna is also considered the author of the *Mahāyāna-vimshaka* (*Twenty Songs on the Mahāyāna*) and of the *Dvādashadvāra-shāstra* (*Treatise of the Twelve Gates*). According to tradition, he is also the author of the *Mahāprajñāpāramitā-shastra*, which is only extant in Chinese translation and probably originated in China. In the → Zen tradition, he is considered the 14th patriarch of the Indian lineage.

Nāgārjuna's major accomplishment was his systematization and deepening of the teaching presented in the → *Prajñāpāramitā-sūtra*. He developed a special dialectic based on a reductio ad absurdum of opponents' positions. Starting from the premise that each thing exists only in virtue of its opposite, he shows that all things are only relative and without essence (*svabhāvatā*), i.e. are empty (→ *shūnyatā*). Nāgārjuna's methodological approach of rejecting all opposites is the basis of the → Middle Way of the Mādhyamikas; it is directly connected with the teaching of the Buddha. This middle position is clearly expressed in the "eight negations": no elimination (→ *nirodha*), no production, no destruction, no eternity, no unity, no manifoldness, no arriving, no departing.

Nāgārjuna's name comes from → *nāga*, "serpent" and *arjuna*, a type of tree. According to tradition, Nāgārjuna was born under a tree and was instructed in the occult sciences by the *nāgas* in their palace under the sea. There, in some caves, he is said to have discovered the Buddhist scriptures.

Typical depiction of Nāgārjuna (Tibetan block print)

Nāgārjuna is the first in the history of Buddhism to have constructed a philosophical "system." With this system he sought to prove the thesis of the unreality of the external world, a point that is presented in the *Prajñāpāramitā-sūtra* as an experiential fact. In this way he laid the foundation for the Mādhyamaka; however, his teaching also exercised considerable influence on the development of other Buddhist schools. Nāgārjuna selected as his point of departure the law of conditioned arising (→ *pratītya-samutāpada*), which for him constitutes the basic nature of the world. He sees it as unreal and empty, since through it no arising, passing away, eternity, mutability, etc. are possible.

Nāgārjuna attempts to show the emptiness of the world through the relativity of opposites. Opposites are mutually dependent; one member of a pair of opposites can only arise through the other. From this he draws the conclusion that such entities cannot really exist, since the existence of one presupposes the existence of the other.

A central notion in his proofs is that of nonessentiality: the things of the phenomenal world possess no essence. An essence is eternal, immutable, and independent of all other essences; but the things of the world of appearance arise and pass away—they are empty.

Thus for Nāgārjuna emptiness means the absence of an essence in things but not their nonexistence as phenomena. Thus it is false to say that things exist or that they do not exist. The truth lies in the middle, in emptiness. The world of phenomena does have a certain truth, a truth on the conventional level (→ *samvriti-satya*), but no definitive truth (→ *paramārtha-satya*). From the point of view of the conventional truth, the world and also the Buddhist teaching have their validity; from the point of view of the definitive truth, all of that does not exist since everything is only appearance. For Nāgārjuna the phenomenal world is characterized by manifoldness (*prapañcha*), which is the basis of all mental representations and thus creates the appearance of an external world. Absolute reality, on the other hand, is devoid of all manifoldness. Absence of manifoldness means → nirvāna. In nirvāna the manifoldness of the world and the law of conditioned arising are effaced. It is by its very nature peaceful.

Nirvāna and the phenomenal world, for Nagarjuna as well as the *Prajñāpāramitā-sūtra*, are fundamentally identical. They are only two forms of appearance of the same reality. That which constitutes the phenomenal world in the aspect of conditionedness and contingency is, in the aspect of unconditionedness and noncontingency, nirvāna. Thus for Nāgārjuna nirvāna consists not of something that can be attained, but rather in the realization of the true nature of phenomena, in which manifoldness comes to rest.

Nāgasena 🅱 a learned monk whose conversations with King Milinda on difficult points of the Buddhist teaching were written down in the → *Milindapañha*. Nāgasena is supposed to have lived in the 1st century C.E.. He came from a brahmin family and entered the Buddhist → *sangha* at the age of fifteen. He studied the teaching in various places, among them → Pātaliputra, where he is said to have attained the stage of an → arhat. He is considered to have been extremely talented: after only one hearing he purportedly memorized the entirety of the → Abhidharma-pitaka. His historicity is widely doubted.

Nagna 🅷 Skt., lit. "naked, bare"; a sect of → *sannyāsins,* whose members go naked as a sign that they have overcome all sexual desire.

Naishkarmya-Siddhi 🅷 (Naiṣkarmya-Siddhi), Skt., lit. *naishkarmya:* "inactivity, nondoing," *siddhi:* "perfection"; the sense is "realization of one's own identity with *brahman* through nondoing"; a work about → Advaita-Vedānta by → Sureshvara, a direct pupil of → Shankara. It consists of four chapters, the first of which counters the view that self-knowledge can be achieved by means of such activities as prayers or meditation or by activity combined with knowledge. The second chapter leads the seeker to a theoretical understanding of the mystical texts of the → Upanishads. The third chapter explains the great precept *Tat tvam asi* ("That thou art"). The fourth chapter proves that the preceding statements are in accordance with the teachings of → Gaudapāda and Shankara. Each book comprises approximately 100 stanzas, each connected to a commentary. (English trans.: *Realization of the Absolute,* London, 1959.)

Nakagawa Sōen 🆉 1907–84, Japanese Zen master of the → Rinzai school; a student and dharma successor (→ *hassu*) of → Yamamoto Gempō. Nakagawa Rōshi, who was for many years the abbot of the Ryūtaku-ji monastery near Mishima (Shizuoka province) was definitely one of the most noteworthy Japanese Zen masters of this century. Like many well-known Zen masters, he was not only of great intelligence but also extraordinarily talented as an artist. He was a master of "the art of life." He was renowned for the way in which, for him, ordinary everyday business spontaneously emerged as a work of art—as, for example, when a telegram message became a haiku, or the serving of coffee a "coffee ceremony." In the West he was primarily known through his visits to the United States and Israel, where he instructed Western students in Zen.

Nala 🅷 1. A king of Nishada. The story of Nala and his consort, the "charming Damayantī," is one of the best-known episodes of the → *Mahābhārata:* in a game of dice, Nala lost his kingdom and all his possessions, including his clothing. Later he bet his wife against the kingdom and won it all back again.

The king's victory is described in a celebrated poem, *Nalodaya,* at one time ascribed to → Kālidāsa; the authorship has since been called into question because of the mannered style of the text. The story of Nala and Damayantī is also told in the popular literary epic *Naishadha-Charita* ("The Deeds of the King of Nishada"), written by the court poet and philosopher → Harsha (twelfth century C.E.). 2. Name of a monkey prince who could make stones float on water. He served in Rāma's army and built the stone bridge that bore Rāma and his troops from India to Ceylon. The bridge was named → Rāmasetu (*setu*: "dam, bridge") or Nalasetu.

Nālandā 🅱 a center of Buddhist and worldly studies in north India. The "Buddhist university," as Nālandā is often called, was founded as a monastery in approximately the 2d century by Shakrāditya, a king of → Magadha. It then developed into a university at which, particularly, famous teachers of → Mādhyamaka taught. Nālandā was for centuries one of the great centers of learning of the world, not least because of its great library. Close connections developed between Nālandā and Tibet, where in 1351 an institution of learning with the same name was built.

According to the account of the Chinese pilgrims → Hsuan-tsang and → I-ching, who visited Nālandā at the height of its activity, 10 thousand monks were resident there and studied the teachings of the Hīnayāna and Mahāyāna, as well as logic, mathematics, medicine, and so on. Important teachers included → Dharmapāla, → Dignāga, Hsuan-tsang, and → Sthiramati. Nālandā is thought to have been destroyed by Muslims in the 12th or 13th century.

Namah 🅷 (Namaḥ), or Namas, Skt., lit. "bow, veneration"; used in connection with a prayer or mantra. In certain combinations the word becomes *namo*, as in → OM NAMO NĀRĀYANĀYA, a greeting offered in homage to one of the forms of Vishnu. Monks also greet one another with these words of homage to God.

Nāmajapa 🅷 Skt.; the repetition of one of the names of God (→ *japa*), which is thus used as a mantra.

Nāman 🅱 Skt. (Pali, nama), lit. "name"; refers to the psychological as opposed to the physical (→ *rūpa*, → *nāmarūpa*) and embraces the four → *skandhas* of feeling, perception, mental formations, and consciousness, which, together with the fifth *skandha*, corporeality, constitute the empirical entity.

Nāman, as the fifth link in conditioned arising (→ *pratītya-samutpāda*) is conditioned by consciousness (→ *vijñāna*) and itself conditions the six sense bases (→ *shadāyatana*). In the Mahāyāna, *nāman* is opposed to "reality," since name can neither grasp nor express the objective world. From this premise the unreality of all phenomena is derived (→ *shūnyatā*).

Nāmarūpa 🅷 🅱 Skt., lit. "name-form."
🅷 A term used to refer to → *māyā, the manifest world, in which everything has a name and shape.*
🅱 a term referring to the empirical personality in its essential components, the mental and physical. Thus it is also a paraphrase for the five → *skandhas*, in which *rūpa* (form) stands for the first *skandha*, and *nāma* (name) for the other four.

Nāmarūpa is the fourth link in the chain of conditioned arising (→ *pratītya-samutpāda*), which is constituted by the entry of consciousness (→ *vijñāna*) into the womb and brings about the arising of a new individual.

Also → *nāman*.

Nampo Shōmyō 🆉 → Shōmyō

Nampo Sōmin 🆉 → Shōmyō

Namu 🆉 Jap.; Japanese pronunciation of the Chinese character by which the Sanskrit word *namas* is translated into Chinese. It means approximately "venerate, praise" and is generally used in relation to the Buddha and the three precious ones (→ *sambō*).

Namu-sambō 🆉 Jap.; taking refuge in the three precious ones (→ *sambō*).

Nānak 🅷 1469–1538, the founder of → Sikhism, the religion of the Sikhs, which attempts to unite Hinduism and Islam in daily life. Guru Nānak taught that one can please Allah *and* Brahma by serving humanity, their creation. Union with God can be attained only through one's own efforts. Nānak's poetry was influenced by the mystic → Kabīr. His religious poems are included in the Sikhs' holy book, the → *Ādi Granth.*

Nan-ch'uan P'u-yuan 🆉 (Jap., Nansen Fugan), 748–835; one of the great Chinese Ch'an (Zen) masters of the T'ang period; a student and dharma successor (→ *hassu*) of → Ma-tsu Tao-i (Jap., Baso Dōitsu). Nan-ch'uan had seventeen dharma successors, among them one of the most important Ch'an masters, → Chao-chou Ts'ung-shen (Jap., Jōshū Jūshin) and → Ch'ang-sha Ching-ts'en (Jap., Chōsha Keijin). Nan-ch'uan appears in examples 14, 19, 27, and 34 of the → *Wu-men-kuan*, and in examples 28, 31, 40, 63, 64, and 69 of the → *Pi-yen-lu.*

Nan-ch'uan already had a period of intensive study of Buddhist philosophy behind him (including the teachings of the → Fa-hsiang, → Hua-yen, and → San-lun schools of Chinese Buddhism) when he came to Master Ma-tsu, under whose guidance he realized profound enlightenment. In the year 795 he built a hut on Mount Nan-ch'uan, from which his name is derived, and lived there for more than thirty years in seclusion. Finally some Ch'an monks persuaded him to come down from Nan-ch'uan, settle in a monastery, and lead students on the way of Zen. It is said that from that time on the students never numbered less than a hundred.

One of the most impressive kōans with Nan-ch'uan is example 40 of the *Pi-yen-lu*:

Lu-keng Tai-fu (Jap., Riku-kō Taifu) said to Nan-ch'uan in the course of their conversation, "Chao the dharma teacher said, 'Heaven and Earth and I have the same root; the ten thousand things and I are one body.' Absolutely wonderful!"

Nan-ch'uan, pointing to a blossom in the garden said, "The man of our times sees this blossoming bush like someone who is dreaming."

From Nan-ch'uan, who is famed for his vivid expressions and paradoxical pronouncements in the course of Zen training, come a number of much-cited Zen sayings. Thus, in apparent contradiction of his master Ma-tsu (for whose statement, → Ta-mei Fa-chang), he said, "Consciousness is not Buddha, knowledge is not the way" (*Wu-men-kuan* 34). Equally well known is the → *wato* from example 27 of the *Wu-men-kuan*: "It is not mind, it is not Buddha, it is not things." For the → *mondō* with his principal student Chao-chou, which arose out of the question, "What is the Way?" → *Heijōshin kore dō.*

Nan-ch'uan's comments and instructions are recorded in the *Ch'ih-chou Nan-ch'uan P'u-yuan-ch'an-shih kuang-lu* (*'Great Collection of the Words of the Ch'an Master Nan ch'uan P'u-yuan from Ch'ih-chou'*).

Nandi H Skt.; 1. one of the great worshipers of → Shiva; he took on the form of a bull, because the human body was not strong enough to bear the devotional ecstasy he experienced; 2. the bull of Shiva. The representation of a bull, carved from stone and milky white in color, is seen outside many temples dedicated to Shiva.

Nangaku Ejō Z Jap. for → Nan-yueh Huai-jang

Nan-hua chen-ching T Chin. → Chuang-tzu

Nan-hua chen-jen T → *chen-jen*

Nan'in Egyō Z Jap. for → Nan-yuan Hui-yung

Nansen Fugan Z Jap. for → Nan-ch'uan P'u-yuan

Nanshū-zen Z Jap. for *nan-tsung-ch'an*, → Southern school

Nan-t'a Kuang-jun Z (Jap., Nantō Kōyū), 850–938; Chinese Ch'an (Zen) master of the → Igyō school; a student and dharma successor (→ *hassu*) of → Yang-shan Hui-chi (Jap., Kyōzan Ejaku) and the master of → Pa-chiao Hui-ch'ing (Jap., Bashō Esei).

Nantō-kōan Z Jap. → Kōan

Nantō Kōyū Z Jap. for → Nan-t'a Kuang-jun

Nan-t'ou Z Chin. for *nantō-(kōan)*, → kōan

Nan-tsung-ch'an Z Chin. → Southern school

Nan-yang Hui-chung Z (Jap., Nan'yō Echū), 675?–775?; early Chinese Ch'an (Zen) master; a student of → Hui-neng. The *Tsu-t'ang-chi* reports that he did not speak a single word till the age of sixteen and would never cross the bridge in front of his parents' house. One day as a Ch'an master was approaching the house, he ran over the bridge to the master and requested him to ordain him as a monk and accept him as a student. The master, who recognized the boy's great potential, sent him to the monastery of Hui-neng. Hui-neng told him that he would be a "buddha standing alone in the world," accepted him as a student and later confirmed him as his dharma successor (→ *hassu*). After long training under Sixth Patriarch Hui-neng, Nan-yang went into seclusion for forty years on Mount Pai-ya (Jap., Hakugai) in Nan-yang (hence his name) in order to deepen his realization of Ch'an. In 761, when Nan-yang was about eighty-five years old, he reluctantly accepted the summons of Emperor Su-tsung and went to the imperial court to become the personal master of Su-tsung and his successor Tai-tsung. As master of two emperors of the T'ang Dynasty, Nan-yang was the first Ch'an (Zen) master to receive the honorific title Teacher of the Country (Chin., → *kuo-shih*; Jap., → *kokushi*); thus in Ch'an (Zen) literature he is generally called Chung-kuo-shih (Jap., Chū Kokushi). We encounter him in example 17 of the → *Wu-men-kuan* and in examples 18, 69, and 99 of the → *Pi-yen-lu.*

One of the most famous kōans in which Teacher of the Country Chung appears is "The Teacher of the Country calls three times" (*Wu-men-kuan* 17):

"Three times the Teacher of the Country called his monastic servant and three times the servant answered.

"The Teacher of the Country said, 'Until now I thought I was turning my back on you. But it's really you who are turning your back on me.' "

Nan'yō Echū Z Jap. for → Nan-yang Hui-Chung

Nan-yuan Hui-yung Z Jap., Nan'in Egyō), also called Pao-ying Hui-yung, d. 930; Chinese Ch'an (Zen) master; a student and dharma successor (→ *hassu*) of → Hsing-hua Ts'ung-chiang (Jap., Kōke Zonshō) and the master of Feng-hsueh Yen-Chao (Jap., Fuketsu Enshō). The way in which Master Nan-yuan placed the high-strung Feng-hsueh under strict training and eventually led him to enlightenment is reported in Master → Yuan-wu K'o-ch'in's (Jap., Engo Kokugon's) introduction to example 38 of the → *Pi-yen-lu.*

Nan-yueh Huai-jang 🅉 (Jap., Nangaku Ejō), 677–744; early Chinese Ch'an (Zen) master; a student and dharma successor (→ *hassu*) of → Hui-neng. He settled on Mount Nan-yueh (Jap., Nangaku), from which his name is derived. Little is known of Nan-yueh other than that he was the student of the sixth patriarch (→ Hui-neng) and the master of Ma-tsu Tao-i (Jap., Baso Dōitsu), one of the greatest Ch'an masters of the T'ang period. One of the few incidents from his life that have been handed down is often cited and frequently misunderstood:

When Ma-tsu was living on Mount Heng, he sat day after day absorbed in meditation (→ *zazen*). Master Huai-jang came by, saw him, and asked what he hoped to attain by sitting. Ma-tsu answered that he hoped to attain buddhahood. Huai-jang then picked up a piece of tile and began to rub it on a stone. When Ma-tsu asked him why he was doing that, Huai-jang answered that he wanted to polish the piece of tile into a mirror. Ma-tsu exclaimed, "How can one make a mirror out of a piece of tile by polishing it?!" Huai-jang replied, "How can one become a buddha by sitting in meditation?"

This famous episode is often misunderstood to the effect that Nan-yueh Huai-jang altogether denied the necessity and worth of the practice of *zazen*; in fact, he was only pointing out to Ma-tsu a wrong attitude toward the practice of *zazen*.

The second main lineage of the Ch'an (Zen) tradition originated in the T'ang period with Nan-yueh Huai-jang (see the Ch'an/Zen Lineage Chart).

Nanzen-ji 🅉 one of the most important Zen monasteries of Kyōto, originally the country seat of the abdicated emperor Kameyama. In 1293 he had it changed to a Zen monastery. Nanzen-ji did not belong to the Five Mountains (→ Gosan) of Kyōto; rather by decree of the shogunate it was placed above the Gosan. It is also known for its landscape garden.

Nārada 🄷, one of the seven great → Rishis and one of the → Prajāpatis. Several hymns in the → *Rigveda* are ascribed to him. The → Purānas contain many stories and legends about him. He is said to have been lord of the → *gandharvas*, the heavenly musicians, and to have invented the *vīnā* (lute). In the *Mahābhārata*, he is associated with Krishna. Above all he is known as the great devotee who composed the → *Bhakti-Sūtra*, a collection of celebrated aphorisms on the love and worship of God. Another work of his, concerning laws, bears the title *Nāradīya-Dharma-Shāstra*. Nārada is regarded as a *nitya-siddha* (→ *nitya*).

Naraka 🄷 🄱 Skt., lit. "hell."

🄷 place of torture and torment, where the souls of the wicked go. → Manu enumerates twenty-one hells, each of which has its own name.

🄱 (Pali, niraya); one of the three negative modes of existence (→ *gati*). The hells are places of torment and retribution for bad deeds; but existence in them is finite, i.e., after negative → karma has been exhausted, rebirth in another, better form of existence is possible. Like the buddha paradises (→ pure land), the hells are to be considered more as states of mind than as places.

Buddhist cosmology distinguishes various types of hells, essentially adopted from Hinduism. There are hot and cold hells divided into eight main ones, among which Avichi is the most horrible, each surrounded by sixteen subsidiary hells. The inhabitants of the hells suffer immeasurable torment for various different lengths of time. They are hacked into pieces, devoured alive by birds with iron beaks, and cut up by the razor-sharp leaves of hell-trees. The hells are ruled by → Yama.

Nāralīlā 🄷 Skt., lit. *nāra*: "man, human being," *līlā*: "play"; the play of God that manifests itself in the human being.

Nara-Nārāyana 🄷 (Nara-Nārāyana), Skt., lit. *nara*: "man," *nārāyana*: "God"; the human soul and God commingled. This representation of God as *narayana* is a symbol for the highest truth, that is, that the Self in man (→ *ātman*) is one with → *brahman;* at the same time, it brings God close to humanity in a vivid and inspiring manner.

In mythology, the name Nara-Nārāyana is associated with two → *rishis* of antiquity, sons of → Dharma and → Ahimsā in their personified forms as divinities. The name is sometimes also applied to → Krishna and → Arjuna.

Narasimha 🄷 (Narasiṃha), Skt., lit. *nara*: "man," *simha*: "lion," or Nrisimha; Vishnu in his fourth incarnation as → *avatāra*, a link between animal and human being in the form of a man-lion. He symbolizes the turning to the mastery of consciousness, which evolves to full waking in the human being.

Nārāyana H (Nārāyaṇa), Skt., lit. *nāra*: "human, having to do with the human (the primal or divine man)," *ayana*: "path, way." *Nārāyana* stands for the divine that manifests itself in man. Thus nārāyana is primarily used to refer to Vishnu, who is incarnated again and again in various forms (→ *avatāra*). However, it is also a term used in general to refer to God. *Sadhus* and saints in India greet one another with OM NAMO NĀRĀYANĀYA ("Honor to God in man!").

In mythology, Nārāyana is said to represent the creator god → Brahmā, because according to → Manu he emerged from the waters (*nāra* in the plural form: "water"), an association that recalls these words by Thales of Milet: "Everything arises from water, everything is maintained by water. Ocean, grant us thy eternal rule." The name Nārāyana first appears in the → *Shatapatha-Brāhmana.*

Nāro Chödrug B (Nāro chos-drug), Tib., lit. "*Six Doctrines of Nāropa.*" A group of → Vajrayāna teachings, especially a set of disciplines into which the Indian → *mahāsiddha* Nāropa was initiated by his teacher → Tilopa. Nāropa transmitted them to → Marpa the Translator, who brought them to Tibet in the 11th century under Nāropa's name. The six doctrines are, after the → Mahāmudrā teaching, the most important meditation techniques of the → Kagyupa school. They consist of the following practices: (1) production of "inner heat" (→ *tumo*), (2) the experience of one's own body as an illusion (→ *gyulü*), (3) the dream state (→ *milam*), (4) perception of the "clear light" (→ *ösel*), (5) the teaching of the in-between state (→ *bardo*), (6) the practice of transference of consciousness (→ *phowa*). These teachings partially coincide with those of the → *Bardo thödol.* The most graphic example of their accomplishment is Milarepa's mastery of inner heat.

The six doctrines of Nāropa were developed in different Tantras and were transmitted by differrent teachers. In a work of Nāropa it is stated that perception of one's own body as illusory and perception of the clear light stem from → Nāgārjuna, the inner heat from Charyapa, the dream-state teaching from Lavapa, and the in-between state and transference of consciousness teachings from a third Tantric master, Pukasiddhi.

Mastery of the six practices leads to particular supernatural powers (→ *siddhi*) and is based on control of the refined energies of the body. These are a product of the incorporation of the body into the process of spiritual development and are described in the Tibetan tradition in terms of three aspects: the energy currents (Tib., *lung*; Skt., → *prāna*) that in various ways, regulate bodily functions; the energy channels (Tib., *tsa*; Skt., → *nāḍī*) in which these energies flow; and a certain energy potential (Tib., *thig-le*; Skt., → *bindu*) that is fundamental for this system.

Through the various techniques of the six doctrines, these energies are activated and applied as a means of attaining enlightenment (→ *bodhi*). The goal is realization of the indissoluble unity of emptiness (→ *shūnyatā*) and emotional fulfillment, or bliss. This experience is described by Milarepa in terms of six blisses:

"When inner heat ignites the entire body—bliss!
When the energy currents focus in the three channels—bliss!
When the current of enlightenment mind flows from above—bliss!
When below the radiant energy potential is fulfilled—bliss!
When masculine and feminine harmonize in the middle—bliss!
When the body is filled with serene ecstasy—bliss!"

Nāropa B (Nā-ro-pa), 1016–1100; along with his teacher → Tilopa, one of the best-known Indian → *mahāsiddhas* and an important holder of the transmission of the → *mahāmudrā* teachings. The practices named after Nāropa (→ *Nāro chödrug*) reached Tibet through Nāropa's student → Marpa and are up to the present day one of the central doctrines of the → Kagyupa school. Nāropa held an important position at the Buddhist monastic university, → Nālandā, before he became a student of Tilopa's. Among his contemporaries was the scholar → Atīsha.

Nāsadāsīya H Skt.; the title of this song is derived from its opening words. It is the celebrated hymn of creation in the *Rigveda* (10.129), which in its seven verses probes the mystery of existence. The word *kāma* ("love") in verse four expresses the poet's profound knowledge of the nature of all things. In verse six he leaves the gods themselves behind, because they "emerged this side of creation." The last verse answers the question of how creation arose: "He who brought forth this creation,/ the observer in the highest heaven,/ who created it or did not create it,/ He knows it!—or perhaps he knows it not."

Nāstika H Skt., lit. "atheistic"; term referring to the unorthodox philosophical schools, which do not believe in the authority of the → Vedas. They are the schools of → Chārvāka, of → Jainism, and of Buddhism.

Nātaka H (Nāṭaka), Skt.; drama with a religious or mythological theme (e.g., → Kālidāsa's *Shakuntalā* and *Vikramorvashīya*) and featuring a god, saint, or ruler as its hero.

Natarāja ◻ (Naṭarāja), Skt., lit. "king of the dance"; → Shiva as king of dancers and lord of the world stage. His cosmic dance portrays his five activities: creation, maintenance, destruction, embodiment, and liberation.

Shiva as Natarāja, Lord of the Dance. (Bronze, 82 cm)

In the famous representations of Natarāja, one of Shiva's feet crushes the demon Mujalaka, the symbol of ignorance and worldliness; the other foot is raised to symbolize the supraconscious state. The dance takes place in materiality, the embodiment of the individual as well as of the cosmos. The circle of flames within which Natarāja dances is the dance of the forces of nature (as opposed to Shiva's dance of wisdom). His dance has also been identified with the syllable → OM.

Navaratna ◻ Skt.; nine famous poets, the "nine jewels" at the court of King → Vikramāditya. They are (1) Dhanvantari, the pearl; (2) Kshapanaka, the ruby; (3) Amara-Simha, the topaz; (4) Shanku, the diamond; (5) Vetālabhatta, the emerald; (6) Ghatakarpara, the lapis lazuli; (7) Kālidāsa, the coral; (8) Varāhamihira, the sapphire; and (9) Vararuchi, not identified with a particular gem.

Navavidhān ◻ Skt. → Keshab Chandra Sen

Nehan ◻ ◻ Jap. for → nirvāna

Nehandō ◻ Jap., lit. "nirvāna hall"; term for the building in a Zen monastery in which sick persons are housed and cared for. Other names for the infirmary are *enjudō* ("hall of prolonging life") and *anrakudō* ("hall of peace and joy").

Nei-ch'i ◻ Chin., lit. "inner breath"; vital energy stored within the body, as opposed to → *wai-ch'i,* the outer breath, which designates the air we inhale. In the Taoist view, a person's *nei-ch'i* corresponds to the primordial breath (→ *yüan-ch'i*) of the cosmos, the primal energy from which Heaven (→ *t'ien*) and Earth arose at the beginning of the world. The primordial *ch'i* enters the human body at birth and in fact forms the mind (→ *shen*), the body itself, the saliva (→ *yü-chiang*) and spermatozoa (→ *ching*). A Taoist practitioner strives to conserve and strengthen his *nei-ch'i* and restore it to the pure state in which it was at the time of birth. If the inner breath is allowed to escape during exhalation this results in a shortening of that person's life span.

Since the time of the T'ang Dynasty Taoist authors have consistently emphasized that the instructions on how to perform breathing exercises such as embryonic breathing (→ *t'ai-hsi*) refer to the inner rather than the outer breath (→ *fu-ch'i,* → *hsing-ch'i,* → *yen-ch'i*). The *nei-ch'i* is stored in the ocean of energy (→ *ch'i-hai*) and circulates in harmony with the outer breath but separate from it. As the outer *ch'i* ascends during exhalation, the inner breath follows it; but they must not mix. In an untrained person the inner breath will leave the body together with the outer. Once the inner *ch'i* is exhausted, death ensues. The Taoist adept, however, swallows the inner *ch'i* before it can leave his body (→ *yen-ch'i*) and during inhalation channels it back to the *ch'i-hai.*

Nei-kuan ◻ also known as *nei-shih,* Chin., lit. "inner viewing"; a Taoist practice in which the practitioner visualizes the inside of his body until the smallest details appear with great clarity before his inner eye. The practice of *nei-kuan* facilitates the circulating of the breath (→ *hsing-ch'i*). In the → Inner Deity Hygiene School it is used for visualizing and contacting the various body deities. The successful practice of *nei-kuan* depends on the elimination of all external disturbances and the effective calming of all thought processes.

Nei-shih ◻ Chin. → *nei-kuan*

Nei-tan ◻ Chin., lit. "inner cinnabar"; the inner elixir, the inner alchemy. In the language of the Taoist School of the Inner Elixir *nei-tan* refers to the development of an immortal soul from the three life-preserving energies: the essence (→ *ching*), the vital energy (→ *ch'i*) and the spirit (→ *shen*). This process often is described in the language of the Outer Alchemy (→ *wai-tan*), which endeavors to produce an elixir of immortality (→ *ch'ang-sheng pu-ssu*) by combining various chemical substances. The Inner Alchemy compares the melting pot of the Outer Alchemy to the human body in which the essence and the life force—corresponding to the chemical substances employed by the Outer Alchemy—are fashioned into a sacred embryo (→ *sheng-t'ai*) with the help of the mind.

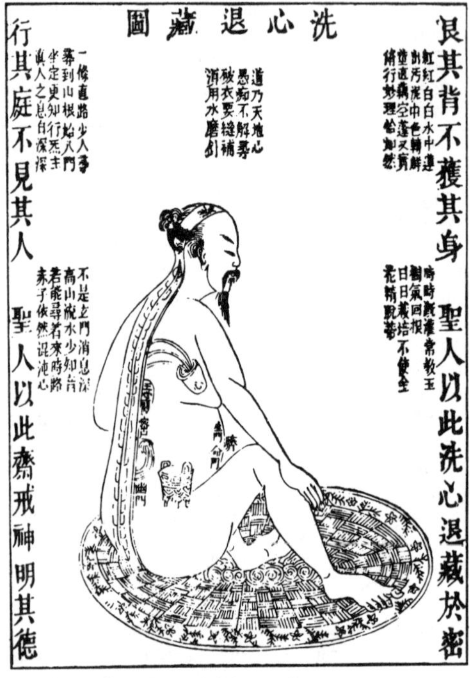

An adept of the Inner Alchemy (*nei-tan*).

In the practice of *nei-tan* the inner amalgamation and sublimation are brought about by taming and sublimating the thought processes of the mind. All processes that normally result in the death of a person can be reversed by concentrating and purifying the life energies within the body, thus making them independent of the world of the senses.

By various meditative breathing techniques the practitioner causes a new being—the so-called sacred embryo—to develop within him. This sacred embryo is synonymous with our idea of an immortal soul and—like the soul—leaves the dying body at the moment of death to ascend to Heaven. Taoists frequently refer to the sacred embryo as the golden flower, which opens when the adept has attained enlightenment. In a philosophical sense the enlightenment of the followers of the inner elixir consists in a return to nothingness. The goal of the Inner Alchemy therefore is the same as that of the philosophical Taoism (→ *tao-chia*) of Lao-tzu or Chuang-tzu: to become one with the Tao by balancing yin and yang (→ yin-yang).

The practice of *nei-tan* began to replace those of the outer elixir during the Sung Dynasty. It was particularly widespread in the School of the Realization of Truth (→ *ch'üan-chen tao*) and its various branches and strongly influenced by Buddhism, especially Zen.

The most famous representatives of the School of the Inner Elixir were → Wei P'o-yang, → Chen T'uan, and → Chang Po-tuan. One of the most important Inner Alchemy texts is the → *T'ai-i chin-hua tsung-chih,* known as *The Secret of the Golden Flower.*

The main teaching of the School of the Inner Elixir states that the three vital energies of man—*ching, ch'i,* and *shen*—have both a material, visible aspect, which is active within the body, and an immaterial, invisible aspect, which is active in the universe. Practitioners of the Inner Alchemy perform meditative breathing exercises with the aim of purifying the essence and transforming it into *ch'i* and thereafter purifying *ch'i* and transforming that into *shen* (*lien-ching hua-ch'i, lien-ch'i hua-shen*). The final stage of the *nei-tan* path consists in purifying the mind and returning to nothingness (*lien-shen fu-hsü*), i.e., integrating the self with the universe.

The strengthening of one's own essence is a prerequisite for the successful practice of *nei-tan.* Frequently, various sexual techniques (→ *fang-chung shu*) are employed to that effect. However, many Taoist scholars categorically reject such practices, the most important of which consists in "returning the essence [semen] to strengthen the brain" (→ *huan-ching pu-nao*).

The actual work of the inner alchemist begins with the creation of channels within himself along which the energy can circulate. The first of these is the so-called lesser celestial circulation (*hsiao-chou-t'ien*), which begins at the heart and from there descends via the middle of the abdomen to the kidneys. In Taoist texts this path of the inner circulation is often related to the five elements (→ *wu-hsing*), the annual seasons, the cardinal points, physical organs, animals, etc.

The lesser circulation forms the basis for the greater, which engages the whole of the body, in that the energy rises from the lower end of the spine along the vertebral column to the top of the head and from there, via the face, chest, and abdominal surface, back down to the end of the spine. The ascending current of energy is referred to as *tu-mai,* or the controlled path. Its most important centers are situated (1) at the lowest point of the spine, (2) at the level of the kidneys, (3) at the halfway point of the vertebral column, and (4) at the connecting point between the spine and the head. The topmost of these centers is the so-called upper cinnabar field (→ *tan-t'ien*), or, more specifically, the → *ni-huan.*

The descending channel is called *jen-mai,* or involuntary path. Its most important centers are the middle and lower cinnabar fields, the yellow castle (*huang-t'ing*) in the middle of the abdomen, and the hall of light (*ming-t'ang*) between the eyes.

Alchemical texts sub-divide the whole circulatory path into twelve sections that are symbolized by hexagrams from the → *I-ching* or by signs corresponding to the twelve months of the year or twelve two-hour periods of the day.

In addition, the texts often describe the ascent and descent of the energy as a fusion of → *k'an* and *li* or of dragon (yang) and tiger (yin), whereby the actual aim of *nei-tan* is realized.

Detailed description of the practice of Inner Alchemy may be found in Chang Chung-yuan 1963; Wilhelm 1938; Miyuki 1984.

Nembutsu 🅱 Jap., recitation of the name of Buddha → Amitābha; meditation practice of the → Pure Land school (→ Jōdo-shū, → Jōdo-shin-shū). The formula for recitation is *Namu Amida butsu* (Jap., "Veneration to Buddha Amitābha"). If the *nembutsu* is done with complete devotion, it can bring about rebirth in the → Pure Land of Amitābha, which is the supreme goal of the practice of this school.

Nempyo sambakyu soku 🅩 Jap., lit., "*Three Hundred Kōans with Commentary*"; a kōan collection with explanations compiled and composed by the Japanese Zen master Dōgen Zenji. (Also → Dōgen Zenji).

Nen 🅩 Jap., colloquial, lit. "idea, thought": a concept that in Zen has a special meaning that is fairly different from its meaning in the colloquial language. The Zen meaning derives from the Chinese character that is read *nen* in Japanese, which is comprised of one element meaning "present" and another element meaning "heart, mind, consciousness" (→ *kokoro*). "Moment of consciousness," "mind directed toward the moment," and "attention" are thus more accurate definitions of the concept as it is used in Zen. A further meaning is "intensive, concentrated, nondualistic thought," a thought that has no object outside itself.

Nenge-mishō 🅩 Jap., lit. "smiling and twirling a flower [between the fingers]"; a Zen expression that refers to the wordless transmission of the → buddha-dharma from → Shākyamuni Buddha to his student Kāshyapa, later called → Mahākāshyapa. The transmission from heart-mind to heart-mind (→ ishin-denshin) is the beginninf of the "special transmission outside the [orthodox] teaching" (→ *kyōge-betsuden*), as Zen calls itself.

The story begins with a sūtra, the *Ta-fan-t'ien-wang-wen-fo-chueh-i-ching* (Jap., *Daibontennō-mombutsu-ketsugi-kyō*). In it it is told that once Brahmā, the highest deity in the Hinduist assembly of gods, visited a gathering of the disciples of Buddha on Mount Gridhrakūta (→ Vulture Peak Mountain). He presented the Buddha with a garland of flowers and requested him respectfully to expound the dharma. However, instead of giving a discourse, the Buddha only took a flower and twirled it, while smiling silently, between the fingers of his raised hand. None of the gathering understood except for Kāshyapa, who responded with a smile. According to the somewhat shortened version of this episode given in the → *Wu-men-kuan* (example 6), the Buddha then said, "I have the treasure of the eye of true dharma, the wonderful mind of nirvāna, the true form of no-form, the mysterious gate of dharma. It cannot not be expressed through words and letters and is a special transmission (outside of) all doctrine. This I entrust to Mahākāshyapa."

The student of the Buddha who after this event was called Mahākāshyapa thus became the first patriarch of the Indian transmission lineage of Ch'an (Zen) (see the Ch'an/Zen Lineage Chart).

Nenge-shunmoku 🅩 Jap., lit. "winking and twirling a flower [between the fingers]"; another expression for → nenge-mishō.

Neo-Confucianism 🅣 → Confucianism, → Chu Hsi

Neo-Taoism 🅣 → *hsüan-hsüeh*

Neti, Neti 🅗 Skt., lit. "Not this, not this"; These frequently cited words from the → *Brihadāranyaka-Upanishad* reject the appearances of the entire universe as mere superimpositions upon → *brahman* and establish that *brahman* alone exists and nothing else. This application of the knowledge that the ultimate reality is "not this, not this" to all manifestations represents in → Advaita-Vedānta a process of negative discrimination that constitutes the intellectual path of the → *jñāni.*

New Lotus school 🅱 → Nichiren school

Ngöndro 🅱 Tib. → body, speech, mind

Nichiren 🅱 1222–82, founder of the → Nichiren school (also New Lotus school) of Japanese Buddhism. For Nichiren the teaching of Buddha found its highest expression in the → *Lotus Sūtra.* It was his conviction that the teaching found there alone could lead mankind to liberation. In his view the essence of the sūtra's message was to be found in its title. Thus the practice that he instituted consisted in the recitation of the title of the sūtra: "Veneration to the *Sūtra of the Lotus of the Good Law*" (Jap., *Namu myōhō renge-kyō*).

Nichiren, who relentlessly criticized all other Buddhist schools, saw himself as the savior of his nation. He wanted to bring about peace in Japan by causing its people to live in accordance with the teachings of the *Lotus Sūtra.* He accused the rulers of supporting "heretical" schools of Buddhism and regarded this as the reason for the difficulties in which the country found itself at this time. As a patriot, he wanted to make Japan the center of the authentic teaching of the Buddha and envisioned its spread to the entire world from there. Because of his unyielding advocacy of his views, Nichiren was condemned to death. He was, however, miraculously saved and then exiled to a small island. In 1274 he was allowed to return to Kamakura.

Nichiren was born on the south coast of Japan, the son of a poor fisherman. He was ordained as a monk at the age of fifteen in a monastery in the vicinity of his home village. Searching for an answer to the question "What is the true teaching of the Buddha?" he went to Kamakura and later to Mount Hiei (→ Hieizan), the main seat of the → Tendai school. The Tendai philosophy, which is based on the *Lotus Sūtra,* seemed to him to come nearest the truth. In 1253, he returned to his home monastery, because he felt that on Mount Hiei the true teaching of the *Lotus Sūtra* had slipped too much into the background. During this period, he elaborated his own doctrine: the teaching of the *Lotus Sūtra* alone can save mankind during a period of religious decline, because it shows the one and only way to liberation. His view that the mere recitation of the title of the sūtra was enough led to Nichiren's expulsion from the monastery. He then began to propagate his teaching on the streets, at the same time vehemently attacking all other schools. He saw the Pure Land of the → Jōdo-shū as hell; in the founder of the Jōdo-shū, Hōnen, he saw the enemy of all the buddhas and the party responsible for the misfortunes of Japan. Zen was for him the expression of diabolical powers; → Shingon meant national ruin, and → Ritsu was high treason. Nichiren was convinced that the peace and welfare of the nation was possible only through the unification of all Buddhist schools in the teaching of the *Lotus Sūtra.*

Exiled to the island of Sado, he composed a number of written works. He began to see himself as the savior of the nation and an incarnation of two → bodhisattvas who, according to the *Lotus Sūtra,* would spread the teachings. He placed special importance on the vows taken by the students of the Buddha in the sūtra, in which they promise to propagate the teachings during bad times and to bear all hardships resulting from this. He required of his followers that they emulate the bodhisattva ideal of self-sacrifice according to his example.

Nichiren school 🅱 (Jap., nichiren-shū, lit. "School of the Lotus of the Sun") also New Lotus school; school of Japanese Buddhism, named after its founder → Nichiren (1222–82). Its teaching is based on that of the *Lotus Sūtra,* the title of which alone, according to Nichiren, contains the essence of the Buddhist teachings. The practice advocated by Nichiren consists in reciting the formula, "Veneration to the *Sūtra of the Lotus of the Good Law*" (Jap., *Namu myōhō renge-kyō*). If this formula of veneration is recited with complete devotion, through it buddhahood can be realized in an instant.

The Nichiren school exhibits strong nationalistic tendencies; it envisions an earthly Buddha realm, which, with Japan as its centerpoint, will embrace the whole world. It stresses the sociopolitical responsibilities of religion.

In the twentieth century, from the original school of Nichiren a number of new schools developed. The *Nichiren-shōshū* ("True School of Nichiren") draws its doctrine from Nikkō, a student of Nichiren's, and venerates Nichiren as "the buddha of the final time." Also, modern Japanese folk religions like → Risshō Koseikai, → Sōka Gakkai, and → Nipponzan Myōhōji are based on the Nichiren school.

The Nichiren school venerates "three great mysteries." The first, devised by Nichiren himself, is the → mandala (*go-honzon*) preserved on Mount Minobu, said to synthesize the teaching of the *Lotus Sūtra.* In the center of the mandala is the pagoda that is the symbol of the truth of the Buddha (→ *tathagata*) in the *Lotus Sūtra.* The pagoda represents the five characters of the title of the *Lotus Sūtra.* Around the "great title" (*daimoku*) the names of bodhisattvas and other beings are arranged in concentric circles. The second mystery is the *daimoku,* the title of the sūtra itself. It is the formula of veneration that embodies the essence of the "lotus teaching". The recitation of this formula brings about a purification of → body, speech, and mind and takes the place of the refuge (→ *trisharana*) in traditional Buddhism. The third mystery is the *kaidan,* a kind of sacred platform that originally served for the ordination of monks but was given a symbolic role by Nichiren—Japan itself is seen as the *kaidan.* This became the central idea of chauvinistic Nichirenism.

Nidāna 🅱 Skt., Pali, roughly, "link"; the twelve links that constitute the chain of conditioned arising (→ *pratītya-samutpāda*). They are (1) → avidyā (ignorance); (2) → *samskāra* (formations, impulses); (3) → *vijñāna* (consciousness); (4) → *nāmarūpa* (the mental and the physical); (5) → *shadāyatana* (the six bases, i.e., the six sense-object realms); (6) → *sparsha* (contact); (7) → *vedanā* (sensation); (8) → *trishnā* (thirst, craving); (9) → *upādāna* (clinging, taking possession of a womb); (10) → *bhava* (becoming); (11) *jāti* (birth); (12) *jarā-maranamh* (old age and death).

Nididhyāsana 🅷 Skt., lit. "contemplate, consider"; meditation on a specific theme as the crowning of one's efforts in study and contemplation. For the attainment of spiritual knowledge → Vedānta views three steps as essential: → *shravana,* reading, hearing, and taking in spiritual truths; → *manana,* the critical testing and contemplation of that received in the stage of *shravana;* and *nididhyāsana,* its realization through meditation.

Nidrā 🅷 Skt., lit. "sleep"; goddess of sleep. Various sources refer to her as a feminine form of → Brahmā or say that she emerged from the → Churning of the Ocean. (See also → Yoga-Nidrā).

Ni-huan 🅃 Chin., lit. "ball of clay"; name given by the → Inner Deity Hygiene School of religious Taoism (→ *tao-chiao*) to the most important area of the upper cinnabar field (→ *tan-t'ien*), in which the Great One (→ T'ai-i), the highest body deity, resides. The term *ni-huan* may, however, also refer to the brain in general or to a deity associated with the brain.

Nijūhasso 🅉 Jap., lit. "twenty-eight patriarchs," also saiten-ni jūhasso; the twenty-eight patriarchs (→ *soshigata*) of the Indian lineage of Ch'an (Zen) from → Mahākāshyapa (also → *nenge-mishō*) to → *Bodhidharma.* (See also Chan/Zen Lineage Chart.)

Nijūshi-ryū 🅉 Jap., lit. "the twenty-four currents"; the twenty-four "schools" of Zen in Japan. Here are included the three major schools—the → Rinzai school, the → Sōtō school, and the → Ōbaku school—as well as the subsidiary lineages of the Rinzai school into which Rinzai Zen in Japan split. These subsidiary lineages are generally named after a large Japanese Zen monastery where they originated and by whose abbot they were transmitted (quite frequently also in the many submonasteries of the main monastery). Thus, for example, there is an Engaku-ji school, a Kenchō-ji school, a Nanzen-ji school, and so forth. These subsidiary lineages of the Rinzai school hardly differ from one another as concerns the essentials of Zen training.

Nikāya 🅱 Skt., Pali, lit. "corpus"; collection of sūtras of the Pali canon (→ Pali, → Tripitaka). The Pali term *Nikāya* is essentially synonymous with the Sanskrit term → *Agama.* The "basket" of scriptures (→ Sūtra-pitaka) of the Pali canon consists of five Nikāyas: → *Dīgha-nikāya,* → *Majjhima-nikāya,* → *Samyutta-nikāya,* → *Anguttara-nikāya,* and → *Khuddaka-nikāya.*

Nīlakantha 🅷 (Nīlakaṇṭha), Skt., lit. *nīla*: "blue," *kantha*: "throat"; an epithet for → Shiva. At the → Churning of the Ocean he is said to have drunk the poison that rose to the surface, in order to protect humanity from its effect. His throat was dyed blue by the poison.

Nimbārka 🅷, Indian philosopher of the eleventh/twelfth century, one of the celebrated commentators on the → *Vedānta-Sūtra,* the chief representative of the philosophy of → Dvaitādvaita-Vedānta and founder of the Rādhā-Krishna sect, a Vaishnava sect (→ Vaishnavism) whose members are called Nimbārkas. They worship Vishnu in his manifestation as the youthful Krishna at play with his beloved → Rāhdha. Because the Vaishnavas strive not for union with the divine but for eternal proximity to him, God is worshiped in his manifest form and in his play (→ *līlā*) in the world of appearances.

Nimbārka's brief commentary on the *Vedānta-Sūtra* bears the title *Vedānta-Pārijāta-Saurabha* ("The Fragrance of the Heavenly Blossom of Vedānta"); it is written in a straightforward manner, with no allusions to the theories of other commentators. He also composed a short work, *Dashalokī,* on the subject of the three realities: → *brahman* (which for Nimbārka is identical with Krishna), consciousness (→ chit), and matter (*achit*).

Ninkyō-Funi 🅉 Jap., lit. "person-phenomenon not-two"; an expression pointing to the fundamental Zen realization of the nondistinctness of subject (person) and object (phenomenon). The erroneous view of being separated as an experiencing subject from an experienced phenomenal world "out there," is an expression of → delusion that Zen training is intended to overcome.

Nipponzan Myōhōji 🅱 Jap.; a Buddhist revival movement named after its main temple. It is also called the Movement of the Wondrous Law of the *Lotus Sūtra*. The movement was founded in 1917 by Fujii Nichidatsu and is based on the teachings of → Nichiren. Nipponzan Myōhōji advocates world peace. Its followers organize marches for peace in which they beat the "drum of Heaven" and recite the name of the → *Lotus Sūtra*. They build "peace pagodas" throughout the world.

The founder separated himself from the existing Nichiren schools and set out on a wandering pilgrimage with the intention, in accordance with a prophecy of Nichiren (who predicted the return of Buddhism to its motherland, India), to spread Nipponzan Myōhōji throughout Asia. During the Second World War Fujii became a radical pacifist. This led to a new orientation of the movement and to its involvement in worldwide activities.

Nirbīja-Samādhi 🅷 Skt., lit. "seedless *samādhi*"; a term used in the philosophy of → yoga to refer to the highest, supraconscious state, in which all thought waves have subsided and all duality is extinguished. It is called "seedless" because it destroys the seeds of future karma (→ *āgāmi-karma* and → *sanchita-karma*), which would otherwise lead to rebirth. In *sabīja-samādhi* ("*samādhi* with seed"), by contrast, this seed is not destroyed. (See also → *samprajñāta-samādhi*.)

Nirdvamda 🅷 (Nirdvaṃdva), Skt., from *nir*: "not," *dvamdva*: "pair of opposites"; the state in which the mind no longer conceives of pairs of opposites such as warm and cold, good and bad.

Nirguna-Brahman 🅷 (Nirguṇa-Brahman), Skt., lit. "Brahman without qualities"; a term in → Vedānta to describe the Absolute, the One without a second, in its qualityless aspect, as contrasted to "*brahman* with qualities" (→ *saguna-brahman*).

Nirgunagunī 🅷 (Nirguṇaguṇī), Skt., from *nir*: "not," *guna*: "quality"; a term from the → Upanishads used to describe the divine in its two aspects. It is a description of the highest being, who is both immanent and transcendent and yet goes beyond both. An example is Krishna in the *Bhagavad-Gītā*.

Nirmānakāya 🅱 🆉 Skt. → *trikāya*

Nirodha 🅷 🅱 Skt., lit. "destruction, dissolution."

🅷 A state of intense concentration, in which the distinction between subject and object ceases (is "annihilated"), so that the mind comes to rest and is conquered.

🅱 *Nirodha* is interpreted in various ways: as the dissolution of suffering in the sense of the third of the → four noble truths; as the elimination of the passions, which are the cause of suffering; and as the ending of rebirth and mortal existence, of feelings and perceptions. *Nirodha* is often equated with → nirvāna. The notion stresses the active elimination of the causes of renewed rebirth (→ *Nirodha-samāpatti*)

Nirodha-samāpatti 🅱 Skt., Pali; attainment of the state of extinction, i.e., the state in which every mental activity is temporarily eliminated. It can be reached after passing through the → four stages of formlessness and only an arhat can attain it. Prerequisites for its attainment are tranquility (→ *shamatha*) and insight (→ *vipashyanā*). The state of extinction can last for several days.

Nirukta 🅷 Skt., lit. "etymology, definition"; one of the → Vedangas. The most important dictionary of early Sanskrit literature (fifth century B.C.E.), it is devoted to the explanation of difficult concepts from the → Vedas and was composed by → Yāska, a predecessor of → Pānini. Based on older, no longer extant Vedic word lists (*nighantu*), it consists of three parts: (1) *Nighantuka*, a collection of words related in meaning; (2) *Naigama*, a collection of words that appear particularly in the Vedas; (3) *Daivata*, words having to do with divinities and sacrificial offerings. The work is simply a list of words and as such is of limited use for the reader. The most valuable part is Yāska's commentary. He explains the words, investigates their origin, and cites texts from the Vedas as examples. The oldest etymological work on the Vedas, it sheds light on the scholarly and religious background of the time, but is difficult to understand due to its exceptionally concise presentation.

Nirupadhishesha-nirvāna 🅱 (Nirupadhiśeṣa-nirvāna), Skt. (Pali, anupadisesa-nibbāna), roughly "nirvāna with no remainder of conditions"; nirvāna in which the aggregates (→ *skandha*), the twelve sense realms (→ *āyatana*), the eighteen elements (→ *dhātu*), and the → *indriyas* are no longer present. This comes about at the death of an → arhat, who is not to be reborn. This type of nirvāna is often also called → *parinirvāna*. (Also → nirvāna).

Nirvāṇa 🅷 🅱 🆉 (nirvāna), Skt., lit. "extinction."

🅷 A state of liberation or illumination, characterized by the merging of the individual, transitory I in → *brahman*. *Nirvāna* frees one from suffering, death and rebirth, and all other worldly bonds. It is the highest, transcendent consciousness, referred to in the *Bhagavad-Gītā* as *brahman-nirvāna*, in the Upanishads as → *turīya*, in yoga as → *nirbīja-samādhi*, and in Vedanta as → *nirvikalpa-samādhi*.

B **Z** (Pali, nibbāna; Jap., nehan); the goal of spiritual practice in all branches of Buddhism. In the understanding of early Buddhism, it is departure from the cycle of rebirths (→ samsāra) and entry into an entirely different mode of existence. It requires complete overcoming of the three unwholesome roots—desire, hatred, and delusion (→ *akushala*)—and the coming to rest of active volition (→ samskāra). It means freedom from the determining effect of → karma. Nirvāna is unconditioned (→ *asamskrita*); its characteristic marks are absence of arising, subsisting, changing, and passing away.

Entry of the Buddha into final *nirvāna*, the *parinirvāna* (relief from eastern India, 10th century)

In → Mahāyāna, the notion of nirvāna undergoes a change that may be attributed to the introduction of the → bodhisattva ideal and to emphasis on the unified nature of the world. Nirvāna is conceived as oneness with the absolute, the unity of samsāra and transcendence. It is also described as dwelling in the experience of the absolute, bliss in cognizing one's identity with the absolute, and as freedom from attachment to illusions, affects, and desires (Also → *parinirvāna*).

In the West nirvāna has often been misunderstood as mere annihilation; even in early Buddhism it was not so conceived. In many texts, to explain what is described as nirvāna, the simile of extinguishing a flame is used. The fire that goes out does not pass away, but merely becomes invisible by passing into space (→ *ākāsha*); thus the term *nirvāna* does not indicate annihilation but rather entry into another mode of existence. The fire comes forth from space and returns back into it; thus nirvāna is a spiritual event that takes place in time but is also, in an unmanifest and imperishable sphere, always already there. This is the "abode of immortality," which is not spatially localizable, but is rather transcendent, supramundane (→ *lokottara*), and only accessible to mystical experience. Thus in early Buddhism, nirvāna is not seen in a positive relation to the world but is only a place of salvation.

In some places in the sūtras an expression is used for nirvāna that means "bliss," but far more often nirvāna is characterized merely as a process or state of cessation of suffering (→ *duhkha*). This should not, however, be regarded as proof of a nihilistic attitude; it is rather an indication of the inadequacy of words to represent the nature of nirvāna, which is beyond speech and thought, in a positive manner. As a positive statement concerning nirvāna, only an indication concerning its not being nothing is possible. For Buddhism, which sees all of existence as ridden with suffering, nirvāna interpreted as the cessation of suffering suffices as a goal for the spiritual effort; for spiritual practice it is irrelevant whether nirvāna is a positive state or mere annihilation. For this reason the Buddha declined to make any statement concerning the nature of nirvāna.

In → Hīnayāna two types of nirvāna are distinguished: nirvāna with a remainder of conditionality, which can be attained before death; and nirvāna without conditionality, which is attained at death (→ *sopadhishesha-nirvāna*, → *nirupadhishesha-nirvāna*).

The view of nirvāna of the individual Hīnayāna schools differs considerably in some aspects. The → Sarvāstivāda sees in nirvāna something positive that is unmanifest and imperishable. It is reached through successively overcoming the passions. For the overcoming of each passion a specific "realm" is posited; thus many many different types of nirvāna exist, which tends to give it a hypostatic quality. In addition, it is only one among many unconditioned → dharmas. For the → Sautrāntikas nirvāna is just the disappearance of the passions, not however an unmanifest and imperishable metaphysical factor.

In the → Vātsīputrīya school, which posits a "person" (→ *pudgala*, → *anātman*) that is not impermanent, nirvāna is a positive state in which the person continues to exist.

For the → Mahāsānghikas, who can be seen as precursors of the Mahāyāna, the nirvāna of remainderless extinction becomes less important than nirvāna with a remainder of conditionality. From this view, later schools developed the conception of "indeterminate extinction" (→ *apratishthita-nirvāna*), in which a buddha renounces remainderless extinction and yet is free of attachment to the world.

In Mahāyāna, because of emphasis on the bodhisattva ideal, attainment of nirvāna slips somewhat into the background. It loses, however, none of its importance, since in no school of the Mahāyāna is bodhisattvahood considered the ultimate goal. Extinction in nirvāna is only postponed by the bodhisattva until all beings are liberated from suffering. Here nirvāna takes on a positive character, since it becomes essentially a state of awareness of one's identity with the absolute. The experience of unity with the absolute is not limited to the person of the experience; rather it is a limitless experience that encompasses all appearances, including one's own body. In this view, there is no essential distinction between samsāra and nirvāna.

Here two types of nirvāna are distinguished: indeterminate (*apratishthita-nirvāna*) and complete (→ *pratishthita-nirvāna*).

Views of nirvāna differ also among the Mahāyāna schools. The → Mādhyamikas see nirvāna as emptiness (→ *shūnyatā*), which they define as "coming to rest of the manifold," since this coming to rest of the manifold means also the cessation or absence of everything relating to a confused projection of the world. Nirvāna is oneness with the inexpressible reality that always exists, only is not recognized. Nirvāna and samsāra are not different if one perceives the world in its true nature, which is emptiness. It is our discriminating mind that prevents us from recognizing this true nature.

The → Yogāchāra posits the nondistinctness of samsāra and nirvāna as well as the unreality of all appearances. Nirvāna for this "mind-only" teaching is the cessation of discrimination, as well as the consciousness that only mind exists and the faith that the objective existence of the phenomenal world represents nothing but a confusion of the mind. This school recognizes two types of nirvāna: that of the arhat, with whom, after death, only absolute being remains. It is a coming to rest but not a consciously experienced bliss; it is seen as inferior in comparison with the second type of nirvāna, that of the Buddha, since the latter entails conscious extinction and conscious exercise of compassion. In this form of nirvāna, which exhibits a positive character and represents conscious unity with all beings, the individual as empirical personality continues in force.

In Zen Buddhism nirvāna is also seen as not separate from this world; it is rather the realization of the true nature of the mind (the mind's essence), which is identical with the true nature of human beings—the buddha-nature (→ *busshō*). This realization is only possible through wisdom, thus nirvāna is often equated with → *prajñā*. In the Zen sense, *prajñā* and nirvāna are two aspects of the same state. Nirvāna is the state in which a person lives who has attained *prajñā* and thus also insight into his own mind or true nature; and *pragñā* is the wisdom of a person who has attained nirvāna.

Nirvāna school 🅑 a strain of early Chinese Buddhism, which originated in the 5th century. It is not a school in the true sense but rather the term refers to a succession of monks who concerned themselves primarily with the teachings of the → *Mahāparinirvāna-sūtra.*

The most important teachings of this sūtra are that → Nirvāna is eternal, joyous, personal, and pure in nature. This contrasts with the view put forward in the → *Prajñāpāramitā-sūtra,* in which nirvāna is described as the realization of emptiness (→ *shūnyatā*). All beings possess → buddha-nature and can attain buddhahood; in this sense the true self is like the → *tathāgata.*

These teachings were studied throughout China but rejected by many as "heretical," since they conflicted with the teachings of the *Prajñāpāramitā-sūtra.* The most outstanding spokesmen of these revolutionary doctrines were → Tao-sheng in the south and Tao-leng in the north. The theses of Tao-sheng, based on the *Mahāparinirvāna-sūtra,* that even → *ichchantikas* possess buddha-nature and the buddhahood is achieved through "sudden" enlightenment, led to many controversies among the learned monks of this time.

The Nirvāna school also originated the practice, so characteristic of Chinese Buddhism, of dividing the teachings of the Buddha into various phases. The *Mahāparinirvāna-sūtra* is considered to be the last of the Buddha's discourses. From this the Chinese developed the notion that the Buddha must have expounded other teachings earlier in his life, and they divided the entire body of teachings according to content into different periods and doctrines, which corresponded to different phases in the life of the Buddha. In the course of development of Chinese Buddhism, nearly every school put forward its own classification. The first division was that into doctrines of "sudden" and "gradual" enlightenment.

Nirvichāra-Samādhi 🅗 (Nirvicāra-Samādhi),

Skt.; a term in the yoga philosophy of → Patañjali, who refers thereby to a state of absorption in which the mind becomes one with the object of concentration. The perception of names and qualities or other forms of cognition no longer disturb the mind, since it intuitively sees through everything in a flash.

Nirvikalpa-Samādhi 🅗 Skt., lit. "changeless *samādhi*"; a term used in → Vedānta to refer to the highest, transcendent state of consciousness, the realization of the concept "I am *brahman*," which until realization exists in the mind only as a thought. In this state there is no longer mind, duality, nor subject-object relationship. It is the highest, *samādhi*-state of nondual union with *brahman.*

Nirvishaya 🅗 (Nirvisaya), Skt., lit. *nir*: "not," *vishaya* "object, world of the senses"; a state in which the consciousness no longer entertains associations with the objects of sense perception.

Nisargadatta Maharaj 🅗 1897–1981, Indian spiritual teacher; his given name was Maruti Kampli. Through his intense longing for spiritual truth he found a guru, and by means of his complete trust in and obedience to the teacher attained enlightenment. In later years he lived modestly as a householder in an impoverished section of Bombay. He never referred to himself as a → *mahātmā*, → *bhagavan*, or → *paramahamsa* and founded no school and no philosophy; he merely spoke about what he himself had experienced: his own real Self (→ *ātman*). The instructions and replies he gave in response to questions from visitors and pupils were pure → Advaita in the sense of → Rāmana Maharshi; in the last ten years of his life, these conversations were collected and translated into English by Maurice Frydman.

Nishkāma-Karma 🅗 (Niṣkāma-Karma), Skt., lit. *nishkāma*: "desireless, selfless," *karma*: "deed"; actions that are undertaken without the expectation of any return; selfless action without expecting the fruits thereof.

Nishthā 🅗 (Niṣṭhā), Skt., lit. "completion, pinnacle"; total submission to or absorption in the object of surrender.

Nissoku-kan 🅩 Jap. → *susokukan*

Nistraigunya 🅗 (Nistraiguṇya), Skt., lit. *nis*: "without," *traigunya*: "the three fundamental qualities"; free from the three qualities (→ *guna*) of nature.

Nīti-Shāstras 🅗 (Nīti-Śāstras), Skt.; ethical scripture, having to do with wise and moral behavior. The traditional method in India of teaching such behavior involves the use of allegories, fairy tales, fables, and legends, usually in prose form, although those maxims considered to be especially worthy of consideration are inserted in verse form.

Nitya 🅗 Skt., lit. "constant, eternal"; the ultimate reality, the eternal Absolute; one who is united with this ultimate reality is called *nitya-mukta,* "one who is liberated and released for all time"; one who is united with *nitya* and yet undergoes rebirth for the sake of the good of humanity is named *nitya-siddha,* "one who is eternally perfect." To this latter category belong → Nārada and → Shukadeva. *Nitya* as the Absolute is contrasted to → *līlā* as the relative, the manifestation of the Absolute as God's "play" in the world of appearances.

Nitya-Karma 🅗 Skt., lit. "duty"; religious ceremonies, such as worship and prayer, that a householder must perform daily so that previous sins may be removed and new ones avoided as far as possible. A → *sannyāsin* is not bound to this duty.

Nitya-Vāk 🅗 (Nitya-Vāc), Skt., lit. *nitya*: "eternal, lasting, constant," *vāc*: "word, speech"; the inner, indivisible, constant sound, the divine word of the → *Rigveda.* (See also → *vāk.*)

Niu-t'ou-ch'an 🅩 → Gozu school

Nīvarana 🅑 (nīvaraṇa) Skt., Pali, lit. "obstruction, hindrance"; refers to five qualities that hinder the mind, obstruct insight, and prevent practitioners from attaining neighboring or complete concentration (→ *samādhi*) and from knowing the truth. The five hindrances are (1) desire (*abhidyā*), (2) ill will (*pradosha*), (3) sloth and torpor (*styāna* and *middha*), (4) restlessness and compunction (*anuddhatya* and *kaukrītya*), (5) doubt (→ *vichikitsā*). The elimination of the five hindrances is the precondition for attaining the five stages of absorption (→ *dhyāna*).

Nivritti-Mārga 🅗 (Nivṛtti-Mārga), Skt., lit. *nivritti*: "return," *mārga*: "path"; the path back inward, to spiritual self-recollection.

Niwa-zume 🅩 Jap., roughly "being left standing in the court"; the time in which a Zen monk who has requested admittance to a monastery, after an initial rejection remains prostrating at the monastery gate in order to prove the earnestness of his longing for spiritual training.

In the Zen tradition it is clear that only a person with a great sense of commitment and a strong "will for the truth" (→ *kokorozashi*) is suitable to undertake the difficult and lengthy path of spiritual training in the search for → enlightenment, a path which demands of each seeker, mentally and physically, the utmost of which he or she is capable. Thus, particularly in ancient times, persons who sought to be admitted to a Zen monastery or to be accepted by a → *rōshi* as his student were often harshly rejected at first in order to test them. If they were discouraged by this rejection, it was clear that their will for truth was not strong enough.

"Being left standing in the court" could last for several days. During this time the monk, prostrating or in a posture of humility, stayed day and night at the gate of the monastery, no matter what the weather, provided that his wish to be accepted into the monastery was an earnest one. This period of trial has a long tradition in Ch'an (Zen). The second patriarch of Ch'an (Zen) in China, → Hui-k'o, was initially rejected by → Bodhidharma when he requested the latter to accept him as a student. According to tradition, Hui-k'o persisted for many days, standing in the snow in bitter cold before the cave in which Bodhidharma was practicing *zazen* "facing the wall" (→ *menpeki*). Bodhidharma paid him no heed. Only when Hui-k'o, as a sign of his earnestness, cut off his own left arm and presented it to Bodhidharma did the latter accept him as a student.

Niyama 🅗 Skt.; the second step of → Patañjali's well-known yoga system, also called Rāja-Yoga. Like → *yama*, the first step, it is part of one's ethical preparation and consists of outward and inward purity, contentment, stringency regarding one's own behavior, study of holy scripture, and submission to God.

Nō 🅩 Jap.; the highly refined dance-drama of Japan, in which the means of expression are reduced to the essential. Like many other Japanese arts, Nō is permeated by the spirit of Zen and strongly marked by it. The originator of the classical form of Nō is considered to be Ze-ami (1363–1443), who was the greatest author of Nō plays and wrote the most important theoretical work on Nō and its aesthetic.

Nöndro 🅑 Tib.; an alternate way of writing *ngöndro*, → body, speech, mind.

Nonself 🅑 → *anātman*

Northern school 🅩 → Southern school

Nōshi 🅩 Jap. → *nōsu*

Nōsu 🅩 also nōshi, Jap., lit. "patchwork robe"; 1. the robe of a Buddhist monk. 2. in Zen a term for a Zen monk (who wears a patchwork robe).

Nrisimha-Tapanīya-Upanishad 🅗 (Nṛsiṃha-Tapanīya-Upaniṣad), Skt., lit. *simha*: "lion," *tapanīya*, from *tapana*: "burning, ascetic suffering"; one of the Vishnu-Upanishads. It contains six books, comprising an exoteric and an esoteric part, the latter found in the last book, also known as the *Nrisimha-Uttara-* ("later, higher") *Tapanīya-Upanishad.* Its fundamental view is of a fourfold identity: → *ātman* equals → OM equals → *brahman* equals Nrisimha (Vishnu in his incarnation as the lion-man → Narasimha); through the medium of the syllable OM, the *ātman*, the individual principle, is equated with the *brahman*, the cosmic principle, and all three are viewed as symbolically present in Nrisimha. This sixth book was reserved for the use of those few who were ready to receive its profound message.

The first five books, also known as the *Nrisimha-Pūrva-*("earlier") *Tapanīya-Upanishad,* are devoted to the early, simple worship of Nrisimha that glorifies Vishnu in his lion form as the emblem of power, thus meeting the people's religious needs with a folk hero in the form of a powerful, divine hero. Paul Deussen describes the distinction between the two parts in this way: "In the first part, the Upanishadic teaching serves the devotion of Nrisimha, while in the second part the worship of Nrisimha serves the Upanishadic teaching."

Nü-kua 🅣 female figure in Chinese mythology. Nü-kua is considered to have created mankind. A text dating from the Han Dynasty states that after Heaven and Earth had separated, Nü-kua began to form human figures out of yellow earth. But this method proved too tedious and time-consuming, so she dipped a rope into mud and then swung it about her so that lumps of mud fell to the ground. The original handmade humans became the wealthy and noble, and those that arose from the splashes of mud the poor and common. In addition, Nü-kua is said to have restored the universal order after a devastating attack by the mythical monster Kung Kung. In this role she is usually represented in the company of → Fu Hsi, her alleged husband. They are shown as a couple in human form but with intertwining dragon tails. Fu Hsi holds a set square, and Nü-kua a compass, symbols of Heaven and Earth.

Nü-kua is also credited with having instituted marriage. In addition, she tamed wild animals and—together with other mythological figures—instructed mankind in the art of building dikes and dams as well as channels for regulating flood water and for purposes of irrigation.

Another myth states that beyond the northwestern

ocean there live ten ghosts who were fashioned from the bowels of Nü-kua.

→ Lieh-tzu gives the following description of Nü-kua's activities: "At one time it was found that the cardinal points were no longer in the proper place. The nine provinces lay exposed. Heaven no longer fully covered Earth, and the Earth in turn supported Heaven only in places. Fire burned continuously. Water flowed incessantly. Wild animals devoured peaceable human beings. Predatory birds carried off old men and children. Then Nü-kua melted colored stones to mend the azure skies. She cut off the legs of a turtle to support the cardinal points. She slayed the black dragon to save the land of Ch'i. On the river bank she piled up the ashes of reeds to dam the overflowing water. And all was calm again and everyone lived in peace" (Christie 1968, p. 84).

Nyānatiloka 🅱 1878–1957, German Buddhist scholar and translator. His original name was Walter Florus Gueth. He came from a Catholic family. After receiving his high school degree, he studied music and became a violin virtuoso. During a trip to Sri Lanka, he came in contact with Buddhism. He went to Burma, where he entered the Buddhist monastic order. He is considered one of the most important Pali scholars. Among his works of translation are *Die Fragen des Milindo* (1919–24) (→ *Milindapañha*), the → *Anguttara-nikāya* (1922), and the → *Visuddhi-magga* (1952). He composed many doctrinal works and a *Buddhist Dictionary* (Colombo, 1972).

Nyāya 🅷 , or Tarkavidyā ("science of debate"), or Vādavidyā "science of discussion"), Skt., lit. "correct" or "logic"; one of the six philosophical systems of Hinduism (→ *darshana*); it is thought to have been established by → Gotama, who presumably lived between the sixth and third centuries B.C.E. Nyāya, the science of logical proof, provides a well-founded system for the philosophical investigation of objects and the subject of human knowledge. Its adherents, known as *niyayikas,* represent Nyāya as a means toward true knowledge of the soul and the aim of human life, according to natural law. *Nyāya* means "to investigate thoroughly" through analytic and logical inquiry. → Vātsyāyana, the classical commentator on the → *Nyāya-Sūtra,* refers to this method as "a critical testing of the objects of knowledge, by means of logical proof."

Nyāya-Sūtra, 🅷 Skt.; the chief work of → Gotama, founder of the → Nyāya philosophy. It is estimated to have been written in the third/fourth contury B.C.E. The principles of Nyāya existed prior to Gotama's time in undifferentiated form. This *sūtra,* divided into five books, each of which contains two subsections, attempts to reconcile the conclusions arrived at by the brahmans (→ *brāhmana*) as a result of logical thinking with their religious and philosophical dogmas. In the third century, → Vātsyāyana composed a commentary on the work (*Nyāya-Bhāshya*), that is still regarded as standard today.

Nyingmapa 🅱 (rnyiṅg-ma-pa), Tib., lit. "School of the Ancients"; one of the four principal schools of → Tibetan Buddhism. The school brings together the oldest Buddhist traditions of Tibet, which were brought to the country from India by → Padmasambhava and the monks Vimalamitra and Vairochana in the 8th century. Since the 15th century there has existed an independent collection of these teachings, which, however, is not included in the official Tibetan canon (→ Kangyur-Tengyur). The Nyingmapas consider → *dzogchen* to be the supreme doctrine; the systematization of the *dzogchen* teaching by → Lonchenpa and his commentary on it are considered authoritative.

The early Nyingmapas were laymen as well as monks. They managed to maintain their tradition in spite of the persecution of Buddhism by Langdarma (836–42). In the 11th century the name *nyingma* ("old") came into use to distinguish their school from the new schools that had developed by then. Three lineages of transmission are recognized in this school: the historical, direct, and visionary lineages.

The historical or *kama* (utterance), lineage includes all teachings that, stemming from → Samantabhadra, were passed down in an uninterrupted transmission from teacher to disciple. Among these are the teachings of the three vehicles (→ *yāna*) that are peculiar to the Nyingmapa school: *mahāyoga, anuyoga,* and *atiyoga* (for the last of these, → *dzogchen*).

The direct, or → *terma,* lineage is associated with those transmissions that were hidden as texts by Padmasambhava, so that at the right time they could be rediscovered and taught anew. The → *Bardo thödol* is one of the best-known *terma* works. Direct spiritual contact with teachers of past generations that result in empowerments for particular teachings constitute the visionary lineage. In this way Lonchenpa received the teachings of Padmasambhava.

Nyoi 🆉 Jap. for → *ju-i*

Nyo-nyo-chi 🆉 Jap., lit. "the wisdom that is like thusness [→ *shinnyo*]"; the wisdom that arises from profound → enlightenment, the realization of one's own buddha-nature (→ *busshō*); also enlightened consciousness.

Nyorai 🆉 Jap. for → *tathāgata*

Nyorai-zō 🅉 Jap., lit. "*tathāgata* treasure-house"; a synonym for the buddha-nature (→ *busshō*) inherent in all beings, the true nature of reality that in unenlightened persons (→ *bonpu-no-jōshiki*) is obscured by → delusion.

Nyorai-zō-shin 🅉 Jap., lit. "heart-mind [→ *kokoro*] of the *tathāgata* treasurehouse"; expression in Japanese Buddhism referring to the view, common to the many Mahāyāna schools, that the mind (heart-mind) of human beings is fundamentally perfect and identical with that of buddha (→ *busshō*).

Nyoze 🅉 Jap., lit. "thus, precisely, just like this"; an expression betokening complete certainty, the absence of any doubt. Used by a master to his student, it means that the student has understood.

Nyūfuni-hōmon 🅉 Jap., lit. "entry through the dharma gate [→ *hōmon*] of nonduality"; awakening to the truth of nonduality, i.e., experience of enlightenment. The expression comes from the → *Vimalakīrtinirdesha-sūtra*, where it appears as the heading of a chapter.

O

Ōbai 🅉 Jap. for → Huang-mei

Ōbaku Kiun 🅉 Jap. for → Huang-po Hsi-yun

Ōbaku school 🅉 with the → Rinzai and → Sōtō schools, one of the three schools of Zen in Japan. It was originated by the Chinese master → Yin-yuan Lung-ch'i (Jap., Ingen Ryūki), who founded the school's main monastery, Mampuku-ji, in the middle of the 17th century in Uji near Kyōto. The Ōbaku school is a subsidiary lineage of the Rinzai school; in present-day Japan it possesses hardly any active monasteries and is thus the least influential of the three schools of Zen in Japan.

Yin-yuan was originally the abbot of Wan-fu-ssu (Jap., Mampuku-ji), a monastery on Mount Huang-po (Jap., Ōbaku) in China. In the year 1654 he came to Japan, where in 1661 Shōgun Tokugawa Tsunayoshi had a monastery in the Chinese Ming style built for him. Yin-yuan gave this monastery the name Ōbaku-san Mampuku-ji. In 1671 → Mu-an Hsing-t'ao (Jap., Mokuan Shōtō), a Chinese monk and student of Yin-yuan's who had accompanied the latter to Japan, founded the Zuishō-ji monastery in the vicinity of Tōkyō, which became a strong force in spreading Zen in this area. Until the Japanese monk Ryūtō was installed as the 14th abbot of this monastery, the lineage stemming from Yin-yuan and Mu-an was continued by Chinese dharma successors (→ *hassu*). In 1876 this lineage was officially recognized as the Ōbaku school. It was first developed as an independent school in Japan and was not, as often supposed because of its name, founded by the great Chinese master → Huang-po Hsi-yun (Jap., Ōbaku Kiun), who was the master of Lin-chi I-hsuan, the founder of the Rinzai school.

Ōbaku-shū 🅉 Jap. → Ōbaku school

Ojas 🄷 Skt., lit. "power, life force"; the highest form of energy in the human body. Through steadfast renunciation and purification, other forms of energy, such as sexuality, are transformed into *ojas* and stored in the brain. They may act as spiritual as well as intellectual power. *Ojas-shakti* refers to the effect of the accumulated *ojas* force, which manifests itself in worldly activities in the case of political, business, or military leaders; at the intellectual level in the case of those who found philosophical systems; and at the highest level of spiritual activity in the case of illumined ones, whereby the energy of *ojas* returns to absolute consciousness.

Ōjin 🅉 Jap. for *nirmānakāya*, → *trikāya*

OM 🄷 🄱 also AUM or *pranava*, Skt.; the most comprehensive and venerable symbol of spiritual knowledge in Hinduism. It also appears in Buddhism (particularly in → Vajrayāna) as a mantric syllable, but has a different sense than in Hinduism.

OM is a symbol of form as well as sound. This syllable is no magic word and is not even considered to be a word; rather it is a manifestation of spiritual power, a symbol that is to be found throughout the East, which betokens the presence of the absolute within → māyā. The worlds of the physical, mental, and unconscious are represented in the letters of the syllable OM by three curves; the supreme consciousness is represented by the point outside and above the rest; this illuminates and reveals the other three. The

The symbol OM

form of OM is a concrete manifestation of the visible truth. No concept or object of this universe is independent. All are permutations of the one consciousness and participate in its nature to various degrees; in this way they are connected with one another.

The OM symbol consists of three curves, a semicircle, and a point and is an enclosed unit. The three curves are connected with one another and grow one out of the other. The point with the semicircle stands by itself. It rules the whole. The symbol stands for three states of consciousness—the waking state, the dream state, and the state of deep sleep—as well as the supreme consciousness or self, which observes and permeates these states. The semicircle under the point is not closed; it symbolizes the infinite and its openness indicates that finite thinking cannot grasp the depth and the height of the point.

The material world of the wakeful consciousness, the level of external activity and thus the most palpable, is symbolized by the large lower curve (1). The level of the dream state, subject to the stimulus not of external objects but only of mental representations, is symbolized by the second, small curve (2), which is, so to speak, between wakefulness and sleep. The upper curve (3) symbolizes the unconscious, which we call deep sleep, but it is also a connective link, for it is closest to the point that represents absolute consciousness. The point is the absolute consciousness that illuminates and governs the three others; it is → *turīya*, "the fourth." Without *turīya*, there would be no thinking, no symbol, and no universe. The point illuminates the three states. It itself lights by its own light and is only experienced by persons who have gone beyond the three curves and attained the point and merged with it. The point can be interpreted variously: as absolute consciousness, as witnessing consciousness behind body and thought, or as liberation from the world of appearance.

Western commentators have equated OM as *aum* with the three deities (→ *trimūrti*); however this exposition is not sufficiently profound.

OM MANI PADME HUM 🅱 Skt., lit. "OM, jewel in the lotus, hum" (Tib., om mani peme hung); Sanskrit formula associated with → Avalokiteshvara, the most important and oldest mantra of Tibetan Buddhism. The simplest explanation of the two words, enclosed by so-called seed-syllables, that mean "jewel in the lotus" is equation of the jewel with enlightenment-mind (→ *bodhicitta*), which arises in the lotus of human consciousness. The complex meaning of this sequence of sounds is connected with the role it plays in → *sādhanas* and must be described in the context of the entire symbology of the → Vajrayāna. For Tibetan Buddhists, these six syllables are an expression of the basic attitude of compassion, and the recitation of them expresses the longing for liberation (→ nirvāna) "for the sake of all sentient beings." For this reason, the six syllables are also associated with the six modes of existence in the wheel of life (→ *bhava-chakra*).

The mantra OM MANI PADME HUM in its Tibetan form

OM MANI PEME HUNG 🅱 Tib. for → OM MANI PADME HUM

OM NAMO NĀRĀYANĀYA 🅷 Skt., lit. "OM! Honor be to God in man!"; a traditional form of greeting among → *sadhus* and saints; also a frequently employed mantra. (See also → *nārāyana*.)

OM TAT SAT 🅷 Skt., lit. "OM! That is Being"; *That* refers to → *brahman, Being* is absolute Being, or *brahman,* but now manifesting as the creation; the sense of the words is that what we perceive as the creation, the world of appearances, is in reality *brahman.* This sacred sentence appears at the beginning of many books. In the → *Bhagavad-Gītā*, every chapter closes with these words.

One-pointedness of mind 🅑 (Skt., ekāgrata; Pali, ekāgattā); focusing (concentration) of mind on a single object. (Also → *samādhi.*)

Ordination 🅑 in the Buddhist sense, acceptance into the → *sangha* of the Buddhist community of monks and nuns, which represents a legal act that must be carried out in the presence of witnesses according to specific rules; a prerequisite is the voluntary declaration of entering into → homelessness. Ordination does not bind the person ordained to the *sangha* for life; leaving the order and returning to it are possible at any time.

Three different types of ordination are distinguished: (1) the lower ordination, through which one becomes a novice (→ *shrāmanera*); (2) the higher ordination, through which a novice is consecrated as a monk (→ *bhikshu*) or nun (→ *bhikshunī*); (3) the "bodhisattva ordination" in the Mahāyāna.

Ordination ceremonies vary greatly from country to country. The first ordination is described in the *Prātimoksha-sūtra.*

Originally entry into the order was accomplished by shaving the hair and beard, putting on the upper and lower yellow robes (→ *trichīvara*), and doing a threefold recitation of the refuge formula (→ *triratna*). However, this simple ceremony was soon felt to be inadequate and gave way to a complicated procedure. In the ordination for the novitiate, the candidate has to appear with shaven head before at least ten (or in areas where Buddhism developed late, five) monks; female novices-to-be need nuns as well as monks as witnesses, otherwise the ordination is invalid. The male novice receives the two-piece robe from the hands of the abbot of the monastery, at which time he is reminded of the impermanence of the body this robe will cover. Then he retires to put on the robe, during which process he recites a formula intended to make him aware that the robe is to be worn as a protection and not an adornment of the body. Then he requests to be granted refuge and takes upon himself the ten → *shīlas*, which the abbot recites and the novice repeats.

In the ordination for full monkhood (*upasampadā*), the novice first goes once more through the lower ordination; then an examiner questions him according to a fixed text concerning his age, origin, illnesses, and so on. The monk-to-be then names his two teachers (→ *āchārya*, → *upādhyāya*) and one of them confers upon him the three-piece robe and the begging bowl. Then follows the description of the behavioral precepts and that of the four violations that lead to expulsion from the *sangha* (→ Vinaya, → *Prātimoksha*). The candidate requests acceptance and the ordination formula is repeated three times. At this point anyone in the community has the right to object. The ceremony is concluded by an address by the abbot. In Mahāyāna countries, after some time the taking of the bodhisattva vow (→ *pranidhāna*) follows. In China, this precedes the → *moxa* ceremony, in which incense is burned on the bald head of the monk; this leaves visible scars.

Orgyen 🅑 → Urgyen

Original face 🅩 → *honrai-no-memmoku*

Ōryō E'nan 🅩 Jap. for → Huang-lung Hui-nan

Ōryō-ha 🅩 Jap. for → Ōryō school

Ōryōki 🅩 Jap., roughly "that which contains just enough"; a set of nesting eating bowls, which Zen monks or nuns receive at their ordination. In a narrower sense *ōryōki* means just the largest of these bowls (also → *jihatsu*), which corresponds to the single eating and begging bowl that the itinerant monks of India immediately after the time of → Shākyamuni Buddha were allowed to possess. In an extended sense, *ōryōki* refers to the ceremonial use of the eating bowls during the silently taken meals in a Zen monastery.

Ōryō school 🅩 (Chin., Huang-lung-p'ai, Jap., Ōryō-ha [Chin., p'ai; Jap., ha, "wing"]); a lineage of Rinzai Zen stemming from the Chinese Ch'an (Zen) master → Huang-lung Hui-nan (Jap., Ōryō or Ōryū E'nan). It belongs to the "seven schools" (→ *goke-shichishū*) of Ch'an (Zen) and was the first school of Zen in Japan, brought there by → Eisai Zenji. It died out both in China and Japan after a few generations. Since the Ōryō lineage developed out of the → Rinzai school, it is also called the Rinzai Ōryō school.

Ösel 🅑 ('od-gsal) Tib., lit. "clear light, luminosity"; 1. the luminosity of mind, the realization of which, as complementing the emptiness (→ *shūnyatā*) of mind, is generally defined as the supreme goal of the → Tantras (→ *mahāmudrā*, → *dzogchen*).

2. One of the "six doctrines of Nāropa (→ *Nāro chödrug*), through the practice of which "light in its essential identity with the mind radiating from oneself [manifests] in the same manner as a lamp illuminates itself and objects without further external means" (G. Tucci).

Ōtani 🅑 Jap. → Jōdo-shin-shū

Ō-Tō-Kan School 🅩 Jap.; lineage of Japanese Rinzai Zen stemming from the three great Zen masters Nampo → Shōmyō (also Daiō Kokushi), → Myōchō Shūhō (also Daitō Kokushi), and Kanzan Egen (also Musō Daishi). The name of this lineage derives from the last characters of *Daiō* and *Daitō* and from the first of *Kanzan*. The important Zen master and great reformer of Rinzai Zen → Hakuin Zenji was a heritor of this lineage.

Outer elixir T → *wai-tan*

P

Pa-chiao Hui-ch'ing Z (Jap., Bashō Esei) a Zen master of about the 10th century who came from Korea and belonged to the → Igyō school. Pa-chiao traveled from Korea to China and became there a student and dharma successor (→ *hassu*) of → Nan-t'a Kuang-jun (Jap., Nantō Kōyū). He was the master of → Hsiang-yang Ch'ing-jang (Jap., Kōyō Seijō). We encounter Pa-chiao in example 44 of the → *Wu-men-kuan*.

The pronouncement of Pa-chiao that is presented here as a kōan is one of the most famous Zen sayings. "Master Pa-chiao said while instructing his students, 'If you have a staff, I'll give you a staff. If you don't have a staff, I'll take your staff away.' "

Padārtha H Skt. → Vaisheshika

Padma H B Skt. → lotus

Padmapāni B → *Avalokiteshvara*

Padma-Purāna H (Padma-Purāṇa), Skt.; one of the *Vishnu-Purānas* (→ Purāna), stylistically characteristic of the → Vaishnavas, particularly the last part, wherein Shiva describes to his wife Pārvatī the essence and qualities of Vishnu, and the two finally worship him together. It is thought to have been composed no earlier than the twelfth century.

The work describes the world and its events when the former was still a golden lotus (*padma*), hence the title. It consists of 55,000 double verses arranged in five books that deal in turn with the creation, the earth, heaven, the underworld, and additional matters. A sixth part presents an essay on the practice of worship of God. The contents are entirely heterogenous; probably the title represents a collection of various independent works.

Padmasambhava B Skt., lit. "the Lotus-born"; contemporary of the Tibetan king Trisong Detsen (755–97) and one of the historically identifiable founders of → Tibetan Buddhism. He left his imprint particularly on the → Nyingmapa school and is venerated by its followers as the "second Buddha." His special task lay in taming the indigenous demons, or the forces of nature embodied in them. The methods of Padmasambhava ranged from the use of ritual implements, such as the → *phurba*, to the mastery of the meditation techniques of → *dzogchen*. In the course of centuries, the figure of Padmasambhava, who continued the tradition of the → *mahāsiddhas*, took on an increasingly legendary character. He is still venerated today in the Himalayan countries under the name *Guru Rinpoche* (Precious Guru).

Padmasambhava, who brought Buddhism to Tibet, and two of his female students (Tibetan block print)

According to legend, Padmasambhava was born in the country of → Urgyen in northwest Kashmir. He quickly mastered all the learned disciplines of his time, especially the teachings of the → Tantras. In the 8th century he made his appearance in history through his mission to Tibet, then under the dominance of nature religion and the → *bön* faith. His campaign in Tibet came to an end with the construction of the Samye Monastery (775). Concerning the remainder of Padmasambhava's stay in Tibet, the sources diverge, giving anywhere from a few months to many years. He transmitted his teachings to twenty five principal students, including the Tibetan king. Especially important among these teachings were the "eight logos." For the benefit of future generations, he also hid a great number of teachings in the form of texts (→ *terma*). The most important female student of Padmasambhava and the author of his biography was → Yeshe Tsogyel.

The followers of the Nyingmapa school celebrate the important events in the life of Guru Rinpoche on the tenth day of each month. Thus on the tenth of the first month they celebrate his renunciation of the world and his meditating in charnel grounds; on the tenth of the second month, his ordination; on the tenth of the third month, his transformation of fire to water in the kingdom of Zahor—and so forth. The best known invocation of Padmasambhava is that in seven lines:

In the northwest of the land of Urgyen
On a blooming lotus flower
You attained supreme wondrous perfection.
You are called the Lotus-born
And are surrounded by a retinue of *dākinīs.*
I follow your example—
Approach and grant me your blessing.

A biography of Padmasambhava is to be found in W. Y. Evans-Wentz 1954.

Padmāsana H Skt.; the "lotus position," a bodily pose in → Hatha-Yoga that is particularly suitable for meditation.

The *Hatha-Yoga-Pradīpika describes padmāsana* as follows: "The right foot is placed on the left hip and left foot on the right hip; then the hands are crossed behind the back, and the big toes are held firmly. The chin is pressed against the chest, and the eyes are directed to the tip of the nose. This is called *padmāsana,* which removes all evil from the *yami* (the practitioner)." This position is also called the "locked position" (*baddha-padmāsana*).

Pagoda B Buddhist architectonic form indigenous to China, Japan, and Korea, which developed out of the Indian → stūpa. Pagodas are usually narrow four- or eight-cornered structures out of stone, brick, or wood, with several stories and prominent eaves. On the very top is a post with a great number of rings.

A pagoda, like a stupa, serves as a container for relics (→ *sharīra*) or as the tomb of a famous master. The core of the pagoda, which contains the relics, can be ritually circumambulated on a stairway. The pagoda also appears throughout East Asia in miniature form as a votive offering vessel, an incense holder, or as the central piece on a domestic shrine.

In the development from the Indian stūpa to the East Asian pagoda, a greater sense of verticality was obtained by the multiplication of levels in the lower part of the structure, creating the impression of a tower. The structural elements that separate the levels are extended into jutting eaves, which taper slightly in width as they approach the top of the pagoda. The hemisphere so characteristic of the stūpa is preserved in the pagoda only as the pediment for the ring-bearing post at the very top.

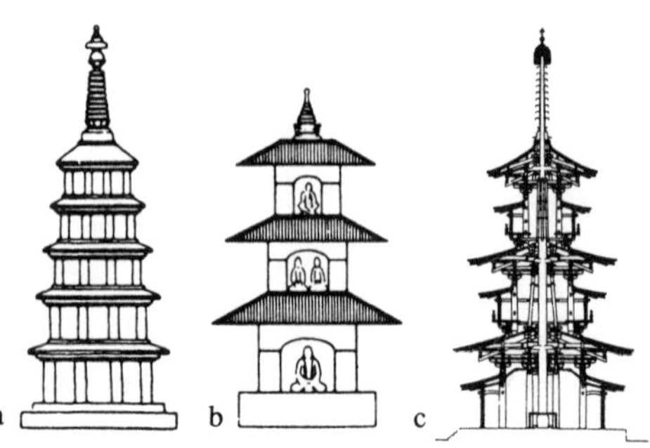

Basic types of Chinese (a, b) and Japanese (c) multistory pagodas (after D. Seckel)

In China the form of the pagoda was already fully developed by the 5th century. Wooden pagodas are known from even earlier times. Chinese pagodas are usually made from brick, stone, or wood and are richly adorned with sculptural forms. Their sweeping rooves are covered with colorful glazed shingles. The roof corners and the rings on top are often hung with small bells, the sound of which symbolically carries the Buddhist teachings in all directions. Inside, Chinese pagodas have either a pillar, around which stairs wind so that the pagoda can be ritually circumambulated, or a central shaft containing buddha figures from which walkways lead to windows in the outer wall. Many pagodas are ornamented on the outside with reliefs of buddha images that symbolize the innumerable buddhas of all worlds.

In addition to functioning as a Buddhist sacred site, a pagoda is intended to exercise a geomantically favorable influence on its locale.

Pagodas, like stūpas, embody a cosmic symbology. The absolute that is personified in the figure of the Buddha is symbolically represented by the central pillar of a pagoda. This central axis of the structure is the center of the universe. Out of it the cardinal directions and their world quarters arise, each of which in the Mahāyāna is associated with a particular buddha. In this way, a pagoda is similar to a → mandala.

Individual stories represent the different worlds (→ *triloka*), the stages of the bodhisattva path

(→ *bhūmi*), or the path to enlightenment in general. The eight-cornered ground plan popular in China symbolizes the wheel of dharma (→ dharma-chakra) with its eight spokes, which in turn refers to the → eightfold path.

Pa-hsien ◼ Chin., lit. "eight immortals"; a group of eight immortals (→ *hsien*), who are among the best known figures of Taoist mythology. The earliest descriptions of them date from the T'ang Dynasty, but their present grouping was not established until the Ming Dynasty. The eight immortals are Li T'ieh-kuai (also called Li Hsüan), Chang Kuo-lao, Ts'ao Kuo-chiu, Han Hsiang-tzu, Lü Tung-pin, Ho Hsien-ku, Lan Ts'ai-ho and Chung Li-ch'üan (also called Han Chung-li). Chang Kuo-lao, Lü Tung-pin, Ts'ao Kuo-chiu and Chung Li-ch'üan are historical figures.

Throughout China the eight immortals are a symbol for good fortune. In addition, they represent eight different conditions of life: youth, old age, poverty, wealth, nobility, the populace, the feminine, and the masculine.

The *pa-hsien* are a favorite theme in artistic representations. They can be found on fans, porcelain, picture scrolls, etc. and also figure prominently in many literary works.

1. *Li T'ieh-kuai* (lit. "Li with the Iron Crutch") is usually portrayed with an iron crutch and a pumpkin containing magic potions. According to tradition, the Royal Mother of the West (→ Hsi Wang-mu) healed an abcess on Li's leg and taught him how to become immortal. She also gave him the iron crutch.

Another legend explains how Li came to have a crippled leg: Lao-tzu had descended from Heaven to initiate Li in the Taoist teachings. Soon after that Li attained immortality and left his body to travel to sacred Mount Hua-hsan. He told one of his pupils to guard his body during his absence but to burn it if he did not return within seven days. After Li had gone six days, this pupil received a message to say that his mother was dying. To enable him to fulfill his duty as a son, he burned the body of his master and went to his dying mother. When Li returned all he found was a heap of ashes and thus was forced to enter the body of a dead beggar, who had a black face, a pointed head, matted hair, a crippled leg, and big protruding eyes. Li did not want to live in such a body but Lao-tzu begged him to accept his fate and presented him with a band of gold to keep his tousled hair in place and with an iron crutch to help him walk.

2. *Chang Kuo-lao* was a Taoist who lived during the T'ang Dynasty. Legend tells us that he owned a white donkey capable of traveling a thousand miles a day. This magic donkey could be folded like a handkerchief and carried in one's pocket. To revive it, Chang had only to sprinkle a handful of water over the handkerchief. Chang's symbol is the so-called fish drum, an instrument for raising a loud noise.

Chang held a high official post and attracted the curiosity of the emperor who had questioned a famous Taoist master about him. This Taoist master told the emperor that he knew the true identity of Chang but was afraid to reveal it, because he had been told that he would fall dead to the ground if he were to do so. However, if the emperor in person were to go barefoot and bareheaded to ask Chang to forgive such a betrayal, Chang could bring him back to life. The emperor promised to do so whereupon the master told him that Chang was an incarnation of the primordial chaos. The master immediately fell dead to the ground. After the emperor had begged forgiveness of Chang he brought the Taoist master back to life by sprinkling water over his body. Soon after, Chang became ill and withdrew to the mountains where he died between 742 and 746 C.E. When his pupils opened his grave they found it to be empty (→ *shih-chieh*).

3. *Ts'ao Kuo-chiu* (d. 1097 C.E.) was the brother-in-law of a Sung Dynasty emperor. His younger brother became a murderer. In shame, Ts'ao withdrew to the mountains and decided to spend his life as a hermit. He is usually portrayed holding a pair of castanets.

According to legend Ts'ao one day encountered Chung Li-ch'üan and Lü Tung-pin, who asked him what he was doing in the mountains. Ts'ao answered that he was following the Way (→ Tao) whereupon they wanted to know where the Way was. Ts'ao pointed at Heaven. Lü and Chung then wanted to know where Heaven was. Ts'ao pointed at his heart. At this Chung Li-ch'üan smiled and said, "The heart is Heaven and Heaven is the Way. I see that you know the original face of things." They then taught Ts'ao how to attain perfection and within a few days he became an immortal.

Another legend says that the emperor gave Ts'ao a golden medal which would allow him to overcome all obstacles. One day, when Ts'ao had to cross the Yellow River, he showed that medal to the ferryman. Thereupon a poorly dressed Taoist priest asked Ts'ao why he—a follower of the Way—stooped to employ such methods. At this Ts'ao begged the priest to cast the medal into the river. The priest took him aside and said, "Have you heard of Lü Tung-pin? I am he and have come to help you attain immortality."

4. *Han Hsiang-tzu* is generally believed to be the nephew of Han Yü, a famous literary figure and statesman of the T'ang Dynasty, who had been entrusted with Hsiang-tzu's education. Han Hsiang-tzu had a stormy temper and possessed various supernatural abilities. He is usually portrayed holding a flute, a bouquet of flowers, or a peach.

Once Han caused peonies of many colors to blossom forth in the middle of winter. On the petals of these peonies appeared the following poem: "Clouds veil the peaks of Ch'in-ling mountain. Where is your home? Deep lies the snow on Lan Pass and the horses will go no further." Han Hsiang-tzu saw a hidden meaning in these lines, but his uncle dismissed them as nonsense. Soon after, Han Yü fell in disgrace with the emperor and was banished. When he reached Lan Pass the snow was so deep that he could make no further progress. Then Han Hsiang-tzu appeared and cleared away the snow. He told his uncle that he would regain his official post and return to the bosom of his family, which prophecy soon came true.

5. *Lü Tung-pin* was born in 798 C.E. in Northern China. His family were civil servants. As a young man he traveled to Mount Lü in the south of the country where he met a fire dragon who presented him with a magic sword that enabled him to conceal himself in Heaven.

On a journey to the capital he came upon the immortal Chung Li-ch'üan, who was warming up some wine. Lü fell asleep and dreamt that he had been promoted to a high official post and possessed enormous wealth. In his dream he lived the life of a rich man for the next fifty years until a crime caused his family to be banished and exterminated. When he awoke from his dream he found that only a few moments had passed. The dream, which has become proverbial in China, brought him to his senses and he decided to forgo an official career and follow Chung Li-ch'üan into the mountains. Chung initiated him into the secrets of alchemy and taught him the art of swordsmanship. At the age of 100 Lü still retained his youthful appearance and was capable of traveling 100 miles in a matter of seconds.

Lü Tung-pin considered compassion to be the essential means of attaining perfection. He transformed the methods of the Outer Alchemy (→ *wai-tan*) into those of the Inner (→ *nei-tan*). To him his sword—his symbol—was not a tool for killing enemies but for conquering passion, aggression, and ignorance. Through his example Lü had a decisive influence on the development of Taoism, and the school of → *ch'üan-chen tao* venerated him as the teacher of its founder.

6. *Ho Hsien-ku* is the only female among the *pa-hsien.* She lived during the T'ang Dynasty and spent her life as a hermit in the mountains. When she was fourteen, a spirit appeared to her in a dream and told her to grind a stone known as "mother of clouds" into powder and eat that powder. She would then become as light as a feather and attain immortality. She followed these instructions and furthermore vowed never to get married. Thereafter she was able to fly from one mountain peak to the next; as she did so she gathered fruit and berries for her mother. She herself no longer had any need of nourishment. One day the emperor summoned her to the court but on her way there she disappeared and became an immortal. Legend further reports that she was sighted several times after her earthly demise.

According to another legend young Ho Hsien-ku lost her way in the mountains while gathering tea and met a → *tao-shih,* who gave her a peach to eat. After that she never again felt hungry. This *tao-shih* is said to have been none other than Lü Tung-pin, the fifth of the eight immortals.

7. *Lan Ts'ai-ho* is sometimes portrayed with female features. He is dressed in rags, wears a belt made of black wood, and wears a boot on one of his feet, the other being bare. In his hand he carries a basket of flowers.

In summer he would wear a thick overcoat but dress lightly in winter. His breath was like hot steam. According to legend he roamed the streets as a beggar, accompanying his songs with castanets. Most of the time he was drunk. When people gave him money he used to string the coins on a cord, which he dragged behind him. One day he stopped at an inn, took off his boot, belt, and cloak, and disappeared into the clouds, riding on a crane.

8. *Chung Li-ch'üan* allegedly lived during the Han Dynasty. His symbol was a fan made of feathers or palm leaves. He is usually portrayed as a corpulent man, bald, but with a beard that reaches down to his navel. In representations of the eight immortals he can also be recognized by the wisps of hair that grace his temples. Reports about his life vary greatly: according to some he was a field marshal, who withdrew to the mountains in his old age; others claim that he was a vice-marshal who, after losing a battle against the Tibetans, fled into the mountains, where five Taoist saints initiated him into the teachings of immortality. Several hundred years later he is said to have taught Lü Tung-pin.

Various legends give conflicting versions as to how he became an immortal: according to one he met an old Taoist master in a forest, who at his request gave him prescriptions on how to attain immortality. As Chung was leaving this venerable master, he turned to cast a last glance at his hut but found that it had vanished.

Another version claims that during a famine Chung produced silver coins by miraculous means and distributed them among the poor, thereby saving numerous lives. One day, a wall of his hermitage collapsed as he was meditating and behind it appeared a jade vessel which contained prescriptions for attaining immortality. He followed these and—to the accompaniment of heavenly sounds—was borne away to the abode of the immortals on a shimmering cloud.

Pai-chang-ching-kuei 🅩 (Jap., *Hyakujō Shingi*); a written work containing the rules for life in a Zen monastery (→ *tera*) established by the Chinese Ch'an (Zen) master → Pai-chang Huai-hai; it was redacted by the monk Te-hui (Jap., Tokuki). The regulations recorded in this work are considered authoritative to the present day.

Pai-chang Huai-hai **Z** also Po-chang Hui-hai, (Jap., Hyakujō Ekai), 720–814; one of the great Chinese masters of Ch'an (Zen) of the T'ang period; a student and dharma successor (→ *hassu*) of → Ma-tsu Tao-i (Jap., Baso Dōitsu) and the master of → Kuei-shan Ling-yu (Jap., Isan Reiyū) and → Huang-po Hsi-yun (Jap., Ōbaku Kiun). Pai-chang founded the Ch'an Zen) monastic tradition by establishing precise rules for the life and daily routine of a Ch'an monastery (see also → *tera*). Ch'an masters and their students had hitherto been "guests" in monasteries of other Buddhist schools and had adhered to the monastic rules of these schools. The rules of Pai-chang made possible the development of independent Ch'an monasteries in which the daily routine was entirely determined by the requirements of the Ch'an style of training.

Following the tradition of → Tao-hsin, the fourth patriarch of Ch'an who founded the first self-supporting community of Ch'an monks, Pai-chang stressed the importance of combining meditative practice (→ *zazen*) with daily work in the monastery and in the fields. From Pai-chang comes the well-known Zen saying: "A day without work, a day without food." He himself lived in accordance with this principle until advanced old age (→ *samu*). Until this time Buddhist monks in China had lived, following the Indian monastic tradition, from offerings gathered by the monks on begging rounds or brought to the monasteries by lay believers. Now the monks of the Ch'an monasteries gained their livelihoods principally through their own manual labor. However, the tradition of making begging rounds (→ *takuhatsu*) was preserved in Pai-chang's rules as a form of spiritual training.

Although the precise written form in which Pai-chang originally set forth his rules has been lost, these rules and their spirit have been preserved in the Zen tradition and are followed today in Zen monasteries.

Pai-chang is not known for his organizational talent alone, rather primarily for his profound Zen realization and his great wisdom, already indicated by the monastic name he received from his first master, Tao-chih. The name is Huai-hai, '[He Who Bears the] Ocean [of Wisdom in His] Bosom." Pai-chang is the author of *Tun-wu ju-tao yao-men-lung*, a fundamental Ch'an text concerning "sudden enlightenment" (→ *tongo*). In this work he shows that the teaching of the → Southern school of Ch'an is in accord with the deepest sense of the great Mahāyāna sūtras.

From this text it is evident that Pai-chang was well versed in the sūtras. Thus even in the school of sudden enlightenment (the Southern school), though the primacy of the enlightenment experience over any "theory" was stressed, great importance was still placed on the study of the sūtras. This text, composed by Pai-chang in dialogue form, begins with the following sentences:

Question: What practice must we practice in order to attain liberation?

Answer: Liberation can only be realized through sudden enlightenment.

Question: What is sudden enlightenment?

Answer: *Sudden* means to liberate oneself in an instant from all delusive thoughts. *Enlightenment* means the insight that enlightenment is nothing that could be attained.

Question: Where should we begin with this practice?

Answer: At the root.

Question: And what is the root?

Answer: The mind [consciousness] is the root.

An English translation of this text is found in J. Blofeld, *The Zen Teaching of Hua Hai on Sudden Illumination* (London, 1962). The sayings and teachings of Pai-chang are recorded in *Hung-chou Pai-chang-shan ta-chih-ch'an-shih yü-lu* (*Record of the Words of the Ch'an Master of Great Wisdom, Pai-chang from Hung-chou*; Chinese short title, *Pai-chang yü-lu*) and in the *Pai-chang kuang-lu*. An English translation of both texts is found in T. Cleary, trans., *Sayings and Doings of Pai-Chang* (Los Angeles, 1978).

Pai-chang appears in examples 2 and 40 of the → *Wu-men-kuan*, as well as examples 26, 53, 70, 71, and 72 of the → *Pi-yen-lu*.

We learn more about the mind of Pai-chang from these kōans than from all historical data concerning his life and significance. Here, for instance, is example 26 of the *Pi-yen-lu*:

A monk asked Pai-chang, "What is there that's extraordinary?"

Pai-chang said, "Sitting alone on [Mount] Ta Hsiung [Jap., Dai Yūhō]."

The monk bowed respectfully. Pai-chang hit him.

Pai-lien-tsung **B** Chin. → White Lotus school

Pai-ma-ssu **B** Chin., lit. "White Horse Monastery"; the oldest Buddhist monastery in China, in the vicinity of Lo-yang. The history of this monastery can be traced back to the first century C.E. It has been rebuilt a number of times. Its present form is from the Ming period. The monastery belongs to the Ch'an (Zen) school.

From inscriptions we learn that here the first sūtras (incuding the → *Sūtra in Forty-two Sections*) were translated into Chinese, by two Indian monks—Matanga and Chu-fa-lan—whose tombs are in the monastery.

The name of the monastery derives from events initiated by → Ming-ti, an emporer of the Han Dynasty. Ming-ti had a dream about a certain deity and sent ministers to the west to learn more concerning this phenomenon. They returned with the *Sūtra in Forty-two Sections*, riding on a white horse. According to another tradition, the two monks Matanga and Chu-fa-lan arrived in Lo-yang riding on a white horse.

Of note are a stele from the T'ang period and a thirteen-story pagoda, which is located outside the monastery walls on the east. In the ancestor hall are statues of the six patriarchs of the Ch'an school. Matanga and Chu-fa-lan are said to have carried out their translation work on the so-called Cool Terrace.

Pai-yün kuan [T] Chin., lit. "Monastery of the White Clouds"; a Taoist monastery (→ *kuan*) in Peking; the main monastery of the School of the Realization of Truth (→ *ch'üan-chen tao*). *Pai-yün kuan* was constructed in 739 C.E. and restored in 1167.

During the 13th century this monastery was the residence of Ch'ui Ch'u-chih, the founder of the northern (or dragon gate) faction of the *ch'üan-chen tao*, who is also buried there. The present layout of the monastery dates from the Ch'ing Dynasty. It is now the headquarters of the Taoist Society of China.

Pai-yün Shou-tuan [Z] (Jap., Hakuun Shutan), 1025–75; Chinese Ch'an (Zen) master of the Yōgi lineage of Rinzai Zen (→ Yōgi school); a student and dharma successor (→ *hassu*) of Yang-ch'i Fang-hui (Jap., Yōgi Hōe) and the master of → Wu-tsu Fa-yen (Jap., Goso Hōen).

Pai-yün-tsung [Z] Chin. → Hakuun school

Pa-kua [T] Chin., eight trigrams; eight signs that form the basis of the *Book of Change(s)* (→ *I-ching*) and from which the sixty-four hexagrams are derived. Each trigram consists of three lines, each of which may be either yin (- -) or yang (—) (→ yin-yang). There are eight possible combinations:

Ch'ien *Tui* *Li* *Chen*

Sun *K'an* *Ken* *K'un*

The most important trigrams are → *ch'ien* and *k'un* because they symbolize the primordial energy from which all phenomena arise. *Ch'ien* is pure yang, pure male energy; whereas *k'un* represents yin or female energy. Their material manifestations are, respectively, Heaven and Earth. The intermingling of *ch'ien* and *k'un* gives rise to the remaining six trigrams.

Two further important trigrams are → *k'an* and *li,* because their configuration remains unchanged when they are turned upside down. Each, when doubled, gives rise to a hexagram bearing the same name.

The *pa-kua* are considered to be images of concrete reality:

Ch'ien, the creative, is strong, Heaven, the father.
K'un, the receptive, is yielding, Earth, the mother.
Chen, the arousing, is movement, thunder, the first son.
K'an, the abysmal, is danger, water or clouds, the second son.
Ken, keeping still, is rest, mountain, the youngest son.
Sun, the gentle, is penetrating, wind or wood, the oldest daughter.
Li, the clinging, is luminous, the sun or lightning, the second daughter.
Tui, the joyous, is joyful, the lake, the youngest daughter.

According to tradition, the eight trigrams originated with the legendary emperor → Fu Hsi: A dragon-horse emerged from the Yellow River, carrying on its back the so-called river diagram (→ *Ho-t'u* and *Lo-shu*); and a turtle, emerging from the River Lo, carried on its back the Lo River diagram. From these two magic number diagrams (similar to magic squares) Fu Hsi derived the *pa-kua.* The ancient historian Ssu-ma Ch'ien, on the other hand, states that the trigrams as well as the hexagrams go back to King Wen, one of the founders of the Chou Dynasty. Fu Hsi established correspondences between these trigrams, the cardinal points, and the seasons. His arrangement of the trigrams is known as the precelestial ordering (top diagram, p. 263). The postcelestial ordering was established by King Wen (bottom diagram).

In addition, the trigrams are of considerable importance in the alchemical teachings of the inner and outer elixir (→ *nei-tan,* → *wai-tan*). → Wei P'o-yang's *Ts'an-t'ung-ch'i* states, "*Ch'ien* and *k'un* are the gate

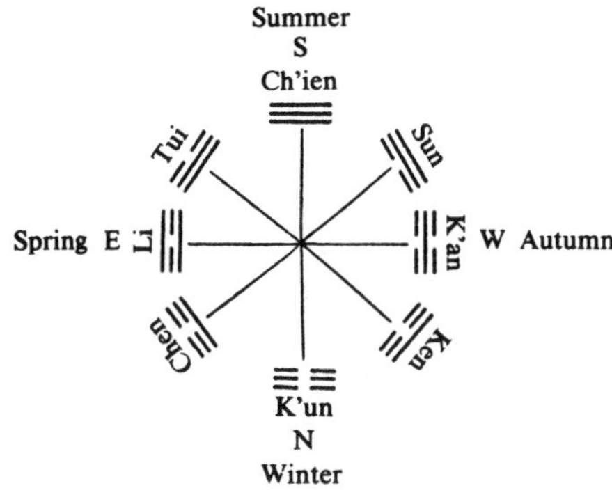

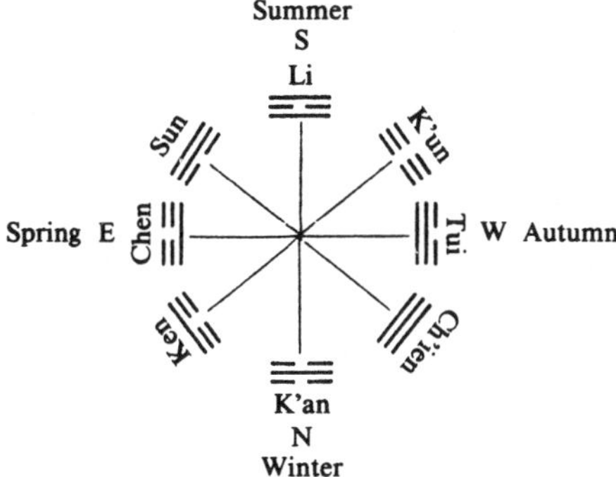

and entrance to change [i.e., the beginning of all transformation] and the father and mother of the remaining signs." *K'an* and *li* are symbolic of the function of *ch'ien* and *k'un,* i.e., the influences of Heaven and Earth. In the language of the alchemists *ch'ien* and *k'un* stand for, respectively, the furnace and the melting pot; and *k'un* and *li* for the various ingredients from which the elixir is produced.

Pali B (Pāli); Indian dialect derived from Sanskrit in which the canonical texts of the Theravāda are composed. Opinions concerning the origin of this dialect differ widely. Rhys-Davids is of the view that Pali was a dialect of → Koshala in the northeast Gangetic basin. Walleser considers it to have been the language of → Pātaliputra (present-day Patna), the capital of → Magadha. Many researchers regard Pali as the variation of the Magadha dialect that is said to have been the language of the Buddha and that may have served as the colloquial tongue of the Magadhan elite. However, inscriptions discovered in Māgadhī exhibit considerable differences from Pali. Lamotte takes the view that Pali was a central Indian dialect, i.e., one of the ancient Prakrit tongues.

Pa-ling Hao-chien Z (Jap., Hayō Kōkan), 10th century; Chinese Ch'an (Zen) master of the → Ummon school; a student and dharma successor (→ *hassu*) of → Yun-men Wen-yen (Jap., Ummon Bun'en). He had the nickname *Garrulous Chien,* because, completely unlike his master Yun-men (who was known for his often literally monosyllabic style of expression), Paling was fond of responding to his students in elegant poetic formulations. Pa-ling had two dharma successors; we encounter him in examples 13 and 100 of the → *Pi-yen-lu.*

Kōan 13 of the *Pi-yen-lu* gives us an impression of the master's way of expressing himself. A monk asks him in this example about the Deva school. This is a reference to Kānadeva, the fifteenth patriarch in the Indian lineage of Ch'an (Zen). Kānadeva was a student and dharma successor of Nāgārjuna, the fourteenth patriarch, one of the greatest philosophers in the Buddhist tradition. Like his master, Kānadeva was an outstanding philosopher and an indomitable foe in the philosophical debates so popular in the Buddhism of his times. The kōan is as follows:

"A monk asked Pa-ling, 'What is the Deva school?'

"Pa-ling said, 'Snow heaped in a silver bowl.' "

Pali school B → Theravāda

Pañchadashi H (Pañcadaśi), Skt., lit. "the fifteen"; a celebrated treatise on the metaphysics of → Advaita-Vedānta, composed by Svāmi → Vidyāranya, a follower of → Shankara. His teaching is entirely in the spirit of Shankara's work. The treatise is divided into fifteen chapters; each group of five chapters has a special theme.

The first five chapters distinguish the various elements and the sheaths surrounding the Self, and also explain the → *mahāvākyas,* the "great precepts." The second group of five chapters has to do with the light of knowledge in its various forms, and the last five chapters are devoted to the subject of bliss, from the bliss of objects to the bliss of yoga to the bliss of the Self. The numerous Indian editions of the text are difficult to understand. The English translation by Hari Prasad Shastri (1954) is clear enough to be accessible to Western readers.

Pañchāgnividyā H (Pañcāgnividyā), Skt., lit. *pañcha*: "five," *agni*: "fire," *vidyā*: "knowledge, teaching"; that is, the "Five Fires Teaching." It describes how the immortal part of man, after his death and the cremation of the body, rises "in a form the color of light" (*Brihad-āranyaka-Upanishad* 6.2.14) as faith to heaven and is sacrificed by the gods five times in succession in the sacrificial fire of heaven, air, earth, man, and woman, whereby it changes from faith to *soma,* from *soma* to rain, from rain to food, from food to seed, from seed to embryo, and so returns to a new existence on earth. This ancient Vedic eschatoloty is the beginning of the teaching of the transmigration of souls, which is carried on in the teaching of the two ways (→ *devayāna* and *dakshināyana* or *pitriyāna*).

Pañcha-mārga B (pañca-mārga), Skt., lit. "five paths"; like the stages of a bodhisattva (→ *bhūmi*), an important description of the spiritual path. In this case, there are five phases: (1) path of accumulation (*sambhāra-marga*), (2) path of preparation (*prayoga-mārga*), (3) path of seeing (*darshana-mārga*), (4) path of meditation (*bhāvanā-mārga*), (5) path of no-more-learning (*ashaiksha-marga*).

The content of the practices to be accomplished on the respective paths are differently defined for the vehicles of the → *shrāvakas,* → *pratyekabuddhas,* and → bodhisattvas. Bodhisattvas reach the first stage of a bodhisattva at the beginning of the path of seeing.

Pañcharātra H (Pañcarātra), Skt., lit. "five days"; 1. a → *soma* sacrifice in which each day for five days the *soma* juice is freshly expressed; 2. name of the sacred books of various Vishnu sects.

Pañchatantra H (Pañcatantra), Skt., lit. *pañcha*: "five," *tantra*: "textbook"; a famous, voluminous collection of moralizing stories and fables in five books from the fifth century, compiled to teach young princes political acumen and proper comportment.

The work was compiled by a brahman named Vishnusharman for the edification of a king's sons. It was enlarged at various times, has often been imitated (→ *Hitopadesha*), and has been translated into many languages. It serves as the source for many widespread and popular tales that have since been incorporated into the popular literary tradition of many regions of the world.

Pañchatapas H (Pañcatapas), Skt.; an unusual form of ascetic practice, in which one sits in the heat of the sun from sunrise to sunset, surrounded by four fires and wholly absorbed in → *japa* and meditation.

Panchen Lama B (paṇ-chen bla-ma), Skt.-Tib., "guru who is a great scholar"; an honorific title conferred by the fifth → Dalai Lama on his master, the abbot of Tashi Lhunpo Monastery. Because the Dalai Lamas from this time on were considered to be incarnations of → Avalokiteshvara, the fifth Dalai Lama declared his guru to be on a higher level as the incarnation of → Amitābha. In contrast to the Dalai Lama, the Panchen Lama, who like the Dalai Lama is reincarnated again and again (→ *tulku*), has no political responsibilities. After the death of a Dalai Lama, the Panchen Lama merely holds the position of the former's spiritual representative. Only in the 20th century did the Panchen Lama also begin to assume political office.

Pāndavas H (Pāṇḍavas), Skt.; the descendents of King → Pāndu. The five Pāndava princes led the great battle against the → Kauravas that is described in detail in the → *Mahābhārata.* Yudhishthira, Bhima, and Arjuna were the sons of Kuntī, Nakula and Shadeva were the sons of Mādrī, the sister of the king of Madras.

Pandit H (Paṇḍita), Skt., lit. "scholar"; a scholar or learned man who studies and interprets sacred texts as an intellectual activity but is seldom interested in the realization of the truths they contain. These truths were revealed to the → *rishis;* the pandits have interpreted and disseminated them. In Hinduism, the hairsplitting arguments of the pandits have generated strange offshoots.

Pāndu H (Pāṇḍu), Skt., lit. "the pale one"; the brother of → Dhritarāshtra. Pāndu was the king of Hastināpura, the kingdom for whose sake the great war of the → *Mahābhārata* was ignited, and the father of the five → Pāndavas, whose fate is described in the epic.

P'ang Yün Z also P'ang-chu-shih (Jap., Hō Un or Hō Koji), 740–808/11, "Layman P'ang," China's most famous Ch'an (Zen) layman; a student and dharma successor (→ *hassu*) of → Shih-t'ou Hsi-ch'ien (Jap., Sekitō Kisen) and → Ma-tsu Tao-i (Jap., Baso Dōitsu) and close friend of the Ch'an master → Tan-hsia T'ien-jan (Jap., Tanka Tennen). The → *mondō* and → *hossen* of Layman P'ang with the great Ch'an masters of his time that are recorded in the *P'ang-chu-shih yu-lu* are a high point of Ch'an (Zen) literature. (English translation: *The Recorded Sayings of Layman P'ang,* trans. R. Fuller-Sazaki et al. [New York, 1971].) P'ang Yun appears in example 42 of the → *Pi-yen-lu.*

P'ang Yun came from a family of minor functionaries and, like his forebears, studied the Confucian classics. However, he became aware of the vacuity of book learning and worldly possessions; one day he packed all his possessions into a boat and sank it in the river in front of his house. Then, accompanied by his talented daughter Ling-chao, he entered into → homelessness. Wandering through China, he visited the great Ch'an masters in order to train himself through his encounters with them.

In his first meeting with Master Shih-t'ou, Pang Yun asked him, "Who is he who is not dependent upon the ten thousand things [all phenomena]?" Immediately, Shih-t'ou held P'ang Yun's mouth shut, and insight dawned on the layman.

Later Shih-t'ou inquired about his everyday affairs. P'ang Yun answered with a poem, which, freely translated, is as follows:

There is nothing special about my daily affairs,
I am simply in spontaneous harmony with them.
Clinging to nothing and also rejecting nothing,
I encounter no resistance and am never separate.
What do I care about the pomp of purple robes—
The pure summit was never sullied by so much as a fleck of dust.
The wondrous action of supernatural forces
I find in hauling water and cutting wood.

Shih-t'ou then confirmed him as his dharma successor, and P'ang Yun went on to Ma-tsu. Him also P'ang asked, "Who is it who is not dependent upon the ten thousand things?" Ma-tsu answered, "This I'll tell you when you drink up the waters of the West River in a single gulp." With these words P'ang Yun came to profound enlightenment.

Pānini 🅗 (Pāṇini), Skt.; the most celebrated Sanskrit grammarian in Hinduism. He lived after the time of the Buddha, probably in the fourth century B.C.E. His chief work is the *Pāninīya,* also called the *Ashtādhyāyī* for its eight (*ashta*) chapters. Still considered a standard work for Sanskrit grammar whose rules are uncontested, it is so highly regarded that it is claimed to have arisen through divine inspiration. Pānini is therefore numbered among the → *rishis.* However, he was not the first grammarian; he drew upon the work of his predecessors. The *Pāninīya* is composed in the form of *sūtras* that are markedly complicated, so that particular study is required to grasp their meaning.

A great difference exists between the Western concept of grammar and that of Hinduism. For Westerners, grammar is simply the means to an end, a way to generally register the use of language. For this reason it may at first seem difficult to understand why Hinduism ascribes such importance to grammar. What do philosophy and enlightenment, the "water of life," have to do with the dry realm of grammar? It must be pointed out that enlightenment is a transcendent experience and as such lies beyond words. Yet the *rishis* attempted repeatedly to clothe their experience in words, in order to lead those searching for the ultimate truth to that same experience. They did so initially in the form of concise intimations that were difficult to comprehend and had to be explicated with commentaries. A well-thought-out, carefully constructed grammar helps to make the language more precise and hence aids in the comprehension of what the language is to express. For this reason great worth is placed on grammar. Even contemporary saints such as → Rāmakrishna examined the meaning of individual words down to their roots and thereby found new possibilities for the explanation of transcendental truths.

Western Indologists have called Pānini's work a natural history of the Sanskrit language. (English trans. by Shrisha Chandra Vasu, Allahabad, 1891.)

P'an-ku 🅣 creator of the world; first human being. According to a myth dating from the 3d century B.C.E., P'an-ku arose out of chaos, which had the form of a chicken's egg. Then the constituent parts of the egg separated into those which were heavy and pervaded by yin (→ yin-yang), which led to the formation of the Earth, and those that were light and pervaded by yang, which caused Heaven to come into being.

P'an-ku holding the World Egg.

Over a period of 13,000 years the distance between Heaven and Earth increased at the rate of ten feet per day. P'an-ku grew at the same rate so that he always filled the space between the two. After his death the different parts of his body were transformed into the various regions of the world. Different sources describe this transformation in various ways.

According to a 6th-century text P'an-ku's head turned into the four sacred mountains. His eyes became sun and moon, his fatty tissues the rivers and oceans, his hair and beard the grasses and trees.

Other traditional texts state that his ears were transformed into rivers, his breath into wind, his voice into thunder, and the pupils of his eyes into lightning.

P'an-shan Pao-chi 🅩 (Jap., Banzan Hōshaku), 720–814; Chinese Ch'an (Zen) master; a student and dharma successor (→ *hassu*) of → Ma-tsu Tao-i (Baso Dōitsu). After receiving the seal of confirmation (→ *inka-shōmei*) from Ma-tsu, P'an-shan settled in northern China on Mount P'an-shan, not far from the present-day border with North Korea. He was one of the few early Ch'an masters to be active in this area. We meet him in example 37 of the → *Pi-yen-lu.*

The story of his first enlightenment experience, as it is recorded in the *Wu-teng hui-yuan*, is noteworthy:

Once when the master was crossing the marketplace, he overheard a customer, who was just buying some pork, say to the butcher, "Cut me a piece of the good stuff."

The butcher folded his arms and said, "Sir, what here is not the good stuff!?"

At these words, the master attained insight.

P'an-shan was not, however, confirmed by his master after this experience. This happened only later, after a significantly deeper realization, which W. Gundert gives an account of in his explanation of the text of example 37 of the *Pi-yen-lu*:

One day he encountered a funeral procession, and from the chant he picked out these words: "For the red orb of the sun, it is a certainty to sink into the west. But the soul—whither will it go?" Behind the coffin walked the son of the deceased, wailing plaintively. Everything was as custom demanded; one could see this almost every day. However, it struck the youth [P'an-shan] with all the force of cosmic law. He saw the cycle of birth and death, and with this the light arose in him that remains untouched by this cycle.

Pansil 🅑 Pali, abbreviation for *pancha-sīla* (→ *shīla*); the five moral rules that all followers of the → Theravāda are obliged to observe. In a broader sense, *pansil* refers to all the formalized texts that are recited on specific occasions like → *pūjās* and → *uposatha* ceremonies: invocation of the Buddha, taking refuge (→ *trisharana*), and the *pansil* in the true sense.

Pao-feng K'o-wen 🅩 (Jap., Hōbō Kokumon), 1025–1102; Chinese Ch'an (Zen) master of the Ōryō lineage of Rinzai Zen (→ Ōryō school); a student and dharma successor (→ *hassu*) of → Huang-lung Hui-nan (Jap., Ōryō E'nan) and the master of → Tou-shuai Ts'ung-yueh (Jap., Tosotsu Jūetsu).

Pao-fu Ts'ung-chan 🅩 (Jap., Hofuku Jūten), d. 928; Chinese Ch'an (Zen) master; a student and dharma successor (→ *hassu*) of → Hsueh-feng I-ts'un (Jap., Seppō Gison). Pao-fu had twenty five dharma successors; we encounter him in examples 8, 23, 76, 91, and 95 of the → *Pi-yen-lu.*

Pao-lin-ssu 🅩 (Jap., Hōrin-ji) a Buddhist monastery in southern China, built in 504, in which → Hui-neng, the sixth patriarch of Ch'an (Zen), lived for some time. Since that time it has been one of the best-known monasteries in China.

Pao-p'u-tzu 🅣 Chin., lit. *"He Who Embraces the Unhewn Block* [→ *p'u*]"; the most important work of → Ko Hung, in which all the methods for attaining immortality known in his time are systematically set out. The expression *unhewn block* stands for artless simplicity, the natural primordial state of man. For that reason *Pao-p'u-tzu* is sometimes translated as *The Master Who Prefers His Simplicity.*

Pao-ying Hui-yung 🅩 → Nan-yuan Hui-yung

Pāpa-Purusha 🅗 (Pāpa-Puruṣa), Skt., lit. *pāpa*: "sin, evil, wrong," *purusha*: "man, human being"; personified wickedness or badness in human form. Compound words beginning with *pāpa* have to do with sin, evil, baseness, perversity, or misfortune. An exception is *pāpa-rahita,* lit. "separated from sin," that is, guiltless, harmless.

Para-Bhakti 🅗 Skt., from *para,* lit. "highest"; synonomous with *mahabhava* and *prema-bhakti.* When → *bhakti,* the love of God, becomes more intense, the state is then called → *bhāva.* The highest state thus reached is called *para-bhakti.* In this state the worshiper completely forgets the surrounding world and even his own body. The average person never attains this state but comes only as far as *bhāva.*

Parabrahman 🅗 Skt., lit. "the highest → *brahman"*; an expression that is actually irrational, since *brahman* itself is absolute being, absolute consciousness, and absolute bliss and cannot be intensified further by a superlative form.

Paramahamsa 🅗 (Paramahaṃsa), Skt., lit. "the highest swan"; 1. a term referring to the highest station of → *sannyāsin.* Also an honorable title that may be given by a guru to a suitable pupil, as in the case of → Yogānanda, who was given this title by his teacher → Yukteshvar. *Pandits* (scholars) and worshipers also called → Rāmakrishna by this name; 2. term for a monk who belongs to a particular school of followers of → Shankara.

Paramānanda 🄷 Skt., lit. "supreme bliss"; the concept of the divine as a state of utter, inexpressible bliss.

Paramapāda 🄷 Skt.; the last step or highest state, the final bliss of absolute consciousness.

Parama-Rishi 🄷 (Parama Ṛṣi), Skt.; term used to refer to the seven great → *rishis* of the Vedic age.

Paramārtha 🄷 🄱 Skt., lit. "supreme reality, supreme truth."

🄷 The goal of the spiritual seeker, by the attainment of which liberation (→ *moksha*) is achieved.

🄱 name of one of the four great translators in Chinese Buddhism. Paramārtha (499–569) was an Indian; he came to China in 546. In the same year, the emperor, who wanted to place him at the head of a translation bureau, invited him to the capital (present-day Nanking). However, political turmoil made this plan impracticable. Paramārtha spent the next years in various places in southern China. Finally he settled in Canton, where, at the request of the prefect of the city, he translated important works of the → Yogāchāra into Chinese. Among these were the → *Abhidharmakosha*, the *Mahāyāna-samparigraha* of → Asanga, the *Vimshatikā* of → Vasubandhu, and the → *Diamond Sūtra*. All told, Paramārtha translated sixty four works in 278 volumes.

His translations made possible the development of the Chinese form of Yogāchāra, the → Fa-hsiang school, by → Hsuan-tsang and K'ueichi. The appearance of the Chinese version of the *Abhidharmakosha* brought about the inception of the so-called → Kosha school in China.

Paramārtha-satya 🄱 Skt. "ultimate truth"; the absolute truth as opposed to the conventional truth (→ *samvriti-satya*) or relative truth of the phenomenal world.

Paramātman 🄷 Skt., lit. "the supreme → *ātman*"; the supreme Self, often also translated as "world soul." As absolute consciousness, it is identical with → *brahman.*

Para-Māyā 🄷 , or Daivi-Maya, Skt.; there are two kinds of → *māyā*: *para-māyā,* or divine *māyā,* wherein the world of appearances is viewed as a manifestation of → *brahman;* and the *māyā* of ego-related identification with the body, wherein only the world of the senses is regarded as real.

Parameshvara 🄷 (Parameśvara), Skt., lit. *parama*: "surpassing everything, transcendent," *īshvara*: "the Lord, God"; the highest Lord of all Being, removed from any possibility of description. By his spiritual control over his own power manifesting in nature, he develops the cycles of the world and the natural evolution of creatures in these cycles. He is the source, father and mother in one, the origin of the Self and of the universe. → Shiva, → Vishnu, and → Indra are often referred to as *parameshvara.* The feminine form of the name, *parameshvarī,* is used for → Durgā and → Sītā.

Pāramitā 🄱 🅉 Skt., lit. "that which has reached the other shore," the transcendental. The *pāramitās*, generally translated as "the perfections," are the virtues perfected by a bodhisattva in the course of his development (→ *bhūmi*). There are six of these: (1) *dāna-pāramitā* (generosity), (2) *shīla-pāramitā* (discipline), (3) *kshānti-pāramitā* (patience), (4) *vīrya-pāramitā* (energy or exertion), (5) *dhyāna-pāramitā* (meditation), (6) *prajñā-pāramitā* (wisdom). Frequently four further virtues are added, which were accepted into the canon later: (7) *upāya-kaushala-pāramitā* (right method or means), (8) *pranidhāna-pāramitā* (vow), (9) *bala-pāramitā* (manifestation of the ten powers, → *dashabala*), (10) *jñāna-pāramitā* (knowledge of the true definition of all dharmas).

Dāna-pāramitā consists of beneficence and giving in both the material and spiritual sense. This includes being compassionate and kind and not keeping accumulated merit for oneself but rather dedicating it to the liberation of all beings (→ *dāna*). *Shīla-pāramitā* includes proper behavior conducive to the eradication of all passions and the securing of a favorable rebirth for the sake of liberating all beings (→ *shīla*). *Kshānti-pāramitā* refers to the patience and tolerance that arise from the insight that all the problems of beings have causes. *Vīrya-pāramitā* is resolute effort that does not permit itself to be diverted by anything. *Dhyāna-pāramitā* here means meditation as the way of cutting through the illusion of an ego and of not experiencing oneself as separate from other beings (→ *dhyāna*). *Prajñā-pāramitā* is the realization of supreme wisdom (→ *prajñā*).

Parāprakriti 🄷 (Parāprakṛti), Skt., lit. *para*: "beyond," *prakriti*: "nature"; the higher, divine nature, the Divine Mother (→ Shakti) who creates the universe.

Parāpratyaksha 🄷 (Parāpratyakṣa), Skt., lit. *para*: "beyond," *pratyaksha*: "perception"; the extrasensory, transcendent faculty of perception that arises as a consequence of → *samādhi.* (See also → *pratyaksha.*)

Para-Purusha 🅗 Skt. → *purushottama*

Parārdha 🅗 Stk., lit. *para*: "beyond," *ardha*: "half"; the spiritual half of the path taken following death, synonymous with → *devayana*, the "way of the gods." According to the Vedas, two possibilities exist for the human soul after death: *devayana*, the path that leads to liberation from rebirth, and → *pitriyāna*, or *dakshinayāna*, the path that leads back to earth after an intermediate stay in Chandraloka, the "realm of the moon."

Para-Shakti 🅗 (Para-Śakti), Skt.; the highest aspect of the Divine Mother (→ Shakti), who stands behind the entire creation.

Parāshara 🅗 (Parāśara), Skt.; after → Manu, → Yajñavalkya, and → Nārada the fourth famous lawgiver, whose writings are often cited in the law books (→ Dharma-Shāstra). It is not certain when he lived. He is thought to have been a pupil of → Kapila and is regarded as a → *rishi;* several hymns in the *Rigveda* are attributed to him.

Parashu-Rāma 🅗 (Paraśu-Rāma), Skt., lit. "Rāma with the Axe"; the first → Rāma and the sixth → *avatāra* of Vishnu. He appeared in order to break the tyrannical rule of the → *kshatriyas*, the warrior caste. His story is told in the *Mahābhārata* and in the Purānas, but he also appears in the *Rāmāyana*, primarily as the opponent of Rāmachandra (i.e., Rāma).

According to the *Māhābharata*, Parashu-Rāma instructed Arjuna in the use of arms and fought a battle with → Bhīshma that ended in a draw. This Parashu-Rāma appeared on earth before Rāma or Rāmachandra, the seventh incarnation of Vishnu, but lived during the same period. The *Rāmāyana* relates that Parashu-Rāma, as a follower of Shiva, was angered when Rāma broke Shiva's bow. He therefore challenged Rāma to a duel that ended in his defeat; as a result, he was denied a place in heaven. The legend reports that he liberated the earth twenty-one times from the dominion of the *ksatriyas* and delivered it over to the brahmans.

Parātpara 🅗 Skt.; the transcendent, infinite, and universal personality, which is at once personal and impersonal, finite and infinite, limited and unlimited, one and many. The opposites contained in the description of *parātpara* indicate that this concept is actually beyond description.

Parāvairāgya 🅗 Skt., lit. "uttermost indifference, dispassion"; the complete detachment of a liberated soul, one who has renounced everything and no longer is moved by the ego. (See also → *vairāgya*.)

Parāvāk 🅗 (Parāvāc), Skt., lit. *para*: "beyond," *vāk*: "language"; 1. the unmanifest vibrations that precede the creation of universal ideas; 2. the eighth of the "inaudible sounds," → *nāda*.

Para-Vidyā 🅗 , or Brahma-Vidyā, Skt.; the direct, absolute knowledge of → *brahman* on the transcendent plane, in contrast to → *apara-vidyā*, indirect knowledge thereof from the level of this world.

The difference between *para-vidyā* and *apara-vidyā* is clearly drawn by the metaphor of a city that one has never seen. One can hear about the city from others, can read about it and look at pictures of it; such behavior represents *apara-vidyā* (indirect knowledge). If one visits the city personally, however, it becomes part of one's own experience, which corresponds to *para-vidyā (direct knowledge).*

Paribhū 🅗 Skt., lit. "encompassing, guiding"; the Lord who pervades all activities in the universe, a concept found in the → Upanishads.

Pārijāta 🅗 Skt.; the mythic coral tree that appeared at the → Churning of the Ocean. It is the delight of the heavenly nymphs, and the fragrance of its blossoms fills the world.

The Pārijāta grew in → Indra's heaven and was the pride of his wife Sachī. When Krishna visited Indra, his spouse Satyabhāmā prevailed upon him to take the tree from Indra. A battle between the two gods and their followers ensued, in which Indra was defeated. The tree was brought to Dvārakā and planted there, but after Krishna's death it returned to Indra's heaven.

Parikalpita 🅑 Skt.; that which is imagined or conceptualized. According to the → Yogāchāra doctrine, that which people take to be the "objective" world is imagined or conceptualized; i.e., this world is illusory and deceptive; it exists only as a semblance but not as a true reality.

Parikara 🅗 Skt., lit. "multitude, entourage"; the multitude of devotees who participate in the divine play (→ *līlā*), each one of whom enjoys the divine bliss of this *līlā* according to his individual nature and receptibility; the individual's religious denomination plays no role in such participation.

Parināmavāda 🅗 (Pariṇāmavāda), Skt., lit. "doctrine of evolution." The doctrine of evolution constitutes an essential element in → Sānkhya theory. According to this teaching, the effect exists in a latent state within the cause and requires only a releasing factor to make it appear. Cause and effect are the undeveloped and developed states, respectively, of one and the same substance. Every form of generation and formation is de-velopment (*udbhāva,* "springing from"), every form of destruction is a (re-) enveloping (*anudbhāva*), or sinking back into the cause; the theory is thus one of evolution and involution.

Parinirvāna 🅱 (parinirvāṇa), Skt. (Pali, parinibbāna); total extinction. Synonym for → nirvāna. *Parinirvāna* is often equated with nirvāna after death (→ *nirupadhishesha-nirvāna*), but can also refer to nirvāna before death (→ *sopadhishesha-nirvāna*). Sometimes *parinirvāna* only means the death of a monk or nun.

Parishad 🅷 (Pariṣad), Skt., approximately "disputation assembly, council"; a school or community of brahmans who furnish counsel regarding the Vedas. The texts that they produce are called Pārshada.

Parishishta 🅷 (Pariśiṣṭa), Skt., lit. "addendum, appendix"; a group of works that still belong to the Vedic period but represent its end and the transition to the → Sūtras. The Indologist Max Müller wrote: "The Parishishtas discuss theological and ceremonial problems and lead into the Sūtras, but treat everything in a general, superficial manner, as if the age had already passed in which students spent ten or twenty years of their lives penetrating the mysteries of the Brāhmana literature and mastering its contents."

Pārvatī 🅷 Skt., lit. "of the mountains"; a name for the consort of Shiva, the Divine Mother (→ Shakti).

Pāsha 🅷 (Pāśa), Skt., lit. "noose, fetter"; the threefold fetter of ignorance that binds us to the body, the mind, and our human life.

Pashyantī 🅷 (Paśyantī), Skt., from *pashya*: "seeing"; a sound that evolves in the direction of the visible; the third, advanced state of → *nada* meditation, in which the meditator perceives the entire universe as filled with sound, as is sometimes indicated by the sentence "*Brahman* is sound." In combination with -*vāk* ("language"), *pashyantī-vāk* means "the seeing word," a reference to the second level of speech, which contains the vision of truth.

Pātāla 🅷 Skt., from *pāta*: "sunken," *tala*: "ground, foundation"; a name for the subconscious level in all human beings, where all kinds of irrational, unacknowledged instincts, impressions, and memories arise to influence our thoughts and actions without our being aware of their source. Many absurd dreams emerge from this subconscious realm.

Pātāla is also used as a name for the regions of the underworld, or hells, that are inhabited by snakes (→ *nāga*), → Daityas, → *yakshas,* and other beings. They are seven in number and are named in the *Vishnu-Purāna*: Atala, Vitala, Nitala, Gabhastimat, Mahātala, Sutala, and Pātāla.

The → *Padma-Purāna* lists the seven regions and their rulers as follows: (1) Atala, governed by → Mahāmāyā; (2) Vitala, ruled by a form of Shiva named Hātakeshvara: (3) Sutala, governed by → Bali; (4) Talātala, governed by Māyā; (5) Mahātala, where the great snakes dwell; (6) Rasātala, inhabited by the Daityas and Yakshas; and (7) Pātāla, the undermost region, where → Vāsuki rules over the snake gods.

The *Shiva-Purāna* names eight Pātālas: Pātāla, Tala, Atala, Vitala, Tāla, Vidhipātāla, Sharkarābhūmi, and Viyaya. The sage → Nārada is said to have visited these regions and to have reported on them.

Pātaliputra 🅱 Skt. (Pali, Pataliputta), present-day Patna; under King → Ashoka, the capital of the → Magadha kingdom and the site of the third → Buddhist council.

Patañjali 🅷 , ca. second century B.C.E.; founder of the yoga philosophy based on → Sānkhya. This yoga is one of the six → *darshanas.* Patañjali defines it as a methodical effort to attain perfection by mastering the various elements of human nature, physical as well as psychic. The physical body, the active will, and the observing mind must all be brought under control. Patañjali emphasizes certain practices designed to free the body from its restlessness and its impurity. If such practices strengthen one's vital power and also prolong youth and one's span of life, such effects occur in the interest of realization of spiritual freedom. Other practices are employed to clarify the mind and bring peace. Patañjali is not interested in metaphysical theory; his concern is to indicate a practical way toward release and liberation by means of disciplined action. To this end he composed the *Yoga-Sūtra.*

Patañjali's system is comprised of the following eight steps: (1) → yama; (2) → niyama. These two steps encompass various ethical and moral practices, considered as prerequisites. (3) → *Āsana,* bodily positions. Their aim is to find a position in which the concentration is not disturbed by the body; (4) → *prānāyāma,* breath control, practiced because the breath greatly influences one's thoughts and emotional state. The third and fourth stage gave rise to the development of → Hatha-yoga; (5) Pratyāhāra, the withdrawal of the senses from sense objects, so that the mind is not diverted; (6) → *Dhāranā,* or concentration; the ability to rest the mind on an object without straying or going out of control; (7) → *Dhyāna* (or → meditation). At this level, it is said, the mind no longer projects its own concepts onto the object of meditation, but instead merges with the object itself; (8) → *Samādhi,* also known as → *turīya,* the supraconscious state, in which duality and the manifest world no longer exist. This yoga is now generally known as Rāja-Yoga. Besides his eightfold path, Patañjali imparted many notes regarding difficulties and impediments in meditation as well as instructions for their elimination.

Whether the Patañjali who composed the *Yoga-Sūtra* is identical wih the Patañjali who wrote the *Mahābhāshya,* a celebrated commentary on → Pānini's grammar, has not been established with any certainty. The *Mahābhāshya* is said to have been composed in the mid-second century B.C.E., whereas estimates of the date of the *Yoga-Sūtra* range from the second century B.C.E. to the fourth century C.E..

Patriarch 🅱 🆉 in Chinese Buddhism, the founder of a school and his successors in the transmission of its teaching.

Also → *soshigata.*

Pa-tuan-chin 🆃 Chin., roughly "eight elegant exercises"; a series of Taoist physical exercises (→ *ch'i-kung*) allegedly dating from the 12th century and originally consisting of eight movements, to which others were added in the course of time.

There are two forms of *pa-tuan-chin:* the northern (difficult) and the southern (easier). The latter are attributed to Liang Shih-ch'ang, the former to Yo Fei, but it is more likely that both have an as yet undiscovered common source.

The eight elegant exercises may be performed in a sitting position or standing up.

The oldest texts list the following eight standing exercises:

1. Grasping Heaven with both hands extended, thereby regulating the "triple heater" (*san-chiao,* an acupuncture meridian).
2. Adopting the position of an archer aiming at an eagle (toward either the left or the right).
3. To regulate and harmonize the pancreas and stomach one should extend one arm upwards:
4. To perceive the difficulties and sorrows of one's past existence one should look behind oneself;
5. Simultaneously rocking the head and the posterior from side to side will expel the fire of the heart;
6. The seven sorrows and one hundred illnesses disappear behind the back.
7. Clenching the fists and making the eyes fierce intensifies the energy.
8. Grasping the tips of the toes with both hands makes kidneys and hips firm. (cf. Pálos 1980).

Pāvamāna 🅷 Skt.; free flow of the clear → *soma* draught, a symbol for the uninterrupted flow of the purified spiritual stream in the depths of consciousness, which greatly aids the seeker by making it possible to return repeatedly to directing all efforts to the goal.

P'ei Hsiu 🆉 → Huang-po Hsi-yun

Pei-tsung-ch'an 🆉 Chin. for Northern school, → Southern school

P'eng-lai 🆃 Chin., lit. "Rampant Weeds"; an island in the East China Sea, which Taoists believe to be inhabited by immortals (→ *hsien*). In Chinese mythology *p'eng-lai* epitomizes bliss, because this is where the legendary mushroom of immortality grows, in search of which numerous expeditions were dispatched as long ago as the 4th century B.C.E. All these expeditions failed, because any ship approaching the legendary island either capsized or was driven off course, or the island itself sank into the sea before the very eyes of the ship's crew. The earliest mention of P'eng-lai in Taoist literature is in the work of → Lieh-tzu (Book 5, Chapter 2). The motive of the search for the mushroom of immortality was an important element in the development of religious Taoism (→ *tao-chiao*).

Lieh-tzu describes the Isle of P'eng-lai as follows: "Up there everything consisted of gold and precious stones; birds and animals shone a glittering white, trees of pearl and coral grew in dense forests, all the flowers were exquisitely fragrant and the fruit deliciously sweet. Anyone eating that fruit felt himself to be liberated from old age and death. Those living there were either fairies or immortals; day and night they would fly in great numbers to visit each other" (Bauer 1974, p. 145).

Ch'in Shih Huang-ti, the first historical emperor of China, dispatched several expeditions to gain possession of the mushroom of immortality. The most famous of these was led by Hsü Fu, who recruited an expeditionary force of three thousand young men. They took with them different kinds of grain as well as plant seeds. However, Hsü Fu never returned: he and his men settled in a fertile region, where he appointed himself king.

P'eng-tzu 🆃 figure in Chinese mythology, representing longevity. Religious Taoism (→ *tao-chiao*) maintains that the Taoist sexual practices for prolonging life (→ *fang-chung hsu*) were introduced by P'eng-tzu.

According to legend he was born during the Hsia Dynasty and by the end of the Yin Dynasty had reached the age of 777 years (over 800 years according to some sources). King Yin appointed him his physician. His outer appearance was that of a youth. To keep young he swallowed mica dust and the ground antlers of a species of elk. He considered it wrong to withdraw from the world and claimed that the enjoyment of its delights would not impede progress along the Way.

His biography is contained in the writings of → Ko Hung, from which we quote the following passage: "Whoever would follow the Way should eat sweet delicious food; dress in light, becoming gowns; and give his sexual desires their due. He may also accept official and honorary posts. His bones will be hard and firm, his face contented and healthy. He will age without becoming decrepit and, always being in the present, prolongs his life span and thus enjoys a long and happy life in human company. Neither cold nor heat, wind, or fog can harm him; while ghosts and other specters will not dare approach him. . . . Neither displeasure nor joy, pain, or fame will move him. Well might such a man be considered an estimable person. An ordinary man should, by virtue of his life energy, reach an age of 120 years, even without resorting to magical potions, providing he looks after himself. Those that die sooner have willfully abused their life energy. Anyone with no more than a slight knowledge of the Way can reach an age of 240 years and—if he knows a little more than that—480 years. If he makes full use of the power of his spirit he need not die at all. . . . The Way of longevity simply consists in never offending against life. In winter one should keep warm, and cool in summer, and never fail to adjust to the inherent harmony of the four seasons: in this way a man attunes his body to the natural flow. In darkened rooms he may enjoy the company of women, thereby banishing lascivious fantasies: in this way his life force is allowed to flow freely. As for owning carriages and official gowns, as well as possessing power and influence, a man should know what is sufficient and have no desires beyond that: in this way he will harness his will. The eight tones and five colors are welcome to delight our eyes and ears: thus are our hearts guided" (Bauer 1974, p. 157).

Petavatthu 🅱 Pali → *Khuddaka-nikāya*

Phadampa Sangye 🅱 → Chöd

Phowa 🅱 ('pho-ba), Tib., lit. "change of place"; one of the six yogas of → Nāropa (→ *Nāro chödrug*), which reached Tibet in the 11th century through → Marpa the Translator. The practice of *phowa* involves a special technique that permits one intentionally to transfer one's consciousness to a pure buddha-paradise, such as that of → Amitābha, at the moment of death. Through the application of certain mantras and meditations (→ *sādhana*), the practitioner of *phowa* prepares himself for this moment. In the West, the *phowa* teachings are primarily transmitted by a representative of the Drigung Kagyu (→ Kagyupa).

Phurba 🅱 (phur-pa), Tib., lit. "nail, wedge"; a dagger for subduing demons introduced into the ritual of Tibetan Buddhism by → Padmasambhava. As a symbol for the direct transmutation of negative forces, it plays a central role in a system of meditative practice that was transmitted by → Yeshe Tsogyel. The actual *phurba* is a three-edged knife with a handle in the shape of half of a → *dorje*.

In Tibetan Buddhist ritual dances, rites associated with the *phurba* are still carried out today. The "soul" of a demon is captured in a doll; the *phurba* is driven into the heart of the doll, absorbing the "soul," while the demonic power is destroyed along with the doll. In the → Vajrayāna outlook, this symbolic act of killing becomes an act of compassion (→ *karunā*), since through the help of the *phurba* the demon is brought to liberation (→ nirvāna).

The origin of the *phurba* is associated with a long → Tantra presented by Padmasambhava at the beginning of his journey to Tibet. A deity personified as a *phurba* plays an important role as a → *yidam* in the → Sakyapa and → Nyingmapa schools; new transmissions, in the form of → *terma* texts, of teachings relating to this deity were discovered in the 19th century (→ Rime).

Phyagchen 🅱 Tib., short form of *phyag-rgya chen-po*, → *mahāmudrā*

Pi-ch'i 🆃 Chin., lit. "holding the breath"; Taoist breathing technique, in which the breath is first harmonized (→ *t'iao-ch'i*), then swallowed (→ *yen-ch'i*), and finally retained for as long as possible.

A beginner may retain his breath for the duration of three to nine heartbeats; this is known as the small round. Advanced practitioners practice the great round lasting 120 heartbeats. At this level it is possible to heal sicknesses in one's body. However, only those who are able to stop their breath for a duration of 1,000 heartbeats are approaching immortality.

When practicing *pi-ch'i* with the aim of curing himself of illness, the adept should begin by concentrating his mind on the sick area of his body and then direct and collect his breath at that point. In this way blockages—the most frequent cause of illness—can be dissolved with the breath. The practitioner then exhales. This process is repeated between twenty and fifty times, i.e., until perspiration appears at the affected area. The practice is continued until all signs of the illness have disappeared.

Pi-hsia yüan-chün 🆃 Chin., lit. "Princess of the

Azure Clouds"; Taoist deity, daughter of the god of Mount T'ai (→ T'ai-shan, → T'ai-yüeh ta-ti). Pi-hsia yüan-chün is also known as the Lady of T'ai-shan (T'ai-shan niang-niang) or the Holy Mother (Sheng-mu). She is the protectress of women and children and in this role is often compared to the Buddhist Kuan-yün. Her temple on top of Mount T'ai continues to be visited by many pilgrims who beseech the Princess of the Azure Clouds to bless them with children.

The veneration of Pi-hsia yüan-chün can be traced back to the time of the Han Dynasty. She is the subject of many legends. Generally she is shown in the company of two female assistants: the Lady of Good Sight, who protects children from eye infections, and the Lady Who Bestows Children (Sung-tzu niang-niang). Often there are six further deities by her side, who have the task of protecting children of different ages. Pi-hsia yüan-chün, her two assistants, and the six subordinate deities form a group known as the "nine ladies" (*chiu niang-niang*) to whom temples (*nai-nai miao*) were dedicated throughout China.

Pi-ku 🅃 Chin., lit. "abstaining from eating grain"; Taoist practice indispensable for the attainment of immortality. The practice is based on the notion that the five types of grain forming the staple diet of the Chinese—i.e., rice, barley, wheat, millet, and beans—also are the nourishment of the three worms (→ *san-ch'ung*), who are the cause of illnesses and thus shorten a person's life span. Another reason why they are considered to be harmful is that they are the essence of Earth. In the Taoist view the physical damage and diseases caused by eating these grains can be passed on from one generation to the next.

Abstinence from eating grain, in order to be successful, must be accompanied by other methods, i.e., the practitioner is not allowed to drink alcohol or eat meat and should avoid all fatty food.

Pingala 🄷 important authority on the subject of Vedic meter. His works are believed to have been composed in the third century B.C.E. The study of versification (prosody) is accorded particular importance in Sanskrit, as it is believed that a → mantra can unfold its full effect only when its syllables are articulated with the correct lengths and emphasis. For this reason, a mantra cannot simply be taken from a book, but rather is given personally to the pupil in oral form by the guru in an initiation ceremony.

Pingalā 🄷 (Piṇgalā), Skt.; one of the important channels that direct the → *prana* to all parts of the body. (See also → *nādī*.) The *pingalā* takes up the *prāna* through the right nostril. This channel of energy is glowing and powerful like the sun; it corresponds to the sympathicus of the sympathetic nervous system. Its counterpart is → *idā*.

Pishāchas 🄷 (Piśāca), Skt.; demon, will o' the wisp, monsters, evil spirits, ranked lower than the → *rākshasas* in the Vedas. They are the lowest and vilest of all beings. Opinions vary regarding their origin.

The *Mahābhārata* and the Brāhmanas describe the *pishāchas* as created along with the → *asuras* and the *rakshasas* by Brahmā, who formed the gods, human beings, → *gandharvas*, etc., from drops of water. From the water that splattered over in the process, the *pishāchas* arose. According to → Manu, they arose from the → Prajāpatis. The Purānas describe them as descendants of → Kashyapa and his wife Pishāchā.

Pitri 🄷 (Pitṛ), Skt., lit. "father," plural "forefathers"; ancestors, manes. The term is used to refer to three classes of beings: (1) deceased ancestors, to whom food and water are offered at certain times; (2) the ten → Prajāpatis, the mystical forefathers of the human race; and (3) the first sons of the gods.

According to legend, the gods had insulted → Brahmā by neglecting to worship him. He pronounced a curse that they would become fools. When they offered atonement, he advised them to allow themselves to be taught by their sons. The sons were instructed regarding the rites and spoke to the gods as their fathers. → Yama, the god of death, is said to have been the king of the *pitris*; as such he bears the name Pitripati ("Lord of the *pitris*").

Pitriyāna 🄷 (Pitṛyāna), Skt., lit. "way of the fathers"; the lower, southernmost path (→ *dakshinayāna*) taken by departed souls in order to reap the reward for their good deeds in the realm of Chandraloka ("moon realm"). Subsequently, they must return to earth in order to satisfy their unfulfilled desires. The higher way is that of → *devayāna* ("way of the gods"), the path of wisdom and spiritual knowledge. One who succeeds in reaching this realm of light attains liberation from the cycle of rebirths.

Paul Deussen refers to *pitriyāna* and *devayāa* as the "two-path teaching," a further development of the ancient Vedic eschatology of the "five fires teaching" (→ *pañchāgnividyā*). The beginnings of reincarnation theory contained in the earlier teaching are consolidated in the "two-path teaching."

Pi-yen-lu 🅉 Chin. (Jap., *Hekigan-roku*), lit. "*Blue-green Cliff Record*"; with the → *Wu-men-kuan*, one of the most important of the great →

kōan collections of Ch'an (Zen) literature and also the oldest. It was composed in its present form in the first half of the 12th century by the Chinese Ch'an (Zen) master → Yuan-wu K'o-ch'in (Jap., Engo Kokugon). It is based on a collection of a hundred koans collected approximately a century earlier by the Ch'an master → Hsueh-tou Ch'ung-hsien (Jap., Setchō Jūken) and provided by him with incidental commentary and "praises" (→ *ju*). These praises, poems in classical Chinese verse form, are not only the most renowned of their genre in Ch'an (Zen) literature, but also are among the greatest of Buddhist-inspired products of the Chinese poetic tradition. Taking Hsueh-tou's text as a basic structure, Yuan-wu added the following components to the text: introductions (Jap., *suiji*), which direct the attention of the reader to the essence of the kōan; commentaries or incidental remarks (→ *jakugo*) on the kōan; explanations (Jap., *hyōshō*) of the kōan; commentaries and explanations of the "praise." Because the text has so many different layers, the *Pi-yen-lu* is one of the most complex texts of Ch'an (Zen) literature. (An English translation is Cleary & Cleary 1978.)

Because of this complexity and the literary refinement of the text, many Zen masters have a higher regard for the *Wu-men-kuan*, which is simpler in form, since in their opinion it gets more directly and less figuratively "to the point." The danger posed by the literary beauty of the *"Blue-green Cliff Record"* was already seen by the Ch'an master → Ta-hui Tsung-kao (Jap., Daie Sōkō), a student and dharma successor (→ *hassu*) of Yuan-wu. When he saw that his students had the tendency to get involved in the qualities of the verbatim text rather than attend to the immediate experience that is its true content, he had all available copies of the *Pi-yen-lu* collected and burned. With all respect for the great work of his master, he was more concerned for the survival of the latter's dharma teaching than for that of his writings.

Fortunately for posterity, however, the greater part of this precious text was preserved in a few, though not entirely complete, copies. From these, the Ch'an layman Chang Ming-yuan was able, in the 14th century, to reconstruct the full text with the exception of a few passages.

Platform Sūtra **Z** → *Liu-tsu-ta-shih fa-pao-t'an-ching*

P'o **T** Chin.; body soul, one of two types of soul that, according to Chinese belief, inhabit every human being. The other is the so-called breath, or spirit, soul (→ *hun*).

Every human being has seven *p'o* souls, which owe their existence to the passive yin energy (→ yin-yang) and regulate the lower body functions. They cling to the human body; if they depart from it, death ensues. In that case the *p'o* souls rejoin the Earth, which is pure yin.

"Point" of a kōan **Z** → *wato*

Prabhākara **H** Founder of one of the first important schools based on the philosophy of → Pūrva-Mīmāmsā. He lived in the early eighth century and concerned himself primarily with the question of right knowledge.

Pradhāna **H** Skt., lit. "undeveloped nature," one of the fundamental principles of → Sānkhya thought, synonymous with → *prakriti*, primal matter, as opposed to the other fundamental principle, → *purusha*, the primal spirit.

Pradyumna **H**, a son of → Krishna and his wife Rukminī; in the presence of his father he was slain during a tumultuous gathering of drunkards. Many legends exist surrounding him; he is said to have been, among other things, a rebirth of Kāma, the god of love.

When Pradyumna was six days old, he was abducted by the demon Shambhara, thrown into the sea, and swallowed by a fish, which was later caught and brought to Shambara's house. When it was about to be drawn, a beautiful child emerged, whom Māyādevī, mistress of the house, took under her care. The sage → Nārada told her who the child was. When Pradyumna grew into manhood, Māyādevī fell in love with him and revealed his origins to him. Thereupon he slew the demon Shambhara following a difficult battle and fled with Māyādevī to the palace of his father, Krishna, who then brought him and his virtuous wife to his mother, Rukminī. He later took a second wife, Kakudmatī, who bore him a son, → Aniruddha. Pradyumna's victory over the Daitya Vajranābha is the subject of the seven-act drama *Pradyumna-Vijaya* by Shankara Dikshita (nineteenth century).

Prahlāda **H** Skt., lit. "refreshment, joy"; a great worshiper of Vishnu whose life is described in the Purānas. He was the son of the → Daitya king Hiranyakashipu.

Prahlāda's father, a follower of Shiva, was enraged by his son's profound devotion to Vishnu and in his anger ordered that Prahlāda be killed. Yet neither the weapons of Daityas nor the fangs of serpents, neither the tusks of elephants nor the fire's flames could harm the boy in any way. In order to deliver Prahlāda from his father's persecution, Vishnu took on his fourth incarnation (→ *avatāra*) as lion-man, and slew Hiranyakashipu. Prahlāda then became king of the Daityas and, according to the *Padma-Purāna*, was ultimately united with Vishnu.

Prajāpati **H** Skt., lit. "lord of creatures"; a title used in the Vedas to refer to → Indra, → Savitri,

Hiranyagarbha, and other divinites. → Manu refers to Brahmā in his role as creator and support of the universe as Prajāpati. Ten → *rishis,* considered to be the spiritual sons of Brahmā, are traditionally named the ten Prajāpatis: Marīchi, Atri, Angiras, Pulastya, Pulaha, Kratu, Vasishtha, Prachetas or Daksha, Bhrigu, and Nārada. Other sources number only seven *rishis,* who are identical with the seven great Rishis. The → *Mahābhārata* speaks of twenty-one Prajāpatis.

Prājña H Skt., the state of deep sleep, in which the activity of mind ceases and the → *jīva* momentarily, but unconsciously, unites with *brahman.* → Vedānta distinguishes four states of consciousness: → *vaishvārana,* the waking condition; → *taijasa,* the dream state; → *prājña*; and → *turīya,* "the fourth." They are discussed in detail in the → *Māndūkya-Upanishad.* The four states *(avasthā) are also known as → jāgrat* (waking), → *svapna* (dreaming), → *sushupti* (deep sleep), and *turīya.*

Prajñā H B Z Skt., lit. "consciousness" or "wisdom."

H Consciousness as the nature of the → *ātman;* according to Paul Deussen, "the objectless subject of consciousness, the highest soul, which has no object outside itself and hence is unconscious; that soul which envelops the individual soul in deep sleep. Hence *prajña,* the soul in deep sleep."

B Z (Pali, pañña; Jap., hannya); wisdom; a central notion of the → Mahāyāna referring to an immediately experienced intuitive wisdom that cannot be conveyed by concepts or in intellectual terms. The definitive moment of *prajñā* is insight into emptiness (→ *shūnyatā*), which is the true nature of reality. The realization of *prajñā* is often equated with the attainment of enlightenment and is one of the essential marks of buddhahood. *Prajñā* is also one of the "perfections" (→ *pāramitā*) actualized by a bodhisattva in the course of his development (→ *bhūmi*).

Also → enlightenment.

Prajñādhāra Z (Jap., Hannyatara); twenty-seventh patriarch in the Indian lineage of Ch'an (→ Zen); also → Bodhidharma.

Prajñānam Brahma H Skt., lit. "Consciousness is *brahman*"; one of the → *mahāvākyas,* the great precepts; it is found in the *Aitareya-Upanishad* of the *Rigveda.* Toward the end of this Upanishad, the following passage appears: "Everything that lives, everything that moves and flies and is still, all this is guided by consciousness, is founded in consciousness; the world is guided by consciousness, consciousness is its foundation, consciousness is *brahman.*

The notion that consciousness is identical with *brahman* presents certain difficulties for the Western reader, who customarily equates consciousness with thinking. → Vedānta distinguishes clearly between thinking consciousness and absolute consciousness and demonstrates that thinking consciousness exists only in the waking and dreaming states, not in deep sleep or → *samādhi,* and hence cannot be ultimately real, whereas absolute consciousness is present in all four states (waking, dreaming, deep sleep, and *samādhi*). In deep sleep we are not aware of its presence, but in *samādhi,* the state in which consciousness is experienced without thought projections, one is united with the absolute consciousness and knows that consciousness is *brahman,* the One without a second.

Prajñāpāramitā-sūtra B also *Mahāprajñāpāramitā-sūtra,* Skt., lit. *"[Great] Sūtra of the Wisdom [→ Prajñā]* That Reaches the Other Shore [i.e., that is transcendental, or liberating]"; term for a series of about forty Mahāyāna sūtras, gathered together under this name because they all deal with the realization of *prajñā.* They represent a part of the → *Vaipulya-sūtras* of the Mahāyāna and probably were composed around the beginning of the Common Era. Some sūtras are preserved in Sanskrit, however most of them have come down only in Chinese or Tibetan translation. Those best known in the West are the → *Diamond Sūtra (Vajrachchedikā)* and the → *Heart Sutra (Mahāprajñāpāramitā-hridaya-sūtra*). Their most important interpreter was → Nāgārjuna.

The *Prajñāpāramitā-sūtras* are marked by a pronounced didactic tendency; in this they resemble the Hīnayāna sūtras. Most of them are dedicated to → Subhūti and are said to have been delivered on → Vulture Peak Mountain.

The oldest part is probably the *Ashtasāhasrikā* in 8,000 verses. It is composed of discussions of the Buddha with several students and constitutes the basis for all the other *Prajñāpāramitā-sūtras* (which vary in length from 300 to 100 thousand verses). It is the most frequently translated and commented upon of these sūtras. The first Chinese translation is from the year 179.

Prajñaptivādin B Skt. → Hīnayāna, → Mahāsānghika

Prajñātman H Skt., snynonymous with → *ātman*

Prakāsha H (Prakāśa), Skt., lit. "light, clarity"; clear, shining radiance, illumination.

Prākrita 🅗 (Prākṛta) Skt., lit. "popular"; vernacular dialects of → Sanskrit that lie somewhere between Sanskrit and the languages of present-day India.

The Prākritas are known chiefly from dramas, in which the roles of kings and brahmans are recorded in Sanskrit, while those of the lower classes employ the various Prākritas. Sometimes they are so garbled that they cannot be identified clearly either as Sanskrit or as one of the vernaculars.

Prakriti 🅗 (Prakṛti), Skt., lit. "nature, matter"; the primal matter of which the universe consists. Its structure is determined by the three → *gunas (tamas, rajas,* and *sattva).* According to → Sānkhya philosophy, *prakriti* (also called → *pradhāna)* is real and creates by proximity to → *purusha* the world of mind and of appearances. For → Advaita-Vedānta, matter has no final reality, since the material world is experienced only in the waking and dreaming states and not in deep sleep or → *turīya.* For Advaita, only that which exists in all four states of consciousness is real.

Pralaya 🅗 Skt., lit. "dissolution." At the end of a → *kalpa* (world cycle) the manifest world dissolves, that is, changes from a manifest to an unmanifest or potential state, from which a new world subsequently emerges. Hinduism does not describe a single creation such as that pictured in the Old Testament, but rather speaks of a repeating cycle of manifestation and nonmanifestation, which latter state contains the possibility of renewed manifestation.

Pramāna 🅗 (Pramāṇa), Skt., lit. "proof"; means of attaining correct knowledge, such as → *pratyaksha* (sensory perception), oral testimony, logical conclusion, the authority of the Vedas, etc.

Prāna 🅗 (Prāṇa), Skt., lit. "breath, breath of life"; the cosmic energy that penetrates and maintains the body and is most overtly manifest in creatures as the breath. → Patañjali discusses *prāna* in the fourth step (→ *pranāyāma*) of his yoga; it also plays an important part in → Hatha-Yoga. The → *Atharvaveda* personifies *prāna,* to whom one of its hymns is devoted.

Hinduism distinguishes between five different *prānas:* (1) *prāna,* the essence of breath, the pure force of life as such; (2) *vyāna,* which guides the circulation; (3) *samāna,* which controls the intake and utilization of food and maintains the balance of the body by the chemical processes of metabolism; (4) *apāna,* which sees to the elimination of waste material from the body and is active in the lower part of the body; and (5) → *udāna,* which works in the upper part of the body and furthers spiritual development by creating a bridge between the physical and spiritual aspects of one's nature.

Pranām 🅗 (Praṇāma), Skt., lit. "a bow"; reverential form of greeting, offered to God as well as to saints and respected persons, in which one either places the palms of the hands together, or touches first the feet of the one being greeted and then one's own forehead, or prostrates oneself before him.

Prānamaya-Kosha 🅗 (Prāṇamaya-Kośa), Skt.; the second of the five → *koshas* (sheaths), the subtle or vital sheath, which animates and holds together the body and mind. For as long as this sheath is present in the organism, it remains alive. Its gross manifestation is the breath.

Pranava 🅗 (Praṇava), Skt.; a term used to refer to the mystical, sacred syllable → OM. If the sound is drawn out when the syllable is pronounced, it is called *dirgha-pranava.*

Prāna-Vidyā 🅗 (Prāṇa-Vidyā), Skt.; knowledge of the life force (→ *prāna*). As a result of such knowledge, the individual life is united with universal life, and the will of the individual merges with the will of God, with the creative energy of → Īshvara, and thereby becomes a dynamic channel for universal life.

Prānāyāma 🅗 (Prāṇāyāma), Skt., lit. "control of → *prāna*"; the fourth step of → Rāja-Yoga. It consists of breathing exercises, which may be combined with the practice of a mantra. The breath is divided into three phases: *pūraka* (inhalation), *rechaka* (exhalation), and → *kumbhaka* (retention of the breath). An introduction to the practice of *prānāyāma* is offered in Iyengar 1981.

Pranidhāna 🅑 (praṇidhāna), Skt.; the bodhisattva vow, which is the first step on the way of a → bodhisattva (→ *bhūmi*). It includes the firm resolution to attain enlightenment (→ *bodhi*) oneself and to liberate all beings by leading them to → nirvāna. The vow is an expression of the "mind directed toward enlightenment" (→ *bodhichitta*). As part of the Mahāyāna, it is taken by laypersons as well as by monks and nuns.

Prāpti-Prāpya 🅗 Skt.; one who has attained everything there is to attain; term used to refer to a liberated soul (→ *jīvanmukta*).

Prārabdha-Karma 🅗 Skt., lit. *pra:* "before,"

ārabdha: "begun," → *karma*: "deed"; the results of deeds that were begun in former lives and are now working themselves out in the present one. Such consequences are the harvest of ripened fruits; the resulting events cannot be prevented, just as one cannot call back an arrow that has already left the bow. Aside from *prārabdha-karma* there are also → *āgāmi-karma* and → *sanchita-karma*.

Prasāda 🅗, or Prasād, Skt.; 1. the favor or benevolence of God; 2. clarity, purity, peace of mind; 3. food sacrifices that are presented to a divinity and then distributed to the worshipers, or food sampled by a holy man. Such *prasāda* is said to contain spiritual powers.

Prāsangika 🅑 Skt., lit. "Making Use of the Consequences"; a subschool of the → Mādhyamikas founded by the Buddhist sage Buddhapālita, a student of → Nāgārjuna.

Prashna 🅗 (Praśna), Skt., lit. "question"; a Vedānta-Upanishad belonging to the → *Atharvaveda*. It treats six questions as posed to the sage Pippalāda.

The six questions concern the following subjects: (1) the origin of matter and life from → Prajāpati; (2) the precedence of → *prāna* before the other life forces; (3) the distribution of *prāna* in the human body; (4) the states of dreaming and deep sleep; (5) meditation on → OM; (6) the "sixteen divisions" of man. The answer to the last question culminates in this passage: "The sixteen divisions are the spokes that radiate from the Self, for this Self is the hub. This Self is the final aim of knowledge. Know this, and you are free from death."

Prashnottara 🅗 (Praśnottara), Skt., lit. "question and answer"; a dialogue between master and disciple, whereby spiritual questions are answered.

Prasthānatraya 🅗 Skt., lit *prasthāna*: "system," *traya* "triad"; a comprehensive term referring to the three basic works of → Vedānta: the Upanishads, the *Bhagavad-Gītā*, and the → *Brahma-Sūtras*.

Prātibhātika 🅗 (Prātibhāṭika), Skt.; apparent reality, which by means of → *viveka* (discrimination) may be recognized as unreal.

Pratibimba-Vāda 🅗 Skt., lit. *pratibimba*: "mirror image," *vāda*: "proposition"; the view that the → *jīva* is a reflection of *brahman* in the realm of ignorance.

Pratiloma 🅗 Skt., lit. "distorted, unnatural"; an expression referring to the ego, whose particular characteristic it is to cut itself off by means of ignorance from the cosmic unity and in so doing to set itself in opposition to the natural order of that unity.

Prātimoksha 🅑 (prātimokṣa), Skt. (Pali, pātimokkha); a part of the → Vinaya-pitaka that contains the 227 disciplinary rules for monks and 348 for nuns and is recited at every → *uposatha* ceremony. At this ceremony, every monk or nun must confess any violations of these rules.

Pratipaksha-Bhavana 🅗 (Pratipakṣa-Bhavana), Skt., lit. *pratipaksha*: "enemy, opponent," *bhavana*: "become, originate"; a practice utilized in → Rāja-Yoga to avoid being disturbed during concentration by base thoughts. Even as they arise, they are countered by strong spiritual thoughts—a means that is also utilized by the Rāja-Yogi in everyday life to maintain his equanimity.

Pratisamkhyā-nirodha 🅑 (pratisaṃkyā-nirodha), Skt.; extinction (→ *nirodha*), intentional and grounded in wisdom and insight, that brings about the termination of defilements and passion (→ *klesha*). This state of extinction is identified with → nirvāna. *Pratisamkhyā-nirodha* is one of the unconditioned (→ *asamskrita*) dharmas of the → Sarvāstivāda and → Yogāchāra.

Pratishthā 🅗 (Pratiṣṭhā), or Ādhāra, Skt., lit. "fundament, basis"; applied to gross matter, the term refers to the earth; applied to human beings, it refers to the three basic principles of body, mind, and life, which together serve as a vehicle for the soul.

Pratishthita-nirvāna 🅑 (pratiṣṭhita-nirvāṇa), Skt., lit. "static nirvāna"; according to the Mahāyāna view, the nirvāna after death, the remainderless extinction of a liberated one, in which all relationship to the world is broken off and there is no activity. It is opposed to → *apratishthita-nirvāna*, in which the liberated one remains in the world. A bodhisattva renounces entry into *pratishthita-nirvāna* so that he can, in accordance with his vow (→ *pranidhāna*), lead beings on the way to liberation.

Pratishthita-nirvāna can be equated with the Hīnayāna nirvāna without remainder of conditionality (→ *niruphadhishesha-nirvāna*). (Also → nirvāna.)

Pratītya-samutpāda 🅑 Skt., (Pali, patichcha-samuppāda), lit. "conditioned arising" or "interdependent arising," often also translated "conditional nexus" or "causal nexus." The doctrine of conditioned arising says that all psychological and physical phenomena constituting individual existence are interdependent and mutually condition each other; this at the same time describes what entangles sentient beings in → samsāra.

The chain of conditioned arising is, together with the → *anātman* doctrine, the core teaching of all Buddhist schools. Attainment of enlightenment (→ *bodhi*) and thus realization of buddhahood depends on comprehending this doctrine.

Pratītya-samutpāda consists of twelve links (→ *nidāna*): (1) ignorance (→ *avidyā*)—lack of recognition of the → four noble truths, ignorance of the suffering-ridden nature of existence—conditions (2) formations or impulses (→ *samskāra*), which precede actions. These can be good, bad, or neutral and are related to physical, verbal, and psychological actions. In turn they condition (3) consciousness (→ *vijñāna*) in the next life of the individual. This consciousness reenters another womb after the death of an individual who has not been liberated and instigates there the arising of (4) "name and form," the psychological and physical factors (→ *nāmarūpa*), i.e., a new empirical being constituted by the five → *skandhas*. Which womb the consciousness chooses is determined by its qualities, which in turn depend upon the formations or impulses. Interdependently with *nāmarūpa*, (5) the six bases (→ *shadāyatana*) arise. These are the six object realms of the senses, which present themselves to the being after its birth, thus conditioning (6) contact (→ *sparsha*) with its environment. This contact invokes (7) sensation (→ *vedanā*), out of which develops, for someone who is ignorant in the Buddhist sense, (8) craving (→ *trishnā*). Ignorance and craving lead, after the death of the individual, to (9) clinging (→ *upādāna*) to a womb, where (10) a new becoming (→ *bhāva*) is set in motion. This is followed by (11) birth (*jāti*), which again comes to an end in (12) old age and death (*jarā-maranam*). The entire chain of conditions thus covers three existences: 1–2 relate to the previous existence, 3–7 to conditioning of the present existence, 8–10 to the fruits of the present existence, and 11–12 to the future life.

The teaching of conditioned arising shows the dependent nature of the streams of physical and psychological existential phenomena conventionally conceptualized as *I, man, animal*, and so on. While the doctrine of *anātman* has the effect of breaking down individual existence into empty, essenceless components, the teaching of conditioned arising works in the direction of synthesis by showing that all phenomena stand in some relationship of conditionedness, a relationship that can be understood in terms of simultaneity as well as succession in time.

Pratītya-samutpāda was interpreted by the various schools from differing points of view. In Hīnayāna, its function is to explain the arising of suffering (→ *duhkha*); here it shows that all composite existence (→ *samskrita*) has cause and condition and thus is without substantiality. This doctrine is then used as the basis for the negation of self (as composite existence). In Mahāyāna conditioned arising is further interpreted to prove the unreality of existence by reason of its relativity. In the → Mādhyamika system, *pratītya-samutpāda* is equated with emptiness (→ *shūnyatā*). Here conditioned arising is taken to show that because of their relativity, appearances have only empirical validity and are ultimately unreal.

In the → Yogāchāra view, only true understanding of *pratītya-samutpāda* can overcome the error of taking what does not exist for existent and what does exist for nonexistent.

The → *Prajñāpāramitā-sūtras* emphasize that *pratītya-samutpāda* does not refer to a temporal succession but rather to the essential interdependence of all things.

Pratyabhijñā 🅷 Skt., lit. recognition; 1. the knowledge of everything that is required for → *moksha* (liberation); knowledge of the identity of the manifest world, the soul, and God; 2. another name for → Shaivism in Kashmir, whose followers incline more toward → Advaita-Vedānta than do those in South India. Here Shiva is the only reality, the infinite, pure Self, the basis of the universe; he appears through the power of his → *shakti* and is the origin of all apparent distinctions. (See also → *trika*.)

Pratyāhāra 🅷 Skt.; the fifth step of → Rāja-Yoga, the withdrawal of the senses from sense objects so that the mind can be directed undisturbed toward the object of meditation; an indispensable condition for concentration (→ *dhārana*), the next step in Rāja-Yoga.

Pratyaksha 🅷 (Pratyakṣa), Skt.; direct perception by means of the senses. For *charvakas* (materialists), it is the only means of true knowledge (→ *pramāna*). The other philosophical schools do not rely solely on sensory perception, but require further means of knowledge.

Pratyeka-buddha 🅱 Skt. (Pali, pachcheka-buddha), lit. "solitary awakened one"; a term for an awakened one (buddha), who due to insight into the twelve → *nidānas* has attained enlightenment on his own and only for himself. Meritorious qualities, such as omniscience (→ *sarvajñatā*), or the ten powers (→ *dashabala*), which characterize a fully enlightened one (→ *samyak-sambuddha*) are not ascribed to him. In the levels of sainthood, he is placed between the → arhats and the buddhas who have attained complete enlightenment.

Sometimes this term is also applied to enlightened ones who live in a time when there is no buddha and have attained enlightenment in a previous existence through insight into conditioned arising (→ *pratītya-samutpāda*).

The *pratyeka-yāna* ("vehicle of the solitary awakened ones") is one of the three vehicles leading to the attainment of nirvāna (→ *triyāna*).

Pravrajyata B Skt. → homelessness

Pravritti H (Pravṛtti), Skt., lit. "origin, arising"; evolution, the unfoldment or manifestation of what was previously latent; the opposite of → *pralaya*.

Prayopaveshana H (Prayopaveśana), Skt.; an ascetic practice wherein one lies before the image of a deity for a prolonged period of time without eating or drinking and prays for the fulfillment of some wish.

Prema-Bhakti H, or Prema, Skt.; the highest form of love of God, wherein the worshiper longs for God as a drowning man longs for air. It is a state similar in spirit to *mahābhāva* and → *para-bhakti*. The bliss that arises from such love is called *premānada*.

Prema-Sāmarthya H Skt.; the power of love, which can do anything; one of the four "perfections of the heart" (→ *kalyāna-shraddha*).

Preta B Skt. (Pali, peta), lit. "departed one"; these so-called hungry ghosts constitute one of the three negative modes of existence (→ *gati*). *Pretas* are beings whose karma is too good for rebirth in the hells (→ *naraka*), but too bad for rebirth as an → *asura*. Greed, envy, and jealousy can, according to the traditional view, lead to rebirth as a *preta*. *Pretas* suffer the torment of hunger, because their bellies are immense but their mouths only as big as the eye of a needle. They are also subject to various other tortures.

Prithā H → Kuntī

Prithivī H (Pṛthivī), Skt.; the earth, personified in the Vedas as the mother of all beings and invoked together with heaven.

According to the Vedas, there are three earths and three corresponding heavens. Our earth is called Bhūmi or → Bhūrloka. In the *Vishnu-Purāna*, she received her name from the mystical figure Prithī, who was like a father to her.

Prīti B Skt. → *bodhyanga*

Prītijushā H Skt. → Ūshā

P'u T Chin., lit. "rough timber, an unhewn block"; simplicity, plainness, innocence. A symbol used by Lao-tzu in the → *Tao-te ching* to describe the original, simple, and unpretentious nature of man. This original human nature is also compared to that of a new-born child (*ying-erh*) or to raw silk (*su*). It is the goal we must regain, because *p'u* is the ultimate destination of the return to our source (→ *fu*). Its predominant characteristic is spontaneous action (→ *wu-wei*) and freedom from desire. The return to this primordial state is only possible by shedding our desires and attachments. Chapter 19 of the *Tao-te ching* (Wei 1982, p. 152) states,

> Display plainness (*su*), embrace simplicity (*p'u*),
> Reduce selfishness and decrease desires.
> Forswear learning
> and vexation will vanish.

Lao-tzu considers the desire for wealth, fame, and sensuous pleasures the main hindrance to our development, because they give rise to envy and hatred. A person who attains true inner simplicity thereby gains power over the whole world (Chap. 32, Feng & English 1972):

> The Tao is forever undefined.
> Small though it is in the unformed state,
> it cannot be grasped.
> If kings and lords could harness it,
> the ten thousand things would naturally obey.
> . . .
> Men would need no more instruction
> and all things would take their course.

Public notice Z → kōan

Pudgala B Skt. (Pali, puggala), roughly "person"; the ego or self, the "substance" that is the bearer of the cycle of rebirth. In Buddhism the existence of an eternal person or "soul" is denied. Buddhism sees in the "person" only a conventional name for an apparent unity, which in reality is composed only of physical and psychological factors that change from moment to moment (→ *skandha*).

The → Vātsīputrīya school understood the *pudgala* as a manifest reality that is neither identical with the *skandhas* nor distinct from them. According to this view, the "person" undergoes changes from one life to another and even continues to exist after → *parinirvāna*. In this way, the Vātsīputrīyas attempted to solve the problem of retribution (→ karma). Their view, however, was rejected by all other Buddhist schools as not in accordance with the dharma.

In addition *pudgala* has the meaning of "person" in a more ordinary sense, as in → *arya-pudgala* (noble one).

Pudgalavādin 🅱 Skt. → Vātsīputrīya

P'u-hsien 🅱 Chin. for → Samantabhadra

P'u-hua 🅩 also P'u-k'o (Jap., Fuke), d. 860; Chinese Ch'an (Zen) master; a student and dharma successor (→ *hassu*) of → P'an-shan Pao-chi (Jap., Banzan Hōshaku). P'u-hua was known for his eccentric behavior; he founded the → Fuke school, which was brought to Japan during the Kamakura period by Shinchi → Kakushin. After his master P'an-shan died, P'u-hua joined the circle of Lin-chi I-hsuan's (Jap., Rinzai Gigen's) followers. In this circle he played the role of a "holy fool," and in the *Lin-chi-lu* (→ Lin-chi I-hsuan) some anecdotes regarding his unconventional lifestyle are recorded.

The incident that marks the transmission of the dharma from Master P'an-shan to P'u-hua is reported by Master Yuan-wu in his commentary on example 37 of the → *Pi-yen-lu*. Here the unique style of P'u-hua comes plainly to the fore:

When he [P'an-shan] felt that he would soon pass away, he said to an assembly of his students: "Is there one among you who can catch my true form from a distance?"

Then each one in the assembly drew a picture and held it up to him. He, however, derided all of them. Then P'u-hua came forward and said, "I could give a remote representation of you."

P'an-shan replied, "Then, old monk, why don't you show it to me?"

Then P'u-hua did a somersault in front of the master and went out. P'an-shan said to the others, "This fellow will again lead people to knowledge with his fool's style" (trans. from Gundert 1967, p. 84)

Pūjā 🅗 🅱 Skt.; worship, ceremony, religious service.

🅗 Ritual worship ceremony with Ganges water, flowers, a bell (*ghantā*), incense, and mantras. During the service, symbolic gestures (→ *mudrās*) are used to draw a mystical circle around the worshiper; this serves to separate him from the transitory world of senses and helps to establish the connection with God. The practitioner is called the *pūjari* or *pūjaka*.

🅱 a ceremony of the → Theravāda that includes offering of food, flowers, incense, water, etc., recitation of the refuge formula (→ *trisharana*), a short meditation, and so on. It typifies the basic form of Buddhist religious service. A *pūjā* is performed, for example, on → *uposatha* days. The details of the form vary from country to country.

Also, certain ceremonies of the → Vajrayāna that include recitation of sacred texts and → mantras, execution of → mudrās, invocation and visualization of deities, as well as presentation of ritual offerings, are called *pūjās*.

P'u-k'o 🅩 Chin. → P'u-hua

Pu-nao 🅣 Chin. → *huan-ching*

Punarājāti 🅗, also Punarāvritti, Punarutpatti, Punarjanman, and Punarjīvātu, Skt.; rebirth. Indian religion and philosophy teach that perfection is not attained by a human being in a single lifetime but is the result of a long chain of experiences over many consecutive lifetimes. Hence the general belief in → karma and rebirth. (Regarding the beginnings of the Hindu doctrine of rebirth, see → *pañchāgnividyā* and → *pitriyāna*.)

Punya 🅱 (puṇya), Skt. (Pali, punna), roughly "merit." This term generally refers to the karmic merit gained through giving alms, performing → *pūjās*, reciting sūtras, and so on, which is said to assure a better life in the future. Accumulating merit is a major factor in the spiritual effort of a Buddhist layperson.

The Mahāyāna criticizes the egoistic accumulation of merit in the Hīnayāna and teaches that accumulated merit should serve the enlightenment of all beings by being transferred to others. The commitment to transfer a part of one's accumulated merit to others is a significant aspect of the bodhisattva vow (→ *pranidhāna*). Perfection in this is achieved in the eighth stage of a bodhisattva's development (→ *bhūmi*).

Punyamitra 🅩 twenty-sixth patriarch of the Indian lineage of Ch'an (→ Zen)

Punyayasha 🅩 eleventh patriarch of the Indian lineage of Ch'an (→ Zen)

Pūraka 🅗 Skt. → *prānāyāma*

Purāna 🅗 (Purāṇa), Skt., "ancient narratives." In contrast to the older → Itihāsas, which describe the legendary deeds of human heroes, the eighteen Purānas and the eighteen Upa-Purānas (Secondary Purānas) that are classified beneath them present legends of the gods. They are steeped in devotion (→ *bhakti*) and therefore constitute the chief scriptures of the worshipers of Vishnu, Shiva, and Brahmā; hence they are divided into Vaishnava-, Shaiva-, and Brāhmana-Purānas. Vedic religion couched its deep spirituality in a nature symbolism that the common people seldom penetrated; for this reason, popular worship was directed toward the outer manifestations of nature. In the Purānas, with their trinity of the three great gods Brahmā (the creator), Vishnu (the sustainer), and Shiva (the destroyer of everything, including all evil and ignorance), the symbolic character of the three divine figures was easier to comprehend and could therefore satisfy the people's inner religious need. Thus the mythological Purānas represent the true storehouse of the Hindu religion and are today still of vital importance for Hindu belief.

The six Vaishnava-Purānas are: *Vishnu-*, → *Bhāgavata-*, → *Padma-*, *Nārada-*, *Garuda-*, and *Varāha-Purāna*. The six Shaiva-Purānas are *Matsya-*, *Linga-*, *Skanda-*, *Kūrma-*, *Shiva-*, and *Agni-Purāna*. The *Agni-Purāna* is sometimes replaced by the *Vāyu-Purāna*, apparently the oldest Purāna. The six Brāhmana-Purānas are *Brahma-*, *Brahmavaivarta-*, *Vāmana-*, *Brahmānda-*, *Mārkandeya*, and *Bhavishya-Purāna*. The most famous and most traditional of the Purānas are the *Vishnu-Purāna* and the *Bhāgavata-Purāna*; the latter tells the story of Krishna and has influenced—and continues to influence—most intensely the beliefs of Hindus.

All the Purānas are written in verse form (between 5,600 and 81,000 couplets) and are in the form of a dialogue between an enlightened master and his disciple, in which dialogues and observations of other characters are inserted. Each Purāna is supposed to contain five characteristics (*pañcha-lakshana*) in the form of the following themes: (1) creation; (2) the destruction and renewal of the world; (3) the genealogy of the gods and heroes; (4) the rule of the various → Manus during the various stages of human development; (5) life and works of the descendants of the Manus. However, not all Purānas adhere to this pattern of *lakshanas*.

The *Vāyu-Purāna* is presumed to go back as far as the sixth century, whereas others may have arisen only in the thirteenth to sixteenth centuries. The one thing that seems certain is that all of them were revised, since each individual Purāna enumerates all the preceding ones.

Aside from the eighteen Purānas and the Upa-Purānas, there are also the → Sthala-Purānas, which tell of the history and the merit of sacred sites (*sthala*); at such places recitation from these Purānas constitutes an important element in the daily worship services.

As a whole, the Purāna complex represents to some extent "a kind of encyclopedia of Hindu religious forms and their countless traditions, which interweave, cross, and overlap one another" (Mario Vallauri).

Purashcharana 🅷 (Puraścaraṇa), Skt., lit. "preparation"; preparation for meditation by the repetition of a → mantra, performed together with sacrificial offerings and other rites prescribed by the Vedas. In one particular form of *purashcharana*, the number of mantras to be repeated increases daily over a specified period and then decreases again. For example, the practitioner may begin at the new moon with 1,000 repetitions, reach 15,000 repetitions by the full moon, and gradually return to 1,000 repetitions by the next new moon. The practice is intended to produce self-control, clarity of mind, and power of concentration.

Pure land 🅱 (Chin., ching-t'u; Jap., jōdo); in Mahāyāna the "pure lands" (also buddha-realms or buddha-paradises), each ruled over by a buddha. Since according to the Mahāyāna there are countless buddhas, countless pure lands also exist. The most important is → Sukhāvatī, the pure land of the west or the western paradise, ruled by Buddha → Amitābha. An eastern paradise is the pure land of → Bhaishajya-guru Buddha ('Medicine Guru Buddha'). The → Abhirati paradise of Buddha → Akshobhya is also in the east. In the south is the paradise of Buddha Ratnaketu, in the north that of Buddha Dundubhīshvara. A further pure land will be brought forth by the future buddha → Maitreya, who presently still dwells in the → Tushita Heaven.

These pure lands are transcendent in nature. They are the hope of believers who wish to be reborn in them. The decisive factor here is not their good → karma but rather the aid of a given buddha, who has taken the vow to help all those to rebirth in his pure land who turn to him in faith. In folk belief these paradises are geographically localizable places of bliss; however, fundamentally they stand for aspects of the awakened state of mind, and the directions (east, south, etc.) have iconographical meanings. The pure lands are not, however, the final stage on the way, but are the stage before → nirvāna, which is to be realized in the ensuing rebirth. Nevertheless, in a pure land, retrogression is no longer possible. (Also → Pure Land school.)

Pure Land school 🅱 (Chin., Ching-t'u-tsung; Jap., Jōdō-shū), also known as the Lotus school. A school of Chinese and Japanese Buddhism, which was founded in the year 402 by the Chinese monk → Hui-yuan and brought to Japan by Hōnen. The goal of the adherents of this school is to be reborn in the → pure land of Buddha → Amitābha, i.e., in the western paradise. This school is characterized by its stress on the importance of profound faith in the power and active compassion of Buddha Amitābha. Amitābha made a vow to cause all beings to be reborn in his pure land Sukhāvatī who trust themselves to him with faithful devotion. Thus, since its adherents count on the external help of Amitābha, the way of the Pure Land school is often regarded as the "way of faith" or the "easy way".

The practice of this school consists primarily in the recitation of Amitābha's name (→ *nembutsu*) and in visualizing his paradise. These practices were adopted by other schools of Chinese and Japanese Buddhism. The sūtras used as the scriptural foundation of the school are the → *Sukhāvatī-vyūha*, the → *Amitābha-sūtra*, and the → *Amitāyurdhyāna-sūtra*. The Pure Land school is presently the school of Buddhism in China and Japan that has the most followers. (Also → Amidism.)

Hui-yuan founded in 402 the so-called White Lotus Society. Monks and laypeople assembled under his supervision before an image of the Buddha Amitābha and vowed to be reborn in the western paradise. Hui-yuan is thus considered the first patriarch of this school. T'an-luan (Jap., Donran), 476–542, contributed considerably to the development of the Pure Land school. He advocated the view that in a time of deterioration of the Buddhist teaching, one's own effort (→ *jiriki*) is insufficient for the attainment of liberation. He rejected the "hard way" of the other schools and fostered the "easy way," in which one places one's trust in the external help (→ *tariki*) of Buddha Amitābha. In his opinion, it is sufficient to recite Amitābha's name with complete devotion to be reborn in the pure land. Shan-tao (Jap., Zendo), 613–81, is considered the actual founder of the organized Pure Land school. He composed important commentaries on the *Amitāyurdhyāna-sūtra*. In his time the school experienced a major upsurge, since its practice, compared with that of other schools, seemed relatively easy.

The recitation of Amitābha's name serves to bring the mind under control. The practitioner commits himself to a certain, usually very large, number of repetitions. This meditation is intended to make it possible to have a vision of Amitābha and his companions → Avalokiteshvara and → Mahāsthāmaprāpta even during this lifetime and to gain foreknowledge concerning the time of one's death. This recitation can be done out loud or silently, with or without concentration on an image of Amitābha. This is the predominant practice of the school. The second type of practice consists of visualizations—particularly the sixteenth variant described in the *Amitāyurdhyāna-sūtra*—which serve to cause Amitābha and his pure land to arise before the spiritual eye of the practitioner. The supreme stage of practice is the contemplation of Buddha Amitābha as not separate from one's own being. The supreme achievement resulting from the spiritual practice of the school is seeing Buddha Amitābha in a vision. This is regarded as a guarantee of being reborn in his pure land. Recitation and visualization are considered the external condition, faith and total devotion toward Amitābha as the inner condition, for a successful practice. Only when both are present is rebirth in the western paradise possible.

Puri 🅗 1. well-known pilgrimage site at the Bay of Bengal; one of the four particularaly holy places in India, site of the celebrated → Jagannātha Temple. The other three holy places are → Dvārakā, → Kedārnāth, and → Rāmeshvara. Puri is also the location of a monastery belonging to the → Shankara tradition; 2. surname given to monks at any of the ten monastic orders of the Shankara tradition. It is appended to the monk's personal name. Other widely known surnames of this sort are Giri and Ānanda; 3. longtime residence of the great saint → Chaitanya.

Pūrna 🅑 → ten great disciples of the Buddha

Pūrnādvaita-Vedānta 🅗 (Pūrṇādvaita-Vedānta), or Pūrnādvaitavāda, Skt.; a modern-day philosophical teaching, represented chiefly by Shrī → Aurobindyo. It attempts to bring together all traditional interpretations of → Vedānta.

Pūrnakāma 🅗 (Pūrṇakāma), Skt., lit. *pūrna*: "fulfilled, perfect, complete," *kāma*: "wish, desire"; one whose wishes have all been fulfilled. One who no longer has any desires creates no new karma; once his karma has worked itself out, such a soul attains perfection and is not reborn.

Pūrna-Yoga 🅗 (Pūrṇa-Yoga), Skt.; total union with the Divine. Shrī → Aurobindo, founder of this system, gave it the name Integral Yoga, because its goal is not solely the ascent of the human spirit to the divine but also the integration of the divine into the world of matter and of everyday life.

Purūravas 🅗, a mythological figure, according to the → *Bhāgavata-Purāna* the source (at the onset of the *tretā-yuga*; see → *yuga*) of the threefold Veda (*Rig-, Sāma-, and Yajurveda*).

A hymn in the *Rigveda* contains a conversation between Purūravas (symbolizing the sun, the eternal light of knowledge) and → Urvashī, an *apsarā*, or water nymph (symbolizing the dawn mist that is drawn by the morning sun and transformed into fog or clouds). Love develops between the two figures. The Indologist Max Müller called the story of Purūravas and Urvashī a myth that uses the relationship between the dawn and the sun as a symbol for the love between mortal man and the immortal. Purūravas is the hero Vikrama in → Kālidāsa's drama of the tale of Vikrama and Urvashī, the *Vikramorvashīya* ("The Hero and the Nymph").

Purusha 🅷 (Puruṣa), Skt., lit. "man, person"; the original, eternal person, the highest being; one of the two forms of reality described in the philosophy of → Sānkhya, in which *purusha* is the Self, the Absolute, pure consciousness. *Purusha* is the "witness," who observes the changes taking place in → *prakriti*, although the universe comes to be only through the union of *purusha* and *prakriti*. In → Vedānta, *purusha* is identical with *ātman* and hence also with *brahman*.

Purusha in its plural form refers to male gods or active divine forces. → Agni is the divine *purusha*, Purusha-Nārāyana is the creator god → Brahmā.

Purushārtha 🅷 (Puruṣārtha), Skt., lit. "goal (*artha*) of the human being (*purusha*)"; the four goals toward which human life may be directed: *artha* (wealth), *kāma* (desire), *dharma* (righteousness, duty), and *moksha* (liberation).

Purusha-Sūkta 🅷 (Puruṣa-Sūkta), Skt., lit. "the song of Purusha"; one of the late hymns of the *Rigveda* (10.90); it is the only one to mention the four castes (→ *varna*). According to Paul Deussen, this hymn forms the conclusion of the philosophy of the *Rigveda*.

In the "Song of Purusha," the creation of the world is described as a sacrifice brought by the gods. As sacrificial offering they took the Primal Person (→ *purusha*), whose limbs were dissected according to ritual tradition; from these limbs emerged the various parts of the world.

Purusha-Yajña 🅷 (Puruṣa-Yajña), Skt., lit. *purusha*: "person," *yajña*: "sacrifice"; the great sacrifice made by man in offering his soul to the Divine.

Purushottama 🅷 (Puruṣottama), or *para-purusha* or *uttama-brahman*, Skt., lit. "highest spirit, highest soul"; a term used to refer to the highest Self. The Self and nature, all being and becoming, all activity and silence in this world are the self-perception of *purushottama* and his manifestation as energy. He is greater than the imperishable (*akshara*) and the perishable (*kshara*) and yet includes these opposites.

Pūrva 🅷 Skt., lit. "earlier than, beginning with"; in Sanskrit literature one encounters repeatedly the expressions *pūrva* and *uttara* ("later than, following, better, higher"). These terms may refer, first, simply to chronological order. However, they point to a deeper meaning. *Pūrva*-texts are almost invariably related to the preparation for the attainment of higher knowledge. Almost all religions have acknowledged the need for such preparation. Most often it consists of ritual worship, but even logical thinking can constituite such preparation, as it develops clarity. If such activity is used for its own ends, however, it becomes an impediment to the higher development to which later (*uttara-*) texts are devoted.

Pūrva-Mīmāmsā 🅷 (Pūrva-Mīmāṃsā), Skt., lit. *pūrva*: "earlier," *mīmāmsā*: "investigation"; one of the six → *darshanas*, dealing with the subject matter of ritual. It preceeds the → Uttara-Mīmāmsā, not only chronologically but in an even more important sense: the purifying action of ritual serves as preparation for the attainment of knowledge (the content of Uttara-Mīmāmsa; see also → Mīmāmsā). The sage → Jaimini is regarded as the founder of Pūrva-Mīmāmsā.

Pūshan 🅷 (Pūṣan), Skt., from *push*: "feed, maintain, further, reveal"; a deity who is often mentioned in the Vedas; many hymns are dedicated to him.

The *Taittirīya-Brāhmana* states that as → Prajāpati created living beings, Pūshan nourished them. In later texts he is identified with the sun or referred to as the brother of → Indra. Pūshan is toothless, since, as the Purānas relate, Shiva in his manifestation as → Rudra once interrupted the sacrificial rites of the gods and on that occasion knocked out Pūshan's teeth.

Pushkara 🅷 (Puṣkara), Skt., lit. "blue lotus"; epithet for → Krishna and → Shiva.

One of the seven mythical continents (Dvīpa), which radiate like the petals of a lotus blossom from the cosmic mountain → Meru and are washed by the waters of seven mythical oceans consisting of salt water, sugar syrup, wine, clarified butter, curds, milk, and fresh water.

Pu-tai 🅱 🆉 Chin., lit. "hempen sack"; Chinese monk said to have lived in the 10th century. His name comes from his wandering through the towns with a hempen beggar's sack on his back. Countless stories are associated with Pu-tai. They depict him as a wonder-working eccentric in whose actions the mind of Ch'an (Zen) is expressed. Only at the time of his death did he reveal his true identity as an incarnation of the future buddha → Maitreya. In Chinese monasteries he is represented as the → Laughing Buddha. Pu-tai is the embodiment of the ideal of Ch'an Buddhism as represented in the *Ten Oxherding Pictures* (→ *Jū-gyū-no-zu*).

Pu-tai, painted by Yin-t'o-lo (14th century)

Pu-tai, whose real name was Ch'i-tz'u, lived in what is now the province of Chekiang. He was highly regarded by the people, since he could predict the weather. If he went to sleep on a bridge or on the street, one could expect good weather. On the other hand, if he wore sandals and looked for shelter, one could count on rain.

His character showed the love of paradox that is typical of Ch'an. To the question how old he was, for example, he would answer, "As old as space." Once when he was in the middle of the marketplace someone asked him what he was doing there. He answered, "I'm looking for people." His person was also surrounded by a sense of the miraculous. He could sleep while snow was falling and no snow would land on him. The pronouncement he made, according to tradition, at the time of his death, revealed his identity as an incarnation of the buddha Maitreya:

Maitreya, truly Maitreya,
Countless times reborn,
From time to time appearing among men,
But by the men of the time unrecognized.

He is said to have reappeared after his death in other parts of China. Gradually monks and laymen, aware of his popularity among the people, began to make pictures of the monk with the hempen sack. The figure of the Laughing Buddha developed out of this. This figure is to be found today in every Chinese monastery.

Pūtanā **H**, a female demon, the daughter of → Bali. She attempted to kill the infant → Krishna by offering him her poisoned breast, but he seized it and sucked out her life instead. This legend, like so many others, conceals a deep symbolism. Pūtanā, the demonic ego that comes from a good family (daughter of the virtuous king Bali), wants to absorb or annihilate the Divine, which the ego takes to be slight in substance (symbolized by the infant). But the reverse takes place: the divine element, the stronger of the two, absorbs the ego and destroys it.

P'u-t'i-ta-mo **Z** Chin. for → Bodhidharma

P'u-t'i-ta-mo-ssu-hsing-lun **Z** (Jap., *Bodaidaruma shigyōron*); an early written work of Ch'an (Zen), which is attributed to → Bodhidharma, the first patriarch of Ch'an (Zen).

P'u-t'o-shan **B** a mountain island in the East China Sea (Chekiang Province), one of the → four famous mountains of China. It is one of the most important centers of Buddhism in China and is considered to be the holy place of the bodhisattva Kuan-yin (→ Avalokiteshvara).

A number of legends explain how P'u-t'o-shan came to be the holy place of Kuan-yin. The name of the island derives from *Potalaka*, an island in the Indian Ocean known as a resort of Avalokiteshvara. In 847 an Indian monk glimpsed in a cave on P'u-t'o-shan a likeness of the bodhisattva. Thereupon he named the island *Potalaka*, which became *P'u-t'o-shan* in Chinese.

According to another legend, around 850 a monk on the island burned all his fingers. Kuan-yin heard his cries of pain. She appeared to the monk and expounded the teaching to him.

A very popular legend tells of a Japanese monk who wanted to bring a Kuan-yin statue from → Wu-t'ai-shan back to his homeland. On the return journey his ship was overtaken by a storm on the high seas. He vowed before the image of Kuan-yin to build a monastery should he be saved and come to land. The ship, as though steered by an unseen hand, headed for P'u-t'o-shan, where the monk was able to go ashore safely. In gratitude he built the Pu-chi monastery. Since that time Kuan-yin has been venerated here as the patroness of seafarers and travelers.

Q

Question and answer Z → *mondō*

R

Rādhā H , or Rādhikā; the playmate of → Krishna, the best known of the → *gopīs* of Vrindāvan. The motif of the tender loveplay (*rasalīlā*) between Rādhā and Krishna is one that permeates Hinduism at every level, from the physical realm to divine transcendence; it is the eternal play between the individual soul and God, as it is found in the mystic traditions of almost all religions. In Hinduism the play between Rādhā and Krishna is a central theme of the → Vaishnavas, whose path of love (→ Bhakti-Yoga) raises the human feeling of love and surrender (symbolized by Rādhā) to love and surrender to God in the form of Krishna. What spiritual heights such love can attain is demonstrated by the life of → Chaitanya, the great Bengali saint of the sixteenth century, who is still venerated by followers today as an incarnation of Krishna.

Rādhākānta H Skt., lit. "Rādhā's lover"; a name for → Krishna. Many Rādhākānta temples are found in India; they are invariably furnished with pictures or sculptures of → Rādhā and Krishna.

Rādhā-Krishna sects H → Nimbārka

Rādhikā H → Rādhā

Rāga H Skt., lit. "passion, fundamental melody"; Indian musical modes; they express specific moods and are associated with precise times of day.

Rāga-Bhakti H Skt. → *bhakti*

Rāhula B son of the Buddha (→ Siddhārtha Gautama). His mother was → Yasodharā. Rāhula was born just at the time that the Buddha came to his decision to leave his family and seek enlightenment (→ *bodhi*). Rāhula entered the → *sangha* as a child of seven and is thus considered the patron or guardian of novices (→ *shrāmanera*). He was ordained by → Shāriputra. Probably he died very young, long before his father. Rāhula is among the → ten great disciples of the Buddha.

Rāhulabhadra Z sixteenth patriarch of the Indian lineage of Ch'an (→ Zen)

Rājagriha B (Rājagṛha), Skt. (Pali, Rājagaha); a city 70 kilometers southeast of Patna on the Ganges river. It was the capital of → Magadha during the reign of → Bimbisāra. In Rājagriha sixteen monasteries, including the Venuva Monastery built under the patronage of Bimbisāra, stood open to the historical Buddha. → Shākyamuni spent several rainy seasons in Rājagriha. Here also the First Buddhist → Council took place shortly after the death of the Buddha. According to tradition the texts of → Sūtra-pitaka and the → Vinaya-pitaka were established at this council.

Rājarishi H (Rājarṣi), Skt., lit. "kingly sage"); a sage belonging to the warrior caste, a → *kshatriya*, who because of his holy life on earth became a → *rishi* and entered → Indra's heaven as a demigod. There were several such *rājarishis*, the best-known being → Janaka.

Rajas H Skt.; the second of the three → *gunas*; it appears in → *prakriti* as activity, striving, greed, restlessness, and daring; it is the force that can overcome indolence (→ *tamas*). When *rajas* dominates a person's deeds and thoughts, he is referred to as *rajasika*, that is, permeated by *rajas*.

Rajatādri H → Kailāsa

Rāja-Yoga H Skt., lit. "the royal yoga"; one of the four most important yogic paths toward union with God; its system is presented by → Patañjali in his → *Yoga-Sūtra*. (The term "Rāja-Yoga," however, was conceived long after Patañjali's time.)

Rāja-Yoga contains the following eight steps: (1) → *yama*; (2) → *niyama*. These two steps encompass various ethical and moral practices, considered as prerequisites. (3) → *Āsana,* bodily poses; their aim is to find a position in which the practice of concentration is not disturbed by the body; (4) → *prānāyāma,* breath control, practiced because the breath greatly influences one's thoughts and emotional states. The third and fourth stage gave rise to the development of → Hatha-Yoga. (5) *Pratyāhāra,* the withdrawal of the senses from sense objects, so that the mind is not diverted; (6) → *dhāranā,* or concentration, the ability to rest the mind on an object without straying or going out of control, (7) → *dhyāna,* or → meditation. At this level, it is said, the mind no longer projects its own concepts onto the object of meditation, but instead merges with the object itself. (8) → *Samādhi,* also known as → *turīya,* the supraconscious state, in which duality and the manifest world no longer exist. An introduction to Rāja-Yoga is found in Vivekānanda 1955c.

Rakan B Z Jap. for → lohan

Rakan Dōkan Z Jap. for → Lo-han Tao-hsien

Rakan Keijin Z Jap. for → Lo-han Kuei-ch'en

Rākshasa H (Ṛakṣasa), fem. Rākshashī, Skt.; more or less evil spirits. Three types are distinguished: (1) harmless beings such as the → *yakshas*; (2) titans, or enemies of the gods; (3) demons and devils, who inhabit cemeteries and harass human beings.

The leader of the third type of *rākshasa* was → Rāvana. The origin of the *rākshasas* is explained in various ways. Some say they emerged from → Brahmā's foot. According to the *Vishnu-Purāna,* they are descendents of → Kashyapa. The *Rāmāyana* relates that God created the water and the *rākshasas* to protect it. In the old epics they were the original inhabitants of India who were subjugated by the Aryans. Many texts exist that describe the individual characteristics and actions of the *rākshasas.*

Rakusu Z Jap., a rectangular piece of fabric composed of "patches," which is worn on a cord around the neck. It symbolizes the patchwork robe of → Shākyamuni Buddha and his disciples and is worn by monks and lay followers of Mahāyāna Buddhism. The *rakusu* is conferred upon one when taking the → *jukai,* the initiation into Buddhism in which one takes the Buddhist vows (→ *jūjūkai*).

Rāma H, or Rāmachandra, Skt.; an → *avatāra* who appeared at the end of the *tretā-yuga* (→ *yuga*) as the seventh incarnation of Vishnu. His significance as an *avatāra* lies in the fact that he developed the quality of → *sattva* in humanity. Rāma and his wife → Sītā are venerated by Hindus as the ideal of man and wife. Rāma's inner, spiritual path is sketched by the legendary sage → Vālmīki in his → *Yoga-Vasishtha.* Above all, however, Rāma is the hero of the monumental epic poem → *Rāmāyana,* whose basic structure is also ascribed to Vālmīki.

Rāma was born as the eldest son of King → Dasharatha of Ayodhyā and his principal wife, Kausalyā. Together with his three brothers he visited the court of King → Janaka. Janaka possessed a bow that had been Shiva's. Whoever could string the bow would be given his daughter Sītā for a wife. Rama strung and broke the bow and married Sitā. As he was to inherit his father's throne, his stepmother, → Kaikeyī, contrived a plot against him, so that her son Bharata became king and Rāma was banished from the kingdom, accompanied by Sītā and his half brother → Lakshmana. Sītā was then abducted by the demon king → Rāvana and taken to → Lankā. In the war that followed, Rāma was aided by the monkey king → Hanumat and succeeded in taking Lankā, killing Rāvana, and freeing Sītā. He later became king of Ayodhyā.

The name Rāma is occasionally used to refer to → Parashu-Rāma, the sixth incarnation of Vishnu, or to → Balarāma, Krishna's older brother.

Rāmakrishna H 1836–1886, a Bengali spiritual leader, worshiped today by many Hindus as an → *avatāra* (divine incarnation). Just as the Hindus consider Jesus to be the *avatāra* of love to humanity, so they view Shrī Rāmakrishna as the *avatāra* who from his own experience bore witness that all religions can lead human beings to God-realization. His most important disciples were Svāmi → Vivekānanda and Svāmi → Brahmānanda.

Shrī Rāmakrishna was born Gadādhar Chattopādhyāyā in Kamarpukur, a village in West Bengal. His parents were poor, and he recieved little schooling. In 1856 he became a priest at the Kālī temple of Dakshineshvara. For twelve years, under the guidance of various gurus, he submitted himself to spiritual practices of assorted religious systems, including Christianity and Islam. Each direction led him to illumination, so that he could declare on the basis of personal experience that the followers of all religions alike could realize the ultimate reality if their surrender to God was sufficiently intense. In one vision he recognized Christ as a divine incarnation. Through the power of his own spiritual realization and with the help of his many disciples, he brought about a renewal of Hinduism, which had lost its influence in the face of material progress and the Christian influence of the British colonial government. In 1886 he initiated several disciples as monks and thus laid the cornerstone for the → Rāmakrishna monastic orders that were subsequently established by → Vivekānanda.

Rāmakrishna Order 🅷 , a monastic order in the tradition of → Shankara; its cornerstone was laid by Shrī → Rāmakrishna shortly before his death (1886), as he initiated several of his chief disciples into monastic life. The actual founding of the order took place on the eve of December 25, 1887, when a number of Rāmakrishna's disciples determined to take up monastic life and founded a monastery under the leadership of Svāmi → Vivekānanda, whose personality was particularly suited to this function. The young monks discovered only later that this had taken place on Christmas Eve, which they saw as a confirmation of their close connection to Christianity, based on Rāmakrishna's spiritual experiences. The main seat of the order is the Belur Math, on the Ganges near Calcutta. In addition, 200 monasteries are scattered throughout India.

In 1900, Svāmi → Brahmānanda, Rāmakrishna's second chief disciple, took over the leadership of the order until his death (1922). He laid stress on the spiritual development of the monks, and under his guidance a number of great spiritual personalities developed. The order's name "Rāmakrishna's Math and Mission" is to some extent misleading, since the order's mission, following Rāmakrishna's instructions, is not assistance offered to one's fellow beings out of pity but the active service of God dwelling in each one of them. Hence the monks are to lead an active life of social service as well as one of contemplation, and many of hte Indian monasteries and centers of the order run hospitals, schools, orphanages, ambulance corps, dispensaries, and libraries.

The monks (*svāmis*) of the Rāmakrishna order visit other countries only at the direct invitation of others; when invited, they come as guest lecturers offering spiritual help and instruction to all seekers, whatever their creed. Usually Vedānta centers or societies spring up around these monks; at present there are approximately twenty such organizations outside India.

Rāmalīlā 🅷 , or Rāmlīlā, Skt., lit. "the play *(līlā)* of Rāma"; a major Hindu festival celebrated annually in North India. It is held in the honor of → Rāma, whose life is shown in scenes performed during the festival.

Rāmana Mahar(i)shi 🅷 1879–1950; one of the greatest spiritual teachers of modern-day India. At the age of seventeen, Shrī Rāmana Maharshi attained a profound experience of his true self (→ *ātman*) without the guidance of a guru and thereafter remained conscious of his identity with the Absolute (→ *brahman*) at all times. After some years of silent reclusion at the holy mountain Arunāchala in South India, he finally began again to speak and to reply to the questions put to him by spiritual seekers all over the world. He followed no particular traditional system of teaching, but rather spoke directly from his own experience of nonduality (→ *advaita*). Rāmana Maharshi wrote virtually nothing; his "teaching" took the form of conversations with visitors seeking his guidance (as transcribed by followers), the brief instructions he left with his followers, and a few religious songs. His method of instruction was to direct the questioner again and again to his true self and to recommend, as a path to realization, a tireless form of self-inquiry featuring the question "Who am I?"

Q: Svāmi, who am I? How can I attain salvation?

R.M.: Through constant self-inquiry with "Who am I?" you will come to know yourself and thereby attain salvation.

Q: Who am I?

R.M.: The true I, or the Self, is not the gross body. Nor is it the five senses of perception, or the organs of action. Neither is it *prāna*, or the mind, nor the state of deep sleep in which nothing more is known.

Q: If I am none of these, then who am I?

R.M.: After all this is negated and you can say "I am not this," what remains is the true I, and that is awareness.

Q: What is the nature of this awareness?

R.M.: It is → *Sat-Chit-Ānanda*, in which there is no longer the least trace of I-thought. It is named *mouna*, silence, or *ātman*, the Self. It is the only thing that really exists. When the triad of world, I, and God is viewed as three separate totalities, they are illusory notions. (Trans. from A. Osborne, *Rāmana Maharshi und der Weg der Selbsterkenntnis.*)

The transcribed conversations of Rāmana Maharshi are known among spiritual seekers the world over and are prized for their great inspirational power, which transcends all religious differences. (See Bibliography.)

Shrī Rāmana Maharshi was born on December 29, 1879, in Tiruchuli, Tamil Nadu (South India), the son of Shundaram Ayyar, a scribe and country lawyer; he was given the name Venkatarāman, abbreviated as Rāmana. At the age of seventeen, he suddenly had an experience of death in which he realized that the body dies but the consciousness is not touched by death. "I" am immortal consciousness. "All these," he later reported, "were no idle speculations. They went through me like a powerful, living truth that I experienced directly, almost without thinking. 'I' [i.e., the true I or Self] was reality, the only reality in this momentary state. All conscious activity that was related to my body flowed into this 'I.' From that moment, all attention was drawn as if by powerful magic to the 'I' or the 'Self.' The fear of death was permanently extinguished. From this time on I remained fully absorbed in the 'Self.' "

After this experience, Venkatarāman lost all interest

in things of the world and ultimately left home without his parents' permission to find his way to the holy mountain of Arunāchala, whose name had fascinated him earlier. There he spent several years in silent Self-absorption, first in a dark corner of a temple in Tiruvannāmalai, at the foot of the mountain, later in various caves on the mountain itself; during this time he totally neglected all care of the body and at one point was virtually chewed up by insects. Even when his mother sought him out and attempted to get him to return home, he did not break his silence but rather acted as though he did not see her. When his followers begged him to make some response to his mother's desperate pleas, he wrote the following impersonal words on a scrap of paper:

"The fate of the soul is determined in accordance with its → *prārabdha-karma.* What is not meant to happen will not happen, however much you wish it. What is meant to happen will happen no matter what you do to prevent it. This is certain. Therefore, the best path is to remain silent."

When Rāmana Maharshi later broke his silence and began to respond to questions about the path to the Self, an → ashram grew up around him in Tiruvannāmalai. There, in 1950, ill with cancer, Rāmana Maharshi passed into → *mahāsamādhi.* The site continues to be visited by spiritual seekers of every nationality as a place of pilgrimage where the presence of the great saint can still be felt.

Rāmānanda 🅗, great saint of the thirteenth century. He was the first to revive the → *bhakti* movement in North India as a reaction against the political conquest of India by the Muslims.

Rāmānanda's liberal views on caste and religious affiliation are seen in his famous statement: "No one should ask about another's caste or hesitate to eat with him. Whoever worships Hari belings to Hari." In other words, whoever is the child of God (→ Hari) is liberated from caste law and the division between Hindus and Muslims. The poet → Kabīr took up Rāmānanda's ideas and spread them throughout India by means of his popular songs.

Rāmānuja 🅗, ca. 1055–1137, celebrated philosopher and → Vaishnava saint of South India; the founder of the philosophy of → Vishishtādvaita-Vedānta (qualified nondualism). His highest ideal was the love of God (→ *bhakti*) as well as the knowledge that all creatures and all inanimate things alike are "forms of God."

After renouncing the world, Rāmānuja lived in Shrirangam until his death. His famous commentary on the → *Vedānta-Sūtra,* the *Shrībhāshya,* is the classic standard book of the Vaishnavas. He also wrote a commentary on the → *Bhagavad-Gītā* and various treatises on his philosophy (→ *Vedāntasāra, Vedārtha-Samgraha, Vedāntadīpa,* etc.).

Rāmasetu 🅗 Skt., lit. "Rāma's bridge"; a coral bridge, which according to legend was built for → Rāma by Nala, chief of the monkeys, to provide a way to reach Ceylon from the Indian subcontinent and conquer → Rāvana. This event is described in the literary epic *Setubandha* ("Bridge-building"), which is presumed to have been composed by → Kālidāsa and King Pravarasena I. The rocks that lie in the channel between India and Ceylon are now known as "Adam's Bridge."

Rāmatāpanīya-Upanishad 🅗 Skt.; an → Upanishad from the *Atharvaveda* in which → Rāma is revered as the highest god and is celebrated by the saint → Yajñavalkya.

Rāmāyana 🅗 (Rāmāyaṇa), Skt., lit. "The Life Story of Rāma"; the oldest epic in Sanskrit literature, attributed to the legendary saint → Vālmīki. The oldest, purest version stems from North India (fourth century B.C.E.) and underwent substantial revisions in Bengal over the course of subsequent centuries. The work contains 24,000 couplets arranged in seven chapters (*kānda*); it describes the life of → Rāma and → Sītā, Sitā's abduction by → Rāvana, the battle with the demons, the return to Ayodhyā, and finally their death and ascent to heaven. The story's adventures, described in broad, dramatic strokes, and its many outstanding characters have made it, next to the *Māhābharata,* the most important source for all genres of Indian literature.

Rāma and Sītā in a chariot; scene from the *Rāmāyana.* (Sandstone relief from Cambodia, 11th century)

The *Rāmāyana* is still widely venerated today in India and Southeast Asia. One of its introductory verses states: "He who reads and repeats the holy, life-giving *Rāmāyana* is liberated from all sin and attains heaven."

The seven *kāndas* are as follows: (1) "Bālalakānda," the story of Rama's childhood; (2) "Ayodhyākānda," Rama's life in the capital city Ayodhyā and his banishment; (3) "Aranyakānda," life in the forest and the abduction of Sītā; (4) "Kishkindhyākānda," Rāma's life with his monkey allies; (5) "Sundarakānda," Rāma's crossing over the bridge to Ceylon; (6) "Yuddhakānda," the battle with Rāvana, the demon king's death, the rescue of Sītā and the return to Ayodhyā; (7) "Uttarakānda," Rāma's life in Ayodhyā, Sītā's banishment, their reunion, death, and ascent to heaven.

Rāmeshvara 🅷 (Rāmeśara), or Rāmeshvaram, Skt.; famous temple built to Shiva and a site of pilgrimage at the southernmost tip of India. Here → Rāma is said to have erected the great → *linga* with the name Rāmeshvara.

Rām-Nam 🅷 Skt., lit. "Homage to Rāma"; a worship service with ancient Hindu songs said to call forth the presence of → Rāma, → Sītā, and → Hanumat. It is held on → Ekādashī.

Rāmprasād 🅷, or Rāmaprasād, 1723–1803, one of the most important Bengali saints and poets of the eighteenth century; a worshiper of the Divine Mother → Kālī, whose songs are sung throughout Bengal even today and are viewed as a source of inspiration for spiritual seekers.

It is said that after the death of his father, Rāmprasād became the bookkeeper for a wealthy man in order to support the family. However, his thoughts were so totally occupied with the Divine Mother that he entered in the account books poems that came to him while he was at work. When his employer was checking the books one day and discovered the poems, he was so moved that instead of reprimanding Rāmprasād he bequeathed to him an income that would provide for his family, so that he could devote himself entirely to spiritual life.

Rankei Dōryū 🅩 Jap. for → Lan-ch'i Tao-lung

Rasa 🅷 Skt., lit. "enjoyment, passion"; the enjoyment of spiritual delight in a state of ecstatic union with the Divine. It is not to be compared with the enjoyment of sense objects, and eludes any description by the use of reason.

Rasalīlā 🅷 Skt. → Rādhā

Rathayātrā 🅷 Skt., lit. *ratha*: "carriage," *yātrā*: "procession"; a festival held in the month of Āshad (mid-June/July), in which the image of a divinity is driven around in a carriage and bystanders attempt to pull themselves into the carriage in order to ride along. The best known of such festivals is that held at the → Jagannātha temple in → Puri.

Ratnakūta-sūtra 🅱 Skt., lit. "*Sūtra of the Heap of Jewels*"; one of the oldest sutras of the Mahāyāna. It is one of the → Vaipulya-sūtras and is a collection of forty-nine independent sūtras. It is completely preserved only in Chinese and Tibetan translations. In the *Ratnakūta-sūtra*, the thought of the → Middle Way is developed, which later became the basis for the Mādhyamaka teaching of → Nāgārjuna. It also contains sūtras on transcendental wisdom (→ *Prajñāpāramitā-sūtra*).

Ratnasambhava 🅱 🅩 (Ratnasaṃbhava), Skt., lit. "Jewel-born One"; one of the five transcendent buddhas. He is associated with the earthly buddha Kāshyapa and the transcendent bodhisattva Ratnapāni. Ratnasambhava is usually depicted making the gesture of wish granting (→ mudrā 6), riding on a lion or a horse.

Ratnasambhava with hands in the Varada Mudrā

Rāvana 🅷 (Rāvaṇa), Skt., the demon king of → Lankā (from which city he had driven his half-brother → Kubera) and the leader of the → *rākshasas;* he was able to take on any shape at will. The *Rāmāyana* portrays him as the embodiment of utter evil.

In order to put an end to the terror wrought by Rāvana, Vishnu incarnated as → Rāma. When Rāvana abducted Rāma's wife, Sītā, a great battle ensued. The outcome remained uncertain until Rāma fitted to his bow an arrow fashioned by Brahmā. The arrow pierced Rāvana's breast, flew into the ocean, was cast back up, and returned to Rāma's quiver. Rāvana sank to the ground dead, and the gods exalted Rāma as Vishnu, who had saved them from Rāvana's destruction.

Realization Z → *kenshō*

Rechaka H Skt. → *prānāyāma*

Refuge B → *kyabdro*

Refuge, threefold B Z → *trisharana*, → *sambō*

Release of the burning mouths B (Chin., fang yen-k'ou); ceremony for the dead. The "burning mouths" are a type of hungry ghost (→ *gati*, → *preta*). This ritual, which is of Tantric origin (→ Mi-tsung), is intended to free the hungry ghosts from their torment and to enable them to be reborn as humans or even in the western paradise (→ Sukhāvatī). It is a very popular ceremony. It is held by families for the welfare of their deceased kin and is also performed within the framework of the → Ullambana festival. This tradition is no longer attached to a particular school.

The ceremony of the release of the burning mouths lasts about five hours and takes place in the evening, since it is then that the hungry ghosts can most easily leave their abodes. The participating monks wear red or gold hats in the form of crowns, use various ritual implements, such as → *dorje* and bell and call on the three precious ones (→ *triratna*) for aid. Then through the power of their magical gestures they break down the gates of hell (→ *naraka*), open the mouths of the hungry ghost and pour into them sweet nectar, i.e., water that has been consecrated by the recitation of → mantras. Thereupon the burning mouths take refuge (→ *trisharana*) and the bodhisattva vow. If the ceremony is successful, the hungry ghosts can immediately be reborn as humans or in the western paradise.

This ceremony is still performed today in Taiwan and Hongkong. It derives from the tradition that → Ānanda had a dream about burning mouths. In order to avoid being reborn as one himself and for the sake of saving all the burning mouths, he turned to the Buddha for help, who then recited certain → *dhāranīs* for the hungry ghosts.

Ri-bi Z Jap., lit. "truth, principle [*ri*]–the secret, the subtle [*bi*]; an expression that appears frequently in Zen literature, meaning a kind of cosmic principle. *Ri* here means the absolute truth, the emptiness (Jap., *ku*; Skt., → *shūnyatā*) or "suchness" (→ *tathatā*) of all things as it is experienced in profound enlightenment. This absolute truth manifests itself spontaneously and unobstructedly in endlessly varied ways in the phenomenal world, always in a fashion consonant with the given circumstances. This spontaneous, unobstructed action of *ri* is called *bi*. In many contexts, *ri-bi* also stands for "subject-object."

The paired notions *ri-bi* recall the Tao-te of Taoism, in which → Tao and → *te* are defined quite similarly to *ri* and *bi*.

Riddhi H B (ṛddhi), Skt., lit. "well-being, wealth [also in terms of power]."

H Name of the wife of → Kubera, god of wealth. The name is also used to refer to → Pārvatī, the wife of Shiva.

B (Pali, iddhi); a term for supernatural, magical powers that are a part of → *abhijñā*. It refers primarily to the power to manifest multiple forms of oneself, to transform oneself into another shape, to become invisible, to pass through solid things, to walk on water, to touch the sun and moon, and to scale the highest heaven; the power of spiritual production (to emanate a mind-made body from one's body); the power of pervading knowledge that enables one to remain unharmed in times of peril; and the power of complete concentration.

These abilities are by-products of various meditation and concentration practices. Exhibiting and exploiting these powers is a violation of monastic discipline, and pretending to possess such powers is grounds for dismissal from the community (→ *sangha*, → Vinaya).

Riddhipāda B (ṛddhipāda), Skt. (Pali, iddhipāda), lit. "ways of power." The following four properties, which bring about concentration (→ *samādhi*) and form the basis for the activation of magical powers, are called "components of miraculous power": concentration (1) of intention (chanda), (2) of will power or exertion (→ *vīrya*), (3) of the mind (→ *chitta*), and (4) of inquisitiveness and daring (*mīmāmsā*).

Rigveda H (Ṛgveda), Skt., lit. "The knowledge *(veda)* laid down in verses *(rig)*"; the oldest and most extensive of the four Vedic text anthologies (→ Vedas); also the oldest evidence of Indian literature. The work was conceived sometime between the twelfth and eighth centuries B.C.E.; it comprises 1,028 hymns, a total of 10,580 verses arranged in ten "song cycles" (mandalas). Most are associated with the name of a particular → *rishi* who is also considered to be the author of the text (e.g., Bharadvāja, → Vāmadeva, → Vasishtha, → Vishvāmitra). Above all, the *Rigveda* contains the hymns that were recited by the *hotar* (the "caller"), one of the four chief priests at the sacrificial rites, in order to invite the gods to pertake of the sacrifice.

Most of the hymns are directed to personifications of natural forces; these are glorified as divinities (e.g., Agni, Indra, Soma, the → Asvins and → Maruts) and thanked for the fruits of the earth and their personal protection. The texts are written in an archaic form of Sanskrit that is extremely difficult to interpret and since the fifth century has given rise to various commentaries (→ Yāska, → Nirtuka). "In spite of all its difficulties the *Rigveda* is one of the most important linguistic, mythological-religious, literary, and cultural documents of humanity. It has maintained its vital religious force in present-day Hinduism, and the inviolable sacrality of its every word has made possible the transmission of its text unaltered through the centuries and is still held as binding by the people of India today." (William Halbfass)

Rime 🅱 (ris-med), Tib., lit. "unbiased"; term for a current in → Tibetan Buddhism that had its origin in east Tibet in the 19th century. It arose from the need to overcome sectarian bias in the evaluation of the doctrinal traditions of the various schools and to accept each tradition on its own merits. The movement was initiated by the → Sakyapa teacher Jamyang Khyentse Wangpo (1820–92). Among his many students, the most important were Chogyur Dechen Lingpa (1829–70) and → Jamgon Kongtrul (1811–99). The fundamental attitude of unbiasedness of the movement is most evident in the person and work of Jamgon Kongtrul. The influence of the Rime movement is still palpable today, especially in the → Karma Kagyu and → Nyingmapa schools. The main concern of the first Rime teachers and the succeeding generations of their students was a clear structuring of doctrinal and practical materials, based on the example of the → Gelugpa school.

From the beginning Tibetan Buddhism has exhibited the two fundamental tendencies of religious tolerance and irreconcilable sectarian strife. The confrontation between the → *bön* teaching and Buddhism at the time of the first spreading of Buddhism in Tibet was marked by a strict concern for mutual delimitation, as was the confrontation between the two religions in the 11th and 12th centuries, particularly in west and central Tibet. A good example of these struggles can be found in the biography of → Milarepa.

On the other hand, a climate of mutual understanding also prevailed, along with an effort towards synthesis. Such an attitude predominated especially in the southern provinces of Tibet and in the east. It was in east Tibet that the Rime movement eventually developed, its appearance being primarily a result of a strengthening of the authority of the Nyingmapa school. This school had developed as an independent tradition by the 14th century through the discovery of so-called "treasures" (→ *terma*). In the following centuries it was the victim of various persecutions and had to defend the authenticity of its teachings. However, through the person of Jigme Lingpa (1730–98) the school gained great influence in east Tibet, which was strengthened further by the founder of the Rime movement, who was regarded as an incarnation (→ *tulku*) of Jigme Lingpa.

However, the process within the Rime movement of reviving transmissions of teachings that had been thought lost and providing them with fresh commentary also embraced the traditions of the other schools. In the Rime collections of texts, works of the Kagyupa, Sakyapa, → Kadampa, and → Chöd lineages are also found. The Rime teachers also advocated revival of the *bön* teachings. In addition to their religious activities they also found time to be politically active as mediators with the central government in Lhasa.

Rinchen Sangpo 🅱 (rin-chen bzan-po), Tib., "Beautiful Jewel"; 958–1055, important personality in → Tibetan Buddhism, whose activity inaugurated the second spreading of the Buddhist teaching in Tibet, with west Tibet as the center. According to tradition he founded 108 different monasteries, of which the most famous was Toling. He achieved renown, however, as a translator of Tantric works. These translations were referred to as "new" to distinguish them from the translations of the Old school (→ Nyingmapa). A detailed account of Rinchen Sangpo's meeting with → Atīsha, whom he accepted as his teacher after initial doubts, has been handed down.

Rinne 🆉 Jap., lit. "wheel [*rin*] that turns in circles [*e*]"; the "wheel of life." This refers to the wheel that spins as the cycle of birth and death (→ samsāra) and the six realms of existence (→ *gati*).

Rinpoche 🅱 Tib. → lama

Rinzai Gigen 🆉 Jap. for → Lin-chi I-hsuan

Rinzai school 🆉 (Chin., Lin-chi-tsung; Jap., Rinzai-shū); one of the most important schools of Ch'an (Zen). It originated with the great Chinese Ch'an master → Lin-chi I-hsuan (Jap., Rinzai Gigen) and was one of the → *goke-shichishū*. At the beginning of the 11th century the Rinzai school split into two lineages, the Rinzai Yōgi lineage (→ Yōgi school) and the Rinzai Ōryō lineage (→ Ōryō school).

The Rinzai school is one of the two schools of Zen still active in Japan. At the end of the 12th century → Eisai Zenji brought Rinzai Ōryō Zen to Japan. It was the first school of Zen to reach Japan; however, it soon died out. The Rinzai Zen that was to flourish anew in Japan was that deriving from the Chinese and Japanese masters of the strict Rinzai Yōgi lineage. This lineage produced great Japanese masters like → Ben'en (also Shōichi Kokushi, 1202–80), → Shōmyō (also Daiō Kokushi, 1235–1309), → Myōchō Shūhō (also Daitō Kokushi, 1282–1338), and Musō Soseki (also Musō Kokushi, 1275–1351), who in the early period of Zen in Japan made essential contributions to the spread of this way of spiritual training. Also later great masters like → Bassui Zenji, → Ikkyū Sōjun, and the reformer of Rinzai Zen in Japan, → Hakuin Zenji, belonged to this lineage of Rinzai Zen.

In the Rinzai school, primarily → *kanna* Zen and thus → kōan practice are stressed as an especially fast way to the realization of → enlightenment (also → *kenshō*, → satori). The → Sōtō school, the other school of Zen still active today in Japan, more heavily stresses → *mokushō* Zen and thus also the practice of → *shikantaza.*

Rinzai-shū 🅉 Jap. → Rinzai school

Rishi 🄷 (Ṛṣi), Skt.; general term used to refer to seers, saints, and inspired poets; in particular it refers to the seers, known as the seven great *rishis*, to whom the hymns of the → Vedas were revealed.

The → *Shatapatha-Brāhmana* names the seven great *rishis* as Gotama, Bharadvāja, Vishvāmitra, Janmadagni, Vasishtha, Kashyapa, and Atri. The → *Mahābhārata* gives the seven as Marīchi, Atri, Angiras, Pulaha, Kratu, Pulastya, and Vasishtha. The *Vishnu-Purāna* adds Bhrigu and Daksha and calls them the nine *Brahma-Rishis.* In addition to these great *rishis*, there are many others.

Risshō Koseikai 🄱 Jap., lit. "Society for the Establishment of Justice and Community for the Rise [of Buddha]"; modern Buddhist folk movement of Japan, which is based on the teachings of → Nichiren. It was founded in 1938 by Niwano Nikkyō (b. 1906) and Naganuma Myōkō (1889–1957).

Characteristic of the Risshō Koseikai is the association of the original Buddhist teaching with faith in the salvational power of the → *Lotus Sūtra*. The focus of worship is the Buddha → Shākyamuni as embodiment of the transcendent truth. Practice consists in recitation of the name of the *Lotus Sūtra*. The Rissho Koseikai administers organizations for social assistance and education and has its own publishing facilities and journals.

The practice places emphasis on the development of the personality of the adherent, based on the model of the bodhisattva ideal. A means to this end are group discussions (*hōza*) in which an opportunity for self-expression and guidance is offered; these have been compared to Christian confession. They are said to bring about inner purification and to act as a stimulus to benevolent action. Another component of the practice is daily veneration of ancestors.

Rita 🄷 (Ṛta), Skt., lit. "truth, divine order"; the living truth that flows and works directly from the Divine.

Ritsu school 🄱 Jap., lit. "discipline school"; school of Japanese Buddhism that developed out of the original Chinese form of this school (→ Lu-tsung). It was brought to Japan in the year 754 by the Chinese monk → Chien-chen (Jap., Ganjin). The school stresses the literal observance of the → Vinaya rules for Buddhist life. It attaches special value to the correct performance of the → ordination ceremony. The Ritsu school survives until the present but has never been of great importance. This can be attributed to a strong tradition of less literal observance of discipline in the other Buddhist schools. These schools attach less value to the rule itself than to the spirit behind it. Another factor in the minimal influence of the Ritsu school was the appearance of a Mahāyāna ordination ceremony in the → Tendai school.

Emperor Shōmu (724–48), who strongly favored the diffusion of Buddhism in Japan, wanted to bring a competent teacher from China to Japan, who would convey deep and thorough knowledge of the disciplinary rules to Japanese monks and nuns. After the arrival of Chien-chen in Japan, the emperor had a monastery specially built for him with an ordination hall attached. The monk → Saichō, who was ordained in this monastery, nevertheless later declared this kind of Hīnayāna ordination not valid and developed a "bodhisattva ordination" according to Tendai teachings, which was purely Mahāyāna and less strictly formal. However, because of strong protest on the part of the other schools, this way of consecrating a monk was not recognized until after Saichō's death. Then it was recognized by imperial decree. Later, other schools, such as → Zen and → Jōdo, adopted this form of ordination.

Rō 🅉 Jap., lit. "twelfth month [of the lunar calendar]"; in ancient China it was customary to make a ceremonial offering, called *la* (Jap., *rō*) at the end of the year. Buddhist monks adopted this term as a designation for the end of the → *ango*, the summer training period. Finally the word took on the meaning of "the number of years a monk has spent in a monastery." Thus it is said that a monk already has so many *ro*.

Rōba Zen 🅉 Jap., lit. "grandmother Zen"; a

term for a particularly mild style of Zen training, the opposite of the "hammer and tongs" method (→ *kentsui*). This mild form of training is used by a Zen master either because it is more appropriate than the "hard" method for certain students, or because, as a result of his character, it is too difficult for him to be as hard on his students as perhaps is necessary.

In the latter case, the expression *rōba Zen* contains a definite, though not unsympathetic, reproach toward the master who "has a soft heart, like a grandmother's for her grandchildren." Ultimately, after all, the supposed harshness of the *kentsui* method is nothing other than an expression of loving compassion if it actually helps Zen students to find *real* happiness and peace of mind (→ *anjin*).

Rōhatsu Z also rōhachi, Jap., lit. "the eighth [day] of the twelfth month"; the day, especially celebrated in Zen, on which according to tradition → Shākyamuni Buddha, sitting in meditation (→ *zazen*) under the → Bodhi-tree, at the first glimpse of the morning star, attained enlightenment.

The written character for *rō*, taken precisely, means the twelfth month of the Asiatic lunar calendar; in present-day Japan, however, *rōhatsu* is nevertheless celebrated on the eighth of December, which only rarely coincides with the eighth day of the twelfth month of the lunar calendar.

Rōhatsu-sesshin Z Jap.; a → *sesshin* done in Zen monasteries in commemoration of the Buddha's enlightenment (→ *rōhatsu*). This sesshin generally runs from the first of December until the morning of the eighth. The last night, on which, unlike on the other nights, the monks do not lie down to sleep, is the *tetsuya*, which roughly means "[sitting] the whole night through."

Rokudo Z Jap. for the "six realms of existence," → *gati*.

Rokuso Z Jap., lit. "Sixth Patriarch"; a popular name for → Hui-neng, the sixth patriarch of Ch'an (Zen) in China. (Also → *soshigata*).

Rokuso Daishi Z Jap. for → Liu-tsu-ta-shih

Rōnō Sotō Z Jap. for → Lao-na Tsu-teng

Rōshi Z Jap., lit. "old [venerable] master"; title of a Zen master. Traditional training in Zen takes place under a *rōshi*, who can be a monk or layperson, man or woman. It is the task of the *rōshi* to lead and inspire his students on the way to → enlightenment (also → *kenshō*, → satori), for which, naturally, the prerequisite is that he himself has experienced profound enlightenment (→ *daigo-tettai*).

In ancient times the title of *roshi* was hard to obtain. The public (rather than the person him- or herself) gave this title to a person who had realized the → dharma of a buddha through his own direct experience, who was able to live this realization in everyday life (→ *mujōdō-no-taigen*), and was capable of leading others to the same experience. In addition, at least a pure, unshakable character and a mature personality were required. To become a fully developed *rōshi*, many years of training under a Zen master were indispensible. Following profound enlightenment and the conferral of the seal of confirmation (→ *inka-shōmei*) by his master, further years of ripening through "dharma contests" (→ *hossen*) with other masters were also customary. In present-day Japan, where true masters have become rare, the standards are less strict. Unfortunately for the authentic Zen tradition, Zen monks are often addressed as *roshi* merely out of respect for their position and age.

Rōshō-no-memmoku Z Jap., lit. "countenance of a newborn girl"; Zen expression for the state of childlike innocence, the "first naturalness." This state is generally soon lost in the course of a person's life and the person falls into → delusion. In order to overcome this delusion, the experience of → *honrai-no-memmoku* is necessary, as well as the deepening of the experience of → enlightenment and the realization of it in everyday life (→ *mujōdō-no-taigen*). If a person realizes enlightenment to the extent that he "no longer leaves any trace behind" (→ *mosshōseki*), then he has won through to a new innocence, the "second naturalness." This innocence is on a "higher level" than the first childlike innocence and distinguishes itself from the latter in that it cannot be lost. Basically, with this "second naturalness" the primordial naturalness is discovered which existed even before the first, but of which the person until this discovery has been unaware.

Ru-chia T Chin. → Confucianism

Rudra H , Skt., lit. "the howling one, the terrible"; in the Vedas, Rudra has many characteristics and many names. He is the howling, terrible god, the god of storms; at times he is identified with the god of fire. Rudra is later identical wih → Shiva in his aspect as destroyer.

In one aspect, Rudra is the destructive divinity who brings illness to human beings and cattle; in another, he is the god of abundant blessings who helps and heals. He is named Mahādeva in the *White* → *Yajur-veda*. He is the father of the Rudras, or → Maruts.

Rūpadhātu B Skt. → *triloka*

Rūpaloka B Skt. → *triloka*

Ryōga-kyō 🅉 Jap. for → *Lankāvatāra-sūtra*

Ryōgon-kyō 🅉 Jap. for → *Shūrangāma-sūtra*

Ryōkan Daigu 🅉 1758?–1831; Japanese Zen monk of the → Sōtō school. Ryōkan was ordained as a monk at the age of eighteen. After four years of training at a small temple near his home town, he entered the Zen monastery Entsū-ji, the abbot of which was Master Kokusen. After twelve years of training under Master Kokusen, he received from the latter the seal of confirmation (→ *inka-shōmei*). Soon thereafter, his master died, and Ryōkan wandered for about five years as a pilgrim through Japan. Finally he settled at a hermitage on Mount Kugami in the vicinity of his birthplace, where he dedicated himself primarily to writing poetry, an art he had learned from his father. Ryōkan's → haiku and → *waka*, and also his poetry in the Chinese style (Jap., *kanshi*), are poetical expressions of Zen realization and are among the most beautiful Zen poems in Japanese literature.

Although an authorized Zen master, he preferred to take no students and to spend his life in solitude and utmost simplicity, which meant putting up with periods of bitter poverty. He is known for his gentle temperament and his love for children, with whom he often, forgetting himself, played for hours during his begging rounds. His poems evince extraordinary purity and "innocence" (→ *mushin*, → *rōshō-no-memmoku*) and an unreserved acceptance, born of nonattachment, of all circumstances. Thus, after a thief had stolen all the meagre possessions from his rude hermit's hut, he wrote the following haiku:

The thief left it there
There in the windowframe—
The shining moon.

Ryōnen 🅉 → Myōzen Ryōnen

Ryōtan Sōshin 🅉 Jap. for → Lung-t'an Ch'ung-hsin

Ryūge Koton 🅉 Jap. for → Lung-ya Chu-tun

Ryūtan Sōshin 🅉 Jap. for → Lung-t'an Ch'ung-hsin

Ryū Tetsuma 🅉 Jap. for → Liu T'ieh-mo

S

Sabīja-Samādhi 🄷 Skt. → *nirbīja-samādhi*, → *samprajñāta-samādhi*

Saddharmapundarīka-sūtra 🄱 🅉 Skt. → *Lotus Sūtra*

Sadguru 🄷 Skt.; the perfect → guru, who has attained illumination and has become one with divine consciousness. He can indicate the way to the realization of truth, and he knows all the obstacles that appear along the way; nevertheless, the pupil must traverse this path for himself.

Sādhakakoti 🄷 Skt.; a term used to refer to those who have become spiritual seekers and have entered the path leading to truth. "Truth" in this context means that one is not the body nor the mind but absolute, immortal consciousness.

Sādhana 🄷 🄱 Skt.; derived from *sādh*, "to arrive at the goal" and meaning roughly "means to completion or perfection."

🄷 Practices that lead to mastery of one of the yogic paths. Examples are → *japa*, meditation, and worship of the → *ishta-deva* (chosen deity). One who practices *sādhana* is called a *sādhaka*.

🄱 In → Vajrayāna Buddhism, a term for a particular type of liturgical text and the meditation practices presented in it. *Sādhana* texts describe in a detailed fashion deities to be experienced as spiritual realities and the entire process from graphic visualization of them to dissolving them into formless meditation. Performing this type of religious practice, which is central to Tibetan Buddhism, requires empowerment and consecration by the master (→ guru) for practice connected with the particular deity involved. Part of this is transmission of the → mantra associated with the deity.

Buddhist writings contain a multitude of *sādhana* texts, which are often brought together in special collections. One of the most important is *Garland of Sādhanas*, which stems from the 12th century and includes 312 *sādhanas* by different authors. Such collections are also to be found in the Tibetan canon (→ Kangyur-Tengyur), and new collections were still being compiled in the 20th century by members of the → Rime movement.

The practice of a *sādhana* can be divided into three sections: the preliminaries, the main part, and the concluding section. At the beginning of the *sādhana* is the fundamental act of taking refuge (→ *kyabdro*) and arousing the "mind of enlightenment" (→ *bodhicitta*). The main part is divided into a "developing phase," the creation of the visualization of the deity, and a "dissolving phase," the contemplation of the supreme reality, emptiness (→ *shūnyatā*). The concluding part is made up of various prayers of aspiration and pronouncements of auspiciousness and blessing.

For the Vajrayāna Buddhist, the visualization of a deity is not a magical action nor an adoration of an entity conceived of as external. It is rather to be regarded as a process of identification with a certain energy principle, of the presence of which the practitioner is convinced. The basic pattern for the visualized deities is provided by the five → *buddhakulas*.

Sādhu [H] Skt., from *sadh*: "to lead to fulfillment"; a holy person, often a monk, who desires to realize God and who has renounced the world.

Sadmaya-Kosha [H] (Sadmaya-Kośa), Skt.; the "sheath" *(kosha)* of being *(sat)* that envelops the → *ātman*. It serves as an aid to the human mind, which can conceive of the *atman* only in this sheath. Without it, *atman* is one with *brahman*, a fact that the teaching of → Vedānta stresses repeatedly.

Saguna-Brahman [H] (Saguṇa-Brahman), Skt., lit. "*brahman* with qualities"; the scriptures distinguish between two aspects of → *brahman:* a higher aspect, that of the qualityless *brahman* (→ *nirguna-brahman*) and a lower aspect wherein for the purpose of veneration *brahman* is accorded qualities (→ *upādhi*). The *Rāmatāpanīya-Upanishad* notes: "*Brahman* is pure consciousness, without parts, without form. In order to help the seeker in his efforts to surrender, symbols and qualities are added to *brahman.*" *Brahman* with qualities (→ *guna*) becomes → Īshvara, the personal god whom one may worship and adore.

Sahaja [H] Skt., lit. "natural"; according to the wise, truth is what is natural and original, whereas ignorance is what has been constructed by the mind. *Sahaja-avasthā* is the "natural state" (→ *avasthā*), the state of consciousness that all → *sādhanas* are meant to lead to; in other words, it is our real self in the state of → *samādhi.* → Rāmana Mahar(i)shi referred to his *samādhi* as *sahaja-samādhi.*

Sahasranāman [H] Skt., lit. "a thousand names"; associated with numerous deities, particularly Vishnu, Shiva, and → Shakti. Many *bhaktas* (lovers of God) repeat daily the thousand names of their → *ishta-deva* as an act of devoted surrender, in order to please one's chosen deity and to come a step closer to union with the deity.

Sahasrāra-chakra [H] [B] Skt. → chakra 7

Sahō kore shūshi [Z] Jap., lit. "The dharma practice [itself] is the taste of the school"; a formulation that comes from the → Sōtō school. Its meaning is that the emphasis on meditative practice (→ *zazen*) is itself the characteristic element of this school of Buddhism. *Zazen* is here seen in the sense of the esoteric definition of → Zen as the direct manifestation of one's own buddha-nature (→ *busshō*) and not as a "method" for the "attainment" of → enlightenment.

Sai Baba of Shirdi [H] died 1918; one of the greatest spiritual figures of modern-day India; he is worshiped in India as an → *avatāra* but is relatively unknown in the West. Among his worshipers are Muslims as well as Hindus; Sai Baba himself stood beyond all religion. He lived and acted from the direct experience of the ultimate reality. His manner of living had much of the "holy fool" about it, for which reason he was regarded uneasily by those of orthodox belief. He made use of → *siddhis,* such as the ability to appear simultaneously in different locations, and worked numerous miracles. He neither wrote nor read, and therefore was taken by many to be illiterate; yet when he deemed it necessary he would demonstrate a profound knowledge of Sanskrit and of scriptural literature. His life and work are described in Osborne, 1972.

Sai Baba of Shirdi should not be confused with the spiritual teacher from South India named Sai Baba who was born in 1926 and lives in his ashram, Prasanti Nilayam, in Puttaparthi. The latter has become known in the West for his healing powers and his → *siddhis* (such as power to make various objects, for example, clocks, materialize); his followers claim that he is a reincarnation of Sai Baba of Shirdi.

Saichō [B] called Dengyō Daishi, 767–822; founder of the monastic center on Mount Hiei and of the Japanese → Tendai school, the teachings of which, along with those of → Hua-yen and of esoteric Buddhism (→ Mi-tsung) he studied in China in the year 804. He emphasizes the universality of the Tendai doctrine and the importance of a morally pure way of life. He fostered the practice of *shikan* (Chin., → Chih-kuan), a form of meditation in which the Tendai monks were instructed in the course of their twelve-year training on Mount Hiei. He wanted to create in his monastery a purely Mahāyāna ordination center. However, this plan failed due to the resistance of other Buddhist schools. Saichō died in 822 on Mount Hiei.

Saichō in conversation with the monk Gyōja (colored woodblock, 15th century)

The Tendai school founded by Saichō differed little from the original Chinese school. It was also based on the → *Lotus Sūtra,* i.e., on the words of the Buddha himself. In Saichō's view, this made it superior to other Buddhist schools, whose doctrines were based essentially on commentaries rather than sūtras.

Also in opposition to the other schools of his time, Saichō stressed the unity and universality of the Tendai teaching: it is universal because all beings possess the ability to attain enlightenment and become buddhas. A further aspect of this universality is to be found in the Tendai view of the essential unity of Buddha and human being; every human being possesses → buddha-nature (also → *busshō*) and is thus a potential buddha. The way to attain buddhahood is, for Saichō, primarily to lead a morally pure life and practice concentration and insight (*shikan*).

Saichō cultivated close relations with the imperial court. Mount Hiei was considered the "center for protection of the nation." Saichō was himself convinced that Mahāyāna Buddhism was the great benefactor and protector of Japan. He distinguished different classes of monks who completed training in his monastery. The most talented were the "treasure of the nation," and these had to remain in the monastery and serve the state through their practice. Less talented ones entered the civil service, taught, or worked in agriculture or in other areas for the welfare of the country.

For the significance of Saichō in Zen, → Tao-hsuan Lu-shih.

Saiin Shimyō 🅩 Jap. for → Hsi-yuan Ssu-ming

Saijōjō Zen 🅩 Jap. → five types of Zen 5

Saiten-nijūhasso 🅩 Jap. → *nijūhasso*

Sākhya-Bhāva 🅗 Skt. → *bhāva*

Sakridāgāmin 🅑 (sakṛdāgāmin) Skt. (Pali, sakadāgāmin), lit. "once-returner"; a term for saints who have reached the second stage of the supramundane path (→ *ārya-mārga,* → *ārya-pudgala*). They are reborn only once more before the attainment of nirvāna. In them the three unwholesome roots—desire, hatred, and delusion (→ *askushala*)—are present only to a slight extent.

Sākshin 🅗 (Sākṣin), Skt., lit. "the observer"; the teaching of → Vedānta speaks of *sākshin-chaitanya* (→ *chaitanya*), the detached observer-consciousness. As one frees oneself, primarily by means of spiritual practices (→ *sādhana*), from identification with the body and one's thoughts and feelings, one realizes more clearly the fundamental observer-consciousness (or, as it is often called, "witness"-consciousness), which perceives everything the individual encounters (joy and sorrow, happiness and misery) but knows it to be the play of → *māyā* and is neither moved nor blinded by it. The observer-consciousness remains unblemished by these events, just as a white cinema screen remains untouched by the image that is projected unto it.

Sakugo 🅩 Jap., lit. "requesting a word"; a question asked by a Zen monk of a master while the latter is making a public presentation of the buddha-dharma (→ *teishō*). Because questions on the essential content of the presentation of a Zen master cannot be answered with mere conceptual-verbal information, such questions can give rise to a → *mondō* or a → *hossen.*

Sakyapa 🅑 (sa-skya-pa), Tib.; a major school of → Tibetan Buddhism named after the Sakya (lit. "Gray Earth") Monastery, located in southern Tibet. In accordance with a prophecy of → Atīsha, the Sakya Monastery was founded in the year 1073, and its abbots, members of the Khön family, devoted themselves primarily to the transmission of a cycle of → Vajrayāna teachings known by the name of "path and goal" (→ Lamdre). This school concerned itself with creating a systematic order for the Tantric writings (→ Tantra), but also turned its attention to problems of Buddhist logic. In the 13th and 14th centuries it had great political influence in Tibet.

The Sakyapas received their form as an independent school mainly from five gurus who lived between 1092 and 1280: Sachen Kunga Nyingpo (1092–1158), his two sons Sonam Tsemo (1142–82) and Drakpa Gyaltsen (1147–1216), his grandson Sakya Pandita (1182–1251), and the latter's nephew Chögyal Phagpa (1235–80). All five teachers were recognized as incarnations of → Mañjushrī. Up to the present day, the principal leaders of the Sakyapa school are of the Khön family.

Of these the greatest influence was exercised by Sakya Pandita, whose erudition embraced all worldly and religious disciplines. His translations from Sanskrit not only made him known in India but also caused a grandson of Genghis Khan to invite him to Mongolia. Sakya Pandita's missionary activities there were so successful that rulership of Central Asia was conferred upon the Sakya school in the year 1249.

In the following centuries the Sakyapas played an important role in the spiritual life of Tibet. Not only were → Tsongkhapa, and through him the → Gelugpa school, influenced by them, but also the school of Jonangpa, no longer extant today, and its most important spokesman Tāranātha (b. 1575), as well as the historian Butön (1290–1364) were strongly influenced by the Sakyapas.

Samādhi 🅗 🅑 🅩 Skt., lit. "establish, make firm."
🅗 A state of consciousness that lies beyond waking, dreaming, and deep sleep, and in which mental activity ceases. It is a total absorption in the object of meditation. If that object is God or the Absolute, the result is union. There are various stages of *samādhi,* of which the highest is → *nirvikalpa-samādhi.*
🅑 🅩 (Jap., sanmai or zanmai); collectedness of the mind on a single object through (gradual) calming of mental activity. *Samādhi* is a nondualistic state of consciousness in which the consciousness of the experiencing "subject" becomes one with the experienced "object"—thus is *only* experiential content. This state of consciousness is often referred to as "one-pointedness of mind"; this expression, however, is misleading because it calls up the image of "concentration" on one point on which the mind is "directed." However, *samādhi* is neither a straining concentration on one point, nor is the mind directed from here (subject) to there (object), which would be a dualistic mode of experience.

The ability to attain the state of *samādhi* is a precondition for absorption (→ *dhyāna*).

Three supramundane (→ *lokottara*) types of *samādhi* are distinguished that have as their goal emptiness (→ *shūnyatā*), the state of no-characteristics (→ *animitta*) and freedom from attachment to the object, and the attainment of → nirvāna. Any other form of *samādhi*, even in the highest stages of absorption, is considered worldly.

Samādhirāja-sūtra 🅑 Skt., lit. *"King of Concentration Sūtra"*; a Mahāyāna sūtra in forty or forty-two chapters, of which only sixteen are extant in the Sanskrit original and the rest only in Chinese and Tibetan translations. Its teaching is related to that of the → *Prajñāpāramitā-sūtra* and deals with the essential identity of all things.

Samantabhadra 🅑 🅩 Skt. (Chin., P'u-hsien; Jap., Fugen), lit. "He Who Is All-pervadingly Good" or "He Whose Beneficence Is Everywhere"; one of the most important bodhisattvas of Mahāyāna Buddhism. He is venerated as the protector of all those who teach the dharma and is regarded as an embodiment of the wisdom of essential sameness, i.e., insight into the unity of sameness and difference.

Samantabhadra in his Tibetan form as Primordial Buddha (Ādi-Buddha)

Samantabhadra is often depicted in the company of → Shākyamuni and → Mañjushrī. He rides on a white six-tusked elephant, which represents the power of wisdom to overcome all obstructions. The six tusks represent overcoming attachment to the six senses.

As a bodhisattva, Samantabhadra is associated with → Vairochana. His symbols are the wish-fulfilling jewel and the lotus or else the scroll on which the text of his meditation sūtra is written.

In China Samantabhadra is venerated as one of the four great bodhisattvas. His sacred place is Mount O-mei, where he is said to have remained after he came to China from India riding on a white elephant.

In the → Vajrayāna Samantabhadra is the primordial buddha (*ādi-buddha*), who represents the experiential content of the *dharmakāya* (→ *trikāya*).

His naked deep blue body symbolizes nothingness (→ *shūnyatā*) and he is iconographically depicted in union (→ *yab-yum*) with his white consort. (Another tradition sees Vajradhara, "the Dharma-Holder," as the symbol of the *dharmakāya*. Vajradhara's appearance is like that of a *sambhogakāya* buddha (→ *trikāya*). He is of central significance in the → *mahāmudrā* teaching.)

Samāpatti 🅱 Skt., Pali; lit. "attainments"; a term referring to the four absorptions (→ *dhyāna*), the four stages of formlessness, and sometimes also the so-called state of extinction (→ *nirodha-samāpatti*).

Samarpana 🅷 (Samarpaṇa), Skt., lit. "offering"; the offering of oneself to God, subjection to his will, the end of any desires for oneself. The → *kundalinī* can be awakened thereby and made to rise.

Samatva 🅷 Skt., lit. "equanimity"; composure, steady conduct under all circumstances, and important virtue in Yoga; it is reached by the overcoming of the opposites of attraction and repulsion to objects of all kinds.

Sāmaveda 🅷 Skt., the → Veda of songs with which the *udgātri* (singer), one of the four chief priests at the sacrificial service, accompanies the preparation and offering of the → *soma* sacrifice. The work comprises 1,549 verses, of which only 78 are not derived from the → *Rigveda.*

Sambhogakāya 🅱 🆉 Skt. → *trikāya*

Sambō 🆉 Jap., lit. "three precious ones"; the three precious ones (Skt., *triratna*, also translated "three treasures" or "three jewels") constitute the foundation of Buddhism. There can be no Buddhist religious life without faith and veneration toward them. In the → Mahāyāna these three are more broadly interpreted than in the → Hīnayāna, where they simply mean → Buddha, → dharma, and → *sangha*. In the context of Zen training, students are introduced to the distinct Mahāyāna understanding of the three precious ones after completing → kōan training. Here there are three levels of meaning of the *sambō*: (1) the three precious ones as one (*ittai-sambō*, lit. "the three precious ones as one body"); (2) the three precious ones as manifestation (*genzen-sambō*); (3) the three precious ones as verification. Although in truth they are one, they are distinguished for the sake of explanation.

1. The three precious ones as one are (a) the buddha Birushana (Skt., → Vairochana), who represents knowledge of the world of nothingness (→ *shūnyatā*, → *enlightenment*), of buddha-nature (→ *busshō*), and of unconditional sameness; (b) the → dharma, i.e., the law of beginningless and endless becoming (or of the great order), according to which causes and conditions underlie all forms of appearance; (c) the interpenetration and interaction of the first two, which constitute that perfect reality that is experienced by enlightened ones.

2. The three precious ones as manifestation are (a) the historical Buddha → Shākyamuni, who through his complete enlightenment realized the truth of the three precious ones in himself; (b) the dharma (as the teaching of the historical Buddha), which contains the spoken words and expositions of Shākyamuni Buddha, in which he clarified the meaning of the three precious ones as one and the way leading to realization of them; (c) the disciples of the Buddha and other contemporary followers, who heard the teaching of the three precious ones as he taught it, believed it, and realized it in their lives.

3. The three precious ones as verification are (a) the iconography of the Buddha that has come down to us; (b) the recorded expositions and discourses of the buddhas (i.e., fully enlightened beings) as they are presently available to us in the → sūtras and other Buddhist texts; (c) the present-day adherents of Buddhism, who practice and realize the saving truth of the three precious ones as one that was first revealed by Shākyamuni Buddha.

The three precious ones are interdependent. One who has not realized the *ittai-sambō* through enlightenment cannot fundamentally grasp the enlightenment of Shākyamuni Buddha, nor is he able to appreciate the limitless preciousness of his teaching. He is unable to relate to images and representations of Buddha as living realities. The *ittai-sambō* would be unknown if Shākyamuni Buddha had not revealed it in his own body and mind and in the way to its realization as he expounded it. Finally, the *ittai-sambō* would be a remote ideal, the life of Shākyamuni Buddha would be a dry historical matter, and the words of the Buddha would be lifeless abstractions if in our time there were no enlightened ones who pursue the way of the Buddha in order to lead and inspire others on this path to self-realization (→ *kenshō*, → satori). Moreover, since each individual embodies the *ittai-sambō*, the ground of the three precious ones is nothing other than oneself.

Samghanandi 🅩 seventeenth patriarch in the Indian lineage of Ch'an (→ Zen)

Samghyathata 🅩 eighteenth patriarch of the Indian lineage of Ch'an (→ Zen)

Samhitā 🅗 (Saṃhitā), Skt., lit. "collection"; descriptive title applied to the collected arrangements of songs and sacrifice-related texts laid down in the various Vedic scriptures.

The Samhitā of the *Rigveda* consists of 1,017 hymns in 10,580 verses; that of the *Sāmaveda* consists of 1,549 verses that (with the exception of 78) also appear in the *Rigveda* but have been altered to suit whatever function they serve. The samhitā of the *White* → *Yajurveda* contains sacrificial passages in both prose and verse form that are taken from the *Rigveda-Samhitā*. The → *Atharvaveda-Samhitā* consists of 760 hymns, of which only about a sixth are taken from the *Rigveda*; the rest occupy an independent position in the body of Vedic mantra-literature.

Sammon 🅩 Jap., also Sanmon, lit. "mountain gate"; the entrance gate of a Zen monastery (*mountain*, since in ancient times monasteries were built on mountains). The *sammon* is usually a massive, multistory, tower-like structure.

Sampai 🅩 Jap., lit. "threefold [*san*] prostration [*hai*]"; expression of veneration through prostration customary in Zen, in which otherwise there is a dearth of ceremonial forms. *Sampai* was probably originally an expression of veneration toward the "three precious ones" (→ *sambō*). Under certain circumstances, also "ninefold prostration," (*kyūhai*) is practiced.

Samprajñāta-Samādhi 🅗 (Saṃprajñāta-Samādhi), Skt., from *samprajñāta*: "conscious"; the yoga philosophy of → Patañjali distinguishes between two stages of → samādhi: *samprajñāta-samadhi* and *asamprajñāta-samādhi*, corresponding roughly to → *savikalpa-samādhi* and → *nirvikalpa-samādhi* in → Vedānta. In *samprajñāta-samādhi*, mental activity as well as → *kleshas* are still present, so that this form of *samādhi* is characterized by germination (*sabīja-samādhi*); that is, the individual's diminished and hidden desires (→ *vāsanās*) still exist in seed form and may reemerge. This form is contrasted to *asamprajñāta* ("supraconscious"), the highest level of *samādhi*, which is without seeds (→ *nirbīja-samādhi*), since all *kleshas* have been overcome, all *vāsnās* extinguished, and all bonds of → karma broken.

Samsāra 🅗 🅑 🅩 (saṃsāra), Skt., lit. "journeying."

🅗 The cycle of birth, death, and rebirth, to which every human being is subject so long as we live in ignorance and do not know our identity with → *brahman*.

🅑 🅩 the "cycle of existences," a succession of rebirths that a being goes through within the various modes of existence (→ *gati*) until it has attained liberation and entered → nirvāna. Imprisonment in samsāra is conditioned by the three "unwholesome roots" (→ *akushala*): hatred (*dvesha*), desire or craving (→ *trishnā*), and delusion (→ *avidyā*). The type of rebirth within samsāra is determined by the → karma of the being. In the Mahāyāna, samsāra refers to the phenomenal world and is considered to be essentially identical with nirvāna.

The essential unity of samsāra and nirvāna is based on the view that everything is a mental representation, and thus samsāra and nirvāna are nothing other than labels without real substance, i.e., they are empty (→ *shūnyatā*). To the extent that one does not relate to the phenomenal aspect of the world but rather its true nature, samsāra and nirvāna are not different from one another.

The chain of existences is without a knowable beginning. The Buddha never indulged in speculations concerning the beginning of samsāra, since he did not regard this as helpful for the attainment of liberation. Departure from samsāra through entry into nirvāna is only possible during rebirth as a human being. In all other forms of existence, beings cannot end the cyclical process because they cannot recognize desire and ignorance as the driving forces of samsāra and thus overcome them.

Samskāra 🅗 🅑 (saṃskāra), Skt., lit. "impression, consequence."

🅗 Impressions, tendencies, and possibilities present in consciousness that have arisen through one's actions and thoughts, including those of earlier births. The sum total of *samskāras* form the person's character.

🅑 (Pali, sankhara); generally translated "formations," "mental formational forces" or "impulses," *samskāra* refers both to the activity of forming and the passive state of being formed (→ *Samskrita*).

Samskāra is the fourth of the → *skandhas* and the second link in the chain of conditioned arising (→ *pratītya-samutpāda*). Formations include all volitional impulses or intentions that precede an action. Since actions can be either physical, verbal, or mental, impulses that are physical, verbal, and mental are distinguished. Their presence is the condition for a new rebirth. If they are absent, no → karma is produced, and no further rebirths take place. In addition they determine the type of rebirth, since they can be good, bad, or neutral, and their quality conditions the consciousness that arises—according to the doctrine of conditioned arising—through them, that seeks a womb after the death of a being, and that brings about the existence of a new empirical person.

Samskrita 🅱 (saṃskṛta), Skt. (Pali, sankhata), roughly "formed, conditioned"; all interdependent and mutually conditioning phenomena, the essential characteristic of which is that they arise, subsist, change, and pass away. Thus everything conditioned is empty, impermanent, without essence (→ *anātman*), and characterized by suffering.

In the Hīnayāna the transitoriness of human life is explained by the conditioned nature of all phenomena. The Mahāyāna applies the concept of *samskrita* to all the material and mental phenomena of the world and thus establishes its doctrine of the emptiness (→ *shūnyatā*) of all dharmas (because of their conditioned character they are considered to be "empty", indeed devoid of all self-nature) and also the "mind-only" teaching of the → Yogāchāra.

The classification of phenomena into conditioned and unconditioned (→ *asamskrita*) varies from school to school.

Samsvedaja 🅷 🅱 Skt. → *chatur-yoni*

Samu 🆉 Jap., lit. "work service"; generally, the physical work that is part of everyday life in a Zen monastery, and particularly the work periods during a → *sesshin*. *Service* is here to be understood in the sense of service to the three precious ones (→ *sambō*). If the work is carried out wakefully, in a manner based entirely on the activity of collected attention and total carefulness, then it is a continuation and another form of meditative practice (→ *zazen*), in which the practitioner learns to maintain the meditative state of mind even in the midst of everyday routine. *Samu* is an important part of Zen training in a monastery according to the monastic rule established by → Pai-chang Huai-hai (Jap., Hyakujo Ekai) in China in the eighth century.

From Pai-chang also stems the Zen saying, "A day without work, a day without food." He himself lived according to this. When the monks of his monastery hid his gardening tools in order to save the aged master the exertion of work, on that day he ate nothing. The tools reappeared and Pai-chang labored and ate once again.

Samudāya 🅱 Skt. → four noble truths

Samudra 🅷 Skt., lit. "ocean"; infinite, eternal existence; streams of higher consciousness that flow from immortality into mortal man.

Samvriti-satya 🅱 (saṃvṛti-satya), Skt., roughly "conventional truth"; the relative truth of the phenomenal world as opposed to the ultimate truth (→ *paramārtha-satya*). The "two truths" are defined differently by different Buddhist schools.

Samyak-prahānāni 🅱 Skt. → four perfect exertions

Samyak-sambuddha 🅱 Skt. (Pali, samma-sambuddha), lit. "fully awakened one"; refers to a being who has attained perfect complete enlightenment, has by himself rediscovered the teaching that leads to liberation after it has disappeared from the world, has fully realized it, and proclaimed it to the world. The enlightenment realized by him is called *samyak-sambodhi* (enlightenment of a perfect buddha). A samyak-sambuddha is characterized by omniscience (→ *sarvajñatā*) and the possession of the ten powers (→ *dashabala*).

Samyak-sambuddha is also one of the → ten epithets of a buddha.

Samyama 🅷 (Saṃyama), Skt., lit. "restraint, self-control"; a term used in the yoga philosophy of → Patañjali to summarize the three final stages of → Rāja-yoga (*dhāranā, dhyana, and samādhi*).

In the third chapter of his → *Yoga-Sūtra*, Patañjali lists the occult powers that can be attained through the mastery of *samyama*, but he ultimately stresses that only the release of all attachment to these powers will lead from the mastery fo *samyama* to the goal of yoga, to enlightenment and union with the Absolute.

Samyojana 🅱 (saṃyojana), Pali, Skt., lit. "fetters"; in the Hīnayāna ten fetters are enumerated that chain a being to the cycle of rebirths (→ samsāra): (1) belief in individuality (→ *drishti*), (2) scepticism (→ *vichikitsā*), (3) clinging to rites and rules, (4) craving or desire (→ *trishnā*, → *kāma*), (5) hatred, (6) craving for refined corporeality, (7) craving for incorporeality, (8) conceit, (9) excitability, (10) ignorance (→ *avidyā*).

One who is free of the first three fetters is a → *shrota-āpanna*. One who has also overcome the fourth and fifth fetters to a great extent has reached the stage of a → *sakridāgāmin*. If one has fully done away with the first five fetters, one is an → *anāgāmin.* Freedom from all ten fetters characterizes an → arhat.

Samyuktāgama 🅑 Skt. → Āgama, → Nikāya, → *Samyutta-nikāya*

Samyutta-nikāya 🅑 Pali (Skt. *Samyuktāgama*), lit. "*Unified Collection*"; the third collection (→ Nikāya, → Āgama) of the Sūtra-pitaka. It consists of numerous short texts dealing with incidents connected with the life and work of the Buddha. They are ordered in a number of ways including according to the occasion for their original recital, according to the speaker to whom they are attributed, according to theme, and so on.

Sanātana-Dharma 🅗 Skt., from *sanātana*: "imperishable, eternal"; the eternal religion or truth of Hinduism. Hindus use this name to characterize their religion because it does not derive from a human founder; rather, the truth was revealed to the → *rishis.* The scriptures (→ *shruti*) are based on these revelations.

Sāñchī 🅑 city in central India where, between the 3d century B.C.E. and the 1st century C.E., the first monuments of Buddhist art originated. These are mainly → stūpas exemplary of the original form of the stūpa, out of which all the other forms developed.

The most renowned is the Great Stūpa of Sāñchī, the core structure of which stems from the 3d century B.C.E. On a circular base is a hemisphere that is flattened toward the top; on top of this is a post that rises through a boxlike latticework structure of stone and has three flat umbrella-shaped forms towards the top. On the base is a narrow processional path that runs around the hemisphere and is surrounded by a stone wall. This can be entered only through gates in the four cardinal directions and thus protects the sacred site from the exterior.

San-chieh school 🅑 (Chin., san-chieh-chiao, lit. "School of Three Stages"); school of Buddhism during the Sui and T'ang periods. The name of this school, founded by Hsin-hsing (540–94), comes from its division of the overall duration of the Buddhist teaching into three stages: (1) the period of true → dharma, during which the words of the Buddha were strictly adhered to—this lasted for 500 years starting with the → *parinirvāna* of the Buddha; (2) the period of the adulterated dharma, during which the true teaching was obscured by pseudo-Buddhist doctrine (1,000 years); (3) the period of degeneration of the dharma, in which the teaching has fallen into discredit and is threatened with extinction (10 thousand years). This third period is purported to have begun around 550 C.E. and to be still continuing.

Hsin-hsing and his followers were convinced that they alone possessed the teaching suitable for this present stage. They stressed the importance of observance of rules (→ *shīla*), altruistic deeds, and ascetic practice (thus, for example, they took nourishment only once a day). Since they accused the other schools, and even the rulers, of advocating "heretical" teachings, the School of Three Stages was officially banned in the year 600 but in fact ceased to exist only after 845.

According to Hsin-hsing, in the first phase the "single vehicle" (→ *ekayāna*) was taught and in the second period, the "three yānas" (→ *triyāna*: → *shrāvaka*, → *pratyekabuddha*, → *bodhisattva*). He saw both as limited methods. According to the School of Three Stages, the third period, which had then already begun, requires a universal teaching such as its own.

The third period is characterized by lack of esteem for the moral and → Vinaya rules, by belief in false teachings, and the mixing of good and evil. Human beings are therefore condemned to be reborn in the hells (→ *naraka*). According to Hsin-hsing's view, in such a phase meditation and monastic life are no longer sufficient. He urged that doctrine be adapted to circumstances and advocated ascetic practice and strict observance of disciplinary rules. His followers did not live in the monasteries themselves but rather in rude shelters in their vicinity. They tried to accommodate themselves as much as possible to the life of simple folk.

According to their view, all the things of the phenomenal world are manifestations of → buddha-nature; thus they saw all beings as future buddhas. In order to give expression to this conviction, followers of this school often prostrated before strangers on the street and even before animals. This exposed them to general derision.

The school of Three Stages also attached special value to almsgiving, through which over the years they accumulated considerable wealth. This permitted them to carry out various beneficent actions. They distributed food, clothing, and money to the needy and used a part of their wealth for the maintenance of monasteries and for the performance of rites.

San-ch'ing 🅣 Chin., lit. "the three pure ones"; the three Taoist heavens (→ *t'ien*) and the three deities inhabiting them.

The first of these is *yü-ch'ing,* the Heaven of Jade Purity, inhabited by → Yüan-shih t'ien-tsun, the Celestial Venerable of the Primordial Beginning. He is also known as T'ien-pao-chün or Lord of the Heavenly Jewel. According to some sources this first and highest heaven also is ruled by → Yü-huang, the Jade Emperor. In popular belief Yü-huang is considered the ruler of Heaven and Earth and thus ranks higher than Yüan-shih t'ien-tsun.

The second heaven—*shang-ch'ing*—is the Heaven of Great Purity and is reserved for Ling-pao t'ien-tsun, the Heavenly Venerable of the Magic Jewel. He is sometimes called Tao-chün, Lord of the Tao, and considered to be the guardian of magical writings (→ *Ling-pao ching*). He has existed since the beginning of the world and it is his task to calculate time, allocate it to the various epochs, and to regulate yin and yang (→ yin-yang).

The third heaven—*t'ai-ch'ing*—is the Heaven of Highest Purity, ruled by Tao-te t'ien-tsun, the Heavenly Venerable of the → Tao and the → *te*. He is identical with T'ai-shang lao-chün, Supreme Master Lao, i.e., Lao-tzu (also → Lao-chün). This heavenly venerable reveals the Taoist teachings contained in the writings guarded by the Heavenly Venerable of the Magic Jewel. He will assume a great variety of forms—e.g., that of Lao-tzu—to bring the people of the "world of dust" closer to the teachings of the Tao.

Sanchita-Karma 🅗 (Saṃcita-Karma), Skt., the accumulated → *samskāras* that an individual has created in previous lives and that await their effect in a future life.

San-ch'ung 🅣 Chin., lit. "three worms"; three transcendental beings whom Taoists believe to inhabit the three cinnabar fields (→ *tan-t'ien*). Having no permanent form, they may take on the appearance of demons or of human beings.

The three worms endeavor to shorten the life of those whose bodies they inhabit and thus prevent them from attaining immortality. They are the cause of a great variety of diseases and also inform Heaven of people's transgressions so that the deities might shorten their lives (→ Ssu-ming). A Taoist adept striving for immortality therefore tries to rid himself of the three worms by abstaining from eating grain (→ *pi-ku*) because grain is their nourishment. As an additional measure, he may meditate and fast on the days when the three worms ascend to Heaven to inform → Yü-huang, the Jade Emperor, of man's good and evil deeds. The meditation and fasting prevent the worms from ascending to Heaven.

The first worm lives in the palace (→ *ni-huan*) of the upper cinnabar field situated in the head. It causes blindness and deafness, loss of teeth and hair, as well as foul-smelling breath and congestion of the nose. The second worm resides in the middle cinnabar field situated near the heart. It causes heart disease, asthma, and melancholy. The third worm inhabits the lower cinnabar field in the region of the navel and causes intestinal malfunctions, skin diseases, rheumatism, and lack of will power.

Sandhyā 🅗 (Saṃdhyā), Skt., lit. "dusk, twilight"; 1. morning and evening devotion, to be offered by every caste-born Hindu, usually associated with the practice of meditation; 2. the beginning of a world-age (→ *yuga*).

Sandōkai 🅩 Jap. for → *Ts'an-t'ung-ch'i*

Sandoku 🅩 Jap., lit. "the three poisons"; the three spiritual poisons: hatred (also anger or aggression), desire (this includes covetousness, greed, attachment, etc.), and stupidity (or ignorance, → *avidyā*). These poison every experience of persons living in → delusion and stupefy their minds to such an extent that they do not become aware of their immanent perfection (→ *busshō*). (Also → *bonpu-no-jōshiki*.)

Sangai 🅑 🅩 Jap. for → *triloka*

Sangai(-yui)-isshin 🅩 Jap., lit. "three worlds [nothing else than] one mind"; a Zen expression indicating that the three worlds (Skt., *triloka*; Jap., *sangai*: world of desire, world of form, world of no-form—in brief, the worlds of unenlightened beings) all arise from the consciousness (heart-mind, Jap., → *kokoro*) of beings and have no separate "objective" existence. The entirety of the phenomenal world is nothing else than the projection of the mind.

Sangha 🅗 🅑 🅩 (saṃgha), Skt., lit. "crowd, host."

🅗 A group of seekers who gather around a master (→ guru) in order to attain, with his help, spiritual knowledge and realization of the highest truth.

🅑 🅩 the Buddhist community. In a narrower sense the *sangha* consists of monks (→ *bhikshu*), nuns (→ *bhikshunī*), and novices (→ *shrāmanera*). In a wider sense the *sangha* also includes lay followers (→ *upāsaka*).

The *sangha* is one of the three precious ones (→ *triratna*, → *sambō*); the way of life of its members is determined by the rules established in the → Vinaya-pitaka.

Sanhāra 🅗 Skt. → *mahāpralaya*

San-hsing 🅣 Chin., lit. "three stars"; three stellar deities or gods of good fortune, which are a favorite motif in Chinese folk art: Fu-hsing (Lucky Star) is most frequently portrayed in the company of a child or in his symbolic form of a bat—a sign of good luck. Lü-hsing (Star of Honor or Status) often appears in his symbolical form of a stag. Shou-hsing (Star of Longevity) has an enormously high bald head. He supports himself on a knotty staff, a symbol of the immortals (→ *hsien*). In his other hand he holds the peach of immortality. Symbolically he is represented by a mushroom or a turtle (→ Shou-lao). The *san-hsing* are historical personalities who were deified in recognition of the special merits they accumulated.

The three gods of good fortune: left, Shou-hsing; center, Lu-hsing; right, Fu-hsing.

Fu-hsing, according to tradition, was a 6th-century government official by the name of Yang Ch'eng. He came from the village of Tao-chou, all the inhabitants of which were of extremely short stature. Every year, the emperor would summon a large number of people from this village to his court, because he loved to surround himself with dwarfs. In consequence, the population of Tao-chou was greatly reduced as the years went on. Yang Ch'eng addressed a petition to the emperor asking him to show consideration for the people of his home town. The emperor was so touched by Yang Ch'eng's petition that he never again summoned them to his court.

There are, however, other historical personalities to whom the function of Fu-hsing is ascribed. The most prominent of these is the 8th-century general Kuo Tzu-i, who saved the T'ang Dynasty from destruction after an uprising. It is said that the Heavenly Weaver—a female mythological figure—appeared to him. When he asked her to grant him fame and fortune, she replied that he himself was the god of wealth. This encounter is the subject of many artistic representations. In popular belief, Fu-hsing is frequently confused with the Ruler of Heaven (→ *san-kuan*).

Lü-hsing, who is also known as Kuan-hsing (Star of State Officials), is supposed to have been Shih Fei, a vassal of the founder of the Han Dynasty. Another tradition identifies Lü-hsing with the god of literature (→ Wen-ch'ang).

Shou-hsing came to be known as Shou-lao in later popular belief and is also called the Old Man of the South Pole. A legend tells of one Chao Yen who, as a child, was told by a physiognomer that he had only nineteen more years to live. He therefore advised the child to go on a certain day to a certain field and take with him a jar of wine and dried meat. In that field he would find two men playing draughts under a mulberry tree. Chao Yen should offer them wine and meat but on no account answer any of their questions. Chao Yen followed the physiognomer's advice.

After they had partaken of the wine and meat offered to them by Chao Yen, the two players discussed how they might best thank the boy for his hospitality. In the end they decided to reverse the digits of the number of years the boy could be expected to live, thus changing the *19* into a *91.* Later the physiognomer told Chao Yen that one of the two players had been the God of the North Pole, who determines the day on which people are born, and the other the God of the South Pole, who fixes the dates of death.

San-hsüan ▮ Chin., lit. "three unfathomables"; neo-Taoist (→ *hsüan-hsüeh*) collective term for the → *Tao-te ching* of Lao-tzu, the → *Chuang-tzu,* and the → *I-ching.*

San-huang ▮ Chin., lit. "three nobles"; three legendary emperors of China, namely → Fu Hsi, → Shen-nung, and Yen-ti. The period during which they are believed to have ruled is variously given as 2852–2697 B.C.E. or 2952–2490 B.C.E. They were succeeded by the five legendary emperors (→ *wu-ti*).

San-i ▮ Chin.,, lit. "the three ones"; three deities who, according to the Inner Deity Hygiene School of religious Taoism (→ *tao-chiao*), guard the three cinnabar fields (→ *tan-t'ien*) situated respectively in the head, near the heart, and in the abdominal region. The *san-i* are in turn ruled by the Supreme One (→ T'ai-i), who dwells in a particular compartment of the upper cinnabar field. The task of the three ones consists in guarding the three cinnabar fields—the focal points of man's life energy—against ghosts and evil breath. They are the enemies of the three worms (→ *san-ch'ung*).

The term *san-i* may also designate the trinity of mind (→ *shen*), life force (→ *ch'i*), and essence (→ *ching*). In Taoist texts from the Han Dynasty the three ones refer to the Celestial One (T'ien-i), the Earthly One (Ti-i), and the Supreme One (→ T'ai-i).

The idea of the three ones originated with a passage of the *Tao-te ching* (chap. 42, Feng & English 1972):

The Tao begot one
one begot two
two begot three
and three begot the ten thousand things.

Due to the tendency of Taoism to personalize abstract concepts, this "one" that arises from the Tao quickly became transformed into a deity, the Supreme One (T'ai-i), who for a long time was the most important deity in religious Taoism. The splitting up of the One into three ones proved necessary as a result of the fusion of two practices, which until then had been independent of each other: (1) meditation aimed at becoming one with the Tao, based on the teachings of → Lao-tzu and → Chuang-tzu, who considered the preservation of → *shou-i* to be indispensable, and (2) the practice of "allowing the breath to circulate" through the cinnabar fields of the body (→ *hsing-ch'i*). Since there are three fields and the ultimate principle of the One resides in each of them it became necessary to assume the existence of three ones, which dwell in three different places but nevertheless form a unity.

Sānīpya 🅷 Skt., lit. "proximity"; the effort of the lover of God to approach his → *ishta-deva;* a step on the path of → Bhakti-Yoga.

Sankalpa 🅷 (Saṃkalpa), Skt., lit. "intention, will"; controlled, self- willed thoughts, in contrast to the mental activity known as *vikalpa* (lit., "doubt, false notion"), which emerges as a countermovement from the subconscious on the basis of one's → *samskāras,* the hidden tendencies that come from earlier experiences. Both types together form the normal activity of thought processes. The yogi attempts to bring all *vikalpas* under control so that the thought processes can be fully mastered. This leads to the state of pure *sankalpa,* unencumbered by *vikalpas.* This is a sign of steadfast wisdom and freedom of will. The yogi who attains → *samādhi* leaves even *sankalpa* behind.

Sānkhya 🅷 (Sāṃkhya), Skt., one of the six orthodox doctrines of philosophy (→ *darshana*) of Hinduism. Founded by → Kapila, it teaches that the universe arises through the union of → *prakriti* (nature) with → *purusha* (consciousness). According to Sānkhya, there are as many souls and units of consciousness (*purushas*) as there are living beings. Concerning its evolutionary theory, → *parināmavāda.*

Sankīrtan 🅷 Skt. → *kīrtana*

San-kuan 🆃 Chin., roughly "three rulers"; three Taoist deities, namely T'ien-kuan (Ruler of Heaven); Ti-kuan (Ruler of the Earth), and Shui-kuan (Ruler of Water). These three play an important part in the religious life of the Chinese. According to popular belief the Ruler of Heaven bestows wealth and good luck, the Ruler of the Earth forgives sins and transgressions, and the Ruler of Water helps the believer to overcome obstacles. In addition, all three keep a register of the good and evil deeds of people.

The veneration of the *san-kuan* goes back to the beginning of religious Taoism (→ *tao-chiao*) because both → Chang Chüeh and → Chang Tao-ling, the respective leaders of the Way of Supreme Peace (→ *t'ai-p'ing tao*) and Five-Pecks-of-Rice Taoism (→ *wu-tou-mi tao*), enlisted their help during healing ceremonies.

At these healing sessions the sick would list their sins—which were considered to be the cause of their illness—on three strips of paper, one for each of the three rulers. The paper strip intended for T'ien-kuan was either burned or deposited on the peak of a mountain; that addressed to the Ruler of the Earth was buried in the ground; and that intended for the Ruler of Water thrown into a river.

Under → K'ou Ch'ien-chih, the *san-kuan* cult was reformed and the three rulers became functionaries of the gods, responsible for supervising rites and rewarding believers. In ancient times, each city had a hall or temple dedicated to the three rulers.

In representations they are not often seen together. When they are, they sit next to each other and are dressed as mandarins. In their hands they hold the register of the good and evil deeds. However, representations showing the Ruler of Heaven on his own are quite common: he is usually shown standing and holding a scroll with the inscription, "The Ruler of Heaven bestows good fortune." For that reason he is also venerated as a god of good fortune (→ *san-hsing*).

San-lun school 🅱 Chin., lit. "School of Three Treatises"; Chinese form of the Indian → Mādhyamaka. The name refers to the three written works fundamental for the school: the *Mādhyamaka-kārikā* and the *Dvādashadvāra-shāstra* of → Nāgārjuna and the *Shata-shāstra* of → Āryadeva. These were translated into Chinese and provided with commentary by → Kumārajīva in the 5th century. Kumārajīva passed these texts on to his students → Tao-sheng, → Seng-chao, and Seng-lang. The last of these delimited the San-lun school from the → Satyasiddhi school and can thus be regarded as its actual founder. In the 6th century the most important representatives of this school were → Fa-lang and → Chi-tsang and under them the San-lun school experienced a major upsurge. In the 7th century it was brought to Japan by Ekwan, a Korean student of Chi-tsang's. After the appearance of the → Fa-hsiang school, the San-lun school decreased in importance.

To the teachings of the Indian → Mādhyamikas, which the Chinese adopted, several purely Chinese ideas were added. The San-lun school postulates that the Buddha taught two different paths: that of the → *shrāvakas*, and that of the → bodhisattvas. The San-lun school is part of the latter. The school also distinguishes three phases of doctrine. The first phase is that of the → *Buddhāvatamsaka-sūtra*, which represents the beginning of the Buddha's teaching career. The teaching of this sūtra was meant for bodhisattvas, but the students at that time were not yet ripe for this kind of instruction. Thus follows the second phase, which extends from the *Buddhāvatamsaka-sūtra* to the *Lotus Sūtra*, includes all the teachings of the Hīnayāna and the Mahāyāna, and is directed toward *shrāvakas*, → *pratyekabuddhas*, and bodhisattvas. The third phase follows the period of the *Lotus Sūtra*; in this period beings were ready to accept the single buddha-vehicle (→ *ekayāna)*.

Sanmai 🅉 Jap. → *zammai*

San-mei-k'o 🅉 Chin. (Jap., *Hōkyō zanmai*), lit. "[*Song of the*] *Treasure House of Mirrorlike Samādhi*"; written work of the Chinese Ch'an (Zen) master → Tung-shan Liang-chieh (Jap., Tōzan Ryōkai) in which he celebrates the experience of the "suchness" (Skt. *tathatā*) of things, thus their true nature or buddha-nature (→ *busshō*). An English translation of the Chinese original is in Cleary 1980b.

Sanmotsu 🅉 Jap., lit. "three things"; when a Zen master (→ *rōshi*) has proved himself after his confirmation as → *shōshi* through further years of leading people on the path of Zen, then *sanmotsu* is conferred on him in a special ceremony, usually in his own *zendō*. This is the last and definitive confirmation that a principal student receives from his master. In earlier days its conferral was subject to very strict standards.

This confirmation is enacted by adding the Zen name of the master being confirmed to each of three paper strips (the "three things") of about 30 times 100 cm, on each of which has been written in a different way the chain of names of the holders of the lineage from Shākyamuni down to the present day.

Sanne Ippatsu 🅉 also ehatsu for short, Jap., lit. "three robes, one bowl"; the three robes (one for summer, one for winter, and an overgarment) and the begging and eating bowls that are the sole possessions of a Buddhist monk.

Sannyāsa 🄷 (Saṃnyāsa), Skt., lit. "renunciation"; 1. the fourth and final stage of life (→ *āshrama*), the highest stage, whereby the Hindu abandons all worldly things and gives up all selfish interests. His efforts are wholly directed toward → *moksha* (liberation) and union with God. One who in spiritual wisdom renounces the world in order to realize God becomes a → *sannyāsin*. Having once become a liberated soul, he sees through the deceptive game of material pleasures and wanders freely everywhere as a living witness to the reality of God, helping others to spiritual knowledge through his own knowledge. 2. The initiation ceremony at which a novice performs his monastic vows and becomes a *sannyāsin*.

Sannyāsa-Upanishad 🄷 (Saṃnyāsa-Upanishad), Skt., an Upanishad belonging to the → *Atharvaveda*, one of seven Upanishads having to do with → *sannyāsa*. (P. Deussen has given these the collective title "Sannyāsa-Upanishads.") This ancient Upanishad describes in five chapters how the householder (→ *grihastha*) becomes a forest hermit (→ *vānaprastha*) and finally, as a *sannyāsin*, renounces the world entirely.

Sannyāsin 🄷 (Saṃnyāsin), or Sannyāsi, from → *sannyāsa;* one who has renounced the world and who lives totally without possessions solely for the realization of liberation (→ *moksha*). The *sannyāsin's* lack of possessions consists not only in total material poverty but also in what Christian mysticism calls the "poverty of spirit," that is, freedom from such dualistic notions as good and bad, desire and repulsion, fear and greed.

The use of such terms as *sannyāsin* or → *bhagavan* by Western followers of modern-day gurus is an example of the impoverished meaning of such words: when a mouse is called an elephant, the word "elephant" loses its value as the unequivocal term for a real elephant, and ultimately language loses its function as a means of communication.

San-pao 🅃 Chin., lit. "three treasures"; the term *san-pao* occurs in the → *Tao-te ching* and refers to love, moderation, and the renunciation of fame and honor.

Chapter 67 of the *Tao-te ching* (Lin 1949) states:
I have Three Treasures;
Guard them and keep them safe:
The first is Love.
The second is, Never too much.
The third is, Never be the first in the world.
Through Love, one has no fear;
Through not doing too much, one has amplitude [of reserve power];
Through not presuming to be the first in the world,
One can develop one's talent and let it mature.
If one forsakes love and fearlessness,
Forsakes restraint and reserve power,
Forsakes following behind and rushes in front,
He is dead!
For love is victorious in attack,
And invulnerable in defence.
Heaven arms with love
Those it would see destroyed.

In religious Taoism (→ *tao-chiao*) the term *san-pao* has varied meanings: (1) similar to the three treasures of Buddhism, it refers to the Way (→ Tao), the Taoist scriptures (→ *Tao-tsang*), and the masters of the Way (→ *tao-shih*). Taoists venerate these three treasures in numerous ceremonies; (2) the three cinnabar fields (→ *tan-t'ien*); (3) the so-called inner treasures: primordial essence (→ *ching*), primordial energy (→ *yüan-ch'i,* → *ch'i*), and the primordial spirit (→ *shen,* → *san-yüan*).

The three outer treasures—as opposed to the inner ones—are the ears, eyes, and mouth.

Sanron school **B** from Jap. sanron, "three treatises"; the Japanese form of the Chinese → San-lun school, which in turn comes from the Indian → Mādhyamaka. This school was brought to Japan by the Korean monk Ekwan in the year 625 and further spread there by two of his students These two set in motion two currents within the Sanron school (→ Jōjitsu school). The Sanron in Japan was never an independently organized school; its teachings were studied by followers of all Buddhist schools because it contained essential elements for an understanding of the → Mahāyāna that served as a theoretical basis for many schools.

The Sanron school was a major influence on Prince Shōtoku (574–622), who unified Japan. Three Korean masters of Sanron taught in his temple. The teachings of this school are reflected in the "constitution" that Shōtoku gave Japan.

San-sheng Hui-jan **Z** (Jap., Sanshō Enen) a Chinese Ch'an (Zen) master of about the 9th century; one of the most outstanding students and a dharma successor (→ *hassu*) of → Lin-chi I-hsuan (Jap., Rinzai Gigen). San-sheng compiled the *Lin-chi-lu* (Jap., *Rinzai-roku*) in which the sayings and teachings of Lin-chi are recorded. We encounter San-sheng in examples 49 and 68 of the → *Pi-yen-lu.*

After San-sheng had taken leave of Lin-chi. he wandered through China seeking to deepen his realization in → *hossen* with other Ch'an masters. One day when he came to → Hsiang-yen Chih-hsien, the following took place:

"Hsian-yen asked San-sheng, 'Where do you come from?'

"San-sheng answered, 'From Lin-chi.'

"Hsiang-yen said, 'Did you bring Lin-chi's sword with you?'

"Even before Hsiang-yen had finished speaking, San-cheng stepped forward, grabbed a cushion and hit Hsiang-yen with it.

"Hsiang-yen said nothing and only smiled."

Sanshō Enen **Z** Jap. for → San-sheng Hui-jan

Sanskrit **H** (Saṃskṛta), Skt., lit. "perfect, complete, made final." Over the course of centuries, the language of the peoples who emigrated from northwestern regions toward India was refined and perfected, in order to lend expression to the mystical truths that were revealed to the → *rishis* in their meditations. A highly differentiated terminology was developed in Sanskrit that comprehends the various stages of meditation, states of consciousness beyond that of everyday experience, and various mental and spiritual processes. Most of these terms have no equivalent in European languages. Today Sanskrit is a "dead" language, as is Latin, but it remains the sacred language of Hinduism, since all of its religious texts, from the Vedas and the Upanishads to the *Bhagavad-Gītā,* are composed in Sanskrit.

As one of the Asian languages, Sanskrit developed an alphabet of its own, Devanāgarī (from *deva*: "God," and *nāgarī*: "city"); the name means that the language has found a home for the words of the gods. Sanskrit became the "language of the gods," since for Hindus an enlightened being has attained divine consciousness and hence speaks like God (a notion that will not be entirely alien to the West if one compares it to Meister Eckehart's statement that "to see God means to see as God sees").

In the transliteration of Devanāgarī into the Roman alphabet, difficulties and discrepancies arose that are still in dispute. There are clear differences, for example, between the English and German principles for transliterating the Devanāgarī characters, and even the scholars in Germany are not in agreement among themselves on all points. Then, too, the sequence of letters is entirely different than that followed in our alphabet. The vowels come first, then the consonants, within which group the unvoiced unvariably precede the voiced: *K* before *G*, *T* before *D*, etc. Sanskrit has no *F*, *Q*, *W*, *X*, or *Z*. The first consonant is *K*, which holds a special meaning (→ Ka).

Sansō Z Jap., lit. "mountain monk"; a formula of humility by which a Zen master (→ *rōshi*) refers to himself.

Santosha H (Saṃtoṣa), Skt., lit. "satisfaction, contentment"; one of the five virtues required for the second stage (*niyama*) of → Rāja-Yoga as listed in the *Yoga-Sūtra* of Patañjali. The other four are *shaucha* (purification), → *tapas* (austerity), *svādyāya* (study of the holy scriptures), and → īshvara-pranidhāna (surrender to God).

San-ts'ai T Chin., lit. "three powers"; a term found in the → *I-ching*, referring to Heaven (→ *t'ien*), Earth, and man. Elsewhere the term *san-ts'ai* also may designate the trinity of Heaven and Earth (taken as one constituent), man, and the ten thousand things (→ *wan-wu*).

In the *Shuo-kua* ("Explanation of the Trigrams") of the *I-ching* (see also → *Shih-i* and → *pa-kua*) it is stated: "Therefore they determined the Tao of Heaven and called it the dark and the light. They determined the Tao of the Earth and called it the yielding and the firm. They determined the Tao of Man and called it love (→ *jen*) and rectitude (→ *i*). They combined these three fundamental powers and doubled them; therefore in the Book of Changes is always formed by six lines" (Wilhelm 1967).

San-tsang B → Hsuan-tsang

San-yüan T Chin., lit. "three origins, three foundations"; in Taoist literature the term *san-yüan* refers to various groupings of three: (1) Heaven, Earth, and Water (→ *san-kuan*); (2) the three cinnabar fields (→ *tan-t'ien*); (3) primordial essence (→ *ching*), primordial energy (→ *yüan-ch'i*), and primordial spirit (→ *shen*); i.e., essence, energy, and spirit in the unborn state to which, according to the Taoist teachings, we must return to attain perfection.

Sanzen Z Jap., lit. "going [to] Zen"; to go to a Zen master (→ *rōshi*) to receive instruction. In the → Rinzai school, *sanzen* became a synonym for → *dokusan*. In the vocabulary of → Dōgen Zenji, *sanzen* generally means the right way of practicing Zen. (Also → Sōsan.)

Sarasvatī H Skt.; lit. a legendary river, located partly underground, which converged in the vicinity of Prayāga with the Ganges and the Yamunā. It was held sacred by the people of India even in ancient Vedic times, when they had not yet reached the Ganges, and was venerated as a goddess who later became Brahmā's consort; 2. the goddess of the "stream of speech," of rhetoric, scholarship, and intuition (the divine word). The inception of → Sanskrit and of its alphabet (Devanāgarī) is attributed to her. She is also the patron of the arts, especially of music.

Sārnāth B city near Benares (today Isipatana), where the historical Buddha → Shākyamuni gave his first discourse after his awakening (→ *bodhi*). This is traditionally referred to as "setting in motion the wheel of the teaching (→ dharma-chakra)."

The 44-meter-high Dhamek stūpa dating from the 4th to 6th centuries still indicates today the spot on which the Buddha gave this first discourse to his five disciples. This stūpa contains as its core a small brick stūpa from the time of King → Ashoka. There was also in Sārnāth a stūpa containing relics of the Buddha; this was torn down in the 18th century. Also of the Mūlagandhakūtī Temple, which marks the Buddha's meditation place, only the foundation walls are preserved.

Sarvabhūta H Skt., lit. "all beings"; all existence, the entire manifest world; another term for → *prakriti*.

Sarvajñatā B Skt., "omniscience"; a term for the knowledge of a buddha (→ *samyak-sambuddha*), which is his definitive attribute.

In thc Hīnayāna omniscence is taken to be knowledge of everything that is necessary for the attainment of liberation, since every other form of omniscence was rejected by the Buddha himself.

In the Mahāyāna *sarvajñatā* is interpreted as the knowledge of all dharmas and their true nature, which is empty (→ *shūnyatā*), and is often equated with wisdom (→ *prajñā*).

Sarvam Khalvidam Brahma H Skt., lit. "Verily, all this is *brahman*," a statement made by saints upon attainment of enlightenment.

Sarvāstivāda B Skt., roughly "the teaching that says that everything *is*"; school of the Hīnayāna that split off from the → Sthaviras under the reign of King → Ashoka. The name of this school comes from its basic premise that everything—past, present, and future—exists simultaneously. The Sarvāstivādin school prevailed primarily in Kashmir and → Gandhāra. It constitutes a transitional stage between the → Hīnayāna and the → Mahāyāna.

The Sarvāstivādins possessed their own canon, composed in Sanskrit, which is partially preserved in Chinese and Tibetan translation. The most important works of this school are the → *Abhidharmakosha* by → Vasubandhu and the *Mahāvibhāshā* (*Great Exegesis*), which was composed under the supervision of → Vasumitra at the council of Kashmir and to which the school owes the name → Vaibhāshika, by which it is also known. The *Mahāvibhāshā* is a summary of the Sarvāstivāda teaching and is the latest of the seven works of the → Abhidharma-pitaka. Another important work is the *Abhidharma-hridaya*, the *Heart of* → *Abhidharma* in ten chapters. The *Vibhāshā* by Kātyāyaniputra is also a summary of the doctrine. The *Loka-prajñapti* gives a description of the mythical universe of Buddhism. On matters of discipline, only the *Vinaya-vibhāshā* is extant.

The teaching of the Sarvāstivāda is a radical pluralism based on denial of the reality of a self as a substance or soul (→ *anātman*) and the affirmation of the existence of momentary entities, the so-called → dharmas.

The Sarvāstivādins postulate seventy-five different dharmas, which (like the ancient notion of atoms) represent final, indivisible units, viewed as real. They distinguished conditioned (→ *samskrita*) and unconditioned (→ *asamskrita*) dharmas. Among the latter are space (→ *ākāsha*), → *apratishthita-nirvāna*, and → *pratishthita-nirvāna*.

The conditioned dharmas are divided into four categories: form or matter (→ *rūpa*); consciousness (→ *vijñāna*); mental factors (→ *chetasika*), meaning all psychological processes; and dharmas, which are neither form nor consciousness, and include, for example, old age, vitality, attainment, nonattainment impermanence, and so on.

According to the Sarvāstivādins, these conditioned dharmas do not come into being but rather exist from beginningless time and only change from a latent to a manifest state. From this the view results that "everything *is*," and that past, present, and future exist simultaneously in a single dharma. In addition, one finds in the Sarvāstivāda an early form of the Mahāyāna teaching of the → *trikāya* and the belief, which continued to grow in importance, in the future buddha → Maitreya.

Sarva-Upanishad-Sāra 🅷 , or *Sarva-Upanishada* or *Sarva-Sāra*, Skt.; an Upanishad belonging to the → *Atharvaveda*, in which twenty-three major concepts of → Vedānta philosophy are listed and explained.

Sat 🅷 Skt.; absolute, eternal, unchanging Being; like → *chit* and → *ānanda*, it is identical with → *brahman*.

Satata-Yukta 🅷 Skt., lit. *satata*: "perpetually," *yukta*: "bound"; ever bound to the divine in consciousness.

Satchidānanda 🅷 (Saccidānanda), Skt., lit. "being-consciousness-bliss," a compound of → *sat*, → *chit*, and → *ānanda*. Because → *brahman*, the Absolute, cannot be described with words, this conceptual approximation is used to inspire the intuition of the seeker of liberation (*moksha*).

Satī 🅷 Skt., lit. "true wife"; a name for the consort of → Shiva. According to the *Vishnu-Purāna*, following a quarrel between her husband and her father, → Daksha, she gave up the body and was reborn as Umā, the daughter of Himavat, the ruler of the Himalayas. In the *Kāshi-Kānda*, a section of the *Skanda-Purāna*, it is said that Satī threw herself on a funeral pyre. Hence the widows who committed voluntary self-immolation following the deaths of their husbands in India were called *satī*.

Satipatthāna 🅱 (satipaṭṭhāna), Pali (Skt. smriti-upasthāna), lit. "four awakenings [foundations] of mindfulness"; one of the fundamental meditation practices of the Hīnayāna, which consists of mindfulness of body, feeling (→ *vedanā*), mind (→ *chitta*), and mental objects, in that order. This method is described in detail in the *Satipatthāna-sutta*, and the Buddha is supposed to have said that by itself it could lead to the realization of nirvāna. *Satipatthāna* is a form of meditation that is very much practiced today, also in the West. It can be practiced in sitting meditation as well as during all activities of life.

Mindfulness of body includes mindfulness of inhalation and exhalation (→ *ānāpānasati*) as well as of bodily posture (walking, standing, sitting, lying), clarity of mind during all activities, contemplation of the thirty-two parts of the body, analysis of the bodily elements (→ *dhātu-vavatthāna*), and → charnel ground contemplation.

In mindfulness of feeling, one recognizes feelings as pleasant, unpleasant, or indifferent, worldly or supramundane, and sees clearly their transitory quality.

In mindfulness of mind, every state of consciousness that arises is noted and recognized as passionate or passionless, aggressive or free from aggression, deluded or undeluded.

In mindfulness of mental objects, one is aware of the conditionedness and inessentiality of things, knows whether or not the five hindrances (→ *nīvarana*) are present, recognizes the personality and the basic elements of the mental process as consisting of the five → *skandhas*, and possesses an understanding of the → four noble truths that corresponds to reality.

In the Mahāyāna, this practice is found in a slightly

altered form: body, feeling, mind, and mental objects are recognized as essentially empty (→ *shūnyatā*).

Satipatthāna-sutta 🅑 (Satipaṭṭhāna-sutta), Pali, lit. "*Discourse on the Awakening of Mindfulness*"; a discourse contained in the → *Majjhima-nikāya* and the → *Dīgha-nikāya* on the method of arousing mindfulness (→ *satipatthāna*), one of the most important forms of meditation in the Hīnayāna.

Satori 🅩 Jap.; Zen term for the experience of awakening (→ enlightenment). The word derives from the verb *satoru*, "to know"; however, it has nothing to do with "knowledge" in the ordinary or philosophical sense, because in the experience of enlightenment there is no distinction between knower and known. The word → *kenshō* is also often used as a synonym for satori.

Satsanga 🅗 (Satsaṃga), or Satsang, Skt., lit. *sat*: "good, true," *sanga*: "company"; the company or intercourse with holy people or conscientious seekers of God.

The presence of a holy person can cause the spark of divine intuition to pass from that soul to those present, and the company of other seekers of God can be of great help to each individual through mutual inspiration. For these reasons, *satsang* is recommended to spiritual aspirants.

Sattva 🅗 Skt.; the noblest of the three → *gunas*, characterized as harmoniousness, uprightness, peaceableness, and composure.

Sattvasamatā 🅑 Skt.; sameness of all beings. The firm conviction that there is no distinction between sentient beings is the basis for the compassion (→ *karunā*) that determines the action of a bodhisattva.

Satya 🅗 Skt., lit. "true, genuine, real"; truth, honesty, one of the five virtues of the first stage (*yama*) of → Rāja-Yoga that are required in the *Yoga-Sūtra* of → Patañjali (2.30-31) and constitute the "Great Vow" (→ *mahāvrata*) made for all eight stages. The other four virtues are *ahimsā* (noninjury of others), *asteya* (not stealing), *brahmacharya* (continence) and *aparigraha* (noncovetousness).

Satyāgraha 🅗 Skt., lit."holding *(graha)* to truth *(satya)*"; Mahātma → Gandhi made this term known the world over with his movement of the same name, as he introduced nonviolent disobedience in the face of injustice.

Satyakāma 🅗 Skt., lit. *satya*: "truth," *kama*: "wish, desire"; 1. the desire for truth; 2. Satyakāma Jabālā, a teacher of the → Veda who was an extraordinary lover of truth. The → *Chāndogya-Unpanishad* discusses in detail his background and his spiritual development. The *Brihadāranyaka-Unpanishad* mentions in several places his statements as a teacher.

Satyakāma was the illegitimate son of Jabālā. He wanted to be accepted by the sage Gotama as a student and asked his mother about his origins. She said that she did not know who his father was, because in her youth she had worked as a servant in many places. When the sage asked him about his family, Satyakāma told him honestly what his mother had said. Gotama was convinced that such honesty could come only from a brahman and took him on as a student. Satyakāma was entrusted with the care of the cows. After he had spent many years with them in the forest and had increased their numbers greatly, he began his journey back and on the way received teachings of *brahman* from a bull, a voice from his evening fire, a swan, and a loon. When he arrived, Gotama exclaimed: "Your face shines like that of a knower of *brahman*. Who has taught you?" "Beings other than men," replied Satyakāma, "but please do you teach me also. Only the knowledge that comes from the teacher leads to the supreme good." The sage taught him everything and left out nothing.

Satyaloka 🅗 Skt.; the realm (*loka*) of the supreme truth (*satya*), of the supreme being, the goal of spiritual work, attainable through purification and meditation. Harmony, peace, and bliss rule there, for the one who reaches this goal knows himself to be one with the Absolute.

Satyasiddhi school 🅑 Skt. (Chin., Ch'eng-shih; Jap., → Jōjitsu), lit. "School of the Perfection of Truth"); school of Chinese Buddhism based on the Indian → Sautrāntikas. The text fundamental for this school is the *Satyasiddhi* of → Harivarman (4th century), which was translated into Chinese by → Kumārajīva in the 5th century.

Important representatives of this school were Seng-t'ao and Seng-sung, both students of Kumārajīva, who spread the teaching of the Satyasiddhi school throughout China. As a result, by the beginning of the 6th century it was one of the most important Buddhist schools in the country. It stood in opposition to the → San-lun school, which accused the masters of the *Satyasiddhi* of falsely explaining the notion of emptiness. The attacks by → Chi-tsang and → Fa-lang, two important representatives of the San-lun school, finally led to a decrease of interest in the Satyasiddhi school.

In the 7th century the Satyasiddhi school was brought to Japan by a Korean monk, where, however, it continued only as a part of the → San-ron school, the Japanese form of the San-lun.

This school is classified as Hīnayāna, since it draws its support directly from the teachings of the Buddha, the sūtras. Its basic premise is the negation of all true existence—neither mind nor matter are real. However, it teaches a twofold truth: the "worldly," conventional truth and the "supreme" truth. The Satyasiddhi school subsumes the phenomenal existence of the → dharmas under the first; these arise in a conditioned manner, are mutable, and exist only for a limited time. From the point of view of the supreme truth all dharmas are empty (→ *shūnyatā*). The Satyasiddhi school thus advocates the view that both the person (→ *pudgala*) and the dharmas are empty. Because of this it is often considered a Mahāyāna school. However, in contrast to the true Mahāyāna, which posits a transcendental emptiness, the emptiness of the Satyasiddhi school can only be reached by destruction or abstraction—every object is dismantled, first into its molecules and then into its atoms, until one finally arrives at emptiness. It is an antithetical emptiness as opposed to the synthetical emptiness of the San-lun school.

Saumyatva 🅗 Skt.; gentleness, goodness. One of the four "perfections of the heart" (→ *kalyāna-shraddha).*

Sautrāntika 🅑 Skt.; Hīnayāna school that developed out of the → Sarvāstivāda around 150 C.E. As its name indicates, the followers of this school draw their support only from the → Sūtra-pitaka and reject the → Abhidharma-pitaka of the Sarvāstivāda as well as its "everything is" theory.

The Sautrāntikas posit the existence of a refined consciousness that constitutes the basis of human life and that persists from one rebirth to the next. In contrast to the → Vātsīputrīyas, who postulate the existence of an entire "person" that persists from one life to the next, the Sautrāntikas see the consciousness as no more than the bearer of the cycle of existence (→ samsāra). Into this consciousness the remaining four → *skandhas* are absorbed at the time of death. This notion of a continuously existing consciousness had a strong influence on the → Yogāchāra school.

The theory of the instantaneity of everything existing is very pronounced in the Sautrāntika school. It sees in each existent nothing more than an uninterrupted succession of moments; duration is only a semblance, an illusion that is produced only by the density of succession of individual moments. → Nirvāna for the Sautrāntikas is a purely negative spiritual event—it is nonbeing. He who has attained release is annihilated.

Savichāra-Samādhi 🅗 (Savicāra-Samādhi), Skt.; a term used in the yoga philosophy of → Patañjali. It refers to a state in which the mind identifies with the object of meditation but is still partially involved with the perception of names, qualities, and cognition. (See also → *nirvichāra-samādhi.*)

Savikalpa-Samādhi 🅗 Skt.; a state of consciousness in which one knows God or → *brahman* but remains in a subject-object relationship with him. In contrast to → *nirvikalpa-samādhi,* this state still contains a trace of duality, which prevents total absorption in God. *Savikalpa-samādhi* may be compared to the *visio Dei* of Christian mysticism.

Savitri 🅗 (Savitr), Skt., lit. "procreator"; 1. in the Vedas, a name for the sun god → Sūrya. Many hymns are directed to him; 2. one of the → Ādityas.

Sāvitrī 🅗 Skt.; 1. a sacred verse from the → *Rig-veda* (3.62.10), generally known as the → Gāyatrī; 2. the consort of → Brahmā, regarded as the personification of the verse; 3. the daughter of King Ashvapati and the beloved of Satyavān. She wished to marry him, although a → *rishi* had warned her that he would live only one year longer. She followed him on the fatal day, and as he lay dying she saw the figure of → Yama, god of death, who had come to fetch her husband. As he carried Satyavān away, she followed him. Her devotion pleased Yama. He therefore offered her three boons, but told her not to ask for her husband's life. Sāvitrī tricked Yama by asking for children, so that Yama finally had to return her husband to life.

Sayadaw 🅑 Burm., "teacher"; Burmese title for a Buddhist monk. This title properly only applies to the abbot of a monastery but is frequently used also as an honorific form of address for monks in general.

Sāyana 🅗 (Sāyaṇa), or Sāyanāchārya, a famous fourteenth-century commentator on the Vedas and the older brother of the South Indian scholar → Vidyāranya.

Both brothers were celebrated scholars who composed not only important commentaries to the Samhitās and Brāhmanas of the Vedas but also original works on grammar and law.

School of the Magic Jewel 🅣 → *ling-pao p'ai*

School of Three Stages B → San-chieh school

Seal of transmission Z → *inka-shōmei*

Seidō Chizō Z Jap. for → Hsi-tang Chih-tsang

Seigan Z Jap. → Shiguseigan

Seirai-no-i Z Jap., lit. "the meaning of coming out of the west"; an expression that refers to the coming of → Bodhidharma from India to China and to the profound meaning, the innermost principle, of the → buddha-dharma transmitted by him. The question concerning coming out of the west, which comes up again and again in Ch'an (Zen) literature, is a question concerning the one truth of Ch'an (Zen) and represents a challenge to a → *mondō* or → *hossen.*

Seiza Z Jap., lit. "sitting in silence"; the traditional Japanese sitting posture in which one kneels sitting on one's heels, the back held straight and erect. *Seiza,* among practitioners of → *zazen,* is an alternative to the lotus posture (→ *kekka-fusa*; Skt., padmāsana), which is more generally considered in the East the most appropiate sitting posture for mediation.

Sekishu Z Jap., lit. "one hand"; a reference in short form to the → kōan, "What is the sound of one hand clapping?" This is the best known kōan stemming from a Japanese Zen master, → Hakuin Zenji. Hakuin saw it, with the kōan (→ *mu*), as one of the most effective *hosshin-kōans,*, i.e., as a kōan particularly suitable for aiding a practitioner working with it to come to a first enlightenment experience (→ *kenshō,* → *satori).*

Sekisō Keishō Z Jap. for → Shih-shuang Ch'ing-chu

Sekisō Soen Z Jap. for → Shih-shuang Ch'u-yuan

Sekitō Kisen Z Jap. for → Shih-t'ou Hsi-ch'ien

Self-realization Z → *kenshō*

Sengai Gibon Z 1751–1837; Japanese Zen master of the Rinzai school. He became a monk at the age of 11 and at 19 went on wandering pilgrimage (→ *angya*). He became a student and dharma successor (→ *hassu*) of Master Gessen Zenji. After his training with Gessen was completed, he went once again on wandering pilgrimage and was appointed in 1790 the 123rd abbot of Shōfuku-ji in Hakata on Kyūshū, which had been founded in 1195 by → Eisai Zenji as the first Zen monastery in Japan.

Sengai was known for his unorthodox but extremely effective style of training Zen students and for his humor. These are qualities that are reflected in his ink paintings and calligraphies, which have come to be appreciated by lovers of art throughout the world.

Seng-chao B 374 or 378–414; important representative of the → San-lun school of Chinese → Mādhyamaka. Seng-chao, who came from Ch'ang-an (present-day Xian), occupied himself initially with the teachings of → Lao-tzu and → Chuang-tzu. After reading the → *Vimalakīrti-nirdesha-sūtra* he became a monk and studied the writings of → Nāgārjuna under → Kumārajīva. His renown as a thinker and writer rests primarily on three treatises: on the immutability of things, on the emptiness (→ *shūnyatā*) of the unreal, and on "→ *Prajñā* is not knowledge." In them he tries to show that the absolute and the relative, the phenomenal and the essential, are not something separate and opposite. The manifoldness of appearances is not based on an immutable substance. For Seng-chao substance and appearance are the same.

His works, which are on the highest literary level, represent a synthesis of Indian and Chinese thought.

The "immutability of things" consists for Seng-chao in the fact that past things are neither "at rest" not identical wih present things, nor do past things develop into present ones through movement. For him neither rest nor movement exists.

His concept of *shūnyatā* is that things both exist and do not exist. Everything arises in a conditioned manner; if the cause of it falls away, a thing ceases to exist. According to Seng-chao's view, things are like a magically created man, which on the one hand is not real; but since it exists as magically created, it is on the other hand not unreal.

In his work on *prajñā,* Seng-chao defines *prajñā* as "knowledge" that has the absolute for object. The absolute, however, is empty and without qualities, and thus cannot in fact be an object. But it is also not separate from things. Thus the sage dwells in the realm of emptiness and nonactivity, but at the same time in the realm of activity.

Senge Z Jap., lit. "entering transformation"; an expression referring in Buddhism to a person's death, particularly that of a Buddhist master. This expression reflects the fact that Buddhism does not regard death as an end but rather only a change in outer form; the essence of a human being, his or her buddha-nature (→ *busshō*), is eternal, i.e., timeless and beyond becoming and passing away.

Seng-ts'an 🅩 (Jap. Sōsan), d. 606?; the third patriarch (→ *soshigata*) of Ch'an (Zen) in China; the dharma successor (→ *hassu*) of → Hui-k'o and the master of → Tao-hsin. Hardly any details are known of the life of the third patriarch. There are, however, many legends about him and his meeting with Hui-k'o. According to one of these legends Seng-ts'an was suffering from leprosy when he met the second patriarch. Hui-k'o is supposed to have encountered him with the words, "You're suffering from leprosy; what could you want from me?" Seng-ts'an is supposed to have replied, "Even if my body is sick, the heart-mind (→ *kokoro*) of a sick person is no different from your heart-mind." This convinced Hui-k'o of the spiritual capacity of Seng-tsan; he accepted him as a student and later confirmed him as his dharma successor and the thirtieth patriarch (third Chinese patriarch) in the lineage of Ch'an (Zen), which begins with → Shākyamuni Buddha.

The incident that marked the "transmission from heart-mind to heart-mind" (→ isshin-denshin) from Hui-k'o to Seng-ts'an is given in the → *Denkō-roku* as follows:

The thirtieth patriarch Kanchi Daishi [*daishi*, "great master"] went (for instruction) to the twenty-ninth patriarch and asked, "The body of the student is possessed by mortal illness. I beg you, master, wipe away my sins."

The patriarch [Hui-k'o] said, "Bring me your sins here, and I'll wipe them away for you."

The master [Seng-ts'an] sat in silence for a while, then said, "Although I've looked for my sins, I can't find them."

The patriarch said, "In that case I've already thoroughly wiped away your sins. You should live in accordance with Buddha, dharma, and *sangha*" [→ *sambō*].

It is said that during the Buddhist persecution of the year 574, Seng-ts'an had to feign mental illness in order to escape execution, and that finally he went into hiding for ten years on Mount Huan-kung. His mere presence there is said to have pacified the wild tigers, which until that time had caused great fear among the local people. The authorship of the *Hsin-hsin-ming* (Jap., *Shinjimei*) is attributed to Seng-ts'an. It is one of the earliest Ch'an writings. It expounds Ch'an's basic principles in poetic form and shows strong Taoist influence. The *Hsin-hsin-ming* begins with a famous sentence, which comes up again and again in Ch'an (Zen) literature (for instance, in example 2 of the → *Pi-yen-lu*): "The venerable way is not difficult at all; it only abhors picking and choosing." In this early Ch'an poem, the fusion, typical for later Ch'an (Zen), of the mutually congenial teachings of Mahāyāna Buddhism and Taoism appears for the first time.

Sengyo 🅩 Jap., lit. "fish weir"; a Zen expression pointing to the fact that the reality sought by the Zen practitioner in direct experience cannot be found in scriptures or techniques of practice. These are at best only supportive means that can help us come to such an experience but that never contain that reality itself. Thus one should never cling to concepts and methods but should "forget" these in order to make oneself available for the experience of true reality (→ enlightenment). The expression stems from the great Taoist sage Chuang-tzu, one of the spiritual forebears of Ch'an (Zen). He writes, "The fish weir is there to catch fish; we should keep the fish and forget the weir. The snare is there to catch rabbits; we should keep the rabbits and forget the snare. Words are there to convey a profound meaning; we should keep the meaning and forget the words" (*Chuang-tzu*, 31).

Senkan 🅩 Jap. for Hsuan-chien, → Te-shan Hsuan-chien

Senshō-Fuden 🅩 Jap., lit. "not transmittable by a thousand sages"; a Zen expression indicating that Zen realization cannot be told. Even a thousand sages could not convey it in words; each person must awaken to it by and for himself. (Also → *fukasetsu*.)

Sentsang 🅑 → Hsuan-tsang

Seppō Gison 🅩 Jap. for → Hsueh-feng I-ts'un

Sesshin 🅩 Jap., lit. "collecting (*setsu*) the heart-mind (*shin*, → *kokoro*)"; days of especially intensive, strict practice of collected mind (→ *zazen*) as carried out in Zen monasteries at regular intervals.

The normal daily routine in a Zen monastery includes, in addition to several hours of *zazen* practice, long periods of physical work, begging rounds (→ *takuhatsu*), and other forms of service to the community of believers. However, during a *sesshin*, which is considered the high point of Zen training, the monks devote themselves exclusively to meditation. Long periods of *zazen* are interrupted only by a few hours of sleep at night, recitations, a short period of work (→ *samu*), and short rest breaks after the midday and evening meals. However, concentration or collectedness of mind in relation to the particular practice that the monk has received from the master (for example, → kōan practice or *shikantaza*) should continue as much as possible without interruption during all these activities. Special inspiration and incentive for the monks during the days of *sesshin* are provided by the → *teishō* of the → *rōshi* and the individual instruction (→ *dokusan*) that monks often receive several times a day.

Sesshu Tōyō Z 1420–1506; a monk of the → Rinzai school who is considered one of the greatest painters of Japan and certainly the most important Zen painter.

Sesson Yūbai Z 1288–1346; Japanese Zen master of the → Rinzai school. He was initially a student of the Chinese master → I-shan I-ning (Jap., Issan Ichinei) at the → Kenchō-ji in Kamakura. In 1307 he went to China, where he soon fell under suspicion as a spy and was imprisoned for ten years. After this, he wandered throughout China seeking out Chinese Ch'an (Zen) masters. In 1328 he returned to Japan and settled at the Manju-ji monastery at the request of Shōgun Ashikaga Takauji. In 1345 he was appointed abbot of → Kennin-ji. With his first master I-shan I-ning he is considered a founder of the Literature of the Five Mountains (→ Gosan-bungaku).

Setchō Jūken Z Jap. for → Hsueh-tou Ch'ung-hsien

Seven Holy Cities H → *nagara*

Shabda H (Śabda), Skt., lit. "sound"; in Sanskrit every sound has two aspects, the gross aspect of the audible sound and the subtle aspect, a vibration that is transcendent in nature. This inner sound is the true *shabda;* also called *sphota,* it rises from the eternal unmoving principle with illuminating force (*shakti*). When its vehicle, the spoken word (*dhvani*), resonates in inner and exterior perfection, it causes the inner force to vibrate, and this power can then impart insight, even to the point of full illumination. (See also → mantra).

Shabda-Brahman H (Śabda-Brahman), Skt.; the world of sound (→ *shabda*) is described in Sanskrit as a manifestation of *brahman.* In the ancient Vedic tongue, *brahman* is the word for "mantra" or "power of prayer." In the later texts of the Upanishads, *brahman* is ultimate transcendence, whereas *shabda-brahman* refers to the "written Veda," that is, the words of the eternal, imperishable → Veda as the manifestation of *brahman.*

Shadāyatana B (ṣaḍāyatana) Skt. (Pali, salāyatana), roughly "six bases or realms"; term referring to the six objects of the sense organs, the objects of seeing, hearing, smelling, tasting, touch, and mental representation (→ *ayātana*).

As the fifth link in the chain of conditioned arising (→ *pratītya-samutpāda*), they are the realms of sense activity that present themselves to the sense organs of a being after its birth and make possible contact (→ *sparsha*) with its environment.

Shaiva H Skt. → Shaivism

Shaiva-Siddhānta H (Śaiva-Siddhānta), Skt., lit. "the highest goal of the Shaivas"; name given to the South Indian movement → Shaivism, which resembles the → Vishishtādvaita-Vedānta (qualified nondualism) of → Rāmānuja in that it postulates neither absolute identity nor absolute disparity between God, the soul, and the world. The highest god is → Shiva with his consort Ambā (the feminine aspect or → Shakti).

The sources of this school derive from Aryan, but also from Dravidian culture, the Vedic figure → Rudra, the Rudra-Shiva cult of the → brahmans, the → *Māhābhārata,* the → *Shvetāshvatara-Upanishad,* and the Shaiva-Āgamas. The most important scriptures of the school are the *Shaiva-Siddānta-Shāstra,* Nīlakantha's commentary on the *Brahma-Sūtras,* and Apyaya Dīkshita's commentary *Shivārkamanidīpika.*

Shaivism H , or Shivaism; one of the three major devotional movements in modern-day Hinduism. The other two are → Vaishnavism and → Shaktism. Shaivas view Shiva as the supreme being and devote themselves to his worship alone. He is for them the creator, the maintainer, and the destroyer of the universe. Shaivism in South India is called → Shaiva-Siddhānta; Shaivism in Kashmir is called → Pratyabhijñā.

Shākhā H (Śākhā), Skt., lit. "branch"; of the Veda, Vedic school. At first the Vedas were transmitted orally from generation to generation; in the process, various Vedic schools developed, so that each of the four Vedas existed simultaneously in various forms (*shākhās*). Above all, each *shakha* had its own → Brāhmana, consisting on the one hand of instruction *(vidhi)* and interpretation *(atharvāda),* the two ritual texts, and on the other hand of Vedānta (end of the Veda, final observation), that is, the Upanishadic text, or dogmatic text. The → Upanishads were originally simply the dogmatic texts of the individual Vedic schools.

Shako Z Jap., lit. "this!"; a cry customary in Zen, which points directly to genuine reality.

Shākta H Skt. → Shaktism

Shakti H (Śakti), Skt., lit. "force, power, energy"; the consort of → Shiva, venerated throughout India under many names (e.g. Ambā, Durgā, Kālī). She is the personification of primal energy, the force of → *brahman,* the dynamic aspect of God through whose agency he creates, maintains, and dissolves. Hindus believe that Shakti's grace is needed in order to grasp the transcendent aspect of God.

Shakti is of particular importance in → Tantra, in which, for example, each → *chakra* is governed by a particular Shakti: Mūladhāra is governed by Kākindī, Svādhishthāna by Rākinī, Manipūra by Lākinī, Anāhata by Kākinī, Vishuddha by Shākinī, and Ājñā by Hākinī. (See also → *kundalinī.*)

Shakti-Sānchāra H (Śakti-Sāṃcāra), Skt., lit. "setting forces in motion"; the awakening of spiritual powers through transference of such faculties from guru to pupil.

Shaktism H (Śaktism), also called Tantrism; one of the three major traditions of worship in modern Hinduism. The other two are → Vaishnavism and → Shaivism. Shāktas worship → Shakti and revere her as the force that makes all life possible and maintains the universe. This is the fundamental creative force whose most primary expression is the sexual energy that unites the polarity of male and female and brings forth new life. Hence the symbols of Shaktism (→ *yoni,* → *linga*) are sexual in nature, and the deities of Shaktism are often represented iconographically in the act of sexual union. As a way toward experience of the Ultimate Reality, Shāktas employ sexual practices (as, for example, those presented in the → *Kāma-Sūtra*) in connection wih practices from → Kundalinī-Yoga. In many sects, the sexual forms of expression are now only symbols of inner meditative processes; union is achieved no longer on the physical level but on the mental level alone (see also → Tantra). An introduction to the intellectual basis of Shaktism can be found in Mookerjee & Khanna 1977.

Shakujō Z Jap., lit. "copper staff"; the priest's staff that is part of the equipment of a Zen monk (→ *unsui*) during pilgrimage (→ *angya*).

The *shakujō* is a wooden staff with a metal cap on which a metal ring is loosely hung so that a jingling noise is made in walking. This noise is intended to warn beetles, snakes, and other small creatures on which the monk might possibly tread of his approach so that they can get out of the way. Thus the monk, whose way of life includes the intention not to cause suffering to any sentient being, will not inadvertently kill or injure them.

Shakuntalā H (Śakuntalā), Skt., an → *apsarā* (heavenly nymph), the mother of King → Bharata. The story of her love for King Dushyanta is told in the famous drama *Shakuntalā,* by → Kālidāsa. Its source is the *Māhabhārata* and the *Padma-Purāna.*

Shakuntalā lived in the hermitage of a *rishi.* When King Dushyanta espied her in the forest, he fell in love with her and prevailed upon her to enter a *gandharva* marriage (a simple declaration of marriage by both parties). Before leaving her, he gave her a ring in token of his pledge. Lost in thoughts of Dushyanta, Shakuntalā neglected to accord proper respect to a holy guest of the hermitage. He pronounced a curse, saying that her lover would forget her, but promised that the curse would be lifted if Dushyanta were to see the ring. On the way to find the king, Shakuntalā bathed in a lake and thereby lost the ring, which was swallowed by a big fish. A fisherman caught the fish and sold it to the king, who remembered Shakuntalā when he saw the ring and took her as his wife, together with the son (Bharata) who had been born to her in the meantime.

Shākya B (Śākya) Skt. (Pali, Sakka); a noble clan from which the historical Buddha → Siddhārtha Gautama came and which ruled one of the sixteen states into which the India of his time was splintered. The Shākyas occupied the area of present-day southern Nepal. Their capital was → Kapilavastu, where the Buddha was born and grew up. The Buddha's father, Suddhodana, was then the king of the Shākya state.

The Shākyas had formed an aristocratic republic, ruled by a council of elders (*sangha*) but to a certain extent dependent upon the state of → Koshala. The clan was nearly entirely wiped out by a hostile Koshalan king during the lifetime of the Buddha.

Many Shākyas entered the Buddhist order when the Buddha returned to Kapilavastu after his enlightenment to teach. The simple barber → Upāli was the first to be ordained as a monk and thus was ranked higher in the *sangha* than the leading personalities of the state.

Shākyamuni B (Śākyamuni) Skt., lit. "Sage of the → Shākya Clan"; epithet of → Siddhārtha Gautama, the founder of Buddhism (→ buddhadharma), the historical Buddha, who belonged to the Shākya clan. Siddhārtha received this epithet after he had separated himself from his teachers and resolved to find the way to enlightenment by himself.

Typical representation of Buddha Shākyamuni with the earth-touching gesture (bhūmisparsha-mudrā)

Shākyamuni is often used in association with *Buddha* (*Shākyamuni Buddha*) in order to distinguish the historical Buddha from other buddhas.

Shama 🅗 (Śama), Skt.; control of the mind; undivided concentration on an object of meditation. In Shankara's → *Tattvabodha* it is one of the "six virtues" (→ *shatkasampatti*).

Shamatha 🅑 (śamatha), Skt., lit. "dwelling in tranquility"; In the → Gelugpa school of Tibetan Buddhism it is stressed that the precondition of "concentration" (→ *samādhi*) is intentional development of "dwelling in tranquility" and "special insight" (→ *vipashyanā*). Dwelling in tranquility calms the mind, while special insight, through analytical examination, leads to vision of genuine reality, which is emptiness (→ *shūnyatā*). *Shamatha* is first developed in preliminary practice and later further refined in connection with *vipashyanā*. Dwelling in tranquility is compared to a still, clear lake in which the "fish of special insight" plays.

The various obstacles that counter the development of *shamatha* are overcome through nine stages of mind, six powers, and four mental activities.

1. The *stages of mind* are (a) directedness of mind toward the object of meditation, (b) stabilization of the mind, (c) continuous renewal of attention, (d) confinement to the object, (e) taming of the mind, (f) calming the mind, (g) refined calm, (h) the mind collected into oneness, and (i) *samādhi*.

2. The *powers* are (a) hearing the teaching (corresponds to 1a), (b) reflection (1b), (c) power of attention (1c–d), (d) clear comprehension (1e–f), (e) concentrated energy (1g–h), and (f) natural confidence (1i).

3. The *mental activities* are: (a) connecting the mind to the object (corresponds to 1a–b), (b) reestablishment of attention (1c–g), (c) uninterrupted attention (1h), (d) dwelling effortlessly (1i).

The concepts of this program of practice come from the literature of the → Yogāchāra school and were put into practice in Tibet as a unified system of meditation. The entire process is often made clear by the use of an image. The two hindering tendencies of torpor and overexcitement are depicted as an elephant and a monkey. In the course of practice, these two are tamed.

Shambhala 🅑 (Śambhala), Skt.; name of a mythical kingdom, the geographical location of which is uncertain, but which according to legend lies northeast of India. It is considered the place of origin of the → Kālachakra teachings and, with all its associations as a "source of auspiciousness," plays a central role in → Tibetan Buddhism. A key part of the myth is that the savior of humanity will come out of Shambhala at a time when the world is dominated by war and destruction.

The various speculations concerning the precise location of Shambhala range from areas of Central Asia to China and the North Pole. The importance of this kingdom has less to do with the possibility of locating it precisely than with the spiritual quality that is associated with it. The Tibetan tradition includes Shambhala among the "hidden valleys," certain places that become accessible at times of urgent need.

The twenty-five teachers who proclaim the Kālachakra teaching also play a role in the Shambhala myth. At the time of the last of these, a golden age will dawn and all negative forces will be overcome. Under the influence of this prophecy, Shambhala has in the course of time become associated with the epic of → Gesar and with the coming of → Maitreya.

The third → Panchen Lama composed a guide for finding this kingdom that was very popular in Tibet and was based on a work preserved in the Tibetan canon (→ Kangyur-Tengyur). A detailed exposition of the Shambhala myth is Bernbaum, *The Way to Shambhala* (1980).

Shāmbhava 🅗 (Śāṃbhava), Skt., from Shambu ("the prosperous"), an epithet for → Shiva; the underlying philosophy of → Tantra, representing the viewpoint that Shiva is impersonal and inactive and brings everything about through his → Shakti.

Shānavāsin 🅉 third patriarch of the Indian lineage of Ch'an (→ Zen).

Shāndilya-Vidyā 🄷 (Śāṇḍilya-Vidyā), Skt.; a comprehensive view, named for the saint Shāndilya. It includes the soul's relationship both to the material world and to the spiritual sources of light and knowledge.

Shang-ch'ing 🅃 Chin. → *san-ch'ing*

Shankara 🄷 (Śaṃkara), or Shankarāchārya, 788–820, one of India's greatest saints and philosophers; his name means "he who brings blessings" and is also an epithet for Shiva in his role as chief of the → Rudras. Shankara was the main representative of → Advaita-Vedānta and the renewer of Hinduism after that tradition had been displaced for a time by Buddhism. Despite the short span of his life, the versatile student of → Gaudapada's student Govindapada composed numerous works. The most important of these are → *Ātmabodha,* → *Tattvabodha,* → *Upadesha-Sahasri,* → *Viveka-Chūdāmani,* and the great commentary on the *Vedānta-Sūtra, Shārīraka-Bhāshya.* He also wrote commentaries on the → *Bhagavad-Gītā,* on ten Upanishads, and on hymns to various gods.

Shankara was born in Kāladi on the coast of Malabar and died in Kedārnāth in the Himalayas at the age of thirty-two. When he was eight years old he renounced the world and began to wander throughout India. He displayed such great wisdom and holiness that he was viewed as an incarnation of Shiva; hence the name Shankara. He founded numerous monasteries in order to spread his teachings through the monks. The chief of these monasteries is Shringeri in South India; the three next important are → Puri in the east, → Dvaraka in the west, and Badrinath in the Himalayas. Shankara was at once a philosopher and a poet, a scholar and a saint, a mystic and a reformer. Several of his pupils wrote works about his life, of which the most important are Vidyāranya's *Shankaradigvijaya* and → Ānandagiri's *Shankaravijaya.*

Shānta 🄷 (Śānta), Skt., lit. "inner peace"; the first of the five → *bhāvas* demonstrated by a lover of God (*bhakta*), a peaceful, serene disposition in which one feels close to God without having formed a particular relationship to Him.

Shāntanu 🄷 (Śāntanu), Skt., a king of the lunar race, father of → Bhīshma and grandfather of → Dhritarāshtra and → Pāndu.

It is said that Shāntnu could grant youth to the elderly with a touch of his hand. He was called Satyavachana ("he who speaks the truth"), and he was praised particularly for his beneficence, kindness, modesty, and devotion to God.

Shan Tao 🅃 → *chu-lin ch'i-hsien*

Shānti 🄷 (Śānti), Skt., lit. "peace"; the inner peace that one attains through the spiritual knowledge that one is not the mortal body but rather imperishable consciousness.

Shāntideva 🄱 (Śāntideva), Skt.; representative of the → Mādhyamika school of the Mahāyāna. According to legend, Shāntideva was a king's son from south India. He flourished in the 7th/8th centuries and was a monk at the monastic university → Nālandā. He was the author of two surviving works, the *Shikshāmuchchaya (Collection of Rules)* and the *Bodhicharyāvatara* (*Entering the Path of Enlightenment*). The latter is still used in → Tibetan Buddhism as a teaching text. (English translation: Matics 1970.)

In this book Shāntideva describes the path of development of a bodhisattva from the first arising of the thought of enlightenment (→ *bodhichitta*) to the attainment of the transcendental knowledge (→ *prajñā*) corresponding to the six "perfections" (→ *pāramitā*). The *Bodhicharyāvatara* is conceived primarily as an introduction for lay persons and beginners. In it Shāntideva explains two methods of meditation intended to help the future bodhisattva to recognize the basis for turning oneself toward other beings and to act from this understanding. One of these methods is the practice of the equality of self and other (*parātmasamatā*); the other is that of exchanging oneself for other (*parātmaparivartana*).

Shāntirakshita 🄱 → Mādhyamika

Shan-wu-wei 🄱 Chin. for Shubhākarasimha, → Mi-tsung

Shao-lin Monastery 🅉 (Chin., Shao-lin-ssu; Jap., Shōrin-ji); Buddhist monastery on → Sung-shan built in 477 by Emperor Hsiao-wen of the Northern Wei Dynasty. The Indian monk Bodhiruchi lived at this monastery at the beginning of the 6th century and there translated numerous sūtras into Chinese. Also in the first half of the 6th century, → Bodhidharma withdrew to Shao-lin after having learned in south China that the time for the acceptance of his dharma teaching in China had not yet come. It is said that Bodhidharma spent "nine years facing the wall" (→ *menpeki*) in silent meditative absorption (→ *zazen*) at Shao-lin monastery before his future dharma successor (→ *hassu*) → Hui-k'o found him there.

Today many people—including Westerners—associate the Shao-lin monastery with the practice of kung-fu, a form of → *ch'i-kung* that is often misunderstood as a combat sport though it was originally a form of spiritual training. According to legend, kung-fu was developed by Buddhist monks of Shao-lin monastery.

Shāriputra 🅱 (Śāriputra), Skt. (Pali, Sāriputta); a principal student of the Buddha. Shāriputra came from a brahmin family. Shortly after the awakening (→ *bodhi*) of the Buddha he entered the Buddhist order together with his childhood friend → Mahāmaudgalyāyana and was soon renowned on account of his wisdom. He is supposed to have died a few months before the Buddha. Images of Shāriputra and Mahāmaudgalyāyana are often found in monasteries next to that of the Buddha. Shāriputra is one of the → ten great disciples of the Buddha.

According to the scriptures, the conversion of Shāriputra, who initially advocated a kind of agnostic scepticism, followed upon his meeting with the monk Assaji. Shāriputra questioned him concerning his beliefs and Assaji answered with the following verse (trans. from Schumann 1976, p.37):

Of *dhammas* arising from causes
The Perfect One has explained the cause.
And also how to bring them to extinction
Is taught by the great *samanna* [→ *shramana*].

Shāriputra, who immediately grasped the meaning of these lines, told his friend Mahāmaudgalyāyana of the incident, and together they requested the Buddha to accept them into the → *sangha*.

Sharīra 🅷 🅱 (śarīra), Skt., lit. "body, husk."
🅷 Perishable form; three sheaths surround the → *ātman*: (1) *sthūla-sharīra,* the gross body, identical with → *annamaya-kosha;* (2) *sūkshma-sharīra,* also called *linga-sharīra,* the subtle body, made up of → *prānamaya-kosha,* → *manomaya-kosha,* and *vijñānamaya-kosha;* (3) *kārana-sharīra,* the casual sheath, identical with → *ānandamaya-kosha.*
🅱 relics of the Buddha → Shākyamuni or of a saint, usually preserved and venerated in → stūpas and → pagodas.

The cult of relics probably began immediately after the death of the Buddha Shākyamuni. His ashes were shared out, which led to conflicts among individual tribes. In the broadest sense, → sūtras, → dhāranīs, and representations of the Buddhas are also relics; they can confer a quality of sacredness on a stūpa or pagoda. According to folk belief, veneration of relics can bring protection from misfortune.

Relics of the historical Buddha have been found in his home city → Kapilavastu and also in → Vaishālī. One of the Buddha's teeth is said to be preserved in a special temple in Kandy in Sri Lanka, and hairs of the Buddha in a pagoda in Burma. The begging bowl of the Buddha is also said to have been preserved. According to the → *Mahāvamsa,* it was brought to Sri Lanka during the reign of → Ashoka, and according to Marco Polo it was transferred from there to China at the command of Kublai Khan.

Sharya 🆉 Jap. → *ajari*

Shaseki-shū 🆉 Jap. → Ichien

Shāstra 🅷 🅱 (śāstra) Skt., lit. "instruction, textbook."
🅷 The → Vedas and all other holy scriptures that are in accord with them; the law books and other scholarly works such as commentaries.
🅱 treatises on dogmatic and philosophical points of Buddhist doctrine composed by Mahāyāna thinkers that systematically interpret philosophical statements in the → sūtras. They are strongly didactic in character. *Shāstras* constitute a considerable part of the Chinese → Tripitaka.

Shatapatha-Brāhmana 🅷 (Śatapatha-Brāhmana), Skt.; the → Brāhmana of the *White* → *Yajurveda.* Attributed to the *rishi* → Yājñavalkya, it is the most complete, most systematic, and most important of the Brāhmanas. Its → Āranyaka is the → *Brihadāranyaka-Upanishad.*

Shatkasampatti 🅷 (Ṣatkasaṃpatti), Skt., lit. *shatka:* "consisting of six," *sampatti*: "attainment, success, achievement"; in → Shankara's work *Tattvabodha,* the "six great virtues," one of the four prerequisites that must be fulfilled by a student of → Vedānta. The other three are → *mumukshutva* (right desire), → *viveka* (discrimination), and → *vairāgya* (detachment). The six great virtues are (1) → *shama,* inner control, that of the mind above all; (2) *dama,* control of the organs of sense; (3) → *uparama,* fulfillment of one's duties (*dharma*); (4) *titikshā,* the patient endurance of all pairs of opposites; (5) → *shraddhā,* faith in the holy scriptures and trust in the → guru; (6) *samādhāna,* the faculty of concentration and of contemplation alone on the Vedantic texts and the words of the guru, as well as the ability to instruct suitable students.

Shaucha 🅷 (Śauca), Skt., lit. "purification, cleanliness"; one of the five virtues required on the second stage (*niyama*) of → Rāja-Yoga, as listed in the → *Yoga-Sutra* of → Patañjali (2.32). The other four virtues are → *santosha* (contentment), → *tapas* (austerity), → *svādhyāya* (study of the holy scriptures), and → *īshvara-pranidhāna* (surrender to God).

Shayata 🅉 Jap. name for the twentieth patriarch in the Indian lineage of Ch'an (→ Zen).

Shen 🅃 Chin., deity, spirit; in Taoism *shen* refers both to the deities that inhabit the universe (and, in the view of some schools, the human body) and to the personal spirit (or mind)—one of the three life energies of man.

The macrocosm, i.e., the universe, is inhabited by 36,000 deities, who, according to the → Inner Deity Hygiene School, exist also within the body of each human being. To attain immortality, the Taoist adept must prevent these deities from leaving his body by the performance of various meditative, breathing, and hygiene exercises. Each of the *shen* has its own name and area of responsibility. The highest *shen* are the three pure ones (→ *san-ch'ing*).

In addition, *shen* designates the personal spirit of a human being, which arises from the union of → *ching*, the essence, with the primordial energy (→ *yüan-ch'i*) of the universe and enters the body with the first breath of a newborn child. This *shen* leaves the body at the moment of death. While in the body, it determines our thoughts and feelings. Its seat is in the upper cinnabar field (→ *tan-t'ien*).

In the Confucianist view *shen* constitutes the spiritual element inherent in the ancestral family tree that is venerated by the relatives of the dead.

In the sense of "mind," *shen*—according to the meditative schools of Taoism—refers to ordinary consciousness (*shih-shen*) and spiritual consciousness (*yüan-shen*). The former consists of the senses, feelings, thoughts, perceptions, etc. accumulated by a person in the course of life. The spiritual consciouness, on the other hand, exists already before birth and is part of the energy that pervades the whole of the universe. After birth, it becomes invisible, because it is covered over by our ordinary consciousness. By meditating (→ *nei-tan*) the Taoist adept is able to reestablish contact with his spiritual consciousness and at the same time eliminate the influence of his ordinary consciousness.

Frequently *shen* is considered to be the opposite of → *kuei*, in that it refers to the heavenly yang spirits as opposed to the yin demons (*kuei*) (→ yin-yang).

Sheng-jen 🅃 Chin., lit. "sage, saint"; one of the names by which → Chuang-tzu describes the ideal man, who has attained perfection (→ *chih-jen*, → *chen-jen*, → *shen-jen*). The *Chuang-tzu* (Book 2, Chapter 1) describes the qualities of a *sheng-jen* as follows:

"For the true sage, beyond the limits of an external world, the so-called 'Eight Predicables' (right and left, relationship and obligation, division and discrimination, emulation and contention) exist, but are not recognised. By the true sage, within the limits of an external world, they are recognised, but are not assigned. And so, with regard to the wisdom of the ancients, as embodied in the canon of *Spring* and *Autumn*, the true sage assigns, but does not justify by argument. And thus, classifying, he does not classify, arguing, he does not argue. The true sage keeps his knowledge within him, while men in general set forth theirs in argument, in order to convince each other. And therefore it is said that in argument he does not manifest himself. Perfect Tao does not declare itself. Nor does perfect argument express itself in words. Nor does perfect charity show itself in act. Nor is perfect honesty absolutely incorruptible. Nor is perfect courage absolutely unyielding. For the Tao which shines forth is not the Tao. Speech which argues falls short of its aim. Charity which has fixed points loses its scope. Honesty which is absolute is wanting in credit. Courage which is absolute misses its object. These five are, as it were, round, with a strong bias towards squareness. Therefore knowledge that stops at what it does not know is the highest knowledge. Who knows the argument which can be argued without words? (Who knows) the Tao which does not declare itself as Tao? He who knows this, may be said to be of god. To be able to pour in without making full and pour out without making empty in ignorance of the power by which such results are accomplished,—this is accounted Light" (Giles 1961).

Sheng-mu 🅃 → Pi-hsia yüan-chün

Sheng-t'ai 🅃 Chin., lit. "sacred embryo"; an embryo or fetus that, according to Taoist beliefs, comes into being by the fusion of the inner *ch'i* (→ *nei-ch'i*, → *ch'i*) and the essence (→ *ching*) in the lower cinnabar field (*tan-t'ien*), where it is nourished by the breath and slowly develops into a new purified body within the physical body. This embryo is the immortal soul of Taoists. When the physical body dies, this pure body departs from its mortal sheath and the practitioner becomes an immortal (→ *hsien*).

In the teachings of the Inner Alchemy (→ *nei-tan*) the development of the sacred embryo is described in great detail—albeit in the language of the Outer Alchemy (→ *wai-tan*)—and is said to have nine stages, which are analogous to the effect of the ninefold-purified cinnabar of the alchemists: (1) the living *ch'i* circulates freely and unimpeded throughout the body; (2) the essence, the semen (*ching*), collects in the lower cinnabar field; (3) the sacred embryo begins to assume the form of a human embryo; (4) the two souls (→ *hun* and → *p'o*) of the sacred embryo come into being; (5) the embryo is fully formed and has various supernatural powers; (6) inner and outer yin and yang (→ yin-yang) reach their highest intensity and the embryo merges with the body of the adept; (7) the five internal organs (→ *wu-tsang*) are transformed by the power of *ch'i* into those of an immortal; (8) an umbilical cord develops, through which the breath is channeled during a practice known as embryonic breathing (→ *t'ai-hsi*); (9) form and → Tao combine and clouds form below the feet of the practitioner, on which he ascends toward Heaven (→ *fei-sheng*), thereby completing the metamorphosis.

Texts that are not as strongly influenced by the Outer Alchemy describe the sacred embryo—at the beginning of its development—as a pearl or a rust-colored drop; → Wei P'o-yang for instance refers to it as a child of a pearl. Other texts speak of a mysterious pearl (*hsüan-chu*). Sometimes the embryo is also compared to a grain of corn or a drop of water. Syncretist movements combining Taoism, Buddhism, and Confucianism compare the Taoist *sheng-t'ai* to the Buddhist *tathagatagarbha* or the *dharmakaya.*

The term *sheng-t'ai* furthermore occurs in the writings of Tsung-mi, a patriarch of the Hua-yen School of Chinese Buddhism. In a passage on the origin of Zen, Tsung-mi speaks of nourishing the spirit (→ *shen*) and allowing the sacred embryo to grow. Ma-tzu Tao-i, one of the most famous Zen masters of the 8th century, also used the term.

Shen-hsiang B → Kegon school

Shen-hsiu Z (Jap., Jinshū), 605?–706; one of the principal students of → Hung-jen, the fifth patriarch of Ch'an (Zen). According to tradition, Shen-hsiu was defeated in the memorable "competition" for the successorship to the fifth patriarch by → Hui-neng, who was later recognized as the sixth patriarch. Shen-hsiu nevertheless claimed the successorship of Hung-jen and founded the Northern school of Ch'an, in which the Ch'an of the earlier patriarchs, which was strongly marked by traditional Indian Meditation Buddhism (→ Dhyāna Buddhism) and relied on the → *Lankāvatāra-sūtra* as its basic scripture, survived for a few more generations.

Shen-hsiu was a Confucian scholar endowed with great intelligence. Driven by inner frustration, he turned to Buddhism and at approximately forty-six years of age found his way to the monastery of Hung-jen on Mount Huang-mei (Jap., Ōbai). Here he became one of the most outstanding students of the fifth patriarch, of which eleven are mentioned in later accounts as important Buddhist masters. After Hung-jen's death, Shen-hsiu left the latter's monastery and wandered through the country for nearly two decades. As concerns his fame and the number of his students, he was already outstripped during these years of wandering by Fa-ju, another student of Hung-jen's. The fact that it was nevertheless Shen-hsiu who was officially recoginized as the spiritual heir of the fifth patriarch until the middle of the 8th century can be attributed to his connection to the imperial court of the time. Shen-hsiu was already over ninety years old and well known as an outstanding Ch'an master and an advocate of strict → *zazen* practice when Empress Wu summoned him to the imperial court—no doubt because she found it politically opportune to patronize a school of Buddhism that deviated from the position of the established schools. Shen-hsiu is said to have answered this summons only reluctantly. Installed as "dharma master of Ch'ang-an and Loyang" (the two imperial capitals), he instructed a huge following of monks and scholars from the whole of north China, whom he deeply impressed by his sharp intellect and the earnestness of his commitment to meditative practice.

Whether or not Shen-hsiu was in actual fact the jealous rogue who sought the life of Hui-neng, as he was later made out to be by the followers of the → Southern school of Ch'an, can hardly be determined today with certainty, since formation of legend concerning the successorship of the fifth patriarch set in quite early. Nevertheless it is historical fact that the Northern school of Ch'an founded by him, probably not least because of its alliance with the T'ang Dynasty rulers, declined and died out after a few generations, whereas the Southern school founded by Hui-neng flourished and brought forth all the important schools and outstanding masters of Ch'an.

Shen-jen T Chin., lit. "spiritual man"; a term used by → Chuang-tzu to describe his ideal man, i.e., one who has realized the Tao (→ *chen-jen,* → *chih-jen,* → *sheng-jen*). According to the *Chuang-tzu,* "the highest man [*chih-jen*] is free of 'I'; the spiritual man (*shen-jen*) is free of action; the realized saint (*sheng-jen*) is free of name" (Wilhelm 1969).

Shen-nung T Chin., lit. "Divine Countryman"; figure in Chinese mythology, one of the three noble ones (→ *san-huang*). He is said to have invented the plow and taught man the art of agriculture as well as the cultivation of forests. Furthermore, he is credited with having introduced the use of medicaments. Lastly, he is considered to be the god of wind, and, as such, was the ideal of various movements in Chinese history that were hostile to civilization and romantically enthused by nature.

Shesha-Nāga H (Śeṣa-Nāga), Skt.; the king of

the → *nāgas* (serpents) and of the lower region, called → *pātāla.*

Shesha-Nāga has a thousand heads; Vishnu rests on his back between creations. When Shesha yawns, he creates earthquakes. At the end of an age (→ *kalpa*) he spits forth fire, which destroys the creation. He is also named Ananta, the endless one, as a symbol for eternity. His hood is called Manidvīpa ("island of jewels"), his palace is Manimandapa ("jewel palace").

Shiban Mangen 🅉 1625?–1710; a Japanese Zen monk of the → Rinzai school who compiled the *Empō dentō-roku*, a work containing the biographies of more than a thousand Zen monks.

Shibayama Zenkei 🅉 1894–1975; Japanese Zen master of the → Rinzai school, one of the outstanding → *rōshis* of modern Japan. Ordained as a monk at fourteen, at twenty he entered the Nanzen-ji monastery in Kyōto. There he underwent training for ten years and finally received the seal of confirmation (→ *inka-shōmei*) from Master Bukai Kono. He taught for eight years at the universities of Hanazono and Ōtani. From 1948 to 1967 he was the abbot of Nanzen-ji and from 1959 also the head of the entire Nanzen-ji school of Rinzai Zen in Japan, to which about 500 Zen monasteries and temples throughout the country belong.

Shibayama Zenkei became known in the West through two books: an English translation of the → *Wu-men-kuan* with his → *teishō* on the individual kōans *(Zen comments on the Mumonkan*, 1974) and a collection of Zen essays, *A Flower Does Not Talk* (1970).

Shichishū 🅉 Jap., lit. "seven schools"; the seven schools of Ch'an (Zen) during the Sung period; → *goke-shichishū.*

Shifuku 🅉 Jap. for → Tzu-fu

Shiguseigan 🅉 also shiguzeigan, for short, guzei or seigan, Jap., lit. "four great vows"; vows that are part of the bodhisattva vow as they are recited three times successively in a Zen monastery after ending the practice of → *zazen.* These vows, which are as old as Mahāyāna Buddhism, are:

1. Beings are countless—I vow to save them all (Jap., *Shujō muhen seigando*).

2. The passions are innumerable—I vow to extirpate all of them (Jap., *bonnō mujin seigandan*).

3. The dharma gates are manifold—I vow to enter all of them (Jap., *Homon muryō seigan-gaku*).

4. The way of the Buddha is unsurpassable—I vow to actualize it (Jap., *Butsudō mujō sei-ganjo*)."

Shih 🅑 Chin. → Hua-yen school

Shih-chieh 🅃 Chin., lit. "separation from the corpse"; a theory in Taoist tradition to explain the physical death of an immortal (→ *hsien*) by postulating that an immortal only appears to change into a corpse before he ascends to Heaven in broad daylight (→ *fei-sheng*).

In such cases, the coffin—when opened sometime after "death"—is found to be empty, or else just contains the staff, sword, sandals, or some other item of clothing of the adept, who has become an immortal.

One Taoist text describes the process of *shih-chieh* as follows: " 'Separation from a corpse' means to present one's body as apparently dead, without in fact being dead. . . . Whenever a dead person's body looks as if it were still alive, i.e., when the skin does not wrinkle, the blood does not drain from the feet, the light of the eyes is not extinguished, . . . whenever such a 'dead' person returns to life after death or causes his corpse to disappear before he is buried, so that nothing but his clothes are left behind in the coffin, while his physical body dissolves of its own account or floats away—in all such cases we may speak of a 'separation from the corpse' " (Bauer 1974, p. 160).

The followers of Taoism could not ignore the fact that even immortals are subject to physical death. Only very few *hsien* are said to have withdrawn to the mountains and lived as hermits for hundreds of years, occasionally revealing their true identity to ordinary mortals. In this way, religious Taoism considered death itself a means of overcoming death: dying became an indispensable prerequisite for a transformation, without which immortality was unattainable.

Shih-i 🅃 Chin., lit. *"Ten Wings";* the commentaries (*i-chuan*) on the → *I-ching,* which explain the main part of the *Book of Change(s)* from a Confucianist point of view.

The *Ten Wings* are: *Tuan-chuan* (*Commentary on the Decisions of Judgments* [2 parts]); *Hsiang-chuan* (*Commentary on the Images* [2 parts]); *Hsi-tz'u*—also called *Ta-chuan*—(*Great Commentary on the Appended Judgments* [2 parts]); *Wen-yen* (*Commentary on the Words of the Text*); *Sho-kua* (*Discussion of the Trigrams* [→ *pa-kua*]); *Hsü-kua* (*Sequence of the Hexagrams*); and *Tsa-kua* (*Miscellaneous Notes*).

The *Tuan-chuan* gives exact interpretations of decisions (judgments) on the basis of the structure and other elements of the hexagrams.

The *Hsiang-chuan* consists of two commentaries: one on the great images and one on the small images. The term *great images* refers to images associated with the two trigrams of each hexagram; *small images* refers to the individual lines of a hexagram. The commentary as a whole is based on the idea that each trigram of a hexagram represents certain images, which reflect the objective conditions prevailing in the world as well as the relevant laws of change. Therefore, a knowledge of the meaning of the trigrams and of their individual lines is indispensable for a genuine understanding of the meaning of the various hexagrams.

The *Hsi-tz'u* is the most important commentary of the *I-ching.* It explains the underlying concepts of the main text and their application in nature and society. The *Hsi-tz'u* is based on the premise that the → Tao arises from the interaction of yin and yang (→ yin-yang) and that the succession of yin and yang—rest and motion, soft and hard, and other opposites—is a basic law of nature.

The *Wen-yen* deals with the hexagrams → *ch'ien* and *k'un,* which are the most important, because they can be considered the basis of all other hexagrams.

The *Sho-kua* explains the eight trigrams (*pa-kua*) with reference to the things and concepts they represent.

The *Hsü-kua* explains the present sequence of the sixty-four hexagrams of the *Book of Change(s).*

The *Tsa-kua* deals with the relationships between pairs of individual hexagrams, although the order followed in this commentary essentially differs from the present arrangement of the hexagrams.

According to tradition, the *Ten Wings* are said to have originated with Confucius (→ K'ung-tzu), but scholars have established that they date from the Warring States Period, i.e., the Ch'in or Han dynasty.

Shihō ■ Jap., lit. "dharma transmission"; → *hassu,* → *inka-shōmei,* → *denkō-roku.*

Shih-shuang Ch'ing-chu ■ (Jap., Sekisō Keisho), 807–88/89; Chinese Ch'an (Zen) master; a student and dharma successor (→ *hassu*) of → Tao-wu Yuan-chih (Jap., Dōgo Enchi). Shih-shuang had several dharma successors, among them → Chang-sho Hsiu-ts'ai (Jap., Chōsetsu Yūsai). The → *Ching-te ch'uan-teng-lu* reports that Shih-shuang received his first consecration as a monk at the age of thirteen from Master Shao-luan, who shaved his head. At the age of twenty-three he received full ordination on → Sung-shan, one of the "sacred mountains" of China. Later he worked in the kitchen of the monastery of → Kuei-shan Ling-yu (Jap., Isan Reiyū).

Here Shih-shuang showed his potential in an encounter with Kuei-shan:

One day Shih-shuang was sifting rice when Kuei-shan said to him, "You shouldn't throw out what our patrons have given us."

Shih-shuang said, "I'm not throwing anything out."

Kuei-shan picked up a grain of rice from the floor and said: "You say you're not throwing anything out; then where does this come from?"

Shih-shuang was unable to reply.

Kuei-shan continued, "Don't underestimate the value of this one grain of rice—a hundred thousand grains come from this one grain."

Shih-shuang said, "A hundred thousand grains come from this one grain, but where does this one grain come from?"

Kuei-shan laughed out loud and returned to his room. In the evening he went up to the hall and said, "[Watch out], all of you! There's a worm in the rice."

Eventually Shih-shuang became a student of Tao-wu. After a period of training under the latter, he "effaced his traces" by hiring himself out as a worker in a pottery workshop in Ch'ang-sha. During the day he worked, at night he sat → *zazen.* Later, after → Tung-shan (Jap., Tōzan Ryōkai) had a monk track him down, his capabilities were recognized and he was requested to become the abbot of the monastery on Mount Shih-shuang (Rock Frost), from which his name derives. He agreed to do this.

Shih-shuang was known for his emphasis on strict meditative training. It is said that his students always only sat and never lay down; thus his monastic community became known as the "assembly of dead trees." The T'ang emperor Hsi-tsung heard of his reputation and sent messengers to him to confer on him the purple robes of a "master of the country"; however, Shih-shuang firmly declined to accept them.

Shih-shuang Ch'u-yuan ■ (Jap., Sekisō Soen) also called Ch'i-ming (Jap., Jimyō), 986–1039; Chinese Ch'an (Zen) master of the → Rinzai school; a student and dharma successor (→ *hassu*) of → Fen-yang Shan-chao (Jap., Fun'yō Zenshō) and the master of → Yang-ch'i Fang-hui (Jap., Yōgi Hōe) and → Huang-lung Hui-nan (Jap., Ōryō E'nan). Shih-shuang became a monk at the age of twenty-two and sought out many well-known Ch'an masters of his time. Although his life, for a Ch'an master's, was quite short, he nevertheless contributed greatly to the revival of Rinzai Zen. Among his dharma successors were several outstanding Ch'an masters, among whom the most important were Yang-ch'i, founder of the → Yōgi school, and Huang-lung, founder of the → Ōryō school. We encounter Shih-shuang in example 46 of the → *Wu-men-kuan.*

The koan is as follows:

"Master Shih-shuang spoke: 'From the tip of a hundred-foot pole, how do you go further?'

"An ancient master said on this point, 'One who sits on a hundred-foot pole, although he may have penetrated it, does not yet fulfill the truth. He must go still one step further and reveal his entire body in the ten directions.' "

Shih-t'ou Hsi-ch'ien ■ (Jap., Sekitō Kisen), 700–790; early Chinese Ch'an (Zen) master; the student and dharma successor (→ *hassu*) of → Ch'ing-yuan Hsing-ssu (Jap., Seigen Gyōshi) and master of Yueh-shan Wei-yen (Jap., Yakusan Igen), → T'ien-huang Tao-wu (Jap., Ten'ō Dōgō), and → Tan-hsia T'ien-jan (Jap., Tanka Ten'en). As in the case of his master Ch'ing-yuan, we know nearly nothing of the life of Shih-t'ou. From the sources we only learn that he was the leading master of a famous center of Ch'an (Zen), which had developed in the Heng mountains in Hunan (lit. "South of the Lake"). Beween this and another great Ch'an center of that time, which had formed in Kiangsi Province (lit. "West of the River") around the great Ch'an master → Ma-tsu Tao-i (Jap., Baso Dōitsu), there was lively exchange. The two great masters often had their students travel back and forth between the two centers so that they could deepen their realization through → *mondō* and → *hossen* with other masters. Ma-tsu warned his students from time to time about the "slipperiness of the clifftop" (Chin., *shih-t'ou*, "clifftop"), which was his way of expressing his high regard for the "indomitable" Ch'an realization of Shih-t'ou. Thus it is said in the Buddhist chronicles of the T'ang period, "West of the river lived Ma-tsu, south of the lake, Shih-t'ou. Between these two the people wandered about, and whoever never met these two masters remained ignorant." Three of the "five houses" of Ch'an stem from Shih-t'ou (→ *goke-shichishū*; cf. the Ch'an/Zen Lineage Chart).

Shika Z Jap., lit. "one who knows about the guests"; originally the monk responsible for the care of guests in a Zen monastery. Today the term generally refers to the head monk in charge of the administration of the monastery. The *shika* is a Zen monk who is advanced on the path and can in many matters function as the representative of the → *rōshi*. Thus it is among his duties to examine the suitability of monks who are seeking acceptance into the monastery during the → *tanga-zume*.

Shikan B Jap. for → Chih-kuan

Shikantaza Z Jap., lit. "nothing but (*shikan*) precisely (*ta*) sitting (*za*)"; a form of the practice of → *zazen* in which there are no more supportive techniques of the type beginners use, such as counting the breath (→ *susoku-kan*) or a → kōan. According to → Dōgen Zenji, *shikantaza* —i.e., resting in a state of brightly alert attention that is free of thoughts, directed to no object, and attached to no particular content—is the highest or purest form of *zazen*, *zazen* as it was practiced by all the buddhas of the past.

The modern Japanese Zen master → Hakuun Ryōko Yasutani says in his *Introductory Lectures on Zen Training*, "Shikantaza ... is the mind of somebody facing death. Let us imagine that you are engaged in a duel of swordsmanship of the kind that used to take place in ancient Japan. As you face your opponent you are unceasingly watchful, set, ready. Were you to relax your vigilance even momentarily, you would be cut down instantly. A crowd gathers to see the fight. Since you are not blind you see them from the corner of your eye, and since you are not deaf you hear them. But not for an instant is your mind captured by these impressions" (Kapleau 1980).

Shiki Z Jap., lit. "consciousness"; Buddhism distinguishes eight classes of consciousness. The first six are the senses of sight, hearing, smell, taste, touch, and thought (intellect). While the intellect creates the illusion of a subject *I* standing apart from an object world, it is not persistently conscious of this *I*. Only in the seventh class of (sub)consciousness (Skt., *manas*) is this awareness of a discrete ego-*I* constant. *Manas* also acts as conveyor of the seed-essence of sensory experiences to the eighth level of (sub)consciousness (Skt., *ālaya-vijñāna*), from which, in response to causes and conditions, specific "seeds" are reconveyed by *manas* to the six senses, precipitating new actions, which in turn produce other "seeds." This process is simultaneous and endless.

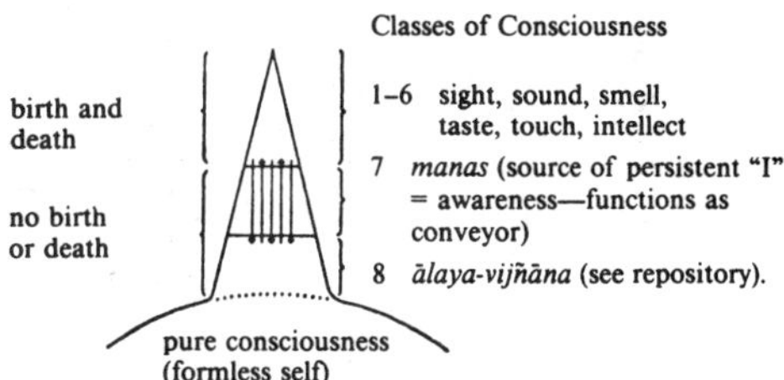

The accompanying diagram, based on a scheme by the modern Japanese Zen master → Daiun Sōgaku Harada, shows the relation of the eight classes of consciousness to birth and death and to birthlessness and deathlessness. The triangular portion stands for the life of the individual, revealing his link to pure consciousness, or formless self. This life is not unlike a wave on the vast ocean; its brief existence seems apart from the ocean—and in a sense it is not the ocean—but in *substance* it is not other than the ocean, out of which it arose, into which it will recede, and from which it will emerge again as a new wave. In just the same way, individual consciousness issues from pure consciousness and in its essential nature is indistinguishable from it. Their common element, the viable Void, is shown in the diagram by the all-pervading white background. (Source: Kapleau, 1980.)

Shikin 🅑 Skt.; buddha of a previous world age; see also → buddha

Shiko Rishō 🅩 Jap. for → Tzu-hu Li-tsung

Shikshā 🅗 (Śikṣā), Skt.; one of the → Vedāngas, the science that deals with correct pronunciation and intonation (phonetics) in the recital of the → Vedas. There are numerous works on this topic. Its significance in Hinduism is discussed further under → *shabda.*

Shīla 🅑 (śīla) Skt. (Pali, sīla), "obligations, precepts"; refers to the ethical guidelines that in Buddhism determine the behavior of monks, nuns, and laypersons and that constitute the precondition for any progress on the path of awakening (→ *bodhi*). The ten *shīlas* for monks and nuns (→ *bhikshu, bhikshunī*) and novices (→ *shrāmanera*) are: (1) refraining from killing, (2) not taking what is not given, (3) refraining from prohibited sexual activity, (4) refraining from unjust speech, (5) abstaining from intoxicating drinks, (6) abstaining from solid food after noon, (7) avoiding music, dance, plays, and other entertainments, (8) abstaining from the use of perfumes and ornamental jewelry, (9) refraining from sleeping in high, soft beds, (10) refraining from contact with money and other valuables. The first five *shīlas* apply also to Buddhist laypersons (→ *upāsaka, upāsikā*), who on certain days like → *uposatha* observe the first eight.

The *shīlas* represent a natural morality; this contrasts with the monastic rules (→ Vinaya), which detail all aspects of behavior according to the requirements of monastic life.

Shīla as morality is one of the three areas covered by the → eightfold path; it is a component of the threefold training (→ *trishiksha*) as well as one of the perfections (→ *pāramitā*).

Shin 🅩 Jap. → *kokoro*

Shinchi Kakushin 🅩 Jap. → Kakushin

Shin fuka toku 🅩 Jap., lit "The mind [*shin,* → *kokoro*] cannot be fixated"; a Zen expression that indicates that all phenomena that arise in our mind are in continual flux and have no lasting reality and also that the one mind, as absolute reality, is ungraspable and trascends all limitations (definition).

Shinge-mubeppō 🅩 Jap., lit. "Outside the mind [*shin,* → *kokoro*] [there are] no other dharmas"; the word *dharma* is used here in the sense of "phenomenon." The expression indicates that nothing exists outside the mind (consciousness, → *shiki*), since all phenomena are projections of consciousness.

Shingetsu Shōryō 🅩 also Shingetsu Seiryō, Jap. for → Chen-hsieh Ch'ing-liao

Shingi 🅩 Jap., lit. "clear standard, clear rule"; term for the rules by which daily life in a Zen monastery (→ *tera*) is regulated; also for the rules for monks and laypersons in the daily life outside a monastery. The suffix *-shingi* crops up in the titles of many Japanese written works that treat aspects of the standards of religious life.

Shingon school 🅑 Jap., lit. "School of the True Word [→ mantra]"; school of esoteric Buddhism founded by → Kūkai (Kobo Daishi), 774–835. Kūkai studied the teachings of the → Mi-tsung in China and systematized them in Shingon. The "School of the True Word" places especially great importance on the "three secrets" (→ body, speech, mind). Every person possesses these three functions, all of which harbor secrets that lead to the attainment of buddhahood.

The rituals connected with the three secrets are passed orally from teacher to disciple in Shingon; this represents a considerable difference from the schools of Buddhism intended for the general public. According to the view of the Shingon school, these esoteric teachings were expounded as absolute truth by → Vairochana, the cosmic buddha, and only the initiated can learn to understand them. Vairochana, who is the central buddha of the school, is the universe itself, without beginning or end. He manifests himself through the perfect harmony of the six elements: earth, water, fire, air, space, and consciousness

According to the teaching of this school, the true meaning of the esoteric teachings cannot be conveyed in words but only through artistic representations. This explains the importance of → mandalas in Shingon.

The Shingon school does not, however, despite its esoteric character, deny the importance of our world and of happiness in the present life. From the correct performance of the various rituals, immediate material benefits can be drawn.

This view tended to favor the arising of superstitious practices and various currents within Shingon have opposed this. The Shingon school is still today one of the largest Buddhist schools of Japan.

The "secret of body" finds expression in various hand gestures (→ mudrā), meditation postures, and the use of certain ritual implements, such as → *vajra* or → lotus, that are associated with one or another buddha or bodhisattva being invoked.

The "secret of speech" is related to the recitation of mantras and → *dhāranīs*; the "secret of mind," to the "five wisdoms," which make the comprehension of reality possible, and to → *samādhi*. Through particular rituals, which are rooted in these three secrets, a connection between the practitioner and a particular buddha is brought about, through which the state of "buddha in me, me in buddha" can be realized; i.e., buddhahood can be attained in this lifetime.

The two mandalas important in Shingon are the *garbhadhātu* mandala and the *vajradhātu* mandala. The first ("womb" mandala) symbolizes the matrix of all things, the principle that is the basis of everything, and represents the static aspect of the cosmos. In the middle of this mandala is Vairochana, sitting on a red lotus blossom on the eight petals of which are the four transcendent buddhas and bodhisattvas.

The *vajradhātu* mandala (mandala "of the diamond realm") symbolizes the active aspect of the cosmos, the wisdom of Vairochana, which arises from the above "principle" and is its spiritual expression. In the center of this mandala also is Vairochana. He sits on a white lotus blossom with the four transcendent buddhas around him. The realms of the two mandalas cannot exist apart from one another.

In an important ceremony of this school, the student must throw a flower onto the mandala and thereafter particularly venerate that buddha on which his flower falls, considering him as his spiritual guide. Other important rites are the ceremonies of → *abhisheka* and → ordination.

Shin-in **Z** Jap., lit. "mind seal"; short form of → *busshin-in*

Shinji Kakushin **Z** → Kakushin

Shinjinmei **Z** Jap. for *Hsin-hsin-ming*, → Seng-ts'an

Shinnyo **Z** Japanese pronunciation of the written character by which the Sanskrit word *tathatā* is translated into Chinese. It is generally translated "suchness" in English. Suchness is the true nature of all things, true reality, which, though it can be directly experienced in → enlightenment, is not thinkable (→ *fukashigi*) and thus eludes all description (→ *fukasetsu*). It is the unity, ungraspable by thought of the relative and the absolute, of attributes and the absence of attributes, of form and emptiness—it is the primordial ground out of which all things arise and at the same time these things themselves. Buddha-nature (→ *busshō*) is seen as *shinnyo* inherent in all beings (including unenlightened ones) and is nearly a synonym of the latter.

Shinran **B** properly Shōnin Shinran, 1173–1262; founder of the → Jōdo-shin-shū of Japanese Buddhism, a student of Hōnen (→ Jōdo-shū). The view of Buddhism advocated by Shinran has but little similarity to the original teaching. The three precious ones of Buddhism (→ *triratna*) are changed to one—the basic vow of the Buddha → Amitābha (Jap., Amida), i.e., the eighteenth of his forty-eight vows. The monastic ideal is dropped—Shinran's followers constituted purely a lay community, and he himself married. According to Shinran's teaching, trying to attain enlightenment through one's own efforts is senseless. His approach is based on the "power of the other" (→ *tariki*), in this case that of Buddha Amida. Liberation is to be attained exclusively through the help and grace of Buddha Amida. Shinran reduces practice to recitation of the name of Amida (→ *nembutsu*), which he views as an expression of gratitide toward this buddha; even this practice becomes superfluous when one's faith in Amida becomes strong enough.

Shinran's teachings were collected by his student Yuiembō and presented under the title *Tannishō*. Yuiembō tried by this means to establish his master's teaching in fixed form in order to forestall factional tendencies among his followers. In Shinran's "Shō-shin nembutsu ge" ("Hymn of the True Faith in *Nembutsu*"), which is recited daily by his followers, the basic points of the practice of the Pure Land school (→ Pure Land, → Pure Land school) are summarized.

Shinran was expelled from the monastic community of Kyōto and banished to a northern province because he lived with his wife and thus violated the monastic rules. He is supposed to have married at the request of Hōnen, so as to show that monastic discipline was not the essential factor in the attainment of enlightenment. This led to a schism among the followers of Hōnen, a large part of whom held to celibacy.

For Shinran, by contrast, renunciation of monastic life was a logical step fully in accord with faith in Amida. Since in his view only trust in the help and limitless grace of Amida can bring about liberation, it is senseless to act as though one could contribute actively to the attainment of this goal through any particular lifestyle.

Shinran, who lived as a social outsider, spent his life

among the common folk. He was concerned to bring his teaching to people who were unable to distinguish between wholesome and unwholesome and addressed himself particularly to "bad" people. According to his view Amida should be more ready to help "bad" people, since they possess nothing more than their faith in Amida, while "good" people are often prey to the erroneous notion that they can contribute something toward their liberation through virtue and merit.

Shinran's version of the *nembutsu* practice also differed from that of related (Pure Land) schools and from that of his master Hōnen. Shinran saw Hōnen's teaching, in which repetition of the name of Amida was intended to strengthen faith in Amida, as a form of reliance on "one's own effort" (→ *jiriki*), which for Shinran did not exist. A single sincere invocation of Buddha Amida is sufficient to bring about participation in Amida's grace, and all further invocations are no more than an expression of gratitude toward him.

Shinran reduced the scriptural basis of his school to the eighteenth vow of Amida and rejected all other sūtras.

Shin school 🅱 Jap. → Jōdo-shin-shū

Shinshō 🅱 Jap. for Shen-hsiang → Kegon school

Shin-shū 🅱 Jap. → Jōdo-shin-shū

Shintō 🅱 🆉 Jap., lit. "Way of the Gods"; original religion of Japan. Shinto has existed as a system of beliefs and rites since around the beginning of the Common Era. In its early form it was a primitive nature religion, consisting in the worship of nature deities. In the 5th and 6th centuries it was strongly influenced by Chinese Confucianism, from which it adopted veneration of ancestors, and by Buddhism, from which it borrowed a number of philosophical ideas and rites. It then took on the form of a complex religious system but played, in relation to Buddhism, only a subsidiary role. In 1868 it was elevated to the status of a state religion in which the emperor was worshiped as a god. In 1945 it lost its rank as state religion. In 1946, the emperor renounced all claim to divinity.

Early Shintō is characterized by belief in a multitude of deities. Every mountain, every river—all forms of nature are associated with a deity (*kami*). The most important deities are father Heaven and mother Earth, who created the Japanese islands and the rest of the deities. Amaterasu Omikami (Heaven-radiant Great Divinity) is the most important of their creations. According to Shintō belief, she was sent into the sky to become ruler over the sun. She sent her grandson down to earth, who laid hold of the islands that comprise Japan and founded an eternal dynasty. This mythological representation of the founding of Japan and the establishment of the imperial lineage is the central feature of Shintō belief.

Until 1868 Shintō was secondary to Buddhism in Japan. Under the influence of Buddhist thought, especially that of the → Tendai and → Shingon schools, many Shintō deities came to be seen as incarnations of buddhas and bodhisattvas or were made into protectors of the Buddhist teachings.

In the Tokugawa period (from the beginning of the 16th until the middle of the 19th centuries), a partial identification of Shintō with the Confucian thought of → Chu Hsi took place. The latter placed particular importance on veneration of the emperor. At the same time various currents within Shintō based on folk belief were further elaborated. Altogether thirteen main currents and numerous subsidiary ones are differentiated, all of which stress ethical behavior. Practices include veneration of mountains and spiritual healing. Rituals stem from the early period of Shintō.

Shippei 🆉 also chikuhei, Jap., lit. "bamboo switch"; a stick about fifty cm in length made of split bamboo wound with cord, which the Ch'an (Zen) masters of ancient China used to spur on their students. In kōans, the *shippei* often plays a role similar to that of the → *hossu*. From the *shippei* the → *kyosaku* later developed.

Shi-ryōken 🆉 Jap., lit. "four ways of seeing"; according to the → Rinzai school, there are four ways to look at the world. These are: (1) there is no subject without an object; (2) the entire world is a mere projection of one's own consciousness; (3) there is a state in which the duality of subject and object is transcended; (4) ultimately there is neither subject nor object. In this order of progression, the four ways of seeing represent a progression from the dualistic state of mind of → *bonpu-no-jōshiki* to the enlightened state of mind (→ enlightenment).

Shishibodai 🆉 Jap. for → Simhabodhi

Shishin Goshin 🆉 Jap. for → Ssu-hsin Wu-hsin

Shishō 🆉 Jap., lit. "teacher, tutor." The training of Zen monks often begins in the early years in a small local temple (→ *tera*) under the supervision of the temple priest. This first guide on the path to → enlightenment, who does not have to be a Zen master (→ *rōshi*), and who is regarded by the monk his whole life long as a kind of spiritual mentor, is known in Zen as *shishō*. In the colloquial language every teacher of an art or handcraft can be called *shishō*.

In earlier times, the future monk was often entrusted to the care of the *shishō* as a child. When the *shishō* thought he was ripe for further training, then he sent him on pilgrimage (→ *angya*) to a Zen monastery.

In both Chinese and Japanese literature there are moving accounts about the return of a monk to his *shishō* after decades of training. In these stories, the monk, who has perhaps in the meantime matured into a master, demonstrates to his first spiritual teacher the depth of his realization of the → buddha-dharma, to the latter's great joy.

Shi-tennō 🅱 Jap. → celestial king

Shitsu-nai 🅩 Jap. → kōan

Shiva 🅗 (Śiva), Skt., lit. "the kind one, the friendly one"; the third divinity in the Hindu trinity (→ *trimūrti*) of Brahmā, Vishnu, and Shiva, in which Shiva functions as the god of dissolution and destruction; as the destroyer of → *avidyā* (ignorance), he is a deity abounding in blessings. His symbol is the → *linga*; he is often portrayed in union with his wife → Shakti, whose symbol is the → *yoni.*

A *linga* with three faces of Shiva.

The name Shiva does not appear in the Vedas. In those texts, Rudra is the name of the same deity, and Shiva, together with the → Rudras, his manifestations, developed from this form. In the *Rigveda*, the word *Rudra* is used for → Agni; his sons are the → Maruts. In the *Rāmāyana*, Shiva is a great god, but more in the sense of a personal god than a supreme divinity. In the *Mahābhārata*, Vishnu is greater at times; in other places Shiva is again the Lord and creator of Brahmā and Vishnu and is worshiped by all gods. Later Shiva became Mahādeva, the great god, the destroyer of ignorance and lord of yogis.

When he is revered as one's "chosen deity" (→ *ishta-deva*), then he is the total divinity, the supreme reality. In relation to his dynamic powers, which are known as Shakti, Pārvatī, → Kālī, or Durgā, Shiva is the transcendent Absolute. Each of these feminine divinities is also characterized as Shiva's "wife," since he is often visualized in sexual union (→ Shaktism) with these embodiments of his "feminine" powers. He has many other names, such as Shambu, Shankara, Īshāna, Vishvanātha, Kedārnāth, and → Natarāja, who is represented in art as Shiva-Natarāja, the dancing Shiva, lord of the universe. He rides on → Nandi, the bull of → *dharma,* and is worshiped as the guru of all gurus, the destroyer of worldliness, the one who grants wisdom and who is the embodiment of renunciation and compassion.

Shivaism 🅗 → Shaivism

Shiva-Linga 🅗 Skt. → *linga*

Shivānanda 🅗 Indian spiritual leader, 1887–1963; he came from a South Indian family of sages, ascetics, and scholars, and was active as a physician from 1912 to 1923, when he gave up his profession and all he owned, wandered through India as a beggar, received instruction from sages, and visited the great pilgrimage sites before becoming initiated as a monk in Hrishī-kesh. There he founded the Divine Life Society (1936) and the Yoga-Vedānta Forest Academy (1948). The most important concerns of these two organizations are the distribution of instructions (in the form of publications) on education, philosophy, and spiritual knowledge without regard for caste or creed. All religions are equally respected and all seekers offered assistance in the form of food, medicine, and knowledge. This was also the motto of the World's Parliament of Religions, which Shivānanda established in 1953. Among his numerous works are *Kundalinī, Yoga* (1935), *Hatha Yoga* (1944), *Concentration and Meditation* (1945), and *Student's Success in Life* (1945).

Shivarātri 🅗 (Śivarātri), Skt., lit. "Shiva's night"; a spiritual vigil in → Shiva's honor; it is observed in spring and is associated with fasting, prayer, and meditation.

Shiva-Samhitā 🅗 (Siva-Saṃhitā), Skt.; a classical work on → Hatha-Yoga; it describes the strict prescripts that a student of this yoga must follow and gives instructions for the accomplishment of these steps.

SHIVO'HAM 🅗 (Śivo'Ham), Skt.; a well-known → mantra: "I am Shiva."

Shloka 🅷 (Sloka), Skt., lit. "call, sound, stanza"; the most important epic meter used in the → Vedas and other classic Sanskrit works (e.g. the *Manābhārata* and the *Rāmāyana*). Probably introduced by → Vālmīki, the form of the stanza is two lines, each consisting of two parts *(pādas)* of eight syllables each.

Shō 🆉 Jap., lit. "nature"; a term meaning "nature" in the sense of fundamental or essential character. It appears in such expressions as → *busshō* (buddha-nature) and → *kenshō* (self-realization, lit. "realization of one's nature").

Shōbō-genzō 🆉 Jap.; "*Treasure Chamber of the Eye of True Dharma*"; the principal work of the great Japanese Zen master → Dōgen Zenji. It is a collection of → *teishō* and writings from the last two decades of his life. The *Shōbō-genzō* is considered the most profound work in all of Zen literature and the most outstanding work of religious literature of Japan.

Shōbō-genzō Zuimonki 🆉 Jap.; a collection of sayings and instructions of the great Japanese Zen master → Dōgen Zenji as recorded by his student Ejō (1198–1280).

Shō-chū-hen 🆉 Jap. → five degrees (of enlightenment) 1

Shō-chū-rai 🆉 Jap. → five degrees (of enlightenment) 3

Shōdō 🆉 Jap., lit. "Way of writing"; one of the Japanese ways of spiritual training (→ *dō*). This "art of writing" is considered in the Far East to be one of the most essential arts, since it is one in which the heart-mind (→ *kokoro*) of the artist expresses itself especially clearly. The common translation "calligraphy" is inaccurate, since the intention in *shōdō* is not to write "beautifully" but rather to communicate one's heart-mind (Jap., *kokoro-o ataeru*). This becomes especially clear in the "calligraphic" works of the Ch'an (Zen) masters of China and Japan (→ *bokuseki*), of whom many practiced the Way of writing and whose works are among the greatest examples of this art.

Shōgen Sōgaku 🆉 Jap. for → Sung-yuan Ch'ung-yueh

Shōichi Kokushi 🆉 → Ben'en

Shōitsu Kokushi 🆉 → Ben'en

Shōji 🆉 Jap., lit. "birth [and] death"; the cycle of birth and death, wandering from one existence to the next; the Japanese expression for → samsāra.

Shōjiki 🆉 Jap., lit. "recitation [before the] meal"; ceremonial recitation before mealtimes in a Zen monastery (→ *tera*).

Shōji soku nehan 🆉 Jap., lit. "Birth [and] death themselves [are] nirvāna"; for a completely enlightened one (→ enlightenment) the phenomenal world and the essential world are not different but rather fully identical— → samsāra (birth and death) and → nirvāna are one.

Shōjō 🆉 Jap. for → Hīnayāna

Shōjō Zen 🆉 Jap. → five degrees (of enlightenment) 3

Shōjū Rōjin 🆉 → Dōkyō Etan

Shōkaku Kokushi 🆉 → Musō Soseki

Shōkan 🆉 Jap. → *shōken*

Shōkei Eki 🆉 Jap. for → Chang-ching Huai-hui

Shōken 🆉 also Shōkan, Jap., lit. "seeing one another"; the first → *dokusan* of a Zen student with his master (→ *rōshi*), in which the seeker after → enlightenment is officially accepted as a student by the *rōshi*. Following a fixed ceremonial, the would-be student seeks out the master in the seclusion of the latter's room, makes an offering to him as a representative of the three precious ones (→ *sambō*), and requests the *rōshi* to guide him on the way of Zen. He explains to the master his motives for seeking instruction, and if the *rōshi* is persuaded of the sincerity of his "will for truth" (→ *kokorozashi*) and feels that he himself is the right master for this person, then he accepts him as a student.

In *shōken* a karmic link is forged between master and student—or better, the presence of such a deep relationship is made manifest. The master thus commits himself to train the student on the path to enlightenment to the best of his ability; and the student, on his side, to follow the master with complete devotion, openness, and honesty so long as both deem it suitable. If there are serious reasons for it, this link can be broken by master or student at any time—no authentic master would attempt to bind a student to himself against the student's will. If it does not come to such a break, the link continues in force—even if the student has long since received → *inka-shōmei* and become a master himself—until the death of the master or student and even beyond that.

Shōkyō Eki 🆉 Jap. for Chang-ching Huai-hui

Shōmyō 🆉 also Nampo Shōmyō (Jōmyō) or Nampo Sōmin, as well called Daiō Kokushi (→ *kokushi*), 1235–1309; early Japanese Zen master of the Yōgi lineage of Rinzai Zen (→

Yōgi school); a student and dharma successor (→ *hassu*) of Chinese Ch'an (Zen) master → Hsu-t'ang Chih-yu (Jap., Kidō Chigu). Shōmyō brought the lineage of Ch'an (Zen) to Japan to which → Hakuin Zenji belonged and contributed greatly toward the establishment of Zen in Japan.

Shōmyō began his training in → Kenchō-ji in Kamakura under → Lan-ch'i Tao-lung, a Chinese master who had settled in Japan. In 1259 he traveled to China, where he experienced enlightenment under Master Hsu-t'ang and received the seal of confirmation (→ *inka-shōmei*) from him. He returned to Japan and was active in Kamakura, on the island of Kyūshū, and in Kyōto as a Zen master. Unlike many another early Zen master (for example, → Eisai Zenji, → Ben'en, → Kakushin) Shōmyō did not mix Zen with elements drawn from the → Tendai or → Shingon schools; rather he transmitted the pure → *kanna* Zen of the strict Yōgi school. Thus later masters of this lineage like → Ikkyū Sōjun and Hakuin Zenji, in whose time Rinzai Zen in Japan was already in decline, appealed to the example of Shōmyō's master Hsu-t'ang and speak of themselves as his true dharma heirs. Shōmyō's most famous dharma successor was → Myōchō Shūhō (also called Daitō Kokushi).

Shōrin-ji 🅉 Jap. for → Shao-lin monastery

Shōshi 🅉 Jap., lit. "genuine master"; the confirmation by which a Zen student who has already received → *inka-shōmei* and who is already leading a *zendō* is recognized by his master as a competent Zen master.

Inka-shōmei confirms that the Zen student has experienced → profound enlightenment and has completed Zen training under his master. However, not every student who is so confirmed reaches the point of opening a *zendō* and functioning as a master. If one considers everything involved in running a *zendō* properly, it is astonishing that even a few traditional lineages have survived until the present day.

Shōsō-funi 🅉 Jap., lit. "Nature [and] form [are] not two"; expression for the nonduality, realized in → enlightenment, of absolute and relative, emptiness and form, absence of qualities and qualities.

Shou 🅃 Chin., lit. "long life"; preliminary stage of immortality (→ *ch'ang-sheng pu-ssu*). An almost magical power attaches to the pictogram for *shou,* which, for that reason, is represented in every conceivable shape.

Taoists believe that a person's life span may be extended by the performance of certain exercises. In this context breathing and physical exercises, meditation, the avoidance of certain food substances, and sexual techniques are of particular significance.

Three ornamental representations of *shou.*

Shou-chu 🅉 → Tung-shan Shou-chu

Shou-hsing 🅃 → *san-hsing*

Shou-i 🅃 Chin., lit. "preserving the One"; Taoist meditation practice, in which deities believed to dwell within the body of the practitioner (→ *shen,* → Inner Deity Hygiene School) are visualized with a view to preventing them from leaving the body. The most frequently visualized deity is the Supreme One (→ T'ai-i), with whom the practitioner tries to unite.

The oldest form of this meditation is described in the → *T'ai-p'ing ching* as a "method for preserving the light of the One": "The method for preserving the light of the One forms the basis of the art of ensuring a long life (→ *ch'ang-sheng pu-ssu*). It enables the practitioner to seek out the deities and cause radiant light to appear from their abode. In order to preserve the light of the One the practitioner should, as soon as he perceives the first flicker of the flame, hold on to that image. At first the flame is red, then it becomes white and—after some considerable time—green. It is a radiant luminosity, which seems to spread ever wider. The practitioner should, however, try to gather and collect it. In this way he will create light throughout his body and drive out all illness. Anyone capable of maintaining this inner luminosity without interruption could be said to have mastered the art of living for 10,000 years" (trans. from Kaltenmark, *Lao-tzu und der Taoismus;* see Kaltenmark 1969).

This form of meditation on light was already known in the early stages of Taoism; e.g., → Lao-tzu often speaks of an inner light. In the → *Huai-nan-tzu* the appearance of light in the antechamber of the heart symbolizes the presence of the Tao.

The inner deities did not become objects of meditation until after the personification of the T'ai-i and its subsequent division into the three ones (→ *san-i*). Later, Taoists came to believe that by means of *shou-i* the essence (→ *ching*) could be spread throughout the body, that the three ones could then be made to become visible, and that the sacred embryo (→ *sheng-t'ai*) comes into being through a transformation of the breath (→ *ch'i*). An adept who succeeds in effecting such a transformation has attained immortality and ascends to Heaven in broad daylight (→ *fei-sheng*).

Shou-lao 🅃 Chin.; Taoist god of long life (→ *ch'ang-sheng pu-ssu*). Shou-lao is the popular name of Shou-hsing (→ *san-hsing*), the stellar deity of longevity. In representations he is usually shown with an enormously enlarged head. He carries a long staff and a pumpkin gourd, which contains the water of life. In his other hand he holds the peach of immortality, on which another symbol of immortality—a crane—is often depicted.

Shou-shan Sheng-nien 🅉 (Jap., Shuzan Shōnen), also Shou-shan Hsing-nien, 926–993; Chinese Ch'an (Zen) master of the → Rinzai school; a student and dharma successor (→ *hassu*) of → Feng-hsueh Yen-chao (Jap., Fuketsu Enshō) and the master of → Fen-yang Shan-chao (Jap., Fun'yō Zenshō).

It was Shou-shan who preserved the Rinzai lineage of Ch'an (Zen) from extinction. His master Feng-hsueh was fearful that the dharma transmission of his "great-grandfather in Ch'an (Zen)" the great master → Lin-chi I-hsuan (Jap., Rinzai Gigen), would die with him, because he had found no suitable dharma successor in his monastery. Then Shou-shan, who was a latecomer to the circle of his students, proved himself a worthy heir. After receiving the seal of confirmation (→ *inka-shōmei*) from Feng-hsueh, he "effaced his traces and hid his light." Only after the chaotic situation in the country caused by the demise of the T'ang Dynasty had stabilized again under the Sung did he show himself as a Zen master and begin to guide students on the way of Ch'an. Of his sixteen dharma successors, it was mainly Fen-yang through whom Rinzai Zen again revived and came to be the leading school of Buddhism in the Sung period. We encounter Master Shou-shan in example 43 of the → *Wu-men-kuan.*

The kōan is as follows: "Master Shou-shan held up his staff during instruction and said while showing it to the monks, "Monks, if you call this a staff, that's an offense. If you call it not-a-staff, that makes no sense. Tell me, monks, what will you call it?"

Shōyō-roku 🅉 Jap. for → *Ts'ung-jung-lu*

Shrāddha 🄷 (Śrāddha), Skt.; a religious ceremony in which food and drink are offered to deceased relatives. In the *Mahābhārata,* when Manu, the progenitor of the human race, appears as a brother of Yama, the god of death, the two brothers are described as *shrāddha-deva.*

Shraddhā 🄷 🄱 (śraddhā), Skt., lit. "belief, faith." 🄷 Belief in what holy scriptures teach, confidence that what they proclaim is the truth; one of the "six great virtues" (→ *shatkasampatti*) from Shankara's *Tattvabodha.*

Shraddhā is a fundamental prerequisite for the search for God; yet faith alone is not sufficient in Hinduism. It remains a "working hypothesis," and is fulfilled only when God or → *brahman* is realized, that is, when the aspirant has attained union with him.

🄱 (Pali, saddhā); the inner attitude of faith and devotion toward the Buddha and his teaching. *Shraddhā* is the basis of the first two elements of the → eightfold path—perfect view and perfect resolve—and is one of the five → *balas*. In the Mahāyāna *shraddhā* plays an even more important role, being regarded as the virtue out of which all the others develop and which opens the door of liberation to even those who do not have the self-discipline to tread the path of meditation. In Buddhism, however, faith in the sense of the "pure faith" of Christianity is out of place. *Shraddhā* consists rather in the conviction that grows in students through their own direct experience with the teaching. Blind faith in the words of the Buddha or a master goes against the spirit of Buddhism, and the Buddha himself warned his followers against it.

Trust and belief in the Buddha → Amitābha is nevertheless the principal factor in the practice of the → Pure Land school, which is often described as a "Way of faith."

Shraddhā is also a basis for entry into the supramundane path. A → *shrota-āpanna* can be either an "adherent of faith" (→ *shraddhānusārin*) or an "adherent of the doctrine" (→ *dharmānusārin*) and can become accordingly either one liberated through faith (*shraddhāvimukta*) or one who sees (*dhrishtiprāpta*).

Shraddhānusārin 🄱 Skt. (Pali, saddhānusārin); an adherent of faith, i.e, one of the two kinds of aspirants to "stream-entry" (→ *shrota-āpanna*). The *shraddhānusārin* enters the supramundane path (→ *ārya-mārga*) not, like the → *dharmānusārin* (adherent of the doctrine), on account of his intellectual understanding of the teaching, but rather on account of his trust and faith (→ *shraddhā*) in the teaching.

Shramana 🄱 (śramaṇa), Skt. (Pali, samanna; Chin., shamen); ascetic, monk. Another name for a Buddhist monk, which was originally applied to those who led an ascetic life.

Shrāmanera 🄱 (śrāmaṇera) or (fem.) shrāmanerikā, Skt.; novice; term for male or female Buddhist novices who have committed themselves through the lower ordination to observe the ten → *shīlas*. Novices are often children. The minimum age for ordination of a *shrāmanera* is seven years; that was the age of the son of the historical Buddha, → Rāhula, the patron of *shrāmaneras*, when he entered the → *sangha.*

Novices are given into the care of monks (→ *bhikshu*) or nuns (→ *bhikshunī*), who instruct them in the teaching and the rules of discipline and guide them on the way. Therefore novices are servants of monks and nuns and relieve them of routine work. A *shrāmanera* or *shrāmanerikā* can be ordained as a monk or nun if he or she has reached the required age, after a probation period of four months.

Shrāvaka 🅑 (śrāvaka), Skt., lit. "hearer"; originally a reference to the personal students of the Buddha or students in general. In the Mahāyāna, it means those students who, in contrast to → *pratyekabuddhas* and bodhisattvas, seek personal enlightenment and can attain this only by listening to the teaching and gaining insight into the → four noble truths and the irreality of phenomena. The supreme goal for them is nirvāna without earthly remainder (→ *nirupadhishesha-nirvāna*). Thus the *shrāvaka* corresponds to the level of the → arhat.

Shrāvakayāna 🅑 (śrāvakayāna), Skt., lit. "vehicle of the hearers"; the first of the three "vehicles" that can lead to the attainment of nirvana (→ *triyāna*). The *shrāvakayāna* leads to arhathood and can be equated with the → Hīnayāna.

Shravana 🅗 (Śravaṇa), Skt., lit. "hearing, learning"; the first of three steps considered necessary in → Vedanta for the attainment of spiritual knowledge. *Shravana* consists of hearing about the supreme truth, reading of it, and learning about it from the holy scriptures. The other steps are → *manana* and → *nididhyāsana.*

Shrī 🅗 (Śrī), Skt., lit. "splendor, beauty, fortune; prosperity, wealth; majesty; venerable one, eminent one"; 1. in the lattermost sense, an honorific title set before the names of deities and human beings; 2. another name for → Lakshmī, the goddess of fortune and beauty.

Shrīharsha 🅗 → Harsha, 2.

Shrīmālādevī-sūtra 🅑 (Śrīmālādevī-sūtra), Skt., "*Sūtra of Princess Shrīmālā*"; Mahāyāna sūtra that was translated into Chinese for the first time in the 5th century. It played an important role in the early period of Buddhism in Japan; Prince Shōtoku is supposed to have composed a commentary on it.

Princess Shrīmālā in this sūtra represents the conviction that the Buddha proclaimed all of his teachings for the sake of the Mahāyāna and that this ultimately includes all three "vehicles" (→ *triyāna*).

Shrīmālā mentions three types of beings who can tread the path of the Mahāyāna: (1) those who realize the most profound wisdom (→ *prajñā*) by themselves; (2) those who realize wisdom through hearing the teaching; (3) beings who have devout faith (→ *shraddhā*) in the → *tathāgata*, though they cannot realize supreme wisdom.

Shrīmat 🅗 (→ Srīmat), Skt., lit. "beautiful, illustrious, auspicious"; a word that implies holiness, fortune, and knowledge; it is set before other names, as in *Shrīmat* → *Bhāgavata-Purāna.*

Shri-Yantra 🅗 Skt., lit. "*yantra* of the illustrious one": the most important → *yantra* in Hindu → Tantra. It consists essentially of nine superimposed triangles converging on a central point (→ *bindu*). The five triangles whose apex points down represent → Shakti, while the four with their apexes pointing upward represent → Shiva.

Basic form of the Shrī-Yantra.

Concerning this *yantra*, Mookerjee and Khanna write: "The Shrī-Yantra is a symbol for the form (*svarūpa*) of Shakti, her powers and emanations, and hence a symbol for the gradual descent of Shakti into the manifest; in other words, it shows the form of the universe (*vishvarūpa*). It is a graphic representation of the cosmic field of creation. Like creation itself, the Shrī-Yantra also came into being through the power of primal desire. The impulse of desire (*kāmakāla*), produced by → *prakriti*, begets a movement (*spanda*) that is expressed in the vibration of sound (→ *nāda*). This manifestation is represented by a dot, or *bindu*. . . . This is the nucleus of concentrated energy, the germ of the primal sound, and the dynamic as well as the static aspect of two (Shiva/Shakti) in one. It contains all possibilities of becoming. . . . The dot becomes a radius, the polarization of Shiva and Shakti is accomplished, the dynamic and static energies enter into correlation with one another, and two further dots appear, thus forming a triad of dots—the primordial triangle, or *mula-trikona.*" (Trans. from German ed. of Mookerjee & Khanna 1977.)

The process displayed in the Shrī-Yantra, that of creation emanating from the *bindu* and proceeding through further steps up to the creation of the manifest world, is followed in reverse order by the devotee who meditates on the Shrī-Yantra, beginning at the material level and going back until the meditator discovers in the *bindu* his formless origin, that which "consists wholly of bliss" (*sarva-ānandamaya*), and becomes one with that origin.

Shrota-āpanna 🅱 (śrotāpanna), Skt. (Pali, sotāpanna), lit. "one who has entered the stream"; the first level of sacred accomplishment in the Hīnayāna (→ *ārya-mārga*, → *ārya-pudgala*), which can be attained by an adherent of faith (→ *shraddhānusārin*) or of the doctrine (→ *dharmānusārin*). A stream-enterer is free from the first three fetters of individualistic view, of doubt, and of clinging to rites and rules (→ *samyojana*) but has not yet freed himself of the passions (→ *klesha*). He must be reborn at least seven times in order to attain liberation, but his rebirths will be only in one of the higher modes of existence (→ *gati*). If he has, however, already partially overcome the inclinations toward sensual pleasure (→ kāma) and aggression, he only has to be reborn two or three times.

Shruti 🅷 (Śruti), Skt., lit. "hearing"; the holy scriptures of Hinduism are divided into *shruti* and → *smriti*. *Shruti* includes all those texts that derive from divine revelation and hence hold absolute authority. These are the → Vedas, whose eternal, sacred sound was "heard" by the → *rishis*. However, of these texts only the → Samhitās, → Brāhmanas, → Upanishads, and certain Sūtras are designated as *shruti*.

Shubhākarasimha 🅱 → Mi-tsung

Shuddhāvaita-Vedānta 🅷 Skt. → Vallabha

Shūdra 🅷 Skt. → *varna*

Shūhō Myōchō 🆉 → Myōchō Shūhō

Shui-kuan 🅃 → *san-kuan*

Shukadeva 🅷 (Śukadeva), or Shuka, Skt.; a great sage, the son of → Vyāsa, the narrator of the → *Bhāgavata-Purāna*. He is considered the ideal → *sannyāsin* and is numbered among the *nitya-siddhas* (→ *nitya*).

Shūmitsu 🆉 Jap. for Tsung-mi, → Kuei-feng Tsung-mi

Shun 🅃 2255–2205 B.C.E. or 2233–2184 B.C.E.; one of the legendary five emperors (→ *wu-ti*) and the successor of → Yao, who, on the suggestion of Four Mountains, the ruler of the four points of the compass, chose Shun to succeed him instead of his son. According to classical texts, Shun was an eastern barbarian, a potter, who cultivated his own fields. He is said to have traveled throughout the four directions and banished the ominous beings guarding their entrances. His successor was Yü the Great (→ Ta-yü).

In the *Analects* (*Lun-yü*) of Confucius (→ K'ung-tzu) and other Confucianist texts, Shun and his predecessor Yao are described as ideal rulers of the golden age and held up as a model for all future kings and emperors.

Shun'o Reizan 🆉 1344–1408; Japanese Zen master of the → Rinzai school. He founded the Kōon-ji monastery in the northwest of Edo (modern Tōkyō) and published in 1405 the Japanese edition of the → *Wu-men-kuan* (Jap., *Mumonkan*) that remains authoritative down to the present day. (Also → *kakushin*.)

Shūnyatā 🅱 🆉 (śūnyatā), Skt. (Pali, sunnatā; Jap., kū), lit. "emptiness, void"; central notion of Buddhism. Ancient Buddhism recognized that all composite things (→ *samskrita*) are empty, impermanent (→ *anitya*), devoid of an essence (→ *anātman*), and characterized by suffering (→ *duhkha*). In the Hīnayāna emptiness is only applied to the "person"; in the → Mahāyāna, on the other hand, all things are regarded as without essence, i.e., empty of self-nature (→ *svabhāva*). All dharmas are fundamentally devoid of independent lasting substance, are nothing more than mere appearances. They do not exist outside of emptiness. *Shūnyatā* carries and permeates all phenomena and makes their development possible. One should not, however, take this view of the emptiness of everything existing simply as nihilism. It does not mean that things do not exist but rather that they are nothing besides appearances. *Shūnyatā* is often equated with the absolute in Mahāyāna, since it is without duality and empirical forms. Beyond that, the individual schools present differing interpretations of *shūnyatā*.

The Mahāyāna illustrates the difference between the Hīnayāna and Mahāyāna views with the following image: in the Hīnayāna, things are like empty vessels, whereas the Mahāyāna denies even the existence of the vessels and thus arrives at total insubstantiality.

In the → *prajñāpāramitā* texts *shūnyatā* is regarded as what is common to all contrary appearances; they stress the nondistinctness of emptiness and form (→ *Heart Sūtra*). For the → Mādhyamikas, things are empty because they arise conditionally (→ *pratītya-samutpāda*). The true nature of the world is *shūnyatā*, which is explained as the "pacification of the manifold." Emptiness means that in relation to the true nature of the world, any manifoldness, i.e., any concept or verbal designation—including nonbeing—is inapplicable. *Shūnyatā* has three functions for the Mādhyamikas: it is the precondition for the arising of beings as well as for the impermanence of beings but also makes possible liberation from → samsāra. Comprehension of emptiness by wisdom (→ *prajñā*) is the realization of → nirvāna.

In the → Yogāchāra, things are empty because they arise from the mind (→ *chitta*). Mind in this school is equated with *shūnyatā*.

The concept of emptiness and the communication of this concept in such a way as to lead to a direct experience of it also played a central role in the introduction of the Mādhyamika teachings to Tibet. In the confrontation between the Indian scholar Kamalashila and the representatives of a school of Ch'an (→ Zen), the main question was whether awakening to supreme reality was by stages or was revealed in a sudden flash of insight. The decision in favor of the gradual way proposed by the Indian party led in the 11th century to the development of a number of philosophical methods, the argumentations of which were eventually recorded in the → Siddhānta literature. Therein all the schools of the "middle teaching" take as their point of departure → Nāgārjuna's thesis of the two truths: (1) the apparent truth (also relative or conventional truth, → *samvriti-satya*), which ordinary people take to be real—fundamentally it does not exist since it only appears through "interdependent arising" (*pratītya-samutpāda*); and (2) the supreme truth (also ultimate or absolute truth, → *paramārtha-satya*), the emptiness (beyond existence and nonexistence) of all phenomena, which cannot be expressed in words but only directly experienced. The differences among the individual Mādhyamika schools lie in their differing views concerning the nature of the two truths and how experience of emptiness is to be attained. The realization of emptiness, which is seen as the goal of religious practice (→ enlightenment), does not come about through philosophical argumentation; however, it becomes directly experiencable in the symbology of the → Tantras. The way to this experience is described especially in the teachings of → *Mahāmudrā* and → *dzogchen*. While emptiness is indicated in traditional Mādhyamaka by saying what it is not, in Mahāmudrā and Dzogchen it is viewed in positive terms. *Shūnyatā* as supreme reality here becomes "openness" that is inseparable from clarity (luminosity).

Shūnyatāvāda B → Mādhyamika

Shūrangama-sūtra B Z (Śūraṃgama-sūtra), Skt. (Jap., *Ryōgen-kyō*); the "*Sūtra of the Heroic One*," which is only extant in Chinese translation, exercised a great influence on the development of Mahāyāna Buddhism in China. It emphasizes the power of → *samādhi*, through which enlightenment can be attained, and explains the various methods of emptiness meditation (→ *shūnyatā*), through the practice of which everyone, whether monk or layperson, can realize the enlightenment of a → bodhisattva. The sūtra is particularly popular in Zen.

Shushna H (Śuṣṇa), Skt.; falsehood, deceit; forces that lead to suffering; they arise from impure thoughts and ego-directed impulses, and act as an impediment to knowledge.

In the *Rigveda*, Shushna is a demon (symbolic of the forces opposing knowledge) who is slain by the god Indra, lord of the sense (→ *indriya*). In other words, through control of the senses the forces that stand opposed to knowledge can all be overcome.

Shussoku-kan Z Jap. → Susoku-kan

Shuzan Shōnen Z Jap. for → Shou-shan Sheng-nien

Shvetaketu H (Śvetaketu), Skt.; 1. a sage in the *Mahābhārata*; 2. a young man whose instruction by his father, → Uddālaka Āruni, is described in the → *Chāndogya-Upanishad*. The teachings he receives about the Self and *brahman* all end with the sentence "Thou art that" (→ *Tat tvam asi*).

Shvetaketu had studied the Vedas with a teacher for twelve years and was proud of his knowledge. When he returned home, his father tested him by asking whether he knew how one hears the unhearable, perceives the unperceivable, and knows the unknowable. When Shvetaketu could not answer, his father explained this knowledge to him with various examples, each one ending with the words "That is the truth. That is the unperceivable essence of all things. That is the Self. And that, O Shvetaketu, *That art thou!*"

Shvetāshvatara H (Śvetāśvatara), Skt.; an Upanishad belonging to the *Black* → *Yajurveda*. It is younger than the → *Katha-Upanishad* and so important that it is cited in all Vedantic treatises (→ Vedānta). The teachings it contains range from theism to → Advaita-Vedānta. → Shankara wrote a commentary on its text.

Shyāmā H (Śyāmā), Skt., lit. "the black one"; a name for → Kālī, the Divine Mother and wife of → Shiva.

Siddha H Skt., lit. "perfect, complete"; a perfected one, one who has attained the supreme goal of spiritual aspiration: liberation (→

moksha); an illumined sage. In the → Purānas, a *siddha* is a semidivine being of great purity and power.

Siddhānta 🅱 Skt., roughly "doctrinal view"; In → Tibetan Buddhism a term for the views of various Indian philosophical schools as established through written accounts and proofs and for compilations of them in compendious works. Such works already existed at the time of the introduction of Buddhism into Tibet, but the → Gelugpa school was the first to present particularly concise versions. The doctrinal opinions themselves are divided into those "outside" (non-Buddhist) and those "inside" (Buddhist). The different systems of the Buddhist teaching examined are the → Vaibhāshika and → Sautrāntika, then the → Yogāchāra and → Mādhyamaka. Among the most important authors of *siddhānta* works are Jamyang Shäpa (1648–1721) and Könchok Jigme Wangpo (1728–1781).

Of primary importance to the authors of these Tibetan textbooks was an understanding of the various interpretations of the teaching of Buddha → Shākyamuni that had developed in India into different systems of Buddhist philosophy. Three types of doctrines were ascribed to the Buddha himself: that of the → four noble truths, which is subsumed under the → Hīnayāna; the → *prajñāpāramitā* teaching, which is the basis of the Mādhyamaka, and the doctrine of right discrimination, the teaching of the Yogāchāra.

The divergence of views can be seen in relation to the fact accepted by all Buddhist schools that all composite phenomena (→ *samskrita*) are impermanent. The Vaibhāshikas conceive of this in the everyday sense that at the time of death all things must pass away. The Sautrāntikas understand by the impermanence of appearances that they change with every instant.

For the followers of the Yogāchāra, the production of phenomena does not depend on the nature of external objects but is rather of the nature of the inner mind. A subschool of the Mādhyamikas says that this is not sufficient—the object is produced partly in virtue of its own nature. Finally the highest school of the Mādhyamikas asserts that appearances arise entirely and solely through the attribution of concepts and labels. This opinion is regarded as the correct one and thus represents the true way to expound the teachings of impermanence.

In this way the *siddhānta* texts review the entirety of Buddhist doctrine, presenting the lower-level systems as a means to penetrate into the higher ones. Especially important is discussion of the concept of "emptiness" (→ *shūnyatā*) and its interpretation by the Mādhyamika subschools.

Siddhārtha Gautama 🅱 🆉 Skt. (Pali, Siddhatta Gotama); founder of Buddhism (→ buddha-dharma), the historical → Buddha. Siddhārtha was born in 566 or 563 B.C.E. into a noble family of the Shākya clan in Kapilavastu, a city in present-day Nepal. His father Suddhodana was the head of the Shākyas; his mother Māyādevī, who brought Siddhārtha into the world in the Lumbinī Grove, died seven days after his birth. Siddhārtha was brought up by his aunt on his mother's side, Mahāprajāpatī. Carefully raised in wealthy circumstances, Siddhārtha married Yashodharā at the age of sixteen. At twenty-nine, after the birth of his son Rāhula, he entered → homelessness and attended on various ascetic teachers, without, however, reaching his goal, spiritual liberation. Thus he gave up the ascetic way of life and turned to meditation. At thirty-five he realized complete enlightenment, awakening (→ *bodhi*). After remaining silent at the beginning—because he was aware of the impossibility of communicating directly what he had experienced in enlightenment—he began at the request of others to expound insights drawn from his experience of enlightenment. He spent the rest of his life moving from place to place teaching, and a great number of disciples gathered around him. Siddhārtha Gautama, who came to be known by the name *Shākyamuni* (Sage of the Shākya Clan), died at the age of eighty after eating some spoiled food.

There are a number of legends concerning Siddhārtha's birth. His mother is said to have dreamed that a → bodhisattva entered her body in the form of an elephant. Siddhārtha was then born from his mother's right hip as she stood holding onto the branches of a tree. The newborn, according to tradition, took seven steps in each direction and then, with one arm stretched toward Heaven and the other toward the Earth, spoke these words: "I am the greatest in the world. This is my last birth. I will put an end to the suffering of birth, old age, and death." In each one of his footsteps a lotus blossom bloomed. One often finds this legend in artistic depictions.

Siddhārtha showed the signs of perfection at the time of his birth, and soothsayers prophesied that he would become either a universal monarch (→ *chakravartin* or an "awakened one" (buddha). Four signs were to show him which of the two ways he was destined for. His father, who wanted Siddhārtha to be his successor, gave him the best possible education and tried to prevent him from coming in contact with any signs that might direct him toward the path of religion. Above all, his father tried to keep him far from all care and misery.

Siddhārtha, however, entered the state of homelessness after he had seen the four signs during four

Siddhārtha Gautama as an ascetic (stone sculpture from Gandhāra, 2d century)

excursions. These were an old man, a sick man, a corpse, and a monk. According to legend, these four figures were the manifestations of gods, who appeared to Siddhārtha in order to guide him on the way to buddhahood. Siddhārtha recognized that the first three symbolized the suffering of the world, while in the monk he saw his own destiny. He set himself the goal of overcoming suffering, and attached himself to several teachers, who in accordance with the view in India at the time, saw asceticism as the only way to realization. The most important of these were Ārāda Kālāma and Rudraka Rāmaputra. However, their teachings did not satisfy Siddhārtha, and he decided to seek salvation on his own. Five disciples followed him. Near death after years of fruitless strict asceticism, he recognized this practice as one that does not lead to the goal and again began to take food. At this point his companions were disappointed and left him.

Then Siddhārtha went to Bodh-gayā, where he sat down under what was later to be known as the → Bodhi-tree, and vowed to persist in meditation until he had solved the riddle of suffering. After forty-nine days, at the age of thirty-five and despite the temptations of → Māra, he attained complete enlightenment. From this moment on, Siddhārtha was a buddha, an awakened one, and he knew that for him there would now be no further rebirth.

Since it was clear to the Awakened One that the essential content of his enlightenment experience could neither be formulated in words nor conveyed to others in any other form, he continued in silent meditation under the Bodhi-tree. When he again encountered his former companions, they saw that he was completely transformed. His radiance was such that though they had at first approached him with suspicion, they were soon convinced that he must have found liberation, as they themselves had striven in vain to do by means of asceticism. They asked him for instruction, and moved by compassion for the suffering of all sentient beings, the Buddha broke his silence.

He began to show the way that leads to the experience of awakening and thus to liberation. For this purpose, on the basis of his enlightenment, he formulated his teachings of the → four noble truths, the law of conditioned arising (→ *pratītya-samutapāda*), and → karma. In the Deer Park of Benares he gave his first discourse; in the Buddhist tradition this is known as "setting in motion the wheel of the teaching." His earlier five companions became his first disciples and formed the core of the → *sangha*. There followed a period of many years of teaching. The Buddha stayed mainly in the region of → Rājagriha and → Vaishālī and moved from place to place living on begged food. The number of his students grew quickly. It was of particular importance for the development of the *sangha* that King → Bimbisāra of Magadha became a lay follower (→ *upāsaka*) of the Buddha and gave him a monastery in the vicinity of Rājagriha, the capital of Magadha. The Buddha's most important students were → Ānanda, → Shāriputra, and → Mahāmaudgalyāyana. The order of nuns (→ *bhikshunī*) was also founded at this time.

The Buddha also had to deal with enemies. His cousin → Devadatta, who wanted to become the head of the community of followers, planned to kill the Buddha; however the plan failed. Devadatta nevertheless brought about a schism among the monks of Vaishālī by advocating an ascetic life in contradiction of the Buddha.

According to the → *Mahāparinibbāna-sutta*, in 486 or 483 B.C.E. the Buddha partook of spoiled food, and lying on his right side and facing west, entered → *parinirvāna*. According to the Pali tradition, the Buddha died on the full-moon day of the month April/May; according to the Sanskit texts, on the full-moon day in November.

The funeral of the Buddha is said to have been accompanied by miracles. The distribution of his relics led to conflicts, since many communities laid claim to them. They are said to have been divided in eight parts and were preserved in → stūpas. Although the historical facts of Siddhārtha Gautama's biography were soon overlaid by legend, today, on the basis of investigation of philological and archaeological evidence, he is accepted as a historical personality and the founder of Buddhism even by sceptical Western scholars.

Siddhi **H** **B** Skt., roughly "perfect abilities."
H Psychic, so-called supernatural ability or abilities that may appear as by-products of spiritual

development if certain powers are developed that open the way to universal spheres. *Siddhis* can be developed deliberately through certain Tantric and yogic practices. Among these occult powers are mind-reading, clairvoyance, materialization, levitation, making things invisible, and entering other bodies. All the great teachers have cautioned against the effort to achieve *siddhis* for their own sake, because such powers, even if they seem to be "supernatural," nevertheless belong entirely to the phenomenal realm and contribute nothing to one's realization of absolute truth, and because attachment to such abilities constitutes a serious obstacle in the way of spiritual development.

Thus the great spiritual teacher → Rāmana Maharshi, for example, warned people repeatedly against attachment to *siddhis* and made no use of them himself, while other great masters, such as → Sai Baba of Shirdi, employed *siddhis* for the welfare of their followers and for their spiritual instruction. However, for those who have not reached a similar level of spiritual development, there is a clear danger of misuse of power in the employment of *siddhis*, which would negate all previous spiritual efforts.

B in the context of Buddhist yoga as it is practiced especially in the → Vajrayāna, perfect mastery over the powers of the body and of nature. The Vajrayāna is acquainted with eight ordinary *siddhis*: (1) the sword that renders unconquerable, (2) the elixir for the eyes that makes gods visible, (3) fleetness in running, (4) invisibility, (5) the life-essence that preserves youth, (6) the ability to fly, (7) the ability to make certain pills, (8) power over the world of spirits and demons. Enlightenment is differentiated from these eight as the sole "extraordinary" or supreme *siddhi*. In the biographies of the eighty-four → *mahāsiddhas*, the attainment of these abilities is described in detail.

Sigan Reisan Z → Ts'ui-yen Ling-ts'an

Sikhism H a religion founded by Guru → Nānak (1469–1538), who wished to create a synthesis of the religious teachings of Hinduism and those of the invading Muslims. Sikhs place no value in mere ritual and reject renunciation of the world as cowardly escapism. They emphasize rather that both Allah and Brahmā are pleased by surrender to God and the loving service of one's fellow human beings. Caste distinctions are not recognized. Sikhs believe in evolution, the law of → *karma*, and reincarnation. Liberation or union with God is made possible only by one's personal efforts. Sikhs greet one another with the words *Sat siri akal* ("God is true; truth is eternal"). Their holy scripture is the → *Ādi Granth*.

Silence of the Buddha B the historical Buddha → Shākyamuni refrained from giving a definitive answer to many metaphysical questions of his time. This is often referred to as the silence of the Buddha.

Again and again his students asked him if a self exists or not (→ *anātman*); if an enlightened one in any way continues to exist after his death; if the world is eternal and unending or not. The Buddha explained that he was silent on these questions because answers to them would in no way further progress on the path—they would not contribute to the overcoming of the passions nor to the attainment of wisdom. He was concerned that occupation with these questions would divert people from the path that leads to liberation from suffering.

The Buddha illustrated his position in the parable of a man who has been hit by a poisoned arrow. The man is immediately taken to a doctor, who wants to pull out the arrow at once. But the wounded man cries out, "The arrow shall not be pulled out until I know who the man is who shot me with it, to what family he belongs, if he is big, small, or of medium size, if his skin is black, brown, or yellow." Just as the man wounded by the arrow would have died before he got the answer to his questions, so the student would be laid low by the suffering of the world before solving these metaphysical problems.

Simhabodhi Z (Jap., Shishibodai); twenty-fourth patriarch of the Indian lineage of Ch'an (→ Zen).

Singh H lit. "the lion," from Skt. *siṃha*; Guru Govind Singh, 1666–1708, the founder of a Sikh brotherhood (→ Sikhism) that fought against the Mogul invaders. After joining the religious community, every Sikh receives the second name "Singh."

Sītā H Skt., lit. "furrow." In the Vedas, Sītā is the personification of agriculture and is worshiped as the divinity who rules over agriculture and the fruits of the earth. In the *Rāmāyana*, she is the daughter of King → Janaka and the wife of → Rāma. Her father said, "As I was plowing the field, a maiden sprang up from behind the plow and hence received the name Sītā, 'the furrow.' She emerged from the earth and was brought up as my daughter."

Rāma won Sītā for his wife because he was able to string Janaka's bow, which had been given to the king by Shiva. Sītā followed Rāma when he was banished and was subsequently abducted by → Rāvana. After

Rāma was victorious in the war that ensued and had won Sītā back, he cast her aside, believing that she had lost her honor. Sītā later called upon Mother Earth to prove her innocence. The ground opened beneath her, and she returned whence she had come.

Sivananda 🅷 → Shivānanda

Sīvathikā 🅱 Pali → charnel ground contemplation

Six houses (and) seven schools 🅱 (Chin., liu-chia ch'i-tsung); currents of Chinese Buddhism in its early phase (4th century), all arising from engagement with the → *Prajñāpāramitā-sūtra* and presenting a particular interpretation of the notion of → *shūnyatā* (emptiness). They developed under the influence of neo-Taoism, which was widely diffused in the learned circles of the time and whose central idea, → *wu* (nothing), was very close to the Buddhist notion of *shūnyatā.*

Buddhist monks tried initially to grasp *shūnyatā* with the help of this aspect of Chinese thought. Since the various interpretations of *shūnyatā* differed considerably from one another, formation of the "six houses and seven schools" came about. The principal of these were the School of Appearances As Such, the School of Stored Impressions, the School of Illusions, the School of the Nonbeing of the Mind, the School of Causal Combination, the School of Fundamental Nonbeing, and the Modified School of Fundamental Nonbeing.

Skanda 🅷 Skt.; the god of warriors, who challenges the ignorant to battle and provides spiritual seekers with strength for their development. Another name for Skanda is → Kārttikeya.

Skandha 🅱 🆉 Skt. (Pali, khanda), lit. "group, aggregate, heap"; term for the five aggregates, which constitute the entirety of what is generally known as "personality." They are (1) corporeality or form (→ *rūpa*), (2) sensation (→ *vedanā*), (3) perception (Skt., *samjñā*; Pali, *sannā*), (4) mental formations (→ *samskāra*), (5) consciousness (→ *vijñāna*). These aggregates are frequently referred to as "aggregates of attachment" (*upādāna-skandha*), since (excluding the case of → arhats and buddhas) craving or desire (→ *trishnā*) attaches itself to them and attracts them to itself; thus it makes of them objects of attachment and brings about suffering.

The characteristics of the *skandhas* are birth, old age, death, duration, and change. They are regarded as without essence (→ *anātman*), impermanent (→ *anitya*), empty (→ *shūnya*), and suffering-ridden (→ *duhkha*).

The aggregate of corporeality (also form or matter) is composed of the four elements (the firm, fluid, heating, and moving [→ *mahābhūta*]), of the sense organs, their objects, and so on. The sensation aggregate consists of all sensations, unpleasant, pleasant, or neutral. Perceptions include perception of form, sound, smell, taste, bodily impressions, and mental objects. The aggregate of mental formations (also translated "psychological powers of form" or "mental impulses") includes the majority of mental activities such as volition, attention, discrimination, joy, happiness, equanimity, resolve, exertion, compulsion, concentration, and so on. The consciousness aggregate includes the six types of consciousness (consciousness of seeing, hearing, smelling, tasting, bodily sensation, and mental consciousness), all of which arise out of contact between the object and the corresponding organ.

The characteristics of suffering and impermanence of the five *skandhas* form a central theme of Buddhist literature. Suffering is based on impermanence and transitoriness; from the impermanence of the personality composed of the five *skandhas*, Buddhism derives the absence of a self (*anātman*). Whatever is characterized by impermanence and thus suffering cannot constitute a self, since according to the Indian view, this entails permanence and freedom from suffering. The knowledge of the "inessentiality" of the *skandhas* already contains the insight that leads to liberation. Nyānatiloka explains what consequences this insight has for the conception of the existence of an ego:

"What is called individual existence is in reality nothing but a mere process of those mental and physical phenomena, a process that since time immemorial has been going on, and that also after death will still continue for unthinkably long periods of time. These five groups [aggregates], however, neither singly nor collectively constitute a self-dependent real Ego-entity, or personality (*atta* [Skt. *ātman*]), nor is there to be found any such entity apart from them. Hence the belief is such an Ego-entity or Personality, as real in the ultimate sense, proves a mere illusion" (Nyānatiloka 1972, p. 83).

Smriti 🅷 🅱 (smṛti), Skt., lit. "recollection, tradition."

🅷 Hinduism distinguishes between two types of holy scripture: → *shruti* (revealed scriptures) and *smriti.* The latter includes all those texts based upon tradition. However, these are regarded as valid only when they are assumed to derive from a *shruti.* The category of *smriti* consists chiefly of the → Vedāngas, the Shrauta- and Grihya-Sūtras, the → *Manu-Samhitā*, the *Mahābhārata*, the *Rāmāyana*, the Purānas, and the → Niti-Shāstras.

🅱 (Pali, sati). The term *smriti*, which in Buddhism is understood as meaning "attention" or "mindfulness," refers to mindfulness of all mental and physical activities. This is the "perfect mindfulness," i.e., the seventh element of the → eightfold path, one of the seven factors of enlightenment (→ *bodhyanga*), and one of the five powers (→ *bala*). It is seen as "perfect" because it serves the goal of Buddhism, the elimination of suffering. Since *smriti* is free from falsifying influences, it can bring insight into the transitory, unsatisfactory, and essenceless nature of all appearances. Such insight is the precondition for the attainment of freedom from suffering, or liberation. It is with this view that mindfulness is practiced in the "four foundations of mindfulness" (→ *satipatthāna*).

Smriti-Shuddhi 🅗 (Smṛti-Śuddhi), Skt., lit. *smriti*: "memory," *shuddhi*: "purification, clarity"; pure memory, which brings immediate awareness of something sought in the mind or the object of meditation.

Snānayātrā 🅗 Skt.; a festival in the month of Jyaishtha (→ Bengali calendar), at which an image of the divinity is bathed (→ Jagannātha).

Sōdō 🅩 Jap., lit. "monks' hall"; a term for a Zen monastery (→ *tera*).

Soe-tae San 🅑 → Won Buddhism

SO'HAM 🅗 Skt., lit. "He am I"; one of the sacred formulas (→ mantra) of nondual → Vedānta, expressing the identity of → *ātman* with → *brahman*.

Sōji-ji 🅩 Jap., one of the two principal monasteries of the → Sōtō school of Zen in Japan. Sōji-ji was founded in the 8th century by the monk Gyōgi as a monastery of the Hossō school (Chin., → Fa-hsiang) of Japanese Buddhism and originally lay in the Ishikawa prefecture. Since → Keizan Jōkin became abbot of this monastery in 1321, it has been a Zen monastery. In 1898, after a fire which completely destroyed it, Sōji-ji was moved to Yokohama, its present location. The other principal monastery of the Sōtō school is → Ehei-ji, founded by → Dōgen Zenji.

Sōka Gakkai 🅑 Jap., lit. "Scientific Society for the Creation of Values"; modern Buddhist mass movement in Japan, founded in 1930 by Makiguchi Tsunesaburō (1871–1944). Its doctrine is rooted in the thought of → Nichiren. Veneration of Nichiren as well as of the "three great mysteries" (→ Nichiren school) and the → *Lotus Sūtra* constitute the basic program of the Sōka Gakkai.

The original name of the movement was Scientific Association for Education That Creates Values. In the context of this association Makiguchi attempted to diffuse his theory of values. According to his view, the useful, beautiful, and good are the principal values through which a happy life, the supreme goal, can be achieved. Under the influence of a colleague, Makiguchi joined the True School of Nichiren, which brought about a deepening of his worldview. Soon his theory of values reappeared along with the veneration of Nichiren and the *Lotus Sūtra*. In 1943 Makiguchi and other leading members of the Sōka Gakkai were arrested because they refused to take part in Shintō rituals (→ Shintō) and were against the merger of existing religious communities. In 1944 Makiguchi died in prison.

Under his successor Toda Josei (1900–1958), Sōka Gakkai became a mass movement. Makiguchi's theory of values decreased in importance, and on the religious side the emphasis shifted from the *Lotus Sūtra* to the figure of Nichiren himself. Thanks to a special method of recruiting members (*shakubuku*), which was devised by Nichiren, the membership numbers climbed quickly. In *shakubuku* (lit. "destroying errors and coming forcefully to conclusions"), "false views" are uncovered by means of Makiguchi's theory of values, and the benefit of venerating the three mysteries is stressed.

In 1960 Daisaku Ikeda (b. 1928) became president of the movement, and in 1964 he founded the political party Kōmeitō (Party of Cleanliness), which advocates Buddhist-oriented democracy and humanistic socialism and is dedicated to decrease in corruption and to general welfare and world peace. This kind of political engagement also derives from Nichiren. The Sōka Gakkai has its own presses, schools, and universities and administers various social institutions.

Sokushin sokubutsu 🅩 Jap.; a famous Zen saying, which in effect means "Basic heart-mind [is] basic Buddha."

Soma 🅗 Skt.; the intoxicating juice of a climbing plant that is offered to the gods and ingested by the brahman priests. The *soma* drink plays a significant role in the → *Rigveda*.

Because *soma* seemed to lend supernatural powers to those who drank it, it was worshiped as a god. Hindus also called it "the wine of immortality" (→ *amrita*). It symbolizes the replacement of commonplace sense-pleasure by divine bliss (→ *ānanda*). It was prepared by a priest, who pressed the stalks of the *soma* plant (*amshu*) between stones. The juice was strained, mixed with beer and milk, and offered to the gods. It is a sweet, brown liquid that induces a temporary state of ecstasy.

Sopadhishesha-nirvāna 🅑 (sopadhiśeṣa-nirvāṇa), Skt. (Pali, savupadisesa-nibbāna); nirvāna with a remainder of conditionality, the nirvāna before death. In this type of nirvāna, all passions (→ *klesha*), which are the fundamental cause of rebirth into a new existence after death, are eliminated. It is attained before death. The aggregates (→ *skandha*) continue to be present, i.e., individuality is still empirically perceivable.

The one who has gained release in *sopadhishesha-nirvāna* is not yet completely free from suffering, since he must still live through the remaining consequences of his old karma. Freedom from suffering is only temporarily possible during certain meditative states. At death the one so released enters into complete nirvāna (→ *nirupadhishesha-nirvāna*), in which his empirical existence, and with it all suffering, comes to an end. *Sopadhishesha-nirvāna* is realized with the attainment of → arhatship.

From this Hīnayāna version of nirvāna, the → *apratishthita-nirvāna* of the Mahāyāna developed. (Also → nirvāna.)

Sōrin 🅉 Jap., lit. "monks' grove"; term for a large Zen monastery (→ *tera*) in which many monks are living.

Sōsan 🅉 Jap. for → Seng-ts'an

Sōsan 🅉 Jap., lit. "general *sanzen*"; a form of → *sanzen*: a ceremonial gathering in a Zen monastery in which a master or an advanced Zen student presents a short discourse and then engages in Zen dialog (→ *hossen*, → *mondō*) with anyone who, putting his insight to the test, asks a question or makes a comment. At times *sōsan* of this nature are held in the presence, and with the participation, of the assembled Zen masters of a lineage. In such a case a particular student is called upon to give an account of himself before being officially recognized as a dharma successor (→ *hassu*) of his master.

The term *sōsan* is also sometimes applied to sessions not having the character of a → *teishō* in which a Zen master gives public instruction on questions of practice.

Soshi 🅉 Jap., lit. "the Patriarch"; an epithet of → Bodhidharma. (Also → *soshigata*.)

Soshigata 🅉 Jap.; the "partriarchs" of the transmission lineage of Ch'an (Zen). The patriarchs are great masters, each of whom received the → buddha-dharma from his master in the "transmission from heart-mind to heart-mind" (→ *hassu*, → *Denkō-roku*) and transmitted it further to his dharma successor(s). In India there were twenty-eight patriarchs in the succession from → Shākyamuni Buddha, and in China six. In this sequence → Bodhidharma counts both as the twenty-eighth in the Indian lineage and as the first in the Chinese.

The sixth Chinese patriarch → Hui-neng never transmitted the patriarchate formally to a successor; thus it came to an end. Nevertheless, Hui-neng had five chief disciples and dharma successors from whom derive all the schools of Ch'an (Zen) that developed in several parallel lineages of transmission after Hui-neng (see the Ch'an/Zen Lineage Chart). The outstanding masters of these lineages in the generations after Hui-neng, both in China and Japan, are often referred to as "patriarchs" out of a sense of veneration and appreciation for their great accomplishments.

Soshi-no shin-in 🅉 Jap., lit. "the mind seal of the patriarchs"; an expression for an experience of → enlightenment confirmed by a master of a living lineage of the Zen tradition. Also an expression for the true nature or buddha-nature (→ *busshō*) or for the genuine tradition of budha-dharma within the transmission lineage of Zen (also → *hassu*, → *inka-shōmei*).

Soshi seirai 🅉 Jap., lit. "the coming of the patriarch out of the west"; a Zen expression that refers to the coming of → Bodhidharma, the first Chinese patriarch of Ch'an (Zen), from India to China.

Soshi Zen 🅉 Jap., lit. "patriarch Zen"; a term for the Ch'an (Zen) of the → Southern school.

Soshun 🅉 Jap. for → Ch'u-chun

Sōtō school 🅉 (Chin., Ts'ao-tung-tsung; Jap., Sōtō-shū); with the → Rinzai school, one of the two most important schools of → Zen in Japan. It belongs to the → *goke-shichishū* and was founded by the great Chinese Ch'an (Zen) master → Tung-shan Liang-chieh (Jap., Tōzan Ryōkai) and his student → Ts'ao-shan Pen-chi (Jap., Sōzan Honjaku). The school was named Ts'ao-tung (Jap., Sōtō) after the first character of the names of the two founders.

In the first half of the 13th century, the tradition of the Sōtō school was brought to Japan from China by the Japanese master → Dōgen Zenji; there, Sōtō Zen, along with Rinzai, is one of the two principal transmission lineages of Zen still active today. While the goal of training in the two schools is basically the same, Sōtō and Rinzai Zen differ in their training methods—though even here the line differentiating the two schools cannot be sharply drawn. In Sōtō Zen, → *mokushō* Zen and thus → *shikantaza* is more heavily stressed; in Rinzai, → *kanna* Zen and kōan practice. In Sōtō Zen, the practice of →

dokusan, one of the most important elements of Zen training, has died out since the middle of the Meiji period.

Southern school 🅉 (Chin., Nan-tsung-ch'an; Jap., Nanshū-zen); the school of Ch'an (Zen) that derives from → Hui-neng, the sixth patriarch of Ch'an, and that produced all the important masters and lineages of transmission of Ch'an (Zen) (also → *goke-shichishū* and the Ch'an/Zen Lineage Chart). The term *Southern school* is used in counterdistinction to the school deriving from → Shen-hsiu, the representatives of which lived in northern China and which is thus called the Northern school. While the latter was still strongly influenced by traditional Indian Meditation Buddhism (→ Dhyāna Buddhism), which had shaped the Ch'an of the patriarchs prior to Hui-neng, the Ch'an of the Southern school represented an unorthodox approach to realization and transmission of the → buddha-dharma, which was strongly marked by indigenous Chinese Taoism and the Chinese folk character. While the Northern school placed great value on the study and intellectual penetration of the scriptures of Buddhism, especially the → *Lankāvatāra-sūtra*, and held the view that enlightenment is reached "gradually" through slow progress on the path of meditative training (→ *zengo*), the Southern school stresses the "suddeness" of the enlightenment experience (→ *tongo*) and the primacy of direct insight into the true nature of existence (→ *kenshō*) over occupation with conceptual affirmations about this.

In many → kōans handed down in the Southern school, we learn of adherents of the Northern school, who armed with their erudition in the scriptures, sought out masters of the Southern school in order to expose their ignorance. However, the adepts of the Southern school made clear with a single question or comment that the erudition of the northerners was impotent to grasp the profound sense of the scriptures and rather hindered the experience of enlightenment than furthered it.

While the Southern school flourished in the T'ang and Sung periods and produced literally hundreds of profoundly enlightened masters, the Northern school declined in a few generations and finally died out altogether. Also → Hui-neng, → Shen-hsiu.)

The Ch'an of the Southern school is also called "Patriarch Ch'an" (Chin., *Tsu-shih-ch'an*; Jap., *Soshi-zen*).

Sōzan Honjaku 🅉 Jap. for → Ts'ao-shan Pen-chi

Sparsha 🄱 (sparśa), Skt. (Pali, phassa), "contact"; refers to the contact between a sense organ and the corresponding sense object along with the participation of consciousness (→ *vijñāna*); such contact calls forth sensation (→ *vedanā*). *Sparsha* represents the simple contact of consciousness with an object—the first awareness of a sense impression before perception of characteristic qualities. Six types of *sparsha* are differentiated: *sparsha* in connection with seeing, hearing, smelling, tasting, touching, and mental function. *Sparsha* belongs to the aggregate of mental formation (→ *skandha*, *samskāra*) and is the sixth link in the chain of conditioned arising (→ *pratītya-samutpāda*).

Sphota 🄷 Skt. → *shabda*

Srishti 🄷 (Sṛṣṭi), Skt., lit. "creation, origin"; the projection or gradual unfoldment of something that lay hidden in its causal form. The term is used primarily in reference to the development of the universe from its seed state.

Ssu-hsiang 🅃 Chin., lit. "four images"; a concept found in the → *I-ching*. Each of the four images—the building blocks of the sixty-four hexagrams—consists of two lines, each of which can be either yin or yang, the former being indicated by a broken line (– –), the latter by a continuous line (——). Yin symbolizes Earth, yang Heaven. The four images, with the permutations of yin and yang lines, represent the four possible combinations of Heaven and Earth, which give rise to the four seasons of the year.

The first image consists of two yang lines ⚌ and is known as *t'ai-yang* (ripe yang); it signifies summer.

The second image consists of a yang line below a yin line ⚍; it is known as *shao-yin* (young yin) and signifies spring.

The third image consists of a yin line below a yang line ⚎, is known as *shao-yang* (young yang), and signifies autumn.

The fourth image consists of two yin lines ⚏, is called *t'ai-yin* (ripe yin), and signifies winter.

By adding a third line (either yin or yang), which is meant to represent man as a link between Heaven and Earth, one arrives at the eight trigrams (→ *pa-kua*), the basic signs of the *Book of Change(s)*.

In another context, however, *ssu-hsiang* may also refer to the four seasons of the year, the four elements (water, fire, wood, and metal), or the four cardinal points.

The *Hsi-tz'u* (→ *Shih-i*) of the *I-ching* states,

"In change there is the supreme ultimate [→ *t'ai-chi*]. It created the two forms [→ *liang-i*]. From them arose the four images, and from these, in turn, the eight trigrams."

Ssu-hsin Wu-hsin Z (Jap., Shishin Goshin), 1044–1115; Chinese Ch'an (Zen) master of the Ōryō lineage of Rinzai Zen (→ Ōryō school); a student and dharma successor (→ *hassu*) of → Hui-t'ang Tsu-hsin (Jap., Maidō Soshin). We encounter Master Ssu-Hsin in example 39 of the → *Wu-men-kuan.*

Ssu-ming T Chin., lit. "Lord of Fate," better known as → Tsao-chün, the hearth deity; one of the most important deities of religious Taoism (→ *tao-chiao*). Ssu-ming determines the life span of each individual. He keeps a register of our transgressions and omissions, of which he informs the Supreme One (→ T'ai-i), at the same time asking him to lengthen or shorten the life span of the individual in question accordingly. Ssu-ming's *Book of Death* contains the names of all who must die; his *Book of Life,* those of the immortals (→ *hsien*).

According to the teaching of the Inner Deity Hygiene School, Ssu-ming—like the Supreme One—lives in one of the compartments of the inner cinnabar fields (→ *tan-t'ien*).

Ssu-ming goes back to the 8th century B.C.E. He is one of the deities with whom shamans—the precursors of the later Taoist → *fang-shih*—made contact. Even then, it was their task to determine the life span of human beings. In the course of time (→ Li Shao-chün), Ssu-ming became identified with the hearth god Tsao-chün, who continues to be the most important deity in Chinese folk religion.

Ssu-shih-erh-chang ching B Chin. for → *Sūtra in Forty-two Sections*

Sthavira B Skt., roughly "adherent of the elders"; one of the two Hīnayāna schools into which the original Buddhist community split at the third → Buddhist council of Pātaliputra. The split took place as a result of disagreements over the nature of an → arhat. A monk named Mahādeva is said to have proposed the following five theses: (1) an arhat is still susceptible to temptation, i.e., he can still have nocturnal emissions of semen; (2) he is not yet free from ignorance (→ *avidyā*); (3) he is still subject to doubt concerning the teaching; (4) he can still make progress on the path of liberation through the help of others; (5) he can still make progess on the path of liberation through enunciating certain sounds and through concentration (→ *samādhi*). The Sthaviras rejected these theses; their opponents, the → Mahāsānghikas, accepted them.

Sthiramati B philosopher of the → Yogāchāra, who lived in the 6th century. He wrote several important commentaries on the works of → Vasubandhu (for example, on the → *Abhidharmakosha*) and → Nāgārjuna, in which he attempted to develop the common ground in the teachings of the Yogāchāra and the → Mādhyamikas. He advocated a moderate idealism.

Sthita-Prajñā H Skt., lit. "firm in knowledge"; a term referring to one who is firmly grounded in spiritual knowledge. Such a one is no longer moved by dual pairs of opposites such as joy and sorrow, gain and loss, fortune and misfortune, victory and defeat.

Sthūla-Sharīra H (Sthūla-Śarīra), Skt., lit. *sthūla*: "gross," *sharīra*: "body, sheath"; the gross outer sheath surrounding the → *ātman*, the self; the body. This sheath is identical with → *annamaya-kosha.* (See also → *kosha,* → *sharīra.)*

Storehouse consciousness B → *ālaya-vijñāna*

Stotra B Skt., lit. "hymn, song of praise"; a song of praise to the Buddha or to great masters or deities of Buddhism. (Also → Kangyur-Tengyur.)

Stūpa B Skt. (Pali, thūpa; Sinh. dagoba; Tib., chöten), lit. "hair knot"; characteristic expression of Buddhist architecture, one of the main symbols of Buddhism and a focal point in temples and monasteries.

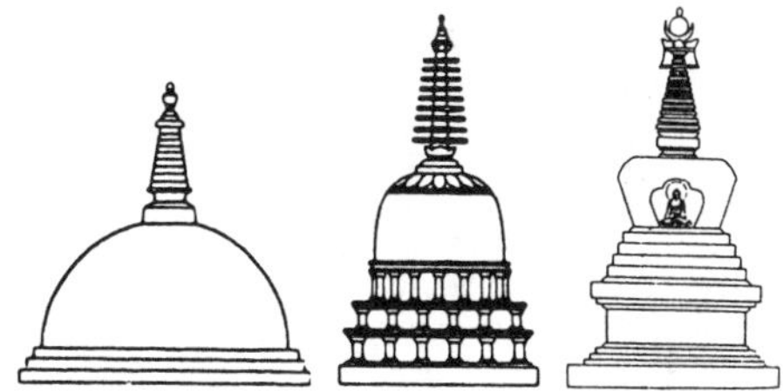

Various forms of the stūpa: basic Indian type, Gandhāra type, and Tibetan form (chöten)

Originally stūpas were memorial monuments over the mortal remains (→ °sharīra) of the historical Buddha and other saints. They also served, however, as symbolic reminders of various decisive events in the life of → Shākyamuni Buddha. Thus stūpas were built at → Lumbinī, → Bodh-gayā, → Kushinagara, → Sārnāth, and so on. At the latest by the time of King → Ashoka (3d century B.C.E.), the veneration of saints had become a general custom; the stūpas from his time are still preserved.

Not every stūpa contains relics in the proper sense; in their place sacred texts and representations are also enshrined, which confer their sacredness on the stūpa. Stūpas are often purely symbolic structures; examples are Borobudur and the three-dimensional mandalas of Tibet.

The veneration of stūpas, in which the Buddha is "present," has been known since the early period of Buddhism. Such veneration is usually expressed by circumambulating the stūpa in the direction of the sun's course but also through other forms of worship (→ *pūjā*). It is not, however, the relics themselves that are venerated; rather the stūpa serves as a support for meditation and as a symbolic reminder of the awakened state of mind.

The original form of the stūpa is preserved in the stūpas of → Sāñchī. On a circular base, there is a hemisphere, flattened at the top; on this, rising through a square stone latticework structure, is a short post with three flat umbrella shapes towards the top. The latticework structure often has the form of a box roofed with slabs. The umbrella shapes are symbols of dignity and veneration. A stone wall with four gates as entrances separates the sacred site from the world around it. The reliquary vessels, which themselves often have the form of a stūpa and are made of precious materials, are usually located at the central axis of the stūpa, on the floor of the hemisphere or at its top.

All stūpa forms and those of the → pagoda, the East Asian variant of the stūpa, are derived from this type of stūpa, which was widespread between the 3d century B.C.E. and the 1st century C.E.

In the second phase of development of the stūpa, which took place in → Gandhāra, the circular base was raised into a cylinder. This was divided into levels. The hemisphere also underwent vertical elongation and became smaller in relation to the base. These changes made room for differentiated architectonic articulation through the use of buddha images, votive statues, and reliefs depicting a story. The top part also became longer and was given more umbrella shapes, which in further course of development came to form a cone-shaped spire.

Between 150 and 400 C.E., the circular base became a square pedestal, which was divided into several levels and was provided with stairways that led up to the circumambulation path. This form of stūpa is also found in Central Asia.

In Sri Lanka and Thailand the basic form with the low circular base is preserved, the hemisphere is elongated vertically and is often bell-shaped. It is topped off with a very narrow, long spire. In Tibet and Lamaist China, the old type with hemispheric body between base and spire continued. The three-dimensional form called *chöten* ("offering container") is regarded in Tibetan Buddhism as a symbol of the body, speech, and mind of the Buddha. Its size ranges from that of small shrine objects to that of monumental structures visible from a distance. When above a certain size, *chötens* are ritually circumambulated. Two of the most important stūpas in Nepal are still today objects of pilgrimage.

The symbology of the *chöten* is based on Mahāyāna doctrine. The four lower levels stand for the four positive states of mind of love, compassion, joy, and equanimity. A secondary pedestal on top of this has ten further levels that ascend to the middle part of the *chöten*; these represent the ten stages (→ *bhūmi*) of the spiritual development of a bodhisattva. The middle part or "body" of the *chöten* symbolizes the awakened mind (→ *bodhicitta*) and in certain cases contains the image of a deity.

Above this middle part rise thirteen umbrella shapes of different sizes; they represent various methods of propagating the Buddhist teaching (→ dharma). On top of these umbrella shapes is a five-petaled lotus, symbol of the properties of the five Buddha families (*buddhakula*). The pinnacle of the stūpa is composed of a sun disk resting on a crescent moon, which symbolizes the cosmic grandeur of the teaching.

There is a further typology of eight kinds of *chötens* that differ only slightly in form, which developed as a reminder of the eight essential acts of the Buddha during his life. The cult of the stūpa as a visible sign of the teaching was introduced into Tibet mainly by → Atīsha, and the *chöten* is still today the symbol of the → Kadampa school.

Subhūti 🅱 student of the Buddha, who stood out through his abilities in the meditation of lovingkindness (→ *maitri, Mettā-sutta*). In the → Prajñāpāramitā-sūtras of the Mahāyāna, it is generally Subhūti who, because of his profound insight, explains the teaching of → *shūnyatā* (emptiness). Subhūti is one of the → ten great disciples of the Buddha.

Suffering in Buddhism 🅱 → *duhkha*

Suibi Mugaku 🅩 Jap. for → Ts'ui-wei Wu-hsueh

Sukhāvatī 🅱 Skt., lit. "the Blissful"; the so-called western paradise, the → pure land of the west, one of the most important of the buddha-fields to appear in the Mahāyāna. It is reigned over by Buddha → Amitābha, who created it by his karmic merit. Through faithful devotion to Amitābha and through recitation of his name, one can be reborn there and lead a blissful life until entering final nirvāna.

Sukhāvatī is described in detail in the sūtras devoted to Amitābha (→ *Amitābha-sūtra,* → *Sukhāvatī-vyūha,* → *Amitāyurdhyāna-sūtra*). Though these descriptions are taken by folk belief to refer to a localizable place, in a profounder sense they are characterizations of a state of mind.

The paradigm for this paradise was primarily Kusavati, the city of the legendary King Mahasudassana, who is frequently mentioned in the Pali canon. Sukhāvatī is set in the west. It is flooded by radiance that emanates from Amitābha. This land is filled with the most exquisite fragrances; it is blossoming, rich, and fruitful. Wondrous flowers and trees of jewels grow there. There are no hells, no beasts, no corpses, no → *asuras.* Through the countryside flow rivers of sweet-smelling waters with bouquets of flowers afloat on them. The rushing of these waters is music.

Those who, by the strength of their faith, are reborn in Sukhāvatī awaken in a lotus flower. All their wishes are fulfilled. There is no sadness, misfortune, pain, or any other unpleasantness. In this buddha-field all beings cleave to the truth of the teaching until their final entry into nirvāna. Their supreme happiness is hearing the teaching proclaimed by Amitābha, who lives in the center of the land and is accompanied by → Avalokiteshvara and → Mahāsthāmaprāpta.

In Sukhāvatī the pleasures of love are absent, since no one is reborn there as a woman.

Sukhāvatī-vyūha **B** Skt., lit. "Sūtra of the Land of Bliss," also called *Aparimitāyur-sūtra* (*Sūtra of Unending Life*); one of the three basic sūtras of the → Pure Land school. It exists in a longer and a shorter (→ *Amitābha-Sūtra*) version; between 147 and 713 C.E., it was translated into Chinese twelve times. This sūtra describes the career of Buddha → Amitābha and the magnificence of his pure land → Sukhāvatī. It begins with a dialogue between → Ānanda and the Buddha in which the latter tells the story of a monk named Dharmākara, who when he was a king, was moved by a discourse of the Buddha to convert to Buddhism and to give up the throne in order to devote himself entirely to the attainment of buddhahood. He took forty-eight vows, including the vow to create, upon attaining buddhahood, a pure land in which all who turned to him full of faith and trust would be reborn and lead a life of peace and happiness until their final entry into nirvāna.

The most important of Amitābha's vows are (1) in the pure land, there will be no inferior modes of existence (→ *gati*); (2) In the pure land there will be no women as all women who are reborn there will transform at the moment of death into men—birth there will take place in a lotus flower, already prepared through the practice of reciting the name of Amitābha; (3) there will be no differences in appearance there—every being is to have a golden body that exhibits the thirty-two marks of perfection (→ *dvātrimshadvara-lakshana*; (4) everyone will possess knowledge of all past existences; (5-6) everyone will possess the "divine eye" and "celestial ear" (→ *abhijñā*); (7-8) every being will possess the ability to move about by supernatural means and to know the thoughts of others, and (17) beings of the worlds in all ten directions, upon hearing the name of Amitābha, will arouse → *bodhichitta* and vow to be reborn in the western paradise after death.

The vows most important for believers are (18) Amitābha will appear at the moment of their death to all beings who have aroused *bodhichitta* through hearing his name and protect their minds from fear; (19) all beings who through hearing his name have directed their minds toward rebirth in his pure land and have accordingly accumulated karmic merit will be reborn in this paradise and (24) after rebirth in the pure land, only one further rebirth will be necessary before entry into nirvāna—falling back is not possible.

Sūkshma-Sharīra **H** (Sūksma-Śarīra), or Linga-Sharira, Skt., lit. *sūkshma*: "subtle," *sharīra*: "body, sheath"; in → Vedānta the second, subtle sheath surrounding the → *ātman.* It consists of thinking, feeling, and desiring, and corresponds to → *prānamaya-kosha,* → *manomaya-kosha,* and *vijñānamaya-kosha.* (See also → *kosha,* → *sharīra.*)

Sumeru **H** **B** Skt., identical with → Meru

Sung-shan **Z** Chin. (Jap., Sūsan, Sūzan); a sacred mountain in the Chinese province of Honan on which many famous monasteries were located, including the → Shao-lin Monastery, known primarily because → Bodhidharma, the first patriarch of Ch'an (Zen) in China, lived there.

Sung Wen-ming **T** Taoist writer and reformer, who lived during the 6th century and—basing himself on the Buddhist model—popularized the idea of celibacy for Taoist monks. He wrote commentaries on the works of → Chang Tao-ling and played a decisive role in the spread of the School of the Magic Jewel (→ *ling-pao p'ai*).

Sung-yuan Ch'ung-yueh **Z** (Jap., Shōgen Sōgaku), 1139–1209; Chinese Ch'an (Zen) master of the Yōgi lineage of Rinzai Zen (→ Yōgi school); a "grandson in dharma" of Master → Hu-ch'in Shao-lung (Jap., Kukyū Jōryū). Through Master Sung-yuan passes the lineage of Ch'an (Zen) that produced → Hakuin Zenji, the great reviver of Rinzai Zen in Japan. We encounter master Sung-yuan in example 20 of the *Wu-men-kuan.*

Master Sung-yuan is chronologically the last Ch'an master to appear in the *Wu-men-kuan.* In example 20 we read, "Master Sung-yuan said, 'How is it that a man of great strength does not lift up his legs?' And he also said, 'It isn't the tongue with which we speak.' "

Sun Ssu-miao **T** 581–682 C.E.; famous Taoist

physician and scholar of the T'ang Dynasty, on whom the Emperor Sung Hui-tsung—in recognition of his medical knowledge—bestowed the title *true human being* (→ *chen-jen*).

Sun Ssu-miao systematized the clinical and diagnostic knowledge of his time, collected prescriptions, and was interested in acupuncture. A well-known collection of breathing exercises, known as *Thousand Ducet Recipes* (*Ch'ien-chin fang*) is attributed to him. In addition, he was the author of treatises on the prolongation of life, a method of meditation known as → *ts'un-ssu,* and a longevity breathing exercise known as "melting the breath" (→ *lien-ch'i*).

Surabhī H, or Kāmadhenu, Skt.; the "cow of plenty" who appeared at the → Churning of the Ocean and fulfilled all wishes. Worshiped as the source of milk and cheese, she is said to have belonged to the sage → Vasishtha.

Sureshvara H (Sureśvara), or Sureshvarāchārya, a sage who was a direct student of → Shankara. His profound inquiries into → Advaita-Vedānta are presented in his work → *Naishkarmya-Siddhi.* Other Advaita-Vedānta works by his hand are *Mānosollasa* and *Vārttika*, in which last his commentaries on various classical texts and Upanishads are summarized.

Sūrya H, or Savitri, Skt.; the sun, the sun god. Sūrya is one of the major divinities in the Vedas and is venerated as the great source of light and warmth.

The texts concerning Sūrya are more poetic than they are precise. Sometimes he is identical with Savitri, at other times he is identified with → Āditya. There are various sun temples in India, the most famous of which is in Konarak near → Puri.

Sūryadvāra H Skt., lit. "gate (*dvāra*) to the sun (*sūrya*)"; here the sun symbolizes spiritual enlightenment, the door to supreme realization.

Sushumnā H (Suṣumnā), Skt.; the most important energy channel (→ *nādī*); it extends from the lower end of the spine to the brain. If the → *kundalinī* is awakened, it rises in *sushumnā*, which represents the precise center between → *idā* and → *pingalā*. (See also → *chakra.*)

Sushupti H (Suṣupti), Skt.; the state of deep sleep, in which neither the mind nor the ego exist and in which we are aware neither of our own body nor of the universe. Sushupti is not unconsciousness but rather the cessation of thought. One of the four → *avasthās*, it is also known in Vedanta as → *prājña.*

Susoku-kan Z Jap., lit. "contemplation of counting the breath"; a meditative practice generally practiced by beginners in → *zazen.* Four types of *susoku-kan* are distinguished: (1) *shutsunyusoku-kan* (counting the exhalations and inhalations; (2) *shussoku-kan* (counting the exhalations); (3) *nissoku-kan* (counting the inhalations); (4) *zuisoku-kan* (following the breath).

The practice of *susoku-kan* helps to achieve the collectedness that is necessary for *zazen.* The modern Japanese Zen master → Hakuun Ryōku Yasutani said about *susoku-kan* in his *Introductory Lectures on Zen Training*, "The easiest practice for beginners is counting incoming and outgoing breaths. The value of this particular exercise lies in the fact that all reasoning is excluded and the discriminative mind put at rest. Thus the waves of thought are stilled and a gradual one-pointedness of mind achieved" (Kapleau 1980).

In this method one collects one's attention on the inbreath on one, on the outbreath on two, on the inbreath on three, and so on up to ten, then begins again with one. One can modify this practice to count only on the outbreath or the inbreath. One continues to count up to ten and begin again with one. In the last of the four techniques, *zuisoku-kan*, with collected mind one follows the movement of the breath without counting. For a person without experience in *zazen*, to concentrate on counting the breath without drifting off into thoughts or losing the thread of the count is not easy. Persistent practice of one of the types of *susoku-kan* has proved itself an excellent basis for more advanced practice on the way of Zen and can even lead to the breakthrough of an enlightenment experience.

Sūtra H B Z Skt., lit. "thread."

H The sūtras reduce the content of the → Brāhmanas, from which they derive, and summarize their text for the purpose of practical application in short, pithy statements that usually cannot be understood without a commentary.

Three types of sūtras are distinguished: (1) the *Shrauta-Sūtras*, which are based on *shruti* texts (divine revelation) and concern the performance of major sacrifices; (2) the *Grihya-Sūtras*, which govern household customs in the event of birth, marriage, and death; (3) the *Dharma-Sūtras*, which indicate the duties of the various castes and life stations. From these are derived the later law books (e.g., that of → Manu). All → *darshanas* (Hindu systems of philosophy) were also originally composed in sūtra form. The best known of these are the → *Vedānta- or Brahma-Sūtras* and Patañjali's → *Yoga-Sūtra.*

B Z (Pali, sutta; Jap., kyō); discourses of the → Buddha. The sūtras are collected in the second part of the Buddhist canon (→ Tripitaka), the → Sūtra-pitaka, or "Basket of the Teachings."

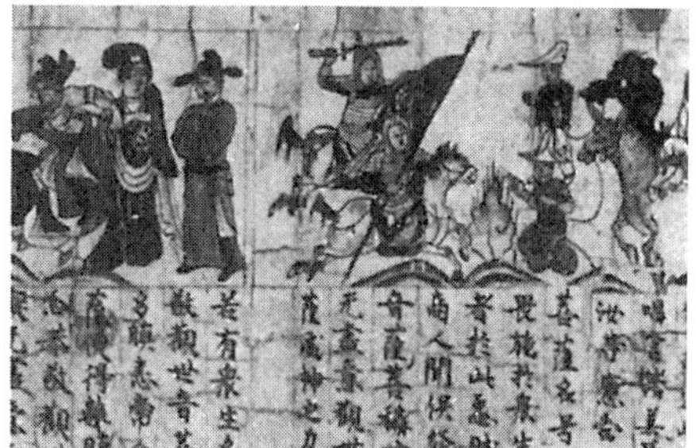

Page from a *Lotus Sūtra* discovered in the caves of Tun-huang (7th century)

The sūtras have been preserved in Pali and Sanskrit, as well as in Chinese and Tibetan translations. According to tradition they derive directly from the Buddha. The sūtras are prose texts, each introduced by the words, *Thus have I heard*. These words are ascribed to → Ānanda, a student of the Buddha. He is supposed to have retained the discourses of the Buddha in memory and to have recited them at the first → Buddhist council, immediately after the death of the Buddha. After these introductory words, the circumstances that occasioned the Buddha to give the discourse are described, as well as the place, the time of year, etc. Then the actual instruction follows, sometimes in the form of a dialog. The style of the sūtras is simple, popular, and didactically oriented. They are rich in parables and allegories. In many sūtras songs (*gāthā*) are interpolated. Each sūtra constitutes a self-sufficient unit.

The Hīnayāna sūtras are divided into "collections," which in the Pali canon are called → Nikāyas and in the Sanskrit version, → Āgamas. The Nikāyas are the → *Dīgha-nikāya*, → *Majjhima-nikāya*, → *Samyutta-nikāya*, → *Anguttara-nikāya*, and → *Khuddaka-nikāya*.

Along with these Hīnayāna sūtras, a great number of Mahāyāna sūtras have also been preserved. They were originally composed in Sanskrit but are for the most part extant only in Chinese or Tibetan translations. They are thought to have been composed between the 1st century B.C.E. and the 6th century C.E. They adopted the external form of the Hīnayāna sūtras—they also begin with the words *Thus have I heard* and a description of the place, occasion, and the persons present. Three types of Mahāyāna sūtras are differentiated: → Vaipulya-sūtras, → *dhāranīs*, and independent sūtras.

As to content, two currents of tradition can be recognized:

1. sūtras based on faith (→ *shraddhā*), which treat buddhology and the → bodhisattva teaching and stress devotion. Their area of origin is probably north India. In these sūtras, no bounds are set to the imagination—buddhas and bodhisattvas perform countless miracles in limitless space and endless time. They are elevated to the level of divine beings—a tendency in the Mahāyāna that accommodates the religious needs of the layfolk but also arises from the nature of the Mahāyāna, with its doctrines of nonsubstantiality and emptiness (→ *shūnyatā*) that come to expression in a view that sees the world as illusory (→ māyā). In such a view, all miracles, like the world of appearance itself, are no more than a product of illusion.

2. Philosophically oriented sūtras that have as their theme emptiness, the central notion of the mahāyāna. These sūtras originated in the eastern part of central India. They were differently interpreted by Mahāyāna thinkers and this provided the impetus for the formation of various schools. The most important independent sūtras are: *Saddharmapundarīka-sūtra (→ Lotus Sūtra)*, → *Lankāvatāra-sūtra*, → *Lalitavistara*, → *Samādhirāja-sūtra*, → *Sukhāvatī-Vyūha-sūtra*, → *Dashabhūmika*, → *Badrakalpika-sūtra*, → *Brahmajāla-sūtra*, → *Gandavyūha-sūtra*, *Shrīmālādevī-sūtra*, → *Amitābha-sūtra*, → *Amitāyurdhyāna-sūtra*, → *Vimalkīrtinirdesha-sūtra*, → *Shūrangama-sūtra*.

Sūtra in Forty-two Sections B (Skt., *Dvāchatvārimshat-khanda-sūtra*), the first sūtra to be translated into Chinese. The *Ssu-shih-erh-chang ching* is said to have been brought to the court by emmisaries of Emperor → Ming-ti who were searching for Buddhist scriptures in the western lands of China (i.e., Central Asia) and to have been translated in the year 67 C.E. by the Indian monks Matanga and Chu-fa-lan. In this sūtra, which was also the first Buddhist written work in the Chinese language, the essential teachings of the Hīnayāna, such as impermanence (→ *anitya*) and desire or craving (→ *Trishnā*), are explained. Many different versions of this sūtra are extant; they differ considerably in places as to content.

Sūtra of Golden Light B (Skt. Suvarna-prabhāsa-sūtra); a Mahāyāna sūtra that played a major role in establishing Buddhism in Japan, because, among other things, it stressed the political aspect of Buddhism and thus was highly regarded by Japan's ruling class.

The sūtra begins with an exposition of the nature of

the Buddha, who exists not only as a mundane personality but also as a universal absolute truth. He is present in everything, and everything existing benefits from his limitless compassion. The sūtra further teaches that the gates to the lotus paradise in which the Buddha dwells are open, since every being can become a buddha. The method recommended by this sūtra for accomplishing such a transformation consists of remorse and self-sacrifice. The high point of the sūtra is a parable in which the Buddha offers himself to a hungry lion.

The main theme of the sūtra is the virtue of wisdom (→ *prajñā*), which discriminates good and evil. Each person, from the ruler to those in the lowest state, must follow this "inner light."

The political aspect finds its clearest expression in the chapter on law, where it says that government and religion are unified by the dharma. Human law must have peace as its highest goal. A king who violates the law is to be punished; so long, however, as he respects the law, his lot is immeasurable well-being. A country in which the teaching of this sūtra has been propagated is protected by the → celestial kings and → *devas*. During the Nara period (8th century) the *Sūtra of Golden Light* was so highly regarded by the rulers of Japan that they founded policy upon it.

Sūtra-pitaka B Z (Sūtra-piṭaka), Skt. (Pali, Sutta-pitaka); lit. "Basket of Writings"; a part of the Buddhist canon (→ Tripitaka). According to tradition the Sūtra-pitaka contains the discourses of the historical Buddha → Shākyamuni (→ sūtra).

The Sūtra-pitaka is preserved in a Sanskrit version composed of four collections (→ Āgama). In the Pali recension, which is the only one to have been completely preserved, it is composed of five collections (→ Nikāya).

Sūtrātman H Skt., lit. "thread-self"; a term referring to the universal soul, which like a thread holds all beings and the universe together. Identical in meaning with → Hiranyagarbha.

Sutta-nipāta B Pali → *Khuddaka-nikāya*

Sutta-pitaka B Pali → Sūtra-pitaka

Suzuki Daisetsu Teitaro Z 1870–1966; Japanese Buddhist scholar, who as one of the best-known modern interpreters of Zen in the West, did a great deal to arouse interest in Zen here. He was a lay student of Master Shaku Sōen from → Engaku-ji in Kamakura and underwent some Zen training. However, he focused primarily on the intellectual interpretation of the Zen teachings and was never confirmed as a Zen master.

Suzuki Shunryū Z 1905–71 Japanese Zen master of the → Sōtō school. In 1958 he went to the United States and founded several Zen centers there, among them Zen Center in San Francisco and the Zen Mountain Center in Tassajara, California, the first Sōtō Zen monastery in the West. Some of his introductory talks on Zen practice are found in Suzuki 1970.

Svabhāva H B Skt., lit. "self-nature";
H One's own inner nature or character, the impulse within each individual to express himself.
B in the Mahāyāna, as a further development of the → *anātman* doctrine of the Hīnayāna, all things are seen as empty of self-nature, i.e., devoid of self-sufficient, independent existence or lasting substance. This, however, does not mean that they do not exist at all but rather that they are nothing but pure appearance and do not constitute the true reality; i.e., they do not possess an essence (*svabhāvatā*). This type of emptiness (→ *shūnyatā*) is known as *svabhāva-shūnyatā* and it is a central notion in the → *prajñāpāramitā* literature and in the teaching of the → Mādhyamika school.

Svadharma H Skt., lit. *sva*: "own," *dharma*: "law"; one's own inner law, which regulates one's thoughts and actions and must be in harmony with divine will.

Svādhishthāna-chakra H B Skt. → Chakra 2

Svādhyāya H Skt.; "self-study," especially study of the → Vedas, but also of other sacred texts. In order to be impressed on the memory, they should be chanted repeatedly (a proven technique for memorization). The Vedas, like most of the scriptures, were originally transmitted orally from teacher to student, who had to learn the texts by heart. *Svādhyāya* is one of the five virtues required at the second stage (→ *niyama*) of → Rāja-Yoga, as listed in the *Yoga-Sūtra* of → Patañjali (2.32). The other four virtues are → *santosha* (contentment), → *shaucha* (purification), → *tapas* (austerity), and → *īshvara-pranidhāna* (surrender to God).

Svāhā H Skt.; a ritual exclamation that follows every sacrificial offering. It means "So be it!" or "May good arise therefrom!"

Svāmi H, or Svāmin, Skt., lit. "Sir," written *Swami* in English and in modern Indian dialects; 1. a mode of address that in general is set before the names of monks; 2. a title of respect that follows the name of a spiritual teacher or a man revered as holy.

Svapna 🅗 Skt.; the dream state experienced in sleep. During this state, the mind acts independent of the body and the outer world. In the waking state, it is considered unreal and illusory. Svapna is one of the four → *avasthās*. In → Vedānta it is called → *taijasa.*

Svar 🅗 Skt.; a → *vyāhriti,* the third word of the → Gāyatrī. From this word, which → Prajāpati spoke at the creation, heaven was created.

Svarloka 🅗 Skt.; the heaven (*svar*) of Indra and the world (*loka*) of light, of pure thoughts and feelings. A name for the pure state of consciousness, which for human beings constitutes true heaven.

Svarūpa-Jñāna 🅗 Skt., lit. *svarūpa*: "essence, nature," *jñāna*: "knowledge"; this expression refers to the → *ātman,* who by nature is *jñāna,* that is, is aware of its identity with *brahman. Jñāna* in this context equals consciousness, for knowledge is not possible without consciousness.

Svayam-Bhagavan 🅗 Skt., lit. *svayam*: "being out of itself," *bhagavan*: "God"; the supreme → *atman*, perceived as the lord of the universe, the one of infinite power, unlimited compassion, immeasurable knowledge, unconditioned love, and indescribable beauty.

Svayambhū 🅗 Skt., lit. "existing out of itself"; all objects in the manifest world exist by the power of the idea concealed within each of them.

In the creation myth of → Manu, Svayambhū is the unexplained first cause from which Brahmā emerged. (See also → Hiranyagarbha.)

Svayamprakāsha 🅗 Skt., lit. "self-illuminating"; the supreme Self, which is self-illuminating and aware of itself as absolute consciousness: this is direct, supreme knowledge.

Svedaja 🅗 Skt., lit. "sweat-born"; in Hinduism the first of the four types of origin of life, that of insects. The other three are the seed-born (plants), egg-born (birds, fish, and amphibians), and womb-born (mammals).

Swami 🅗 → *svāmi*

Swastika 🅗 🅑 Skt., derived from *svasti*, "happiness, well-being."

🅑 The ancient sign of the swastika is interpreted in Buddhism as a symbol of the wheel of the teaching (→ dharma-chakra) or of the Buddhist teaching in general.

In China the swastika is the symbol of the number 10,000, i.e., the factor of limitlessness or eternity that was revealed in the teaching of the Buddha. Thus in Chinese depictions of the Buddha, it is placed on the chest at the level of the heart.

In Zen it symbolizes the "seal of buddha-mind" (→ *busshin-in*) that was transmitted from patriarch to patriarch.

🅗 An auspicious figure of a cross, a mystical sign found everywhere on temples and objects of art.

Syādvāda 🅗 Skt., lit. *syat*: "it may be," *vāda*: "teaching"; a concept taken from → Jainism: the theory of multiple possible viewpoints of reality. Every judgment is subjective and subject to conditions and limitations, and various differing statements regarding the same reality can be correct when each is viewed from its own perspective.

T

Tādātmya 🅗 Skt., lit. "essential unity"; the essential unity of the self with → *brahman*; the spiritual knowledge that one is not the body and the mind but eternal, immortal → *ātman* (Self), which is identical with → *tat* ("that"), i.e., *brahman.*

Tagore, Devendranāth 🅗 (Beng.: Thākur), 1817–1905; father of the great poet Rabīndranāth Tagore; next to Rāja Rammohan Roy, founder of the → Brāhmo-Samāj, he was the chief organizer of that socioreligious reform movement. His penetrating mind, his spiritual level, and his aristocratic appearance made him a model for educated Bengalis, who addressed him respectfully as "Mahar(i)shi" (great seer). A Sanskrit scholar, he derived inspiration exclusively from the → Upanishads. He was also an unrelenting opponent of iconolatry and fought the infiltration of Christian ideas into the Brāhmo-Samāj.

Tagore, Rabīndranāth 🅗 (Beng.: Thākur), 1861–1941, the most important modern-day Indian poet; son of Devendranāth Tagore, the long-standing leader of the → Brāhmo-Samāj. In the language of his native Bengal as well as in English, he wrote novels, plays, and political-pedagogical works, but above all poetry, of which more than forty collections were published. Among his chief lyrical-mystical works is *Gītānjali*, featuring conversations between the human soul and God (Vishnu). His novel *Gorā* is a kind of modern-day → *Mahābhārata*. In 1911 Tagore founded a school for philosophy and art, which he named Shāntiniketan ("abode of peace"); in 1951 it became a state university. In 1913 Tagore received the Nobel Prize for literature.

Ta-hui Tsung-kao 🅩 (Jap., Daie Sōkō), 1089–1163; Chinese Ch'an (Zen) master of the Yōgi lineage of Rinzai Zen (→ Yōgi school); the outstanding student and dharma successor (→ *hassu*) of Master → Yuan-wu K'o-ch'in (Jap., Engo Kokugon). It was he who had all available copies of the → *Pi-yen-lu*, composed by his master, collected and burned when he saw that his students clung to the words of the text rather than concerning themselves with the immediate experience of his master's dharma teaching. (Fortunately for posterity, however, the greater part of this precious text was preserved in a few, though not entirely complete, copies.)

Ta-hui was a passionate champion of kōan training (→ kōan); and his controversy with Sōtō master → Hung-chih Cheng-chueh (Jap., Wanshi Shōgaku) concerning the advantages of the → *kanna* Zen of the → Rinzai school over the → *mokushō* Zen advocated by the → Sōtō school, which was obviously conducted in a friendly spirit, brought about the final shaping of kōan training and its definite establishment as a part of Rinzai Zen training. Master Ta-hui required his students to enter into the words of the ancient masters handed down as kōans without at all attempting to resolve them through reasoning. This is a method of training that since that time has proved its effectiveness countless times as a technique of Zen training.

Ta-i 🅣 Chin. → T'ai-i

Taiba Hōjō 🅩 Jap. for → Ta-mei Fa-ch'ang

T'ai-chi 🅣 Chin., lit. "ridge beam"; a term denoting the supreme ultimate. The concept occurs in the → *I-ching*, where it refers to ultimate reality, the primordial ground of being from which everything arises. The notion of *t'ai-chi* is of particular importance in neo-Confucianist philosophy (→ Chu Hsi). Essentially *t'ai-chi* is synonymous with → T'ai-i, the Supreme One.

The *I-ching* states, "Thus there is in the changes the great primordial beginning [*t'ai-chi*], which produces the two original energies [→ yin-yang]. These in turn produce the four images [→ *ssu-hsiang*], from which arise the eight trigrams [→ *pa-kua*]."

In neo-Confucianism *t'ai-chi* denotes the fusion of the two basic principles of the universe, namely → *li*, the normative, structural principle, and → *ch'i*, the formative primordial substance, matter. *T'ai-chi* itself is unlimited; since it contains *li* it is capable of giving rise to all things. This creative process is marked by alternating phases of rest and activity—rest being characteristic of yin, activity of yang. *T'ai-chi* combines these two. The alternation of the two energies produces the five elements (→ *wu-hsing*), which form the basis of all material existence.

T'ai chi ch'uan 🅣 Chin., lit. the "fist (-fighting method) of the supreme ultimate (→ *t'ai-chi*)"; a form of meditation based on physical movements and a method of self-defense.

The origins of T'ai chi ch'uan are said to go back to the 14th century. It is practiced by performing a sequence of soft, flowing, and slowly executed movements, which coordinate mind and body—i.e., consciousness, breath, and the body as such—and thereby produce a harmonization of the energies of yin and yang (→ yin-yang). T'ai chi ch'uan enhances the general state of health of the practitioner, dissolves tensions in the body, and removes blockages in the energy meridians. There are at present five main styles, the best known being the Yang style, named after its originators Yang Lu-ch'an and Yang Ch'eng-fu.

T'ai chi ch'uan is normally practiced alone, but there is a method known as *t'ui-shou* (roughly "pushing hands"), which involves a partner. T'ai chi ch'uan can also be performed with a lance, knife, or sword.

T'ai-ch'ing 🅣 Chin. → *san-ch'ing*

T'ai-chi-t'u 🅣 Chin., lit. "diagram of the supreme ultimate (→ *t'ai-chi*)"; a cosmological diagram created by the neo-Confucianist philosopher Chou Tun-i (1017–73 C.E.) to describe the process of how the ten thousand things (→ *wan-wu*) arise from the supreme ultimate (*t'ai-chi*), which he considered to be identical with → *wu-chi*, the unconditioned. From it arise the two energies of the → yin-yang, which in turn give rise to the four seasons, the five elements (→ *wu-hsing*), and the ten thousand things.

In his diagram Chou Tun-i connects Confucianist ideas with those of religious Taoism.

Chou Tun-i's commentary on the *t'ai-chi-t'u* states, "The unconditioned also is the supreme ultimate. The supreme ultimate moves and thereby creates yang. After this movement has reached its extreme, it returns to rest. Through this rest yin is created. When this rest has reached its extreme, it once again transforms into movement; thus movement and rest alternate and give rise to each other. When yin and yang act separately, the two energies [→ *liang-i*] can be clearly perceived. By the fusion of yin and yang the two energies become transformed into the five elements—fire, water, wood, metal, and earth [→ *wu-hsing*]. These five 'breaths' [→ *ch'i*], i.e. the elements, spread out in harmonious order and the four seasons come into being. The five elements are the same as yin and yang; yin and yang are the same as the supreme ultimate. The supreme ultimate originally is the unconditioned. When the five elements are brought into existence, each of them has its characteristic nature. The reality of the unconditioned, and the essences of the two energies and of the five elements, in miraculous fashion are one. The *ch'ien* principle becomes the masculine, and the *k'un* principle the feminine [→ *ch'ien* and *k'un*]. By their combination, the two energies yin and yang create the ten thousand things. By their unceasing production and reproduction, the ten thousand things transform themselves and are never exhausted."

T'ai-hsi T Chin., lit. "embryonic breathing"; a Taoist meditation practice for prolonging life. *T'ai-hsi* consists in learning to breathe like an embryo in the mother's body. Essentially it is a combination of holding the breath (→ *pi-ch'i*) and then allowing it to circulate (→ *hsing-ch'i*), thereby creating an immortality body, which is nourished by the breath (→ *shen-t'ai*). When the adept dies, this embryo separates from the corpse (→ *shih-chieh*) and the practitioner becomes an immortal (→ *hsien*).

At first the adept must learn to hold his breath. By daily practice he will manage to do so for ever longer periods—three, five, seven, nine (etc.) heartbeats until he can do so for approximately one thousand heartbeats. At this point, the practitioner can cure himself of any illnesses by means of the breath and is said to be approaching immortality. As the breath is held, it is directed through the body of the practitioner. This is done by a technique known as inner vision (→ *nei-kuan*). Normally, the air we inhale only reaches as far as the heart, entrails, liver, and kidneys; the Taoist practitioner, however, endeavors to direct it to the lower cinnabar field (→ *tan-t'ien*) situated in the region of the navel, and from there right down to the soles of his feet. The breath should then be made to rise along the spine to the brain, i.e., the upper cinnabar field, from there to the chest (middle cinnabar field), and from there, via the lungs, back to the throat. When it reaches the throat the breath is gradually swallowed. In this way the practitioner nourishes himself by the breath.

Kuan-yin surrounded by magic formulae for producing embryonic breathing.

While the practitioner directs the breath through his body he endeavors to produce as much saliva (→ *yü-chiang*) as possible, by pressing his tongue against the palate. This accumulated saliva is swallowed, together with the breath. Breath and saliva are considered to be the best nourishment for those who strive for immortality: it is said that their body becomes light and transparent, so that they are able to ride on the clouds.

To realize the importance of embryonic breathing as a Taoist practice, it is necessary to remember that in the Taoist view man consists of breath, i.e., energy (→ *ch'i*). The body of a human being is formed by coarse Earth energies, while the life energy of a person circulates between Heaven and Earth. To attain immortality it is necessary to transform the coarse energies into pure energy. For that reason, practitioners of *t'ai-hsi* must also refrain from eating grain (→ *pi-ku*) because it is believed to consist of coarse energy.

Over the centuries, the Taoist understanding of embryonic breathing has radically changed. At first it was believed that the "breath" that is allowed to circulate through the body was the actual air the practitioner inhales. Since the time of the T'ang Dynasty, however, relevant texts state that what circulates through the body is the inner breath (→ *nei-ch'i*), which is synonymous with the primordial breath (→ *yüan-ch'i*) and corresponds to the energies that give rise to Heaven and Earth. This primordial breath the adept must preserve within his body. Normally it escapes through the mouth. The practitioner of *t'ai-hsi* therefore tries to store it in the lower cinnabar field and prevent it from mingling with the ordinary outer breath, i.e., the air he inhales. Both these breaths move synchronously within the body: as the outer breath rises during exhalation, the inner breath ascends from the lower cinnabar field; and as the outer breath sinks during inhalation, the inner breath descends to the lower cinnabar field.

The practice of allowing the inner breath to circulate begins by swallowing it (→ *yen-ch'i*), thereby preventing it from leaving the body together with the outer breath. After that the inner breath is collected and channeled toward the lower cinnabar field (also called → *ch'i-hai*, "ocean of the breath") via the alimentary tract, and from there through the whole of the body. The practitioner may also allow the inner breath to circulate freely without directing it in any way. This method is known as "melting the breath" (→ *lien-ch'i*).

T'ai-hsu 🅱 1889–1947; important Chinese monk who was a main participant in the revival and reformation of Buddhism in China though revitalization of the → *sangha*, adaptation of study of the Buddhist teaching to modern needs, and reorganization of the monastic system. He is the founder of the Buddhist Society of China, which in 1947 had over four million followers, and the Institute for Buddhist Studies, in existence since 1922, which played a major role in the revival of the → Fa-hsiang school. T'ai-hsu emphasized the compatibility of the Fa-hsiang teachings with modern science and in this way attracted a large number of young intellectuals. One of his most important achievements was a harmonious blending of the philosophies of the Fa-hsiang, → Hua-yen, and → T'ien-t'ai schools. Through this he accomplished his goal of developing a synthesis of the most important schools of Chinese Buddhism.

T'ai-hsu entered the Buddhist monastic order at the age of sixteen and dedicated himself primarily to study of the → *Shūrangama-sūtra* and the teachings of the T'ien-t'ai and Hua-yen schools. Later he specialized in the Fa-hsiang school. In 1911 he became abbot of a monastery in Canton and a member of the Pan-Chinese Buddhist Society. He became active in the defense and reformation of Buddhism and its monastic system and called for a rise in the level of education of members of the *sangha*. Through his activities a renewal movement was set in motion. In 1918 he founded the periodical *Hai-chao-yin* (*Roar of Sea Waves*), which was for more than thirty years the foremost Buddhist periodical in China. In Paris he created the Institute for Buddhist Studies and thus initiated the propagation of the Buddhist teachings in the West by Chinese monks. In 1931 he built an institute in Szechuan province for the study of Tibetan Buddhism.

T'ai-i 🆃 Chin., lit. "the Supreme One," also called Ta-i, "the Great One"; a Taoist concept that has undergone many changes of meaning in the course of its development. In philosophical Taoism (→ *tao-chia*) T'ai-i denotes the original cause of all appearances and thus is synonymous with → Tao.

The → Inner Deity Hygiene School considered the Supreme One to be the most important deity within the human body. As abstract concepts became personified, T'ai-i became → *san-i*, the highest deity of religious Taoism (→ *tao-chiao*).

Frequently, T'ai-i is synonymous with → *t'ai-chi*.

The origin of the notion of a Supreme One goes back to a time when shamanism was practiced in China. In the *Nine Songs* (*Chiu-ko*), which contain shamanistic ideas of the 4th and 3d century B.C.E., sacrifices to the Supreme One are already mentioned. In philosophical Taoism the idea of the "one" or "unique" can be traced back to the → *Tao-te ching*, Chapter 42 of which states, "Out of Tao, One is born; Out of One, Two; Out of Two, Three; Out of Three, the created universe (the Ten Thousand Things)" (Lin 1949).

The → *Chuang-tzu*, too, mentions the concept of T'ai-i or Ta-i. The following quote is from the *Spring and Autumn Annals* (→ *Lü-shih ch'un-ch'iu*): "T'ai-i produces the two forms; the two forms cause yin and yang (→ yin-yang) to arise." In a philosophical sense, the concept of T'ai-i constitutes an attempt at postulating a unity that forms a common ground of the multiplicity of appearances. At first the Supreme One was understood to be that which existed before the ten thousand things (→ *wan-wu*) came into being; later it was taken to be that in which the opposite qualities of yin and yang are united.

During the Han Dynasty the Supreme One was venerated as part of the triad of the three ones (→ *san-i*) and became a personalized deity. In the 2d century B.C.E. the Taoist magician Miu Chi introduced the T'ai-i cult to the ruler's court. Sacrifices were made to the Supreme One in the Palace of Long Life. The followers of this cult believed that the Supreme One was assisted by → Ssu-ming (Lord [or Ruler] of Fate). T'ai-i became the highest deity, and was said to dwell in the polar star, while the five legendary emperors—as rulers of the five cardinal points—became subjects of T'ai-i. The followers of the later Inner Deity Hygiene School believed that the Supreme One resides in the brain—specifically, in one of the nine compartments of the upper cinnabar field (→ *tan-t'ien*)—and from there rules the triad of the three ones. An adept of this school would endeavor to visualize T'ai-i as the supreme deity within his body and make contact with it so as to prevent it from leaving the body, thereby removing the inevitability of death.

Other schools venerate T'ai-i together with the god of the sun.

T'ai-i chin-hua tsung-chih 🅃 Chin., lit. *"Teaching of the Golden Flower of the Supreme One"* (→ T'ai-i); 17th-century Taoist text in the tradition of one of the great movements of religious Taoism—the School of the Realization of Truth (→ *ch'üan-chen tao*). The *Teaching of the Golden Flower* is a synthesis of the meditative breathing exercises of the Inner Elixir School (→ *neitan*) and Chinese Zen (Ch'an) Buddhism.

The *T'ai-i chin-hua tsung-chih* became relatively well known in the West, owing to an (incomplete) translation (with a commentary by C. G. Jung) by the German sinologist Richard Wilhelm under the title *Das Geheimnis der goldenen Blüte* (English: *The Secret of the Golden Flower;* see Wilhelm 1938). In the original illustrations to this text, C. G. Jung saw parallels to symbols of psychic processes described by him. A complete translation of the text into German has been made by the Japanese Taoist scholar Mokusen Miyuki (1984).

The central feature of the *T'ai-i chin-hua tsung-chih* is the circulation of light *(fan-chao)*. The (inner) light corresponds to pure yang (→ yin-yang), i.e., the true precelestial (→ *hsien-t'ien*) breath. The practitioner causes this light to circulate (→ *hsing-ch'i*) within his body and ultimately to crystallize, forming the "golden flower." By this method the mortal body can give birth to a new immortal being, the sacred embryo (→ *sheng-t'ai*).

The correct circulation of the light brings about a "return to the source" (→ *fu*), "where form and spirit have not yet separated within consciousness into knowing and understanding. This process is quite simply a search for a wholeness that existed within our body before Heaven and Earth came into existence" (trans. from the German version based on Mokusen Miyuki).

Some of the practical instructions for this form of meditation are similar to those for Buddhist shamatha/vipashyana (peaceful abiding/insight) meditation.

T'ai-i tao 🅃 Chin., lit. "Way of the Supreme One"; a school of religious Taoism (→ *tao-chiao*). The *t'ai-i tao* was founded in the 12th century C.E. by Hsiao Pao-chen and is related to an earlier movement, the → *cheng-i tao* (Way of Right Unity), whose priests conducted ceremonies to cure diseases by the use of talismans (→*fu-lu*), magic formulae, and exorcism. The *t'ai-i tao* also contained Confucianist elements. Its followers were committed to strict obedience of monastic rules. It became extinct during the middle period of the Yüan Dynasty.

Taijasa 🄷 Skt., lit. "full of light"; term used in → Vedānta for the dreaming state, one of the four → *avasthās*, identical with → *svapna*. The three other states of consciousness are known in Vedānta as → *prājña* (deep sleep), → *vaishvānara* (waking state), and → *turīya* ("the fourth"). They are discussed in detail in the *Māndūkya-Upanishad.*

The consciousness of a dreaming person generally creates mental pictures and notions, which are not identical with those created during the waking state but originate there and reappear as transformed and displaced experiences from the day. These are to be distinguished from the visionary dreams that are inspired by higher levels of consciousness.

Taikō Koke 🅉 Jap. for → Ta-kuang Chu-hui

Tailadhāra 🄷 Skt., lit. "stream of oil"; oil that pours forth continuously in a silent stream; often used as a symbol of the subconscious that flows forth without ever breaking off its connection to God—a desirable and useful condition for the *sādhaka* (→ *sādhana*).

T'ai-p'ing ching 🅃 Chin., lit. *"Book of Supreme Peace";* a Taoist text existing in a number of differing versions, one of which has been ascribed to → Yü Chi. Only fragments of this text have been preserved. It formed the doctrinal basis of a school known as the Way of Supreme Peace (→ *t'ai-ping tao*) and dealt with all aspects of ancient Taoist teachings on such subjects as → yin-yang and the five elements (→ *wu-hsing*). In addition, it contained descriptions of deities and one of the earliest forms of Taoist meditation (→ *shou-i*) known to us.

T'ai-p'ing tao 🅃 Chin., lit. "Way of Supreme Peace"; early Taoist school founded between 172 and 178 C.E. by → Chang Chüeh. It derived its name from its basic doctrinal text, the → *T'ai-ping ching.*

As a result of his spectacular methods of healing, Chang Chüeh attracted a vast following. In this he was helped by the extremely poor living conditions of the peasants, who not only had suffered epidemics and natural disasters but were also cruelly oppressed by the rulers of the Han Dynasty. Chang Chüeh's healing methods were based on magic. To be healed a believer had to confess his or her sins—which Chang Chüeh considered to be the root of their afflictions—at public mass ceremonies. A further important ritual of the *t'ai-p'ing tao* was fasting ceremonies (→ *chai*). In addition, the priests or officials of this school made use of talismans (→ *fu-lu*), holy water (*fu-shui*), magic formulae, etc. The *t'ai-p'ing tao* tried to explain some of its practices by a willfully convenient interpretation of the *Tao-te ching.* In actual fact, its teachings are very similar to those of Five-Pecks-of-Rice Taoism (→ *wu-tou-mi tao*). As a mass movement the *t'ai-p'ing tao* was furthermore of political importance. Its followers were organized on a strictly hierarchical basis which, moreover, fulfilled certain military functions. Its influence extended over eight provinces, subdivided into thirty-six districts, with between seven thousand and ten thousand followers in each. Every one of these districts was under the charge of a "general," while Chang Chüeh and his brothers were the leaders of the *t'ai-p'ing tao* as a whole. Chang named himself *celestial duke-general.* His two brothers bore the titles *terrestrial duke-general* and *people's duke-general,* respectively.

In 184 C.E. 36,000 followers of the Way of Supreme Peace rose against the central government. The rebels wore yellow head bands, which is why this rebellion is recorded in Chinese history as the Rising of the Yellow Turbans (*Huang-chin*). Although the rebellion was put down, and Chang Chüeh and his two brothers were executed, the Yellow Turbans for some considerable time remained a political power whose influence was by no means negligible.

Chang Chüeh announced the dawning of a new age and promised the people to establish a utopian order of the kind described in the *T'ai-p'ing ching.* This new age was to commence when the Blue Heaven (i.e., the rule of the Han Dynasty) was succeeded by the Yellow Heaven (i.e., the Way of Supreme Peace), which venerated → Huang-ti, the Yellow Emperor, as one of its founders. This was to happen in 184 C.E. The Rising of the Yellow Turbans was motivated by a desire for equality, but in the end the followers of Chuang Chüeh did not consider equality without peace worth fighting for.

T'ai-shan ◼ the most important of China's sacred mountains. It is situated in Shantung Province in eastern China and for that reason also known as the Sacred Mountain in the East. From earliest times T'ai-shan has been a focal point of the religious life of the Chinese people; its deity, the Great Emperor of the Eastern Peak (→ T'ai-yüeh ta-ti) is one of the most famous Taoist gods. His daughter Sheng-mu, the Sacred Mother—patroness of women and children—also plays an important role in the faith of the people.

The Great Emperor of the Eastern Peak is generally believed to rule over Earth and mankind. He is subordinate only to the Jade Emperor (→ Yü-huang). His most important task is to determine the dates of a person's birth and death.

During the early centuries of our era T'ai-yüeh ta-ti was furthermore venerated as a deity of the dead; the soul of a person was believed to come from T'ai-shan and return there after that person's death. These souls were said to assemble on a hill at the foot of T'ai-shan, known as Hao-li-shan. Nevertheless, T'ai-shan's importance in the role of the Great Emperor of the Eastern Peak by far exceeded his significance as a deity of the dead, because the Jade Emperor had also entrusted him with the regulation of all worldly affairs.

Mount T'ai-shan is 1,545 meters high. Its top is reached via an ascending terrace of approximately 7,000 steps, known as the Stairway to Heaven. It is lined by temples dedicated to important Taoist deities; on its peak stands the temple of the Jade Emperor. Over the centuries, many artists have been drawn to this mountain and have left their inscriptions in the rock face at the side of the stairway. Last but not least, T'ai-shan is famous for its breathtakingly beautiful sunrise.

T'ai-shang kan-ying p'ien ◼ Chin., lit. *"Treatise on Action and Recompense";* Taoist text from the time of the Sung Dynasty, mainly emphasizing the moral side of Taoism. Its central theme is the rewarding of good actions and the punishment of evil deeds by Heaven, on the basis of reports submitted by the three worms (→ *san-ch'ung*) and the Ruler of Fate (→ Ssu-ming). A person's life is shortened in proportion to the sins he or she has committed: a serious transgression costs 12 years, a lighter one 100 days. By performing 300 good deeds, a believer can become a terrestrial immortal (→ *hsien*), and after 1,300 good deeds, a celestial immortal.

The text lists a number of virtues that are not specifically Taoist and seems to have been influenced by Buddhist and Confucianist moral concepts.

Among the sins that are punished are contradicting your teacher, father, or older brother; refusing to obey an order; and slander. It is a woman's duty to obey and respect her husband. These demands show a strong Confucianist influence. In addition, a Taoist should not be dishonest, cruel, boastful, or false; he must not commit adultery and must always respect those older than him. Nor is he allowed to kill animals. These prohibitions reflect the Buddhist influence.

T'ai-shang lao-chün 🅃 Chin., lit. "Supreme Master Lao"; → Lao-chün

T'ai-shang tao-chün 🅃 Chin., lit. "Supreme Master of the → Tao," also called Ling-pao t'ien-tsun (lit. "Celestial Venerable of the Magic Jewel"); one of the highest deities in religious Taoism (→ *tao-chiao*). T'ai-shang tao-chün dwells in the Heaven of High Purity, one of the three pure heavens (→ *san-ch'ing*). He is also the patron of the second section (*tung*) of the Taoist canon (→ *Tao-tsang*).

Occasionally T'ai-shang tao-chün is identified with T'ai-shang lao-chün. Both are considered to be incarnations of the Taoist teachings—the Tao. Another such incarnation was → Lao-tzu, whose task it was to instruct mankind in the wisdom of the Tao.

T'ai-shan niang-niang 🅃 → Pi-hsia yüan-chün

T'ai-shih 🅃 Chin., 1. roughly "nourishing the embryo"; Taoist method of prolonging life; preliminary exercise for embryonic breathing (→ *t'ai-hsi*). When practicing *t'ai-shih* the Taoist adept, while inhaling, collects saliva (→ *yü-chiang*) in his mouth, by pressing his tongue against the palate. He then rolls back his head and swallows the accumulated saliva in three gulps, allowing it to ascend and feed the brain (→ *huan-ching pu-nao*) and to descend and moisten the five (internal) organs (→ *wu-tsang*).

2. lit. "great beginning"; the primordial beginning of the world—a state existing before form came into being (→ *Huai-nan-tzu*).

Taishō issaikyō 🄱 Jap., modern edition of the Chinese → Tripitaka, redacted in 1924–34 by the Japanese researcher in Buddhism, Takakusu. It is a hundred-volume work with 3,360 → sūtras and other writings.

The main part consists of fifty-five volumes with twenty-one volumes of sūtras; three volumes of → Vinaya texts; eight volumes of → Abhidharma; twelve volumes of Chinese commentary; four volumes on the individual schools of Chinese and Japanese Buddhism; and seven volumes of historical accounts, biographies, and catalogs. In addition the Taishō issaikyō contains thirty volumes of works by Japanese writers and fifteen volumes of illustrations and indexes.

Tai-sō-yu 🅉 Jap., lit. "essence-[or substance]-form-action"; this expression describes three levels of reality that are fundamentally one; for purposes of explanation, however, different aspects of the single reality are differentiated. They correspond to the levels symbolized by the "three bodies of a buddha" (→ *trikāya*).

Taittirīya-Upanishad 🄷 (Taittirīya Upaniṣad), Skt.; a work belonging to the *Black* → *Yajurveda*. It is divided into three → *vallī*: 1. the Shikshā-Vallī is concerned with instructions for the students regarding the correct pronunciation and intonation of blessings and prayers; 2. the Ānanda-Vallī discusses the → *ātman* and its incomprehensibility by the mind as well as → *brahman*, which is described here as → *Satchchidānanda*. The text explains how knowledge of the identity of → *ātman* and *brahman* leads to bliss (→ *ānanda*); 3. the Bhrigu-Vallī contains the teaching given to → Bhrigu by his father, Varunan, on the paths that lead to knowledge of *brahman*.

Taittirīya is the name of a late school of the *Black Yajurveda* (the older schools of this Veda are → Kathaka and Maitrāyanīya). Like the other two schools, the Taittirīya combines in its → Samhitā sacrificial formulas (mantras) and instructions for their use (*brāhmanam*). The two Upanishads of this school, the *Mahānārāyana* and the *Taittirīya*, both of them among the known and important Upanishads, are attached as → Āranyakas.

T'ai-yüeh ta-ti 🅃 Chin., lit. "Great Ruler of the Eastern Peak" (→ T'ai-shan); the most important and most popular of Taoist mountain deities. He is considered to be the ruler of Earth and mankind. His superior is the Jade Emperor (→ Yü-huang). His task consists in regulating human affairs and determining the time of a person's birth and death. In addition, he keeps a register of the lives and reincarnations of people and has the power to decide their social position, wealth, and progeny.

T'ai-yüeh ta-ti is usually portrayed in imperial dress. His facial expression is impersonal. In the houses of Taoist families, however, it is not his image that is venerated but his seal or amulets dedicated to him, which are said to have the power to dispel evil spirits.

To help him fulfill all these responsibilities, he has at his disposal an enormous administration that is a faithful copy of the actual administration of the state. There are separate departments to deal with various aspects of life: one for births, another for deaths, a third to determine a person's fate in the light of his good or bad deeds, etc. Additional offices are responsible for the various professions, natural phenomena, illnesses, and so on. The administrative staff is recruited from among the dead, but the performance of such functions may also be entrusted to living persons.

Taizui Hōshin 🅉 Jap. for → Ta-sui Fa-chen

Tajō-ippen 🅉 Jap., lit. "precisely [sitting, being] of one piece"; transcending duality in the practice of → *zazen*. A term of the → Sōtō school, in which *zazen* itself is seen as the realization of the buddha-nature (→ *busshō*) inherent in human beings, rather than as a "means" for "attainment" of → enlightenment. (Also → Zen, esoteric, and → *shikantaza*.)

Takuan Z Jap. 1. A dried radish pickled in salt and bran, which is part of the daily diet in a Zen monastery.

2. The name given to himself by the Japanese Zen master Sōhō (1573–1645) and by which he is generally known. Takuan, who belonged to the → Rinzai school, was one of the most important personalities in Japanese Zen at the beginning of the Tokugawa (or Edo) period. Takuan became a monk as a child and trained under the Zen masters Enkan Kokushi Shūshuku and Mindō Kokyō; from the latter he received → *inka-shōmei*. In 1609 he became abbot of → Daitoku-ji in Kyōto and in 1638 moved at the request of the Shōgun Tokugawa Iemitsu to Shinagawa near Edo (later called Tōkyō), where he became the first abbot of the Takai-ji monastery. Takuan was not only an outstanding Zen master but also made a name as a poet of → *waka*, as a painter, and as a master of the way of writing (→ *shōdō*) and of the way of tea (→ *chadō*). He was the master of the swordsman Yogyu Munenori, whom he instructed in a famous letter on the spirit of the way of the sword (→ *kendō*) concerning the unity of Kendō and Zen.

Ta-kuang Chu-hui Z or Ta-kuang Chu-tun (Jap., Daikō [Taikō] Koke), 836/37–903; Chinese Ch'an (Zen) master; a student and dharma successor (→ *hassu*) of → Shih-shuang Ch'ing-chu (Jap., Sekisō Keisho). We encounter Ta-kuang in example 93 of the → *Pi-yen-lu*.

Takuhatsu Z Jap., lit. "request [*taku*] with the eating bowl [*hachi* or *hatsu*]"; the traditional religious begging round of Buddhist monks as still practiced by Zen monks today.

In *takuhatsu* the monks generally go in groups of ten or fifteen, one behind the other, and recite sūtras in front of houses for the benefit of the residents. Believers and well-wishers, when they hear the sūtras, make donations, either in the form of money, which they toss into the monks' wooden bowls, or of uncooked rice, which the monks collect in a sack. Recipient and giver then bow to one another in mutual gratitude with humility and respect.

The frequent translation of *takuhatsu* by "begging round" is not entirely accurate, since here both parties are "recipients." The notion on which *takuhatsu* is based is as follows: the monks, who are guardians of → dharma, offer it to the public by means of their own example; in exchange for this they are supported by those who trust in the truth of the dharma. In addition, from the traditional Buddhist point of view almsgiving is considered a virtue, which increases good → karma. The monks through *takuhatsu* provide the public with an opportunity to practice this virtue.

Tala H Skt.; a state of darkness, self-concealment, and self-distortion. The seven *talas* are the lower realms of the → *lokas*; these are the seven unworthy conditions, sometimes also called hells.

Their names are (1) *atala*, the nonmaterial world, a state of mental dissolution; (2) *vitala*, the material impulse; yet dark and unformed, it is a state in which the spiritual remains obscured due to the lack of effort; (3) *sutala*, a material plane governed by desires and passions; (4) *rasātala*, the manifest world of sensory pleasures; (5) *talātala*, a no longer purely material realm of senses and licentiousness; (6) *mahātala*, the great realm of shadow existence, where the ego and selfishness hold sway; (7) *pātāla*, the subconscious in every being, the source of irrational and ignorant instincts as well as impulses and memories whose cause one cannot fathom. The various → Purānas give different divisions of *tala*; the *Vishnu-* and *Padma-Purāna* name seven regions, whereas the *Shiva-Purāna* gives eight, each with differing meanings.

Ta-luo-t'ien T Chin. → *t'ien*

Tamas H Skt., lit. "darkness, blindness, ignorance"; one of the three → *gunas* that together form the structure of → *prakriti*. It constitutes the dull, inactive forces in nature, which manifest as ignorance, inactivity, incompetence, confusion, and darkness. *Tamas* is the lowest level of the three *gunas*.

Ta-mei Fa-ch'ang Z (Jap., Daibai [Taiba] Hōjō), 752–839; Chinese Ch'an (Zen) master; a student and dharma successor (→ *hassu*) of → Ma-tsu Tao-i (Jap., Baso Dōitsu) and the master of → Hang-chou T'ien-lung (Jap., Kōshū Tenryū). Ta-mei appears in example 30 of the → *Wu-men-kuan*.

Ta-mei had already studied Buddhist philosophy for more than thirty years when he came to Ma-tsu. When he met the great master of "sudden enlightenment" (→ *tongo*), Ta-mei, all of whose studying had not revealed the nature of → buddha-dharma, asked him, "What is Buddha?" Ma-tsu answered, "The mind is Buddha." With these words, Ta-mei experienced enlightenment.

After he had received the seal of confirmation from Ma-tsu (→ *inka-shōmei*), Ta-mei secluded himself on a mountaintop and for thirty years deepened his realization through solitary practice of *zazen* before he himself began to lead students on the way of Ch'an.

Tan 🅩 Jap., lit. "slip [of paper]"; the assigned sitting place of a monk in a Zen monastery where he practices → *zazen*. The name of the monk is written on a slip of paper that is hung above his place; thus this place is called *tan*. The term *tan* is also applied by extension to the wooden platforms, just a meter or slightly less in height and about two meters deep, which run along the two long walls of the → *zendō* of a Zen monastery. During the day the monks sit *zazen* on these and during a → sesshin they also sleep on them at night.

Tan 🅣 Chin., lit. "cinnabar"; the most important substance used in Taoist alchemy. The followers of the Outer Alchemy (→ *wai-tan*) strive to produce purified cinnabar, the ingestion of which is said to have a life-prolonging effect. The most powerful type of cinnabar has been recycled nine times (*chiu-huan-tan*), because its life-prolonging power increases in proportion to the number of transformations it undergoes.

In his *Pao-p'u-tzu* the great Taoist alchemist → Ko Hung describes the properties of cinnabar as follows: "If a person ingests cinnabar that has been transformed once, it will take him three years to become an immortal (→ *hsien*). The same goal can be reached in two years by ingesting cinnabar that has been transformed twice and in one year if it has been transformed three times. Cinnabar of the fourth transformation allows the practitioner to become immortal within six months; and fifth-generation cinnabar, within a hundred days. Anyone who ingests cinnabar of the sixth transformation will become immortal after only forty days. In the case of cinnabar that has been transformed seven times, this process takes only thirty days, and a mere ten days if the practitioner ingests eight-fold purified cinnabar. The most powerful type of cinnabar, however, is one that has been transformed nine times: it renders a person immortal within three days. During these 'transformations' various other substances are added, which are difficult to obtain, especially in restless times such as these. In addition, it is necessary to tend the fire or furnace with extreme care in order to adjust its strength during the various phases of the operation."

In the symbolic language of the Inner Alchemy (→ *nei-tan*), cinnabar represents the energy of combined yin and yang (→ yin-yang) which is set alight in the lower cinnabar field (→ *tan-t'ien*) by means of various meditative breathing techniques. This practice ultimately results in the spiritual immortality of the Inner Alchemy practitioner.

T'an-ching 🅩 Chin. → *Liu-tsu-ta-shih fa-pao-t'an-ching*

Tanden 🅩 Jap., lit. *tan*, "one, single, simple, unique, individual";

Tanden 🅩 Jap. for the Chinese *tan-t'ien*, lit. "cinnabar field"; another term for → *hara*. *den*, "transmission"; a term for the genuine transmission of the → buddha-dharma within the tradition of Zen. *Tanden* can be translated "transmission of the one," but also as "the one [or single] transmission" (also → *ishin-denshin*).

Tanga 🅩 also tanka, Jap., lit. "staying until the morning"; overnight stay in a Zen monastery of a wandering priest or a monk on pilgrimage (→ *angya*). Every monastery has special guest rooms for this purpose, the *tanga-ryō*.

In present-day Japan it is customary during → *niwa-zume* to have monks enter the monastery in the evening and spend the night in the *tanga-ryō*. The next day after breakfast, however, they must resume waiting at the monastery gate or in the entrance hall until they are finally admitted to the monastery for → *tanga-zume*.

Tanga-zume 🅩 Jap., lit. "staying in the guest room"; a period of trial for a monk who is requesting to be accepted into a monastery, which follows the → *niwa-zume*. In *tanga-zume* a monk must spend a week alone in a guest room of the monastery practicing → *zazen*.

He is observed during this time by an elder monk who provides him with food. In addition he goes every morning to the head monk, who is in charge of the administration of the monastery (→ *shika*), and thanks him for his hospitality. This gives the *shika*, who is himself a monk advanced on the path of Zen, an opportunity to get acquainted with the aspirant and to test his suitability.

Tangen Ōshin 🅩 also Tangen Shin'o, → Tan-yuan Ying-chen

Tan-hsia T'ien-jan 🅩 (Jap., Tanka Tennen), 739–824; Chinese Ch'an (Zen) master; a student and dharma successor (→ *hassu*) of → Shih-t'ou Hsi-ch'ien (Jap., Sekitō Kisen) and the master of → Ts'ui-wei Wu-hsueh (Jap., Suibi Mugaku). We encounter Tan-hsia in example 76 of the → *Pi-yen-lu*.

As Master Yuan-wu reports in his commentary on example 76 of the *Pi-yen-lu*, Tan-hsia, whose birthplace and family are unknown, studied the Confucian classics and planned to take the civil service examination in the capital, Ch'ang-an. On the way there he met a Ch'an monk, who asked him what his goal was. "I've decided to become a functionary," said Tan-hsia. "What does the decision to become a functionary amount to compared with the decision to become a buddha?" replied the monk. "Where can I go if I want to become a buddha?" Tan-hsia then asked. The monk suggested that he seek out the great Ch'an master → Ma-tsu Tao-i (Jap., Baso Dōitsu), whereupon Tan-hsia unhesitatingly set out to do so. Ma-tsu soon sent him on to Shih-t'ou, under whom he trained for some years. He went on to become one of Shih-t'ou's dharma successors.

Later he returned to Ma-tsu. Having arrived in Ma-tsu's monastery he sat himself astride the neck of a statue of → Mañjushrī. As the monks, upset by the outrageous behavior of the newcomer, reported this to Ma-tsu, the latter came to see Tan-hsia and greeted him with the words, "You are very natural, my son." From this incident Tan-hsia's monastic name *T'ien-jan* (the Natural) is derived. After the death of Ma-tsu, Tan-hsia went on wandering pilgrimage and visited other great Ch'an masters of the time in order to train himself further in → *hossen* with them. At the age of eighty-one, he settled in a hermitage on Mount Tan-hsia, from which his name is derived. Soon up to 300 students gathered there around him and built a monastery. Four years after his arrival on Mount Tan-hsia, he suddenly said one day, "I'm going on a journey once again." He picked up his hat and his pilgrim's robe and staff. When he had put on the second of his pilgrim's sandals, he passed away before his foot again touched the ground.

There are many stories about Tan-hsia, who was a close friend of the Ch'an layman → P'ang-yun, telling of his unconventional behavior. The most famous of these stories tells that once during his wandering years he spent the night in a Ch'an temple. The night being cold, he took a buddha image off the shrine, made a fire with it, and warmed himself. When the temple priest took him to task for having violated a sacred statue, Tan-hsia said, "I'll get the bones of the Buddha [for relics] out of the ashes." "How can you expect to find Buddha's bones in wood?" asked the priest. Tan'hsia replied, "Why are you berating me then for burning the wood?!"

Tan-hsia Tzu-ch'un Z (Jap., Tanka Shijun), d. 1119; Chinese Ch'an (Zen) master of the → Sōtō school; a sixth-generation dharma heir of → Yun-chu Tao-ying (Jap., Ungo Dōyō) and the master of → Hung-chih Cheng-chueh (Jap. Wanshi Shōgaku) and → Chen-hsieh Ch'ing-liao (Jap., Shingestsu Shōryō). Tan-hsia was the "great-grandfather in dharma" of → Dōgen Zenji.

Tanka Z Jap. → *tanga*

Tanka Shijun Z Jap. for → Tan-hsia Tzu-ch'un

Tanka Tennen Z Jap. for → Tan-hsia T'ien-jan

Tankū Z Jap., lit. "just emptiness," → futan-kū

Tanmātra H Skt., lit. "primal matter"; the fundamental principles or subtle elements from which the gross elements (→ *mahābhūtas*) derive.

There are five *tanmātras*: (1) *shabda* (sound); (2) *sparsha* (touch); (3) *rūpa* (sight); (4) *rasa* (taste); (5) *gandha* (smell). The five *mahābhūtas* (gross elements) are (1) *ākāsha* (ether, space); (2) *vāyu* (air); (3) *tejas* (fire); (4) *apas* (water); (5) *prithivī* (earth).

Tannishō B Jap. → Shinran

Tan-t'ien T Chin., lit. "cinnabar fields," elixir field; three regions of the human body through which the vital energy (→ *ch'i*) flows: the upper cinnabar field is situated in the brain, the middle one near the heart, and the lower in the region of the navel.

Some Taoist schools believe that these three vital centers of the human body are inhabited by deities (→ Inner Deity Hygiene School, → *shen*) and harmful beings (→ *san-ch'ung*).

The lower cinnabar field—sometimes equated with the "ocean of breath" (→ *ch'i-hai*) is of particular significance in connection with various practices aimed at the prolongation of life, because it is the place where not only the → *ch'i* but also a man's semen (→ *ching*) and a woman's menstrual flow are accumulated (see also → *huan-ching,* → *nei-tan,* → *t'ai-hsi,* → *wai-tan*).

Each of the three cinnabar fields consists of nine compartments arranged in two rows (one of five and one of four). The only descriptions in existence refer to the various compartments of the upper cinnabar field. Among the most important of these is one referred to as government palace (*ming-t'ang-kung*), which, according to the teachings of the Inner Deity Hygiene School, is the dwelling place of → Huang-lao-chün and his retinue. In the central compartment—known as the palace of → *ni-huan* (or *ni-wan* after the Sanskrit Buddhist term *nirvana*)—resides the highest body deity, the → T'ai-i, or Supreme One.

Tantra H B Skt., lit. "weft, context, continuum."

H Next to the Veda, the Upanishads, the Purānas, and the *Bhagavad-Gītā*, Tantra is one of the fundamental elements in → *sanātana-dharma*, the "eternal religion" of Hinduism. Its central theme is the divine energy and creative power (→ Shakti) that is represented by the feminine aspect of any of various gods; personified as a *devī*, or goddess, she is portrayed as his wife, above all as the wife of → Shiva. Corresponding to the particular form taken by Shiva, his Shakti may be a fortune-granting figure, such as Maheshvarī, Lakshmī, Sarasvatī, Umā, or Gaurī, or may be a terrifying figure, such as Kālī or Durgā.

The term *Tantra* also refers to a group of texts and a practice that are fraught with danger for anyone who is not prepared to be subjected to strict spiritual discipline. Two Tantric schools have evolved: (1) the impure, perilous path of Vāmāchāra ("left-hand path"), devoted to licentious rites and sexual debauchery; and (2) the → Dakshināchāra ("right-hand path"), featuring a purification ritual and a strict spiritual discipline that requires absolute surrender to the Divine Mother in her multifarious forms.

A Tantric diagram of the body, showing the chakras and the major channels of energy (*nādīs*).

Each of the Tantric texts is supposed to contain five themes: (1) the creation of the world; (2) its destruction or dissolution; (3) the worship of God in his masculine or feminine aspect, i.e., the worship of one of the numerous male or female divinities; (4) the attainment of supernatural abilities; (5) the various methods of achieving union with the Supreme by means of the appropriate form of meditation. These means consist of the various older yoga disciplines such as → Karma-Yoga, → Bhakti-Yoga, → Kundalinī-Yoga, and other yogic paths.

The Tantric texts are usually in the form of a dialogue between Shiva, the divine lord, and his Shakti, divine energy. They attempt to raise all of humanity to the level of divine perfection by teaching human beings how to awaken the cosmic force that lies within (→ *kundalinī-shakti*) by means of particular rites and meditation practices.

The Tantric rites require the use of five elements: (1) *madya*, wine; (2) *mānsa*, meat; (3) *matsya*, fish; (4) *mudrā*, parched grain and mystical gestures; (5) *maithuna*, sexual intercourse. An introduction to Hindu Tantra is Agehananda Bharat. 1965.

B in → Tibetan Buddhism, a term for various kinds of texts (medical Tantras, astrological Tantras, etc.), however, primarily a general concept for the basic activity of the → Vajrayāna and its systems of meditation. The expounding of the Tantras is attributed to Buddha → Shākyamuni in his *dharmakāya* (→ *trikāya*) manifestation. In this case, *Tantra* means "continuum" or "system." This tradition, which is strongly oriented toward man's experiential potential, describes spiritual development in terms of the categories of ground, path, and fruition. The ground is the practitioner; the path is the path of meditation, which purifies this ground; the fruition is the state that arises as an effect of Tantric practice. All forms of Tantra relate to these three phases.

The Tibetan tradition speaks of four classes of Tantra: *kriyā-tantra* (action Tantra), *charyā-tantra* (elaboration Tantra), *yoga-tantra*, and *anuttara-yoga-tantra* (supreme yoga Tantra). The criteria for this classification are the differences in the spiritual capacities of practitioners and the corresponding effectiveness of the means for leading them to enlightenment. Among the most important works of the supreme yoga Tantra are the *Guhyasamāja-tantra* and the → *Kālachakra-tantra*.

The "ancient Tantras" of the → Nyingmapa school divide the supreme yoga Tantra into three further categories: *mahā-*, *anu-*, and *ati-yoga* (→ *dzogchen*). These Tantras take the purity of mind that is always already present as the basis for their practice. The best-known of them is the *Guhyagarbha-tantra*. The polarity-oriented thought of the Tantras finds its strongest expression in a many-layered sexual symbology. Transcendence of the duality of the masculine principle (skillful means, → *upāya*) and the feminine principle (wisdom, → *prajñā*) through the union of the two is given as the key characteristic of the supreme yoga Tantra.

An introduction into the Tantra of Tibetan Buddhism is Hopkins 1977.

Tantra-Yoga **H** Skt., synonymous with → Kundalinī-Yoga

Tantrism **H** → Shaktism

Tan-yuan Ying-chen **Z** or Tan-yuan Chen-ying (Jap., Tangen Ōshin or Tangen Shin'ō), 8th/9th century Chinese Ch'an (Zen) master; a student and dharma successor (→ *hassu*) of Nan-yang Hui-chung (Jap., Nan'yō Echū). Little is known of Tan-yuan; he is the servant of Teacher of the Country Chung in example 17 of the → *Wu-men-kuan* (on this, → Nan-yang Hui-chung) and appears also in example 18 of the → *Pi-yen-lu*. From his master Nan-yang, a student of the sixth patriarch of Ch'an (Zen), → Hui-neng, Tan-yuan received a secret system of instructions based on ninety-seven symbols, each inscribed in a circle (on this, → Igyō school). Tan-yuan in turn transmitted it to → Yang-shan Hui-chi (Jap., Kyōzan Ejaku), one of the founding fathers of the Igyō school of Ch'an, before he passed away at an advanced age.

Tao ◼ Chin., lit. "Way"; central concept of Taoism (→ *tao-chia,* → *tao-chiao*) and origin of its name. The Tao also is the central feature of the *Tao-te ching* and the → *Chuang-tzu.*

Although the original meaning of the pictogram for Tao is "Way," it can also denote "Teaching." From earliest times the term has been used in the sense of human behavior and moral laws—the Way of man; this certainly is its meaning in Confucianist texts. The *Tao-te ching* of → Lao-tzu is the first text to ascribe a metaphysical meaning to the term, in the sense that it is seen as the all-embracing first principle, from which all appearances arise. It is a reality that gives rise to the universe. Lao-tzu referred to it as the Tao only because there was no other adequate term available. In the translation of Chang Chung-yuan (1963):

There was something complete and nebulous
Which existed before the Heaven and Earth,
Silent, invisible,
Unchanging, standing as One,
Unceasing, ever-revolving,
Able to be the Mother of the World.
I do not know its name and call it Tao.

The Tao then is nameless, unnamable. Chapter 1 of the *Tao-te ching* (Feng & English 1972) states:

The Tao that can be told
is not the eternal [→ *ch'ang*] Tao.
The name that can be named
is not the eternal name.

The Tao is the mother who gives birth to and nourishes the ten thousand things (→ *wan-wu*). It is the primordial source of all being. In Chapter 6 of the *Tao-te ching* it is compared to a "mysterious female" whose gateway is the root of Heaven and Earth. (During the later phases of Taoism this passage was frequently quoted by Taoist adepts to justify certain sexual practices [→ *fang-chung shu*] as a means of becoming one with the Tao.)

All things, furthermore, return to the Tao. This is a universal law. Enlightenment (→ *ming*) in a Taoist sense is the realization of this universal law of the return of all things to the Tao (→ *fu*). This return is something to which the Tao itself is subject: "Return is the movement of the Tao."

Chapter 14 of the *Tao-te ching* describes the Tao as invisible, inaudible, unfathomable, the form of the formless and eternal. The function of the Tao is being; its essence is nonbeing. It is the Great One, in which all opposites are canceled.

That which you look at but cannot see
Is called the Invisible.
That which you can listen to but cannot hear
Is called the Inaudible.
That which you grasp but cannot hold
Is called the Unfathomable.
None of these three can be inquired after,
Hence they blend into one.
Above no light can make it lighter,
Beneath no darkness can make it darker.
Unceasingly it continues
But it is impossible to be defined.
Again it returns to nothingness.
Thus it is described as the Form of the Formless,
The Image of the Imageless.
Hence it is called the Evasive.
It is met with but no one sees its face;
It is followed but no one sees its back.
To hold to the Tao of old,
To deal with the affairs at hand,
In order to understand the primordial beginnings,
That is called the rule of Tao.
(Chang Chung-yuan 1963)

The Tao acts spontaneously and in accordance with its nature (→ *tzu-jan*). Its effect and activity are without intent (→ *wu-wei*), yet there is nothing that remains undone. In the phenomenal world, the Tao manifests through its power, its "virtue" (→ *te*), which all things receive from the Tao and by which they become that which they are.

All Taoists strive to become one with the Tao. This cannot be achieved by trying to understand the Tao intellectually; the adept becomes one with the Tao by realizing within himself its unity, simplicity (→ *p'u*), and emptiness.

This requires intuitive understanding, which Book 22, Chapter 2 of the *Chuang-tzu* describes as follows: "*Tao* may be known by no thoughts, no reflections. It may be approached by resting in nothingness, by following nothing, pursuing nothing. . . . The Sage teaches a doctrine which does not find expression in words" (Chang Chung-yuan 1963). The Tao thus is realized by abiding in silence, and the way to silence is found by "letting go": "To search for knowledge means to acquire day after day; to seek the Tao means to let go day after day." In the *Tao-te ching* silence corresponds to the return to the source; by abiding in stillness all inner and outer activity comes to rest and all limitations and conditions fade away. This is when the celestial light shines forth, allowing us to behold our true selves and realize the absolute (*Chuang-tzu* 23.2).

This process of submerging oneself in stillness is also described in Chapter 16 of the *Tao-te ching* (Chang Chung-yuan 1963):

Devote yourself to the utmost Void;
Contemplate earnestly in Quiescence.
All things are together in action,
But I look into their non-action.
For things are continuously moving, restless,
Yet each is proceeding back to its origin.
Proceeding back to the origin means Quiescence.
To be in Quiescence is to see "being-for-itself."

Taoism has developed a number of practices to facilitate the realization of the Tao. Both the *Chuang-tzu* and the *Tao-te ching* contain guidelines for producing a state of meditative absorption. In this context breathing exercises are particularly important, either as a preliminary practice or as a means of enhancing the meditative process. They were developed by the School of the Inner Elixir (→ *nei-tan*).

Even in pre-Confucianist China the Tao was a symbol for human ideals, and a great variety of philosophical schools subsequently incorporated it into their system. In this context Chuang-tzu makes the following observation: "There are many masters in the school of philosophy in the world of today. Each of them claims to have found the correct answer. When we ask, 'Where is the philosophy of the ancient *Tao*?' we may answer, 'It is in every system' " (Chang Chung-yuan 1963).

The early Chinese Buddhists made use of Taoist terminology to express their ideas and saw the Tao as the Way to nirvāna. There is also a famous Zen saying, "The wondrous Tao consists in carrying water and chopping wood."

Tao-an 🅱 312–85; the most important Chinese Buddhist scholar of the 4th century. His main contribution to the development of Chinese Buddhism was his joining of two aspects of Buddhist practice: → *prajñā* and → *dhyāna*. He is considered the founder of an early school of Chinese Buddhism, which developed out of his engagement with the → *Prajñāpāramitā-sūtra*. This was the school of fundamental nonbeing (→ six houses and seven schools).

Tao-an also compiled the first catalog of sūtras, listing those already available in Chinese translation at that time, regulated the conferral of monastic names, and, lacking a complete → Vinaya-pitaka, established guidelines for the communal life of his followers. In addition he is considered the originator of the cult of → Maitreya. Because of his emphasis on the importance of meditation practice, he is regarded as one of the fathers of → Dhyāna Buddhism in China, and by many as the actual founder of Ch'an (→ Zen).

Tao-an was born in northern China into a Confucianist family. By the age of twelve, however, he had already become a novice in the Buddhist monastic order. He studied under → Fo T'u-teng the various *prajñāpāramitā* texts and the sūtras dealing with the practice of *dhyāna*. He composed commentaries on these texts very early on in his life, and this was the beginning of his teaching activity.

The school of fundamental nonbeing, founded by him, saw in this nonbeing the basis for every phenomenal process. Liberation from all spiritual fetters can only be attained through the mind's dwelling in nonbeing.

Tao-an also recognized the inadequacy of the Vinaya rules as then known in China. Thus he established his own guidelines for rites of veneration of the Buddha (for example, circumambulation of statues), methods of expounding the sūtras, communal meals, and the → *uposatha* ceremonies.

Tao-an laid the groundwork for the development of the cult of Maitreya (which was soon to give place to that of → Amitābha) through his custom of gathering with his students before an image of Maitreya and supplicating for rebirth in the → Tushita Heaven.

Tao-chia 🆃 Chin., philosophical Taoism; one of two streams of Taoism, the other being religious Taoism (→ *tao-chiao*). Philosophical Taoism bases itself on the writings of → Lao-tzu (→ *Tao-te ching*) and → Chuang-tzu, who are considered to be its founders, → Lieh-tzu and → Yang Chu being their acknowledged successors.

Followers of philosophical Taoism strive to achieve mystical union with the → Tao by meditation and by following the nature of the Tao in thought and action. Unlike the adherents of religious Taoism, they are not interested in attaining physical immortality.

The term *tao-chia* was first used during the Han Dynasty and refers to the central meaning of Tao as the Way. The Tao is thus understood to be the all-embracing principle from which all things arise. The ideology of philosophical Taoism is strongly marked by political considerations. A central feature is the concept of *wu-wei* —spontaneous, unmotivated action—which philosophical Taoism emphasizes as a model for rulers. From an ethical point of view, philosophical Taoism is the opposite of → Confucianism, whose cardinal virtues of humanity (→ *jen*) and uprightness (→ *i*) it rejects, because they veil the true nature of man and impede the Tao.

The political ideas of philosophical Taoism soon were adopted by other philosophical schools, but during the Han Dynasty philosophical Taoism lost a great deal of influence when Emperor Wu-ti (156–87 B.C.E.) proclaimed Confucianism the official state religion. At the same time, however, the teachings of philosophical Taoism spread among the people and played a decisive role in the later development of religious Taoism, which venerates the deified Lao-tzu as its founder.

During the Wei and Chin dynasties the *tao-chia* experienced a revival in the form of neo-Taoism (→ *hsüan-hsüeh*), which combined Confucianist and Taoist ideas. In addition, philosophical Taoism played an important part in the establishment of Buddhism in China: it has been said that the Chinese form of Zen (Ch'an) could not have flowered if philosphical Taoism had not prepared the ground for it. The philosophical ideas of Lao-tzu and Chuang-tzu live on in the hearts and minds of the Chinese people and find their most immediate expression in Chinese painting and poetry.

Tao-chiao ■ Chin., religious Taoism; one of the two streams of Taoism, the other being philosophical Taoism (→ *tao-chia*). The *tao-chiao* embraces all Taoist schools and movements whose aim consists in the attainment of immortality (→ *ch'ang-sheng pu-ssu*). The most important of these are: the → Inner Deity Hygiene School, Five-Pecks-of-Rice Taoism (→ *wu-tou-mi tao*), the Way of Supreme Peace (→ *t'ai-p'ing tao*), the School of the Magic Jewel (→ *ling-pao p'ai*), the Way of Right Unity (→ *cheng-i tao*), and the Way of the Realization of Truth (→ *ch'üan-chen tao*).

The methods employed to attain immortality range from meditation to alchemical practices, physical exercises, breathing exercises, and sexual practices.

Religious Taoism is the product of several philosophical and religious movements. The teachings of → Lao-tzu, → Chuang-tzu, and → Lieh-tzu (350–250 B.C.E.), which form the basis of philosophical Taoism, also left their mark on the *tao-chiao*. In addition, there already existed a hygiene school whose followers strove to lengthen their life by certain breathing practices (→ *hsing-ch'i*) and physical exercises (→ *tao-yin*). There also was the doctrine of the five elements (→ *wu-hsing*), formulated toward the end of the 4th century B.C.E. by → Tsou Yen, whose followers searched for the elixir of immortality (→ *wai-tan*, → *nei-tan*). Another influence was the search for the isles of the immortals (→ P'eng-lai, → Fang-chang, → Ying-chou), which were first mentioned in Lieh-tzu's writings.

Between ca. 220 and 120 B.C.E. the teachings of the various movements became intermingled. This development was prompted by the activities of the Taoist magicians (→ *fang-shih*) (also → Li Shao-chün). That also was the time when various deities began to be venerated within the *tao-chiao* (→ Tsao-chün, → T'ai-i, → *san-i*).

During the early centuries of our era, the Inner Deity Hygiene School and other religious mass movements came into being. Western scholars often refer to these as the Taoist church. In fact, they constitute the actual *tao-chiao*.

In the first half of the 2d century B.C.E. → Chang Tao-ling founded what became known as Five-Pecks-of-Rice Taoism. His followers venerated Lao-tzu as their founder and quoted the → *Tao-te ching* as a doctrinal source. Its leaders or patriarchs called themselves celestial masters (→ *t'ien-shih*). Not long after that → Chang Chüeh established the School of the Way of Supreme Peace, whose followers—the so-called Yellow Turbans—in 184 C.E. rebelled against the central government. Both these schools made use of talismans (→ *fu-lu*) and conducted mass fasting and healing ceremonies (→ *chai*, → *ho-ch'i*). This accounts for their extraordinary popularity.

In 140 C.E. → Wei P'o-yang wrote his celebrated *Chou-i ts'an-t'ung-ch'i*, considered to be the oldest alchemical text preserved for posterity. In publishing his encyclopedic *Pao-p'u-tzu*, → Ko Hung tried to unite the various streams of religious Taoism. The *Pao-p'u-tzu* is a systematically arranged compendium of methods and practices aimed at becoming an immortal (→ *hsien*). Around the same period the School of the Magic Jewel became established and, in the course of time, displaced the Inner Deity Hygiene movement.

In the 5th century C.E. → K'ou Ch'ien-chih strove to carry out a reform by ridding Taoism of the damaging influence of the Chang lineage (→ *t'ien-shih*) and proclaiming a number of moral rules. This led to the foundation of the Northern Way of the Celestial Masters, while Lu Hsiu-ching, basing himself on the teachings of the Chang clan, founded the Southern Way of the Celestial Masters.

During the 6th century the alchemists abandoned their search for an outer elixir and turned toward the teachings on the inner elixir; this led to a gradual fusion of the practices of the followers of the inner elixir, the inner breath teachings (→ *nei-ch'i*), and Zen Buddhism. Later, → Chang Po-tuan became one of the most prominent proponents of this syncretist movement.

In the 7th century the Emperor T'ang Wu-tsung de facto proclaimed Taoism a state religion: each district had to have its own Taoist temple. The Taoist canon (→ *Tao-tsang*) was compiled—and first appeared in print—during the Sung Dynasty. Taoism reached its greatest flowering under this imperial protection.

Under the Yüan Dynasty the Southern and the Northern Way of the Celestial Masters and various other movements merged to form the Way of Right Unity. In 1167 C.E. → Wang Ch'un-yang founded the School for the Realization of Truth, which incorporated Buddhist teachings and elements of Confucianism.

Some smaller schools—such as the Way of the Supreme One (→ *t'ai-i tao*)—came into being during the transition period between the Chin and Yüan dynasties, but were very short-lived. The survivors were the two great movements of the *ch'üan-chen tao* and *cheng-i tao.* The main doctrines of religious Taoism are based on the → Tao, which is understood as emptiness and the primordial ground of all being. From it arise the cosmos, the five elements, → yin-yang, and the ten thousand things (→ *wan-wu*). Among its objects of veneration are the three pure ones (→ *san-ch'ing*), which are seen as personifications of the Tao, and the celestial venerables (→ *t'ien-tsun*), the most important of whom is Tao-te t'ien-tsun, i.e., Lao-tzu.

The followers of religious Taoism strive to attain physical immortality. Among the practices directed at realizing that aim are *tao-yin,* embryonic breathing (→ *t'ai-hsi*), *nei-tan* (inner elixir), *wai-tan* (outer elixir), *fu-lu* (talismans), → *pi-ku* (abstention from eating grain), and sexual practices (→ *fang-chung shu*). The most important ceremonies are communal fasts (→ *chai*), collective confession, and healing sessions and rituals for the veneration of deities.

Tao-hsin 🅉 (Jap., Dōshin) 580–651; the fourth patriarch (→ *soshigata*) of Ch'an (Zen) in China; the student and dharma successor (→ *hassu*) of → Seng-ts'an and the master of → Hung-jen. He is supposed to have met the third patriarch when he was not yet twenty years old and to have distinguished himself through his special predilection for meditation. It is said that he practiced → *zazen* with an intensity and devotion unequaled by any patriarch since → Bodhidharma.

An account of the incident that marked the transmission of the → buddha-dharma from Seng-ts'an to Tao-hsin is given in the *Denkō-roku*:

"The thirty-first patriarch [-fourth Chinese patriarch], Daii Zenji [honorific title of Tao-hsin] bowed to Kanshi Daishi [honorific title of Seng-ts'an] and said, 'I entreat you, master, have compassion for me; please grant me the dharma-gate of liberation.'

"The patriarch [Seng-ts'an] said, 'Who has you tied up?'

"The master [Tao-hsin] said, 'There is nobody who has me tied up.'

"The patriarch said, 'Then why are you seeking liberation?'

"With these words the master experienced great enlightenment."

Tao-hsin, whose given name was Ssu-ma, came from Honan. He left his home at the age of seven in order to study Buddhism and met Seng-ts'an a few years later. He proved an excellent student. After Seng-ts'an had transmitted the patriarchate to him, he told Tao-hsin to take up residence at a monastery on Mount Lu and instruct students in the → *Lankāvatāra-sūtra,* which had been important in Ch'an since → Bodhidharma and in the practice of → *zazen.* After some time on Lu-shan, Tao-hsin, following a sign, moved to a neighboring mountain called Shuang-feng ('Twin Peaks'). Soon many students gathered around him there, which encouraged him to establish a self-sufficient monastic community. This provided the model for future Ch'an (Zen) monastic communities. In the course of the thirty years that he spent on Shuang-feng, it is said that he had about him at a given time up to 500 students. While the patriarchs preceding him were strongly influenced by the orthodox Mahāyāna tradition and the sūtras, Tao-hsin already showed a tendency that was to be characteristic of the later Ch'an (Zen) tradition—dismissal of scholarly erudition and emphasis on the primacy of meditative practice.

Thus in a still-extant work of his, we read: "Sit eagerly in meditation [*zazen*]! Sitting is the basis.... Shut the door and sit! Don't read the sūtras, don't talk to people. When you practice like that and work at it for a long time, the fruit is sweet—as [it is for the] monkey [who] takes the nut from the nutshell. Such ones are but few!" (trans. from Dumoulin, *Zen—Geshichte and Gestalt*, Bern, 1959).

Among the many students of Tao-hsin, Hung-jen, the future fifth patriarch, was especially outstanding for his profound realization of the dharma teaching of his master. Toward the end of his life, Tao-hsin gave him the task of building a mausoleum on the slopes of Shuang-feng. When this was finished, Tao-hsin entered it and, sitting absorbed in meditation, passed away.

Tao-hsuan 🄱 → Lu-tsung

Tao-hsuan Lu-shih 🅉 (Jap., Dōsen Risshi), 702–60; Chinese master of the → Vinaya school, who in 732 arrived in the then Japanese capital Nara and there taught not only the doctrine of the Vinaya school but also those of the → Hua-yen school of Buddhism and of the Northern school of Ch'an (Zen) (→ Southern school).

He was a third-generation dharma successor (→ *hassu*) of → Shen-hsiu and instructed the Japanese monk Gyōhō (722–97) in Ch'an (Zen) meditation. Gyōhō in turn instructed the monk → Saichō (767–822) in → *zazen.* Saichō—who later went to China, studied the teachings of the T'ien-t'ai school there, and later, after his return to Japan, founded the → Tendai school there—also met in China a master of the → Gozu school of Ch'an. As a result of these contacts with Ch'an, elements of it were introduced into the practice of the Tendai school. Thus in the early period of Zen in Japan (12th/13th centuries), it was primarily the Tendai monasteries that took in the first Zen masters and provided them with a working situation.

T'ao Hung-ching ▣ 456–536 C.E.; Taoist scholar and physician; a follower of → Ko Hung. By applying the strict Confucianist hierarchy of the state to the world of the immortals (→ *hsien*) and deities (→ *shen*), T'ao Hung-ching was the first to classify the Taoist deities. In his writings he endeavored to establish a connection between Confucianism, Buddhism, and Taoism.

T'ao Hung-ching lived on Mount Mao, where he was taught the secret of talismans (→ *fu-lu*) and other magical practices. In his search for life-prolonging substances he visited all the famous Taoist mountains. He was well known for his profound knowledge in relation to the → yin-yang, astrology, and geomancy. His prophecies concerning future events of national importance frequently turned out to be correct, as a result of which the emperor invited him to court on several occasions, but T'ao refused to leave the mountains. However, the emperor's respect for him was so great that he sought him out in his hermitage to benefit from his counsel. Because of this role as imperial advisor T'ao became known as the "Prime Minister in the Mountains."

In addition, T'ao Hung-ching possessed great knowledge of medicinal herbs, which he classified systematically, thus making an important contribution to Chinese pharmacology.

T'ao Hung-ching's hierarchy of the deities and immortals consisted of seven levels, each of them ruled by a main deity residing at the center of that particular level. There are numerous deities on each level, their importance diminishing proportionate to their distance from its center. Beyond the fifth level some of the figures have no specific location assigned to them.

Each level corresponds to a celestial palace, in which the deities and immortals of that particular level reside. The first level is that of pure jade; its central deity is the Celestial Venerable of the Primordial Beginning (→ Yüan-shih t'ien-tsun). On the third level we find the major figures of Chinese mythology, such as → Yao, → Shun, and Yü the Great (→ Ta-yü) but also such historical figures as Confucius (→ K'ung-tzu). Here → Lao-tzu ranks as an immortal of the left wing but—under another name—also holds the central place on the fourth level, with → Chang Tao-ling among those placed to his left.

Tao-I ▣ → Ma-tsu Tao-i

Taoism ▣ collective term used in the West for two essentially different movements of Chinese philosophy and religion, namely philosophical Taoism (→ *tao-chia*), whose most important representatives were → Lao-tzu and → Chuang-tzu, and religious Taoism (→ *tao-chiao*), which consisted of various schools. Philosophical Taoism is a mystical teaching about the → Tao, i.e., the Way, and → *wu-wei* (unmotivated action), whereas the main characteristic of the various streams of religious Taoism consists in their teachings on how to attain immortality (→ *ch'ang-sheng pu-ssu*).

(Also → *cheng-i tao,* → *ch'üan-chen tao,* → Lieh-tzu, → *nei-tan,* → *wai-tan,* → *wu-tou-mi tao.*)

Tao of the Celestial Masters ▣ → *t'ein-shih*

Tao-sheng ▣ 355–434; important Chinese monk and founder of the → Nirvāna school of early Chinese Buddhism. He was an associate of → Kumārajīva, with whom he worked on the translation of the → *Lotus Sūtra* and the *Vimalakīrtinirdesha-sūtra.* Tao-sheng advocated a number of revolutionary theses that had great influence on the future development of Buddhism in China. He took the position that all beings without exception, even → *ichchantikas,* possess → buddha-nature and that this can be realized through sudden enlightenment. He propounded a synthesis of the teachings of the → *Mahāparinirvāna-sūtra* and the → *Prajñāpāramitā-sūtra.* None of his works are extant; they have been handed down only in fragments from compendiums and commentaries.

Tao-sheng was a man of extraordinary talent. He was already a recognized teacher when ordained as a monk. In 397–401, he was at → Lu-shan, an important center of Buddhist studies. In 405 he went to the capital Ch'ang-an, where he collaborated with Kumārajīva and developed his sensational theses, which led to his expulsion from the monastic community there. Though Tao-sheng's theses are confirmed in the *Mahāparinirvāna-sūtra,* this was not fully translated into Chinese at the time he formulated them. After the publication of the translation, Tao-sheng was reinstated.

His conviction that *ichchantikas* possess buddha-nature and can attain buddhahood was based on the Mahāyāna view that all beings possess buddha-nature and that this is only obscured by ignorance. Buddha-nature as realized in sudden enlightenment represents a complete realization of truth. However, preliminary practice is necessary for this. Tao-sheng based his view of sudden enlightenment on the notion that enlightenment means oneness with the supreme truth, which is indivisible. From this he drew the conclusion that this indivisible factor could not be realized in enlightenment gradually. In enlightenment, in his view, one realizes that → samsāra and → nirvāna are not separate and that the reality of buddha-nature is not different from the world of appearances.

For Tao-sheng, buddha-nature as interpreted in the *Mahāparinirvāna-sūtra* and the emptiness (→ *shūnyatā*) of the *Prajñāpāramitā-sūtra* are one and the same.

Both are devoid of characteristics, indivisible, and transcend all forms. Buddha-nature and *shūnyatā* are nothing other than nirvāna, a state in which there is no separation between subject and object. Tao-sheng also denied the existence of a → pure land of Buddha, since Buddha is not separate from our world but rather is found in every being.

Tao-sheng spent the last years of his life again on Mount Lu. One day in the year 434, he delivered one of his famous discourses. As he was about to leave the teaching seat, he suddenly dropped his staff—sitting erect, he had passed into nirvāna.

Tao-shih ◼ Chinese scholar(s) and priest(s) of religious Taoism (→ *tao-chiao*). From approximately the 4th century C.E., the *tao-shih* have been the leaders of Taoist congregations. Their office was passed on by inheritance. They were responsible for supervising all religious matters such as the various rituals and ceremonies (→ *chai*) and assisted members of their flock in times of difficulty by the use of talismans (→ *fu-lu*), spells to ward off demons and evil spirits, etc.

The *tao-shih* of the School of Right Unity (→ *cheng-i tao*) lived with their families near a monastery (→ *kuan*) and were ruled by a celestial master (→ *t'ien-shih*). Those of the School of the Realization of Truth (→ *ch'üan-chen tao*) lived in strict celibacy. The office and title of the *tao-shih* originated with a religious movement known as Five-Pecks-of-Rice Taoism (→ *wu-tou-mi tao*). *Tao-shih* usually wore a long gray or black gown with wide sleeves. They allowed their hair to grow and pinned it up in a knot. At ceremonies they wore a robe consisting of 240 segments arranged on 10 strips of material. This robe was gathered around the waist by a belt adorned with images of clouds. On their head they wore a five-pointed crown.

Tao-shih living in a monastery were subject to strict monastic discipline. They had to observe a large number of fast days, and their daily life was governed by five rules of behavior: they were not allowed to kill, had to abstain from eating meat and drinking alcohol, were forbidden to lie or steal, and could not marry or enter any other kind of sexual relationship.

Beyond this basic moral code, monastic Taoism had additional sets of ten, twenty-seven, or more rules. The School for the Realization of Truth divided these into three stages according to their difficulty: on the first stage the *tao-shih* had to obey rules relating to the "dawning of truth" (*ch'u-chen chieh*) and were referred to as "noble ones in transformation." The second stage contained three hundred rules relating to the intermediate goal (*chung-chi chieh*), and aspirants on this level were known as "noble persons of virtue." *Tao-shih* on the highest level had to observe the rules relating to a celestial immortal (*t'ien-hsien*) and were known as "noble persons in the → Tao." These rules and guidelines governed both the personal behavior of monks as well as the life of the monastic community as a whole. They related to dress, diet, the use of monastic facilities, the performance of religious practices, the relationship between teacher and student, ways of assisting people on their spiritual path toward enlightenment, etc. At the ordination of a *tao-shih* a certain number of fully ordained *tao-shih* had to be present. Analogous to Buddhist practice, *tao-shih* took refuge in the Tao, the Taoist scriptures (→ *Tao-tsang*), and the Taoist masters.

Tao-te ching ◼ Chin., lit. *"The Book of the Way and Its Power"*; a work attributed to → Lao-tzu. It consists of five thousand pictograms and for that reason is often referred to by the Chinese as *Text of the Five Thousand Signs*. The *Tao-te ching* forms the basis of both philosophical Taoism (→ *tao-chia*) and religious Taoism (→ *tao-chiao*). According to tradition, it was written by Lao-tzu during the 6th century B.C.E., but scholars now take the general view that it cannot have come into existence before the 4th or 3d century B.C.E. The oldest existing copy dates from between 206 and 195 B.C.E.

According to legend the *Tao-te ching* was given by Lao-tzu to → Yin Hsi, the Guardian of the Mountain Pass, before continuing on his journey toward the West. It consists of eighty-one short chapters, the first thirty-seven of which form *The Book of the Way* (→ Tao), and the remaining forty-four the *Book of the* → *Te*. The reason for this somewhat arbitrary division is that Chapter 1 deals with the Tao and Chapter 38 with the *te*. The *Tao-te ching* contains, apart from Taoist ideas, teachings of other philosophical movements. Its central philosophy, however, revolves around two concepts: the Tao or (Way), and the *te* (virtue or power). Further central ideas of the *Tao-te ching* are → *wu-wei* (unmotivated action) and → *fu* (the return of all things to their origin or source).

The *Tao-te ching* sees the Tao as the all-embracing ultimate principle, which existed before Heaven and Earth. It is unnamable and cannot be described; it is the mother of all things; it causes everything to arise, yet acts not. Its power (*te*) is that which phenomena receive from the Tao and which makes them what they are.

The goal of philosophical Taoism consists in becoming one with the Tao by realizing within oneself the universal law of the return of everything to its source (→ *fu*). For this the aspirant must acquire the emptiness (→ *wu*) and simplicity (→ *p'u*) of the Tao and abide in nonaction (*wu-wei*). According to the *Tao-te ching,* the latter quality is also characteristic of the exemplary ruler, whose virtues it describes in some detail: the ideal ruler is one of whom the people are unaware, because he interferes as little as possible in the natural flow of things. He lays down the barest minimum of laws, whereby the number of transgressors is reduced, and attaches no value to the traditional Confucianist virtues of uprightness (→ *i*) and humanity (→ *jen*). He endeavors to diminish wishes and desires by reducing their objects, so that the hearts of the people may not be confused and simplicity—*p'u* —may be realized. Originally the *Tao-te ching* was known simply as the *Lao-tzu;* later it received its present title from an emperor of the Han Dynasty. By the designation *ching* it was raised to the same level as the Confucianist classics. More than fifty commentaries—reflecting a great variety of views—on the *Tao-te ching* have been preserved. It is quoted and referred to not only by Taoist movements but also by the Yin-Yang School (→ *yin-yang chia*), scholars of constitutional law, and followers of the → *I-ching.*

Religious Taoism (→ *tao-chiao*) venerates Lao-tzu, under his title of → Lao-chün, as its founder and bases its teaching on the main concept of the *Tao-te ching,* i.e., the Tao. For that reason, the followers of the *tao-chiao* consider it one of the sacred books: Chang Tao-ling and his descendants instructed their followers in its teaching and applied its principles. In addition, the basic text of the → *t'ai-p'ing tao,* the → *T'ai-p'ing ching,* refers to the *Book of the Way and Its Power* as its philosophical basis. Alchemists such as → Wei P'o-yang and → Chang Po-tuan quote the *Tao-te ching* in justification of their practices, and rulers like the Han emperor Wen-ti, the T'ang emperor Hsüan-tsung, and the Ming emperor T'ai-tzu made its doctrine the basis of their rulership.

Tao-tsang 🅣 Chin., Taoist canon; a collection of writings that form the basis of Taoist doctrine. The oldest sections of the *Tao-tsang* date from the 5th century C.E.; the present complete version of the canon stems from the time of the Ming Dynasty and consists of 1,476 works in 5,486 volumes. The individual works contained in it do not bear the names of their authors and are undated.

Apart from purely Taoist works dealing with all aspects of the doctrine, the *Tao-tsang* also contains texts on medicine, botany, astronomy, etc. According to tradition, most of the purely Taoist texts were revelations and thus represent a means of communication between the deities (→ *shen*) and mankind. This explains the belief that a proper understanding of the ancient Taoist texts makes it possible to penetrate the secrets of immortality.

Various works about Taoist deities and immortals (→ *hsien*) existed already at the beginning of the common era, and the catalogs of such writings compiled during the 5th and 6th centuries must be considered precursors of the *Tao-tsang,* the actual compilation of which began in the 8th century when—according to varying sources—3,744, 5,700, or even 7,300 volumes were compiled. This first canon achieved wide dissemination but was no longer extant by the end of the 10th century. In 1010 C.E. the then emperor entrusted a Taoist scholar with making a new compilation, which originally consisted of 4,359 volumes. A few years later this was expanded to 4,565 volumes, divided into three main sections and four subsections: the three main sections are known as *tung,* which, literally translated, means "grotto" (many of the texts were believed to have been concealed in grottos) but can also be understood as "penetrating a secret." Each *tung* is preceded by a text revealed by an important deity of the Taoist pantheon. The first section thus stands under the sign of the Celestial Venerable of the Primordial Beginning (→ Yüan-shih t'ien-tsun), the second under that of the Supreme Lord of the Tao (→ T'ai-shang tao-chün), and the third under the Supreme Master Lao (T'ai-shang lao-chün), i.e., Lao-tzu himself. In time, however, the view that all three sections were revealed by Lao-tzu gained ground and finally became firmly established.

Between 1111 and 1118 C.E. this last version was once again expanded and finally printed in 5,481 volumes. It has become the model on which all subsequent editions of the *Tao-tsang* were based. Due to the hostilities between the Taoists and Buddhists during the Yüan Dynasty, many Taoist scriptures were burned so that part of the canon was irretrievably lost.

Tao-wu Yuan-chih 🅩 (Jap., Dōgo Enchi), 768/69–853; Chinese Ch'an (Zen) master; a student and dharma successor (→ *hassu*) of → Yueh-shan Wei-yen (Jap., Yakusan Igen) and the master of → Shih-shuang Ch'ing-chu (Jap., Sekisō Keisho). We encounter Tao-wu in examples 55 and 89 of the → *Pi-yen-lu.* In the → *Ching-te ch'uan-teng-lu* we find the following → *hossen* between Tao-wu and his master Yueh-shan:

"One day Yueh-shan asked the master [Tao-wu], 'Where are you coming from?'

Tao-wu said, 'From a walk in the mountains.'

Yueh-shan said, 'Quick, say a word [of dharma] without leaving this room.'

Tao-wu said, 'The ravens in the mountains are as white as snow. The fish in the pond swim incessantly to and fro.'

In example 89 of the *Pi-yen-lu,* we find a → *mondo* between Tao-wu and → Yun-yen T'an-sheng (Jap., Ungan Donjō), another student and dharma successor of Yueh-shan:

"Yun-yen asked Tao-wu, 'The great compassionate bodhisattva makes use of many hands and eyes. How is that?'

"Tao-wu said, 'It is as with someone who in the middle of the night reaches behind him to straighten his pillow.'

"Yun-yen said, 'I understand.'
"Tao-wu said, 'What did you understand?'
"Yun-yen said, 'His whole body is hands and arms.'
"Tao-wu said, 'What you've said is well spoken, but it says only eight-tenths.'
"Yun-yen said, 'What does the master think then?'
"Tao-wu said, 'His whole body is hands and arms.' "

Tao-yin 🅃 Chin., lit. "stretching and contracting [of the body]"; Taoist practice of guiding the breath, consisting of a combination of physical and breathing exercises that promote and facilitate the circulation of the breath within the body by resolving tensions and blockages. *Tao-yin* may also be practiced as simply a health exercise; according to the Taoist view it dispels illness as well as bad → *ch'i* and prolongs life. Taoist adepts practice it as a preliminary exercise for → *hsing-ch'i* ("letting the breath circulate").

The various sequences of performing *tao-yin* exercises are said to have originated with immortals (→ *hsien*) such as → P'eng-tzu or Lü Tung-pin (→ *pa-hsien*).

Nowadays it is usual to perform a sequence of eight exercises. During their performance it is essential that all physical movements as well as ways of relaxing and tensing and the actual flow of the breath itself are followed with wakeful attention. The eight exercises are as follows (cf. Pálos 1984, p. 175):

1. "Clapping the teeth together and drumming" (→ *k'ou-ch'ih*, → *t'ien-ku*).
2. "Turning to the left, looking to the right" and vice versa: the head and shoulders are moved in opposite directions to loosen and relax that region of the body.
3. "Stirring the ocean and swallowing the saliva": the tongue is rotated around the cavity of the mouth and then pressed against the palate, thereby promoting the production of saliva, which is then swallowed (→ *yü-chiang*).
4. "Massaging the area around the sacrum with both hands": after rubbing his hands to warm them, the practitioner massages the area on either side of the sacrum in a downward direction with both his hands. This exercise relieves back pain and menstrual difficulties.
5. "Stretching the arms": the hands are made into fists as the arms are extended sideways, then moved back in the direction of the body as if pulling something toward it. This exercise is beneficial for people who suffer from a warped spine.
6. "Double winds": the practitioner rotates shoulders and arms in forward and backward directions while his hands (made into fists) rest against his chest. This stimulates the organ of breathing.
7. "Raising the palms (of the hands)": both arms are extended to the front with the palms of the hands turned upward, then the forearms are angled so that the palms are opposite the face This exercise harmonizes the activity of the stomach and intestines.
8. "Relaxed muscles, loose joints": the practitioner extends his legs from a sitting position, inclines his head forward, at the same time extending his arms to grab his toes. This exercise relaxes the body and stimulates the circulation.

Tapas 🄷, or Tapasyā, Skt., lit. "glow, heat, austerity, mortification"; intensive spiritual exercises, undertaken in the burning desire to realize God, or → *brahman*. Tapas is one of the five virtues required at the second stage (→ *niyama*) of → Rāja-Yoga. The other four are → *shaucha* (cleanliness, purity), → *santosha* (contentment), → *svādhyāya* (study of the holy scriptures), and → *īshvara-pranidhāna* (surrender to God.)

In the hot climate of India, heat became a symbol of struggle and mortification. Through *tapas*, the ego-directed quality of *rajas* in a human being can be transformed into a higher, spiritual force that may help the aspirant to attain his spiritual goal through a process of burning surrender and concentration.

In Vedic cosmology, the world is "incubated" (→ Hiranyagarbha) by *tapas* (heat); this imagery also contains the notion of self-mortification in that the creation represents an act of self-expression. The *Shatapatha-Brāhmana* states: "In the beginning, Prajāpati was alone. He desired: 'I will be (many), I will reproduce.' He labored, he practiced *tapas*; from him who labored and practiced *tapas* were the three worlds created, earth, heaven, and the space between. He hatched out these three worlds."

Tārā 🄱 Skt. (Tib., Dolma), lit. "savior"; an emanation of the bodhisattva → Avalokiteshvara, said to arise from his tears in order to help him in his work. She embodies the feminine aspect of compassion and is a very popular deity in → Tibetan Buddhism. The cult of Tārā was propagated in the 11th century, primarily by → Atīsha. Since that time, veneration of Tārā as a → *yidam* has been quite widespread. There are twenty-one forms of Tārā, which are differentiated iconographically by color, posture of the body, and differing attributes, and can in addition appear in either a peaceful or wrathful → form of manifestation. The most frequently encountered forms are Green Tara and White Tara. The two consorts of the Tibetan king Songtsen Gampo (7th century) are regarded as having been embodiments of these two Tārās. (See illustration on p. 364.)

A study on the importance of Tārā in Tibetan Buddhism is Beyer 1973.

Tariki 🄱 🅉 Jap., lit. "power of the other"; liberation through the power of another. Referred to here is the power of Buddha → Amitābha, who,

Green Tārā (Tibetan blockprint)

according to the conviction of the → Pure Land school, liberates all those who recite his name with devotion and have absolute trust in him and causes them to be reborn in his pure land (→ Sukhāvatī).

Tariki is used in counterdistinction to → *jiriki* ("one's own power"). From the point of view of this distinction, Zen, particularly, is seen as a Jiriki school.

Tarkavidyā 🅗 Skt. → Nyāya

Tārkikā-Buddhi, 🅗 Skt., lit. *tārkikā*, from *tarka*: "refutation, argument," *buddhi*: "intelligence, intellect"; an intellect that likes to argue endlessly. Such behavior is rejected by → Vedānta, since a counterargument can be found for every argument and no spiritual use is derived from this.

Ta-shih 🅩 Chin., lit. "great master"; → *daishi*.

Ta-sui Fa-chen 🅩 (Jap., Taizui Hōshin), ca. 9th century; Chinese Ch'an (Zen) master; a student and dharma successor (→ *hassu*) of Ch'ang-ch'ing Ta-an (Jap., Chōkei Daian, 8th/9th century), who was in turn a dharma successor of → Pai-chang Huai-hai (Jap., Hyakujō Ekai). We encounter Ta-sui in example 29 of the → *Pi-yen-lu*.

Before Ta-sui came to Ch'ang-ch'ing, he trained under → Tung-shan Liang-chieh (Jap., Tōzan Ryōkai), → Kuei-shan Ling-yu (Jap., Isan Reiyu), and other Ch'an masters. After his enlightenment he secluded himself on Mount Ta-sui and did not come down for ten years. He is said to have lived there in the trunk of a big hollow tree. Later monks gathered around him and he began to instruct them.

Tat 🅗 Skt., lit. "that"; the sages in the Vedas often use *tat* as a substantive standing for the unpronounceable principle, the unfathomable secret, the infinite Absolute, or God. Teachers who wished to initiate their pupils into the supreme knowledge of → Vedānta said to them: → *Tat tvam asi* ("Thou art that").

Tathāgata 🅑 🅩 Skt., Pali. lit. "the thus-gone [thus-come, thus-perfected] one"; refers to one who on the way of truth has attained supreme enlightenment (→ *samyak-sambuddha*). It is one of the → ten titles of the Buddha, which he himself used when speaking of himself or other buddhas.

In the Mahāyāna the *tathāgata* is the Buddha in his *nirmānakāya* (→ *trikāya*) aspect. He is both the perfected man who can take on any form and disposes of the ten powers of a buddha (→ *dashabala*) and the cosmic principle, the essence of the universe, the unconditioned. He is the intermediary between the essential and the phenomenal world. In the absolute sense, *tathāgata* is often equated with → *prajñā* and → *shūnyatā*.

Tathatā 🅑 Skt., "suchness"; central notion of the Mahāyāna referring to the absolute, the true nature of all things. *Tathatā* is generally explained as being immutable, immovable, and beyond all concepts and distinctions. "Suchness" is the opposite of "that which is apparent"—phenomena. It is formless, unmade, and devoid of self-nature (→ *svabhāva*). *Tathatā* as the thus-being of things and their nonduality is perceived through the realization of the identity of subject and object in the awakening (→ *Bodhi*) of supreme enlightenment. *Tathatā* is similar in meaning to → *tathāgata-garbha*, → buddha-nature, *dharmakāya* (→ *trikāya*), → *dharmatā*.

Tattva 🅗 Skt., lit. "truth, true being, fundamental principle"; *tat* as "that" refers to that which is essential in all things, hence *tattva* is the "is-ness" or true being. Every Indian philosophy contains a certain number of *tattvas* as the basis of its system of thought.

In → Vedānta, *tattva* is viewed as a compound of *tat* and *tvam*, which suggests the statement "That (eternal → *brahman*) art thou (if you know yourself to be the → *ātman*)." In the philosophy of → Sānkhya, there are twenty-five *tattvas* or fundamental principles: → *avyakta*, → *buddhi*, → *ahamkāra*, five → *tanmātras*, five → *māhābhūtas*, five *buddhīndriyas*, five → *karmendriyas*, → *manas*, and → *purusha*.

Tattvabodha 🅗 Skt., lit. "the knowledge of truth"; a classic work by → Shankara on the philosophy of → Advaita-Vedānta. A relatively short essay, it discusses the → *jīva*, its connection to → Īshvara, and the possibility of its knowing itself as the → *ātman*, as well as its identity with → *brahman*.

Tattva-Jñāna 🅗 Skt.; the knowledge of the principle in all things. *Tattva* is the essence, the "is-ness" of all things, and *jñāna* is the wisdom that arises from this knowledge.

Tat Tvam Asi 🅗 Skt., lit. "That thou art," that is, "the Absolute is in essence one with yourself"; one of the best known and most important → *mahāvākyas*, the great precepts of → Vedānta, contained in the → *Chāndogya-Upanishad*.

When the teacher wishes to transmit the ultimate truth to a student by means of this sentence, certain prerequisites are required on the part of the student: First of all, one must be aware that "that" refers only to → *brahman*, the Absolute, the Eternal, the Immutable. Second, one must know what is meant by "thou," a term that can be interpreted in many ways, both materially and spiritually. The student must know through personal experience that he or she is neither the body nor the mind, but rather the → *ātman*, birthless, deathless, absolute consciousness, beyond all duality and identification with the body. One who knows the self addressed as "thou" to be the *ātman* can attain enlightenment, for *atman* and *brahman* are the same. Such enlightenment cannot be brought about intellectually or effected by efforts in the realm of causality.

Ta-tung chen-ching 🅣 Chin., lit. *"True Book of the Great Secret"*; a text of the → Inner Deity Hygiene School, dating from the 2d–4th centuries C.E. Its thirty-nine chapters—each of which was revealed by a different deity—describe in esoteric language and considerable detail the most important deities of the body, thus helping the practitioner to recognize them when he encounters them in his meditative visualizations. The highest such deity is the Supreme One (→ T'ai-i).

Ta-yü 🅣 Chin., lit. "Yü the Great," also known as the "Master of the Way"; mythological founder of the Hsia Dynasty. Because he is said to have stopped a great deluge by making holes through the mountains and thus producing outlets through which the waters, which had already risen up to Heaven, could drain away, Ta-yü is sometimes referred to as the creator of the world. In addition it is believed that he traversed the nine provinces of the world (the figure nine is a symbol of wholeness) and made the land arable by regulating the course of the waters and connecting the nine provinces with each other. To this task he applied such energy that he began to walk with a limp. His limping gait became the model for the "step of Yü" (→ *Yü-pu*), a shamanic dance performed by Taoist masters.

According to legend, Great Yü received the river diagram (→ *Ho-t'u* and *Lo-shu*) from a turtle that emerged from the Yellow River.

Another tradition states that during his work Yü would turn himself into a bear. Every day his wife would bring him his food as soon as he beat his drum. One day he was breaking up rocks, the fragments of which crashed against each other, producing a sound like a drum. His wife came running with the food and fled again when she beheld a bear. Yü pursued her, but she ran on until she fell exhausted to the ground and turned to stone. As she was pregnant at the time, the stone continued to grow. At the end of the tenth month Yü opened her petrified body with a stroke of his sword and his son Ch'i (lit. "the Opener") was born.

Te 🅣 Chin., lit. "virtue, power"; the energy of the → Tao; the inherent principle, i.e., the qualities or nature each thing receives from the Tao, making it what it is, and through which it manifests in the phenomenal world. In addition, *te* signifies the virtue attained by realizing the Tao.

The *Tao-te ching* accords to *te* the same attributes as to the Tao itself: it is deep, profound, mysterious; it enables man to return to childlike innocence, natural simplicity (→ *p'u*).

Confucius (→ K'ung-tzu) considers *te* to be a quality possessed by noble and civilized human beings and argues that a sage, because of his *te*, becomes a cultural ideal and a model for his fellowmen.

Concerning the Tao and *te*, Chapter 51 of the *Tao-te ching* (Feng & English 1972) states,

All things arise from Tao.
They are nourished by Virtue [*te*].
They are formed from matter.
They are shaped by environment.
Thus the ten thousand things all respect Tao and honor Virtue.

Respect of Tao and honor of Virtue are not demanded,
But they are in the nature of things.
Therefore all things arise from Tao.
By Virtue they are nourished,
Developed, cared for,
Sheltered, comforted,
Grown, and protected.
Creating without claiming,
Doing without taking credit,
Guiding without interfering,
This is the Primal Virtue.

Teishō Z Jap., lit. "recitation offering, presentation"; in Zen the "presentation" of Zen realization by a Zen master (→ *rōshi*) during a → *sesshin.*

The word is derived from *tei*, "carry, offer, show, present, proclaim" and *shō*, "recite, proclaim." The *rōshi* offers the *teishō*—which generally has a → kōan or an important passage in Zen literature as its theme—to the buddha in the presence of the assembly of practitioners. It is not an explanation, commentary, or exposition in the usual sense and certainly not a lecture in the academic sense. Thus the frequent translation of *teishō* by "lecture" is misleading, and "presentation" is more accurate. No one is being lectured here, and purveyance of factual knowledge is not the point. The *rōshi*'s offering is free from everything conceptual. It is an immediate demonstration of his genuine insight into the theme treated and for that reason can touch the deepest mind of its hearers.

Tejas H Skt., lit. "brilliance, glow"; 1. a light that sometimes surrounds the head of one who is meditating or that of a spiritual master; known in the West as an "aura"; 2. fiery spirit, one of the four "perfections of the heart" (→ *kalyāna-shraddhā*).

Tejobindu-Upanishad H (Tejobindu-Upaniṣad), Skt., lit. "the dot that signifies the power of *brahman*"; a Yoga-Upanishad of the → *Atharvaveda.* Its name, taken from the word with which the text begins, refers to the dot in the written symbol for → OM, which symbolizes the power of *brahman.* In only fourteen verses the Upanishad covers the main elements of → Vedānta.

The text is clearly divided into five sections. The first section discusses the difficulty of meditation (→ *dhyāna*); the second lists the requirements to be fulfilled by one who is called to meditation; the third concerns *brahman* as the object of meditation; the fourth speaks of the nature of *brahman*, which is not to be grasped by reason; the fifth describes the → *jīvanmukta*, the one who is released while still in the body.

Tekiden Z Jap., lit. "authorized transmission"; the transmission, confirmed by → *inka-shōmei*, of → *buddha-dharma* from a Zen master (→ *rōshi*) of a living Zen lineage to his student (→ *hassu*). (Also → *sanmotsu.*)

Tempyō Z Jap. for → T'ien-p'ing

Ten contemplations B → *anussati*

Tendai school B Japanese form of the Chinese → T'ien-t'ai school, brought to Japan from China in the 8th century by → Saichō (Dengyō Daishi). There are no essential doctrinal differences between the Chinese and Japanese forms of the school. An important representative of the Tendai school was → Ennin.

In Japan there were three subschools of Tendai: Sammon, Jimon, and Shinsei. The central focus in the Shinsei school is veneration of Buddha → Amitābha.

Tendai Tokushō Z Jap. for → T'ien-t'ai Teshao

Ten disgusting objects B → *ashubha*

Tendō Nyojō Z Jap. for T'ien-t'ung Ju-ching

Ten epithets of a buddha B stereotypic descriptions of a buddha to be found in many sūtras: perfect (→ *tathāgata*), holy one or saint (→ *arhat*), fully enlightened (→ *samyak-sambuddha*), gifted in knowledge and conduct, well-gone one, knower of the worlds, unsurpassable teacher of men, teacher of gods and men, awakened one (buddha), sublime one.

Ten great disciples of the Buddha B Z the ten most important students of the Buddha, who are frequently mentioned in the sūtras of the → Mahāyāna: (1) → Mahākāshyapa, who is considered the first patriarch of the Indian lineage of Ch'an (→ Zen); (2) → Ānanda, who "heard much," the second Indian patriarch of Ch'an (Zen)—with Mahākāshyapa he is often represented next to the figure of the Buddha; (3) → Shāriputra, who was distinguished by his wisdom and in the → Hīnayāna sūtras is the most important disciple of the Buddha; (4) → Subhūti, the expounder of the emptiness (→ *shūnyatā*) of existents; (5) Pūrna, the expounder of the → dharma; (6) → Mahāmaudgalyāyana, who was distinguished by his supernatural powers—he and Shāriputra constitute the most important pair of disciples in the Mahāyāna; (7) Katyāyana, the master of discussion and exegesis; (8) Aniruddha, the master in the use of the "heavenly eye" (→ *abhijñā*); (9) → Upāli, who was responsible for disciplinary and ritual questions; (10) → Rāhula, the son of the Buddha and master of esoteric activities.

Tengyur 🅑 Tib. → Kangyur-Tengyur

Tenjin 🅩 also Tenshin, Jap., lit. "enlightenment [*ten-tenjiru,* "to illuminate"] of the mind [*jin* = *shin,* → *kokoro*]"; Zen expression for a refreshment, a small snack, also for a particular kind of small cake eaten as a snack.

Zen monks coming back from → *takuhatsu* are sometimes invited by laypeople who are supporters of their particular monastery into their houses to eat. The food presented to the monks on such an occasion, which has a function similar to donations during *takuhatsu,* is also called *tenjin.*

Tenjō tenge yuiga dokuson 🅩 Jap., lit. "Above Heaven [and] under Heaven I alone [am] worthy of honor;" a pronouncement said to have been made by → Shākyamuni Buddha after his complete → enlightenment. It bears witness to an awareness of the identity of *I* (one's own true nature or buddha-nature [→ *busshō*], not to be confused with → ego) with the true nature of the entire universe. There is only one true nature, and nothing else. One who has realized this, has, as the Zen expression says, "swallowed the universe."

Tennō Dōgo 🅩 Jap. for → T'ien-huang Tao-wu

Ten Oxherding Pictures 🅩 → *Jūgyū(-no)-zu*

Ten powers 🅑 → *dashabala*

Tenryū 🅩 Jap. for T'ien-lung, → Hang-chou T'ien-lung

Tenryū-ji 🅩 Jap.; one of the great Zen monasteries of Kyōto, built by Shōgun Ashikaga Takauji in 1339. Its first abbot was → Musō Soseki, who also designed the famous landscape garden of the monastery. Tenryū-ji is one of the "Five Mountains (→ Gosan) of Kyōto.

Ten Wings 🅣 → *Shih-i*

Tenzo 🅩 Jap.; term for the head cook, or kitchen master, of a Zen monastery. This position is considered one of the most responsible in the monastery and thus it is generally held by an advanced elder monk.

In ancient China a number of monks who later became great Ch'an (→ Zen) masters, served as *tenzo*: for example, → Kuei-shan Ling-yu, → Tung-shan Shou-ch'u, and → Hsueh-feng I-ts'ung. The activity of the *tenzo* is distinguished from that of an ordinary cook primarily by the mental attitude on which it is based. The *tenzo* sees his work as service to the three precious ones (→ *sambō*) and as an opportunity for spiritual training. If he fully considers the needs of the monks in terms of quantity and quality of food, if he makes each move with wakeful attention, avoids all waste, comports himself properly with regard to foodstuffs and utensils, then his kitchen work becomes an exercise in maintaining the mind of Zen in everyday life.

The great Japanese Zen master → Dōgen Zenji composed a small work, *Tenzo kyokun* (*Instruction for the Kitchen Master*) on the duties and mental attitude of a *tenzo.*

Tera 🅩 Jap. also *O-tera* or, after a name, *-dera* or *-ji,* where → *-ji* is the Sino-Japanese way of reading the character for *tera*; temple or monastery. It may be a complex of buildings, composed of main hall, lecture hall, the founder's room, and the living quarters of the monks, on premises entered through a massive towerlike gateway. However, it may also be a small single structure. If monks live in a *tera,* then the translation "monastery" is appropriate; if it only used for prayer, then it is a "temple."

Of all the Buddhist schools of Japan today, only Zen still maintains an authentic monastic system. It is organized on fundamental principles laid down by → Pai-chang Huai-hai in China in the 8th century. Simplicity and frugality distinguish this monastic life. The object of the training in a Zen monastery is not only → enlightenment (also → *kenshō,* → satori) but also cultivation of fortitude, humility, and gratitude—in other words a strong character. Monastic training is comprised chiefly of daily → *zazen,* periodic → sesshins, physical work (→ samu), and → *takuhatsu.*

In the Zen school novices must spend an average of three years in a Zen monastery before they are eligible to serve as priests in temple or monastery. Such priests, however, are by no means Zen masters (→ *rōshi,* → *hassu,* → *inka-shōmei*). Temples and monasteries in present-day Japan are often hereditary within a family of priests. This can only lead to deterioration in the Zen tradition in the case where such priests lack enlightenment.

Terma 🅑 (gter-ma), Tib., lit. "treasure." In Tibetan Buddhism, a term for religious texts, which during the first spread of Buddhism in Tibet during the 8th century were hidden in secret places, so that at the right time they would be discovered and newly expounded by qualified persons—the *tertön.* These are regarded as authoritative works primarily by the → Nyingmapa school but also by the → Bön school and later by the → Rime movement. The preservation of religious literature in hidden places is a practice handed down from an earlier period in India. Thus → Nāgārjuna is said to have found teachings, which he later propagated, in the realm of the serpent spirits (→ *nāga*), where they were being guarded from falling into the wrong hands.

The Nyingmapas possess by far the most voluminous *terma* literature, of which the most important works derive from → Padmasambhava and his female companion → Yeshe Tsogyel. These works are based not only on Indian sources but also on teachings from the land of → Urgyen. According to his biography, Padmasambhava hid his works in 108 different places in Tibet, in caves, statues, etc. Among the best-known *terma* texts are just this biography of Padmasambhava and the *Tibetan Book of the Dead* (→ *Bardo thödol*). In addition, works on astrology and the basic text on Tibetan medicine were transmitted as *terma*.

Between the 10th and 14th centuries, discoverers of *terma* periodically appeared, whose discoveries often took place through dreams and visions. Receiving an indication or clue in this manner, they reconstituted the works so found and furnished them with commentaries. Among the many *tertön*, the Nyingmapas give the highest place to the five "kings of the treasure finders," among whom Urgyen Pema Lingpa (1445–1521) is regarded as an incarnation of → Longchenpa.

In some cases, works once discovered were rehidden, as the time was not yet ripe for their propagation. These texts are known as "twice-hidden treasures."

Tertön 🅱 Tib. → terma

Te-shan Hsuan-chien 🅩 (Jap., Tokusan Senkan), ca. 781–867; great Chinese Ch'an (Zen) master; a student and dharma successor (→ *hassu*) of → Lung-t'an Ch'ung-hsin (Jap., Ryūtan Sōshin). Te-shan had nine dharma successors, among whom → Yen-t'ou Ch'uan-huo (Jap., Gantō Zenkatsu) and → Hsueh-feng I-ts'un (Jap., Seppō Gison) are the best known. As the master of Hsueh-feng, from whom both the → Ummon school and the → Hōgen school derive, he was one of the forefathers of these schools and one of the most important Zen masters of the T'ang period. He appears in examples 13 and 28 of the → *Wu-men-kuan* and in example 4 of the → *Pi-yen-lu*.

Te-shan was a Buddhist scholar from Szechuan. His given name was Chou, and since he was especially well versed in the teachings of the → *Diamond Sūtra* and had composed a learned commentary on it, he was called Diamond Chou. In this sūtra it is said that it requires thousands of world ages for a person to attain buddhahood. When Te-shan heard that there was a Buddhist school in the south (the → Southern school) that asserted that "[one's own] mind is Buddha," he packed up his commentaries and headed south with the intention—as he thought—of refuting this false teaching. On the way he met an old woman, who made clear to him with a single comment that he, the great scholar, had not really grasped the deep meaning of the *Diamond Sūtra*. When Te-shan asked her about a master who had realized this deep meaning, she sent him to Master Lung-t'an. (For more on this, see Master Yuan-wu K'o-ch'in's commentary on example 4 of the *Pi-yen-lu*.)

In example 28 of the *Wu-men-kuan*, we hear of Te-shan's enlightenment under Master Lung-t'an:

> Once Te-shan was asking Lung-t'an for instruction late into the night. Lung-t'an said, "It is the middle of the night. Will you not retire?" Te-shan took his leave, raised the door hanging, and went out. As he saw the darkness outside, he turned around and said, "Dark outside."
>
> At this Lung-t'an lit a paper torch and handed it to him. Te-shan was about to take it when Lung-t'an blew it out.
>
> All of sudden Te-shan had a moment of insight. He prostrated.
>
> Lung-t'an said, "What truth did you see?"
>
> Te-shan said, "From now on this one here [I] will not harbor doubts about the words of the old master [famous everywhere] under Heaven."
>
> The next day Lung-t'an ascended the high seat and said, "Among you there is a fellow with fangs like a sword-tree and a mouth like a bowl full of blood. If you hit him, he won't turn his head. One day he'll settle on some lonesome peak and establish our way there."
>
> Then Te-shan took his commentaries [on the *Diamond Sūtra*], went to the front of the dharma hall and said, "Even if we have mastered the profound doctrine, it is only like placing a hair in vast space; even if we have exhausted the essential wisdom of the world, it is only letting a drop fall into a great abyss." He picked up his commentaries and burnt them. Then he bowed and departed.

After thirty years of living in hiding, Te-shan finally yielded with reluctance to pressure from the governor of Wu-lin in Honan to assume the leadership of the monastery on Mount Te-shan, from which his name is derived. Te-shan became famous for his use of the stick (→ *shippei*, → *kyosaku*) in training his students (also → Bōkatsu). The following remark of his has been handed down: "Thirty blows if you speak; thirty blows if you remain silent!"

Tetsuya 🅩 Jap., lit. "[sitting] through the night"; the last night of the → Rōhatsu sesshin.

Tha 🅗 Skt. → Hatha-Yoga

Thākur 🅗 Bengali for → Tagore

Thangka 🅱 (thaṅ-ka) roughly "picture, painting." In → Tibetan Buddhism, a scroll painting framed in silk, which fulfills various religious functions. The themes of iconography are fixed by tradition and are based on three principles: expression, proportion, detail. Commissioning the painting of a *thangka* and the painting itself are considered highly meritorious actions.

The images are painted on linen with vegetable- and mineral-based pigments. In some cases they serve as visual reminders of general Buddhist teachings—examples are the wheel of life (→ *bhava-chakra*) or the depictions of the previous existences of the Buddha (→ *jātaka*). In other cases *thangkas* play an important ritual role—as, for example, detailed paintings of central personalities of a particular school being used for taking refuge (→ *kyabdro*). However, the most important role of the *thangka* is connected with the performance of *sādhanas*, where the picture functions as support for memory in the process of visualization. Painted → *mandalas* fulfill the same purpose.

Up to the 16th century, various traditions of *thangka* painting developed in Tibet. Among the best-known is the *karma sgar bris* style of the → Karma Kagyu.

Thangtong Gyelpo B (Thaṅ-stoṅ rgyal-po), Tib., lit. "king of the wilderness." A famous teacher of → Tibetan Buddhism in the 15th century, of whom it is said that he died at the age of 125.

One of his most important contributions is a text on the practice of meditation (→ *sādhana*) on → Avalokiteshvara. This text is still used today in the → Karma Kagyu school, and commentaries on it were written in the 19th century by teachers like Jamgon Kongtrul and the 15th Karmapa, Khachab Dorje. Thangtong Gyelpo built bridges held by iron chains throughout Tibet, and the school founded by him bore the epithet Iron Bridge School. He is also considered the father of various aspects of Tibetan folk culture—for instance, drama—and there is also a tradition of the → Chöd teaching that derives from him. For the → Nyingmapa school, Thangtong Gyelpo was important as a "treasure finder" (→ *terma*).

Theosophical Society H an esoteric organization founded in New York in 1875 by Helena Petrovna Blavatsky and Colonel Henry S. Olcott, who was also its first president. In 1882 the organization's headquarters were moved to Adyar, a suburb of Madra, India; its name thereafter became the Adyar Theosophical Society. Its goals include the intense study of the ancient world religions for the purpose of deriving a universal ethical code. The society was at first closely connected with Buddhism, but from 1894 on it drew close to Hinduism. The society's publishing house contributed much to the dissemination of Hindu philosophy in the West.

Thera B Pali; monks (→ *bhikshu*) who have either belonged for many years to the order or who have distinguished themselves through particular wisdom or erudition as exemplified in the following four qualities: honorable character, perfect mastery of the most important teachings of Buddhism, excellence in the practice of meditation (→ *dhyāna*), awareness of having attained liberation through elimination of spiritual defilements.

Thera-gāthā B Pali → *Khuddaka-nikāya*

Theravāda B Pali, lit. "teaching of the elders of the order"; Hīnayāna school (also called the Pali school) belonging to the → Sthavira group, which developed from the → Vibhajyavādin school. It was founded by Moggaliputta Tissa (→ Buddhist council) and brought to Ceylon in 250 B.C.E. by → Mahinda, where it was propagated by the monks of the Mahāvihāra monastery. Conflicts over disciplinary questions led to schisms within the Theravāda. Today the Theravāda is widespread in the countries of Southeast Asia (Sri Lanka, Burma, Thailand, Kampuchea, Laos, etc.).

Theravāda, today the only surviving school of the Hīnayāna, regards itself as the school closest to the original form of Buddhism. Its canon, composed in Pali, comes according to the view of the Theravādins, directly from the mouth of Buddha (→ Tripitaka). The teaching of the Theravāda consists essentially of the → four noble truths, the → eightfold path, the doctrine of conditioned arising (→ *pratītya-samutpāda*), and the doctrine of → *anātman*. The emphasis in the Theravāda is on the liberation of the individual, which takes place through one's own effort (in meditation), and through observance of the rules of moral discipline (→ *shīla*) and leading a monastic life. The → arhat is the ideal figure of the Theravāda.

In the Theravāda, which exhibits a strongly analytical bent, the → Abhidharma is of great importance. Important noncanonical works of this school are the → *Visuddhi-magga* and the → *Milindapañha*. Among its outstanding dogmatic theorists are → Buddhaghosha, → Dhammapāla, → Anuruddha, and → Buddhadatta.

Therī B Pali; eldest nun in a community of Buddhist nuns (→ *bhikshunī*), reckoned from the time of entry into the → *sangha*. (Also → *thera*.)

Therī-gāthā 🅱 Pali → *Khuddaka-nikāya*

Third Eye 🅷 🅱 → chakra 6.

Thirty-two marks of perfection 🅱 → *dvātrimshadvara-lakshana*

Threefold refuge 🅱 → *trisharana*

Three jewels 🅱 → *triratna*

Three liberations 🅱 also, three gates of nirvāna (Skt., vimoksha; Pali, vimokka); a meditation practice that prepares the way to nirvāna through realization of emptiness (→ *shūnyatā*), formlessness (→ *animitta*), and passionlessness. The three liberations are the recognition of ego and all dharmas as empty; the recognition of all dharmas as formless and devoid of distinctions; the recognition of existence as unworthy of desire since it is characterized by suffering.

Three precious ones 🅱 → *triratna*

Three truths 🅱 → T'ien-t'ai school

Three woeful paths 🅱 → *apāya*

Three worlds 🅱 → *triloka*

Throne of the Buddha 🅱 takes for the most part three forms: the lion throne, the lotus flower, Mount → Meru represented with the shape of an hourglass. The lion symbolizes the might of a ruler and also embodies the victorious power of the Buddhist teaching.

The lotus flower is a symbol of purity but is also considered a cosmic symbol. It is attributed to the Buddha as a universal spiritual ruler and an embodiment of the absolute. This form of the Buddha's seat appears first in → Gandhāra in the 3d/4th century, particularly in depictions of the Buddha expounding the teachings.

The third type is common primarily in China and Japan. It is a rectangular or round pedestal that is broadened at the top and bottom and tapered toward the middle, thus giving the form of an hourglass. This throne symbolizes the world mountain, Mount Meru.

Sometimes the Buddha is also depicted sitting on the body of a nine-headed serpent, who holds his heads protectively over the Buddha. This form, which was widespread in lower India, derives from the story of the Buddha's visit to a serpent king (→ *nāga*). In another variant, two deer, usually holding the wheel of teaching (→ dharma-chakra) between them, kneel before the throne. This recalls the first expounding of the teaching in the Deer Park in → Sārnāth near Benares.

Ti 🆃 Chin., lit. Lord, God, also known as Shang-ti (Supreme Lord); the oldest Chinese designation for a supreme being. In legend, Ti is the primordial ancestor of the people of Shang (2d millennium B.C.E.). The meaning of *Ti* in Taoist texts varies.

On the basis of oracular inscriptions, scholars have established that in ancient times Ti was considered one of the highest rulers and was credited with supernatural powers as well as the ability to influence natural phenomena such as rain, drought, the harvest, etc. He was furthermore thought to direct and determine the fate of people, but was not venerated as a lord of fate in religious rites. Later *Ti* became an honorary title for royal ancestors.

At the time of Confucius the terms *Ti* and *Shang-ti* had already been replaced by *t'ien* (Heaven). In the *Chuang-tzu, Ti* is used in the sense of "God"; for example, death is referred to as the "loosening of the bands by Ti." The *Tao-te ching* considers Ti to be subordinate to the → Tao. Other philosophers considered Ti to have been a personal god.

T'iao-ch'i 🆃 Chin., lit. "harmonizing the breaths"; Taoist breathing technique performed as a preliminary to other breathing exercises (→ *fu-ch'i*, → *hsing-ch'i*, → *lien-ch'i*).

The practitioner of *t'iao-ch'i* assumes the prescribed posture (usually the lotus position) and begins by inhaling and exhaling three times to dissolve any blockages. He then calms his mind and endeavors to forget his body. He continues to breathe calmly and deeply, exhaling the contaminated breath through his mouth and inhaling the pure breath through the nose. This cycle is repeated six or seven times.

Tibetan Book of the Dead 🅱 → *Bardo thödol*

Tibetan Buddhism 🅱 also called Lamaism in Western literature, a form of Mahāyāna Buddhism practiced not only in Tibet but also in the neighboring countries of the Himālaya. The specific nature of Tibetan Buddhism comes from the fusion of the monastic rules of the → Sarvāstivāda and the cultic methodology of the → Vajrayāna. The foundations of Tibetan Buddhism were laid in the 8th century under the protective rulership of King Trisong Detsen (755–97) by the Indian scholar Shāntirakshita and by → Padmasambhava. This so-called first spreading of Buddhism in Tibet ended in the middle of the 9th century. The → Nyingmapa school bases its instruction on the traditions initiated during this period. After a time of politically motivated persecution of Buddhism, the 11th century brought a revival. Among others, the → Kagyupa and → Sakyapa schools developed, and a major part of the Buddhist writings of India were translated into Tibetan (→ Kangyur-Tengyur). Starting at the end of the 14th century, the Gelugpa school arose and developed and became the last of the four principal schools of Tibetan Buddhism. Each of these great doctrinal traditions is distinguished by its own synthesis of philosophical theories and practical applications of them in meditation.

Before the introduction of Buddhism, a kingdom supported by the → Bön religion dominated Tibet. Under King Songtsen Gampo (620–49) the Tibetan royal house converted to Buddhism. Following a revival of the Bön religion, under King Langdarma (838–42) a persecution of Buddhism and its ordained followers took place. Exempt from this was only the so-called "white community," composed of married laypeople who wore white robes. Their tradition became the basis of the Nyingmapa school.

The second spreading of the Buddhist teaching started from west Tibet as a result of the missionary activity of → Atīsha. The newly aroused interest in Buddhism, a central feature of which was authority and validity of teachings based on direct transmission from teacher to student, led to the founding of the main monastery of the Sakyapa school (1073) and to the journeys of → Marpa the Translator, father of the Kagyupa school. The development of the monastic tradition and intensive efforts to perpetuate the teachings of Indian Buddhism were definitively shaped by individual Buddhist masters (→ lama), who conferred upon Tibetan Buddhism its own form and character. The most important master was the reformer → Tsongkhapa, who reorganized the various traditions into a new overview and, with the founding of Ganden Monastery (1409), brought the Gelugpa school into existence.

Though other doctrinal traditions—for example, that of → Chöd—produced a noteworthy literature, they did not develop a monastic culture and thus eventually merged into the main schools. The basis for their approach was a movement, running parallel to the monastic tradition, that was modeled on the ideal of the Indian → *mahāsiddhas.*

With the rules of discipline (→ Vinaya), the Mahāyāna teachings of → Nāgārjuna and → Asanga are the great pillars of Tibetan Buddhism. Logic is regarded as an aid to the understanding of doctrine. Finally, the Tantras emphasize the realization of theory in direct experience.

T'ien 🅃 Chin., lit. "Heaven"; religious Taoism (→ *tao-chiao*)—following the example of Buddhism—recognizes thirty-six heavens, arranged on six levels and inhabited by different deities.

The lowest level consists of the six heavens of desire. This is followed by the eighteen heavens of the world of forms. Above these are the four heavens of formlessness, followed by the four heavens of Brahma. On the penultimate level are the heavens of the three pure ones (→ *san-ch'ing*), which are inhabited by the celestial venerables (→ *t'ien-tsun*) and are the most important heavens in Taoism. The highest Taoist heaven is the *ta-luo-t'ien,* the Heaven of the Great Web. The descriptions of this supreme heaven in ancient texts vary considerably: some describe it as empty (uninhabited), others as the seat of the Celestial Venerable of the Primordial Beginning (→ Yüan-shih t'ien-tsun). This last and highest heaven separates the universe from the great darkness.

The *Tao-te ching* considers *t'ien* to be synonymous with the → Tao. The *Lü-shih ch'un-ch'iu* states, "Heaven is invisible and begets, Earth is visible and forms." In the *I-ching,* Heaven is symbolized by the hexagram *ch'ien* (→ *ch'ien* and *k'un*) and corresponds to pure yang (→ yin-yang). It represents the male principle, as opposed to Earth, which is yin and female.

T'ien already was a central concept in Chinese thought during the Chou Dynasty. It referred to a supreme being, which influenced man's destiny by virtue of a celestial mandate (→ *t'ien-ming*). Heaven preserved order and calm, but also caused catastrophes and punished human transgressions. This supreme being reveals itself only to those who cultivate their innermost self and their virtue. The *Shih-ching* (*"Book of Songs"*)—a Confucianist classic—states, "Heaven in producing mankind annexed its laws to every faculty and relationship. Man possessed of this nature should strive to develop its endowment to perfection" (Chang Chung-yuan 1963, p. 63).

In Confucianism, *t'ien* generally means "God" but can also refer to the material sky, to fate, or to nature. When *t'ien* designates an ethical principle, it is considered the highest such principle in the universe.

Heaven is also symbolically represented by the so-called Pi disc—a round disc, the outer rim of which is twice as wide as the diameter of the circular hole at its center.

Furthermore, the emperor is referred to as "Son of Heaven" (T'ien-tzu) and considered to be a mediator between Heaven and man, because he combines in himself both secular and sacred power. His sacred power he receives from Heaven in the form of his celestial mandate.

T'ien-huang Tao-wu 🅉 (Jap., Tennō Dōgo), 738/48–807, Chinese Ch'an (Zen) master; a student and dharma successor (→ *hassu*) of → Shih-t'ou Hsi-ch'ien (Jap., Sekitō Kisen) and the master of Lung-t'an Ch'ung-hsin (Jap., Ryūtan Soshin).

T'ien-i 🅃 Chin. → *san-i*

T'ien-ku ▮ Chin., lit. "heavenly drum"; Taoist health exercise. To "beat the heavenly drum," the practitioner places the palms of his hands over his ears in such a way that the fingertips touch behind his head. He then presses upon the middle finger of his right hand with the index finger of his left and allows the latter to slide off the former, so that it knocks against the back of his head, producing a sound similar to that of a drum.

This exercise is performed before various breathing exercises and is said to prevent harmful influences.

T'ien-kuan ▮ → *san-kuan*

T'ien-lung ▮ → Hang-chou T'ien-lung

T'ien-ming ▮ Chin., lit. "celestial mandate"; the mandate by virtue of which the Son of Heaven, i.e., the Chinese emperor, rules. The notion of a celestial mandate has been traced back to the Yin and Chou dynasties. The ruler received his mandate directly from heaven, whereby his rule was legitimized and at the same time made subject to certain limitations. It was the task of the ruler to recognize the signs of heavenly wrath and heavenly approval and act accordingly. Abnormal or unusual natural phenomena were considered to be an indication of heavenly disapproval, which compelled the ruler to reexamine and correct his rulership so as to bring it once again into harmony with the will of heaven.

This understanding of the idea of a celestial mandate is also found in the philosophy of Confucius (→ K'ung-tzu). He took *t'ien-ming* to be the will of Heaven—a power directed at a specific aim. In *Analects* (*Lun-yü*) 2.4 we read, "At the age of fifty, I knew the will of Heaven."

T'ien-ping ▮ (Jap., Tempyō), 8th/9th century; Chinese Ch'an (Zen) master; a student and a fourth-generation dharma successor (→ *hassu*) of → Hsueh-feng I-ts'un (Jap., Seppō Gison). We encounter Master T'ien-ping in example 98 of the → *Pi-yen-lu*.

T'ien-shih ▮ Chin., lit. "celestial master"; title borne by all Taoist masters who were genealogical descendants of → Chang Tao-ling. The *t'ien-shih* were the leaders of Five-Pecks-of-Rice Taoism (→ *wu-tou-mi tao*) and its successor, the School of Right Unity (→ *cheng-i tao*).

The title *celestial master* has been passed on within the Chang family to this day. Up to the time of the Communist takeover the *t'ien-shih* lived on → Lung-hu-shan in Kiangsi Province; the present holder of the title lives in Taiwan.

Western scholars often wrongly translate *t'ien-shih* as "Taoist pope." From its very beginnings, religious Taoism (→ *tao-chiao*) did not recognize a central authority in charge of all schools and factions. Instead, each monastery or congregation had its own hierarchical structure. In some cases, several monasteries (→ *kuan*) were ruled by the leader of the school to which they belonged, but in most cases the abbot, i.e., the → *tao-shih*, held the highest position in the hierarchy. The authority of a *t'ien-shih* was formal rather than factual. He issued two types of diplomas, which he awarded to *tao-shih* in recognition of their office. Thereafter, these *tao-shih* were able to settle with their families in a place of their choice and there performed their spiritual functions, which mainly consisted of casting out demons and warding off evil spirits.

T'ien-shu ▮ Chin., lit. "celestial writing"; Taoism distinguishes between two types of *t'ien-shu:* (1) natural *t'ien-shu* (Chinese pictograms that resemble clouds in the sky and can only be understood by those who have realized the → Tao) and (2) Taoist texts written in so-called cloud script (→ *yün-chuan*).

T'ien-t'ai school ▮ Chin., lit. "School of the Celestial Platform"; school of Buddhism that received its definitive form from → Chih-i (538–97). Its doctrine is based on the → *Lotus Sūtra*, thus it is often called the Lotus school.

The T'ien-t'ai school sees → Nāgārjuna as its first patriarch, because its doctrine of three truths is derived from Nāgārjuna's thesis that everything that arises conditionally is empty (→ *shūnyatā*). The school takes as a premise that all phenomena are an expression of the absolute, of "suchness" (→ *tathatā*), and this is expressed in the teaching of the three truths, which distinguishes the truth of emptiness; of temporal limitation, i.e. of the phenomenal world; and of the middle.

The first truth says that → dharmas possess no independent reality and thus are empty.

The second truth says that a dharma has the temporally limited apparent existence of phenomena and can be perceived by the senses.

The third truth is a synthesis of the first and second. It is the truth of the "middle," which stands above the two others and includes them. This truth of the middle is equated with suchness, the true state that is not to be found elsewhere than in phenomena. According to this truth, phenomena and the absolute are one.

This view stresses the notions of totality and mutual interpenetration. The whole and its parts are one, all dharmas are merged with one another to such an extent that each also contains the others. Emptiness, phenomenality, and the middle are identical and are aspects of a single existence: "The whole world is contained in a mustard seed," and "One thought is the 3,000 worlds," as the masters of this school express it. By the latter saying is meant that one thought embodies the universality of all things.

The practice of the school consists of meditation based on the methods of → *chih-kuan.* It contains esoteric elements such as → mudrās and → mandalas.

The T'ien-t'ai school is generally considered a syncretistic school, since it synthesizes all the extremes and one-sided views of other schools. This is seen in the school's classification of the teaching of Buddha into "five periods and eight teachings." It is considered universal because it advocates the notion of universal liberation, which is possible because all beings and things possess → buddha-nature and because they all make use of available means for the realization of enlightenment. The most important works of the T'ien-t'ai school are *Mahā-shamatha-vipashyanā* (Chin., *Mo-he chih-kuan*), *Six Wondrous Gates of Liberation* (Chin., *Liu-miao-fa-men*), and various commentaries on the *Lotus Sūtra*, all by Chih-i.

The school was brought to Japan in the 9th century by → Saichō, a student of the 10th patriarch of the school, Tao-sui. There it is known under the name → Tendai and is one of the most important Buddhist schools.

The main practice of *Chih-kuan* has two aspects: *chih* is concentration or collectedness and brings us to recognize that all dharmas are empty. In this way the further arising of illusions is prevented. *Kuan* (insight, contemplation) causes us to recognize that though dharmas are empty, they have apparent, temporary existence and fulfill the function of conventionality. The classification of sūtras and the teachings of Buddha into five periods and eight teachings by Chih-i represents an attempt to systematize the teachings of Buddha and to explain through a division in terms of chronology and content the arising within Buddhism of different doctrines and ways of solving metaphysical problems. It shows that the T'ien-t'ai school, more than any other, is eager to unify all forms of Buddhism within itself. It provides a place for the most widely different sūtras and regards the → Hīnayāna as well as the Mahāyāna as an authentic doctrinal expression of the Buddha.

The division into five periods is based on chronological criteria: the period (1) of the → *Buddhāvatamsaka-sūtra,* (2) of the → Āgamas, (3) of the → Vaipulya-sūtras (the first stage of Mahāyāna), (4) of the → *Prajñāpāramitā-sūtra,* (5) of the → *Lotus Sūtra* and the → *Mahāparinirvāna-sūtra.*

The first phase of the Buddha's teaching, which lasted three weeks, is represented according to Chih-i by the *Buddhāvatamsaka-sūtra,* which the Buddha is supposed to have taught immediately following his enlightenment. His students, however, did not understand the principal idea of the sūtra, that the universe is the expression of the absolute. Thus the Buddha decided to teach the Āgamas (second period). In these, he did not teach the complete truth, but went only so far as the understanding of his students permitted. He presented the → four noble truths, the → eightfold path, and the teaching of conditioned arising (→ *pratītya-samutpāda*). This phase lasted twelve years.

In the third period, which spanned eight years, the Buddha taught the first level of the Mahāyāna. In it he stressed the superiority of a → bodhisattva over an → arhat and the unity of Buddha and sentient beings, of absolute and relative. The fourth period, which lasted twenty-two years, contains the teachings of the *Prajñāpāramitā-sūtra,* i.e., of *shūnyatā* and the nonexistence of all opposites.

In the fifth and last period, which corresponds to the last eight years of Buddha's life, he emphasized the absolute identity of all opposites. The three vehicles (→ *triyāna*) of the → *shrāvakas,* → *pratyeka-buddhas,* and bodhisattvas have only temporary or provisional validity and merge into a single vehicle (→ *ekayāna*). According to the T'ien-t'ai view, in this last period, that of the *Lotus Sūtra,* the Buddha expounded the complete and perfect teaching.

This represents a chronological division of the teaching. Yet the school holds the view that the Buddha also taught the teachings of the five periods simultaneously, and this leads to a systematization of the Buddha's teaching into eight doctrines, four of which are to be considered from the point of view of method and four from the point of view of content.

The first group includes:

1. The sudden method, which is to be used with the most talented students who understand the truth directly. This is the method of the *Buddhāvatamsaka-sūtra.*

2. The gradual method, which progresses from elementary to more complex doctrines and includes the Āgama, Vaipulya-sūtra, and *Prajñāpāramitā-sūtra* periods. The *Lotus Sūtra* is not included here, since its approach is neither sudden nor gradual; rather it contains the ultimate truth taught by the Buddha.

3. The secret method, which was used by the Buddha only when addressing one person, in which case he was understood only by this person. Other people could have been present, but owing to the supernatural power of the Buddha, they would not have been aware of each other or of what he said to them individually.

4. The indeterminate method, in which, though the individual students were aware of each other, they heard and understood his words in different ways.

The last two methods were used by the Buddha when he wanted to instruct students of different capacities at the same time.

Then there are the four categories that are differentiated from the point of view of content:

1. The teachings of the Hīnayāna, meant for *shrāvakas* and *pratyeka-buddhas.*

2. The general teaching, which is common to Hīnayāna and Mahāyāna and is meant for *shrāvakas, pratyeka-buddhas,* and lower-level bodhisattvas.

3. The special teaching for bodhisattvas.

4. The complete, "round" teaching, that of the → Middle Way of mutual identification.

The period of the *Buddhāvatamsaka-sutra* includes special and "round" teachings, that of the Āgamas only the teachings of the Hīnayāna, the Vaipulya phase all four doctrines; the *Prajñāpāramitā-sūtra* contains "round" but also general and special teachings. Only the *Lotus Sūtra* can be regarded as really "round" and complete.

T'ien-t'ai Te-shao 🅉 (Jap., Tendai Tokushō), 891–972; Chinese Ch'an (Zen) master; a student and dharma successor (→ *hassu*) of → Fa-yen Wen-i (Jap., Hōgen Bun'eki) and the master of → Yung-ming Yen-shou (Jap., Yōmyō Enju).

T'ien-ti 🅃 Chin., lit. "Heaven and Earth"; conventional expression to designate the universe (→ *wan-wu*).

T'ien-tsun 🅃 Chin., lit. "celestial venerable"; title accorded to the highest deities in religious Taoism (→ *tao-chiao,* → *shen*). The most important *t'ien-tsun* are the Celestial Venerable of the Primordial Beginning (→ Yüan-shih t'ien-tsun), the Celestial Venerable of the Magic Jewel (Ling-pao t'ien-tsun), and the Celestial Venerable of the Tao and the Te (Tao-te t'ien-tsun, → *san-ch'ing*). In addition, the Jade Emperor (→ Yü-huang) is venerated as a *t'ien-tsun.*

The celestial venerables of Taoism are modeled on the bodhisattvas of Mahāyāna Buddhism. The title *t'ien-tsun* began to be attached to Taoist deities around the 3d century C.E., at which time Buddhism became a growing influence in Chinese religion, so that Taoists felt impelled to create a counterpart to the Buddhist idea of a bodhisattva.

The celestial venerables—like bodhisattvas in popular belief—descend from Heaven to teach mankind or intimate their knowledge and wisdom to lower-ranking deities or immortals (→ *hsien*), who in turn explain them to ordinary humans. This is how man is believed to have come into possession of the sacred Taoist writings and of the prescriptions for attaining immortality. When Buddhism first came to China, the title *t'ien-tsun* became attached to the Buddha himself, but was later withdrawn in favor of *shih-tsun* ("terrestrial venerable") to avoid confusion.

T'ien-t'ung Ju-ching 🅉 (Jap., Tendō Nyojō), 1163–1228; Chinese Ch'an (Zen) master of the → Sōtō school; a student and dharma successor (→ *hassu*) of Tsu-an Chih-chien (Jap., Sokuan Chikan, 1105–1192) and the master of the great Japanese master and founder of Japanese Sōtō Zen, → Dōgen Zenji.

T'ien-wang 🄱 Chin. → celestial kings

Ti-i 🅃 Chin. → *san-i*

Ti-kuan 🅃 → *san-kuan*

Tilopa 🄱 (Ti-lo-pa), Tib., roughly "Man Who Crushes Sesame"; 989–1069; one of the most renowned → *mahāsiddhas* and the first human teacher in the → *mahāmudrā* lineage. He unified various Tantric systems of India and transmitted these methods to his student → Nāropa. Under the latter's name (→ *Nāro chödrug*), these teachings were propagated in Tibet and attained great importance, particularly for the → Kagyupa school. The name Tilopa derives from the fact that the great *mahāsiddha* earned his living by producing sesame oil.

Ti-lun school 🄱 Chin., lit. "School of the Treatise on the → Bhūmis"; school of early Chinese Buddhism, which was based on a commentary by → Vasubandhu on the → *Dashabhūmika.* This commentary was translated into Chinese in 508 by → Bodhiruchi, Ratnamati, and Buddhasanta. A branch of this school became the predecessor of the → Hua-yen school.

The Ti-lun school adopted the basic philosophy of the → Yogāchāra, particularly the theory of the storehouse consciousness (→ *ālaya-vijñāna*), concerning which there were different views within the school. The northern branch, represented by Tao-ch'ung, a student of Bodhiruchi, took the position that the storehouse consciousness is not real—it is false and separate from suchness (→ *tathatā*)—and → buddhanature is first acquired upon attaining buddhahood; thus it is not inborn. The southern and more important branch of the school under Hui-kuang, a student of Ratnamati, saw the storehouse consciousness as real and identical with suchness, and buddha-nature as inborn. Out of this southern branch, the Hua-yen school developed; the northern branch was absorbed by the Fa-hsiang school.

Ting Shang-tso 🅉 (Jap., Jō Jōza), ca. 9th century; Chinese Ch'an (Zen) master; a student and dharma successor (→ *hassu*) of → Lin-chi I-hsuan (Jap., Rinzai Gigen). We encounter Head Monk Ting in example 32 of the → *Pi-yen-lu* (→ Lin-chi I-hsuan).

Tirthankara 🄷 (Tīrthaṅkara), Skt., lit. "fordmaker," or *jina;* → Jainism recognizes twenty-four *tīrthankaras,* or masters, who have conveyed the principles of Jain belief over the centuries. The last such teacher was → Mahāvīra, who founded Jainism as a religious community.

Parshva, the twenty-third *tīrthankara* (8th century B.C.E.).

Mahāvīra and his eleven disciples were the first to turn against the brahmans. Their teaching is called India's unorthodox religion, as it rejects the brahmanic sacrificial rites as well as the authority of the → Vedas. Jainism requires that one practice austerities for at least twelve years.

Titikshā 🅗 Skt. → *shatkasampatti*

Ti-ts'ang 🅑 Chin. (Skt. → Kshitigarbha), lit. "Womb of the Earth"; 1. one of the four great → bodhisattvas in Chinese Buddhism, who according to folk belief, liberates those who dwell in the various hells (→ *naraka*). The mountain associated with him is Chiu-hua-shan in south China, where he is said to have lived during the T'ang period as a Korean prince. After his death his body did not decay. A temple was built over it, which still exists today.

Ti-ts'ang is depicted as a monk. In his right hand is a metal staff with six jingling rings on it, which opens the gates of the hells for him. In the left hand he holds a wish-fulfilling jewel, the radiance of which illuminates the hells and calms the sufferings of the damned. Sometimes Ti-ts'ang wears a crown of the type worn by Chinese monks during funeral ceremonies. Sometimes he is also depicted sitting on a lotus throne.

An endlessly long time ago, Ti-ts'ang was a brahmin, who took a vow before the buddha of that time also himself to become a buddha but not before he had liberated all beings from the cycle of life and death (→ *samsāra*). In one of his countless existences, he was a girl whose mother killed sentient beings for food. After the mother's death the daughter meditated for a long time, until she heard a voice commanding her to recite the name of Buddha. She entered an ecstasy and reached the gates of hell, where she learned that she had saved her mother from the torments of hell through her meditation.

Ti-ts'ang, through his supernatural power, can take on six different forms in order to help the beings of the six modes of existence (→ *gati*). In a special ceremony, which is generally held on the hundredth day after the death of the relative of a monk, the monk invokes Ti-ts'ang in front of an ancestor tablet erected on behalf of the deceased and supplicates him to guide the deceased to the pure land of Buddha → Amitābha. Then follows the recitation of a mantra through which the deceased is summoned back so that he or she can hear the teachings expounded. The ceremony ends with the invocation of Amitābha and Ti-ts'ang.

2. Chinese Ch'an (Zen) master, → Lohan Kuei-ch'en.

Tōhō Anshu 🅩 also Tōhō Anju, Jap. for → T'ung-feng An-chu.

Tokudo 🅩 Jap., lit. "attainment of going-beyond"; 1. name of a ceremony in which a Buddhist monk is ordained or a layperson is initiated into Buddhism. It includes taking the Buddhist vows (→ *jūjūkai*). The monk's ordination is called *shukke-tokudo*; the lay initiation, *zaike-tokudo*. 2. An expression for the experience of → enlightenment.

Tokusan Senkan 🅩 Jap. for → Te-shan Hsuan-chien

Tongo 🅩 Jap., lit. "sudden [ton] enlightenment [*go* → satori]"; the teaching of sudden enlightenment, associated with the → Southern school. It is contrasted with the teaching of gradual enlightenment (→ *zengo*) associated with the Northern school. The distinction between "sudden" and "gradual" is, however, a superficial one—deeper Zen realization makes evident that there is no contradiction between the two. Thus

Hui-neng, the sixth patriarch of Ch'an (Zen) in China, who is considered the founder of the school of sudden enlightenment, stresses again and again in his → *Liu-tsu-ta-shih fa-pao-t'an-ching* that sudden and gradual are not in the dharma: "In the dharma there is neither sudden nor gradual. Because of delusion or enlightenment, it goes slow and fast."

Tōsan Shusho 🅉 Jap. for → Tung-shan Shou-chu

Tosetsu Jūetsu 🅉 Jap. for → Tou-shuai T'sung-yueh

Tōsu Daidō 🅉 Jap. for → T'ou-tzu Ta-t'ung

Tou-mu 🅃 Chin., lit. "Mother of the Great Wagon"; Taoist deity. Tou-mu supervises a register in which the life and death of each person is recorded. She is venerated by all who hope for a long life and personifies compassion.

It is quite common for a whole hall of a Taoist temple to be dedicated to her. She is portrayed sitting on a lotus throne and has four heads, with three eyes in each, and eight arms—four on each side of her body. In her hands she holds various precious objects. Tou-mu is also venerated by Chinese Buddhists.

Tou-shuai Ts'ung-yueh 🅉 (Jap., Tosetsu Jūetsu), 1044–91, Chinese Ch'an (Zen) master of the Ōryō lineage of Rinzai Zen (→ Ōryō school); a student and dharma successor (→ *hassu*) of → Pao-feng K'o-wen (Jap., Hōbō Kokumon). From Master Tou-shuai come the famous "three barriers" of example 47 of the → *Wu-men-kuan.*

The kōan is as follows:

"The purpose of going to forsaken places to practice *zazen* is to seek your true nature. Where is your true nature now, in this instant?

"When you have experienced your true nature, can you liberate yourself from birth and death? How can you liberate yourself when your eyesight gives out?

"When you have liberated yourself from birth and death, you know the place you're going to. When your body has broken down into the four elements, where do you go then?"

T'ou-tzu Ta-t'ung 🅉 (Jap., Tōsu Daidō), 819–914; Chinese Ch'an (Zen) master; a student and dharma successor (→ *hassu*) of → Ts'ui-wei Wu-hsueh (Jap., Suibi Mugaku). We encounter him in examples 41, 79, 80, and 91 of the → *Pi-yen-lu.* As the → *Ching-te ch'uan-teng-lu* tells us, T'ou-tzu left his home at an early age to practice Buddhist meditation. He had his first enlightenment experience as a monk of the Hua-yen school of Chinese Buddhism. Later he became a student of Ts'ui-wei, under whom he experienced profound enlightenment.

A → *mondō* with his master recorded in the → *Ching-te ch'uan-teng-lu* is as follows:

"One day as Ts'ui-wei was walking around the dharma hall, T'ou-tzu came up to him and asked, 'Master, how do you show people the secret meaning of coming out of the west [→ *seirai-no-i*]?'

"Ts'ui-wei paused for a moment.

"T'ou-tzu asked again, 'Please, master, instruct me.'

"Ts'ui-wei said, 'Do you want me to pour another bucket of putrid water over you?'

"T'ou-tzu prostrated with gratitude and withdrew."

After long years of wandering, during which Tao-tzu trained further in → *hossen* with other masters, he secluded himself in a hermitage on Mount T'ou-tzu, from which his name is derived. After the great Ch'an master → Chao-chou Ts'ung-shen (Jap., Jōshū Jūshin) sought him out there (a part of the *hossen* between the two masters is recorded as example 41 of the *Pi-yen-lu*), T'ou-tzu's fame spread, Ch'an monks gathered around him, and he guided them for more than thirty years on the way of Ch'an.

In example 80 of the *Pi-yen-lu* we find him in a *mondō* with a wandering Ch'an monk:

"A monk asked Chao-chou, 'Does an infant use his sixth sense or not?'

"Chao-chou said, 'He plays ball on the rushing water.'

"Later the monk asked T'ou-tzu, 'What does it mean "to play ball on the rushing water?"'

"T'ou-tzu said, 'Consciousness, consciousness doesn't stop flowing.' "

Tōzan Ryōkai 🅉 Jap. for → Tung-shan Liang-chieh

Tōzan Shusho 🅉 Jap. for → Tung-shan Shou-chu

Traidhātuka 🄱 Skt. → *triloka*

Trailanga Svāmi 🄷 a sage who lived in Benares in the nineteenth century, in a temple on Manikarnikā-Ghat, the great cremation site on the Ganges.

He had recognized that the world's differences cannot be resolved by speeches and discussions: to participate in discussions is to be conscious of the world's diversity. After his enlightenment, in which he experienced his unity with the universe and all living beings, Trailanga Svāmi took a vow of silence. → Rāmakrishna, who visited him in Benares, expressed his conviction that he was a true → *paramahamsa.*

Trailokya 🄱 Skt. → *triloka*

Trātaka 🄷 (Trāṭaka), Skt.; direction of the eyes toward a spot between the eyebrows, or concentration upon a specific object; also, staring without blinking the eyes; a → *kriyā*-practice employed in → Hatha-Yoga.

Tretā-Yuga 🅗 Skt. → *yuga*

Trichīvara 🅑 Skt., "three-part robe"; refers to the robe of a Buddhist monk or nun. It consists of the undergarment (*antara-vāsaka*), a cloth wound about the loins and thighs, made of five pieces of fabric; the overgarment (*uttarāsanga*), which is also pieced together from several pieces of cloth; it is worn for daily begging rounds, ceremonies, and so on; and the cloak (*sanghāti*), which is worn only on festive occasions and is put together from 9–25 pieces. The robe is usually of wool but can be of silk or other materials. The customary color is ochre yellow; however, this varies greatly from country to country. The Chinese monks, for example wear blue or brown, Tibetan monks red, and Japanese monks black robes. They are pieced together from several pieces of cloth because originally the clothing of monks and nuns were a patchwork of rags as a sign of poverty.

Triguna 🅗 Skt.; the three → *gunas*

Trigunātīta 🅗 , or Traigunyātīta, Skt., synonymous with → *gunātīta*

Trika 🅗 Skt., lit. "forming three"; a term referring to the doctrine of recognition in northern → Shaivism, consisting of three elements: (1) The world originates solely from the desire of the supreme god (→ Shiva). He creates the impression that the world exists independently of him, while in reality it takes on form only within him and through his mere desire and will. (2) Only through Shiva's grace can human beings attain the "recognition" that one's true being (→ *ātman*) has ever been one with the supreme reality (Shiva, → *brahman*). (3) One who comes to this recognition is qualified to lead others to this same recognition.

The chief works of this threefold Vedantic teaching (→ Vedānta) include Vasugupta's *Shiva-Sūtra* (ninth century C.E.) and *Spanda-Kārikā* along with the *Vritti* of his pupil Kalata; Somananda's *Shivadrishti* (900 C.E.); Utpala's *Pratyabhijñā-Sūtra* (930 C.E.); Abhinavagupta's *Paramārthasāra, Pratyabhijñāvimarshini,* and *Tantrāloka,* as well as Kshemarāja's *Shivasūtravimarshinī and Spandasandoha.*

Trikāla-Jñāna 🅗 Skt., lit. *trikāla*: "three times" (i.e., past, present, and future), *jñāna:* "knowledge"; when the → *kundalinī* rises through the various → *chakras*, various → *siddhis*, or occult powers, are attained. A *trikāla-jñāni* is able to know the past, the present, and the future. (See also → *chakra*).

Trikāya 🅑 🅩 Skt., lit. "three bodies"; refers to the three bodies possessed by a buddha according to the Mahāyāna view. The basis of this teaching is the conviction that a buddha is one with the absolute and manifests in the relative world in order to work for the welfare of all beings. The three bodies are:

1. *Dharmakāya* (body of the great order); the true nature of the Buddha, which is identical with transcendental reality, the essence of the universe. The *dharmakāya* is the unity of the Buddha with everything existing. At the same time it represents the "law" (→ dharma), the teaching expounded by the Buddha.
2. *Sambhogakāya* ("body of delight"); the body of buddhas who in a "buddha-paradise" enjoy the truth that they embody.
3. *Nirmānakāya* ("body of transformation"); the earthly body in which buddhas appear to men in order to fulfill the buddhas' resolve to guide all beings to liberation.

The *dharmakāya* was initially identified with the teaching expounded by the historical Buddha → Shākyamuni. Only later was it brought together with the other two bodies to form a series. It is timeless, permanent, devoid of characteristics, free from all duality; it is the spiritual body of the buddhas, their true nature, which all buddhas have in common. Various names are applied to the *dharmakāya* depending on whether it is being taken as the true nature of being (*dharmatā, dharmadhātu, tathatā, bhūtatathatā, shūnyatā, ālaya-vijñāna*) or as the true nature of the buddhas (*buddhatā*, buddha-nature, *tathāgatagarbha*). In many schools the *dharmakāya* is regarded as something impersonal, in others as something personal (for example, → *Lankāvatāra-sūtra*, → *Buddhāvatamsaka-sūtra*). The *dharmakāya* is realized through → *prajñā.*

The *sambhogakāya* is the result of previous good actions and is realized, as a result of a bodhisattva's accumulated merit, in enlightenment. It exhibits the thirty-two major marks (→ *dvātrimshadvara-lakshana*) and the eighty minor marks of a buddha and can be perceived only by bodhisattvas who have attained the last stage (→ *bhūmi*) of a bodhisattva's development. This "body of delight" represents the Buddha as an object of devotion. The descriptions of the buddhas introduced in the Mahāyāna sūtras refer to this aspect. The buddhas in their → *sambhogakāya* manifestations populate the buddha-fields (→ Sukhāvatī, → Abhirati); to be reborn in these buddha-fields is the hope of many Buddhists (→ Pure Land school, → Jōdo-shū).

The *nirmānakāya* is embodied in the earthly buddhas and bodhisattvas projected into the world through the meditation of the *sambhogakāya* buddhas as a result of their compassion. The task of the *nirmāna-kāya* manifestations is to expound the teaching. They are guides on the way to liberation from suffering, but cannot bring beings to this liberation directly. Like all human beings, they are subject to the misery of illness, old age, and death, but possess the divine eye and divine hearing. The individuality of *nirmānakāya* buddhas dissolves after their deaths.

The teaching of the three bodies of a buddha seems to have first reached full development with → Asanga, but derives originally from the views of the → Mahāsānghikas, who did much to shape Mahāyāna Buddhology. For them the emphasis was on the supramundane, absolute nature of a buddha; the figure of the historical Buddha faded increasingly into the background. The buddha is physically and spiritually pure, possesses eternal life and limitless power. Buddhas as experienced by human beings are, according to this view, only magical projections of mind, which appear among men in order to liberate them.

The notion of endless space filled with countless worlds plays a major role in the development of this doctrine. In order for all the beings in all the worlds to be liberated, the number of liberators must be greatly increased. This explains the great number of bodhisattvas.

In Zen the three bodies of buddha are three levels of reality, which stand in reciprocal relationship to each other and constitute a whole. The *dharmakāya* (Jap., *hosshin*) is the cosmic consciousness, the unified existence that lies beyond all concepts. This substrate, characterized by completion and perfection, out of which all animate and inanimate forms as well as the moral order arise, is embodied in → Vairochana (Jap., Birushana).

The *sambhogakāya* (Jap., *hōjin*) is the experience of the ecstasy of enlightenment, of the dharma-mind of the Buddha and the patriarchs, and of the spiritual practices transmitted by them. It is symbolized by → Amitābha (Jap., Amida).

The *nirmānakāya* (Jap., *ōjin*) is the radiant, transformed buddha-body personified by → Shākyamuni Buddha.

The reciprocal relationship between the three bodies is illustrated in Zen by the following analogy: the *dharmakāya* can be compared to medical knowledge; the *sambhogakāya* to the education of the doctor through which he gains this knowledge; and the *nirmānakāya* to the application of this knowledge in treating patients, who through it are changed from sick to healthy persons.

In the → Vajrayāna the *trikāya* concept serves to express different experiential levels of enlightenment. The *dharmakāya* stands for the fundamental truth of emptiness (→ *shūnyatā*), the all-pervading supreme reality, enlightenment itself. The *sambhogakāya* and the *nirmānakāya*, the "form bodies," are seen as means for conveying the experience of the absolute. In → Tibetan Buddhism, the body, speech, and mind of the master (→ guru) are equated with the three bodies and symbolized by the mantra *om ah hum*.

The all-pervading and all-embracing power of the *dharmakāya* is here embodied as → Samantabhadra. The → *mahāmudrā* and → *dzogchen* teachings are intended to lead to this holistic experience of the limitless openness of mind. The *sambhogakāya* represents the qualities of the *dharmakāya* and is considered to arise directly out of it. Its forms are expressed in iconography as the five → *buddhakulas*, which in → *sādhanas*, as visualized deities, become a means of communication with the highest reality. This "body of delight" can manifest in either peaceful or wrathful forms (→ forms of manifestation), including the various → *yidams* and → *dharmapālas*.

The *nirmānakāya* is the intentional embodiment of the *dharmakāya* in human form. Though in Mahāyāna this generally means the historical Buddha Shākyamuni, in the Vajrayāna the *nirmānakāya* is any person who possesses the spiritual capabilities of a teacher who has previously died (→ *tulku*).

The three bodies are not different entities but rather constitute a unity that is called the *svābhāvikakāya* ("essence body"). In certain → Tantras, a further level of experience is described—the emotional fulfillment of existence or *mahāsukhakāya* ("body of great bliss").

Trilakshana **B** (trilakṣana) Skt. (Pali, tilakkhana), "three marks"; refers to the three marks of conditioned arising: impermanence (→ *anitya*), suffering (→ *duhkha*), and egolessness (→ *anātman*).

Trilochana **H** (Trilocana), Skt., lit. "three-eyed"; a name for → Shiva.

The *Mahābhārata* states that once, after Shiva had been practicing austerities in the Himalayas, his wife playfully passed her hands over his eyes and a third eye with an enormous flame appeared on his forehead. The effect of this eye was destructive. It transformed → Kāma, the god of love, to ashes.

Triloka **H** **B** Skt., lit. "three worlds, three spheres."
H The three worlds of Hindu cosmology, → Svarga (heaven), Bhūmi (earth), and Pātāla (the underworld, hell).
B also *trailokya, traidhātuka.* Three different worlds or spheres that constitute → samsāra and within which the cycle of existences of all beings in the six modes of existence (→ *gati*) takes place. The three spheres are:

1. Kāmaloka (sphere of desire, also Kāmadhātu); here sexual and other forms of desire predominate. Kāmaloka includes the realms of existence of hell

beings (→ *naraka*), humans, animals, the six classes of gods (→ *deva*), and of the *asuras*.

2. Rūpaloka (sphere of desireless corporeality or form, also Rūpadhātu); here desire for sexuality and food falls away, but the capacity for enjoyment continues. This sphere contains the gods dwelling in the dhyāna heaven. Rebirth in this sphere is possible through practice of the four absorptions (→ *dhyāna*).

3. Arūpaloka (sphere of bodilessness or formlessness, also Arūpadhātu); this realm is a purely spiritual continuum consisting of the four heavens in which one is reborn through practice of the → four stages of formlessness.

Trimārga 🅗 Skt., lit. "triple path"; the combination of the three yogic paths: → Karma-Yoga, → Bhakti-Yoga, and → Jñāna-Yoga. Because → Rāja-Yoga is simply a later term for the yogic path described by Patañjali in his → *Yoga-Sūtra*, it is not included in this group.

Trimūrti 🅗 Skt., lit. "three-form"; the Hindu trinity of the three gods → Brahmā, → Vishnu, and → Shiva, who symbolize the principle of creation, maintenance, and destruction. *Trimūrti* is represented as a body with three heads, Brahmā in the center, Vishnu to the left, and Shiva to the right. In the Vedas this trinity preceded the trinity of → Agni, → Vāyu, and → Sūrya. A well-known stone sculpture of the *trimūrti* is located in a cave on the island of Elefanta, near Bombay.

The Hindu trinity: Shiva, Vishnu, Brahmā.

Brahmā is the embodiment of *rajas* (→ *guna*), that is, of passions and desires, by whose means the world came into being. Vishnu is the embodiment of *sattva*, the qualities of mercy and goodness, by means of which the world is maintained. Shiva is the embodiment of *tamas*, the qualities of darkness, rage, and destructive fire, by means of which the world will be destroyed. The trinity represents three in one and one in three, just as the Vedas are divided into three (Samhitā, Brāhmana, and Sūtra) and yet are one. All are contained within the one being that is the true self of all things.

The → *Padma-Purāna*, a Vaishnava work and thus one that accords prominence to Vishnu, states: "At the onset of creation, as the supreme Vishnu wished to form the entire world, he became threefold: the creator, the maintainer, and the destroyer. In order to form this world, the supreme spirit produced from his right side Brahmā. In order to maintain the world, he created from his left side Vishnu. To destroy it he gave rise to Shiva from his middle. Some men worship Brahmā, others Vishnu, and yet others Shiva. Since these three are one, the devout should draw no distinction between them." Worship of Brahmā has almost entirely diminished, whereas Vishnu and Shiva are each venerated by followers with great devotion as the supreme spirit.

Tripitaka 🅑 (Tripitaka) Skt. (Pali, Tipitaka), lit. "Three Baskets"; canon of Buddhist scriptures, consisting of three parts: the → Vinaya-pitaka, → Sūtra-pitaka, → Abhidharma-pitaka. The first "basket" contains accounts of the origins of the Buddhist → *sangha* as well as the rules of discipline regulating the lives of monks and nuns. The second is composed of discourses said to have come from the mouth of Buddha or his immediate disciples and is arranged into five "collections: → *Dīgha-nikāya*, → *Majjhima-nikāya*, → *Samyutta-nikāya*, → *Anguttara-nikāya*, → *Khuddaka-nikāya*. The third part is a compendium of Buddhist psychology and philosophy.

The Vinaya-pitaka contains some of the oldest parts of the canon, which originated in the first decades after the death of the Buddha. After the split into individual schools, the Abhidharma-pitaka, which differs from school to school, was added. This marked the end of the unified tradition. Each school possessed its own canon; however, the differences between the various versions were minimal. Not very much has been preserved of the various different versions.

Only the so-called Pali canon, so named for the language in which it was composed, has been preserved intact. This is probably derived from the canon of the → Sthaviras of central India. The Vinaya-pitaka and Sūtra-pitaka of the Pali canon were written down, according to tradition, at the first → Buddhist council (480 B.C.E.), at which → Upāli was questioned concerning discipline and → Ānanda concerning doctrine. Their answers constituted the basis for these two "baskets." According to many sources, the Abhidharma-pitaka originated at this time also. In addition we possess the greater part of the → Sarvāstivāda canon, which was composed in Sanskrit and was authoritative in northwestern India.

Of the scriptures of the other schools—for example,

the → Mahāsānghika and → Dharmaguptaka schools—only Chinese translations are extant. The Chinese canon, which was authoritative for China and Japan, is derived from that of the Dharmaguptakas. Its organization is less strict than that of the Pali canon and in the course of time it was often altered. The oldest catalog, from 518 C.E., mentions 2,113 works. This canon was printed for the first time in 972. (Also → Taishō Issaikyō, → Kangyur-Tengyur.)

Triputi 🄷 (Triputi), Skt., lit. "threefold sheath"; the threefold manifestation of the one supreme reality in time and space, divided into subject, object, and the relationship between the two. Well-known examples of this triad are the knower, the known, and the knowledge between, or the lover, the beloved, and the love between. *Triputi* as an illusory notion is discusses in detail in the → *Drig-Drishya-Viveka.*

Triratna 🄱 Skt. (Pali, tiratna), lit. "three precious ones"; also three jewels; the three essential components of Buddhism: → Buddha, → dharma, → *sangha*, i.e., the Awakened One, the truth expounded by him, and the followers living in accordance with this truth. Firm faith in the three precious ones is the stage of "stream-entry" (→ *shrota-āpanna*). The three precious ones are objects of veneration and are considered "places of refuge." The Buddhist takes refuge in them by pronouncing the threefold refuge formula, thus acknowledging himself publicly to be a Buddhist (→ *trisharana*). Contemplation of the three precious ones comprises three of the ten contemplations (→ *anussati*). (Also → *sambō.*)

Trisharana 🄱 (triśaraṇa), Skt. (Pali, tisarana), lit. "threefold refuge"; taking refuge in the three precious ones (→ *triratna*)—Buddha, dharma, and *sangha*—by reciting the threefold refuge formula through which a follower of Buddhism acknowledges himself as such. Therein he takes refuge in the Buddha as teacher, in the teaching (dharma) as "medicine," and in the community (*sangha*) of companions on the path. Taking refuge is part of daily practice. (Also → *sambō.*)

In China taking refuge is part of the ordination of a layperson (→ *upāsaka, upāsikā*), in which the layperson, either by himself or together with others, recites the refuge formula under the supervision of a monk and then receives a dharma name. This constitutes official acceptance into the Buddhist *sangha.*

In Pali the refuge formula is *Buddham saranam gachchami, dhammam saranam gachchami, sangham saranam gachchami* ("I take refuge in the Buddha, I take refuge in the teaching, I take refuge in the community").

Trishiksha 🄱 (triśikṣa) Skt. (Pali, tisso-sikkhā), lit. "threefold training"; the three inseparable aspects of the practice of Buddhism are (1) training in moral discipline (*adhishīla-shiksha*, → *shīla*), (2) training the mind (*adhicitta-shiksha*, → *samādhi*), (3) training in wisdom (*adhiprajñā-shiksha*, → *prajñā*). These three areas of training cover the entire Buddhist teaching.

By training in discipline is meant avoidance of karmically unwholesome activities. Training the mind is done by meditation—concentration or samādhi; training in wisdom is the development of *prajñā* through insight into the truths of Buddhism. These three elements are interdependent. Cultivation of only one of them cannot lead to the intended goal—liberation (→ *vimukti*).

Trishnā 🄷 🄱 (tṛṣṇā), Skt., lit. "thirst, craving, longing, desire."

🄷 Thirst for life, or the longing for sense objects, which can and must be overcome with the help of spiritual exercises (→ *sādhana*), because *trishnā* is an impediment in the path of spiritual development.

🄱 (Pali, tanha); a central notion of Buddhism. *Trishnā* is the desire that arises through the contact between a sense organ and its corresponding object. It is the cause of attachment and thus of suffering (→ *duhkha*); it binds sentient beings to the cycle of existence (→ samsāra). Overcoming and giving up *trishnā* is possible through guarding the sense organs in such a way that in contact with a sense object passion and desire no longer arise. This leads to the end of suffering.

Examining *trishnā* from different points of view, the following classifications are made:

1. Sensual desire (Skt., *kāma-trishnā*), craving for existence (Skt., *bhava-trishnā*), and craving for self-annihilation are distinguished. These three kinds of craving or desire comprise the content of the second of the → four noble truths, the truth of the origin of suffering. They occasion actions and already carry a result characterized by suffering within them.

2. In relation to sense objects, desire for form, sound, odor, taste, touch, and mental impressions are distinguished.

3. In relation to the three worlds (→ *triloka*) sensual desire, desire for fine-material existence (Skt., *rūpa-trishnā*), and desire for formless existence (*arūpa-trishnā*) are distinguished.

In the context of the chain of conditioned arising (→ *pratītya-samutpāda*), *trishnā* is conditioned by → *vedanā*, sensation, and in turn itself calls forth taking possession of a womb (→ *upādāna*).

In the early phase of Buddhism, *trishnā* by itself was

regarded as the cause of suffering and therefore of imprisonment in the cycle of existence. However, elimination of suffering was an insufficient explanation for liberation from the cycle, and a further teaching, that of egolessness (→ *anātman*) was brought in: the fact that the personality is seen as an independent self-existing *I* or ego (→ *ātman*) leads to placing special value on everything connected with it, and this is what gives rise to desire or craving. Liberation results from everything that is erroneously regarded as pertaining to an independently existing ego being recognized as inessential—this causes desire to fall away.

Trishula 🅗 (Triśula), lit. "trident"; → Shiva's famous emblem, frequently seen in representations of him. The → *sādhus* among Shiva devotees often carry a triad, which they set up when performing → *pūjā*.

Trivikrama 🅗 Skt., lit. "Triple Step"; an epithet of → Vishnu, in reference to the three steps that he is said to have taken (the meaning of which is interpreted variously).

An ancient Vedic commentary states that Vishnu traversed the entire universe in three steps: with the first step (as the fire god, → Agni), he covered the earth; with the second step (as the wind god, → Vāyu), the air; and with the third step (as the sun god, → Sūrya), the heavens. According to another explanation, the three steps symbolize the rising, the zenith, and the setting of the sun. The celebrated commentator → Sāyana spoke of them as Vishnu's three steps in his incarnation (→ *avatāra*) as the dwarf → Vāmana.

Triyāna 🅑 Skt., lit. "three vehicles"; three vehicles that bring one to the attainment of nirvāna: *shrāvaka-yāna*, *pratyeka-yāna*, and *bodhisattva-yāna* (→ *shrāvaka*, → *pratyeka-buddha*, → bodhisattva). The → Mahāyāna equates the *shrāvaka-yāna* with the → Hīnayāna, which leads to arhatship (→ arhat); the *pratyeka-buddha-yāna* with the "middle vehicle" (→ *mādhyama-yāna*), which leads to buddhahood attained for one's own sake; and the *bodhisattva-yāna* with the Mahāyāna, which after countless lives of self-sacrifice leads to supreme buddhahood.

In the → *Lotus Sūtra* these three vehicles are viewed as parts of the single vehicle or buddha vehicle (→ *ekayāna*), which is taught to students in these three different forms depending on their abilities. In this sūtra they are symbolized by carts drawn by goats, reindeer, and oxen respectively.

Trungpa, Chögyam 🅑 (1940–87) contemporary Tibetan master of the → Kagyupa and → Nyingmapa schools, one of the most influential exponents of → Tibetan Buddhism in the West, characterized by his ability to expound the buddha-dharma in terms of the everyday lives of his listeners. Following the Chinese invasion of Tibet, he escaped to India in 1959. In 1963 he was awarded a fellowship to study at Oxford University. In 1970 he went to North America where he taught until his death. He founded the Vajradhātu organization, which has several thousand followers worldwide. Among his many books on Buddhism is *Cutting Through Spiritual Materialism*. His book *Shambhala: The Sacred Path of the Warrior* is on the basic teachings of → Shambhala. Two volumes of his poetry have also been published.

Ts'ai-shen 🅣 Chin.; a god of prosperity, one of the most important deities of religious Taoism (→ *tao-chiao*) and in the syncretist folk religion of China. In Taoism, the personality venerated as Ts'ai-shen traditionally is Chao Hsüan-t'an Yüan-shuai, i.e., General Chao of the Dark Terrace, who is said to have lived during the Ch'in Dynasty and allegedly attained enlightenment on top of a mountain. Legend further relates that → Chang Tao-ling, during his search for the life-prolonging elixir, asked for the assistance of a protective deity, whereupon the Jade Emperor (→ Yü-huang) sent him General Chao.

As a deity of prosperity, Ts'ai-shen has various magical powers: he is capable of riding a black tiger, warding off thunder and lightning, fighting illnesses, and ensuring profit from commercial transactions.

Ts'ai-shen is usually portrayed with a black face and a thick moustache. On his head he wears a cap made of iron and he holds a weapon, also of iron.

A great number of personalities, apart from General Chao, are venerated as *ts'ai-shen*. In fact, he holds a central position in popular faith and is venerated by most families, although no specific cult has formed around him. Poorer families content themselves with writing the two signs of his name on a piece of paper, which they affix to the door of the most important room in their house. Richer families may own a statue of him. On his birthday (the sixteenth day of the third month) it is customary to sacrifice a cockerel to him, the blood of which is smeared all over the doorstep of the house.

Sometimes two figures are venerated as *ts'ai-shen* —one military, the other civilian—whose roles may differ from one region of the country to the next.

"Ts'an-t'ung-ch'i" 🅩 Chin. (Jap., "Sandōkai"), lit. "Coincidence of Difference and Sameness"; poem of the Chinese Ch'an (Zen) master → Shih-t'ou Hsi-ch'ien (Jap., Sekitō Kisen) celebrating the enlightened state of mind that transcends all duality (→ enlightenment). The "Ts'an-t'ung-ch'i" is chanted up to the present day in Zen monasteries, particularly those of the → Sōtō school. A translation from the Chinese original is found in Thomas Cleary, *Timeless Spring* (New York, 1980).

Tsao-chün ■ Chin., lit. "Lord of the Hearth"; a Taoist hearth and kitchen deity, who, to this day, holds the most important place in Chinese folk religion. A picture of Tsao-chün is fixed above the hearth and venerated by the whole family on the days of the new and full moon.

From his place above the hearth Tsao-chün notes everything that happens in the house and reports on this to the Jade Emperor (→ Yü-huang) on each New Year's Day. For that reason it is customary to smear honey around the mouth of the deity on New Year's Eve, hoping that this will prompt him to submit a favorable report to Yü-huang.

On color prints Tsao-chün is usually surrounded by a host of children, because he also acts as protector of the family.

According to legend Tsao-chün was already venerated in the 2d century B.C.E. One tradition states that he granted eternal youth and freedom from want to the Taoist magician → Li Shao-chün, who promised to pass on these gifts to the Emperor Hsiao Wu-ti (140–86 B.C.E.) if he were to pass a law to protect the cult of the hearth deity. Li caused the deity to appear to the emperor at night, whereupon the emperor offered a sacrifice to Tsao-chün, hoping to gain possession of the pill of immortality and be initiated into the secret of turning base metal into gold. When the emperor's hopes were not fulfilled, Li Shao-chün tried another ruse: he wrote signs on a piece of silk, which he fed to an ox, and prophesied that when this ox was slaughtered a miraculous message would be found. The emperor, however, recognized Li's handwriting and had him punished. Nevertheless, the cult of Tsao-chün had already become established at court and has been part of Chinese folk religion ever since.

One legend still circulating among the people tells of a man called Chang Lang, who was married to a very virtuous woman, who brought good fortune and blessings upon his house: "One day he left her for the sake of a flighty young girl, and the rejected wife returned to her parents. From then on Chang Lang was plagued by bad luck. The young girl turned from him, he became blind and was forced to support himself by begging. One day, his search for alms brought him to the house of his former wife, but he was not aware of this. She, however, recognized him, invited him in, and served him his favorite dish. This reminded Chang of his lost happiness and, with tears running down his face, he related to her his sad tale. She ordered him to open his eyes and, as if by a miracle, he regained his eyesight and recognized her. Deeply ashamed at the way he had treated her, he was unable to remain in her presence and jumped into the hearth, not realizing that it was lit. The wife attempted to save him, but could only salvage one of his legs. Since then, the fire tong or poker is known in popular language as "Chang Lang's leg." Chang's wife mourned for him, fixed a small plaque above the hearth in which he lost his life, and made sacrifices to him. That was the beginning of his veneration as a hearth deity" (trans. from E. Unterrieder, *Glück ein ganzes Mondjahr lang* [Klagenfurt, 1984], 12).

Ts'ao Kuo-chiu ■ → *pa-hsien*

Ts'ao-shan Pen-chi ■ (Jap., Sōzan Honjaku), 840–901. Chinese Ch'an (Zen) master; a student and dharma successor (→ *hassu*) of → Tung-shan Ling-chieh (Jap., Tōzan Ryōkai). Together with his master Tung-shan, Ts'ao-shan founded the Ts'ao-tung school (Jap., → Sōtō school) of Ch'an (Zen), the name of which is derived from the first characters of the names of the two masters. The Sōtō school is one of the two schools of Zen still active in Japan today. We encounter Ts'ao-shan in example 10 of the → *Wu-men-kuan*. His teachings and sayings are contained in the *Fu-chou Ts'ao-shan Pen-chi-ch'an-shih yu-lu* (*Record of the Words of Ch'an Master Ts'ao-shan Pen-chi from Fu-chou).*

Ts'ao-shan, who in his youth studied the Confucian classics, left his home at the age of nineteen and became a Buddhist monk. At twenty-five he received full ordination. He lived in the monastery on Ling-shih Mountain in Fu-chou and often visited the public discourses on → buddha-dharma of Master Tung-shan in Kiangsi. One day a → *mondō* took place between Tung-shan and Ts'ao-shan through which the master recognized Ts'ao-shan's potential and accepted him as a student.

Under Tung-shan, Ts'ao-shan came to profound enlightenment. As he took his leave of Tung-shan, the following exchange took place, which is recorded in the → *Ching-te ch'uan-teng-lu*:

Tung-shan said, "Where are you going?"

Ts'ao-shan said, "To where there's no change."

Tung-shan said, "How can you go to where there's no change?"

Ts'ao-shan said, "My going is no change."

After his departure from Tung-shan, Ts'ao-shan wandered through the country and instructed people in the buddha-dharma in accordance with the circumstances that presented themselves. Finally he was invited to take up residence in a monastery on Ts'ao-shan (Mount Ts'ao), from which his name derives. Later he lived on Mount Ho-yu; in both places a great host of students gathered about him.

In example 10 of the → *Wu-men-kuan*, we see Ts'ao-shan in a → *hossen* with his student Ch'ing-jui (Jap., Seizei):

A monk once came to Master Ts'ao-shan [and said], "Ching-jui [himself] is very lonely and miserable. Please be so kind as to help me to get ahead."

Ts'ao-shan said, "Āchārya [→ *ajari*] Jui!"

Ch'ing-jui said, "Yes!?"

Ts'ao-shan said, "You have already drunk three cups of superb wine from the house of Pai of Ch'uan-chou, and still you're saying that you haven't wet your lips!"

Ts'ao-tung-tsung Z Chin. for → Sōtō school

Tso-ch'an Z Chin. for → *zazen*

Tsogchen B Tib. → *dzogchen*

Tsongkhapa B (Tsoṅ-kha-pa), Tib., lit. "Man from Onion Valley"; the renowned reformer and scholar (1357–1419) who founded the → Gelugpa school and created one of the most important doctrinal traditions of → Tibetan Buddhism. Born in a time when the redaction of the the Tibetan canon (→ Kangyur-Tengyur) had been completed, Tsongkhapa was in a position to work through these teachings thoroughly. He presented the results of this process in two principal works, the *Lamrim chenmo* (*Great Discourse on the Stages of the Path*, also translated *Stages to Enlightenment*) and the *Ngagrim chenmo* (*Great Discourse on the Secret Mantra*). The great monasteries of Tibet, such as Drepung, Sera, and Ganden, were a result of Tsongkhapa's activity.

Born in northeast Tibet, in Amdo, Tsongkhapa became familiar with religion at an early age. He took layman's vows at the age of three from the fourth → Karmapa, Rolpe Dorje (1340–83). He studied all branches of knowledge under numerous teachers and was exposed especially to the teachings of the → Sakyapa and → Kadampa schools.

Tsongkhapa's outstanding ability as a scholar of wide knowledge is evident in his works, which fill eighteen volumes, and which were used as textbooks by succeeding generations. He especially stressed the study of five branches of knowledge, the mastery of which requires thorough study of the Buddhist teachings, critical examination of them, and realization of them through meditation.

He attributed the right philosophical view and proper logic to the "middle doctrine" (→ Mādhyamaka) and the appropriate instruction on meditation to the → *Prajñāpāramitā-sūtra* and the → Abhidharma; the proper way of life is achieved through the disciplinary rules of the → Vinaya.

To Tsongkhapa four great actions are ascribed: the restoration of an important sculpted image of → Maitreya; insistence on observance of the Vinaya; the establishment of the Mönlam, a new year's festival; and construction of certain monastic buildings.

The reformer Tsongkhapa (Tibetan blockprint)

Tsou Yen T 3d century B.C.E.; most famous representative of the Yin-Yang School (→ *yin-yang chia*). According to the great historian Ssu-ma Ch'ien, Tsou Yen's method consisted in first examining small things and then gradually widening his analysis to larger things until he reached the limitless. He applied the doctrine of the five elements (→ *wu-hsing*) to history and geography; classified the country's rivers, mountains, valleys, animals etc.; and maintained that the area of China accounted for less than one eightieth of the surface area of the world, which he described as consisting of nine continents surrounded by a large ocean.

Tsou Yen developed a new view of history, by relating political and social events to the sequence of the five elements: the Yellow Emperor (→ Huang-ti) had ruled under the element earth, which was conquered by the wood of the Hsia Dynasty. This in turn was vanquished by the element metal of the Shang Dynasty and that by the element of fire, under whose sign the Chou Dynasty ruled. The fire would—according to Tsou Yen—be succeeded by the water of the next dynasty, which would then be followed by another dynasty, once again ruled by the element earth.

Tsou Yen's philosophy of history is described in

Book 13, Chapter 2 of the → *Lü-shih ch'un-ch'iu,* although his name as such is not specifically mentioned: "Whenever a ruler or king is about to appear, Heaven reveals this to mankind through happy omens. At the time of the coming of the Yellow Emperor, Heaven caused a large earthworm and a gigantic cricket to appear. The Yellow Emperor said, 'The might of earth is victorious.' Because of this, he chose yellow as his supreme color and took the earth as a model for his actions. At the time of Yü (→ Ta-yü) Heaven prevented grasses and trees from yellowing or shedding their leaves in autumn or winter. Thereupon Yü said, 'The might of wood is victorious.' Because of this, Yü chose green as the ruling color and let wood be the example that determined his actions. At the time of T'ang (the founder of the Shang Dynasty) Heaven first caused a metal blade to appear in water, whereupon T'ang said, 'The might of metal is victorious.' As a result of this, T'ang chose white as the superior color and made metal the guiding principle of his actions. At the time of King Wen (the founder of the Chou Dynasty) Heaven first caused a red crow to appear, which held a red envelope in its beak and settled on the earth altar of Chou. Thereupon King Wen said, 'The might of fire is victorious.' Because of this, he made red the superior color and in his actions followed the example of fire. One day, the rule of fire will surely be succeeded by the might of water. Before that happens, Heaven will reveal that the might of water is victorious. The future ruler will then choose black as the superior color and model his actions on the characteristics of water. When the might of water is manifest and the ruler and people fail to seize the fateful moment, might will pass to the element earth" (Wilhelm 1979, p. 160).

Tso-wang 🅣 Chin., lit. "sitting [and] forgetting"; Taoist method of meditation descriptive of the highest stage of Taoist absorption. The practitioner of *tso-wang* does not meditate on an object, but rather allows his mind to float freely without intervening. In this way, he abides in nonaction (→*wu-wei*) and becomes one with the → Tao. He leaves behind all forms and limitations and is free of wishes and desires.

The → *Chuang-tzu* (Book 6, Chapter 7) describes *tso-wang* as follows: "On a third occasion Wen Hui met Confucius and said, 'I am getting on.' 'How so?' asked the Sage. 'I have got rid of everything,' replied Wen Hui. 'Got rid of everything!' said Confucius eagerly. 'What do you mean by that?' 'I have freed myself from my body,' answered Wen Hui. 'I have discarded my reasoning powers. And by thus getting rid of body and mind, I have become One with the Infinite. This is what I mean by getting rid of everything.' 'If you have become one,' cried Confucius, 'there can be no room for bias. If you have passed into space, you are indeed without beginning or end. And if you have really attained to this, I trust to be allowed to follow in your steps' " (Giles 1961).

Ts'ui-wei Wu-hsueh 🅩 (Jap., Suibi Mugaku), 9th century, Chinese Ch'an (Zen) master; a student and dharma successor (→ *hassu*) of → Tan-hsia T'ien-jan (Jap., Tanka Tennen) and the master of → T'ou-tzu Ta-t'ung (Jap., Tōsu Daidō). We encounter him in example 20 of the → *Pi-yen-lu.* Little is known of Ts'ui-wei, other than that like his master Tan-hsia, he was a personage free from the fetters of convention and abhorred scholarly knowledge. On this account he was also known as Wu-hsueh, "the Uneducated." He had five dharma successors, of whom especially T'ou-tzu became known as a great Ch'an master.

Ts'ui-yen Ling-ts'an 🅩 (Jap., Suigan Reisan), 9th–10th century; Chinese Ch'an (Zen) master; a student and dharma successor (→ *hassu*) of → Hsueh-feng I-ts'un (Jap., Seppō Gison). Ts'ui-yen had two dharma successors, concerning whom—as concerning their master—as good as nothing is known. We encounter Ts'ui-yen in example 8 of the → *Pi-yen-lu.*

Ts'ung-jung-lu 🅩 Chin. (Jap. *Shōyō-roku*), roughly "Book of Equanimity"; collection of a hundred kōans, compiled in the 12th century by the Chinese Ch'an (Zen) master → Hung-chih Cheng-chueh (Jap., Wanshi Shōgaku). The title is derived from the name of this master's hermitage, the Cloister of Equanimity. More than a third of the kōans of the *Ts'ung-jung-lu* are identical with kōans in the → *Pi-yen-lu* and the → *Wu-men-kuan.* An English translation by Thomas Cleary appeared under the title *The Book of Equanimity* (New York, 1985).

The fact that Master Hung-chih, who belonged to the → Sōtō school and who is often represented as an enemy of the kōan practice (→ *kanna* Zen) of the → Rinzai school, himself compiled such a collection of kōans makes clear that the differences of opinion and in training methods of the two schools were not so great in ancient China. Sōtō Zen also made use of the kōan as an outstanding means of training.

Tsung-mi 🅑 780–841, fifth and last patriarch of the → Hua-yen school of Chinese Buddhism. Tsung-mi advocates in his works a combination of the philosophy of the Hua-yen school and the practice of the Ch'an (Zen) school. He explained the complicated theories of Hua-yen, particularly those of Fa-tsang, in an understandable fashion. His treatise, the *Original Nature of Humanity* (Chin., *Yuan-jen lun*) became one of the standard works for the training of Buddhist monks in Japan. In it he presents the teachings of the individual Buddhist schools of his time systematically and critically and distinguishes them from other spiritual currents.

Tsung-mi grew up in a Confucianist family. In 807 he intended to take the examinations for a career as a civil service functionary. However, he met a Ch'an (Zen) master who so impressed him that he became a monk. First he studied the teachings of Ch'an. However after he had read a commentary on the *Buddhāvatamsaka-sūtra*, he became a student of Ch'eng-kuan, and important representative of the Hua-yen school. Soon thereafter, he began his teaching career, in which he concentrated on expounding this sūtra. Nonetheless, his whole life long he was also intensively engaged with the practice of Ch'an. His reputation as a Hua-yen master was so great that he was invited to the imperial court several times and was honored with the title *master of the purple robe*. For his importance in the Ch'an (Zen) tradition of Buddhism, → Kuei-feng Tsung-mi, his Ch'an name.

Ts'ung-shen 🅩 → Chao-chou Ts'ung-shen

Ts'un-shen 🅣 Chin. → Ts'un-ssu

Ts'un-ssu 🅣 Chin., lit. "maintaining the thought [the attention]"; Taoist method of meditation, in which the practitioner contemplates a certain object. The most common objects of meditation are the three jewels (→ *san-pao*); the Tao, i.e., the Taoist writings—above all the writings on the Magic Jewel (→ *Ling-pao ching*)—and the Master (in this case, → Lao-chün). A variant of *ts'un-ssu* consists in trying to visualize the deities (→ *shen*) said to inhabit the body of each human being (→ Inner Deity Hygiene School). This method is known as *ts'un-shen* (lit. "maintaining the deities"; → *nei-kuan*). It specifically aims at attaining longevity by the production of pure energy.

Tukārām 🅗 1608–1649, the most important religious poet in the western Indian literary tradition of the Marāthī language. His numerous short songs, called *abhangs*, describe his spiritual experiences. Despite the protests of the educated brahman caste, his so-called *kīrtanas* (sung sermons) enjoyed great popularity among the common people as well as the ruling class.

Tukārām came from a prosperous family of grain merchants from Dehu, near Poona. However, he devoted himself entirely to his religious practices and to poetry and hence felt himself bound to poverty, so that he refused the fees offered to him by the rich for his time. In his songs he speaks of the pain of separation from God, from the comfort received when God takes him by the hand like a child, and finally of the joy he experiences in having overcome the senses and having found union with God.

"Like the Bengali saint → Chaitanya, who is related to him in many ways and by whom he may have been directly influenced, he is said to have found his death in a remarkable manner: As he stood on the banks of the Indrāyanī with his followers, singing hymns in ecstasy, he suddenly vanished from their sight and was seen no more" (H. von Glasenapp).

T'u-ku na-hsin 🅣 also called *t'u-na,* Chin., lit. "disposing of the old and acquiring the new"; Taoist breathing exercise, in which the stale breath is expelled as completely as possible through the mouth, whereupon the practitioner inhales fresh air through his nose, endeavoring to fill the lungs to their maximum capacity. This allows him to expel the dead breath (*ssu-ch'i,* → *ch'i*) and then absorb the living breath (*sheng-ch'i*)—an essential precondition for the attainment of immortality. *T'u-na* is one of several methods of nourishing the body, or life (→ *yang-hsing,* → *yang-sheng*). As he expels the stale air, the adept may produce six different sounds, each of which acts upon a particular internal organ and is said to have specific healing powers.

Exhaling and at the same time making the sound *ch'i* strengthens the lungs and can cure tuberculosis. The sound *ho* strengthens the heart and also is a cure for headaches. The sound *hsü* acts on the liver and dispels a phlegmatic temperament. *Hu* acts on the pancreas and lowers the temperature when the patient is suffering from a fever. *Ch'ui* acts on the kidneys and is a prophylactic against catching cold. *Hsi* influences the alimentary tract, the stomach, and the urogenital system and relieves rheumatic pain.

Tulku 🅑 (sprul-sku) Tib., lit. "transformation body"; in → Tibetan Buddhism, a term for a person who, after certain tests, is recognized as the reincarnation of a previously deceased person. This conception developed out of the → *trikāya* teaching and was first applied in Tibet with the discovery of the second → *karmapa*, Karma Pakshi (1204–83). The *tulku* was seen as an important means for assuring the spiritual and political continuity of monastic institutions. In addition to those of the four heads of the principal schools of Tibetan Buddhism, there were a great number of *tulku* lineages in Tibet.

The power to determine the circumstances of one's rebirth was already mentioned in the → Mahāyāna teachings as a special ability. It is one of the properties that distinguishes a bodhisattva in the eighth stage (→ *bhūmi*) of his spiritual development. This, along with the concept of the *nirmānakāya* (→ *trikāya*)—in whom the supreme reality becomes manifest as a physical phenomenon—constitutes the doctrinal basis of the *tulku* teaching.

The principle of intentional rebirth was first elaborated in all its aspects in the → Karma Kagyu school. It especially served the uninterrupted transmission of the → *mahāmudrā* teachings. The potential of a child recognized as a *tulku* was intensively nurtured, in such a way that eventually the *tulku* mastered the entire doctrinal tradition and could in turn transmit it to the reincarnation of his own teacher. However, the political dimension also played a certain role, which can be seen in the example of a → dalai lama. The most important contemporary *tulkus* are Dalai Lama Tendzin Gyatso (b. 1935), head of the → Gelugpas; Karmapa Rigpe Dorje (1924–82), head of the Kagyupas; Dudjom Rinpoche (1904–86), head of the → Nyingmapas; and the Sakyapa, Sakya Trizin (b. 1945).

Tulsīdās 🅗, or Tulasīdās, 1532–1623, the greatest Indian poet of his time. His Hindi version of Vālmiki's → *Rāmāyana* is still today the most beloved and influential book in North and central India. His *Rāmcharit-Mānas* ("The Holy Sea of Rāma's Deeds") has shaped the moral and spiritual life of millions of Hindus. Of the thirty-seven works ascribed to Tulsīdās, only twelve are known with certainty to have been composed by him. His second great work, the *Vinaya-Patrikā* (" the petition"), discloses in its moving hymns his devotion-filled heart.

Tulsīdās was born the son of a brahman in a village in the province of Uttar Pradesh (North India). Because of an unfavorable constellation at his birth, he was abandoned and was brought up by a → *sādhu*. Ultimately, he married a woman whom he loved passionately. One day, as he followed her uninvited to her parents' house, she turned him back with the words, "If you had half as much love for Rāma as you do for this perishable body, all your sorrows would be over and you would attain enlightenment." Through these sharp but wise words Tulsīdās was brought to understand the unreality of the world. He renounced his wife and consecrated his entire life to Rāma as manifestation of the supreme reality. Many legends have been woven around his life.

The *Rāmcharti-Mānas* is not simply a Hindi translation of Vālmiki's great Sanskrit epic. In Tulsīdās's version, Shiva tells the story of Rāma to his wife Pārvatī. This story is at first concealed within Shiva, just as the great lake Sarovara lies hidden near Mount → Kailāsa, Shiva's home. Only when Pārvatī questions Shiva about the true nature of Rāma does this hidden lake emerge from his innermost being for the benefit of humanity.

Tumo 🅑 (gtum-mo) Tib., lit. "inner heat." One of the six doctrines of Nāropa (→ *Nāro chöd-rug*), which have become known in the West particularly through the biography of → Milarepa. Through regulation of the rhythm of the breath, concentration on the navel center (→ chakra), visualization of certain syllables, as for instance *ram* and *ham* (→ mantra), it is possible for the practitioner to raise his body temperature at will to such a point that he is, in a sense, "burning." This technique, developed from the methods of Indian yoga, in Tibet not only was a special means for attaining enlightenment but was also used for protection against the extreme cold.

T'ung Chung-shu 🅣 Chin. → Confucianism

T'ung-feng An-chu 🅩 (Jap., Tōhō Anshu [Anju]), 9th century; Chinese Ch'an (Zen) master; a student and dharma successor (→ *hassu*) of → Lin-chi I-hsuan (Jap., Rinzai Gigen). We encounter him in example 85 of the → *Pi-yen-lu.* Like a number of Lin-chi's dharma successors, he lived as a hermit.

Tung-shan Liang-chieh 🅩 (Jap., Tōzan Ryōkai), 807–69; Chinese Ch'an (Zen) master. He is considered the student and dharma successor (→ Hassu) of → Yun-yen T'an-sheng (Jap., Ungan Donjō) and was the master of → Ts'ao-shan Pen-chi (Jap., Sōzan Honjaku), → Yueh-chou Ch'ien-feng (Jap., E'shū Kempō, and → Yun-chu Tao-ying (Jap., Ungo Dōyō). Tung-shan Liang-chieh (not to be confused with → Tung-shan Shou-chu) was, together with Ts'ao-shan Pen-chi, the founder of the → Sōtō school and was one of the most important Ch'an masters of the T'ang period. He formulated the → five degrees (of enlightenment), which play an important role in Zen training up to the present (they follow completion of → kōan training in the → Rinzai school). The dharma expositions of Tung-shan Liang-chieh are recorded in the *Shui-chou Tung-shan Liang-chieh-ch'an-shih yu-lu* (*Record of the words of Ch'an Master Tung-shan Liang-chieh from Shui-chou*), which was compiled in the 17th century by the monk Yuan-hsin (1571–1646) and others. We encounter Tung-shan Liang-chieh in example 43 of the → *Pi-yen-lu.*

When Tung-shan Liang-chieh was still a novice training in a monastery of the → Vinaya school of Buddhism, he asked his master the meaning of a line from the → *Heart Sūtra.* The master could give no answer. Thus Tung-shan set out to seek an answer to this burning question from Ch'an masters. At the age of twenty-one he received full ordination on → Sung-shan, then wandered as a pilgrim throughout the country seeking out great Ch'an masters. First he came to → Nan-ch'uan P'u-yuan (Jap., Nansen Fugan), who after a talk with Tung-shan recognized his potential and accepted him as a student. After a period of training, he continued his wandering and came to → Kuei-shan Ling-yu (Jap., Isan Reiyū). After a time, the latter sent him on to Yun-yen T'an-sheng, whose most outstanding student he became and under whom he had his first experience of enlightenment.

When Tung-shan took leave of Yun-yen, as we read in the → *Ching-te ch'uan-teng-lu,* Tung-shan asked him, "How should I describe your dharma if someone asks me about it after you have passed away?" Yun-yen answered, "Just say, 'Just that, that!' " This was an answer that Tung-shan did not understand. When, however, during his further travels, he was wading a river and glimpsed his reflection in the water, he experienced profound enlightenment (→ *daigo-tettei*) and suddenly understood.

At about fifty years of age, Tung-shan became the abbot of a monastery on Mount Hsin-feng. Later he settled on Mount Tung-shan (from which his name is derived), where numerous students gathered around him. He guided them on the path of Ch'an until, in his sixty-third year, sitting in meditation, he passed away.

An example of Tung-shan's teaching style is found in example 43 of the *Pi-yen-lu*:

A monk asked Tung-shan, "Cold and heat come and go. How can one avoid them?"

Tung-shan said, "Why don't you go where there's no cold and heat?"

The monk said, "Where is the place where there is no cold and heat?"

Tung-shan said, "When it's cold, the cold kills the *āchārya* [you]; when it's hot, the heat kills the *āchārya.*"

Tung-shan Shou-chu 🅩 (Jap., Tōsan [Tōzan] Shusho, 910–90; Chinese Ch'an (Zen) master; a student and dharma successor (→ *hassu*) of → Yun-men Wen-yen (Jap., Ummon Bun'en). He should not be confused with → Tung-shan Liang-chieh, who lived on Mount Tung-shan in Kiangsi. The Mount Tung-shan on which Tung-shan Shou-chu carried out his activities as a Ch'an master and from which his name is derived lay in the north of Hupeh province.

Tung-shan Shou-chu came from Shensi in northwestern China. He traveled more than 2,000 kilometers on foot to reach Kwangtung province in southeastern China, where he met Master Yun-men. Considering the uneasy times and the trackless stretches of country he had to cross, this was an impressive proof of his "will for truth" (→ *kokorozashi*).

The story of the enlightenment of Tung-shan Shou-chu is found in example 15 of the → *Wu-men-kuan.*

The kōan is as follows:

"Once when Tung-shan came to Yun-men for instruction, Yun-men asked, 'Where are you coming from?'

"Tung-shan said, 'From Ch'a-tu.'

"Yun-men said, 'Where were you during the summer?'

"Tung-shan said, 'In the Pao-tzu [monastery] in Hunan [lit. "south of the lake"].'

"Yun-men said, 'When did you leave there?'

"Tung-shan said, 'On August 25.'

"Yun-men said, 'I'll spare you sixty blows.'

"The next day Tung-shan came to Yun-men and asked, 'Yesterday I suffered the master's sparing me sixty blows. I don't know where my fault lay.'

"Yun-men said, 'Oh, you rice bag! Why do you wander around west of the river and south of the lake!'

"At these words Tung-shan experienced profound enlightenment." (On "west of the river and south of the lake," → Shih-t'ou Hsi-ch'ien.)

Besides what we learn in examples 15 and 18 of the *Wu-men-kuan* and in Master Yuan-wu's commentary on example 12 of the → *Pi-yen-lu* (which is identical to *Wu-men-kuan* 18), hardly anything is known of Tung-shan Shou-chu. However, his famous answer to the question "What is Buddha?" is one of the most renowned "one-word limits" (→ *ichiji-kan*) in Ch'an (Zen):

A monk asked Tung-shan, "What is Buddha?"

Tung-shan said, "Three pounds of hemp [Jap., *masagin*]!"

Tung-shan wu-wei 🅩 Chin., lit. "five degrees of Tung-shan"; → five degrees (of enlightenment).

Tun-huang 🅑 oasis town in the province of Kansu in northwestern China, where there are famous caves known by the name of Mo-kao-k'u. It is the largest preserved complex of Buddhist cultic caves in the world. The earliest are from the beginning of the 5th century. Today 492 caves are still preserved. The complex extends on five levels over a distance of one kilometer. The caves are primarily famed for their frescoes, which cover a surface area of 45,000 square meters. In addition they contain over 2,400 painted statues. In one of the caves (no. 16), thousands of written scrolls, for the most part sūtras, were discovered. These are of incalculable value for research into the Buddhism of Central Asia and China. The frescoes illustrate stories from the sūtras or depict individual buddha-figures as well as scenes from everyday life. The paintings dating from before the end of the 6th century show incidents from the life of Buddha → Shākyamuni; in those dating from the T'ang period on, frescoes of the western paradise (→ Sukhāvatī) predominate. Other motifs are the Buddha → Maitreya and illustrations from the → *buddhāvatamsaka-sūtra,* the → *Lo-*

tus Sūtra, and the → *Vimalakīrtinirdhesha-sūtra*.

The statues represent buddhas, bodhisattvas (especially the thousand-armed → Avalokiteshvara and → Ti-ts'ang), → *lohans*, different types of deities, and other mythological figures.

The Mo-kao grottoes, which had been filled by desert sand, were discovered by a farmer in 1900. He excavated grotto 16, in which over 40,000 written scrolls (documents, sūtras, Taoist and Confucianist scriptures and paintings) and ritual implements were found. These were left behind by monks who had been living in the caves when they took flight. The farmer, who was not aware of the worth of these objects, sold a part of them. In 1907 there was an expedition of Westerners to Tun-huang. Sir Aurel Stein bought up 150 pieces of silk brocade, over 500 paintings, and 6,500 sūtra scrolls. In 1908 Paul Pelliot, a French Sinologist, left Tun-huang with 6,000 scrolls. Englishmen and Japanese followed. The greater part of the art treasures are now in Western museums.

The basic form of the caves is rectangular or square. The earliest grottoes, from the Wei-dynasty period (middle of the 4th to middle of the 5th centuries), consist of rooms of moderate size with apses in which statues are located. The later ones are made up of several rooms. The statues stand for the most part in the middle of the rooms on a pedestal or on the back walls of the caves. During the Sung period, the caves were connected to each other by balconies and ladders. The walls are divided in sections and have paintings in temperas of themes from the → *Jātaka* tales and of the buddha realms.

The figures from the Wei-dynasty period show clear Indian influence and are characterized by a flat, linear style. They have broad faces and long noses, expressive eyebrows, and radiate a sense of majestic strength. The robes are light and thin. Ornamentation consists of symmetrical forms, foliage motifs, and animals from Chinese mythology. The statues of the Sui-dynasty period (581–618), besides buddhas and bodhisattvas, for the first time depict → Ānanda. In this period a marked Sinicization begins. The figures, with their large heads and upper bodies, have an unproportioned effect and are conspicuous for their rich ornamentation.

The paintings from the T'ang period (618–907) are realistic and lifelike. Robes and jewelry are worked out in detail. From this period come the colossal statues. The largest buddha-figure is 33.25 meters high. The frescoes show scenes from the sūtras; often only a bodhisattva is depicted—evidence of the importance of the veneration of bodhisattvas during this period. Also the earliest → mandalas are found here. From the later periods hardly any caves in their original state are preserved. Most of them have undergone much later alteration, in which, however, no essentially new elements were introduced.

T'un-t'o 🅩 Chin. → *yü-chiang*

Turīya 🅗 Skt., lit. "the fourth"; the superconscious state of illumination, called the fourth because it transcends the three famliar states (→ *avasthā*) of waking, dreaming, and deep sleep. This state of absolute consciousness is beyond thought, causality, and identification with the body; it is indescribable. From the psychological point of view, it is called *turīya*; its philosophical name is → *brahman*. The → *Māndūkya-Upanishad*, which contains an analysis of the various states of consciousness, describes *turīya* as "neither subjective nor objective experience, neither knowledge of the senses, nor relative knowledge, nor derived knowledge." It is positively described as "pure, unified consciousness, unspeakable peace" and "the nature of the → *ātman*" (See also → *brahma-chaitanya*.)

Tushita 🅑 (Tuṣita), Skt., lit. "contented ones"; the heaven inhabited by the "contented gods" (→ *deva*). The Tushita Heaven is the abode of all buddhas who need be reborn on Earth only once more, in order to work through the last remains of karma. Thus it is considered the seat of the future buddha → Maitreya.

Tushita as the heaven of Maitreya was an object of longing for China's believers, who wished to be reborn there. They saw in Maitreya a kind of savior, one who would not only proclaim the teaching but also liberate the world from need and suffering and bring it to a state of untroubled joy. Rebirth in Tushita Heaven could be attained by taking refuge in Buddha Maitreya and reciting his name. However, in the course of historical development, Tushita slipped into the background as the paradise of → Amitābha became more prominent as the goal of believers (→ pure land, → sukhāvatī).

Tu-shun 🅑 also called Fa-shun, 557–640, first patriarch of the → Hua-yen school. Soon after he had begun teaching, the adherents of the → Ti-lun school became his followers. This marked the beginning of the Hua-yen school.

In his youth Tu-shun joined the army but became a monk at the age of eighteen and began the practice of → *dhyāna*. Later he specialized in the → *Buddhāvatamsaka-sūtra*. He originated the theory of the "ten secret gates." These contain the basic teachings of Hua-yen and were later reworked by Fa-tsang, the actual founder of the school.

Because he was supposed to have performed many

miracles, he was called the Bodhisattva of → Tun-huang. The ruling emperor conferred on him the honorific title of *imperial heart* and put a considerable sum at his disposal for defrayal of his living expenses.

T'u-t'an-chai ▣ Chin. → *chai*

T'u-ti ▣ Chin.; deity subordinate to a city god (→ *ch'eng-huang*) and in charge of a specific district or building. Each area, street, temple, or public building of a Chinese town has its own protective deity. Sometimes the functions of a *t'u-ti* are delegated to famous historical personalities.

The responsibilities of the *t'u-ti* are the same as those of the *ch'eng-huang*, i.e., to keep a register on the lives and deaths of the inhabitants in the districts or area under their protection. For that reason they must be informed of all deaths; when someone dies, weeping women visit the temple or shrine of the deity and present incense and paper money. In addition, rich harvests depend on the good will of the *t'u-ti*.

Tu-yen-lung ▣ → Ming-chao Te-chien

Tvashtri ▣ (Tvaṣṭṛ), Skt., lit. "carpenter"; in the *Rigveda* this divinity is the ideal artist, the divine artisan, the lord of all skills. He sharpens and carries the great iron axe and fashioned → Indra's thunderbolt.

The *Shatapatha-Brāhmana* says of Tvashtri: "He created a multitude of beings, he gave form to heaven and earth and all things. He is the lord of the universe, the first-born protector and leader; he knows the regions of the gods. He maintains the worshipers and watches over their sacrificial rites. Like other gods he delights in the hymns of his worshipers, whom he showers with fortune." In the → Purānas, Tvashtri is identified with → Vishvakarma, the architects of the gods, and sometimes with → Prajāpati.

Twice-hidden treasures ▣ → *terma*

Tyāga ▣ Skt., lit. "giving up, letting go"; renunciation, selfless action that is not concerned with fruits or results; a basic principle of → Karma-Yoga. The eighteenth chapter of the *Bhagavad-Gītā* treats this concept in detail as Krishna explains to → Arjuna what true renunciation is. One who practices it is called a *tyāgin*.

Tzu ▣ Chin., lit. "ancestor." The veneration of ancestors has a central role in Chinese religion. Ancestors continue to be part of each family in the form of ancestral plaques. They protect the members of the family and provide a link between the living and the higher worlds. On certain days sacrifices are made to them.

The ancestral plaques are kept in the family shrine. They are about four to five inches wide and twice as long, with the name and possibly the title—sometimes also the dates of birth and death of the departed—engraved on them. Rich families keep these plaques in a separate ancestral temple; families in more modest circumstances usually place them against the north wall of the house. They are surrounded by candles and incense.

The plaques are arranged according to the rank of the ancestors within the family hierarchy: by the side of the plaque of a male ancestor stands that of his main wife. The larger the number of plaques a family possesses, the greater its pride and prestige.

On the days of the new moon and full moon, the ancestors are venerated in small ceremonies, at which the head of the family lights candles and incense and bows to the ancestral plaques. There are other cermonies of a more complex nature, which differ from one family to the next but are usually held on the birthday or date of death of the ancestor in question. On these occasions it is not at all uncommon to serve the departed ancestor a complete meal.

Tzu-fu ▣ (Jap., Shifuku), 9th/10th century; Chinese Ch'an (Zen) master of the Igyō school; a "grandson in dharma" of → Yang-shan Hui-chi. Very little is known of Tzu-fu. Nonetheless he must have been an outstanding master, since he was one of the few masters within the Igyō school selected to be initiated into the use of the ninety-seven circle symbols (→ Igyō school). We encounter Tzu-fu in examples 33 and 91 of the → *Pi-yen-lu*. In both examples he makes use of one of the circle symbols as a means to express his realization of living truth.

Tzu-hu Li-tsung ▣ (Jap., Shiko Rishō), roughly 800–880; Chinese Ch'an (Zen) master; a student and dharma successor (→ *hassu*) of → Nan-ch'uan P'u-yuan (Jap., Nansen Fugan). Tzu-hu appears in Master Hsueh-t'ou's praise (→ *ju*) to the examples 17 and 96 of the → *Pi-yen-lu*.

Of Tzu-hu Li-tsung it is said that he had the following warning sign placed at the entrance to the monastery of which he was the → *rōshi*: "Beware. On Tzu-hu [Mountain] there lives a dog. He eats up people's heads, hearts, and feet. Whoever hesitates or argues here loses body and life."

Tzu-hu is also known for once having let the profoundly enlightened nun → Liu T'ieh-mo (Jap., Ryū Tetsuma), who was feared in the Ch'an circles of the time on account of her sharp tongue, taste the stick.

Tzu-jan ▣ Chin., lit. "being such of itself," natural, spontaneous; a concept of philosophical Taoism (→ *tao-chia*). Everything that is spontaneous and free of human intention or external influences is *tzu-jan*. It is something in harmony with itself. It denotes the highest realization of being and absolute loyalty to itself.

Tzu-jan is closely related to → *wu-wei,* unmotivated action, in that it could be said to be both its aim and norm.

Chapter 25 of the *Tao-te ching* defines *tzu-jan* as follows: "There are four great ones in the universe, and one of them is man. Man conforms to Earth, Earth to Heaven, Heaven to the → Tao and the Tao to nature [lit. "suchness"]."

According to the Japanese *Tao-te ching* scholar Akira Öhama, *tzu-jan* is a spontaneous energy inherent in the Tao, and thus the self-unfoldment of its effect: "The Tao acts like an immanent energy, a mysterious presence within the world of the ten thousand things (→ *wan-wu*). Therefore the individual effects of the ten thousand things—if they are not prevented from following their own nature—are in accordance with the *tzu-jan* of the Tao. What matters, is not the self-conscious intentional striving for oneness with the Tao, but rather the fact that human action is identical with the Tao that is present and acting in man. That is *tzu-jan"* (Béky 1972, p. 126).

U

U-ango 🅉 Jap. → *ango*

Uchchishta 🄷 (Ucciṣṭa), Skt., lit. "left over"; the remains of food from a sacrificial offering. According to the Vedic view, it contains divine forces (→ *prasāda*).

Paul Deussen calls attention to a hymn in the *Atharvaveda* (11.7) according to which all names and shapes in the world are due to the *uchchishta,* that is, to the remainder that is left after all names and forms are removed. The inner self of the human being, described in the hymn three times as "that in me" and once as "the brilliance in me," is also traced back to the *uchchishta.* Both of these, the "remainder" of the world and the "remainder" in the inmost self, cannot be grasped by the mind, for they transcend it. In these thoughts the hymn is a direct precursor of the Upanishadic doctrine (→ Upanishads) of the → *ātman.*

Udāna 🄱 Skt. a specific form of → *prāna$ J: the upward-flowing prāna* current that binds the physical and metaphysical parts of our being and, when activated, furthers spiritual development. Through it, the soul leaves the body at the time of death.

🄱 → *Khuddaka-nikāya*

Udbhijja 🄷 Skt., lit. "sprouting from the earth," seed-born; the second of the four types of origin of life, that of plants. The other three are sweat-born (insects), egg-born (birds, fish, and amphibians), and womb-born (mammals, human beings); see also → *chatur-yoni.*

Uddālāka Ārunī 🄷 a sage; his celebrated instructions to his son → Shvetaketu regarding the unity of everything (identity of *ātman* and *brahman*) are in the → *Chāndogya-Upanishad.*

Uddhava 🄷 a friend and confident of Krishna. He was Krishna's cousin, since his father, Devabhāga and Krishna's father, Vasudeva, were brothers. In the eleventh *skandha* (chapter) of the → *Bhāgavata-Purāna,* Uddhava receives full instructions from Krishna, similar to those received by → Arjuna in the → *Bhagavad-Gītā.*

Udgātri 🄷 (Udgātṛ), or Udgātar, Skt.; one of the four chief priests in a sacrificial ceremony. His function is to declaim the prayers and hymns of the → *Sāmaveda,* which declamation or singing is called *udgītha.* The *Chāndogya-Upanishad* equates the *udgītha* with the sacred syllable → OM.

Uktha 🄷 Skt.; a hymn of praise in the → *Rig-veda.* The *Kaushītaki-Upanishad* calls it the most beautiful, most glorious, and most powerful hymn" and equates it with → *brahman.*

Ullambana 🄱 Skt.; festival of the hungry ghosts (→ *preta*); holiday in Chinese Buddhism, celebrated on the fifteenth day of the seventh month. On this day ceremonies are held in which food, flowers, paper money, clothes, and so on are offered and sūtras are recited in order to soothe the torments of the deceased in the lower realms of existence (→ *gati*). This holiday was celebrated for the first time in 538 and is still celebrated today.

The origin of this ceremony is to be found in the legend of → Maudgalyāyana, who thanks to his "divine eye" (→ *abhijñā*) saw that his mother had been reborn as a hungry ghost and wanted to save her. The Buddha told him that only the combined effort of all

Buddhist monks could soothe the sufferings of the tormented. From this tradition developed the custom of offering food, clothing, and so on to the hungry ghosts. These offerings are said to liberate seven generations of the ancestors of the offerer from all suffering. The combination of the Buddhist worldview and the Chinese folk custom of ancestor veneration explains the tremendous popularity of this festival in China, in which not only Buddhists but also Taoists and Confucianists participate.

Since the T'ang period, the Ullambana festival is one of the few days on which the treasures of the monasteries are on view for the public. In the Sung period, the holiday increasingly took on a quality of a real folk festival. It lasted for days, during which, for example, plays with Maudgalyāyana's story as the main theme were performed.

Ultimate truth B → *paramārtha-satya*

Umā H, a name for the wife of → Shiva. As Umā-Haimavatī ("descended from Himalaya") she is a symbol of the supreme pinnacle of being, the supreme force of the One (→ *brahman*), the Divine in his supreme manifestation.

Umā is first mentioned in the → *Kena-Upanishad*, where she appears as mediator between Brahmā and the other gods. She is the daughter of → Himavat, the king of the Himalayas. Shiva, as her husband, bears the name Umāpati ("Umā's spouse").

Umban Z Jap. → *umpan*

Ummon Bun'en Z Jap. for → Yun-men Wen-yen

Ummon school Z (Chin., Yun-men-tsung; Jap., Ummon-shū); a school of Ch'an (→ Zen) originated by the great Chinese Ch'an master → Yun-men Wen-yen (Jap., Ummon Bun'en). It belonged to the "five houses" (→ *goke-shichi-shū*) of Ch'an and produced, among others, the great master → Hsueh-tou Ch'ung-hsien (Jap., Setchō Jūken), who collected the kōans later published by → Yuan-wu K'o-ch'in (Jap., Engo Kokugon) in the → *Pi-yen-lu* and provided them with celebrated "praises" (→ *ju*). Hsueh-tou was the last important master of the Ummon school, which began to decline in the middle of the 11th century and died out altogether in the 12th.

Umpan Z also umban, Jap., lit. "cloud-platter"; a flat gong of bronze used in Zen monasteries to give various signals. The name comes from the fact that the flat bronze piece has the shape of a cloud (also → *unsui*) and its surface is often decorated with cloud motifs.

Percussive devices like the *umpan*, → *han*, or → *inkin* are used in Zen monasteries, in which the monks—especially during → sesshins—maintain complete silence, to indicate the various periods and activities of the day. The sound of bells or gongs, of wooden planks or clackers, have a special effect on the consciousness of practitioners in the silence that prevails in a Zen monastery. The effect of the sudden sound of such instruments on the collected heart-mind (→ *kokoro*) of the practitioner of *zazen* can, depending on his or her momentary state, lie anywhere between "refreshing" and "shattering" and can even provide a moment of breakthrough leading to an experience of enlightenment (→ *kenshō*, → satori).

Ungai Shichi Z Jap. for → Yun-kai Shou-chih

Ungan Donjō Z Jap. for → Yun-chu Tao-ying

Unnō Z Jap., lit. "cloud robe"; another word for → *unsui*.

Unsui Z Jap., lit. "cloud water." Novices in a Zen monastery are called *unsui*, and ornaments in a Zen monastery and temples are often in the form of stylized clouds and water motifs. Aimlessly coming and going, moving freely, forming and changing in accordance with external circumstances, disappearing without reluctance like clouds; like water soft and flowing around every obstruction without hesitation; like water in relation to a container, fully adapting to any situation—these are the characteristics of living in the mind of Zen. Another word for *unsui* is → *unnō*.

Taking clouds and water as a model for one's way of life is a notion that derives from Taoism, which had as strong a shaping effect on Ch'an (Zen) as Buddhism did. Countless Taoist poets have celebrated the "white cloud" as a symbol of a liberated existence. The 11th-century Taoist scholar Nan Yao wrote in his *Tao-cheng*:

"Of all the elements, the sage should choose water as his teacher. Water is all-victorious. . . . Water evades all confrontations with a kind of deceptive modesty, but no power can prevent it from following its predestined course to the sea. Water conquers through humility; it never attacks but nevertheless wins the final battle. The sage who makes himself like water is distinguished by his humility. He works through passivity, acts through nonaction, and thus conquers the world." (trans. from German trans. of J. Blofeld, *Wheel of Life*)

Upādāna B Skt., Pali; all attachments that create bonds that bind beings to existence and drive them from rebirth to rebirth. Objects of attachment are constituted by the five → *skandhas*, which are thus often referred to as *upādāna-skandha*. In the context of the chain of conditioned arising (→ *pratītya-samutpāda*), attachment or craving (→ *trishnā*) has as its effect "taking possession of a womb" and thus instigates the arising of a new existence (→ *bhava*).

The → *Abhidharmakosha* distinguishes four kinds of *upādāna*; sensual attachment, attachment to views, attachment to rites and rules, and attachment to belief in an individuality (→ *anātman*).

Upādāna-skandha 🅱 Skt. → *skandha*

Upadesha-Sahasri 🅷 (Upadeśa-Sahasri), Skt., lit. *upadesha:* "instruction, teaching," *sahasri:* "thousandfold"; one of the chief works of → Shankara. The first part is composed in prose, the second part in poetry.

The prose section comprises only three chapters. They discuss the method leading to the enlightenment of the student, knowledge of the immutable, nondual Self (→ *atman*), and give instructions for the repetition and spiritual penetration of sacred texts. The verse section expounds the nature of consciousness, the "witness," and the mind, and ends with an explanation of the precept → *Tat tvam asi*" ("That thou art"). For spiritual aspirants and students of → Vedānta, the work is of great importance.

Upadesha-Vākya 🅷 (Upadeśa-Vākya), Skt., lit. *upadesha:* "instruction, teaching," *vākya:* "speech, sentence"; the words used by the → guru to initiate a student into the truth. They must be words that come from the guru's own realization; a construction of purely academic words will have no effect.

Upādhi 🅷 Skt., lit. "addition"; a limiting attribute. This concept of → Vedānta refers to all names and forms of ignorance that are taken up by the → *ātman* when it is identified with the body, mind, senses, and ego. *Upādhi* refers to everything that is superimposed on and conceals → *brahman.*

Upādhyāya 🅱 Skt.; Buddhist teacher responsible for observance of rites, rules, and discipline in a monastic community. (Also → *āchārya.*)

Upagupta 🆉 fourth patriarch in the Indian lineage of Ch'an (→ Zen).

Upāli 🅱 student of the → Buddha. Upāli was originally a barber to the → Shākya princes but held a higher rank within the → *sangha,* since he was ordained by the Buddha before the princes. His earlier profession led to his being the one to shave the heads of the monks. Tradition sees in him the specialist in questions of discipline and ritual. In the first → Buddhist council, it was Upāli who was questioned concerning regulations. His responses were the basis for the codification of the → Vinaya-pitaka. He was one of the → ten great disciples of the Buddha.

Upanayana 🅷 Skt., lit. "initiation, taking up"; the ceremony of investment with the sacred thread, by means of which the son of a brahman is permanently taken into the brahman caste (→ *varna*). He takes an oath to practice purity, truthfulness, and self-control, and is initiated into the → Gāyatrī mantra. He is then permitted to practice ritual worship (→ *pūjā).*

Upanishads 🅷 (Upaniṣad), Skt., lit. *upa:* "near," *ni:* "down," *sad:* "sit," "to sit down near to," that is, at the feet of the guru, in order to receive the confidential, secret teaching. The Upanishads form the final portion of the → *shruti* (the revealed part of the Veda) and the principal basis of → Vedānta, the philosophical conclusion derived from the Vedas. They are distinguished, valued highly by seekers of wisdom, for their transcendent breadth and powerful freedom of thought. Like creeping plants (→ *valli*), they lean against the preceding sections of the Veda to which they belong and yet preserve total independence and freedom from priestly dogma. Central to the Upanishads is the significance of → *ātman* and → *brahman*, knowledge of the identity of these two, and the meaning of the sacred syllable → OM.

Of the twelve most important Upanishads, the *Aitareya* and *Kuashītaki* belong to the → *Rigveda,* the → *Chāndogya* and → *Kena* belong to the → *Sāmaveda,* the *Taittirīya, Katha, Shvetāshvatara, Brihadāranyaka,* and *Īshā* belong to the → *Yajurveda,* and the *Prashna, Mundaka,* and *Māndūkya* belong to the *Atharvaveda.*

Each of the four Veda was taught in various → *shakhas* ("branches"), that is, Vedic schools. The older Upanishads were originally the dogmatic textbooks of the individual Vedic schools. However, the Upanishads of the *Yajurveda* and above all of the *Atharvaveda* no longer have any reference whatever to a particular Vedic school. The school of the *Shvetāshvatara-Upanishad,* for example, is completely unknown, and the Upanishads of the *Atharvaveda* are apocryphal in character for the most part.

Each Shākhā has its own → Brāhmana, to which an → Āranyaka is appended that in turn contains the Upanishad. The Brāhmana and Aranyaka arose with a view to the Brahmanic life stages (→ *āshrama,* 2), according to which it fell to those in the second stage (→ *grihasta*) to carry out the sacrificial rites. For the third stage (→ *vānaprastha*) was reserved the process of internalization of these ceremonies. In the place of a physical sacrifice, which an older person often could no longer carry out, came the mental review of the deep, mystical meaning of the Veda. At this level, the man who had learned the Upanishadic text at the first stage (→ *brahmacharya*) was finally capable of understanding its profound insights into the nature of the world and one's own self.

The teachings of the Upanishads are frequently clothed in stories. In many of these great sages visit the courts of kings, who become their pupils and ask for instruction in the way to discover the supreme truth.

Upa-Purāna H Skt. → Purāna

Uparama H, or Uparati, Skt., lit. "cessation"; that which helps to quiet the mind so that one may concentrate undisturbed. Included are the fulfillment of one's duty (→ *dharma*), because unfulfilled duties disturb the mind, and the practice of tolerance regarding other religious beliefs. Uparama is one of the "six virtues" (→ *shatkasampatti*) listed in Shankara's work → *Tattvabodha* among the requirements for a student of Vedānta.

Upāsaka B (fem., upāsikā), Skt., Pali, lit. "one who sits close by"; Buddhist lay adherent who through the threefold refuge (→ *trisharana*, → *sambō*) acknowledges himself as such and vows to observe the five → *shīlas*.

According to the Hīnayāna view, laypersons are still far from the final goal of liberation, since they are not ready to give up their worldly life and its pleasures. Still they can accumulate merit (→ *punya*), especially through the practice of generosity (→ *dāna*), and this enables them to be reborn as monks or nuns and still later as → arhats. In this way they can advance on the way to nirvāna.

In the Hīnayāna, the lay adherents are the bearers of the Buddhist cult through making offerings of food, clothing, music, processions, and so on. The monastic community expects that the lay adherents will care for the material welfare of the monks and nuns.

In the Mahāyāna, lay followers are of greater importance, since the possibility of their attaining liberation is no longer discounted. The ideal figure of the Mahāyāna, the → bodhisattva, is a layperson.

In China formal ordination of lay adherents, usually as part of a ceremony for ordaining monks, is common. Lay ordination consists of vowing to observe the five *shīlas*. In case for any reason one or more of these *shīlas* cannot be observed, it is possible to take on oneself only the remaining ones. As a sign of ordination, *upāsakas* are burned three or more times on the inside of the arm. Lay adherents usually go on to take the bodhisattva vow (→ *pranidhāna*) after lay ordination.

Upasampadā B Skt. → ordination

Upāsana H Skt.; veneration and worship of God in one of his numerous forms or manifestations. in the → Upanishads, *upāsana* consists of meditation; according to → Rāmānuja it plays an essential role in the process of intensification of one's love for God (→ *bhakti).*

Upāsana-Kānda H (Upāsana-Kāṇḍa), Skt.; occasionally the division of the → Vedas into a *karma-kānda* (section on action) and a *jñāna-kanda* (section on knowledge) is supplemented by a third section, the *upāsanda-kānda* (section on worship), dealing with devotion, prayer, meditation, and loving surrender to God; it is of particular importance for → Bhakti-Yoga. The rites, ceremonies, and forms of worship contained in this section are called *upāsana-vākya.*

Upaveda H Skt.; secondary Veda, Veda in the sense of a science. The Upavedas are not counted among the → *Shrutis* as the Vedas are.

There are four Upavedas: (1) *Āyurveda* (on medicine); (2) *Gandharvaveda* (on music and dance); (3) *Dhanurveda* (on archery); (4) *Sthāpatyaveda* (on architecture).

Upāya B Skt.; skill in means or method. 1. The ability of a → bodhisattva to guide beings to liberation through skillful means. All possible methods and ruses from straightforward talk to the most conspicuous miracles could be applicable. This ability, which is one of the → *pāramitās*, is perfected by the bodhisattva in the seventh stage of his development (→ *bhūmi*).

Avalokiteshvara, whose thousand arms symbolize his "skillful means" (upāya)

2. Skill in expounding the teaching. Many

schools of the Mahāyāna (→ T'ien-t'ai, → Hua-yen) hold the view that the historical Buddha made use of *upāya* by teaching in accordance with the capabilities of his students, first teaching only the Hīnayāna, which is regarded as incomplete, and then only toward the end of his life teaching the complete Mahāyāna, especially the → *Lotus Sūtra.*

Upāya is the activity of the absolute in the phenomenal world, which manifests as compassion (→ *karunā*). *Upāya*, the principle of the manifold, is contrasted with wisdom (→ *prajñā*), which represents universal unity. From the standpoint of enlightened understanding, i.e., looking with the eye of wisdom, bodhisattvas do not perceive individual suffering beings, since nothing exists other than the *dharmakāya* (→ *trikāya*), the absolute. However, when regarding the universe from the point of view of compassion, they recognize suffering, which arises from attachment to forms, everywhere. In order to liberate beings from their suffering-ridden state, they devise all possible means helpful toward the attainment of nirvāna. These are supported by the limitless compassion of the *dharmakāya.*

Upāya-Pratyaya 🅗 Skt., lit. *upāya:* "approach, arrival," *pratyaya:* "reason, cause"; the merging of the individual consciouness, mental consciousness, in the final cause, absolute consciousness (→ *brahman*), resulting in → *samādhi.*

Upekshā 🅗 🅑 (upekṣā), Skt., lit. "not taking notice, disregard."
🅗 Not simply the act of overlooking others' faults or errors, but also the act of critically considering how one would behave in a similar situation, in order to learn from such examination for oneself and for others.
🅑 (Pali, upekkhā); equanimity, one of the most important Buddhist virtues. *Upekshā* refers to (1) a state that is neither joy nor suffering but rather is independent of both; (2) the mind that is in equilibrium and elevated above all distinctions. In Buddhist texts *upekshā* is usually found in the second sense. *Upekshā* is one of the seven factors of enlightenment (→ *bodhyanga*) and one of the four → *brahma-vihāras.*

Uposatha 🅑 Pali, lit. "fasting"; an observance taking place on days of the quarter-moon. *Uposatha* is one of the most important observances in the Southeast Asian countries of Theravāda Buddhism. It is a day of religious reflection for laypersons leading a worldly life, who at this time devote themselves to stricter practice. The lay people gather at a monastery where they participate in worship and expositions of the teaching and vow to observe the rules of moral discipline (→ *shīla*). Many of them observe eight *shīlas* on *uposatha* days, fast, and spend the day in meditation. In addition, on full- and new-moon days the monastic disciplinary code (→ *Pratimoksha*) is recited before the assembly of monks.

Monks are obliged to take part in the uposatha ceremonies, which take place in a special room in the monastery (→ *vihāra*) that must be large enough to accomodate the local community of monks. If a monk is prevented from attending, he must make a declaration to another monk that he is not aware of having violated any rule of the *Pratimoksha.* The ceremony cannot take place if a monk does not attend for any reason other than illness. Monks who have committed a violation must communicate this to another monk before the beginning of the ceremony. During the *uposatha* ceremony, the *Pratimoksha* is recited by the head of the monastery, who calls three times for the monks to confess their faults. Laypersons, novices, nuns, and monks who have been expelled from the order are not permitted to attend this ceremony.

Ūrdhva-Budhna 🅗 Skt., lit. *ūrdhva:* "upward, over," *budhna:* "depths, bottom"; a term referring to the force residing in language (→ *vāk*), whose vibrations can raise the vital energies from the depths and enable human beings spiritually to surpass their own limitations by enlightening their minds.

One has only to consider how praise lifts a person up, whereas an insult can injure and repulse. This effect is produced not by the wod alone but by the power of the vibration that gives the word its life.

Urgyen 🅑 (u-rgyan or o-rgyan), Tib. (Skt., Oddiyana); a mythical realm that in Tibetan Buddhism is considered the birthplace of → Padmasambhava and the dwelling place of the → *dākinīs.* Geographically, it is placed in an area between Afghanistan and Kashmir, approximately in the Swat valley of present-day Pakistan. The oldest Buddhist Tantras, however, speak of Urgyen as a holy site located in Bengal in northeast India. In both of these traditions Urgyen is considered the place of origin of certain Tantric teachings. One of the eighty-four → *mahāsiddhas*, Indrabhūti, is considered to have been the king of Urgyen.

Urvashī 🅗 (Urvaśī), Skt.; a heavenly nymph of extraordinary beauty, first mentioned in the *Rigveda.*

Urvashī provoked the wrath of → Mitra and → Varuna, who damned her to life on earth. She became the wife of → Purūravas. The love story of Urvashī and Purūravas is told by → Kālidāsa in his drama *Vikramorvashīya.*

Ūshā 🅗 a → Daitya princess, daughter of → Bāna and granddaughter of → Bali. She is also called Prītijushā.

In a dream, Ushā fell in love with a prince; by the help of her friend Chitralekha she knew him to be → Aniruddha. Chitralekha brought him to her by means of her occult powers, but her father, Bāna, abducted him by magic and held him prisoner. When Krishna, → Pradyumna, and → Balarāma heard of this and wanted to free him, a great battle broke out, at the end of which Aniruddha returned to Dvārakā with Ushā as his wife.

Ushas 🅗 (Uṣas), Skt., lit. "dawn"; the goddess of the dawn, daughter of heaven and sister of the → Ādityas. Only a few Vedic hymns are dedicated to her, but these few belong to the most tender, beautiful, and poetic of the hymns.

Ushas is the friend of mankind. She appears as a lovely maiden who takes the place of her sister, Night, and climbs ever higher out of the mist of the eastern sky, bathing heaven and earth in waves of light. She enters every house, disdaining neither old nor young as she grants prosperity to the inhabitants. Herself eternally youthful, she nevertheless allows human beings to grow old.

Utkata-Karma 🅗 (Utkaṭa-Karma), Skt., *utkata,* lit. "excessive, full"; → *karma* that is due and hence must come into operation; also, deeds and thoughts that can no longer be reversed or changed, just as an arrow that has left the bow cannot be taken back or changed in its course. Synonymous with → *prārabdha-karma.*

Utsāha 🅗 Skt.; power, vitality, endurance, constant wakefulness. Only by endurance, persistent exertion, and one's own tenacious efforts is it possible to advance along the spiritual path. Therefore, *utsāha* is an essential quality.

Uttara 🅗 Skt. → *pūrva*

Uttarabodhi-mudrā 🅑 Skt. → mudrā 7

Uttara-Mīmāmsā 🅗 (Uttara-Mīmāṃsā), Skt., lit. *uttara:* "later, subsequent," *mīmāmsā:* "discussion"; Uttara-Mīmāmsā is one of the six → *darshanas.* Generally referred to as → Vedānta, it succeeds the philosophy of → Pūrva-Mīmāmsā not only chronologically but in terms of its content. Uttara-Mīmāmsā is concerned with the attainment of knowledge, which in general must be preceded by purification, such as that which Pūrva-Mīmāmsā brings about through the performance of ritual. (See also → Mīmāmsa.)

Uttarayāna 🅗 Skt. → *devayāna*

V

Vāch 🅗 Skt. → *vāk*

Vachchagotta 🅑 (Vaccagotta); 1. one of the forty-one "great monks" mentioned in the → *Anguttara-nikāya,* who were among the direct students of Buddha → Shākyamuni. Vachchagotta was renowned as a meditation master and is supposed to have had many magical powers.

2. A wandering ascetic by the same name, who, as reported in the → *Samyutta-nikāya,* asked the Buddha if there was such a thing as self or not. The Buddha declined to answer this question.

Vādavidyā 🅗 Skt. → Nyāya

Vāhana 🅗 Skt., lit. "vehicle"; means of conveyance as employed by the majority of Hindu gods; iconography accords to each god a *vāhana* in the form of a more or less fantastic animal, as show in the table below:

Divinity	*Vāhana*
Agni	Ram
Brahmā	Swan (→ *hamsa*)
Durgā	Lion or tiger
Ganesha	Rat
Indra	Elephant
Kārttikeya	The peacock Paravāni
Shiva	Bull (→ *nandi*)
Varuna	Fish
Vāyu	Antelope
Vishnu	the "bird" → Garuda
Yama	Buffalo

Vaibhāshika 🅑 (Vaibhāṣika), Skt., lit. "adherents of the Mahāvibhāshā"; term for the late phase of the → Sarvāstivāda. It is derived from the names of the two works (*Mahāvibhāshā* and *Vibhāshā*) considered fundamental by this school.

They are two important commentaries on the → Abhidharma of the Sarvāstivāda school.

Vaidhī-Bhakti 🅗 Skt. → *bhakti*

Vaikhari-Japa 🅗 Skt. → *japa*

Vaikuntha 🅗 (Vaikuṇṭha), Skt.; Vishnu's paradise, variously described as located on Mount → Meru or in the northern ocean. Vishnu himself is sometimes called Vaikuntha, as is Indra.

Vaipulya-sūtra 🅑 Skt., lit. "Extensive Sūtra"; extensive Mahāyāna sūtras, sometimes even collections of independent sūtras, each having a particular aspect of the teaching as its subject. Among the Vaipulya-sūtras are the → *Prajñāpāramitā-sūtra,* the → *Buddhāvatamsaka-sūtra* (short name, *Avatamsaka-sūtra*), and the → *Ratnakūta-sūtra.* In addition, in the Chinese canon are found the → *Mahāparinirvāna-sūtra,* the *Mahāsamnipāta-sūtra,* and the → *Lotus Sūtra.*

Vairāgya 🅗 Skt.; lit. "absence of passion," in the West often erroneously translated as "renunciation," which latter condition generally requires a deliberate restraint. *Vairāgya,* by contrast, is understood in → Vedānta as a process of naturally growing away from the transient things of this world because one has discovered the immortal reality that is *brahman.* One who delights in the study of holy texts needs no self-control to give up children's books; such a student has outgrown them. Shankara's work → *Tattvabodha* lists *vairāgya* as one of the four prerequisites for the spiritual aspirant. The other three are → *viveka,* → *mumukshutva,* and → *shatkasampatti.* One who has attained *vairāgya* is called a *vairāgi.*

Vairochana 🅗 🅑 🅩 (Vairocana), Skt., lit. "He Who Is Like the Sun."
🅗 or Virochana; an → *asura,* the son of → Prahlāda and father of → Bali. The *Chāndogya-Upanishad* (8.7-8) describes his attempt, together with Indra, to find the Self (→ *ātman).*

The gods and the demons wanted to discover the Self and thus sent Indra and Vairochana to → Prajāpati to ask for instruction. Prajāpati taught them with the words "That which is seen reflected in the eye, that is the Self." They then asked, "Is that which is reflected in water the Self?" "Yes, that is the Self reflected there," answered Prajāpati. "Look at your reflection in the water, and if there is anything you do not understand, tell me about it." The two students looked at themselves in the water. Vairochana believed that he now knew the Self and returned to the *asuras,* whereas Indra had doubts and continued to put questions to Prajāpati until he had received total certainty regarding the Self and consequently attained enlightenment.

This passage describes one of the characteristic distinctions between the demonic and the godly natures referred to by Krishna in the *Bhagavad-Gītā.* Those of demonic nature are satisfied with the outer appearance, the outer world, while those of godly nature find no rest until they attain enlightenment.

🅑 🅩 one of the five transcendent buddhas. He is associated with the transcendent bodhisattva → Samantabhadra and the earthly buddha Krakuchchanda. Vairochana is often depicted making the gesture of supreme wisdom (→ mudrā). His symbols are the wheel of the teaching (→ dharma-chakra) and the sun.

Vairochana with hands in the mudrā of supreme wisdom

In about the 10th century, a further elaboration took place in the Mahāyāna Buddhist doctrine of the transcendent buddhas and the bodhisattvas associated with them. A supreme buddha, or so-called *ādi-buddha,* was introduced. He was considered the absolute, the personification of dharmakāya (→ *trikāya*). Vairochana, as the first of the transcendent (or *dhyāni*) buddhas, was in the course of time identified with this *ādi-*, or primordial, buddha.

In Japan Vairochana (Jap., Birushana) is regarded as a sun buddha and is at the center of a system in which the four other *dhyāni* buddhas circle him like planets (→ Shingon school).

Vaishālī 🅑 (Vaiśālī) Skt., (Pali, Vesāli); an important city in the early phase of Buddhism (present-day Basarh), 40 kilometers northwest of modern Patna between the Ganges and the

Himālayas. Vaishālī was the capital of the Lichchavis, who belonged to the Vajjī Confederation, which → Ajātasattu wanted to attack. → Shākyamuni frequently visited Vaishālī, where the courtesan Ambapāli had given him a → *vihāra.* Here he is said to have pronounced a number of important discourses. In 386 B.C.E., the second Buddhist → council was held in Vaishālī.

In 1958 a bowl was discovered in a stūpa that contained remainders of bone, ashes, and various burial offerings. This may possibly be the Lichchavis' share of the Buddha's relics.

Vaishampāyana 🅗 (Vaiśampāyana), a celebrated sage; student of the great → Vyāsa, who taught him the *Mahābhārata,* which Vaishampāyana later recited at a festival to King Janamejaya. The → *Harivamsha* is also said to have been transmitted by him.

Vaisharadya 🅑 Skt. → four certainties

Vaisheshika 🅗 (Vaiśeṣika), Skt., lit. "referring to the distinctions (→ *vishesha*)"; the oldest of the six orthodox Hindu philosophical systems (→ *darshana*). Founded by → Kanāda, it divides the multiplicity of nature into six categories, the *padārthas,* and is scientifically rather than philosophically oriented. However, Vaisheshika maintains the view that through the fulfillment of particular duties one may come to know the six *padārthas,* and that this knowledge leads to bliss.

The six *padārthas* are (1) *dravya* (substance, matter); (2) *guna* (quality, characteristic); (3) *karma* (activity); (4) *sāmānya* (universality); (5) *vishesha* (distinctiveness); (6) *samavāya* (inherence, concomitance, the relation between a whole and its parts, between substance and quality, between the general and the particular). The six *padārthas* are no mere concepts; rather they are real essences (*artha*) described by the corresponding word (*pada*). Kanāda presents his system in the *Vaisheshika-Sūtra,* which consists of ten *adhyāyas* (chapters).

Vaishnava 🅗 (Vaiṣṇava), Skt.; an adherent of → Vaishnavism, one of the three chief forms of deity worship in modern Hinduism. The chief scriptures of the Vaishnavas are the Vaishnava-Purānas (→ Purānas).

Within Vaishnavism there are various subgroups, according to the aspect of Vishnu that is worshiped: the → Rāmānujas, who venerate Īshvara as the supreme being; the → Nimbārkas and the Vallabhāchāryas, worshipers of Krishna and Rādhā; the Mādhavas, who worship Vishnu as the supreme being; the Rāmānandins, who worship Rāma and Sītā. Their greatest poets were → Kabīr and → Tulsīdās; the latter composed the Hindi version of the *Rāmāyana.*

Vaishnavism 🅗 (Vaíṣṇavism), or Vishnuism; one of the three great forms of deity worship in modern Hinduism. The other two are → Shaivism and → Shaktism. → Vaishnavas view Vishnu as the supreme being and worship him in his various incarnations (→ *avatāra*), above all as Rāma and Sītā.

Vaishvānara 🅗 (Vaiśvānara), or Virāj, Skt., lit. "referring to all human beings," a term that in → Vedānta refers to the waking state of human beings in general. In reference to an individual, it is called *vishva.* One of the four → *avasthās,* it is synonymous with → *jagrat.* The three other states of consciousness are known in Vedānta as → *prajñā* (deep sleep), → *taijasa* (dreaming sleep), and → *turīya* ("the fourth"). The *Māndūkya-Upanishad* discusses these in detail.

Vaishvānara governs the individual's body, mind, and sensations in the waking state. In the *Rigveda, vaisvānara* means sun and fire; hence → Agni is occasionally called by the same name.

Vaishvānara-Vidyā 🅗 (Vaiśvānara-Vidyā), Skt., lit. *vaishvānara:* "relating to all, encompassing all," *vidyā:* "knowledge"; the knowledge that the universal Self is living in all beings; the certainty that all are one with universal consciousness.

Vaishya 🅗 Skt. → *varna*

Vaivasvata 🅗 Skt., lit. "the sun-born"; the seventh → Manu, that of the present age. He was the son of → Vivasvat and the father of Ikshvāku, founder of the solar race of kings, and was one of the compilers of the → *Manu-Samhitā.* Krishna mentions him in the *Bhagavad-Gītā* (4.1).

Vajra 🅗 🅑 🅩 Skt.

🅗 1. → Indra's flash of lightning or his "thunderbolt," said to have been made from the bones of the seer Dadhīchi. It is a weapon circular in shape with a hole in the center. It has many names, such as "the splitter," "the bellowing one," "the destroyer"; 2. the son of → Aniruddha. His mother is the Daitya princess → Ūshā. Shortly before his death, Krishna made him king of the Yādavas.

🅑 🅩 (Tib., *dorje*); "diamond" or "adamantine." The *vajra* has a different meaning in Buddhism than in Hinduism, where the *vajra* is Indra's "thunderbolt." In Buddhism it is not a weapon but a symbol of the indestructible; for this reason it is translated "diamond" or "adamantine"; the translation "thunderbolt" is false in the Buddhist context. Here it stands for true reality, emptiness (→ *shūnyatā*), the being or essence of everything existing. This emptiness is indestructible like diamond, i.e., imperishable and unborn or uncreated. The spotless purity and translucency of the diamond symbolizes the perfect spotlessness of emptiness, untainted by all the appearances that arise out of it. It is that aspect of reality referred to in Zen in the saying regarding the countless phenomena, "There's not a thing there." This emptiness, however, is not different from things, from all phenomena. It is one and identical with them. This cannot be conceptually "understood" but can be experienced in → enlightenment.

The *vajra* as symbol of the absolute

For the particular meaning of the *vajra* in Tibetan Buddhism, see → *dorje*.

Vajradhara 🅱 Skt. → Samantabhadra

Vajradhātu mandala 🅱 Skt. → Shingon school

Vajrapradama-mudrā 🅱 Skt. → mudrā 10

Vajrasattva 🅱 Skt., lit. "Diamond Being"; in → Vajrayāna Buddhism, the principle of purity and purification. Vajrasattva embodies the capacity to eliminate spiritual impurities of all kinds, particularly neglected commitments toward one's teacher and ones' own spiritual development. Vajrasattva is a *sambhogakāya* (→ *trikāya*) manifestation; he unifies all the five buddha-families (→ *buddhakula*) within himself in the same way that the white color of his body (in iconography) unifies all the five colors. With his right hand he holds a → *dorje* to his heart, which signifies his indestructible essence. His left hand, holding a bell (→ *drilbu*), rests on his hip; this is an expression of his compassion. The hundred-syllable mantra associated with him is used in all schools of Tibetan Buddhism for purification of the mind.

Vajrayāna 🅱 Skt., lit. "Diamond Vehicle"; a school of Buddhism, that arose, primarily in northeast and northwest India, around the middle of the first millenium. It developed out of the teachings of the → Mahāyāna and reached Tibet, China, and Japan from Central Asia and India along with the Mahāyāna. This movement arose from a need to extend the worldview of Buddhism to inveterate "magical" practices and is characterized by a psychological method based on highly developed ritual practices. The Vajrayāna had its origin in small groups of practitioners gathered around a master (→ guru). The accessibility of Vajrayāna through written texts (→ Tantra) as well as its assimilation by monastic institutions was a relatively late development in this movement. Because of the use of certain sacred syllables (→ mantra), Tibetan Buddhism also refers to the Vajrayāna as the Mantrayāna.

The teachings of the Vajrayāna formed an esoteric tradition that combined elements of yoga and of the ancient Indian nature religion with original Buddhist thought. Decisive influences came from northwest India that led to a pronounced symbology of light. This strongly affected the sexual cult from the northeast that determined the iconography of the Vajrayāna.

The Vajrayāna was initially transmitted only orally, but later, between the 6th and 10th centuries, coherent doctrinal systems developed. Among its most important written works are the *Guhyasamāja-tantra* and the → *Kālachakra-tantra*. The formulations found in these texts respectively document the beginning and the end of this phase. Along with the complex writings of the Tantras, the spiritual songs of the → *mahāsiddhas* on the experience of *mahāmudrā* are also important vehicles of the tradition. These teachings became firmly established as part of Buddhism around the time it was being transmitted to Tibet. In Tibetan Buddhism an understanding of the → *prajñāpāramitā* teachings as they were taught by → Nāgārjuna and → Asanga is seen as a precondition for mastery of Vajrayāna methods. Thus the *prajñāpāramitā* teachings are also called the "causal vehicle" and the Vajrayāna teachings, the "fruition [effect] vehicle."

A decisive role is played in the Vajrayāna by initiations, given by an authorized master that empower the practitioner for meditative practice connected with a specific deity and also necessarily place him or her under an obligation to carry out such practice. Among the techniques transmitted in such initiations, which have as their goal the sublimation of the individual as a totality, are recitation of mantras, contemplation of → mandalas, and special ritual gestures (→ mudrā).

For Vajrayāna Buddhists, the elimination of all duality—the experience of fundamental unity in enlightenment—is symbolized by the → *vajra.*

Vāk 🅷, or Vāch (Vāc), Skt., lit. "speech, voice, language"; in the → Vēdas she is the bearer of revelation. The *Rigveda* sings praises to sacred Speech, embodied in the Vedic word, as the primal creative force that sustains all gods. The ancient Hindu scriptures describe in their poetic language how the universe was sung into existence by → Brahmā's divine thoughts, which streamed forth from him through Vāk, the divine voice.

Such passages are reminiscent of the opening words of the Gospel of John: "In the beginning was the Word." In the *Shatapatha-Brāhmana,* → Prajāpati creates the water, from which the earth and all living beings emerge, by means of speech, which showers over the entire world. Thus Vāk is often personified as a goddess, the mother of the universe, and is also identified with → Sarasvatī, the goddess of eloquence and erudition.

Over the course of time, the sacred meaning of Vāk diminished, and → Manas vied with her for the leading position. Prajāpati, who had created them both, was to decide which one would be dominant. He conceded the place to Manas, the intellect, because speech merely proclaims what Manas has previously thought. Here speech has dropped to the level of everyday language and has lost its creative significance.

Vākyanu-Sādhana 🅷 Skt.; meditation *(sādhana)* on the → *mahāvākyas,* the great precepts of the → *shrutis,* and penetration of their profound meaning.

Vākyavritti 🅷 (Vākavṛtti), Skt., lit. "the interpretation *(vritti)* of the sentence *(vākya),*" the interpretation of → *Tat tvam asi* ("That thou art"); a short but important work of → Advaita-Vedānta by Shankara, it explains in fifty-three stanzas (*shlokas*) the eminent meaning of the axiom *Tat tvam asi.*

This sentence is the cornerstone of Vedānta. The identity *(asi)* of *tat* (that) and *tvam* (thou) cannot be substantiated by reason, but can be known only by direct experience. Shankara's short treatise is meant for those who wish to experience the truth of this identity and enjoy its indescribable peace.

Vallabha 🅷, or Vallabhāchārya, a → Vaishnava saint and philosopher of the fifteenth century. His philosophy, known as Shuddhādvaita-Vedānta (*shuddha,* lit. "unadulterated, pure, original") stands between → Shankara's Advaita-Vedānta and → Rāmānuja's Vishishtādvaita-Vedānta.

Shuddhādvaita views the relationship between the soul and the world as real rather than as an apparition of → *māyā.* The soul is a subtle form of *brahman,* which is unchanged by the influence of *māyā*; only the aspect of bliss (→ *ānanda*) appears to be veiled. In its original (*shuddha*) state, the soul is identical with *brahman.* A worshiper of Krishna, Vallabha held → *bhakti* to be the chief means of liberation, but recognized also the usefulness of → *jñāna.* His chief works, in which he presents a theistic interpretation of Vedānta that diverges from those of Shankara and Rāmānuja, are *Anubhāsya, Siddhānta-Rahasya,* and *Bhāgavatatīkāsubodhini.* He also composed an important commentary on the → *Vedānta-Sūtra.*

Vallī 🅷 Skt., lit. "creeping plant"; a striking term used to refer to the way in which an → Upanishad conforms closely to the → Brāhmana with which it is associated and yet retains its total independence down to its very roots. In particular, the three sections of the *Taittirīya-Upanishad* are characterized as *vallī.*

Vālmīki 🅷 author of the famous Sanskrit epic poem → *Rāmāyana,* which he is said to have "seen," in the words of the Vedas. He includes descriptions of himself in the text, as if he had participated in certain events himself. Thus, for example, he describes himself as having given shelter to → Sītā when she was banished and as having raised her twins, Kusha and Lava.

Vālmīki is considered the first literary poet (*ādikavi*) of India to be known by name, and although he was clearly not the sole composer of the *Rāmāyana,* he is indubitably the author of the characteristic epic meter known as the → *shloka,* which was used for the epic about Rāma as well as for most of the *Mahābhārata.* The epic work → *Yoga-Vasishtha* is also said to be by Vālmīki.

In his youth Vālmīki, under another name, managed to stay alive by thievery. One day he fell upon → Nārada and was about to rob him. "Take everything I have," said Nārada, "but first let me ask you a few questions. Why are you living the life of a robber? Aren't you aware that you are committing sins that will reap you punishment?" "Yes," answered the thief, "but my family will share the burden of my guilt." "Have you asked them if they would do so?" "No, but I'm sure they will." Thereupon Nārada challenged the robber to leave him tied to a tree and meanwhile to question his family about the matter. When the thief told his relatives how he had been making his living, none wanted to share his guilt and the consequences of his acts. His eyes were opened and he repented; returning to Nārada, he freed the sage and embarked upon an intensely spiritual life. He meditated until an anthill (*vālmīki*: "ant") rose around his body, and was later venerated as a sage.

Vāmāchāra 🅗 or Vāmāmārga, Skt. → Tantra

Vāmāchāris 🅗 Skt.; an adherent of Vāmāchāra → Tantra

Vāmadeva 🅗 a Vedic → *rishi*, held to be the composer of → *Rigveda 4*. In one of his hymns he speaks of himself before his birth. The commentator → Sāyana notes: "Even as he waited in the womb, the Rishi Vāmadeva wished not to be born in the normal manner. He determined to enter the world through his mother's side." In another hymn Vāmadeva writes: "I shot forth like a hawk." A commentator explained this line thus: "He took on the shape of a hawk and emerged from the womb by means of yogic powers, for he had devine knowledge from the moment of conception."

Vāmadeva is also the name of a sage in the → *Mahābhārata* who owned two horses, called *vājas*, of fabulous speed. Vāmadeva is also an epithet for → Shiva as well as one of the → Rudras.

Vāmana 🅗 Skt., lit. "dwarf"; Vishnu's fifth incarnation as the → *avatāra* of the *tretā-yuga* (→ *yuga*). As early as the *Rigveda*, Vishnu is prominent for his heroic "three steps" (→ *trivikrama*). The *Vāmana-Purāna*, supposed to have been composed in Benares in the fourteenth century, contains a report in Brahmā's words comprising 7,000 stanzas on Vishnu's dwarf incarnation. The work, however, expresses admiration equally for Vishnu and Shiva.

Vāmana took his famed three steps when the gods had begged Vishnu for help against the Daitya king → Bali, who had gained the rule of the three worlds by dint of his great piety and ascetic practices and now threatened the dominance of the gods. Vishnu took on the form of the dwarf Vāmana and tricked King Bali with his three steps.

Vānaprastha 🅗 Skt., lit. "forest abode"; the third stage of life (→ *āshrama*, 2) for a Hindu, whereby a man who has fulfilled the duties of a householder and has served the community withdraws to the forest in order to devote himself entirely to the study of philosophy and the scriptures and to the intense practice of meditation.

Varada-mudrā 🅑 Skt. → mudrā 6

Varna 🅗 (Varṇa), Skt., lit. "color, caste"; a social class system introduced by the Aryans upon their invasion of India. It is made up of four major castes: (1) the brahmans (*brāhmanas*), the educated class of priests, philosophers, scholars, and religious leaders; (2) the *kshatriyas*, or warrior caste, comprising politicians, generals, officers, and civil authorities; (3) the *vaishyas*, or merchants and farmers, also called the providers; (4) the *shūdras*, the workers and servants. The lowest level of Hindu society is made up of the pariahs, the untouchables, who stand outside the caste system. Members of the three upper castes are also called → *dvija* ("twice-born"). The *Bhagavad-Gītā* teaches that one who views the fulfillment of those duties entailed by caste as a sacrifice to God can surmount caste and other karmic limitations and achieve the spiritual perfection that is the birthright of every human being.

The earliest mention of caste is found in a late hymn from the *Rigveda* (→ Purusha-Sūkta). The division probably evolved only because of the various occupations of different groups. According to Vedic tradition, the division into castes was intended to eliminate competition within society. The fact that the brahmans occupied the foremost level indicates that renunciation and wisdom were prized above warmongering, wealth, or physical proficiency. In previous centuries there had been no strict division of castes, and over a long period of time these four chief castes, working together harmoniously, were able to maintain a social balance. Not until the Mogul emperors invaded India with Islamic teachings and other colonial powers threatened the country's social structure were ironclad prescripts slapped on to the old orthodox system to bring about a strict division between castes. The reform movement of the nineteenth century and Gandhi's work led to the direction taken by India's present government to gradually dismantle the caste system and to integrate the untouchables into society.

Varuna 🅗 (Varuṇa), Skt., lit. 1. "the all-encompassing" (*varas:* "breadth, space"); 2. "ocean, sun"; one of the oldest Vedic gods, the personification of the all-encompassing heavens, creator and preserver of heaven and earth, or the king of the universe, of gods and men; the supreme divinity, to whom special honor is accorded. In later times he became lord of the sun gods (→ Ādityas); still later he became the god of oceans and rivers, a position he still occupies today.

In the Vedas, Varuna is connected not directly to water but to water in the elements of ether and earth. Cosmic functions are attributed to him. He allows the sun to shine on the firmament. The wind that roars through the air is his breath. He created the beds of rivers, which by his command flow and pour their waters into the oceans without allowing them to overflow. By his laws the moon shines and the stars appear in the night sky, only to disappear mysteriously the next dav. Nothing happens without his knowledge; no creature can move without him. He observes truth and duplicity in human beings, he initiated Rishi → Vasishtha into the secret knowledge that is not revealed to fools. He has unlimited control over the fate of human beings, knows the answer to everything, and is merciful even to sinners. He is the wise guard of immortality. The characteristics and functions that are ascribed to Varuna raise him far above all other Vedic gods. In the → Purānas he is the lord of waters, his favorite site is Pushpagiri, the "flower mountain." He owns an umbrella named Ābhoga, fashioned from a cobra's hood; no water can penetrate it. Numerous legends are associated with his name, some of which are reminiscent of the classic legends about Neptune.

Vāsanānanda 🅗 Skt.; the joy and bliss (*ānanda*) that are left behind by the imperishable impressions (*vāsanā*) of spiritual experiences.

Vāsanās 🅗 🅑 Skt., lit. "conception, longing, impression."

🅗 submerged and hidden desires, attractions, and ambitions, which can surface again at any given moment. These are closely related to → *samskāras*, to some extent make up a portion of them and are occasionally taken as synonymous with them.

🅑 → *ālaya-vijñāna*

Vasishtha 🅗 (Vasiṣṭha), a famous sage (brahman), the author of *Rigveda* 7. A great rivalry arose between him and the sage → Vishvāmitra, who was originally a → *kshatriya*. The relationship between the two clearly reflects the conflict raging at that time between the brahmans and the *kshatriyas*, who were frequently wise rulers and did not wish to be given instructions by the often arrogant brahman priests. Vasishtha and Vishvāmitra ultimately settled their differences, after the latter had risen to the rank of *brahman* through his intense spiritual practice.

According to → Manu, Vasishtha was one of the seven great → *Rishis* and one of the ten → Prājapatis who descended from Brahmā. Nevertheless, a hymn in the *Rigveda* refers to him as the son of → Varuna. In another hymn he is described as protector of dwellings: He once spoke to a dog who had barked at him as he tried to enter Varuna's house. The dog became silent and fell asleep. Hence these stanzas are recited when thieves and robbers are feared.

Vasishtha owned → Surabhī ("the cow of abundance"), who could fulfill his every wish; Vishvāmitra envied Vasishtha for this possession. There are numerous legends and stories about Vasishtha, almost all of which involve his conflict with Vishvāmitra; they are described in detail in the *Rāmāyana*. He was the family priest of King Dasharatha, → Rāma's father. A Sanskrit text called → *Yoga-Vasishtha*, ascribed to Vālmīki, relates the instructions given by Vasishtha to his student Rāma.

Vasubandhu 🅑 🅩 outstanding scholar of the → Sarvāstivāda and → Yogāchāra schools, who is also considered the twenty-first patriarch of the Indian lineage of Ch'an (Zen). The question of the historical personality of Vasubandhu raises a number of problems. He was born in modern Peshawar, lived in Kashmir, and died in Ayodhyā. He is thought to have been the brother and student of → Asanga, the founder of the Yogāchāra. Asanga is said to have converted him to Mahāyāna Buddhism. Vasubandhu might have lived in the 4th or the 5th century. The Indologist E. Frauwallner posits two Vasubandhus, the Yogāchārin (Vasubandhu the Elder, 4th century) and the Sarvāstivādin (Vasubandhu the Younger, 5th century).

The Sarvāstivādin was the author of the → *Abhidharmakosha*, one of the most important works of this school. The Yogāchārin Vasubandhu is considered the cofounder of the Yogāchāra school with his brother Asanga. A number of works of fundamental importance for this school are ascribed to him, among them the *Vimshatikā-vijñaptimātratāsiddhi* (*Proof That Everything Is Only Conception in Twenty Verses*), for short, the *Vimshatikā*. It is extant both in the Sanskrit original and a Chinese translation; it is a summary of the Yogāchāra doctrine.

He was also the author of the *Trimshikā*, a poem made up of thirty songs, which also expounds the Yogāchāra teaching; and of a number of commentaries on works by Asanga and on important Mahāyāna sūtras such as the → *Dashabhūmika*, → *Diamond Sūtra*, → *Lotus Sūtra*, and the → *Sukhāvatī-vyūha*.

Vāsudeva 🅗 the father of Krishna. His sister was → Kuntī, the mother of the → Pāndava princes. In the *Bhagavad-Gītā* Krishna is called Vāsudeva. According to the *Mahābhārata*, the name means that Krishna resides (Skt. *vāsanat*) in all beings.

Vāsudeva married seven sisters, the youngest of whom was → Devakī, Krishna's mother. After the death of Krishna and → Balarāma, Vāsudeva also died, and four of his wives immolated themselves with his corpse. Vāsudeva was also named Ānaka Dundubhi, because the gods, realizing that he would be the father of the divine Krishna, sounded the drums (*dundubhi*) of heaven at his birth.

Vāsuki 🅗 the king of the *nāgas*, or serpents, who live in Pātāla, a region of the underworld. The gods and → *asuras* used his body to encircle Mount Mandara during the → Churning of the Ocean.

Vasus 🅗 Skt.; a group of eight gods who are known as the servants of → Indra. In Vedic times they were personifications of natural phenomena. They are Āpas (Water), Dhruva (the North Star), Soma (Moon), Dharā (Earth), Anila (Wind), Anala (Fire), Prabhāsa (Light), and Pratyūsha (Dawn).

Vātsalya 🅗 Skt., lit. "tenderness"; the tender love of parents for their child; one of the five dispositions (*bhāvas*) of a lover of God on the path of → Bhakti-Yoga.

Vātsīputrīya 🅑 Skt.; follower of a Buddhist school that split off from the → Sthaviras about 240 B.C.E.. Another name of this school is Pudgalavāda. It is the school of ancient Buddhism that diverged most from the orthodox view of the teaching. The founder of the school, Vātsīputra, a Brahmin who was originally a Sthavira, propounded the thesis that there is a person (→ *pudgala*) or individuality that is neither identical with the five aggregates (→ *skandha*) nor different from them. It is the basis of rebirth, warrants retribution for actions (→ karma), and even continues to exist in → nirvāna. This school was one of the largest of its time, yet it encountered fierce resistance from representatives of other schools, because the "person" of the Vātsīputrīyas was regarded as nothing other than a new version of the → ātman, the soul, the existence of which was considered to have been denied by the Buddha.

Vātsyāyana 🅗 a fourth-century scholar who also wrote on erotic themes. He is the author of the → *Kāma-Sūtra* and of the *Nyāya-Bhāshya*, the classic commentary on the *Nyāya-Sūtra* of → Gotama.

Vāyu 🅗 Skt., lit. "air, wind"; the god of winds. In the Vedas he appears together with Indra and shares a chariot with him, whereby Indra is the charioteer. Few hymns are dedicated to him. Three gods appear in the Vedas joined in a special relationship to one another: → Agni, whose place is on earth; Vāyu, who inhabits the air; and → Sūrya, whose place is in the heavens.

Vāyu is said to have emerged from the breath of → Purusha. In the *Bhāgavata-Purāna* he is challenged by → Nārada to break off the tip of Mount → Meru. He created a powerful storm that lasted for a year, but Vishnu's bird, → Garuda, protected the mountain with his wings, so that the storm's gusts were helpless. Nārada advised him to attack the mountain in Garuda's absence. He did so, broke off the tip and hurled it into the sea, where it became the island of → Lankā. Vāyu has various epithets, such as "bearer of fragrances" and "the eternally moving one."

Veda 🅗 → Vedas

Vedanā 🅑 Skt., Pali; "sensation" or "feeling"; the general concept for all feelings and sensations. In terms of qualities, it can be divided into three categories (pleasant, unpleasant, and neutral) and five classes (mentally pleasant and unpleasant, physically pleasant and unpleasant, and indifferent). With regard to the six sense organs, sensations conditioned by impressions of sight, hearing, smelling, tasting, touching, and mental impressions are differentiated. *Vedanā* is the second of the five → *skandhas* and the seventh link in the chain of conditioned arising (→ *pratītya-samutpāda*); it is conditioned by contact (→ *sparsha*) and in turn calls forth craving (→ *trishnā*).

Vedānga 🅗 (Vedāṇga), Skt., lit. "limbs of the Veda"; supplementary texts to the → Vedas, so that they can be correctly read, understood, and applied. Mainly composed in Sūtra prose style, the Vedāngas are like textbooks that cover the six Vedic auxiliary sciences: (1) phonetics (→ *shikshā*); (2) prosody (→ *chandas*); (3) grammar (*vyākarana*); (4) etymology (→ *nirukta*), with an especially famous work of the same name by → Yāska; (5) astronomy (→ *jyotisha*); (6) sacrificial rites (→ *kalpa-sūtra*). The Vedāngas belong to the body of Hindu scriptures called → *smriti*.

Vedānta 🅗 Skt.; a compound of → Veda and *anta:* "end"; the end, that is, the conclusion of the Vedas, as contained in the → Upanishads. Their scattered revelations and profound insights, which above all have to do with *brahman* and *ātman* and the interrelationship of the two, are summarized by Bādarāyana in his → *Vedānta-Sūtra,* which forms the basis of the philosophy of Vedānta (→ Uttara-Mīmāmsā). Radhakrishnan wrote in the introduction to a chapter on the *Vedānta-Sūtra* in his work *Indian Philosophy* (1962): "Of all the Hindu systems of thought, the Vedantic philosophy is the most closely connected to Indian religion, and in one or another form it influences the worldview of every Hindu thinker of the present time."

Three chief branches of Vedānta have developed: (1) → Advaita-Vedānta (nondualism), whose major teachers are Gaudapāda, Shankara (the most important), Padmapāda, Sureshvara, and

Vidyāranya; (2) → Vishishtādvaita-Vedānta (qualified nondualism), whose chief representative is → Rāmānuja; and (3) → Dvaita-Vedānta (dualistic Vedānta), whose chief representative is → Madhva.

Vedānta-Paribhāshā 🅷 (Vedāntaparibhāṣā), Skt.; a work on → Advaita-Vedānta, by Dharmarāja, who lived in South India in the seventeenth century C. E. and who belongs to the school of → Padmapāda. The book contains eight chapters and deals with the various methods of knowledge, the great Vedic precepts (→ *mahāvākya*), and the various states of consciousness. It stresses the authority of the Vedic scriptures and views enlightenment as the supreme goal of life.

Vedāntasāra 🅷 Skt., lit. "heart of the Vedānta"; 1. a work by → Rāmānuja; 2. a work by Sadānanda (fifteenth century) that because of its clarity and precision is one of the most widely read works in → Vedānta. Among other things it describes the concealing power of ignorance and the superimposition upon the Self of gross and subtle sheaths, and discusses in detail the great Vedic precepts (→ *mahāvākya*) and the state of the → *jīvanmukta,* one who is released while still in the body.

Vedānta-Sūtra 🅷 , or *Brahma-Sūtra,* Skt.; scholars have set the date of origin of this *sūtra* variously between 400 B.C.E. and 200 C.E. The Indologist Max Müller held it to be older than the → *Bhagavad-Gītā.* Scholars are also at variance regarding the work's author. Many point to → Vyāsa, others to Bādarāyana, and still others believe that these two are the same person. In any event, the author has summarized in this work, which forms the basis of → Vedānta philosophy, the insights and revelations concerning *brahman* and *ātman* that are scattered throughout the Upanishads. The alternate name, *Brahma-Sūtra,* refers to the fact that *brahman* is its central topic.

The *Vedānta Sūtra* consists of 555 fragments, most comprising no more than two or three words, which are unintelligible without explanation. Hence numerous commentaries exist, the most important of which are by → Shankara, → Rāmānuja, → Bhāskara, → Nimbārka, → Madhva, and → Vallabha.

The author of the *sūtra* accepts two views of *brahman:* (1) *brahman* understood as absolute, impersonal intelligence (Nirvishesha, → *chinmātra*); (2) *brahman* viewed as a personal god (*savishesha*). It is not apparent from the sūtra how the author reconciles these two views; the sūtra merely assures us, calling upon the → *shruti* as its basis, that *brahman* has itself become the universe and yet remains transcendent, which explains how it could serve as a basis for each of the various directions of Vedānta, from Advaita- to Dvaita-Vedānta. The work is divided into four chapters. The first covers the theory of *brahman* as the central reality; the second replies to objections against this position and criticizes the theories of opponents; the third indicates ways and means to attain knowledge of *brahman;* the fourth discusses the fruits or effects of this knowledge.

Vedas 🅷 Skt., lit. "knowledge, sacred teaching"; taken collectively, the oldest texts of Indian literature, to which orthodox Hindus ascribe superhuman origins and divine authority. This vast complex of scriptures, in length constituting six times the bulk of the Bible, is divided into four parts: (1) the → *Rigveda,* the Veda of poetry; (2) the → *Sāmaveda,* the Veda of songs; (3) the → *Yajurveda,* the Veda of sacrificial texts; (4) the → *Atharvaveda,* the Veda of Atharvan, a priest of the mystical fire ceremony.

Each of these four Vedas can be subdivided into three genres according to its content, manner of presentation, and date of origin: (a) the → Samhitā (collection); (b) the → Brāhmana (ritual explication); to these are appended the → Āranyakas ("forest" texts), and certain to the → Upanishads also belong to the Brāhmanas; (c) the → Sūtra (manual, guide). With regard to its propositions, each Veda is also divided into a → Karma-Kānda, or section on practices, and a → Jñāna-Kānda, or section on knowledge.

The four Vedas initially served the chief priests as manuals for the texts and correct application of hymns and formulas used in the sacrificial cult. To perform a complete sacrifice, four different chief priests were needed: (1) the *hotar* ("caller"), who recited the verses of the hymns to invite the gods to partake of → *soma* or some other sacrificial offering. He used the *Rigveda*; (2) the *udgâtar* ("singer"), who accompanied the preparation and offering of the *soma* with singing. He used the *Sāmaveda*; (3) the *adhvaryu* (general priest), who carried out the sacred rite and thereby murmured the appropriate verses and formulas (*yajus*). His manual was the *Yajurveda*; (4) the high priest, whose duty was the supervision and direction of the sacrifice as a whole. However, he was not particularly connected to the *Atharvaveda* in any way.

A vast stretch of time must be postulated for the inception of the Vedas as a whole (from 1500 B.C.E.), for at first they were transmitted orally from generation to generation, whereby the various → *shākhās* ("branches") arose in relation to the various schools that studied the Vedas. There are various accounts of the origins of the Vedas, but all agree that the knowledge they hold was revealed to the → *rishis* during states of deep contemplation. Hence the Vedas are also referred to as → *shruti* ("that which was revealed").

Vedavyāsa 🅗 Skt., lit. "collector of the Vedas"; a name for → Vyāsa, although it is also used to refer to many others who compiled aphorisms or narratives.

Vesak 🅑 also Vesakha, Pali; most important holiday in the countries of → Theravāda Buddhism, which is celebrated on the full-moon day in May. This day commemorates at once the birth, enlightenment, and → *parinirvāna* of the Buddha. The Vesak celebration consists of presentations of the teaching, contemplation of the life of Buddha, processions around sacred sites, shrines, and monasteries, chanting, and so on. The meaning of the Vesak festival goes beyond mere historical commemoration; it is a reminder of the necessity, and of the possibility, for each person to become enlightened.

Vibhajyavādin 🅑 Skt., lit. "Defender of What Is To Be Differentiated"; Hīnayāna school that split off from the → Sthaviras around 240 B.C.E. From this school the → Mahīshāsikas and the → Theravāda were produced. Its doctrine is opposed in many points to the → Sarvāstivāda. The school of the Vibhajyavādins probably died out by the end of the 7th century.

Vibhanga 🅑 Skt. → Abhidharma

Vibhīshana 🅗 (Vibīṣaṇa), or Bibhīshana, Skt., lit. "terrible, intimidating"; a brother of → Rāvana, but in contrast to his brother, Vibhīshana was noble and virtuous. He became Rāma's ally.

Like his brother, Vibhīshana had won favor with Brahmā and was granted a wish. He asked never to be forced to perform an unworthy action, not even under extreme circumstances. As he rejected the behavior of the → *rākshasas,* he quarreled with Rāvana and fled from his persecution to Mount Kailāsa. Shiva then advised him to ally himself with Rāma, who received him as a friend and set him on the throne of Lankā after Rāvana's death.

Vibhūti 🅗 Skt., lit. "acute, powerful; revelation, power"; 1. abilities and powers arising from practices such as those listed in the *Yoga-Sūtra* of → Patañjali (3.16-55), e.g., knowledge of past and future, the ability to read thoughts, knowldege of earlier births and of the hour of one's own death. For the most part these powers and those called → *siddhis* are identical; 2. the manifestations of divine power in the form of knowledge, love, energy, and strength. Among human beings, these *vibhūtis* are seen in spiritual teachers, brilliant scientists, and artists. Such figures have the same effect as → *avatāras,* but within a smaller sphere: They help others to develop spiritually.

Vichara 🅗 (Vicāra), Skt., lit. "discrmination, examination, investigation"; all material and spiritual problems must be examined and investigated. The highest form of investigation is the attempt to discover why immortal consciousness (→ *ātman*) mistakes itself for a mortal body (→ *jīva*). One who solves this problem attains enlightenment. The → *Pañchadashi* repeatedly demands that one take up this type of *vichāra.* Shastri remarks in a note to one verse from this work (9.14): "The intellectual process of *vichāra* reaches its apex in one-pointed contemplation (→ *nididhyāsana*). Pure *nididhyāsana* is a means to direct knowledge (→ *para-vidyā*)."

Vichikitsā 🅑 (vicikitsā), Skt. (Pali, vicikichchā); doubt, uncertainty, scepticism, one of the five hindrances (→ *nīvarana*) and one of the three fetters (→ *samyojana*) eliminated during the first stage of the supramundane path (→ *ārya-mārga,* → *shrota-āpanna*). In Buddhism this doubt or uncertainty is defined as "without wish to cure.... It has the characteristic of doubt. Its function is to waver. It is manifested as indecisiveness, or it is manifested as taking various sides. Its proximate cause is unwise attention. It should be regarded as obstructive of theory" (Nyanamoli 1976, vol. 2, p. 533).

Videha 🅗 Skt., lit. "released from the body"; 1. an epithet of King → Janaka, indicating that he had freed himself from bondage to the world; 2. the name of Janaka's realm and people, in present-day North Bihar; its capital is Mithilā.

Videhamukti 🅗 Skt., lit. *videha:* "bodiless," *mukti:* "liberation"; liberation through the knowledge that one is not the body but rather absolute consciousness (→ *ātman*).

Vidhātri 🅗 (Vidhātṛ), Skt., lit. "creator"; a name used for → Brahmā, → Vishnu, and → Vishvakarma.

Vidvat-Sannyāsa 🅗 (Vidvat-Saṃnyāsa), Skt., lit. "renunciation of the enlightened one," a concept that in fact is self-contradictory, since an enlightened one does not need to renunciate anything: such a person's desires have vanished, and there is no longer any attachment to the objects of the senses. Here the term "renunciation" means to view events with detachment.

Vidyā H Skt., lit. "knowledge, teaching"; Hinduism distinguishes two types of *vidyā*: 1. lower knowledge (→ *apara-vidyā*), intellectually acquired knowledge; 2. higher knowledge (→ *para-vidyā*), intuitive, spiritual experience, which leads to enlightenment, liberation, and realization of the supreme reality.

Vidyā-Māyā H Skt. → *māyā*

Vidyāranya H (Vidyāraṇya), or Madhāvāchārya, a fourteenth-century philosopher who espoused Shankara's philosophy of → Advaita-Vedānta and with his → *Pañchadashi* created a standard work of this Vedānta school. Other of his important works are *Jīvanmukti-Viveka* and *Vivarana-Prameya-Samgraha.*

In worldly life Vidyāranya was minister at a South Indian court, but then renounced the world and became a monk. Vidyāranya, his monk's name, means "forest of erudition."

Vidyā-Shakti H (Vidyā-Śakti), Skt., lit. *vidyā:* "knowledge," *shakti:* "force"; the force of *brahman,* which leads the → *jīva* out of ignorance (→ *avidyā*) to the realization of *brahman.*

Vigraha H Skt., lit. "form"; the divine represented as form. An image that is consecrated by → mantras and glorified through the veneration and worship of God-seekers itself becomes a divinity. Hence *vigraha* cannot be translated as "idol" or "graven image."

Once, at the court of a mahārāja, as Vivekānanda heard the ruler's Western-educated adviser storming against the idolatry of his countrymen, the spiritual leader silently took down a large photograph of the mahārāja from the wall and said to the adviser, "Spit on this!" As the man paled and turned away from the portrait, Vivekānanda continued, "If a piece of paper under glass is the Mahārāja for you, why shouldn't others see God in an image? Both are merely symbols used by human imagination."

Vihāra B Skt., Pali, lit. "sojourning place"; residence for monks, to which they can also retire for meditation. The first *vihāras* were houses placed at the disposal of the historical Buddha → Shākyamuni for the growing monastic community (→ *sangha*).

Vijātīya-Vritti H (Vijātīya-Vṛtti), Skt., lit. *vijātīya:* "heterogenous, contrary," *vritti:* "thought wave"; turbulent thoughts that have no place in meditation and by their uncontrollable nature prevent any real concentration. They constitute one of the greatest obstacles to meditation.

Vijayā H Skt.; the last day of the festival of Durgā-Pūjā, when an image of the goddess Durgā is lowered into water. Vijayā is still today a special holiday for Hindus, a day on which greetings and good wishes are exchanged.

Vijñāna H B Skt., lit. "consciousness, knowing."

H The highest state of spiritual realization, whereby the enlightened soul perceives → *brahman* not in a special state of → *samādhi* but in the midst of the manifest world, which is now nothing other than a manifestation of *brahman.* → Vedānta refers to this supreme knowledge as "seeing *brahman* with open eyes"; one who has realized this is called a *vijñānin.*

B (Pali, viññāna); the six kinds of consciousness (i.e., those of the five sense organs and mental consciousness), each of which arises from contact of an object with the organ corresponding to a given sense. *Vijñāna* is the fifth of the five → skandhas and the third link in the chain of conditioned arising (→ *pratītya-samutpāda*).

Vijñāna is the central psychological "organ." It is, however, put on an equal footing with the five other organs of perception in order to avoid its being seen as the basis of a personality of self (→ *anātman,* → *pudgala*). *Vijñāna* is only one of the components of the empirical personality.

Vijñānakāya B → Abhidharma

Vijñānamaya-Kosha H Skt. → *kosha*

Vijñānavāda B Skt. → Yogāchāra

Vijñaptimātratā-siddhi B Skt. → Hsuan-tsang

Vikalpa H → *sankalpa*

Vikāra H Skt., lit. "transformation"; the actual transformation of one substance into another, as milk is transformed to cheese. The primal source of all substances is → *prakriti,* from which the entire manifest creation emerges in a process of transformation. *Vikāra* is a concept in the Sānkhya teaching of → *parināmavāda.*

Vikramāditya H a famous king who ruled over Ujjayinī, one of the seven holy cities of India (→ *nagara*). The Samvatsara era that began in 56 B.C.E. bears his name. Literature blossomed at his court, where he assembled nine illustrious poets and scholars, the "nine gems," namely Dhanvantari, Kālidāsa, Vararuchi, Kshapanaka, Amara-Simha, Vetālabhatta, Ghatakarpara, Shanku, and Varāhamihira.

Vikshepa H (Vikṣepa), Skt., lit. "scattering, dispersion"; one of two ways in which → *avidyā* (ignorance) operates in its inability to perceive *brahman*. In general, *avidyā* refers to ignorance in the sense of inability to distinguish between the real and the unreal, the eternal and the transient. However, when *brahman* is not known, *avidyā* operates as follows: (1) the true nature of *brahman* is not known, and (2) what is not known is covered over (→ *āvarana*) by something else. This second aspect is referred to as *vikshepa* or *adhyāropa* (lit. "false covering"). → Shankara gives as illustration the example of the rope (*brahman*) that in the dark is not simply not known to be a rope but is covered over (*viksehpa* or *adhyāropa*) by the idea of a snake (the manifest world).

Vimalakīrtinirdesha-sūtra **B** **Z** (Vimalakīrtinirdeśa-sūtra), Skt., lit. "*Discourse of Vimalakīrti*"; important work of Mahāyāna Buddhism, which had great influence especially in China and Japan. It was composed about the 2d century C.E. The original has been lost. A number of Chinese translations exist, of which the most important is that of → Kumārajīva (406). The name of the sūtra is derived from that of its principal character, Vimalakīrti, a rich adherent of the Buddha, who lives in the midst of worldly life yet treads the path of the → bodhisattva. The popularity of this sūtra is due to its stress on the equal value of the lay life and the monastic life.

The *Vimalakīrtinirdesha-sūtra* is an illustration of the Buddhist way of life as a path to liberation and of the practical application of insight into the emptiness (→ *shūnyatā*) of existence. Zen holds this sūtra in particularly high regard.

The sūtra tells the story of Vimalakīrti, who is lying sick in bed. The Buddha wants to send his students to get news of his condition. However, all decline; they are ashamed because of Vimalakīrti's superior wisdom and do not feel able to face him. Finally → Mañjushrī agrees to go, and the rest follow along. Asked how he is feeling, Vimalakīrti explains his illness in the following words:

Mañjushrī, my sickness comes from ignorance and the thirst for existence and it will last as long as do the sicknesses of all living beings. Were all living beings to be free from sickness, I also would not be sick. Why? Mañjushrī, for the bodhisattva, the world consists only of living beings, and sickness is inherent in the living world. Were all living beings free from sickness, the bodhisattva also would be free from sickness. For example, Mañjushrī, when the only son of a merchant is sick, both his parents become sick on account of the sickness of their son. And the parents will suffer as long as that only son does not recover from his sickness. Just so, Mañjushrī, the bodhisattva loves all living beings as if each were his only child. He becomes sick when they are sick and is cured when they are cured. You ask me, Mañjushrī, whence comes my sickness; the sicknesses of the bodhisattvas arise from great compassion.

Then follow expositions of the most important teachings of the Mahāyāna: the transcendent nature of a buddha and especially the nonduality of true reality, which Vimalakīrti expounds through silence. The content of this sūtra has inspired many artistic depictions. Scenes from it can be found in the caves of → Lung-men and Yun-kang in China. An English translation of this work is Thurman 1976.

Vimalamitra **B** → *dzogchen*

Vimukti **B** Skt. (Pali, vimutti); liberation, release from suffering through knowledge of the cause of suffering and the cessation of suffering, i.e., through realization of the → four noble truths and elimination of the defilements (→ *āsrava*). *Vimukti* is the extinction of all illusions and passions. It is liberation from the karmic cycle of life and death (→ samsāra) and the realization of → nirvāna.

Vinaya-pitaka **B** (Vinaya-piṭaka, Skt., Pali, lit. "Basket of Discipline"; third part of the → Tripitaka, containing the rules and regulations for the communal life of monks and nuns. The Vinaya-pitaka has been preserved in various versions (e.g., the Vinaya-pitaka of the → Theravāda, of the → Dharmaguptaka, of the → Sarvāstivāda).

The Vinaya-pitaka consists of three parts: (1) *Bhikshuvibhanga* (*Explanation of the Rules for Monks*), (2) *Bhishunīvibhanga* (*Explanation of the Rules for Nuns*), and (3) *Khandaka*.

The *Bhikshuvibhanga* consists of eight chapters: (a) *pārājika*, final expulsion of monks who have been guilty of murder, theft, or sexual offense, or who have unsuitably extolled their own sanctity; (b) *sanghāvashesha* (Pali, *sanghādisesa*), provisional expulsion of monks who have committed one of the thirteen principal faults, such as slander, instigating dissatisfaction, touching a woman, and so on; (c) *aniyata*, "indeterminate" faults; (d) *naihsargika* (Pali, *nissaggiya*), thirty cases of "giving up" dishonestly acquired things like clothes, food, medicine, etc.; (e) *pātayantika* (Pali, *pāchittiya*), ninety cases of "penance exercises" for minor violations such as insults, disobedience, lying; (f) *pratideshanīya* (Pali, *pātidesanīya*), four faults related to mealtimes; (g) *shikshakaranīya* (Pali, *sekhiya*), manners; (h) *adhikaranashamatha*, guidelines for resolution of conflicts.

2. The *Bhikshunīvibhanga* contains the same chapters as the section for monks. The rules for nuns, however, are considerably more numerous.

3. The *Khandaka* contains regulations, organized differently in the different Vinaya-pitakas, concerned with the daily life of monks and nuns (specifications for the → *uposatha* ceremonies, dress, food, behavior during the rainy season, entering → homelessness, etc.). To the Vinaya-pitaka also belongs the → *Prātimoksha*, a summary of the rules for monks and nuns, which is read at the *uposatha* ceremony. Individual monks and nuns are required to confess any violations of rules publically.

Vinaya school 🅑 🅩 a school of Buddhism in China and Japan that primarily stresses strict observance of the rules laid down in the Vinaya-pitaka, the third part of the Tripitaka. Here the life of monks and nuns is regulated in every detail of its moral, ethical, and spiritual aspects, and the precise forms for life in a monastery, ordination ceremonies, and so on, are given. In the great Buddhist monasteries of China and Japan, which often housed masters of more than one Buddhist denomination, generally a Vinaya master (Skt., → *upādhyāya*) was responsible for the ordination of monks.

Also → Lu-tsung, → Ritsu school.

Vinaya-vibhāshā 🅑 Skt. → Sarvāstivāda

Vipāka 🅑 Skt., Pali, lit. "ripen, fruit"; in the teaching concerning → karma, *vipāka* is understood to mean the ripening of the "fruit" (*phala*) of an act. When this fruit is ripe, it takes effect in one way or another on the actor. The ripening of actions can take place in this life or also in the next or even a later rebirth. It is considered positive for an act to ripen in the present life.

Viparīta-Bhāvana 🅗 Skt., lit. *viparīta:* "wrong, reversed," *bhāvana:* "notion"; the false belief, the erroneous conviction that the visible world of appearances is the only reality.

Viparyaya 🅗 Skt., lit. "error, misunderstanding"; an incorrect view that is born of ignorance but after prolonged study is recognized as such.

Vipashyanā 🅑 (vipaśyanā), Skt. (Pali, vipassanā); insight, clear seeing; intuitive cognition of the three marks of existence (→ *trilakshana*), namely, the impermanence (→ *anitya*), suffering (→ *duhkha*), and egolessness (→ *anātman*) of all physical and mental phenomena. In Mahāyāna Buddhism, *vipashyanā* is seen as analytical examination of the nature of things that leads to insight into the true nature of the world—emptiness (→ *shūnyatā*). Such insight prevents the arising of new passions. *Vipashyanā* is one of the two factors essential for the attainment of enlightenment (→ *bodhi*); the other is → *shamatha* (calming the mind).

Vipashyin 🅑 Skt.; the Buddha of an earlier world age; see also → buddha 1.

Vipassanā 🅑 Pali → *vipashyanā*

Vīrabhadra 🅗 Skt.; a creature produced by → Shiva, "a being like the flames of destiny," terrifying in form and of mighty power. The caves of Elephanta (on the island of Gharapuri, near Bombay) and Ellora (near Aurangabad) contain sculptures of him.

Daksha, a son of Brahmā, made a great sacrifice to Vishnu and invited many gods, but overlooked Shiva. In his anger, Shiva created Vīrabhadra to disturb the ceremony and drive away the gods. Vīrabhadra was accompanied by a huge troop of demigods, also created by Shiva, and a catastrophic scene ensued. In terror Daksha bowed before the enraged figure of Shiva and acknowledged his superiority. This legend presumably springs from the rivalry between the followers of Vishnu and those of Shiva. Vīrabhadra is worshiped primarily in western India.

Virāj 🅗 Skt., lit. "splendid, ruling"; a term used in Vedānta to refer to → *saguna-brahman,* which as Īshvara permeates and governs the entire manifest creation.

Viraja-Homa 🅗 Skt., lit. *viraja:* "passionless," *homa:* "to sacrifice in fire"; the sacrifice of all things belonging to this manifest world with its roots in → *ajñāna* (ignorance of reality), in the fire of discrimination (→ *viveka*). This is possible only for one who has entered the path of total renunciation (→ *sannyāsa*). The sacrifice is called *viraja* because it liberates one from → *rajas,* the → *guna* of greed and passion. It is the ritual of purification for those who have surrendered everything.

Vīrashaiva 🅗 Skt. → Lingāyat

Virāt 🅗 or Viraj, Skt. → *vaishvānara*

Virochana 🅗 Skt. → Vairochana

Vīrya 🅑 Skt. (Pali, viriya); exertion, energy, will power; energy the basis of which is indefatigable exertion to bring about wholesomeness and avoid unwholesomeness, and to transform impure into pure.

Vīrya is identical with the sixth element of the → eightfold path and the → four perfect exertions; *vīrya* is also one of the five powers (→

bala), one of the → *pāramitās*, one of the seven factors of enlightenment (→ *bodhyanga*), and one of the → *indriyas*.

Visamvāda-Bhrama 🅷 (Visaṃvāda-Bhrama), Skt., lit. *visamvādin:* "contradictory, false," *bhrama:* "error"; an error that arises by mistaking something that exists for something other than what it is. → Shankara offers the pertinent example of the rope that in the darkness is taken for a snake.

Vishāda 🅷 (Viṣāda), Skt., lit. "despondency, dejection"; the state in which Arjuna finds himself at the beginning of the *Bhagavad-Gītā*, a formidable obstacle on the path of spiritual development. This state can be traced to the identification with the body and to notions of one's limitations and shortcomings, all of which is viewed by → Vedānta as a major weakness.

Vishaya-Chaitanya 🅷 (Viṣaya-Caitanya), Skt., lit. *vishaya:* "world of the senses," *chaitanya*: "consciousness"; the consciousness that is used by the mind and body to allow the objects of the manifest world to appear; according to → Vedānta, these objects are all projections of the mind.

Vishaya-Shakti 🅷 (Viṣaya-Śakti), Skt., lit. "force of the world of the senses"; the mysterious force that turns our thoughts outward and impels us again and again to the objects of sense perception, even when we wish to turn inward.

Vishesha 🅷 (Viśeṣa), Skt., lit. "difference, particularity"; the fifth of the six *padārthas* (categories) of → Vaisheshika, the oldest of the six orthodox systems (→ *darshana*) of Hindu philosophy. The name of the system is derived from this term.

Vishishtādvaita-Vedānta 🅷 (Viśiṣṭādvaita-Vedānta), Skt., qualified nondualism, from *advaita:* "not-duality, nondualism," and *vishishta,* derived from *vishesha:* "particularity, specificity"; Advaita-Vedānta with a quality, to wit: that of plurality, the view that the world is founded on a spiritual principle (→ *brahman*), from which the individual soul and inanimate nature are essentially distinct. The founder of this branch of Vedānta, → Rāmānuja, focuses attention on the relationship between God and the world. He espouses the view that God is real and independent, but emphasizes that individual souls and the world are equally real but not independent, since their reality resides fully in, and is dependent upon, the reality of God. Personal values are subordinate to the impersonal supreme reality, but for the lover of God (→ *bhakta*), truth, beauty, and goodness possess a reality that cannot be reconciled with the impersonal abstraction of *advaita*. This discord led Rāmānuja, who was himself a *bhakta,* to establish Vishishtādvaita-Vedānta.

Vishnu 🅷 (Viṣṇu), Skt.; one of the chief deities of Hinduism. In the *Rigveda* he is the "worker" (*vish*: "to work"), a sun god, but stands out only through the heroic "three steps" with which he crosses the universe. They symbolize the rising, apex, and setting of the sun. The apex, "Vishnu's supreme step," refers to the abode of the blessed. Although he is mentioned only infrequently in the *Rigveda,* he subsequently develops into a powerful deity, with whom other divine figures such as Hari and Nārāyana merge, so that their names become his epithets. In the epic period he alternates with → Brahmā and → Shiva as the supreme deity; he is worshiped primarily in the Ganges area, whereas Shiva's province is the region of the Himalayas. A balance between the three gods is first achieved in the Purānas in the form of the → *trimūrti,* wherein Vishnu is the sustainer beside Brahmā as creator and Shiva as destroyer. Vishnu is the guardian of → *dharma;* whenever the world is out of joint, he hurries to its aid and incarnates himself as an → *avatāra* in order to show humanity new directions for further development. His worshipers, the Vaishnavas, established → Vaishnavism, now one of the three great forms of theistic worship in Hinduism.

Like → Shakti, Vishnu also has a "thousand names" (*sahasranāma*), the repetition of which is a meritorious act of devotion that is performed daily by many Vaishnavas. Worship of Vishnu is joyous in character. His wife is → Lakshmī, his heaven Vaikuntha, and his vehicle the bird Garuda. He is portrayed as a handsome youth with four arms (multiple arms is always the sign of a deity). One hand holds a conch shell, the second a missile weapon, the third a club, and the fourth a lotus. The sacred river Ganges issues from his foot. His bow is called Shārnga, his sword is Nandaka. Sometimes he sits on a lotus blossom, his wife Lakshmī at his side; at other times he rests on the serpent Shesha or rides mounted on his powerful bird Garuda.

Vishnu-Purāna 🅷 (Viṣṇu-Purāṇa), Skt.; one of the six Vaishnava- Purānas, the chief scriptures of the → Vaishnavas.

Vishuddha-chakra 🅷 🅱 Skt. → chakra 5

Vishva 🅷 Skt. → *vaishvānara*

Vishnu in his incarnation as the boar Varāha. (Relief from the Vishnu temple in Belur)

Vishvabhū 🅱 Skt.; buddha of a previous world age; also → buddha 1

Vishva-Devās 🅷 (Viśva-Devās), or Vishve-Devās, Skt., lit. "all gods." Originally in the *Rigveda* this word meant all the gods together. In this regard, Paul Deussen mentions a peculiarity of the deity worship in the *Rigveda.* He states that the Vedic system of belief is not a type of polytheism in which each god possesses a separate individuality and is ranked in a particular order in relation to the other gods; rather, each is supreme unto himself. For the devotee who approaches one god and calls to that one, all other gods vanish; only the chosen one exists. Hence the same feats—creating the earth, supporting the firmament, leading forth the sun, and so on—are attributed first to one god and then to another, and ultimately all are united in the form of → Soma or → Brahmanaspati. It is as though consciousness of the unity of the divine were present at the deepest level of spirit and as though this divine consciousness itself were using the various deities merely as a vehicle to express itself.

This notion of unity finds magnificent realization in the song of unity of the blind sage Dīrghatama (*Rigveda* 1.164) and the famous hymn of creation (*Rigveda* 10.129; → *Nāsadāsīya*). Under the influence of a growing systemization, the Vishva-Devās later evolved into a particular group of nine or ten deities.

Vishvakarma 🅷 (Viśvakarma), Skt., lit. "all-creating"; in the *Rigveda,* the personified activity of creation, the "all-creator." Vishvakarma is celebrated as such in the *Rigveda* in two hymns in which he transforms himself into the world without needing to resort to any material outside of himself. He is at once the primal actor and primal matter. In the epics and the Purānas he is the adviser, builder, and armorer of the gods, the inventor of the sciences of architecture and mechanics.

Vishvāmitra 🅷 (Viśvāmitra), a famous sage, said to be the chief author of *Rigveda* 3; he was born a → *kshatriya,* but through intensive austerities rose to the *brahman* caste and became one of the seven great → *Rishis.* The many legends that have grown up around his name almost always feature his quarrel with the brahmanic *Rishi* → Vasishtha. Both figures played an important role in the Vedic period as the brahmans wrestled with the *kshatriyas* for predominance.

Vishvāmitra was the son of Gāthin and was therefore also called Gādthinandana. Of his birth the *Vishnu-Purāna* relates that Gathin had a daughter Satyavatī, who was married to a *brahman.* Since she was a *kshatriya,* in order to beget a son with the qualities of a *brahman* her husband served her a special food that would have this effect. At the same time he gave her mother a dish by means of which she would bear a son with the qualities of a warrior. The dishes were inadvertently exchanged, and the mother bore Vishvāmitra, a *kshatriya* with the qualities of a *brahman,* while Satyavatī bore Jamadagni, the father of → Parashu-Rāma, the warlike *brahman* who would destroy the *kshatriyas.* The *Mahābhārata* and the *Rāmāyana* relate that the gods were dismayed by Vishvāmitra's strict asceticism and sent the nymph Menakā to seduce him. She succeeded, and → Shakuntalā was born to her. The holy man was so ashamed that he withdrew to the mountains and took up yet more severe austerities.

Vishvanātha 🅷 (Viśvanātha), Skt., lit. "lord of the universe"; 1. one of the chief deities at → Kāshī (Benares). The Shiva temple there bears his name; 2. author of the *Rāghava-Vilāsa* (a narration of the life of → Rāmā) and the *Sāhita-Darpana* (a treatise on the poetic art). He is also called Vishvanātha Kavirāja.

Vishvarūpa-Darshana 🅗 (Viśvarūpa-Darśana), Skt.; the vision of the universal divine form. In the eleventh chapter of the *Bhagavad-Gītā*, Krishna shows himself to Arjuna, at the latter's behest, in his all-embracing, universal form.

Vishvasrij 🅗 (Viśvasṛj), Skt., lit. "all-creator"; a name for → Brahmā, who symbolizes the creative aspect in the → trimūrti, the Hindu trinity.

Vishveshvara 🅗 (Viśveśvara), or Vishvesha, Skt., lit. "lord of the universe"; 1. an epithet for → Shiva; 2. the → *linga,* which is worshiped in Benares as a symbol of Shiva.

Visions 🅩 → *makyō*

Visuddhi-magga 🅑 Pali, lit. "*Path of Purity*"; the most important postcanonical work of the → Theravāda. It was composed in the 5th century by → Buddhaghosha. The *Visuddhi-magga* systematically presents the doctrine of the Mahāvihāra subschool of the Theravāda. It is divided into three parts with twenty-three chapters: chapters 1–2 deal with moral discipline (→ *shīla*), chapters 3–13 with meditation or concentration (→ *samādhi*), and chapters 14–23 with wisdom (→ *prajñā*). The part that deals with concentration describes in detail the meditation methods and objects of meditation used in the Theravāda to make development of concentration possible and also describes the fruits of meditation. The section on *prajñā* presents the fundamental elements of the Buddhist teaching (four noble truths, *pratītya-samutpāda*, eightfold path). An English translation is Nyanamoli 1976.

Vitala 🅗 Skt.; the second of seven states of the lower world (→ *tala*), also called the underworld, or hell. Its counterpart in the upperworld is *tapar-loka* (→ loka), the realm of intensive practice of → *tapas* (austerities). *Vitala* belongs to the world of dense matter. In it the spiritual world is obscured, because no conscious efforts are undertaken in the form of spiritual practices to overcome the heavy veil of ignorance that blots out all light.

Vīta-Rāga 🅗 Skt., lit. *vīta:* "past, fallen back," *rāga:* "passion"; freedom from passions, which have fallen away through the overcoming of egoism and purification of the mind.

Vitarka-mudrā 🅑 Skt. → mudrā 2

Vitarkas 🅗 Skt., lit. "doubt"; thoughts that are capable of destroying the personality. They stem from the demonic tendencies in the human being; such tendencies give rise to destructive thinking that engenders depression, immoral thoughts, and thoughts of suicide.

Vivarta 🅗 Skt., lit. "transformation"; in contrast to the real transformation of → *vikara, vivarta* is the apparent transformation of one substance into another, especially that of *brahman* into the manifest world (by which *brahman* itself remains untouched, being immutable). *Vivarta* is a concept of → Advaita-Vedānta.

Vivasvat 🅗 an → Āditya, the father of → Yama and → Manu. Krishna mentions him in the *Bhagavad-Gītā* (4.1).

Viveka 🅗 Skt., lit. "discrimination"; in spiritual terms, the ability to discriminate between the real and the unreal, the eternal and the transient. In Shankara's work → *Tattvabodha,* it is one of the four prerequisites for a spiritual aspirant. The other three are *vairāgya, numukshutva,* and → *shatkasampatti. Viveka* is the central theme of the → *Viveka-Chūdāmani*, one of Shankara's chief works.

Viveka-Chūdāmani 🅗 (Viveka-Cūḍāmaṇi), Skt., lit. "the crest jewel of discrimination"; an important work on → Advaita-Vedānta by → Shankara, it discusses the distinction between reality and the world of appearances. English trans. Prabhavananda & Isherwood 1947.

Vivekānanda 🅗 , Svāmi, 1863–1902 (given name: Narendranāth Datta), the most important disciple of → Rāmakrishna. He sat for six years at the feet of his master, who had recognized at their first meeting that this student would carry forth into the world his message of the unity and truth of all religions, a truth he himself had experienced. After Rāmakrishna's death, Vivekānanda initially lived with a group of monk-disciples; in 1887 he founded with them the → Rāmakrishna Order, which he led until shortly before his death. He subsequently wandered through India as a *sadhu* for some years and came to know both the material poverty and the spiritual wealth of his homeland. In 1893, with the financial support of a disciple (the Mahārāja of Khetri), Vivekānanda traveled uninvited to the World's Parliament of Religions in Chicago. Appearing as the last speaker on the program, he made a deep impression on those present. When the parliament had ended he went on to hold lectures in many of the states and established the Vedanta Society in New

York. On the way back to India, he visited England, France, and Switzerland. He spent two years in India, then returned to the West in 1899, visiting first London and then New York. Because of failing health, he returned to his homeland in 1900, where he devoted himself entirely to the Rāmakrishna Mission, an international mission founded by the Rāmakrishna Order to serve God in one's needy fellow human beings, according to Rāmakrishna's teaching. On July 4, 1902, in Belur Math, he left the body while in → *samādhi.*

Vivekānanda was born in Calcutta, the son of Vishvanāth Datta, a lawyer and skeptic, and was named Narendranāth. His grandfather had renounced the world at an advaced age. His mother was deeply religious and introduced him early on to the spiritual treasures of his homeland, the Vedas, Purānas, and epics. Naren, as he was called, was a highly intelligent student with an unusually fine memory. Throughout school and at the university he was tortured by the question of whether God really existed. He asked theologians, teachers, scholars, and holy men whether they had seen God, but the answer was always negative or evasive. When he first met Rāmakrishna he asked the same question and received the reply "Yes, I have seen God just as I see you before me, only much more real." With this a connection was established that despite Naren's skepticism lasted throughout his life and turned him into the herald of Rāmakrishna's message of Vedānta.

Vivekānda wrote a number of books on the yogic paths, including *Jñāna Yoga, Raja Yoga,* and *Karma Yoga and Bhakti Yoga.*

Vividisha-Sannyāsa 🅷 (Vividiṣa-Saṃnyāsa), Skt.; the renunciation *(sannyāsa)* of a spiritual seeker, which requires that a difficult decision be made. The aspirant cannot serve two masters; to attain the eternal, one must surrender what is short-lived and impermanent. As difficult as it is to renounce the objects of sense perception, so great is the potential reward: liberation.

Vraja 🅷 Skt. → Vrindāvan

Vrindāvan 🅷 (Vṛndāvana), or Brindāban, Brindāvan, Vraja, or Braja, Skt.; a sacred forest, which is situated still today by the river Yamunā near Mathurā, the birthplace of Krishna. Krishna spent his youth in Vrindāvan, where he played with the *gopīs,* the cowherding maidens, especially with → Rādhā. The play of Krishna and Rādhā has deep symbolic significance in Hinduism as the divine play of the soul with its Lord, comparable to the divine love (*minne*) described by medieval German mystics. Hence Vrindāvan is a particularly sacred place for → Vaishnavas, who equate it symbolically with the heart, the arena of the divine play.

Vrishti 🅷 (Vṛṣṭi), Skt., lit. "rain"; the rain of universal light, the stream of enlightening thought. Vrishti is the manifestation of the superconscious, or spiritual fullness, in our life.

Vritra 🅷 (Vṛtra), Skt., lit. 1. "storm cloud"; 2. a demon who was vanquished by Indra; the dark cloud of indolence and ignorance, symbolizing the force that opposes enlightenment, is personified in the serpent demon Vritra, who obscures, veils, and holds from humanity the light of knowledge. He is slain by Indra, the god of heaven and of light, which symbolizes how the light of divine knowledge destroys the demon of darkness, ignorance, and indolence within us.

In the → *Rigveda,* Vritra is the demon of drought, who holds the rain cow imprisoned in his cloud castle. Indra must battle him repeatedly and must cleave the castle with his thunderbolt to release the cow so that she may restore the earth with her rain. This legend symbolizes the dry periods in one's spiritual quest that appear from time to time (mentioned frequently by Christian mystics), which must be withstood until the divine light intervenes to give the seeker new life.

Vritti 🅷 (Vṛtti), Skt., lit. "wave (of thought)"; all thoughts of the waking consciousness and the dream state, which wash over the consciousness like waves. Such mental oscillations arise ceaselessly within us and veil absolute consciousness.

Vritti-Jñāna 🅷 (Vṛtti-Jñāna), Skt.; knowledge won by the activity of the mind. Because of its attachment to the duality of subject and object, the mind divides the One into many and thereby spreads the manifest world before us. Knowledge at the level of mind is bound to the empirical world and is therefore limited.

Vulture Peak Mountain 🅱 🆉 (Skt., gridhrakūṭa); a mountain in the neighborhood of the city of Rājagriha that was a favorite sojourning place of → Shākyamuni Buddha. According to tradition Buddha expounded the → *Lotus Sūtra* on Vulture Peak Mountain.

According to a saga the name of this mountain derives from an event in which → Māra in the form of a vulture attempted to divert → Ānanda from his meditation. See also → *nenge-mishō.*

Vyāhriti 🅷 (Vyāhṛti), Skt.; the utterance of certain brief formulas, especially the three sacred sacrificial utterances of → Prajāpati: *bhūr, bhuvar, svar,* also known as the "three clear ones." These three mantric syllables were taken by the Vedic creator-god from the three → Vedas *(Rigveda,*

Yajurveda, and Sāmaveda) ascribed to him. From *bhūr* he created the earth, from *bhuvar* space, and from *svar* heaven. They are the opening words of the → Gāyatrī.

The above is related in the *Aitareya-Brāhmana,* which further states that Prajāpati created the three letters A, U, and M from the three sacred utterances and joined them to make the sacred syllable OM.

Vyākarana 🅗 Skt. → Vedānga

Vyakta 🅗 Skt., lit. "the perceivable"; what has been developed or brought into manifestation, the world of appearances, a product of → *prakriti.* Its opposite is *avyakta* (the unmanifest).

Vyākulata 🅗 Skt.; passionate, uncontrollable zeal, the irresistable craving of an individual to realize God. → Rāmakrishna said, "One who longs for God as a drowning man longs for air will assuredly see God."

Vyāpakatva 🅗 Skt., lit. *vyāpaka:* "permeating, extending," and *tva:* "thou" (the same word as *tvam* in → *Tat tvam asi*); in Kashmir Shaivism (→ Pratyabhijñā) the spiritual experience that everything is permeated by Shiva as the supreme god and sole reality; knowledge of the identity of the manifest world, the soul, and God.

Vyāsa 🅗 Skt.; the name of many of the authors and "collectors" *(vyāsa)* of Sanskrit works, above all of Veda-Vyāsa, the compiler of the → Vedas, who is named Shāshvata ("the imperishable") for the immortality of his work; also the name of the compiler of the → *Mahābhārata,* the founder of → Vedānta, and the compiler of the → Purānas. The Purānas mention no fewer than twenty-eight *vyāsas,* who are said to have appeared on earth at various times in order to compile the Vedas and to disseminate them.

Vyatireka 🅗 Skt., lit. "contrast, paricularity"; a method of classification of objects in Hindu philosophy by distinguishing them in one of the following ways: 1. difference of kind, as between a cow and a horse; 2. difference within the same kind, as between a black cow and a white one; 3. differences within the same object, as between the trunk, branches, and leaves of a tree.

Vyāvahārika 🅗 Skt.; conventional, relative reality; the way of thinking of those who identify with the body and who take the relative, gross world to be the only reality.

W

Wai-ch'i 🅣 Chin., lit. "outer breath"; the air we inhale, as opposed to the inner breath (→ *nei-ch'i*) that corresponds to the cosmic primordial energy (→ *yüan-ch'i*) within the human body.

Up to the time of the T'ang Dynasty Taoists believed that in breathing exercises such as holding the breath (→ *pi-ch'i*) or circulating the breath (→ *hsing-ch'i*) it was the outer breath that was held or circulated. The practitioner would therefore endeavor to retain the inhaled air for as long as possible and/or make it circulate throughout the body. These practices were not exclusively Taoist in that they also played an important part in Chinese medicine.

During the middle T'ang Dynasty exercises such as *pi-ch'i* and *hsing-ch'i* were reinterpreted as a result of which it was accepted that it was not the outer but the inner breath that was held or made to flow through the body. The dangerous practice of holding the breath—at times for as long as two hundred heartbeats—thus became redundant. In addition, this new understanding of Taoist breathing exercises made it possible to distinguish them from the purely health-promoting exercises recommended by Chinese medicine.

Wai-tan 🅣 Chin., lit. "outer cinnabar"; the "outer elixir," the "outer alchemy." One of two branches of Taoist alchemy, the other being → *nei-tan,* Inner Alchemy. *Wai-tan* practitioners strive to produce a pill of immortality (→ *ch'ang-sheng pu-ssu*) by the transformation of chemical substances. The most important ingredients during the working of the outer elixir are cinnabar (*tan*) and gold. The latter was used because of its durability, the former—red mercury ore—because of its color and chemical properties.

The followers of the Outer Alchemy believed that a person's life force was identical with the so-called primordial energy (→ *yüan-ch'i*) or cosmic energy. A reduction or loss of a person's *yüan-ch'i* would therefore result in illness or death. The *yüan-ch'i* itself was understood to be a special mixture of yin and yang (→ yin-yang). According to the doctrine of the Outer Alchemy, only cinnabar and gold were capable of restoring within the organism that primordial state in which yin and yang combine and thus become indistinguishable from each other.

The most important Taoist alchemists were → Wei P'o yang and → Ko Hung. As Taoism developed, the view that immortality could be attained by ingesting a pill or drug was gradually replaced by the doctrine and teachings of the Inner Elixir School.

The practitioner of the Outer Alchemy produces his elixir over a fire in a cauldron, by which method transformations normally occurring in nature are accelerated. A series of reductions and recyclings produces purified cinnabar, the efficiency of which increases proportionate to the number of such recyclings. The most powerful immortality drug is said to be cinnabar that has been purified nine times (*chiu-huan-tan*): anyone ingesting it is believed to be capable of ascending to Heaven in broad daylight (→ *fei-sheng*). Ko Hung describes the properties of gold and cinnabar as follows: "Cinnabar becomes transformed when heated. The longer the period it is heated, the more miraculous the transformation it undergoes. Gold, on the other hand, retains its nature even when placed into fire, melted a hundred times or buried in the ground to the end of time. The ingestion of these two substances brings about a sublimation of the body. . . . Even the cheapest and coarsest type of cinnabar is infinitely superior to the most excellent medicinal plants. If you incinerate plants they turn into ashes. Granules of cinnabar, on the other hand, give rise to granules of mercury when heated; a further sublimation once again produces cinnabar" (chap. 4 of Ko Hung's *Pao-p'u-tzu;* trans. from Kaltenmark, *Lao-tzu und der Taoismus;* see Kaltenmark 1969).

Waka 🅉 Jap.; traditional Japanese poetic form with fixed line lengths of 5–7–5–7–7 syllables. Like → haiku poems, *waka* poetry is pervaded by the mind of Zen and is the form often chosen by Zen masters when they want to give expression to their realization of Zen.

Wakuan Shitai 🅉 Jap. for → Huo-an Shih-t'i

Wang Ch'un-yang 🅃 → *ch'üan-chen tao*

Wang Hsiao-yang 🅃 → *ch'üan-chen tao*

Wang Jung 🅃 → *chu-lin ch'i-hsien*

Wang Pi 🅃 226–49 C.E.; a representative of neo-Taoism (→ *hsüan-hsüeh*) and one of the most important commentators on the *Tao-te ching* and the *Book of Change(s)* (→ *I-ching*).

Wang Pi's edition of the *Tao-te ching* has remained authoritative to this day. In his commentary he takes the view that the → Tao is equivalent to emptiness (→ *wu*): "Although we say of the Tao that it is nonbeing, we must not forget that all things owe their perfection to the Tao. The assumption that the Tao is being still does not permit us to perceive its form."

Thus *wu* is considered to be the primordial ground of all being: "All things in this world arise from being. But the origin of being is rooted in nonbeing. To realize true being it is necessary to return to nonbeing."

Wang Pi's commentary on the *I-ching* describes it as a book of wisdom rather than one of oracles, and thereby cleanses it of the inflated interpretations of the Yin-Yang School (→ *yin-yang chia*).

Wanshi Shogaku 🅉 Jap. for → Hung-chih Cheng-chueh

Wan-wu 🄱 🅃 🅉 Chin., lit. "ten thousand things or beings"; a conventional expression descriptive of the totality of phenomena within the universe. *Ten thousand* here simply means "innumerable" or "all."

Wasan 🅉 Jap., lit. "song of praise"; generally a Buddhist song of praise in which a buddha, bodhisattva, patriarch (→ *soshigata*), or other Buddhist theme is celebrated. In the area of Zen, the best-known work of this genre is "Song in Praise of Zazen" by the great Japanese Zen master → Hakuin Zenji (→ *Hakuin Zenji zazen-wasan*), in which the fundamental importance of the practice of → *zazen* for the discovery of the ever-present buddha-nature is expressed.

Wato 🅉 Jap., lit. "word-head"; the point, punch line, or key line of a → kōan, the word or phrase in which the kōan resolves itself when one struggles with it as a means of spiritual training. A kōan can have only one, or several, *wato*, and the *wato* can consist of a single word (→ *ichiji-kan*) or be a long expression.

Way of Supreme Peace 🅃 → *t'ai-p'ing tao*

Way of the Realization of Truth 🅃 → *ch'üan-chen tao*

Wei Ch'eng 🅃 Chin. → *men-shen*

Wei-lang 🅉 → Hui-neng

Wei P'o-yang 🅃 2d century C.E.; one of the most important representatives of Taoist alchemy and author of the oldest known treatise on alchemy, the *Chou-i ts'an-t'ung-ch'i* (roughly "On the Uniting of Correspondences"), which deals with the production of the elixir of immortality (→ *ch'ang-sheng pu-ssu*). In this work Wei P'o-yang also makes reference to certain elements and concepts of the *Book of Change(s)* (→ *I-ching*). Its language is highly esoteric and allows a variety of interpretations. For that reason, it has come to be understood both as a recipe for producing the outer elixir and as a method of creating or developing the inner elixir. In the opinion of some Taoist practitioners it also contains references to certain sexual practices (→ *fang-chung shu*). In later Taoism, however, it is generally seen as a text of the Inner Alchemy. The *Chou-i ts'an-t'ung-ch'i* owes its fame in part to a commentary by the 12th-century neo-Taoist philosopher → Chu Hsi.

Another commentator (→ Yü Yen) sees its central notion as follows: Man makes use of the secret energies of Heaven and Earth to produce for himself the great elixir of the golden liquid and thus is part of Heaven and Earth from their very beginning. . . . Whenever Heaven combines with Earth man should strive to acquire and make use of the secret energies of the creative activities of yin and yang.

A well-known anecdote protrays Wei P'o-yang as a follower of the Outer Elixir School:

"One day Wei P'o-yang went into the mountains with three of his pupils in order to prepare the elixir. When it was ready they first fed it to a dog, which immediately fell dead to the ground. Wei P'o-yang then asked his pupils whether he, too, should ingest the elixir and follow the dog [into death]. His disciples turned the question back on him, and he replied, 'I have abandoned the ways of the world and my family and friends to go and live in the mountains. It would be shameful to return without having found the Tao of the sacred immortals (→ *hsien*). To die from the elixir can be no worse than to live without it. So I must partake of it.' He did so and fell dead to the ground. One of the three pupils followed his example but the other two went back into the world. When they had gone, Wei P'o-yang, his pupil, and the white dog came back to life and despatched a letter to the two that had left, thanking them for their kindness. When they received the message their hearts were filled with sadness and regret." (Trans. from Colgrave 1980.)

Wei-shan Ling-yu 🅉 → Kuei-shan Ling-yu

Wei-t'o 🄱 Chin. (Skt., Veda); image in Buddhist monasteries of China, found in the hall of the → celestial kings with the statue of the → Laughing Buddha. Wei-t'o, one of the generals of the Guardian of the South, wears full warrior's armor. His head is adorned with a helmet and in his hand he holds either a → *vajra* or a war club, with which he annihilates enemies of the Buddhist teaching. Thus he is a guardian of the teaching.

Wei-t'o is said to have seen the Buddha face to face at the moment when the Buddha charged him with the protection of the → dharma. Thus his statue stands facing the image of the Buddha in the main hall of the monastery. In most monasteries Wei-t'o is invoked in the course of daily worship. Often the selection of a new abbot of the monastery is symbolically attributed to him. Strips of paper containing the names of the individual candidates are placed before his image in a vase. The retiring abbot or a representative draws one of the strips, but in so doing is only a medium for the will of Wei-t'o.

Wei-yang-tsung 🅉 Chin. → Igyō school

Wen-ch'ang 🅃 Taoist god of literature. In reality, Wen-ch'ang is a constellation of six stars in the vicinity of the Great Bear. It is said that when these stars are bright, literature flourishes. However, the stellar deity Wen-ch'ang, according to legend, repeatedly descended to Earth and manifested himself in human form. Taoists texts mention seventeen separate existences of Wen-ch'ang on Earth. He is above all venerated by people who require help with their entrance examinations for an official career. Wen-ch'ang is believed to be the author of extensive literary works, which were revealed to man in various, miraculous ways.

Many educated Chinese put up a plaque—or, more rarely, a picture—showing Wen-ch'ang dressed as a mandarin and holding in his hand a wish-fulfilling scepter (→ *ju-i*). He is usually portrayed in the company of K'uei-hsing (also a stellar deity) and Chu-i, the Red-robed One. The former is responsible for issuing official testimonials, while the latter acts as the patron of ill-prepared candidates for official examinations.

Wen-shu 🄱 Chin. name for → Mañjushrī, one of the "four great bodhisattvas" of China. The place in China where he is said to have appeared and expounded the teaching is Mount Wu-t'ai-shan (→ four famous mountains), which remains today a place of pilgrimage for Chinese Buddhists who wish to pay homage to Wen-shu. (For iconographical representation, → Mañjushrī.)

According to Chinese tradition, Wen-shu was chosen by → Shākyamuni Buddha to proclaim the teaching in China. He is said to have taught during the reign of Emperor → Ming-ti and to have been personally venerated by him.

Wen-ta 🅉 Chin. for → *mondō*

Western paradise 🄱 → Sukhāvatī

White Lotus school 🄱 (Chin., Pai-lien-tsung); a school of Pure Land Buddhism, founded by Mao Tzu-yuan in the 12th century. The White Lotus school was an association of monks, nuns, and laypersons, whose objective was by regularly invoking the Buddha → Amitābha and observing the → *shīlas* to create good karma,

Wen-ch'ang listening to sages in the company of Chu-i and K'uei-hsing.

overcome all passions, and be reborn in the pure land. A unique feature in the practice of the White Lotus school was daily "penance." The members were strict vegetarians and also did not take wine, milk, or onions.

This school of Buddhism was soon discredited as being linked with demons, and was banned several times; nevertheless it survived. Later on → Maitreya, the future buddha, was venerated along with Amitābha; non-Buddhist elements also penetrated the school. Thus the White Lotus school became a secret society and played an important role in the rebellions and peasant insurrections of the 13th–15th centuries.

Mao Tzu-yuan, a monk of the T'ien-t'ai school, quite early became interested in the teachings of the Pure Land school. The example of → Hui-yuan inspired him to found the White Lotus school. The goal of its adherents was to be reborn in the pure land, which was understood not as a geographical place but as a state of mind. Amitābha, ruler of the pure land, is the true nature of man. Even if one cannot give up worldly ties and undertakes no strict practice other than reciting the name of Amitābha, according to Mao's view, a rebirth in the pure land is possible.

White Lotus Society B → White Lotus school, → Pure Land school

Will for truth Z → *kokorozashi*

Won Buddhism B Kor. *won*, lit. "circular"; modern Buddhist folk movement in South Korea, founded by Soe-tae San (1891–1943).

The practice of Won Buddhism has two aspects: realization of → buddha-nature and "timeless and placeless Zen." This means that the adherents of Won Buddhism seek to see the Buddha in all things and to live in accordance with this insight. This type of meditation is called timeless and placeless because it does not depend on specific meditation periods and halls, but is to be practiced always and everywhere.

In Won Buddhism only one meditation object is used—a black circle on a white field, which symbolizes the cosmic body of Buddha, the *dharmakāya* (→ *trikāya*). The name of the school is derived from this circle.

Won Buddhism is not a purely monastic religion. Monks are permitted to marry. There are no specific ceremonies and rituals; an attempt is made to adapt to the needs of modern men and women. Thus the most important sūtras were translated into easily understandable Korean. The followers of Won Buddhism are active in social and charitable work. In the postwar years they established numerous kindergartens, schools, and universities.

Soe-tae San spent many of his youthful years in ascetic practice, until in 1915 he attained "great enlightenment." Nine disciples attached themselves to him to practice and study the Buddhist teachings. In 1924 he founded the Association for the Study of the Buddha-Dharma, which, however, remained quite limited in its effect during Japanese colonial rule. Only in 1946 were his teachings propagated, under the name Won Buddhism, throughout South Korea. Today Won Buddhism has many followers.

World Fellowship of Buddhists (WFB) B international association of Buddhists founded in 1950 by the Sinhalese Buddhist scholar Malalasekera. The objective of the World Fellowship of Buddhists is to propagate the Buddhist teaching and seek reconciliation between the different currents within Buddhism.

The WFB has a flag of six colors with the wheel of dharma (→ dharma-chakra) on it as a symbol of the teaching. It has declared the full-moon day in May to be Buddha Day. The World Fellowship of Buddhists periodically holds world conferences. The first one took place in 1950 in Sri Lanka. It puts out a journal called *World Buddhism*. Its main seat is in Bangkok.

Wu 🅉 Chin. for → satori

Wu 🅃 Chin., lit. "nonbeing," emptiness; a basic concept in Taoist philosophy; the absence of qualities perceivable by the senses. *Wu* is the essential characteristic of the → Tao, but may also refer to a Taoist so imbued with the Tao that he has become free of all desires and passions, i.e., empty.

Chapter 11 of the *Tao-te ching* (Feng & English 1972) describes the nature of emptiness as follows:

Thirty spokes share the wheel's hub;
It is the centre hole that makes it useful.
Shape clay into a vessel;
It is the space within that makes it useful.
Cut doors and windows for a room;
It is the holes which make them useful.
Therefore profit comes from what is there;
Usefulness from what is not there.

Chapter 5 (ibid.) states:

The space between heaven and earth is like a bellows.
The shape changes but not the form;
The more it moves, the more it yields.

Wu-an P'u-ning 🅉 (Jap., Gottan Funei), 1197–1276, Chinese Ch'an (Zen) master of the → Rinzai school; a student and dharma successor (→ *hassu*) of → Wu-chun Shih-fan (Jap., Bushun [Wujun] Shiban).

Wu-an went to Japan in 1260, where he was active for some years in the → Kenchō-ji monastery. He guided the Shōgun Hōjō Tokiyori to an enlightenment experience (→ *kenshō*) and founded the Shōden-ji monastery in Kyōto. Later he returned to China, where he died on a pilgrimage. In Japan he received the posthumous honorific title of *shūgaku zenji*.

Wu-ch'ang 🅃 Chin., lit. "five constants"; the five cardinal virtues of Confucianism (→ K'ung-tzu), which regulate human behavior: → *jen* (humanity, fellow feeling), → *i* (uprightness), → *li* (rites and customs), *chih* (wisdom, insight) and *hsin* (trust). See also → *wu-lun*.

Wu-chen pien 🅃 Chin., lit. *"Treatise on Awakening to the Truth"*; best-known work of the alchemist → Cheng Po-tuan (983–1082 C.E.), containing his interpretation of the doctrine of the inner elixir (→ *nei-tan*), which became the doctrinal basis of the later Southern School of → *ch'üan-chen tao*.

The hundred chapters of the *Wu-chen pien* are written in verse and describe the various methods for producing the inner elixir. Chang Po-tuan rejected the outer elixir (→ *wai-tan*). He was convinced that every human being contained it within himself, so that there was no need to collect medicinal herbs or perform hygiene exercises.

Chang Po-tuan taught that to produce the inner elixir, the practitioner must know the nature of true lead (yang) and true mercury (yin) (→ yin-yang). Yang must catch and absorb yin—a process described in the *Wu-chen pien* as the marriage of yin and yang. The alchemist adept, lying on his bed at midnight or at the time of the winter solstice, causes the two energies (yin and yang) to combine in his abdomen with the help of → *ch'i*, the vital energy, and thus produces an embryo (→ *sheng-t'ai*) that grows in proportion to the increase in yang. In this way the alchemist practitioner can become an immortal (→ *hsien*).

Wu-chi 🅃 Chin., lit. "peak of nothingness"; the limitless, unconditioned, primordial, formless, and invisible, to which everything returns (→ *fu*). The Taoist philosopher Chou Tun-i considered *wu-chi* to be synonymous with the *t'ai-chi* (→ *t'ai-chi-t'u*).

Wu-ch'in-hsi 🅃 Chin. → Hua T'o

Wu-chi-t'u 🅃 Chin. → Ch'en T'uan

Wu Chiu 🅉 (Jap., Ukyū), ca. 8th–9th century; Chinese Ch'an (Zen) master; a student and dharma successor (→ *hassu*) of → Ma-tsu Tao-i (Jap., Baso Dōitsu). Wu Chiu appears in example 75 of the → *Pi-yen-lu*. He was one of the first Ch'an masters to make use of the stick (→ *shippei*, → *kyosaku*) in the training of Ch'an monks.

Wu-cho 🅉 (Jap., Mujaku) 821–900, Chinese Ch'an (Zen) master of the → Igyō school; a student and dharma successor (→ *hassu*) of → Yang-shan Hui-chi (Jap., Kyōzan Ejaku). In his youth he traveled through the country seeking out various Ch'an masters. The occurrence reported in example 35 of the → *Pi-yen-lu* is said to have taken place during this pilgrimage.

The name Wu-cho "no attachment," was conferred upon the master by the Chinese emperor during the time after his enlightenment under Yang-shan when he was active as a Ch'an master.

Wu-chun Shih-fan 🅉 (Jap., Bushun [Mujun] Shiban), 1177–1249; Chinese Ch'an (Zen) master of the → Rinzai school. He was the master of the Japanese Zen master → Ben'en, who helped establish Zen in Japan.

Wu-chun was one of the most outstanding Ch'an masters of his time. He was the abbot of important

Chinese monasteries, among them the Wan-shou monastery on Mount Ching in Chekiang province, the first of the Five Mountains (Chin., Wu-shan; Jap., → Gosan) of China.

Wu-feng Ch'ang-kuan 🅩 (Jap., Gohō Jōkan), ca. 8th–9th century; Chinese Ch'an (Zen) master; a student and dharma successor (→ *hassu*) of → Pai-chang Huang-hai (Jap., Hyakujō Ekai). We encounter him in examples 70 and 71 of the → *Pi-yen-lu*.

Wu-hsin 🅩 Chin. for → *mushin*

Wu-hsing 🅣 Chin., lit. "five movers," also known as *wu-te* (lit. "five virtues"); the five elements. Five phases of transformation, or five energies, that determine the course of natural phenomena. These five elements—water, fire, wood, metal, and earth—are not to be understood as real substances but rather as abstract forces and symbols for certain basic characteristics of matter: e.g., it lies in the nature of water to moisten and to flow downward; of fire to heat and to rise; of wood to bend and straighten again; of metal to be cast or hammered into various forms; and of earth to be fertile. At the time of the Warring States Period, the notion arose that the elements not only give rise to each other but also may help conquer or destroy each other (*hsiang-sheng hsiang-k'o*): wood can give rise to fire, fire to earth, earth to metal, metal to water, and water to wood. At the same time water will conquer fire, fire vanquishes metal, metal can destroy wood, wood can conquer the earth, and earth overcomes water. This theory, furthermore, is of relevance in Chinese medicine.

Within a more complicated system of correspondence, the five elements are related to the seasons of the year, the cardinal points, colors, flavors, numbers, internal organs, and other groupings.

During the 4th and 3d centuries B.C.E., the doctrine of the five elements constituted an independent school. The most important representative of this school was → Tsou Yen (3d century B.C.E.), who applied the theory of the five elements to the area of politics by relating the course of history to their interdependence and succession. At the time of the Han Dynasty the Five Elements School combined with the Yin-Yang School (→ *yin-yang chia*) and has since been considered part of the latter.

The succession of the four seasons is reflected by the interdependence of the five elements: in spring, wood is dominant and gives rise to fire, the element of summer. Fire gives rise to earth, which is characteristic of the center, i.e., the third month of summer. Earth, in turn, gives rise to metal which dominates autumn, and metal to the water of winter.

Furthermore, each element has its corresponding color, flavor, and cardinal point: the north and that which is black and salty correspond to water. Fire is related to the south, the color red, and to that which tastes bitter. The east, the color green, and that which tastes sour correspond to wood. The qualities of metal are related to the west, the color white, and that which tastes sharp; and water corresponds to the color yellow, that which tastes sweet, and to the center, which, in the Chinese view of the world, is the fifth cardinal point.

In the microcosmic realm, the five elements are connected with various organs of the body and with certain emotions. These correspondences are of great importance in Chinese medicine. Wood is related to the eyes, the sinews, the gall bladder, the liver, and anger; fire to the tongue, the blood vessels, the small intestine, the heart, and the feeling of joy; earth to the mouth, the muscles, the stomach, the pancreas, and worrying; metal to the nose, the hairs of the body, the large intestine, the lungs, and sadness; and water to the ears, the bones, the bladder, the kidneys, and fear.

In addition, the five elements are said to be connected with the planets Mercury, Venus, Mars, Jupiter, and Saturn as well as the signs of the Chinese lunar calendar.

The Yin-Yang School allocated numbers to the five elements: one and six to water, two and seven to fire, three and eight to wood, four and nine to metal, and five and ten to earth. Even numbers are said to be Earth numbers and odd numbers Heaven numbers. In this sense the odd numbers are characteristic of what gives rise to an element, and the even numbers of what brings it to fruition or perfection. These relationships are also of significance in connection with the *Book of Change(s)* (→ *I-ching*).

According to the historical view of Tsou Yen, the succession of the various dynasties imitates that of the elements: Earth, under whose sign the legendary Yellow Emperor (→ Huang-ti) ruled, was conquered by the wood of the Hsia Dynasty; this in turn was vanquished by the metal of the Shang Dynasty; and Tsou Yen was of the opinion that the fire of the Chou Dynasty, during which he lived, would be conquered by the water of the next dynasty and that by the earth of a further dynasty, thereby initiating a new cycle. Each ruler of a dynasty adopted the color of, and ruled in accordance with, the quality of its corresponding element and furthermore adapted the calendar, the color of fabrics, etc. to it.

Wu-hsueh Tsu-yuan 🅩 (Jap., Mugaku Sogen), 1226–86, Chinese Ch'an (Zen) master of the → Rinzai school; he trained under, among others, → Wu-chun Shih-fan (Jap., Bushun Shiban) and became abbot of the Chen-ju monastery of T'ai-chou. In 1279 the Shōgun Hōjō Tokimune invited him to Kamakura in Japan. There, succeeding → Lan-ch'i Tao-lung (Jap., Rankei Dōryū), he became abbot of → Kenchō-ji Monastery. He later founded → Engaku-ji monastery, of which he also become abbot. Kenchō-ji and Engaku-ji belong to the → Gosan of Kamakura, the most important monasteries of this important Japanese center of Zen. Posthumously, he received the honorific titles of → *bukkō kokushi* (also *bukkō zenji*) and *emman jōshō kokushi*.

Wu-lun 🅸 Chin., lit. "five relationships"; five types of relationship—between (1) parent and child, (2) ruler and subject, (3) husband and wife, (4) older and younger brother, and (5) friend and friend—which, according to the Confucianist model of society, form the basis of human interaction (→ *wu-ch'ang*).

Wu-men Hui-k'ai 🅩 (Jap., Mumon Ekai), 1183–1260; Chinese Ch'an (Zen) master of the Yōgi lineage of Rinzai Zen (→ Yōgi school); a student and dharma successor (→ *hassu*) of → Yueh-lin Shih-kuan (Jap., Gatsurin Shikan) and the master of Shinchi → Kakushin, who brought the Ch'an of the Yōgi school and the → *Wu-men-kuan* published by Wu-men to Japan. Wu-men, who is considered the most outstanding Rinzai master of his time, is today primarily known for having composed the *Wu-men-kuan*, i.e., for having compiled its forty-eight kōans and having furnished them with commentaries and "praises" (→ *ju*).

Wu-men was born in Hang-chou. Since Hang-chou had been one of the centers of Ch'an in China since the T'ang period, it is likely he came in contact with Ch'an at an early age and eventually sought instruction in it. His first master was Kung Ho-shang; later he came to Master Yueh-lin, who submitted him to strict training. He gave Wu-men the kōan → *mu*, and Wu-men struggled six years with it without coming to a breakthrough. Finally he was so desperate that he swore not to sleep any more until he had solved the kōan. He uninterruptedly practiced → zazen with this kōan. When he got sleepy, he went to the entryway of the meditation hall and hit his head against a wooden pillar in order to stay awake.

One day when the great drum was struck to indicate midday, he suddenly realized profound enlightenment. Then he wrote a poem, which begins with the words "Out of the clear sky with the sun brightly shining, suddenly a thunderclap. . . ."

After Master Yueh-lin had examined him and confirmed his enlightenment experience, he wrote another poem in a short verse form with five-syllable lines. It went as follows:

Mu Mu Mu Mu Mu
Mu Mu Mu Mu Mu
Mu Mu Mu Mu Mu
Mu Mu Mu Mu Mu

Later he was highly regarded throughout China as a Ch'an master. In 1288 he completed the *Wu-men-kuan*, with the → *Pi-yen-lu*, one of the two most renowned kōan collections. In the following year it was printed for the first time.

Emperor Li-tsung appointed Wu-men abbot of a large Ch'an monastery near the capital in 1246 and conferred on him the honorific title of *buddha eye*. Toward the end of his life, he withdrew to a small monastery in the mountains. Despite his fame and the deference and honor accorded to him on every hand, he remained until his death an extremely humble man, who continued to wear only a simple, coarse robe and, in the spirit of → *Pai-chang Huai-hai (Jap., Hyakujō Ekai)* he always participated in the manual labor of the monastery. His death poem was as follows:

Emptiness is unborn
Emptiness does not pass away.
When you know emptiness
You are not different from it.

Wu-men-kuan 🅩 Chin. (Jap., *Mumonkan*), lit. "the *Gateless Gate*"; one of the two most important kōan collections in Ch'an (Zen) literature; the other is the → *Pi-yen-lu*. The *Wu-men-kuan* was compiled by the Chinese Ch'an (Zen) master → Wu-men Hui-k'ai (Jap., Mumon Ekai). It is composed of forty-eight kōans, which Wu-men collected and arranged. He provided each kōan with a short insightful commentary and with a "praise" (→ *ju*) and published the collection in 1229. In 1254 the *Wu-men-kuan* was brought to Japan by the Japanese master → Kakushin, a student and dharma successor (→ *hassu*) of Wu-men. In 1405 Shun'ō Reizan (1334–1408), a fourth-generation dharma heir of Kakushin, published at Kōon-ji monastery the Japanese edition of this work that is considered authoritative down to the present day. Shibayama Zenkei, *Zen Comments on the Mumonkan*, trans. Sumiko Kudo (New York 1974), is noteworthy for the → *teishō* added to the examples of the ancient masters by the important modern Zen master → Shibayama Zenkei. Another English translation is *Two Zen Classics*, trans. Katsuki Sekida (New York, 1977).

The *Wu-men-kuan* begins with the renowned kōan → *mu*, with which Master Wu-men himself came to profound enlightenment. It is especially suitable as a *hosshin* kōan, i.e., as a kōan that can help a practitioner to a first enlightenment experience (→ *kenshō*, → satori). It is still given today to many beginners on the Zen path as their first kōan. Since the *Wu-men-kuan*'s most famous kōan is used with beginners and since from a literary point of view it is much plainer than the *Pi-yen-lu*, it is often considered less profound than the latter. This overlooks that a kōan like *mu* can be understood anew on ever deeper levels of enlightenment and that the *Wu-men-kuan* also contains examples (for instance, example 38) of *nantō* kōan, those that are especially difficult to resolve.

Kōans originated as an immediate expression of the Ch'an (Zen) realization of the ancient masters—realization that is not conceptually graspable (→ *fukasetsu*), not "understandable." Its nature is paradoxical, i.e., beyond concept. Thus Ch'an and Zen texts are among the most difficult to translate in world literature. Even for someone who has achieved perfect mastery of Chinese or Japanese, it is just about impossible for one who does not have a profound realization of Zen to come up with an appropiate translation (i.e, one usable for Zen training) of a kōan. Thus most European translations of the *Wu-men-kuan* and other Ch'an and Zen texts suffer from the fact that though the translaters may be philologically competent, they do not possess the "Zen eye."

The reader of Ch'an and Zen texts who finds kōans strange or alienating, must keep in mind that kōans are by definition ununderstandable, inaccessible to the reasoning mind—precisely because they are challenges to transcend logical-conceptual mind. Even in cases where illuminating interpretations of kōans present themselves, from the standpoint of Zen they are false if they are thought out and will be quickly exposed as such by any Zen master. Texts like the *Wu-men-kuan* are aids in Zen training and should not be regarded either as literature or as a historical record. For a person practicing → *zazen* with a kōan, it is not the point to be informed about what a Chinese Ch'an master experienced or said hundreds of years ago, but rather to realize himself here and now the living truth toward which the kōan points. Many of the kōans in the *Wu-men-kuan* and other collections might appear superficially as amusing anecdotes—not rarely Ch'an or Zen masters have a profound sense of humor—but, the power of these kōans to enlighten, which alone is important for Zen, becomes evident only within the context of Zen training under the guidance of a → *rōshi.*

Wu-shih ■ Chin., lit. "five corpses"; five types of contaminated (impure) energy found in the five internal organs of the human body (to which the colors red, green, white, yellow, and black are allocated). Because the presence of these impure energies within the body reduces a person's life span, a Taoist practitioner wishing to attain immortality must eliminate the five corpses by meditative practices and fasting.

Wu-shih ch'i-hou ■ Chin., roughly "five periods and seven time spans"; various stages and phases on the meditative path of a Taoist practitioner, ranging from a simple pacifying of the mind to the highest state of spiritual realization. They are, in summary, as follows:

1. The mind is moving, restless, and only rarely still.
2. The mind begins to be less restless.
3. Calm and movement hold each other in balance.
4. The mind is calm most of the time and only rarely moves, and the practitioner concentrates on an object of meditation.
5. The mind abides in pure stillness; it is no longer kept in motion by external impressions.

After these five *wu-shih* the practitioner passes through the following seven *ch'i-hou:*

1. Worry and sorrow subside, as do the passions and the practitioner realizes the → Tao.
2. The outer appearance of the adept becomes like that of a child, his body supple and his mind at peace, and the practitioner possesses supernatural powers.
3. The practitioner is assured of a long life and reaches the level of an immortal (→ *hsien*).
4. He purifies his body and perfects the energy (→ *ch'i*) and thus attains the level of the true man (→ *chen-jen*).
5. He purifies the energy and perfects the mind (spirit) (→ *shen*) and reaches the level of a saint (→ *shen-jen*).
6. He purifies the mind and brings it into harmony with all forms, thereby reaching the level of a perfected human being.
7. The adept has passed beyond all rites and rules and is free of all motivated action, the highest realization in Taoist practice.

Wu-t'ai-shan ■ Chin., lit. "Five-Terrace Mountain"; one of the → four famous mountains of China, located in Shansi province. It is one of the most important pilgrimage sites for Chinese Buddhists, who venerate the bodhisattva → Wen-shu (Skt., Mañjushrī) on Wu-t'ai-shan, where he is said to have expounded the teaching of Buddha. The mountain is also an important center of Mongolian Buddhism. The first monasteries were built here in the 4th–5th centuries; by the 6th century over 200 were already in existence. Of these about fifty-eight are preserved today.

The belief that this bodhisattva was active on Wu-t'ai-shan is also widespread in India and Nepal. It is based on a passage in the → *Buddhāvatamsaka-sūtra*, where it says that Mañjushrī will appear in a northeastern country and expound the teaching. Similar passages are found in other texts.

Wu-te ■ Chin. → *wu-hsing*

Wu-ti ■ Chin., lit. "five emperors"; legendary emperors said to have ruled China between 2697 and 2205 B.C.E. or—according to an alternative calendrical calculation—2674 and 2184 B.C.E. The five are the Yellow Emperor (→ Huang-ti), Chuan Hsü, Ku, → Yao, and → Shun. The belief in their existence is based on historical speculations dating back to the 2d and 1st centuries B.C.E.; Confucius—who lived earlier than that—only mentions Yao and Shun. Their grouping into five reflects the Chinese system of cosmological correspondences. Since the number five is also related to the five elements (→ *wu-hsing*), one element is allocated to each of the five emperors.

Wu-tou-mi tao 🅃 Chin., lit. "Five-Pecks-of-Rice Taoism"; early Taoist school (→ *tao-cniao*), founded by → Chang Tao-ling between 126 and 144 C.E. in Szechwan in western China. It remained active up to the 15th century. The reason for the school's name stems from the practice that anyone wishing to join it had to make a payment of five pecks of rice to the → *tao-shih. Wu-tou-mi tao* is also known as the School of the Celestial Masters (→ *t'ien-shih*) because the heads of this school bore the title *celestial master.* Five-Pecks-of-Rice Taoism is based on the teachings of Lao-tzu, who is venerated by his followers as → T'ai-shang lao-chün. The root text of the school is the → *Tao-te ching,* which it interprets in a way specifically suited to its practices and requirements.

Like other Taoist movements of the period, Five-Pecks-of-Rice Taoism, in its religious rituals, placed particular emphasis on the healing of illnesses that it believed to be a consequence of evil deeds. In this context mass confessions at which believers recited a catalog of their transgressions to the three rulers (→ *san-kuan*)—Heaven, Earth, and Water—were of particular significance. Other practices of Five-Pecks-of-Rice Taoism were ritual fasts (→ *chai*), the use of talismans (→ *fu-lu*), orgiastic feasts (→ *ho-ch'i*), and ceremonies for the dead.

The followers of the *wu-tou-mi tao* were organized on a strictly hierarchical pattern. The bulk of the congregation was made up of so-called demon soldiers, who were led by the presenters of liquid sacrifices (Chin., *chi-chiu*), each of whom was in charge of a particular district. The top position in the hierarchy was held by the celestial master (*t'ien-shih*).

After the death of its founder, the leadership of the school passed to Chang Heng and from him, in turn, to → Chang Lu, who, toward the end of the Eastern Han Dynasty, established in the northern part of the country a state structure in which there was no separation between politics and religion. The religious hierarchy thus was at the same time a military one. This form of government continued until the year 215 C.E. During the subsequent centuries Five-Pecks-of-Rice Taoism spread among the peasantry and played an important part in several peasant uprisings at the time of the Chin Dynasty.

In the 5th century → K'ou Chien-chih, under whose influence Taoism was proclaimed a state religion, assumed the ancient title of *celestial master* and endeavored to liberate Taoism from the negative influences of → Chang Chüeh by introducing various Confucianist ideas, as a result of which good deeds and hygiene exercises became an integral aspect of *wu-tou-mi tao* practice. This new form of Five-Pecks-of-Rice Taoism is also known as the Northern Branch of the Tao of the Celestial Masters.

In the south of the country the most influential representative of Five-Pecks-of-Rice Taoism was Lu Hsiu-ching, who incorporated Buddhist ideas and rites and thus founded the southern branch of the school. He also established strict rules on how to conduct the various ceremonies. During the T'ang and Sung dynasties, the *wu-tou-mi tao* merged with other Taoist movements such as the School of the Magic Jewel (→ *ling-pao p'ai*) and later became absorbed by the Way of Right Unity (→ *cheng-i tao*), a movement embracing several schools.

Wu-tsang 🅃 Chin., lit. "five [internal] organs." Taoist doctrine distinguishes between two groups of internal organs, namely the six containers (→ *liu-fu*) and the five organs (lit. "entrails"), i.e., the lungs, the heart, the pancreas, the liver, and the kidneys. The Taoist system of correspondences between the microcosm and the macrocosm accords to these five organs corresponding phases of transformation (→ *wu-hsing*), colors, seasons, flavors, etc.

Wu-tsu Fa-yen 🅉 (Jap., Goso Hōen), ca. 1024–1104, Chinese Ch'an (Zen) master of the Yōgi lineage of Rinzai Zen (→ Yōgi school); a student and dharma successor (→ *hassu*) of → Pai-yun Shou-tuan (Jap., Hakuun Shutan) and the master of → K'ai-fu Tao-ning (Jap., Kaifuku Dōnei) and → Yuan-wu K'o-ch'in (Jap., Engo Kokugon). We encounter Master Wu-tsu in examples 35, 36, 38, and 45 of the → *Wu-men-kuan.*

Wu-tsu literally means "fifth patriarch"; Master Wu-tsu was not, however, the fifth patriarch of Ch'an (→ Hung-jen), but rather a later Ch'an master who was named after Mount Wu-tsu (better known as Mount → Huang-mei), where the fifth patriarch once resided and taught.

Wu-tsu became a monk at the age of thirty-five. He first studied the sūtras and the writings of the → Yogāchāra school of Buddhism. He was not satisfied, however, by philosophical study, and turning to Ch'an, he sought out various masters. Finally he stayed with Master Pai-yun. He experienced enlightenment one day as he listened to Master Pai-yun giving instruction to another student on the kōan → *mu.* In example 36 of the *Wu-men-kuan*, Master Wu-tsu asks a question that has often been cited in Ch'an (Zen) literature: "If you meet a master on the way, you should greet him neither with words nor silence. So tell me, how should you greet him?"

Wu-tsung B T, 814–46 C.E.; T'ang Dynasty emperor, a fanatical supporter and champion of Taoism. He surrounded himself with Taoist priests (→ *tao-shih*) and alchemists, organized communal fasts (→ *chai*) and attempted to produce life-prolonging elixirs.

In 842 C.E. following the promptings of his Taoist advisors, he passed a series of laws to suppress Buddhism. This led to a persecution of Buddhists that reached its peak in 845 C.E.; no less than 260,000 Buddhist monks and nuns were forced to leave their monastic establishments. The art treasures of forty-six hundred monasteries were impounded and even Buddhist families were forced to surrender statues of the Buddha and other ritual objects to imperial officials.

Wu-wei Z Chin. → five degrees (of enlightenment)

Wu-wei T Z Chin., lit. "nondoing"; unmotivated, unintentional action. A concept of the → *Tao-te ching,* designating nonintervention in the natural course of things; spontaneous action that, being completely devoid of premeditation and intention, is wholly appropriate to a given situation. *Wu-wei* is said to be the attitude of a Taoist saint.

In Chapter 48 of the *Tao-te ching* (Feng & English 1972), Lao-tzu describes *wu-wei* as follows:

In the pursuit of learning, every day something is acquired [as regards our efforts and expectations].
In the pursuit of Tao, every day something is dropped [as regards our business and desires].
Less and less is done
Until non-action is achieved.
When nothing is done, nothing is left undone.
The world is ruled by letting things take their course.
It cannot be ruled by interfering.

Wu-wei therefore does not denote absolute nonaction but rather a form of action that is free of any desires, intention, or motivation.

A Taoist adept, by following the ideal of *wu-wei,* imitates the Tao, the universal effectiveness of which is a consequence of *wu-wei:*

Tao abides in non-action,
Yet nothing is left undone. [Ibid.]

A Taoist therefore endeavors to imitate the Tao by not intervening in the course of things, thereby permitting all things to unfold in accordance with their own nature. *Wu-wei* may essentially be understood as action confined to what is natural and necessary.

The *Tao-te ching* furthermore applies the notion of *wu-wei* to the way a ruler acts. In this context, Lao-tzu illustrates the effectiveness of unmotivated action by the example of a ruler of whose existence the people, ideally, would not even be aware. Only by abiding in *wu-wei* is it possible for a ruler to have power and influence.

Chapter 37 of the *Tao-te ching* (ibid.) describes how someone following the ideal of unmotivated action would rule:

If kings and lords observed this, the ten thousand things [→ *wan-wu*] would develop naturally.
If they still desired to act, they would return to the simplicity of formless substance.
Without form there is no desire.
Without desire there is tranquility.
In this way all things would be at peace.

This view is also shared by Confucius. In the *Analects* (*Lun-yü*) 15.4 we read, "The Master said, 'If there was a ruler who achieved order without taking any action, it was, perhaps, (the legendary emperor) Shun. There was nothing for him to do but to hold himself in a respectful posture and face due south' " (Lau 1979).

In addition, the ideal of nonaction is a central characteristic of Chinese Zen (*Ch'an*) Buddhism.

Y

Yab-yum 🅱 Tib., lit. "father [and] mother"; term for masculine and feminine deities in sexual union, a frequent image in Tibetan art. In the symbology of the → Vajrayāna, this image expresses the unity of the masculine principle (→ *upāya*) and the feminine principle (→ *prajñā*). The *yab-yum* motif, which appears in sculpted images and painted → *thangkas*, serves primarily as an aid to concentration in fusing the masculine and feminine energies within the practitioner himself in → *sādhana* practice.

Masculine and feminine principles in union (Tibetan blockprint)

Yajña 🅷 Skt., lit. "sacrifice"; 1. an epithet for → Vishnu; 2. in the → Purānas, the son of Ruchi and husband of → Dakshinā. He had the head of a stag and was killed by → Vīrabhadra in the performance of a sacrifice. Brahmā brought him to the realm of planets and made him a constellation, that of the stag's head.

Yājñavalkya 🅷 a famous sage at the court of King → Janaka. His family name was Vājasaneya. He was the founder of a school of the *White* → *Yajurveda* (the so-called Vājasaneyins), the author of the *Vājasaneyi-Samhitá*, the *Dharma-Smriti*, and the *Shatapatha-Brāhmana*, whose → Āranyaka includes the → *Brihadāranyaka-Upanishad*. This Upanishad contains Yājñavalkya's famous instruction to Maitreyī (one of his two wives) and also his dispute with the brahman philosophers at the court of King Janaka, in particular his conversation with the woman Gargī, in which Yājñavalkya emerged the victor.

Yajurveda 🅷 Skt.; the Veda (→ Vedas) of sacrificial formulas to be chanted during the performance of the sacred rite by the *adhvaryu*, one of the four chief priests at the sacrifice. A distinction is made between the archaic *Black Yajurveda*, compiled from 1000 B.C.E. by four schools in five books with varying versions (Samhitās), and the later and more unified *White Yajurveda*, said to derive extensively from the sage → Yājñavalkya.

The *Black Yajurveda* is also called "unordered" or "mixed," because in it mantric formulas for use in rites alternate with prose sections containing theological interpretations (Brāhmanas), whereas the "ordered" *White Yajurveda* consists of mantras alone. Only partial translations into English exist.

Yakkogin-no-zen 🅩 Jap., lit. "quicksilver Zen"; a "Zen" that is only an imitation of Zen in external appearance; it is not genuine Zen, as quicksilver is not genuine silver.

Yakō Zen 🅩 Jap., lit. "wild-fox Zen"; the Zen of persons, who, though they possess no genuine Zen realization, pretend to be enlightened and deceive other people by imitating outer forms and mouthing truths concerning which they have no real understanding. The fox in China, where this image comes from, was the animal demons rode upon or was itself a demon who could take on human form in order to lead people into error.

Yaksha 🅷 🅱 (yakṣa), Skt.

🅷 A group of supernatural beings, servants of → Kubera, the god of wealth. They have no special characteristics, are not violent, and are therefore called *punyajana* ("good beings"). As their master, Kubera bears the epithet Punyajaneshvara. → Kālidāsa's poem *Meghadūta* ("The Cloud Herald") is spoken by a *yaksha*.

🅱 (Pali, yakka); beings mentioned in the Buddhist canon who are divine in nature and possess supernatural powers. In many cases *yakshas* are wild demonic beings who live in solitary places and are hostile toward people, particularly those who lead a spiritual life. They often disturb the meditation of monks and nuns by making noise.

Yakuseki **Z** Jap., lit. "medicine stone"; the last meal of the day in a Zen monastery; it is taken in late afternoon.

The name comes from the earlier practice of monks of placing a heated stone on their bellies in order to soothe their grumbling stomachs. This came about because in the orthodox Buddhist code of behavior, the midday meal was the final meal of the day. Later the stone was replaced by a simple meal made of leftovers from the midday meal.

Yama **H** **B** Skt.

H 1. lit. "self-control," the first of the eight stages of → Rāja-Yoga. It consists of five ethical practices: nonjury of others (*ahimsā*), truthfulness (*satya*), not stealing (*asteya*), continence (*brahmacharya*), and noncovetousness (*aparigraha*). These must be practiced in thought, word, and deed; 2. the author of the law book *Dharma-Shāstra*; 3. the god of death. The *Katha-Upanishad* describes his instruction of → Nachiketa.

Yama (Chin. Yen-lo) is the son of → Vivasvat and the twin brother of → Yamunā. Yama and Yamunā are regarded as the first human pair. In the older hymns of the *Rigveda* those who are good are permitted by the grace of the gods after death to continue life with them under Yama's supervision. In later hymns Yama is the first man, who has found the way to the luminous heights of heaven and there reigns sovereign in the realm of the blessed. In order to come to him, the soul must pass Yama's pair of dogs, who guard the entrance to heaven and do not permit all seekers to enter (*Rigveda* 10.14). Here, too, is the first hint of the judgment seat that Yama later occupies. The dove is his messenger of death. He also has slings and nets, symbolizing the horrors of death. He bears such epithets as "the perfect one" and "king of righteousness."

B in Buddhist mythology the ruler of the hells (→ *naraka*). Yama was originally a king of → Vaishālī, who, during a bloody war, wished himself the ruler of hell. In accordance with this wish he was reborn as Yama. His eight generals and his retinue of 80 thousand accompany him in the hell realm. Three times a day he and his helpers have molten copper poured in their mouths as a punishment. This will last until their evil deeds have been expiated. Yama sends human beings old age, sickness, and approaching death as his messengers to keep them from an immoral, frivolous life. Yama resides south of → Jambudvīpa in a palace made of copper and iron. Yamī, Yama's sister, rules over the female inhabitants of the hells.

Yamaka **B** Skt. → Abhidharma

Yamamoto Gempō **Z** 1866–1961; one of the most outstanding Zen masters of modern times, often called the "twentieth-century Hakuin." Yamamoto Gempō was a foundling. In his early twenties, threatened by complete blindness, he left his wife and property, went on pilgrimage, and eventually entered a Zen monastery. At the age of forty-nine he received the seal of confirmation (→ *inka-shōmei*) from Master Sōhan of Empuku-ji monastery. He restored the Ryūtaku-ji monastery near Mishima in Shizouka province, of which → Hakuin Zenji had once been abbot, and was himself the abbot there for many years. At the age of eighty-two he reluctantly accepted an appointment as abbot of the Myōshin-ji monastery in Kyōto.

Yamamoto Gempō was virtually an illiterate until middle age because of his life circumstances and bad eyesight. His eyesight somewhat improved during his spiritual training, and later he became one of the most renowned modern masters of the way of writing (→ *shōdō*). He is also known for his eccentric lifestyle, his love of rice wine, and his fondness for women. He was one of the first Zen masters to travel throughout the world: to India, Africa, Europe, and the United States.

Yamaoka Tesshū **Z** 1836–88; a profoundly realized Zen layperson (Jap., *kōji*). He was without doubt the greatest master of the way of the sword (→ kendō) in 19th-century Japan, an outstanding painter and calligrapher, and one of the most important Japanese statesmen of his time. At the beginning of the Meiji Restoration, the reestablishment of imperial power after long dominance by the shōgunate, he was instrumental in forestalling a test of power between the allies of the emperor and the followers of the Shōgun Saigō Takamori that would have resulted in civil war. The life and work of Yamaoka Tesshū are described in Stevens 1984.

Yami **B** Skt. → Yama

Yamunā **H**, alsos Jamunā or Jumnā, Skt.; a tributary of the Ganges, personified as the daughter of → Vivasvat. She and her twin brother → Yama are held to be the first human couple.

Yāmunāchārya **H** (Yāmunācārya), a king, scholar, and South Indian → Vaishnava saint of the tenth century, who renounced his throne in order to become a monk. He taught that submission to God's will is the highest ideal of human life.

Yāna **B** Skt., lit. "vehicle"; the concept, already developed in Hīnayāna Buddhism, of a vehicle in which the practitioner travels on the way to enlightenment (→ *bodhi*). The different vehicles correspond to views of the spiritual "journey" that differ as to the basic attitude of the practitioner and the means of making progress on the way. According to → Tibetan Buddhism, the choice of vehicles depends on the spiritual maturity of students and the capability of masters. Here three vehicles are distinguished: → Hīnayāna, → Mahāyāna, and → Vajrayāna. From the standpoint of the → Vajrayāna, all three vehicles can be practiced at once; this view is reflected in the term → *ekayāna* ("one vehicle").

At the time of the first spreading of the Buddhist teaching in Tibet, different ways of dividing up the vehicles existed, of which the division into nine vehicles survived in the → Nyingmapa school and was adopted in the 19th century by the → Rime movement. According to this system, the following belong to the exoteric teaching: (1) the vehicle of the → *shrāvakas*, (2) that of the → *pratyeka-buddhas*, and (3) that of the bodhisattvas; i.e., Hīnayāna and Mahāyāna. The esoteric teaching is divided into two categories, the outer and the inner → Tantras. The outer Tantras are the three classes of Tantra also recognized by the other schools, which are included in the following vehicles: (4) *Kriyā-tantra* (action Tantra), (5) *charyā-tantra* (elaboration Tantra), and (6) *yoga-tantra*. The further division of the supreme *yoga-tantra* into three inner Tantras is unique to the Nyingmapa school. These vehicles are (7) *mahā-yoga*, (8) *anu-yoga*, (9) *ati-yoga (→ dzogchen)*.

According to the Nyingmapa doctrine, the first three vehicles were transmitted by Buddha → Shākyamuni, a manifestation of the *nirmānakāya* (→ *trikāya*). The source of the outer Tantras is the *sambhogakāya* manifestations, for example → Vajrasattva. The inner Tantras have their origin in → Samantabhadra, a manifestation of the *dharmakāya*. This conception also influenced the number of stages (→ *bhumi*) in the spiritual development of a bodhisattva. According to the Nyingmapa system, there are not, as in Mahāyāna Buddhism, ten such stages, but rather sixteen, as in this system nine, rather than three, vehicles are differentiated.

Yang-ch'i Fang-hui 🅩 (Jap., Yōgi Hōe), 992–1049; Chinese Ch'an (Zen) master of the → Rinzai school; a student and dharma successor (→ *hassu*) of → Shih-shuang Ch'u-yuan (Jap., Sekisō Soen) and the master of → Pai-yun Shou-tuan (Jap., Hakuun Shutan). Yang-ch'i founded the → Yōgi school of Rinzai Zen, which bears his name. It is one of the two lineages into which the tradition of the Rinzai school divided after Master Shih-shuang. The strict Ch'an of the Yōgi lineage was brought to Japan by Chinese and Japanese masters and still flourishes there today.

Yang-ch'i-p'ai 🅩 Chin. for → Yōgi school

Yang-ch'i-tsung 🅩 Chin. for → Yōgi school

Yang Chu 🅣 Taoist philosopher of the 4th/3d century B.C.E. His writings have not been preserved, but his basic teachings are contained in the → *Chuang-tzu,* the → *Lü-shih ch'un-ch'iu,* and various other works. There is a chapter devoted to him in the → *Lieh-tzu,* but its authenticity has not been established beyond doubt.

Yang Chu was an opponent of Confucianism (→ K'ung-tzu). His basic ideas are those of appreciating life and respecting the self. He considered it a primary duty to preserve and protect life so that its inherent truth might be nourished. External things, therefore, should not be allowed to corrupt life and the individual. It has been said of him that he would not sacrifice a single hair, even if thereby he could save the whole world. For that reason, his philosophy is sometimes described as extremely egotistical or hedonistic.

Yang Chu exclusively concentrates on man's life in this world and maintains that death constitutes the absolute end of this life. For that reason, he recognizes no ideals. In his view, any form of human ambition and striving—be it for fame or moral perfection—will only distract a person from life, which is the only boon and must be lived as fully as possible. Therefore an individual should unreservedly surrender himself to his natural impulses and inclinations and follow them without any thought of the consequences. Yang Chu categorically opposes any external intervention in human affairs. As a result, he rejects culture as such, and considers social standards as mere arbitrary conventions. His philosophy is thus diametrically opposed to that of Confucius.

Yang-hsing 🅣 Chin., lit. "nourishing the life principle"; collective term for all Taoist exercises and practices aimed at prolonging life and attaining immortality. This includes all practices whose purpose it is to nourish the body (→ *yang-sheng*) or the mind (→ *yang-shen*).

Yang-shan Hui-chi 🅩 (Jap., Kyōzan Ejaku), 807–83 or 813/14–90/91; one of the great Ch'an (Zen) masters of China; a student and dharma successor (→ *hassu*) of → Kuei-shan Ling-yu (Jap., Isan Reiyū) and the master of → Nan-t'a Kuang-jun (Jap., Nantō Kōyū). Yang-shan was one of the most important Ch'an masters of his time; his great abilities brought him the nickname Little Shākyamuni. Already before he was twenty years old, he had visited several great Ch'an masters, among them → Ma-tsu Tao-i (Jap., Baso Dōitsu) and Pai-chang Huai-hai

(Jap., Hyakujō Ekai), and had made himself a name as an outstanding student of Ch'an. Under Kuei-shan he realized profound enlightenment. As his master's dharma successor of equal accomplishment, he is considered the cofounder with his master of the → Igyō school of Ch'an, which derives its name from the first character of the names of the two men. By Master → Tan-yuan Ying-chen (Jap., Tangen Ōshin), under whom he had his first enlightenment experience, he was initiated into the use of the ninety-seven circle symbols that were later to play a major role in the Igyō school.

The → *hossen* and → *mondō* of Yang-shan with his master Kuei-shan and other Ch'an masters, recorded in the *Yuan-chou Hui-chi-ch'an-shih yu-lu* (*Record of the Words of the Ch'an Master Yang-shan Hui-chi from Yuan-chou*), are considered outstanding examples of Ch'an (Zen) mind. Yang-shan appears in example 25 of the → *Wu-men-kuan* and examples 34 and 68 of the → *Pi-yen-lu.*

Yang-shan already wanted to become a monk at the age of fifteen, but his parents held him back. At the age of seventeen he finally cut off two of his fingers and presented them to his parents as a sign of his resolve. They then permitted him to go ahead. After having sought out a number of great Ch'an masters and, under them, having opened his dharma eye to a certain extent, he found in Kuei-shan the master who ideally suited him and who could guide him to profound enlightenment. Between Kuei-shan and Yang-shan there prevailed such a harmony of temperament and of spiritual outlook, that it was said of them: "Father and son sing with one mouth."

Yang-shen ■ Chin., lit. "nourishing the mind [or spirit]"; Taoist practice aimed at attaining immortality. The purpose of *yang-shen* consists in using meditation as a means of preventing the deities inhabiting the human body from leaving it (→ Inner Deity Hygiene School).

This method of Taoist meditation involves a concentration of the practitioner's attention on so-called body deities, thereby causing them to appear in great detail before the inner eye. In this way, these deities are guarded and prevented from leaving the body, so that it is impossible for death to occur. If *yang-shen* is practiced in combination with techniques aimed at nourishing the body (→ *yang-sheng*), immortality is attained. At first, the practitioner only perceives insignificant inner deities, but as he perseveres with his practice, he gradually succeeds in making contact with the highest deities of the upper cinnabar field (→ *tan-t'ien*) in the brain.

A more advanced stage of nourishing the mind is reached when the practitioner is able to keep the mind free of all attachments and external distractions. This is considered to be the right method of becoming one with the Tao. For anyone experiencing such indissoluble unity, physical immortality becomes a matter of minor importance. A practitioner at this level possesses supernatural powers, and his actions are devoid of all intention and motivation (→ *wu-wei*). This is the path pointed out by Lao-tzu and Chuang-tzu.

Sometimes other forms of meditation, such as → *tso-wang,* → *ts'un-ssu,* and → *shou-i* are considered forms of *yang-shen.*

Yang-sheng ■ Chin., lit. "nourishing life," also "nourishing the body"; Taoist exercises aimed at attaining immortality. This includes the various breathing exercises such as "allowing the breath to circulate" (→ *hsing-ch'i*), "melting the breath" (→ *lien-ch'i*), "absorbing the breath" (→ *fu-ch'i*), "swallowing the breath" (→ *yen-ch'i*), "embryonic breathing" (→ *t'ai-hsi*), and an exercise known as "expelling the old and taking in the new" (→ *t'u-ku na-hsin*). In addition, abstention from eating grain (→ *pi-ku*) and various gymnastic exercises (→ *tao-yin*) as well as sexual practices (→ *fang-chung shu*) fall under the general heading of *yang-sheng.*

Many Taoists believe these exercises to be indispensible for prolonging life and attaining immortality. Philosophical Taoism (→ *tao-chia*), on the other hand, attaches only secondary importance to such practices, because it is of the opinion that the meditative technique known as "nourishing the mind" (→ *yang-shen*) alone is able to bring the practitioner to immortality.

Yantra ■ Skt., lit. "support, instrument"; a mystic diagram, used as a symbol of the divine as well as of its powers and aspects, employed above all in → Tantra. The → Karma-Kānda, the portion of the Vedas that deals with practice, discusses the performance of sacrifices, rites, and charms. To support their execution, cult images, *yantras* and *mandalas* constructed of geometric shapes, were later developed. In the meditation practices of Tantra (e.g., in Kundalinī-Yoga), these play an important role as "supports"; they are models for "visualizations," whereby the mediator inwardly pictures various aspects and powers of the divine. The best known of all *yantras* is the → Shrī-Yantra. (See p. 426 for Kālī-Yantra.)

Heinrich Zimmer offers a further meaning of the word *yantra*: "The *yantra* is so named because it brings about the vanquishment *(niyantrana)* of all evil that arises from desire, anger, and other errors. Hence one should draw an auspicious *yantra* along with the

The Kālī-Yantra.

surrounding frame and develop it before one's inner eye, once one has learned everything useful to know about it from the mouth of the teacher."

Yao 🅣 2333–2234 B.C.E. or—according to an alternative calendrical calculation—2356–2255 B.C.E.; one of the legendary five emperors (→ *wu-ti*). Yao is said to have established the calendar and introduced official posts, the holders of which were responsible for making proper use of the four seasons of the year. Instead of his son he made → Shun his successor and subjected him to a series of severe tests, extending over a period of three years, before entrusting the rule of the country to him. According to legend, ten suns appeared in the sky and threatened to scorch the earth to a cinder when Shun seated himself on the throne after the death of Yao. However, Shen I, the heavenly archer, was able to shoot nine of them out of the sky with the help of his magic bow.

Tradition further relates that Yao, assisted by Shen I, restored order in the realm, after a monster had devastated the south of the country by violent storms. For that reason, he is known as the Tamer of the Winds. With the help of another mythological figure—i.e., Kun, the great-grandson of the Yellow Emperor (→ Huang-ti)—he fought to dam the floods of the Yellow River, which were threatening to reach Heaven.

Yao-shan Wei-yen 🅩 → Yueh-shan Wei-yen

Yasha 🅑 Skt. → Buddhist councils

Yashodā 🅗 (Yaśodā), Skt.; → Krishna's foster mother. She protected the young god from the demon → Pūtanā and according to numerous Vedic legends is considered the guardian of children.

Yashodharā 🅑 (Yaśodharā); wife of → Siddhārtha Gautama the historical Buddha and mother of his son → Rāhula.

Yāska 🅗 the author (fifth century B.C.E.) of the → *Nirdkta,* the oldest extant gloss on the Vedic hymns. Yāska lived before → Pānini, who drew upon his predecessor's work. However, Yāska was not the first to compile an etymological dictionary of this kind; he himself refers to various predecessors.

Yasutani Rōshi 🅩 → Hakuun Ryōko Yasutani

Yatāman 🅗 Skt., lit. "controlling oneself"; 1. the restraint of thoughts and emotions; 2. control of one's true self (→ *ātman*) over the body, mind, and sensations, with which it is no longer identified.

Yathābhūtam 🅑 Skt., Pali; knowledge in accordance with reality; knowledge of true reality, of "suchness" (→ *tathatā*, → *bhutatathata*).

Yati 🅗 Skt., lit. "ascetic"; term used to refer to a truth-seeker who aspires to the supreme truth and thereby becomes a → *sādhu.*

Yātrā 🅗 Skt., lit. "festivity, procession"; 1. a great religious festival featuring songs and offerings, such as the festivals at which huge images of deities are carried through the streets; 2. a rural theater performance with a religious theme.

Yayāti 🅗 the fifth king of the lunar race. He had two wives, Devayānī and Sarmishtā. The former bore him Yadu, the latter Puru; these are the forefathers of the Yādava and Paurava clans.

Many stories are told of Yayāti's amorous adventures, especially in the *Vishnu-Purāna.* He was once invited to heaven by Indra, who sent his charioteer, Mātali, to drive him there. On the way they engaged in conversation about philosophy, which so affected Yayāti that upon his return to earth he liberated his subjects from passion and mortality. → Yama then complained that people were no longer dying, and Indra sent Kāma, the god of love, and his daughter Ashruvindumatī to rewake passion in Yayāti's breast. The → *Harivamsha* relates that Indra gave Yayāti a heavenly chariot, in which he conquered the earth in six nights and even subdued the gods. He later became a hermit and after death entered heaven.

Yaza 🅩 Jap., lit. ya=*yoru,* "night"; *za,* "sitting"; → *zazen* after the usual time for going to sleep in a Zen monastery.

Yellow Turbans 🅣 → *huang-chin,* → *t'ai-p'ing tao*

Yen-ch'i T Chin., lit. "swallowing the breath"; Taoist breathing exercise forming part of embryonic breathing (→ *t'ai-hsi*). The breath swallowed during this exercise is the inner *ch'i* (→ *nei-ch'i*), which, during exhalation, accompanies the outer *ch'i* (→ *wai-ch'i*) from the lower cinnabar field (→ *tan-t'ien*) as far as the throat. However, if damage to the practitioner's health is to be avoided, the inner *ch'i* must not be allowed to escape. For that reason, the practitioner—as the outer breath leaves through his throat—quickly closes his mouth, "beats the heavenly drum" (→ *t'ien-ku*), swallows the inner *ch'i* together with the accumulated saliva (→ *yü-chiang*), and directs it back to the "ocean of breath" (→ *ch'i-hai*). When the breath has been swallowed three times in succession, the *ch'i-hai* is full.

The purpose of this exercise therefore consists in preventing the inner *ch'i* from leaving the body and instead accumulating it in the "ocean of breath"—this being the only way of attaining immortality.

A particularly effective method is that of following the practice of *yen-ch'i* by an exercise known as "allowing the breath to circulate" (→ *hsing-ch'i*) or by "melting the breath" (→ *lien-ch'i*).

Yen-kuan Ch'i-an Z (Jap., Enkan Seian [Saian]), roughly 750–842, Chinese Ch'an (Zen) master; a student and dharma successor (→ *hassu*) of → Ma-tsu Tao-i (Jap., Baso Dōitsu). Yen-kuan appears in example 91 of the → *Pi-yen-lu*.

Yen-lo B Chin. for → Yama

Yen-t'ou Ch'uan-huo Z (Jap., Gantō Zenkatsu), 828–87; Chinese Ch'an (Zen) master; a student and dharma successor (→ *hassu*) of → Te-shan Hsuan-chien (Jap., Zuigan Shigen). Yen-t'ou appears in example 13 of the → *Wu-men-kuan* and in examples 51 and 66 of the → *Pi-yen-lu*.

Yen-t'ou was known for his clear eye and his sharp mind. When Te-shan died, Yen-t'ou was thirty-five years old. After he had lived in solitude for a time, students began to gather around him and he became the abbot of a large monastery. It was a chaotic period during the decline of the T'ang dynasty; robber bands attacked the monastery. The monks, forewarned, fled; only Master Yen-t'ou remained in the monastery. The robbers found him sitting in meditation. Disappointed that they had found no booty, they murdered the master. When they stabbed him, Yen-t'ou is supposed to have uttered a cry that could be heard for ten Chinese leagues (*li*); it is renowned in the tradition as "Yen-t'ou's cry." This cry has presented a knotty problem to many a later Zen student, whose conception of the life and death of a Zen master this story did not match. This was the case also for the great Japanese master → Hakuin Zenji. Only when Hakuin had realized enlightenment did he understand, and he cried out: "Truly, Gantō [Yen-t'ou] is alive, strong, and healthy!"

Yeshe Tsogyel B (Ye-shes Mtsho-rgyal) Tib., lit. "Princess of the Wisdom Lake," 757–817; intimate companion of → Padmasambhava and the most important female figure in the tradition of the → Nyingmapa school. Named for a miracle that occurred at the time of her birth, the rising of a nearby lake, this daughter of the noble Kharchen family attracted the attention of Tibetan king Trison Detsen when she was only twelve years old. At the king's court she also met the Indian scholar Shāntirakshita. Padmasambhava took her as his consort and transmitted to her particularly the teachings of the → *phurba* cycle. Yeshe Tsogyel codified countless of her guru's teachings in → *terma* texts and also composed his biography. In the last part of her life she was active mainly in east Tibet. She is venerated up to the present day as a → *dākinī*.

Yidam B (yid-dam), Tib., lit. "firm mind"; in → Vajrayāna Buddhism, a term for a personal deity, whose nature corresponds to the individual psychological makeup of the practitioner. *Yidams* are manifestations of the → *sambhogakāya* and are visualized in meditative practice (→ *sādhana*), i.e., perceived with the inner eye. They can take on either a peaceful or wrathful → form of manifestation, and each belongs to a particular buddha family (→ *buddhakula*). Among the most widely invoked *yidams* are → Chenresi, Green → Tārā, and others who appear only in strictly secret teachings, such as Dorje Phagmo (Diamond Sow).

Tibetan Buddhism does not particularly regard *yidams* as protective deities (as the personal deities [*ishtadevatā*] are considered in Hindu Tantra); rather their function is as an aid in the transformative process in which the practitioner comes to acknowledge his or her own basic personality structure. The *yidams* also serve to bring the practitioner to a sense of intimate connection with the traditional lineage whose teaching he or she follows.

The *yidams* can be classified according to their basic qualities as follows:

	peaceful: *bhagavat*	active
Male Yidam	semiwrathful: *dāka*	sympathy
	wrathful: *heruka*	(compassion)
	peaceful: *bhagavatī*	knowledge of

Female Yidam	semiwrathful: *dakīnī*	supreme
	wrathful: *dākinī*	reality

In the Tibetan pantheon, male and female deities are also represented in union (→ *yab-yum*), as, for example, the male deities Chakrasamvara and Vajrabhairava with their consorts. In this way an extremely complex iconography was developed.

Ying-chou ■ Chin., lit. "world-ocean continent"; one of three islands in the East China Sea believed to be abodes of the immortals (→ *hsien*) and representative of the very epitome of bliss (→ P'eng-lai, → Fang-chang).

Yin Hsi ■ also known as Kuan-yin-tzu; the Guardian of the (Mountain) Pass encountered by Lao-tzu on his journey to the West. At Yin Hsi's request, Lao-tzu embodied his teachings in a written work consisting of five thousand pictograms and containing his thoughts on the Tao and its → *te.* This has become known as the *Tao-te ching.* Lao-tzu is said to have continued on his journey toward the West. Yin Hsi, as a result of his encounter with Lao-tzu, became an important figure in religious Taoism and was admitted to the Taoist pantheon as an immortal (→ *hsien*). He is furthermore credited with the authorship of the *Kuan-yin-tzu,* which describes and explains various Taoist techniques of meditation.

According to legend, Yin Hsi lived as a recluse. One of his practices consisted in absorbing the essences of the sun and moon (→ *fu jih-hsiang*). It is said that as Lao-tzu came toward him, Yin Hsi was able to tell by his → *ch'i* that he was a true man (→ *chen-jen*). Later he followed Lao-tzu to the West and—like him—disappeared without a trace.

Yin-yang ■ Chin.; two polar energies that, by their fluctuation and interaction, are the cause of the universe. Yin and yang are polar manifestations of the Tao of the supreme ultimate (→ *t'ai-chi*), their concrete manifestations being Earth and Heaven.

From the intermingling of yin and yang arise the five elements (→ *wu-hsing*); they in turn are the basis of the ten thousand things (→ *wan-wu*). This manifestation of all phenomena is seen as a cyclic process, an endless coming into being and passing away, as everything, upon reaching its extreme stage, transforms into its opposite. The underlying shared characteristic of yin and yang therefore consists in giving rise to this continuous change, which is said to be the movement of the Tao.

The composition of the hexagrams found in the *Book of Change(s)* (→ *I-ching*), from which the concept yin-yang stems, also reflects the view that all things and situations arise from a combination of yin and yang. The two hexagrams → *ch'ien* and *k'un* represent, respectively, pure yang and pure yin; all other hexagrams are combinations of these basic energies.

Originally the word *yin* designated the northern slope of a mountain, i.e., the side facing away from the sun—and was further associated with cold, turgid water and a cloud-covered sky. *Yang* denoted the mountain slope facing the sun and was associated with brightness and warmth.

The system of correspondences between the microcosm and the macrocosm attributes further properties and phenomenal associations to yin and yang: yin is the feminine, the passive, the receptive, the dark, the soft. Symbols of yin are the moon, water, clouds, the tiger, the turtle, the color black, the north, lead, and all even numbers.

Yang corresponds to what is masculine, active, creative, bright, and hard. Symbols of yang are the sun, fire, the dragon, the color red, the south, mercury, and all odd numbers. Yin and yang are represented by a well-known symbol.

Yin-yang symbol

The symbol stands for the universe composed of yin and yang, which form a whole only in combination. The two spots in the symbol indicate that each of the two energies—at the highest stage of its realization—already contains the seed of, and is about to transform into, its polar opposite.

The first known mention of yin-yang occurs in Chapter 5 of the *Hsi-tz'u* (→ *Shih-i*) of the *Book of Change(s)*, which states, "One yin, one yang, that is the Tao." In Book 5, Chapter 2 of the → *Lü-shih ch'un-ch'iu* (*Spring and Autumn Annals*) the arising of all things from yin and yang—the light and the dark—is described as follows: "The Great One produces the two poles [i.e., Heaven and Earth], which in turn give rise to the energies of the dark (yin) and the light (yang). These two energies then transform themselves, one rising upwards and the other descending downwards; they merge again and give rise to forms. They separate and merge again. When they are separate, they merge; when they are merged, they separate. That is the never-ending course of Heaven and Earth. Each end is followed by a beginning; each extreme by a transformation into its opposite. All things are attuned to each other. That from which all beings arise and from which they have their origin, is known as the Great One; that which gives them form and perfection, is the duality of darkness and light" (Wilhelm 1979).

The energies of yin and yang are furthermore of great importance in traditional Chinese medicine. The body is healthy only when yin and yang hold each other in balance. Too much yang causes heightened organic activity; too much yin, an inadequate functioning of the organs.

Yin-yang chia ■ Chin., lit. "School of → Yin-Yang"; Chinese philosophical school that flourished at the end of the Warring States Period (3d century B.C.E.). Originally *yin-yang chia* referred only to teachings that were based on the premise that the universe arises from the interplay of yin and yang. During the Han Dynasty, the meaning of the concept was widened, when the followers of the *yin-yang chia* began to incorporate the teachings about the five elements (→ *wu-hsing*).

The theoretical basis of the Yin-Yang School is to be found in the commentaries on the *Book of Change(s)* (→ *I-ching*)—the so-called *Ten Wings* (→ *Shih-i*)—which tradition attributes to Confucius.

According to the *yin-yang chia,* the universe arises from the fusion of the masculine and the feminine—i.e., yang and yin—which in the *I-ching* are symbolized, respectively, by the trigrams *ch'ien* (Heaven) and *k'un* (Earth), from which all other trigrams arise. Each trigram corresponds to a particular natural energy (→ *pa-kua*).

Specifically, the doctrine of the *yin-yang chia* is based on the eight trigrams of the *I-ching,* which correspond to different natural phenomena and interhuman relationships:

Ch'ien is Heaven, the Ruler and Father, and representative of pure yang.
K'un is Earth, the Mother, and representative of pure yin.
Chen is Thunder, the eldest son.
Sun is Wind and Rain, the eldest daughter.
K'an is Water and Clouds, the second son.
Li is Fire and Lightning, the second daughter.
Ken is the Mountain, the youngest son.
Tui is the Lake, the youngest daughter.

The Yin-Yang School also tried to explain the mystery of the universe numerologically, allocating to Heaven (yang) the odd numbers 1, 3, 5, 7, and 9 and to Earth (yin) the even numbers 2, 4, 6, 8, and 10, which are said to complete each other. Later, the *yin-yang chia* made use of numbers to relate the energies of yin and yang to the five elements.

Yin-yuan Lung-ch'i ■ (Jap., Ingen Ryūki), 1592–1673; Chinese Ch'an (Zen) master of the → Rinzai school, abbot of the Wan-fu monastery (Jap., Mampuku-ji) on Mount Huang-po (Jap., Ōbakusan) in China. Yin-yuan went to Japan in 1654 and founded there the → Ōbaku school. He received from the Japanese imperial house the posthumous title *daiko fushō kokushi* (→ *kokushi*). His teachings and sayings are recorded in the *Ōbaku-hōgo*, the *Fushō-kokushi-kōroku*, and the *Ingen-hōgō*.

Yoga ■ ■ Skt., lit. "yoke." In Hinduism this has the sense of harnessing oneself to god, seeking union with him. Since any path to knowledge of god can be called yoga, there are in Hinduism many names for the different yogic paths that accommodate the basic makeup of individual seekers. Those Hindu paths that are best known in the West and that have been most thoroughly elaborated are: → *karma-yoga*, selfless action; → *bhakti-yoga*, devout love of god; → *rāja-yoga*, the "royal yoga," which is identical with the yoga of → Patañjali, one of the six → *darshanas*; Tantric → *kundalinī-yoga;* → *jñana-yoga*, the path of abstract knowledge.

In the West the term *yoga* usually refers to → hatha-yoga, which is based on physical exercises (→ *āsana*) in conjunction with breathing exercises (→ *prānāyāma*). This "physical" yoga, however, is regarded in India only as a practice preparatory for the spiritual forms of yoga that work with various meditation techniques.

As a way to knowledge of god, yoga in its broadest sense is not confined to India. All seekers for the experience of fundamental unity (the so-called) mystical experience), whether they are Indian shamans or Christian mystics, are yogis in this sense. Thus the Tantric practices of → Tibetan Buddhism are also called yoga, and its great saints (for example, → Milarepa) are called yogis.

Yoga-Bhrashta ■ (Yoga-Bhraṣṭa), Skt., lit. *brashta:* "past, vanished, released, freed"; the spiritual training of a yogi; methodically followed, it leads to liberation.

Yogāchāra ■ (Yogācāra), Skt., lit. "application of yoga" (also called the Vijñānavāda, lit. "the School That Teaches Knowing"); school of Mahāyāna Buddhism founded by → Maitreyanātha, → Asanga, and → Vasubandhu.

According to the central notion of the Yogāchāra, everything experienceable is "mind only" (*chittamātra*); things exist only as *processes* of knowing, not as "objects"; outside the knowing process they have no reality. The "external world" is thus "purely mind." Just as there are no things qua objects, there is also no subject who experiences. Perception is a process of creative imagination that produces apparently outer objects. This process is explained with the help of the concept of the "storehouse consciousness" (→ *ālaya-vijñāna*). In addition the teaching of the three bodies of a buddha (→ *trikāya*) took its definitive form in the Yogāchāra. Apart from the founders, important representatives of the school were → Sthiramati and → Dharmapāia, both of whom originated new currents within the Yogāchāra school (→ Fa-hsiang school, → Hossō school).

The name of the Yogāchāra school stems from the fact that its followers placed particular value on the practice of "yoga," which here is used in a quite general way to mean meditative practice that perfects all the qualities of a future buddha, a bodhisattva.

The mechanism of the arising of the external world is explained in the Yogāchāra in the following manner: In the *ālaya-vijñāna*, which is the ground of knowledge and the storehouse of all previous impressions, seeds (*bīja*) develop, which produce mental phenomena. As the storehouse of all seeds, the *ālaya-vijñāna* is the determining factor for the process of ripening (→ *vipāka*) by which the Yogāchāra explains the development of → karma. In the storehouse consciousness, the seeds affect each other in such a way that their interaction creates the deception that something really exists. The *ālaya-vijñāna* is often compared to a stream, the water of which perpetually renews itself and after the death of an individual being continues to flow, providing continuity from one existence to the next.

The individual forms of sense consciousness are produced by the activity of the seeds and the mind (→ *manas*). The latter is "tainted" and is considered the main factor in the arising of subjectivity. It creates the illusion of an *I*, or ego, where in fact only psychological phenomena exist, that is, only experience, no experiencing subject. That which is knowable by the mind—phenomena—is of threefold nature: conceptualized (*parikalpita*), dependent (*paratantra*), and perfect (*parinishpanna*). The conceptualized phenomena are mere imagination, false conceptions. They are dependent because they arise in dependence upon other factors. They are perfect in their true or ultimate nature, which is emptiness (→ *shūnyatā*), also known as "suchness" (→ *tathatā*). The characteristic of "suchness" is nonduality. Realization of this true nature is enlightenment (→ *bodhi*). It is immanent in all things. "Suchness" is sometimes also called the buddhā-self; on this account the Yogāchāra was accused of substantialism.

The path to liberation in the Yogāchāra, in continuance of ancient Buddhism, is divided into four stages and presumes practice of the → *pāramitās* and concentration (→ *samādhi*): (1) preliminary path—here the bodhisattva undertakes the teaching of "mind only"; (2) path of seeing (→ *darshana-mārga*)—in this stage the bodhisattva gains a realistic understanding of the teaching, attains knowledge beyond concepts, and enters upon the first of the ten stages (→ *bhūmi*) of the development of a bodhisattva, realizing higher intuitive knowledge, in which subject and object are one; on the path of seeing, the elimination of the defilements (→ *klesha*) begins as well as the "conversion of the ground"; (3) path of meditation (*bhāvanā-mārga*):—here the bodhisattva passes successively through the ten stages and develops the insight already attained further; liberation from defilements and "conversion of the ground" continue; (4) path of fulfillment—in this last stage all defilements are eliminated and the "conversion of he ground" is completed, putting an end to the cycle of existence (→ samsāra); the bodhisattva has actualized the "body of the great order" (*dharmakāya*, → *trikāya*).

The Yogāchāra school reached its zenith in the 6th century. A center of the school was the monastic university → Nālandā in northern India. There Dharmapāla taught an absolute idealism and concentrated on the doctrine of "nothing but conception."

Along with the school of Nālandā existed the school of Valabhī, which was founded by Gunamati and had its most important representative in Sthiramati. The latter advocated a moderate idealism and attempted to reconcile the teaching of the Yogāchāra with that of → Nāgārjuna. The focal point of his thought was the notion of emptiness (→ *shūnyatā*). A rapprochement of Yogāchāra thought with that of the → Sautrāntikas produced the logical epistemology school of → Dignāga and his student → Dharmakīrti.

Opponents of the Yogāchāra were the followers of the Mādhyamika school, which fiercely criticized the Yogāchāra system, in which it saw a revival of substantialistic thought.

Yogāchārabhūmi-shāstra 🅱 Skt., lit. *"Treatise on the Stages of the Yogāchāra"*; fundamental work of the → Yogāchāra school, which according to tradition was composed by → Asagna and was transmitted to him by the future buddha → Maitreya. The most recent research attributes it to → Maitreyanātha. It is one of the most voluminous works of Buddhist literature and presents the complete teaching of the Yogāchāra. The Sanskrit original is preserved only fragmentarily, however complete translations exist in Chinese and Tibetan.

The work is composed in prose with short sections of verse and is divided into five parts: (1) the seventeen stages (→ *bhūmi*), presenting the progression on the path to enlightenment with the help of the Yogāchāra teaching—this is the main part; (2) interpretations of the these stages; (3) explanation of those sūtras from which the Yogāchāra doctrine of the stages draws support; (4) "classifications" contained in these sūtras; (5) topics from the Buddhist canon (→ sūtra, → Vinaya-pitaka, → Abhidharma). A short version of this work, also composed by Asanga, is the *Āryashā-*

sana-prakarana (*Proof of the Sacred Doctrine*), of which there are two Chinese translations, one by → Paramārtha, the other by → Hsuan-tsang.

Yogānanda 🅗, Paramahamsa, 1893–1952; the name literally means "the bliss of yoga." Yogānanda was born in Gorakhpur to a → *kshatriya* family. His given name was Mukunda Lal Ghosh. In 1914, following his spiritual inclinations, he entered a monastic order and took the name Yogānanda. His guru, → Yukteshvar, initiated him and invested him with the title Paramahamsa. In 1917 he established in Ranchi a yoga school, which he named Satsanga-Brahmacharya-Vidyālaya. In 1920 he attended a meeting in the United States and remained there to hold lectures in the major states. In 1925 he founded a Yoga Institute in Los Angeles, where he also taught and established the Self-Realization Fellowship (S.R.F.). In 1935 he traveled through Europe (where among other things he visited Therese Neumann in Konnersreuth) to India, where he met with → Rāmana Maharshi, Mahatma → Gandhi, and → Ānandamayī Mā. When his guru died in 1936, Yogānanda was by his side. That same year, he returned by way of England to California, where in 1937 he founded a larger ashram in Encinitas. Over the next years numerous S.R.F. centers arose, both in the United States and in Europe, to teach the path of → Kriyā-Yoga advocated by Yogānanda. Since Yogānanda's death the work of the S.R.F. has been carried on by his students.

Yogānanda's life and teaching are described in his *Autobiography of a Yogi* (1946), one of the most popular books in the West on Indian spirituality.

Yoga-Nidrā 🅗 Skt., from → yoga and *nidrā:* "sleep"; 1. the so-called yogic sleep, in which the body is totally relaxed and hence appears to be asleep, while the yogi is fully conscious but unaffected by thoughts (→ *vritti*), since he is free of desires and distractions; 2. one of the various bodily postures (→ *āsana*) of → Hatha-Yoga.

Yoga-Shakti 🅗 (Yoga-Śakti), Skt.; the powers (→ *shakti*) gained through → yoga that enable the aspirant to overcome all obstacles and achieve union with God, or the Absolute.

Yoga-Sūtra 🅗 Skt.; a collection of aphorisms by → Patañjali. With this work he established the philosophy the branch of → yoga now generally known as → Rāja-Yoga; it is one of the six orthodox systems (→ *darshana*) of Hinduism.

The *Yoga-Sūtra,* the oldest textbook on the system of yoga, has four parts. The first part discusses the state of → *samādhi;* the second indicates the means whereby this goal may be attained; the third speaks of the supernatural powers (→ *siddhi*) that can be gained by yogic practices; the fourth describes liberation. The work is generally presumed to have been composed in the second century B.C.E., although some scholars date its origin to the fourth century C.E.

Yoga-Vasishtha 🅗 (Yoga-Vasiṣṭha), Skt.; a work attributed to → Vālmīki, in which the sage → Vasishtha teaches his pupil Prince → Rāma how one may come to the immutable reality that is veiled by the fleeting world of sensory impressions. The work comprises 32,000 verses. A short selection of extracts is available in English translation by Hari Prasad Shastri under the title *The World within the Mind (1937; 1980).*

Yogeshvara 🅗 (Yogeśvara), Skt., lit. a compound of *yoga:* "union" and *īshvara:* "lord, God"; 1. a term referring to one who is united with God (e.g., a title for Krishna in the *Bhagavad-Gītā*) or one who has attained enlightenment; 2. a term referring to one who has become a "master of yoga" (i.e., has gained supernatural powers through the practice of yoga; see → *siddhi*).

Yōgi-ha 🅩 Jap. for → Yōgi school

Yōgi Hōe 🅩 Jap. for → Yang-ch'i Fang-hui

Yoginī 🅗 Skt.; 1. a female yogi; 2. witch, sorceress. Eight Yoginīs, female demons, serve the goddess → Durgā.

Yōgi school 🅩 (Chin., Yang-ch'i-tsung or Yang-ch'i-p'ai; Jap. Yōgi-shu or Yōgi-ha [Chin., *p'ai* and Jap. *ha*, "wing"]); a school of Ch'an (Zen) originating with the Chinese Ch'an master → Yang-ch'i Fang-hui (Jap., Yōgi Hōe). It is one of the "seven schools" (→ *goke-shichishū*) of Ch'an (→ Zen) in China and is the more important of the two lineages into which the → Rinzai school split after → Shih-shuang Ch'u-yuan (Jap., Sekisō Soen). As a traditional lineage of Rinzai Zen, it is also called the Rinzai-Yōgi lineage.

The Yōgi school produced important Ch'an masters like → Wu-men Hui-k'ai (Jap., Mumon Ekai), the compiler of the → *Wu-men-kuan*, and his dharma successor (→ Kakushin), who brought the Ch'an of the Rinzai-Yogi lineage to Japan, where as Zen it still flourishes today.

As Ch'an gradually declined in China after the end of the Sung period, the Rinzai-Yōgi school became the catchment basin for all the other Ch'an schools, which increasingly lost importance and finally vanished. After becoming mixed with the Pure Land school of Buddhism, in the Ming period Ch'an lost its distinctive character and ceased to exist as an authentic lineage of transmission of the buddha-dharma "from heart-mind to heart-mind" (→ *ishin-denshin*).

Yojana 🅑 Skt.; ancient Indian land measure that frequently appears in Buddhist writings. It is based on the distance that an army can march in a day, i.e., 15–20 kilometers.

Yōka Gengaku 🅩 Jap. for → Yung-chia Hsuan-chueh

Yōmyō Enju 🅩 Jap. for → Yung-ming Yen-shou

Yoni 🅗 Skt., lit. "womb, origin, source;" the origin or primal source of all being. The *yoni* is represented by a triangle with its apex pointing downward, signifying the female sexual organ, which in turn symbolizes the mystery of the cosmos. This symbol, by itself or conjoined with the → *linga,* is venerated by the Shaktas (the worshipers of → Shakti).

Yōsai 🅩 → Eisai Zenji

Yü 🅣 → Ta-yü

Yüan-ch'i 🅣 Chin., lit. "primordial breath"; the primordial energy in which yin and yang (→ yin-yang) are still closely intermingled and which gives rise to the whole universe—i.e., the multiplicity and variety of the ten thousand things (→ *wan-wu*).

The *yüan-ch'i* corresponds to the inner *ch'i* (→ *nei-ch'i*) found in the human body. The → *Yün-chi ch'i-ch'ien* states, "Before the breaths became separated in order to take on form, they were entangled and resembled an egg. They formed a perfect whole—the Great One [→ T'ai-i]. The *yüan-ch'i* [i.e., the egg-shaped energy forming a whole] ascended in a pure state and became Heaven; when it was already turbid it descended and became Earth."

In addition, the concept of *yüan-ch'i* is of great importance in traditional Chinese medicine.

According to traditional Chinese medicine, the *yüan-ch'i* is produced in the "portal of destiny" (→ *ming-men*) near the kidneys and accumulated in the lower cinnabar field (→ *tan-t'ien*) or the Ocean of Breath (→ *ch'i-hai*). From there it follows the path of the threefold meridian and disperses to all parts of the body, ensuring the proper functioning of the five organs (→ *wu-tsang*) and the six containers (→ *liu-fu*). By absorbing the *yüan-ch'i* of the cosmos and strengthening it within the body, a person may considerably lengthen the life span.

Yuan-chueh-ching 🅩 Chin. (Jap., *Engaku-kyō*), "*Sutra of Perfect Enlightenment*"; a sūtra that was translated into Chinese by the Buddhist monk Buddhatrāta in the year 693. In it twelve bodhisattvas, among them → Mañjushrī (Jap., Monju) and → Samantabhadra (Jap., Fugen), are instructed in the nature of perfect → enlightenment. This sūtra had great influence on Ch'an (Zen).

Yüan-shih t'ien-tsun 🅣 Chin., lit. "Celestial Venerable of the Primordial Beginning"; one of the highest deities of religious Taoism (→ *tao-chiao*). Yüan-shih t'ien-tsun is one of the three pure ones (→ *san-ch'ing*) and resides in the Heaven of Jade Purity. He is believed to have come into being at the beginning of the universe as a result of the merging of the pure breaths. He then created Heaven and Earth.

At the beginning of each age or aeon he transmits the *Scriptures of the Magic Jewel* (→ *Ling-pao ching*) to subordinate deities, who in turn instruct mankind in the teachings of the Tao. He rescues souls caught in the various hells and sets them free. Originally, the Celestial Venerable of the Primordial Beginning headed the administration of Heaven but—like a wise ruler—entrusted that task to his assistant, the Jade Emperor (→ Yü-huang), whose importance later came to exceed that of Yüan-shih t'ien-tsun.

The earliest mention of Yüan-shih t'ein-tsun occurs in the writings of the alchemist → Ko Hung. Gradually, he came to take the place of → Huang-lao-chün, the most important deity of early Taoism, who now occupies a subordinate place in the celestial hierarchy.

Yüan-shih t'ien-tsun is said to be without beginning and the most supreme of all beings, in fact, representative of the principle of all being. From him all things arose. He is eternal, invisible, and limitless. He is the source of all truths contained in the *Scriptures of the Magic Jewel.* An alternative description of the celestial hierarchy states that the Celestial Venerable of the Primordial Beginning resides in the *ta-luo-t'ien* (→ *t'ien*) above the heavens of the three pure ones.

Yuan-wu K'o-ch'in 🅩 (Jap., Engo Kokugon), 1063–1135, Chinese Ch'an (Zen) master of the Yōgi lineage of Rinzai Zen (→ Yōgi school); a student and dharma successor (→ *hassu*) of → Wu-tsu Fa-yen (Jap., Goso Hōen) and the master of → Hu-kuo Ching-yuan (Jap., Gokoku Keigen), → Hu-ch'in Shao-lung (Jap., Kukyū Jōryū), and → Ta-hui Tsung-kao (Jap., Daie Sōkō). Yuan-wu was one of the most important Ch'an masters of his time. With masters like him and the twenty-years-younger → Wu-men

Hui-k'ai (Jap., Mumon Ekai), also in the tradition of the Yōgi school, Ch'an reached the last peak of its development in China before the dharma transmitted by the patriarchs (→ *soshigata*) from heart-mind to heart-mind (→ *ishin-denshin*) was brought to Japan. There it continued to flourish, while in China it gradually declined.

Master Ta-hui, one of Yuan-wu's chief students, played a major role in shaping kōan practice. → Hakuin Zenji, the great renewer of Rinzai Zen in Japan, was in the lineage of transmission stemming from Yuan-wu. Yuan-wu himself is known primarily as the editor of the → *Pi-yen-lu*, together with the → *Wu-men-kuan* one of the two best-known kōan collections. His instructions, incidental remarks (→ *jakugo*), and explanations on the hundred kōans collected and provided with "praises" (→ *ju*) by Master Ch'ung-hsien make the *Pi-yen-lu* one of the greatest works of Ch'an (Zen) literature and one of the most helpful for training students.

Son of a family from Szechuan, the heads of which had been Confucian scholars for generations, as a child he learned the Confucian classics by heart. He was attracted to Buddhism at an early age and entered a Buddhist monastery, where he devoted himself to the study of the sūtras. After nearly dying from an illness, he came to the conclusion that mere scholarly erudition could not bring one to the living truth of the buddha-dharma. Thus he set out to find an enlightened Ch'an master. As an → *unsui*, he traveled to south China, where he eventually found and stayed with Master Wu-tsu, whom he served as an attendant for many years. Even after he had realized profound enlightenment under Wu-tsu and had received from him the seal of confirmation (→ *inka-shōmei*), he stayed with him to train further until the master's death.

Then he set out for the north, where he was appointed by high state officials and finally by Emperor Hui-tsung himself to the abbacy of various large Ch'an monasteries. The conquest of north China by the Kitan drove him once again to south China. However, he soon returned to his home province and was active there as a Ch'an master until his death.

Yü Chi ■ also known as Kan Chi, d. 197 C.E.; Taoist scholar, well versed in the teaching on the five elements (→ *wu-hsing*), magic, and medicine. Yü Chi worked as a miracle healer in eastern China, effecting cures by the use of incense and holy water.

Around 145 C.E. he wrote the *T'ai-p'ing ch'ing-ling shu* (*The Book of Supreme Peace and Purity*, → *T'ai-p'ing ching*) which became the doctrinal basis of the School of Supreme Peace (→ *t'ai-p'ing tao*). According to legend, Yü Chi is not the actual author of this work, but is said to have come into its possession in a miraculous manner. In 197 C.E. he was murdered by his relatives.

Yü-chiang ■ Chin., lit. "jade liquid"; euphemism for saliva. In Taoist health exercises saliva is considered to be an important substance that has to be carefully preserved within the body, because its loss—e.g., by spitting—can result in a dangerous reduction of vitality. For that reason a practice known as *t'un-t'o* ("swallowing the saliva") frequently forms part of Taoist breathing exercises. When the practitioner has swallowed the accumulated saliva in small quantities, it ascends to nourish the brain and then descends to moisten the five organs (→ *wu-tsang*). In Taoist terminology this process is known as "feeding the embryo" (→ *t'ai-shih*). By swallowing his saliva, a practitioner may also succeed in expelling the three worms (→ *san-ch'ung*). Furthermore, the practice is said to strengthen the teeth, the growth of hair, and general resistance to illness.

Swallowing the saliva—which, according to the Taoist view, is produced in two containers below the tongue—is best practiced at dawn. The practitioner adopts a sitting position, closes his eyes, dispels all disturbing thoughts, and claps his teeth together twenty-seven times (→ *k'ou-ch'ih*), causing the cavity of the mouth to fill with saliva. He rinses his teeth with it and, after swallowing it, guides it—by the power of the mind—first to the brain and then downward to the "ocean of breath" (→ *ch'i-hai*). In this way the "three foundations" (→ *san-yüan*) are nourished.

Yü-ch'ing ■ Chin. → *san-ch'ing*

Yudhishthira ■ (Yudhiṣṭhira), Skt., the oldest and best beloved of the five → Pāndavas; he is described as composed, dispassionate in judgment, and of uncorruptible righteousness. He was celebrated as a ruler, not as a warrior. When King → Dhritarāshtra named him successor to his throne in the place of his own son Duryodhana, a great battle ensued between the Pāndavas and → Kauravas that is described in the *Mahābhārata*.

Upon learning of Dhritarāshtra's decision, Duryodhana and the other Kauravas were jealous. They invited Yudhishthira to join them in a game of dice. Duryodhana's uncle, a gambler and swindler, saw to it that Yudhishthira lost everything—his kingdom, himself, his brothers, and his wife were all banished from the realm. Duryodhana attempted to trap them by setting fire to their house, but → Bhīma thwarted the plan. When the Pāndavas later attempted to return, they were stopped by the Kauravas, and a great battle then broke out. Following the Pāndavas' victory, Yudhishthira was restored to his throne; he was a just and benevolent ruler whose subjects lived without fear of war or disorder and were thus able to devote themselves entirely to their religious duties. When → Krishna died, Yudhishthira named Parikshit, a grandson of → Arjuna, as his successor, and the five brothers, renouncing the world, withdrew to the Himalayas. The story of their journey there is beautifully told in the final verses of the *Mahābhārata.*

Yueh-an Shan-kuo 🅉 (Jap., Gettan Zenka), 1079–1152, Chinese Ch'an (Zen) master of the Yōgi lineage of Rinzai Zen (→ Yōgi school); a student and dharma successor (→ *hassu*) of → K'ai-fu Tao-ning (Jap., Kaifuku Dōnei) and the master of → Lao-na Tsu-teng (Jap., Rōnō Sotō). We encounter Master Yueh-an in example 8 of the → *Wu-men-kuan.*

Yueh-chou Ch'ien-feng 🅉 (Jap., E'shū Kempō); Chinese Ch'an (Zen) master of the T'ang period; a student and dharma successor (→ *hassu*) of → Tung-shan Liang-chieh (Jap., Tōzan Ryōkai). We encounter him in example 48 of the → *Wu-men-kuan.*

Yueh-lin Shih-kuan 🅉 (Jap., Gatsurin [Getsurin] Shikan), 1143–1217; Chinese Ch'an (Zen) master of the Yōgi lineage of Rinzai Zen (→ Yōgi school); a student and dharma successor (→ *hassu*) of → Lao-na Tsu-teng (Jap., Rōnō Sotō) and the master of → Wu-men Hui-k'ai (Jap., Mumon Ekai).

Yüeh-shan Wei-yen 🅉 also Yao-shan Wei-yen (Jap., Yakusan Igen), 745–828 or 750–834, Chinese Ch'an (Zen) master; a student and dharma successor → *hassu*) of → Shih-t'ou Hsi-ch'ien (Jap., Sekitō Kisen) and the master of → Tao-wu Yuan-chih (Jap., Sekitō Kisen) and → Yun-yen Tan-sheng (Jap., Ungan Donjō). From the → *Ching-te ch'uan-teng-lu* we learn only that he left home at the age of seventeen and was ordained as a monk in 774 on Heng mountain by the Vinaya master Hsi-ts'ao (→ Vinaya). He is without doubt the most prominent of the students who were sent back and forth between Shih-t'ou and → Ma-tsu Tao-i (Jap., Baso Dōitsu) (on this, → Shih-t'ou Hsi-ch'ien).

In the → *Denkō-roku* we learn of the incident that marked the transmission of the dharma from Shih-t'ou (Sekitō) to Yueh-shan:

The thirty-sixth patriarch Kōdō Daishi [honorific title for Yueh-shan] went to Sekitō and said, "I almost know the teachings of the three vehicles and of the twelve branches of doctrine. Once I heard that in the south there existed direct instructions on the mind of men that make men into buddhas and bring them to realize their nature. That is not yet clear to me. Bowing, I request the master to have compassion on me and instruct me."

A student comes to *dokusan* with Master Yüeh-shan Wei-yen (Ch'an painting by Ma Kung-hsien, 12th century)

Sekitō said, "When you say 'It is this,' then you miss it. This and not-this, both miss *it.* What do you think about that?"

The master [Yueh-shan] did not know what to answer.

Sekito said, "Your karma does not connect you to this place. [Ch'an masters often used the expression *this place* to refer to themselves.] Go for a little while to Baso Dōitsu [Ma-tsu]."

The master obeyed the command, went to Baso, paid homage to him, and once again asked his earlier question.

The patriarch [Ma-tsu] said, "Sometimes I make it raise its eyebrows and blink its eyes, and sometimes I make it not raise its eyebrows and blink its eyes. Sometimes that which raises its eyebrows and blinks its eyes is *that!* Sometimes that which raises its eyebrows and blinks its eyes is *not-that!* What do you think about that?"

With this the master experienced great enlightenment. He prostrated.

The patriarch said, "What kind of thing has become clear to you that you prostrate yourself?"

The master said, "When I was with Sekitō, it was like a gnat crashing into an iron ox."

The patriarch said, "You've got it now. Keep it well. But your master is Sekitō." When, at the age of eighty-four, Yueh-shan saw his end approaching, he cried out, "The dharma hall is collapsing! All you [monks], hold it up!" Then he raised a hand and said, "You monks don't understand my words," and passed away.

Yuga 🅗 Skt.; term referring to any of the four ages of the world, whose time is reckoned in divine years, which must be multiplied by 360 to obtain the sum of human years. Each cosmic age is preceded by a "dawn" (*sandhyā*) and is followed by a "dusk" of equal length (*sandhyānsha*). Each of these two periods constitutes one-tenth of the respective *yuga.* The four *yugas* are (1) Krita- or Satya-Yuga (1,728,000 human years); (2) Tretā-Yuga (1,296,000 years); (3) Dvāpara-Yuga (864,000 years); (4) Kali-Yuga (432,000 years). The total of 4,320,000 human years (12,000 divine years) equals one *mahā-yuga,* or "great age." Two thousand *mahā-yugas* equal one day and one night in the life of Brahmā (→ *kalpa*).

This ingenious system is not yet mentioned in the *Rigveda*; it first appears in → Manu and the *Mahābhārata,* where the four ages are described as follows: Krita is the ideal or golden age, in which neither hate nor envy, care, nor fear exist. There is only *one* God, *one* Veda, *one* law, and *one* ritual. The castes have varying tasks, and each fulfills its duty selflessly. The performance of sacrifices begins in the Tretā-Yuga, when righteousness declines by one quarter. The sacrifices necessitate rites and ceremonies. The actions of human beings are marked by intentionality; people expect rewards in exchange for their rituals and offerings, and the sense of duty declines. In the Dvāpara-Yuga, righteousness is reduced by one half. There are now four Vedas, which are studied only by the few. Ritual is predominant; only few still abide by the truth. Desires and diseases surface, and injustice grows. In the Kali-Yuga, righteousness has dwindled to one quarter of its original substance. Spiritual efforts slacken off, knowledge is forgotten, evil dominates. Disease, fatigue, anger, hunger, fear, and despair gain ground; humanity has no goal. This last age is said to have begun in 3102 B.C.E. and is consequently still underway.

According to Svāmi Shrī → Yukteshvar, a great modern-day Indian spiritual figure, this calculation of the *yugas* is erroneous. His work *The Holy Science* sets forth a method of calculation according to which the *yugas* are considerably shorter. The calculations referred to above, which are those accepted by present-day scholars, are based in Yukteshvar's opinion on errors committed by Sanskrit scholars who were born in the dark age of the Kali-Yuga and therefore no longer understood the old traditions. Yukteshvar's method is based on astrological cycles.

Yü-huang 🅣 Chin., lit. "Jade Emperor"; one of the most important deities in Chinese folk religion and religious Taoism (→ *tao-chiao*); one of the three pure ones (→ *san-ch'ing*). Yü-huang personally determines all that happens in Heaven and on Earth. For this purpose he has at his disposal an enormous celestial administration, which is a faithful replica of the terrestrial administration of the Chinese Empire. Each deity has a clearly defined responsibility. At the beginning of each year all the deities report to the Jade Emperor after ascending to his palace, which is situated in the highest of all the heavens. Depending on how well the deities have lived up to their responsibilities, the Jade Emperor may promote them to higher positions or transfer them to other departments.

The Jade Emperor's earthly representatives are the deity of Mount T'ai (→ T'ai-yüeh ta'ti), the city deities (→ *ch'eng-huang*), the hearth deity (→ Tsao-chün), and the local deities (→ *t'u-ti*). Yü-huang is usually portrayed sitting on a throne, dressed in the ceremonial robes of an emperor, which are embroidered with dragons. On his head he wears the imperial headdress, from the front and back of which dangle thirteen strings of pearls. In his hand he holds a ceremonial plaque. His stern facial expression is meant to express calm and dignity. In the Taoist celestial hierarchy Yü-huang originally was the assistant of the Celestial Venerable of the Primordial Beginning (→ Yüan-shih t'ien-tsun), who later resigned from his post in favor of the Jade Emperor, thereby making him the most important deity in the Taoist pantheon.

According to legend, Yü-huang was the son of a king. Before he was born, his mother had a dream in which → Lao-chün handed her a child. After the death of his father the young prince ascended to the throne but abdicated his office after only a few days to withdraw to the mountains and study the Tao. Upon attaining perfection, he devoted the remainder of his life to the sick and poor, instructing them in the Tao. After 3,200 world periods he became a golden immortal and after a further hundred million aeons, the Jade Emperor.

The cult of Yü-huang began in the 11th century C.E. In the year 1005 C.E. the then emperor—Sung Chen-tsung—was forced to conclude a humiliating treaty with a foreign power and thus was in danger of losing the support of the people. To pacify them, the emperor posed as a visionary and claimed to be in direct communication with Heaven. He further stated that an immortal (→ *hsien*) had appeared to him in a dream, handing him a letter from Yü-huang, who promised that the founder of the dynasty would appear to him. With the fulfillment of this promise began the veneration of the Jade Emperor, to whom Sung Hui-tsung, in 1115 C.E., erected the first temple, and on whom he bestowed the title *Shang-ti* (God).

Yü-huang's palace is situated in the highest Taoist heaven, known as *ta-luo-t'ien* (→ *t'ien*). From there he rules the whole of the universe, i.e., the subordinate heavens, the Earth, and the lower regions. His palace is guarded by a figure known as the Transcendental Official (*Ling-kuan*), who was so widely venerated during the 15th century that a separate temple was dedicated to him in Peking.

Yü-huang had a large family: one of his sisters was the mother of Erh-lang, who dispels evil spirits by setting the Hounds of Heaven (*t'ien-kou*) on them; one of his wives is the so-called horse-headed deity, who rules over silkworms; and one of his daughters, known as the "Seventh Lady" (Ch'i ku-niang), is venerated by all girls wanting to know whom they will marry.

The immeasurably vast administration of the Jade Emperor contains ministries responsible for various natural phenomena and aspects of human existence, such as thunder, wind, water, fire, time, sacred mountains, war, literature, wealth, medicine, epidemics, etc. Each of these ministries is run by a president with a large number of subordinates. However, only very few of these have become significant in the religious life of the Chinese people.

These divine officials look after the spiritual and material welfare of mankind and are punished by Yü-huang if they neglect their duties. In reality, however, all these tasks were the responsibility of the terrestrial administration under the emperor. In other words: if the deity responsible for rain neglected its duties, it was "warned" by an imperial official, who would try to persuade it by logical arguments to live up to its responsibilities. If this intervention did not bring the desired result, the deity would be threatened with the loss of its rank. As a last resort, its noble title would be withdrawn by imperial decree. These changes in the celestial hierarchy and the appointment of new deities were confirmed by Taoist priests (→ *tao-shih*) at special religious ceremonies.

Yuige Z Jap. lit. "poem [ge, Skt., gāthā] left behind [yui]"; a verse left behind by a Zen master for his students at the time of his death.

In these—mostly short—poems, masters express their Zen realization "in a nutshell" in order to inspire their students and to encourage them not to flag in their efforts on the Zen way, even after their master's passing away (→ *senge*).

Yü-jen T Chin., lit. "feather man"; alternative designation for a Taoist priest (→ *tao-shih*). Originally, feather men were flying immortals (→ *hsien*), whose bodies were covered with a coat of feathers. As a result of the Taoist belief that *tao-shih,* after attaining immortality (→ *ch'ang-sheng pu-ssu*), ascend to Heaven in broad daylight (→ *fei-sheng*), they also came to be referred to as *yü-jen.*

Yukta H Skt.; a human being who has attained union with the world soul that permeates the entire universe, and who is free from all attachment to the things of this world.

Yukteshvar H 1855–1936, Indian spiritual teacher; his full name is Jñānāvatār Svāmi Shrī Yukteshvar Giri. "Giri" indicates that he was a member of a Shankara order. His teacher was the holy man Lahiri Mahāsaya. In the West Yukteshvar became known above all as the guru of → Yogānanda Paramahamsa. He is the author of *Kaivalya-Darshana* (see Yuktesvar 1957), a work that shows "the fundamental concordance between the little-understood Book of Revelation and India's → Sānkhya philosophy" (Yogānanda).

Yün-chi ch'i-ch'ien T Chin., lit. *"Cloud Book Cassette and Seven Strips of Bamboo";* an 11th-century Taoist encyclopedia consisting of 122 volumes. The special containers of Taoist scriptures are known as "cloud book cassettes"; the seven strips of bamboo refer to the four main parts and seven subsections of the Taoist canon (→ *Tao-tsang*). The *Yün-chi ch'i-ch'ien* contains a complete survey of Taoist exercises aimed at prolonging life and of meditation practices up to the time of the Sung Dynasty.

It is an extremely extensive work, providing additional information on all aspects of religious Taoism, such as biographies of immortals (→ *hsien*), instructions for hygiene and breathing exercises, descriptions of the methods of the Inner and Outer Elixir Schools (→ *nei-tan,* → *wai-tan*), sexual techniques (→ *fang-chung shu*), magical practices (→ *fang-shih*), fasting ceremonies, etc. A further aspect of the *Yün-chi ch'i-ch'ien*'s importance for Taoist scholars is that it contains passages or chapters of Taoist works that are no longer extant.

Yün-chuan T Chin., lit. "cloud writing"; a style of writing used in religious Taoism (→ *tao-chiao*). *Yüan-chuan* resembles a script known as seal script. Its curved lines are an imitation of cirrus clouds, hence its name.

Cloud writing is difficult to read and can only be understood by initiates. It is often found on talismans and amulets (→ *fu-lu*) and is said to be imbued with miraculous properties, such as the power to cure sickness and ward off evil spirits and demons.

Yun-chu Tao-ying 🅉 (Jap., Ungo Dōyō), d. 901/2; Chinese Ch'an (Zen) master; a student and dharma successor (→ *hassu*) of → Tung-shan Liang-chieh (Jap., Tōzan Ryōkai). Yun-chu is the student of Tung-shan who continued the lineage of the → Sōtō school founded by Tung-shan and → Tsao-shan Pen-chi (Jap., Sōzan Honjaku). → Dōgen Zenji was a later dharma heir of this lineage and Sōtō Zen in Japan continues its tradition today.

Yung-chia Hsuan-chueh 🅉 (Jap., Yōka Genkaku), 665–713; early Chinese Ch'an (Zen) master, who is considered a student of → Hui-neng. He left in his youth to become a Buddhist monk and studied all the important Buddhist writings. He was especially well-versed in the teachings of the T'ien-t'ai school (Jap., Tendai school, → Mikkyō) of Buddhism. He was also instructed in the practice of meditation (→ *zazen*) according to the tradition of this school. He is said to have perfectly realized this in "walking, standing, sitting, and lying" (→ *gyō-jū-za-ga*). When he heard of Hui-neng, he sought him out in Pao-lin monastery in Ts'ao-ch'i.

According to the → *hossen* recorded in the → *Ching-te ch'uan-teng-lu* between Hui-neng and Yung-chia, Hui-neng barely had the chance to confirm Yung-chia's profound enlightenment. He asked Yung-chia, who wanted to leave immediately, at least to stay the night at his monastery. He did, and thus is also known as the "master of the enlightenment of staying for one night."

Yung-chia combined in his teaching of the buddha-dharma the philosophy of the T'ien-t'ai school and the practice of Ch'an. He also introduced into the theoretical superstructure of the latter the dialectic of the → Mādhyamika. His writings are preserved in the *Collected Works of Ch'an Master Yung-chia Hsuan-chueh.*

Yung-ming Yen-shou 🅉 (Jap., Yōmyō Enju), 904–75; Chinese Ch'an (Zen) master; a student and dharma successor (→ *hassu*) of → T'ien-t'ai Te-shao (Jap., Tendai Tokushō). Yung-ming, who survived his master only by three years, was one of the last important masters of the → Hōgen school of Ch'an.

Yun-kai Shou-chih 🅉 (Jap., Ungai Shichi), 1025–1115; Chinese Ch'an (Zen) master of the Ōryō lineage of Rinzai Zen (→ Ōryō school); a student and dharma successor (→ *hassu*) of → Huang-lung Hui-nan (Jap., Ōryō E'nan).

Yun-kang 🄱 Chin., lit. "cloud hill"; grotto complex in the vicinity of the northern Chinese city of Ta-t'ung (Shansi province). It dates from the period between 460 and 540 and is one of the greatest monuments of Buddhist art in China. Today fifty-three caves exist in a cliff that extends over more than one kilometer. These contain a total of 50 thousand images of buddhas, bodhisattvas, and various deities. The largest buddha statue reaches a height of seventeen meters and is one of the largest in China.

The first grottos date from 460. The first phase of work took place under the supervision of the monk T'an-yao, under whom grottoes 16–20 were chiseled from the rock. The motivation behind these labors was to create an indestructible symbol of the Buddhist teaching. The ground plan of the first caves is oval. In the second phase (caves 5–10), the caves took on a rectangular form. In the middle of each of the caves is found a buddha statue; most of them depict the buddha sitting, accompanied by standing companions. On the walls, at the entrance, and on the dome are found many small buddha images, depictions of deities, illustrations of stories from the sūtras, and ornamental decorations. The most important caves are numbers 5 and 6, in which the life story of Buddha → Shākyamuni, from his birth to his attainment of enlightenment, is depicted. In other caves are illustrations relating to the → *Vimalakīrtinirdesha-sūtra.* The latest caves date from the Sui Dynasty period (589–618).

The grottoes of Yun-kang are an expression of remorse for the persecution of Buddhism under Emperor Wu in the year 466 and a symbol of the protection his successor lavished on Buddhism. We learn from inscriptions that the project was financed by the imperial court and by lay followers in order to achieve various aims. By fashioning the grottoes it was hoped to secure welfare and long life for the realm and its rulers and for the ancestors of the patrons rebirth in the pure land. It was also wished to contribute toward the strengthening of Buddhism among the Chinese folk.

The art of Yun-kang is strongly influenced by that of India (→ Gandhāra) and Central Asia. The buddha images make a stiff, often rigid, impression; the bodhisattvas, on the other hand, are more lively and lifelike. Various ornaments, such as dragons, birds, lotus flowers, and the aureoles around the heads of the buddhas, are already purely Chinese elements.

Yun-men Wen-yen 🅉 (Jap., Ummon Bun'en), also called K'uang-chen, 864–949; Chinese Ch'an (Zen) master; a student and dharma successor (→ *hassu*) of → Hsueh-feng I-ts'un (Jap.,

Seppō Gison) and the master of → Hsiang-lin Ch'eng-yuan (Jap., Kyōrin Chōon), → Tung-shan Shou-chu (Jap., Tōsan Shusho), and → Pa-ling Hao-chien (Jap., Haryō Kōkan). Yun-men was one of the most important Ch'an masters and the last of the "Ch'an giants" in the history of Ch'an in China. We encounter him in examples 15, 16, 21, 39, and 48 of the → *Wu-men-kuan*, and the examples 6, 8, 14, 15, 22, 27, 34, 39, 47, 50, 54, 60, 62, 77, 83, 86, 87, and 88 of the → *Pi-yen-lu*. The most important of his sayings and teachings are recorded in the *Yun-men K'uang-chen-ch'an-shih kuang-lu* (*Record of the Essential Words of Ch'an Master K'uang-chen from Mount Yun-men*).

On the incident that led to Yun-men's first enlightenment under Master Mu-chou, see → Mu-chou Ch'en-tsun-ma. Yun-men, who himself had more than sixty dharma successors, was known, like Master Mu-chou, as a particularly strict Ch'an master. He founded the Yun-men school (Jap., → Ummon school) of Ch'an, which belonged to the "five houses" (→ *goke-shichishū*) of the Ch'an tradition in China, and survived until the 12th century. The dharma heirs of Yun-men played a major role in the preservation of Ch'an literature for later generations. The best-known of them is Yun-men's "great-grandson in dharma," the great master → Hsueh-tou Ch'ung-hsien (Jap., Setchō Jūken), who collected a hundred examples of the ancient masters and provided them with "praises" (→ *ju*). These master → Yuan-wu K'o-ch'in (Jap., Engo Kokugon) later made the basis of his edition of the → *Pi-yen-lu*.

Yun-men was among the first of the great Ch'an masters to use the words of preceding masters as a systematic means of training monks. This style of training eventually developed into kōan practice (→ *kanna* Zen, → Ta-hui Tsung-kao), one of the most effective methods of Ch'an (Zen) training. Yun-men also often gave "another answer" or an "other word" (Chin., *pieh-yu*; Jap., *betsugo*) than the one given in the → *mondō or* → *hossen* cited by him. Then he again posed a question and answered it himself instead of his students with a "word taking their part" (Chin., *tai-yu*; Jap., *daigo*), as in example 6 of the → *Pi-yen-lu*. The answer given in this example became one of the most renowned sayings of the Ch'an (Zen) tradition: "Yu-men said while giving instruction, 'I'm not asking you about the days before the fifteenth. But about the days after the fifteenth, come forward with a word and speak!' Taking their part, he said himself, 'Day for day a good day.' "

Sometimes he combined the "word taking their part" with the "other word" and in a later explanation gave another answer to a question that he himself had previously posed and answered "taking their part."

Master Yun-men's sayings and answers are highly prized in the Ch'an (Zen) tradition. No other master's words are so frequently cited in the great kōan collections as his. It is said that his words always fulfill three important qualifications of a "Zen word": (1) his answers correspond to the question posed "the way a lid fits a jar"; (2) they have the power to cut through the delusion of his students' dualistic way of thinking and feeling like a sharp sword; (3) his answers follow the capacity for understanding and momentary state of mind of the questioner "as one wave follows the previous one."

Yun-men's pregnant answers often consist of only one word and are among the most renowned "one-word barriers" (→ *ichiji-kan*) in the Ch'an (Zen) tradition.

Such "one-word barriers" are Yun-men's "*Kan*!" in example 8 of the *Pi-yen-lu* (→ *ichiji-kan*) and his famous → *kan-shiketsu* from example 21 of the *Wu-men-kuan*. A further example of Yun-men's *ichiji-kan* is found in example 77 of the *Pi-yen-lu*:

> A monk asked Yun-men, "What are the words of the venerable buddhas and the great patriarchs?"
>
> Yun-men said, "Dumplings!"

Yun-men was, however, not only a master of words but also of the wordless gesture, as example 22 of the *Pi-yen-lu* shows:

> Hsueh-feng said while instructing the monks, "On South Mountain there's a turtle-nosed snake. You should all certainly have a look at it."
>
> Ch'ang-ch'ing [Hui-leng] said, "Today there are many here in the dharma hall who are about to lose their body and life."
>
> A monk reported this to → Hsuan-sha [Shih-pei].
>
> Hsuan-sha said, "There is just Brother Leng [Ch'ang-ch'ing] who can understand that. But however that may be, I am not of that opinion."
>
> The monk asked, "What is your opinion then, Master?"
>
> Hsuan-sha said, "What does he need the South Mountain for?"
>
> Yun-men took his staff, threw it down in front of him, and made a gesture of fear."

Yun-men, who made such skillful use himself of the words of the ancient masters, was at the same time very mistrustful of the written word, which could all too easily be understood literally but not really grasped. Thus he forbade his students to write his sayings down. We owe it to one of his followers, who attended his discourses wearing a paper robe on which he took notes in spite of the ban, that many of the imperishable sayings and explanations of the great Ch'an master have been preserved.

Yun-yen T'an-sheng ▣ (Jap., Ungan Donjō), 781?–841, Chinese Ch'an (Zen) master; a student and dharma successor (→ *hassu*) of → Yueh-shan Wei-yen (Jap., Yakusan Igen) and the master of the great Ch'an master → Tung-shan Liang-chieh (Jap., Tōzan Ryōkai). In the → *Ching-te ch'uan-teng-lu* we learn that he left his home at an early age and was first trained by → Pai-chang Huai-hai (Jap., Hyakujō Ekai), under whom, however, he did not yet experience enlightenment. After having served Master Pai-chang for twenty years, till the latter's death, Yun-yen entered the monastery of Yueh-shan. There his dharma eye opened and he was confirmed by Yueh-shan as his dharma successor. Later he went to live on Mount Yun-yen ("Cloud Crag") in Hunan, from which his name is derived. We encounter Yun-yen in examples 70, 72, and 89 of the *Pi-yen-lu*.

In the *Ching-te ch'uan-teng-lu* we find a number of examples of → *mondō* between Yun-yen and his famous student and dharma successor Tung-shan, among them the following:

One day Yun-yen said to the assembly of monks, "There is a son of a certain family. If you ask him a question, there's nothing he couldn't answer."

Tung-shan said, "How many scriptures were in his house?"

The master said, "Not a single word."

Tung-shan said, "Then where did he know so much from?"

The master said, "Night and day he never slept."

Tung-shan said, "Could I ask him something else?"

The master said, "Even if he could say it, he wouldn't say it."

When Yun-yen felt his end approaching, he summoned the head monk and told him to prepare a feast for the monks. On the evening of the next day, he passed away (→ *senge*).

Yü-pu ▣ Chin., lit. "step of Yü" (→ Ta-yü); magic Taoist dance said to have originated with Great Yü, the founder of the Hsia Dynasty and Master of the Waves. The dance is performed by Taoist masters (→ *tao-shih*), often in a state of trance. It enables them to get in touch with supernatural forces and thus serves to dispel evil spirits and demons. The "step of Yü" is considered to be the most ancient form of Taoist magic.

The legends about the origin of *Yü-pu* vary; one states that Yü observed this manner of walking in birds who were trying to crack open pebbles. According to another, Great Yü overexerted himself when he was taming the waves and thereafter walked with a limp. The dance is thought to be an imitation of his limping gait. Yet other traditions state that Yü was taught this sequence of steps by the heavenly spirits to give him power over the forces of nature.

Yu-wang Cho-an ▣ (Jap., Ikuō Setsuan); Chinese Ch'an (Zen) master, → Dainichi Nōnin.

Yü Yen ▣ 1258–1314 C.E.; Taoist scholar famous for his interpretation of the *Book of Change(s)* (→ *I-ching*) and an expert in alchemy. In his writings, Yü Yen combines Taoist and neo-Confucianist ideas. He is the author of commentaries on the *I-ching*, the *Chou-i ts'an-t'ung-ch'i* of → Wei P'o-yang, and other texts.

Z

Zabuton ▣ Jap., lit. "sitting mat"; a mat usually filled with kapok and covered with dark blue fabric, on which → *zazen* is practiced. The *zabuton* is square and just big enough for a Japanese sitting in the lotus position (→ *kekka-fusa*) to fit bottom and knees on it.

Zadan ▣ Jap., lit. "sitting, to cut through"; cutting through all deluded thoughts and feelings (→ delusion), i.e., the dualistic worldview, through the practice of → *zazen*. Another term for *zadan* is → *zazetsu*.

When the projections of unenlightened mind (→ *bonpo-no-jōshiki*) are cut through, one can realize the true nature of reality, emptiness (Jap., *ku*; Skt., → *shūnyatā*), which is the basis of all phenomena, bearing and producing them. So long as one remains attached to the phenomenal aspect of reality and holds it for the only reality, the essential is hidden by phenomena. In the practice of *zazen* the ground of the projections that obscure the true nature of reality is systematically removed, until the dualistic worldview held intact by them finally completely collapses. This is the "great death" (→ *daishi*) of → ego, which alone can lead to the "great rebirth" or "great life," i.e., to enlightenment in everyday life (→ *mujōdō-no-taigen*).

Zafu 🅩 Jap., lit. "sitting cushion"; a round cushion of black fabric, firmly stuffed with kapok, that is used for → *zazen*. This *zafu* is the cushion referred to in the famous Zen saying, "At some time you must die on the cushion" (→ *daishi*).

Zage 🅩 Jap., lit. "sitting summer"; another word for → *ango*.

Zagu 🅩 Jap., lit. "sitting thing"; originally a light sitting mat that was among the six permissible possessions of a Buddhist monk (Jap., *roku-motsu*). If a monk was traveling on pilgrimage, he carried this mat folded under his robe. In Zen this became a cloth, the so-called "Zen cloth," which today is used mainly on certain ceremonial occasions, when, for example, a Zen master spreads it out on the floor so that he can make a prostration on it. The *zagu*, thus used, plays a role in an ancient kōan.

Zaike 🅩 Jap., lit. "householder"; a person who lives in his house, a Buddhist layperson as opposed to a monk; a monk can also be called a "homeless one."

Zammai 🅩 also sanmai, Jap.; Japanese pronunciation of the word *samādhi*. In Mahāyāna Buddhism, *samādhi* generally designates equilibrium, tranquility, and collectedness of mind; in Zen, beyond that, *zammai* designates a completely wakeful total absorption of the mind in itself. It is a nondualistic state of mind in which there is no distinction between subject and object, inner and outer, in which, in other words, there is no "mind" of the meditator (subject) that is directed toward an object of meditation or concentrated on a "point" (so-called one-pointedness of mind); in *zammai* subject and object are one.

From the standpoint of complete → enlightenment, *zammai* and enlightenment are identical, i.e., the same in nature. From the point of view of the stages that lead to enlightenment (→ satori, → *kenshō*), however, *zammai* and enlightenment are different; that is, a transitory experience of the state of *zammai*, which can occur under certain circumstances in the life of any person, is not yet the same thing as enlightenment.

Zasetsu 🅩 Jap., lit. "sitting, to kill"; the elimination of → delusion in the practice of → *zazen*. Another word for → *zadan*.

Zazen 🅩 Jap., (Chin., tso-ch'an), lit. *za*, "sitting" and *zen*, "absorption"; meditative practice taught in Zen as the most direct way to → enlightenment (also → satori, → *kenshō*). *Zazen* is not meditation in the usual sense, since meditation includes, at least initially, the focusing of the mind on a "meditation object" (for example, a mandala or a graphic representation of a bodhisattva) or contemplating abstract properties (for instance, impermanence or compassion). *Zazen*, however, is intended to free the mind from bondage to any thought-form, vision, thing, or representation, however sublime or holy it might be.

A monk practices *zazen* on a wooden platform (*tan*) in a Zen hall (*zendo*)

Even such aids to *zazen* practice as → kōans are not meditation objects in the usual sense; the essential nature of a kōan is paradox, that which is beyond conception.

In its purest form *zazen* is dwelling in a state of thought-free, alertly wakeful attention, which, however, is not directed toward any object and clings to no content (→ *shikantaza*). If practiced over a long period of time with persistance and devotion, *zazen* brings the mind of the sitter to a state of totally contentless wakefulness, from which, in a sudden breakthrough of enlightenment, he can realize his own true nature or buddha-nature (→ *busshō*), which is identical with the nature of the entire universe.

As is already clear from the presence of the word *zen*, i.e., "absorption," in its name, *zazen*, "sitting in absorption," is the alpha and omega of Zen. Without *zazen*, no Zen. Kōans like that in which a great Ch'an master tells his student "through sitting [*zazen*] one can't become a buddha" (on this, → Nan-yueh Huai-jang) are occasionally completely misunderstood to mean that these masters considered *zazen* ultimately unnecessary, since one is already a buddha. Now the affirmation that all beings are, from the beginning, buddhas is indeed a central affirmation of Buddhism and of Zen; however, Zen stresses that it makes a great—in fact a decisive—difference whether one merely gullibly takes this affirmation to be true or whether one experiences this truth in its deepest sense directly and immediately oneself. Such an experience is the "awakening" to which the practice of *zazen* is intended to lead.

As the first patriarch of Ch'an (Zen) in China (→ Bodhidharma) already demonstrated through his nine years of sitting in absorption facing the wall (→ *menpeki*) at the Shao-lin Monastery, *zazen* is the central practice of Zen and is prized by all Zen masters as the "gateway to complete liberation," as → Dōgen Zenji said. In his → *Zazen-wasan* ("*Song in Praise of Zazen*"), the great Zen master → Hakuin Zenji sings:

Zazen as taught in the Mahāyāna:
No praise can exhaust its merit.
The six *pāramitās*, like giving of alms, observing the precepts and other good deeds, differently enumerated,
They all come from *zazen*.
Whoever even gains the merit of practicing *zazen* once,
Eliminates immeasurable guilt accumulated in the past.

Zazen-kai 🅉 Jap., lit. "*zazen* meeting"; a meeting of followers of Zen to practice → *zazen* together, to hear the presentation of the buddha-dharma by a → *rōshi*, and to have → *dokusan*.

Zazen-wasan 🅉 Jap. → "Hakuin Zenji zazen-wasan"

Zazen Yōjinki 🅉 Jap., "*Precautions To Be Taken in Zazen*"; a well-known work on the practice of *zazen*, composed in the 14th century by → Keizan Jōkin, a patriarch of the Japanese → Sōtō school of Zen.

Zemban 🅉 Jap., lit. "Zen board"; a wooden board used by Ch'an (Zen) monks in ancient times. During long periods of intensive training in which the monks practiced → *zazen* uninterruptedly without lying down to sleep, they set the Zen board on their hands (resting one on top of the other) and supported the chin on it in order not to fall forward when, in spite of all efforts, they nodded off.

The Zen board is mentioned in a number of ancient kōans, for instance, example 20 of the → *Pi-yen-lu*, in which the Ch'an masters → Ts'ui-wei Wu-hsueh (Jap., Suibi Mugaku), → Lin-chi I-hsuan (Jap., Rinzai Gigen), and → Lung-ya Chu-tun (Jap., Ryūge Koton) appear:

Lung-ya asked Ts'ui-wei, "What is the meaning of the patriarch's coming from the west [→ seirai-no-i]?"

Ts'ui-wei said, "Give me the Zen board."

Lung-ya handed Ts'ui-wei the Zen board. Ts'ui-wei took it and hit him.

Lung-ya said, "If you hit me, I'll let you hit me. In short, the patriarch's coming from the west has no meaning."

Later Lung-ya asked Master Lin-chi, "What is the meaning of the patriarch's coming from the west?"

Lin-chi said, "Hand me that cushion."

Lung-ya picked up the cushion and passed it to Lin-chi. Lin-chi took it and hit him.

Lung-ya said, "If it comes to hitting, I'll let myself be hit. In brief, the patriarch's coming from the west has no meaning."

Zembyō 🅉 also Zenbyō, Jap., lit. "Zen sickness"; 1. an expression for deceptive sensations and appearances (→ *makyō*) that can come up during the practice of → *zazen*; 2. any attachment to one's own enlightenment experiences; also attachment to emptiness (Jap., *ku*; Skt., → *shūnyatā*) is a Zen sickness. It is an especially pronounced form of *zembyō* when someone develops great pretensions about his experience on the Zen path and thus considers himself someone special. Also when it is all too obvious that someone has experienced enlightenment (on this, → *mosshōseki*), this condition also is referred to as Zen illness.

Zen 🅑 🅉 Jap.; an abbreviation of the word *zenna* (also *zenno*), the Japanese way of reading Chinese *ch'an-na* (short form, *ch'an*). This in turn is the Chinese version of the Sanskrit word → *dhyāna*, which refers to collectedness of mind or meditative absorption in which all dualistic distinctions like *I/you*, *subject/object*, and *true/false* are eliminated. Zen can be defined both exoterically and esoterically.

Exoterically regarded, Zen, or Ch'an as it is called when referring to its history in China, is a school of Mahāyāna Buddhism, which developed in China in the 6th and 7th centuries from the meeting of → Dhyāna Buddhism, which was brought to China by → Bodhidharma, and Taoism. In this sense Zen is a religion, the teachings and practices of which are directed toward self-realization (→ *kenshō*, → *satori*) and lead finally to complete awakening (→ enlightenment) as experienced by → Shākyamuni Buddha after intensive meditative self-discipline under the

Bodhi-tree. More than any other school, Zen stresses the prime importance of the enlightenment experience and the uselessness of ritual religious practices and intellectual analysis of doctrine for the attainment of liberation (enlightenment). Zen teaches the practice of → *zazen*, sitting in meditative absorption as the shortest, but also the steepest, way to awakening.

The essential nature of Zen can be summarized in four short statements: (1) "(a) special transmission outside the [orthodox] teaching" (→ *kyōge-betsuden*); (2) nondependence on [sacred] writings" (→ *furyū-monji*); and (3) "direct pointing [to the] human heart" (→ *jikishi-ninshin*); leading to (4) realization of [one's own] nature [and] becoming a buddha" (→ *kenshō-jobutsu*). This pregnant characterization of Zen is attributed by tradition to Bodhidharma, its first patriarch; however, many modern scholars suspect that it originated rather with the later Ch'an master → Nan-ch'uan P'u-yuan (Jap., Nansen Fugan).

According to legend the "special transmission outside the orthodox teaching" began with the famous discourse of Buddha → Shākyamuni on → Vulture Peak Mountain (Gridhrakūta). At that time, surrounded by a great host of disciples who had assembled to hear him expound the teaching, he is said only to have held up a flower without speaking. Only his student Kāshyapa understood and smiled—as a result of his master's gesture he suddenly experienced a breakthrough to enlightened vision and grasped the essence of the Buddha's teaching on the spot (on this, also → *nenge-mishō*). With this, the first transmission from heart-mind to heart-mind (→ *ishin-denshin*) took place. The Buddha confirmed → Mahākāshyapa, as his enlightened student was called henceforth, as the first Indian patriarch in the lineage of transmission. In Zen, which is often also called the "School of Buddha-Mind," sudden enlightenment (→ *tongo*) has played a central role.

It is said that the → buddha-dharma was passed down in an unbroken chain of transmission to the twenty-eighth Indian patriarch, Bodhidharma. The Indian period and its lineage of transmission, which was first mentioned in later Chinese texts, is regarded as legendary by historians, since there are no historical documents concerning it. For Zen itself, the historicity of the early patriarchs is irrelevant, since the authenticity of the enlightenment experience, which can be easily tested by an enlightened master (if he has not grown slack), is the matter of primary concern. What is important here is living truth rather than the dry, thinglike reality of documents and dates to which scientific researchers would like to reduce a richer, more global reality that they do not understand.

When Bodhidharma brought Dhyāna Buddhism from India to China at the beginning of the 6th century, he became the first patriarch of the lineage of Ch'an (Zen). In the course of further transmission of the teaching, down to the 6th patriarch → Hui-neng (638–713), there developed out of the combination of the spiritual essence of Dhyāna Buddhism and the teaching and approach to life of Taoism, which was congenial to Buddhism in many ways, what today we call Zen. This is primarily the teaching of the → Southern school stemming from Hui-neng, which stressed the doctrine of sudden enlightenment (*tongo*). Another school of Ch'an, the Northern school, which was originated by → Shen-hsiu, a "rival" of Hui-neng, and taught gradual enlightenment (→ *zengo*), survived for only a short time.

With Hui-neng and his immediate dharma successors (→ *hassu*) began the great period of Ch'an, which especially during the T'ang period but also in the beginning of the Sung period produced a large number of great masters. Among these were extraordinary masters such as → Ma-tsu Tao-i, (Jap., Baso Dōitsu), → Pai-chang Huai-hai (Jap., Hyakujō Ekai), → Te-shan Hsuan-chien (Jap., Tokusan Senkan), → Tung-shan Liang-chieh (Jap., Tōzan Ryōkai), → Chao-shou T'ung-shen (Jap., Jōshū Jūshin), and Lin-chi I-hsuan (Jap., Rinzai Gigen). These masters largely shaped the training methods that became typical of Ch'an. The lineage of the Southern school of Ch'an split into "five houses, seven schools" (→ goke-shichishu); these were currents within the Ch'an tradition that differed in details of training style but not in essential content. They are the → Sōtō school, the → Ummon school, the → Hōgen school, the → Igyō school, and the → Rinzai school; subschools of Rinzai are the → Yōgi school and the → Ōryō school (see also the Ch'an/Zen Lineage Chart).

Of these traditions, two, those of the Rinzai school and the Sōtō school, reached Japan, in the 12th century and at the beginning of the 13th century, respectively. Both schools are still active there today. While Ch'an in China declined after the Sung period and then, through admixture with the → Pure Land school of Buddhism during the Ming period, ceased to exist altogether as an authentic lineage of transmission of the buddha-dharma "from heart-mind to heart-mind," in Japan, as Zen, it began to flourish anew. → Dōgen Zenji, who brought the Sōtō tradition to Japan, and → Eisai Zenji, Shinchi → Kakushin, → Shōmyō, and others in the Rinzai tradition, together with a few Chinese Ch'an masters who were invited to Japan, founded the Zen tradition. A school founded in Japan in the middle of the 17th century by the Chinese master, → Yin-yuan Lung-ch'i (Jap., Ingen Ryūki), the → Ōbaku school, is today practically without importance, having only one active monastery, the → Mampuku-ji in Uji near Kyōto. One of the most outstanding figures in Zen was → Hakuin Zenji, who reformed Japanese Rinzai Zen in the 18th century after a period of deterioration and helped it to revive and flourish once again.

Since for some decades Westerners have also been seeking guidance on the Zen way in Japan, nowadays Japanese masters teach the dharma also in Europe and the United States, and there are already a number of Western dharma successors. Thus we might be seeing a further step in Zen's migration across the continents. The fact that recently Westerners have progressed from superficial intellectual interest to genuine Zen practice under the guidance of authorized masters encourages one to think that Zen can also set down roots in the West and bear fruit there.

Esoterically regarded, Zen is not a religion but rather an indefinable, incommunicable (→ *fukasetsu*) root, free from all names, descriptions, and concepts, that can only be experienced by each individual for him- or herself. From *expressed forms* of this, all religions have sprung. In this sense Zen is not bound to any religion, including Buddhism. It is the primordial perfection of everything existing, designated by the most various names, experienced by all great sages, saints, and founders of religions of all cultures and times. Buddhism has referred to it as the "identity of → samsāra and → nirvāna." From this point of view *zazen* is not a "method" that brings people living in ignorance (→ *avidyā*) to the "goal" of liberation; rather it is the immediate expression and actualization of the perfection present in every person at every moment.

Zenbyō 🅩 → *zembyō*

Zendō 🅩 Jap., lit. "Zen hall" (also dōjō, "way hall")' a large hall or room, in monasteries a special structure, in which → *zazen* is practiced.

Even though a *zendō* built in the traditional style is very conducive to the practice of *zazen*, Zen masters stress repeatedly that the practice of Zen fundamentally does not require a special room in a quiet, idyllic environment —though such circumstances are naturally helpful and even indispensible for beginners in *zazen*. As → Dōgen Zenji said, *Waga shin kore dōjō*, "Your own heart, that is the practice hall."

Zen'en 🅩 Jap., lit. "Zen garden"; a Zen monastery (→ *tera*), another term for → *zenrin*.

Zengen Chūkō 🅩 Jap. for → Chien-yuan Chung-hsing

Zengo 🅩 Jap., lit. "gradual enlightenment"; the teaching of gradual enlightenment (also referred to as "step-by-step" or "stage-by-stage") associated with the Northern school of Ch'an (Zen) in China, as opposed to the teaching of sudden enlightenment (→ *tongo*), which characterizes the → Southern school (→ Zen).

Zenji 🅩 Jap., lit. "Zen master (*ji=shi*, "master")"; honorific title having the sense of "great [or renowned] Zen master." It is a title that is generally conferred posthumously; several masters, however, received this title during their lifetimes.

Zenjō 🅩 Japanese pronunciation of the Chinese character by which the Sanskrit word → *dhyāna* was translated into Chinese (Chin., *ch'an-na*). The term refers to the state of meditative absorption or the practice related with it. As → *zazen*, it is the basic practice of Zen. (Also → Zen).

Zenke 🅩 Jap., lit. "Zen house, Zen family"; 1. a Zen temple or monastery (→ *tera*). 2. The "family" of followers of Zen, the monks, nuns, and laypersons belonging to the great school of the authentic tradition of Zen (→ *goke-shichi-shu).*

Zenkō Kokushi 🅩 → Eisai Zenji

Zenna 🅩 Jap. → Zen

Zenno 🅩 Jap. → Zen

Zenrin 🅩 Jap., lit. "Zen forest"; the community of Zen monks or a Zen monastery.

Zenrin-kushū 🅩 Jap., lit. "*Collection of Sayings from the Zen Forest*"; an anthology, published in 1688 by the Zen layman Ijūshi, of sayings from the sūtras, from the writings of the great Chinese Ch'an (Zen) masters, from Confucian and Taoist texts, as well as lines from poems of great Chinese poets. It is based on a shorter collection of sayings compiled at the end of the 15th century by the Japanese Zen master Tōyō Eichō, a seventh-generation dharma successor (→ *hassu*) of → Kanzan Egen. The *Zenrin-kushū* consists of about 6,000 entries, which are organized according to the number of written characters in the sayings. Since the time of → Hakuin Zenji, who became acquainted with this work in his youth, it has been a favorite source of → *jakugo* in Rinzai Zen. An English translation of 1,234 sayings from the *Zenrin-kushū* is Shigematsu 1981.

Zenshū 🅉 Jap. for → Ch'an-tsung

Zensu 🅉 Jap., lit. "child of Zen"; a student of Zen who is being guided on the Zen way by a master (→ *rōshi*).

Zuigan Shigen 🅉 Jap. for → Jui-yen Shih-yen

Zuisoku-kan 🅉 Jap. → *susokukan*

Ch'an/Zen Lineage Chart

The chart on the following pages shows only the most important masters and acknowledged lineages of transmission, from Buddha Shakyamuni up to the transplantation of the Ch'an tradition to Japan. In Japan the lineages divided into so many branches that this type of graphic representation is no longer possible. (The names of masters of most importance for the history of Ch'an/Zen are printed in bold type.)

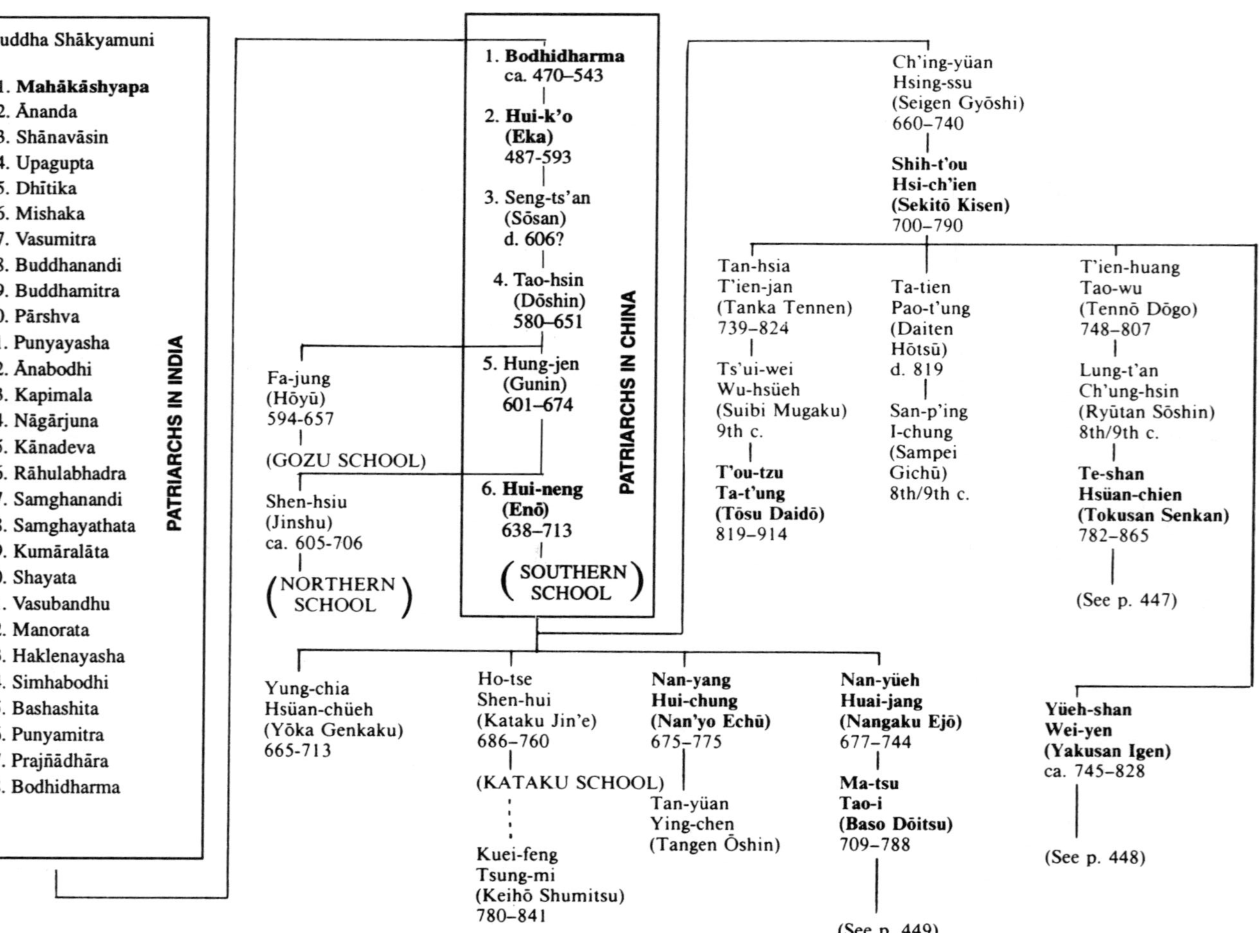
Buddha Shākyamuni
1. Mahākāshyapa
2. Ānanda
3. Shānavāsin
4. Upagupta
5. Dhītika
6. Mishaka
7. Vasumitra
8. Buddhanandi
9. Buddhamitra
10. Pārshva
11. Punyayasha
12. Ānabodhi
13. Kapimala
14. Nāgārjuna
15. Kānadeva
16. Rāhulabhadra
17. Samghanandi
18. Samghayathata
19. Kumāralāta
20. Shayata
21. Vasubandhu
22. Manorata
23. Haklenayasha
24. Simhabodhi
25. Bashashita
26. Punyamitra
27. Prajñādhāra
28. Bodhidharma
PATRIARCHS IN INDIA
1. Bodhidharma ca. 470–543
2. Hui-k'o (Eka) 487-593
3. Seng-ts'an (Sōsan) d. 606?
4. Tao-hsin (Dōshin) 580–651
5. Hung-jen (Gunin) 601–674
6. Hui-neng (Enō) 638–713
(SOUTHERN SCHOOL)
PATRIARCHS IN CHINA
Fa-jung (Hōyū) 594-657
(GOZU SCHOOL)
Shen-hsiu (Jinshu) ca. 605-706
(NORTHERN SCHOOL)
Ch'ing-yüan Hsing-ssu (Seigen Gyōshi) 660–740
Shih-t'ou Hsi-ch'ien (Sekitō Kisen) 700–790
Tan-hsia T'ien-jan (Tanka Tennen) 739–824
Ts'ui-wei Wu-hsüeh (Suibi Mugaku) 9th c.
T'ou-tzu Ta-t'ung (Tōsu Daidō) 819–914
Ta-tien Pao-t'ung (Daiten Hōtsū) d. 819
San-p'ing I-chung (Sampei Gichū) 8th/9th c.
T'ien-huang Tao-wu (Tennō Dōgo) 748–807
Lung-t'an Ch'ung-hsin (Ryūtan Sōshin) 8th/9th c.
Te-shan Hsüan-chien (Tokusan Senkan) 782–865
(See p. 447)
Yung-chia Hsüan-chüeh (Yōka Genkaku) 665-713
Ho-tse Shen-hui (Kataku Jin'e) 686–760
(KATAKU SCHOOL)
Kuei-feng Tsung-mi (Keihō Shumitsu) 780–841
Nan-yang Hui-chung (Nan'yo Echū) 675–775
Tan-yüan Ying-chen (Tangen Ōshin)
Nan-yüeh Huai-jang (Nangaku Ejō) 677–744
Ma-tsu Tao-i (Baso Dōitsu) 709–788
(See p. 449)
Yüeh-shan Wei-yen (Yakusan Igen) ca. 745–828
(See p. 448)

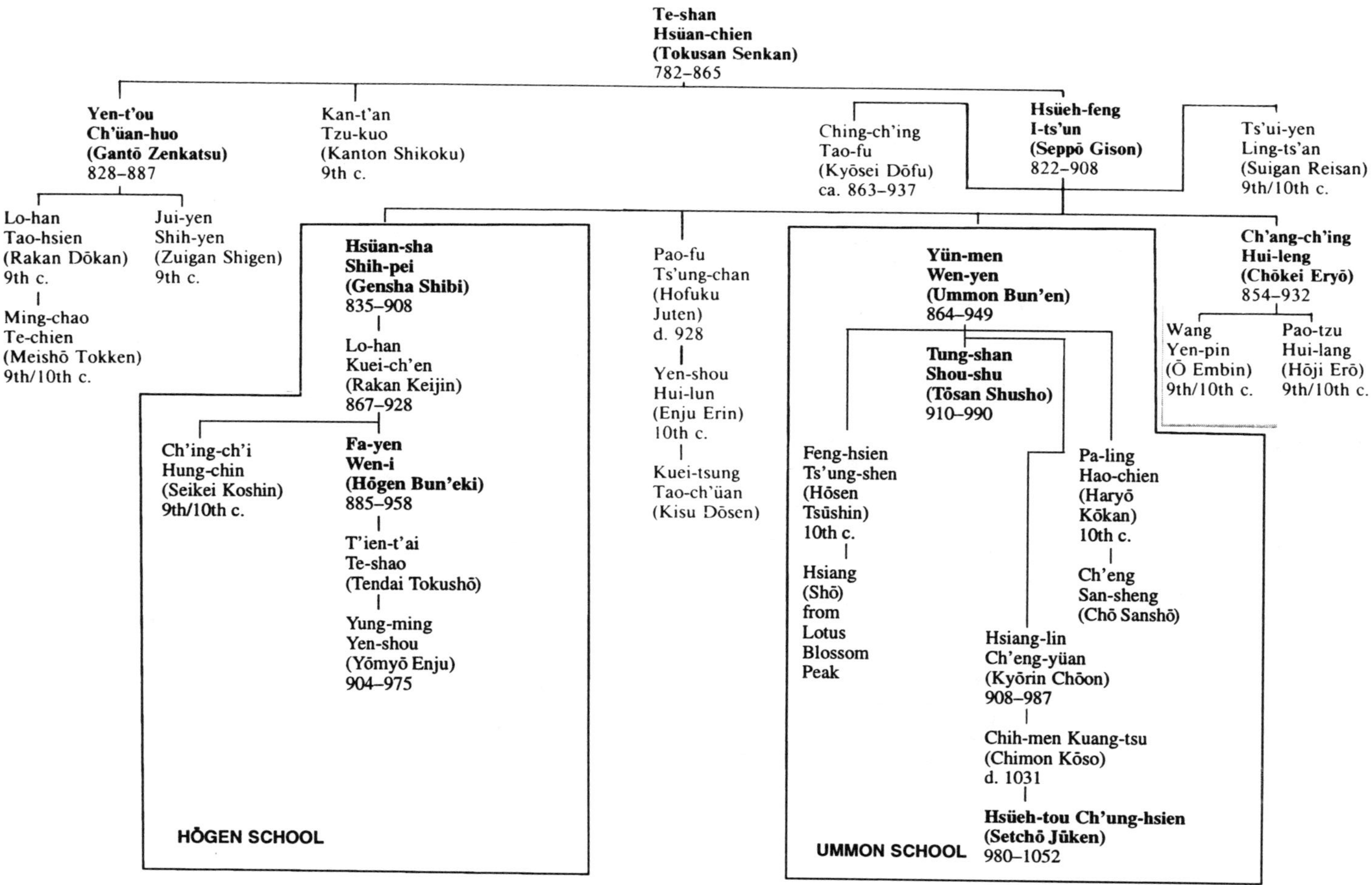
Te-shan Hsüan-chien (Tokusan Senkan) 782–865
Yen-t'ou Ch'üan-huo (Gantō Zenkatsu) 828–887
Kan-t'an Tzu-kuo (Kanton Shikoku) 9th c.
Ching-ch'ing Tao-fu (Kyōsei Dōfu) ca. 863–937
Hsüeh-feng I-ts'un (Seppō Gison) 822–908
Ts'ui-yen Ling-ts'an (Suigan Reisan) 9th/10th c.
Lo-han Tao-hsien (Rakan Dōkan) 9th c.
Jui-yen Shih-yen (Zuigan Shigen) 9th c.
Ming-chao Te-chien (Meishō Tokken) 9th/10th c.
Hsüan-sha Shih-pei (Gensha Shibi) 835–908
Lo-han Kuei-ch'en (Rakan Keijin) 867–928
Ch'ing-ch'i Hung-chin (Seikei Koshin) 9th/10th c.
Fa-yen Wen-i (Hōgen Bun'eki) 885–958
T'ien-t'ai Te-shao (Tendai Tokushō)
Yung-ming Yen-shou (Yōmyō Enju) 904–975
HŌGEN SCHOOL
Pao-fu Ts'ung-chan (Hofuku Juten) d. 928
Yen-shou Hui-lun (Enju Erin) 10th c.
Kuei-tsung Tao-ch'üan (Kisu Dōsen)
Yün-men Wen-yen (Ummon Bun'en) 864–949
Tung-shan Shou-shu (Tōsan Shusho) 910–990
Feng-hsien Ts'ung-shen (Hōsen Tsūshin) 10th c.
Hsiang (Shō) from Lotus Blossom Peak
Pa-ling Hao-chien (Haryō Kōkan) 10th c.
Ch'eng San-sheng (Chō Sanshō)
Hsiang-lin Ch'eng-yüan (Kyōrin Chōon) 908–987
Chih-men Kuang-tsu (Chimon Kōso) d. 1031
Hsüeh-tou Ch'ung-hsien (Setchō Jūken) 980–1052
UMMON SCHOOL
Ch'ang-ch'ing Hui-leng (Chōkei Eryō) 854–932
Wang Yen-pin (Ō Embin) 9th/10th c.
Pao-tzu Hui-lang (Hōji Erō) 9th/10th c.

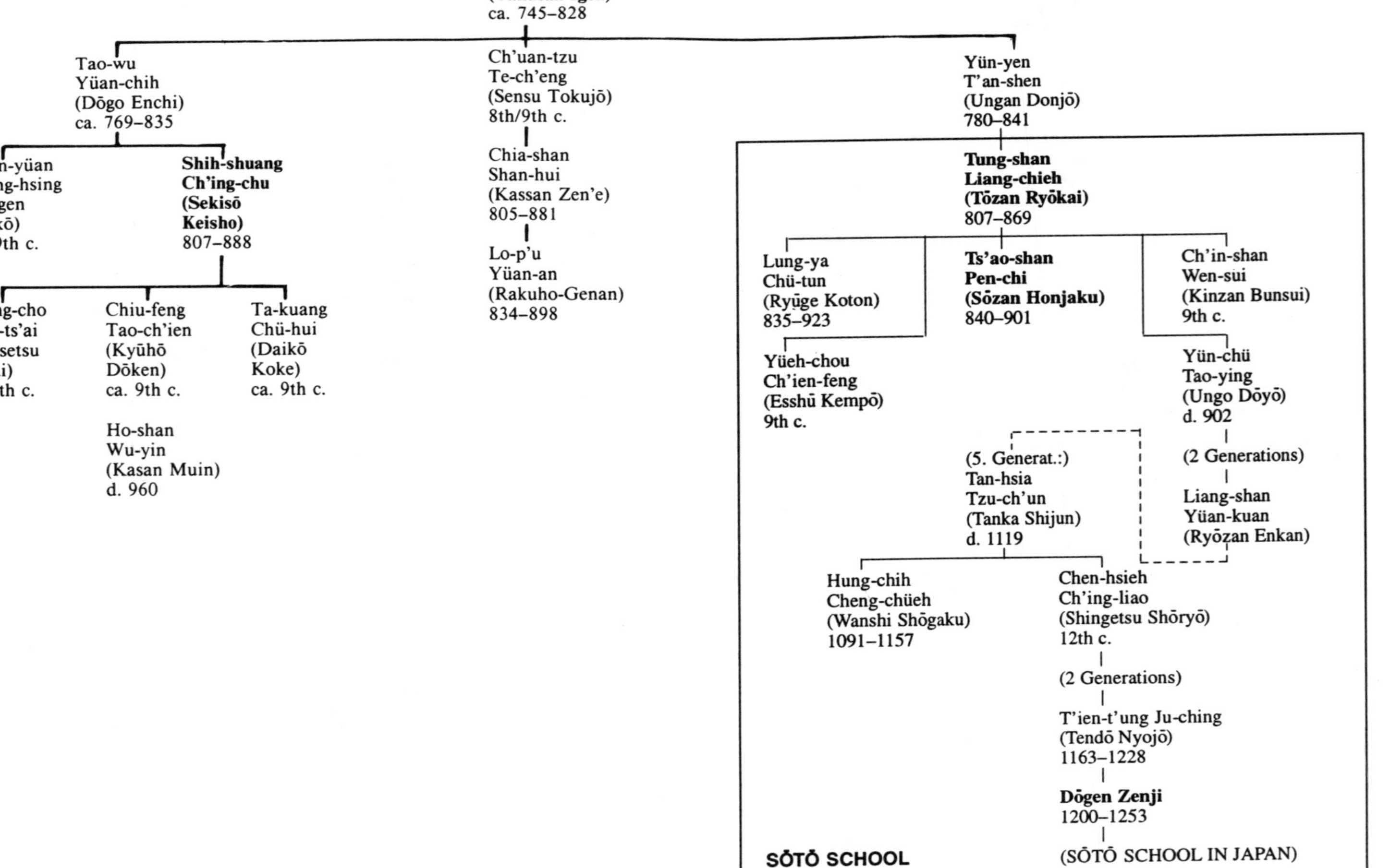
Yüeh-shan Wei-yen (Yakusan Igen) ca. 745–828
Tao-wu Yüan-chih (Dōgo Enchi) ca. 769–835
Chien-yüan Chung-hsing (Zengen Chūkō) 8th/9th c.
Shih-shuang Ch'ing-chu (Sekisō Keisho) 807–888
Chang-cho Hsiu-ts'ai (Chōsetsu Yusai) ca. 9th c.
Chiu-feng Tao-ch'ien (Kyūhō Dōken) ca. 9th c.
Ho-shan Wu-yin (Kasan Muin) d. 960
Ta-kuang Chü-hui (Daikō Koke) ca. 9th c.
Ch'uan-tzu Te-ch'eng (Sensu Tokujō) 8th/9th c.
Chia-shan Shan-hui (Kassan Zen'e) 805–881
Lo-p'u Yüan-an (Rakuho-Genan) 834–898
Yün-yen T'an-shen (Ungan Donjō) 780–841
Tung-shan Liang-chieh (Tōzan Ryōkai) 807–869
Lung-ya Chü-tun (Ryūge Koton) 835–923
Yüeh-chou Ch'ien-feng (Esshū Kempō) 9th c.
Ts'ao-shan Pen-chi (Sōzan Honjaku) 840–901
Ch'in-shan Wen-sui (Kinzan Bunsui) 9th c.
Yün-chü Tao-ying (Ungo Dōyō) d. 902
(2 Generations)
Liang-shan Yüan-kuan (Ryōzan Enkan)
(5. Generat.:) Tan-hsia Tzu-ch'un (Tanka Shijun) d. 1119
Hung-chih Cheng-chüeh (Wanshi Shōgaku) 1091–1157
Chen-hsieh Ch'ing-liao (Shingetsu Shōryō) 12th c.
(2 Generations)
T'ien-t'ung Ju-ching (Tendō Nyojō) 1163–1228
Dōgen Zenji 1200–1253
(SŌTŌ SCHOOL IN JAPAN)
SŌTŌ SCHOOL

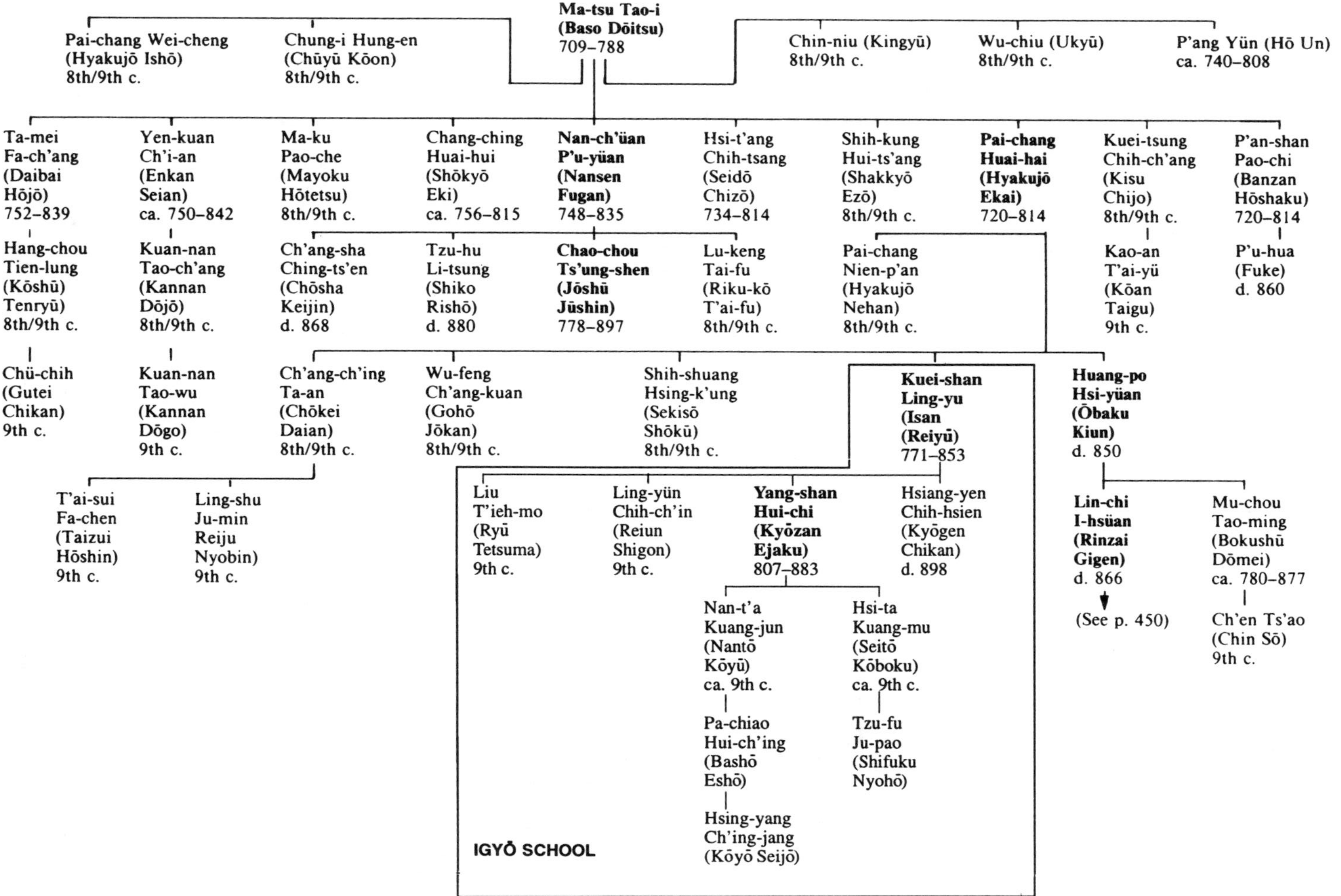
Ma-tsu Tao-i
(Baso Dōitsu)
709–788
Pai-chang Wei-cheng
(Hyakujō Ishō)
8th/9th c.
Chung-i Hung-en
(Chūyū Kōon)
8th/9th c.
Chin-niu (Kingyū)
8th/9th c.
Wu-chiu (Ukyū)
8th/9th c.
P'ang Yün (Hō Un)
ca. 740–808
Ta-mei
Fa-ch'ang
(Daibai
Hōjō)
752–839
Yen-kuan
Ch'i-an
(Enkan
Seian)
ca. 750–842
Ma-ku
Pao-che
(Mayoku
Hōtetsu)
8th/9th c.
Chang-ching
Huai-hui
(Shōkyō
Eki)
ca. 756–815
Nan-ch'üan
P'u-yüan
(Nansen
Fugan)
748–835
Hsi-t'ang
Chih-tsang
(Seidō
Chizō)
734–814
Shih-kung
Hui-ts'ang
(Shakkyō
Ezō)
8th/9th c.
Pai-chang
Huai-hai
(Hyakujō
Ekai)
720–814
Kuei-tsung
Chih-ch'ang
(Kisu
Chijo)
8th/9th c.
P'an-shan
Pao-chi
(Banzan
Hōshaku)
720–814
Hang-chou
Tien-lung
(Kōshū
Tenryū)
8th/9th c.
Kuan-nan
Tao-ch'ang
(Kannan
Dōjō)
8th/9th c.
Ch'ang-sha
Ching-ts'en
(Chōsha
Keijin)
d. 868
Tzu-hu
Li-tsung
(Shiko
Rishō)
d. 880
Chao-chou
Ts'ung-shen
(Jōshū
Jūshin)
778–897
Lu-keng
Tai-fu
(Riku-kō
T'ai-fu)
8th/9th c.
Pai-chang
Nien-p'an
(Hyakujō
Nehan)
8th/9th c.
Kao-an
T'ai-yü
(Kōan
Taigu)
9th c.
P'u-hua
(Fuke)
d. 860
Chü-chih
(Gutei
Chikan)
9th c.
Kuan-nan
Tao-wu
(Kannan
Dōgo)
9th c.
Ch'ang-ch'ing
Ta-an
(Chōkei
Daian)
8th/9th c.
Wu-feng
Ch'ang-kuan
(Gohō
Jōkan)
8th/9th c.
Shih-shuang
Hsing-k'ung
(Sekisō
Shōkū)
8th/9th c.
Kuei-shan
Ling-yu
(Isan
(Reiyū)
771–853
Huang-po
Hsi-yüan
(Ōbaku
Kiun)
d. 850
T'ai-sui
Fa-chen
(Taizui
Hōshin)
9th c.
Ling-shu
Ju-min
Reiju
Nyobin)
9th c.
Liu
T'ieh-mo
(Ryū
Tetsuma)
9th c.
Ling-yün
Chih-ch'in
(Reiun
Shigon)
9th c.
Yang-shan
Hui-chi
(Kyōzan
Ejaku)
807–883
Hsiang-yen
Chih-hsien
(Kyōgen
Chikan)
d. 898
Lin-chi
I-hsüan
(Rinzai
Gigen)
d. 866
(See p. 450)
Mu-chou
Tao-ming
(Bokushū
Dōmei)
ca. 780–877
Ch'en Ts'ao
(Chin Sō)
9th c.
Nan-t'a
Kuang-jun
(Nantō
Kōyū)
ca. 9th c.
Hsi-ta
Kuang-mu
(Seitō
Kōboku)
ca. 9th c.
Pa-chiao
Hui-ch'ing
(Bashō
Eshō)
Tzu-fu
Ju-pao
(Shifuku
Nyohō)
Hsing-yang
Ch'ing-jang
(Kōyō Seijō)
IGYŌ SCHOOL

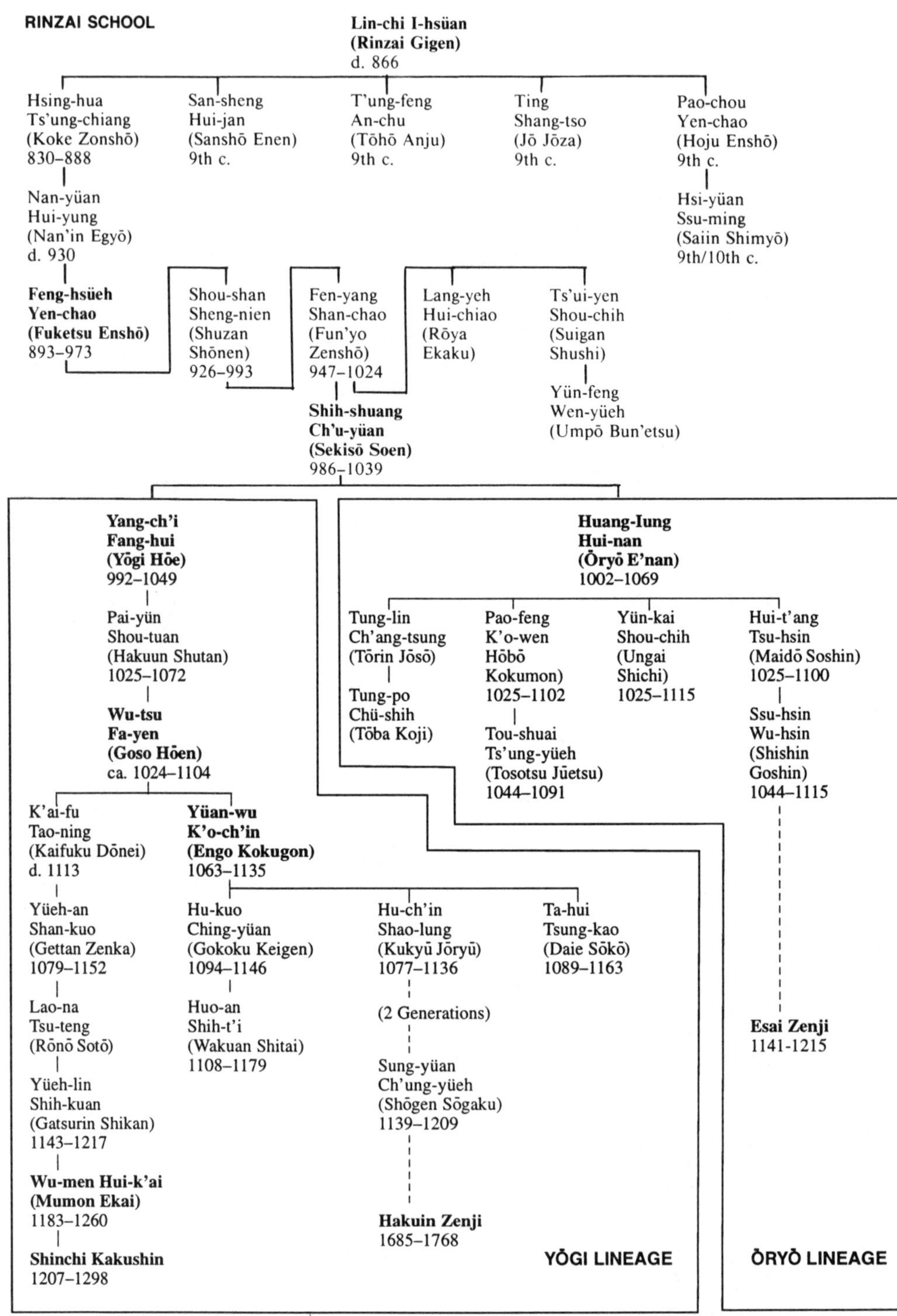
RINZAI SCHOOL
Lin-chi I-hsüan (Rinzai Gigen) d. 866
Hsing-hua Ts'ung-chiang (Koke Zonshō) 830–888
San-sheng Hui-jan (Sanshō Enen) 9th c.
T'ung-feng An-chu (Tōhō Anju) 9th c.
Ting Shang-tso (Jō Jōza) 9th c.
Pao-chou Yen-chao (Hoju Enshō) 9th c.
Nan-yüan Hui-yung (Nan'in Egyō) d. 930
Hsi-yüan Ssu-ming (Saiin Shimyō) 9th/10th c.
Feng-hsüeh Yen-chao (Fuketsu Enshō) 893–973
Shou-shan Sheng-nien (Shuzan Shōnen) 926–993
Fen-yang Shan-chao (Fun'yo Zenshō) 947–1024
Lang-yeh Hui-chiao (Rōya Ekaku)
Ts'ui-yen Shou-chih (Suigan Shushi)
Yün-feng Wen-yüeh (Umpō Bun'etsu)
Shih-shuang Ch'u-yüan (Sekisō Soen) 986–1039
Yang-ch'i Fang-hui (Yōgi Hōe) 992–1049
Pai-yün Shou-tuan (Hakuun Shutan) 1025–1072
Wu-tsu Fa-yen (Goso Hōen) ca. 1024–1104
K'ai-fu Tao-ning (Kaifuku Dōnei) d. 1113
Yüeh-an Shan-kuo (Gettan Zenka) 1079–1152
Lao-na Tsu-teng (Rōnō Sotō)
Yüeh-lin Shih-kuan (Gatsurin Shikan) 1143–1217
Wu-men Hui-k'ai (Mumon Ekai) 1183–1260
Shinchi Kakushin 1207–1298
Yüan-wu K'o-ch'in (Engo Kokugon) 1063–1135
Hu-kuo Ching-yüan (Gokoku Keigen) 1094–1146
Huo-an Shih-t'i (Wakuan Shitai) 1108–1179
Hu-ch'in Shao-lung (Kukyū Jōryū) 1077–1136
(2 Generations)
Sung-yüan Ch'ung-yüeh (Shōgen Sōgaku) 1139–1209
Hakuin Zenji 1685–1768
Ta-hui Tsung-kao (Daie Sōkō) 1089–1163
YŌGI LINEAGE
Huang-lung Hui-nan (Ōryō E'nan) 1002–1069
Tung-lin Ch'ang-tsung (Tōrin Jōsō)
Tung-po Chü-shih (Tōba Koji)
Pao-feng K'o-wen Hōbō Kokumon) 1025–1102
Tou-shuai Ts'ung-yüeh (Tosotsu Jūetsu) 1044–1091
Yün-kai Shou-chih (Ungai Shichi) 1025–1115
Hui-t'ang Tsu-hsin (Maidō Soshin) 1025–1100
Ssu-hsin Wu-hsin (Shishin Goshin) 1044–1115
Esai Zenji 1141-1215
ŌRYŌ LINEAGE

Bibliography

Buddhism *Primary Sources*

Abhidhamma Pitaka. See Rhys-Davids 1974.

Abhidharmakosha. See Lamotte 1976*a*; Vallée-Poussin 1923–1926.

Akshayamati Pariprichchā. See Chang 1983.

Anguttara Nikāya. See Woodward 1932–1936.

Ashokadatta Vyākarana. See Chang 1983.

Ashtasāhasrikā Prajñāpāramitā Sūtra. See Conze 1958*a*, 1973*b*.

Ashtashataka Prajñāpāramitā Sūtra. See Conze 1955.

Ashvaghosha. *See* Suzuki 1900; Weller 1926, 1928.

Asmussen, Jes Peter (trans.). 1961. *The Khotanese Bhadracaryādeśanā.* Copenhagen.

Atīsha. *See* Sherburne 1983.

Aung, Shwe Zan, and Rhys-Davids, Caroline (trans.). 1915. *Points of Controversy,* Pali Text Society Translation Series 5. Oxford.

Avatamsaka Sūtra. See Buddhāvatamsaka Sūtra.

Babbitt, Irving. 1936. *The Dhammapada.* New York & London.

Batchelor, Stephen, and Sherpa Tulku (trans.). 1979. *A Guide to the Bodhisattva's Way of Life.* Dharamsala, India.

Bays, Gwendolyn. 1983. *The Voice of Buddha* (2 vols.). Boulder, Colo.

Beyer, Stephan. 1974. *The Buddhist Experience.* Encino, Calif.

Blofeld, John (trans.). 1947. *The Sutra of Forty-two Sections.* London.

Bodhi, Bhikkhu. 1978. *The Discourse on the All-Embracing Net of Views: The Brahmajāla Sutta and Its Commentaries.* Kandy, Sri Lanka.

Brahmajāla Sūtra. See Bodhi 1978, Weller 1971.

Buddhavamsa. See Horner 1974–1975.

Buddhāvatamsaka Sūtra. See Asmussen 1961, Chang 1971, Hurvitz 1969.

Burlingame, Eugene Watson. 1921. *The Dhammapada.* Cambridge, Mass.

Chalmers, Sir Robert (trans.). 1926–1927. *Further Dialogues of the Buddha* (2 vols.). London.

Chan, Wing-tsit (trans.). 1963. Treatise in Thirty Verses on Consciousness-Only, translated in "Buddhist Idealism: Hsuan-tsang of the Consciousness-Only School." In Wing-tsit Chan (ed.), *A Source Book of Chinese Philosophy,* chap. 23. Princeton, N.J.

Chandragarbha Prajñāpāramitā Sūtra. See Conze 1973*b*.

Chandragomin. *See* Tatz 1985.

Chandrakīrti. *See* Sprung 1979.

Chang, Garma C. C. (trans.). 1971. *The Buddhist Teaching of Totality.* London.

______. 1977. *The Hundred Thousand Songs of Milarepa* (2 vols.). Boulder, Colo.

______ (ed.). 1983. *A Treasury of Mahayana Sutras.* Philadelphia.

Chariyāpitaka. See Horner 1974–1975.

Chihman, Upāsikā (trans.). 1936. *The Two Buddhist Books of Mahayana.* Hong Kong.

Conze, Edward (trans.). 1955. *Prajñāpāramitās: Selected Sayings from the Perfection of Wisdom.* London.

______. 1958*a*. *Aṣṭasāhasrikā Prajñāpāramitā.* Calcutta.

______. 1958*b*. *Buddhist Wisdom Books.* London.

______. 1961–1964. *Pañcavimśati-Sāhasrika: The Large Sutra on Perfect Wisdom* (2 vols.). London.

______. 1968. *Buddhist Scriptures.* Baltimore, Md.

______. 1973*a*. *The Perfection of Wisdom in Eight Thousand Lines.* Berkeley, Calif.

______. 1973*b*. *The Short Prajñāpāramitā Texts.* London.

Cowell, Edward B. (trans.). 1895–1907. *The Jātaka* (6 vols.). Cambridge.

Dahlke, Paul (trans.). 1919–1923. *Suttapitaka: Das Buch der buddhistischen Urschriften* (3 vols.). Berlin.

Dhammapada. See Babbitt 1936, Burlingame 1921, Müller 1881, Radhakrishnan 1966, Silacara 1915, Sparham 1983, Thera 1954, Wagiswara & Saunders 1912, Woodward 1921.

Dhammasangani. See Rhys-Davids 1974.

Dharmakīrti. *See* Stcherbatsky 1962.

Dhvajāgra Mahāsūtra. See Waldschmidt 1959.

Diamond Sūtra. See Vajrachchedikā Prajñāpāramitā Sūtra.

Dīgha Nikāya. See Rhys-Davids & Rhys-Davids 1977, Edmunds 1899–1903.

Dīpamkarashrījñāna. See Eimer 1978.

Dowman, Keith (trans.). 1984. *Sky Dancer: The Secret Life and Songs of the Lady Yeshe Tsogyel.* London.

Dvāchatvārimshat Khanda Sūtra. See Blofeld 1947, Hackman 1927, Hsüan Hua 1977, Soyen Shaku & Suzuki 1906.

Edmunds, Albert J. (trans.). 1899–1903. *A Dialogue on Former Existence and on the Marvellous Birth and Career of the Buddhas between Gotamo and His Monks.* Philadelphia.

Eimer, Helmut (trans.). 1978. "Bodhipathapradīpa." *Asiat. Forschungen* 59.

Ensink, Jacob (trans.). 1952. *The Question of Rāstrapāla.* Zwolle, Netherlands

Evans-Wentz, W. Y. (ed.). 1928. *Tibet's Great Yogi Milarepa.* London.

———. 1960. *The Tibetan Book of the Dead.* New York.

Fausböll, V. (trans.). 1924. *The Sutta-Nipāta.* Oxford. (Delhi, 1965)

Frauwallner, Erich (trans.). 1969. *Philosophie des Buddhismus.* Berlin.

Fremantle, Francesca, and Chögyam Trungpa (trans.). 1987. *The Tibetan Book of the Dead: The Great Liberation through Hearing in the Bardo.* Boston & London.

Gampopa. *See* Guenther 1986.

Gangottarā Pariprichchā. See Chang 1983.

Geham, H. S. (trans.). 1942. *Petavatthu: Stories of the Departed.* London.

Geiger, Wilhelm (trans.). 1925, 1930. *Samyutta-Nikaya: Die in Gruppen geordnete Sammlung* (2 vols.). Munich.

Goddard, Dwight. 1931. *The Buddha's Golden Path.* London.

Guenther, Herbert V. (trans.). 1963. *The Life and Teaching of Naropa.* London.

———. 1969. *The Royal Song of Saraha: A Study in the History of Buddhist Thought.* London.

———. 1975–1976. *Kindly Bent to Ease Us: A Translation of Longchenpa's "Trilogy of Finding Comfort and Ease."* 3 vols. Emeryville, Calif.

———. 1986. *The Jewel Ornament of Liberation* by sGam.po.pa. Boston & London.

——— and Kawamura, Leslie (trans.). 1975. *Mind in Buddhist Psychology.* Emeryville, Calif.

Hackman, H. F. L. (trans.). 1927. "Dvāchatvārimshat-Khanda-Sūtra." *Acta Orientalia* 5.

Hare, E. M. (trans.). 1944. *Woven Cadences of Early Buddhists.* London; editions 1945, 1947.

Heart Sutra. See Mahāprajñāpāramitā Hridaya Sūtra.

Hopkins, Jeffrey, and Lati Rimpoche (Rinbochay/Rinpochay) (trans.). 1975*a*. *The Buddhism of Tibet and the Key to the Middle Way by Tenzin Gyatso.* London.

———. 1975 *b*. *The Precious Garland and the Song of the Four Mindfulnesses by Nāgārjuna and the Seventh Dalai Lama.* London.

———. 1977. *Tantra in Tibet: The Great Exposition of Secret Mantra.* London & Boston.

———. 1980. *Compassion in Tibetan Buddhism by Tsong-ka-pa.* London.

Horner, I. B. (trans.). 1954–1959. *The Collection of the Middle Length Sayings (Majjhima-Nikāya),* Pali Text Society Translation Series 29, 30, 31 (3 vols.). London.

———. 1974. *A General Explanation of the Vajra Prajñā Pāramitā Sūtra.* London.

———. 1974–1975. *Minor Anthologies of the Pali Canon* (Sacred Books of the Buddhists, pts. 3 and 4). London.

Hsüan Hua (trans.). 1974. *The Wonderful Dharma Flower Sutra.* San Francisco.

———. 1977. *General Explanation of the Buddha Speaks: Sutra in Forty-Two Sections.* San Francisco.

Hurvitz, Leon N. (trans.). 1969. "The Vow to Live the Life of Samantabhadra." In W. T. DeBary (ed.), *The Buddhist Tradition.* New York.

———. 1976. *Scripture of the Lotus Blossom of the Fine Dharma.* New York.

———. 1977. "Mahāprajñāpāramitā-Hridaya-Sūtra." In Lewis R. Lancaster (ed.), *Prajnaparamita and Related Systems.* Berkeley, Calif.

Huth, Georg (trans.). 1891. *Prātimoksha-Sūtra: Die tibetische Version der Naihsargika-prāya citikadharmas.* Strassburg.

Inada, Kenneth K. (trans.). 1970. *Nāgārjuna: A Translation of His Mūlamadhyamakakārika.* Tokyo.

Itivuttaka. See Moore 1908.

Jātaka. See Cowell 1895–1907.

Kalzang, Thubten, et al. (trans.). 1973. *Three Discourses of the Buddha.* Patna, India.

Kāshyapa Parivarta. See Weller 1962–1970.

Kathavatthu. See Aung & Rhys-Davids 1915.

Katō, Bunnō; Tamura, Yoshirō; & Mīyasaka, Kōjirō (trans.). 1975. *The Threefold Lotus Sutra.* New York.

Kaushika Prajñāpāramitā Sūtra. See Conze 1955.

Kawamura, Leslie (trans.). 1975. *Golden Zephyr: The Garland of White Flowers. A Commentary on Nāgārjuna's "A Letter to a Friend."* Emeryville, Calif.

Khuddakapātha. See Seidenstücker 1910.

Lalitavistara. See Bays 1983.

Lamotte, Étienne (trans.). 1976*a*. *Abhidharmakosha.* Löwen.

———. 1976*b*. *The Teaching of Vimalakīrti.* London.

Lankāvatāra Sūtra. See Suzuki 1932.

Law, Bimala Churn (trans.). 1924. *Designation of Human Types,* Pali Text Society Translation Series 12. Oxford.

Lēvi, Sylvain (trans.). 1932. *Mahākarmavibhanga.* Paris.

Lhalungpa, Lobsang P. 1984. *The Life of Milarepa.* Boston & London.

Longchenpa. *See* Guenther 1975–1976.

Lotus Sutra. See *Saddharmapundarīka Sūtra.*

Luk, Charles (Lu K'uan Yü) (trans.). 1966. *The Śūrangama Sūtra.* London.

———. 1972. *The Vimalakīrti Nirdeśa Sūtra.* Berkeley, Calif.

Mahākarmavibhanga. See Lévi 1932.

Mahāparinirvāna Sūtra. See Yamamoto 1973–1975.

Mahāprajñāpāramitā Hridaya Sūtra. See Conze 1958*b*, Hurvitz 1977, Rabten 1983, Thomas 1952, Wayman 1977.

Majjhima Nikāya. See Chalmers 1926–1927, Horner 1954–1959.

Marpa. *See* Nalanda 1986.

Matics, Marion L. (trans.). 1970. *Entering the Path of Enlightenment.* New York.

Milarepa. *See* Chang 1977, Evans-Wentz 1928, Lhalungpa 1984.

Milindapañhā. See Rhys-Davids 1963.

Moore, Justin Hartley (trans.). 1908. *Sayings of the Buddha, The Iti-Vuttaka.* New York; 2d ed. 1934.

Müller, F. Max. 1881. *The Dhammapada.* Oxford. Reprint Delhi 1965.

Muralt, Raoul V. (ed.). 1973. *Meditations-Sūtra des Mahāyāna-Buddhismus* (2 vols.). Obernhain.

Murano, Senchū (trans.). 1974. *The Lotus Sutra.* Tokyo.

Nāgārjuna. *See* Hopkins & Lati Rimpoche 1975*b*, Inada 1970, Kawamura 1975, Streng 1967.

Nalanda Translation Committee (trans.). 1986. *The Life of Marpa the Translator.* Boston & London.

Ñānamoli, Bhikkhu (trans.). 1962. *The Guide,* Pali Text Society Translation Series 33. London.

Nārada, U. (trans.). 1962*a*. *Discourse on Elements,* Pali Text Society Translation Series 34. London.

______. 1962*b*. *Pitaka Disclosure,* Pali Text Society Translation Series 35. London.

______. 1969. *Conditional Relations,* Pali Text Society Translation Series 37, 42. London.

Nāropa. *See* Guenther 1963.

Nettipakarana. See Ñānamoli 1962.

Neumann, Karl Eugen (trans.). 1956. *Die Reden Gotamo Buddhos.* Vol. 1. *Mittlere Sammlung.* Zurich.

______. 1957*a*. *Die Reden Gotamo Buddhos.* Vol. 2. *Längere Sammlung.* Zurich.

______. 1957*b*. *Die Reden Gotamo Buddhos.* Vol. 3. *Sammlung der Bruchstücke. Die Lieder der Mönche und Nonnen: Der Wahrheitspfad.* Zurich.

Nyanamoli, Bhikku, trans. 1976. *The Path of Purification (Visuddhimagga)* by Bhadantacariya Buddhaghosa. 2 vols. Berkeley.

Nyanatiloka, Bhikkhu (trans.). 1921. *Das Wort des Buddha.* Munich.

______. 1952. *Visuddhi-Magga.* Constance.

Oldenberg, Hermann (trans.). 1922. *Reden des Buddha.* Munich.

Pañchashatikā Prajñāpāramitā Sūtra. See Conze 1973*b*.

Pañchavimshatisāhasrikā Prajñāpāramitā Sūtra. See Conze 1961–1964.

Patthāna. See Nārada 1969.

Paul, Diana (ed.). 1985. *Women in Buddhism.* Berkeley, Calif.

Petakopadesa. See Ñānamoli 1962.

Petavatthu. See Geham 1942, Horner 1974–1975, Stede 1914.

Prajñāpāramitā Pañchashatikā Sūtra. See Conze 1973*b*.

Prajñāpāramitā Sūryagarbha Sūtra. See Conze 1973*b*.

Prajñāpāramitā Vajraketu Sūtra. See Conze 1973*b*.

Prajñāpāramitā Vajrapāni Sūtra. See Conze 1973*b*.

Prātimoksha Sūtra. See Huth 1891, Prebish 1975.

Pratītyasamutpādādivibhanga Nirdesha Sūtra. See Frauwallner 1969.

Prebish, Charles S. 1975. *Buddhist Monastic Discipline: The Sanskrit Prātimokṣa Sūtras of the Mahāsaṃghikas and Mūlasarvāstivādins.* University Park (Pa.) & London.

Price, A. F. (trans.). 1947. *The Jewel of Transcendental Wisdom.* London.

______ and Wong Mou-lam. 1985. *The Diamond Sutra and the Sutra of Hui Neng.* Boston.

Puggalapannatti. See Law 1924.

Rabten, Geshe. 1983. *Echoes of Voidness.* Annapolis, Md.

Radhakrishnan, S. 1966. *The Dhammapada.* New York.

Rājadesha Sūtra. See Kalzang 1973.

Rāshtrapāla Paripichchā. See Ensink 1952.

Ratnarāshi Nāma Mahāyānasūtra. See Chang 1983.

Rhys-Davids, Caroline (trans.). 1974. *Abhidamma Pitaka: A Buddhist Manual of Psychological Ethics,* Pali Text Society Translation Series 41. London.

Rhys-Davids, T. W. (trans.). 1963. *The Questions of King Milinda.* New York.

______ and Rhys-Davids, C. A. F. (trans.). 1977. *Dialogues of the Buddha* (3 vols.). London & Boston. Orig. pub. London 1899–1921.

Robinson, James B. (trans.). 1979. *Buddha's Lions: The Lives of the Eighty-Four Siddhas.* Berkeley, Calif.

Rockhill, William W. (trans.). 1884. *The Life of the Buddha.* London.

Saddharmapundarīka Sūtra. See Hurvitz 1976; Katō et al. 1975; Murano 1974.

Samantabhadra Prajñāpāramitā Sūtra. See Conze 1973*b*.

Samyutta Nikāya. See Geiger 1925–1930.

Saraha. *See* Guenther 1969.

sGam.po.pa. *See* Guenther 1986.

Shālistambha Sūtra. See Frauwallner 1969.

Shāntideva. *See* Batchelor & Sherpa Tulku 1979, Matics 1970.

Sherburne, Richard (trans.). 1983. *A Lamp for the Path and Commentary by Atīśa.* London.

Shīlasamyukta Sūtra. See Kalzang 1973.

Shrīmālādevī Sūtra. See Chang 1983, Wayman 1973.

Shūrangama Sūtra. See Luk 1966.

Silacara, Bhikku. 1915. *The Dhammapada, or Way of Truth.* London.

Sokei-an (trans.). 1945. *The Prajñā-Pāramitā-Sūtra.* New York.

Soyen Shaku, and Suzuki, D. T. (trans.). 1906. *Sermons of a Buddhist Abbot.* Chicago.

Sparham, Gareth (trans.). 1983. *The Tibetan Dhammapada.* New Delhi.

Sprung, Mervyn (trans.). 1979. *Lucid Exposition of the Middle Way: The Essential Chapters from the Prasannapadā of Candrakīrti.* London.

Stcherbatsky, E. T. 1962. *Buddhist Logic.* New York.

Stede, Wilhelm (trans.). 1914. *Die Gespenstergeschichten des Peta Vatthu.* Leipzig.

Steinkellner, Ernst (trans.). 1973. "Buddha-Parinirvana-Stotra." *Wiener Zeitschrift für der Kunde des Morgenlandes,* 17.

Streng, Frederick J. 1967. *Emptiness: A Study in Religious Meaning.* Nashville, N.Y.

Strong, D. M. (trans.). 1902. *The Udāna.* London.

Sumatidārikā Pariprichchā. See Paul 1985.

Surata Pariprichchā. See Chang 1983.

Suttanipāta. See Fausböll 1924, Hare 1944.

Suzuki, Daisetsu Teitaro (trans.). 1900. *Acvaghosha's Discourse on the Awakening of Faith in the Mahāyāna.* Chicago.

———. 1932. *The Lankāvatāra-Sūtra.* London.

Svalpākasharā Prajñāpāramitā Sūtra. See Conze 1955.

Tarthang Tulku (trans.). 1983. *Mother of Knowledge: The Enlightenment of Ye-shes mTsho-rgyal.* Berkeley, Calif.

Tatz, Mark (trans.). 1985. *Candragomin. Difficult Beginnings: Three Works on the Bodhisattva Path.* Boston.

Thera, Narada. 1954. *The Dhammapada.* London.

Theragāthā and *Therīgāthā. See* Neumann 1957*b*.

Thittila, P. (trans.). 1969. *The Book of Analysis,* Pali Text Society Translation Series 39. London.

Thomas, E. J. (trans.). 1952. *Perfection of Wisdom.* London.

Thurman, Robert A. F. (trans.). 1976. *The Holy Teaching of Vimalakīrti: A Mahāyāna Scripture.* University Park, Pa., & London.

Trikāya Sūtra. See Rockhill 1884.

Tsongkhapa. *See* Hopkins and Rimpoche 1977, 1980; Wayman 1978.

Udāna. See Strong 1902.

Udānavarga. See Willemen 1978.

Udayanavatsarāja Pariprichchā. See Paul 1985.

Vajrachchedikā Prajñāpāramitā Sūtra. See Conze 1958*b*, Hsüan Hua 1974, Price 1947, Price & Wong 1985, Sokei-an 1945.

Vallée-Poussin, Louis de la (trans.). 1923–1926. *L'Abhidharmakośa de Vasubandhu.* Paris.

Vasubandhu. *See* Chan 1957, Frauwallner 1969, Vallée-Poussin 1923–1926.

Vibhanga. See Thittila 1969.

Vimalakīrtinirdesha Sūtra. See Lamotte 1976*b*, Luk 1972, Thurman 1976.

Vimanavatthu. See Horner 1974.

Visuddhi Magga. See Nyanatiloka 1952.

Wagiswara, W. D. C., and Saunders, K. J. 1912. *The Buddha's "Way of Virtue."* New York. (London, 1920)

Waldschmidt, Ernst (trans.). 1959. "Dhvajāgra-Mahāsūtra." *Nachr. d. Akad. d. Wiss.* Göttingen.

Walleser, Max (trans.). 1911. *Die mittlere Lehre des Nagarjuna.* Heidelberg.

Wangyal, Geshe (trans.). 1982. *The Prince Who Became a Cuckoo.* New York.

Wayman, Alex (trans.). 1973. *The Lion's Roar of Queen Srimala.* New York.

———. 1977. "Mahāprajñāpāramitā-Hridaya-Sūtra." In *Prajñāpāramitā and Related Systems,* ed. Lewis R. Lancaster. Berkeley, Calif.

———. 1978. *Calming the Mind and Discerning the Real: Buddhist Meditation and the Middle View.* New York.

Weller, Friedrich (trans.). 1926–1928. *Das Leben des Buddha von Aśvaghoṣa* (2 vols.). Leipzig.

———. 1962–1970. *Kāshyapa-Parivarta* (2 vols.). Berlin.

———. 1971. "Das Brahmajālasūtra des chinesischen Dīrghagama." *Asiatischen Studien.* 25.

Willemen, Charles (trans.). 1978. *The Chinese Udānavarga,* Mélanges Chinoise et Bouddhique, 19.

Woodward, Frank Lee (trans.). 1921. *The Buddha's Path of Virtue.* Madras & London.

———. 1932–1936. *The Book of the Gradual Sayings (Anguttara-nikāya) or More-Numbered Sutras* (5 vols.). London.

Yamamoto, Kōshō (trans.). 1973–1975. *The Mahāyāna Mahāparinirvāna-Sūtra* (2 vols.). Karinbunko, Japan.

Yeshe Tsogyel (Ye-shes mTsho-rgyal). *See* Dowman 1984; Guenther & Kawamura 1975; Tarthang Tulku 1983.

Buddhism *Secondary Sources*

Anderson, Walt. 1983. *Der tibetische Buddhismus als Religion und Psychologie.* Bern.

Arnold, Paul. 1971. *Unter tibetischen Lamas: Chronik einer geistigen Erfahrung.* Berlin.

Bacot, Jacques. 1947. *Le Bouddha.* Paris.

Bareau, André. 1964. *Die Religionen Indiens,* vol. 3. Stuttgart.

Bechert, Heinz, and Gombrich, Richard. 1984. *the World of Buddhism.* London.

Beckh, Hermann. 1980. *Buddha und seine Lehre.* Stuttgart.

Bernbaum, Edwin. 1980. *The Way to Shambhala.* Garden City, N.Y.

Beyer, Stephan. 1973. *The Cult of Tara: Magic and Ritual in Tibet.* Berkeley, Calif.

Birnbaum, Raoul. 1979. *The Healing Buddha.* Boulder, Colo.

Blofeld, John. 1959. *Wheel of Life.* London. (Boston, 1988)

______. 1970. *The Way of Power.* London.

______. 1977. *Mantras: Sacred Words of Power.* London.

______. 1980. *Gateway to Wisdom: Taoist and Buddhist Contemplative and Healing Yoga Adapted for Western Students of the Way.* London & Boston.

______. 1983. *Selbstheilung durch die Kraft der Stille.* Bern.

Burang, Theodor. 1974. *Tibetische Heilkunde.* Zurich.

Chan, Wing-tsit. 1953. *Religious Trends in Modern China.* New York.

Chang, Garma C. C. 1979. *Mahamudra-Fibel.* Vienna.

Ch'en, Kenneth S. C. 1964. *Buddhism in China.* Princeton, N.J.

Clifford, Terry. 1986. *Tibetan Buddhist Medicine and Psychiatry: The Diamond Healing.* York Beach, Me.

Conze, Edward. 1951. *Buddhism: Its Essence and Development.* New York & Oxford.

______. 1962. *Buddhist Thought in India.* London.

Dalai Lama (Tenzin Gyatso). 1968. *The Opening of the Wisdom-Eye.* Bangkok.

Dargyay, Eva K., and Geshe Lobsang (eds.). 1980. *Das tibetische Buch der Toten.* Bern.

David-Neel, Alexandra. 1932. *Magic and Mystery in Tibet.* New York. (New Hyde Park, N.Y., 1965)

______. 1934. *Meister und Schüler: Die Geheimnisse der lamaistischen Weihen aufgrund eigener Erfahrung.* Leipzig.

______. 1937. *Vom Leiden zur Erlösung: Sinn und Lehre des Buddhismus.* Leipzig.

______. 1939. *Buddhism: Its Doctrines and Its Methods.* London.

______. 1959. *Initiations and Initiates in Tibet.* New York.

______. 1962. *Immortalité et réincarnation.* Paris.

______. 1967. *The Secret Oral Teachings in Tibetan Buddhist Sects.* San Francisco.

______. 1980. *Ralopa: Der Meister geheimer Riten.* Bern.

De Bary, William T. (ed.) 1969. *The Buddhist Tradition in India, China and Japan.* New York.

Dowman, Keith, 1986. *The Divine Madman.* London.

Dumoulin, Heinrich. 1966. *Östliche Meditation und christliche Mystik.* Freiburg.

______ (ed.). 1970. *Buddhismus der Gegenwart.* Freiburg.

______. 1982. *Begegnung mit dem Buddhismus.* Freiburg.

Eimer, Helmut. 1976. *Skizzen des Erlösungswegs in buddhistischen Begriffsreihen.* Bonn.

Evans-Wentz, W. Y. (ed.). 1935. *Tibetan Yoga and Secret Doctrines.* London.

______. 1954. *The Tibetan Book of the Great Liberation.* London. (New York, 1968)

Finckh, Elisabeth. 1975. *Grundlagen tibetischer Heilkunde.* Ülzen.

Frauwallner, Erich. 1953–1956. *Geschichte der indischen Philosophie* (2 vols.). Salzburg.

______. 1969. *Die Philosophie des Buddhismus.* Berlin.

Glasenapp, Helmuth von. 1940. *Entwicklungsstufen des indischen Denkens.* Halle.

______. 1946. *Die Weisheit des Buddha.* Baden-Baden.

______. 1956. *Der Pfad zur Erleuchtung.* Düsseldorf.

Govinda, Anagarika Brahmacari. 1937. *The Psychological Attitude of Early Buddhist Philosophy and Its Systematic Representation According to Abhidhamma Tradition.* Allahabad. (London, 1961)

______. 1959. *Foundations of Tibetan Mysticism, According to the Esoteric Teachings of the Great Mantra, Om Mani Padme Hūm.* London. (New York, 1960)

______. 1966. *The Way of the White Clouds: A Buddhist Pilgrim in Tibet.* London. (Boston, 1988)

______. 1976. *Psycho-Cosmic Symbolism of the Buddhist Stupa.* Berkeley, Calif.

______. 1977. *Schöpferische Meditation und multidimensionales Bewusstsein.* Freiburg.

______. 1980. *Mandala: Der heilige Kreis.* Zurich.

______. 1983. *Buddhistischen Reflexionen.* Bern.

Greschat, Hans Jürgen. 1980. *Die Religion der Buddhisten.* Stuttgart.

Grönbold, Günter. 1985. *Der buddhistische Kanon: Eine Bibliographie.* Wiesbaden.

Guenther, Herbert V. 1969. *Yuganaddha: The Tantric View of Life* (rev. ed.). Banaras. 1st ed. 1952.

______. 1976. *Philosophy and Psychology in the Abhidharma.* Berkeley, Calif.

———. 1984. *Matrix of Mystery: Scientific and Humanistic Aspects of rDzogs-chen Thought.* Boulder & London.

Guenther, Herbert V., and Trungpa, Chögyam. 1988. *The Dawn of Tantra.* Boston.

Gyatso, Geshe Kelsang. 1980. *Meaningful to Behold: View, Meditation and Action in Mahayana Buddhism, An Oral Commentary to Shantideva's Bodhisattvacharyavatara.* Ulverston, Cumbria.

———. 1982. *Clear Light of Bliss: Mahamudra in Vajrayana Buddhism.* London.

———. 1984. *Buddhism in the Tibetan Tradition: A Guide.* London.

Hedinger, Jürg. 1985. *Aspekte der Schulung in der Laufbahn eines Bodhisattva.* Wiesbaden.

Humphreys, Christmas. 1959. *Karma and Rebirth.* London.

Ikeda, Daisaku, 1976. *The Living Buddha.* New York.

Jamgon Kongtrul. 1986. *The Torch of Certainty.* Trans. Judith Hanson. Boston & London.

Jaspers, Karl. 1978. *Lao-tse, Nagarjuna: Zwei asiatische Metaphysiker.* Munich.

Karwath, Walter. 1971. *Buddhismus für das Abendland.* Vienna.

Katz, Nathan (ed.). 1983. *Buddhist and Western Psychology.* Boulder, Colo.

Khetsun Sangpo Rinbochay. 1982. *Tantric Practice in Nying-Ma.* London.

Kornfield, Jack. 1977. *Living Buddhist Masters.* Santa Cruz.

Lati Rimpoche (Rinbochay). 1980. *Mind in Tibetan Buddhism.* London.

———. 1983. *Meditative States in Tibetan Buddhism: Concentrations and Formless Absorptions.* London.

Lati Rimpoche, and Hopkins, Jeffrey. 1979. *Death, Intermediate State, and Rebirth in Tibetan Buddhism.* London.

Lauf, Detlev I. 1979. *Geheimlehren tibetische Totenbücher.* Freiburg.

Lehmann, Johannes. 1980. *Buddha: Leben, Lehre, Wirkung.* Gütersloh.

Lhündup Söpa, Geshe. 1976. *Practice and Theory of Tibetan Buddhism,* trans. Jeffrey Hopkins. London.

Lommel, Andreas. 1984. *Kunst des Buddhismus.* Freiburg.

Losang, Rato Khyongla Nawang. 1977. *My Life and Lives: The Story of a Tibetan Incarnation.* New York.

Lu K'uan Yü (Charles Luk). 1969. *Secrets of Chinese Meditation.* London.

Malasekera, G. P. (ed.). 1961 ff. *Encyclopedia of Buddhism.* Colombo.

Meier, Erhard. 1984. *Kleine Einführung in den Buddhismus.* Freiburg.

Mi-pham-rgyal-mtsho, 'Jam-mgon 'Ju. 1973. *Calm and Clear,* trans. Tarthang Tulku. Emeryville, Calif.

Murti, Tirupattur R. V. 1980. *The Central Philosophy of Buddhism.* London.

Nyanaponika. 1984. *Geistestraining durch Achtsamkeit: Die buddhistische Satipatthana-Methode.* Constance.

Nyanatiloka, Bhikkhu. 1956. *Der Weg zur Erlösung.* Constance.

———. 1972. *Buddhist Dictionary: A Manual of Buddhist Terms and Doctrines.* Colombo.

Nydahl, Ole (ed.). 1979. *Der Diamantweg.* Vienna.

Oldenberg, Hermann. 1971. *Buddha: His Life, His Doctrine, His Order.* Delhi.

Pallis, Marco. 1980. *A Buddhist Spectrum.* London.

Pálos, Stephan. 1968. *Lebensrad und Bettlerschale.* Munich.

Percheron, Maurice. 1975. *Buddha, in Selbstzeugnissen und Bilddokumenten.* Reinbek.

Rabten, Geshe. 1979. *Mahamudra, der Weg zur Erkenntnis der Wirklichkeit.* Zurich.

———. 1980. *The Life and Teaching of Geshe Rabten.* London.

Rahula, Walpola. 1959. *What the Buddha Taught.* New York. (2d ed., 1974)

Rhys-Davids, T. W., and Stede, William. 1979. *The Pali Text Society's Pali-English Dictionary.* London.

Rivière, Jean M. 1985. *Kalachakra: Initiation tantrique du Dalai Lama.* Paris.

Rousselle, Erwin. 1959. *Vom Sinn der buddhistischen Bildwerke in China.* Darmstadt.

Sangharakshita, Bhikshu. 1980. *A Survey of Buddhism.* Boulder, Colo.

Schlingloff, Dieter, 1962–1963. *Die Religion des Buddhismus* (2 vols.). Berlin.

Schluchter, Wolfgang (ed.). 1984. *Max Webers Studie über Hinduismus und Buddhismus.* Frankfurt.

Schumann, Hans Wolfgang. 1974. *Buddhism.* Wheaton, Ill.

Seckel, Dieter. 1980. *Kunst des Buddhismus.* Baden-Baden.

Snellgrove, David. 1980*a*. *A Cultural History of Tibet.* Boulder, Colo.

———. 1980*b*. *The Nine Ways of Bon.* Boulder, Colo.

———. 1981. *Himalayan Pilgrimage: A Study of Tibetan Religion.* Boulder, Colo.

Soni, R. L. 1980. *The Only Way to Deliverance.* Boulder, Colo.

Tarthang Tulku. 1973. *Calm and Clear.* Emeryville, Calif.

———. 1977*a*. *Gesture of Balance: A Guide to Awareness, Selfhealing, and Meditation.* Emeryville, Calif.

———. 1977*b*. *Time, Space and Knowledge: A New Vision of Reality.* Emeryville, Calif.

———. 1979. *Psychische Energie durch inneres Gleichgewicht.* Freiburg.

———. 1980. *Selbstheilung durch Entspannung: Die tibetische Heilkunst des Kum Nye.* Bern.

______. 1985. *Der verborgene Geist der Freiheit.* Basel.

Tatz, Mark, and Kent, Jody. 1977. *Rebirth: The Tibetan Game of Liberation.* Garden City, N.Y.

Trungpa, Chögyam. 1985*a*. *Meditation in Action.* Boston & London.

______. 1985*b*. *Journey without Goal.* Boston & London.

______. 1987*a*. *Cutting through Spiritual Materialism.* Boston & London.

______. 1987*b*. *Glimpses of Abhidharma.* Boston & London.

______. 1987*c*. *Mudra.* Boston & London.

______. 1988. *The Myth of Freedom.* Boston & London.

Tucci, Giuseppe. 1972. *Geheimnis des Mandala.* Weilheim.

______ and Heissig, Walter. 1970. *Die Religionen Tibets und der Mongolei.* Stuttgart.

Waldschmidt, Ernst. 1929. *Die Legende vom Leben des Buddha.* Berlin.

Walleser, Max. 1904. *Die philosophischen Grundlagen des älteren Buddhismus.* Heidelberg.

______. 1904–1927. *Die buddhistische Philosophie in ihrer geschichtlichen Entwicklung* (4 vols.). Heidelberg.

Wangyal, Geshe. 1975. *Tibetische Meditationen.* Zurich.

Welch, Holmes, 1973. *The Practice of Chinese Buddhism.* Cambridge, Mass.

Zago, Marcello, 1984. *Der Buddhismus.* Aschaffenburg.

Zimmer, Heinrich. 1973. *Yoga und Buddhismus.* Frankfurt.

______ (ed.). 1985. *Buddhistische Legenden.* Frankfurt.

Zürcher, Erik. 1972. *The Buddhist Conquest of China* (2 vols.). Leiden.

Hinduism *Primary Sources*

Ashtavakra Gītā. See Shastri 1978.

Ātmabodha. See Leggett 1978, Menon 1964, Nikhilananda 1956.

Barnett, Lionel D. (trans.). 1905. *Bhagavadgita, or The Lord's Song.* London.

Bhagavad Gītā. See Barnett 1905, Bolle 1979, Edgerton 1972, Gotshalk 1985, Hill 1966, Iyer 1985, Lal 1965, Miller 1986, Nikhilananda 1944, Purohit 1977, Radhakrishnan 1974, Ryder 1929, Telang 1882, Zaehner 1966.

Bhakti Sūtras. See Sturdy 1976.

Bhoosnurmath, S. S., and Menezes, L. M. A. (trans.). 1968–1969. *Sūnyasampādane* (vols. 2 and 3). Dharwar, India.

Bloomfield, Maurice (trans.). 1897. *Hymns of the Atharva-Veda,* Sacred Books of the East, vol. 42. Oxford.

Bolle, Kees W. (trans.). 1979. *The Bhagavadgītā: A New Translation.* Berkeley, Calif.

Bose, Abinash Chandra (trans.). 1966. *Hymns from the Vedas.* New York.

Buck, William (trans.). 1973. *The Mahābhārata.* Berkeley, Calif.

______. 1976. *Ramayana: King Rama's Way.* Berkeley, Calif.

Bühler, Georg (trans.). 1969. *The Laws of Manu,* Sacred Books of the East, vol. 25. New York (reprint).

Buitenen, J. A. B. van (trans.). 1973. *The Mahābhārata.* Chicago.

Chandiramani, G. L. (trans.). 1971. *Pantschatantra: Das Fabelbuch des Pandit Wischnu Scharma.* Düsseldorf & Cologne.

Cowell, E. B., and Gough, A. E. (trans.). 1914. *Mādhavāchārya, Sarvadarshana-Samgraha.* London.

Danielson, Henry (trans.). 1980. *The Essence of Supreme Truth: Paramārthasāra.* Leiden.

Dutt, Romesh C. (trans.). 1975. *The Rāmāyana: Epic of Rama, Prince of India.* Bombay.

Dvivedi, M. N. (trans.). 1980. *The Yoga-Sūtras of Patañjali.* Delhi.

Edgerton, Franklin (trans.). 1972. *The Bhagavad Gītā.* Cambridge, Mass.

Feuerstein, Georg (trans.). 1979. *The Yoga-Sūtra of Patañjali.* Folkstone, Eng.

Ghate, V. S. 1926. *The Vedanta Bhardarkar.* Poona.

Goldman, Robert P. (trans.). 1984. *The Rāmāyana of Vālmīki: An Epic of Ancient India.* Princeton.

Gotama. *See* Vidyabhushana 1911–1923.

Gotshalk, Richard (trans.). 1985. *The Bhagavad Gītā.* Delhi.

Graul, Karl (trans.). 1969. *Tamulidische Schriften zur Erläuterung des Vedanta-Systems.* Osnabrück.

Griffith, Ralph T. H. (trans.). 1963. *The Ramayan.* Banaras.

______. 1973. *The Hymns of the Rigveda* (4 vols.). Delhi. (orig. pub. Banaras 1889–1892)

Hill, W. Douglas P. (trans.). 1966. *The Bhagavadgītā.* Madras & New York.

Hohenberger, A. 1960. *Ramanuja: Ein Philosoph indischer Gottesmystik,* Bonner Oriental. Studien No. 10. Wiesbaden.

———. 1964. *Ramanuja's Vedantadipa,* Bonner Orient. Studien No. 14. Wiesbaden.

Hume, R. E. (trans.). 1931. *The Thirteen Principal Upanishads.* Oxford.

Iyer, Raghavan (trans.). 1985. *The Bhagavad Gita, with the Uttara Gita.* London & Santa Barbara.

Jacobi, Hermann (trans.). 1964. *Jaina Sutras* (2 vols.). Delhi. Orig. pub. as vols. 22 and 45 of Sacred Books of the East, Oxford 1884–1895.

Jaimini. *See* Jha 1916, Thadani 1952.

Jha, Ganganatha (trans.). 1916. *Jaimini: Pūrva-Mīmāmsā-Sūtra.* Allahabad.

———. 1984. *The Nyāya-Sūtras of Gautama.* Delhi.

Jnananda Bharathi, Swami (trans.). 1983. *Pañchadasi.* Madras.

Joshi, S. D., and Roodbergen, J. A. F. (trans.). 1980. *Patanjali's Vyakarana-Mahabhasya.* Poona.

Lal, P. (trans.). 1965. *The Bhagavadgita.* Delhi.

———. 1980. *The Mahabharata of Vyasa.* New Delhi.

Leggett, Trevor. 1978. *The Chapter of the Self.*

Mādhava. *See* Jnananda 1983.

Mādhavāchārya. *See* Cowell and Gough 1914.

Mādhavānanda, Svāmi. 1948. *Mīmāmsā Paribhāsā of Kṛṣṇa Yajvan.* Belur Math.

Mahābhārata. See Buck 1973, Buitenen 1973, Lal 1980, Narayan 1978.

Mazumdar, Shudha (trans.). 1974. *Ramayana.* Bombay.

Menon, V. P. N. (trans.). 1964. *Atma Bodha.* Palghat.

Miller, Barbara Stoler (trans.). 1986. *The Bhagavad-Gita: Krishna's Counsel in Time of War.* New York.

Mīmāmsā Sūtra. See Jha 1916, Thadani 1952.

Mitra, Vihârilâla (trans.). 1976–1978. *The Yoga-Vāsishtha-Mahārāmāyana of Vālmīki* (4 vols.). Banaras. Orig. pub. Calcutta 1891–1899.

Mukerji, P. N. (trans.). 1983. *Yoga Philosophy of Patañjali.* Albany, N.Y. 1st ed. Calcutta 1981.

Müller, Max (trans.). 1884. *The Upanishads,* Sacred Books of the East, vols. 5 and 15. Oxford.

———. 1964. *Vedic Hymns* (2 vols.). Delhi; orig. pub. as vols. 32 and 46 of Sacred Books of the East, Oxford 1891–1897.

Nandimath, S. C.; Menezes, L. M. A.; and Hiremath, R. C. (trans.). 1965. *Sūnyasaṃpādane,* vol. 1. Dharwar.

Nārada. *See* Sturdy 1976.

Narasimha Ayyangar, M. B. (trans.). 1979. *Vedāntasāra of Bhagavad Rāmānuja.* Madras.

Narayan, R. K. (trans.). 1978. *The Mahabharata.* New York.

Nikhilananda (trans.). 1944. *The Bhagavad Gita.* New York.

———. 1949. *The Upanishads* (4 vols.). New York.

———. 1956. *Atmabodha.* Frankfurt.

Nyāya Sūtras. See Jha 1984, Vidyabhushana 1911–1923.

O'Flaherty, Wendy Doniger (trans.). 1981. *The Rig Veda: An Anthology.* New York.

———. 1984. *Dreams, Illusion, and Other Realities.* Chicago.

Otto, Rudolf (trans.). 1917. *Siddhānta des Ramanuja.* Jena.

Pañchadashi. See Jnananda 1983.

Pañchatantra. See Chandiramani 1971.

Patañjali. *See* Danielson 1980, Dvivedi 1980, Feuerstein 1979, Joshi & Roodbergen 1980, Mukerji 1983, Prabhavananda & Isherwood 1953, Prasada 1978, Shearer 1982, Taimni 1961, Yardi 1979.

Prabhavananda, Swami, and Isherwood, Christopher (trans.). *Shankara's Crest-Jewel of Discrimination.* 1947. Hollywood, Calif. (3d ed. 1978)

———. 1953. *How to Know God: The Yoga Aphorisms of Patanjali.* New York; 2d ed. 1969.

Prasada, Rama (trans.). 1978. *Patanjali's Yoga Sutras.* New Delhi.

Purohit, Swami (trans.). 1977. *The Bhagavad Gita.* New York.

Radhakrishnan, Sarvepalli (trans.). 1953. *The Principal Upanishads.* London.

———. 1974. *The Bhagavad Gītā.* Bombay.

Raghunathan, N. (trans.). 1981. *Srimad Vālmīki Rāmāyana* (3 vols.). Madras.

Rāmānuja. *See* Hohenberger 1960, 1964; Narasimha Ayyangar 1979; Otto 1917; Sampatkumaran 1969; Thibaut 1962.

Rāmāyana. See Buck 1976, Dutt 1975, Goldman 1984, Griffith 1963, Mazumdar 1974, Raghunathan 1981, Subramaniam 1981.

Rig Veda. See Griffith 1973, Müller 1964, O'Flaherty 1981, Satya Prakash Sarawata & Vidyalankar 1977, Wilson 1977, Zaehner 1966.

Ryder, Arthur W. (trans.). 1929. *The Bhagavad-Gita.* Chicago.

Sampkatkumaran, M. R. (trans.). 1969. *The Gitabhashya of Ramanuja.* Madras.

Sarvadarshana Samgraha. See Cowell & Gough 1914.

Satya Prakash Saraswata, Swami, and Vidyalankar, Satyakam (trans.). 1977. *Ṛgveda Samhitā* (8 vols.). Delhi.

Schang, Doris (trans.). 1980. *Shankara: Bhaja Govindam.* Stühlingen.

Shankara. *See* Prabhavananda & Isherwood 1947, Schang 1980.

Shastri, Hari Prasad (trans.). 1978. *Ashtavakra Gita.* London.

Shastri, V. L. (trans.). 1948. *One Hundred and Ten Upanisads.* Bombay.

Shearer, Aliastair (trans.). 1882. *Effortless Being: The Yoga Sutras of Patanjali.* London.

Shūnyasampādane. See Bhoosnurmath & Menezes 1968–1969, Nandimath et al. 1965.

Siddhānta. See Otto 1917.

Smith, H. Daniel (trans.). 1968. *Selections from Vedic Hymns.* Berkeley.

Sturdy, E. T. (trans.). 1976. *Nārada Sūtra: An Inquiry into Love (Bhakti Jijnāsā).* New Delhi.

Subramaniam, Kamala (trans.). 1981. *Ramayana.* Bombay.

Taimni, I. K. (trans.). 1961. *The Science of Yoga: The Yoga-Sūtras of Patañjali.* Wheaton, Ill.

Telang, Kāshināth Trimbak (trans.). 1882. *The Bhagavadgītā, with the Sanatsugātīya and the Anugītā.* Oxford.

Thadani, N. V. (trans.). 1952. *Mimamsa: The Secret of the Sacred Books of the Hindus.* Delhi.

Thibaut, George (trans.). 1962. *The Vedānta Sūtras* (3 vols.). Delhi; orig. pub. as vols. 34, 38, and 48 of Sacred Books of the East, Oxford 1890–1904.

Upanishads. See Hume 1931, Müller 1884, Nikhilananda 1949, Radhakrishnan 1953, Shastri 1948.

Uttara Gītā. See Iyer 1985.

Vālmīki. *See* Mitra 1976–1978, O'Flaherty 1984, *Rāmāyana.*

Vasu, Shrisha Chandra (trans.). 1981. *Pāninīya.* Allahabad.

Vedāntadipa. See Hohenberger 1964.

Vedānta Sūtras. See Thibaut 1962.

Vedas. See Bloomfield 1897, Bose 1966, Griffity 1963, Müller 1964, Smith 1968.

Vidyabhushana, S. (trans.). 1911–1923. *The Nyāya Sūtras of Gotama.* Allahabad.

Vidyāranya. *See* Jnananda 1983.

Wilson, H. H. (trans.). 1977. *Rig-Veda Samhita: A Collection of Ancient Hindu Hymns of the Rig-Veda* (7 vols.). New Delhi.

Yardi, M. R. (trans.). 1979. *The Yoga of Patañjali.* Poona.

Yoga Vāsishtha. See Mitra 1976–1978, O'Flaherty 1984.

Zaehner, R. C. (trans.). 1966. *Hindu Scriptures.* London & New York. (Rev. ed, 1972)

Hinduism *Secondary Sources*

Abhedananda, Swami. 1943. *How to Be a Yogi.* Calcutta.

______. 1946. *The Sayings of Ramakrishna.* Calcutta.

Abhishiktananda. *See* Le Saux.

Abs, P. Joseph. 1923. *Indiens Religion: Der Sanatana-Dharma.* Bonn.

Agehananda Bharati, Swami. 1965. *The Tantric Tradition.* London. (Rev. ed., New York, 1975)

Allen, Marcus. 1981. *Tantra im Westen.* Dachsberg.

Ānandamayī Ma, Sri. 1982*a. Matri Vani* (2 vols.). Calcutta.

______. 1982*b. Words of Sri Anandamayi Ma.* Calcutta.

Aurobindo, Sri. 1938. *The Message of the Gita.* London.

______. 1949. *The Human Cycle.* Pondicherry.

______. 1950*a. The Ideal of Human Unity.* Pondicherry.

______. 1950*b. Kalidasa.* Pondicherry.

______. 1952*a. Hymns to the Mystic Fire.* Pondicherry.

______. 1952*b. Speeches.* Pondicherry.

______. 1953*a. The Future Poetry.* Pondicherry.

______. 1953*b. The Mind of Light.* New York.

______. 1953*c. Sri Aurobindo on Himself and on The Mother.* Pondicherry.

______. 1954. *Savitri.* Pondicherry.

______. 1955*a. Bases of Yoga.* Pondicherry.

______. 1955*b. The Divine Life.* Pondicherry.

______. 1956*a. On the Veda.* Pondicherry.

______. 1956*b. Vyasa and Valmiki.* Pondicherry.

______. 1957. *More Poems.* Pondicherry.

______. 1957–1958. *Letters on Yoga* (3 vols.). Pondicherry.

______. 1959*a. Essays on the Gita.* Pondicherry.

______. 1959*b. The Foundations of Indian Culture.* Pondicherry.

______. 1959*c. The Hour of God.* Pondicherry.

______. 1959*d. Thoughts and Aphorisms.* Pondicherry.

______. 1961. *Evening Talks with Sri Aurobindo.* Pondicherry.

______. 1963. *The Future Evolution of Man: The Divine Life on Earth.* London.

______. 1970–1973. *Sri Aurobindo* (Works; 30 vols.). Pondicherry.

______. 1971. *The Synthesis of Yoga* (2 vols.). Pondicherry.

______. 1972*a. Light to Superlight.* Calcutta.

______. 1972*b. The Mother.* Pondicherry.

______. 1973. *The Essential Aurobindo.* New York.

______ and The Mother. 1959. *A Practical Guide to Integral Yoga.* Pondicherry.

Avalon, Arthur. *See* Woodroffe.

Besant, Annie. 1954. *Yoga: The Hatha Yoga and the Raja Yoga of India.* Madras.

Bhandarkar, R. G. 1913. *Vaisnavism, Saivism, and Other Minor Religious Systems.* Strassburg.

Bhave, Vinoba. 1960. *Talks on the Gita.* London.

Bishop, Donald H. (ed.). 1975. *Indian Thought.* New Delhi.

Bohm, Werner. 1980. *Die Wurzeln der Kraft: Chakras—Die Kraft der Lotosblumen.* Bern.

Bose, A. C. 1960. *The Call of the Vedas.* Bombay.

Brunton, Paul. 1935*a*. *A Search in Secret India.* New York. (Reprint, 1977, 1981)

______. 1935*b*. *The Secret Path.* New York.

______. 1936. *A Message from Arunachala.* New York.

______. 1937. *Discover Yourself.* New York.

______. 1939. *Indian Philosophy and Modern Culture.* New York.

______. 1941. *The Hidden Teaching beyond Yoga.* New York.

______. 1969*a*. *A Hermit in the Himalayas.* London.

______. 1969*b*. *The Wisdom of the Overself.* London.

Bruteau, Beatrice. 1971. *Worthy to the World: The Hindu Philosophy of Sri Aurobindo.* Cranbury.

Chattopadhyaya, D. 1959. *Lokayata: A Study in Ancient Indian Materialism.* New Delhi.

Chaudhuri, Haridas. 1965. *Integral Yoga.* London.

Chetananda, Swami. 1979. *Meditation und ihre Methoden im Vedanta.* Wiesbaden.

Chinmoy, Sri. 1974*a*. *Death and Reincarnation: Eternity's Voyage.* Jamaica, N.Y.

______. 1974*b*. *Yoga and the Spiritual Life.* Jamaica, N.Y.

Colaco, Paul. 1954. *The Absolute in the Philosophy of Aurobindo Ghose.* Rome.

Conio, Caterina. 1984. *Der Hinduismus.* Aschaffenburg.

Das, A. C. 1958. *A Modern Incarnation of God.* Calcutta.

Dasgupta, Surendranath. 1947. *A History of Sanskrit Literature* (vol. 1): *Classical Period.* Calcutta.

______. 1962. *Indian Idealism.* Cambridge.

______. 1963. *A History of Indian Philosophy* (5 vols.). Cambridge.

Date, V. H. 1970. *Brahma Yoga of the Gītā.* Bombay.

De Bary, William T. 1964. *Sources of the Indian Tradition.* New York.

Deussen, Paul. 1894–1908. *Allgemeine Geschichte der Philosophie, mit besonderer Berücksichtigung der Religionen* (3 vols.). Leipzig.

______. 1966. *The Philosophy of the Upanishads* (trans. of vol. 2 of Deussen 1894–1908). New York. (Orig. pub. 1906)

______. 1980. *Vier philosophische Texte des Mahabharata.* Bielefeld.

Deutsch, Eliot. 1969. *Advaita Vedanta: A Philosophical Reconstruction.* Honolulu.

______ and Buitenen, J. A. B. van (eds.). 1971. *A Source Book of Advaita Vedanta.* Honolulu.

Devamata, Sr. 1977. *Indische Klostertage.* Wiesbaden.

Dhavamony, Mariasusai. 1971. *Love of God According to the Saiva Siddhānta.* Oxford.

Distelbarth, Margret, and Fuchs, Rudolf. 1982. *Umgang mit der Upanishad: Ishavasya-Upanishad.* Gladenbach.

Diwakar, R. R. 1962. *Mahayogi Sri Aurobindo.* Bombay.

Donnelly, Morwenna. 1956. *Founding the Life Divine: Introduction to the Integral Yoga of Sri Aurobindo.* New York.

Douglas, Nik, and Slinger, Penny. 1985. *Das grosse Buch des Tantra.* Basel.

Dowson, John. 1950. *A Classical Dictionary of Hindu Mythology and Religion, Geography, History and Literature.* London.

Dunn, Jean (ed.). 1982. *Seeds of Consciousness: The Wisdom of Sri Nisargadatta Maharaj.* New York.

Easwaran, Eknath. 1981. *Dialogue with Death: The Spiritual Psychology of the Katha Upanishad.* Petaluma, Calif.

Eliade, Mircea. 1958. *Yoga: Immortality and Freedom.* Princeton.

Embree, A. T. (ed.). 1966. *The Hindu Tradition.* New York.

Farquhar, J. N. 1918. *Modern Religious Movements in India.* New York.

Feuerstein, Georg A. 1974*a*. *The Essence of Yoga.* London.

______. 1974*b*. *Introduction to the Bhagavad Gītā.* London.

______. 1975. *Textbook of Yoga.* London.

______ and Miller, Jeanine. 1971. *A Reappraisal of Yoga.* London.

Frauwallner, Erich. 1953–1956. *Geschichte der indischen Philosophie* (2 vols.). Salzburg.

Gail, Adalbert. 1969. *Bhakti im Bhagavatapurana.* Wiesbaden.

Gandhi, Mohandas Karamchand. 1955. *My Religion.* Bombay.

Garber, William. 1967. *The Mind of India.* New York.

Garrison, Omar. 1964. *Tantra: The Yoga of Sex.* New York.

Gehrts, Heino. 1975. *Mahabharata: Das Geschehen und seine Bedeutung.* Bonn.

Ghate, V. S. 1960. *The Vedānta.* Poona.

Glasenapp, Helmuth von. 1948. *Der Stufenweg zum Göttlichen.* Baden-Baden.

______. 1958. *Indische Geisteswelt.* Baden-Baden.

______. 1961. *Die Literaturen Indiens.* Stuttgart.

______. 1962. *Von Buddha zu Gandhi.* Wiesbaden.

Gonda, J. 1972. *The Vedic God Mitra.* Leiden.

Goudriaan, Teun, and Gupta, Sanjukta. 1981. *Hindu Tantric and Sakta Literature.* Wiesbaden.

Hacker, Paul. 1951. *Die Schüler Śaṅkaras.* Wiesbaden.

Hanefeld, Erhardt. 1976. *Philosophische Haupttexte der älteren Upanisaden.* Wiesbaden.

Harharananda, Swami. 1983. *Kriya Yoga: Einführung in den geistigen Weg Sri Yukteswars und Yoganandas.* Munich.

Hauer, J. E. 1983. *Der Yoga: Ein indischer Weg zum Selbst.* Südergellersen.

Hinze, Oscar Marcel. 1983. *Tantra Vidya: Wissenschaft des Tantra.* Freiburg.
Hiriyanna, M. 1951. *Outlines of Indian Philosophy.* London.
———. 1967. *Essentials of Indian Philosophy.* London.
Inhoffen, Hubertus von. 1983. *Yoga: Wissen der Vergangenheit—Wissenschaft der Zukunft.* Munich.
Isherwood, Christopher. 1951. *Vedanta and the West.* New York.
Iyengar, B. K. S. 1976. *Light on Yoga.* London. (New York, 1977)
———. 1981. *Light on Prāṇāyāma: The Yogic Art of Breathing.* New York.
Kapur, Daryai Lal. 1982. *Gespräche mit Sawan Singh: Die Sant-Mat-Philosophie und der Surat-Shabd-Yoga.* Freiburg.
Keilhauer, Anneliese, and Keilhauer, Peter. 1983. *Die Bildsprache des Hinduismus.* Cologne.
Keith, A. B. 1975. *A History of the Sāmkhya Philosophy.* Delhi.
Khanna, Madhu. 1979. *Yantra, the Tantric Symbol of Cosmic Unity.* London.
Kinsley, David R. 1975. *The Sword and the Flute: Kālī and Krsṇa.* Berkeley.
Krishna, Gopi. 1975. *Höheres Bewusstsein: Die evolutionäre Kundalini-Kraft.* Freiburg.
———. 1985*a*. *Kundalini: The Evolutionary Energy in Man.* Boston & London.
———. 1985*b*. *Über Bewusstseinserweiterung, Meditation und Yoga.* Stuttgart.
Krishnamurti, J. 1927. *The Kingdom of Happiness.* New York.
———. 1953. *Education and the Significance of Life.* New York.
———. 1954. *The First and Last Freedom.* New York.
———. 1963. *Life Ahead.* New York.
———. 1970*a*. *The Only Revolution.* New York.
———. 1970*b*. *Think on These Things.* New York.
———. 1970*c*. *The Urgency of Change.* New York.
———. 1971. *The Flight of the Eagle.* New York.
———. 1972a. *The Impossible Question.* New York.
———. 1972*b*. *You Are the World.* New York.
———. 1973*a*. *The Awakening of Intelligence.* New-York.
———. 1973*b*. *Beyond Violence.* New York.
———. 1975*a*. *Beginnings of Learning.* New York.
———. 1975*b*. *Freedom from the Known.* New York.
———. 1977. *Truth and Actuality.* London.
———. 1978. *The Wholeness of Life.* London.
———. 1979. *Exploration into Insight.* London.
———. 1980*a*. *The Collected Works of Krishnamurti.* San Francisco.
———. 1980*b*. *From Darkness to Light.* San Francisco.
———. 1980*c*. *Meditations.* London.
———. 1983. *The Flame of Attention.* London.
———. 1985. *The Way of Intelligence.* Madras.
Lemaître, Solange. 1984. *Ramakrishna and the Vitality of Hinduism.* Woodstock, N.Y.
Le Saux, Henri (Swami Abhishiktananda). 1974. *Guru and Disciple.* London.
———. 1975. *The Further Shore: Sannyasa and the Upanishads.* Delhi.
———. 1979. *Das Feuer der Weisheit.* Bern.
Lord, A. B. 1960. *Singer of Tales.* Cambridge, Mass.
Macdonnell, A. A. 1971. *The Vedic Mythology.* New Delhi.
Mahadevan, T. M. P. 1957. *The Philosophy of Advaita.* Madras.
Majumdar, R. V. 1951. *The Vedic Age.* London.
Mishra, Rammurti S. 1963. *The Textbook of Yoga Psychology.* Garden City, N.Y.
Mookerjee, Ajitcoomar. 1971. *Tantra Asana.* Basel.
———. 1984. *Kundalini: Die Erweckung der inneren Energie.* Basel.
——— and Khanna, Madhu. 1977. *The Tantric Way: Art, Science, Ritual.* London.
Mukerji, Dhan Gopal. 1927. *The Face of Silence.* New York.
Muktananda, Paramhamsa. 1978. *Play of Consciousness: Chitshakti Vilas.* San Francisco.
———. 1979*a*. *Kundalini: The Secret of Life.* South Fallsburg, N.Y.
———. 1979*b*. *Von der Natur Gottes: Der Siddha-Yoga-Weg zum höchsten Ziel.* Freiburg.
———. 1983. *I Am That.* South Fallsburg, N.Y.
Murty, Satchidananda. 1959. *Revelation and Reason in Advaita Vedanta.* New York.
Nandimath, S. C. 1942. *A Handbook of Vīraśaivism.* Dharwar.
Narayanananda, Swami. 1950*a*. *The Primal Power in Man or the Kundalini Shakti.* Rishikesh.
———. 1950*b*. *The Way to Peace, Power, and Long Life.* Rishikesh.
———. 1951*a*. *The Ideal Life and Moksha.* Rishikesh.
———. 1951*b*. *The Mysteries of Man, Mind and Mind-Functions.* Rishikesh.
Nicolas, Antonio T. de. 1960. *Der Hinduismus.* Munich.
———. 1972. *Vivekananda: Leben und Werk.* Munich.
———. 1978. *Meditations through the Ṛg Veda.* Boulder, Colo.
Nisargadatta Maharaj. 1973. *I Am That.* Bombay.
Nityabodhananda, Swami. 1964. *Wahrheit und Toleranz.* Stuttgart.
———. 1965. *Science du yoga.* Paris.
———. 1967. *Mythes et religions de l'Inde.* Paris.
Osborne, Arthur (ed.). 1968. *The Collected Works of Ramana Maharshi.* Tiruvannamalai.
———. 1972. *The Incredible Sai Baba.* London.

Otto, Rudolf. 1934. *Die Urgestalt der Bhagavad-Gita.* Tübingen.
______. 1935. *Die Lehrtraktate der Bhagavad-Gita.* Tübingen.
Pandit, Sri Madhav P. 1959*a*. *Kundalini Yoga.* Madras.
______. 1959*b*. *The Teaching of Sri Aurobindo.* Madras.
______. 1967. *Guide to the Upanishads.* Pondicherry.
______. 1976. *The Yoga of Works.* Pondicherry.
______. 1979. *The Yoga of Knowledge.* Pomona, Calif.
______. 1984. *Verborgene Aspekte im Leben.* Südergellersen.
Paradkar, M. D. 1970. *Studies in the Gītā.* Bombay.
Pelet, Emma von. 1930. *Worte des Ramakrishna.* Leipzig.
Prabhavananda, Swami, and Manchester, Frederick. 1963. *The Spiritual Heritage of India.* Garden City, N.Y.
Prem, Sri Krishna. 1938. *The Yoga of the Bhagavad Gita.* London.
Radha, Swami Sivananda. 1985. *Kundalini Yoga for the West.* Boston.
Radhakrishnan, Sarvepalli. 1924. *The Philosophy of the Upanishads.* London.
______. 1927*a*. *The Brahma Sutra: The Philosophy of Spiritual Life.* London.
______. 1927*b*. *The Hindu View of Life.* London. (Rev. ed., 1961)
______. 1962. *Indian Philosophy.* New York & London.
Rajagopalachari, P. 1977. *Der Meister.* Bern.
Raju, P. Y. 1971. *The Philosophical Traditions of India.* London.
Ramakrishna, Sri. 1934. *Teachings of Ramakrishna.* Mayavati.
______. 1949. *Sayings.* Mylapore.
______. 1981. *Das Vermächtnis.* Bern.
______. 1983. *Leben und Gleichnis.* Bern.
______. 1984. *Setzt Gott keine Grenzen.* Freiburg.
Ramana Maharshi. 1957. *Self-Enquiry.* Tiruvannamalai.
______. 1968. *The Collected Works of Ramana Maharshi,* ed. Arthur Osborne. Tiruvannamalai.
______. 1988. *The Spiritual Teaching of Ramana Maharshi.* Boston.
Ramanujan, A. K. 1963. *Speaking of Shiva.* Harmondsworth.
Renou, Louis. 1965. *The Destiny of the Veda in India.* New Delhi.
______. 1968. *Religions of Ancient India.* New York.
Rolland, Romain. 1924. *Mahatma Gandhi.* New York.
______. 1965*a*. *The Life of Ramakrishna.* Calcutta & Hollywood.
______. 1965*b*. *The Life of Vivekananda and the Universal Gospel.* Calcutta.
Roy, A. 1940. *Sri Aurobindo and the New Age.* London.
Roy, Dilip Kumar & Devi, Indra. 1977. *Der Weg der grossen Yogis.* Frankfurt.
Sadhu, Mouni. 1962. *Samadhi.* London.
______. 1967. *Meditation.* London.
Saradananda, Swami. 1956. *Sri Ramakrishna: The Great Master.* Madras.
Saraswati, Swami K. 1984. *Die Bhagavadgita im täglichen Leben.* Südergellersen.
Sarma, D. S. 1941. *What Is Hinduism?* Mylapore.
______. 1967. *Hinduism through the Ages.* Bombay.
Sarma, K. Lakshma. 1958. *Maha Yoga: Die Lehren Sri Ramana Maharshis.* Frankfurt.
Sastri, T. V. Kapali. 1947. *Lights on the Veda.* Madras.
______. 1951. *Further Lights: The Veda and the Tantra.* Pondicherry.
Satprem. 1981. *Der Mensch hinter dem Menschen.* Bern.
______. 1984. *Sri Aurobindo, or the Adventure of Consciousness.* New York.
Schluchter, Wolfgang (ed.). 1984. *Max Webers Studie über Hinduismus und Buddhismus.* Frankfurt.
Schreiner, Peter. 1984. *Begegnungen mit dem Hinduismus.* Freiburg.
Shivānanda. *See* Sivananda.
Siddheswarananda, Swami. 1966. *Meditation According to Yoga-Vedānta.* Puranattukara.
Singh, Mohan. 1985*a*. *Botschaft eines Yogi: Universaler Einklang im Yoga.* Bern.
______. 1985*b*. *Mystik und Yoga der Sikh-Meister.* Bern.
Sivānanda, Swami. 1929. *Practice of Yoga.* Madras; Sivananda-nagar 1970.
______. 1935. *Kundalini Yoga.* Madras; Rishikesh 1950.
______. 1944. *Hatha Yoga.* Rishikesh.
______. 1945*a*. *Concentration and Meditation.* Rishikesh.
______. 1945*b*. *Students' Success in Life.* Rishikesh.
______. 1951. *Yoga for the West.* Rishikesh.
______. 1954. *Self-Realisation.* Ananda Kutir.
Speyer, J. S. 1914. *Die indische Theosophie.* Leipzig.
Stevenson, Mrs. Sinclair. 1970. *The Heart of Jainism.* New Delhi.
Stutley, Margaret, and Stutley, James. 1977. *Dictionary of Hinduism.* London.
Subba Row, T. 1959. *Der Philosophie der Bhagavad Gita.* Munich.
Tagore, Rabindranath. 1913. *Sādhanā: The Realisation of Life.* New York.
Taimni, Iqbal K. 1961. *The Science of Yoga.* Wheaton, Ill.
______. 1984. *Bhakti Yoga, der Yoga der Hingabe.* Munich.
Tattwananda, Swami. 1960. *The Quintessence of Vedānta.* Kalandy.
Thirleby, Ashley. 1979. *Das Tantra der Liebe.* Bern.

Thompson, Edward J. 1926. *Rabindranath Tagore: His Life and Work.* Oxford.

Tipperudraswami, H. 1968. *The Vīraśaiva Saints.* Mysore.

Torwesten, Hans. 1980. *Ramakrishna und Christus.* Planegg.

______. 1981. *Ramakrishna: Schauspieler Gottes.* Frankfurt.

______. 1985. *Vedanta: Kern des Hinduismus.* Freiburg.

Tyberg, Judith M. 1976. *The Language of the Gods: Sanskrit Keys to India's Wisdom.* Los Angeles.

Vivekānanda, Swami. 1955*a*. *Jnana-Yoga.* New York.

______. 1955*b*. *Karma-Yoga and Bhakti-Yoga.* New York.

______. 1955*c*. *Rāja-Yoga.* New York.

______. 1957-1959. *The Complete Works* (8 vols.). Calcutta.

______. 1977. *What Religion Is.* Calcutta.

Vogl, Carl. 1921. *Sri Ramakrischna, der letzte indische Prophet.* Munich.

Wolf, Otto (ed.). 1957. *So spricht Aurobindo.* Munich and Planegg.

______. 1967. *Sri Aurobindo.* Reinbek.

Woodroffe, John George (Arthur Avalon). 1919. *The Serpent Power.* London. (New York, 1974)

______. 1951. *The Garland of Letters (Varnamālā): Studies in the Mantra-Shāstra.* Madras.

______. 1964. *Mahamaya, the World as Power: Power as Consciousness.* Madras.

______. 1969. *Śakti and Śākta.* Madras.

Yesudian, Selvarajan, and Haich, Elisabeth. 1975. *Raja-Yoga: Yoga in den zwei Welten.* Munich.

Yogānanda, Paramhansa. 1923. *Songs of the Soul.* Boston.

______. 1952. *The Master Said.* Los Angeles.

______. 1958. *Scientific Healing Affirmations.* Los Angeles.

______. 1959. *Metaphysical Meditations.* Los Angeles.

______. 1969. *Autobiography of a Yogi.* Los Angeles. (Orig. pub. 1946)

______. 1973. *Whispers from Eternity.* Los Angeles. (Orig. pub. 1959)

______. 1974. *The Science of Religion.* Los Angeles. (Orig. pub. 1953)

Yukteswar Giri, Jnanavatar Swami Sri. 1957. *Kaibalaya Darshanam, the Holy Science.* Ariadaha, India.

Zaehner, R. C. 1962. *Hinduism.* London & New York.

Zimmer, Heinrich. 1946. *Myths and Symbols in Indian Art and Civilization.* Princeton.

______. 1951. *Philosophies of India.* Princeton.

______. 1978. *Maya: Der indische Mythos.* Frankfurt.

______. 1979. *Die indische Weltmutter.* Frankfurt.

______. 1983. *Yoga und Buddhismus.* Frankfurt.

______. 1985. *Der Weg zum Selbst: Leben und Lehre des Shri Ramana Maharshi.* Cologne.

Taoism *Primary Sources*

Blofeld, John (trans.). 1965. *I Ching: The Book of Change.* London.

Chai, Ch'u, and Chai, Winberg. 1965. *The Sacred Books of Confucius, and Other Confucian Classics* (6 vols.). New Hyde Park, N.Y.

Chang Chung-yuan (trans.). 1975. *Tao: A New Way of Thinking. A Translation of the Tao Te Ching.* New York.

Chia Yü. See Wilhelm 1981*a*.

Chuang-tzu. See H. A. Giles 1961, Graham 1981, Legge 1962, Watson 1968.

Confucius (Konfutse). *See Chia Yü, Lun Yü, Shih Ching, Shu Ching.*

Feng, Gia-fu, and English, Jane. 1972. *Tao Te Ching.* New York. (London, 1973.)

Giles, Herbert A. (trans.). 1961. *Chuang Tzu: Taoist Philosopher and Chinese Mystic.* London.

Giles, Lionel (trans.). 1910. *Sun Tzu: The Art of War.* London.

______. 1912. *Taoist Teachings from the Book of Lieh Tzu.* London.

Graham, A. C. (trans.). 1978. *Later Mohist Logic, Ethics, and Science.* London & Hong Kong.

______. 1981. *Chuang Tzu: The Inner Chapters.* London.

Huang Ti Nei Ching Su Wen. See Veith 1966.

I Ching. See Blofeld 1965, Legge 1964, Wilhelm 1967.

K'ung Tzu. *See* Confucius.

Lao-tzu. *See Tao Te Ching.*

Lau, D. C. (trans.). 1963. *Lao Tzu: Tao Te Ching.* London.

______. 1979. *The Analects (Lun Yü).* New York.

Legge, James (trans.). 1861–1872. *The Chinese Classics.* Hong Kong; London 1875–1876.

______. 1962. *The Texts of Taoism* (2 vols.). New York.

______. 1964. *The Sacred Books of China* (6 vols.). Delhi. (Orig. pub. Oxford 1879–1885)

Li-chi. See Chai & Chai 1965, Legge 1964.

Lieh-tzu. See L. Giles 1912, Wilhelm 1981*b*.

Lin Yutang (trans.). 1948. *The Wisdom of Laotse.* New York.

______. 1949. *The Wisdom of China.* London.

Lun-yü. See Lau 1979; Legge 1861–1872, 1964; Waley 1938; Ware 1950.

Lü Shih Ch'un Ch'iu. See Wilhelm 1979.

Mei, Yi-Pao (trans.). 1929. *The Ethical and Political Works of Motse.* London.

Meng-tzu. See Legge 1861–1872, 1964.

Miyuki, Mokusen (trans.). 1984. *Die Erfahrung der goldenen Blüte* [The Secret of the Golden Flower]. Bern.

Mo Ti. *See* Graham 1978, Mei 1929, Watson 1967.

Shih Ching. See Legge 1861–1872, 1964.

Shu Ching. See Legge 1861–1872, 1964.

Sun Tzu. See L. Giles 1910.

T'ai Hsüan Ching. See Walters 1983.

T'ai I Chin Hua Tsung Chih. See Wilhelm 1938.

T'ai Shang Kan Ying P'ien Ku. See Legge 1962.

Tao-te Ching. See Chang 1975; Feng and English 1972; Lau 1963; Legge 1962, 1964; Lin 1948; Waley 1958; Wei 1982; Wing 1986.

Veith, Ilza (trans.). 1966. *The Yellow Emperor's Classic of Internal Medicine.* Berkeley.

Waley, Arthur (trans.). 1938. *The Analects of Confucius.* London & New York.

———. 1958. *The Way and Its Power: A Study of the Tao Te Ching and Its Place in Chinese Thought.* New York.

Walters, Derek (trans.). 1983. *The T'ai Hsüan Ching: The Hidden Classic. A Lost Companion of the I Ching.* Wellingborough, Engl.

Ware, James R. (trans.). *The Best of Confucius.* Garden City, N.Y.

Watson, Burton (trans.). 1967. *Basic Writings of Mo Tzu, Hsün Tzu, and Han Fei Tzu.* New York.

———. 1968. *The Complete Works of Chuang Tzu.* New York.

Wei, Henry. 1982. *The Guiding Light of Lao-tzu.* London.

Wilhelm, Richard (trans.). 1938 (repub. 1975). *The Secret of the Golden Flower,* trans. Cary F. Baynes. New York. (London, 1962)

———. 1967. *The I Ching, or, Book of Changes,* trans. Cary F. Baynes. Princeton, N.J.

———. 1969. *Dschuang Dsi: Das wahre Buch vom südlichen Blütenland.* Dusseldorf and Cologne.

———. 1979. *Frühling und Herbst des Lü Bu We.* Düsseldorf & Cologne.

———. 1981*a*. *Kungfutse: Schulgespräche (Gia Yü).* Düsseldorf and Cologne.

———. 1981*b*. *Liä Dsi: Das wahre Buch vom quellenden Urgrund.* Dusseldorf and Cologne.

———. 1982. *Mong Dsi: Die Lehrgespräche des Meisters Meng K'o.* Dusseldorf and Cologne.

Wing, R. L. (trans.). 1986. *The Tao of Power.* Wellingborough, England.

Taoism *Secondary Sources*

Bauer, Wolfgang. 1974. *China und die Hoffnung auf Glück.* Munich.

Béky, Gellért. 1972. *Die Welt des Tao.* Freiburg & Munich.

Blofeld, John. 1973. *The Secret and the Sublime: Taoist Mysteries and Magic.* London.

———. 1974. *Beyond the Gods: Taoist and Buddhist Mysticism.* London.

———. 1978. *Taoism: The Road to Immortality.* Boulder, Colo.

———. 1979. *Taoism: The Quest for Immortality.* London.

———. 1983. *Selbstheilung durch die Kraft der Stille.* Bern.

Carus, Paul. 1907. *Chinese Thought.* La Salle, Ill.

Chan, Wing-tsit. 1979. *Commentary on Lao-Tzu.* Honolulu.

Chang Chung-yuan. 1963. *Creativity and Taoism.* New York.

Christie, Anthony. 1968. *Chinesische Mythologie.* Wiesbaden.

Colegrave, Sukie. 1980. *Yin und Yang* (German translation of *The Spirit in the Valley*). Bern.

Cooper, J. C. 1977. *Der Weg des Tao.* Bern.

———. 1981. *Yin & Yang: The Taoist Harmony of Opposites.* Wellingborough, England.

———. 1984. *Chinese Alchemy.* Wellingborough, England.

Delius, Rudolf von. 1930. *Kungfutse: Seine Persönlichkeit und seine Lehre.* Leipzig.

Diederichs, Ulf (ed.). 1984. *Erfahrungen mit dem I Ging.* Cologne.

Doré, Henri. 1911–1938. *Recherches sur les superstitions en Chine* (18 parts). Shanghai.

Durdin-Robertson, Lawrence. 1976. *The Goddesses of India, Tibet, China and Japan.* Clonegal.

Eberhard, Wolfram. 1986. *A Dictionary of Chinese Symbols.* London & New York.

Eisenberg, David. 1985. *Encounters with Qi: Exploring Chinese Medicine.* New York.

Fung Yu-lan. 1953. *A History of Chinese Philosophy.* Princeton, N.J.

Granet, Marcel. 1934. *La pensée chinoise.* Paris.

———. 1950. *Chinese Civilisation.* London.

———. 1975. *The Religion of the Chinese People.* New York.

Gulik, Robert van. 1961. *Sexual Life in Ancient China.* Leiden.

Homann, Rolf. 1971. *Die wichtigsten Körpergottheiten des Huang-t'ing-ching.* Göppingen.
Hook, Diana ffarington. 1980. *The I Ching and Its Associations.* London & Boston.
Jaspers, Karl. 1966. *Anaximander, Heraclitus, Paramenides, Plotinus, Lao-tzu, Nagarjuna.* New York.
Jou, Tsung Hwa. 1980. *The Tao of Tai-chi Chuan.* Piscataway, N.J.
______. 1983. *The Tao of Meditation.* Piscataway, N.J.
Kaltenmark, Max. 1969. *Lao Tzu and Taoism.* Stanford.
Kielce, Anton. 1985. *Taoismus.* Munich.
Lai, T. C. 1972. *The Eight Immortals.* Hong Kong.
Legeza, Laszlo. 1975. *Tao Magic.* London.
Li, Dun Jen. 1975. *The Civilization of China.* New York.
Lu K'uan Yü (Charles Luk). 1969. *Secrets of Chinese Meditation.* London. (New York, 1964)
Malek, Roman. 1985. *Das Chai-chieh lu: Materialien zur Liturgie im Taoismus.* Frankfurt & New York.
Maspéro, Henri. 1981. *Taoism and Chinese Religion.* Amherst, Mass.
Needham, Joseph. 1954–1965. *Science and Civilization in China* (5 vols.). Cambridge, England.
______. 1977. *Wissenschaftlicher Universalismus: Über Bedeutung und Besonderheit der chinesischen Wissenschaft.* Frankfurt.
Opitz, Peter J. (ed.). 1968. *Chinesisches Alterum und konfuzianische Klassik.* Munich.
Pálos, Stephan. 1980. *Atem und Meditation.* Bern.
______. 1984. *Chinesische Heilkunst.* Bern.
Porkert, Manfred. 1978. *China: Konstanten im Wandel.* Stuttgart.
Rawson, Philip, and Legeza, Laszlo. 1973. *Tao: The Eastern Philosophy of Time and Change.* Farnborough, Hampshire, England.
Robinet, Isabelle. 1979. *Méditation taoiste.* Paris.
Rossbach, Sarah. 1983. *Feng Shui: The Chinese Art of Placement.* New York.
Saso, Michael. 1968. *The Teachings of Taoist Master Chuang.* New Haven.
Schipper, Kristof. 1982. *Le corps taoiste.* Paris.
Schluchter, Wolfgang (ed.). 1982. *Max Webers Studien über Konfuzianismus und Taoismus.* Frankfurt.
Sherrill, Wallace A., and Wen Kuan Chu. 1977. *An Anthology of I Ching.* London.
______. 1976. *The Astrology of the I Ching.* New York & London.
Simbriger, Heinrich. 1961. *Geheimnis der Mitte: Aus dem geistigen Vermächtnis des alten China.* Düsseldorf & Cologne.
Siu, R. G. H. 1974. *A Neo-Taoist Approach to Life.* Cambridge, Mass.
Sivin, Nathan. 1968. *Chinese Alchemy: Preliminary Studies.* Cambridge, Mass.
Skinner, Stephen. 1982. *The Living Earth Manual of Feng Shui: Chinese Geomancy.* London & Boston.
Smith, D. Howard. 1974. *Confucius.* Frogmore, England.
Twam, Kim. 1982. *Geheime Übungen taoistischer Mönche.* Freiburg.
Unterreider, Else. 1984. *Glück ein ganzes Mondjahr lang.* Klagenfurt.
Watts, Alan. 1975. *Tao: The Watercourse Way.* New York.
Welch, Holmes. 1957. *The Parting of the Way.* London.
Werner, E. T. C. 1961. *A Dictionary of Chinese Mythology.* New York.
Wilhelm, Hellmut. 1960. *Change: Eight Lectures on the I Ching.* New York.
______. 1972. *Sinn des I-Ging.* Düsseldorf & Cologne.
Wing. R. L. 1979. *The I Ching Workbook.* New York.
Zenker, E. V. 1941. *Der Taoismus der Frühzeit.* Vienna.
Zöller, Josephine. 1984. *Das Tao der Selbstheilung.* Bern.

Zen *Primary Sources*

Bankei Eitaku. *See* Waddell 1984.
Blofeld, John (trans.). 1958. *The Zen Teaching of Huang Po on the Transmission of Mind.* London.
______. 1962. *The Zen Teaching of Hui Hai on Sudden Illumination.* London.
Chan, Wing-tsit (trans.). 1963. *The Platform Sutra.* New York.
Chang Chung-yuan (trans.). 1969. *Original Teachings of Ch'an Buddhism, Selected from the Transmission of the Lamp.* New York.
Ching Te Ch'uan Teng Lu. See Chang 1969.
Chao Chou Ch'an Shih Yü Lu. See Hoffman 1978.
Cleary, Thomas (trans.). 1978*b*. *The Original Face: An Anthology of Rinzai Zen.* New York.
______. 1978*c*. *Sayings and Doings of Pai-Chang, Ch'an Master of Great Wisdom.* Los Angeles.
______. 1980*a*. *Record of Things Heard from the Treasury of the Eye of the True Teaching.* Boulder, Colo.
______. 1980*b*. *Timeless Spring: A Soto Zen Anthology.* New York.
______. 1986. *The Book of Serenity.* New York.
______, and Cleary, J. C. 1978*a*. *The Blue Cliff Record.* Boulder, Colo.

Cook, Francis Dojun. 1978. *How to Raise an Ox: Zen Practice as Taught in Zen Master Dogen's Shobogenzo.* Los Angeles.

Deshimaru, Taisen (ed.). 1979. *Shinjinmei, von Meister Tozan.* Berlin.

______. 1980. *Sandokai, von Meister Sekito.* Berlin.

______. 1981. *Hokyozanmai, von Meister Tozan.* Berlin.

Fuller Sasaki, Ruth (trans.). 1975. *The Record of Linchi.* Kyoto.

______, Yoshitaka Iriya, and Fraser, Dana R. (trans.). 1971. *The Recorded Sayings of Layman P'ang.* New York.

Genjō Kōan. See Maezumi 1978.

Gundert, Wilhelm (trans.). 1964/73. *Bi-Yän-Lu: Meister Yüan-wu's Niederschrift von der Smaragdenen Felswand.* Munich.

Hakuin Zenji. *See* Shaw 1963, Yampolski 1971.

Han Shan. *See* Lu 1966, Red Pine 1983, Snyder 1965, Watson 1970.

Hoffmann, Yoel (trans.). 1977. *Every End Exposed: The 100 Perfect Kōans of Master Kidō.* Brookline, Mass.

______. 1978. *Radical Zen: The Sayings of Jōshū.* Brookline, Mass.

Hsin Hsin Ming. See Deshimaru 1979.

Hsü T'ang Yü Lu. See Hoffmann 1977.

Huang Po Shan Tuan Chi Ch'an Shih Ch'uan Hsin Fa Yao. See Blofeld 1958.

Hung Chou Pai Chang Shan Ta Chih Ch'an Shih Yü Lu. See Cleary 1978*c*.

Ikkyu Sōjun. *See* Shuichi & Thom 1979.

Kyōun Shū. See Shuichi & Thom 1979.

Lin Chi Lu. See Fuller Sasaki 1975; Schleogl 1975.

Liu Tsu Ta Shih Fa Pao T'an Ching. See Lu 1960–1962; Wing 1963; Wong 1953.

Lu K'uan Yü (Charles Luk) (trans.). 1960–1962. *Ch'an and Zen Teachings* (3 vols.). London.

______. 1966. *The Śūraṅgama Sūtra,* with a commentary by Han Shan. London.

______. 1972. *The Vimalakīrti Nirdeśa.* Berkeley.

______. 1974. *The Transmission of the Mind outside the Teaching,* vol. 1. London.

Maezumi, Hakuyu Taizan. 1978. *The Way of Everyday Life: Zen Master Dōgen's Genjokoan with Commentary.* Los Angeles.

Masunaga, Reihō (trans.). 1972. *A Primer of Sōtō Zen: A Translation of Dōgen's Shōbōgenzō Zuikmonki.* London.

Nishiyama, Kosen, and Stevens, John (trans.). 1975–1983. *Shōbōgenzō: The Eye and Treasury of the True Law* (3 vols.). Tokyo.

Orategama. See Shaw 1963, Yampolski 1971.

Pai Chang Kuang Lu. See Cleary 1978c.

P'ang Chü Chih Yü Lu. See Fuller Sasaki 1971.

Pi Yen Lu. See Cleary 1978*a,* Sekida 1977.

Red Pine. 1983. *The Collected Songs of Cold Mountain.* Port Townsend, Wash.

Renondeau, G. (trans.). 1965. *Le Bouddhisme japonais: Textes fondamentaux de quatre grands moines de Kamakura: Hōnen, Shinran, Nichiren et Dōgen.* Paris.

Ryōkan Daigu. *See* Stevens 1979, Watson 1977.

San Mei K'o. See Cleary 1980*b,* Deshimaru 1981.

Schleogl, Irmgard (trans.). 1975. *The Record of Rinzai.* London.

Sekida, Katsuki (trans.). 1977. *Two Zen Classics: Mumonkan and Hekigan-roku.* New York.

Shaw, R. D. M. (trans.). 1963. *The Embossed Tea Kettle: Orate Gama and Other Works of Hakuin Zenji.* London.

Shibayama Zenkei. 1974. *Zen Comments on the Mumonkan.* Trans. Sumiko Kudo. New York.

Shigematsu, Sōiku (trans.). 1981. *A Zen Forest: Sayings of the Masters.* New York.

Shōbōgenzō. See Cook 1978, Nishiyama & Stevens 1975–1983.

Shōbōgenzō Zuimonki. See Cleary 1980*a,* Masunaga 1972, Renondeau 1965.

Shuichi Katō and Thom, Eva (trans.). 1979. *Ikkyu Sojun: Im Garten der schönen Shin.* Düsseldorf & Cologne.

Snyder, Gary (trans.). 1965. *Cold Mountain Poems.* Portland, Ore.

Stevens, John (trans.). 1979. *One Robe, One Bowl: The Zen Poetry of Ryōkan.* New York.

Thurman, Robert A. F. (trans.). 1976. *The Holy Teaching of Vimalakīrti: A Māhāyana Scripture.* University Park, Pa., & London.

Ts'an T'ung Ch'i. See Cleary 1980*b*; Deshimaru 1980.

Ts'ung Jung Lu. See Cleary 1986.

Tun Wu Ju Tao Yao Men Lung. See Blofeld 1962.

Vimalakīrti Nirdesha Sūtra. See Lu 1972, Thurman 1976.

Waddell, Norman (trans.). 1984. *The Unborn: The Life and Teaching of Zen Master Bankei.* San Francisco.

Watson, Burton (trans.). 1970. *Cold Mountain: 100 Poems by the T'ang Poet Han-Shan.* New York.

______. 1977. *Ryôkan: Zen Monk-Poet of Japan.* New York.

Wing, Tsit-chan (trans.). 1963. *The Platform Sutra.* New York.

Wong Mou-lam (trans.). 1953. *The Sutra of Wei Lang (Hui Neng).* London. (Berkeley, 1969)

Wu Men Kuan. See Sekida 1977, Shibayama 1974, Yamada 1979.

Yamada, Kōun (trans.). 1979. *Gateless Gate.* Los Angeles.

Yampolski, Philip B. (trans.). 1971. *The Zen Master Hakuin: Selected Writings.* New York.

Zenrin Kushū. See Shigematsu 1981.

Zen *Secondary Sources*

Aitken, Robert. 1978. *A Zen Wave: Bashō's Haiku and Zen.* New York.

______. 1982. *Taking the Path of Zen.* San Francisco.

______. 1984. *The Mind of Clover: Essays in Zen Buddhist Ethics.* San Francisco.

Bancroft, Anne, 1979. *Zen: Direct Pointing to Reality.* London & New York.

Benoit, Hubert. 1951. *The Supreme Doctrine: Psychological Studies in Zen Thought.* New York.

Benz, Ernst. 1962. *Zen in westlicher Sicht: Zen-Buddhismus, Zen-Snobismus.* Weilheim.

Blyth, Reginald Horace. 1949–1952. *Haiku* (4 vols.). Tokyo.

______. 1960–1970. *Zen and Zen Classics* (5 vols.). Tokyo.

______. 1963–1964. *A History of Haiku* (2 vols.). Tokyo.

Brinker, Helmut. 1985. *Zen in der Kunst des Malens.* Bern.

Buksbazen, John Daishin. 1977. *To Forget the Self.* Los Angeles.

Chang Chung-yuan. 1963. *Creativity and Taoism.* New York.

Chang, Garma Chen-chi. 1959. *The Practice of Zen.* New York.

Davidson, A. K. 1982. *Zen Gardening.* London.

Deshimaru, Taisen. 1977. *Zen et les arts martiaux.* Paris.

______. 1978. *Zen-Buddhismus und Christentum.* Berlin.

______. 1979. *Za-Zen: Die Praxis des Zen.* Berlin.

Dumoulin, Heinrich. 1963. *A History of Zen Buddhism.* New York. Boston, 1959.

______. 1976. *Der Erleuchtungsweg des Zen im Buddhismus.* Frankfurt.

Dürckheim, Karlfried von (ed.). 1979. *Wunderbare Katze und andere Zen-Texte.* Bern.

______. 1987. *Zen and Us.* New York.

Enomiya-Lassalle, Hugo M. 1973. *Zen: Way to Enlightenment.* London.

______. 1974*b*. *Zen-Buddhismus.* Cologne.

______. 1974*a*. *Zen Meditation for Christians.* LaSalle, Ill.

Grames, Eberhard, and Müller, Michael (ed.). 1985. *Zen.* Hamburg.

Groening, Lies. 1985. *Die lautlose Stimme der einen Hand: Zen Erfahrunginen einem japanischen Kloster.* Reinbek.

Hammitzsch, Horst. 1980. *Zen in the Art of the Tea Ceremony.* New York.

Hasumi, Toshimitsu. 1960. *Zen in der japanischen Kunst.* Munich & Planegg.

______. 1986. *Zen in der Kunst des Dichtens.* Bern.

Herrigel, Eugen. 1960. *The Method of Zen.* New York.

______. 1971. *Zen in the Art of Archery,* New York.

Herrigel, Gustie L. 1958. *Zen in the Art of Flower Arrangement.* London.

Hisamatsu, Hoseki Sen'ichi. 1984. *Die Fülle des Nichts.* Pfulligen.

Hoffmann, Yoel. 1975. *The Sound of the One Hand.* London.

Hoover, Thomas. 1977. *Zen Culture.* New York.

______. 1980. *The Zen Experience.* New York.

Humphreys, Christmas. 1984. *Zen Buddhism.* London.

Ital, Gerta. 1978. *Meditationen aus dem Geist des Zen.* Freiburg.

______. 1987. *Master, the Monks, and I: A Western Woman's Experience of Zen.* Wellingborough, England.

Izutsu, Toshihiko. 1982. *Toward a Philosophy of Zen Buddhism.* Boulder, Colo.

Kammer, Reinhard. 1978. *Zen and Confucius in the Art of Swordsmanship.* London.

Kapleau, Philip (ed.). 1980. *The Three Pillars of Zen: Teaching, Practice, and Enlightenment.* New York.

Kennett, Jiyu. 1972. *Selling Water by the River: A Manual of Zen Training.* New York.

______. 1976. *Zen Is Eternal Life.* Emeryville, Calif.

Legget, Trevor. 1960. *A First Zen Reader.* Rutland, Vt.

______. 1964. *The Tiger's Cave: Translations of Japanese Zen Texts.* London.

______. 1978. *Zen and the Ways.* London.

______. 1985. *The Warrior Koans.* London.

Lu K'uan Yü (Charles Luk). 1969. *Secrets of Chinese Meditation.* London.

Maezumi, Hakuyu Taizan, and Glassman, Bernard Tetsugen. 1976. *On Zen Practice* (2 vols.). Los Angeles.

______. 1978. *The Hazy Moon of Enlightenment.* Los Angeles.

Merton, Thomas. 1961. *Mystics and Zen Masters.* New York.

______. 1968. *Zen and the Birds of Appetite.* New York.

______. 1975. *Weisheit der Stille.* Bern.

Miura, Isshū, and Fuller Sasaki, Ruth. 1965. *The Zen Koan.* New York.

Mountain, Marian. 1982. *The Zen Environment: The Impact of Zen Meditation.* New York.

Munsterberg, Hugo. 1978. *Zen-Kunst.* Cologne.

Ōhasama, Shūeji, and Faust, August. 1925. *Zen: Der lebendige Buddhismus in Japan.* Gotha & Stuttgart.

Ōmori, Sōgen, and Terayama, Katsujō. 1983. *Zen and the Art of Calligraphy.* London.

Reps, Paul. 1976. *Ohne Worte, ohne Schweigen.* Bern.

Sasaki, Joshu. 1974. *Buddha Is the Center of Gravity.* San Cristobal, N.M.

Schleogl, Irmgard. 1975. *The Wisdom of the Zen Masters.* London.

Sekida, Katsuki. 1975. *Zen Training: Methods and Philosophy.* New York.

Shibayama Zenkei. 1970. *A Flower Does Not Talk.* Trans. Sumiko Kudo. Rutland, Vt.

Shimano, Eido. 1982. *Der Weg der wolkenlosen Klarheit.* Bern.

Sokei-an, Shigetsu Sasaki. 1985*a*. *Sokei-an's Übertragung des Zen.* Zurich.

______. 1985*b*. *Der Zen-Weg zur Befreiung des Geistes.* Zurich.

Stein, Hans Joachim. 1985. *Die Kunst des Bogenschiessens: Kyūdō.* Bern.

Stevens, John. 1989. *The Sword of No-Sword: Life of the Master Warrior Tesshu.* Boston & London.

Stryk, Lucien; Ikemoto, Takashi; and Takayama, Taigan (ed.). 1973. *Zen Poems of China and Japan.* Garden City, N.Y.

Sung Bae Park. 1983. *Buddhist Faith and Sudden Enlightenment.* Albany, N.Y.

Suzuki, Daisetz (Daisetsu) Teitaro. 1930. *Studies in the Lankavatara Sutra.* London.

______. 1934. *The Training of a Zen Monk.* Kyoto.

______. 1935. *A Manual of Zen Buddhism.* Kyoto; New York 1960.

______. 1949. *Introduction to Zen Buddhism.* London & New York. (New York 1964)

______. 1950–1953. *Essays in Zen Buddhism,* Series 1-3 (3 vols.). London.

______. 1955. *Studies in Zen.* London.

______. 1962. *The Essentials of Zen Buddhism.* New York.

______. 1969. *The Zen Doctrine of No-Mind.* London.

______. 1970. *Zen and Japanese Culture.* Princeton.

______. 1971. *What Is Zen?* London.

______. 1972. *Living by Zen.* London.

______. 1987. *The Awakening of Zen.* Boston & London.

Suzuki, D. T.; Fromm, Erich; and De Martino, Richard. 1960. *Zen Buddhism and Psychoanalysis.* New York.

Suzuki, Shunryū. 1970. *Zen Mind, Beginner's Mind.* New York.

Uchiyama, Kosho. 1976. *Zen für Küche und Leben.* Freiburg.

Van de Wetering, Janwillem. 1975. *The Empty Mirror: Experiences in a Japanese Zen Monastery.* Boston.

______. 1975. *A Glimpse of Nothingness: Experiences in an American Zen Community.* New York.

Viallet, François A. (Karl Friedrich Boskowits). 1971. *Zen, l'autre versant.* Tournai.

______. 1978*a*. *Einladung zum Zen.* Olten and Freiburg.

______. 1978*b*. *Zurück mit leeren Händen: Zen-Erfahrung.* Olten & Freiburg.

Watts, Alan. 1958. *The Spirit of Zen.* New York.

______. 1961. *Zen-Buddhism: Tradition und lebendige Gegenwart.* Reinbek.

______. 1972. *This Is It.* New York.

Wood, Ernest. 1957. *Zen Dictionary.* New York.